A New Testament Commentary

Based on the Revised Standard Version

General Editor
G. C. D. HOWLEY

Consulting Editors
F. F. BRUCE
H. L. ELLISON

LONDON
PICKERING & INGLIS LTD.

PICKERING & INGLIS LTD.
29 LUDGATE HILL, LONDON, E.C.4
26 BOTHWELL STREET, GLASGOW, C.2

Printed in Great Britain

PREFACE

BIBLICAL studies can never remain static, for the passage of time brings fresh light to bear upon the text, whether in historical and other factual data as a result of new discoveries, or through the insights of scholars and others who apply themselves to pondering the Word of God. The present climate of theological thought is one in which widely different currents are discernible, both liberal and conservative. The purpose of this Commentary is to provide a basis for the exegesis of Scripture which endeavours to be up-to-date and scholarly. The nature of the work precludes the placing of emphasis on devotional or hortatory elements; it is concerned rather with a close examination of the text as it stands. While the viewpoint is conservative, it will not (we hope) appear to be obscurantist. We desire to place in the hands of Christians of all types or denominations a volume that takes its stand upon the historical and orthodox belief in the authority of Holy Scripture.

We have tried to avoid being merely academic; our aim is to appeal to the non-expert in theological matters as well as to those who have had a fuller training in the 'queen of the sciences'. While we have tried to be up-to-date throughout, it is well understood that in some matters of a technical kind finality may, perhaps, never be reached, owing to the new factors that come to light from time to time.

The articles that precede the commentary proper cover a wide range of subjects, and we hope they will prove a valuable addition to the study of the sacred text. The contributors maintain an objective and positive attitude in their work, each man being free to express his own mind on the matters he deals with, and no attempt has been made to press their contributions into a uniform mould. A comparison of the different contributions will quickly reveal, for example, that there is some diversity of viewpoint on such matters as the North/South Galatian theories, the fulfilment of the prophecy of Joel 2: 28-32 regarding the Pentecostal outpouring of the Holy Spirit, etc.

We have been careful to learn from others; no true Biblical scholarship can ever be isolationist. We share the rich heritage of the Church Universal, and realize that 'others have laboured, and (we) have entered into their labour'. All the contributors to this volume are associated with the churches of the Christian Brethren; but it is no part of our aim to express a 'denominational' point of view, but rather to provide a further tool for the reverent handling of the New Testament. It is the impulse to help the rising generation to think biblically that has sent us to this work.

The work has taken much time and thought in busy lives, and it has suffered some delay because of many interruptions, arising from the claims of other work, as well as from a considerable time spent overseas by the General Editor. But a sense of the need for, and the importance of, such a work has proved sufficient recompense for the labours involved. The contributors (one of whom passed away while the work was in process) are all men who are devoted to the study and ministry of the Word of God—ministers, lecturers, teachers, missionaries, scholars.

5

It was part of the original plan to confine our task to the New Testament for the time being, in view of the pressure of time and work.

It has been thought wise to use the Revised Standard Version as our basic text, since this is the English version which is coming to be the most widely accepted throughout the world. We express our thanks to the National Council of the Churches of Christ in U.S.A. for permission to use this text. We are grateful also to all who have shared in the project, as contributors, readers, and in other ways. The General Editor wishes particularly to record his appreciation of all the help he has received from the Consulting Editors, Professor F. F. Bruce and Mr. H. L. Ellison. We send this work forth, seeking the blessing of God upon it and upon all who consult its pages or ponder its contents.

G. C. D. HOWLEY

CONTENTS

7

CONTENTS

LIST OF CONTRIBUTORS

LESLIE C. ALLEN, M.A., Ph.D., Lecturer in Old Testament Language and Exegesis, London Bible College. *Romans.*

ERNEST G. ASHBY, B.A., B.D., M.A., formerly Head of Religious Education, Tottenham Grammar School. *Colossians, Philemon.*

F. F. BRUCE, M.A., D.D., Rylands Professor of Biblical Criticism and Exegesis, University of Manchester. *Revelation, The Fourfold Gospel, The General Letters.*

T. CARSON, M.A., DIP.ED., Language Master, Cumberland High School, Sydney, Australia. *James.*

DAVID J. A. CLINES, M.A., Lecturer in Biblical Studies, University of Sheffield. *2 Corinthians, The Language of the New Testament.*

F. ROY COAD, F.C.A., Bible Teacher and Author. *Galatians, The Apostolic Church.*

PETER E. COUSINS, M.A., B.D., Senior Lecturer in Divinity, Gipsy Hill College, London. *1 and 2 Thessalonians.*

DAVID J. ELLIS, B.D., Principal Lecturer and Head of Divinity Department, Trent Park College, Barnet. *The Gospel of John, The New Testament Use of the Old Testament.*

H. L. ELLISON, B.A., B.D., Author, formerly Missionary and Bible College Lecturer. *The Gospel of Matthew, The Religious Background of the New Testament (Jewish).*

GEORGE E. HARPUR, Bible Teacher and Convention Speaker. *Ephesians.*

GERALD F. HAWTHORNE, B.A., M.A., B.TH., PH.D., Associate Professor of Greek, Wheaton College, Wheaton, Illinois, U.S.A. *Hebrews.*

The late H. C. HEWLETT, Bible Teacher and Convention Speaker in New Zealand. *Philippians.*

J. M. HOUSTON, M.A., B.SC., D.PHIL., Fellow and Bursar of Hertford College, Oxford, University Lecturer in Geography. *An Environmental Background to the New Testament.*

G. C. D. HOWLEY, Bible Teacher, Editor of 'The Witness' and Convention Speaker. *The Authority of the New Testament, The Letters of Paul.*

WALTER L. LIEFELD, TH.B., M.A., PH.D., Professor of New Testament, Chairman of the Division of New Testament, Trinity Evangelical Divinity School, Deerfield, Illinois, U.S.A. *The Development of Doctrine in the New Testament.*

PAUL W. MARSH, B.D., Bible Reading Editor, Scripture Union, London. *1 Corinthians.*

ALAN R. MILLARD, M.A., M.PHIL., Librarian, Tyndale Library for Biblical Research, Cambridge. *Archaeological Discoveries and the New Testament.*

ALAN G. NUTE, Bible Teacher and Convention Speaker. *1 and 2 Timothy-Titus.*

R. W. ORR, M.P.S., D.B.A., Missionary and Bible Teacher. *1, 2 and 3 John.*

DAVID F. PAYNE, B.A., M.A., Lecturer and Head of Department of Semitic Studies, The Queen's University of Belfast. *2 Peter, Jude, The Text and Canon of the New Testament.*

G. J. POLKINGHORNE, DIP.TH., Civil Servant in Customs and Excise, and Bible Teacher. *I Peter.*

LAURENCE E. PORTER, B.A., Head of Divinity Department and School Librarian, Bootle Grammar School, Lancs. *The Gospel of Luke.*

HAROLD H. ROWDON, B.A., PH.D., Lecturer in Church History and Christian Ethics, and Senior Resident Tutor, London Bible College. *The Historical and Political Background of the New Testament, The Religious Background of the New Testament (Pagan).*

STEPHEN S. SHORT, M.B., CH.B., M.R.C.S., L.R.C.P., B.D., A.L.B.C., Bible Teacher and Convention Speaker. *The Gospel of Mark.*

ERNEST H. TRENCHARD, B.A., A.C.P., Director of 'Literatura Biblica', Madrid, Missionary and Author. *The Acts of the Apostles.*

ABBREVIATIONS

OLD TESTAMENT, NEW TESTAMENT AND APOCRYPHA

OT		NT		Apoc.	
Gen.	Genesis	Mt.	Matthew	1 Esd.	1 Esdras
Exod.	Exodus	Mk	Mark	2 Esd.	2 Esdras
Lev.	Leviticus	Lk.	Luke	Tob.	Tobit
Num.	Numbers	Jn	John	Jdt.	Judith
Dt.	Deuteronomy	Ac.	Acts	Ad. Est.	Additions to
Jos.	Joshua	Rom.	Romans		Esther
Jg.	Judges	1 C.	1 Corinthians	Wis.	The Wisdom of
Ru.	Ruth	2 C.	2 Corinthians		Solomon
1 Sam.	1 Samuel	Gal.	Galatians	Sir.	Ecclesiasticus
2 Sam.	2 Samuel	Eph.	Ephesians	Bar.	Baruch
1 Kg.	1 Kings	Phil.	Philippians	S 3 Ch.	Song of the Three
2 Kg.	2 Kings	Col.	Colossians		Holy Children
1 Chr.	1 Chronicles	1 Th.	1 Thessalonians	Sus.	Susanna
2 Chr.	2 Chronicles	2 Th.	2 Thessalonians	Bel	Bel and the
Ezr.	Ezra	1 Tim.	1 Timothy		Dragon
Neh.	Nehemiah	2 Tim.	2 Timothy	Man.	The Prayer of
Est.	Esther	Tit.	Titus		Manasseh
Job	Job	Phm.	Philemon	1 Mac.	1 Maccabees
Ps.	Psalms	Heb.	Hebrews	2 Mac.	2 Maccabees
Prov.	Proverbs	Jas	James		
Ec.	Ecclesiastes	1 Pet.	1 Peter		
Ca.	Song of Solomon	2 Pet.	2 Peter		
Isa.	Isaiah	1 Jn	1 John		
Jer.	Jeremiah	2 Jn	2 John		
Lam.	Lamentations	3 Jn	3 John		
Ezek.	Ezekiel	Jude	Jude		
Dan.	Daniel	Rev.	Revelation		
Hos.	Hosea				
Jl	Joel				
Am.	Amos				
Ob.	Obadiah				
Jon.	Jonah				
Mic.	Micah				
Nah.	Nahum				
Hab.	Habakkuk				
Zeph.	Zephaniah				
Hag.	Haggai				
Zech.	Zechariah				
Mal.	Malachi				

BOOKS AND JOURNALS

Ant.	Josephus, *Antiquities of the Jews*	Jos.	Josephus
AOFG	C. F. Burney, *The Aramaic Origin of the Fourth Gospel*, 1922	*LAP*	J. Finegan, *Light from the Ancient Past*[2], 1960
Arndt	Arndt-Gingrich, *Greek-English Lexicon of the New Testament*, 1957	*MM*	Moulton and Milligan, *The Vocabulary of the Greek Testament*, 1930
BJRL	*Bulletin of the John Rylands Library*	*MNT*	*Moffatt New Testament Commentary*
BNTC	*Black's New Testament Commentary*	*NBC*	*New Bible Commentary*, 1953
CBSC	*Cambridge Bible for Schools and Colleges*	*NBD*	*New Bible Dictionary*, 1962
		NCB	*New Clarendon Bible*
CGT	*Cambridge Greek Testament*	*NIC*	*New International Commentary*
EB	*Expositor's Bible*	*NLC*	*New London Commentary*
EGT	*Expositor's Greek Testament*	*NTS*	*New Testament Studies*
Ep. Barn.	*The Epistle of Barnabas*	*NTT*	E. Stauffer, *New Testament Theology*, 1955
EQ	*Evangelical Quarterly*		
ExpT	*Expository Times*	*SB*	(or Strack-Billerbeck) H. L. Strack
HDB	Hastings' *Dictionary of the Bible*, 5 vols., 1898-1904		and P. Billerbeck, *Kommentar zum Neuen Testament aus Talmud und Midrasch*, 6 vols., 1922-61
HE	*Historia Ecclesiastica* (Eusebius)		
IB	*Interpreter's Bible*	*TB*	*Babylonian Talmud*
ICC	*International Critical Commentary*	*TC*	*Torch Commentary*
ISBE	*International Standard Bible Encyclopaedia*[2], 5 vols., 1930	*TNTC*	*Tyndale New Testament Commentary*
		WC	*Westminster Commentaries*

GENERAL ABBREVIATIONS

ad. loc.	at the place	Heb.	Hebrew
Aram.	Aramaic	*ibid.*	in the same book (or passage)
art.	article	lit.	literally
AV	Authorised Version	*loc. cit.*	in the passage already quoted
c.	about (of time)	LXX	Septuagint
cent.	century	mg	margin
cf.	compare	MS(S)	manuscript(s)
ch(s).	chapter(s)	*MT*	Massoretic Text
cntd.	continued	n.	note
Comm.	commentary	NEB	New English Bible
comp.	compare	*op. cit.*	in the work cited above
d.	died	p(p).	page(s)
ed.	editor (or edited)	*q.v.*	which see
e.g.	for example	RSV	Revised Standard Version
esp.	especially	RV	Revised Version
E.T.	English Translation	*scil.*	that is to say
EVV	English versions	*s.v.*	under the word
f(f).	following	tr.	(or trans.) translated or translation
Gk.	Greek	v(v).	verse(s)

PART ONE

GENERAL ARTICLES

THE AUTHORITY OF
THE NEW TESTAMENT

G. C. D. HOWLEY

'The Christian community was in essence not "bookish": it had been called into existence by a series of events well remembered; it lived under the continued personal guidance, as it believed, of the central figure of those events; and the time would not be long, so it imagined, before he would return to sight. Its authority was "the Lord and the Apostles".' These words of C. F. D. Moule[1] draw attention to an interesting fact concerning the early Christians. The churches were for the most part composed of people who were not 'bookish', and the community as a whole partook largely of that nature. Yet Christians have always been 'people of the Book', and in this matter they claim a spiritual ancestry reaching right back to the first generation of the Church.

What were the books to which they turned? How did they originate? What did they accomplish? Their holy books were those which had been fulfilled in the great facts centred in their Founder and Head, Jesus Christ. Their spiritual life was centred in Him, and their witness was always pointing to Him. They looked back to the history of the people of God before Christ's advent, and realized their continuity with them. As Moule further says of the early Church: 'The only book it needed was the collection of scriptures already recognized by the Jews, in which the Christians now found explanation and confirmation of their own convictions, while conversely, they found the scriptures explained and confirmed in an entirely new way by the recent events'.[2]

If the early Christians inherited the sacred books of the Hebrews, it was because they found them to be introductory to the period in which they lived. The vital link between the two periods was their acknowledgment of Jesus as their Messiah. 'It is exactly the concept of messiahship which demands both continuity with the old order and its fulfillment. Messiahship is essentially unintelligible apart from the presupposition of the old covenant and it remains unrealized unless it ushers in the new

covenant . . . . The divine messiahship of Jesus is then the basic fact behind the formation of the New Testament.'[3] This messianic awareness was something that characterized the Old Testament writings; and within the life of the early Church the same awareness marked their faith. They had learned from the Old Testament something of the ways of God in redeeming His people, and the promises bound up in the prophets concerning the Coming One who should deliver His people.

In Jesus the first Christians had found the reality to which the Old Testament shadows led on. They found themselves living in the age of fulfilment, and looked back to the earlier centuries as those of promise. They believed that in the fulness of the time God had sent forth His Son . . . to redeem. H. Cunliffe-Jones expresses the fact excellently: 'If Jesus Christ does not make plain the meaning of the Old Testament revelation, then His mission is false and the claims Christians have made for Him are mistaken. But in fact the Christian theologian, acknowledging the authority of the Bible in its witness to the revelation of God, must both acknowledge the faith of the Old Testament as the revelation of the one God of Christian worship and also treat the Old Testament as something inherently incomplete, with the key to its own understanding not given in itself, so that its real meaning is only made plain in Jesus Christ'.[4]

If these Christians believed that Jesus had brought to them the fulfilment of God's ancient promises, it is plain also that they recognized the importance of His teaching, through which He had brought them God's message. At all costs they desired to preserve a faithful record of His words and works. Harnack once said that 'the earliest motive force, one that had been at work from the beginning of the Apostolic Age, was the supreme reverence in which the words and teaching of Christ Jesus were held'. If Judaism had reverenced the writings of Moses, it is not surprising that

15

Christians should hold the words of One infinitely greater than Moses as supreme in importance; nor that, when His words had been written down, they should give high place to those records. In Jesus Christ God had spoken to men, and His great redemptive purposes had been and were being worked out in Him: this was the good news the Church existed to proclaim. In a very real sense, then, the words and works of Jesus Christ lie directly behind the writing of the New Testament books. The oral message led on quite naturally, and inevitably, to the written record of that message.

The function of the writers in apostolic times was to witness to Christ. This they did as men who had enjoyed a personal experience of Him. Some of the writers had known Him during His earthly ministry, while others had come to know Him at some time subsequent to His death and resurrection. They had a diversity of spiritual experience but in each case it was something that rang true in the minds of those who encountered either them or their writings. There was a certain boldness about those new writings. One of the earliest letters of Paul closes with the solemn charge, 'I adjure you by the Lord that this letter be read to all the brethren' (1 Th. 5: 27). The expectation that his letters would be read publicly in the assemblies for worship and instruction indicated that the apostle rated their importance highly. And that this custom was not confined to Thessalonica is seen from the injunction to interchange two of his other letters so that each church might benefit from what had been written primarily to another community (Col. 4: 16). Nor was there anything out of place in this assumption of authority. They were the apostles of Christ, commissioned by Him and acting on His behalf, having derived their authority directly from Him. Small wonder, then, that they expected their writings to be read in the public assemblies of the churches, even if this tended to give those letters equal prominence to the Old Testament scriptures which would habitually be read on such occasions. Justin Martyr, writing in the mid-second century, may be regarded as acquainted with Christian custom over a wide area, and in his *Apology* (I. 67) says: 'On the day called Sunday all those who live in the towns or in the country meet together; and the memoirs of the apostles and the writings of the prophets are read, as long as time allows. Then, when the reader has ended, the president addresses words of instruction and exhortation to imitate these good things'. The fact to note is that Justin assumes equal authority for the apostolic and the prophetic writings; and it is fair to assume that this recognition was general in the churches of his generation.

There were many writings in circulation among the early Christians, but only a proportion of them received general acceptance in the churches as possessing apostolic authority. C. H. Dodd sums up the situation thus: 'The Church read as Scripture those writings which it felt to be most vitally related to the spiritual impulse that created it . . . . So far as we are able to compare the writings of the original Canon with their competitors, especially with those which were ultimately excluded, there can be no doubt that as a whole they stand, spiritually, intellectually, and aesthetically, on an altogether higher plane'.[5] The books that were recognized among the churches received this acknowledgment by their own merit. As for the rest, they lacked the direct and immediate note of inherent authority and, as has many times been said, nobody excluded them from the body of New Testament writings: they excluded themselves.

We are now in a position to see why the term, 'The New Testament', is used of the second part of the Biblical literature. A. H. McNeile rightly says that 'This title, as applied to the collection of sacred Christian writings, is often used with no clear understanding of its meaning'.[6] The word 'Testament' comes into our English Bible from the Latin *testamentum* which means 'covenant' or 'testament', while the Greek *diathēkē* carries the same meanings. As McNeile further says: 'There were two eras in the world's history, in which there were two *diathēkai*, the one involving slavery, the other freedom . . . . What we call the Old and the New Testaments are two collections of writings containing the divine message, which belong respectively to the two dispensations'.[7] If we replace the word 'Testament' with 'Covenant' we see at once that these books bring us into the atmosphere of the new era which was inaugurated by the coming of Christ into the world. Here we breathe the pure air of primitive Christian faith and thought.

The facts to which the Christians' books bore witness were not merely connected with life on a temporal plane, though they were deeply involved in life's problems. The writings in question contained the record of a divine revelation to men. Herein also lay part of their continuity with the Old Testament, for the earlier books recorded God's revelation to His people. Judaism received the older writings as from God; and the Church regarded the apostolic books similarly as the record of His full and final revelation in Christ. The Bible affirms that at certain points in history God disclosed Himself to men, this revelation being therefore both historic and personal. It was not, however, merely a revelation in deed but also in the necessary word to explain the deed, or, as Dodd puts it, 'events plus interpretation'. We fall from the level of apostolic thought if we think of this revelation as only given in divine action. Surely God must reveal the meaning of His acts? On this point B. B. Warfield commented acutely: 'It is easy to talk of revelation by deed. But how little is capable of being revealed by even the mightiest deed unaccompanied by the explanatory word?'[8] If we regard the divine revelation as only in action, are we not in danger of mere subjectivism when we turn to examine the writings that contain that revelation?

There is a pattern discernible throughout scripture in which we perceive the hand of God at work in the salvation of men. In the Old Testament it is shown in the event of the Exodus, with all that sprang from it in the subsequent history of Israel. It has been said that 'the saving character of God is the thread, and that election is the instrument employed to effect the saving purpose of God', as seen throughout the Old Testament. The last and greatest act, however, takes us beyond that period, to the point where we see God the Saviour at work, now to redeem and deliver, not from Egypt or Babylon, but from Satan, sin and death. 'His deeds bear the stamp of salvation, and their doer the character of a saviour.'[9] It may be well while on this point, to consider a wider assessment of this principle. 'As the divine saving pattern is the link between prophecy and fulfilment, and insight into this pattern constitutes the ground of prophecy, so it is this same pattern that constitutes the ground and criterion for legitimate typology'.[10]

How is this divine revelation to be received? The simple answer is, by faith. There have been many who have demanded that we bring the Bible to the bar of human reason, but (to quote some wise words of Pascal here) there are 'two forms of excess: to exclude reason, and not to admit anything but reason'; and again, 'Reason's last step is the recognition that there are an infinite number of things which are beyond it; it is merely feeble if it does not go so far as to grasp that. If natural things are beyond it, what are we to say about super-natural?'[11] Such words may check an excess of enthusiasm in applying human reason to the Bible beyond a certain point. It is in this very matter, we judge, that some have missed the way in handling the Bible. It is true that God

addresses man as a rational and moral being, and also, as Alan Richardson expresses it, 'we must use our reason and common sense when we seek to find God's message for us in the Bible'.[12] But he well adds the following: 'we must remember that its message for us can be understood only by means of a "diviner light". Biblical faith . . . is uncompromisingly opposed to all forms of rationalism—the view that the human reason is, in virtue of its own inherent perfection, a competent and impartial judge of truth and falsehood in all matters, whether secular or religious'.[13] This is a necessary balance. To that witness we add that of R. R. Williams: 'The revelation in the Bible is not to be tested and verified by the reason, but appropriated by the heart and conscience. When that is done the reason can be given its fullest play, with complete assurance'.[14]

Space does not allow a detailed survey of the views of scholars and theologians of the past hundred years or so, but mention needs to be made of some of those trends. The modern debate embraces the Liberalism of the nineteenth century and beyond which was marked by a strong vein of subjectivism. T. W. Manson summed Liberalism up in words that cannot be misunderstood: 'The upshot is that Liberalism was predisposed against a God who intervenes in the world, or in history, whether by deed or word; and predisposed in favour of an interpretation of religion which would make it no more than an element in human civilization, the sum of man's deepest and gradually achieved convictions about ultimate Reality and absolute values'.[15] Man's thought about God took the place of God's revelation of Himself, and such views contain within themselves the seeds of their own destruction.

What of the post-Liberal era? This has been marked by the development of the theology associated with the names of Karl Barth, Emil Brunner and other scholars. From the stream of neo-orthodoxy flow many of the elements in contemporary theology. In discussing the relationship of the new theology to the intellectual climate of today, Francis A. Schaeffer comments upon the passing of the older Liberalism: 'So it was not so much neo-orthodoxy which destroyed the older form of liberalism, even though Karl Barth's teaching might have been the final earthquake which shook down the tottering edifice; rather it had already been destroyed from within'.[16] There is a danger that, in thinking of the Bible as merely the earthen vessel in which is to be found the treasure of God's revelation as He makes Himself known in personal encounter—

B

as is the case with neo-orthodoxy—insufficient serious attention may be given to Holy Scripture itself. Can we afford to regard as unimportant the framework through which God has been pleased to communicate His revelation? The standpoint of this volume is that both form and content are important. The words of S. T. Coleridge have sometimes been quoted as a guide in discovering or hearing the Word of God, 'Whatever finds me bears witness for itself that it has proceeded from a Holy Spirit'.[17] What is this but making the test of what is or is not of the Holy Spirit within ourselves? It is but another form of bringing the Word of God to the bar of the human mind, and we have already considered the weakness of this approach.

A new form of Liberalism has arisen in recent years associated with the names of theologians such as Rudolf Bultmann and Paul Tillich. Though their approaches differ, they affirm that the Christian message needs translating into terms modern man can understand. We are told that in the form in which it is found in the New Testament it is mythological, and the mythological draperies must be removed before we can perceive the real meaning of Christianity. This element of myth is found in the image of God, the virgin birth, the resurrection and ascension of Jesus. The Bible history of redemption must be 'demythologized'; we will then be left with the real Christian faith. Tillich tells us that we must forget everything traditional that we have learned about God. It is admitted by many that there is a great deal of confused language in some of these modern views; are we wrong in assuming some confusion of thought also? Certainly such views depart from the historic faith at various points, besides tending to bewilder many persons.

'There is a measure of continuity in Christian thought', writes Bernard Ramm, contending that it is important to take the history of theology seriously because it possesses manifestations of the teaching ministry of the Holy Spirit. He gives three reasons why the interpreter must pay due regard to the history of theology: (a) the Holy Spirit is the Teacher of the Church; (b) the present Church is the inheritor of all the great scholarship of the past; (c) theological and ecclesiastical crises drive men to think deeper and clearer than they do in ordinary circumstances.[18] So long as Christian thought has been based on Holy Scripture it has been within the scope of the ministry of the Holy Spirit, of whom Christ said, 'He will teach you all things, and bring to your remembrance all that I have said to you' (Jn 14: 26). The Lord had brought the Word of God to men during His ministry,

and He promised that this ministry would be continued by the Holy Spirit. The apostolic age saw the fulfilment of this promise, as the Christian writings came into being, meeting the needs of the young churches. Then came the Patristic period, during which Christianity became established. In the doctrinal disputes of the period, appeal to the authority of the Bible was sufficient; while during the long period of the Middle Ages, even though the Bible was not in the hands of ordinary people, we are told that in their preaching, the friars chose and announced their texts with care. 'The handbooks for preachers insist on this: the text must be from the authentic canonical scripture . . . no word is to be added, no tense or number changed, nor an unfamiliar translation employed.'[19]

The allegorizing of scripture was common. Master Rypon of Durham declares that 'Holy Scripture is not merely to be understood according to its literal or grammatical sense, but with equal truth according to the mystical or moral sense'. Stephen Langton tells us that 'Jerusalem can mean four things: the city overlooking the valley of Cedron in Palestine (that is the literal and historical place), allegorically the Church Militant, anagogically the Church Triumphant, and tropologically the faithful soul'.[20] This varied interpretation of scripture may have run wild at times, but bound up with it was a recognition of the Bible as the revelation of God. The Church of the Middle Ages had many faults, some of them glaring evils, but even though the Bible was overloaded with the interpretations of the Church, it was always regarded as the Word of God.

To the fact of divine revelation we must add that of the illumination which marks those who receive the Word of God by faith. (This is indicated by such passages as 1 C. 2: 6-16; 2 C. 3: 12—4: 6, and 1 Jn 2: 20, 27.) Psalm 36: 9 shows the relationship of revelation to illumination: 'For with thee is the fountain of life; in thy light do we see light'—the light of illumination flowing from the light of the revelation. The objective revelation of God needs to be supplemented by an internal work of the Holy Spirit, bringing the experience of illumination. The natural man is a stranger to this experience, as Paul clearly states: 'The unspiritual man does not receive the gifts of the Spirit of God, for they are folly to him, and he is not able to understand them because they are spiritually discerned' (1 C. 2: 14).

It may be asked, how can we tell when the revelation of God came to an end? Or does it continue today in the same way as in Biblical times? The New Testament is the primary witness to the events associated with the supreme revelation of God in the person of His Son Jesus Christ. It is this event that effects the redemption of the world, therefore the apostolic witness is the final word of objective revelation. 'To ask for more revelation than this is to misunderstand the entire philosophy of special revelation. Special revelation is the knowledge-correlate of divine redemption. When redemption reaches its climax, special revelation reaches its climax. With the end of the events of redemption comes the end of special revelation. Hence the word of the apostles in witness to Jesus Christ, the climax of redemption and special revelation, is the end of revelation . . . The New Testament written by the apostles is the delegated authority of the Lord Jesus'.[21] This expresses quite clearly what we believe to be the truth of the matter. When the need for special revelation ceased, then the revelation found completeness.

What made these books unique was their quality of inspiration. By this we do not refer to anything parallel to the masterpieces of literature that have been given to the world through the centuries. Their writers were 'inspired' in another sense, but not in the strict Biblical meaning of the term. 'The prophets have the timeliness which belongs to genius' one writer states: and while this is true, it is not the whole truth. They had something more, 'the burden of the word of the Lord'. 'Inspiration may be regarded in one aspect as the correlative of revelation', wrote B. F. Westcott in 1851; 'Both operations imply a supernatural extension of the field of man's spiritual vision, but in different ways.' Inspiration was a direct intelligible communication of God's will to chosen messengers. The word *theopneustos* (2 Tim. 3: 16), 'inspired by God', means 'God-breathed', in Warfield's definition 'produced by the creative breath of the Almighty'.[22] If this definition is correct, it indicates that inspiration does not merely attach to the men, but to the product of their work, the inspired books. The reasonableness of this view may be seen when we consider the purpose of the writings, to bring the knowledge of God to man.

Does this, then, imply a form of mechanical dictation which would make the writers of the Biblical books mere 'typewriters'? So far from this being the case, all the evidence goes to show that the men who wrote the sacred books were in full possession of their faculties at the time of writing. The different personalities of the writers shine out in all they write. Each man writes according to his distinctive experience of God; his style is his own entirely, and strong differences mark the literary talents of the different authors: he uses his own vocabulary and emphasis, so that one writer will use words and phrases that are seldom found in the other books. So far from the personalities of the writers being suppressed at the time they were engaged in their tasks, we may rather conceive that their powers would be heightened as they were under the control of the Holy Spirit.

The testimony of 2 Peter is equally plain, and, we may add (because of the non-Petrine viewpoint on authorship which is held by many scholars), whatever the authorship or date of this letter, it exhibits a high view of the doctrine of inspiration. 'First of all you must understand this, that no prophecy of scripture is a matter of one's own interpretation, because no prophecy ever came by the impulse of man, but men moved by the Holy Spirit spoke from God' (2 Pet. 1: 20 f.). The New English Bible renders v. 21: 'men they were, but, impelled by the Holy Spirit, they spoke the words of God'. The prophetic word did not originate in mere human thought or intuition, it was not created by human initiative, for the men who wrote became at that time the divine spokesmen, they were 'moved by the Holy Spirit'. There was a combination of divine and human elements at work in the writing of the books of the Bible—God and man: the moving power and the living instrument. As Westcott said: 'We have a Bible competent to calm our doubts, and able to speak to our weakness . . . . It is authoritative, for it is the voice of God; it is intelligible, for it is in the language of men'. Inspiration is, thus, dynamical and not mechanical. Even in God's hand, man does not become a mere machine. The mysterious interpenetration of the divine and the human elements in Holy Scripture resulted in a unity which is rightly called the Word of God.

The testimony of these scriptures is in harmony with the general viewpoint of the New Testament writers. They do not appear to regard inspiration as attaching only to the religious teachings of the Bible, or merely to its ideas or truths, but also to the form in which they were presented. The remarkable assurance that characterizes Paul's account of his own ministry (cf. 1 C. 2: 6-16) pervades the whole body of literature. If those men of God were borne along by the Holy Spirit, then the Spirit of God is in a sense the Author of scripture, and also (to borrow some words of F. F. Bruce), 'in Abraham Kuyper's phrase, the Perpetual Author, continually speaking through the Word to the believing reader and unfolding fresh meaning from it'.[23] The Spirit and the Word are essentially conjoined, the scriptures functioning through the ministry of the Holy Spirit, while the Spirit functions through the medium of the Word. This was without doubt the belief of the Reformers. In emerging from the shackles of the Pre-Reformation era they rediscovered for themselves the living character of scripture. While in some details their views differed, in regard to the Bible they appear to have stood close together.

Divine inspiration does not entail holding rigid ideas that could not face up to the evidence. For example, our Lord spoke in Aramaic, but the record of His words is preserved in the Gospels, written in Greek. The many differences between the Hebrew text of the Old Testament and the Septuagint are to some extent reflected in the quotations from that version in the New Testament. As D. W. Gooding says: 'The Septuagint is not an original composition but a translation, and a translation that has often been revised in order to make it represent the original Hebrew more faithfully'. And further: 'The wide differences between the Greek and the Massoretic texts obviously date from times earlier than all our extant Greek evidence'.[24] The speeches recorded in The Acts of the Apostles are without doubt given in summary form, as Luke himself indicates following his report of Peter's sermon at Pentecost, 'And he testified with many other words and exhorted them, saying, "Save yourselves from this crooked generation"' (Ac. 2: 40). What has been recorded contains every essential element for faith, and for the written record of God's revelation. In this connection, Philip E. Hughes said, in a valuable address on 'The Reformers' View of Inspiration', given at the Oxford Conference of Evangelical Churchmen in 1960: 'Of course the words of Holy Scripture are of vital importance. They are the units of meaning and the means of communication. But they are significant only in combination. Words isolated from their context have lost their significance and are not sacrosanct. What is essential is the truth which the words unitedly reveal'.

'The question of authority . . . in its religious form, is the first and last issue of life', wrote P. T. Forsyth. 'As soon as the problem of authority really lifts its head, all others fall to the rear.'[25] The problem of the seat of authority in religion is a perennial one, for while one person may find what he is seeking, another will be wandering in spirit, looking for safe anchorage. The historic answers to this question point variously to the Church, to Reason, or to the Bible, the latter being the anchorage found by the Reformers. It has sometimes been suggested that they elevated the Bible to the place of final authority because they looked for something to replace the authority of the Church. In other words, they found a substitute to fill the vacuum created by the abandonment of the authority of the Papacy. Perhaps another view of the situation might be that what they did was to re-establish in its rightful place that which had always been regarded with some degree of reverence, the Bible itself. In this they did justice to Holy Scripture, while, as a secondary issue, man's need for authoritative guidance was met.

This recognition of the authority of scripture was fundamental in the moulding of the Reformed Churches, and it is necessary to affirm this truth in the face of modern pessimism and a general reaction against authority in many spheres of life. We must recognize and retain the authority of the scriptures because they are for us the normative account of the beginnings of Christianity; further, the written documents act as a check on the many vagaries, both of doctrine and of conduct, that otherwise could choke spiritual life; but also because God does speak to men in every age through scripture. We have already seen that this Biblical insight marked the teaching of the Reformers. In a recent symposium on Biblical authority for today, representatives of widely different churches contributed chapters on fundamental considerations. In each case (with one exception which was for reasons of the more limited scope of the article) the writers emphasized the internal witness of the Holy Spirit as a prominent element in their overall conception of scripture. In this they are on common ground with the Reformers.

In his *Prologue to the Book of Genesis* Tyndale wrote: 'The Scripture is the touchstone that trieth all doctrines, and by that we know the false from the true'. Cranmer said that even in regard to 'learned and godly-minded' persons, they were to be believed 'no further than they can show their doctrine and exhortation to be agreeable with the true Word of God written. For that is the very touchstone which must, yea, and also will, try all doctrine or learning, whatsoever it be, whether it be good or evil, true or false'. This was the general standpoint of the great leaders of the Reformation. But in no sense did they look upon the scriptures as something static, rather they perceived them to be living oracles, the oracles of God. It was the ministry of the Holy Spirit on which they depended, in His testimony within their hearts and lives. A modern scholar draws the same lesson: 'The proof of its authority lies in its continued power to speak, and the limits of the literary history cannot limit God's power to make use of what true word He will, in speaking to the soul of man'.[26]

There is an instinct of authority in the Biblical writers, and in the books they produced. This authority characterized the writings from the moment of their origin, as will be seen from the necessity for immediate attention that marks, for example, the New Testament letters. The idea of authority is rooted in the fact of divine revelation, and because the readers of those books believed them to convey God's message, they were brought into the obedience of Christ as they received and acted upon that message. This submission to the Word of God was in no way hostile to freedom. On the contrary, it was the way through which Christians found that His service is perfect freedom. The same passage that affirms Holy Scripture as being 'God-breathed' goes on to show the essentially pragmatic nature of scripture, as profitable for several eminently practical reasons (2 Tim. 3: 16 f.), bringing Christian people to maturity of life and experience. Every part of life is affected by the penetration of God's Word, as was the case in the first days of Christianity when the apostolic letters dealt with the plainest and most matter-of-fact everyday things from the standpoint of the will of God for His people. Not that the New Testament writings brought men and women into legalistic bondage, or hedged them around with commands and prohibitions. Those documents were never intended to be regarded merely as a collection of precedents, to be followed blindly, but rather as providing guiding-lines for daily life in their outlining of spiritual principles.

God has expressed His authority by divine self-revelation; and this revelation has found its supreme manifestation in the person of the Lord Jesus Christ, the Son of God. His whole life bore the stamp of divine authority. It was seen in the moral perfection of His life, for (to quote again from C. H. Dodd), 'the effect He produced upon men with whom He came in contact—the effect indeed which He still produces upon men—is such that we cannot think He had any unresolved discords in His own soul'.[27] Throughout His earthly ministry the Lord showed an awareness of His unique relationship to God, and of His own authority. In contrast to the teachers of that age, He affirmed with assurance of the truth of His words, and His right to say them, 'I say unto you . . .'. The living Word Christ brought to men was itself the revelation of God, and in His life, death and resurrection He spoke that Word and demonstrated that it was a Word of salvation for men. It is to Christ risen and ascended to heaven that we look as the One in Whom all authority is vested by God. He is, therefore, the ultimate and final authority for all believers.

From these facts, therefore, we find the authority of the New Testament. It bears the stamp of apostolic authority in its witness to Christ. This witness of the apostles is made good to men today by the internal witness of the Holy Spirit, of whose function Jesus said, 'He will glorify me, for he will take what is mine and declare it to you' (Jn 16: 14). It is in the fellowship of the church that Christians can enter into much of the reality of this inner testimony of the Spirit, as they come under the Word of God within the sphere where Christ, crucified and risen, is worshipped. Yet not only in relation to church life, but also as individuals, believers are brought into the power of a personal relationship and communion with Christ, as they respond by faith to the Holy Spirit's witness to their spirits (cf. Rom. 8: 16).

In the final chapter of his book, *The Authority of Scripture*, J. K. S. Reid says that the authority with which the Bible is credited needs to be carefully defined: 'It will have, for one thing, to rest on something other than internal but trivial characteristics or impressive but external guarantee'. He suggests it will have to be permanent, simple, universal, categorical and acceptable. The response Christians will give is, of course, that all of these things mark the authority of the New Testament (with which we are particularly concerned). It is permanent, covering all life and not patchy or fragmentary in its bearing; it is simple, open to all people and to be understood by all; it is universal, for its teaching fits into every kind of human life (even as every kind of person finds that he can fit into its framework); it is categorical, straightforward in its instruction and its challenge and brooking no evasion; and it is acceptable, in that it can secure the assent of those who feel its impact. God's will is 'good, acceptable, and perfect', writes Paul to the Romans, and the New Testament, as the medium whereby He communicates to us the knowledge of His will, can bring us into a rich spiritual experience in which we 'stand mature and fully assured in all the will of God' (Col. 4: 12).

The events recorded in and attested by the New Testament writings are unique. The life that is associated with the Christian gospel is also unique in its ideal expression, seen first in Jesus Christ, and then, by the Holy Spirit, in those who believe on Him and are members of His Body, the Church. To this end the apostles bore their witness; and to this end the

Holy Spirit witnesses in the hearts of believers everywhere, through the instrumentality of the written Word of God, to bring them into the fullness of the knowledge of God. 'Thus for the New Testament, as for the Old', wrote John Baillie, 'God is One who is directly known in His approach to the human soul. He is not an inference but a Presence. He is Presence at once urgent and gracious. By all whom He seeks He is known as a Claimant; by all whom He finds, and who in Christ find Him, He is known as a Giver. The knowledge of God of which the New Testament speaks is a knowledge for which the best argument were but a sorry substitute and to which it were but a superfluous addition. "He that hath seen me hath seen the Father; and how sayest thou then, Shew us the Father?" '. [28]

REFERENCES

1   *The Birth of the New Testament* (London, 1962), p. 181.
2   *op. cit.*, p. 182.
3   N. B. Stonehouse: 'The Authority of the New Testament', *The Infallible Word* (London, 1946), p. 108.
4   *The Authority of the Biblical Revelation* (London, 1954), p. 48.
5   *The Authority of the Bible* (London, 1928), p. 196.
6   *An Introduction to the Study of the New Testament* (Oxford, 2nd edition, 1953), p. 1.
7   *op. cit.*, p. 2.
8   *Biblical and Theological Studies* (London, 1952 edition), p. 17.
9   J. K. S. Reid: *The Authority of Scripture* (London, 1927), p. 249.
10 *op. cit.*, p. 251.
11 *Pensées*, IV. 267.
12 *Christian Apologetics* (London, 1947), p. 222.
13 *op. cit.*, p. 223.
14 *Authority in the Apostolic Age* (London, 1950), p. 122.
15 'The Failure of Liberalism to Interpret the Bible as the Word of God', *The Interpretation of the Bible* (London, 1944), p. 95.
16 *The God Who is There* (London, 1968), p. 52.
17 *Confessions of an Enquiring Spirit*, Letter I.
18 *The Pattern of Authority* (Grand Rapids, 1957), pp. 57 ff.
19 'The Faith of the Middle Ages', *The Interpretation of the Bible* (London, 1944), pp. 26 f.
20 *op. cit.*, pp. 35 f.
21 Ramm, *op. cit.*, pp. 54 f.
22 *The Inspiration and Authority of the Bible* (London, 1951), p. 296.
23 'The Scriptures', *The Faith — A Symposium* (London, 1952), p. 18.
24 *The Account of the Tabernacle* (Cambridge, 1959), pp. 1 f.
25 *The Principle of Authority* (London, 1913), p. 1.
26 H. Wheeler Robinson: *The Bible in its Ancient and English Versions* (Oxford, 1940), p. 299.
27 *The Authority of the Bible* (London, 1928), p. 240.
28 *Our Knowledge of God* (Oxford, 1939), p. 126.

BIBLIOGRAPHY

ABBA, R., *The Nature and Authority of the Bible* (London, 1958).

DODD, C. H., *The Bible To-day* (Cambridge, 1946); *According to the Scriptures* (London, 1952).

DUGMORE, C. W. (ed.), *The Interpretation of the Bible* (London, 1944).

GELDENHUYS, NORVAL, *Supreme Authority* (London, 1953).

HENRY, C. F. H. (ed.), *Revelation and the Bible* (London, 1959).

JAMES, M. R., *The Apocryphal New Testament* (Oxford, 1924).

REID, J. K. S., *The Authority of Scripture* (London, 1957).

RICHARDSON, A. and SCHWEITZER, W. (ed.), *Biblical Authority for Today* (London, 1951).

ROBINSON, H. W. (ed.), *The Bible in its Ancient and English Versions* (Oxford, 1940; New (revised) edition, 1954).

ROWLEY, H. H., *The Unity of the Bible* (London, 1953).

SMALLEY, BERYL, *The Study of the Bible in the Early Middle Ages* (Oxford, 1941; New (revised) edition, 1952).

STONEHOUSE, N. B. and WOOLLEY, PAUL (ed.), *The Infallible Word* (London, 1946).

WARFIELD, B. B., *The Inspiration and Authority of the Bible* (London, 1951).

THE TEXT AND CANON OF THE NEW TESTAMENT

DAVID F. PAYNE

I. CANON

Introduction

Orthodox Christians everywhere today take it for granted that Holy Scripture consists of two parts, or Testaments, between them containing 66 books. We should be disconcerted, to say the least, if on purchasing a new Bible we found that it omitted any of these 66 or included any extra books. Some Bibles, to be sure, include the Old Testament Apocrypha, but those that do so normally indicate the fact clearly on the outside cover. But the New Testament, which is here our concern, is never added to. It is probable that the percentage of Christians who have any acquaintance with New Testament apocryphal books is very small indeed.

We possess, then, a New Testament of 27 books, which in the ordinary English Bible always appear in the same order. This is the Canon of the New Testament; we find in it 5 narrative books, 21 letters, and a single book of quite a different character, aptly called The Apocalypse or Revelation; and in them we acknowledge the supreme and complete guide for Christian doctrine and faith.

But the apostles themselves had no such written rule of faith and conduct. Their Bible, and that of the Jews to this day, consisted of the Old Testament; this was the Canon of Holy Writ accepted by Jesus Himself, and referred to simply as 'the scriptures' throughout the New Testament writings. It was not until the year A.D. 393 that a church council first listed the 27 New Testament books now universally recognized. There was thus a period of about 350 years during which the New Testament Canon was in process of being formed. It is our purpose here to trace the developments of those years.

The Canon and Authority

The Greek word *kanōn*, as used by the early church fathers, had a number of meanings and uses, two of which are relevant to this study. From a basic sense of a ruler or measuring rod, with its markings, there derived the metaphorical meanings 'list' and 'rule' (i.e. 'standard'). It is

important to note that the first sense is that intended in the phrase 'Canon of Scripture'. The New Testament Canon is simply the list of books contained in the New Testament; the books on this list are 'canonical', all others are 'uncanonical'. But the second meaning is easily confused with the first, since the canonical books are those which alone we find authoritative, presenting the 'rule' of faith and conduct. The Canon and the authority of the New Testament are thus closely related topics; but it is misleading to equate the terms 'canonical' and 'authoritative', because the Canon is not an authoritative list of books, but a list of authoritative books. Each book of the New Testament was authoritative from the beginning; but none of them could be called canonical until collections and lists of such books were made. The only authority the Canon wields is that of its component parts.

The New Testament Documents

The great majority of the New Testament books were penned between A.D. 50 and 100. The writers were apostles and their associates, and were men specially fitted and commissioned to convey to mankind the Word of God as revealed in the acts and the teachings of the Lord Jesus. They both spoke and wrote with authority, adapting the message of Christ to the needs of the hearers and readers. It seems that some apostolic writings had only temporary or local value, and were not therefore preserved; one letter (at least) written by Paul to the church at Corinth has disappeared (cf. 1 C. 5:9), and possibly a letter by him to Laodicea too (unless the reference in Col. 4:16 is to what we know as the Letter to the Ephesians). Nor was all the oral ministry of the apostles put into written form and preserved. John explicitly states his principles of selection of material worth recording (Jn 20:30 f.); and we may conclude that our New Testament is the authoritative apostolic message suited to the needs of posterity. It is highly probable that apocryphal works do contain, here and there, genuine additional information about Jesus and the apostles; but in the canonical books we have all we need to know for salvation and instruction in righteousness.

The First Collections

Some of the New Testament books were expressly addressed to individuals, some to churches or groups of churches; and even those which reveal nothing about the intended recipients, and seem to have been meant for more general use, must have circulated in a very limited area in the first place. But the self-evident authority and value of them all quickly made them prized possessions, and they were copied and re-copied for an ever widening public. The earliest 'canon' was that possessed by the church at Thessalonica soon after A.D. 50, and consisted of two letters, both by Paul; but we may surmise that in due course a copy of his letter to neighbouring Philippi was added to their 'canon', while doubtless copies of their own two prized letters were sent to the Philippian church. Paul himself gave the initial impetus for such a practice in Asia Minor (cf. Col. 4: 16).

By about the year 90, many churches possessed a collection of Paul's letters, and early in the second century the four Gospels were brought together (conceivably from original 'homes' in Syria, Italy, Greece and Asia Minor respectively). It is generally agreed that Luke's two books, the third Gospel and Acts, were originally two parts of a single work; the incorporation of the first part of his history in the fourfold Gospel left the second part to fend for itself, but it was well able to stand on its own merits, and besides it served admirably as an introduction to the collection of Paul's letters. The second century churches, then, had two collections of inspired and authoritative books, above and beyond the Old Testament Scriptures, 'the Gospel' and 'the Apostle'. Acts was also recognized, and the other New Testament books too, although they were not all known and used so widely. (The Syriac speaking churches, for instance, ignored 2 Pet., 2 and 3 Jn, Jude and Rev. until the sixth century.) By now some Christian writings which do not figure in our New Testament were in existence, and enjoyed a certain popularity, usually purely local; we may instance the Epistle of Clement and the *Shepherd* of Hermas. The former is a genuine letter of one of the apostolic fathers, and like all such bowed to the authority of the apostles and their writings. Such works neither demanded nor received true canonical status, even though they might be reckoned among a church's literary treasures. The *Shepherd* was an allegorical work, which has often been compared with Bunyan's *Pilgrim's Progress*; it enjoyed a similar popularity in the early church.

We should remember that books were rare and expensive, and few individuals in the early church can have afforded a Christian library; hence Christian writings of any value, canonical or not, were owned by the local church and publicly read there. But we need not doubt that it was clearly recognized which books were truly inspired and authoritative, and which were of lesser value.

The Influence of Heresies

Another category of Christian literature sprang up in the second century, and to it belong most of the books in the New Testament Apocrypha. It consists mainly of religious fiction, and the majority of such works were penned under false names; Gospels, Acts, Letters and Apocalypses were written and attached to a variety of apostolic names, notably Peter's. As a rule the spuriousness of such documents is immediately evident, and few of them can have misled the majority of church leaders and congregations. But not all were simply essays in fiction; some were deliberately promulgated in the endeavour to support with apostolic authority heretical teachings. Such works constituted a real danger to simple Christians, and it is not surprising that church leaders began to feel it necessary to define the New Testament Canon, in order to ensure that such insidious propaganda should not be read in church.

One outstanding heretical teacher of the mid-second century, however, sought to limit the Canon, rather than add to it. This was Marcion, a native of Asia Minor who challenged the orthodox churchmen in Rome from about A.D. 140. He rejected the Old Testament, since he considered the God revealed in it to be a much inferior deity to the God about Whom Jesus had taught. Everything in the New Testament that smacked of the Old, or appeared to support its concepts and theology, was therefore anathema to Marcion. Small wonder, then, that he limited his canon to writings of Paul, the Apostle to the Gentiles, and Luke, the only Gentile among the Biblical writers (so far as we know). His Bible consisted of Luke's Gospel, and the Pauline Letters with the exception of those to Timothy, Titus, and the Hebrews. He excluded Acts, since it told of some activities of apostles other than Paul; to Marcion, all the other apostles were Judaizers who had adulterated the truth of the Gospel. But even the eleven books he did accept required expurgation, he felt, and he revised them in the light of his own theological views.

Orthodox church leaders, sensible to the dangers of such heretical doctrines, found themselves with a twin responsibility; they must ensure that nothing contrary to God's revealed will should be read or taught in the churches, and at the same time they must take care not to exclude any writings that bore the impress of divine inspiration. So from this time onwards Christian writings were subjected to a close scrutiny. It was only natural that some individuals and churches and groups of churches should err on the side of excessive caution, while others proved not cautious enough; but the degree of unanimity churchmen exhibited over the next century or two is remarkable. In the event, the Canon of the New Testament, as we know it, was defined not by church council, still less by papal decree, but by the consensus of Christian opinion everywhere. In this we may well see the hand of God—He who inspired the Biblical writers in the first place, guided those responsible for its safe keeping and transmission as well. Another important reason for the unanimity was that to Christians everywhere the New Testament books plainly exhibited their divine authority. The church never *gave* the New Testament writings any authority; it merely acknowledged the authority they already possessed.

After Marcion

Orthodox churchmen realized that the apostles had written with particular authority, for they had accompanied the Lord Jesus and heard His instruction at first hand. Marcion's claim that Paul was the only true apostle was accordingly rejected out of hand. *All* the apostles had spoken and written with authority. So apostolic authorship became an important criterion, though by no means the only one, or the Gospels of Mark and Luke would never have ranked with those of Matthew and John. Some care was taken to detect forgeries. The fragmentary Muratorian Canon testifies to these two interests; emanating from Rome towards the end of the second century, it gives a list of New Testament books, and says something about their origins and authenticity. It explicitly excludes several works bearing Paul's name which were recognized as Marcionite and other gnostic forgeries. It contains fully 22 of our 27 New Testament books; its only surprise inclusions are the apocryphal Wisdom of Solomon and Apocalypse of Peter, although it admits that the latter was disputed. The *Shepherd* of Hermas is mentioned as wholesome but not authoritative.

From much the same date, we have the testimony of Irenaeus. His views are of special interest, because he was widely travelled, and was acquainted with the views of church leaders in more than one region. In his writings, he refers to and quotes from all our New Testament books except five shorter ones. It is quite possible that he knew and recognized at least

some of these five as well; the lack of reference to them could well be accidental. Irenaeus made use of the Letter to the Hebrews, but he considered it of lesser worth and standing than the rest of the New Testament books known to him. Many writers of the early Christian centuries were dubious about this letter; its place in the Canon was not assured until it became universally held to be Paul's work. But it is an exaggeration to state that Hebrews was accepted for no better reason than that Paul's name became attached to it; it was rather the intrinsic value of the book that ensured its ultimate acceptance everywhere.

From the first half of the third century we have the testimony of Tertullian (of Carthage and Rome) and Origen (of Alexandria and Caesarea). Both of them accepted Hebrews as canonical, though neither writer attributed it to Paul; Tertullian claimed that the author was Barnabas, while Origen thought that some disciple of Paul must have written it. As for the rest of the New Testament (and incidentally it was Tertullian who first used this title for the Christian Canon), it is clear that by now all the books we know, with the exception of James and 2 Peter, were accepted nearly everywhere. There was no unanimity regarding these two letters as yet; but Eusebius, early in the fourth century, could say that while some still disputed the canonicity of one or two of the smaller letters, the majority of Christians accepted them. In A.D. 367, the bishop of Alexandria, Athanasius, in a letter announcing the date of Easter, listed exactly the 27 books with which we are familiar. Thirty years later the Synod of Carthage ratified this list.

Some areas, mostly of rather heterodox views, were slow to fall into line with other Christians; the Syriac church, in particular, held aloof till the sixth century (see above). But since then all branches of the Christian church have recognized the same New Testament Canon, not because of any decree, but because of the unmistakable authority and inspiration of these 27 books.

We may conclude that it seems reasonable to suppose that He who inspired the New Testament writers also overruled in the transmission of the text and in the formation of the Canon. And thus we may confidently believe that we have in our hands the Word of God, complete and unadulterated.

II. TEXT

Introduction

Marcion's challenge to his contemporaries is still a fair one: have we the New Testament books exactly, word for word, as they were penned by their authors? This is obviously a vital question; yet at first sight there seem grounds for pessimism about it, since we do not possess the autograph of any New Testament book, and although we have between four and five thousand Greek MSS of the New Testament (in whole or part), no two of them agree exactly. It is the task of textual criticism to examine these many copies and to decide which of the many variant readings are original. It is clearly an immense task, and one which can never be fully completed, if only because of the fact that new MSS keep coming to light. Textual criticism calls for critical and subjective judgments; on the other hand, it is an objective discipline to the extent that in nearly all cases of variant readings the original wording must be represented somewhere in the MSS available. There is evidence in abundance, in fact; the chief problem is that of weighing it accurately.

The problems faced by the New Testament textual critic might be compared with those that would confront someone who set about reconstructing the original wording of English hymns simply by examining a number of current hymnbooks. The compilers of some hymnbooks (notably *Songs of Praise* and the *Little Flock* collection, despite their very different character) have pursued a thorough policy of revision, and the investigator would soon discover that such books would need to be used very cautiously. It is interesting to note that some similar principles of revision were adopted by early copyists of New Testament documents and by compilers of English hymns more recently. Both groups wanted to 'improve' their material in various respects. (See below, *Variant Readings*.) It would be a serious mistake to suppose that the more accurate hymnbooks presented a completely unrevised text of every hymn. And it would be an equally serious error to imagine that the earlier the date of publication the more accurate the hymnbook. These two rather natural assumptions must be avoided by every textual critic.

The Evidence

(*a*) **The Greek Manuscripts.** The witnesses, in view of their numbers, have to be marshalled into some sort of order. They have been classified in various ways. The age of the MSS is one important aspect; hand-written copies known to us date from the early second century down to and well into the age of printing. It is clear that the earlier they are, the less corrupt the text ought to be, since generations of copyists would inevitably add error to error, alteration to alteration. (But it should be noted that some early MSS were carelessly transcribed, while

some very later MSS were copied directly from early and excellent witnesses.) Some MSS were dated by those who copied them; but in any case various tests, especially the study of ancient hand-writing (palaeography), can establish the approximate age of any ancient Greek document; till the ninth century it was invariably the custom to use capital letters only, each letter separate and distinct, but thereafter a flowing script was gradually introduced. MSS using the former method are known as 'uncials', those in flowing script as 'cursives' or 'minuscules'. From the fourth century onwards, the common form of MS was the parchment (vellum) codex, the precursor of the modern book. Till then, codices made of papyrus were the norm. The original New Testament documents were probably written on papyrus scrolls; but scrolls had to be unrolled for reading purposes, and would have been too cumbersome for documents longer than Luke's Gospel, so in the papyrus scroll era the New Testament could never circulate as a whole.

The MSS of the New Testament in Greek can usefully be classed in three categories, then, papyri, uncials and cursives. Late papyri are however less important than early uncials, and in turn, some cursives of good pedigree are more valuable than some late uncials; the value of a MS depends on the value of that from which it was copied.

(*b*) **Lectionaries.** Besides Greek MSS of the New Testament or its component parts, there are three other sources of evidence. The first of these are the lectionaries—MSS containing New Testament passages arranged in accordance with the church calendar, to be read publicly at services. Of the four types of witness, this has been the least studied to date.

(*c*) **Versions.** From very early Christian days it has been the practice to translate the New Testament into other languages, and the early versions of the New Testament are therefore important witnesses to the Greek text. The most valuable versions are those in Latin, Syriac and the Coptic dialects; before A.D. 500 the New Testament had been translated into Armenian, Georgian and Ethiopic as well. But the value of this type of evidence is limited by two considerations: first, a translation can bear witness only to the *meaning* of the original, not to its exact words; and secondly, these versions in turn have a textual history, which requires detailed examination. There are extant far more MSS of the Latin than the Greek New Testament. Indeed, in the fourth century, there were so many variations in the Old Latin versions that Pope Damasus commissioned Jerome to make a careful revision, which we know as the Vulgate;

but the history of variant readings in the Latin New Testament did not cease with its publication—in fact, the Vulgate was afterwards 'corrupted' by intrusions from the Old Latin texts it was intended to supersede.

The Syriac equivalent of the Vulgate, the Peshitta, was published at much the same time. Behind it lay the Old Syriac versions. Earlier still, the four Gospels had been woven into a harmony called the Diatessaron by a man called Tatian (*c.* A.D. 180). Unfortunately no copy of it remains, except in translation, but it seems to have affected the later text of the Syriac Gospels, and perhaps the Gospels text in other languages too.

(*d*) **Patristic Quotations.** The early church fathers quoted scripture very freely, and bear witness to the text they knew. But a new problem faces us here; we have no way of telling when they were quoting accurately, when they were quoting (perhaps inaccurately) from memory, or when they were themselves 'improving' the text. Furthermore, these writings too have their own textual history, as they were copied and recopied; and since not all the fathers wrote in Greek, the factor of translation is again a problem. The special value of patristic evidence is that we know exactly when and where the fathers lived; as we shall see, knowledge of locale as well as date can be useful.

Variant Readings

It may fairly be asked why there should be so much variation in the MSS. The first reason is simply that until printing was invented, a number of variations from one MS to another were bound to occur, however careful the scribes. All ancient documents which passed down from hand to hand demonstrate the difficulties of such transmission. Such accidental changes (mis-spellings, mis-readings, omissions and repetitions) can usually be readily identified and corrected by the expert.

But in the New Testament far more variations were deliberately introduced, by scribes who thought (not always without justification) that they should 'correct' what they found written in front of them. Such alterations were intended to improve the grammar, sense, or the theology. Another type of 'improvement', sometimes unconsciously done, was the assimilation of similar or parallel passages; thus a copyist thoroughly familiar with Matthew's Gospel would frequently introduce 'Mattheanisms' into Mark's Gospel.

Sometimes scribes made considerable additions to the text, on the basis of extra material known to them; this happens particularly in the Gospels and Acts. Two such additional passages amount to twelve verses each in length (see Appendix A).

It will be seen that the textual critic has not only to attempt to reconstruct the original readings, but also to explain the reasons for the alterations.

Criteria

How is the investigator to decide which readings are original? There are certain basic principles which may be applied. First, it is the case that the true text is usually shorter than its 'improvements', since scribes tended to expand the text in an effort to clarify it. Secondly, it is often true that the original reading is the one that seems at first sight least probable, for difficult and 'improbable' statements were precisely those that needed altering and amending. Copyists rarely made easy sentences difficult! Thirdly, the expert can employ linguistic, stylistic, and doctrinal analysis; the New Testament writers have clearly recognizable characteristics. Finally, the textual critic must be guided by the best MSS available.

On the negative side there are certain errors to be avoided. It must not be thought that the true reading can be elicited by taking the majority verdict of the MSS; on the contrary, it is now certain that the majority of MSS belong to the least reliable textual 'type'. But the mistake to be avoided at all costs is that of reconstructing the text according to one's own theological presuppositions. The authenticity of a verse must never be defended simply because it happens to be a useful peg to hang a doctrine on.

History of the Text

We can only guess at the history of New Testament transmission in the first two or three centuries A.D., in the light of later phenomena. It seems that the majority of variant readings crept into the text during this period. Among the early Christians there were probably few trained scribes, so mistakes in copying will have been plentiful; and it was only in the earliest period that there were 'floating' traditions about Jesus and the apostles, which could be inserted in the texts.

In due course there emerged a number of distinct textual families, which scholars have come to associate with several great centres of early Christianity. (The MSS in any one family are not exact replicas of one another, but they tend to show similar characteristics, recognizable to experts.) It seems that at these centres a careful revision of the text was made at one time or another, in an early effort to get rid of the multiplicity of variant readings, and to impose a standard text. Thus a measure of uniformity resulted, as MSS were copied and recopied from these basic standard texts. The families generally recognized today are commonly called Alexandrian, Western, Caesarean, Syriac and Byzantine. The Byzantine was the latest of these, and the one which eventually became standard throughout Christendom. Naturally enough, it was used for the earliest printed Greek New Testaments. Erasmus prepared the first Greek New Testament for the press (1516); in a revision of it by Stephanus published in 1633, the printing house (Elzevir) could claim that the Greek text used was accepted by everyone—the much publicized 'Received Text'. But gradually more and more MSS of great age have come to light, and by the nineteenth century it became apparent that the Received Text must be set aside, and attempts made to reconstruct the original text. Several scholars made their contributions to the new science, but the outstanding names are those of B. F. Westcott and F. J. A. Hort, whose text (1881) and whose principles of action have remained fundamental for more recent researches.

The Families

Setting aside the Byzantine text, Westcott and Hort had to choose between the Alexandrian and Western families (the Caesarean and Syriac families were not viewed as distinct from the Western until the present century). The Western MSS are characterized by frequent additions and interpolations, which Westcott and Hort decided could rarely be original; and so they treated the Alexandrian MSS (especially Codices Vaticanus and Sinaiticus, both dating from the early fourth century) as the superior text. They dubbed this text 'neutral'; but it is now clear that it was as much a revised text as any other. Papyri found since 1930 antedate the revisions (probably none of which was made much before A.D. 300) which resulted in the various families, and their affinities are clearly mixed. Today, therefore, textual experts do not lean too heavily on any one family, but use the best individual MSS available and apply all suitable criteria to each individual variant reading; sometimes even Byzantine readings have been accepted as original after all.

Conclusion

A great deal of intensive research yet remains to be done in the field of New Testament textual criticism; considerable uncertainty about the exact wording often remains, although the vast majority of variant readings have no appreciable effect on the meaning, especially in translation. It is to be noted that all the research of the last 150 years has not presented us with a radically different Bible; not one article of the Christian creed has been overthrown by newly accepted readings. We may perhaps lose favourite verses, such as 'all things work together for good . . .' (Rom. 8: 28, AV), but usually the same thought

can be found elsewhere in Scripture. (Many of us feel happier to think that 'God'—cf. RSV or NEB—rather than 'things' is at work.) But on the other hand, views and doctrines based on single verses and more particularly on single words, are always liable to be upset by textual criticism.

Those who value the Word of God must be grateful to those scholars who so painstakingly strive to know and show the exact words of Scripture as originally written; and we must always be willing to accept the facts they elicit and set before us, often by the medium of up-to-date translations of the Bible.

Appendix A

Some examples of variant readings, comparing AV with RSV.

(*a*) Mt. 6: 13; Lk. 11: 4. The final sentence of the Lord's Prayer (as we know it), derived from 1 Chr. 29: 11, was obviously a liturgical addition in Matthew; it can command only Caesarean and Byzantine support. Luke's version originally finished at the word 'temptation', but some Western and the Caesarean MSS harmonized it with Matthew's.

(*b*) Mk 16: 9-20. This section is omitted by the principal Alexandrian authorities, included by the Caesarean, while the Syriac and Western MSS are divided. The style is not that of Mark; and there is no reason why if genuine it should have been omitted by so many MSS. It must have been a very early, and indeed valuable, independent summary of resurrection appearances, subsequently added to Mark's record.

(*c*) Jn 5: 4. This verse is omitted by the Bodmer Papyrus, the Alexandrian MSS, and the leading Western MS. It is clearly an interpolation, designed to lay a foundation for the paralytic's remarks in verse 7. Whether the additional sentence records fact or superstition is a question outside the scope of textual criticism.

(*d*) Jn 7: 53-8: 11. The story of the woman taken in adultery is left out, or placed elsewhere (even in Luke's Gospel!), by all but Western and many late MSS. While the story may well be true, stylistic analysis indicates that John was not the writer.

(*e*) Eph. 1: 1. There are some grounds for thinking that this Letter was originally intended to circulate; this view is perhaps supported by the fact that the words 'in Ephesus' are omitted by the Chester Beatty Biblical Papyrus II (P46) and the leading Alexandrian MSS.

(*f*) 1 Jn 5: 7 (AV). The most spurious verse in the AV! The sentence has not even the support of the Byzantine family—it is found in just a few very late MSS. Erasmus included it in his printed text only with reluctance and under pressure. It must have been interpolated to give an explicit Biblical expression of a Trinitarian formula.

Appendix B

Some famous manuscripts.

(*a*) A fragment of papyrus (P52), now in the John Rylands Library, Manchester, containing a few verses from Jn 18, is the earliest extant New Testament MS; it dates from A.D. 100-150.

(*b*) A very valuable papyrus (Bodmer II; P66), now at Geneva, was only published in 1956-58. It contains John's Gospel, though with gaps.

(*c*) The Chester Beatty Biblical Papyri I, II and III (P45, P46, P47), housed mainly in Dublin, date from the third century, and cover most of the New Testament, though with gaps. The text of Mark is of the Caesarean family.

(*d*) The fourth century Codex Sinaiticus (‎א), in the British Museum, includes the whole New Testament. Its text is Alexandrian.

(*e*) The fourth century Codex Vaticanus (B), in the Vatican City, has all the New Testament except the Pastoral Epistles, Philemon and Revelation. Its text is Alexandrian.

(*f*) The early fifth century Codex Alexandrinus (A), in the British Museum, includes the whole New Testament, with some gaps. It seems to be a precursor of the Byzantine textual family.

(*g*) Codex Bezae (D), in Cambridge University Library, the chief witness to the Western text, dates from the fifth or sixth century. It contains the Gospels and Acts, with some gaps.

BIBLIOGRAPHY

On the Canon:

BLACKMAN, E. C., *Marcion and his Influence* (London, 1948).

FILSON, F. V., *Which Books belong in the Bible?* (Philadelphia, 1957).

GRANT, R. M., *The Formation of the New Testament* (London, 1965).

On the Text:

FOX, A., *Meet the Greek Testament* (London, 1952).

KENYON, F. G., *The Text of the Greek Bible* (rev. edn., London, 1949).

METZGER, B. M., *The Text of the New Testament* (Oxford, 1964).

ROBERTSON, A. T., *Studies in the Text of the New Testament* (New York, 1926).

TAYLOR, V., *The Text of the New Testament* (London, 1961).

TWILLEY, L. D., *The Origin and Transmission of the New Testament* (Edinburgh, 1957).

On both:

BRUCE, F. F., *The Books and the Parchments* (London, 1963).

McNEILE, A. H., *Introduction to the Study of the New Testament* (London, 1953).

SOUTER, A., *The Text and Canon of the New Testament* (2nd edn., London, 1954).

See also relevant articles in *The New Bible Dictionary* (ed. J. D. DOUGLAS, London, 1962) and *Peake's Commentary on the Bible* (rev. ed., M. BLACK and H. H. ROWLEY, London, 1962).

THE LANGUAGE OF
THE NEW TESTAMENT

DAVID J. A. CLINES

The language of the NT writings, at least in their present form, is Greek. But Greek has been for more than three thousand years a living language, and subject throughout this period to a multitude of changes, so that the Greek of each century is recognizably different from that of the previous one. The NT, belonging as it does to the first century A.D., is written in the Greek of that period, known as 'Koinē' or Common Greek.

DEVELOPMENT OF THE KOINĒ

The dominating trends in the development of the Greek language were largely dictated by the political history of the Greek people. In the pre-classical period of Greek, Greece consisted of geographically isolated, politically auto-nomous city-states; the variety of the Greek dialects was merely an expression of this insularity.

The first movement towards a common dialect for all the Greeks was made by one such city-state, Athens. Its founding, early in the fifth century B.C., of a Greek naval confederacy spread the influence of Attic, its own dialect, far beyond the walls of the city: the adminis-tration of the league, as well as the transactions of Athenian merchants throughout the Aegean, was conducted in Attic, which gained thereby considerable status as a *lingua franca*. Athens' political supremacy was short-lived, but the fifth century was also witnessing in Athens an unparalleled flowering of culture which earned for it, far more permanently than did its fleet, the title of 'the Greece of Greece'. By the end of the century, Attic could boast of being the paramount dialect of Greece; was it not the language of Sophocles, Aristophanes, Thucy-dides, to name but three representative giants?

It was in this role as purveyor of culture and literature that Attic was adopted into the court of the Macedonian kings. And it was one of their number, Alexander the Great (356-323 B.C.), who made Greek an imperial language, first by imposing a unity upon the Greeks which they had never been able to achieve by their own efforts, and secondly by his remarkable eastern conquests which carried him, and Greek language and civilization, as far as India. Not only was Greek the administrative language of this now enormous empire, which encompassed Asia Minor, Syria, Palestine, Mesopotamia, and the lands to the east as far as the Indus, as well as Egypt and Greece itself, but also his garrisons and colonies throughout the empire were natural centres for the dissemination of the language. By the time of Roman expansion outside Italy and the eventual incorporation of the greater part of Alexander's empire into the Roman Empire, Greek was firmly entrenched as the official, and often as the vernacular, language everywhere in the Near East.

Not all, by any means, of Alexander's soldiers and settlers were Attic-speakers, and though Attic enjoyed the sanction of the Macedonian court, in the mêlée of Greek dialects that was to be heard in the empire, some of Attic's idiosyncrasies, which sounded strange to the ears of most Greeks, were eliminated in favour of features more charac-teristic of the other dialects. The resultant idiom was in fact a compromise between the strongest (Attic) and the majority.

Besides this blending of the Greek dialects, there were other forces at work towards establishing a new set of distinctive charac-teristics for the common language. By the time of the NT, most of the speakers of the Koinē were non-Greeks, and to many of them Greek was a second language; hence inevitably a certain diminution of the precision and elegance of the classical Attic tongue.

What would have appeared the most startling change to the ears of a fifth-century Athenian could he have been confronted with a Greek-speaker of the first century A.D. would have been that from a tonic accent to a stress accent; traces of a tendency towards a stress accent are discernible in Greek of pre-Koinē times, but the difficulties of non-Greeks with an unaccustomed tonal system must have hastened the process (an Englishman used to a stress accent in English finds the tone system of Chinese equally difficult).

Other changes in the vocabulary and grammar of Greek, often significant for the interpretation of the NT, had taken place; the following examples illustrate how inaccurate a reading of the NT solely in the light of classical Greek must be. There is a general tendency toward the weakening of meaning: *trōgō*, which meant 'gnaw' in Attic, means simply 'eat' in colloquial Koinē; *ekballō* 'cast out' can mean 'lead forth' in Koinē (e.g. Mk I: 12). Compound verbs replace simple ones: *peripateō* 'walk' is now used where simple *pateō* once sufficed. There is increasing failure to draw the precise distinctions so characteristic of the classical language. Thus partially synonymous words tend to become confused, so that, for instance, no firm line can be drawn in the NT between *kalos* and *agathos* 'good', or between *phileō* and *agapaō* 'to love'. Superlative is at times used for comparative, and diminutives without special diminutive force. The meaning of particles, prepositions, and conjunctions, and the classical distinction between the tenses of the verb have all become blurred. Partly in reaction to these confusions, and partly perhaps in response to the needs of non-Greeks, there is an emphasis on clarity which a Greek of classical times would feel to be otiose: personal pronouns are inserted to make subject and object of a verb explicit, though in classical Greek they are regularly omitted when they may be understood from the context; the use of certain prepositions (*eis, en, ek*) has been greatly increased to make everywhere explicit prepositional notions which in classical Greek were felt to be implicit in the verb. Simplicity is everywhere a dominant motif, most noticeably perhaps in the sentence-structure of Koinē writings; it is a far cry from the complexity of the Thucydidean or Demosthenic period to the simple sentences of the Gospel of Mark. But the same tendency has been at work less obtrusively in the virtual disappearance of the optative mood, and in the elimination of many anomalous nouns and verbs, difficult to non-Greeks because not regularly declined or conjugated. Thus the normal word for 'ship', *naus*, occurs but once in the NT (in Acts), for its place has been taken by the regularly declined *ploion;* difficult verbs of the type of *histēmi* 'set up' are being replaced by new formations like *histanō*, which conforms to a more regular pattern.

It remains to remark that the foregoing tendencies appear for the most part further worked out in modern Greek. The synonymity of *kalos* and *agathos*, for instance, has resulted in the virtual elimination of *agathos* as superfluous; the increasing use of the prepositions has made the dative case unnecessary, and except in a few stereotyped expressions it no longer survives.

RELATIONSHIP OF NT GREEK TO KOINĒ

It must be observed that the term Koinē covers a wide variety of strata of language, both spoken and written. Of course, it is impossible for us to be informed of the exact nature of the spoken language, yet extant letters and other documents composed unreflectingly by people of little literary training approximate closely enough to the spoken language. At the other end of the spectrum from popular language is the formalized literary Koinē of writers like the historians Polybius, Diodorus Siculus, Plutarch, and Josephus. (The works of other authors of the period, such as Dionysius of Halicarnassus and Lucian, who wrote in an artificial Atticizing style, are useless for the study of the Koinē, except in so far as they unwittingly betray traces of the current vernacular in spite of their intended adherence to archaic models.) At what point in the gradation from literary Koinē to the language of the common man the NT stands is a disputed matter; but it is generally agreed that, along with the *Discourses* of the philosopher Epictetus, the NT has most in common with the popular language of the non-literary papyri. A more precise setting of the NT as a whole cannot be made, for there is a considerable range within the NT itself from the most literary parts (Hebrews, parts of Luke-Acts) to the least (Revelation).

Semitisms

The language of the NT, although basically the non-literary Koinē of the first century A.D., is set apart from it to some extent by distinctive features, most of which it shares with other examples of 'biblical Greek' (principally the Septuagint version of the OT [the LXX]; also the pseudepigrapha). These features, termed Semitisms, were introduced into the NT in two ways: (i) as quotations from the LXX or adaptations to its style (ii) as direct translation from a Semitic original.

(i) Most Jews of the first century A.D. read their Bible in Greek (i.e. the LXX), for Hebrew and Aramaic were little used outside Palestine. (The letter to the Hebrews was written in Greek!) Hence Jewish Christians especially would naturally find their vocabulary and style when speaking of religious subjects to be largely fashioned by the familiar phrases of the LXX. But the LXX is not always a model of good Greek style; some portions are, for reverential reasons, scrupulously literal renderings of the

Hebrew, and hence far from idiomatic Greek. Thus there are taken into the NT expressions that are really Hebrew idiom in Greek clothing.

It was even possible for a writer who knew neither Hebrew nor Aramaic to adapt his style to that of the LXX and thus write a Semiticizing Greek. Such appears to have been the case with Luke, the opening chapters of whose Gospel in particular abound with Semitisms. These are perhaps due to a Semitic source which he is translating, but there appear to be other instances where Luke, uninfluenced by Semitic sources, has yet written in Septuagintal style. (Similarly John Bunyan could write in Authorized Version English, which is full of Hebraisms, without knowing any Hebrew himself.)

(ii) It is plain that the sayings of Jesus recorded in Greek in the Gospels were originally uttered in Aramaic (or perhaps in Hebrew), and that therefore there has been translation from one to the other at some stage in their transmission. So it is not surprising that above all other parts of the NT the words of Jesus display evidence of their Aramaic originals. Thus a passage like Mt. 11: 28-30, when retranslated into Palestinian Aramaic, exhibits not only poetical structure, but also alliteration and even rhyme, and shows incidentally that the model our Lord chose for His addresses was the poetical 'sermon' of the Hebrew prophets.

More, however, than the sayings-material in the Gospels shows traces of its Semitic origin. Some scholars have postulated Aramaic documents behind all the Gospels and Acts, but the evidence does not compel us to go so far, and is fully satisfied if we see in Matthew, Mark, and John men who thought in Semitic and wrote in Greek, and in Luke a Greek writing in the familiar style of the LXX, with reference to Aramaic sources as occasion demanded. A good case can be made out that parts at least of Revelation have been translated from Hebrew, or perhaps from Aramaic. Of the rest of the NT writers it may be said that their Greek, though generally idiomatic, often bears a Semitic colouring.

It should be remarked that an expression in the NT may be a Semitism even although it can be paralleled in extra-Biblical Greek. In some cases an expression, while not foreign to the idiom of the Greek language, but rarely attested, has become in the NT a living expression, under the influence of a Semitic idiom. Thus the Semitic nature of the expression lies not in its existence, but in the frequency of its occurrence.

It is often not easy to distinguish between a Hebraism and an Aramaism; for first, the two languages have many idioms in common; and secondly, the Aramaic of the period is best known from targums (explanatory translations of the OT), so that what appears to be an Aramaic expression may be only a literal translation of a Hebrew one. So no attempt is made here to unravel the intricate evidence; rather, various Semitisms are grouped together to illustrate the effect of its Semitic background on the NT.

(*a*) *Parataxis* (the use of co-ordinate, rather than subordinate, clauses). This stylistic characteristic is common to Hebrew and Aramaic, and is especially frequent in Mark. For example, Luke says, 'Having left our homes we have followed you' (18: 28); Mark, 'we have left everything and followed you' (10: 28). But simplicity of style is a general characteristic also of Koinē; the Semitic element lies probably in the frequency of its use.

(*b*) *Parallelism*, well-known in Heb. poetry, is found in many sayings of Jesus, *e.g.* Mt. 5: 45; Lk. 12: 48.

(*c*) *Adjectival Genitive*. Hebrew, being poor in adjectives, often expressed an adjectival notion by appending a noun in a genitival relation; thus 'a man of wealth' means 'a wealthy man', and 'the hill of my holiness' means 'my holy hill'. In NT some clear cases are: 'the son of his love' for 'his beloved son' (Col. 1: 13), 'the power of his might' for 'his mighty power' (Eph. 1: 19), 'the mammon of unrighteousness' for 'unrighteous mammon' (Lk. 16: 9), 'the body of this death' for 'this mortal body' (Rom. 7: 24), 'men of (God's) good-will' for '(God's) chosen people' (Lk. 2: 14). But it is not always easy to decide whether the Semitic idiom is being used; does 'the wealth of his glory' mean 'his glorious wealth' (Eph. 3: 16)?

(*d*) *The 'Infinitive Absolute' construction*. The 'absolute' form of the Heb. infinitive is used with a finite form of the same verb to express emphasis or duration, *e.g. môt tāmût* 'dying (infin.) thou shalt die'='thou shalt surely die' (Gen. 2: 17). This idiom occurs in NT in quotations from LXX (*e.g.* 'blessing I will bless you', Heb. 6: 14), and also a few times in Luke: 'with desire I have desired' (*epithymiā epethymēsa*) = 'I have earnestly desired' (Lk. 22: 15); 'with a commandment we commanded' (*parangeliā parēngeilamen*)='we strictly enjoined' (Ac. 5: 28). Cf. also Ac. 4: 17 (*v.l.*); 23: 14; Jn 3: 29. The idiom can be paralleled from classical sources, but seems to be a Septuagintalism in Luke.

(*e*) *Indefinite Third Person Plural*. Where in English we might use the passive or 'one' when the subject of the verb is indefinite (cf. French *on*, German *man*), Heb. and Aram. tend to use a third person plural verb (like English 'they say' = 'indefinite persons *or* people in general say'). Thus in Jn 15: 6, 'they gather them (the branches) and cast them into the fire', we do not need to ask who 'they' are; it merely = 'are gathered'. Cf. also Lk. 12: 20 'this night they (indefinite) require thy soul'; 6: 38 (where both passive and third person plural are used); Mk 10: 13; Mt. 5: 15. In classical Gk. this construction is used mostly with verbs of saying (so also in modern Gk.), but under the influence of Aram., which avoids the passive, its use is extended in NT.

(*f*) '*And it came to pass that . . .*' Perhaps the most conspicuous Semitism in the NT, it has a similar connotation in the Gospel narratives as it does if used today: it is a direct reminiscence of Biblical language. It is not idiomatic Gk., but a literal translation of the common Heb. phrase *way^ehî w^e* (lit. 'and it befell and . . .').

(*g*) '*Not all*' = '*none*'. In place of the usual Gk. word for 'none, no one', we sometimes find 'not all', formed on the model of a Heb. idiom (*e.g.* 'all plants of the field were not as yet' = 'not one plant was yet', Gen. 2: 5). Similarly *ou pas* in NT: 'all flesh would not be saved' = 'no flesh would be saved' (Mt. 24: 22). So also Rom. 3: 20; 1 C. 1: 29; Ac. 10: 14; 2 Pet. 1: 20. But not every instance of 'not all' requires this interpretation; 'not every one who says Lord, Lord' (Mt. 7: 21) means exactly what it means in English, 'some, but not all'.

(*h*) '*Answered and said*'. Various tautological formulas for introducing discourse are modelled on the Heb. idiom which prefixes direct speech with 'saying'. Hence in NT we find the types 'he answered and said' (*e.g.* Jn 1: 48) (often in Jn, seldom in Mk and Lk., never in Mt.), 'he answered, saying' (Lk. 3: 16), 'answering, he said' (Mt. 3: 15) (not common in Jn). On the same pattern 'saying' is used with other verbs, such as 'witness' (Ac. 13: 22), and 'write' (Lk. 1: 63).

(*i*) *Various pleonasms*. Heb. is given to describing activity with a wealth of detail we find unnecessary, though perhaps picturesque, *e.g.* 'he opened his mouth and spoke', 'he arose and went', 'he lifted up his eyes and saw'. The influence of this manner of speech is seen in the following examples: 'a grain of wheat, which a man took and sowed' (Mt. 13: 31), 'I shall arise and go' (Lk. 15: 18); cf. Mt. 13: 33, 46; 25: 16; Ac. 5: 17. Very frequently 'begin' is used pleonastically, especially in Mark (*e.g.* 1: 45; 5: 17; 6: 7), but it is not pleonastic in *e.g.* Ac. 1: 1 (Acts continues what Jesus *began* to do and teach).

The Semitic background of the NT is also claimed to appear in certain places where the putative Semitic original explains a difficulty in the present Greek text. Much ingenuity has been employed in the study of such passages, but in the absence of the originals it is a hazardous task, and there is hardly a proposed solution that commands general agreement. Some examples are:

(*a*) Lk. 1: 39 (*eis polin Iouda*) seems to mean 'into the city Judah', which is curious because Judah is a province, not a city. It is suggested that *polin* 'city' represents the Aram. *m^edînah* which had meant 'province', but in the 1st cent. A.D. was coming to mean 'city'. Hence the word was ambiguous, and it is suggested that the translator (Luke or his source) chose the wrong sense. But it is easier to suppose that *eis polin Iouda* means 'into *a* city of Judah'.

(*b*) Lk. 12: 49b should mean 'How I wish it were kindled!' But the introductory word *ti* means 'what', which is almost unintelligible (RV 'what will I, if it is already kindled?'). However, the Aram. *mā'* can mean both 'what' and 'how', and it is possible that the ambiguity there is the source of the error in translation. Yet *ti* can mean 'how' in modern Gk., and it may be that it can bear this meaning in the NT also.

(*c*) Mt. 7: 6 reads 'Do not give dogs what is holy; and do not throw your pearls before swine'. It is suggested that 'holy' is a misunderstanding of the original Aram. *q^edāšā'* 'ring' as *qudšā'* 'holy' (the two words would be written identically in Aram., viz. *qdš*, but pronounced differently). 'Ring' would then be in parallelism with 'pearls': 'Do not give a ring to dogs, and do not throw your pearls before swine'. This is an attractive restoration of the original form of the saying; it may be noted, however, that many would prefer to speak not of a 'misunderstanding' by the evangelist, but of his 'interpretation' of the meaning of 'ring' as 'what is holy'.

The most obvious influence of a Semitic background on the NT, namely, Hebrew and Aramaic words transliterated into Greek, must also be mentioned. From Hebrew we have: *allēlouia, amēn, batos* 'bath' (a Heb. 8–9 gallon measure), *geenna, korban* 'gift', *koros* 'kor' (a Heb. 10–12 bushel measure), *manna, pascha* 'passover', *sabaōth, sabbaton* 'sabbath', *satanas, hyssōpos*. From Aramaic (though some of these originally were Hebrew): *abba* 'father', *elōi* 'my God', *ephphatha* 'be opened', *korbanas* 'temple treasury', *lama sabachthani* 'why hast thou forsaken me', *mammōnas* 'mammon', *maran atha* 'our Lord has come' or *marana tha* 'our Lord, come!', *rabbi* 'my master', *rabbouni* 'my lord', *raka* 'fool, empty-head', *saton*

33

'measure' (a Heb. 1½ peck measure of grain), *sikera* 'strong drink', *talitha koum(i)* 'little girl, get up!' Most of the Heb. terms survive in English, being technical terms of religion; the Aram. phrases and words from the Gospels are preserved as such, being the *ipsissima verba* of our Lord.

THE LANGUAGE OF INDIVIDUAL WRITERS

Reference has already been made to the wide variety of styles and levels of Koinē Greek in which the NT is written, and we come now to examine the styles of the individual writers in more detail.

Mark writes in a simple, straightforward style which is equally evident in Greek and in English translation. The abundant use of parataxis (*e.g.* 1: 9-13) is typical of unsophisticated writing in any language, but in the case of Mark it may also be a reflection of the Semitic speech of his reputed informant, Peter. The historic present tense (*e.g.* 2: 15, 17, 18), an element in Mark's well-known vivid style (it occurs usually at or near the beginning of a paragraph when a new scene is introduced), can be paralleled from Gk. of all times, but again may be influenced by the use in Aram. of the participial sentence. Other Semitic traces are to be found in his common use of the periphrastic present tense ('he is eating' instead of usual Gk. 'he eats'), which was just possible in Gk., but frequent in Aram. (Only Luke has a higher proportion of periphrastic presents; his are in imitation of LXX style, Mark's are through mental translation from Aram.) The word-order in Mark's sentences frequently reflects the Semitic style: while it is possible (and common with verbs of saying) to put the verb first in normal Gk., in Semitic the verb regularly comes first; so often in NT, and especially in Mark. Mark's Greek also contains a number of Latin loanwords: *e.g.*, from military and official terminology: *praitōrion* 'praetorium', *legiōn* 'legion', *kentyriōn* 'centurion', *Kaisar* 'Caesar', *phragelloō* 'to whip' (from vulgar Lat. *fragellum* 'whip'=*flagellum*), *spekou-latōr* 'spy, scout, executioner'; from commercial terminology: *modios* 'peck-measure', *dēnarion* 'denarius', *kodrantēs* 'quadrans' (the smallest Roman coin, one sixty-fourth of a denarius); and a Latin idiom, *to hikanon poiein* (15: 15) liter-ally = Lat. *satisfacere* 'to satisfy'. The deduction to be made from Mark's use of these Latinisms is not, as some have suggested, that Mark is translated from a Latin original, but that he reproduces faithfully the vernacular of the Roman Empire.

Luke writes at times in an elevated and elegant style (*e.g.* the polished opening period of the Gospel, 1: 1-4; also the well-phrased sentence, Ac. 15: 24-26), at others in imitation of the LXX or in a very ordinary Koinē (*e.g.* Lk. 1: 5 plunges immediately into Septuagintal style; the more Semitic passages appear to be either where he is dependent on an Aram. source or where he feels a Septuagintal style to be appropriate). But in general he is more conscious of style than most of the NT writers; thus in his use of Mark's material he often makes corrections and improvements in the language. Various connective particles (*te*, *de*, *oun*) and asyndeton are employed in place of Mark's ubiquitous and sometimes wearying *kai* 'and' (*e.g.* Lk. 8: 34-39; Mk 5: 14-20). He appears to go out of his way to choose a Gk. equivalent for Mark's Latin loanword, no doubt regarding the native Gk. word as more literary than the vernacular loanword. For example, *heka-tontarchēs* 'centurion' (23: 47) for Mark's *kentyriōn* (15: 39), *phoros* 'tax' (20: 22) for Mark's *kēnsos* (Mk 12: 14; also Mt. 22: 17); cf. also *epigraphē* 'title' (23: 38) instead of John's *titlos* (19: 19). Other instances of his substitutes for Mark's more colloquial vocabulary: *pais* (8: 54) 'child' for Mark's *korasion* (5: 41) 'little girl', post-classical diminutive of *korē* 'girl'; *limnē* (5: 1) 'lake' for Mark's *thalassa* (1: 16) 'sea' in classical Gk. but also 'inland lake' in Koinē; *agō* (4: 1) 'to lead' for Mark's *ekballō* (1: 12) 'to cast forth' in classical Gk. but also 'to lead out' in 1st cent. Koinē, though still colloquial. Luke uses *esthiō* exclusively for 'to eat', while Matthew (sometimes) and John (always) use the more colloquial *trōgō* ('to gnaw' in classical Gk.). Almost half of the NT occurrences of the obsolescent optative mood are found in Luke; he also perpetuates the use of the future infinitive and the future participle of purpose, which are rare elsewhere in Koinē. He keeps the classical word *heteros* 'other of two' along with *allos* 'other' which in Koinē is usurping the meaning of *heteros* (Mark never uses *heteros* [it occurs in the non-Markan ending, Mk 16: 12], and John only once); but he does not always observe the classical distinction between the two, and in *e.g.* Lk. 8: 6 he writes incorrectly *heteros*, though Mark had already used the correct *allos* (4: 5).

Matthew employs 'a correct if rather colour-less Greek which avoids the vulgar forms without displaying a mastery of the literary syntax' (J. H. Moulton). While with Mark he uses the less formal words *korasion* 'little girl' and *ekballō* 'to take out', he shows little sign in his language of his Semitic origin, and avoids in fact not a few of Luke's deliberate Hebraisms (*e.g.* *enōpion* 'before the face of' =

Heb. *lipnê;* the periphrastic present, common in Luke and Mark, is rare in Matthew). He alone of all NT writers distinguishes correctly between *eis* 'into' and *en* 'in' (Mk 1: 39, for instance, has 'preaching into (*eis*) the synagogues'; in modern Gk. *eis* has absorbed the functions of *en*, and the process is already at work in Koinē).

John's Greek is, even more than Mark's, the most colloquial in the NT, and also the furthest advanced in the direction of modern Gk. For example, Attic *piezō* 'squeeze, press hard' is only in Lk. 6: 38, but the Doric equivalent *piazō* is colloquial for 'seize' (8 times in John, 4 in the rest of the NT), and hence modern Gk. *pianō* 'seize'; *opsarion* and *prosphagion*, which meant in classical Gk. 'relish, tidbit' (*i.e.* cooked food eaten with a meal), mean in colloquial Koinē 'fish' (both words only in John), and modern Gk. for 'fish' is *psari*, from *opsarion*. John's simple and repetitive style is *de l'homme même*, and is not indicative of any difficulty with the language, in which he finds himself completely at home.

Revelation is the work of an author, according to C. F. D. Moule, 'who writes like a person who, nurtured in a Semitic speech, is only just learning to write in Greek. He is capable of horrifying grammatical blunders and patently Semitic idioms, but is not thereby prevented from achieving extraordinary power and sometimes a quite unearthly beauty'. So striking, indeed, is the difference between the Greek of Revelation and the Greek of John's Gospel and Letters, that many have found it difficult to believe that both styles of Greek are from the pen of one writer; but the difficulty may be overcome by assuming that John's original Aramaic (or Hebrew) has been translated into Greek by a scribe with very meagre knowledge of (or respect for) grammar. The most patent solecisms of Revelation are failures to observe grammatical concord, *e.g.* 'from Jesus Christ (genitive case), the faithful and true witness (nominative case)' (the latter phrase should also have been in the genitive); 'saying' is often used without regard to the case or person with which it should agree (very possibly on the model of the indeclinable Heb. *lē'mōr* 'saying'). The use of prepositions is interesting: instrumental *en* = 'by' (like Heb. *bᵉ*) is particularly frequent; so also *enōpion* 'before' (= Heb. *lipnê*); *syn* 'with' (frequent only in Luke and Paul) has yielded to *meta* 'with' (which, in the form *me*, alone survives in modern Gk.); the classical *hypo* with the accusative case for 'under' has been replaced by the compound adverb *hypokatō* (a formation typical of Koinē). Not all instances, however, of grammatical anomalies are to be attributed to the author's Semitic background, for many may be paralleled in the least literary of the papyri from Egypt; lack of grammatical concord, especially with participles, can be observed in mediaeval Greek, and perhaps the author of Revelation is, in this instance, but an early witness to a long history of confusion which culminated in the indeclinable participle of modern Greek (*blepontas* is 'seeing', in whatever case, person, or gender).

Paul is capable of a lively and forceful idiomatic Greek. His style is often tortuous and cumbrous, but equally often rhythmic and natural. A few examples will suffice to show that he writes an educated Greek: the well-known classical idiom of a neuter adjective for an abstract noun appears in the NT almost exclusively in Paul (*e.g. to chrēston* 'the good, kind thing' = 'goodness, kindness', Rom. 2: 4; *to mōron* = 'foolishness', 1 C. 1: 25); he uses the optative mood more frequently than any other NT author. Semitisms of grammar are virtually non-existent in his writings (though see 'not all = none' and 'adjectival genitive' above); but on every page there may be found many words which reveal their Semitic content by forcing their interpreter to turn to his LXX rather than his classical lexicon for a correct understanding of them (*e.g. eirēnē* 'peace', *diathēkē* 'covenant', *euangelion* 'gospel', *epistrephō* 'convert', *eidōlon* 'idol', *peripateō* 'walk' (in the moral sense).

Hebrews is the most literary of the books of the NT; Origen recognized it as 'more Greek' than any of Paul's letters. An instructive example of the author's adherence to classical models is his avoidance of hiatus (in some circles it was considered inelegant to use a word beginning with a vowel if the previous word ended in a vowel, certain unavoidable words excepted). Other instances of his careful grammar are: use of neuter adjective for abstract noun (*e.g. to asthenes* 'weakness', 7: 18); future infinitive and future participle (both only in Acts and Hebrews in NT); the conjunction *hina* is used only in its classical sense 'in order that', although Koinē was introducing *hina* clauses in various functions, notably to replace the infinitive, a process well nigh complete in modern Gk. The more formal classical particles like *men . . . de* 'on the one hand . . . on the other hand' are rare in the NT, but Hebrews, together with Acts and some Pauline letters, has examples of this combination; the only NT occurrence of the classical and literary *dēpou* 'of course, as you know' is in Heb. 2: 16; *hothen* 'whence' (= 'for which reason') occurs 6 times in Hebrews and elsewhere in the NT only in Acts and Matthew (once each); Attic *kathaper* 'as' appears only in Hebrews and Paul. The author of Hebrews is very evidently steeped in the language of the LXX, but its Greek does little harm to his; some Semitic touches are: 'spoken by (*en*, lit. 'in', like Heb. *be*) the prophets' (1: 1), 'an evil heart of unbelief' (3: 12) (adjectival genitive).

James is not unaware of classical style; witness the classical locutions *age nyn* 'come now!' (4: 13; 5: 1) (nowhere else in NT), *chrē* 'it is necessary' (replaced in the rest of NT by *dei*), *eoika* 'seem' (only here in NT), and *tis* 'a certain' in the classical sense of 'a kind of' (1: 18) (thus only elsewhere in Luke and Hebrews). His unhesitating and vivid choice of words declares him an expert in the Greek tongue, and few traces of Semitism can be detected. His fondness for *idou* 'behold' has been thought reminiscent of the omnipresent *hinnēh* in the OT; there is an imitation of the 'infinitive absolute' in a description of Elijah (5: 17): 'with prayer he prayed' (*proseuchē prosēuxato*) (a deliberate Septuagintalism?). 'A hearer of forgetfulness' (1: 25) for 'a forgetful hearer' likewise cannot but be Semitic.

Peter is not the ignorant fisherman sometimes imagined — 'unlearned' (*agrammatos* 'without letters') in Ac. 4: 13 does not mean 'illiterate', but 'without formal theological training'. The Greek of 1 Peter is not necessarily therefore due to Silvanus, but rather implies Peter's long familiarity with the language (his brother Andrew had a Greek name!). That he had been brought up on the LXX is evident from his numerous quotations from it and reminiscences of its language. But apart from these direct influences of the LXX on his writing, few Semitisms can be traced; 'children of obedience' (1: 14), and perhaps the participle used as an imperative (*e.g.* 3: 7 ff.) (also in Paul) may be cited. 2 Peter has been described as Atticizing and bookish, and it is striking that it contains no quotations from the LXX, only a handful of allusions to it, and barely one Semitism (*en empaigmonē empaiktai* 'mockers with mocking' [3: 3] may be an 'infinitive absolute' construction).

Jude similarly shows himself familiar with the Koinē, and shares with 2 Peter a predilection for the long and sonorous word. He appears equally innocent of Semitisms.

BIBLIOGRAPHY

Dictionaries

ARNDT, W. F., and GINGRICH, F. W., *A Greek-English Lexicon of the New Testament and other Early Christian Literature* (Chicago/Cambridge, 1957) (the best for general use).

MOULTON, J. H., and MILLIGAN, G., *The Vocabulary of the Greek Testament illustrated from the papyri and other non-literary sources* (London, 1930) (not a NT dictionary proper, but illuminates the NT from Koinē usage).

KITTEL, G., (ed.), *Theologisches Wörterbuch zum Neuen Testament* (Stuttgart, from 1933); at present being translated by G. W. Bromiley under the title *Theological Dictionary of the New Testament* (vols. 1-5, Grand Rapids, Michigan, 1964-9). A massive treatment of NT theological terms; 7 complete vols. have so far been published, covering *alpha* to *sigma*.

SOUTER, A., *A Pocket Lexicon to the Greek New Testament* (Oxford, 1916).

Grammars

FUNK, R. W., *A Greek Grammar of the New Testament and other Early Christian Literature: a revision of F. Blass and A. Debrunner, 'Grammatik des neutestamentlichen Griechisch'* (Cambridge, 1961) (an excellent grammar, convenient to use).

MOULTON, J. H., *A Grammar of New Testament Greek* (3 vols., Edinburgh, 1906, 1919-29, 1963 (vol. 3 on syntax being by N. Turner)).

MOULE, C. F. D., *An Idiom Book of New Testament Greek* (2nd edn., Cambridge, 1959).

WENHAM, J., *The Elements of New Testament Greek* (Cambridge, 1965). Replacing H. P. V. Nunn's Grammar, this is probably the best grammar for beginners; it includes exercises and vocabulary.

Other works

BLACK, M., *An Aramaic Approach to the Gospels and Acts* (3rd edn., Oxford, 1968).

BARCLAY, W., *A New Testament Wordbook* (London, 1955).

BARCLAY, W., *More New Testament Words* (London, 1958).

BARR, J., *The Semantics of Biblical Language* (Oxford, 1961).

HILL, D., *Greek Words and Hebrew Meanings* (Cambridge, 1967).

TURNER, N., *Grammatical Insights into the New Testament* (Edinburgh, 1965).

WILCOX, M., *The Semitisms of Acts* (Oxford, 1965).

ARCHAEOLOGICAL DISCOVERIES AND THE NEW TESTAMENT

A. R. MILLARD

The NT, being based upon events which took place in history, can be associated with historical information from other sources. These may be employed to supplement data in the NT and to verify it. Too often they are used by Christians attempting to 'prove' Scriptural statements, or by sceptics to discredit them. A balanced approach will remember that the NT is also an ancient document, deserving as much respect as any other writing surviving from antiquity. Of course, its particular nature will be taken into account, as will that of any text, but this does not permit one to jettison every awkward passage, any more than it allows uncritical acceptance of every word. While we are not saying that the NT is to be read solely as an historical work, our attention is directed to this general aspect in the present study.

Less value is attached by most people to archaeological discoveries relating to the NT than to those relating to the OT, because so much written information has survived from the era of Roman world rule. Moreover, the NT contains a smaller amount of narrative which might be associated with monumental remains. Thus it is not surprising that NT archaeology is frequently concerned with details, at first sight of small worth.

Documents

One category of those details is the precise meaning of words, idioms, and figures of speech. For centuries the NT stood isolated; while it could be understood with much greater surety than the Hebrew of the OT, through comparison with other Greek books, no works were known composed in quite the same form of Greek. Then, about a century ago, documents written in ink on *papyrus* (ancient equivalent of paper) desiccated in the desert sand, and others written on less perishable potsherds (*ostraca*), were unearthed in Egypt. At first they came in a trickle, the chance treasure troves of peasants and looters all over the land, then in a flood from official excavations in the rubbish heaps of several towns that flourished in the millennium 300 B.C. to A.D. 700. They were tax returns, census records, and other humdrum remnants of imperial bureaucracy, and the papers of citizens, their letters and accounts, wills and legal deeds, and some of the books they used to read. So many were obtained that a vast quantity remain unpublished; those available in catalogues need intensive further study.

Isolated examples may be amusing, pathetic, amazingly up-to-date, or may impart historically valuable information. The material as a whole is vitally important, for its language is virtually identical with New Testament Greek, that is, it reveals the language of the NT to be, basically, the language of daily life, of commerce and of government. (See 'The Language of the New Testament', pp. 30 ff.) One result is the clarification of many passages in AV by exhibition of rare words in new contexts. So legal use perhaps delimits the 'substance of things hoped for' of Heb. 11: 1 as 'the title-deeds of things hoped for', and the expression rendered 'I have all and abound' (Phil. 4: 18) and 'they have their reward' (Mt. 6: 2, 5, 16) is revealed as the formula for quitting a claim, paying in full. (On the meaning of *hypostasis* in Heb. 11: 1, see also F. F. Bruce: *The Epistle to the Hebrews*, 1964, p. 278.) The 'earnest' of Eph. 1: 14 (AV) is seen to be a payment in advance, deposit, or first instalment, of a sum due later. In a contract of apprenticeship is a penalty clause in case of slackness or truancy, and the term for that is the 'disorderly' (AV) of 2 Th. 3: 6 ff. (RSV 'idleness'). That same letter and others speak of the Lord's coming, the *parousia*. Orders from senior officers to municipal bodies require them to make elaborate preparations for the coming of the emperor (like the medieval 'royal progress'), employing *parousia* for the state visit.

37

In Lk. 17: 21 stands the enigmatic clause 'the kingdom of God is in the midst of you'. 'Within you' is a credible rendering of the Greek phrase, but study of the papyri and of other examples of Greek literature has demonstrated that 'to hand, within reach' was the everyday meaning. A doctor wrote asking for a woollen jacket to be sent to him 'so that I may have it with me' in a letter of *c.* A.D. 270. In Luke this produces a sense which is arguably more in agreement with the tenor of other NT passages.

The papyri yield many further linguistic secrets, and, more than these, they offer a vast number of facts on many aspects of life. While the Egyptian context should be remembered, much can be transferred to the Palestinian scene, or to any other province of Rome in the east Mediterranean region. In the sphere of government light is thrown on the census procedure and the problems concerning the date of the Lord's birth (see below, p. 40). A notice of A.D. 104 ordering persons to register in their home districts has survived, such as caused Joseph and Mary to go to Bethlehem, their ancestral home, and there are several actual census returns. Evidence is plentiful, also, of the resentment aroused by the oppressive taxes levied by Rome and the system of farming out the collections to grasping 'publicans' like Zaccheus. Important official letters, written by clerks, amanuenses, from dictation, or transcribed from shorthand notes (several systems of shorthand are attested, and some manuals have been recovered), were authenticated by the high-ranking sender adding the words of greeting in his own handwriting. Paul took this action when he felt a need to assert his apostolic authority and the genuineness of his words (*e.g.* Gal. 6: 11; 2 Th. 3: 17). Seals were impressed upon the outside of rolled-up letters and documents and upon consignments of goods as a guarantee against falsification or tampering.

More personal correspondence abounds. In one letter a 'prodigal son' begged for his mother's pardon, he was ashamed to return home because of his ragged clothing, and admitted that his condition was his own fault. In different vein, an absent husband wrote to his wife affectionately, urging her to care for their child, yet instructing her to expose (to death) a girl baby should she give birth to one. Christianity offered a quite opposite ethic, demanding a very real conversion. Other social customs repugnant to Christians (and to others nowadays through their influence) appear in the papyri beside allusions to diverse religious beliefs, Egyptian, Greek, Jewish, Roman, and mystery cults, all

rivals and enemies of the new faith. (See 'The Religious Background, Pagan', p. 67.)

Official and legal papers normally bear a date, following one or two of the several systems in use, so from careful scrutiny of their handwriting and other characteristics, charts can be drawn to show the changing styles of script over the centuries. From them the undated texts can be allocated approximate dates by minute comparison. The value of this exercise is proved when copies of NT books are disinterred, since their worth in textual criticism largely depends upon their age. Works of literature rarely bear a date themselves.

Several pieces of NT books (and some of the OT in Greek) were found in the rubbish heaps, the oldest being a fragment of John's Gospel said to date from the decades prior to A.D. 150 (now in the Rylands Library, Manchester). More complete copies, parts of small libraries, found elsewhere in Egypt, comprise one or more books copied in the years around A.D. 200 and during the subsequent centuries (the Chester Beatty Collection, Dublin, and the Bodmer Collection, Geneva, are two major groups). To date nearly fifty Greek NT papyri are known as old as, or older than, the famous Sinai and Vatican codices (*c.* A.D. 350). Some of them enable us to read many parts of the text as it was copied little more than a century after the last books were composed. (See 'Text and Canon, II: Text', pp. 25.) An interesting sidelight is the suggestion that our current book form was brought into general use for literary works by the early Christians; hitherto it had been a secondary form, used only for notes and technical handbooks, the usual scroll being too cumbersome for speedy reference. The multiplicity of NT manuscripts testifies to the centrality of the written word in early Christian life.

The other major collection of ancient 'papers' is the Dead Sea discovery. Aspects of language and society arise here; the theological value is discussed later (p. 41). They are by far the oldest Jewish books of their kind, showing just how the OT appeared in the Gospel period, and how one sect of religious zealots treated it. Like the papyri they provide a contemporary source for elucidating the meanings of words, especially words with ritual or legal Jewish undertones. Hebrew, Aramaic, Nabataean and Greek are the languages represented in the texts from Qumran and the slightly later ones from caves farther down the coast (*c.* A.D. 130). Hebrew was in use more extensively than suspected before, perhaps partly in patriotic fervour. The impression that many Palestinians were bilingual or trilingual which the NT conveys receives support. The very number of the Biblical scrolls (many score, and dozens of copies of certain books), some obviously used heavily, may presuppose a highly literate society (notice that a country carpenter could read, according to Lk. 4: 16). A potsherd unearthed in the ruins of the communal building at Qumran, where the Scrolls' owners evidently met, carries a student's exercise in writing the Hebrew alphabet. The same ruin contained smashed remnants of writing-benches for the scribes, and their inkwells. Undoubtedly schools existed in many other areas, apart from special centres like Qumran. Various mundane activities were carried out in the building, making it a good fount for knowledge of daily work. Thus we learn about the smithy and the potter's workshop, about a fuller's plant, a tannery (primarily, maybe, for preparing the vellum to be made into scrolls) and, in a separate place, a complete farm.

Sites

No question has ever arisen over the sites of the major cities in the NT stories. Jerusalem, Damascus, Rome stand to this day. Numerous smaller towns are difficult to locate, despite traditional identities, or sometimes because of them, for a lost town or monument can be 'found' for the pious by the more mercenary! Here the study of texts joins with ground survey and excavation to establish the terrain and occupancy of one or another site, balancing each segment of evidence in reaching a conclusion. Often the two former researches may be ambiguous, but the actual digging decisive.

Emmaus has had three candidates for its name, each of different merit, but only one agreeing in its distance from Jerusalem with the sixty furlongs given by the majority of good manuscripts of Lk. 24: 13 (other manuscripts have one hundred and sixty furlongs, the distance of the Emmaus mentioned in 1 Mac. 3: 40; 4: 1 ff.). This site, el-Qubeibeh, produced relics of the New Testament period when excavated; the traditional site at Amwas did not.

The remote town of Derbe in Anatolia (Ac. 14: 21, etc.) was an out-of-the-way backwater in Paul's day, and no one had known its exact whereabouts for centuries before 1956. In that year an inscription was deciphered relating to the citizens of Derbe in A.D. 157, and, in 1958, another was found bearing the name of a bishop of Derbe. From these stones the town can be identified with their place of origin, near Kerti Hüyük, lying about thirty miles farther east than had been surmised for the site of Derbe. Now maps of Paul's journeys may be drawn more accurately.

Cities are seldom forgotten, scenes of brief events often. In Palestine the first generation Christians did not concern themselves with the places of the gospel story, although they could say where they were if necessary; their interest lay in the fact of the story. Forty years after the Crucifixion the Roman military occupation would have hindered the sanctification of sites, and the key Jerusalem church was scattered. Not until the latter half of the second century is there any indication of a special aura attached to a scene of Christian history, and that is Peter's tomb beneath the Church of St. Peter in Rome. During the fourth century, following Constantine's 'conversion', pilgrims began flocking to the Holy Land, and undoubtedly there were dozens of holy places to be seen then.

Chief among the sacred sites was the Holy Sepulchre in Jerusalem, more appropriately called the Church of the Resurrection in those days. The authenticity of the spot ornamented by Constantine's great church (now mostly rebuilt and altered) has been disputed by many people. However, its claim is strengthened by the recent excavations in Jerusalem and the hints they give of the route of the city wall. Proof will never be found for that particular tomb, yet it is clear now that that area lay within a Jewish cemetery beyond the city wall. (The 'Garden Tomb' is an increasingly implausible rival; the skull formation of the adjacent rock cannot be so old.)

Excavated remains coupled with a text from the Dead Sea Scrolls assure the position of the Bethesda Pool north of the Temple area, and also solve the problem of its name, obscured by scribal variants from a very early date. The widely used spelling Bethesda is nearest the Aramaic, which means 'place of flowing water' according to the most authoritative of recent studies, and is written with a grammatical termination showing that there were two of them, as the excavation found.

While only parts of the substructure of Herod's Temple remain in Jerusalem, something of its magnificence, calling forth the disciples' awed exclamation (Mk 13: 1), is reflected in the shrine Herod built for Abraham's tomb at Hebron. His masons were responsible for the greater portion of the fine outer wall still standing there.

A vivid relic of Herod's Temple is the 'Stone of Forbidding', a block inscribed in Greek with a warning that any Gentile who passed it would be responsible for his resulting death. The precinct wall of the inner courts contained several notices like this; a complete one is in a museum in Istanbul, part of a second is preserved in Jerusalem. That wall Paul and Trophimus were supposed to have penetrated

(Ac. 21: 28 f.), but it no longer had any real significance, as Paul hinted later (Eph. 2: 14).

In the Holy City it is natural to endeavour to connect every discovery with the Scriptures, so archaeology can raise more questions and give rise to opposing theories. Many scholars adjudge the broad stone pavement laid bare beneath the Convent of the Sisters of Zion in Old Jerusalem as authentically Gabbatha, the courtyard upon which Pilate condemned Jesus (Jn 19: 13). The massive stones laid before A.D. 70, and the soldiers' games scratched upon them impress every visitor. Yet there is no proof that the Fortress of Antonia, to which the paving apparently belonged, served as Pilate's praetorium on the occasion of Jesus' trial. Herod's palace on the opposite, west, side of the city (now the Citadel), is an equally reasonable site. Excavations have not yielded a solution.

Finally, we notice that several allusions in the Letters to the Seven Churches (Rev. 2: 3) have been illumined by archaeological exploration. Local landmarks and characteristics metaphorically conveyed the Lord's message to each church. Laodicea's rebuke was couched in terms of her water supply. As no main source arose in the city, the water was drawn from hot springs at a distance and conveyed through stone pipes, arriving tepid, 'neither hot nor cold', suitable only as an emetic.

People

'Not many powerful, not many noble . . .' (1 C. 1: 26): Paul's survey of Church society reveals the reason why few NT figures are known from extant remains. Inevitably rulers are attested by monuments and coins, yet the name of Pontius Pilate exists on no more than a single inscribed stone, from Caesarea. The pomp of Herod the Great re-echoes in dedications to pagan deities found in Greece, as well as in the fashionable temples he built in the non-Jewish parts of his kingdom. Similarly, memorials from other provinces contain the names of Roman officials, and their manifold titles are seen to correspond appropriately with the various ranks given them by the author of Acts. Thus the authorities at Thessalonica were *politarchs* (Ac. 17: 6), a title confirmed by a number of inscriptions concerning that city, while Publius was called 'chief man' (lit. 'first man') in Malta (Ac. 28: 7), which texts show to be his correct designation in Greek and Latin. A firm date in Paul's career is provided by an imperial decree engraved at Delphi early in A.D. 52 during the year of office exercised by the proconsul Gallio, the period when the apostle was in Corinth (Ac. 18: 11-17). Perhaps we may recognize in Paul's friend Erastus the city-treasurer of Corinth (Rom. 16: 23) the Erastus

who gave a pavement to the city, a munificence recorded in Latin on stones now uncovered.

Two prominent persons named by Luke receive meagre external testimony to their existence. Sergius Paulus, proconsul of Cyprus (Ac. 13: 7), is attested in the date-formula, alone, of a stone from Paphos of A.D. 55, and Lysanias, tetrarch of Abilene (Lk. 3: 1), was not otherwise known until attention was turned to a dedication by one of his freedmen dated *c.* A.D. 20 which had been found at Abila, north of Damascus, and to one mentioning his rule as contemporary with Tiberius (A.D. 14-37). Previously Luke had been accused of error, since the only Lysanias of Abilene then known was executed by Antony and Cleopatra in 36 B.C.

When instances like these can be cited favouring Luke's historical accuracy, his unsupported statements become more creditable. To discount the record of the census held at the time of Jesus' birth, while Quirinius was governor of Syria (Lk. 2: 2) is to discard an ancient source for which no other can be substituted. In fact, a recent study (L. Dupraz: *De l'Association de Tibère au Principat à la Naissance du Christ*, 1966) reinterprets related documents widely believed to invalidate Lk. 2: 2 with the result that a governorship of Quirinius between 7 and 5 B.C. becomes feasible, although Luke's remark is the most explicit evidence. (See also 'Historical and Political Background, Chronology', pp. 62 f.)

Archaeology can often inform on the mundane matters of life. Statuary helps to envisage appearance and modes of dress, and some representations of women exhibit the elaborate coiffure disliked by the apostles. Humble household artefacts, the pots and pans that comprise the bulk of an archaeologist's material evidence, have their place in building up a general picture of daily life. Occasionally they have a special relevance, like the common pottery oil-lamp illustrating metaphors and parables. Long-necked perfume bottles are unexciting finds in themselves, but they lend colour to one incident. The woman at Simon's banquet (Mk 14: 3) apparently had one of these (AV 'box' is misleading). In her haste to honour the Lord she did not trouble to open the sealed mouth, but snapped the neck, releasing the unguent and rendering the container useless. Attempts at polishing ancient metal mirrors explain Paul's comparison with our present understanding of Christ (1 C. 13: 12), because their surfaces could never give a clear reflection.

The tombs of the dead form a profitable source of information. Many Jewish cemeteries of the years prior to A.D. 70 have been explored in the neighbourhood of Jerusalem. One type of rock-cut tomb agrees with that described in the resurrection narratives in its construction. Examples can be seen to-day, one of the best being the 'Tomb of the Kings' in northern Jerusalem. There the low entrance conforms to Jn 20: 5 (many tombs have rather larger entries); the stone cover lies to one side, in a slot cut to allow for rolling it across. Inside these tombs the body was laid on a rock-cut shelf, above floor level. After decomposition, the bones were normally gathered into stone chests (ossuaries) for their final rest. Names written on the chests found in such tombs include some also met in the NT, among them Elizabeth, Mary, Sapphira, Lazarus, Jesus son of Joseph—none, of course, necessarily identifiable with the Biblical figures. There is a possibility that two chests of *c.* A.D. 50 bear brief prayers addressed to the risen Jesus.

In this connection may be included the 'Nazareth Decree'. On a marble slab, said to originate in Nazareth, is a Greek inscription ordaining that tombs remain undisturbed, and that anybody found guilty of demolishing one, moving the remains, or breaking the seals should be executed. No date or name is given, but the heading 'ordinance of Caesar' displays its imperial warranty. The question is, which Caesar. Palaeographical study points to a date between 50 B.C. and A.D. 50, other arguments favour Claudius (A.D. 41-54) who was concerned at Jewish-Christian disputes according to the biographer Suetonius. Were the text pre-resurrection in date it would underline the heinousness of the offence of which the Temple authorities attempted to accuse the disciples; were it later it would seem to emphasize the spread of the resurrection faith, and of efforts to quench it.

Another possible witness to early Christianity is the famous word-square:

```
ROTAS
OPERA
TENET
AREPO
SATOR
```

Specimens are listed from a third or fourth century A.D. structure at Cirencester, from a third century town on the Euphrates (Dura), and from Pompeii, destroyed by Vesuvius' eruption in A.D. 79. A case can be made for a Jewish origin in translating portions of Ezekiel 1 and 10 into Latin. More convincing is the unravelling of the letters around the central N to form the initial words of the Lord's Prayer in Latin, with the Latin equivalents of Alpha and Omega (observe the cruciform TENET, too):

```
          A
          P
          A
          T
          E
          R
A PATERNOSTER O
          O
          S
          T
          E
          R
          O
```

The preceding paragraphs summarize a few examples of archaeological discoveries in the realms of material culture and history. Matters of faith and doctrine cannot be subject to inquiry on the same level by reason of their character. However, two great finds made since the Second World War do impinge upon the study of religious thought in the background of the NT. These are the Dead Sea Scrolls, writings of a Jewish sect flourishing from the second century B.C. until *c.* A.D. 68 in the Judaean wilderness, and the Nag Hammadi Texts, thirteen volumes of Gnostic origin found in Egypt, copied about A.D. 400 and after. As neither group of manuscripts is published in entirety all discussion should retain an element of caution; new evidence can so swiftly upturn fashionable theories. In the case of the Dead Sea Scrolls this point is particularly valid because the more exciting documents have naturally attracted wide attention. Taking one or two texts and making sensational claims for them is an abuse of a wonderful treasure.

Among the non-Biblical scrolls are long-forgotten books which enlarge our knowledge of Jewish thought and beliefs in the Gospel period. In general it can be said that they serve to re-emphasize the OT foundation of Judaism and Christianity, weakening theories of extensive Persian and Greek influence on them. Peculiar practices and doctrines (asceticism, celibacy, frequent baptism, the priestly line, calendar, eschatology, exclusivism) marked off the sect from the main stream of Judaism, nevertheless it remained essentially Jewish, looking for the coming of the Messiah (or Messiahs), performing punctiliously rites of purification and worship. (See 'Religious Background, the Jewish Religious Parties', p. 75.) In their psalms and their Biblical exegesis these men approach the sentiment of some NT passages, and while they also believed that 'salvation' was available to their followers and none beside, in their exclusivism they went further, almost severing themselves from the world at large. Unlike the Christians, their missionary activity appears to have been minimal; applications from prospective members were awaited rather than invited. Despite that, their society continued for about two centuries at Qumran and probably in other centres. Parallels drawn between Christian organization and the hierarchical structure laid down in the Scrolls have their appeal for those who seek the origins of the Church. No proof of borrowing can be adduced; the parallels turn out to be superficial when viewed against the contradictory motives and beliefs underlying the institutions. So little does survive from that age in Judaea that it is sensible to extract every morsel of information from whatever is found, and improbable theories spring fast from the field.

The Jewish flavour of Mt. 5—Christ's enunciation of the Law in the light of His advent—is enhanced by linguistic echoes in the Scrolls. 'Poor in spirit', to take a single phrase, clearly meant 'the spiritually loyal', those who held faithfully to the covenant. A different product is a text with Nero Caesar spelt in Hebrew letters which, if given numerical values, have a sum of 666 (cf. Rev. 13: 17 f., with note *ad loc.*). It is as Jewish writings two centuries earlier than the compilation of the main rabbinic traditions (the Mishnah) that the Scrolls give their richest contribution to the vari-coloured world of the NT. It is instructive to read these records of a movement that failed beside those of a faith still flourishing.

Gnosticism has also been gleaned in the search for seminal concepts that flowered as Christianity, even although its early history has been extremely obscure. The Nag Hammadi books are translations into Coptic of Greek works written between A.D. 150 and 300, and include major compositions from various Gnostic parties. They indicate, by quotation, that the NT books were mostly recognized as canonical by A.D. 150 or thereabouts, and that Gnostics borrowed extensively from them. More important, they contradict the contentions that Paul's and John's writings adopt Gnostic ideas in formulating or explaining their doctrine (as members of the Bultmann school have argued), ideas which, it is said, require to be purged away before pristine Christianity can be seen. They illustrate the perversion of the Christian faith into one of the earliest heresies. Gnosticism claimed a monopoly of divine revelation, and the attainment of this knowledge (*gnosis*) was the aim of the Gnostic. For him

matter was evil; release therefrom could be gained by following Jesus who broke the power of the physical realm and showed the way to the spiritual. (See 'The Religious Background, Pagan', pp 69 f.) Some of the writings imitate NT forms to propound new doctrines. 'The Gospel of Thomas' is a string of sayings purportedly delivered by Jesus to Thomas Didymus. Some rephrase familiar texts; others are utterly strange; a few may be authentic. Other books speak of the state of the world, the strata of celestial society, the resurrection, sometimes cast in letter-form. Here is an ancient example of the common tendency to exalt man and to add his ideas to the revelation once given.

By the unearthing of these two libraries of ancient writings NT studies have been given a new impetus. Along with the other archaeological evidence, they have brought in a phase in which old theories are being critically reviewed, and in which a more serious consideration is being given to the words of the gospel and their truth.

BIBLIOGRAPHY

The material is very scattered. Many relevant articles appear in *The Biblical Archaeologist*, published quarterly since 1938 by the American Schools of Oriental Research, Room 102, 6 Divinity Avenue, Cambridge, Mass. See also relevant articles in *NBD*.

BARRETT, C. K., *The New Testament Background* (London, 1957).

BLAIKLOCK, E. M., *Out of the Earth* (London, 1957).

BRUCE, F. F., *Second Thoughts on the Dead Sea Scrolls*[3] (Exeter, 1966).

DEISSMANN, A., *Light from the Ancient East*[4], E.T. (London, 1927).

FINEGAN J., *Light from the Ancient Past*[2] (Princeton and Oxford, 1959).

GRANT, R. M. and FREEDMAN, D. N., *The Secret Sayings of Jesus* (London, 1960).

HARRISON, R. K., *Archaeology of the New Testament*. Teach Yourself Books (London, 1963).

HELMBOLD, A. K., *The Nag Hammadi Gnostic Texts and the Bible* (Grand Rapids, 1967).

KIRSCHBAUM, E., *The Tombs of St. Peter and St. Paul*, E.T. (London, 1959).

METZGER, H., *St. Paul's Journeys in the Greek Orient*, E.T. (London, 1955).

MILLIGAN, G., *Here and There among the Papyri* (London, 1922).

MOULTON, J. H., *From Egyptian Rubbish Heaps* (London, 1916).

PARROT, A., *Golgotha and the Church of the Holy Sepulchre*, E.T. (London, 1957).

PARROT, A., *The Temple of Jerusalem*, E.T. (London, 1957).

PFEIFFER, C. F. (ed.), *The Biblical World* (London, 1967), especially articles 'Bethesda', 'Emmaus', 'Nag Hammadi Gnostic Texts', 'Oxyrhynchus Papyri', 'Pontius Pilate'.

RAMSAY, W. M., *The Bearing of Recent Discovery on the Trustworthiness of the New Testament* (London, 1915).

THOMPSON, J. A., *The Bible and Archaeology* (Grand Rapids and Exeter, 1962).

UNGER, M. F., *Archaeology and the New Testament* (Grand Rapids, 1962).

VAN UNNIK, W. C., *Newly Discovered Gnostic Writings*, E.T. (London, 1958).

AN ENVIRONMENTAL BACKGROUND TO THE NEW TESTAMENT

J. M. HOUSTON

Four miles to the east of Naples lie the excavated ruins of Herculaneum, perhaps the most perfectly preserved of the Roman towns. On the upper floor of one of the largest houses there is a modest apartment that was rented possibly by some craftsman or merchant. There, on a white stuccoed panel, is imprinted a large cross.[1] If associated with a Christian family, it demonstrates the existence of the Christian faith in this small town of 4-5,000 inhabitants before it was engulfed in mud-flows from the eruption of Vesuvius in A.D. 79. More vivid still is the *graffito* on the wall of a house in the Palatine district of Rome. Here the representation of the Crucifixion is a blasphemy (fig. 1). Christ is depicted with an ass's head, suspended on a

Fig. 1

cross. Alongside it, there reads in illiterate scrawl with contemptuous scorn: 'Alexamenos worships God'.[2] Perhaps a slave, Alexamenos was

certainly the butt of his fellows for being a Christian. At opposite ends of the Roman world there is also evidence of the spread of Christianity. At the Roman fort of Dura Europos built on the Euphrates a house-church has been excavated. A room, later enlarged with two more to hold possibly a hundred people, together with baptistery and murals of Biblical scenes, has been unearthed, dating from the third century.[3] At Lullingstone villa near Eynsford in Kent, England, one small room clearly used as a chapel has on the wall a monogram with the letters 'Alpha and Omega'. It dates from the fourth century.[4]

Here, then, is archaeological evidence of the rapid spread of Christianity. While the abundant testimony to personal faith can be read in the thousands of epigrams in the Roman catacombs, the essential simplicity of the primitive church may be inferred from the meagre evidence of these house-churches. It is not until the age of Constantine and the acceptance of Christianity as the official religion of the state, that ecclesiastical architecture is developed and archaeological finds become abundant.

The simple atmosphere of these household meetings is vividly recaptured in Ac. 20: 7-8 when the Apostle Paul visited Troas. Biblical discourse, before the Breaking of Bread, harked back probably to the synagogue with its ministry of the Word. Christian life, however, centred around a novelty, the celebration of the Lord's Supper, as described in 1 C. 11: 23-26. Originally in Jerusalem, the Christian Jews used a communal meal as the setting for the Breaking of Bread, or Eucharist. It was the Lord's Supper.

Even when the Christians formed only a small minority in the local community, they were scattered in the town and they did not form ghettoes. In the second century, Tertullian objected to the accusation that the Christians were anti-social and a caste apart. 'How is it that we are called a burden to the community, we who live with you, who eat the same food, wear the same clothing, have the same furniture and other necessities of life? We are not Brahmans or Indian yogis, dwellers in the woods, and exiles from civil life . . . We live in this world with you, making use of your forum, meat market, baths, inns, shops, farms, markets, and every other commercial venture. We sail, serve in the army, go on vacations and trade with you. We mix with you and even publish our works for you to use'.[5]

The inscriptions of the catacombs testify clearly to this.[6] Christians occupied all walks of life, all grades of society and diverse cultures. This is itself legitimate reason for having some background to the geographical, political, social and religious environments of Primitive Christianity. There is also the challenge of Polybius that has been taken up now by many generations of classical scholars. 'Can anyone be so indifferent or idle', he asked, 'as not to care to know by what means and under what kind of polity, almost the whole inhabited world was conquered and brought under the dominion of the single city of Rome, and that too within a period of not quite fifty-three years?' That is not quite our challenge, but rather the quest of how a small community of Jesus' disciples in Jerusalem could scatter and multiply in this Roman world. What facilities did they have? What problems did they face in their society? What differences of environment, of culture, of modes of life, did they have? These are immense questions and no one can be a professional in attempting to answer them all. Nor are we sure that in the criticism of evidence due weight is attached correctly. We never can think exactly as those in the past were influenced to think.

THE CLASSICAL WORLD

It was probably the pagans at Antioch who first called the followers of Christ 'Christian'. It was the Emperor Nero who first made membership of this group a crime, distinguished Christians from Jews and proclaimed their faith to be illicit. It was Pliny the Younger, in his report to the Emperor Trajan, who first produced an imperial edict concerning the treatment of all Christians. Thus it was in, and by, the conflict with Rome that Christianity became more formalized until eventually hostility was changed to public favour and acceptance in A.D. 312. The rise of the Catholic Church was thus the first world-wide religious organization to be accepted officially within the Roman Empire.[8]

However, the indirect contribution made by Rome to the spread of Christianity was much more important. It presented Christian missionary enterprise with the gifts of justice, good roads, a uniform coinage and a common language. Never before or since have such gifts been provided more opportunely. It was as the Apostles realized, 'the fulness of the times'.[9]

i. Pax Romana

The concept of a world empire was not new in 31 B.C. when the Roman Republic was finally transformed into an imperial dictatorship. Much earlier, the great hydraulic societies of the Near East had developed the massive organization of technical co-division of labour, efficient transport and despotism, in the irrigated plains of Egypt and Mesopotamia. Then arose the Persian Empire with its proud symbol of a highway between Susa and Ephesus 1,800 miles away. Alexander the Great bridged the Dardanelles to link Greece with an Asiatic empire that stretched to the Himalayas and the Gobi desert. It was left, however, to the Romans to be first to convert the Mediterranean Sea and its surrounding lands into one empire. This waterway gave cohesion to a vast domain, forming the axis of an ellipse that stretched 2,300 miles from the Straits of Gibraltar to the Syrian coast. Wherever possible, the borders were geographical: the transition between the deciduous and coniferous forest zones of the Rhine and upper Danube; the desert border of the Sahara; and the Euphrates in the east.

After two centuries of uncertainty, the Augustan era was heralded as a new age of peace. It was a peace guarded by an army of less than three hundred thousand men, but the Roman roads enabled its twenty-seven legions to be concentrated at trouble spots.[10] Travel by Roman roads was indeed better organized in the time of Paul's missionary work than in Wesley's tour of England eighteen hundred years later. Not until modern times was there the same security from pirates on the high seas.[11] Thus political unity was achieved through good communications. The letters of Paul give us some idea of how thought could travel throughout the Empire, even by men who were not wealthy by Roman standards. True, Roman peace may be exaggerated as Paul's own encounter with robbers would attest. Moreover, imperial propaganda through the coinage did not give the missionaries all the free hand they might have wished. 'Whose is this image and superscription? And they said unto Him, Caesar's'.[12] Likewise the events of Paul's life in Syria were to be re-examined and judged 1,500 miles away in Rome.

ii. Citizenship

For the government of his empire, Augustus wisely refrained from hastening a unified legislation. He combined a strong central government with many forms of local independence. This is seen vividly in the Gospels in the administration of Judaea; a governor directly responsible to the Emperor in Judaea proper and Samaria; a native ruler like Herod the tetrarch in Galilee and Transjordan. There were cities which possessed the full Roman franchise; *coloniae* that had been settled by Roman citizens and *municipia* where citizenship had been given to a previously autonomous community.[13] The spread of Roman citizenship was restricted to those who could genuinely represent the Roman way of life. At its apogee there were 5,627 civic bodies in the Empire, each a 'package' arrangement containing those physical facilities of forum, baths, theatres, stadium, library, shops, etc., that were required to Romanize the populace.[14] Thus Paul was proud to be both a citizen of Tarsus—'no mean city'—and of Rome.

iii. Commerce

Roman law and roads, together, laid the foundation for much mercantile enterprise. Rome came to depend on the import of some 180,000-190,000 tons of wheat each year, employing a fleet of up to 2,000 vessels.[15] Much of the grain was brought from Sicily and Egypt. The eighth hill of Rome, Monte Testaccio, is eloquent testimony of the oil trade with Andalusia, for it was the rubbish heap built up of broken *amphorae*. The silver mines of Cartagena enriched the coinage. The finest pottery came from Southern Gaul. During the first two centuries, Roman enterprise linked the commerce of the Indian Ocean with that of the Mediterranean.[16] The Nile delta became a conservatory, where exotics like rice, bananas, sugar cane, citrus fruits, etc., could be first cultivated away from their native hearth of south-east Asia. The range of commodities traded, notably by Greek and Syrian merchants, is catalogued in Revelation: 'cargoes of gold and silver, jewels and pearls, cloths of purple and scarlet, silks and fine linen, all kinds of scented woods, bronze, iron and marble, cinnamon and spice, incense, perfumes and frankincense, wine, oil, flour and wheat, sheep and cattle, horses, chariots, slaves, and the lives of men. The fruit you longed for'.[17]

With such commerce we also meet Christian traders such as Lydia in Philippi, three hundred miles away from her native city. Among Christian travellers, apart from Paul and his companions, we meet Phoebe journeying to Rome from Corinth; Epaphroditus travelling from Rome to Philippi; Aquila and Priscilla are recorded at Rome, Ephesus, Corinth and again in Ephesus.[18]

Roman coinage had a political propaganda value rather like the varied issues of postage stamps today. But a common coinage was of inestimable value. It facilitated in the Primitive Church the ready assistance of charity between the Greek churches and Judaea, recorded in

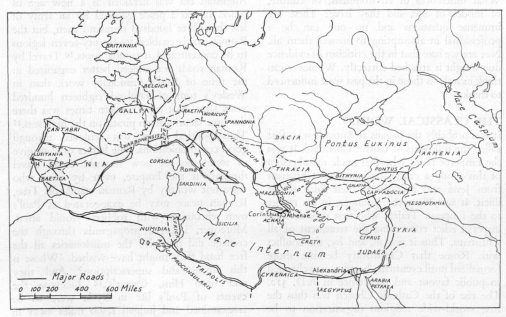

The major roads in Roman times.

2 Corinthians.[19] With its mixed government and at the threshold of varied cultures, the Palestine of the Gospels, however, reflects a mixed lot: the Roman *as*,[20] *quadrans*,[21] and *denarii;*[22] Greek talents,[23] *didrachma, drachmas*[24] and *stater;*[25] *lepta* and *mina*.[26] No wonder money-changers are mentioned in Jerusalem. The impact of a decree from Caesar Augustus that all the world should be enrolled in A.D. 6 had not yet standardized the Palestine 'hoards' of the period.

iv. A Common Language

The Lord's rule to the disciples: 'Go into all the world', was also facilitated by the use of a common language. All the documents of the NT were written in Greek and even the Gospel tradition, formed in the first instance in Aramaic, has been transmitted in a Greek dress.[27] This was called by the grammarians the 'Common Dialect' to distinguish it from regional dialects of Greek. It was the *lingua franca* of the common people, only a few of whom were Greeks.[28] The name 'Greek' was no longer a national but a cultural term, as for example in Mk 7: 26: 'A Greek woman, Syro-Phoenician by race'.

The importance of Greek, circulated with Hellenistic culture in the Mediterranean world, was more than the convenience of a common language. With the balanced, humanistic ideal of the development of the whole man, Greek had a richer vocabulary than Latin. As Lucretius acknowledged: 'It is a hard task to set clearly in the light the dark discoveries of the Greeks, above all when many things must be treated in new words because of the poverty of our tongue and the newness of the themes'.[29] For in every branch of knowledge Hellenistic scholars had reached new conclusions by the application of reason.

It was this living, universal language that had already contributed to the rebirth of the Hebrew Scriptures in the Septuagint. After the Greek translation of the OT in Alexandria had begun in the third century B.C., the diffusion of the Scriptures in the vernacular was not dissimilar to the impact made by Wyclif in the fourteenth and Coverdale in the sixteenth century. From an appeal to the Scriptures, Paul was able to demonstrate that Christ is the real content of them.[30] The apostolic appeal to the Septuagint is itself evidence of its knowledge by Hellenized Jews.

v. The Diaspora

Wherever the pioneer Christian missionaries went, they had a ready-made audience among the scattered colonies of Hellenized Jews. Their number is only an intelligent series of guesses, such as Philo made in Egypt. Perhaps 7 per cent. of the total population of the Roman world, or some 4-4.5 million Jews, existed in the reign of Tiberius.[31] There were about a million of them in Egypt, rather more in Syria and perhaps less than 700,000 in Palestine. There were at least 10,000 in Rome, with other large colonies in the great mercantile cities of Greece and Asia Minor. Beyond the Empire, they were also massed in Mesopotamia and Media. As Josephus observed: 'There is not a community in the entire world which does not have a portion of our people'.[32] During the struggles for power, Julius Caesar had received the support of the Jews, and his decrees on their behalf have been called their Magna Carta.[33] For three more centuries they enjoyed special privileges, including the full freedom of worship.

As a revealed religion, Judaism took itself seriously. The unique importance of the Law was emphasized, in whose observance a Jew had no ulterior motive but the love of God and obedience to His Word. Moral purity was stressed. For the first time in its history, Judaism had begun to blossom out from being a national faith to a world religion. Proudly the Jew felt he had something to proclaim to the whole world.[34] As Harnack has indicated, the Christian was indebted to the Jews for six reasons: A field tilled all over the Empire; religious communities already formed in the towns; the background of the Holy Scriptures and liturgy; the habit of regular worship and the control of private life; impressive apologetics on behalf of monotheism, ethics and God's purposes in history; and the feeling that witness was a duty.[35] So great was the debt, as Paul well appreciated (Rom. 9: 1-5; 10), that at first Christianity appeared to be no more than a sect of Judaism. But in the uproar that followed, the division became sharper and bitterer, until John the Apostle could speak vehemently of 'those who say that they are Jews, and are not, but are a synagogue of Satan'.[36] We have the reference in Suetonius's biography of Claudius that the Emperor 'expelled from Rome the Jews who persisted in rioting at the instigation of Chrestus', perhaps between A.D. 41 and 49.[37] Among those driven out were Aquila and Priscilla (Ac. 18: 2).

CHRISTIANITY IN PAGAN SOCIETY

Another and even more menacing conflict was that between Christianity and pagan society. This was largely fought out in the field of private life. The ordinary pagans thought of the Christian as essentially anti-social, and on this basis their relations must often have been very strained.

i. Social Life

Roman society was divided fairly rigidly into social classes. All free-born were separate from slaves who originally had no legal rights or even personality. Many were treated like brute-beasts. The aristocracy of senators and knights had legal protection that favoured the miscreant much more than in the lower classes. As a fellowship of brotherly love, where in Christ there was neither slave nor free, the freedom of spirit and personal dignity realized would appreciably affect pagan households. Already Jewish slaves were unpopular as they insisted on the observance of the seventh day and refused to eat pagan food. Their ready redemption by fellow Jews was often accepted with alacrity. Similar trends might well have developed with Christian slaves, although Paul's letter to Philemon clearly indicates the Christian leaders had no intention of deliberately upsetting the *status quo*.

Slavery degraded marriage, for it introduced concubinage into family life. Not the slightest stigma was attached to it by public opinion, and the average Roman lacked any ideal to counter this practice. Seneca reveals the state of affairs: 'No woman need blush to break off her marriage since the most illustrious ladies have adopted the practice of reckoning the year not by the names of the consuls but by those of their husbands. They divorce in order to remarry. They marry in order to divorce'.[38] Another cause of this laxity was the diminution of the stern discipline of the *pater familias* since the days of the Republic. Women were in many cases as emancipated as they are now, and such feminism tended to emulate man's vices. Children tended to be spoilt. At the same time infanticide was common, an unwanted baby being 'exposed', often left on the rubbish heap to die of hunger, cold or be devoured by the dogs. Paul's picture of pagan society in Romans chapter one is no exaggeration of its morals.

The boredom and leisure of the populace could be dangerous to the state. It was in the political interest, therefore, that the chariot races of the circus diverted the passions of the masses with their thrills and gambling. In the theatre, slices of pagan life were served up, hot and spicy, nearing the limit of even Roman conventions. The amphitheatre with its gladiatorial spectacle of human slaughter was foul and debased.[39] The baths where the citizens took their daily afternoon wash were the most innocent of daily pleasures, but even here the social life and the opportunities for promiscuity made them feared by the Christians.[40] The one main meal of the day, in the evening, was the occasion of much drunkenness and gluttony. Clubs were an important feature of Roman life where further licence was found. Faced by all

these features of daily life, the Christians had to reject a great deal. No wonder they were viewed as kill-joys, whose negativism did so much to stir the wrath of the pagans. When the Christians were thrown to the lions it would cause pagan satisfaction that they were both forced to attend the very amphitheatre they had denounced and also provided a Roman holiday at their martyrdom.

ii. Economic Life

The Augustan peace had fostered trade immensely. The spirit of materialism dominated life in the cities. Private enterprise was open and individual fortunes were amassed. The blatant display of luxuries and the waste of money by the rich, caused blind discontent among the masses.[41] Sycophancy was ostentatious and beggary rapacious. The paying of homage to patrons and superiors involved each day a merry-go-round of salaams. Trade was split into a multitude of specialist lines, and Rome alone had over 150 corporations, which Augustus co-ordinated by careful legislation.

Living in such a hostile environment, the collective forbearance of the Christians could readily touch the pockets of the pagan tradesmen until it hurt them.[43] At Philippi and Ephesus, Paul was attacked by the men whose business had suffered by the preaching of the gospel. When the meat market with its sales of cheaper meat that had been offered to the idols was boycotted, the effect would be felt in poorer Christian homes. Many Christians, however, must have found it very difficult to decide how far to compromise with pagan society. Between Paul's advice on the eating of sacrificial meat and John's denunciation of the Nicolaitans, there must have existed many fine and difficult decisions to make.

iii. Religion

The materialism of Roman life contributed to the decay of pagan religion. Priesthood could not be held with a secular office, and as every man of good family had business in the provinces, few would be attracted. Many temples in the Augustan era fell into neglect.[44] Moreover, the old gods of the household, under the Republic, had been associated originally with the spirits of nature and of the needs of agriculture. Their relevance to city life was less obvious. Roman religion had little to offer in the way of emotional appeal, and of the explanation of life and its immediate problems. The Roman stood on the narrow base of 'right and duty', of observance of traditional cults, rather than with a concern for personal belief.[45] The thoughtful who viewed the gods as mere superstitions, had nothing to replace them, and as the practice of ceremonial cults was all that society demanded, their inner thoughts might never be revealed.

As the migration of peoples intensified with the expansion of the Empire, mystic cults of the East—of Osiris, Mithras and numerous lesser superstitions—were introduced.[46] The intellectual muddle of 'gods many, lords many' could not be overcome, despite some efforts at syncretism. The only questions asked concerning their adoption by the State were three: Would they upset the existing cults? Were they politically unsafe? Were they morally undesirable?[47] As grossly immoral rites were associated with the Eastern cults, especially that of Isis, their worship on occasion was stopped, but never permanently. Added to the amalgam were demonology, astrology, magic and mystery religions.

From the time of Augustus onwards, there appeared also the worship of the Emperor. In the Provinces of the Eastern Mediterranean, the cult had a spontaneous growth, and their peoples readily accepted godhead in their rulers. In Italy, however, the idea of ascribing divinity in any sense to a man was repugnant.[48] There, the 'deification' of the Emperor meant little more than a certain sacrosanctity to the office and the observance of loyalty, flattery and whatever sycophancy would be tolerated.

iv. Persecution of the Christians

It is well attested that the first Roman persecution of the Christians occurred after the Fire of Rome in A.D. 64. Nero might well have chosen the Jews as a scapegoat for the event, had not the Empress Poppaea Sabina been particularly sympathetic to the Jews. Instead, he used the Christians. From then until the Decian persecution of A.D. 250-1, the persecution went on automatically, if sporadically. It is fallacious to distinguish between 'good' and 'bad' Emperors, according to their treatment of the Christians. Until the third century, it was the provincial governor who played the more significant rôle. As Pilate had yielded Jesus to the cries of the Jews, so too later governors were often influenced by public outcry against the Christians.[49] At Ephesus and elsewhere the apostle Paul had seen how the mob could be whipped up into a frenzy, and after Nero's persecution the Christians were a conspicuous sally for public discontent, wherever there was a disaster. As Tertullian said: 'If the Tiber overflows or the Nile doesn't, if there is a drought or an earthquake, a famine or a pestilence, at once the cry goes up, "The Christians to the lions"'.[50] The monotheistic exclusiveness of the Christians was believed to alienate the gods, and in the closely-knit structure of Roman

life this was considered a danger to all—state and individuals.

The Jews were recognized to be different. They were atheists on licence, because their customs were venerable with age and could be overlooked because of their antiquity. But the Christians had actually departed from their ancestral rites. The negative attitude towards the pagan way of life created deepest resentment, and for those who wished to stir up trouble for the Christians it only needed to be pointed out that their practices were treasonable.[51] They worshipped a man who had been condemned to death in Judaea for a treasonable offence. Their loyalty to the state was doubtful because they refused to swear an oath by the Emperor's Genius. They were always talking about the end of the world. One of their writers had spoken in bitter hatred of Rome, prophesying its doom in the thin disguise of Babylon. As Trajan instructed Pliny, governor of Bithynia, procedure was simple. Whoever acknowledged that he belonged to Christ and recanted not the Name, could be punished with death. Perhaps at Pergamum some had been put to death for refusal even to worship the Emperor,[55] but normally this test was not applied. The Name they bore was usually the sole charge. Yet it was this intense idealism of the Early Church to die for their faith, that gave them such dynamic power. As Tertullian exclaimed: 'The blood of the Christians is seed',[54] seed that flourished with an increasing missionary harvest.

v. Philosophy

There was, finally, the encounter the Christians constantly faced with philosophy. Its emphasis on man's needs was more pragmatic than much modern philosophy, and it was popularized by open-air preachers. On Paul's visit to Athens we read that certain philosophers of the Epicureans and of the Stoics encountered him[55] in a city where the founders of both movements had taught.

The serious followers of Epicurus are misrepresented in associating them with desire only for physical pleasures;[56] rather peace of mind was their quest. Like some modern psychiatrists, the Epicureans considered religion was the chief enemy to eradicate, for it only stirred up fears of the mind and what we would term today 'guilt-complexes'. They denied the existence of life after death so there could be no substance for fear in hell or the after-life. The universe merely consisted of the chance association of atoms and void. Happiness, which was the great good for man to attain, could be achieved through the cultivation of the quiet mind and of friendships. Evil was avoided by justice. Thus Epicureanism was a gospel of

C

escape, of ignoring the problems, and not facing them.

Much more important in the Western Mediterranean was Stoicism, which suited the Roman temperament and dominated Rome for three centuries.[57] Zeno had diagnosed desire as the fundamental sickness of man, of which other evils were symptoms. An earlier philosopher, Heraclitus, had discovered Reason to be both in the centre of human life and in the Universe. By allowing personal reason to be in harmony with cosmic Reason, or Nature, man could be self-sufficient and defy evil. Such a faith could put steel into disillusioned Romans but it gave scope only for the mind, not the emotions. It gave support to the cosmopolitanism of Roman law, for if the Greek was the genius of beauty, the Jew the genius of righteousness, the Roman was the genius of law. Hence Stoicism had great power in the Roman world, and it was advocated by some of its finest men.

However, the abnormal opportunities for self-indulgence in the period brought decay to even the noblest system of thought. Epicureanism popularized turned to vice. Stoicism's elastic ability to come to terms with the gods gave popular superstitions a spurious respectability. Moreover it tended to widen the gulf between state morals and individual immorality. Christianity succeeded for the masses in its unique capacity to meet the social needs of the age.[58] That God should be righteous, yet still love the sinner, must have been a potent attraction. Ideas were put into practice and not simply discussed. Hospitality to the stranger, the warm and friendly fellowship of house-churches,[59] the consistent practice of ethical ideals in family life, must all have met the social needs of many a convert.

REGIONAL ENVIRONMENTAL FEATURES

In the physical and social environments of Primitive Christianity that both repelled and fostered the growth of its communities, there were also nuances and even marked differences. After all, the territory of the Roman Empire was vast and its habitats, peoples and cultures of varied character. Four regional contexts may be distinguished: Judaea, Syria, Asia Minor and the cities of Greece and Rome. Egypt, with its great Jewish community in Alexandria, might be a fifth, but little is known of it in the first century and it is not a relevant NT background.[60]

i. Judaea

A fundamental distinction in Mediterranean environments that has lasted since classical times is that of town and country, the former progressive and commercial, the latter conser-

vative and agricultural. Now the scenery of the Gospels is essentially rural despite reference to our Lord's ministry at Jerusalem, notably during the Passion Week. The rural world of the Gospels is also of limited extent, involving journeys on foot of no more than three days from west to east, and perhaps a week from north to south. Its so-called 'towns', many of ancient origin, have been for long no more than rural centres fostering the agricultural needs of a district. It was only Hellenistic influence that grafted on rural Palestine 'towns' in the Roman sense; such were Caesarea, founded in

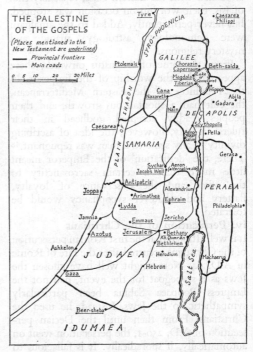

THE PALESTINE OF THE GOSPELS
(Places mentioned in the New Testament are underlined)
Provincial frontiers
Main roads
0 5 10   20   30 Miles

22 B.C., and Tiberias, c. A.D. 18. The Hellenistic 'cities' of the Decapolis on the east side of Palestine remained small throughout the first century.

With its higher rainfall and deeper soils, Galilee was particularly well populated. Some of its numerous villages according to Josephus had 15,000 inhabitants or more. Of the 47 synagogues known to have existed in Roman Palestine, about 33 were in Galilee. Mark describes accurately the custom of these larger centres with their synagogues administering a district or toparchy;[61] its officials are alluded to in the parable of the talents. This hierarchical system of village administration is very ancient, and there are comparable allusions to it in Vedic literature, in India.[62] Judges rather than city magistrates are referred to, and the court life of petty, rural monarchs is described. There is the example of a single village defying the authority of such a 'king'. Scenes from the countryside are frequent in the parables and other sayings of our Lord. As Sherwin-White has noted: 'The absence of Graeco-Roman colouring is a convincing feature of the Galilean narrative and parables. Rightly, it is only where the scene changes to Jerusalem that the Roman administrative machine manifests itself, in all three accounts, with the procurator and his troops and tribunal, and the machinery of taxation'.[63]

Judaean Christians must at first have been largely country-folk, to whom were added Hellenistic town-dwellers, notably in Jerusalem. Their distinct outlook led to a cleavage and the appointment of seven guardians of the poor, all having Greek names. Chief among them was Stephen, stoned as the first martyr because of his implication that the cultus of the Temple no longer mattered. This view was also shared by some of the Diaspora who were not Christians. Like Huss, Stephen died for an issue he could not foresee. It is likely that the Jewish Christians, still orthodox in their observance of the Law, were left alone by the authorities. There were already various parties within the commonwealth of Israel, such as the Pharisees, Sadducees, Zealots and Essenes. In the minds of orthodox Jews, the Nazarenes were admitted probably as yet another group, whose absurd claim to know the Messiah personally was largely undermined by His crucifixion. Their only danger was a political one, for in an age of threatened revolt the Nazarenes' daily prayer for a 'kingdom' and their expectation of the return of their Messiah could be conflagratory propaganda for hotheads. Perhaps it was for this reason that in A.D. 62, in the interregnum between the Roman procurators Festus and Albinus, the high priest caused James, leader of the Jerusalem community, and others to be stoned. Four years later, extremists took over the city and Jerusalem was destroyed by the Romans in A.D. 70.

Meanwhile, at the Council of Jerusalem in *c*. A.D. 49, the distinction between Gentile Christians and Jewish Christians had been faced and settled somewhat vaguely. Philip's mission in Samaria, and Peter at Caesarea, had involved the Nazarenes in this difficult problem of Jewish-Gentile relations. Paul's own activities caused greatest embarrassment to the orthodox. By A.D. 64 Rome, however, had clearly distinguished between Jews and Christians, and by A.D. 70 they had diverged in Palestine. Those engaged in missionary enterprise and a universal church now looked north to Syria and west to the Mediterranean world. Those

orthodox, anxious to conserve their Jewish roots, migrated to Pella in Transjordan after the death of James.[64] There, they are lost sight of, although traces of them are found down to the Muslim conquest.

ii. Syria

Much more Hellenized was Syria to the north. Great highways from Damascus south to Arabia, and from Antioch east to Mesopotamia, laid it open to much cultural influence from the Orient. It traded with the Mediterranean and beyond, through its Phoenician ports. It boasted some of the greatest cities of classical times, Antioch 'the Vienna of the Near East', Damascus rich in irrigated lands.[65] It was to this cosmopolitan, city life that the first missionaries came from Jerusalem, Barnabas the Cypriot, Simeon Niger, Lucius of Cyrene, Manaen and Paul.[66] At Antioch, the third city of the Empire, there was the first Gentile community of Christians. So distinct were they from the Jews that their pagan opponents nick-named them 'Christians'.[67] Antioch was also the point of departure for the first mission to the Gentiles and a base of operations for men like Barnabas, Paul and Silas. Possibly, too, it was from Antioch that the gospel was first taken to Rome, for through its seaport of Seleucia there was constant communication with the west.

The Judaism of Syria appears to have been different from that of Palestine.[68] It is no wonder that in its mixed communities questions like circumcision were ignored until delegates from Jerusalem, three hundred miles away, disturbed the peace. In this area of diverse cultures and easy ways, syncretistic tendencies were encouraged. We have the example of false prophets like Simon Magus. Together with Samaria and Alexandria, this was a great spawning ground of Gnosticism. It is a tradition that Luke was a native of Antioch. Some think Matthew's Gospel was written in Syria and that perhaps James wrote his letter for the benefit of Syrian believers. Geographically and theologically, Syria proved to be a bridgehead between Judaea and Asia Minor.

iii. Asia Minor

The task of evangelism in Asia Minor might have seemed much more formidable. Its great size of 200,000 square miles, its remote high interior and the illiterate paganism of its country folk were all major obstacles.[69] There is, however, clear evidence that the apostolic missions were carefully and strategically planned. Paul's Syrian base of Antioch, his Cilician birthplace of Tarsus where he had lived for some years after his conversion, his Roman citizenship and, above all, his clear understanding of the call to evangelize the Gentile world, placed him in a strong position to penetrate Asia Minor.[70] This he did by use of both sea-routes and the highways of the interior. The road net-work was the legacy of Persian, Seleucid and Roman engineering, and he kept to the major highways.[71] Also, he and his companions concentrated attention on the major cities with the Graeco-Roman culture, and it was not until later that the country districts were evangelized.

Along the south coast was the province of Cilicia, with poor communications. Here the Tarsus range narrows the coastal plain and is a formidable obstacle, best traversed through the Cilician Gates north of Tarsus. As in Cyprus, Cilicia had early received contact from Christian missionaries, but there is little subsequent reference to it. To the east, Cappadocia was more isolated and scarcely reached with the Gospel. The central districts of Pamphylia, south

where the great overland routes terminated. Ephesus, the richest city and chief seaport, was also the great missionary headquarters of the apostle. Within easy reach there were twelve churches established, seven of which are enumerated in John's letters to the churches.

The documents of these churches, Ephesians, Colossians, 1 Peter and the Johannine writings—especially the rich allusions of Revelation[72]—clearly demonstrate specific dangers that faced these communities. Judaizing teachers that dogged Paul's footsteps are alluded to frequently, notably in the letter to the Galatians and most harshly later still in John's Apocalypse. Converts who reverted to paganism or compromised with pagan ways are recognized, perhaps in the guise of the 'Nicolaitans'.[73] Later, Pliny refers to those who had renounced their Christian faith some twenty years previously.[74] The worship of the Emperor, traditional to the Asians, was a

Asia Minor.

Galatia and Lycaonia were contacted in the mission of Paul and Barnabas. Although the synagogues were first visited, the Gentile church of Pisidian-Antioch was one of the earliest successes in the pagan world. The northern province of Bithynia was later to become one of the strongholds of Christianity as Pliny's concern attests. Paul was guided, however, to turn his footsteps westwards. The province of Asia was the wealthiest and most urbanized of Asia Minor, stretching along the west coast

severe test of some communities, notably at Pergamum, a royal city and seat of the Proconsul.[75] Syncretism, and the spread of Gnosticism were recognized, especially in 1 John, as a growing threat.[76] The affluent society, in rich trading centres, was also a cause of spiritual decadence, in Ephesus and notably so in Laodicea. Thus in the apostolic age, the very environment where Christianity had been most successfully established, was also most in peril.

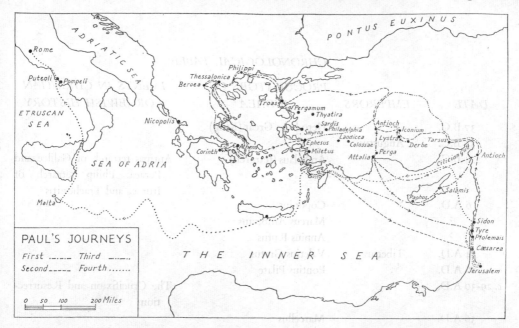

PAUL'S JOURNEYS

First .... Third _____
Second _____ Fourth ....

0   50   100   200 Miles

iv. The European Churches

In Asia Minor Christianity, although introduced first into the cities, spread by the end of the first century into the villages of the countryside. Village churches became an important feature of Phrygia; and Bithynia has already been mentioned.[77] However, in Europe the Christian communities remained for much longer concentrated in cities. Probably Paul may have founded three churches in the province of Macedonia: Philippi, a Roman military colony; Thessalonica, now Salonica, the seat of the Proconsul and chief seaport; and Berea, a regional centre. From their inception they had been in touch with Asia Minor. Consequently the same perils, notably Gnosticism, that endangered Antioch and Asia also affected Philippi. In Achaia, Paul had laboured longer, with scant results in Athens, but with some success in Corinth, then the greatest city of Greece, and at its seaport of Cenchreae. The First Epistle of Clement, sent to it c. A.D. 96, indicates that it had become a very large church, but affected by schism.[78] Many foreign Christians visited it, so that news of discord travelled quickly. Perhaps from it the gospel had been taken to Crete.[79] But the cause of the disunity which gave such bad testimony to the Church Universal was conflict between officialdom and the Spirit.

In the Western Mediterranean, Rome is the only church of which we have any data, although there was also a community at the Neapolitan seaport of Puteoli before Paul's arrival. The beginnings of Christianity in Gaul and North Africa may have taken place also in the first century. The church at Rome was started through unknown missionaries. There, at the end of his life, Paul worked for several years unhindered, if not free. Some converts had been made in the imperial household, but as the Emperor had some 20,000 slaves alone, it is clear that many might not have been freedmen. Tradition also maintains that Peter came and died in Rome; as John indicates in his Gospel, he was crucified.[80] The persecution of the Roman Christians in A.D. 64 is briefly mentioned by Suetonius[81] and at length by Tacitus.[82] It was then, perhaps, that both apostles were martyred.

If the Roman church was particularly vulnerable to persecution, the imperial household was also open to influence by Christianity through its servants. There is thus evidence that in Domitian's reign, relatives of the Emperor were themselves accused and condemned for being Christians. But this church served non-Latin, that is Greek-speaking, peoples whose cosmopolitan character enabled it to maintain a universal rather than parochial character, and in the break-down of paganism Christianity was to offer a new hope for the World.

CHRONOLOGICAL TABLE

DATE	EMPERORS	PROCURATORS OF JUDAEA	EVENTS IN CHRISTIAN OR JEWISH HISTORY
37 B.C.		Herod the Great (King)	
31 B.C.	Augustus		
4 B.C.		Archelaus (tetrarch)	Antipas tetrarch of Galilee and Peraea. Philip tetrarch of Ituraea and Trachonitis
6 A.D.		Coponius	
?		Marcus Ambivius	
?		Annius Rufus	
14 A.D.	Tiberius	Valerius Gratus	
26 A.D.		Pontius Pilate	
c. 29-30 A.D.			The Crucifixion and Resurrection
36 A.D.		Marcellus	
37 A.D.	Caligula	Marullus	Herod Agrippa succeeds Philip and Antipas
40 A.D.			Caligula desecrates the Temple
41 A.D.	Claudius	Herod Agrippa (King)	Death of James, son of Zebedee. Death of Herod. Paul's missionary journeys, 41-54
45 A.D.		Cuspius Fadus	
46 A.D.		Tiberius Alexander	Famine
48 A.D.		Ventidius Cumanus	
49 A.D.			The Apostolic Council
51-52 A.D.			Gallio, proconsul of Achaea
52 A.D.		Felix	
54 A.D.	Nero		
59 A.D.?		Porcius Festus	
61 A.D.?		Albinus	Death of James, the Lord's brother
64 A.D.		Gessius Florus	Fire of Rome and persecution of Christians
66 A.D.			The Jewish Revolt
69 A.D.	Vespasian		
70 A.D.			Destruction of Jerusalem
79 A.D.	Titus		
81 A.D.	Domitian		Further persecution of Christians
96 A.D.	Nerva		
98-117 A.D.	Trajan		

REFERENCES

1. Istituto Geografico de Agostini, *Herculaneum and the Villa of the Papyri*, 1963, pp. 25-26.
2. Gough, M., *The Early Christians*, London, 1961, p. 83.
3. Rostovtzeff, M. I., *Excavations at Dura Europos, Preliminary Report on fifth season of work*, Oxford, 1934.
4. Meates, G. W., *Lullingstone Roman Villa*, London, 1955.
5. Tertullian, *Apologeticus*, 42, 1-3.
6. Hertling, L. and Kirschbaum, E., *The Roman Catacombs*, London, 1960, pp. 177-195.
7. Quoted by F. R. Cowell, *Cicero and the Roman Republic*, London, 1961, p. XI.
8. Ehrhardt, A., 'The adoption of Christianity in the Roman Empire', *Bull. John Rylands Library*, 45, 1962, pp. 97-114.
9. Gal. 4: 4.
10. Mattingly, H., *Roman Imperial Civilization*, London, 1957, pp. 137-160.
11. See Charlesworth, M. P., *Trade-Routes and Commerce of the Roman Empire*, Cambridge, 1924.
12. Mt. 22: 20.
13. Caird, G. B., *The Apostolic Age*, London, 1955, p. 9.
14. Houston, J. M., *The Western Mediterranean World*, London, 1964, p. 110.
15. Cowell, *op. cit.*, p. 117.
16. See Warmington, E. H., *The Commerce between the Roman Empire and India*, Cambridge, 1928.
17. Rev. 18: 12-14, NEB.
18. The travels of Aquila and Priscilla may be traced as follows:—Rome, Ac. 18: 2; Corinth, Ac. 18: 2; Ephesus, Ac. 18: 19; 1 C. 16: 19; Rome, Rom. 16: 3 f.; Ephesus again, 2 Tim. 4: 19.
19. 2 C. 8-9.
20. Mt. 10: 29.
21. Mk 12: 42; 14: 5.
22. Mk 6: 37.
23. Mt. 18: 23-34.
24. Lk. 7: 41; 10: 35; 12: 6; 15: 8.
25. Mt. 10: 29; 17: 24-27.
26. Lk. 19: 12-20; 21: 2.
27. See Beare, F. W., 'New Testament Christianity and the Hellenistic World' in *The Communication of the Gospel in New Testament Times*, A. Farrer *et alii*, London, 1961, pp. 57-73.
28. Lietzmann, H., *A History of the Early Church*, translated by B. L. Woolf, London, 1961, p. 89.
29. Lucretius, *De rerum natura* i. 136-139.
30. Rom. 1: 2 f.
31. Harnack, A., *The Mission and Expansion of Christianity in the first three centuries*, translated by J. Moffatt, new edit., New York, 1962, pp. 1-11.
32. Josephus, *Bell.* ii. 16, 4.
33. Leon, H. J., *The Jews of Ancient Rome*, Philadelphia, 1960, pp. 9-10.
34. Rom. 2: 19 f.
35. Harnack, *op. cit.*, p. 15.
36. Rev. 2: 9; 3: 9.
37. Leon, *op. cit.*, p. 25.
38. Seneca, *De Beneficiis*, iii. 16, 2.
39. See Carcopino, J., *Daily Life in Ancient Rome*, translated by E. O. Lorimer, London, 1962, pp. 223-270.
40. Mattingly, *op. cit.*, p. 176.
41. Cowell, *op. cit.*, pp. 326-340.
42. Ac. 16: 19; 19: 19, 25.
43. See Blaiklock, E. M., *The Christian in Pagan Society*, London, 1951.
44. Fowler, W. Warde, *Social Life in Rome in the age of Cicero*, London, new edit., 1963, pp. 319-352.
45. Halliday, *op. cit.*, pp. 171-182.
46. See Halliday, W. R., *The Pagan Background of Early Christianity*, London, 1925.
47. Barrow, R. H., *The Romans*, London, 1949, p. 144.
48. Ibid., p. 145.
49. Ste. Croix, G. E. M. de, 'Why were the early Christians Persecuted?', *Past and Present*, 26, 1963, pp. 6-31.
50. Tertullian, *Apologeticus*, 40. 1-2.
51. Frank, Tenney, *Aspects of Social Behaviour in Ancient Rome*, Cambridge, Mass., vol. 2, 1932, p. 115.
52. Pliny, *Epistles* x, 96 and 97.
53. Rev. 2: 13.
54. Tertullian, *Apologeticus*, 50.
55. Ac. 17: 18.
56. Festugière, A. J., *Epicurus and his Gods*, translated by C. W. Chilton, London, 1955.
57. Bailey, C., *Phases in the Religion of Ancient Rome*, London, 1933, Ch. 7.
58. See excellent study of A. D. Nock, *Early Gentile Christianity and its Hellenistic Background*, London, Torchbook edit., 1964.
59. Judge, E. A., *The Social Pattern of Christian Groups in the first century A.D.*, London, 1960.
60. Lietzmann, H., *A History of the Early Church*, translated by B. L. Woolf, London, 1953, p. 275.
61. Mk 8: 26-27.
62. Desai, A. (edit.), *Rural Sociology in India*, 1960, p. 160.
63. Sherwin-White, A. N., *Roman Society and Roman Law in the New Testament*, Oxford, 1963, pp. 127 ff.
64. See Bruce, F. F., *The Spreading Flame*, London, 1958, p. 70.
65. Jones, A. H. M., *Cities of the Eastern Roman Provinces*, Oxford, 1937.
66. Ac. 11: 19 f.; 13: 1.
67. Ac. 11: 26.
68. Weiss, J., *Earliest Christianity*, translated by F. C. Grant, New York, 1959, vol. 2, pp. 756-766.
69. See Sir Wm. M. Ramsay, *The Historical Geography of Asia Minor*, London, 1890.
70. See Sir Wm. M. Ramsay, *St. Paul the Traveller and Roman Citizen*, London, 1896.
71. Metzger, H., *St. Paul's Journeys in the Greek Orient*, translated by Prof. S. H. Hooke, London, 1955, p. 13.
72. See Sir Wm. M. Ramsay, *The Letters to the Seven Churches*, London, 1904.
73. Blaiklock, E. M., *The Christian in Pagan Society*, *op. cit.* (n. 43).
74. Pliny, *Epistles, loc. cit.*
75. Case, S. J., *The Evolution of Early Christianity*, London, 1914, pp. 195-238.
76. See Grant, R. M., *Gnosticism and Early Christianity*, London, 1959.
77. Weiss, *op. cit.*, vol. 2, pp. 780-782.
78. For convenient English translation see Lake, K., *The Apostolic Fathers*, I, 9-121.
79. Tit. 1: 5 f.
80. Jn 21: 18.
81. Suetonius, *Nero*, 16.
82. Tacitus, *Annals*, 15. 44.

BIBLIOGRAPHY

Atlases

Atlas of the Classical World, edit. by A. A. M. Van der Heyden and H. H. Scullard (London, 1959).

Atlas of the Early Christian World, F. Van der Meer and C. Mohrmann, translated and edited by M. F. Hedlund and H. H. Rowley (London, 1959).

Bibliography

BAYNES, N. H., *The Early Church and Social Life*, *Hist. Assoc.* 1927, 16 pp.

TENNEY, M. C., *New Testament Survey* (London 1961), pp. 433-453.

General Works

BLAIKLOCK, E. M., *The Christian in Pagan Society* (London, 1951).

BLAIKLOCK, E. M., *Rome in the New Testament* (London, 1959).

BRUCE, F. F., *The Spreading Flame* (London, 1958).

CADOUX, C. J., *The Early Church and the World* (Edinburgh, 1925).

CAIRD, G. B., *The Apostolic Age* (London, 1955).

CARY, M., *The Geographic Background of Greek and Roman History* (Oxford, 1949).

GLOVER, T. R., *The Conflict of Religions in the Early Roman Empire* (London, 1909).

GUIGNEBERT, C., *The Jewish World in the Time of Jesus*, tr. S. H. Hooke (London, 1939).

HALLIDAY, W. R., *The Pagan Background of Early Christianity* (Liverpool, 1925).

HARNACK, A., *The Mission and Expansion of Christianity*, tr. J. Moffatt (London, 1908).

LAKE, K., and CADBURY, H. J., *The Beginnings of Christianity*, vol. V. (London, 1933).

MATTINGLY, H., *Christianity in the Roman Empire* (London, 1955).

MOMIGLIANO, A. (edit.), *Paganism and Christianity in the Fourth Century* (Oxford, 1963); see especially article by A. H. M. Jones, 'The Social Background of Christianity'.

MOORE, G. F., *Judaism in the First Centuries of the Christian Era* (Cambridge, Mass., 1927).

NOCK, A. D., *Early Gentile Christianity against its Hellenistic Background* (New York, 1928).

NOCK, A. D., *Conversion* (Oxford, 1933).

OAKLEY, H. CAREY, 'The Greek and Roman Background of the New Testament', *Vox Evangelica* No. 1, 1962, pp. 2-3.

WORKMAN, H. B., *Persecution in the Early Church* (London, 1906; new edit., 1960).

WRIGHT, G. E., *An Introduction to Biblical Archaeology*, pp. 147-198 (London, 1959).

THE HISTORICAL AND POLITICAL BACKGROUND AND CHRONOLOGY OF THE NEW TESTAMENT

HAROLD H. ROWDON

The Historical and Political Background

Though a glance at an atlas of the world shows that the Roman Empire covered only a fraction of the inhabited earth, yet in the first century A.D. it was regarded—with justice—as a world empire of a new order. Rome, a city situated on the western side of the Italian peninsula, had gained control not only of Italy, Gaul, Spain, and North Africa in the west, but also of all the lands bordering the eastern coasts of the Mediterranean Sea. That sea had become a Roman lake, the security of which required further expansion to the river-boundaries of the Rhine, Danube and Euphrates. Not even far-off Britain was omitted.

Palestine was situated in the extreme east of the Roman world, in the large area stretching from Greece to Egypt where Greek culture and the common dialect of the Greek language had spread as a result of trade and colonization even before Alexander the Great had swept all before him in military triumph. There, too, Rome had established her sway. Already in control of Greece and the west of Asia Minor by the end of the second century B.C., Rome waged war for a quarter of a century against Mithridates of Pontus and his allies until, at the end of 64 B.C., Pompey, who had already achieved fame by clearing the Mediterranean of the pirates who infested it, brought peace to the eastern hinterland of that sea by establishing the Roman province of Syria. Among the client kingdoms where native dynasties were entrusted with control and made responsible for peace, order and the prompt payment of taxes was Judaea, which was part of Herod the Great's kingdom where Jesus was born at Bethlehem.

For centuries Rome had been organized as a republic. The Roman senate, largely composed of former magistrates who had been elected to office by the people, though theoretically only an advisory body, had become the real ruler of the empire in the second and third centuries B.C. and had acted as a conservative force against political development. During the last century of the republic, its supremacy had been challenged again and again by military commanders, the greatest of whom, Julius Caesar, defeated the senatorial forces in civil war and became dictator. His autocratic rule deeply offended the Roman nobility and led to his assassination in 44 B.C. Caesar's nephew, Octavian, employed greater diplomacy and while professing to restore the republic in 27 B.C. actually transformed it into an empire, and was later granted the honorific title of 'Augustus'.

The theory of Roman government rested on the concept of *imperium*, the authority to command obedience. This was given to the emperor whose direct authority extended to most of the provinces where troops were stationed. The senate was entrusted with the government of the rest of the empire, with the exception of a few client-kingdoms, mainly in the east. The emperor's powers were nominally limited in time and required renewal, and there was no guarantee that Octavian would have successors. Nevertheless, the arrangement proved to be more than a delicately balanced constitution of limited duration.

Since the emperor was responsible for the frontiers and the more disturbed areas, whereas the senate administered internal and settled provinces, the emperor was empowered to act as *imperator*, commander-in-chief of the armed forces. His authority ran in senatorial provinces as well as his own. His tribunician powers eventually gave him powers of legal veto and appellate jurisdiction (Ac. 25: 11 may be explicable on other grounds, but shows the line of development by which, eventually, 'appeal to Caesar' replaced the traditional 'appeal to the people'). His *auctoritas* gave immense prestige to his pronouncements so that soon imperial instructions by edict, mandate or rescript came to acquire the force of law. Octavian's family name was Caesar; he was given the title of honour, Augustus, which signifies something set apart for the service of the gods; and the term, *Princeps*, by which he was designated, though it defined him merely as first citizen, came to elevate him above all others. The fact that he normally resided at Rome, and the gradual steps taken to dignify his person and office—later to culminate in the cult of emperor worship—underlined and enforced his supremacy. The long reign of Caesar Augustus —he lived until A.D. 14—also served to establish the new order which was able to survive a succession of somewhat second-rate or sinister emperors.

Augustus's elderly stepson, Tiberius, who reigned from A.D. 14-37, lacked the tact and prestige of Augustus. Gaius Caligula succeeded. He was a megalomaniac who was assassinated in A.D. 41. Claudius (A.D. 41-54) was not without ability, but suffered from a physical defect which may have been the result of Parkinson's disease or a spastic condition (Blaiklock). A letter of Claudius, written in A.D. 41 to the people of Alexandria, forbade the Jews there 'to admit Jews who come down from Syria or Egypt. . . . Otherwise I will by all means take vengeance on them as fomentors of what is a general plague infecting the whole world'. In A.D. 49, Claudius expelled the Jews from Rome (Ac. 18: 2) because of the disorders arising 'at the instigation of one Chrestus' (Suetonius). These may be uncertain allusions to Christianity, but there is no doubt that Claudius's adopted son, the infamous Nero who became emperor in A.D. 54, inflicted savage punishments on Christians in Rome, Peter and Paul probably among them. Nero, who had a passion for Greek art and culture, was dissolute and irresponsible and alienated almost every section of the community. His act of suicide in A.D. 68 was followed by a period of bitter civil strife, mainly in A.D. 69, the 'year of the four emperors'.

Vespasian emerged, an able and competent administrator who brought order out of chaos (A.D. 69-79). The new Flavian dynasty continued with Titus, son of Vespasian and conqueror of Jerusalem, who reigned A.D. 79-81, and ended with Domitian, the younger brother of Titus, who was emperor A.D. 81-96. Roman writers, such as Tacitus, portray Domitian as suspicious, sinister and cruel. Christian traditions single him out as the next great persecutor of the Church after Nero. The Apocalypse was doubtless written under the shadow of Domitian as well as with memories of Nero.

The Roman Empire comprised some 40 provinces at the end of the first century A.D. Senatorial provinces were ruled by proconsuls who were responsible to the senate by whom they were appointed. Their appointment was normally for one year, though this might be renewed. In Paul's day, Sergius Paulus was proconsul of Cyprus (Ac. 13: 7) and Gallio proconsul of Achaia (Ac. 18: 12). Imperial provinces were governed by senatorial legates appointed by the emperor with the title of propraetor, or by *equites* with the title of prefect or procurator: all these were responsible directly to the emperor and held office at his pleasure.

A number of Roman provinces figure in the New Testament. Spain (Rom. 15: 24) and, possibly, Gaul (2 Tim. 4: 10) receive a brief mention, but the action of the New Testament took place almost entirely in the eastern part of the empire. Illyricum (Rom. 15: 19), now western Yugoslavia, was subdued largely by Augustus and was subsequently enlarged and divided into Pannonia and Dalmatia (2 Tim. 4: 10). Augustus formed Greece into two provinces: Macedonia (Ac. 16: 9) with its capital at Thessalonica, and Achaia (Rom. 15: 26) where Corinth was the chief city. Colonies of veteran soldiers were established at numerous places, such as Philippi, and several Greek cities, including Athens, remained free cities with treaty rights.

In Asia Minor there were only three provinces in 27 B.C. Asia (Ac. 20: 4) contained many Greek cities. Roman jurisdiction was exercised through nine or more assizes (Ac. 19: 38) presided over by the proconsul. Bithynia (Ac. 16: 7) was administered with Pontus (1 Pet. 1: 1) as a single province. Cilicia, as a separate province, disappeared during the early empire and was administered with Syria (Gal. 1: 21) until A.D. 72 when it was reconstituted. In 25 B.C. Galatia became an imperial province, embracing not only the old ethnic kingdom of Galatia but also parts of Pontus, Phrygia, Lycaonia, Pisidia, Paphlagonia and Isauria (Gal. 1: 2). Cappadocia (1 Pet. 1: 1) was constituted a province by Tiberius in A.D. 17. Pamphylia (Ac. 13: 13) and Lycia (Ac. 27: 5) were organized as a jointprovince by Claudius in A.D. 43. The island of Cyprus had been a Roman province since 58 B.C. It became a senatorial province in 27 B.C. and was therefore ruled by a proconsul in New Testament times (Ac. 13: 7).

Syria (Gal. 1: 21) was the eastern province most important for the security of the empire since it lay adjacent to the Euphrates frontier. Four legions were regularly stationed in the province and the governor, always a man of experience, was responsible for the safety of nearby provinces. Needless to say, Augustus classed Syria as imperial. Antioch became one of the chief cities of the whole empire, and the bastion of the east.

The kingdom of Judaea (Mt. 2: 1) bordered on Syria. When the east was settled by Pompey, Galilee, Samaria, Judaea and Peraea east of the Jordan were entrusted to Hyrcanus II as high priest and ethnarch, and the cities of the north-east were incorporated into the administration of the Syrian province. Subsequently, Herod, son of Antipater, Hyrcanus's minister, journeyed to Rome, ingratiated himself with the future Augustus, and was granted by the Roman senate the dignity of King of Judaea. He had to fight for his position, for he was bitterly opposed in Judaea, not only by reason of his Roman patronage, but also because he was of Idumaean, non-Jewish blood. By 37 B.C. he was able to enter Jerusalem and commence his rule. His marriage to Mariamne, the heiress of the Jewish priestly house, was a bid to win the favour of the Jews.

Herod retained the favour of Augustus and secured some extension of his rule. During a vigorous reign of some 33 years he suppressed the old aristocracy and established a new nobility of royal officials, fostering the party of the Herodians who may have viewed him in a messianic light (Mt. 22: 16; Mk 3: 6; 12: 13). Herod was a great builder who (c. 20 B.C.) commenced the reconstruction of the Temple at Jerusalem (Jn 2: 20). This was intended as a sop to the Jews, but Herod also constructed the port of Caesarea in token of his affection for Rome. Ruthless and cruel, Herod sustained his policies with the aid of astute diplomacy and armed force backed by the power of Rome.

When Herod the Great died in 4 B.C. his kingdom was parcelled out to three of his sons who survived his murderous intrigues. Philip received the remote territories north-east of the Sea of Galilee where he reigned in peace for over 30 years. Herod Antipas received Galilee together with Peraea east of Jordan and the minor title of tetrarch. He built Tiberias, named in honour of the emperor, but lived as a professing Jew and entertained a certain respect for John the Baptist (Mk 6: 20). Though married to the daughter of Aretas, King of Nabataea, Herod Antipas succumbed to the attractions of Herodias, daughter of one of his half-brothers and wife of another. This liaison involved Herod Antipas in war with Nabataea. During the course of this war he celebrated his birthday in the stronghold of Machaerus (according to Josephus) where Salome, Herodias's daughter, danced and brought John the Baptist to his death (Mt. 14: 6-12; Mk 6: 21-29). Antipas was defeated and had to appeal to Rome for help. On the death of the emperor, Tiberius, who had trusted him to the extent of using him as a mediator between Rome and Parthia, Antipas, urged on by Herodias, petitioned Gaius Caligula for the title of king. Instead, he was banished to Gaul as the result of a charge of treasonable conduct brought against him by his nephew, Herod Agrippa I, who was given his territories as a reward (A.D. 39).

The major part of Herod the Great's kingdom —Judaea and Samaria—was bequeathed to his son, Archelaus. He became so unpopular as to provoke numerous uprisings which eventually necessitated the intervention of the Governor of Syria, Varus (cf. Mt. 2: 22). It became necessary for Archelaus to journey to Rome in order to defend his position against the counter-claims of relatives, such as Herod Antipas, and the representations of the Jewish people (cf. Lk. 19: 11-27). Strangely, Archelaus was confirmed in power by Augustus, though without the royal title. He proved an incompetent ruler and a deputation of Jews and Samaritans secured his banishment in A.D. 6.

Judaea was then placed under a Roman procurator who was loosely subordinate to the Syrian legate but directly responsible to the emperor. The procurator's headquarters were in Caesarea, though in times of unsettled conditions, such as the Jewish feasts, he might reside in Jerusalem. He had a small force of 3,000 men, raised in Palestine from the non-Jewish section of the population. One cohort was stationed in Jerusalem in the castle of Antonia overlooking the Temple. The procurator was responsible for law and order and taxation, but otherwise the internal government and legal administration of the land was largely in the hands of the Jews. Yet Judaea seethed with discontent. In A.D. 6-7, the 'census' almost produced general rebellion, and men like Judas of Galilee (Ac. 5: 37) led 'underground' movements which fostered hatred and bloodshed.

The early procurators of Judaea are of little importance for the background to the New Testament apart from the appointments they made to the office of high priest. When Quirinius reorganized the province of Judaea in A.D. 6 he deposed the high priest who had been nominated by Archelaus and appointed Annas, the son of Seth (Jn 18: 13, 24; Ac. 4: 6). Annas remained high priest during the procuratorships of Coponius (A.D. 6-9), Marcus Ambivius (A.D. 9-12) and Annius Rufus (A.D. 12-15).

When Valerius Gratus became procurator in A.D. 15 he deposed Annas in favour of Ishmael, the son of Phobi. Ishmael was followed in quick succession by Eleazar, son of Annas, Simon, the son of Kami, and Joseph Caiaphas who was son-in-law to Annas. Caiaphas remained high priest for 18 years, including the ten years of Pilate's procuratorship, until Vitellius, legate of Syria, deposed him in A.D. 36. He was followed by two sons of Annas: first Jonathan, and then, after a year, Theophilus. It was costly in bribes both to secure office and to retain it, and only wealthy families such as that of Annas could afford the luxury.

Pontius Pilate held the office of procurator from A.D. 26-36. Time and again he provoked Jewish hostility, almost to breaking point. He issued copper coinage bearing heathen symbols to the great scandal of the Jews, but withdrew it from A.D. 31. He ordered the Roman standards with their representations of the Emperor to be taken into Jerusalem under cover of darkness, but eventually removed them. He hung votive shields dedicated to the Emperor in Herod's palace in Jerusalem, but withdrew them on orders from Rome. He financed the building of an aqueduct to bring water into Jerusalem from the sacred Corban fund, and quelled by treachery the tumult that resulted. The same mixture of truculence, cowardice and subtlety may be discerned in Pilate's dealings with Christ. The unhappy man was recalled to Rome in A.D. 36 after a massacre of Samaritans had taken place (cf. Lk. 13: 1).

Marcellus (A.D. 37) and Marullus (A.D. 37-41) followed Pilate, and then for a few years the whole of the territory which had formed the kingdom of Herod the Great was ruled by Herod Agrippa I, his grandson. Agrippa, who was high in the favour of the mad emperor, Caligula (he was able to dissuade him from setting up a statue of himself in the Temple of Jerusalem), was granted in A.D. 37 the northeastern territories which had been ruled by Philip. Two years later, when Herod Antipas was exiled at Agrippa's instigation, the latter was given Galilee and Peraea. Upon the accession of the Emperor Claudius in A.D. 41, Agrippa received virtually all the territory that his grandfather had ruled. King Agrippa I ingratiated himself with the orthodox Jews and persecuted the Christian Church (Ac. 12: 1-19). His ambitions were cut short in A.D. 44 by a sudden disease, described by Josephus in terms similar to those of Ac. 12: 23, and authority over the whole land passed to another succession of Roman procurators.

The first to be appointed was Cuspius Fadus (A.D. 44-46). He claimed the right to appoint high priests which had recently been exercised by Agrippa and which was a source of income as well as influence. In response to Jewish representation the Emperor ruled that it should go to Agrippa's brother, Herod, king of Chalcis. After his death in A.D. 48 it was given to Agrippa's son, Herod Agrippa II, who retained it until the outbreak of the Jewish War in A.D. 66. Soon after Fadus became procurator one, Theudas (not to be confused with the Theudas of Ac. 5: 36), laid claim to miraculous powers and raised one of the messianic followings which were soon to become a feature of the times.

Tiberius Julius Alexander became procurator in A.D. 46 at a time of famine (Ac. 11: 28). As an apostate Jew—his uncle was the famous Jewish philosopher, Philo—his action in crushing a Jewish rising led by two sons of Judas of Galilee was especially unpopular. Other risings followed during the procuratorship of Cumanus (A.D. 48-52).

Antonius Felix who became procurator, probably in A.D. 52, was a man of humble origin. He had once been a slave in the household of Claudius's mother, Antonia. Nevertheless he married well and his third wife was Drusilla, the daughter of Herod Agrippa I. Felix tried to deal with the problem of disorder in Judaea, but this did not endear him to large sections of the people who regarded insurgents as patriots.

Among the rebel leaders of the time was an Egyptian who claimed to be a prophet and led a following of about 4,000 to the Mount of Olives, promising them that at a signal the walls of the city would fall flat and enable them to march in and seize the city. Instead, he and his followers were scattered by Felix's troops. A few years later, Paul was mistaken for this Egyptian (Ac. 21: 38). Some of the extremist Jews began to practise assassination, stabbing their victims with daggers which they carried concealed in their cloaks. They became known as *sicarii* (dagger-men), a word which is translated 'Assassins' in Ac. 21: 38.

One of the notorious high priests of this period was Ananias, the son of Nedebaeus (A.D. 47-58). His greed was such that he seized and sold those parts of the temple sacrifices which were the perquisites of the ordinary priests who, in consequence, were brought to the point of starvation. Ananias presided over the scandalous meeting of the Sanhedrin that examined Paul (Ac. 23: 1-9).

Felix, whom Tacitus described as 'a master of cruelty and lust' (cf. Ac. 24: 25) was recalled by Nero about A.D. 59 and was succeeded by Porcius Festus, a worthier representative of Rome (Ac. 25).

Festus consulted the remaining member of the Herodian house who figures in the New Testament. Agrippa, son of Herod Agrippa I, was considered too young to succeed his father. Later he was made king of Chalcis, a Lebanese territory. In A.D. 53 he exchanged Chalcis for the territory north-east of the Sea of Galilee over which his father had ruled. Nero granted him further accessions of territory, including the cities of Tiberias and Bethsaida Julias. In gratitude, he changed the name of his capital from Caesarea Philippi to Neronias. Herod Agrippa II was 'a Herod of the better sort' (Blaiklock) who was consulted by Festus regarding the charges brought against Paul (Ac. 25: 13-26: 32). He strove, though without success, to avert the catastrophe of the great rebellion against Rome, A.D. 66-70.

Festus died in office, c. A.D. 62, and a three months' interval elapsed before his successor, Albinus, arrived. This enabled the high priest, Annas II, to put a number of his enemies to death. The most notable of these was James the Just, leader of the Christian Church in Jerusalem. This apparently shocked many in Jerusalem who revered James for his asceticism and piety and who later said that the fall of Jerusalem was not unconnected with the judicial murder of James.

Albinus was followed by Gessius Florus (A.D. 65-66). Discontent had been increasing for some time and non-payment of taxes had become chronic. In A.D. 66 Gessius Florus appropriated a large sum from the funds of the Temple. His ruthless crushing of the riots that followed led to a revolt in which the mob gained virtual control of Jerusalem. The Roman garrison had to be withdrawn from the city. The rebels stormed the Dead Sea fortress of Masada and the revolt soon became nation-wide.

The Jewish forces in Galilee, where the full pressure of the Roman punitive expedition might be expected, were put under the command of a young priest, Joseph. In February A.D. 67 Nero appointed Vespasian to reduce Palestine to obedience, and Joseph was unable to withstand the Roman forces. Instead, he surrendered to the enemy and later ingratiated himself with the future emperor, becoming his friend and secretary. As Flavius Josephus, he found time to write his famous volumes on Jewish history. By June A.D. 68 only a few strongholds, including Jerusalem, remained in Jewish hands.

Jerusalem gained an unexpected respite as a result of Nero's suicide in that month. Little could be done in the year of the four emperors to reduce Palestine to full obedience. Meanwhile zealots of several factions, bitterly opposed to each other, crowded into Jerusalem to their mutual discomfort. Remembering her Master's warning (Mt. 24: 16), the Christian community fled to Pella, a Greek city of the Decapolis.

When Vespasian became emperor he made his son, Titus, commander in Palestine. By the spring of A.D. 70 Jerusalem was invested. At the cost of fearful bloodshed, the city was reduced to the accompaniment of bitter strife among the defenders themselves. City and Temple were destroyed. Other Jewish strongholds were taken one by one, the last being Masada, the Dead Sea fortress which held out until April A.D. 73.

Judaea remained a separate province with its procurator directly responsible to the legate commanding the tenth legion which was stationed at Jerusalem. The Sanhedrin, high priesthood and temple worship were abolished and the tax formerly payable by Jews to the Temple funds was diverted to the temple of Jupiter.

Though the province was the normal unit of administration in the Roman Empire, the most vital element in governmental, social and economic affairs was undoubtedly the city. Rome itself, the hub of empire, was a city and city life was fostered throughout the empire as a matter of policy. In the East this was no innovation, for the Greeks who equated city life with civilized life had established a large number of colonies, such as the cities of the Decapolis east of Jordan.

Rome recognized the right of cities to municipal self-government. The citizens, met in lawful assembly (Ac. 19: 39) or in less official ways, were often a force to be reckoned with, but power resided in the magistrates who were increasingly drawn from the ranks of the well-to-do. The Roman law which they administered served as one of the most vital unifying factors in the empire (Ac. 19: 38-40).

Cities served as centres of culture and refinement as well as of entertainment provided through the varied facilities of baths and theatres. Their strategic importance for commerce is perhaps linked with the fact that every city of significance came to have its Jewish community. They served as foci for the surrounding countryside, providing not only market facilities in their splendid *fora* but also stimulus to religion in their costly temples and protection from enemies behind their ample walls. The common Greek which was the language of commerce made intercourse easy, even between men of different races. Small wonder that Paul made the cities the centre of his missionary endeavours!

Social life in the cities posed severe problems for Christians. In addition to the immorality which was commonplace and often hallowed by association with religion, the ubiquitous guilds produced situations fraught with dilemma. These 'voluntary associations of people with common interests' (Oakley) were of many kinds: guilds of artisans and traders, burial clubs and social clubs of all descriptions may be mentioned. The banquets held by such associations in heathen temples and the civic feasts produced acute dilemmas for conscientious Christians (1 C. 8: 10; 10: 19-22).

Cities were of different kinds. *Coloniae* were cities settled by Roman citizens, often veterans from the army who received the franchise on discharge. *Municipia* were cities that had been autonomous communities and, under Roman rule, were given the freedom of Rome. Municipal office might carry with it Roman citizenship which was also given to individuals in recognition of outstanding services to the empire. Under certain circumstances, Roman citizenship might apparently be purchased (Ac. 22: 28). It was granted sparingly until A.D. 212. It conferred both financial (cf. Mt. 17: 25, 26) and legal (Ac. 16: 37) immunities and was regarded as a high honour (Ac. 16: 21, 38; 22: 28). Citizenship of any city, especially if it possessed some claim to fame, was a source of pride (Ac. 21: 39).

Cities which remained independent were allowed to issue their own coinage, an important concession since, apart from other considerations, coinage was universally regarded as an instrument of propaganda. In general, imperial coinage was in use throughout the empire, though the Jews were allowed to mint their own coinage for the Temple tax and also for the use of strict Jews who would not touch a coin bearing the imperial image and superscription (cf. Mt. 22: 15-22). Taxation was an ever-present reminder of the claims of Rome. It was partly in the hands of *publicani* who were regarded in fiery Judaea as collaborators with the hated occupying power as well as financial exactors who unscrupulously lined their own pockets.

Slavery was a universal institution. Legally, the slave had no rights and was regarded as the chattel of his master. Under the influence of Stoicism a more generous attitude began to appear. In the guilds, slaves were allowed to associate on an equal footing with free men, and it became possible for a slave to buy his freedom with the savings which his master allowed him to accumulate (cf. Gal. 3: 28; Col. 3: 11; Phm. 16).

The provinces and cities of the empire were linked together by a magnificent transport system. Roads radiated from Rome, built originally for military purposes and maintained by military labour. The central government assumed major responsibility for the upkeep of roads and for the maintenance of the *cursus publicus*, a system of communications for official purposes. Rest houses were provided at intervals of 25 miles and changes of horses more frequently, though only for the use of imperial couriers. Brigandage was ruthlessly suppressed, though it was not unknown (Lk. 10: 30; 2 C. 11: 26). Travel by sea was made relatively easy after Pompey had cleared the Mediterranean of pirates. A corn fleet sailed at regular intervals to convey corn from Alexandria to Rome (Ac. 27: 6, 38), but sailing was dangerous in autumn and almost impossible in winter (Ac. 27: 9). Goods, persons and ideas travelled freely in the Roman world, as is abundantly clear from the pages of the New Testament.

The Chronology of the New Testament

To an age in which historical research has become a highly specialized study that has developed in a distinctive direction, the New Testament is disconcertingly bare of information which would enable us to turn its historical data into the form of history with which we are familiar. In New Testament times there was no fixed point of reference similar to our dating scheme of B.C.-A.D. Indeed, historians of those days were not unduly concerned to provide a closely-knit narrative of events linked together in chronological sequence. Moreover, the Biblical writers were more concerned to show the relation of the events they recorded to the eternal purposes of God than they were to write historical narratives in the form to which we are accustomed.

This is not to say that the accuracy of the historical data of the New Testament is in question. There is every reason for confidence in the reliability of the sacred record, and the instances where cavil is possible are few. But the task of trying to transpose the New Testament into another form from that in which it was written is a difficult task. It is well worth attempting because of the very great help which it gives to the endeavour which the attentive reader ought to make to see the sacred story as an integrated whole, set in the history of the first century A.D.

The starting-point is naturally the birth of Jesus. This took place during the reign of Herod the Great (Mt. 2: 1), that is, before 4 B.C. Luke tells us that the great event occurred at the time when a census was being taken at the behest of Caesar Augustus and when Quirinius (Cyrenius) was governor of Syria (Lk. 2: 1, 2). We know that Quirinius was governor of Syria in A.D. 6-7 when a census that was being taken in Palestine provoked the revolt of Judas of Galilee (Josephus; Ac. 5: 37). Some scholars have therefore concluded that Luke has made a mistake.

Among the possible explanations, the most likely is the one elaborated by Stauffer. He argues that there is a certain amount of evidence which suggests that Quirinius served as a kind of commander-in-chief in the east for most of the period 12 B.C. to A.D. 16. In this respect he would be in the tradition of men like Pompey and Marcus Antonius. During part of the period Quirinius acted as governor of Syria but at other times an imperial procurator served under him as governor of the province. Stauffer further argues that the census that Quirinius made was not an ordinary census but a *descriptio prima* taken as a basis for the levying of taxation. The first stage would take the form of a registration of all taxable persons and objects and (like the English Doomsday Book) would involve a lengthy process and much opposition. Eventually it would be possible for the final assessment to be made. According to Stauffer, the census of A.D. 7 was such an assessment, made on the basis of the registration which had been commenced some long time earlier.

When was it commenced? Mt. 2: 2 shows that it was at the time when an astronomical phenomenon was observed. Stauffer has drawn attention to two ancient records, one forecasting the conjunction of the planets Jupiter and Saturn in the constellation of the Fishes for 7 B.C., the other declaring that this would signify that 'there will appear in Palestine in this year the ruler of the last days.' Contemporary evidence and astronomical calculations suggest that this conjunction did occur in the year forecast. It is therefore possible to suggest that the birth of Christ during the opening stages of the census procedure took place in the year 7 B.C. (A difficulty to this view is the fact that the word used in Mt. 2: 2 is that for a single star.)

The baptism of Jesus took place when He was about thirty years of age, but this is clearly a round figure (Lk. 3: 23). This event took place after the beginning of the ministry of John the Baptist, though it is not clear whether there was any appreciable interval. This is unfortunate for our present purpose since Luke plainly states that John's ministry began in the fifteenth year of the reign of Tiberius (Lk. 3: 1, 2). Yet even this clear statement is capable of different interpretations. Tiberius's reign used to be reckoned

from the beginning of his co-regency with Augustus, but it is now thought that it should be reckoned from the death of Augustus which took place on 19 August A.D. 14. If so, then John the Baptist commenced his ministry in A.D. 28 or 29 and Jesus was baptized soon after.

A month or two later, after the call of the first disciples, the marriage in Cana and a short stay in Capernaum (Jn 1: 35-2: 12), Jesus went to Jerusalem for the first passover of His ministry (Jn 2: 13). This was probably the passover of A.D. 30. The remark made by the Jews on this occasion that the Temple had taken forty-six years to build (Jn 2: 20) does not fix the date with precision. We know that Herod began to 'build' the Temple *c.* 20 B.C., but some time may have been spent in preparation before the actual work of building commenced. Furthermore, the remark recorded in Jn 2: 20 need not imply that the work had recently been completed. All that it tells us with certainty is that Jesus visited Jerusalem for the first passover of His ministry at least 46 years after 20 B.C.

The length of Jesus's ministry is another open question, though it seems likely that it extended for just over three years. It has been suggested that the length was no more than a single year. This view was originally put forward on the ground that Lk. 4: 19 (Isa. 61: 2) refers to the acceptable 'year' of the Lord. The evidence of the synoptic gospels does not explicitly exclude this view, though the amount of activity they record could hardly have been fitted into a single year. The fourth gospel flatly contradicts it. Some maintain that the ministry covered two years as John's gospel suggests at first sight by its allusions to three passovers (Jn 2: 13; 6: 4; 11: 55). But it is more likely that the ministry of Jesus lasted for three years.

It is true that there is no direct mention of a fourth passover or of any other fact to compel such a view, but the indirect evidence of both the fourth and the synoptic gospels suggests that the interval between the two passovers of Jn 2: 13 and Jn 6: 4 was more than a single year. Jesus and His disciples spent some time in Judaea after the first passover (Jn 4: 1-3). Indeed, it appears that they did not return to Galilee until the following winter, four months before harvest time (Jn 4: 35; it is unlikely that this was a proverbial saying since the interval between sowing and reaping was six months). Jn 5: 1 implies some further lapse of time before Jesus returned to Jerusalem for a feast, the name of which is not given. It is unlikely that this was the feast of Purim which was observed in February/March. It may have been the passover of March/April or even a later feast, such as

Pentecost or Tabernacles. If so, the passover of Jn 6: 4 would be that of the following year. That this was the case is confirmed by the amount of activity recorded in the synoptic gospels as taking place between the commencement of our Lord's Galilean ministry and the passover observed about the time of the feeding of the five thousand, which is that of Jn 6: 4. No fewer than three evangelistic tours, as well as that of the Twelve and sundry other activities, are recorded (Mt. 4: 12-14: 13; Mk 1: 16-6: 32; Lk. 4: 31-9: 10).

The ministry of Jesus ended, as it had begun, under the procuratorship of Pontius Pilate. Pilate was procurator A.D. 26-36. The death of Jesus did not take place near the beginning of this period, for independently of the above discussion of the dating of His ministry, the events referred to in Lk. 13: 1 and 23: 12 seem to require that Pilate had been procurator for some time. True there are traditions going back to Tertullian that date the crucifixion A.D. 29, but there are difficulties to this dating, even if we were to push back the period of the ministry.

It seems clear that Jesus died on a Friday at the time of the paschal full moon, and the tradition of Tertullian and others places that Friday on 25 March. But astronomical calculations indicate fairly decisively that the paschal full moon of A.D. 29 was in April.

The gospels require that the Friday in question was either 14 or 15 Nisan. Since the date of the month Nisan was fixed by the full moon, astronomers have been able to calculate that 15 Nisan was a Friday in A.D. 27 and 14 Nisan was a Friday in A.D. 30 and 33. In view of the evidence already adduced to suggest that the ministry of Jesus extended from A.D. 30 to 33, we may conclude that it is at least likely that the crucifixion took place in A.D. 33.

There is no reason to think that the period between Pentecost and the conversion of Paul was unduly protracted, though the precise length of the interval is unknown. It has been asserted that the stoning of Stephen could not have taken place while Pilate was procurator and must therefore be dated after A.D. 36. But fanaticism is unpredictable and may be unloosed at any time, regardless of consequences.

A tradition was preserved by Irenaeus to the effect that the interval between Pentecost and the conversion of Paul was 18 months, and this may not be very wide of the mark. A clue is given in the New Testament where Paul stated that three years after his conversion he left Damascus (Gal. 1: 18), presumably on the occasion when the governor under King Aretas attempted to seize him (2 C. 11: 32 f.). Damascus was in Roman hands, certainly until

A.D. 33 and probably until 37. Since Aretas died in A.D. 40 he probably gained possession of Damascus between A.D. 37 and 40. During this time, therefore, and probably nearer the beginning than the end, Paul escaped from Damascus. Since this was three years after his conversion, this must have taken place soon after A.D. 34, if not in that year.

After his departure from Damascus in precipitous haste Paul spent 15 days in Jerusalem (Gal. 1: 18) before retiring to Syria and Cilicia (Gal. 1: 21) where he remained in obscurity for an unspecified period until Barnabas went to seek him out (Ac. 11: 25). Barnabas brought him to Antioch where he remained a year (Ac. 11: 26). The two men were then deputed by the church at Antioch to carry aid to the brethren in Judaea who had been stricken by famine. This took place at an unspecified time during the reign of Claudius (Ac. 11: 27-30). A.D. 45 was a year of disastrous harvests in the eastern Mediterranean area, as we learn from Egyptian papyri, and it is therefore likely that this famine-visit, as it has been called, was made by Paul and Barnabas late in A.D. 45 or early in 46. That this was so is confirmed by the fact that Luke interrupts his narrative at the point of the visit in order to relate the persecution of the Church by Herod Agrippa I and the death of the king (Ac. 12: 1-23) which took place 'about that time' (Ac. 12: 1). Herod died in A.D. 44.

Paul's first missionary journey probably took place during A.D. 46 and 47. There is nothing in the narrative to suggest a protracted stay at any of the numerous places visited (Ac. 13: 4-14: 26). It is stated, however, that the missionaries stayed a long time at Antioch after their return (Ac. 14: 28).

The so-called Council of Jerusalem took place after the end of the first missionary journey and before the beginning of the second (Ac. 15). Since the commencement of the second journey can be dated with some certainty late A.D. 49 or early 50 at the latest (see next paragraphs), it seems clear that the Council took place in A.D. 49. If, as is reasonable, this Council is to be identified with that of Gal. 2: 1-10, and if the statement in Gal. 2: 1 is taken to mean that this took place 14 years after Paul's conversion, the conclusion that the Council of Jerusalem took place in A.D. 49 is strengthened.

The view that Paul's second missionary journey lasted from late A.D. 49 or early 50 to the autumn of A.D. 51 rests upon the following data. The journey began not long after the Council had ended (Ac. 15: 33-36). After spending an unspecified time visiting the churches in Syria and Cilicia and the newly-founded churches of Asia Minor, Paul and his companions 'went through' the region of Phrygia and Galatia. If the churches addressed in the letter to the Galatians were churches in the ethnic region of Galatia (according to the North Galatian theory) rather than the churches of southern Asia Minor in the Roman province of Galatia (according to the South Galatian theory), then the brief statement in Ac. 16: 6 must be taken to mean a period of evangelistic activity. Paul then crossed to Europe and, after short stays in Philippi, Thessalonica, Beroea and a short visit to Athens he remained in Corinth for rather more than 18 months (Ac. 18: 11, 18).

It was towards the end of this period that there occurred the Gallio incident, the dating of which can be set with some precision. The Jews in Corinth brought their accusations against Paul to Gallio, undoubtedly soon after he became proconsul of Achaia (Ac. 18: 12). An inscription at Delphi shows that Gallio's year of office began in midsummer of either A.D. 51 or 52. If, as seems likely, it was the former, Paul must have arrived in Corinth early in A.D. 50 and remained there until the summer of 51, when he returned to Antioch via Ephesus and Jerusalem before the onset of winter made sea travel impossible.

This timing is confirmed by the fact that when he arrived in Corinth Paul met Aquila and Priscilla who had recently been forced to leave Rome in consequence of Claudius's edict expelling Jews from Rome (Ac. 18: 2). Since it was probably in A.D. 49 that the edict was issued, it is most likely that Aquila and Priscilla would have reached Corinth early in A.D. 50, not long before Paul arrived.

Paul's third missionary journey was his longest. It followed soon after the conclusion of the second and probably commenced in A.D. 52. After an unspecified period spent in ministering to the churches of Galatia and Phrygia (Ac. 18: 23; cf. 19: 1), Paul spent the greater part of three years at Ephesus (Ac. 19: 8, 10, 21 f.; 20: 31); visited Macedonia and stayed three months in Achaia (Ac. 20: 1-3); and may have journeyed as far as Illyricum (Rom. 15: 19). One of his great concerns on this journey was to gather an offering from the Gentile churches for the poor saints at Jerusalem.

He was anxious to be at Jerusalem by Pentecost (Ac. 20: 16); the year was A.D. 56 or 57. There he was apprehended. He was subsequently examined by Felix (Ac. 24). Two years later, probably in A.D. 59, Festus succeeded Felix (Ac. 24: 27). Arraigned before Festus, Paul made his appeal to Caesar (Ac. 25: 10), and after the hearing before Herod Agrippa II (Ac. 26)

Paul sailed for Rome in the autumn (Ac. 27: 9).

For two years, A.D. 60 and 61, Paul remained a prisoner in Rome (Ac. 28: 20). Subsequent events are shrouded in uncertainty. Possibly the case against Paul went by default, or, more likely, insufficient evidence was brought against him, and he was released. The Pastoral Letters indicate that Paul undertook fresh missionary work before his death which probably took place at Rome before the death of Nero in A.D. 68, and possibly in A.D. 64 at the time of the Neronian persecution.

Peter was miraculously released from prison prior to the death of Herod Agrippa I in A.D. 44 (Ac. 12: 3-19). He left Jerusalem for a time (Ac. 12: 17), but subsequently returned and was present at the Council of Jerusalem (Ac. 15: 7). He visited Antioch (Gal. 2: 11) and may have been at Corinth (1 C. 1: 12). He probably paid at least one visit to Rome. Tradition is strong to the effect that he, as well as Paul, suffered death in Rome. The significance of 1 Pet. 5: 13 is debatable, though Peter may well have used 'Babylon' as an 'apocalyptic' designation for Rome. Almost certainly he fell a victim to Nero's cruelty.

James, the Lord's brother, who became the outstanding Christian leader in Jerusalem (Ac. 12: 17; 15: 13) was stoned to death, probably in A.D. 62. The death of John which, according to tradition, occurred about A.D. 100 marks the close of the apostolic age.

RULERS OF JUDAEA

Herod the Great (King)	37-4 B.C.
Archelaus (Tetrarch)	4 B.C.-A.D.6

Procurators

Coponius	A.D.6-9
Marcus Ambivius	9-12
Annius Rufus	12-15
Valerius Gratus	15-26
Pontius Pilate	26-36
Marcellus	37
Marullus	37-41

King

Herod Agrippa I	41-44

Procurators

Cuspius Fadus	44-46
Tiberius Julius Alexander	46-48
Ventidius Cumanus	48-52
Antonius Felix	52-59
Porcius Festus	59-62
Albinus	62-65
Gessius Florus	65-66

ROMAN EMPERORS

Augustus	27 B.C.–A.D. 14
Tiberius	A.D. 14–37
Gaius (Caligula)	37–41
Claudius	41–54
Nero	54–68
Galba	68–69
Otho	69
Vitellius	69
Vespasian	69–79
Titus	79–81
Domitian	81–96

A SUGGESTED CHRONOLOGY OF THE NEW TESTAMENT

The Birth of Jesus	7 B.C.
The Baptism of Jesus	A.D. 29 or 30
The Death and Resurrection	33
The Conversion of Paul	34 or 35
Paul's First Missionary Journey	46–47
The Council of Jerusalem	49
Paul's Second Missionary Journey	49–51
Paul's Third Missionary Journey	52–56 or 57
Paul's First Imprisonment in Rome	59–61
The Death of James	62?
The Death of Peter	64?
The Death of Paul	64?
The Death of John	c. 100?

THE FAMILY OF HEROD

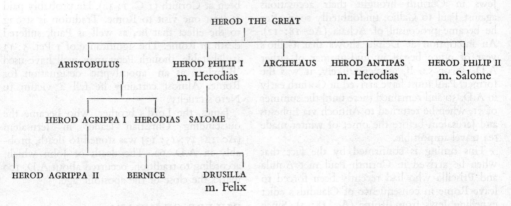

BIBLIOGRAPHY

BLAIKLOCK, E. M., *The Century of the New Testament* (London, 1962).

BLAIKLOCK, E. M., *Cities of the New Testament* (London, 1965).

CHARLESWORTH, M. P., *The Roman Empire* (London, 1951).

GLOVER, T. R., *The World of the New Testament* (Cambridge, 1933).

JUDGE, E. A., *The Social Pattern of Christian Groups in the First Century* (London, 1960).

MATTINGLY, H., *Roman Imperial Civilisation* (London, 1957).

OAKLEY, H. C., 'The Greek and Roman Background of the New Testament', *Vox Evangelica* (London, 1962).

OGG, G., *Chronology of the Public Ministry of Jesus* (Cambridge, 1940).

OGG, G., *Chronology of the Life of St. Paul* (London, 1968).

SHERWIN-WHITE, A. N., *Roman Society and Roman Law in the New Testament* (Oxford, 1963).

WELLS, J. and BARROW, R. H., *A Short History of the Roman Empire* (London, 1950).

THE RELIGIOUS BACKGROUND OF THE NEW TESTAMENT (PAGAN)

HAROLD H. ROWDON

The century of the New Testament was an age of faith. True, the old forms of religion were effete, being more appropriate to city states or at most a small empire than to the world empire that had been created by Rome. Nevertheless at the local level religious fervour found expression in the practice of magic and the veneration of traditional deities who could be equated with, or at least related to, the great gods of Greece and Rome.

Religion was used as a device of government —Augustus restored no fewer than 82 temples in Rome—while emperor worship, which began as a spontaneous movement, was fostered as a means of creating a sentiment of loyalty to the empire as well as to the emperor. New forms of religious life, of which the mystery religions of the East are a well-known example, spread throughout the empire. Philosophical faiths, both old and new, won devotees.

The religions of the first century A.D. shared, to a greater or lesser extent, numerous common features. Usually there was an underlying belief in some form of religious dualism. Though pagan religions were often amoral, if not immoral, there was frequently a strong sense of the conflict between good and evil, or at least between forces benevolent and malevolent to man. Again there was usually an unquestioned acceptance of the possibility of magical control over things and persons. This appears not only in the practice of magic but also in the belief that the punctilious observance of the appropriate religious rites avails to secure the favour of the god in question. At the same time there was usually belief in the activity of Chance or Fortune operating through Fate or Destiny which was in the control of gods, demons or men. The assumption was almost unquestioned that human destiny was ultimately fixed by the stars to which, with the sun, personal existence was ascribed. Needless to say, the reality of the miraculous was generally taken for granted, and unbounded confidence was reposed in

sacred writings especially if these were ancient mysterious or cryptic.

The world of the New Testament was the Roman world which, although restricted to the area surrounding the Mediterranean Sea, was virtually co-extensive with civilization. It is therefore appropriate to conduct a brief survey of public religion from the standpoint of Rome.

Roman state religion, like that of Greece with which it was associated, was polytheistic in character and was largely concerned with the maintenance of right relationship with the gods. The deities of the Roman pantheon included Jupiter, often lauded as 'greatest and best'; Mars, legendary parent of the Roman people, and mighty in war; Minerva, goddess of all who worked with brain or hand; and Vesta, goddess of the undying hearth fire, and symbol of home-life and the family.

The worship of these gods was largely formal and was associated with temple, altar and image. It was also basically civic, particularly on the great festal days when all were expected to take part in the rites. In view of the fact that the family was the basic unit in Roman society, it is not surprising that religion was more strongly entrenched there than in the context of civic worship which was often formal to a degree. *Lares* and *Penates*, symbolic of hearth and home, drew forth the religious devotion of the family.

In the countryside, where religion was more conservative, rustic shrines were erected wherever there was some special sense of the presence of life and power and mystery (the divine *numen*), whether it were a spring, a grove of venerable trees or a range of lofty mountain peaks. To these shrines offerings of milk, cheese, grain or even a few flowers would be brought: the nymphs who inhabited such places must be honoured, and along with them, Faunus god of woodlands, Sylvanus god of unconquered nature, and the like. There were also Terminus who protected fields and boundaries, and the various deities who protected crafts and trades.

The gods who must be approached by the way of sacrifice might also communicate with their devotees by means of dreams, oracles and the answering of prayers. Indeed, if the gods failed to respond to propitiation by answering prayer not only would the promised tribute be withheld but the worshipper might react in disillusionment and turn away to other deities.

An important characteristic of first-century religion was its capacity for syncretism. The way for this had been prepared by the striking development of the Greek Empire and the tendency within Hellenistic religion to identify the deities of different peoples and to fuse their cults. Indeed, the religion of the Hellenistic age has been described by F. C. Grant as being like a chain of lakes with many tributaries. Rome likewise, as she conquered the world, followed the same policy of bringing together the religions as well as the nations under her presidency.

As a result Jupiter and the gods of Rome were equated with Zeus and the gods of Greece. The process may have gone further, for it is likely that when the men of Lystra hailed Barnabas and Paul as Zeus and Hermes (Ac. 14: 11-13) they had in mind not the great deities of Rome but local deities whom they had equated with them. It was not always a question of conquered peoples desiring to acquire the benefits in the power of the gods of their conquerors. The victorious Romans felt it necessary for the gods of a country they had subdued to be honoured since they might be 'Roman gods in native dress' (Charlesworth) and in any case, if they were gods, they must wield some power in their own domains at least. 'Always call on the gods for aid', said a second-century Roman emperor of a philosophical turn of mind (Marcus Aurelius).

During the course of the first century a fresh religious sentiment was fostered in an endeavour to further the unity and well-being of the Roman world. Yet emperor-worship was scarcely a novelty. It was not unknown in the Middle East; Alexander the Great had been given divine honours; and, in any case, since some of the gods of the pagan world were thought to have been men before they became gods and might appear again in human guise, the line between the human and the divine was thin in certain places.

Emperor-worship underwent gradual development, especially in the West where it was eventually fostered for political purposes. At first the emperor was regarded as the representative, if not the incarnation of, the *genius* or presiding spirit of his dynasty; and as *princeps* he represented Rome itself. He was the guardian of the state, the defender of peace and order, the preserver of the empire, its *soter* or saviour. As such it was an easy step for highly revered emperors, such as Augustus and Vespasian, to be included in the roll of those whom the state worshipped as *divus* or divine. For an emperor to demand worship during his lifetime was long regarded as an aberration worthy only of a Caligula or a Domitian.

Yet the increasing pomp and ceremony with which Roman emperors were surrounded made them appear more and more removed from the ranks of ordinary mortals. Men came to worship or take oaths by the *genius* or spirit of living emperors, though emperor-worship was restricted to acts or words of reverence or praise and did not extend to the addressing of prayer or receiving advice in dreams. Especially in the provinces, emperor-worship served as a unifying factor, a sentiment of loyalty to the *status quo*. Joint dedications to a local god and the emperor were frequent, and worship of the emperor was often coupled with that of Rome. The acute embarrassment which this came to present to the Christian may be seen reflected in the pages of the Apocalypse.

One of the most powerful solvents of established religion was provided by the development of philosophical thought. True, Greek religion had declined for other reasons also—disillusionment with the standards of divine conduct, the dissolution of the Greek city-states with which Greek religion had been so closely linked, and the attendant growth of individualism on the one hand and a world-view of things on the other. Yet all this was connected with the rise of philosophical schools of thought which discredited not only Greek religion but also that of Rome.

There was a certain amount of genuine Platonism in the first century: the rise of Neo-Platonism did not come in force until the third century. Platonism 'stood for a view of reality as spiritual, ideal, invisible: the external visible objects in the universe being only copies or shadows of the invisible realities' (F. C. Grant). Such a view produced an attitude of renunciation and asceticism, for the body came to be looked upon as little more than the temporary abiding place of the soul. An interior type of piety was developed which sought to lessen the attachment of the soul to the body, and eventually in Neo-Platonism rigorous asceticism was advocated as a means of releasing the soul from the down-drag of the body.

Attention has been drawn to the contrast between earthly shadows and heavenly realities which is a theme in the Letter to the Hebrews (cf. 2 C. 4: 18) and to passages such as 2 C. 5: 1-8.

But the similarities are superficial: the richness and quality of the Biblical thought make it altogether distinctive.

The Epicurean philosophy taught that pleasure should be the object of life. Though in common parlance the Epicurean view gave rise to the motto, 'Let us eat and drink, for tomorrow we die', yet the pleasure that was sought was not necessarily or even characteristically that which is the product of bodily sensations. The pleasure that was sought was happiness. This, it was maintained, depended on peace of mind. Since religion tended to undermine such happiness with its fear of the supernatural and its bogy of punishment after death the Epicurean was anti-religious. For him the universe consisted of atoms and space. Chance ruled everything and there was no providential oversight by Fate or the gods. At death the soul disintegrated, so there need be nothing to fear thereafter. The existence of pain was not denied but Epicurus declared in a famous phrase that if sharp it is short and if long it is light. Pain, he declared, can always be offset by the memory of past happiness.

The disciples of Epicurus formed scattered groups which followed a common life under careful regulation. There they practised, though only among themselves, their prime virtue of friendship. Paul met Epicureans at Athens (Ac. 17: 18). Though they had gods of their own—beings of supernatural beauty and power living in paradises somehow protected from the general decay—the Epicureans were generally classed, with Christians, as atheists since they denied the existence of the traditional deities.

Cynicism—even more than Epicureanism a household word in the twentieth century—was an attitude held quite widely in the first century. The Cynic affected a lofty disregard for everything external to himself. True nobility, he held, lay in man's mind and not in external trappings. The great aim in life should be to prove that a man can do without things and yet be happy, healthy and wise. Cynicism easily led to contempt for authority and morality as well as religion. Yet the Cynics were never sufficiently numerous to be dangerous, and Vespasian dismissed them as 'barking curs'.

The most important philosophical attitude of the time was undoubtedly that of Stoicism. According to Wendland the hallmark of the Hellenistic age, Stoicism was the one product of Greek intellectual enquiry to assume significant proportions in the western part of the Roman world. Cicero, Seneca and, in the second century, Marcus Aurelius, the philosopher-emperor, were among those who propagated it.

The problems to which Stoicism addressed itself were those which traditional religion had failed to solve and which other philosophies were grappling with. They have been well defined as 'how to behave in a world that had grown so large, and where man seemed so small and unattached, how to meet the onset of fortune (whether good or bad) without flinching, how to face death and bereavement, how to remain master of your soul' (Charlesworth).

The answers which Stoicism provided to these questions stemmed from a view of the universe which may be defined as 'pantheistic materialism'. 'God is Nature, is Fate, is Fortune, is the Universe, is the all-pervading Mind' (Seneca). The fiery ether which was regarded as the divine and basic substance of the universe was identified with that reason or intelligence which constitutes man as man whoever he may be. The ethical ideal of Stoicism was a life in which a man does what is appropriate to his nature. This 'law of nature' is known to all men everywhere. What is needed is for men to be men by living according to that reason which is the law of their being. If they do, they will not give way to passion, unreasonable grief or cowardice, or any display of emotion: they will be free, within the fortress of their own minds, to follow the law of their being and thus to achieve the goal of 'self-sufficiency' by the twin way of 'apathy' and 'self-discipline'. Such was the logic of Stoicism. Though highly critical of traditional religion, Stoicism was able to come to terms with it by means of an allegorical interpretation of the old offensive religious myths.

The use by Paul of ideas such as conformity to nature, sufficiency, things being 'not convenient', and the like, have caused some to argue that he was influenced by Stoicism. Certainly Paul was not averse to using terms in current use: but he invariably filled them with new meaning. The vastly different presuppositions of Christianity and Stoicism (monotheism in contrast with pantheism, for example) require that Paul's thought should run in a direction far removed from that of Seneca. 'In many cases, where the parallels are most close, the theory of a direct historical connection is impossible; in many others it can be shown to be quite unnecessary; while in not a few instances the resemblance, however striking, must be condemned as illusory and fallacious' (Lightfoot). It is not really surprising that Marcus Aurelius, despite his lofty sentiments, should have despised Christians and countenanced their persecution.

A good deal of uncertainty still exists over the precise nature of Gnosticism and its rôle in the first century. It is certain that it constituted a serious threat to the Christian Church in the second century. Nor is there much doubt that it did not exist in the first century in a developed form. But the precise nature of Gnosticism is still a matter for scholarly debate. It seems to have been essentially eclectic, drawing its ideas from many sources. Whether Greek, oriental or Jewish ideas predominated in the final amalgam, it seems clear that many of the notions which contributed to it were common coin in the first century.

Among such ideas were the following: the dualistic basis of approach; the idea of intermediaries between a transcendent deity and a world which, being material, must needs be evil; the emphasis on the redemption of the spiritual element in man from the material body and world in which it has become imprisoned; the claim that initiation into *gnosis* (knowledge) is the way of freedom and release; the ascetic way of life which some gnostic sects required and the antinomianism which others permitted or even advocated. These were ideas current in the first century, some of them in systems of thought which have been summarized above.

Paul had occasion to warn against these very things. Dualism stands condemned in 1 Tim. 4: 1-5. The worship of angelic intermediaries is reproved in Col. 2: 18 and indirectly in Col. 1: 15-17. Over-emphasis on knowledge is deprecated in Col. 2: 8 and 1 C. 8: 1-3, and undue asceticism in Col. 2: 20-23. The incipient Gnosticism opposed by Paul seems to have been associated with Judaism (Col. 2: 16 f.).

The various schools of philosophy had their popularizers in wandering philosophers who peddled their wares just as religious teachers often did. Paul found it necessary to distinguish himself and his companions from such (1 Th. 2: 3-6).

Traditionally there was ample place in the Greek and Roman worlds for the practice of private religion. This normally supplemented the official religion, though if a suppliant were disappointed he might turn to private religion as a virtual substitute for the public cult which henceforth would be for him a purely perfunctory duty. With the increasing failure of the imperial cult to satisfy their spiritual aspirations men turned to new or developed forms of private religion.

Private religion might take the form of magical practices. In these, spiritual aspirations mingled with the grossest requests for material and physical satisfaction. There was no clear-cut line of demarcation between magic and religion: divination, for example, was a recognized element in the latter. Magical papyri containing prayers and hymns might be utilized (Ac. 19: 19)

and magical curses and imprecations uttered. The use of astrology and grossly superstitious practices figured in popular religion, especially among the lower classes of society.

Minor deities, less remote than the Olympians and the gods of the Pantheon, might be approached in private devotions. Asclepius, god of healing, was a universal favourite. Diana of the Ephesians (Artemis) enjoyed a widespread appeal (Ac. 19: 27). Sometimes fasts and purifications were employed in the hope of attaining to the vision of a god.

Perhaps the most remarkable feature of first-century religion, apart from the spread of Christianity, was the proliferation of new cults from the East, and particularly the growing popularity of the Mystery Religions. These new cults spread largely because of the failure of traditional religion to satisfy the growing religious consciousness of an age which was one not only of world empire but also of widespread individualism.

The Mystery Religions offered salvation on the basis of a divine revelation and the assurance of divine aid to redeem individuals from this life through 'rebirth for eternity'. Symbolic purifications and sacramental meals provided initiation into the 'mystery' and lent colour and some degree of plausibility. There was usually a monotheistic slant, the god of the cult being either the supreme deity or his son, consort or loyal friend. The appeal was individualistic, addressed to the soul in its solitariness, even if the individual was brought into a religious fellowship with social implications. There might be ethical implications also, often in the direction of ascetic renunciation.

The Mystery Religion was no innovation. The worship of Demeter at Eleusis had constituted a local religion of this kind in the days of ancient Greece. Several of the best-known Mystery Religions were introduced to Rome before the beginning of the Christian era, though the first century saw their widespread dissemination.

There were striking differences as well as common features in the various Mystery Religions. That of the Egyptian Isis was 'widespread, genteel, mystical and very feminine' (F. C. Grant). Isis, not alone, claimed that the names of other deities were titles that were rightly hers and that their functions really belonged to her. She was the great mother goddess of the world. The sacred mystery of her cult was the dismemberment of her consort, Osiris, by his enemy, Set; the search for the scattered limbs undertaken by the faithful Isis; and their restoration. The dignified processions; the services in her temples with lustrations and offerings of incense instead of bloody sacrifices; the open shrine; the hymns and sacred liturgy: all were capable of inspiring both excitement and devotion. Mattingly has described Isis as in many ways a prototype of the Virgin Mary.

The worship of Cybele, the great mother of Anatolia, and her young consort, Attis, was of a very different sort. It had originated in Phrygia where, in mad hypnotic dances, its devotees had mutilated themselves in honour of Cybele and her divine lover. It spread far and wide. In Rome, the temples of Cybele with their eunuch priests eventually gained acceptance, despite the sacrament of the *taurobolium* in which the initiate was apparently promised rebirth through drenching in the blood of a bull.

Mithraism, though it became the most popular of the mystery religions with a special attraction for soldiers, was not widespread until the second and third centuries. Of Persian origin, Mithraism was based on the myth of the cosmic struggle between Ahura-Mazda, the force of truth and light, and Ahriman, the force of falsehood and darkness. Mithras, champion of truth and light, had slain the great bull for the salvation of the world, and a bas-relief at the far end of the cave, real or artificial, in which meetings of his cult were held, depicted his exploits. Mithraism offered a fellowship in which members were pledged by initiation ceremonies and common meals to loyalty towards each other. Initiates could rise through various grades and were given the promise of a blessed life in the hereafter.

The similarities between the Mystery Religions and Christianity are obvious : the differences are more significant. In particular, the Mystery Religions did not posit an historical figure as saviour. There is no proof of any influence exerted by the ideas of the Mystery Religions upon Christianity. Indeed it has been asserted that one might as easily argue that there was influence in the opposite direction.

In the Roman world, religion came within the scope of state control: it was not regarded as merely a matter of personal conviction. Both religious and political considerations demanded this. On the one hand, the favour of the gods was thought to depend on the faithful observance of the cult by all subjects; on the other, the integrity of the empire was thought to be safeguarded by the universal observance of the imperial religion. But Rome was remarkably tolerant. Provided a man performed his duty in regard to the official *religio* he was free to choose his own *superstitio*, provided that it was neither antagonistic to the official cult, politically subversive nor offensively immoral. Unofficial religions which offended on any of these counts

were likely to be proscribed, like Druidism in Gaul and Britain.

The extent to which Roman toleration might go is seen in the case of Judaism. Here was a religion that was uncompromisingly monotheistic and characterized by nationalistic fervour and proselytizing zeal. Yet it secured a *modus vivendi*. This was partly due to the face-saving consideration that the Jews offered sacrifice to their deity on behalf of the emperor. More significant, perhaps, was the fact that the Jews were of vital importance for the commercial prosperity of the empire. Above all, the Jews were a closely-knit community established throughout the empire, and to prohibit their worship would have caused widespread trouble of a kind that the Romans were always reluctant to provoke. The toleration granted to Judaism was somewhat uneasy, however, and might be forfeited by Jewish rebellions or by popular outcries against the Jews (cf. Ac. 18: 2).

At first Christianity shared the toleration granted to Judaism. Thus at Corinth Gallio regarded Christianity as a sect of that religion and would take no cognizance of it (Ac. 18: 12-17), and neither Festus (Ac. 25: 25) nor Agrippa (Ac. 26: 31, 32) regarded Paul's beliefs as reprehensible. But the Jews themselves were not slow to accuse Christians of political or religious subversion (Ac. 17: 6, 7; 18: 13), and Gentiles whose material interests were injured by the growth of Christianity (Ac. 16: 19-22; 19: 23-28) drew attention to the religious anomalies of Christianity.

Before the end of the New Testament period Christianity, which had become more and more distinct from Judaism, was regarded by those who had no intimate knowledge of its adherents as undesirable on political, religious, social and even moral grounds. Its attitude to pagan religion was sufficiently appreciated and its political and moral outlook was sufficiently misunderstood to render it the object of mingled fear and scorn. The crazed emperor, Nero, who was widely suspected of having wantonly set fire to Rome, was able to divert attention to the Christians by means of the persecution of A.D. 64.

In his first letter, Peter warned the Christians of Asia Minor of the sufferings that they must expect (1 Pet. 2: 12, 19 ff.; 3: 14; 4: 12 ff.) and urged them to silence by their display of good works the ignorance of their enemies who shared that ignorance, it may be noted, with celebrated Roman authors. (Tacitus described Christianity as a 'pernicious superstition', and Suetonius called it 'a novel and mischievous superstition'.)

Towards the end of the first century further persecution broke out at Rome as the result of the malevolence of Domitian. In other parts of the empire, and at all times, Christians were exposed to the hazard of persecution (Rev. 2: 13). Christianity was without legal sanction, and there were precedents for persecution. Moreover a hostile individual or mob might force the hand of a reluctant magistrate by creating a situation of public disorder, as at Ephesus in the time of Paul (Ac. 19).

BIBLIOGRAPHY

GRANT, F. C., *Hellenistic Religions* (New York, 1953).

ANGUS, S., *The Mystery Religions and Christianity* (London, 1925).

WALLS, A. F., 'Gnosticism', *NBD*.

LIGHTFOOT, J. B., *Saint Paul's Epistle to the Philippians*, pp. 270-328 (London, 1903). First published, 1868.

BARRETT, C. K., *The New Testament Background: Selected Documents* (London, 1956).

THE RELIGIOUS BACKGROUND OF THE NEW TESTAMENT (JEWISH)

H. L. ELLISON

In NT times Jewry was divided into three fairly distinct sections:

(a) those in Palestine and inland Syria;

(b) those in Mesopotamia and Persia—at the time they were outside the Roman empire;

(c) those in Mediterranean countries generally. The second group does not enter the NT story directly (but cf. Ac. 2: 9). Hence it will not be mentioned further. The third group is dealt with partly in the article in passing, partly in a special section at the end.

THE EFFECTS OF THE BABYLONIAN EXILE

To understand the Jewish religious world in the NT period, we must look back to the return from the Babylonian exile in 538 B.C. and to certain outstanding events in the Inter-Testamental Period.

The return from exile and the years immediately following involved the Jews in a number of disappointments, the greatest of which was that political independence was not restored and the house of David did not regain the throne. Förster may be correct in maintaining that the pious had realized even in exile that return would not bring national independence with it, but if that is so, they formed a minority of the exiles, and most will have thought that the rebuilding of the Temple in 519 B.C., at the insistence of Haggai and Zechariah, would be followed by political freedom, but nothing happened to justify even the smallest hopes. The nature of the Persian empire was such that revolts might lead to a change of ruler but not to local independence.

Some 70 years later an event happened which vitally affected Judaism down to the present day. It seems clear that under the Monarchy the Law of Moses was largely the possession and concern of the priests and ruling classes. The ordinary man knew as much of it as was recited at the pilgrim feasts or as he was commanded to keep. In approximately 440

B.C. Ezra, aided by Nehemiah, presented the Law to the people as something which it was each individual's responsibility to keep; the tears of Neh. 8: 9 were mainly tears of joy. Though this is not definitely stated, the theory behind Ezra's action was undoubtedly that the exile and subsequent lack of independence had been caused primarily by neglect of the Law, and that if all Israel (not merely its priests and elders) kept the Law as it should be kept, the fulness of God's blessing would come on His people.

Ezra's reformation meant that from that time on the religious life of the Jew changed very gradually from a temple ritual to an ordered system of life, which increasingly embraced all its aspects. It was very soon assumed that though the Law did not contain specific commandments covering every possible aspect of life, yet principles could be deduced from it on which the necessary new commandments could be based. The revelation at Sinai was *torah* (instruction), not merely a law-book.

This enabled the majority who had remained in Babylonia and who came only rarely to Jerusalem to follow the same pattern of life as was becoming standard in Palestine. That Ezra should have come expressly from Babylonia to introduce the new pattern into Palestine shows how conscious the Eastern dispersion was that it was only the keeping of the Law that really stood between them and assimilation to their pagan surroundings.

Just over a century later the conquests of Alexander the Great made Palestine part of the Greek world. This did not bring political independence with it, but it caused the spread of a large number of Jews into the Greek cities, old and new, of the eastern Mediterranean, especially Alexandria. This new dispersion, which very rapidly adopted Greek as its language, was kept from assimilation only by its observance of the Law and by its continuance of the pattern of life observed in Palestine.

73

The Greek civilization carried by Alexander into Asia and Egypt is usually called Hellenism (its adjective is Hellenistic); the form of Gk. used by it, which differed considerably from classical Attic Gk., we call *Koinē*. Hellenism, like all Gk. culture, was based on cities, and so was slow to influence the countryside. In addition, it presupposed a leisured, slave-owning class of citizens. For that reason the Jews of Palestine, who were mostly poor farmers, were slow to be influenced, even though a number of pagan, Hellenistic cities were founded in the country. For all that the influence of Hellenism on the Jews was far-reaching, both positively and negatively.

SOME INFLUENCES OF HELLENISM

There was no real division felt between the Jews of the East and those of Palestine and Syria, apart from those living in Hellenistic cities like Syrian Antioch. They all spoke Aramaic, a Semitic language akin to Hebrew; they all formed part of the traditional Asiatic world that had changed little down the centuries; they were mostly farmers or artisans. In the Hellenistic world the typical Jew spoke Greek; Paul was an exception; he was 'a Hebrew born of Hebrews' (Phil. 3: 5), i.e. although he knew Greek his home language was Aramaic. Further he was with few exceptions a city dweller—here Paul conformed to the pattern—and tended to be far more of an individualist than the Palestinian Jew, though not to the degree we are so familiar with today.

While the Law was read in Hebrew in the synagogues of the Western dispersion—fragments of MSS with the Hebrew written in Greek letters are still in existence; cf. also the second column of Origen's Hexapla (cf. *NBD* p.1, 260a)—it had to be followed by a translation into Greek. By 50 B.C. the whole OT had been translated in a rendering traditionally called the Septuagint (LXX). The first Greek translations of the Law go back in all probability to before 200 B.C., though the traditional story found in *The Letter of Aristeas* is merely pious propaganda. The recasting of Hebrew religious thought into Greek meant subtle changes in outlook, which were hardly felt when Hebrew had to be turned into Aramaic; these also laid them the more open to the influence of Hellenism.

The greatest fascination of Hellenism for the Asiatic was its apparent freeing of man's mind. In the old systems the whole of human activity moved in a totalitarian religious setting. Hellenism freed large areas of thought from the control of the gods. Even before Palestinian Jewry was brought into full contact with it, its influence may be seen at work.

This may best be seen by comparing *Proverbs* with *Ecclesiastes*, which we must date not too long before 200 B.C., and even more with *The Wisdom of Jesus ben Sira* (*Ecclesiasticus*), which in its Hebrew original dates from *c.* 180 B.C. The strain of intellectual rationalism in the latter is the more remarkable, as Ben Sira seems to have been an outspoken enemy of Hellenistic thought. At this period there entered Judaism a strain of rationalism it has never lost. One sign of it is the introduction of 'all your mind' (Lk. 10: 27; Mk 12: 30) into the quotation from Dt. 6: 5.

Among Hellenistic Jews this led to clearer and sharper thought. It was no chance that in Palestine and the East Christianity was able to remain within Jewry until after A.D. 90, and even then the breach was more political and national than theological. But in the Mediterranean world it seems to have been a clear-cut either-or from the first. There was the added factor that in the Greek dispersion the Jew felt the keeping of the Law far more a matter of spiritual life or death than did the Palestinian Jew, for whom it was rather the highest religious privilege.

There is no saying how much Judaism might have been penetrated and corrupted by Hellenism had it not been for another of its facets. Hellenism looked on itself as a system given by the gods to unite and revive a fragmented and weary world. To accomplish this it adopted a system we call syncretism. Instead of decrying and seeking to abolish the Asiatic gods and goddesses, it identified them with the Greek gods of Olympus. A city would continue to worship its old deities but under new names and with a Greek slant. For a short time new life really seemed to flow into the outworn systems. We must note two results, one minor, one major, for Jewry.

In the first century B.C. there entered the Mediterranean lands from further east dualistic systems, which were as much philosophies as religions. In the syncretistic society already described they were made welcome, the more so as they did not try to displace the accepted cults but, as was explained, sought to give them deeper meaning. Just because of their appeal to reason and special, esoteric knowledge, these *Gnostic* systems, as we call them, made a great appeal to some Hellenistic Jews, and even to some in Palestine. They felt they could follow them without any disloyalty to the religion of Moses. Most of the incipient Gnosticism combated in the Pauline letters is to be attributed to Jewish sources.

THE STRUGGLE AGAINST HELLENIST DOMINANCE

Among the heirs of Alexander the Great the most powerful was Seleucus I, who ruled (312-281 B.C.) from Syria to India. This wide-stretching empire was already showing signs of collapse, when Antiochus the Great (223-187 B.C.) was defeated by the Romans at Magnesia (190 B.C.) and had to accept crippling peace conditions. When Antiochus Epiphanes (175-163 B.C.) came to the throne, it was clear that a major effort had to be made to unify his kingdom, or it would crumble away in his hands. He considered himself to be an incarnate manifestation (the force of Epiphanes) of Olympian Zeus and so decided to use Hellenistic religion as the unifying mortar for his kingdom.

His policy coincided with the rise to power in Jerusalem of a small group of rich men, mainly from the more important priests, who wanted to turn Jerusalem into a Hellenistic city. The outcome was that in 167 the Temple was rededicated to Olympian Zeus, with whom Antiochus, after the normal syncretistic fashion, identified Yahweh. An attempt was made to ensure that all Jews sacrificed to Zeus. Circumcision and the possession of portions of the OT Scriptures were made capital offences. One test used was to make Jews eat pork.

It it useless speculating about the motives of those Jews that supported his policy. Probably he went very much further than they had expected, but having once started, they could not draw back. More important is to realize to what extent Hellenism had affected some Jewish circles.

The policy of Antiochus led to vigorous armed resistance. Three years later (164 B.C.) the Temple was cleansed and in 142 B.C. Judaea became independent for the first time since Josiah. Though freedom was won by desperate courage and sordid intrigue, it was gained more through the break-up of the Seleucid empire than through Judaea's own strength. So when Rome appeared on the scene in 63 B.C., the independence of the Jewish state quickly ended, not to be renewed until our own days. An understanding of the effects of the century from Antiochus Epiphanes to Rome is vital for the background to the NT.

Every conscious approximation to Greek thought was made impossible. Whatever the reasons found for refusing social contacts with Gentiles (cf. Ac. 10: 28; 11: 3), probably the main motive lay in a deep fear of dangerous influences.

THE JEWISH RELIGIOUS PARTIES

The Sadducees probably had considerable sympathy for the ideological position of the rich Jewish Hellenists in the time of Antiochus Epiphanes; certainly they were in some ways their successors. But they never ventured to go outside the framework of the Law, even if their interpretation of it was often other than that of the Pharisees. They were drawn mainly from the richer landed aristocracy and the leading priestly families, so never found sympathy among the masses. (It should be remembered that none of their writings have come down to us, so we are dependent for our knowledge of them mainly on statements by the Pharisees, their deadly enemies; so dogmatism in judging them is out of place.)

The lamentable failure of the Hasmonean priest-kings, both morally and politically, so disgusted the better elements of the population that they abandoned all thought of political independence until God Himself should intervene. They were known at first as the *Hasidim* (probably God's loyal ones), but comparatively early in this period they split into at least two parties.

The more radical section we know as the Essenes, and our main information about them is gleaned from the Qumran discoveries. They denied the right of Simon the Hasmonean (143-134 B.C.) to the high-priesthood, which they considered belonged to the descendants of Onias III, deposed by Antiochus Epiphanes. When John Hyrcanus and especially Alexander Jannai added moral unworthiness to the lack of hereditary right, the Qumran group despaired of reformation, decided they were in the last days, turned their backs on the Temple and people and withdrew to the wilderness to await the final struggle between good and evil. They were essentially a secret society, which is one reason why they are not mentioned in the NT, and had little direct influence on the people. The very fact of their protest and existence must, however, have had wide-reaching effects. Their special form of Biblical interpretation was in some way a preparation for that of the NT. Their very existence as an influential, dissident sect within Jewry made it easier for the early Church to be tolerated for a time. After A.D. 70, when their movement dissolved with all its dreams shattered, many of them joined the Church with disastrous theological results for the Hebrew Christians, most of whom were not strong enough to resist the fanatical concepts for which the Essenes stood.

In some relationship to the Essenes stood the writers of apocalyptic and pseudonymous literature, the best known of which is the collection found in *The Book of Enoch*. We know virtually nothing about them; though they shared much of the Essene outlook, it is unlikely that they are to be identified with them. Their theories of fixed times and seasons, of cosmic conflicts centred on this earth and of a mighty struggle between good and evil soon to be ended with the triumph of God, did much to create the fanaticism that was the chief cause of the fall of the Jewish commonwealth and Temple; they left their lasting mark also on popular Christianity.

The other section of the *Hasidim* came to be known as the Pharisees. They were normally utterly rigorous with themselves, but were prepared to compromise where the common man was concerned, for they had not completely given up hope of national reformation. The Essenes looked down on them and called them 'Seekers after smooth things'. This was unfair. Their meticulous tithing policy, which largely cut them off from those whose tithing methods they suspected, and often caused them serious financial loss, showed that they had not chosen an easy way or one that brought them personal gain. What they did was to base themselves on statements like '*All the commandment which I command you this day you shall be careful to do, that you may live and multiply . . .*' (Dt. 8: 1) and insist that the Law must be so interpreted that the ordinary poorer citizen could keep it. This was one of the main reasons why they had the support of the majority in the time of Christ. Josephus gives their numbers in the time of Herod the Great as 6,000; the other groups mentioned will have been smaller still.

John Hyrcanus (134-104 B.C.) reconquered the south of Judaea. It had been settled by Edomites during and immediately after the Babylonian exile and was in consequence called Idumaea. He gave the inhabitants the choice of death or Judaism; most preferred the latter. Aristobulus I (104-103 B.C.) did the same to Galilee, where most were probably descended from the northern tribes. In each case there was produced a population more fanatical than pious. The Idumaeans played an important part in the revolt against Rome. In Galilee there was armed resistance to Roman nominees after the fall of the Hasmonean house (63 B.C.). Herod, while still only procurator of Galilee (c. 47 B.C.) had major trouble in his province, and when he was made King of the Jews by the Romans much of the main opposition was again in Galilee. By his death these men, under the name of Zealots or Cananaeans (cf. Mk 3: 18—Cananaean is the Aramaic equivalent of Zealot) had become a major

influence in Palestine and, at least in Galilee, soon became more popular than the Pharisees. This is easy to understand. Fighting Romans, killing tax-collectors, robbing foreign caravans and making Jewish merchants contribute to their war chest was more satisfying than just keeping the Law and waiting for God's time for salvation. Another reason for the increasing popularity of the Zealots was that they were comparable with the Levellers and Fifth-Monarchy men of the Commonwealth in England. They sought not merely freedom from foreign rule but also a social revolution which would give the poor their rights.

It was mainly they who wished to make Jesus king by force (Jn 6: 15) and who hailed Him as Messiah on the first Palm Sunday (Mk 11: 9, 10). The question about the tribute money (Mk 12: 14) was intended to discredit Him in their eyes, unless He answered in a way that would make Him appear dangerous to the Romans. It was they who precipitated the revolt against Rome and made any compromise solution impossible. They even hastened the destruction of Jerusalem by destroying the stocks of food in it (Jos. *War*, V. i. 4) probably believing that God *was bound* to intervene at the eleventh hour, and so the sooner the crisis came the better.

It is clear there were also a number of other smaller sects, many of them in the lower Jordan valley and Transjordan. Josephus (*Life* 2) tells of one Banus, who lived 'in the wilderness, wearing clothes from trees, and frequently bathing himself with cold water by day and night for purification'. He was doubtless typical of many others.

When we remember that there were also communities from the Greek diaspora in Jerusalem, who maintained their separate language and identity (cf. Ac. 6: 1, 9), it should be clear to us that no really unitary Jewish religious background to the NT existed.

THE SYNAGOGUE AND THE STUDY OF THE LAW

The Pharisees did not go as far as the Essenes and turn their backs on the Temple, but they were deeply disgusted by the venal and corrupt priests who controlled it—this is no judgment on the priests in general but on a few families who held all the real power and were able to pocket most of the revenue. Their answer was to build up the influence of the Synagogue. Its roots go back possibly to the Babylonian exile, but there is no evidence that it was influential in Palestine until near the beginning of the first century B.C. It began by offering the possibility of the study of the Law by the ordinary man, and—little though that was the original purpose—it laid the foundations of a service for the worship of God virtually divorced from the sacrificial ritual of the Temple.

The Pharisees quickly recognized the possibilities offered by the Synagogue for spreading their own concepts and for decreasing the power of the priestly Sadducees. Thanks to their efforts there was probably by 50 B.C. a synagogue in every Palestinian village with a Jewish population of any size. Attached to the synagogue was a school, where the boys learned to read. It was not there to encourage literacy—girls were seldom taught—but to ensure that each man could read the Law.

The original purpose of the Synagogue was expressed by the reading of the Law (to which was later added a prophetic passage) on the Sabbath, and also on Mondays and Thursdays, the regular market days. If there was one present capable of doing it, the passage read could be expounded. Soon there was added to the reading a simple service of praise and prayer. Its heart consisted of the *Shema* (Dt. 6: 4, very early expanded to Dt. 6: 4-9; 11: 13-21; Num. 15: 37-41), the Ten Commandments (dropped about A.D. 100, when Christians stressed them to the exclusion of the remainder of the Law) and the *Amidah*, or *Shemoneh Esreh* ('Eighteen Benedictions'), a great complex of praise, petition and thanksgiving (cf. *NBD* p. 1,228b). Various factors soon led to daily services in larger communities, but they could be held only if there were ten males over thirteen years old present.

It should be noted that the officers of the Synagogue were only administrative. There were one or three elders and a *hazzan*, who was responsible for order, acted as attendant (Lk. 4: 20), and was normally the schoolmaster. Anyone who had the knowledge and piety could lead the congregation in worship.

The Rabbi was an expert in the Law, to whom all difficult cases were brought and who tried to guide others in their studies of it. The only privilege of the priests in the Synagogue was in the public reading of the Law and the pronouncing of the Benediction (Num. 6: 24-26). This helps to explain why the apostolic church knows no sacerdotal caste.

Very few Palestinian Jews living at any distance from Jerusalem will have attended the Temple services, except at the three great feasts of Passover, Pentecost and Tabernacles, and it is not likely that the poorer will have attended all three—there is no mention of Christ's having been in Jerusalem for Pentecost. Those who lived in the Dispersion could often manage only one or two visits in a lifetime.

So of necessity the Synagogue had largely displaced the Temple for the ordinary man, even before the latter's destruction.

Though most knew the Psalter off by heart, the main purpose of Bible study was to discover the demands of the Law on the individual and community. Not long after Ezra it was agreed that it contained 613 commandments, 365 of them negative and 248 positive. The *Hasidim* then made a hedge about these commandments, i.e. they made new laws, not a few based on old traditions, the keeping of which would guarantee the keeping of the original commandments. Though at first they were unable to enforce these new laws, increasingly after the struggle with Hellenism they were accepted by the bulk of the people. They represent 'the traditions of the elders' attacked by Christ.

Even with the traditions these basic commandments did not cover the whole of life. So from *c.* 100 B.C. a complete code of law was slowly developed, based on the principles of the Torah, as they were understood by the Pharisees. Their full formulation is found in the Talmud. Since many of the new demands ran counter to the traditional legislation administered by the Sadducees, they could not be enforced until after A.D. 70. It is often impossible for us to know what the actual law in force in the time of Christ was. Until recently commentaries took for granted that the trial of Jesus offended not only against natural justice but also against specific Jewish law. It is now known that these Talmudic laws were not in force, and indeed some may never have been more than theoretical. The complete Pharisaic system was not accepted by the common people until *c.* A.D. 150 and that after a most bitter struggle.

SOME SPECIAL PROBLEMS OF THE DISPERSION

Julius Caesar had granted the Jews freedom to observe the Sabbath and to gather in synagogues, exemption from military service and the right to live according to their own laws. In addition, provided a non-Jew or a Roman citizen was not involved, they could judge their law suits before their own courts both in Palestine and in the Dispersion generally.

In Palestine such rights could be taken more or less for granted, but in the Dispersion they were exceptional and precious; indeed without them it might have been almost impossible to live openly as Jews. The Roman world did not welcome Sabbath keeping, and was strongly opposed to any faith that would release its adherents from military service or the more onerous municipal or state offices.

So while no effort was made to reduce Jewish privileges, it was expected that they would not increase their numbers by proselytizing. Hence in Acts we meet far more 'God-fearers' (RSV 'devout persons'), people who had accepted Jewish principles without becoming Jews, than proselytes, who ranked as full Jews. Quite apart from their attitude to his teaching, the Hellenistic Jews considered that Paul was endangering their privileges by attracting too many non-Jews into what was still regarded as a Jewish sect.

It should be obvious that it was not possible for the average Hellenistic Jew to keep the finer points of the Law in the way a Pharisee would in Palestine. This rendered him the more zealous about those points which he could keep, and the more bitter about anyone who would seek to abrogate them.

Mention was made earlier of those Hellenistic Jews who were influenced by Gnostic speculation. There were others who deliberately adopted various heathen superstitions, going at times as far as a real syncretistic worship. Examples of these tendencies may be found in Ac. 13: 6-11; 19: 13-16 and 19: 19, to which may be added Simon, a Samaritan (8: 9, 10).

THE TENSION OF THE TIME

During the time of Christ's ministry the Jewish people were coming to the end of their tether. The century of political independence under the Hasmonean priest-kings had ended by their being more firmly under the heel of Rome than they had ever been under their Persian or Greek rulers. The collapse of the Hasmonean house had brought terrible suffering with it. Klausner (*Jesus of Nazareth*, p. 144) estimates that in the thirty years from the death of Queen Shalom-Zion (Salome Alexandra) in 67 B.C. till Herod the Great was fully in power as king in 37 B.C. 'far more than a hundred thousand Jews were killed. And these were the pick of the nation, the healthiest, mainly the young men, and the most enthusiastic, who had refused to suffer the foreign yoke'. In 31 B.C. an earthquake killed about 30,000 (Josephus, *Ant.* XV. v. 2, *Wars* I. xix. 3); there were famine and pestilence in 25 and 24 B.C. (Josephus, *Ant.* XV. ix. 1). After Herod's death thousands more perished in a vain attempt to get rid of his house. Herod bled the land white to pay for his grandiose building schemes in Jerusalem, Sebaste (Samaria), Caesarea, his great fortresses like Machaerus and Masada, and even outside his borders in Tyre and Sidon, Rhodes, Athens, Pergamon and other cities. There is no evidence that taxation grew less after his death, though the money was squandered on even less profitable schemes. F. C. Grant (*The Economic Background of the Gospels*, 1926) reckons that the Romans and the Temple together accounted for thirty to forty per cent., and possibly more, in income tax on the people.

In addition to what the Jew suffered from his rulers must be reckoned the whips of his own countrymen. There is ample evidence that the bulk of the land and commerce was in the hands of a relatively small section of the population, and that they normally used their position with scant humanity (cf. Jas 2: 6; 5: 1-6).

Consequently something had to happen. The folly of a Roman procurator loosed the whirlwind of the revolt against Rome (A.D. 66-73). This swept away Sadducees and Zealots, Qumran Essenes and apocalyptists alike. Jewry had to choose between the infant Church with its message of a crucified and risen Messiah and the Pharisees with their cult of the Law. For a short time it seemed that the Church might triumph, but for the Hebrew Christian the Law was normally too precious to be let go. So the zeal of the Pharisee triumphed over a divided loyalty to the Messiah Jesus. By A.D. 90 the Hebrew Christian found himself being squeezed out of the community of Jewry, whatever his attitude to the Law.

BIBLIOGRAPHY
(Simpler works are marked *)

General
*BRUCE, F. F., *Israel and the Nations* (Exeter, 1964).
FÖRSTER, W., *Palestinian Judaism in New Testament Times* (Edinburgh, 1964).
KLAUSNER, J., *Jesus of Nazareth* (London, 1929).
*PEROWNE, S., *The Life and Times of Herod the Great* (London, 1956).
PFEIFFER, R. H., *History of New Testament Times* (New York, 1949).

Religion
*EDERSHEIM, A., *The Temple: Its Ministry and Service as they were at the Time of Christ* (London, 1874; reprinted 1960).
MOORE, G. F., *Judaism* (Cambridge, Mass., 1927-30).
PARKES, J., *The Foundations of Judaism and Christianity* (London, 1960).

Qumran
BLACK, M., *The Scrolls and Christian Origins* (London, 1969).
*BRUCE, F. F., *Second Thoughts on the Dead Sea Scrolls* (London, 1961).
BURROWS, M., *The Dead Sea Scrolls* (London, 1955).
BURROWS, M., *More Light on the Dead Sea Scrolls* (London, 1958).
*VERMES, G., *The Dead Sea Scrolls in English* (Harmondsworth, 1962).
Reference may be made to articles in NBD and other Bible Dictionaries. Further authorities will be found mentioned in the works cited. Certain older works are not mentioned as not being any longer reliable.

THE DEVELOPMENT
OF DOCTRINE
IN THE NEW TESTAMENT

WALTER L. LIEFELD

To read the NT is to take an exciting journey of discovery. The point of departure is, in the words of Mark, 'the beginning of the gospel of Jesus Christ, the Son of God' (Mk 1: 1). Journey's end is a vantage point from which the Christian looks ahead exclaiming 'Come, Lord Jesus!' (Rev. 22: 20). The journey is taken in the confidence that after centuries of fragmentary communication, God has spoken with finality in His Son (Heb. 1: 1 f.). This word by and about the Lord Jesus Christ needs to be interpreted as the growing church is increasingly able to comprehend its significance (Jn 16: 12-15). The history of redemption has reached its climax in Christ who 'offered for all time a single sacrifice for sins' (Heb. 10: 12). Yet the message of the cross not only has to be carried across the world, but needs to be understood in all its implications and applied to Christian life. The central event of history lies not in the future but in the past (Heb. 9: 28), but instead of living in a new world with enemies conquered and sin restrained (a popular Messianic expectation), the Christian is now a citizen of two worlds, an inhabitant of two ages, daily awaiting the future consummation.

The actual writing of the NT took place in but a fraction of the time spanned by the OT. Yet the doctrinal progress, against a changing background of circumstances, is remarkable. The Gospel of John (which itself reveals new dimensions of Christology unseen in the Synoptics) relates a promise of the Lord Jesus regarding this development of doctrine: 'I have yet many things to say to you, but you cannot bear them now. When the Spirit of truth comes, He will guide you into all truth' (Jn 16: 12 f.). In saying that His disciples could not yet 'bear' this further truth, Jesus probably had reference in part to the fact that they needed the strengthening experience of witnessing His resurrection after the sorrowful experience of the cross. They also needed to receive the Holy Spirit at Pentecost, who would bring into their experience the reality of the truth He would teach them. It is certainly also true that the significance of this further revelation could be understood only as the disciples experienced the opportunities and problems of the first Christian decades. Also one must bear in mind that revelation was given in accordance with God's orderly plan.

The NT, then, like the OT, contains a progressive revelation given by God in various contexts of experiences. Some of the most important doctrinal statements are introduced in response to questions, such as Jn 14: 5-9, or problems, as Phil. 2: 1-13. The growing church itself was full of questions, and provided both the occasion and the context of a developing theology.

In taking this fact into consideration, however, one must avoid some prevalent misconceptions. We cannot say, for example, that the church *created* the teachings of Jesus, as is sometimes claimed on the basis of form-critical studies. A study of the environment within which the Gospels were formed helps us to understand the selection and form of the teachings of Jesus, but this is quite a different thing from asserting that the early church formulated material to meet their own needs and then read it back into Jesus' life.

Likewise, one must not assume that the progress of doctrine in the NT is the same thing as an evolutionary development. Attempts have sometimes been made to place NT materials on a linear scale extending from the 'simple beginnings' of the teachings of Jesus in the Synoptics to the 'higher theology' of John or the later Letters. Certainly there was a maturing of thought. Yet recent studies have emphasized both the depth of the theology of the early Jerusalem church and the early date of much NT material. A simple linear development is also ruled out by the fact that various aspects of divine truth were being unfolded simultaneously in many different places and circumstances. The questions posed by the pagans at Ephesus, the new Christians at Corinth, and the Jews in Jerusalem required different formulations of the Christian message.

Recognition of these varying matrices, however, has occasioned other unsatisfactory hypotheses. The postulations of the 'Tübingen school' regarding an antithesis between Peter and Paul have still not been completely abandoned. The idea that Paul was significantly influenced by Hellenistic thought and the mystery religions is also still being circulated, in spite of the fact that research has demonstrated the exaggeration and anachronisms inherent in some of the suggested comparisons. The Gentile churches did not develop in isolation from the Jerusalem church and its influence. Also the differences between Palestinian and Diaspora Judaism are now acknowledged to have been much smaller than formerly thought, especially in light of the extensive Hellenization of Palestine. Still it must also be noted that the very success of the Christian mission in penetrating by stages beyond Palestinian Judaism into the Diaspora and then into the pagan world called for reformulations of the message.

A realistic reconstruction of the process of development will therefore take into account both the unity and diversity of the NT life and thought. Theologians have long sought for a unifying theme in the NT as, for example, love or the kingdom. Recent stress has been put on 'salvation-history'. Understood rightly as the redemptive acts of God in history and their interpretation in the Scriptures, this is not just a theme but the historical reality in which the church was actually taking part. Our Lord Jesus Christ Himself is certainly the focal point of all the NT. The early church was called on to explain the implication of their message not only regarding the person of Christ, and His death, resurrection and ascension, but also their own very existence as a church: their identity, mission, and destiny.

THE NATURE OF THE DEVELOPMENT

How may we trace the stages of development of NT doctrine? One way, obviously, is to study the successive books in their canonical order. This is the method followed in the famous Bampton lectures given a hundred years ago by Thomas Dehany Bernard, entitled in their published form, *The Progress of Doctrine in the New Testament*. He chose this approach, as his preface explains, in preference to a survey of the development of specific doctrines. He begins by contrasting the Gospels with the rest of the NT, asserting that in the former Christ is the source of doctrine, in the latter He is the subject. The Gospels, he suggests, create a sense of need, give a pledge of revelation to come, provide an initial deposit of material to be

drawn on, and provide a safeguard to the later development. This approach has value in that it honours the canonical order and provides helpful thoughts for the person who reads the NT books consecutively. Doctrine can thus be studied book by book and by authors to see their individual theological contributions. The following brief summary will suffice to illustrate this.

Starting with the Gospels, we find that each of them is a distinctive theological composition, a fact stressed again by recent scholarships after long neglect by those who saw the Gospels mainly as editorial rearrangements of the traditions about Jesus. Matthew, in presenting Him as the promised Messiah, draws not only on specific OT predictions, but employs a method of interpretation then common, to show that in Christ the full significance of OT history (especially the Exodus) is realized. Even the order in which he presents the teachings of Jesus reflects his orientation to Jewish methods of teaching. He shows the Lord Jesus as giving final meaning to the law and as introducing the Kingdom.

Mark's shorter (and probably earlier) work is a gospel of action. The Son of Man performs healings, trying to avoid public identification with the inadequate popular concept of the Messiah. His death for sinners is clearly predicted several times, and a major part of the book describes the event. Luke, both in his Gospel and in the book of Acts, enlarges on the sovereign acts of God in Christ, through the Holy Spirit, toward the accomplishment of His will in the spread of the gospel by the church. John, the beloved disciple, combines an emphasis on the divine Sonship of Christ, to whom many 'signs' or confirmatory miracles clearly point, with a stress on His true humanity. He is the sent One, who has both descended to earth and ascended again, whose power and love are now being realized among men by the Spirit. These themes are found in the Letters as well as in the Gospel of John.

Among the doctrines developed in the Pauline Letters are those of God as Creator, just and merciful; of Christ as Son and Redeemer; of the Holy Spirit as a motivating and powerful force in the believer's life; of the gospel of grace; of the church; and of the place of the Jews and their heritage. Hebrews deals further with the Jewish religion and the superiority of Christ and His work over all that had been said and done in the days of the law and the prophets. James reaffirms the Biblical doctrine of God, His Word and human responsibility, and shows that a professed faith unsubstantiated by deeds proves itself to be no faith at all. Peter, writing under the stress and unbelief of the times, displays what is really of value in this life: Christ Himself, His death, His example, His Word and His promises. The later writings of the NT emphasize the importance of sound doctrine, holy life and steadfast hope in the promised return of Christ.

This development of doctrine in the NT is founded on the teachings of Jesus, along guidelines He laid down during His ministry and, perhaps especially, in His private instruction of the disciples between His resurrection and ascension. One must keep in mind, however, that while the Gospels preserve these foundational words of the Lord Jesus, they were not the first NT books to be composed. Nor are the rest of the books in chronological order. Therefore a consecutive reading of the NT does not convey the doctrinal development as it actually took place in the early church. A survey of the books in order is therefore not completely adequate for a study of the development of doctrine. An alternate approach is the consideration of individual doctrines. Yet it is immediately apparent that the NT does not present a systematic treatment of doctrine, nor can individual doctrines be isolated from each other or from the life and developing needs of the early church.

In recent years much attention has been given to the context of the growing church as providing an understanding of its maturing theology. This context includes not only the church itself but its environment. The Jewish sects, the successive cultures penetrated by the gospel, the various heresies which challenged orthodoxy are all a part. Knowledge of this background is continually being increased from such discoveries as the Dead Sea Scrolls and the Nag Hammadi documents. Much of the NT can be understood better when seen as a response, engendered and guided by the Holy Spirit, to the questions asked of and by the Christian community. The most important of these questions centred about the person and work of Christ. The resurrection had implications which could not humanly have been anticipated before it took place. If Christ and His work were to be proclaimed, they must first be understood. The missionary task of the church necessitated the marshalling of facts and meaning of the gospel in terminology understandable by each successive audience. The cross had to be explained as well as preached, and this doctrine is constantly being augmented throughout the NT. The gospel preaching did not, however, always find a favourable response. The adverse reaction of many Jewish people raised significant ques-

tions: What would become of those who did not accept their Messiah? Were they still the people of God? What was the relationship of the Christian to the Jewish community, to the OT law, the temple, the priesthood? What support for the answers could be found in the OT? If God was now carrying on His purposes through the church instead of through Israel, what was the relationship of Jewish and Gentile believers? What was the nature and destiny of the church? How was it to worship, to serve, to be governed? What place did the church have in salvation-history? The Messiah had come, but had clearly left some important prophecies unfulfilled. He had promised to return, but time was passing with no sign of this taking place. How were Christians to live while waiting for their Lord? In what ways were converts from paganism to change their former way of life? What should be done about the increasing opposition felt from pagans, Jews and heretical Christians? These are a few of the issues that called for further revelation. Some of them will be discussed further below.

The doctrinal answers to these questions were not independently conceived, but went back, as we have suggested, to the teaching of the Lord Jesus Himself. Scholars have been concerned not only to go back to the Gospels, but to ascertain what were the earliest formulations of doctrine in the preaching and teaching of the early church. C. H. Dodd is generally recognized as the one who gave impetus to this study with his reconstruction of the early *kērygma*, or preaching.

The *kērygma* is the essential message of the gospel. It is expressed, for example, in 1 C. 15: 3 ff., and includes the fact of the death of Jesus the Messiah in accordance with OT prophecies, his burial and resurrection, and the fact that his death was an offering given for our sins in voluntary obedience to God. It also included a brief summary of the earthly ministry of the Lord Jesus, and an explanation, based on OT texts, of the reason why the Messiah had to suffer, His vindication by the resurrection, and His future glory. This message is found in the early chapters of Acts, in Peter's message to Cornelius in Ac. 10: 34-43 and in Paul's preaching to the Thessalonians in Ac. 17: 1-3.

Another early doctrinal element was the confession, the personal affirmation that a new convert made to his faith in Christ and his loyalty to Him. It was not only a testimony to conversion but a doctrinal predication regarding Christ. Such a confession is probably seen in Rom. 10: 9. The confession here is

The Development of Doctrine

'Jesus is Lord'. In Mk 8: 29 and parallels the apostles confess that Jesus is the Christ. The Gospel of John was written to demonstrate that Jesus was the Christ, the Son of God (Jn 20: 31). These confessions form a basis for later Christological teaching.

There are also fuller credal statements which are now acknowledged by many scholars to be among the earliest strands of the NT. They may appear in a hymnic style. Some find in the use of the relative pronoun, 'who', a key to the credal statements. So Phil. 2: 6-11, which relates the humiliation and exaltation of Christ begins, 'who being in the form of God . . .', and Col. 1: 13 ff., 'who hath delivered us . . . in whom we have redemption . . . who is the image of the invisible God . . .' etc. 1 Tim. 3: 16 may well be another example of an early credal statement. The best manuscripts have the word 'who' instead of the word 'God', and the creed therefore began evidently, 'who was manifest in flesh . . .' See also Heb. 1: 1-4 and 1 Pet. 2: 22 ff.

Another early element may well have been a collection of moral and ethical exhortations given to new converts. This suggestion is based on a comparison of passages containing such similar expressions as 'put off', 'be subject', 'watch', and 'resist' (e.g. Col. 3: 5-4: 5; Eph. 4: 17-6: 9; 1 Pet. 2: 11-3: 9). A study of these passages and others shows that there is a great similarity in the content of the injunctions. In each case there is some reference to new life in Christ, and attention is given to the relationship of Christians to each other, in their families, to the government, between servants and masters, between husbands and wives, and parents and children.

Such elements of early Christian teaching as have been summarized above undoubtedly form part of what is known in the NT as the 'tradition'. This word (sometimes also used in a bad sense) is a frequent one in the writings of the apostle Paul (e.g. 2 Th. 2: 15; 3: 6; 1 C. 11: 2; Col. 2: 6; 1 Tim. 6: 20; 2 Tim. 1: 14). There is little ground for the idea that Paul superimposed his own complex theological system, different in spirit and content, upon the simple teaching of the Lord Jesus. Instead, he speaks of doctrines and practices which he had 'received' (1 C. 11: 23; 15: 1), and one can find in Paul's writings echoes of the words of the Lord Jesus (cf. e.g. Rom. 12: 14, 17, 21 with Mt. 5: 38 ff.; Rom. 13: 7-10 with Mt. 22: 15-22, 34-40; Rom. 14: 10 with Mt. 7: 1; Rom. 14: 13 with Mt. 18: 7; Rom. 14: 14 with Mt. 15: 11). There is therefore a continuity in the doctrinal development, from the teachings of Christ through the initial affirmations of the early church and the theological contribution of Paul and others, to the final corpus of doctrine in the NT. We shall now briefly survey a few representative themes.

THE PERSON AND WORK OF CHRIST

The most urgent need of the early church was a better understanding of the person and work of the Lord Jesus. Some questions were answered by the very fact of His death, resurrection and ascension, but many others were raised. Since belief in Christ was the *sine qua non* of Christianity, the confession, 'Jesus is the Christ' or 'Jesus is Lord' was, as we have seen, an early and basic doctrinal affirmation. Further evidence of the early identification of Jesus as divine Lord is found in 1 C. 16: 22. Here the transliteration of the Aramaic *maranatha* (which, according to the way the word is divided, may mean either 'may the Lord come' or 'the Lord is coming') testifies to the early belief of the young Aramaic-speaking church at Jerusalem. The Aramaic expression was evidently in such common use that Paul transliterated it rather than use a translation. It testifies to their belief both in the Lord and in His return. The word 'Lord', though common in the Gospels, was evidently not often used as a title during His earthly ministry. However He is so designated in Mk 11: 3, and in Mk 12: 36 the word occurs in a quotation from Ps. 110: 1.

The early chapters of Acts tell us that shortly after His resurrection the Christians declared that Jesus had been exalted by God and designated both 'Lord' and 'Christ' (Ac. 2: 33-36). He is also declared to be the Prince of Life (Ac. 3: 15; 5: 31) and the prophet predicted by Moses (Ac. 3: 22; 7: 37). The apostle Paul began his Christian career by seeking to persuade his Jewish associates that Jesus was the Christ, the Son of God (Ac. 9: 20-22).

The original preaching of the church regarding Jesus, according to the book of Acts, laid stress on His rôle as the suffering Servant of Isaiah. Although this was not the major theme of the Gospels, Mt. 12: 17 ff. applies Isa. 42: 1-3 to Jesus. The thought is also certainly present in the saying of the Lord Jesus that the Son of Man came to serve and give His life a ransom for many (Mk 10: 45). The preaching of Peter, who stands behind Mark's Gospel and who represents the early Palestinian missionary effort, stresses Jesus' rôle as servant. This is evident not only from his writings (1 Pet. 2: 21-25) but also from his preaching (Ac. 3: 13, 26; cf. Ac. 4: 27, 30).

It is clear then that as the doctrine concerning the Lord Jesus developed, stress was first of all

82

laid upon His exaltation as Lord and Messiah, and on His suffering in obedience to the will of God. The allusions in 1 Peter to Isaiah 53 undoubtedly reflect the common use of that passage by Jewish Christians.

In the great Letter to the Romans Paul begins with the affirmation that Jesus is the royal Messiah, the Lord, and the Son of God, as demonstrated by His resurrection (Rom. 1: 3 f.). From these essentials, the doctrine of Christ is expanded as the Holy Spirit leads Paul to a fuller realization of their implication. So Paul strongly declares the pre-existence of Christ. This is done not only in such typological references as 1 C. 10: 4 ('the rock was Christ') and in passages where His pre-existence is implied (Gal. 4: 4; Rom. 8: 3), but also in definite statements such as 2 C. 8: 9, 'though he was rich, yet for your sake he became poor', and 1 C. 15: 47 'the second man is from heaven'. The pre-existence of Christ is also stressed in the Christological summaries of Col. 1: 15-20; Phil. 2: 5-11. Furthermore the Lord Jesus is now in heaven where He intercedes for the believers (Rom. 8: 34), and where those who have been raised spiritually with Him should focus their attention (Eph. 1: 3; Col. 3: 1).

Not only did the Lord Jesus come from and return to heaven, but he has a universal cosmic rôle as creator of all things and rightful head of the universe (Col. 1: 13-18; Eph. 1: 10; Phil. 2: 10). The Letter to the Colossians was written to combat a heresy which lowered the dignity of Christ and therefore it is especially this Letter which expresses His pre-eminence (1: 18).

As these doctrines are stressed, expressions multiply which clearly associate Christ with God Himself (Rom. 1: 7; 1 Th. 1: 11; 2 C. 13: 14). OT passages which refer to God are applied to Christ. Thus Rom. 10: 11 may be compared with Isa. 28: 16; Rom. 10: 13 with Jl 2: 32; 1 C. 2: 16 with Isa. 40: 13; and Phil. 2: 10 with Isa. 45: 23. It also becomes apparent that the concept of Christ as the Son of God is not merely an 'official' or functional Messianic expression, but that it has a more intimate meaning. Thus God sends 'his own Son' (Rom. 8: 3) and permits 'his own Son' to die (Rom. 8: 31). Although other interpretations are possible, Rom. 9: 5 would seem to make the identification complete.

In the Pauline writings the rôle of Christ as the second Adam is also developed. It is He who undoes the evil brought about through the failure of the first Adam and who is the representative of the believer (Rom. 5: 12-21; 8: 29; 1 C. 15: 45-47). In the Pastoral Letters the

Lord Jesus is described as our Saviour, Mediator and Ransom (1 Tim. 2: 3-6), and as the giver of eternal life (2 Tim. 1: 10). His Messiahship and resurrection are unassailable truths which are to give encouragement to the Lord's servants (2 Tim. 2: 8). The Greek of Tit. 2: 13 suggests the identification of Christ as God (cf. 2 Pet. 1: 1).

During the period in which the various Letters were being written, the Holy Spirit was leading in the formation of the four Gospels. The need for written records of the life and teachings of Jesus increased as the gospel was carried across the Empire and as converts needed instruction. The church has traditionally, and correctly, seen in them four portraits of the Lord Jesus carefully drawn for different audiences. Although the Gospels do not always make theology explicit, the core of Christology is here, expressed in such terms as Messiah, Son of Man, Lord and Son of God. By presenting vivid descriptions of the gracious deeds of Jesus, they provide far more than would have been given in mere doctrinal affirmations. They portray Him who was possessed of true humanity, and yet spoke with absolute authority, laying claim to Deity and Lordship over men. He is seen as unequalled in the glory of His personal character, not only with respect to the absence of sin, but, positively with respect to the presence of all moral virtues in perfect balance. His passion and resurrection form a major part of each book.

The Gospel of John concentrates on fewer discourses and miracles of Christ, but through these expands our concept of Him. We realize that He is the 'Word', who has eternally existed in the divine relationship, Creator of all things, who came as the full and perfect expression of the truth and grace of God. In the Johannine Letters stress is laid not only on Jesus as the Son of God but on His true manhood, in opposition to the heresy which denied this fact (1 Jn 1: 3, 7; 3: 23; 4: 2 f.; 5: 1, 5, 10, 13; 2 Jn 7, 9). In the book of Revelation the future vindication and glory of Christ are described. In that apocalyptic work we are told of the future great conflict and the ultimate victory of the Lord Jesus Christ. Against the backdrop of the cosmic events of the last times, He whose personal history encompasses all else from beginning to end appears from heaven as final victor.

THE MEANING OF THE CROSS
We have seen how the basic Christological affirmations of the early confessions and *kērygma* were expanded in the NT writings. Just as the implications of the facts regarding the nature of Christ were spelled out, so were those of the

fact of His death. We have seen that a basic statement is found in 1 C. 15: 1 ff. Here Paul speaks of the fact of Jesus' death and of its connection with our salvation. The early Christian preaching as found in the book of Acts does not explicitly state the place of the cross in the realization of our salvation. Yet although the theology of the cross is not developed, its centrality is affirmed. The death of Christ is seen as completely within the foreknowledge and plan of God (Ac. 2: 23). This fact can be stated with confidence because of the resurrection. Just as Christ Himself was vindicated through the resurrection so the place of the cross in God's plan is established. Jesus is therefore exalted as Saviour (Ac. 5: 31). The Christian message reflected in Acts stresses first of all repentance (2: 38; 3: 19). The unrepentant are to be judged by the very one whom they have rejected, the risen Christ (Ac. 10: 42; 17: 31). Forgiveness is only through His name, the efficacy of which is demonstrated by a miracle of healing (Ac. 3: 12 ff.; 4: 10 ff.; cf. 10: 43 and 16: 30).

Before considering the way in which the doctrine of salvation is developed in the Letters we should take note of the foundation which was laid in the teaching of Jesus. It is noteworthy that John the Baptist, Jesus Himself, and His disciples all began their public ministry with a call to repentance (Mt. 3: 1 f.; 4: 17; Mk 6: 12). Jesus followed His call to repentance with an exhortation to 'believe in the gospel' (Mk 1: 15). These books which contain the teachings of Jesus are themselves properly called 'Gospels'. They contain the essentials of the message not only by but about Christ. The need of man for salvation is frequently stressed in the sayings of Jesus. The Sermon on the Mount expresses throughout the culpable failure of man and the consequences of his evil. Although self-righteous Pharisees are singled out for censure, the guilt of all men is made clear. Even fathers who give good gifts to their children are by nature 'evil' (Mt. 7: 11). External righteousness cannot hide internal sin.

Equally stressed, however, is the forgiveness which Christ seeks to bestow upon men. His authority in this respect is challenged and defended (Mk 2: 5-12). Not only is Jesus' authority to forgive mentioned, but also the means by which He was to actualize the promise. The confession at Caesarea Philippi was followed by the first of a series of passion predictions (Mt. 16: 21 and parallels). Other hints of His approaching death are given. Among these is the statement in Mk 10: 45 (cf. Mt. 20: 28) that the Son of Man would give His life a ransom for, or in place of, many. The

institution of the Lord's Supper provides the most significant setting for a further explanation of His death, as Jesus makes it clear that His blood was to be shed for the forgiveness of sin (Mt. 26: 28).

As the apostle Paul repeated the essential elements of the gospel in his missionary preaching, his inquiring mind began to penetrate further implications of the death and resurrection of Christ. As questions and objections were raised by his hearers, he prayerfully went to the OT Scriptures, and at the same time sought out contemporary modes of expression to explain the significance of the gospel. In the Letter to the Romans Paul carefully forged out the implications of the gospel message. Although the theme of Christ's vindication and victory, and the fact of reconciliation and redemption through the cross of Christ, are prominent in Paul's writings, it is the concept of justification by grace through faith which is Paul's most notable contribution. Rom. 3: 21-26 is a summary of this doctrine, culminating in the statement that through the cross of Christ God was able to maintain His own righteousness while yet declaring the believer in Jesus free from guilt. The holiness and justice of God are vindicated. Human guilt makes self-effort useless, and salvation is solely through the death of Christ, appropriated by faith. The theme of the death of Christ, signified in verse 25 by the word 'blood', is repeated elsewhere. Christ was delivered up for our trespasses (Rom. 4: 25). He died for the ungodly and for sinners (Rom. 5: 6, 8). He was made sin for us (2 C. 5: 21). We are justified (Rom. 5: 9), redeemed (Eph. 1: 7) and reconciled to God through His blood (Rom. 5: 9; Eph. 1: 7; 2: 13; Col. 1: 20). Christ gave Himself for our sins (Gal. 1: 4) and even incurred the curse of the law for us (Gal. 3: 13).

Since God, who had concluded all men under sin, has judged sin in the person of His own Son on the cross (Rom.), brought the law to fulfilment with the death of Christ (Gal.), and reconciled Jew and Gentile together by the gracious act of the cross (Eph.), His great salvation is available through one means only: faith. The doctrine of faith is by no means new with Paul, for it was stressed by Jesus. However it is now emphasized as the sole essential for salvation (Rom. 3: 28; Eph. 2: 8).

The saving work of Christ is further expressed in the Pastorals in His designation, noted above, as Mediator (1 Tim. 2: 5), Ransom (1 Tim. 2: 6), and Saviour (2 Tim. 1: 10; Tit. 2: 13 f.; 3: 6). In Tit. the gospel of the saving grace of God is urged as a motivating force toward purity of life.

The early Christian *kērygma* is amplified also in the writings of Peter. The word for 'gospel' itself is found in 1 Pet. 1: 12; 4: 6, 7. Peter's recollection of the cross is still fresh, as is seen by his reference to the blood of Christ (1 Pet. 1: 2, 19). Writing sometime after the event and during the period of some stress, Peter has made assessments of relative value (as people in distress often do). The word 'precious' and its cognates appear several times in his writings and the blood of Christ is so designated. The death of Christ is seen as substitutionary, as He 'bore our sins in his body on the tree' and 'died for sins once for all, the righteous for the unrighteous', and also as an example of patient endurance of wrong (1 Pet. 2: 21-24; 3: 18). The suffering of Christ is thus seen to bear upon the Christian's moral life (1 Pet. 4: 1 ff.). The Christian must learn to draw upon the benefits of the cross as he lives in the lengthening period between the first coming of Christ and His return, which will bring the consummation of salvation (1 Pet. 1: 6 ff.).

The writer of the Letter to the Hebrews stresses the rôle of Christ as both priest and sacrifice. The death of Christ not only satisfies the typology of the OT sacrifice, but signals its end. The finality of the sacrifice of Christ is emphasized in chapters 9 and 10. The readers are urged on this basis, and in the view of the fact that God has established a new covenant which supersedes the old, to rely completely on Jesus as the 'pioneer and perfecter of our faith' (12: 2).

The completed work of Christ upon the cross is augmented by His present intercession in heaven. This further revelation is given by the writer of Heb. (7: 23-25), by Paul (Rom. 8: 34) and by John (1 Jn 2: 1). The latter passage refers to Christ as an 'advocate' (the same word applied in the Gospel of Jn 14: 16, 26 to the Holy Spirit) and goes on to speak of Him as the 'propitiation' for our sins. These two concepts in conjunction stress the need of a Saviour to avert the just wrath of a holy God. (It is important to remember here that such language is not intended to represent God as being petulantly angry with His creatures in the pagan sense and requiring to be placated, but as Himself in love providing the atonement for the removal of their guilt and of the retribution which it attracts. The RSV renders the word 'expiation'.)

The book of Revelation provides us with vivid reminders of the cross. Christ 'has freed us from our sins by his blood' (1: 5). The symbol of the Lamb is prominent in the book both as representative of a sacrificial victim (5: 6 ff.) and, unexpectedly, as a victorious conqueror (6: 1; 7: 9 ff.; 8: 1; 14: 1 ff.; 19: 7 ff.; 21: 9 ff.). This new rôle of the Lamb is expressed most dramatically in the expression 'the wrath of the Lamb' (6: 16). Judgment falls on all whose names are not in the Lamb's book of life (20: 15; 21: 27). The Apocalypse concludes with a description of the Holy City, in which the Lamb is both temple and light (21: 22 f.).

THE NEW PEOPLE OF GOD

In presenting their case to the Jewish people, it was not enough for the Christians simply to state the claim of Jesus of Nazareth to be the Messiah. They also had to overcome objections to this claim, objections which were largely focused on the cross. In short they had to explain why God allowed His own Son, the Messiah, to die. The problem was compounded by the fact that His execution was by the worst conceivable method, the cross, which, as a form of hanging, incurred the OT curse (Dt. 21: 23), and by the fact that the alleged Messiah was rejected by the covenant people and betrayed by one of His own circle.

The Christians approached this problem by a selective use of OT passages which proved that the Messiah first had to suffer (Ac. 17: 3). Paul, however, went even further than this by using the curse of hanging as a strong element in his presentation of the gospel in Gal. Quoting Dt. 27: 26, he shows that those who choose to live under the law but fail to keep it are under a curse. By becoming a curse Himself, Christ bore that curse which was due to us (Gal. 3: 10-14). Furthermore he adds a point not calculated to win Jewish approval, that this vicarious acceptance of the curse by Christ brings the blessing promised in the OT to Gentiles (Gal. 3: 14).

Another problem which faced the Christians at the very beginning of their missionary effort was the place of the Jewish temple and ritual. The issue had already been raised by a misinterpretation of the remarks of Jesus regarding the destruction of the 'temple' (meaning His body), remarks which were introduced into Jesus' trial (Mt. 26: 61). The Jerusalem believers, according to Ac. 2: 46; 3: 1, attended the temple. Soon, however, opposition crystallized. Stephen was accused of detrimental comments against it, and made it an issue in his defence (Ac. 6: 12 ff.; 7: 44-50). The suggestion that there existed links between Stephen, the 'Hellenists' of Acts and the Essenes may have inadequate support, but the issue of the temple was indeed widespread. Hebrews, as we have seen, takes the position that the OT temple rites fulfilled their purpose. It finds the value of the building in its usefulness as a type of the real sanctuary into which Christ has entered (Heb. 9). John sees a substitute for the temple in the person of Jesus Himself, noting that the 'Word' was present among us in the 'tabernacle' of the body of Jesus (1: 14). Paul states that God's present temple is the Church both as a corporate group and as individuals (Eph. 2: 19-22; 1 C. 3: 16 f.; 2 C. 6: 19 f.).

Likewise the sacrifices of the OT era and the services of the priesthood had no intrinsic value apart from their foreshadowing of the perfect work of Christ, whereby He was both priest and victim (Heb. 8-10). Continuation of the temple cult was therefore futile (Heb. 10: 18). In fact not only had individual provisions of the old covenant been rendered obsolete, but the entire covenant had been superseded by a new one. This was, the writer hastens to affirm, already envisioned in the OT (Heb. 10: 16 f.), but it is new, not only as a covenant but (in the other sense of the Greek word *diathēkē*) as a testament or will. As such it necessitated the death of the 'testator', a further reason for the death of Christ (9: 15 ff.).

What is now the relationship of the Christian to the OT law? The answer to this has its roots in the teaching of the Lord Jesus Himself. In the Sermon on the Mount He makes it clear that He did not come to destroy the law (Mt. 5: 17 ff.), but at the same time He affirms His own authority with respect to its interpretation. It is quite clear that Jesus intended the moral imperative of the law to be obeyed. This is echoed in the Letter of James which contains many allusions to the Sermon on the Mount. Paul said, 'love is the fulfilling of the law' (Rom. 10: 13), a statement in keeping with Jesus' teaching (Mt. 22: 34-40 and parallels). The Gospels show Jesus as fulfilling the law in His teaching, and in His life He also fulfilled the prophecies of the OT, especially with respect to His death (Lk. 4: 21; Mt. 26: 54). Jesus' charge against the Pharisees was not that they observed it too punctiliously, but that they did not obey it consistently and contradicted its spirit (Mt. 5: 20; 23: 23 ff.).

However, the law involved more than the moral aspect, and it seems clear that the Jewish people did not make a firm distinction between this and the so-called 'ceremonial' injunctions. Therefore it was necessary that eventually within the NT there should be a clear statement regarding the place of the whole law in the New Covenant. This definitive statement was made by Paul. He showed that the law could never bring righteousness, and that Christ was the end of the law in this respect, offering that righteousness which comes by faith in Him (Rom. 10: 1-13). Paul's own experience, like that of all men who consciously face the demands of the law, is that it at best brings the knowledge of sin (Rom. 7: 13). The law served its purpose up to the time of Christ when He, having fulfilled it Himself, bore the curse it brought upon sinful mankind and thereby annulled it for those who would believe in Him (Gal. 3: 21-26; Eph. 2: 14-16). The kind of life the law required is now produced not by an external code but by the indwelling Spirit (Gal. 5: 16-25; Rom. 8: 4).

All these issues lead to a basic question: Who now are the people of God? Initially, of course, the Christian believers were Jews who had found the fulfilment of their ancient faith in the person of their Messiah Jesus. It might have been supposed that they could continue as a Jewish sect. According to the early chapters of Acts, as we have noted, the Christians continued in their temple worship. Their teaching, however, occasioned not only disagreement but opposition. The Synoptic Gospels indicate that Jesus had enjoyed, for the most part, the support of the 'common people' with opposition stemming mainly from the Pharisees and the Sadducees. Likewise Acts describes the early opposition as coming from the Sadducean chief priests (Ac. 4: 1-6), while the Christians enjoyed a good reputation among the Jewish people as a whole (Ac. 2: 47). As the missionary enterprise moves forward, however, Luke notes increasing resistance. In the synagogue at Antioch Paul speaks of the unbelief of 'those who live in Jerusalem and their rulers'. As the narrative of Acts continues, antagonism to the gospel comes from the 'Jews' as a group (Ac. 13: 50). The situation is described in the same terms in the Gospel of John where in 7: 1, for example, the threat to Jesus' life comes not from the Pharisees or Sadducees but from 'the Jews' in Judaea.

Thus it became necessary to deal with the fact that the Christians were a people apart. Even though the author of Acts is careful to point out the Jewish origin of Christianity (and may in part be seeking to demonstrate that as a daughter religion Christianity should enjoy the rights granted the Jews), it is clear even in this work that the division is decisive. The book closes with Paul applying Isa. 6 to contemporary Jews, 'this people's heart has grown dull . . .' followed by the concluding statement 'let it be known to you then that this salvation of God has been sent to the Gentiles; they will listen' (Ac. 28: 25-29).

Under these conditions several problems presented themselves. Paul expresses one of them in Rom. 11: 1, 'has God rejected His people?'

In his reply he does not minimize the seriousness of the unbelief of Israel, but describing Israel as branches broken off from an olive tree, he affirms his belief that God is able to replace the branches (Rom. 11: 23-32). Paul makes it very clear, however, that during the present time it is the Christian church which constitutes the people of God; all Christians are spiritually heirs of Abraham. 'There is neither Jew nor Greek . . . you are all one in Christ Jesus. And if you are Christ's, then you are Abraham's offspring, heirs according to promise' (Gal. 3: 28 f.).

Also significant is the fact that Peter applies the description of Israel in Exod. 23: 22 to the Christians: 'But you are a chosen race, a royal priesthood, a holy nation, God's own people' (1 Pet. 2: 9). The words of Hos. 2: 23 are now fulfilled: 'Once you were no people but now you are God's people' (1 Pet. 2: 10).

The Letter to the Ephesians provides further revelation to guide the Christians in their quest for self-understanding and for an articulate expression of their identity over against both Judaism and paganism. Here Paul describes a 'mystery' (divine truth unknowable except by revelation, but now openly proclaimed). Through the cross God not only reconciled men to Himself, but He also united Jew and Gentile in a 'new man' (Eph. 2: 15). This is part of God's eternal plan to exalt Christ as head of the universe (1: 10). The Church then takes its place as part of a plan of God 'who accomplishes all things according to the counsel of His will'. In view of the sovereign work of God in history and through the cross it is clear that salvation is to be viewed as connected with God's workmanship, i.e., of grace and not of our own works (2: 8-10).

The Church is therefore an organic union of all believers (Eph. 3 and 4). This union must be expressed, whatever personal sacrifice is necessary, in the practical unity of Christians (4: 1 f.). Christians share a common life in Christ. They are spiritually united to each other because they are vitally united to Him. This intimate relationship is frequently described by Paul as being 'in Christ' (an expression which borders on, but does not pass over into, mysticism). Jesus had taught His disciples that He would build His Church, that He would be spiritually present, and that believers would be united in divine love (Mt. 16: 18; 18: 20; Jn 17: 20-26). Paul shows that the unity of the Church with its Lord is so unique that it may be described as that of a living body and its head (Eph. 4: 11-16; 1 C. 12: 12-27). Other descriptions of the Church illuminate its varied functions: flock (Lk. 12: 32; Ac. 20: 28), the

planting (1 C. 3: 19), the household (Eph. 2: 19 f.), the temple (1 C. 3: 16), the bride (Eph. 5: 25 ff.), and, when deviation from Christian doctrine was becoming more overt, 'the household of God . . . the pillar and bulwark of the truth' (1 Tim. 3: 15).

ACCORDING TO THE SCRIPTURES

As the young church sought to gain self-understanding and to meet the challenges put to it, the OT was diligently searched. It yielded substantiation for their Messianic affirmations, the gospel message, their stance toward Judaism, and their eschatological hope. Their use of the Scriptures derives from the example and teaching of the Lord Jesus. According to the Gospels Jesus made frequent use of the Scriptures not only in His teaching but in His personal experience of temptation (Mt. 4: 1-11) and in controversies with Jewish leaders. At one point His rejoinder was 'is not this why you are wrong, that you know neither the Scriptures nor the power of God?' (Mk 12: 24). In this same controversy passage Jesus is seen referring to a Messianic Psalm (Ps. 110: 1). In the fourth Gospel He not only bases a reply on the OT, but He adds the words 'Scripture cannot be broken' (Jn 10: 35). Our Lord clearly stated that He was purposefully acting to fulfil the Scriptures (Lk. 4: 16-21; Mt. 26: 54, 56). The Scriptures are found not only on the lips of Jesus but in the comments of the writers. This is particularly true of Matthew. His use of OT verses to illumine events in the life of Jesus may occasionally seem strained to the modern reader. Several things must be borne in mind, however. The type of exegesis by which some NT writers applied OT Scriptures to contemporary events is similar to a known type (called Midrash *pesher*) and has parallels in the Qumran literature. Second, the Gospel of Matthew was undoubtedly written after the Christians already had some experience in the use of the OT Scriptures in debate with Jews. Like other NT writers, Matthew felt the creative liberty of the Spirit in adapting the Scriptures to the recent events which provided their greatest fulfilment. In doing this, he, as well as the other NT authors, had the precedence and the instruction of the Lord Jesus on the road to Emmaus (Lk. 24: 25-27) and perhaps during the period between His resurrection and ascension, when He 'interpreted to them in all the Scriptures the things concerning himself'. We have already seen how an appeal was made to the Scriptures to substantiate the claim that Jesus was the Messiah and to explain His seemingly paradoxical death. Paul had recourse to the Scriptures to explain the gospel and such a crucial matter as the Christian attitude to the law. The Letter to the Hebrews draws heavily on the Biblical descriptions of the institutions of priesthood and sacrifice. The early Jerusalem church drew heavily on the Scriptures, as is seen in Acts, James and 1 and 2 Peter.

There are several ways in which the OT Scriptures were used. One is the use of proof texts. This is seen in the reference to different verses which mention a stone: Ps. 118: 22; Isa. 28: 16; 8: 14; Dan. 2: 34 f. They appear singly and in combination in Mk 12: 10 f.; Lk. 20: 17 f.; Ac. 4: 11; Rom. 9: 33; 1 Pet. 2: 6 ff. These instances suggest that such verses were in common use by the Christians. Some have even postulated the existence of a collection of such verses or *testimonia*. This hypothesis has been aided, but certainly not proved, by the similar use of the Scriptures by later Christian apologists; it may also be illustrated by the collections of *testimonia* among the Qumran texts in the previous century.

Other ways in which the Scriptures were used may be described under the general term 'typology'. There are instances where a one-to-one comparison is made as, for example, in 1 C. 5: 7 where Jesus is described as our 'passover', 1 C. 10: 1 ff. where the supernatural rock in the wilderness is identified with Christ, and Heb. 7, which compares Christ directly with Melchizedek. Beyond these specific instances there is also the underlying assumption of the NT writers that the experiences of Christ were foreshadowed in that of Israel and of individual OT saints. In Matthew one may discern the 'Exodus motif'. Israel came forth from Egypt; so did Christ, and therefore it is said 'out of Egypt have I called My Son' (Mt. 2: 15). Moses and Christ both had a wilderness experience, gave a Law, and so forth. It is, of course, all too easy to read far more typology into the Bible than is intended. The whole subject has been receiving some renewed attention lately in theological works.

THE NEW AGE
At the beginning of His ministry, the Lord Jesus illustrated the newness of His gospel by reminding His audience that men do not put new wine in old wineskins (Mk 2: 22). According to John, His first miracle was the changing of water into wine, followed by the cleansing of the temple and the teaching of the new birth (Jn 2: 1-3; 14). By these words and actions the new age is introduced. This was anticipated in the infancy narratives of Matthew and Luke, as the expectations of believing Jews were finally realized in the birth of their Saviour-

Messiah. It is taught expressly in the words of the Lord Jesus that 'the law and the prophets were until John; since then the good news of the kingdom is preached' (Lk. 16: 16). So the Lord Jesus, when He began His ministry in Galilee, declared, 'The time is fulfilled, and the kingdom of God is at hand; repent, and believe in the gospel' (Mk 1: 14).

The nearness and power of the kingdom were seen in the mighty works of Christ, primarily in His exorcisms. Then, as the claims of the King were pressed, and the initial surge of response changed into varied attitudes of misunderstanding or unbelief, Jesus withdrew from the Galilean crowds, eventually to confirm in the minds of the disciples His divine nature and mission. At the confession 'You are the Christ, the Son of the living God', He proceeded to reveal His intention to establish the Church, following His death and resurrection (Mt. 16: 13-23). The Church is mentioned only one other time in the Gospels, this also in Matthew (18: 17). As we have just seen, the doctrine of the Church is elaborated in the Letters. In contrast, the kingdom, which is a major theme of the teaching of Jesus in the Synoptics, receives little emphasis in the Letters. This is understandable in view of the fact that the kingdom was announced and 'inaugurated' as the reign of Christ over His people, but that it will not have its eschatological consummation until the future appearing of Christ. Some Scriptures, such as Mt. 8: 11 f.; 19: 28; 26: 29; the Olivet discourse of Mt. 24 and parallels, and the parables of Mt. 13 and 25, along with the parable of the nobleman in Lk. 19: 11-27, indicate unmistakably that a full future expression of the kingdom must be awaited. Other verses, as Mt. 12: 28 (cf. Lk. 11: 20); Mt. 11: 12 (cf. Lk. 16: 16), and those that speak of people receiving and entering the kingdom, suggest that in a real sense the kingdom is present. The apostles preached the kingdom (so Paul in Ac. 20: 25) and believers knew that they were now in 'the kingdom of his beloved Son' (Col. 1: 13). A connection (but not identification) clearly exists between the kingdom and the Church, as is indicated in the relationship of the words 'Christ' (or Messiah), 'church', and 'kingdom' in Mt. 16: 16-20. It was also clear that they were living in an eschatological tension 'between the times'. God was not only going to *break into* history (in the sense common to the apocalyptic writers), but He was also doing something *now in* history (in the sense of the prophetic tradition). This is the period of God's activity, not just an interlude between acts.

The consummation lay in the future. The

book of Revelation provides graphic descriptions of this, and 1 C. 15: 24 ff. gives a hint of the state of things under the ultimate rule of God. The early believers were sure both that the central event of history had already occurred, and that their Lord would 'appear a second time, not to deal with sin but to save those who are eagerly waiting for him' (Heb. 9: 28). However, they were left without certainty as to the time of His return. Their attention was to be given to His work now (Lk. 19: 13), which consisted mainly of witnessing for Him (Ac. 1: 8). They were to maintain an attitude of alertness in the expectation of His return (Mt. 25: 1-13; 1 Th. 5: 1-11). The evil world was still about them, but they could now live a victorious life based on Christ's own triumph over evil (Col. 2: 15; 2 C. 2: 14).

As the years passed, Christians probably became more aware that the time before the return of Christ was of indefinite duration. Such events as Caligula's impudent attempt to have his image set up in the holy place in Jerusalem (A.D. 40) and the destruction of the Temple (A.D. 70) must have stirred speculation and drawn attention to the Olivet discourse. Much discussion has centred about the question as to whether Paul initially expected the return of Christ during his lifetime and then, adapting his thinking to the possibility that he would die before the second advent, changed his doctrinal stance in this regard. 1 Th. 4 glows with the expectation of the return of Christ. 2 Thessalonians introduces more eschatological detail. In the Corinthian correspondence Paul includes himself among those who may not live to Christ's return (1 C. 6: 14; 2 C. 4: 14; 5: 1-9). Philippians shows the author's readiness to die, along with his hope of Christ's return (1: 21 ff.; 3: 20 f.). Such a change in attitude is, of course, partly explained by the practical fact that imminent death was a frequent possibility in Paul's experience. More important is the fact that a change in Paul's personal outlook does not necessarily constitute a modification of doctrine. The evangelical view of inspiration differentiates between an author's personal attitude and the infallible doctrine which he is led to express in the Scriptures. (Paul makes this explicit himself in another connection in 1 C. 7: 25.)

The increasing span of time from the resurrection event was, of course, a major problem to some. This is seen in one of the later books of the Bible, 2 Peter, which challenges those who scoff saying 'where is the promise of His coming?' (2 Pet. 3: 1-13). The Christian, however, is to live in view of the coming of his Lord, conducting himself in a godly way (2 Pet. 3: 11 ff.; Tit. 2: 11 ff.), aware that whether he lives until the Lord's return or whether his earthly home is dissolved, he has a heavenly dwelling, will be with his Saviour, and will have his present life evaluated by the Lord (2 C. 5: 1-10).

Meanwhile, pending the consummation, converts were being won who needed instruction in the business of daily Christian living. A body of ethical teaching, built on a doctrinal foundation, was developed. Mention has been made of the form of instruction which was evidently common among Christians. This teaching involved the Christian's moral life, his relationship to unbelievers, and his relationship to other Christians (Eph. 4: 17 ff.; 5: 21 ff.; Col. 3: 5 ff.; 1 Pet. 2: 11 ff.; 5: 5). Paul reminds his Thessalonian congregation that he had given them ethical 'instruction' before, and urges them on to personal consecration. The believer is not to live without restraint, even though he is not under the Mosaic Law, for the 'law of love' now controls him (Rom. 13: 8-10; Jas 1: 22-25; 2: 8-13). He lives under the influence of the Holy Spirit, who accomplishes in his life what the law, hindered by the flesh, could not produce (Rom. 8: 2 ff.; Gal. 5: 13-26). The 'old man' came to his end at conversion; his deeds are to be forsaken and the flesh considered crucified with Christ (Rom. 6: 1-11; Eph. 4: 22-24; Col. 3: 5-10). Thus the intent of the OT law, expounded by Christ, could now be realized. So the believer is to live during this present age as a child of the new age, a son of the light, a son of the day (1 Th. 5: 5).

THE PATTERN OF SOUND WORDS

Among the factors which stimulated the development of doctrine in the NT were the adverse circumstances faced by the early Christians. We have already seen that the unbelief and opposition of the Jewish people called for both a defensive apologetic and a positive formulation of doctrine by the Christians. The same was true with regard to resistance to the gospel on the part of Gentiles. This is seen in the book of Acts where Paul turned demonstrations of pagan unbelief into opportunities for a declaration of the creative and saving activity of God (Ac. 14: 11-18; 17: 16-34). The latter of these is the well known address by Paul on the Areopagus. Their erroneous ideas about God are refuted by summaries of the Biblical doctrine of God, culminating in an appeal to repentance based on the responsibility men now have to the resurrected One who has the authority of judgment.

It has long been recognized that not only

the speeches of Acts but the entire book itself is an apologetic directed to the Roman mind, if not to the Roman government itself. Luke is careful to show, as he did with respect to the trial of Jesus, that whenever Christianity confronted a judicial representative of Rome it was acquitted. In another apologetic, this time in opposition to the many fraudulent peddlers of religion who were travelling from city to city, begging for money and practising immorality in the name of their religion, Luke is concerned to set in contrast the irreproachable ministry of Paul. This is naturally also the concern of the apostle himself, and he occasionally writes in vindication of his methods. Thus we find him working honestly at his trade (Ac. 18: 3), not accepting financial support from those to whom he preached the gospel (1 C. 9: 15-23), and giving himself totally to those whom he sought to win (1 Th. 2: 1-12). It may seem strange to some that NT writers seem to attack the morals of their opponents as well as their doctrine (*e.g.* Phil. 3: 17-19). It is simply a fact of the ancient world, however, that itinerant preachers in general had a poor reputation and also that arguments between sects commonly included charges of hypocrisy and immorality. It is to this fact that we are indebted for some of the examples and exhortations in the NT on behalf of purity in the life of God's servants.

In Paul's address to the Ephesian elders in Ac. 20 he warns against false teachers who would actually invade the church itself. This was the concern of the Christians for many decades. The struggle against doctrinal perversion and heresy produced some of the clearest expressions of doctrine in the NT. Among the most troublesome antagonists were those who opposed seeking Gentile converts and accepting them fully without their submitting to certain Jewish customs. These Judaizing legalists, against whom Paul wrote Galatians, evoked from him a summary of the purpose of the law and his declaration of Christian liberty, to which we have already alluded.

Against another developing system of thought later known as Gnosticism, a higher knowledge, deprecating the created world, and lowering Christ to an inferior position in a world of intermediary beings, Paul presented a lucid and powerful Christology. So we were given the Colossian Letter. Employing the heretics' own vocabulary, he demonstrated that Christ embodies the fulness of God and is due the place of pre-eminence, and that God's creation is for our proper use and pleasure.

Those Letters which were apparently the last to be written reflect the growing problem posed by false teachers. The repetition in 2 Peter of the charge of immorality against these heretics serves to underscore the fact that similar charges by Paul were not an expression of personal vindictiveness but were justified by the facts. We are the beneficiaries of the controversy, for in 2 Peter some significant expressions of doctrine have been called forth by the conflict. First is the exhortation to Christian maturity and holiness (1: 3-11). Second is the invaluable passage regarding the inspiration and historical validity of the Scriptures. 'For we did not follow cleverly devised myths . . . We have the prophetic word made more sure . . . Men moved by the Holy Spirit spoke from God' (2 Pet. 1: 16-21). Next is a revelation of the judgment which will be brought against the opponents of the truth (2: 1-22). Finally, the scoffing of those who used the delay of the *parousia* as an occasion for denying the truth of God's promise occasions further revelation concerning the consummation of God's purposes in earth and heaven: '. . . the coming of the day of God, because of which the heavens will be kindled and dissolved, and the elements will melt with fire. But according to his promise we wait for new heavens and a new earth in which righteousness dwells' (3: 11-13). Encouragement is also given on the basis of God's patient grace, 'not wishing that any should perish but that all should reach repentance' (3: 9, cf. v. 15). The conclusion of the book includes a valuable reference to the writings of Paul, in which they are classed with 'the other scriptures' (3: 16).

The Johannine Letters contain strong warnings against a heresy which came to be known as docetism. This was a denial that the Son of God actually lived in a real body, a proposition based on the wrong assumption that the body, being material, is evil. Therefore, these Letters stress the fact that Christ actually, and not only in appearance, lived and died in a material body. 'That which was from the beginning, which we have heard, which we have seen with our eyes, which we have looked upon and touched with our hands, concerning the word of life . . . we proclaim to you also' (1 Jn 1: 1, 3). 'By this you know the Spirit of God: every spirit which confesses that Jesus Christ has come in the flesh is of God, and every spirit which does not confess Jesus is not of God' (4: 2 f.; cf. 2 Jn 7). Stress is also laid, as we have seen already, on the deity of Christ. These Letters breathe the air of the latter days of the NT period when 'many deceivers have gone out into the world' (2 Jn 7).

Not only is further doctrine unveiled in

response to such heresies, but the claim is increasingly pressed that there was a body of doctrine already revealed which could not be altered. This is highly important as it sets a limit upon the revelation of new truth, and affirms the existence of a commonly recognized corpus of doctrinal propositions. The very fact that some were charged with deviation testifies to the existence of a body of truth from which deviation was possible. Jude, whose Letter is in many ways similar to 2 Peter, writes against those who indulged the flesh, and set themselves against the very person of Christ (Jude 4). In his attack on these dangerous persons he appeals to his hearers to 'contend for the faith which was once for all delivered to the saints' (Jude 3). The finality of the revelation in Christ is thus affirmed. A similar position is taken in 2 Peter who reminds the Christians 'of these things, though you know them and are established in the truth that you have' (2 Pet. 1: 12). Apostates were guilty of having turned from 'the holy commandment' (2 Pet. 2: 21).

There is a significant sequence of verses in the Pastoral Letters. Instruction is given to Timothy so that he 'may know how one ought to behave in the household of God, which is the church of the living God, the pillar and bulwark of the truth' (1 Tim. 3: 15). This is followed by the Christological creed: 'He was manifested in the flesh, vindicated in the spirit, seen by angels, preached among the nations, believed on in the world, taken up in glory' (1 Tim. 3: 16). Immediately after this is the statement that 'the Spirit expressly says that in later times some will depart from the faith by giving heed to deceitful spirits and doctrines of demons' (1 Pet. 4: 1). The 'truth' and the 'faith' have thus come to signify the body of revealed doctrine (cf. 2 Tim. 2: 15; 1 Pet. 1: 22).

In 2 Timothy, Paul likewise encourages fidelity to the revelation already given: 'Do your best to present yourself to God as one approved, a workman who has no need to be ashamed, rightly handling the word of truth' (2 Tim. 2: 15). In the face of opposition Timothy is urged to follow the example of the apostle Paul as regards behaviour (3: 10-13), and to hold to the inspired Scripture which he had learned from childhood (3: 14-17). Paul urges him to 'preach the word' (4: 2), and asserts that he himself has 'kept the faith' (4: 7). This latter statement exhibits the use of the word 'faith' in the sense of a body of doctrine which was seen in Jude 3. This doctrine he had passed on to Timothy, who was to 'follow the pattern of the sound words which you have heard from me . . . Guard the truth which has been entrusted to you . . .' (1: 13 f.).

The word here translated 'pattern' is used in the sense of a standard, and is a cognate of the word translated 'standard' in Rom. 6: 17: 'the standard of teaching to which you were committed'. Paul had also insisted on fidelity to 'the traditions which you were taught by us' in the earlier Thessalonian correspondence (2 Th. 2: 15).

We have seen that there was a continuum of teaching which had its origin in the very words of the Lord Jesus and which was transmitted through the earliest generations of Christians including Paul himself. This was to be considered a 'standard' and an unalterable 'faith' to which Christians were to adhere, and for which they were to contend. No liberty could be taken after the Canon was completed to supplement or modify the standard of accepted truths.

BIBLIOGRAPHY

BERNARD, T. D., *The Progress of Doctrine in the New Testament* (London, 1864; reprinted, Grand Rapids, 1949).

BONSIRVEN, J., *Theology of the New Testament*. Eng. trans. (London, 1963).

BULTMANN, R., *Theology of the New Testament*. Eng. trans. Two vols. (London, 1951, 1955).

CULLMANN, O., *Christ and Time*. Eng. trans. (London, 1951).

CULLMANN, O., *The Early Church*. Eng. trans. (London, 1956), pp. 59-140.

CULLMANN, O., *The Christology of the New Testament*. Eng. trans. (London, 1959).

CULLMANN, O., *Salvation in History*. Eng. trans. (London, 1967).

DODD, C. H., *The Apostolic Preaching and Its Developments* (London, 1936; rev. ed. 1944).

DODD, C. H., *According to the Scriptures* (London, 1952).

HUNTER, A. M., *Paul and His Predecessors* (London, 1961).

HUNTER, A. M., *Interpreting the New Testament* (London, 1951).

LINDARS, B., *New Testament Apologetic* (London, 1961).

MARTIN, R. P., *Worship in the Early Church* (London, 1964).

MORRIS, L., *The Cross in the New Testament* (Exeter, 1965).

MOULE, C. F. D., *The Birth of the New Testament* (London, 1962).

MOUNCE, R. H., *The Essential Nature of New Testament Preaching* (Grand Rapids, 1960).

NEUFELD, V. H., *The Earliest Christian Confessions* (Grand Rapids, 1963).

RICHARDSON, A., *An Introduction to the Theology of the New Testament* (London, 1958).

RYRIE, C. C., *Biblical Theology of the New Testament* (Chicago, 1959).

SAUER, E., *The Triumph of the Crucified*. Eng. trans. (London, 1951).

STAUFFER, E., *New Testament Theology*. Eng. trans. (London, 1955).

TASKER, R. V. G., *The Old Testament in the New Testament* (London, 1946; rev. ed. 1954).

THE FOURFOLD GOSPEL

F. F. BRUCE

The Gospel and the Gospels

We talk familiarly about the four gospels, the apocryphal gospels, and so forth, using the word 'gospels' quite freely in the plural. But this usage would not have been understood in the church of apostolic days, nor yet for nearly a century after the apostolic age. The first known occurrences of the word 'gospels' in the plural in this later sense come in the second half of the second century—in Justin Martyr, Claudius Apollinaris, Clement of Alexandria, Irenaeus, and the Muratorian Canon. Justin (*First Apology* 66. 3) speaks of the memoirs of the apostles 'which are called gospels' (Gk. *euangelia*), while elsewhere (*Dialogue with Trypho* 10.2; 100.1) he speaks comprehensively of the 'gospel' (*euangelion*). Clement (*Stromata* iii. 13) refers to 'the four gospels (*euangelia*) which have been handed down to us'. Irenaeus (*Heresies* iii. 11. 8) speaks not only of 'the fourfold gospel' (*euangelion*) but also of the 'gospels' (*euangelia*). Similarly the Muratorian Canon, while it calls Luke's record 'the third book of the gospel' (singular), refers to John's as 'the fourth of the gospels' (plural). From the way in which some of these writers oscillate between the singular and the plural, it may be inferred that the plural 'gospels' was just coming into use. Earlier writers use the singular, whether they refer to a single gospel-writing or to a collection of such writings. And the use of the comprehensive singular to denote the fourfold record continued for long after the earlier attested occurrences of the plural. To the early Christians there was only one gospel, 'the gospel of God concerning his Son' (Rom. 1: 1-3), variously recorded by Matthew, Mark and the others. The overall caption for the fourfold account was the singular *Euangelion*; the four writings included under that caption were particularized as 'according to Matthew', 'according to Mark', and so on. Even outside the canonical four, such a document as *The Gospel according to the Hebrews* was regarded by those who acknowledged it as the self-same gospel of Christ, in the form in which it was recorded among the 'Hebrews'.

It is noteworthy that none of our four canonical gospel-writings calls itself a 'gospel', and that all four are, strictly speaking, anonymous. In both respects they differ from a number of uncanonical writings of the second and later centuries, which style themselves 'gospels' and claim the authorship of an apostle or other leading light of the first Christian generation. The authorship of the canonical four must be determined, as far as is possible, by internal and external evidence; more important than individual authorship is the truth of the gospel to which all four evangelists bear witness.

In the New Testament the gospel is, first, the proclamation by Jesus that the kingdom of God has drawn near, and, second, the subsequent proclamation by the disciples that in the humiliation and exaltation of Jesus the kingdom of God has been inaugurated, and that forgiveness and life eternal have been secured by Him for all believers. The second phase of the gospel arises inevitably out of the first; indeed, Jesus Himself distinguished the two phases. There was a limited phase in which the presence of the kingdom of God was manifested by His casting out of demons and similar mighty works (cf. Lk. 11: 20; 17: 20 f.); but the present limitations would be removed when the kingdom of God came 'with power' before the eyes of some of His hearers (Mk 9: 1). The passion and triumph of Jesus, which formed the basic subject-matter of the apostolic witness, crowned His ministry and embodied and confirmed all that He had taught about the kingdom of God.

The background of the noun *euangelion* and its related verb *euangelizomai* ('bring good news'), as used in the New Testament, must be sought in the second part of the book of Isaiah—in Isa. 40: 9; 52: 7; 60: 6 and 61: 1. The good news of Zion's liberation, celebrated in Isa. 40: 9 ('O thou that tellest good tidings to Zion . . .'), is interpreted in the New Testament as adumbrating the good news of a greater liberation, just as the voice of Isa. 40: 3 calling for the preparation of a way across the desert for the God of Israel to lead His exiles home is interpreted of another voice which, on the eve of the ministry of Jesus, called for repentance in preparation for the advent of the Coming One (Mk 1: 3). The words of Isa. 52: 7 ('How beautiful upon the mountains are the feet of him who brings good tidings . . .') are to the same effect as those of Isa. 40: 9, and are applied by Paul in Rom. 10: 15 to the preachers of the gospel of Christ.

But more important still for New Testament usage is Isa. 61: 1, where an unnamed speaker (identified in the New Testament with the Servant of the LORD in preceding chapters of Isaiah) introduces himself by saying: 'The Spirit of the Lord GOD is upon me, because the LORD has anointed me (made me Messiah) to bring good tidings to the poor.' In Lk. 4: 17-21 Jesus is depicted as reading this scripture in the Nazareth synagogue and applying it to Himself, and the narrative of Jesus' reply to John the Baptist's message from prison records how He emphasized as the conclusive argument for His being indeed the Coming One of whom John had previously spoken the fact that 'the poor have good news preached to them' (Mt. 11: 5; Lk. 7: 22).

The Oral Gospel
For the first thirty years or so after the death and resurrection of Christ, the necessity for a written account of His ministry was not greatly felt. So long as eyewitnesses of the saving events were alive who could speak with confidence of what they had seen and heard, the living voice sufficed by way of testimony. Even when the good news was told by men and women who had not had direct contact with Christ in the days of His flesh, they could always appeal to the authority of those who spoke with first-hand knowledge. And this attitude of mind was long in dying out. As late as A.D. 130 Papias, bishop of Hierapolis in Phrygia, tells us how eagerly he used to interview those who knew the apostles and their associates and ask them what the apostles really said, for he felt that in this way he was in much closer touch with the original gospel facts than he could ever be by reading a written record.

We are not thrown back on our imagination when it comes to envisaging the forms in which the material later written down in our gospels was preserved and transmitted orally during the first generation after the death and resurrection of Jesus. Certain lines of evidence are available to us.

(*a*) **The Words of Jesus.** When Jesus first 'came into Galilee, preaching the gospel of God', the burden of His message was that the appointed time had now arrived and the kingdom of God had drawn near; He urged His hearers to repent and believe the good news (Mk 1: 14 f.). His preaching was no bolt from the blue; it was the fulfilment of the promise of God communicated in earlier days through the prophets. Now at length God had visited His people; this was

the burden not only of Jesus' preaching but of His mighty works (Lk. 7: 16), which were signs that the domain of evil was crumbling before the onset of the kingdom of God (Mt. 12: 22-29; Lk. 11: 14-22). The same theme runs through the parables of Jesus, which call His hearers to decision and watchfulness in view of the advent of the kingdom.

In addition to His public ministry, Jesus took care to give His disciples systematic instruction in a form that they could easily commit to memory. His debates with the Pharisees and other opponents, too, led to pronouncements which, once heard, would not be readily forgotten, and which in fact stood His disciples in good stead later on when they were confronted with controversial issues in which it was helpful to recall their Master's ruling.

(*b*) **The Apostolic Tradition.** There are several references in the New Testament letters to the 'tradition' (Gk. *paradosis*) received by the apostles from their Lord and delivered by them in turn to their converts. This tradition, in the fullest sense, comprises the apostles' witness to 'all that Jesus began to do and teach, until the day when he was taken up' (Ac. 1: 1 f.). Their witness was borne and perpetuated in many ways—especially in missionary preaching, in the instruction of converts, and in Christian worship.

i. Missionary Preaching
Some idea of the outline of the early Christian preaching (*kērygma*) can be gathered from the Pauline and other letters and from the speeches in Acts.

The Pauline letters were written to people who were already familiar with the *kērygma*; any reference to the *kērygma* in them, therefore, will be incidental and reminiscent. In 1 C. 15: 3 ff., for example, Paul reminds his readers of the most important features of the message which had brought them salvation on his first visit to Corinth: 'that Christ died for our sins in accordance with the scriptures, that he was buried, that he was raised on the third day in accordance with the scriptures, and that he appeared to Cephas (Peter), then to the twelve. Then he appeared to more than five hundred brethren at one time, most of whom are still alive, though some have fallen asleep. Then he appeared to James, then to all the apostles. . . .'

The message thus summarized Paul says that he himself had 'received' from others (*parelabon*) before he 'delivered' it in turn (*paredōka*) to the Corinthians. The others from whom Paul 'received' this outline were probably the two individuals mentioned in it by name, Peter and James, whom he met when he paid a short visit to Jerusalem in the third year after his conversion (Gal. 1: 18 f.). Brief as it is, it contains more than a recital of the bare facts that a certain person died, was buried, rose from the dead and appeared thereafter to a number of people who knew him. These facts are interpreted: the person referred to was the Christ, i.e. the expected Messiah of Israel; his death was in some sense endured for the sins of others; and his death and resurrection alike took place in accordance with the prophetic writings of the Old Testament. From incidental references in the same letter we learn that the death of Christ was inflicted by crucifixion, a fact which scandalized many who heard the gospel story: the very idea of a crucified Messiah was a 'stumbling-block to Jews and folly to Gentiles' (1 C. 1: 23). From other letters of Paul we learn that Jesus was born a Jew and lived under the Jewish law (Gal. 4: 4), that He was not only a descendant of Abraham but also a member of the royal house of David (Rom. 1: 3), that while He died the Roman death by crucifixion, yet some responsibility for His death rested with Jews (1 Th. 2: 15). If we are allowed to regard 1 Tim. 6: 13 as Pauline, we learn there that He appeared before one Pontius Pilate and witnessed a good confession, although (according to 2 Tim. 4: 1) He Himself was the divinely appointed judge of living and dead. Having been raised from the dead, He was now exalted at God's right hand (Rom. 8: 34; Eph. 1: 20; Col. 3: 1). Before His tribunal, says Paul, 'we must all be made manifest' (2 C. 5: 10). This judgment is linked with His future appearance, an event to be accompanied by the resurrection of the dead and the receiving of immortality by those then living (1 C. 15: 52 f.; 1 Th. 4: 16). That Paul's *kērygma* contained some account of this consummation of the divine redemption at the advent of Christ is evident, *e.g.*, when he writes to his Thessalonian converts, reminding them how, at their conversion, they 'turned to God from idols, to serve a living and true God, and to wait for his Son from heaven, whom he raised from the dead, Jesus who delivers us from the wrath to come' (1 Th. 1: 9 f.).

Paul insisted (1 C. 15: 11) that his gospel was basically the same as that preached by the other apostles. It is not surprising, therefore, to find in 1 Peter the same facts presented as the foundation of the *kērygma*: the death and resurrection of Messiah (1 Pet. 1: 3), His exaltation to God's right hand (3: 22), His glory yet to be revealed (5: 1)—all presented as the fulfilment of Old Testament prophecy and as basic for the bestowal of God's salvation.

The writer claims to be a witness of Christ's sufferings, and describes the saving events, especially Christ's patient endurance of undeserved ill-treatment and death, so vividly that

(in C. H. Dodd's words): 'That in general its thought follows the apostolic preaching is clear, and we could easily believe that in places its very language is echoed. . . . We shall not be so ready as some critics have been to put all this down to "Pauline influence". It is a clear echo of the preaching which lies behind Paul and the whole New Testament' (*The Apostolic Preaching and its Developments*, 1936, pp. 97 f.).

The same general pattern of redemptive events is the underlying premiss of other New Testament letters, notably Hebrews and 1 John, and also of the Apocalypse. In the primitive message, then, to which these various documents bear witness, the following elements can be distinguished: (1) God has visited and redeemed His people by sending the promised Messiah, at the time of the fulfilment of the divine purpose revealed in Old Testament scripture. (2) The Messiah came, as was prophesied, of Israel's race, of Judah's tribe, of David's royal seed, in the person of Jesus of Nazareth. (3) As the prophets had foretold, He died for men's sins upon a cross, was buried, and (4) rose again the third day, as many eyewitnesses could testify. (5) He has been exalted in glory at the right hand of God, while (6) His Holy Spirit has been sent to those who believe in Him, and (7) Christ Himself is to return to earth to judge the living and the dead and to consummate the work of redemption, both for His people and, through them, for all creation. (8) On the basis of these facts remission of sins and the life of the age to come are offered to all who repent and believe the good news; those who repent and believe are further baptized into Christ's name and incorporated into a new community, the church of Christ.

The speeches ascribed to Peter and Paul in the first half of Acts are probably not the free invention of the historian, but reliable summaries of the early apostolic preaching. Of these speeches the most important are those delivered by Peter in Jerusalem on the day of Pentecost (Ac. 2: 22-36) and in Caesarea in the house of Cornelius (10: 36-43), and that delivered by Paul some years later in the synagogue of Pisidian Antioch (13: 17-41). Further fragments of the *kērygma* can be traced in 3: 13-26; 4: 10-12; 5: 30-32 and 8: 32-35. In all these we find the same message as is reflected in the Pauline and other letters. The message itself is called the good news; it is announced as the fulfilment of Old Testament prophecy; its subject is Jesus of Nazareth, a descendant of David, whose public life began during the ministry of His forerunner, John the Baptist, and whose mission was divinely attested by His works of mercy and power. He was betrayed to His enemies, handed over to the Romans by the Jewish rulers, and consequently crucified (this is referred to more than once in language reminiscent of Dt. 21: 23: 'a hanged man is accursed by God'). He was then taken down from the cross and buried, but raised by God the third day, the apostles constantly emphasizing their eyewitness testimony to His resurrection. The resurrection, they claimed, declared Him to be Lord and Messiah, exalted to God's right hand, whence He had sent forth His Spirit upon his followers. He was to return to assume His divinely given office as judge of quick and dead; meanwhile the call to those who heard the gospel was to repent, believe, be baptized and receive the remission of sins and the gift of the Holy Spirit.

Acts and the letters tell us the same story. The message was essentially the same no matter who the preacher was. Stereotyped religious teaching was the regular practice throughout the world in those days and the gospel formed no exception.

A similar outline of the *kērygma* has been discerned as the framework on which the body of Mark's Gospel has been built, or (one might say) the thread on which Mark has strung his several units of gospel material. It is noteworthy that Mark begins where the outlines of the *kērygma* begin, with the activity of John the Baptist, and that it ends with an account of the passion and resurrection of Christ which (as in the other Gospels) receives what might appear from a purely biographical point of view to be a disproportionate amount of space. But this is a prominent feature of the *kērygma* in all the forms in which we can trace it.

ii. Early Christian Teaching

Some occasional samples of the instruction of converts appear in the letters, from which it is plain that the basis of this teaching was what Jesus Himself had taught. Thus in giving instruction about marriage Paul quotes Jesus' commandment forbidding divorce (1 C. 7: 10); he similarly quotes His ruling about the maintenance of gospel preachers (1 C. 9: 14). But there is evidence of more systematic instruction by the catechetical method; and as the number of converts increased, especially in the course of the Gentile mission, 'schools' for the training of instructors would have become almost a necessity, and digests of the teaching of Jesus would inevitably have been drawn up, orally if not in writing. We may envisage such a life-setting for the 'sayings collection' on which Mt. and Lk. drew, and at a later date the Matthaean gospel itself has been viewed as taking shape in such a school.

iii. Early Christian Worship

In worship too the works and words of Jesus were bound to be recalled. In the earliest days of the faith those who had known Jesus could scarcely avoid saying to one another, when they met informally or at the stated occasions of fellowship and worship, 'Do you remember how our Master . . .?' In particular, the Lord's Supper provided a regular opportunity for re-telling the story of His death, with the events immediately preceding and following it (1 C. 11: 26). The institution of the Lord's Supper, incidentally, like the outline of the redemptive events in 1 C. 15: 3 ff., is narrated by Paul as something which he 'received' (by a tradition stemming from the Lord Himself) before he 'delivered' it to his converts (1 C. 11: 23 ff.). Not only did the Supper bring the Lord to remembrance; each occasion on which Christians ate the bread and drank the cup was an anticipation of His coming again.

The passion narrative, indeed, being told and retold both in Christian worship and in missionary preaching (cf. 1 C. 2: 2; Gal. 3: 1), took shape as a connected whole at an early date —a conclusion which is otherwise established by the form-criticism of our existing Gospels. By the form-critical method an attempt is made to isolate and classify the various self-contained units which have been brought together in the written Gospels and to envisage the living situations in which they originated and were preserved in the oral stage of transmission. The value of the form-critical method is greatest when what was originally one and the same unit of teaching or narrative can be shown to have come down along two separate lines in two different 'forms'—a situation which appears repeatedly when one compares a Synoptic account with its Johannine parallel. We are thus helped to envisage the material of such a unit as it was before it began to be transmitted.

The Written Gospels

The beginning of gospel writing, as we might expect, coincides with the end of the first Christian generation. As 'those who from the beginning were eyewitnesses and ministers of the word' (Lk. 1: 2) were removed by death, the necessity of a permanent written record of their witness would be more acutely felt than before. It is just at this point that second-century tradition places the beginnings of gospel writing, and rightly so: all four of our canonical Gospels are probably to be dated within the four decades A.D. 60-100. We need not suppose that the transmission of the apostolic witness had been exclusively oral before A.D. 60—some at least of the 'many' who, according to Lk. 1: 1, had undertaken to draw up an orderly account of the evangelic events may have done so in writing before A.D. 60—but no document of an earlier date has survived except in so far as it has been incorporated in our written Gospels.

Several strands of tradition can be distinguished in the four Gospels. In this respect, as in some others, John stands apart from the other Gospels and is best considered independently. The other three Gospels are inter-related to the point where they lend themselves excellently to 'synoptic' study—*e.g.*, as when their text is arranged in three parallel columns, so that their coincidences and divergences can be conveniently examined. For this reason they are commonly known as the 'Synoptic Gospels'—a designation first apparently given to them by J. J. Griesbach in 1774.

(*a*) **The Synoptic Gospels.** A comparative study of Mt., Mk and Lk. leads to the recognition that there is a considerable body of material common to all three, or to two out of the three. The substance of 606 out of the 661 verses of Mk (Mk 16: 9-20 being left out of the reckoning) reappears in abridged form in Mt.; some 380 of the 661 verses of Mk reappear in Lk. This may be stated otherwise by saying that, out of the 1,068 verses of Mt., about 500 contain the substance of 606 verses of Mk, while out of the 1,149 verses of Lk., some 380 are paralleled in Mk. Only 31 verses of Mk have no parallel in either Mt. or Lk. Mt. and Lk. have each up to 250 verses containing common material not paralleled in Mk; sometimes this common material appears in Mt. and Lk. in practically identical language, while sometimes the verbal divergence is considerable. About 300 verses of Mt. have no parallel in any of the other gospels; the same is true of about 520 verses in Lk.

There is no short cut to a satisfactory account of this distribution of common and special material in the Synoptic Gospels. There is no *a priori* reason for holding one gospel to be earlier and another later, for holding one to be a source of another and the latter to be dependent on the former. Nor will the objectivity of statistical analysis guarantee a solution. A solution can be obtained only by the exercise of critical judgment after all the relevant data have been marshalled and the alternative possibilities assessed. If unanimity has not been reached after a century and a half of intensive synoptic study, it may be because the data are insufficient for the purpose, or because the field of enquiry has been unduly restricted. Yet certain findings command a much greater area of agreement than others.

One of these is the priority of Mk, and its use as a principal source by the other two Synoptic evangelists. This finding, which may be said to have been placed on a stable basis by

Carl Lachmann in 1835, depends not merely on the formal evidence that Mt. and Mk sometimes agree in order against Lk., Mk and Lk. more frequently against Mt., but Mt. and Lk. never against Mk (which could be explained otherwise), but rather on the detailed comparative examination of the way in which common material is reproduced in the three Gospels, section by section. In the overwhelming majority of sections, the situation can best be understood if Mk's account was used as a source by one or both of the others. Few have ever considered Lk. as a possible source of the other two, but the view that Mk is an abridgement of Mt. was held for a long time, largely through the influence of Augustine. But where Mt. and Mk have material in common, Mk is fuller than Mt., and by no means an abridgement; and time after time the two parallel accounts can be much better explained by supposing that Mt. condenses Mk than by supposing that Mk amplifies Mt. While Mt. and Lk. never agree in order against Mk, they do occasionally exhibit verbal agreement against Mk, but such instances mainly represent grammatical or stylistic improvements of Mk, and are neither numerous nor significant enough to be offset against the general weight of the evidence for the priority of Mk.

The common Markan element in the Synoptic tradition is the more important because of the close relation between the framework of Mk and the apostolic preaching. It is interesting, too, to recall in this connection the tradition which points to Peter as the authority behind Mark's account. The earliest witness to this tradition is Papias, who records it on the authority of someone whom he calls 'the elder': 'Mark, the interpreter of Peter, wrote down accurately all the words or deeds of the Lord of which he [Peter] made mention, but not in order . . .' (quoted by Eusebius, *Ecclesiastical History* iii. 39. 15). This tradition is corroborated by internal evidence in some parts of Mk's narrative. One of the most interesting pieces of evidence in this regard is presented by what has been called 'Turner's mark' (a feature of Mark's usage the significance of which was pointed out in a series of studies by C. H. Turner). 'Time after time a sentence commences with the plural, for it is an experience which is being related, and passes into the singular, for the experience is that of discipleship to a Master' (C. H. Turner, *The Gospel according to St. Mark*, 1930, p. 9). One example comes in Mk 1: 21, '*they* went into Capernaum; and immediately on the sabbath *he* entered the synagogue and taught.' Where the other Synoptic evangelists reproduce such passages, they tend to replace the initial plural 'they' by the singular 'he' (cf. Lk. 4: 31, '*he* went down to Capernaum . . . *he* was teaching them on the sabbath'). If the reader will now take one step further and put back Mk's third person plural into the first person plural of the narrator, he will receive a vivid impression of the testimony that lies behind the Gospel: thus in 1: 29, 'we came into our house with James and John: and my wife's mother was ill in bed with a fever, and at once we tell him about her' (*ibid.*). In a study of the contexts in which this feature appears, T. W. Manson suggested that the following sections of Mk may reasonably be recognized as Petrine: Mk 1: 16-39; 2: 1-14; 3: 13-19; 4: 35-5: 43; 6: 7-13, 30-56; 8: 14-9: 48; 10: 32-52; 11: 1-33; 13: 3-4, 32-37; 14: 17-50, 53-54, 66-72 (*Studies in the Gospels and Epistles*, 1962, p. 42). This excludes, for example, the ministry and death of John the Baptist (1: 1 ff.; 6: 17-29) and the greater part of the passion and resurrection narrative (14: 55-65; 15: 1-16: 8), for which other sources of information were accessible.

The material common to Mk and one or both of the other Synoptic gospels consists mainly of narrative. (The principal exceptions to this are the parables of Mk 4 and the eschatological discourse of Mk 13.) On the other hand, the non-Markan material common to Mt. and Lk. consists mainly of sayings of Jesus. One might also say that the Markan material relates what Jesus did; the non-Markan material, what Jesus taught. We have here a distinction comparable to that commonly made (albeit to an exaggerated degree) between apostolic 'preaching' (*kērygma*) and 'teaching' (*didachē*). The non-Markan material common to Mt. and Lk. is conventionally and conveniently labelled 'Q'. In the commentaries on the separate gospels in this volume the label 'Q' is used as a short-hand designation for this material.

This body of material, extending to between 200 and 250 verses, might have been derived by the one evangelist from the other, or by both from a common source. Few, if any, can be found to suggest that Mt. derived it from Lk., although theoretically it might be easier to sustain this thesis than that Lk. derived it from Mt. This latter supposition continues to receive diminishing support in some quarters where tradition counts for much, but it is specially vulnerable because it implies that Lk. reduced to relative disorder the orderly arrangement in which the 'Q' material appears in Mt., without giving any plausible reason why this should have been done.

The supposition that the 'Q' material was derived from a common source by Mt. and Lk. involves fewer difficulties than any alternative supposition.

When we attempt to reconstruct this postulated common source, we must beware of thinking that we can do so in anything like a complete form. Yet what we can reconstruct of it reminds us forcibly of the general pattern of the prophetical books of the Old Testament. These books commonly contain an account of the prophet's call, with a record of his oracles set in a narrative framework, but with no mention of his death. So the 'Q' material appears to have come from a compilation which began with an account of Jesus' baptism by John and His wilderness temptations; this forms the prelude to His ministry, and is followed by groups of His sayings set in a minimum of narrative framework; but there is no trace of a passion narrative. There are four main groups of teaching, which may be entitled (i) Jesus and John the Baptist; (ii) Jesus and His disciples; (iii) Jesus and His opponents; (iv) Jesus and the future.

Since our only means of reconstructing this source is provided by the non-Markan material common to Mt. and Lk., the question whether Mk also made some use of it cannot be satisfactorily answered. That it is earlier than Mk is probable; it may well have been used for catechetical purposes in the Gentile mission based on Antioch. The fact that some of the 'Q' material in Mt. and Lk. is almost verbally identical, while elsewhere there are divergences of language, has sometimes been explained in terms of there being two distinct strands of tradition in 'Q', but a much more probable account is that 'Q' was translated more than once into Greek from Aramaic and that Mt. and Lk. sometimes use the same translation and sometimes different ones. In this regard it is apposite to recall the statement of Papias (quoted by Eusebius, *Hist. Eccl.* iii. 39. 16) that 'Matthew compiled the *logia* in the Hebrew (Aramaic) speech, and everyone translated them as best he could.' *Logia* ('oracles') would be a specially appropriate term for the contents of such a compilation as we have tried to recognize behind the 'Q' material.

What other sources were utilized by Mt. and Lk. is an even more uncertain question than the reconstruction of the 'Q' source. Mt. appears to have incorporated material from another sayings-collection, parallel to 'Q', but preserved in Judaea rather than in Antioch—the collection conveniently labelled 'M'. To this material may be assigned certain sections in the Sermon on the Mount (Mt. 5: 17-24, 27 f., 33-39; 6: 1-8, 16-18; 7: 6); the parables of the tares (13: 24-30, 36-43), of the hidden treasure (13: 44), of the pearl of great price (13: 45 f.), and of the dragnet (13: 47-50), of the unforgiving servant (18: 23-35), of the labourers in the vineyard (20: 1-16), of the obedient and disobedient sons (21: 28-32), of the marriage feast (22: 1-14), of the ten virgins (25: 1-13) and of the sheep and the goats (25: 31-46); the two 'church' sayings, with their references to binding and loosing (16: 17-19; 18: 15-20); and parts of the lament over the scribes and Pharisees in ch. 23 (verses 2 f., 5-10, 15-22). This and other special material is interwoven by Mt. with the Markan and 'Q' material so as to yield a well-arranged document, comprising both narrative and teaching, in which incidents and sayings dealing with the same general subjects are for the most part found together. In consequence, to anyone who keeps the general structure of this Gospel in mind it is usually easy to decide where a saying of Jesus on a particular subject is most likely to appear. The sayings are grouped together in the five great discourses which form the most conspicuous feature of the structure of Mt.; each of the discourses is introduced by an appropriate narrative section, mostly, but not entirely, derived and abridged from Mk. The greater part of Mk 1: 2-6: 13 is thus embodied in Mt. 3: 1-13: 58, but the sequence of this part of Mk has been completely rearranged in Mt., possibly in order that each section of narrative in Mt. may provide a suitable introduction to the discourse that follows it. The remainder of the Markan account (Mk 6: 14 ff.) is reproduced in Mt. 14: 1 ff. without such rearrangement.

How far Mt. has rearranged the sequence in which he found his 'Q' material is naturally much more difficult to decide. It is noteworthy, however, that the best parallel arrangement of the 'Q' and 'M' material is to set 'Q' in Luke's order alongside 'M' in Matthew's order (which, of course, is the only order in which 'M' is available to us).

The arrangement of sources in Lk. is quite different from that in Mt. Whereas each section of Mt. presents an interweaving of material from all the sources, Lk. arranges Markan and non-Markan material in alternate blocks. Thus we have Lk. 3 narrating the ministry of John the Baptist in alternate non-Markan and Markan sections; this is followed by Lk. 4: 2-30 (non-Markan); 4: 31-44 (Markan); 5: 1-11 (non-Markan); 5: 12-6: 19 (Markan); 6: 20-8: 3 (non-Markan); 8: 4-9: 50 (Markan); 9: 51-18: 14 (non-Markan); 18: 15-43 (Markan); 19: 1-27 (non-Markan); 19: 28-38 (Markan); 19: 39-44 (non-Markan); 19: 45-22: 23 (largely, but not entirely, Markan). Then comes the passion narrative, parallel to that in Mk, but plainly drawing upon other

sources of information peculiar to Luke among the evangelists: we may think of the words of Jesus to Peter and the other disciples in Lk. 22: 27-38; the angel and the bloody sweat in Gethsemane (22: 43 f.); the appearance before Herod Antipas (23: 5-16); the weeping women on the way to the cross (23: 27-31); the prayer for forgiveness (23: 34), and the incident of the penitent robber (23: 39-43). The resurrection narrative, after the women's discovery of the empty tomb (24: 1-8), is also peculiar to Luke (24: 9-53).

Luke has been pictured as inserting blocks of Markan material into a narrative (sometimes called 'Proto-Luke') which he had already drawn up. Whether this earlier and shorter draft had been published by itself is almost impossible to determine. One of the most striking features of his use of Mk is his omission of the contents of Mk 6: 45-8: 26. The point in Lk. where we might have expected to find his parallels to this Markan section is between verses 17 and 18 of Lk. 9; but we find none. This is commonly referred to as Luke's 'great omission'. This section of Mk appears to reproduce, on largely Gentile territory, a sequence of events similar to that found in the preceding section, Mk 4: 35-6: 44 (cf. Lk. 8: 22-9:17, except that Lk. does not reproduce the narrative of Mk 6: 14-29), where the setting is distinctively Jewish. The earlier of these two Markan sections includes the feeding of the five thousand (Mk 6: 31-44); the other includes the feeding of the four thousand (Mk 8: 1-10). Augustine distinguished these two feedings as signifying our Lord's communication of Himself to the Jews and to the Gentiles respectively; and to some extent the same kind of distinction may be recognized between the two Markan sections in which these feeding narratives appear. (Early in the second of these two Markan sections comes our Lord's abrogation of the food-laws and other ceremonial ordinances which constituted such a barrier between Jews and Gentiles.) But why should the Gentile Luke, with his interest in the Gentile mission, omit this section if this is its significance? Perhaps because he was deliberately reserving the theme (as distinct from the detailed contents) of this section for his second treatise, where (from Ac. 10 onwards) the communication of Christ to the Gentiles is his main subject.

The non-Markan material in Luke's account of the ministry may best be described as 'Q' amplified by material peculiar to Lk. (which we can conveniently label 'L'). Luke, as he traced the course of events accurately from the beginning (cf. Lk. 1: 3), perhaps took around with him a copy of the sayings-collection which underlies 'Q' and enlarged it by means of information which he was able to acquire from the household of Philip in Caesarea and from many other quarters, thus compiling the preliminary draft which was later expanded further by the insertion of Markan blocks.

Some of the most memorable elements in the Synoptic accounts belong to Luke's special material. They include the Baptist's advice to his hearers, including tax-collectors and soldiers (Lk. 3: 10-14); Jesus' sermon at Nazareth (4: 16-30); the miraculous draught of fishes (5: 1-11; cf. Jn 21: 1-11 for a post-resurrection parallel); the raising of the widow's son at Nain (7: 11-17); the incident of the penitent woman and the parable of the two debtors (7: 36-50); the parable of the good Samaritan (10: 30-37); the visit to Martha and Mary (10: 38-42); the parables of the friend at midnight (11: 5-8), of the rich fool (12: 13-21), of the great supper (14: 16-24), of the lost coin (15: 8-10), of the prodigal son (15: 11-32), of the unjust steward (16: 1-12), of Dives and Lazarus (16: 19-31), of the importunate widow (18: 1-8) and of the Pharisee and the tax-collector (18: 9-14); the healing of the ten lepers (17: 11-19), and the story of Zacchaeus (19: 1-10), in addition to the peculiarly Lukan features of the passion and resurrection narratives already mentioned. When we consider how poor we should have been without all this, we may have some idea of our indebtedness to this evangelist for his labour of love in collecting and recording the material for his Gospel.

Luke is a literary artist with a sense of historical setting; he is also keenly interested in the broad humanitarian aspects of Jesus' teaching and action. While even his record cannot be called a biography in the modern sense, he shows more interest in biographical touches for their own sake than the other evangelists do. His Gospel therefore is often felt to be the most readable and appealing of the four for men and women today.

The nativity narratives which introduce Mt. and Lk. lie outside the general scheme of Synoptic criticism; with regard to them some dependence on Semitic documents cannot be excluded. Each of the two is independent of the other.

It must be emphasized that, fascinating and instructive as gospel source-criticism is, the gospels themselves are much more important than their putative sources. It is interesting to consider what sources the evangelists may have used; it is better to consider what use they made of their sources. Each of the Synoptic gospels is an independent whole, no mere scissors-and-paste compilation; each has its own view of

Jesus and His ministry, and each has its special contribution to make to the full-orbed picture of Jesus with which the New Testament presents us.

(b) **The Fourth Gospel.** One of the last survivors of Jesus' closest associates continued to think long and deeply about the meaning of all that he had seen and heard. Much that had once been obscure became clearer to his mind with the passage of time.

What first were guessed as points, I now knew stars,

And named them in the Gospel I have writ.

He himself experienced the fulfilment of the promises recorded in his gospel, that the Holy Spirit would bring the teaching of Jesus to the disciples' remembrance, make its significance plain to them, and guide them into all the truth. In his old age he realized more than ever that, although the conditions of life in Palestine which had formed the setting for Jesus' ministry before A.D. 30 had passed away beyond recall, that ministry itself was charged with eternal validity. In the life of Jesus all the truth of God which had ever been communicated to men was summed up and made perfect; in Him the eternal Word or self-expression of God had come home to the world in a real human life. But if this was so, the life and work of Jesus could have no merely local, national or temporary relevance. So, towards the end of the first century, he set himself to tell the gospel story in such a way that its abiding truth might be presented to men and women who were quite unfamiliar with the original setting of the saving events. The Hellenistic world of his old age required to be told the regenerating message in such a way that, whether Jews or Gentiles, they might be brought to faith in Jesus as the Messiah and Son of God, and thus receive eternal life through Him. Yet he would not yield to any temptation to restate Christianity in terms of contemporary thought in such a way as to rob it of its essential uniqueness. The gospel is eternally true, but it is the story of events which happened in history once for all; John does not divorce the story from its Palestinian context in order to bring out its universal application, and at the heart of his record the original apostolic preaching is faithfully preserved.

The content of Jn represents a good primitive tradition which was preserved independently of the Synoptic lines of tradition, not only in the memory of the beloved disciple but in a living Christian community, quite probably in the milieu from which at a rather later date came the Christian hymnbook called the *Odes of Solomon*. (This collection of over forty poems belongs probably to the second century and is the oldest surviving Christian hymnbook; it has been preserved in a Syriac version. The hymns, many of which seem to have a baptismal reference, breathe high spiritual devotion and poetical genius; in a number of respects, and especially in their doctrine of the Logos, they present affinities with this gospel.) The large area of common background which Jn shares with the Qumran texts is but one among recent discoveries which have helped to impress upon us that the Johannine tradition has its roots in Jewish Palestine, however much the requirements of a wider Hellenistic audience were borne in mind when this gospel was given its literary form at the end of the first Christian century.

As for the feeling sometimes expressed that there is an essential difference between the Christ who speaks and acts in the fourth gospel and the Christ who speaks and acts in the Synoptics, it is relevant to reflect that many have testified that John leads them into an even deeper and more intimate appreciation of the mind of Christ than do the other three. The members of the Christian Industrial League, an organization which carries on a gospel witness among the tough characters of Skidrow, in the heart of Chicago's 'Loop' area, say 'that in their work they have found that St. John's gospel is the best for dealing with these tough, hard men. Its straight, unequivocal words about sin and salvation somehow go home and carry conviction to the most abandoned, while its direct invitation wins a response that nothing else does' (A. M. Chirgwin, *The Bible in World Evangelism*, 1954, p. 113). Or we may listen to a testimony from a very different source, the late Archbishop William Temple, theologian, philosopher and statesman: 'The Synoptists may give us something more like the perfect photograph; St. John gives us the more perfect portrait . . . the mind of Jesus Himself was what the Fourth Gospel disclosed, but . . . the disciples were at first unable to enter into this, partly because of its novelty, and partly because of the associations attaching to the terminology in which it was necessary that the Lord should express Himself. Let the Synoptists repeat for us as closely as they can the very words He spoke; but let St. John tune our ears to hear them' (*Readings in St. John's Gospel*, 1940, pp. xvi, xxxii).

When we read one of the earlier gospels, we sometimes get the impression that in the story which we are reading there is more than meets the eye, something beneath the surface, which if we only could grasp it would give fuller meaning to the record. This is specially true of Mark's gospel. But when we come to John's record, he brings this deeper truth to the surface,

so that what was formerly implicit now becomes explicit: the ministry of Jesus was the activity of the eternal Word of God, who had become incarnate as man for the world's salvation. The mighty works of Jesus were 'signs' through which those who had eyes to see might behold the glory of God dwelling among men in the person of His Son. In Him every other revelation which God had ever given of Himself reached its fulfilment and culmination: to see Christ was to see the Father; He was the way, the truth and the life, apart from whom none could come to God. John thus supplies the key to the understanding of the gospel story as told by the other evangelists.

John's aim in presenting this record has been realized, not only among Jewish and Gentile readers of the Hellenistic world at the end of the first century A.D., but throughout successive generations to our own day. As he introduces us to Jesus as the perfect revealer of God, as love incarnate, as the embodiment of that life which has ever been the light of men, his record still comes home with the self-authenticating testimony which characterizes eternal truth, as it constrains twentieth-century readers to endorse the statement of those men who first gave the evangelist's words to the public: 'we know that his witness is true.'

The Gospel Collection

The gospels of Mark, Matthew and John appear to have been associated at first with three early centres of Christian witness—Rome, Antioch and Ephesus. Luke's twofold work was not originally written for church use but as a work of apologetic for the more unprejudiced members of the Roman official and middle classes. But at an early date after the publication of the fourth Gospel, the four canonical gospels began to circulate as a collection and have continued to do so ever since. Who first gathered them together to form a fourfold corpus we do not know, and it is quite uncertain where the fourfold corpus first became known—claims have been made for both Ephesus and Rome. Catholic and Gnostic writers alike show not only acquaintance with the fourfold gospel, but recognition of its authority. The Valentinian *Gospel of Truth* (*c.* A.D. 140-150), recently brought to light among the Gnostic writings from Chenoboskion in Egypt, was not intended to supplement or supersede the canonical four, whose authority it presupposes; it is rather a series of meditations on the 'true gospel' which is enshrined in the four (and in other New Testament books). Marcion (*c.* A.D. 144) stands out as an exception in his repudiation of Mt., Mk and Jn, and his promulgation of Lk. (edited by himself) as the only authentic *euangelion.* The documents of the anti-Marcionite reaction (*e.g.* the anti-Marcionite prologues to the gospels and, later, the Muratorian canon) do not introduce the fourfold gospel as something new but reaffirm its authority in reply to Marcion's criticisms.

In the half-century following A.D. 95 Theodor Zahn could find only four gospel citations in surviving Christian literature which demonstrably do not come from the canonical four. That the 'memoirs of the apostles' which Justin says were read in church along with the writings of the prophets were the four gospels is rendered the more probable by the fact that such traces of gospel material in his works as may come from the pseudonymous gospels of Peter or Thomas are slight indeed compared with traces of the canonical four.

The situation is clearer when we come to Justin's disciple Tatian, whose gospel harmony or *Diatessaron* (compiled *c.* A.D. 170)—a rearrangement of the fourfold record so as to form one continuous narrative—remained for long the favourite (if not the 'authorized') edition of the gospels in the Assyrian church. Apart from a small fragment of a Greek edition of the *Diatessaron* discovered at Dura-Europos on the Euphrates and published in 1935, our knowledge of the work has until recently been indirect, being based on translations (some of them secondary or tertiary) from the Syriac text. But in 1957 a considerable portion of the Syriac original of Ephrem's commentary on the *Diatessaron* (written about the middle of the fourth century) was identified in a parchment manuscript in Sir A. Chester Beatty's collection; further study of this text promises to throw valuable light on the early history of the *Diatessaron.*

Tatian began his compilation with Jn 1: 1-5, and perhaps ended it with Jn 21: 25. It was the fourfold gospel that supplied him with the material for his harmony; such occasional intrusions of extra-canonical material as can be detected (possibly from the *Gospel according to the Hebrews*) do not affect this basic fact any more than do the occasional modifications of the gospel wording which reflect the vegetarian dogma of Tatian's Encratite group.

The supremacy of the fourfold gospel which Tatian's work attests is confirmed a decade or so later by Irenaeus. To him the fourfold character of the gospel is one of the accepted facts of Christianity, as axiomatic as the four quarters of the world or the four winds of heaven (*Heresies* iii. 11. 8). His contemporary Clement of Alexandria is careful to distinguish 'the four gospels which have been handed down to us' from uncanonical writings on which he draws

from time to time, such as the *Gospel according to the Egyptians* (*Stromata* iii. 13). Tertullian (*c.* A.D. 200) does not even draw upon such uncanonical writings, restricting himself to the canonical four, to which he accords unique authority because their authors were either apostles or men in close association with apostles. (Like other western Christian writers, he arranges the four so as to make the two 'apostolic' gospels, Mt. and Jn, precede Lk. and Mk.) Origen (*c.* A.D. 230) sums up the long-established catholic attitude when he speaks of 'the four gospels, which alone are undisputed in the Church of God beneath the whole heaven' (*Comm. on Mt.*, quoted by Eusebius, *Hist. Eccl.* vi. 25. 4). (Origen, like Irenaeus before him, arranges the four in the order with which we are familiar today.)

The four evangelists, writing from their distinct points of view, concur in presenting us with a comprehensive, sufficient and heart-compelling portrayal of Jesus as Messiah of Israel and Saviour of the world, Servant of the LORD and Friend of sinners, Son of God and Son of man. Their fourfold record coincides in its character and purpose with the mission of the church in the world; the explicit aim of the fourth gospel is equally applicable to the other three: 'these are written that you may believe that Jesus is the Christ, the Son of God, and that believing you may have life in his name' (Jn 20: 31).

BIBLIOGRAPHY

ALAND, K., and others, *The Gospels Reconsidered* (Oxford, 1960).

DODD, C. H., *The Apostolic Teaching and its Developments* (London, 1936).

DODD, C. H., *History and the Gospel* (London, 1938).

DODD, C. H., *The Interpretation of the Fourth Gospel* (Cambridge, 1953).

DODD, C. H., *Historical Tradition in the Fourth Gospel* (Cambridge, 1963).

GUTHRIE, D., *New Testament Introduction: The Gospels and Acts* (London, 1965).

HIGGINS, A. J. B., *The Reliability of the Gospels* (London, 1952).

HIGGINS, A. J. B., *The Historicity of the Fourth Gospel* (London, 1960).

KELLY, W., *Lectures Introductory to the Study of the Gospels* (London, 1874).

LÉON-DUFOUR, X., *The Gospels and the Jesus of History* (London, 1968).

MANSON, T. W., *The Teaching of Jesus* (Cambridge, 1935).

MANSON, T. W., *The Sayings of Jesus* (London, 1949).

MANSON, T. W., *Studies in the Gospels and Epistles* (London, 1961).

ROPES, J. H., *The Synoptic Gospels* (Cambridge, Mass., 1934).

SOLAGES, B. DE, *A Greek Synopsis of the Gospels* (Leiden, 1959).

STREETER, B. H., *The Four Gospels* (London, 1924).

TASKER, R. V. G., *The Nature and Purpose of the Gospels* (London, 1944).

TAYLOR, V., *The Formation of the Gospel Tradition* (London, 1933).

THE APOSTOLIC CHURCH

F. ROY COAD

The Christian Church was born out of historical happenings: happenings in which it is conscious of a unique intervention of God in the history of mankind.

That fact justifies yet another examination of those events. Because God revealed Himself to real men in an historical situation, the story of the apostolic church can never lose its relevance. Nor can it ever lose its interest, so long as men seek to discover what it was, in everyday terms, to have known the earthly presence of Christ or the ardour of the first days of His Church.

The Paradox of the Church

For a basic conception of the Church we turn naturally to the teaching of our Lord Jesus Christ: yet we do so only to be confronted by the startling fact that the Church seems almost wholly absent from His teaching. Instead, He speaks much of the Kingdom of God—a kingdom which is no organized body, but something to be received, and received 'like a child' (Lk. 18: 17; Mt. 18: 3, 4). This Kingdom presents a twofold aspect. It is something imminent and inward, to be received in the present in quiet humility; but it is also to appear in the future as a culminating event of supernatural glory. These two aspects of the Kingdom, present and final, are united in a short parable which is recorded only in Mark's Gospel (Mk 4: 26-29).

Yet, as Jesus taught, He consciously gathered around Himself a community of disciples, who later formed the nucleus of the apostolic church. That community He related directly to the central theme of the Kingdom: 'Fear not, little flock, for it is your Father's good pleasure to give you the kingdom' (Lk. 12: 32). The promise contrasts with a judgment pronounced on the leaders of Israel: 'The kingdom of God will be taken away from you and given to a nation producing the fruits of it' (Mt. 21: 43).

The Lord Jesus identified the community, then, with the flock of the Lord, the faithful remnant of the covenant people of God (Jer. 23 and 31; Ezek. 34): and yet He placed it in marked contrast to the existing expression of that covenant people. Second, the little flock is to be the recipient of the Kingdom, and thus shares from the start that twofold nature which we have

noticed: it is *eschatological*, that is, stamped with the character of the end things, and yet it is of immediate and present import. This dual character is confirmed by the whole context of Lk. 12: 22-56. Third, Jesus's words imply a tension between the community and its environment: a fear, which is set against a new and intimate relation with its Father-God.

These features are developed in the classic passage of Mt. 16: 13-28, the only passage recorded from the mouth of our Lord which unambiguously names the Church, but before tracing them we must notice in that passage another reference back to Old Testament thought, in the question 'Who do men say that the Son of man is?' There, Jesus adopts the representative identity of the Son of man of Dan. 7, the regal personage who in Himself incorporates the whole *people of the saints of the Most High* (Dan. 7: 13, 14, 27) (see K. L. Schmidt, *The Church*, pp. 39-41 and notes; and Cullmann, *The Early Church*, pp. 128, 130). He is the representative head, awaiting the body; the king awaiting his people. Peter's confession, 'You are the Christ, the Son of the living God,' appears as the counterpart to this identification, and therefore expresses the characteristic feature of that people of the Most High. Over against the representative Son of man, there stands the representative confessor of Christ, chosen of the Father ('flesh and blood has not revealed this to you, but my Father who is in heaven'): the pattern of all who should exercise a like response to Christ. It is of such, men who are called, chosen and faithful, that the people of the Most High will consist. That Peter appears in representative rather than in personal capacity is confirmed by his rejection in verse 23, demonstrating that Peter in himself was nothing—a rejection which was to have a later parallel at Antioch (Gal. 2: 11) (even if Peter is considered to appear in personal capacity, it remains that the whole Church is Peter's successor; see E. Schweizer, *Church Order in the NT*, pp. 4 f.). Peter's representative position is analogous to that which is occupied by Abraham, the father of the faithful, and a parallel to Abraham may well be hidden in the reference to Peter as the rock, a reference echoing Isa. 51: 1, 2. (Despite the many alternative explanations, the author feels compelled by the plain sense of the passage to understand Peter as the rock. See article *Peter* in *NBD*.)

We now trace those features already noticed in Lk. 12: 32. Behind the word 'church' used in Mt. 16: 18, there lies a word already familiar to Jewish thought as the designation of the congregation of Israel. So Jesus, in this passage also, identifies His Church with that community, and yet distinguishes it; for this is 'my church', and the building is in the future and is to be His own activity, its membership deriving from the same personal response and confession of Himself which Peter had shown.

Here also, the Church is related directly to the Kingdom. By an act of deliberate divine renunciation, in the committal of the keys, the Church (Peter again being representative; see Mt. 18: 18) is marked as the main earthly instrument of the Kingdom (E. Schweizer, *op.* and *loc. cit.*, has a very different and less robust interpretation). The twofold nature of the Kingdom appears in the Church. The present binding and loosing on earth is to be consummated in the binding and loosing in heaven (see also Jn 20: 23). The revelation of the Son of man in His kingdom is imminent for the chosen (28), and yet it is also future, hidden from the world (20) and awaiting the ultimate unveiling (27). The Church is a final thing, impregnable to the powers of death (18).

In this passage also the Church is seen in tension with its environment. If the keys of the Kingdom are committed to it, it is not for earthly glory, but at the cost of that same renunciation and suffering which the Son of man himself must endure (vv. 21-24; cf. 17: 22; 20: 22 f.; Lk. 17: 22-25; etc.).

The Church thus envisaged is, then, a community founded upon a personal confession of Christ, and sharing the elusive dual quality of the Kingdom: it is, in fact, the instrument of that Kingdom on earth, and exists in consequence in constant tension with its environment. This community is a *little flock* and an *ekklēsia*, as was the chosen people of Israel, and is thus a continuity of the congregation of the people of God, but it is also distinct and of the future ('my church' and 'I will build'). In it the last things of God find an anticipatory fulfilment.

It is after we have traced our Lord's intentions for the community that we recognize that His teaching contains provisions for its continuity which are in character with its nature. There is the presence of the Paraclete for the continual support and increase of its life, and the new foundation commandment of mutual love (Jn 13-16). There are provisions for the self-discipline of the community (Mt. 18: 15-22), and paradoxical rules of an anti-hierarchy (Mt. 20: 25-28). There are also ordinances expressive of its unity: the fellowship of the Last Supper and of the new covenant which it enshrines; and, at the very end, the command to baptize, significantly embodying a trinitarian formula (Mt. 28: 19).

Here, then, is a basic conception of the Church. Its existence lies in its relationship to the Father, a relationship established by personal response to and confession of Christ. Provision for its continuity is not in an organizational structure, but in the abiding of the Holy Spirit, while the relations of its members to each other are the paradoxical reverse of institutional. Its rites emphasize not office, but fellowship and identification. It is the fulfilment of the ideal of the old covenant, and yet a new thing. Its nature is essentially eschatological: it is the anticipatory fulfilment of God's final act, in the present world the holder of the keys of the Kingdom, but, like the Kingdom, the seed springing up in token of the reaping to come. For this reason it is in perpetual tension with its environment: it is in the world, but it is of the world to come.

[Note: In connection with the treatment of the Kingdom here, it may be noted that Cullmann, *op. cit.*, pp. 109-120, distinguishes on the basis of 1 C. 15: 24 between the 'regnum Christi' (the present era) and the 'kingdom of God' ('purely future'). Cullmann nevertheless emphasizes the tension between present and future in the Church.]

Growth to Self-Awareness

After the shattering events of passion week and its sequel, the community of disciples eventually collected in Jerusalem. One central motive united them: a consciousness of a commission to testify to the acts of God which they had witnessed. Those who later recorded that consciousness realized that from the earliest times it held latent a potential which extended far beyond the traditional boundaries of Judaism (Mt. 28: 19; Ac. 1: 8). Yet this wide calling was sensed but uncertainly as yet. Until the outburst of Pentecost, the seed lay dormant, the little community's only development being the filling of the vacancy in the apostolate left by Judas's suicide; a careful completion of the number of the twelve which was essentially Jewish in its inspiration (see Lk. 22: 28-30).

This Jewish atmosphere persists after Pentecost, in the early addresses of Peter. That which has happened is the crisis of Judaism. Although response requires an act of repentance and of renunciation of their generation, with which the act of baptism is associated (Ac. 2: 38-40), yet that renunciation is not a rejection of their whole background. The converts devote themselves to the apostles' teaching and fellowship, but they do so while still attending the temple together (Ac. 2: 42-46). The promise is 'to you and to your children and to all that are far off, every one whom the Lord our God calls to him', but the precise scope of those words remains uncertain. This could be only a reform within Judaism; but an infinitely wider vision is dawning. In Ac. 3, Jesus is 'the Christ appointed *for you*' (20), and the proclamation is strictly within the national ideal: yet the promise quoted from Gen. 22: 18 hints at wider horizons. Jesus has been sent 'to you first': this implies others to follow (25, 26).

In Ac. 4: 12 there appears the exclusive claim to salvation in Christ alone. Then, in the context of the solemn act of judgment of Ac. 5, the community is first named a 'church' with all that implies in realization of a separate ethos (11). (The AV of Ac. 2: 47 arises from a variant reading now usually rejected.) The second appearance of the word is on the occasion of the great persecution, by Jews, which followed the death of Stephen (Ac. 8: 1). So the fires of judgment and persecution forged the Church's realization of its separate destiny, and compelled it to its world-wide mission. How slow this process was is apparent from Ac. 24: 14, where, in Jerusalem itself, 'the Way' is still, a quarter of a century later, regarded as a Jewish sect.

Here then is no carefully constructed society, shaped according to the constitutional pattern of a founder, but rather a growing and developing organism, growing out of its circumstances and being shaped by the reaction of its own inherent life to its environment (see Eph. 4: 16; 1 Pet. 2: 5). So it continues throughout the Church's later expansion. A matter as vital as that of the acceptance of Gentiles to equal membership is resolved only by broadening experience and by painful controversy. The situation as to the assimilation of Gentiles differs from church to church at any one time. It is the same with forms of government. Officers are appointed, and their functions determined, as need arises, and the structure of authority differs from place to place.

Most interesting of all are the indications of differing views on the polity of the Church itself. Around Jerusalem a sense of unity grew in a church which was necessarily fragmented by sheer numbers and lack of meeting places, and the result is that the Church over a considerable district is regarded as a unity (Ac. 9: 31, not AV). Paul, on the other hand, writes with the experience of smaller churches in scattered towns, and his outlook is in consequence more nearly

congregational, even when applied to those same Judean congregations (Gal. 1: 22, and see v. 2, but note v. 13). (Hort, *The Christian Ecclesia*, pp. 144-149, emphasizes that the concept of the universal church appears in Pauline teaching only at a later date, in Eph. and Col.)

These facts suffice to illustrate important factors for guiding study of the apostolic church. We cannot look for any single prescribed pattern of church order or government, nor is there any suggestion that we should do so. Indeed, such a model would be contrary to the very nature of the Church. We do find two important features. The first is that of an obvious growth and development within the period of the New Testament itself, and the second is that of diversity at any one time between different churches.

[Note: These are of course the two theses of Streeter, *The Primitive Church*, ix. But they are much older than Streeter, as witness the two following quotations from Henry Craik of Bristol (*NT Church Order*, 1863): 'A more fully developed church organization and official position were introduced as occasion called for them. . . . We hear nothing at first of Presbyters or Overseers, and the office of the Deaconship appears to have been suggested by the pressure of urgent necessity . . . the possession of spiritual gifts led to the development of rulers, teachers and evangelists, during the apostolic period' (p. 24).

'It appears to me that the early Churches were not, in all places, similarly constituted' (p. 4).]

New Life in Christ

Those who composed the Church stood in a new and profoundly different relationship to God from any that had previously been known. True, they could trace their kinship with the faithful of preceding ages, and their covenant of faith to Abraham himself; but their own relationship to God was based on two radically new experiences. These experiences were individually realized, but they were essentially corporate in their nature. There was the new experience of union with God in and through Christ; a union which had sharply separated those who knew it from 'the world' which did not, while at the same time uniting them indissolubly among themselves. This first experience received its highest devotional expression in the writings of John and its profoundest theological exposition in the letter to the Ephesians. The second experience bore more particularly on the practical outworking of their faith. It was that experience of the indwelling Spirit of God which is such a marked feature of the history recorded in the Acts of the Apostles, and which forms the experiential foundation of the note of assurance in the letters of Paul. These two experiences transcended all known divisions of society. By one Spirit they had all been baptized into one body—Jews and Greeks, slaves and free—and had all been made to drink of one Spirit (1 C. 12: 13).

In the letters to the Ephesians and Colossians these two experiences blend with the early insights concerning the eschatological nature of the Church, and mature into a vision which transcends the temporal world. In an earlier writing of the New Testament, the transcendence of God had been stressed—'to whom be the glory *eis tous aiōnas tōn aiōnōn*' (Gal. 1: 5). Much later, in the second letter to Timothy, the calling in Christ is portrayed as a product of this transcendence: part of the age-old purpose of God *pro chronōn aiōniōn*, and is related to the revelation of life and immortality: but it is set in the immediate context of the here-and-now of witness and suffering (2 Tim. 1: 8-12). In the Ephesian letter, however, the here-and-now itself has receded from sight in the greater shining of the glory of eternity. The Church is there a central feature of the divine plan for all created things and for the fullness of time. This purpose centres in Christ, but in Christ as 'the head over all things for the church, which is his body, the fullness of him who fills all in all' (Eph. 1: 3-23). The relationship of Church to Christ is as that of wife to husband (Eph. 5: 22-33). The witness of the here-and-now is emphatically present, but it is immeasurably broadened and enlarged, for 'the unsearchable riches of Christ' include this, 'that through the church the manifold wisdom of God might now be made known to the principalities and powers in the heavenly places' (Eph. 3: 7-12).

Yet those two experiences, of unity and of the Spirit, were no visionary distractions, but they were basic to a new dimension of practical living. John's experience of union with Christ was expressed in vivid terms, intimately related to the present as well as to eternity. The experience is an eating and drinking of Christ, a believing in Him which brings the gift of eternal life and the resurrection at the last day: and yet that bread of which men eat is 'that which comes down from heaven, and gives life to the world' (Jn 6), and the result of believing is that one should be a present source of 'rivers of living water' (Jn 7: 38). The life in Christ is a present experienced indwelling of the Godhead (ch. 14), a union of the branches with the vine (ch. 15). That indwelling implies the present enlightenment of the Spirit (14: 26), an enlightenment which has a direct relevance to sin and righteousness and judgment in this present world (16: 4-15); and the union of the branches with the

vine is for the immediate purpose of present fruitfulness. Such fruitfulness is in fact the proof of true discipleship (15: 8). Union with God in Christ might provoke the hostility of the world, but it brought with it a new and direct responsibility within and toward the world. Its effects are expressed in varying practical outworkings: in witness, in enlightenment, in effective prayer and in conduct towards fellow men. 'I have given you an example, that you also should do as I have done to you' (Jn 13: 15). Above all, the union with God in Christ was to issue in a visible unity among those who shared it. Jesus had come to die, that He might 'gather into one the children of God who are scattered abroad' (Jn 11: 51, 52), and that unity was to be the supreme witness to the world (Jn 17: 23).

[Note: In passing, the following extract from Robinson's *Guide to Tottenham* (1840 edition) is of interest, as giving the view of the early Brethren assembly then meeting at Brook Street: 'They consider that Christ appointed that all His disciples should form *one visible church* . . .']

The letter to the Hebrews gives this experience of union with Christ a new and heart-warming aspect. Not only is human life lifted to a transcendent fellowship with the Father and His Son Jesus Christ, as John emphasized in his first letter, but in the incarnation the Son has shared in humanity and partaken of the same nature: 'that is why he is not ashamed to call them brethren' (Heb. 2: 11-18). In the Church, not only do men share the things of God—but God partakes in the things of humanity.

In a similar manner, the second experience, that of the Spirit, was seen as directed to the future consummation—'the guarantee of our inheritance until we acquire possession of it' (Eph. 1: 14): but essentially the experience was of immediate and practical import. 'You shall receive power when the Holy Spirit has come upon you; and you shall be my witnesses . . .' (Ac. 1: 8). It is to the evident practical working of that Spirit—the 'miracles' worked among the Galatians—that Paul can point in justification of the gospel which he preached: and those *dynameis* included the practical virtues of love, joy, peace, patience, kindness, goodness, faithfulness, gentleness and self-control (Gal. 3: 5; 5: 22, 23).

The intensity of the early Church's realization of these two aspects of its relation to the Godhead, cannot be illustrated more effectively than by two quotations which are the more striking for their incidental character. The first, the union with Christ, is contained in the words addressed to Saul, the persecutor of the Church: 'I am Jesus, whom you are persecuting' (Ac. 9:

5). Persecution of the Church was persecution of Jesus Himself. The second, the experience of the Spirit, appears in the letter which contained the findings of the Council of Jerusalem: 'It has seemed good to the Holy Spirit and to us . . .' (Ac. 15: 28). The desires of the Spirit and of the Church were one.

The Fellowship of the Common Life

When a convert joined himself to a community of the early church, he entered upon a profoundly new type of human relationship. The fellowship of the local congregation entered into every aspect of his life. 'If one member suffers, all suffer together; if one member is honoured, all rejoice together. Now you are the body of Christ and individually members of it' (1 C. 12: 26, 27).

This sense of community and of mutual responsibility made the genuine unity of the congregation a matter of supreme importance (Eph. 4: 1-7). Unity demanded mutual forbearance and a tolerance strong enough to overcome the inevitable differences among members (Rom. 15: 5; 1 C. 1: 10-13; Phil. 2: 1-5, etc.). It was to be demonstrated in a genuine sharing of burdens and problems (Rom. 15: 1; Gal. 6: 2); in a fellowship of witness and a sympathetic participation in the sufferings and dangers of one another (Phil. 1: 27-30; Rev. 1: 9). Nor was this sense of unity confined to the local congregation. The churches from the beginning maintained a lively interest in the progress of other Christian communities, and were encouraged to a sense of solidarity, which was turned to the practical relief of the necessities of other churches (Ac. 11: 22-30; 15: 3; 1 Th. 2: 14; Rom. 15: 25-27; 1 C. 16: 1-4; 2 C. 8; etc.). Letters were shared among the churches (Col. 4: 16), and teachers were supported while they were working among other communities (2 C. 11: 8; Phil. 4: 16). A warm hospitality was shown to visiting Christians, a brotherly hospitality often experienced by Paul and his companions during the journeyings recorded in the Acts, and forming a regular and important feature of the life of local congregations (see Rom. 16: 23; Heb. 13: 2; 3 Jn 5-8).

The cement of this unity was love—the 'royal law' of Christ (Jas 2: 8). In one of the latest of the writings of the New Testament, when

What first were guessed as points, I now knew stars,

And named them in the Gospel I have writ.

—(Browning, A Death in the Desert),

it was these two elements, unity and love, which were brought out as the basic principles of our Lord's testament for the community which would arise from those He was leaving behind Him (Jn 13-17).

Unity and love were cultivated by ungrudging hospitality, by the holding of possessions not for selfish ends, but with a sense of personal stewardship for one another (1 Jn 3: 16, 17; 1 Pet. 4: 8-10). All barriers between individuals, of nationality, sex, or social class, were to be overridden in the new loyalty of Christ (Gal. 3: 28; Col. 3: 11; Jas 2: 1-4).

It was a radical new ethos, and in an attempt at its expression the early Jerusalem church turned to a not unfamiliar pattern within its own society, the pattern of community of goods (Ac. 4: 32-37). But the ideals and the vision of the faith of Christ could never remain confined within the inevitably narrowed horizons of such a community. The failure of the idealistic attempt was inevitable. Its chief result, after the first deceptive well-being of the participants (Ac. 4: 34), may have been that chronic impoverishment of the Jerusalem church which haunts the later pages of the New Testament (see F. F. Bruce, *The Book of the Acts*, p. 109 note).

After this first failure, the Church approached this problem also in a pragmatic fashion. In Thessalonica an early misunderstanding of Christian ideals again led to social ills, against which Paul felt obliged to intervene in language of severity (1 Th. 4: 9-12 with 2 Th. 3: 6-15). By the time of the first letter to Timothy, some at least of the churches had worked out the social expression of Christian love into a code which was capable of enduring expression. We are given a picture of a community carefully organized to provide for the needs of its poor, and quietly working out the new ideals of brotherhood, in the manner of the Kingdom, from within the existing framework of society (1 Tim. 5: 1-6: 10).

Community life implies the need for discipline also. If each member bore responsibility for the welfare of the others, then that obligation brought with it the need for a personal self-discipline extending to the most elementary actions of life. 'If your brother is being injured by what you eat, you are no longer walking in love' (Rom. 14: 15, and see 1 C. 8: 12, 13). Yet even this principle was not to be applied in such a way as to pander to the bigot (1 C. 10: 25-30, although different versions indicate the ambiguity of this passage). Discipline must also require open repudiation of the flagrant evil-doer (1 C. 5: 11-13), and it called also for adequate and just machinery within the community itself for the settlement of grievances (1 C. 6: 1-8).

It is a fascinating task to trace the scattered references which show us the early churches in their gatherings for worship and the service of God. The sharing of the common life was of the essence of the community, and from the day of Pentecost this *koinōnia* had been the distinctive feature of the Church: 'they devoted themselves to the apostles' teaching and fellowship, to the breaking of bread and the prayers . . . and all who believed were together and had all things in common . . . and day by day, attending the temple together and breaking bread in their homes, they partook of food with glad and generous hearts, praising God and having favour with all the people' (Ac. 2: 42-47). For their meeting places, the temple courts, private homes, a hired schoolroom, an upper chamber, were all put to service as need arose. The Jewish tradition of religious community life, the synagogues of the dispersion, possibly aspects of Gentile organization, were all available to be drawn upon. The Church took tribute from each, but shaped what it took to the purposes of its own destiny, transforming the conception of office by its new law of humility.

In Ac. 12 a group of disciples, at a moment of crisis, engages in prayer in the house of Mark's mother: a type of cottage meeting which must have been a common feature of the life of the unwieldy and scattered church in Jerusalem. By contrast, Ac. 15 introduces us to a formal conclave on a matter of deep importance. In Ac. 20 a group of disciples is found gathering for the breaking of bread on the first day of the week: apparently a regular gathering, for Paul seems to have prolonged his stay in Troas in order to attend. At it the visiting apostle is expected to, and does, preach at length. In contrast, in Ephesus, Paul holds daily sessions of discussion and teaching through a period of two years (Ac. 19: 9, 10), and in so doing builds up a powerful church.

The regular gathering together of Christians for their mutual fellowship and edification, for public reading of Scripture and for preaching and teaching, often under the guidance of a visiting teacher or apostle (1 Tim. 4: 13), was early seen as one of the vital features of the life of a local church. So, from a different tradition, there comes the exhortation not to neglect their meeting together (Heb. 10: 25), and this aspect of the *koinōnia* is surely not lacking from the exhortation of ch. 13: 16 of the same book (see Gk.).

It is in the first letter to the Corinthians that we are given the most detailed insight into early church meetings: and, disorderly as much of the conduct at Corinth may have been, Paul gives no indication that the general tenor of their activities was not typical: in fact his opening words, although ambiguous, indicate that what he had to say would be widely relevant among the churches. In many of the gatherings of that church each member was expected and encouraged to make a personal contribution to the worship: 'when you come together, each one has a hymn, a lesson, a revelation, a tongue, or an interpretation' (1 C. 14: 26—it should be added that the interpretation which reads this verse as a rebuke to the Corinthians is, in view of the context, a little odd!). The apostle was concerned to remedy the abuses which this freedom engendered, but his exhortations were directed to the exercise of a proper self-control, rather than to the restriction of vocal activity to a handful of members. The regulatory principles are to be edification (26) and order (40): the latter in a sense which may indicate some pre-arrangement (*kata taxin*).

In Corinth, we find that the celebration of the Lord's Supper had become a regular and frequent feature of the gatherings of the church. It is possible indeed that it formed a part of every gathering (11: 17-21), and thus had become sadly interwoven with the merely social (not to say convivial) incidents of their meeting together. The apostle's exhortations are directed to emphasizing the solemnity of the occasion, rather than to restricting the frequency of the observance.

There were yet more sombre occasions of meeting, when the church found it necessary to exercise its discipline. In 1 C. 5 we are shown the church assembled for this purpose—'and my spirit is present, with the power of our Lord Jesus, you are to deliver this man to Satan for the destruction of the flesh, that his spirit may be saved in the day of the Lord Jesus.' The ardent unity of the early Church, and its intense sense of the indwelling Spirit, laid upon such an act of excommunication an awful significance.

It would appear that women were accustomed to taking a prominent part in activities of the early Church. This is a notoriously controversial subject, and what follows represents a personal interpretation of the NT evidence. Paul's early and emphatic denial of sex distinctions in Christ (Gal. 3: 28) would have encouraged feminine gifts, as would the frequent and important contribution made by influential women as the Church expanded (Ac. 1: 14; 9: 36 ff.; 12: 12; 16: 13-15; 17: 4, 12; 18: 2, 26). Their contributions were not confined to the exercise of guidance behind the scenes. At a late date we find no hint of disapproval when Paul found the daughters of Philip prophesying (Ac. 21: 8, 9): a fact of the greater interest when his earlier instructions to the Corinthian church are remembered. Differences of function in the churches arose in principle only from the gift bestowed on the individual, and not from distinctions of rank or of sex (cf. 1 C. 12).

Yet, in the licentious centres of Gentile civilization liberty could deteriorate into licence. Certainly the results in Corinth were unhappy. Once again, the church was forced under God to adapt its order to the circumstances of the society in which it moved. Although the participation of women in prayer and prophecy was still contemplated (1 C. 11: 5), it became necessary to restrict their liberty, both in matters of dress (1 C. 11: 4-16) and in public worship (1 C. 14: 33-35). In other aspects of service in the churches, women continued to take prominent part (see Rom. 16: 1; Phil. 4: 3; 1 Tim. 3: 11; 5: 10; Tit. 2: 3 ff.).

By the date of the first letter to Timothy, this aspect also of the churches' life had found a stable form of regulation. That female participation in public prayer was still contemplated may well be indicated. The contrary has been deduced from the use of the word 'males' in the Gk. of 1 Tim. 2: 8: yet surely this is a contrast to the 'women' of v. 9. The passage, taken as a whole, implies that as men were to adorn their prayers with holy characters, so women should adorn theirs with modesty in dress and in conduct. Female participation in teaching or in authoritative rule was forbidden (1 Tim. 2: 11-15). That these rules were not universally applied, and equally that in the first century they were often highly desirable, was demonstrated by the unsavoury happenings a generation later in Thyatira (Rev. 2: 20; see p. 639).

[Note: It may be held, with Lightfoot, that the 'Jezebel' reference is symbolic; but the question would still remain as to how such a symbol came to be used if such female activity was completely unknown.]

It is the Apocalypse which introduces a novel element into any discussion of the worship of the early church. For, contrary to all that we would expect from the other records of the New Testament, the visions of the seer introduce an element of magnificence and imaginative form that startles and entrances (Rev. 4: 7-5: 14; 7: 9-12; 19: 1-8). As the music of the calls to worship and of the thunderous responses dies away, we are left to wonder about the experiences and forms of worship which had shaped the prophet's vision. What experiences of public worship had led him to illustrate the ultimate in human worship in forms such as these? To that question, the remainder of the New Testament affords us no answer.

Government and Gifts

To one who knew only the New Testament, it would be astonishing that discussion of the Church should so often be preoccupied with conceptions of the ministry. Still less could it seem possible that the very term 'the Church'

should become confined to its officers, or that conceptions of the Church itself should turn upon this doctrine.

Yet perhaps some such development was inevitable. As the Church grew, its whole environment demanded a strong and coherent structure of authority to meet the pressures of persecution, the pretences of upstart demagogues, speculation and false doctrine, and the requirements of discipline. The very structure of authority so developed would ultimately generate pressures and interests which would lead to its perpetuation for its own sake. Later, when persecution had ended, doctrine would too easily follow the desires for power which are endemic in human nature. It would be for the Church to experience in its own being the paradox that in saving life, life would be lost, and that in losing life it would be saved.

Amongst the earliest believers, the twelve apostles held an especial position. They were 'the apostles whom He had chosen' (Ac. 1: 2): those who had been with Jesus and were the especial witnesses of their Lord's resurrection and the recipients of His teaching (Mk 3: 14; Ac. 1: 3, 21, 22). In this respect at least their position was unique and unrepeatable (for a discussion of the uniqueness of the apostolate, see Cullmann, *op. cit.*, pp. 75-87).

Upon these twelve, then, there probably fell the brunt of the early leadership. The sudden expansion of the Church after Pentecost made their task impossible, and to meet the problem special administrators were appointed (Ac. 6: 1-6). The subsequent development of this office is lost in oblivion (although it is still a distinguishing mark a generation later—Ac. 21: 8), but at least two of them soon progressed to become active in the Word of God.

Side by side with the administrative tasks for which men could be chosen and appointed, other gifts were forcing themselves to the fore. Some of these were natural gifts of leadership and eloquence, of intellect and personality. Enhanced by the energies of the Spirit, such gifts were of supreme importance to the Church. But there were other gifts also, more sensational and more obviously inspirational, gifts of tongues and prophecies and healings. In them was seen a palpable evidence of the working of the Spirit, and those who exercised them would attract a measure of deference which was often unhealthy, and which led to Paul's words of correction at Corinth (1 C. 12: 27-13: 3).

It was likely therefore that the authoritative structure of the Church would develop along two lines. On the one hand, gifts of leadership and intellect would produce ordered systems, which would make use of natural administrative abilities. These systems would differ in accordance with local circumstances. On the other hand, inspirational gifts would be unpredictable and erratic, not easily subjected to control, and impatient of regulation.

In Jerusalem development was from the beginning of the more ordered type. It is true that inspirational gifts were prominent. Ecstatic utterances were known, and recognized as basically similar to the experience of Pentecost, even if not identical in character (Ac. 10: 44-47; also cf. Ac. 2: 8-11 with 1 C. 14: 6-13). The evangelization of Samaria produced 'signs and great miracles' (Ac. 8: 13), while the gift of prophecy was also prominent (Ac. 11: 27).

Nevertheless, these gifts were exercised in an ordered context. When the twelve were scattered, a settled authority was needed to replace them, and accordingly we find that elders appear at Jerusalem during the period of years covered by Ac. 11, where previously there had been 'apostles and brethren' (Ac. 11: 1, 30). It is to be noted that in the letter of James, deriving from Jerusalem, the only reference to a possibly miraculous gift sees that gift as exercised strictly within the authority of the body of elders (Jas 5: 13-15). No indication is given of the circumstances or manner of appointment of these elders in Jerusalem. On the analogy of Ac. 6, we might suppose that they were chosen by popular election, ratified by the apostles: a mode which was different from that later adopted by Paul and Barnabas in the South Galatian churches (Ac. 14: 23; cf. Tit. 1: 5).

These elders at Jerusalem soon received considerable authority within the church, acting equally with the apostles (Ac. 15). Beyond their authority, James the Lord's brother also assumed a personal prominence. He was already in a prominent position in Ac. 12: 17 and Gal. 1: 19, although this was not yet a solitary position (Gal. 2: 9). In Ac. 15 his voice is decisive in discussion. In Ac. 21, some seven years later, he appears in a position of primacy similar to that which tradition assigns to him. Yet despite these developments, it is plain from the letter of James that the position of teacher was still open to all whose gifts qualified for it and who understood its solemnity (Jas 3: 1).

Developments among the churches influenced by Paul were of a different character. At Antioch the only leadership of which we know was that of prophets and teachers (Ac. 13: 1). By contrast, the churches in South Galatia were furnished with elders at an early stage of their history (Ac. 14: 23). Yet the letter to Galatia which followed soon afterwards makes no reference to those elders, in a matter of doctrine where we might have expected an appeal to them, and it is possible (though unlikely) that their functions were mainly administrative. At Corinth it would appear that the appointment of elders was at first omitted: if elders did exist there, it is remarkable that a letter dealing with disciplinary matters as closely as First Corinthians should make no reference to them, and it is difficult to reconcile the exhortation of 1 C. 16: 15, 16 with the existence of previously appointed elders. Perhaps the appearance of gifts in that church, as they had appeared in the other great city of Antioch, led the apostles to rely on the example of that church at the first. At Thessalonica, there were 'those who labour among you and are over you in the Lord and admonish you' (1 Th. 5: 12). Considerable emphasis is placed on the eldership at Ephesus (Ac. 20: 17-38): it is interesting to recall that the first letter to Corinth was written towards the end of Paul's long stay in Ephesus (Ac. 19), and we might speculate whether the emphasis on the eldership at Ephesus derived something from the unhappy experiences of an elder-less Corinth. For the Ephesian elders were certainly not mere administrators: they were *episkopoi* ('bishops') and shepherds and guardians of the flock.

[Note: For the identity of 'bishops' and 'elders' in the NT see J. B. Lightfoot, *Philippians*, pp. 95-99. On the non-appointment of elders by Paul see E. Schweizer, *op. cit.*, 7k.]

The letter to the Philippians indicates a still more formal structure. There *episkopoi* are accompanied by *diakonoi* (Phil. 1: 1), a structure which probably provides separately for the functions of administration and of spiritual oversight. If the Philippian letter dates from Paul's Roman imprisonment, this further development would arise naturally from the tendencies already noted. If, as some think, the letter was written from an earlier imprisonment in Ephesus, it would be contemporary with the first letter to Corinth, and the developed church order in Philippi would be a remarkable contrast to Corinth. It is probable that Paul had left Luke to care for the church at Philippi (as the 'we' passages in Acts indicate): might we connect the two things? For it is Luke whose writings evince an interest in the practical matters of church administration that is largely absent from the earlier Pauline letters, until the Corinthian troubles arose. Was it the orderly mind of the historian of the primitive church which influenced the later structure of the Pauline churches?

[Note: With this cf. E. Schweizer, who places Luke's view of the Church firmly within the historical and hence tending to the hierarchical view, over against Paul. (*Op. cit.*, 5.7d.20d.)]

The Ephesian and Philippian structures proved to be durable. By the time of the Pastoral Letters, the ordering of the churches, like so many other aspects of their life, had developed in places a stable and formalized character, basically similar to that of the earlier letter to Philippi. In 1 Timothy, the Ephesian church now has both *episkopoi* and *diakonoi*, and the *diakonoi* must serve a probationary period (1 Tim. 3: 10). The Pastorals add one further interesting feature, for they contemplate that a teacher might reside in a district (the residence here being temporary) and during that residence might appoint elders (and, where they are needed, deacons), and also exercise a considerable personal authority. In the examples of Timothy and Titus, this authority derived directly from that of the founder-apostle. It should also be noted that it is implied that the absence of elders is a definite defect, to be remedied (Tit. 1: 5).

The remaining books of the New Testament add to the general picture. Hebrews knows of 'leaders . . . who spoke to you the word of God,' who are to be obeyed 'for they are keeping watch over your souls, as men who will have to give account' (Heb. 13: 7, 17). It might be that the early teachers are here the *de facto* leaders, as in early Antioch. 1 Peter has 'elders' who are responsible shepherds with a definite charge, although the context is completely open, and the persons concerned might be at any point from that of older men exercising authority simply as such, to that of monarchical elders of individual churches (1 Pet. 5: 1-5).

It is the third letter of John, however, which adds two fresh facets to our knowledge. From it we learn of the existence of travelling preachers (5-8), who are also referred to by Jude (3, 4), the latter indicating vividly some of the dangers to which the system gave rise. John's letter also indicates, in the person of Diotrephes, the growth of autocratic rule over the churches; and this evokes a reaction which is still more interesting in its claim to a more than local authority on the part of John 'the elder'. It must be noticed therefore that John does not denounce the monarchic position as such, but that he might even hint, in Demetrius, at a suitable replacement for the obdurate Diotrephes (3 Jn 9-12) (see R. W. Orr, 'Diotrephes: The First Gnostic Bishop?', in *Evangelical Quarterly*, 33, 1961, p. 172).

Thus, alongside the settled and more ordered service of elders and deacons, largely but not exclusively local, there appears to have arisen another ministry, not localized, and consisting of travelling teachers as well as of men claiming to exercise the more inspirational gifts of pro-

phecy. It is possible that these are the 'apostles' of Rev. 2: 2, where the title was claimed with little regard to the spiritual realities, and conceivably of Rom. 16: 7 (see also 2 C. 8: 23; Phil. 2: 25 and Hort, *op. cit.*, pp. 64 f.). It was a system that gave ample freedom to the charlatan, and yet in 3 John such teachers are specifically upheld against a domineering local leader.

We are thus brought closer to the world of the immediately post-apostolic era; the world of the Didache, with its travelling teachers honoured above the local officers, and of the letters of Ignatius, with the single 'bishop' presiding in each Asian church, and their elders and deacons. The trends in development are thus confirmed by those writings, but we have little need of extra-Biblical evidence in tracing the clouds which were already gathering over the Church. The opening chapters of Revelation indicate the corruptions which developed in both streams of ministry: while elsewhere hints of speculation and wild imaginings (*e.g.* Col. 2; 1 Tim. 1: 3-5; and see 1 C. 11: 18, 19), foreshadow the need which would arise for strong hands to take hold of the churches when Jerusalem and the apostles had gone for ever.

How and when this occurred remains unknown, but by the middle of the second century the order of many churches had been systematized and transformed. Bishop Lightfoot considered that there are good grounds for believing that developments in the direction of monarchical government within individual churches had taken place within the lifetime and with the knowledge of the apostle John ('The Christian Ministry', in *Philippians*, pp. 206, 228, 234). It may well be so; but the impressions which we derive from the writings of the first century will probably always depend upon the background from which we approach them, and it is dangerous to assume that our knowledge of some of the churches is characteristic of all (cf. 'When there were some eight hundred bishops in the Province of Africa in the fifth century they must have been a great deal more like Presbyterian ministers than Anglican metropolitans.' [John Oman on 'The Presbyterian Churches' in *Evangelical Christianity, Its History and Witness*, 1911, p. 67]).

It remains to consider the indications of a degree of centralization in the early Church, which some have deduced from the account of the council of Jerusalem in Ac. 15. It is possible that much of Paul's letter to the Galatians is a protest against just such claims to a central authority. Be that as it may, the evidence of Ac. 15 and 16 must remain inconclusive. On the one hand, there is clear recognition of an especial value residing in the judgment of the apostles and elders of Jerusalem on the points in question, and with that judgment there is linked not only the remainder of the church there, but also the authority of the Holy Spirit Himself. On the other hand, it is plain that Jerusalem was being asked to pronounce on a dispute which had been raised by teachers coming from within its own ranks, as the judgment itself recognizes. It is therefore unsafe to base any firm inferences on the incident. The careful self-limitation of the judgment in its claims to authority is of especial significance.

To this survey of the practices of the New Testament church, it is necessary to add some general observations.

First, it is misleading to distinguish too sharply between the inspirational and the more natural gifts, as though only the former were truly charismatic. Both alike are *charismata* (Rom. 12: 6-8), gifts of bounty, as free as the new life of God itself (Rom. 6: 23). (In view of Rom. 12, where *diakonia* is one of the *charismata*, it is surely correct to read the threefold *charismatōn*, . . . *diakoniōn* . . . *energēmatōn* of 1 C. 12: 4-6 as parallel descriptions of the whole range of gifts, rather than as a division into classes. See Schweizer, *op. cit.*, 22b, c, d.) All gifts are the direct provision by God for the nourishment of the Church's life, traced at times to the operation of the Head of the Church Himself, and at others to the direct working within the Church of the Holy Spirit (Rom. 12: 4-8; 1 C. 12; Eph. 3: 5; 4: 7-12). (J. B. Lightfoot, *op. cit.*, p. 185; Hort, *op. cit.*, p. 145 and ch. 10.)

Second, there is no idea of a limited priesthood. All believers alike were priests before God (1 Pet. 2: 5; Rev. 1: 6; 5: 10). The teaching of Hebrews is relevant here. (See J. B. Lightfoot, *Philippians*, p. 119, on *leitourgia*. The universal priesthood is 'the fundamental idea of the Christian Church'.)

Third, there is no limitation of the exercise of spiritual gifts, or of the administration of the sacraments, to those with governmental authority. True, elders are responsible for guarding and feeding the flock (Ac. 20: 28; 1 Pet. 5: 2), and the *episkopos* is to be an apt teacher (1 Tim. 3: 2 and see 1 Tim. 5: 17) and to provide for a proper succession to his teaching (2 Tim. 2: 2): but governments are among the gifts, not conditions precedent to their exercise (1 C. 12: 28). Perhaps the example of Corinth (1 C. 14: 26) is too invidious to provide a safe foundation, but there are other passages which are equally explicit. Paul is satisfied that the Romans are 'able to instruct one another' (Rom. 15: 14). Grace was given to each according to the measure of Christ's gift (Eph. 4: 7). Each had

received a gift, and was to employ it for the benefit of one another, as good stewards of God's varied grace (1 Pet. 4: 10). Indeed, it was the gifts which determined the authority: both governmental and otherwise, they were recognized as carrying with them an authority which demanded respect and obedience (1 C. 16: 16; 2 C. 10: 8; 1 Tim. 1: 20; 5: 19; Heb. 13: 17; 1 Th. 2: 6; 5: 12, 13), and which was capable of severe disciplinary action, particularly over false teachers (1 C. 5: 3-5; 3 Jn 9-10; Tit. 1: 13).

Fourth, the gifts are not poured out on men without regard to natural talent: rather, the Holy Spirit takes up and enlarges a gift which is already there. It is the men themselves, within whom the gift is operative, who are seen as the gifts to the Church in Eph. 4: 11. The natural corollary is that each man must soberly estimate his own gift: while he might earnestly desire the best, the welfare of the Church demands that there should be a proper self-assessment, and a proper self-control and a decent order (Rom. 12: 3; 1 C. 13: 1-3; ch. 14). The impulse of the moment was not the indispensable sign of the movement of the Spirit.

For this reason, it was often the custom of the churches to recognize the possession of gift formally and with solemnity. The laying on of hands was at times associated with the dedication of an experienced leader to a special task (Ac. 13: 3; cf. 6: 6), but there is also an indication in the letter to Timothy of the direct association of the laying on of hands with the gift itself (1 Tim. 4: 14; 2 Tim. 1: 6). The context shows that this bestowing of gift through the laying on of hands was a formal recognition of a gift which already existed, for it had been pointed out by prophetic utterance (1 Tim. 1: 18) (whose utterance, is not clear).

Fifth, the use of a gift brought with it a right to the pecuniary support of the church (1 C. 9: 14; 1 Tim. 5: 17, 18). As yet, there were no possibilities of complete maintenance, and Paul himself worked regularly for his own and others' support (Ac. 20: 34; 1 Th. 2: 9; 2 Th. 3: 8); but the right was inherent in the service of God. To demand scriptural precedent for the regular payment of a spiritual teacher, or for the endowment of his support, is to demand an anachronism; but of the principle itself the relevant passages leave not a shadow of doubt.

It is inevitable that an element of hindsight should enter into discussion of the gifts and government of the New Testament Church. We are liable to read into the record the systems with which we are familiar, or to react against them and to see only their denial. Both attitudes are essentially wrong. The New Testament Church was a living, vigorous community, inhibited from no order or arrangement which ministered to its life, but bound by no bonds of administration where these would restrict or restrain it. No system is in itself necessarily wrong, but equally no system can claim for itself an exclusive validity. The Church could rejoice over its gifts, as the earliest disciples had rejoiced on the first glad day of Pentecost: 'He has poured out this which you see and hear' (Ac. 2: 33; see Heb. 2: 4). A ministry, whatever authority it may claim, which no longer bears the fruits of that grace of Christ is a valid ministry no longer.

Conclusion

'The household of God, which is the church of the living God, the pillar and bulwark of the truth' (1 Tim. 3: 15). 'The time has come for judgment to begin with the household of God; and if it begins with us, what will be the end of those who do not obey the gospel of God?' (1 Pet. 4: 17). In those two verses, the paradox of the Church presents itself again. On the one hand, we have the chosen Church, the Church which is the bearer of the keys of the Kingdom and the sharer of the new life of God: on the other, the Church which lies under the judgment of God, even as all the world must lie.

> Lord, when we cry Thee far and near
> And thunder through all lands unknown
> The gospel into every ear,
> Lord, let us not forget our own.

—(Chesterton, *Hymn for the Church Militant*).

Yet—and here is the Church's hope and its glory, and its final difference from that world— even while it lies under that judgment, the Church is the body of Christ. It is crucified with Christ, and dead to the law through the body of Christ (Gal. 2: 20; Rom. 7: 4). The judgment of God must fall, time and again, in temporal manner: but the Church's ultimate judgment is suffered and accomplished and displayed for ever in the eternal awful Act at Golgotha. Both the verses last quoted appear primarily in the context of individual experience: and, just because of that individual experience of entering and enduring the terror of judgment in Christ, so those who have shared it are knit for ever to Him and to each other. The experience of that dying they express in individual baptism: their continuing identification with it in the corporate Supper.

The Church is part of God's final act. For that reason, we shall never reach the ultimate truth concerning its being, as we shall never reach the final truth concerning God Himself. Even our experience of the truth in our own existence is partial: we are too close to our own experience, and too distant from that of our predecessors. So every attempt at understanding the Church

is inadequate. The classic distinction between the visible and the invisible church is probably misleading. (Brunner, *The Misunderstanding of the Church*, ch. 1, and see K. L. Schmidt, *The Church*, pp. 65 f. Compare with this J. N. Darby: 'To escape from this anomaly, believers have sought to shelter themselves under a distinction between a visible and an invisible church; but I read in scripture—"Ye are the light of the world." Of what use is an invisible light?' [*Reflections on the Ruined Condition of the Church* (1841), p. 5].) Even the distinction between the local and the universal church does not do full justice to the Biblical usage (K. L. Schmidt, *op. cit.*, pp. 68 f.). Adaptable as any work of God, the *ekklēsia* is apparent where two or three are gathered, no less (although in a different manner) than in the universal Church. Again, the Church in Scripture (as E. Schweizer has shown) appears both as a heavenly body, taken out of time and history, in timeless union with God: and also as a body in history, part of God's continuous working. We picture it yet again from the standpoint of the individual, to whom this world is but a passing thing: and we picture it as the church militant, in the world as long as the world endures, and with no *raison d'être* except in relation to the world. We call it 'an extension of the incarnation'; yet, if we use that to justify a priestly succession, we are reminded that God incarnate was a layman.

These things are not irrelevant to the present situation. For no unity can be true unity of the Spirit which fails to recognize that the wind blows where it wills. Those Christian bodies which have been called out of organized church history, as an expression of the total independence of the Spirit from any regulation entrusted to man, can never express the fulness of truth, for their very calling denies them that. But that which they have is of vital importance to the continued life of the Church of God: any movement or union which ignores or despises them, does so at its peril. Meanwhile, we must continually return to the Scriptures and to the Act of God which they record: for there alone can be our final authority for understanding in our own situation that which is needful to us concerning the life and fellowship of the Church of God.

> There shall always be the Church and the World
> And the Heart of Man
> Shivering and fluttering between them, choosing
>   and chosen,
> Valiant, ignoble, dark, and full of light
> Swinging between Hell Gate and Heaven Gate.
> And the Gates of Hell shall not prevail.
> Darkness now, then
> Light.   —(T. S. Eliot, *The Rock*.)

APPENDIX

(The author is grateful to Mr. H. L. Ellison for suggesting that an alternative view of the development of the eldership in the apostolic church should be mentioned. Mr. Ellison puts forward the following as arguable propositions:

1. In Palestine, Christian services from the first were an adaptation of the Synagogue pattern (this can hardly be denied when we remember the strong synagogue influence we find in the Christian pattern in the third and following centuries—it must have come in from the first).

2. The influence of the *presbyteros*, i.e. *senex*, older man of worthy character, is basic in the synagogue set up.

3. Therefore we may assume the influence of *presbyteroi* in both the Palestinian churches and in every *diaspora* church where there were numerous Jewish Christians from the first. If they had been brought in at a given moment, it is hard to believe that Luke would not have mentioned this.

4. The actual importance of the *presbyteroi* will depend on the amount of charismatic gift present. This would explain why they are not mentioned in Jerusalem until the scattering of the apostles, in Antioch in a matter which depended on revelation, and in Corinth where the charismatics seem to have taken the bit between their teeth.

5. A view is held by many that while every *episkopos* was a *presbyteros*, not every *presbyteros* was an *episkopos*. In other words, *episkopoi* were *presbyteroi* with special administrative duties.

This would go a long way to explain the rapid rise of the monarchical episcopate.

6. Incidentally, Clement of Rome was almost certainly a disciple of Paul's, and when he wrote to Corinth on behalf of the Roman church rebuking them for removing their elders, he had no idea that Corinth was ever elderless at the beginning.)

BIBLIOGRAPHY

BANNERMAN, D. D., *The Scripture Doctrine of the Church* (Edinburgh, 1887).

BRUNNER, E., *The Misunderstanding of the Church* (London, 1952).

CRAIK, H., *New Testament Church Order* (London and Bristol, 1863).

CULLMANN, O., *The Early Church* (London, 1956).

HORT, F. J. A., *The Christian Ecclesia* (London, 1897). (1898 edn. quoted.)

LANG, G. H., *The Churches of God* (London, 1959).

LIGHTFOOT, J. B., Dissertation on 'The Christian Ministry' in *Philippians* (London, 1868). (1908 edn. quoted.)

MORRIS, L., *Ministers of God* (London, 1964).

NEWBIGIN, L., *The Household of God* (London, 1953).

SCHLATTER, A., *The Church in the New Testament Period* (1926, Eng. trans., London, 1955).

SCHMIDT, K. L., *The Church* (1938, Eng. trans., London, 1950).

SCHWEIZER, E., *Church Order in the New Testament* (1959, Eng. trans., London, 1961).

STIBBS, A. M., *The Church Universal and Local* (London, 1948).

STREETER, B. H., *The Primitive Church* (London, 1929).

General:

BRUCE, F. F., *The Spreading Flame* (London, 1958).

LATOURETTE, K. S., *A History of Christianity* (London, 1954).

LIGHTFOOT, J. B., ed., *The Apostolic Fathers* (London, 1891).

E

THE LETTERS OF PAUL

G. C. D. HOWLEY

PAUL THE MAN

A passage in a second-century document, *The Acts of Paul and Thecla*, is fascinating in that it is the origin of the only tradition we possess concerning the physical appearance of the apostle Paul. It reads: '. . . And he saw Paul coming, a man little of stature, thin-haired upon the head, crooked in the legs, of good state of body, with eyebrows joining, and nose somewhat hooked, full of grace: for sometimes he appeared like a man, and sometimes he had the face of an angel'.[1] It is impossible to judge the accuracy of this description—it may be a legend —nor does it really matter. Whatever the likeness of Paul may have been, the New Testament is stamped with evidences of his personality and work. His likeness is there in a more important sense. 'Apart from Jesus Christ, St. Paul is the greatest figure in the history of Christianity', said A. H. McNeile;[2] to which we may add a further comment by the same writer: 'The Christianity of today is broadly speaking the Christianity of St. Paul'.[3] This conclusion is undoubtedly correct, for it was the ministry of Paul, under God, that made Christianity of universal importance.

What was it that brought about this vital change, as compared with the limited outlook that marked the Jerusalem apostles at the first? To answer this we must consider something of the life, history and development of the person whose first mention in the New Testament is, 'A young man named Saul' (Ac. 7: 58). Saul was a native of Tarsus, one of the three university cities of that age (the others were Alexandria and Athens). A Jew by birth, and proud of his pure-blooded Jewish ancestry, he was possibly educated in Tarsus in early years, though Ac. 22: 3 suggests that he might have been sent to Jerusalem for education when quite young. He would have an understanding of his background in the Hellenistic environment of Tarsus, realizing what it had imparted to him; but his Jewish heritage was the paramount element in shaping his outlook. He was born to Roman citizenship, a fact of which he was justly proud; and this gave him certain privileges in life from the first, as well as influencing his attitudes in certain situations, as

some events in his life make clear. Paul was, as has been said, a citizen of the world of that time, blending elements in his person of Hebrew, Greek and Roman life. He was the right kind of person for the immense task God planned for him, and we can therefore understand the import of the words spoken by the Lord to Ananias: 'he is a chosen instrument of mine to carry my name before the Gentiles and kings and the sons of Israel' (Ac. 9: 15).

The name Paul is used for the first time in Ac. 13: 9 ('Saul, who is also called Paul'), and from that time his Jewish name gave place to his Roman *cognomen* Paul, the environment of his service being largely in the Roman world. The subsequent history of his ministry makes clear how fully he accomplished the divine plan for his life. W. M. Ramsay used to speak of 'the charm of Paul', and this charm must have shown itself from his youth. Our first glimpse of him is as a young man, and yet one already prominent and trusted in Jewish circles in Jerusalem. His assignment to root out the disciples, 'by authority from the chief priests' (Ac. 26: 10) gives evidence of the extent to which the religious leaders reposed trust in him. He was without doubt regarded as one of the coming men, a certain leader for Judaism within the next few years. Yet all this was to fail of realization. God had something far greater in store for Paul.

Saul's encounter with the risen Christ on the road to Damascus was the crisis that completely altered the course of his life. The angry young man had systematically persecuted the believers in Jerusalem and Judea, and he was on his way to carry on the same savage work in Damascus when 'a light from heaven flashed about him'. This light was that of the glory of Christ Himself, and it was destined to penetrate to the very depths of Saul's personality, leaving him a new man. He saw the Lord, he heard Christ's voice, and from the moment of his question, 'Who are you, Lord?' and the receiving of the answer, 'I am Jesus, . . .', his whole outlook was changed. From that time, the one presiding element in his life was the love of Christ. It was this that controlled him henceforth. His whole life developed from this fresh centre, the reality of the risen Lord Jesus Christ. Describing his conversion years afterwards he spoke of God's outworking purpose: '. . . when he who had set me apart before I was born, and had called me through his grace, was pleased to reveal his Son to me . . .' (Gal. 1: 15). The divine intervention and the revealing of Christ to Saul was to prove a crucial moment in the early days of Christianity.

From the first the new disciple began to serve the Lord, preaching and witnessing boldly amongst those who looked with wonder at this erstwhile proud Pharisee. His early witnessing was to grow into a full-blooded, reasoned declaration of the faith, a mingling of proclamation of the truth coupled with clear and brilliant teaching of all that Christianity meant for mankind. It has been said that Paul spent the rest of his life interpreting to others the significance of his pivotal experience on the Damascus road; and there is truth in this statement. Christ's appearance to him was to mean that he would spend his life expounding the deeper meanings of the resurrection, not just as a fact of history but even more as an essential element in understanding the meaning of the Christian life. Paul's personal relationship with Jesus Christ was the one thing that mattered henceforth. As he said in later years: 'to me to live is Christ' (Phil. 1: 21). This demonstrated itself in many ways, one of which was his description of himself as a 'servant' (*doulos*, slave) of Jesus Christ (Rom. 1: 1; Phil. 1: 1, etc.). He who had been so self-confident now rejoiced in being the willing subject, the slave, of Christ. Life was now to be worked out in terms of obedience to his heavenly Master. Paul's period of retreat in Arabia (not defined as to its length) will have given him time to adjust his mind to his new life; and the longer time spent later in Tarsus must have given him the preparation he needed for his great life work.

THE LETTERS

Letter-writing was common in the Apostolic Age. There is little need for us to explore this realm here; and readers should refer to the article on 'Archaeology and the New Testament'. The question, 'Epistles or Letters?' has intrigued scholars during the past century. Perhaps it would be true to say that some of Paul's letters fall into the category of letters, pure and simple, while others are more in the style of 'epistles', pastoral or encyclical letters intended for wide circulation. To take extremes, Philemon falls into the former class, Romans perhaps into the latter. Of Paul and the other New Testament letter writers Stephen Neill wrote: 'They do not write exactly as Plato or Demosthenes wrote; but they knew what they wanted to say, and went straight to their object with that directness and economy of words which is the indispensable condition of great writing. There is an immense difference between the vigour and general correctness of the New Testament writers, and the halting, broken jargon of so many writers of the papyri'.[4]

There are thirteen letters in the New Testament that bear Paul's signature. They could be viewed as merely a bundle of old letters; but old letters age in more ways than appearance. They cease to be relevant; their writers and their original readers are past and gone. The messages they carried no longer apply. How different is the case, however, when we begin to examine this bundle of letters! Without particularizing for the moment, they scintillate with life; they speak to the heart; they penetrate to the conscience; they possess an ageless quality that makes them always up-to-date. Even now that the immediate circumstances that brought them into being have become ancient history, the abiding principles of their teaching give them importance. It has been well said: 'We should not find in these letters such a living reflection of their writer if they were not, in the main, real letters, sent to definite persons under actual circumstances, evoked by particular needs, and representing, as a true letter always does, what the writer would have wished to say by word of mouth, if absence had not prevented him from doing so (II Cor. x, 11)'.[5] Indeed, the reflection of the personality and essential experience of the author provided by the letters gives us all that we need of insight into the heart of this great man of God. A famous missionary of two generations ago, Dan Crawford, used to speak of 'the Pauline gleam'. We can discern that gleam throughout this collection of letters.

The arrangement of the letters of Paul in the New Testament is in general that of their length. When we rearrange them into their chronological order, fitting them as far as possible into their life-setting within the record of the Acts of the Apostles, they begin to yield up more of their treasures; they become self-explanatory, to a greater extent than when this background is ignored. The letters can be divided into four groups, and this is perhaps the more usual way of considering them. The criteria for this are their subject-matter and style. If we accept this division, we would arrange them in this fashion:

Eschatological. 1 and 2 Thessalonians.
Evangelical. 1 and 2 Corinthians, Galatians, Romans.
Captivity. Ephesians, Colossians, Philemon, Philippians.

Pastoral. 1 Timothy, Titus, 2 Timothy.

(G. G. Findlay, in discussing Paul's earlier letters, made this comment; 'The Thessalonian letters contain very little that bears directly on what we are accustomed to call *the doctrines of salvation* . . . In the second group of St. Paul's writings, . . . the case is entirely altered. Here the cross meets us at every turn . . . . Christ's atonement forms their central and dominant theme, as His second advent that of the epistles to the Thessalonians. For this reason we entitle them collectively *the evangelical epistles* . . .'. *The Epistles of Paul the Apostle*, pp. 54 f.)

A difficulty arises, however, if we place Galatians as the first of Paul's extant letters; for plainly it is related much more closely to Romans than to the Thessalonian letters. We shall probably find a clearer and easier approach to the letters if we regard them as dividing into three rather than four groups. Viewed stylistically they undoubtedly fall into four groups, but this grouping loses something of its strength immediately Galatians is removed from its traditional place. If we take the letters, then, as three groups, and place the first six letters in one group, they may be described in the words of F. B. Clogg, 'the Epistles of Paul the Traveller',[6] or with A. D. Nock, 'the letters written on journeys'—'The Travel Letters'.[7]

The Travel Letters. These letters are essentially missionary letters, filled with the spirit of love and understanding towards those recently converted to the Christian faith, and marked by strong concern where they seem to be in any danger, either through conduct unworthy of disciples of Christ, or teaching calculated to turn them aside from the purity of the apostolic faith. Paul's letters normally open with thanksgiving and prayer for his readers, and his feeling of affection and regard for them is plainly seen in his constancy of spirit in prayerful remembrance of them. It was indeed from this deep desire for their welfare that his letters sprang.

It is fascinating to observe the differences of place, people and experience that are reflected in these missionary letters, as also the variation in the mood of the writer from time to time. We note the fickle Galatians, the sturdy loyalty of the Macedonians, the pride of the Corinthians; and see Paul's anxiety, indignation or satisfaction as he faced and sought to meet their varying needs. Much has been written about Paul's style, and it may be well to bear in mind that a man's style may differ as he encounters different circumstances. In ordinary modern life we would expect this, why not, therefore, in the writings of the Apostolic Age? Paul can be persuasive,

controversial, logical, contemplative, ecstatic, as the mood or the need takes him. His use of the thought-forms of his age, that were familiar to his readers, made his letters *real*, they 'rang a bell' in the minds of his readers. Here was nobody who beat the air: he had a purpose in writing, objectives to attain, and he used every means within his not inconsiderable powers of literary ability to bring his readers to a right frame of mind, so that they would submit to the teaching given them and accept his apostolic direction. Paul was a preacher of the great truths of Christianity. He did not—like some moderns—occupy his time with secondary matters except as they impinged upon the vital matters being expounded. If we survey the main themes dealt with in this group of travel letters, these are typical of his teaching: the Cross in Christian experience (Galatians), conversion and the Christian hope (Thessalonians), the common life of the body of Christ (1 Corinthians), the apostolic ministry (2 Corinthians), the gospel of God (Romans). Our author is never lost for words, but his words are always profitable. His exposition of the scope of the gospel lifts his Roman letter to the heights; while we discern his deep feelings of love and concern for the Galatian, Thessalonian and Corinthian Christians, even though at times he has to chide some of them sharply. Further, the apostle never fails to make clear all that is involved in Christian discipleship. His plain-spoken words to the Thessalonians, and the Corinthians, give evidence of his original preaching of the gospel among them as always being shot through with explanation of what it would mean to become a Christian in the society of that age.

The Captivity Letters. Luke is an exact writer; he is also at times a tantalizing one! Never do his readers feel more frustrated than when he rings down the curtain with Paul's arrival in Rome, followed by his two-year sojourn there 'at his own expense' (Ac. 28: 30). What happened after the termination of this period? All kinds of questions arise in our minds when we reach that point in our reading. We assume in this article that the answer lies in what is revealed in the 'Prison Letters'. Space hardly permits an investigation of the place of origin of the four letters usually set at this point of time, but we assume just now that they emanated from Paul's Roman captivity. The ultimate spiritual value of the letters of the captivity does not depend upon their place of origin; they are like an overflowing well of light and truth, leading ever closer to what Paul calls 'the fulness of Christ'.

Some may discern certain differences of style or emphasis in this group of letters, as compared with those of Paul's active missionary journeys. This could be exaggerated, but it is true that with his altered situation, Paul applied himself to using his captivity for the furtherance of the cause of Christ. And this he did most successfully. A century ago J. B. Lightfoot believed that Philippians was written first, of the four captivity letters, with Ephesians, Colossians and Philemon being written later. Nowadays many scholars believe that the group of three, Ephesians, Colossians and Philemon preceded Philippians, which, they think, was written towards the end of the two years in Rome. There are many scholars today who do not believe that Philippians was written in Rome. This is referred to briefly in the Introduction to the commentary on the letter. If there are grounds for regarding Paul as a mystic, they are based upon these letters. Though a prisoner, he displays a profound penetration into the deep things of God. Not for nothing does the writer speak of his ministry to make known the 'unsearchable riches of Christ' (Eph. 3: 8). If anything, Paul knows his Master better and expounds Him more richly in this period of his life. There are other developments too: for not only does he bring us a rich teaching about Christ, but this is closely related to the new life of Christians, life 'in Christ'.

Albert Schweitzer has an interesting passage concerning Paul's mystical doctrine of Christ: 'Of what precise kind then is the mysticism of Paul? It occupies a unique position between primitive and intellectual mysticism. The religious conceptions of the Apostle stand high above those of primitive mysticism. This being so, it might have been expected that his mysticism would have to do with the unity of man with God as the ultimate ground of being. But this is not the case. Paul never speaks of being one with God or being in God. He does indeed assert the divine sonship of believers. But, strangely enough, he does not conceive of sonship to God as an immediate mystical relation to God, but as mediated and effected by means of the mystical union with Christ . . . . In Paul there is no God-mysticism; only a Christ-mysticism by means of which man comes into relation to God . . . . This "being-in-Christ" is the prime enigma of the Pauline teaching: once grasped it gives the clue to the whole'. (Schweitzer added elsewhere that while this was true of Paul, he was the only Christian thinker who knew only Christ-mysticism, unaccompanied by God-mysticism: 'In the Johannine theology both appear alongside of one another and intermingled with each other'.)[8]

In these letters, not only is Christ viewed as risen and glorified; the Christian shares in His resurrection and triumph. He is 'in Christ'. A. M. Hunter expresses it thus: 'When a man was baptized "into Christ", he passed into His possession, became "in him". Whatever else it means, "in Christ" must mean "in communion with Christ". This experience was basic to Paul's Christianity, as it still is to any Christianity worthy of the name . . . . The Christian, we may say, lives in a Christ atmosphere . . . . Yet this, while true, is but half the truth . . . . We have to say then that the phrase means not only "in communion with Christ" but also "in the community of Christ". It implies membership in the Church, which is Christ's Body'.[9] Deissmann regards the phrase as describing 'the most intimate fellowship imaginable of the Christian with the living spiritual Christ'.[10] To refer to yet another witness, W. D. Davies says: 'The formula which Paul most frequently used to describe the nature of the Christian man was that he was "in Christ". We have already seen that by this Paul meant that the individual who accepted Christ was part of a new humanity of which He was the head; that he was being ingathered into the true Israel of God. It agrees with this that there are passages where to be "in Christ" is clearly to be in the Church. In short *en Christō* is a social concept, to be *en Christō* is to have discovered the true community'.[11]

If the earlier letters reveal Paul as the ardent pioneer missionary, the captivity group show us not only the theologian but the pastor-teacher at work, or, as F. W. Beare sums up this important aspect of his work, 'his work as Spiritual Director'.[12] We find Paul at work in this way throughout his life, and through all his letters; this ministry cannot be confined to any one group of letters. Yet the depth of his teaching at this time, when seen in combination with his down-to-earth application of truth, brings us face to face with a great master in pastoral care. Here is no ponderous autocrat at work, trying to pressure people into certain avenues of thought or life; neither, on the other hand, do we find any suggestion of practical talk without sufficient substance behind it to strengthen his words. There is, as always, a remarkable balance in the messages Paul delivers to churches or to individuals. If we link the captivity letters with Luke's reference to this period in Ac. 28: 30 f., they give us Paul's own explanation of how he set about 'preaching the kingdom of God and teaching about the Lord Jesus Christ'—and what fruitful service it was!

The Pastoral Letters. In this final group of letters traditionally attributed to Paul, we meet the veteran, serving in conjunction with his younger but trusted colleagues Timothy and Titus. It is evident that, as Paul drew near to the close of his ministry, he was concerned to provide for a continuance of the apostolic teaching through men who would share in such a succession. Timothy and Titus were in that succession; but it would not end with them. It was to continue into the next generation, as he made clear by his instructions to Timothy: '. . . and what you have heard from me before many witnesses entrust to faithful men who will be able to teach others also' (2 Tim. 2: 2). The two men were very different types of persons: Titus appears to have been strong, able to cope with complex situations; Timothy was more diffident, perhaps holding back at times from the full thrust of his ministry. Something of this order seems hinted at by the way in which Paul seeks to encourage him in his service (cf. 1 Tim. 4: 14; 2 Tim. 1: 6).

It is not easy to fit the Pastoral letters into the framework of Luke's narrative in the Acts. The view that has held the field until comparatively recent years is that after the two years in Rome, Paul was released, and travelled for some time, seeking—ever watchful as he was—to strengthen and consolidate the churches against the time to come. He himself was well aware that his period of service was limited, and his concern was for the churches, that they should hold their own, and make advance, after his departure. Further, his affection for his co-workers made him desirous of strengthening their hands, so that later, without his support, they would continue the work of the earlier years, and Christianity would continue to expand. The present writer regards these letters as the proper climax of Paul's life. Here, it is true, Paul does not engage in a rich instruction in truth as in the letters of his captivity. But what matters that? His task is different; and while the letters may not contain long passages of teaching, they are filled with allusions to the doctrine that had characterized his ministry over the years. Allusions they may be, but nonetheless significant.

A further consideration is that the tasks before Timothy and Titus were of an administrative nature, so of necessity, Paul has much to say of detailed instruction, even if at times it seems pedestrian in character. Dealing with simple, everyday matters can be pedestrian in modern church life, yet it has to be done, so that provision is made for the many diverse needs of the persons concerned. With reference to the affirmation of some scholars that the letters contain a 'lowered theology, shorn of the watchwords of the apostle's previous teaching', E. K. Simpson refutes this by replying: 'These

criticisms are altogether wide of the mark. For doctrinal edification lies outside the immediate scope of the Pastorals; they comprise executive counsels blended with the ethical. Moreover, no chasm yawns between Christian doctrine and Christian practice'.[13]

The second letter to Timothy is an affectionate call to fidelity, as the apostle sees that his end is near. The tenderness of the bond between the two men is evidenced throughout the letter, and Paul's references to his own earlier service is intended to encourage the younger man. If the two earlier letters of this group were written during Paul's period of freedom, this was composed during his last imprisonment, when his status and condition were very different from the time of his honourable confinement in a hired apartment. Now he is 'suffering and wearing fetters, like a criminal' (2 Tim. 2: 9). His exact whereabouts had to be ascertained by Onesiphorus—'he searched for me eagerly and found me'—his mind is now set on his departure; he is ready; his work is done. And so Paul writes the finale to his life-story.

Chronological Outline

The following chronological outline may be accepted as a working arrangement (even for those letters whose location in the course of Paul's ministry is reasonably certain there is a margin of doubt of a year or two on either side of the dates suggested).

THE TRAVEL LETTERS

Galatians	Written from Antioch in Syria, A.D. 48.
1 Thessalonians	Written from Corinth, A.D. 50.
2 Thessalonians	Written from Corinth, A.D. 50.
1 Corinthians	Written from Ephesus, A.D. 54-55.
2 Corinthians	Written from Macedonia, A.D. 55-56.
Romans	Written from Corinth, early A.D. 57.

THE CAPTIVITY LETTERS

Colossians	Written from Rome, A.D. 60-61.
Ephesians	Written from Rome, A.D. 60-61.
Philemon	Written from Rome, A.D. 60-61.
Philippians	Written from Rome, A.D. 61-62.

THE PASTORAL LETTERS

Titus	Written from Ephesus, after A.D. 62.
1 Timothy	Written from Macedonia, after A.D. 62.
2 Timothy	Written from Rome, A.D. 64-65.

PROBLEMS

We are well aware that the foregoing survey of the thirteen letters traditionally attributed to Paul has been anything but complete. Its very brevity has demanded that many matters of interest and importance have had to be omitted from our consideration. Certain problems, however, have been deliberately ignored, so that they could be looked at separately at this point.

Galatians. Two matters that have engaged the attention of scholars with regard to this letter are the identity of its recipients, and the time when it was written. The two problems are closely related. Earlier scholarship believed that Paul wrote to churches in North Galatia, and that this region is referred to in Ac. 16: 6 and 18: 23. The travel and researches of Sir William Ramsay convinced him that Paul wrote to the churches founded during his first missionary journey, i.e., Pisidian Antioch, Iconium, Lystra, and Derbe, cities which were all within the Roman province of Galatia. Ramsay further affirmed that the references in Acts should read 'the Phrygio-Galatic region' (16: 6), the part of Phrygia that was in the province of Galatia; and 'the Galatic region and Phrygia' (18: 23), where 'the Galatic region' is Lycaonia Galatica.[14] There is no record in Acts of any missionary activity in the north of the province. The matter is fully discussed by Guthrie,[15] while an objective account is also given by R. A. Cole.[16] Suffice it to say that this volume contains both viewpoints, the writer on Acts accepting the northern theory, while the commentary on Galatians regards the southern theory as the correct one.

If the letter was addressed to the churches of Paul's first journey, it follows that it might well have been written shortly after the conclusion of that journey. It could have been produced at a time between the return of the travellers to Antioch in Syria, and the Council of Jerusalem, that is, during the interval in time between Ac. 14: 28 and 15: 1. There are reasons for believing this may have been the case. Cole says: 'If we follow the Southern theory concerning its destination, then we could place the Epistle very early indeed'.[17] The conclusion that we may legitimately reach, but suggest without dogmacy, is that this is the first of the extant letters of Paul, written not long before the Jerusalem conference, in A.D. 48 or 49.

2 Corinthians. Was this letter written as we find it now in our Bibles, or is it composite, being actually made up of three letters or fragments of letters? An article by R. V. G. Tasker in the *Expository Times* for November 1935 entitled 'The Unity of 2 Corinthians'

defended the unity of the letter. During the intervening years we have not found any sufficient reason for moving from that position. Tasker developed this theme in his Introduction to his commentary on the letter.[18] Allan Menzies in his excellent commentary on the letter also defends its integrity, and in the course of a thorough discussion of the matter says, 'If we take the Epistle as it lies before us, we find it not unintelligible'.[19] A powerful supporter of the unity of the letter is found in the Danish scholar Johannes Munck, who roundly affirms, with reference to the 'fragmentary' theory that 'this assumption will not hold water'.[20] Munck provides a learned and lengthy chapter on the subject (chapter 6) to which interested readers may refer. The matter is also dealt with in the Introduction to the commentary in this volume, so that we may leave further discussion at this point. We do not pretend to have done justice to both sides of the argument, but for ourselves accept the unity of the letter, believing that it makes sense as it stands. (For further study, see Guthrie, *op. cit.*)

The whole subject of the Corinthian correspondence is both fascinating and complex. There were a number of letters that passed between Paul and the church in Corinth, and the two letters preserved in the New Testament are but a part of all that was written. It should be said, however, that we believe that what was preserved was all that was essential for the Christian Church, and that any lost letters were allowed to go into oblivion because they contained nothing that was not already found in other apostolic letters, nothing therefore that added anything to the content of the Christian faith. One letter preceded 1 Corinthians (cf. 5: 9); then, after a letter (and possibly a delegation) being received by Paul from Corinth (cf. 7: 1), came 1 Corinthians. Paul seems to have paid a visit to Corinth some time after this was written (cf. 2 C. 1: 23—2: 1; see also 12: 14; 13: 1). It was of a painful character, and was followed later by a severe letter (cf. 2 C. 2: 4). When Titus came to him with encouraging news from Corinth, Paul wrote 2 Corinthians. This brief summary oversimplifies a situation that was at the time not at all simple, but it may be regarded as a short sketch, however inadequate, of the events associated with our two letters to Corinth.

The Pastoral Letters. The Introduction to the commentary includes a survey of some aspects of the problem of the authorship of these letters. We do not propose, therefore, to go over the ground, except on a few matters. Firstly, we discount theories that suggest that any writer used Paul's name falsely, even to spread the teachings of the apostle more widely. There is a reference to a hoped-for visit Paul wanted to make to Timothy in Ephesus (1 Tim. 3: 14; 4: 13). And 2 Timothy includes a request for Timothy to come to Paul in Rome. What possible point would such references have were the letters written long years after the death of Paul? We concur with the judgment of C. F. D. Moule when he says: 'Some may say that this is an obvious device to lend verisimilitude, and I know that judgments of this sort are difficult to assess objectively. I can only say that to me it seems a piece of gratuitous irony and in bad taste'.[21] In his Manson Memorial Lecture here quoted, Professor Moule put forward a new theory towards a solution of the problem of the Pastorals. The lecture, delivered in Manchester in November 1964, offered the suggestion that these letters were written, in fact, in the lifetime of Paul and with his express sanction. 'My suggestion is, then, that Luke wrote all three Pastoral epistles. But he wrote them during Paul's lifetime, at Paul's behest, and, in part (but only in part), at Paul's dictation.'[22] He accepts the view that Paul was released at the end of his two years in Rome. Following some comments about the general situation thus envisaged, he adds: 'This means a thoroughgoing reinstatement of the old-fashioned theory of a journey to Crete and perhaps to Spain and all the rest of it. But why not? Objections are fashionable, but not, I think, cogent'.[23] The interest in such a theory is that it associates the letter firmly with Paul's life and affairs, and accepts it as genuinely Pauline in character. For ourselves, we accept the Pauline authorship of the letters. The problems touched upon in this section are merely a few of those that have a continuing interest for New Testament scholars. We hope that it may be enough to stimulate fresh enquiry and to establish faith.

DISTINCTIVE ELEMENTS IN PAUL'S THEOLOGY

There is a notable phrase in Philippians where Paul expresses one object in Christian witness as being 'the defence and confirmation of the gospel' (1: 7). It can be said that his letters all had this objective, whatever their immediate cause. The truths the apostle proclaimed were held close to his heart, and his constant desire was to further their acceptance among men. As we survey his letters, certain elements of truth stand out as being prominent in his thinking. Paul was a man of affairs, able to grasp and sum up varying situations. He observed the needs of men, in relation to mankind as a whole, and in relation to God.

He believed that his gospel provided the solution to world problems of the day. There was separation between God and man—but his message of justification met this need. He saw all around him the evidence that peace between man and man was non-existent—his doctrine of the Body of Christ met this lack. At every point Paul's teaching was related to life—life as it then was, but so wisely presented was his teaching that it relates immediately to life in any or every generation. Such considerations will save us from ever regarding Pauline theology as merely academic. With this in mind, we may turn our attention to some of the salient features of his doctrine.

Justification. Paul was brought up to understand the gravity of sin, and its universal character. The revelation of God in the Old Testament would impress upon him the reality of the wrath and the judgment of God. The age-old problem of how men could be just with God found its solution in his own reconciliation to God through Christ. He realized the guilt of man, including his own people the Jews. But he had met with Christ, and his outlook was changed. 'He had to urge that their painful efforts to win merit in God's sight were rendered needless by the wondrous exhibition of the very meaning of God in the cross of His Son. So that his central doctrine of Justification by faith is not a scholastic abstraction, formulated to round off an artificial theory.'[24] The answer to man's plight was found in the divine provision in Christ. His atoning work provided the means whereby the sin of man could be forgiven—a note that stood to the front of all Paul's preaching. Further, this message was in sharp contrast to the mould of thought that shaped the minds of multitudes of Jews under the old covenant. 'For God has done what the law, weakened by the flesh, could not do: sending his own Son in the likeness of sinful flesh and for sin, he condemned sin in the flesh . . .' (Rom. 8: 3). This teaching was not original to Paul. 'Jesus himself taught a doctrine of justification of sinners by the outgoing righteousness of God . . . . It is implicit in his conception of himself as the instrument of God's salvation for penitent sinners: "I came not to call the righteous, but sinners" . . .'.[25]

As to the faith that marks the justified, this is beautifully described by C. K. Barrett: 'The hearing of faith (which is certainly not an attitude that man is able of himself freely to adopt, but is a gift from God, made possible in the Holy Spirit) is itself a reversal of the rebellious dissatisfaction of Adam, who was not content to accept the place God assigned him, but set out to secure a better place for himself . . . . It is not that faith is in Pauline or any other proper usage a shibboleth, or an "Open Sesame" which operates as a magic formula. It is not even that faith is an indispensable agent or instrument which by itself effects justification or salvation. It is simply that faith is a description (from the human side) of the relationship with God for which God created man, in which man lets God truly be God, and lets himself truly be man, that is, the obedient creature of the loving God'.[26]

The Body of Christ. Paul used several images to express the truth of the Church, the community of Christians. His conception of the Church as the Body of Christ gave a touch of life and reality to this doctrine. There is a noticeable development in the apostle's teaching on this subject. 'In 1 Cor. the head, so far from being superior to the other members, is not distinguished from them: it is merely one organ among many'[27]—whereas in the captivity letters Christ is named as 'the head of the body, the church' (Col. 1: 18). There is no conflict between these two conceptions; the difference lies in the language, the essential truth conveyed by the metaphor of the Body of Christ is communicated in both cases. From the first days of Christianity the oneness among believers created by the Holy Spirit showed itself in many ways. The early chapters of Acts stress this as a joyful reality in the church in Jerusalem (Ac. 2: 44, etc.). What was true all the time from Pentecost onward found a distinctive interpretation in the Pauline doctrine of Christ's Body. They were indeed one, sharing a common life, making their contribution to the community, exercising their spiritual gifts for the edification of others, and in a thousand ways manifesting the bond that united them in Christ. In the face of all the separating factors in first-century society, Paul affirms that Christ had 'broken down the dividing wall of hostility' (Eph. 2: 14), bringing men together who once had been apart, even at enmity.

The Holy Spirit. In pre-Pauline Christianity the outpouring of the Holy Spirit at Pentecost was recognized as the sign of the Age of Fulfilment. It is the teaching of Paul, however, that gives colour to the whole outlook of the New Testament on the Spirit of God. In his witness to the truth of the gospel certain distinctive insights concerning the Holy Spirit characterized his doctrine. He taught that it is by the Spirit the ministry of the risen Christ is communicated to believers, in particular because it is through the Holy Spirit that Christians are incorporated into the Body of Christ. He revealed the way in which our present experience is linked up with the life that is to be, because the Holy Spirit is the earnest, the guarantee of glory yet to come. His frequent need to guide the converts along avenues proper to discipleship took him again and again to the basic fact that by the Spirit's indwelling and abiding presence with them, the believers possessed a resource whereby they could live for the glory of God and produce spiritual fruit in Christian character.

The Person of Christ. In three passages (Rom. 5: 12-21; 1 C. 15: 20-23, 45-50) Paul draws certain parallels and contrasts between Adam and Christ, 'the last Adam'. He shows the baneful effects of the one act of disobedience of Adam, contrasting it with the beneficial effects of the one act of obedience of Christ, in His obedience unto death. Man's relationship with Adam condemns him to death; but the link the renewed man has with Christ gives him the promise of life eternal. As now men bear the stamp of Adam, so Christians will ultimately 'bear the image of the man of heaven' (1 C. 15: 49). In Christ, the last Adam, man is recovered from the effects of the Fall, and given the pledge of his final entry into the presence of God. And what is the pledge? It is that Jesus Christ is risen, and we shall rise again in Him. Yet another phase of Paul's doctrine of Christ is his teaching concerning Christ and the universe. The cosmic significance of Jesus Christ means that, while Christians may rejoice in a personal knowledge and experience of Him, His influence stretches far beyond any one individual life, beyond His place in the whole Church: it is universal in its scope. In reply to the false teachers who gave Christ a lesser place than God, Paul revealed His place in the universe, declaring that, in view of the place of the Son in relation to the Father, His creative activity and the fact that 'in him all things hold together', His glory is established beyond all argument; as Paul sums up, 'that in everything he might be pre-eminent' (Col. 1: 18 f.). In refuting the error that unsettled the Colossian Christians, Paul expounded the nature of Christ, 'to show that he completely overshadows all the angelic powers that could be imagined, and that they can have nothing to offer men which is not already secured to them in Christ'.[28] It is plain that Paul envisaged a conflict continuing in the invisible, planetary world. There were 'principalities, . . . powers, spiritual hosts of wickedness in the heavenly places' (Eph. 6: 12) engaging in a ceaseless warfare against God and His hosts. Christ is superior to them all, Paul affirms; further, He has defeated them by His Cross. His cosmic rôle is brought into the open; His supremacy is

E*

established beyond all cavil. From this flows the teaching that calls upon Christ's people to show by their behaviour the new life in Christ they enjoy.

Bound up with the fact of Christ's assured triumph is the promise of a full deliverance for the whole creation—to be reconciled to God by the Cross—and its freedom from its age-old 'groaning in travail'. The existing world order is to give place to a new order, from which the marks of sin will be eliminated. 'The final Judgement—"the day of wrath and revelation of the righteous judgement of God"—remains still in the future; the concluding act of the great world-drama has yet to take place; and there are "enemies" still to be subdued . . .'.29 The apostle declares that in the final summing-up of all things, evil will be judged and Christ's glory will be manifested. The Christian will figure with his Lord in the great events of the end-time: 'When Christ who is our life appears, then you also will appear with him in glory' (Col. 3: 4). The hope of resurrection for the believer in Christ is no vague, uncertain thing, but already pledged to him in the fact of Christ's resurrection from the dead. The ultimate for all who belong to Christ is the fulfilment of God's purpose, the realization of their destiny, for they have been 'predestined to be conformed to the image of his Son' (Rom. 8: 29). Attaining to perfect likeness to Christ is the glorious hope of the believer in Him.

Some General Observations. We have noted some of the settled ideas that characterize the ministry of Paul, and the fact that in some realms of thought a development is traceable. We have seen also how doctrine and experience are so intertwined that Paul is never like a person evolving theories that have no relation to life and everyday affairs. His balanced thought is everywhere in evidence. Many years ago an important contribution to the study of the apostle Paul was written by C. A. Anderson Scott, *Christianity According to St. Paul*. In this book he stated: 'St. Paul's conception of Christianity can best be studied under the aspect of Salvation'.30 The term 'Salvation' was considered to be 'the most comprehensive term for what the Apostle found in Christ'.31 Salvation or deliverance is found in one form or another in most religions. But how it is attained or experienced is often an uncertain thing, lost in obscure doctrines. Christianity, on the other hand, came into the open with its offer of forgiveness in Christ. Paul was recognized as its leading exponent in his day, teaching the reality of salvation in Christ. He viewed it as a fact of the past, as a progressive experience, with its consummation in the future.

Scott's book was first published in 1927. In 1954 A. M. Hunter published *Interpreting Paul's Gospel*, and in its Preface said: 'To unlock the wards of Paul's theology, I have unashamedly borrowed the key (the word "salvation") which Anderson Scott, a quarter of a century ago, so successfully employed in his *Christianity According to St. Paul*, in many ways still the best book on Paul's theology we have'.32 The weight thus laid upon the term salvation is surely right. The concept of salvation, deliverance, lights up the whole of Scripture, linking Old and New Testaments as the developing 'Salvation-Story', and finding its full interpretation in Christ. The great apostle was the privileged 'chosen instrument' of God to make it known universally.

PAUL'S PERMANENT INFLUENCE

There is no doubt about the remarkable originality of the mind of Paul. Ronald Knox well said: 'And St. Paul's was no ordinary mind; sensitive, yet fearless, logical, yet poetic, infinitely tender with the scruples of others, yet unflinching in its honesty. A delicate instrument, it will interpret the melody of Christian thought in its own way. We must listen patiently, allowing him his own choice of language, not trying to fix on his words a meaning which has since become technical, not allowing our minds to be disturbed by the echoes of later controversies. You must come to St. Paul with fresh eyes if you are to feel his magic.'33 In giving thought to the abiding influence of Paul upon Christianity, we may first bear in mind that, despite his great originality, his debt to his predecessors was a real one. The Christian message did not originate in Paul; he shared it in common with the rest of the apostles. He drew upon some words of the Lord to enforce his teaching at various points (*e.g.* Ac. 20: 35; 1 C. 7: 10; 9: 14; 11: 23; 1 Tim. 5: 18). He used the Old Testament as pointing to the truth of the apostolic gospel (Rom. 1: 2; 1 C. 15: 3, etc.). 'The apostle's conception of Christ obviously owed much to the Christology of those who preceded him as Christians, as did also his doctrine of the Spirit.'34

In his own day he was a bulwark for the truth of God. Even another apostle has to be corrected if the vital principles of the gospel are at stake (Gal. 2: 11). While gladly admitting Paul's debt to others, as we have done above, we must not fall into the mistake of 'cutting him down to size', of losing the greatness of the man. This is exactly what H. J. Schoeps thinks happened in the early Church. Paul's letters, though devoutly read, 'seldom found understanding'. 'No other apostle had such a vividly marked theology, a personality of such sharp outline . . . . The church was not in a position to digest such a towering figure.'[35] Today this is no longer the case: Christians of all persuasions and throughout the world have come to see his permanent significance. Throughout the centuries of Church history Paul's teaching has proved formative, at many of the main turning-points in Christian history, and in some of the principal exponents of its truths. Whether we think of Augustine, Luther, Wesley or Karl Barth, Paul's voice has been heard throughout the years. We cannot do better in concluding this study than draw upon some words written a few years ago by Donald Coggan, the present Archbishop of York: 'I would say that whenever there has been a renewed grasp of the truths at the heart of St. Paul's gospel, then there has been a revival of true religion . . . . And if you ask me why I believed that history pointed this lesson so clearly, my reply would be that I believe St. Paul was the greatest exponent of the mind of Christ who ever lived. His language differed very greatly from that of his Master, but his great doctrines were derived from Him. There lay his secret, and there it still lies for you to rediscover, if you will.'[36]

REFERENCES

1 M. R. James, *The Apocryphal New Testament* (Oxford, 1924), p. 273.
2 *St. Paul: His Life, Letters and Christian Doctrine* (Cambridge, 1932), p. ix.
3 *op. cit.*, p. v.
4 *The Interpretation of the New Testament 1861-1961* (Oxford, 1966), p. 150.
5 H. N. Bate, *A Guide to the Epistles of Saint Paul* (London, 1926), p. 5.
6 *An Introduction to the New Testament* (London, 1937), p. ix.
7 *St. Paul* (London, 1938), p. 145.
8 *The Mysticism of Paul the Apostle* (London, 1931), pp. 3, 5.
9 *Interpreting Paul's Gospel* (London, 1954), pp. 37 f.
10 *Paul: A Study in Social and Religious History* (London, 1926), p. 140.
11 *Paul and Rabbinic Judaism* (London, 1962), p. 86.
12 *St. Paul and His Letters* (London, 1962), p. 134.
13 *The Pastoral Epistles* (London, 1954), p. 12.
14 W. M. Ramsay, *St. Paul the Traveller and the Roman Citizen* (London, 1895), p. 104.
15 *New Testament Introduction: the Pauline Epistles* (London, 1961), pp. 72-88.
16 *The Epistle of Paul to the Galatians (TNTC)* (London, 1965), pp. 15-23.
17 *op. cit.*, p. 21.
18 *The Second Epistle of Paul to the Corinthians (TNTC)* (London, 1958), pp. 23-35.
19 *The Second Epistle of the Apostle Paul to the Corinthians* (London, 1912), p. xxxvii.
20 *Paul and the Salvation of Mankind* (London, 1959), p. 170.
21 *The Problem of the Pastoral Epistles: A Reappraisal* (Reprinted from the Bulletin of the John Rylands Library, Vol. 47, No. 2, March 1965), p. 447.

22 *op. cit.*, p. 434.
23 *op. cit.*, p. 451.
24 H. A. A. Kennedy, *The Theology of the Epistles* (London, 1919), p. 63.
25 Alan Richardson, *An Introduction to the Theology of the New Testament* (London, 1958), pp. 81 f.
26 *From First Adam to Last* (London, 1962), p. 103.
27 D. E. H. Whiteley, *The Theology of St. Paul* (Oxford, 1964), pp. 191 f.
28 F. W. Beare, *St. Paul and His Letters* (London, 1962), p. 109.
29 A. E. J. Rawlinson, *The New Testament Doctrine of the Christ* (London, 1926), p. 147.
30 *Christianity According to St. Paul* (Cambridge, 1927), p. 16.
31 *op. cit.*, p. 17.
32 *Interpreting Paul's Gospel* (London, 1954), p. 9.
33 *Saint Paul's Gospel* (London, 1953), p. 9.
34 A. M. Hunter, *Paul and His Predecessors* (London, 1961), p. 150.
35 H. J. Schoeps, *Paul* (London, 1961), p. 273.
36 *Five Makers of the New Testament* (London, 1962), pp. 21 f.

BIBLIOGRAPHY

BARRETT, C. K., *From First Adam to Last* (London, 1962).
BATE, H. N., *A Guide to the Epistles of Saint Paul* (London, 1926).
DAVIES, W. D., *Paul and Rabbinic Judaism* (London, 1962).
DEANE, A. C., *St. Paul and His Letters* (London, 1942).
DEISSMANN, A., *Paul: A Study in Social and Religious History*, E. T. (London, 1912; 2nd edition, 1926).
DODD, C. H., *The Meaning of Paul for Today* (London, 1920; Fontana edition, 1958).
HUNTER, A. M., *Interpreting Paul's Gospel* (London, 1954); revised as *The Gospel According to St. Paul* (London, 1966).
HUNTER, A. M., *Paul and His Predecessors* (London, 1961).
KENNEDY, H. A. A., *The Theology of the Epistles* (London, 1919).
LIGHTFOOT, J. B., *Biblical Essays* (London, 1893).
LIGHTFOOT, J. B., *Dissertations on the Apostolic Age* (London, 1892).
LIGHTFOOT, J. B., *Notes on Epistles of St. Paul* (London, 1895).
McNEILE, A. H., *St. Paul: His Life, Letters and Christian Doctrine* (Cambridge, 1932).
MUNCK, J., *Paul and the Salvation of Mankind*, E. T. (London, 1959).
NOCK, A. D., *St. Paul* (London, 1938).
RAMSAY, W. M., *St. Paul the Traveller and the Roman Citizen*, 14th edn. (London, 1920).
RAMSAY, W. M., *The Teaching of Paul in Terms of the Present Day* (London, 1913).
SCHOEPS, H. J., *Paul: The Theology of the Apostle in the Light of Jewish Religious History*, E. T. (London, 1961).
SCOTT, C. A. A., *Christianity According to St. Paul* (Cambridge, 1927).
SCOTT, C. A. A., *Footnotes to St. Paul* (Cambridge, 1935).
SMITH, DAVID, *The Life and Letters of St. Paul* (London, 1919).
WHITE, ERNEST, *Saint Paul: the Man and His Mind* (London, 1958).
WHITELEY, D. E. H., *The Theology of St. Paul* (Oxford, 1964).

THE GENERAL LETTERS

F. F BRUCE

Their Designation and Canonicity

In the Authorized Version, as earlier in the Geneva Bible of 1560, five letters have the word 'general' included in their titles—'The General Epistle of James', 'The First Epistle General of Peter', 'The Second Epistle General of Peter', 'The First Epistle General of John' and 'The General Epistle of Jude'. This distinctive adjective is translated from Gk. *katholikē* (Lat. *catholica*), whence in the Rheims New Testament of 1582 (following Jerome's Vulgate) two of these letters have the word 'catholic' included in their titles—'The Catholic Epistle of James the Apostle' and 'The Catholic Epistle of Jude the Apostle' (in R. A. Knox's version these are entitled respectively 'The Universal Epistle of the Blessed Apostle James' and 'The Universal Epistle of the Blessed Apostle Jude').

Whether the rendering 'catholic', 'general' or 'universal' be used, its significance in the titles of these letters is plain enough: unlike other letters which are addressed to specific churches or persons, these are addressed to a wider and more indefinite circle ('the twelve tribes in the Dispersion', 'the exiles of the Dispersion' in several Roman provinces, 'those who have obtained a faith of equal standing with ours' or 'those who are called, beloved in God the Father and kept for Jesus Christ'), and one of them (1 Jn) has no formal address whatsoever.

This is not the only meaning, however, which the word has borne in this context. At one time seven 'catholic letters' in all were listed, including 2 and 3 Jn as well as 1 Jn. But if 2 and 3 Jn were called catholic letters, it could not be on account of any indefiniteness in their addresses, for 2 Jn is addressed 'to the elect lady and her children' and 3 Jn 'to the beloved Gaius'. At an early date the word 'catholic' as applied to these letters appears to have been understood not only as 'addressed to the Church Catholic' but also, occasionally at least, as 'acknowledged by the Church Catholic'. Sometimes one of these meanings was uppermost, sometimes the other.

Eusebius (*Hist. Eccl.* ii. 23, 25) mentions that the Letter of James was reckoned 'the first of the letters called catholic. But we should observe [he goes on] that some regard it as spurious, since not many of the ancients have made mention of it; the same is true of the letter called Jude's, which is also one of the seven called catholic. Nevertheless we know that these letters have been used publicly along with the rest in most churches.' Eusebius's personal estimate of the canonicity of certain New Testament books was more conservative than that of the church at large in his day (*c.* A.D. 325). But he seems to connect the epithet 'catholic' as used of these seven letters with their being publicly accepted in most churches.

The first person known to us who used this epithet of any of these letters was one Apollonius, towards the end of the second century. In a treatise against the Montanists he accuses Themison, one of their number, of having 'dared, in imitation of the apostle, to compose a catholic letter for the instruction of those whose faith was better than his own' (Eusebius, *Hist. Eccl.* v. 18. 5). (In imitation of which apostle? Of Peter, perhaps, since 2 Pet. is addressed 'to those who have obtained a faith of equal standing with ours', whereas Themison, according to Apollonius, wrote for those who had obtained a faith of *better* standing than his. If this surmise is sound, this would be our earliest external evidence for 2 Pet.) About the same time (*c.* A.D. 190) the Muratorian list of New Testament books, drawn up at Rome, mentions the Letter of Jude and two of John's as being *in catholica*, meaning presumably that they were accepted in the Catholic Church. Clement of Alexandria, who also wrote late in the second century, is said by Eusebius (*Hist. Eccl.* vi. 14. 1) to have given, in his *Hypotyposeis*, 'concise accounts of all the canonical scriptures [of the New Testament], not omitting even those that are disputed—I mean the Letter of Jude and the rest of the catholic letters, and the Letter of Barnabas and the Apocalypse ascribed to Peter.' It is a natural, if not certain, inference from Eusebius that Clement expounded all seven of the catholic letters. Clement may well have called them 'catholic' himself; indeed, in another of his works he applies the epithet to the apostolic letter of Ac. 15: 23-29 (*Stromata* iv. 15).

In the generation after Clement, Origen applies the epithet 'catholic' to 1 Pet. and 1 Jn (and possibly to Jude), and also to the Letter of Barnabas. His disciple, Dionysius of Alexandria, also speaks of 1 Jn as John's 'catholic letter'—perhaps in contrast to 2 Jn and 3 Jn which name particular addressees (Eusebius, *Hist. Eccl.* vii. 25. 7).

After Eusebius we find the Council of Laodicea (A.D. 363) and Athanasius of Alexandria (A.D. 367) explicitly including the 'seven catholic letters' in their lists of New Testament books. Among the Latin Fathers, from Jerome (347-420) onwards, the Greek adjective was sometimes transliterated (thus Jerome speaks of the Letter of James as being *de septem catholicis* 'one of the seven catholic letters') but it was sometimes rendered by the adjective *canonicus*, also of Greek origin (thus Jerome in another place speaks of 'the seven letters which are called "canonical"'). Several later Latin writers adopted the practice of referring to the seven *canonical* letters rather than the seven catholic letters. This was an awkward designation for them, as all the New Testament letters could be called canonical; in so far as the term was applied distinctively to the seven, it marked them out as canonical not in contrast to the other letters but in addition to the others.

These seven are all the New Testament letters not included in the Pauline corpus. (Hebrews, although not a Pauline letter, was included in the Pauline corpus in the east from the second century onwards, in the west from the fourth century onwards.) The Pauline letters received canonical recognition earlier than the others; hence, when the others are called 'catholic' in the sense of canonical (acknowledged by the Church Catholic), they are so called because they, as well as the Pauline letters, are entitled to this designation.

A powerful stimulus to the church's definition of the authoritative writings of the new covenant was provided *c.* A.D. 140 by Marcion's publication of his twofold Christian canon—the *Euangelion* (his edition of Lk.) and the *Apostolikon* (his edition of ten Pauline letters—all those bearing Paul's name except the three Pastorals.) The publication of this canon made it urgently necessary for the leaders of the apostolic churches to say precisely what the true Christian canon was, since they condemned Marcion's as false. In general they replied that (unlike Marcion) they did not reject the Old Testament, but retained it, acknowledging alongside it, as its proper fulfilment, the New Testament; that they acknowledged the fourfold Gospel, not a single mutilated gospel-writing (as Marcion did); that they acknowledged the

Acts of the Apostles, which provided independent testimony both for Paul's apostleship (which Marcion accepted) and for that of the Twelve (which Marcion refused); that they acknowledged thirteen Pauline letters, not ten only; and that, in addition to the Pauline letters, they acknowledged the letters of other apostles and 'apostolic men' (men who were either disciples of the apostles or otherwise closely associated with them). It is these other letters that came to be called the 'catholic letters'. Not that they lacked canonical recognition before Marcion's time; two of them at any rate, 1 Pet. and 1 Jn, were quoted as authoritative documents by Polycarp of Smyrna earlier in the same century. But from now on their status as a well-defined group within the New Testament writings was assured. Some of them took longer to win general acceptance than any other New Testament books, but they were all acknowledged in the Greek and Latin churches by the end of the fourth century; the Syriac churches were slower in following suit.

Before it became the practice to include the whole New Testament (or the whole Bible) in a single codex, it was quite common to include Acts and the Catholic Letters in one codex—a companion codex to the Gospel-codex, the Pauline codex and the Apocalypse codex. Even after the whole New Testament (or the whole Bible) was included in a single codex, the Catholic Letters commonly continued to follow immediately after Acts. Thus in the *Codex Sinaiticus* the Gospels are followed by the Pauline corpus, which is followed in turn by Acts and the Catholic Letters; in the *Codex Vaticanus* Acts and the Catholic Letters come after the Gospels and before the Pauline Letters. It is this last order which is followed in Westcott and Hort's edition of the Greek New Testament, as in earlier critical editions of the nineteenth century. The arrangement with which we are most familiar, where the Catholic Letters come between Hebrews and Revelation, is that of the Latin Bible.

Their Teaching

What distinctive contribution do these seven letters make to the New Testament scriptures? With all their differences of viewpoint and content one from another, they give us a valuable picture of non-Pauline Christianity. Outside the Gospels, Paul dominates the New Testament. Thirteen of the twenty-one letters bear his name, and more than half of Acts is taken up with his apostolic career. The Catholic Letters (with Hebrews), set alongside the letters of Paul, enable us to get a stereoscopic view of first-century Christianity.

For all the individuality of his personality and

his ministry, Paul insists that the gospel which he and the Twelve proclaimed was basically one nd the same: 'Whether then it was I or they, so we preach and so you believe' (1 C. 15: 11). He knew that others were giving currency to a message which they called the gospel, but it was so different from the true gospel that he refused to recognize it as a gospel at all (Gal. 1: 6 ff.; cf. 2 C. 11: 4). When the true gospel was proclaimed from unworthy motives—out of a desire, for example, to rub salt into his wounds when he was in prison and unable to engage freely in apostolic activity—he could thank God, because the unworthiness of the motives or the messengers could not detract from the glory of the message (Phil. 1: 15-18). But the most exalted messenger could not make a false message the true gospel, not even if he were an angel from heaven (Gal. 1: 8).

Can we accept Paul's claim that the gospel preached by James the Lord's brother, and by Peter and the rest of the Twelve, was fundamentally the same as he himself preached? The evidence of the Catholic Letters encourages us to believe that we can. It is, of course, open to those who wish to emphasize the difference between Paul and those others to say that Pauline influence can be traced in some of the Catholic Letters, especially in 1 Pet. But in fact there is not nearly so much Pauline influence in them as has often been maintained. What has frequently been called Pauline influence should in most cases be regarded as derived from that common fund of primitive preaching and teaching which Paul shared with the Twelve and others who were in Christ before him. This is particularly true in 1 Pet., where 'the reader is aware of an atmosphere which seems in some respects nearer to that of the primitive Church, as we divine it behind the early chapters of Acts, than anything else in the New Testament' (C. H. Dodd, *The Apostolic Preaching and its Developments*, 1936, p. 97).

1 Peter

There is some reason to think that a good part of 1 Pet., from 1: 3 to 4: 11, is a baptismal address in literary form, intended for 'newborn babes' in the spiritual sense who require to be taught what their manner of life in a pagan environment must henceforth be. Their Lord must be their supreme example, not least when they are called upon to suffer unjustly or challenged to defend their Christian hope. 'Since . . . Christ suffered in the flesh, arm yourselves with the same thought, for whoever has suffered in the flesh has ceased from sin' (1 Pet. 4: 1). The language is different, but the sense is much the same as Paul's when he urges his readers to

reckon themselves 'dead to sin and alive to God in Christ Jesus', since 'he who has died is freed from sin' (Rom. 6: 11, 7). Only, when Peter speaks of the sufferings of Christ we catch the note of an eyewitness (1 Pet. 5: 1) as we do not in Paul's writings.

The situation in 1 Pet. is two or three years later than what we find in Paul's last letters to churches. As Paul enjoins obedience to the powers that be since 'rulers are not a terror to good conduct, but to bad' (Rom. 13: 3), so Peter enjoins submission to the emperor and governors appointed by him: 'who is there to harm you', he asks, 'if you are zealous for what is right?' (1 Pet. 2: 13 ff.; 3: 13). But the situation in this letter is changing before our eyes. In 1 Pet. 3: 14 suffering for righteousness' sake is a remote possibility; in 4: 12 ff. suffering for the name of Christ has become an imminent certainty. Imperial law, which in the fifties of the first century had indirectly protected a Christian missionary like Paul through its benevolent neutrality, as in the outstanding case of Gallio (Ac. 18: 12-17), was now turning hostile, so that in effect Christians had to suffer for the very fact that they professed the Christian name (and it would make little practical difference if lawyers said that they were suffering not for the name itself but for crimes invariably associated with the name). In this turn of affairs Peter sees a token of the impending judgment of the end-time; as in Ezekiel's day (Ezek. 9: 6), so now, it is the house of God that experiences His judgment first. Such suffering as Christians are now compelled to endure must, however, be accepted by them as a sharing in the suffering of Christ, and a harbinger of their sharing in His glory on the day of revelation (4: 13 f.; 5: 1).

James

The Letter of James reflects a phase of first-century Christianity more detached from imperial policy than 1 Pet. It is addressed 'to the twelve tribes in the Dispersion', i.e. to Christians, and more particularly Christians of Jewish birth, throughout the world; but its background is Palestinian. The people addressed acknowledge 'our Lord Jesus Christ' as 'the glory', i.e. the incarnate manifestation of the glory of God (Jas 2: 1; the thought is not unlike that of Jn 1: 14); the name of Jesus is the 'honourable name' by which they have been called (2: 7). They must beware of the temptation to think that orthodoxy of doctrine will compensate for the lack of works of mercy and faith (2: 14 ff.). (We may compare Paul's description of justifying faith in Gal. 5: 6 as 'faith working through love'.) They must beware, too, of a quarrelsome spirit (4: 1 ff.). If the letter is to be dated in the period preceding A.D. 62, when the

Zealots were increasing their hold on popular sympathy in Palestine, many of the Palestinian believers must have been in danger of embracing the Zealot outlook, in place of the self-effacing charity inculcated by Jesus. The dominant attitude to the law in their environment was that of the 'all or nothing' school of Shammai, according to which a 99 per cent. success in law-keeping was really a failure: 'whoever keeps the whole law but fails in one point has become guilty of all of it' (2: 10). After A.D. 70 the milder school of Hillel became dominant, especially under Rabbi Aqiba (d. 135), whose interpretation implied in practice that a 51 per cent. righteousness would suffice to open the way to paradise: 'a man who is more than half good is not half bad' (I. Zangwill). The people addressed do not belong for the most part to the wealthy land-owning classes, although they have to be warned against showing deference to a wealthy man just because he is wealthy. It is the wealthy land-owners who oppress and prosecute them, and speak ill of the name of Jesus (2: 6 f.). But a fearful fate lies in store for these wealthy oppressors; the blistering attack on them in 5: 1 ff. is well up to the standard of the great prophets of Israel, and the prediction of wretchedness and ruin for them was amply fulfilled in the years following the revolt against Rome in A.D. 66. The party of the Sadducees, who are principally in view in James's attack on the rich, disappeared for good in those years. But as in 1 Pet. 4: 17 ff., so for James the present distress and impending disasters are signs of the last days: let humble believers wait patiently for the coming of the Lord, for 'the Judge is standing at the doors' (5: 3, 7 ff.).

While in English James's letter reads like a series of extracts from OT prophecy, in Greek it reminds one of the moral disquisitions of a philosopher with a feeling for good style. The Greek of the letter may be the result of careful literary revision. The letter passes suddenly from one subject to another, sometimes returning later to one which has already been touched upon. But the opening verses provide something like an index of contents to the main divisions of the letter: the reference to trials in 1: 2 is amplified in 1: 12-17; the words about steadfastness and all-round completeness in 1: 3 f. anticipate the general teaching of chapter 2; what is said about true wisdom in 1: 5-8 is expanded in chapters 3 and 4, and the encouragement to the lowly and warning to the rich in 1: 9-11 are taken up and applied in chapter 5.

The Johannine Letters

The other catholic letters make us aware of a number of the doctrinal and ethical currents and cross-currents in the church's life in the later decades of the first century and beginning of the second.

The Johannine letters probably come from the province of Asia—the western part of the region to which 1 Pet. was sent. From 1 Jn we gather that there had been a considerable secession from the churches in that area in favour of a new and attractive form of teaching which its champions presented as an advance on what had been taught already. What were the criteria by which it might be known for certain whether this new teaching was right or wrong?

If, as is practically certain, the author of 1 Jn is 'the elder' by whom 2 Jn and 3 Jn were composed, he was in a position to be specially helpful to younger friends who were perplexed by the new teaching and recent secession. For he was known as 'the elder' probably not in any official sense but because he was a survivor from the first Christian generation—he belonged to those who had witnessed the saving events and followed Jesus during His Palestinian ministry. He could therefore give a well-informed answer to the question: Is this new teaching a faithful interpretation of the original gospel? No, said the elder, it is not. The original gospel—'that which was from the beginning'—is the message in which you were brought up, not this new teaching which some are finding so attractive. I know, because I was there; and I am writing to share with you what I saw and heard, together with my companions, in those early days when 'the eternal life which was with the Father . . . was made manifest to us' (1 Jn 1: 2). So, 'let what you heard from the beginning abide in you' (2: 24). (The message which John says was 'from the beginning' is manifestly the same in essence as that proclaimed by Paul.)

That was one criterion; another was something which they could judge for themselves. The new teachers claimed to have reached an advanced stage in spiritual experience where they were beyond good and evil; they maintained that they had no sin, not in the sense that they had attained moral perfection but in the sense that what might be sin for those in a less mature stage of inward development was no longer sin for the perfectly spiritual man: for him ethical considerations had ceased to be relevant. To this the elder replies that ethical considerations can never cease to be relevant to the gospel. Since God is light, those who have fellowship with Him must live in the light; their character must be marked by goodness and truth—this is the Johannine counterpart to the injunction of 1 Pet. 1: 15, 'as he who called you is holy, be holy yourselves in all your conduct'. Since Christ was pure and righteous, those who name

His name must be pure and righteous too, and above all else they must love one another, in accordance with His commandment and example. The new teachers were not outstanding for love; on the contrary, they limited their illumination to an élite minority of specially gifted souls. But in the gospel the true illumination is for all believers without distinction: 'you, no less than they, are among the initiated; this is the gift of the Holy One, and by it you all have knowledge' (1 Jn 2: 20, NEB).

Moreover, these new teachers' interpretation of the gospel was so false that it had no right to be called Christian: they denied the incarnation, denied that Jesus Christ had come in a real human body. Whether this was maintained by argument or imparted by prophetic utterance, no matter; it must be refused. Prophetic utterance need not come from the Spirit of God; it might come from some other spirit. Such utterances must be tested by their witness about Christ; if they refused to confess His true incarnation, then they proceeded manifestly from 'the spirit of antichrist' (1 Jn 4: 3).

In this new teaching we can recognize adumbrations of second-century Gnosticism, which manifested itself in a rich variety of forms, but consistently maintained a sharp dualistic opposition between spirit and matter which menaced the Christian doctrines of creation, incarnation and resurrection. One of the forms it took was Docetism, which taught that the humanity (and therefore also the death) of Christ was only apparent, not real. Towards the end of the first century Cerinthus (traditionally the heresiarch whom 'the elder' more particularly opposed) taught that the Christ-spirit came upon the man Jesus at His baptism and left Him just before His death on the cross. This may explain the insistence in 1 Jn 5: 6 that Jesus Christ 'came by water and blood, . . . not with the water only but with the water and the blood' (i.e. the Christ who was baptized is the Christ who truly died).

In 2 Jn the elder urges the church to which he is writing to give no countenance or hospitality to people who come with this subversive teaching; in 3 Jn he has to complain that in one of the churches over which he exercises spiritual authority his own messengers have been refused hospitality—although this may have been for reasons of personal rivalry rather than of doctrinal divergence. But in respect of church administration and theological debate alike we find ourselves in these letters on the eve of well-known second-century developments.

Jude and 2 Peter

The remaining catholic letters, Jude and 2 Pet., attack a form of incipient Gnosticism which,

regarding matter as morally neutral, refused all ethical restraint on bodily actions. Jude describes those who take this line as 'ungodly persons who pervert the grace of our God into licentiousness' (Jude 4); in 2 Pet. they are condemned as misinterpreters of the gospel of free grace who argued, in terms earlier reprobated by Paul, that they should 'continue in sin that grace may abound' (Rom. 6: 1), as 'ignorant and unstable' persons who 'twist to their own destruction' the writings of 'our beloved brother Paul' (2 Pet. 3: 15 f.). Their antinomian excesses may be inferred from the fact that the judgment in store for them is viewed as being foreshadowed by the fall of the angels who were captivated by the daughters of men and by the destruction which overtook the cities of the plain (Jude 6 f.; 2 Pet. 2: 4 ff.)

These libertines called themselves 'spiritual' (Gk. *pneumatikoi*), but their lives showed them to be 'devoid of the Spirit' (Jude 19). When Jude says that they 'set up divisions' (19), he probably has in mind their classification of mankind into the 'spiritual' (themselves), the 'psychic' (those whom they hoped to win to their way of thinking) and the 'carnal' (the rank outsiders, including all who were incurably wedded to the apostolic gospel). In fact, says Jude, it is they themselves who are 'psychic' ('worldly', RSV)—but he uses the word, as Paul does in 1 C. 2: 14, of 'the unspiritual (RV 'natural') man' who 'does not receive the gifts of the Spirit of God, for they are folly to him, and he is not able to understand them because they are spiritually discerned.' Just as the false teachers in 1 Jn are called 'antichrists' so here the libertines are called 'loudmouthed boasters' (Jude 16), 'uttering loud boasts of folly' (2 Pet. 2: 18), in language which echoes Daniel's description of the little horn with 'a mouth speaking great things' (Dan. 7: 8) and of the wilful king who is to 'speak astonishing things against the God of gods' (Dan. 11: 36)—OT figures on which the NT antichrist is modelled.

While 2 Pet. incorporates the substance of Jude, it adds further teaching of its own for the stabilizing of Christians who were in danger of being shaken from their foundations by current winds of change: in particular, it deals with the problem posed for some by the deferment of the parousia by reminding them that God does not reckon time as men do, and that if the day of the Lord is postponed, it is to provide men with a further opportunity for repentance: had not Paul himself said that 'God's kindness is meant to lead you to repentance' (Rom. 2: 4)? But this divine kindness must not be abused: the day of the Lord will certainly come, with the dissolution of the present world-order and the introduction of 'new heavens and a new earth in which righteousness dwells' (2 Pet. 3: 13). And those who look for such a consummation must live lives of righteousness and peace here and now. The catholic letters are at one with the Pauline letters, and with the whole New Testament, in their emphasis on the ethical implications of the gospel.

BIBLIOGRAPHY

MOFFATT, J., *The General Epistles. MNT* (London, 1928).

DODD, C. H., *The Johannine Epistles. MNT* (London, 1946).

GUTHRIE, D., *New Testament Introduction: Hebrews to Revelation* (London, 1962).

WILSON, R. McL., *The Gnostic Problem* (London, 1958).

WILSON, R. McL., *Gnosis and the NT* (Oxford, 1968).

JONAS, H., *The Gnostic Religion* (Boston, 1958).

GRANT, R. M., *Gnosticism and Early Christianity* (New York, 1959).

EHRHARDT, A. A. T., 'Christianity before the Apostles' Creed', *Harvard Theological Review* 55 (1962), pp. 73-120, reprinted in *The Framework of the NT Stories* (Manchester, 1963), pp. 151-199.

ELLIOTT-BINNS, L. E., *Galilean Christianity* (London, 1956).

STREETER, B. H., *The Primitive Church* (London, 1929).

See also bibliographies appended to commentaries on the various General Letters in this volume.

THE NEW TESTAMENT USE OF
THE OLD TESTAMENT

DAVID J. ELLIS

AN AUTHORITATIVE COURT OF APPEAL

The fact that the New Testament refers constantly to the Old Testament, both directly and indirectly, is clear from a casual reading of the Bible. Even the traditional system of marginal references, in spite of its obvious limitations, shows how frequently the NT writers made the scriptures of the OT their authoritative court of appeal.

It is axiomatic that the NT depends on the OT largely for its proper understanding, and that the books of the OT look to those of the NT for their ultimate fulfilment, not only in the prescribed realm of prophecy, but also in their entire mission and message. H. H. Rowley has said that 'it [NT] gathers up the Old Testament into the unity of the Christian Bible, but to illumine the Old with its own light. For the New Testament must be finally normative for the Christian understanding of the Old' (*The Re-discovery of the OT*, 1945, p. 11).

Of the one thousand or more direct references to or quotations of the OT in the NT, the greater majority seem to have been taken from the Septuagint. B. F. C. Atkinson ('The Textual Background of the Use of the OT by the New', *Journal of Transactions of the Victoria Institute*, 79, 1947, pp. 39–60) puts the figure at six out of every seven, and others would not vary widely in their judgment on the matter. Besides these direct references, however, there are many *allusions* to the OT in the NT which may be nothing more than a rhetorical device employed by some writer of the NT to give liveliness to a certain argument or train of thought. This literary method was common enough in Bible times, and can still be used effectively today. Nor should we be surprised that such a method was employed by NT writers, because both they and the characters of their pages would be men and women whose minds were usually soaked in the language of Scripture. Luke, for example, records the words addressed to Mary by aged Simeon (Lk. 2: 35) where it seems that when he said 'and a sword will pierce through

your own soul also' he had nothing else than the wording of Ps. 37: 15 running through his mind. It does not seem that an explicit reference to this scripture has any vital part to play in the story; in fact, the original context of the psalm is retributive and has nothing whatever to do with the circumstances described in the nativity passage.

The NT writers apparently relied much upon memory. This fact must be taken into account when surveying their use of the OT. But the greater number of their references, even allusions, are fairly recognizable, though with varying degrees of accuracy and inaccuracy. It is one of the chief merits of the treatment of this subject by R. V. G. Tasker (*The OT in the NT*, 2nd edn., 1954) that he has helped us to recognize these references, scarcely apparent at times, and here and there nothing more than a mere phrase. But their identity, nonetheless, becomes clearer on examination of their texts and contexts. Atkinson (*op. cit.*, p. 40) has pointed out that this factor does not lend to much classification of OT quotations, except that the Psalms, in general, seem to have been more accurately quoted than most other parts of the OT. The reason for that fact would not be far to seek. Here, perhaps, it should be mentioned that there are clearly many quotations, which, in spite of their variations from one NT book to another, would appear to have been obtained from a prior collection of quotations, on account of their frequent usage in certain contexts. This question will be examined later.

In making reference to the OT, the NT writers clearly regarded it as their authority. The full consensus of the attitude taken by NT writers shows that they regarded the OT as the Word of God without question or reserve (Heb. 4: 12 f.). So Paul, for example, claims that 'the scripture says . . .' (Rom. 10: 11; cf. Isa. 28: 16) and uses his reference as an authority for making an unassailable premiss, backed up by further appeal to the OT (Rom. 10: 13; cf. Jl 2: 32). This use of the OT by running together several passages is quite common in Paul, for as E. Earle Ellis has put it, 'the Scripture is adduced as a final authority and one divinely planned whole, whose significance is bound up inseparably with the New Testament Covenant Community of Christians' (*Paul's Use of the OT*, 1957, p. 25; cf. also F. F. Bruce, 'Promise and Fulfilment in Paul's Presentation of Jesus' in *Promise and Fulfilment*, essays presented to S. H. Hooke, 1963, pp. 36-50). This 'high' view of the Scriptures is reinforced in the NT by categorical statements concerning the nature of inspiration which it was believed the OT carried. So 2 Pet. 1: 20 is in no doubt about the matter. 'First of all you must understand this, that no prophecy of the scripture is a matter of one's own interpretation (Gk. *idias epilyseōs*), because no prophecy ever came by the impulse of man, but men moved by the Holy Spirit spoke from God'. We may find the diffident attitude expressed by C. F. D. Moule on this statement (*The Birth of the NT*, 1962, p. 60) one with which it is difficult to concur. For the juxtaposition of ideas seems clear enough. Our author seems to be saying that just because OT prophets and writers transmitted their messages under the direct influence of the Holy Spirit, it follows that their words can only be properly interpreted by the enlightening help of that same Spirit. And there can hardly be the thought in the writer's mind here that one's own interpretation might be set against the collective authority of the Church.

More than this, however, the fact of inspiration in the OT is made clear by the *mode of reference* which NT writers often employ. It seems evident here that they were following the example set by our Lord Himself in His view of the OT scriptures. Jesus (Mk 12: 36, cf. Mt. 22: 43) speaks of David (Ps. 110: 1) as 'inspired by the Holy Spirit'. In the earliest Christian preaching, Peter designates the utterances of David in the same manner as that 'which the Holy Spirit spoke . . .' (Ac. 1: 16-20; cf. Ps. 69: 25; 109: 8). Paul preaches in the same strain, and warns his congregation (Ac. 28: 25 ff.) that their refusal to heed the voice of the Scripture is indeed something foretold by Isaiah the prophet *in the Holy Spirit* (cf. Isa. 6: 9 f.). Such references as these, therefore, serve to underline that authority with which the NT brings its message out from the OT.

PRINCIPLES OF INTERPRETATION

These questions, however, raise the important matter with regard to the precise way in which the NT writers understood the OT, and how, in consequence, they adduced their references

from the OT for the matter in hand. Is their use of the OT uniform, or was each one free to follow his own predilections? Did they inherit any formally accepted principle of Biblical interpretation, or did they bring some fresh, inspired understanding of the OT to light within their message? Moule has shown (*op. cit.*, pp. 58 ff.) that to understand the earliest Christian use of the OT three decisive factors have to be borne in mind. (i) Pre-Christian Judaism had certain stereotyped methods of exegesis. (ii) Jesus Himself inherited some of these, it is plain, though He turned them inside out with perfect originality. (iii) And on to His controlling attitude towards the OT the early Church placed its conviction that 'the Spirit of Christ' who had inspired and guided the prophets of old, was now freshly active in Christ's people, awakening their minds to a vitally new understanding of the Scriptures.

Jewish exegetes believed that the very text of their Scriptures was inspired. Either that text was to be correctly understood through the channel of rabbinical schools of interpretation, or else, as was freely claimed by others, the individual reader could, by leaning solely upon the help of God, derive a perfect understanding of the meaning of Scripture. 2 Pet. 1: 20 f., indeed, may well have been addressed to such a situation. The basic presupposition all the way through, however, was that the revelation of God in the OT was final and complete. (The Targums, however, were by their nature interpretative translations of the Hebrew text, developed from certain oral traditions. Their influence is probably to be seen, here and there, in the NT interpretation of the OT, a notable example being Mk 4: 11 f. [cf. Mt. 13: 13]; cf. Isa. 6: 9 f., where we may possibly read 'who see, indeed . . .' instead of Mark's 'so that they may indeed see' or instead of Matthew's 'because seeing they do not see . . .'. Similar influences may lie behind Lk. 4: 18 f. [Isa. 61: 1 f.] and Eph. 4: 8 [cf. Ps. 68: 1]. For the importance of the Targums, cf. F. F. Bruce, *The Books and the Parchments*, 3rd edn., 1963, pp. 133 ff.)

But finality and completion do not rule out the possibility of fulfilment. If one thing marked the use of the OT by the Lord Jesus it was a profound sense of consummation. So, at Nazareth, when in the synagogue he declares 'Today this scripture has been fulfilled in your hearing' (Lk. 4: 17-21), and the early Christians were not slow to follow up this dramatic appeal to the OT. J. A. Fitzmyer ('The Use of Explicit Old Testament Quotations in Qumran Literature and the New Testament', *New Testament Studies*, 7, 1961, pp. 297 ff.)

has demonstrated how these early Christians believed that they were living in the last days, and how, accordingly, they were bound to understand the OT in eschatological terms. Peter, for example, on the day of Pentecost maintains that it 'was spoken by the prophet Joel: "And in the last days it shall be, God declares . . ."' and apparently alters the Septuagint reading, unless he is conflating a small phrase from Isa. 2: 2. But whatever it is, it is clear that he has quoted this prophecy concerning the outpouring of the Spirit in order to set the events of Pentecost, as a turning point in the purpose of God, at the dawn of the age of the Messiah. This also means that Peter saw the Pentecost events as revelatory, which therefore could rightly be understood only by appeal to OT scriptures. But such apocalyptic tendencies were by no means confined to early Christians. The use of the OT made by the Qumran sect goes along similar lines, but with significant differences which leave the NT use of the OT still unique. It was characteristic of the Qumran commentators to provide a running commentary (Heb. *pesher*) along with the text they were citing. Something approaching this can be detected here and there in the NT (*e.g.*, Mt. 26: 31; cf. Mk 14: 27; Lk. 4: 21; Jn 13: 18; Ac. 2: 16, etc.). Generally speaking the men of Qumran saw in a given passage a number of ideas which were germane to their own preferences of interpretation, and for which they consequently sought a contemporary application and justification. The *Habakkuk Commentary* is a classic example of this.

But in contrast NT commentators usually appeal to a passage in its entirety, seeking to understand and underline its fundamental message. So in Ac. 15: 15 ff. James, referring to Am. 9: 11 f., sees in the resurrection and exaltation of the Lord the fulfilment of that prophet's oracle concerning the restoration of the Davidic house. Some attention to the matter of contextual considerations on the part of the NT has been given by S. L. Edgar ('Respect for Context in Quotations from the OT', *New Testament Studies*, 9, 1962, pp. 55–62). He concludes, having allowed for factors in translation, that in many of such quotations there seems to be little point, or else, at best, the quotation has been made in the interests of pushing home some basic religious tenet. Among a number of instances of this Edgar draws our attention, for example, to the use made by Paul of Isa. 28: 16 in Rom. 10: 11, *viz.*, 'No one who believes in him will be put to shame'. We may put aside the question of Paul's rendering of the Isaiah passage at this point, except to point out Paul's addition of

'all' (Gk. *pas*) to indicate the universality of salvation. Or, again, Paul's use of Isa. 52: 5 (in Rom. 2: 24) Edgar maintains has been freely adduced to show the effects upon the heathen of the helplessness of God's people. This may be true of the original context of the Isaiah passage, but, as Lindars and others have shown, there is a shift of application in perfect accord with the change of circumstances. Says Lindars (*New Testament Apologetic*, 1961, p. 22): 'It is the Jews' failure to keep the Law which [now] causes the scandal, rather than God's failure to act'.

The difference in exegetical method between Qumran and the NT is seen even more clearly in the attitude which each adopts towards the old Israel in relation to the new situation. For the men of Qumran the old order, after a temporary period of substitutionary offerings and the like, would be restored in a purified form, and their community life, indeed, was built around the expectation of establishing a ritualistic system without delay when the new age dawned. But with the NT it is different. The Church is the new Israel (Gal. 6: 16). Its members constitute a 'chosen race, a royal priesthood . . .' (1 Pet. 2: 9). Just as the Passover and Exodus had heralded the birth of a chosen race in the OT, so now the exodus of the Christ (Lk. 9: 31) and His paschal death (1 C. 5: 7) have brought into existence this new nation in the purpose of God. No longer can it be imagined, affirms the NT, that the old order is to be revived, purified and re-established. The new order is, indeed, linked with the old in God's purpose, in that the promise given to Abraham (Rom. 4) is fulfilled in all, Jews and Gentiles alike, who are now united to Christ by faith. And to this the prophets of the OT give their witness. It is not surprising, therefore, that the difference between Qumran exegesis and NT exegesis of the OT should finally be crystallized in certain messianic passages. F. F. Bruce shows (*Biblical Exegesis in the Qumran Texts*, 1960, pp. 75 f.) that both the men of Qumran and the earliest Christians saw that the OT pointed forward to the coming of a great prophet, a prominent priest, and a majestic king. The difference of interpretation, however, between the two is clearly that in Qumran the three figures are kept distinct till the end of the age, whereas in the NT they are all three clearly seen as perfectly fulfilled in the Lord Jesus (Heb. 1: 1 ff., 8 f.). 'Here, then, is the key to that distinctive interpretation of the Old Testament which we find in the New Testament. Jesus has fulfilled the ancient promises, and in fulfilling them He has given them a new meaning . . . more comprehensive and far-reaching than was foreseen before He came' (Bruce, *op. cit.*, p. 77).

Our Lord's use of the OT is marked by frequent appeal to certain well-known prophetic passages which were also employed by others in the NT. Possibly the most distinctive of these are His references to the Son of Man. A. J. B. Higgins (*Jesus and the Son of Man*, 1964, pp. 185 ff.) has recently tabulated three categories in Jesus' sayings concerning this figure. There are those which concern his earthly activity (*e.g.* Mk. 2: 10; Lk. 9: 58 [Mt. 8: 20]; 19: 10), others which speak of his sufferings (*e.g.*, Mk 8: 31; Lk. 24: 7), and others which announce his forthcoming glorification (*e.g.*, Mk 8: 38; Lk. 12: 40 [Mt. 24: 44]; 21: 36; Mt. 24: 30). In spite of many different views on these quotations it seems clear that the historical-eschatological figure of Dan. 7: 13 is in mind, and that other possible literary sources do not fit the various NT contexts so well. 'Who is this Son of man?' (Jn 12: 34) asked Jesus' hearers on one occasion. To them, the twin ideas of the eternity of the Messiah, and the suffering of the Son of man, to which Jesus had plainly referred, were mutually exclusive. But the Lord teaches that it is by way of death that His 'lifting up' must take place. The coming of the Danielic Son of man is made actual at His crucifixion, as, indeed, Jesus also indicated, the world would also stand judged (Jn 12: 31). However much the symbol in Dan. 7 may primarily refer to a faithful group within Israel, Jesus clearly applied the symbol to Himself as the Representative of that people, humiliated for the moment, but later to be glorified. And in view of this it is difficult to accept Higgins's statement that 'Jesus said nothing whatever about himself as the Son of man. He referred to him as if to a future advocate, witness or judge. He also spoke of His own mission . . . But in his teaching on these matters the idea of the Son of man played no part' (*op. cit.*, pp. 199 f.).

THE USE OF 'TESTIMONIES'

Similar unravelling of prophetic passages can be seen in Jesus' great saying concerning 'the very stone which the builders rejected . . .' (Mk 12: 10; Mt. 21: 42; Lk. 20: 17 f.; cf. Ps. 118: 22 f.). Jesus' claim to be the Messiah is well-founded by the fact that the religious experts, to whom 'builders' refers, instead of recognizing Him for what He was, rejected Him, who was that stone most vital for the erecting of a new edifice. It was the presence of such 'stone passages' which primarily led Rendel Harris (*Testimonies*, 1916-1920), largely following E. Hatch (*Essays in Biblical Greek*, 1889) to postulate books of

Testimonies from which he believed NT writers probably adduced their authority for the message of Jesus as the Messiah. Such books of *Testimonies* are known to have been used by Cyprian of Carthage and others of the early Fathers, and Harris believed that at least one such may underlie the OT quotations in the NT. It is clear, of course, that there are certain passages which recur with significant variations or connections with other OT texts. The 'stone passages' are one example. Whatever may be said with regard to the recurrence of these quotations, it is clear that their usage in different parts of the NT was for different expositional purposes, and that, indeed, the various contexts show how differing doctrinal emphases are underlined by their presence.

We have already seen that our Lord's use of a 'stone passage' (Ps. 118: 22) is purely for the purpose of confounding the claim of religious leaders who rejected His authority. Peter, however, uses the same reference (Ac. 4: 11 f.) to show that the resurrection was an event at one with the mood of the Psalm. Another important use of the same reference is in 1 Pet. 2: 1-10 where it is conflated with Isa. 8: 14 and 28: 16. The two latter 'stone passages' are employed as a commentary on the first. Christ, writes Peter, was the 'stone' rejected by men but exalted by God. Yet the significance of the events in His life is that He was (and is) 'chosen and precious' (1 Pet. 2: 6) and therefore worthy of trust. But to unbelievers He becomes 'a stone that will make men stumble . . . (1 Pet. 2: 8). And here, it may be added, the stone seems to be even more firmly and closely identified with the Person of our Lord, as against the possible analogical use of the text by Jesus Himself.

Barnabas Lindars argues that, by their text forms and functions in their NT contexts, such 'testimonies' reflect a final 'atomistic' stage of selection, in which they are detached from their original setting, and by this means he seeks to add greater weight to the *Testimonies* theory (*op. cit.*, pp. 272 ff.; cf. also L. Morris, *The New Testament and the Jewish Lectionaries*, 1964, pp. 53-63). But such selection might not be so arbitrary as might at first appear. Even the 'formula quotations' suggested by K. Stendahl (*The School of St. Matthew*, 1954, pp. 162 f.) in his examination of the use of the OT made by Matthew and John, could be accounted for as a compilation of texts, sometimes combined with others, to form their own commentary, as we have already said. It can certainly be shown that a *proof text* has been commonly abbreviated by a number of NT writers, as in the case of the use made by Matthew, John and

Revelation, of Zech. 12 (Mt. 24: 30; Jn 19: 37; Rev. 1: 7; cf. Zech. 12: 10-14). Lindars has examined this example thoroughly (*op. cit.*, pp. 122-127). He sees, apart from an initial desire on the part of the NT to free the required text from its original context, certain differences of application. So, Matthew restricts himself to the apocalyptic suddenness of Christ's appearing in triumph, causing the unbelieving Jews to wail. Thus he separates Zechariah from the Passion story as such. John, on the other hand, retains the Passion significance entirely, and with the additional evidence of Ps. 34: 20 sees in the OT a prediction of the wounding of the Saviour's side with the spear (not as Matthew who uses the same text to refer to the wailing at the appearance of the 'sign of the Son of man'). And in Revelation we have almost a total occupation with the return of Christ and the grief shared by humanity at the sight of His wounds—not like Matthew, again, who warns a somewhat smaller body who might feel responsibility for the actual crucifying of Jesus.

Zechariah, indeed, figures prominently in the Passion Narrative, and its place among the *Testimonies* might well be all-important. What is important, clearly, regarding its place in the Gospels is, as F. F. Bruce has said that 'the Evangelists saw such a clear correspondence between the prophetic *testimonia* and the events to which the apostles and their colleagues testified . . .' ('The Book of Zechariah and the Passion Narrative', *Bulletin of the John Rylands Library*, 43, 1960-61, p. 353).

The Lord also referred to popular expectations concerning Elijah *redivivus*, and applied them to the person and mission of John the Baptist (Mk 9: 13; Mt. 17: 12; cf. Mal. 4: 5) and related them also to His own forthcoming sufferings at the hands of the elders, chief priests and scribes. But more than this, Jesus may well have implied that what the prophet had had to say concerning the coming Day of the Lord was to be inaugurated through His Passion.

That Jesus used certain well-known OT passages is clear. It would not be surprising, therefore, to find that the writers of the NT followed His example in this. Does it follow, however, that these facts are only explicable by positing the existence of books of *Testimonies*? Rendel Harris concluded that they were only understandable on some such hypothesis, since many of these recurring quotations, often in forms differing from the Septuagint, were grouped together in sequences, and even cited, occasionally, as having come from a single OT author (*e.g.*, Mt. 27: 9 f. cited as 'Jeremiah'; but cf. Zech. 11: 12 f.; Jer. 32: 6-15) so as to

suggest that they were once contained in a single collection. Harris's case has been somewhat supported by the Qumran discoveries in that the Scrolls from the Dead Sea have brought to light certain messianic collections (4Q *Testimonia*) and certain other expository or homiletic collections (*midrashim*) besides specifically selected collections of texts with pesher commentary (4Q *Florilegium*), which would show that such collections did exist among some pre-Christian communities. (Lindars, however, would not see anything in these Qumran documents comparable to Harris's *Testimonia* because it is not certain whether they were for public use or were only private collections of *memoranda*.)

C. H. Dodd has examined the use of OT quotations in the NT very closely, and in his valuable work on the subject (*According to the Scriptures*, 1952) he has indicated some of the difficulties lying behind Harris's suggestions, not least the mystery that, if such *Testimonia* collections did exist and were used by the early Christians in the formation of the NT, they have apparently disappeared. And Harris's attention to the non-Septuagintal quotations is not quite so fundamental as might appear since these are not so numerous, either where *one* agrees with the Septuagint, or where *both* disagree. On the contrary, Dodd has shown that there are obviously some books, or parts of books, of the OT which are very frequently laid under quotation in the NT. These quotations are usually quite short, however, and rarely do we find that some passage is quoted at length. But closer examination will show that there are also large tracts of OT territory which hardly, if ever, appear in the NT. And again, a particular cluster of quotations may all be used by a single NT writer, *e.g.*, Exodus and Leviticus will be seen again and again in the Letter to the Hebrews. This fact may, of course, be accounted for by the predilections of the author of Hebrews, but where, in other circumstances, references begin to accumulate from a variety of NT books it would suggest that certain parts of the OT were of special interest to the writers of the NT. Dodd has clearly shown, too, that there is, in fact, a fairly large body of lengthy quotations which suggests that, from a very early date, Christians appealed to a body of *Scripture* for the preaching of their message.

PATTERNS OF FULFILMENT

A striking and obvious example of lengthy or detailed quotation is that of the use made by NT writers of Isa. 53. There are some twelve verses in our text of this chapter, and one only of these possibly does not appear in the NT either by direct reference or indirect allusion. No one author quotes Isa. 53 very extensively, and it is rare for more than a single writer in the NT to quote the same verse. Philip (Ac. 8: 32 f.) uses two verses, but in a situation which indicates that he had the entire chapter before him. The rest of Isa. 53 appears, or is alluded to, in all four Gospels, Romans, Philippians, Hebrews, and 1 Peter. Dodd claims that, in fact, if all of the original text of Isa. 53 had been lost it would not necessarily have been irretrievable, but possible to restore almost the whole chapter in Greek translation. This shows that however the NT writers might seem, on the face of it, to have selected their material for shortened quotations very carefully, yet this chapter *considered as a whole* had outstanding significance for the understanding and presentation of the Christian message on the part of its first preachers.

Moreover it is apparent that the NT use of Isa. 53 is coloured by an interpretation which sees in that passage a 'plot', to use Dodd's own word, which is repeated substantially, yet with minor variations, in most of the OT passages quoted *in extenso* by the NT. In general this plan marks out the submission and suffering of one person, or group of persons, clearly intended to portray the Servant of the Lord. This Servant submits to insults and suffering, and finally, death, or, if the picture be of a nation, extinction. But this loving obedience is rewarded with triumphant exaltation through the grace of God.

There are at least two other passages, apart from Dan. 7, which speak of the Son of Man, and which reveal the same basic pattern. Ps. 80 vividly describes, with the aid of colourful imagery, the experiences of the people of God in prosperity and adversity. The vine which formerly flourished is ravaged by wild beasts, until the poet exclaims 'Turn again, O God of hosts! Look down from heaven, and see: have regard for this vine . . .' (Ps. 80: 14). But after this the picture changes, and the prayer becomes 'let thy hand be upon the man of thy right hand, the son of man whom thou hast made strong for thyself' (v. 17). The psalm is never expressly quoted, yet we can see how, and where, it has supplied some of the standing imagery of the NT. The same expression occurs in Ps. 8: 4, a passage several times quoted directly in the NT (cf. Mt. 21: 16; 1 C. 15: 27; Eph. 1: 22), yet only extensively in one place (Heb. 2: 6 ff.). There 'son of man' stands for humanity, and the writer sees the crown of glory, which God destines man to wear, as having already been awarded to Jesus Christ.

Joel is fairly often quoted in the NT, particularly ch. 2-3. The Day of the Lord is heralded by the emergence of a renovated people of God, possibly seen as the Son of man, or Servant in another guise.

Already we have seen that the Book of Zechariah is extensively quoted in the narrative of events towards the close of our Lord's earthly life. In particular the two oracles (Zech. 9-11; 12-14), whose interrelation is not certain, essentially constitute an apocalyptic message concerning the Day of the Lord. First there is the kingly figure who enters Zion, meek and riding upon an ass (Mt. 21: 4 f.; cf. Mk 11: 1-10; Jn 12: 14 f.), and then the scene closes with all the nations coming up to worship at Jerusalem in honour of God their King. In the middle, however, there is a wealth of material much used by the Evangelists for corroboration of events during Passion Week. Basically, in the prophecy's original setting there is the picture of Israel, as the flock of God, passing through several stages of rebellion against God, incurring the punishment she richly deserves, in the course of which the shepherd is smitten and the flock scattered. So in spite of suffering which is deserved there is a glimpse of a leader who is humiliated, but who comes through in triumph. Lindars (*op. cit.*, pp. 110-134) has given close attention to the passage and has shown that the Evangelist sifted his material in order to demonstrate that the very details of Passion Week—the triumphal Entry (cf. Zech. 9: 9), the treachery of Judas (cf. 11: 12 f.) and the scattering of the sheep (13: 7)—indicate that the messianic claim of Jesus is built into the twin patterns of atonement and the wrath of God. The text of Zechariah is abbreviated to draw attention solely to the point at issue in the Passion story namely, that each event in that story was decisive, and played a vital part in the final drama. in which the 'blood of the covenant' (Zech. 9: 11; Mt. 26: 28) preceded the inauguration of the kingdom (Mt. 26: 29; Zech. 9: 10).

Each of these scriptures mentioned is a record or commentary on events which happened in the course of the history of Israel. Moreover the way that these prophets, of different periods, interpret the history of their own times, and forecast the future in its light, shows that they understood that the entire course of that history demonstrated certain fundamental principles upon which God worked His plan for the nation. The Day of the Lord was to be the culmination of vision to which they appealed. And it is from Acts 2 onwards that we see how the early Church recognized that the Day of the Lord had dawned in fact, in the events of the humiliation, death and resurrection of Christ (cf. Peter's quotation and application of Jl 2: 31 on the day of Pentecost). So to make clear this conviction, and to justify it, the NT writers appealed, in their turn, to prophetic passages which spoke both of the Day of the Lord and of the events which led up to it. The hope and fears of the prophets were at last realized and consummated in Christ. So, Peter, in bringing the message of Christ to Cornelius, announced that Christ is 'ordained by God to be judge of the living and dead. To him give all the prophets witness' (Ac. 10: 42 f.). Dodd concludes, therefore, that the whole body of prophetic passages as adduced by NT writers, Luke, Acts, John, Paul, the author of Hebrews, and 1 Peter, provided the 'sub-structure' of their theology, which they believed underlined the fact that the events of history, which took place under Pontius Pilate, nevertheless could be seen also as a demonstration of 'the definite plan and foreknowledge of God' (Ac. 2: 23).

ALLEGORY AND TYPE

Mention must be made, however, of two uses to which the OT was distinctively put by NT writers which have so far been omitted from this discussion. In the world of the NT there was a widely accepted method of interpreting ancient literature, which, though regarded as authoritative, presented certain problems for the commentator. This was the allegorical method of interpretation. It was employed by Jewish exegetes, largely under the leadership of Philo of Alexandria. Its purpose was not so much to give the would-be expositor a freedom which was best served by a very fruitful imagination, but to avoid certain difficulties which the traditional text presented to the Greek mind, and also to give some weight to philosophical ideas with which, of course, the original authors of the text can hardly have been acquainted. Perhaps it is surprising, at first sight, that such a method is not more frequently found in the NT than appears to be the case. Paul's treatment of the episode of Hagar and Ishmael (Gal. 4: 21-31) is, as the apostle expressly states, allegorical (Gal. 4: 24, Gk. *hatina estin allēgoroumena*). Hagar stands for Sinai, the mountain of the law, and Ishmael, her son, for the Jews as the sons of the law. Isaac, the promised child, resembles the Church, afflicted under suffering, and the whole argument of Galatians up to this point in the letter, *viz*., the antipathy of faith and the law, is thus pictured. Then Paul, as we have already seen, runs together other passages (*e.g.*, Isa. 54: 1) to serve as a commentary on the whole section.

In the allegory it is not the original historical context (Gen. 16 and 21) or the original intention of its author that is expounded (see p. 453). This means that the OT supplies certain imagery which alone is sufficient for the later re-inforcement of some NT idea. But the idea itself is not derived *from* the OT. Paul, it may well be, is answering certain objections from Jewish circles which had presumably employed some allegorical method against his own mode of exegesis, so that he turns round the argument by the very means used by his opponents. This alone should be sufficient warning for the modern exegete with regard to a dangerous form of biblical interpretation.

Moreover, the fact that such examples of true allegory are uncommon in the NT makes it fairly evident that another method of OT exegesis used by NT writers, similar to it, should, however, be kept distinct. This is the *typological* method. E. Earle Ellis (*op. cit.*, p. 126) rightly says of Paul's employment of this method that ' "type" used as an exegetical method has . . . a much more restricted meaning than *typos* would suggest . . .'. We may disagree, however, with Ellis's designation of the Hagar-Ishmael episode as typological. There a number of other figures would have served Paul's argument, and in any case, as we have already suggested, he does not take much of the original historical situation into account. But with restricted typology it is different. Adam, in a unique setting, becomes a type of which Christ is the antitype (Rom. 5); that Christ is a new and better 'Adam' is what he has in mind to say, and that Christ's saving work is extended in its effects to all men, just as Adam's sin extended in its effects beyond him. Thus, Adam 'was a type of the one who was to come' (Rom. 5: 14). (There is the further correlation between Adam and Christ in that both stand at the head of a course of events: Adam, at the beginning of history; Christ, at the beginning of salvation-history. In the same way, in 1 C. 15: 20 ff., to be 'in Adam' is to belong to the natural order. To be 'in Christ' [cf. Rom. 5: 17] is to receive all the blessings of the new age. Cf. J. Munck, *Paul and the Salvation of Mankind*, 1959.)

Again, the Paschal Lamb (Exod. 12) is yet another type of Christ 'our paschal lamb' (1 C. 5: 7) in that historical events associated with that sacred meal both have their counterpart, as well as direct fulfilment, in Christ. Further (1 C. 10), Paul uses the word 'type' to denote an association between the OT and the Christian message. Twice over he uses it in 1 C. 10: 'Now these are warnings (Gk. *typoi*) for us . . .' (1 C. 10: 6), and 'These things happened to them as a warning . . .' (v. 11,

Gk. *typikōs*). E. E. Ellis (*op. cit.*, p. 126) associates this passage with other strict typological exegesis in Paul and elsewhere. But the sense of Paul's words in this passage, brought out well by the RSV, would suggest that he was comparing Israel's sin with that kind of sin which seems to beset God's people in every age, so that just as Israel fell by the wayside in the desert by reason of her unbelief and disobedience, so also today, Christian people, for the selfsame reason, are tempted to fall on one side from the path of holy and obedient living in accordance with the will of God. This means no more than that Paul is saying that Israel's trouble turns out, on reflection, to be a *typical* trouble, and that there is no further significance than this for his use of the term *typos*, which, elsewhere, however, might have a much more technical connotation.

There is an important example of explicit typology in Hebrews. Apart from some cases of imprecise typology (*e.g.*, Moses, ch. 3; Aaron, ch. 5, etc.) it is with the figure of Melchizedek (ch. 7) that the writer works out his thesis with some care. As is his custom, the author first quotes a psalm—in this case the much-quoted Ps. 110—and then enlightens this quotation by reference to OT narrative, here Gen. 14. First in significance for Hebrews is the name *Malki-sedeq* 'king of righteousness' and 'king of peace', the latter being treated as another rendering for the original 'Salem' for Jerusalem (Gen. 14: 18). F. F. Bruce ('Hebrews' in *Peake's Commentary*, 1962, p. 1,013) suggests also that 'the collocation of righteousness and peace is naturally found suggestive' (cf. Isa. 32: 17) to the writer (cf. also F. C. Synge, *Hebrews and the Scriptures*, 1959). Further, however, Melchizedek is a priest for ever, another typological factor, and the indication that the circumstances of his birth and death are not mentioned in the OT combines to make this mysterious OT priest a most fitting type of Christ, whose priesthood knows no end, and the suggestion of the author of Hebrews is re-inforced in his exposition by appeal to yet another strange fact that Levi, who 'was in the loins of his ancestor' (Heb. 7: 10) paid Melchizedek tithes in the person of Abraham, thus suggesting that the priesthood which Melchizedek typified is greater even than that of Levi.

In the NT there are two instances of the use of the term 'antitype' as a definitive expression (Heb. 9: 24; 1 Pet. 3: 21). The first of these presents little difficulty to the modern commentator. Christ, says the writer, has not entered into an earthly sanctuary, 'a copy of the true one' (Gk. *antitypa tōn alēthinōn*) but into heaven itself. The antitype here is substantive. Both the earthly sanctuary and the heavenly counterpart represent the same spiritual original, namely, entrance into the holy presence of God.

But the type-antitype relationship in 1 Pet. 3: 21 is not so clear, though E. G. Selwyn (*The First Epistle of Peter*, 2nd edn., 1961, pp. 298 f.) has made out a good case for taking baptism 'which corresponds to this', i.e. the flood water, to mean that the Flood only faintly indicated that perfect salvation which is dramatized in baptism.

It will be seen, therefore, that with typological interpretation in the NT there was a certain amount of flexibility. Yet throughout we may discern a number of basic principles underlying typological exegesis. The type always has its own place and meaning independently of what it may prefigure. Thus the Flood brought disaster to mankind in Gen. 7 but salvation to those who found refuge in the Ark. Or, the paschal lamb of Exod. 12 brought to fulfilment the promise of deliverance to the captive people of Israel, even apart from the greater sacrifice which it came to symbolize. Thus the NT writers never destroyed the historical sense of OT scripture in order to establish some spiritual lesson from its pages. Nor did they find some intricate hidden meaning in the original text before them, but a plain and straightforward meaning. And they seem to have confined the typological method to discover prophetic indications of fundamental doctrines affecting the Person of Christ, or the life and practice of the NT Church. The value of such basic 'rules' will be apparent to the modern commentator.

In spite of Dodd's wish to limit the texts from which the primitive preachers may be thought to have preached and reasoned, he would not, of course, limit their acquaintance with the general substance of the OT. Indeed, examination of typological interpretation in Paul's writings and elsewhere shows how the minds of the NT writers could range over a vast area of the OT. And this fact, whilst assuring us of their knowledge of the OT, also serves as a brake against finding unnecessary typological material where it was not originally intended. It is quite possible, even in modern times, for a writer to have an idea or an image in his mind effectively enough to shape what he says without his being aware of it at all. Whether or not, for example, our Lord's words 'I will give you the keys of the kingdom of heaven' (Mt. 16: 19) is a deliberate allusion, as Tasker (*The Old Testament in the New Testament*, 2nd edn., 1954) would suggest, to Isa. 22: 22, it is certain that the one text has contributed to the formation of the other. (More explicit reference to the Isaiah text, however, is made in Rev. 3: 7.)

THE 'AMEN' TO GOD'S PURPOSES

What is clear in the NT use of the OT is that, from a multiplicity of OT quotations, the NT writers brought their message to bear upon a certain series of undisputed facts comprising the gospel story. The diversity and richness of their use of the OT scriptures, woven together into a single strand, enabled them to affirm with confidence that these scriptures demonstrated 'the definite plan and foreknowledge of God' (Ac. 2: 23) and its consequent fulfilment. Climactically, the NT writers saw fulfilled in Christ the involved and very diverse prophecies concerning the Servant of the Lord and the Son of man. If the former figure be understood as basically the nation of Israel in its entirety, then Christ is the true Israel, and all who are 'in Christ' are heirs to the promises, though we should, possibly, hesitate to go further, as L. C. Allen does ('The Old Testament in Romans I-VIII', *Vox Evangelica* III, 1964, p. 23), to project the image so as to include Paul as a special emissary of the gospel. The Son of man figure, whether he be taken as an individual representing the whole people or not, is clearly understood in the NT as a prophetic pre-figuring of Christ, who, as Man, would by suffering, death and exaltation achieve all that God designed for humanity.

For the NT writers the Passion of our Lord was decisive for any proper understanding of the prophetic adumbration of the NT message. Indeed, there are a number of passages which speak of Christ's pre-existent activity in such a manner as makes Him both subject and object of OT prophecy. Paul identifies the rock (Exod. 17: 6) with Christ (1 C. 10: 4). And the prophets, writes Peter, who foretold of the grace which should be shown us, were moved by 'the spirit of Christ within them when predicting the sufferings of Christ and the subsequent glory' (1 Pet. 1: 11).

The great stream of the scriptures, therefore, broadens with the emergence of the NT. But it is an extension of that former revelation, and at the same time, the guarantee which authenticates its normative importance (2 Tim. 3: 14-17). And of course, the divine inspiration given to the writers of the NT was such that, as C. F. D. Moule puts it, 'they came to scripture from an already given experience, and had only to read in its main contours and its living story the confirmation that what they had experienced was not alien, though so new; it was the climax, the culmination, the "Amen" to all God's purposes (2 C. 1: 20)' (*The Birth of the New Testament*, 1962, p. 70). And there can, after all, be no greater authority for the preaching of the Christian message, in any age, than that Christ's saving work was completed 'in accordance with the scriptures' (1 C. 15: 3 f.).

BIBLIOGRAPHY

ALLEN, L. C., 'The Old Testament in Romans I-VIII' (*Vox Evangelica* III, 1964).

BRUCE, F. F., *The Books and the Parchments* (London, 1950; 3rd edition, 1963).

BRUCE, F. F., *Biblical Exegesis in the Qumran Texts* (London,) 1960.

DODD, C. H., *According to the Scriptures* (London, 1952).

ELLIS, E. E., *Paul's Use of the Old Testament* (Edinburgh, 1957).

GUILDING, A., *The Fourth Gospel and Jewish Worship* (Oxford, 1960).

HARRIS, J. R., *Testimonies* i, ii (Cambridge 1916, 1920).

HEBERT, A. G., *The Authority of the Old Testament* (London, 1947).

LINDARS, B., *New Testament Apologetic* (London, 1961).

MCNEILE, A. H., *The Old Testament in the Christian Church* (London, 1913).

MANSON, T. W., *The Servant-Messiah* (Cambridge, 1953; reprinted 1961).

MANSON, T. W., *The Teaching of Jesus*, 2nd edition (Cambridge, 1935; reprinted 1963).

MORRIS, L., *The New Testament and the Jewish Lectionaries* (London, 1964).

MOULE, C. F. D., *The Birth of the New Testament* (London, 1962).

MOWINCKEL, S., *He That Cometh*, Eng. trans. by G. W. Anderson (Oxford, 1956).

ROBINSON, H. W., *The Cross in the Old Testament* (London, 1955).

STAUFFER, E., *New Testament Theology*, Eng. trans. by John Marsh (London, 1955).

STENDAHL, K., *The School of St. Matthew* (Uppsala, 1954).

SUNDBERG, A. C., *The Old Testament of the Early Church* (Oxford, 1964).

TASKER, R. V. G., *The Old Testament in the New Testament*, 2nd edition (London, 1954).

WENHAM, J. W., *Our Lord's View of the Old Testament* (London, 1958).

PART TWO
THE NEW TESTAMENT

THE GOSPEL ACCORDING TO MATTHEW

H. L. ELLISON

Preliminary Remarks

Mt. raises so many wider problems, to which must be added others affecting all four gospels, that the exegesis has had to be kept as short as possible. Wherever practicable the reader is referred to the treatment of parallels in other gospels. Writers are cited by name only; the title of the work will be found in the Bibliography. All points of Jewish practice and teaching have been checked with Strack & Billerbeck (cited as *SB*); hence citations are rarely necessary.

Authorship

The reader should turn first to the essay on *The Fourfold Gospel*. Mt. is strictly anonymous, i.e. we derive the name from early Christian tradition and usage, not from any hints in the gospel (for 9: 10 cf. comment *ad loc.*). This tradition is of doubtful value, for though it was firmly established by the time of Irenaeus (*c.* 180), it seems in every case to go back to Papias (*c.* 130). He affirms, 'Matthew compiled the oracles (*ta logia*) in Heb. and everyone translated them as best he could'. 'Oracles' is not a normal name for a gospel, and the present Gk. text of Mt. is certainly no ordinary translation. If Matthew had re-written his gospel in Gk., Papias would surely have said so.

If we accept the view that the writer of Mt. used Mk, it becomes virtually impossible to see our Mt. in Papias's tradition. It seems preferable to assume that the anonymous writer combined Mk with other material, mainly Matthew's 'oracles', which will have contained chiefly teaching; thus Matthew's name has been linked with the gospel as a whole.

This view is supported by Tasker, pp. 11-17.

Stonehouse, in a thoroughly conservative study, though he supports Matthew as author, agrees that he used Mk (ch. 2) and denies the gospel is a translation (ch. 3). Guthrie (pp. 31-42, 126-132) reaches similar conclusions, after giving most of the rival views.

Date and Purpose

Except where Mt. is considered the earliest gospel it is normally dated between 75 and 80. Its author, who could have known Matthew, if he was not the apostle, was a member of a church, possibly that of Antioch, where Jewish Christians were numerous, but he did not write exclusively for them. The gospel was intended to serve the church as a teaching manual. This explains its exceptional fivefold structure (see below).

This fivefold division gave rise recently to the view that we have here a Christian Pentateuch, with the Sermon on the Mount taking the place of the Law-giving at Sinai. It is now realized that Mt. breaks the fetters of any such artificial categories, including the older ones of Jewish Gospel, Royal Gospel, etc. Rather, to the Church, to whom the privileges of Israel have been extended, is presented a rounded picture of its King.

Already Papias commented on the lack of chronological order in Mk, and Cole, p. 35, shows convincingly that this derives from Peter's purposes as a teacher. What Mk did for the narrative, Mt. carried further and did to the teaching as well, adding extra illustrative material to the great centres of teaching. All the teaching is Christ's, but we must not assume that it was necessarily all given in the context in which we now find it.

ANALYSIS

Prologue: Birth and Infancy (1: 1-2: 23)

I i Narrative: Proclamation and Appearance of the Messiah (3: 1-4: 25)
    ii Teaching: The Sermon on the Mount (5: 1-7: 29)

II i Narrative: Miracles in Galilee (8: 1-9: 34)
    ii Teaching: The Mission of the Twelve (9: 35-11: 1)

PROLOGUE: BIRTH AND INFANCY (1: 1-2: 23)

The Genealogy (1: 1-17)

Cf. Lk. 3: 23-38. It may be taken for granted that both genealogies are of Joseph, that in Mt. showing his legal claim to the throne, that in Lk. giving his actual descent. The view that Lk. gives Mary's genealogy conflicts with the language, seems to have been unknown in the early Church and first achieved prominence *c.* 1490 (*HDB*, II, p. 138b). For the reconciliation of the genealogies cf. *NBD*, p. 459; Machen, pp. 202-209.

The main purpose of the genealogy is probably less to prove Jesus' legal claim to the Davidic throne, and more to show that he was not merely a revealer of divine truth but far more the climax of a divinely guided historical process. The mention of the four women (3, 5, 6), all of them unattractive by orthodox Jewish standards, will have been to counter discreditable rumours about Jesus' birth circulating in Jewish circles.

The device of breaking up the genealogy into three groups of 14 names stresses the natural divisions of the history, gives an aid to memory, and stamps the name of David on each, for the value of the letters of his name in Heb. adds up to 14. The omission of three names in v. 8 is for the sake of the pattern and quite consistent with Jewish practice (cf. Williams, I, p. 16). In the last section there are strictly only thirteen names, for Jechoniah belongs to the second. It is probable that in the Heb. original of the genealogy Jehoiakim was misread as Jehoiachin in v. 11 (so Schniewind).

The Birth of Jesus (1: 18-25)

Humanly speaking Jesus' claim to the Davidic throne depended on the willingness of Joseph, the legal heir, to accept Him as his son. Hence Mt. gives only Joseph's version of the story. For a brief discussion on the Virgin Birth cf. comments on Lk. 1: 26-38; see also Machen. Here let us note that apart from the divine activity in conception, Christ's birth was completely normal. He was not conceived

until Mary was married; betrothal was legally marriage (24, **he took his wife**). Joseph was His father in every way except procreation. Long-distance foretelling of names is exceptional in prophecy. **23. Emmanuel** is intended to give the significance of the child's birth, not his name. Except for those who approach it with minds made up, **but knew her not until she had borne a son** (25) seems incompatible with the doctrine of the perpetual virginity of Mary.

A Harmony of the Nativity Stories.

The popular interpretation of the story of the wise men, bringing them hard on the heels of the shepherds, makes it impossible to harmonize Lk. and Mt. When we follow the clue of 2: 16 and realize that Jesus was born anything from a year to two before their visit, there is not much difficulty.

Joseph was a citizen of Bethlehem, possibly owning a small piece of ground there; that is why he went there for the census (Lk. 2: 4), that and his knowledge that the Messiah must be born there. After the presentation in the Temple, they returned to Nazareth (Lk. 2: 39). Joseph will have sold up there and returned to Bethlehem, believing that the Messiah must grow up in David's town. After they had settled down the wise men came, and then the story unfolded as in Mt.

The Visit of the Wise Men (2: 1-12)

The **wise men** (*magoi*) were astrologers, who believed that the movements of the heavenly bodies and the destinies of men were linked. They 'observed the rising of his star' (2, NEB) and connected it with the birth of the expected Jewish king. Too little is told us to allow us to decide what sort of a star it was and why they linked it with the birth of the Messiah. There is no suggestion that **the star . . . went before them** (9) until the final stretch of the journey, nor are we told how it could do so.

The story is prophetic of what was to happen. 'This time Magi forestalled Israel, who possessed the clear prophetic word' (Schlatter). They must have heard of Israel's hope through Jews, but they had to tell Israel that it had been fulfilled.

It was God's will that His Son, who is prophetically called Israel (Isa. 49: 3), should recapitulate the history of Israel (2: 15), so He had to go to Egypt. For this the gifts of the Magi were divinely provided. The **gold** paid the cost of the journey, the **frankincense and myrrh**, easily carried and fetching very high prices in Egypt, provided for their first needs there.

The Road to Nazareth (2: 13-23)

We do not know how long they stayed in Egypt, for we do not know how long before Herod's death (4 B.C.) Christ was born. The quotation from Hos. 11: 1 causes no difficulty, when we realize that Mt. is saying that Jesus was recapitulating the history of His people, but what are we to say of v. 18 with its quotation of Jer. 31: 15? This stands shortly before the joy of the promise of the New Covenant (Jer. 31: 31-34). Even so, when the Maker of the Covenant came, He had to be preceded by sorrow. **22. Archelaus:** Son of Herod: cf. *The Historical Background*, p. 59.

Nazareth is mentioned in a synagogue poem of the seventh century based on much older material, but it has no place among the hundreds of Galilean place names in both Josephus and the rabbinic writings. Built a little higher up the hill than most of the modern town it stood near the junction of three secondary roads, but it was little more than a village, overshadowed by its neighbours (cf. Dalman, ch. III).

23. 'He shall be called a Nazarene' is not really a direct OT quotation. It serves three purposes. (i) It links with Isa. 11: 1, *'and a branch (nēṣer) shall grow out of his roots'* and through it with all passages indicating the humble origin of the Messiah. (ii) Through the humbleness of Nazareth it reminds us of passages like the Servant Songs in Isa. 40-55. (iii) In his spelling of Nazareth Mt. intends to remind us of the Nazirite (Num. 6: 1-21) and hence of Jesus' single-minded devotion to God. For the prophecies in this ch. as a whole cf. *The New Testament Use of the Old Testament* (pp. 130 ff).

I. i. THE PROCLAMATION AND APPEARANCE OF THE MESSIAH (3: 1-4: 25)

The Ministry of John the Baptist (3: 1-12)

See comments on Lk. 3: 1-18. The fierceness of the attack on the Pharisees and Sadducees (7, cf. *The Religious Background*, p.p. 75 f) was because as religious leaders they should have been familiar with the heart of John's message even before he began to preach.

The Baptism of Jesus (3: 13-17)

See comments on Mk 1: 9-11. Jesus was 'born under the law' (Gal. 4: 4); since John was God's messenger, He had to **fulfil all righteousness** (15) by accepting his baptism, though he did not need it.

The Testing (4: 1-11)

See comments on Mk 1: 12 f.; Lk. 4: 1-13. It should be noted that *peirazō* (to tempt) and *peirasmos* (temptation) mean in secular Gk. to test and testing. It is only our fallen nature that turns our necessary testing into temptation. Hence we should use the popular rendering only when the context makes it unavoidable. There is no obvious lesson to be deduced from the different order of testings in Mt. and Lk.

The First Message in Galilee (4: 12-17)

See comments on Mk 1: 14 f.

Note on 'The Kingdom of Heaven' (17). In this period the pious Aram. speaking Jew avoided not only the revealed name of Yahweh (Jehovah), by substituting *Adonai* (Lord), but also *Elohim* (God), for which he used especially *ha-shem* (the Name), *maqom* (Space) and *shamayim* (heaven). The last of these is found especially in the expression *malkuth shamayim* (the kingdom of heaven).

The attempt to find some difference in meaning between the kingdom of God and the kingdom of heaven is one of the less profitable exercises in NT exegesis we have inherited. The repeated parallelisms between the kingdom of heaven in Mt. and the kingdom of God in Mk and Lk. should in themselves have shown that they were identical; the rabbinic use proves it. Jesus will normally have used 'kingdom of heaven'; Mt. preserved it, with the exception of 12: 28; 19: 24; 21: 31, because his readers will have been familiar with it. Mk and Lk. felt it necessary to substitute 'kingdom of God' so as to be certain of being understood.

Kingdom (*malkuth, basileia*) is primarily 'sovereignty', kingly rule and power. It is something which has always existed, but in its fulness it is yet future. It entered the world in a new way with the coming of the King (Mk 1: 15) and will be experienced in all its fulness, when at the name of Jesus every knee shall bow (Phil. 2: 10).

There are a few passages where it is used more in our sense of the sphere in which God's sovereignty is exercised. Even here, however, the stress on God's sovereignty is normally prominent.

The Call of the First Disciples (4: 18-22)

See comments on Mk 1: 16-20.

A Summary of Early Activity in Galilee (4: 23-25)

Since this is a summary, there are no exact parallels, but cf. Mk 1: 39; 3: 7 f.; Lk. 4: 44; 6: 17 ff.

I. ii. THE SERMON ON THE MOUNT (5: 1-7: 29)

For over a century an intensive comparison has been made between Christ's teaching and that of the earlier rabbis. It has been conclusively shown that there is very little in the Sermon which cannot be in measure paralleled from rabbinic writings, and the discussion has often degenerated into a question of priority, as though the rabbis would have borrowed consciously from Jesus. The similarities are due to both basing their teaching on the OT. But while the rabbinic parallels are obtained by sifting hundreds of thousands of words, the brief compass of the Sermon stands unique in its power to shake those who are prepared to expose themselves to its concentrated shock.

No attempt is made here to discuss the relationship of these chapters with 'the Sermon on the Plain' (Lk. 6: 17-49). There are no grounds for assuming that all recorded here by Mt. must have been spoken on one occasion, or that Jesus did not repeat Himself, sometimes with considerable variations.

The Beatitudes (5: 3-12)

Cf. Lk. 6: 20-23. The contrast between the Sermon and the Law-giving at Sinai is at its greatest here. The latter begins with the Ten Commandments, which give the fundamental laws governing the behaviour of those that would be in covenant relationship with God. The Beatitudes are addressed to those who show by their lives that they have achieved what the Decalogue demands. So far from being a new law, as some 'dispensationalists' believe, the Sermon describes the life of those who by grace have passed beyond law.

For v. 3 cf. Isa. 11: 4; 57: 15; 61: 1; for v. 4 Isa. 61: 1; for v. 5 Ps. 37: 11; for v. 6 Isa. 55: 1 f.; for v. 8 Ps. 24: 3 f.

Salt and Light (5: 13-16)

Cf. Lk. 11: 33; 14: 34 f. The stress continues on character rather than works. Salt and light function in virtue of what they are, not what they do. It is probably the preservative rather than the seasoning value of salt which is here being stressed. **13. if salt has lost its taste:** This is usually explained by the salt being the outside layer of rock salt, where the salinity has been lost by the action of sun and rain (NBD, p. 1,125b), or that it had been adulterated (M'Neile; Filson suggests both). Neither really suits the context. Rather the physically impossible (Schniewind) shows that the disciple without a salty effect has never been a true one. Note that our **light** (16) is not our **good works**, but the means by which people see that they are good.

Jesus and the Law (5: 17-20)

Jesus then turned to His relationship to the already extant revelation of God. The threefold division of Scripture (Lk. 24: 44) had not yet become general (SB), so here the **prophets** (17) mean all the books of the OT apart from the **law.** He had come to fulfil (plēroō) all of them, but since His great conflict with the Pharisees would be about the law, He confined His remarks to it. The law was a revelation of God's will and would therefore stand **till heaven and earth pass away** (=until all is accomplished, 18). To relax a commandment (19) is to claim authority over God.

20. The **righteousness of the scribes and Pharisees** was inadequate because, with all its zeal, it represented a merely human interpretation of God's demands through the law. Jesus' interpretation, so far from destroying, fulfilled. First He really kept the law (and this righteousness is imputed to us); second He revealed 'the full depth of meaning that it was intended to hold' (M'Neile). When His Spirit indwells us, we have His interpretation written on our hearts.

On Murder (5: 21-26)

Cf. 12: 57 ff. The principle that anger and scorn are in God's sight as evil as the murder they can easily lead to was recognized by the rabbis, but Jesus supplied a new note of seriousness. His words are not easy to follow. **Judgment** must bear the same meaning in vv. 21, 22; it will refer to the local Jewish courts of 23 members. Then **the council** (22) will be the 71 member Sanhedrin in Jerusalem, the supreme court. **22 mg. Whoever says Raca to his brother:** Raca, an Aram. word, means 'empty head', and is often mentioned in rabbinic writings as a common term of abuse; mōre (**you fool!**) is not Gk. here but Aram. and equivalent to 'godless fellow'. Jesus means that the local court *should* try anger as much as murder, while the denial of a man's self-respect *should* concern the supreme court. To deny a man's moral standing before God is so serious that only the Heavenly Court is competent to deal with it. Of course, human courts seldom deal with these matters, but that will not prevent the Heavenly Court from doing its duty. To give another a just charge against us is so serious that putting the matter right is more important than worship (23). To say that vv. 25 f. refer to a man's relationship to God is an example of perverse allegorical ingenuity.

22. the hell (geenna) **of fire:** In the OT the place of the dead, both good and bad, is called Sheol, rendered Hades in the NT. With the growth of belief in the resurrection during the Inter-Testamental period, we find in the Bk. of

Enoch (*c.* 150–100 B.C.) the concept of a 'hell' for sinners after the final judgment. This was soon universally called Ge-Hinnom, short for Ge-ben-Hinnom, the Valley of (the son of) Hinnom—in Gk. *ge(h)enna.* Literally this was the valley south of Jerusalem, where child sacrifices had been offered under Ahaz and Manasseh, which from the time of Josiah became the place where the rubbish of Jerusalem was tipped and burnt. In the later first century A.D. a group of Pharisees considered that Gehenna had a purifying rôle for lesser sinners consigned there; in the second century it was expanded to mean also a sort of purgatory before the final judgment. These latter uses are not found in the NT.

On Adultery and Divorce (5: 27-32)

Cf. 19: 9; Mk 10: 11 f.; Lk. 16: 18. For the OT fornication and adultery are not two stages of one sin but different types of sin. The former is expressly condemned only in its more aggravated forms, though it is always regarded with disfavour. The latter was a fundamental sin against the family, and so against society, and carried the death penalty with it (Lev. 20: 10; Dt. 22: 22). The pious Jew regarded all sexual sin, whether of act or thought, with abhorrence. If Jesus concentrated on the more serious offence, He was not in any way condoning the lesser.

The popular opinion that the rabbis were very lax about divorce comes from an ignorance of their exegetical methods. The disciples of Shammai (1st cent. A.D.) rendered Dt. 24: 1 as in RSV; their rivals, the disciples of Hillel, understood it as 'anything offensive'. On the basis of this they said that burning her husband's food would be ground enough for divorce, or if he saw someone more beautiful (Aqiba, died 135). But this was only expounding the law as they understood it. In fact they deprecated divorce, and there is no evidence that it was common.

Jesus' use of **adultery** (28) implies that the man and woman were debarred from being married. Presumably *gynē* (**woman**) bears here, as so often, the meaning 'wife' (so *Arndt*). The sin, even in thought, is so serious that it would be worth while to cripple oneself to avoid it. This would seem to answer in anticipation the modern argument that adultery and fornication are, under certain circumstances, natural and necessary for fulness of life.

Christ's saying on **divorce** has caused so much controversy, that we must confine ourselves to a statement of facts. (*a*) Jesus was addressing people whose characters are depicted in 5: 3-10. He was not placing the unregenerate Gentile under greater restrictions than had already been laid on the Jew (Dt. 24: 1-4).

(*b*) Since the Gospels did not circulate in one *codex* until the 2nd. century, we must not read into **except on the ground of unchastity** (*porneia*) a meaning so important that those possessing only Mk or Lk. would seriously misunderstand Christ's words. (*c*) *Porneia* is never used in LXX or NT of simple adultery. The Orthodox Church has understood it to mean here repeated acts of adultery, which make the wife no better than a harlot. (*d*) From the fact that it carried the death penalty, it may be argued that adultery automatically ends a marriage, but this cannot be inferred from this passage. (*e*) Only three, not mutually exclusive, meanings of the exceptive clause seem to have claims to consideration: (i) that of the Orthodox Church, which should know the meaning of the Gk.; (ii) that unconfessed pre-marital sin is indicated, i.e. the marriage was entered on under false pretences; (iii) that marriage within the prohibited degrees is intended, as in Ac. 15: 20, 29—the idea that the early Gentile Christians were given to sexual promiscuity is foolish and uncharitable. **32. makes her an adulteress:** Under the social conditions of the time it was almost impossible for a younger woman to live an independent single life.

On Swearing (5: 33-37)

23: 16-22 is considered here also. The telling of the complete truth at all times is so fraught with danger, that it is possible only to the one who trusts completely in God. Once my word is not regarded as reliable, I shall try to establish my veracity by the use of oaths; but these tend rapidly to become mechanical and virtually meaningless. The rabbis tried to counter this by laying down oaths which could be relied on. Jesus is concerned here, not with the demands of authority that under certain circumstances an oath be taken, but with that perfect honesty which will make oaths unnecessary. I, as a Christian, am entitled to expect that those who know me will accept my word, if I am invariably truthful. Why should a judge, or other authorized person, who does not know me, accept my uncorroborated statement that I am a Christian and release me from an oath, or affirmation, which is an oath under another name? Jewish jurisprudence, in any case, did not know our evidence given on oath. The only cases where one was required were those like Exod. 22: 10 f.

In an oath I call on God, or someone or something else, to bear witness to the truth of my statement and, if necessary, bring disaster on me. But I cannot control **heaven, earth, Jerusalem,** or even my **head.** It is still worse when I make a distinction between oath and oath (23: 16-22). I may deceive the man unversed

F

in these subtleties and so profane holy things. These differences are not found in second-century rabbinic writings. It is probable that this is one of the cases where Jesus' rebuke was taken to heart; cf. comment on 15: 4 f.

On True Love (5: 38–48)

Cf. Lk. 6: 27–36. Any and every effort to explain these verses in terms of law is bound to fail. We are simply given a picture of how the regenerate will behave, if they respond to their new nature. We should render v. 48, 'Ye therefore shall be perfect, as your heavenly Father is perfect' (RV). This is merely a variant of Lev. 19: 2, '*You shall be holy; for I the LORD your God am holy*'. Buber says on this (p. 128), 'more in the form of a promise than in the form of a demand'. Experience has shown that it is not difficult for a Christian to carry out this section spontaneously, but it is almost impossible as the result of deliberate action.

The law, **an eye for an eye and a tooth for a tooth** (38; Exod. 21: 24; Lev. 24: 20; Dt. 19: 21), does not command revenge, but moderation in revenge, which should not exceed the damage done. While the high-priestly party among the Sadducees still applied the law literally at this time, most Pharisees insisted on the monetary equivalent's being paid. The context shows that **Do not resist one who is evil** (39) means that one should not seek justice for *oneself*. There is no suggestion that by inaction or silence we should encourage injustice to others. Nor is it implied that we should not lay our case in the Divine Judge's hands. Four practical cases are envisaged. (i) Positive injustice: 'If someone slaps you on the right cheek' (39, NEB). Injured honour as well as physical pain are involved. Not passive but active acceptance is advocated. (ii) Possible injustice: **if anyone would sue you** (40). His action, though apparently unjust, might prove to be well founded. The **coat** (*chitōn*) is the long inner shirt, the **cloak** (*himation*) the much more valuable outer garment, which by law could not be taken (Exod. 22: 26 f.). (iii) Official burdens: 'If a man in authority makes you go one mile' (41, NEB). *Angareuō* is the Persian, possibly Babylonian, loanword (*Arndt*) for the age-old system of unpaid service that those in official service were entitled to demand. It was looked on as slave-service, and therefore degrading. To go a second mile would relieve another from the burden. (iv) Unreasonable claims: the context suggests that the beggar and borrower would deprive one of what one needs oneself. What of it, if the other is really in need? Ac. 3: 6 illustrates one way of carrying out this precept.

43. You shall love your neighbour and hate your enemy: It is normally assumed that Jesus was placing beside narrow Jewish national love for their own people (**your neighbour**) a wider love embracing the Gentiles (**your enemy**) as well, but this is improbable. It is true that the rabbis always interpreted Lev. 19: 18 as referring to fellow-Jews, as indeed it does. Controversy only concerned which classes of Jews might legitimately be excluded from its scope (cf. Lk. 10: 29). But nowhere do we find in their writings the suggestion that all Gentiles were enemies and to be hated. The nearest to it is the exceptional passage in *Sifra* (89b), which says, commenting on Lev. 19: 18a, 'Against others you may be revengeful or bear a grudge'. By **hate your enemy** Jesus was putting into words the ordinary accepted attitude towards all regarded as enemies, whether Jews or Gentiles. Here, as so often in the NT, the emotional side of love is not under consideration. The parable of the Good Samaritan is the classic example of what Jesus meant by loving one's enemy, and here even a greeting is seen as an example of it (47).

The very illustration of the Father's love (45) is an indication of the type of being **perfect** (48) that Jesus was teaching. If they were holy (see above) and mature sons of the Father, they would, as sharers of His Spirit, partake in His impartial love of men. The NT does not suggest that we receive more from God, but what we receive can be rightly applied and used (cf. Rom. 8: 28). The perfection is not sinlessness, but a complete control by God's Spirit.

On True Religion (6: 1–18)

The character described in ch. 5 will express itself in outward actions, which collectively we call 'religion' (Jas 1: 26 f.) or **piety** (1, *dikaiosynē*, lit. righteousness). The quality of these actions does not depend on whether men see them, but on whether men are intended to see them; those whom Jesus was rebuking undoubtedly did them for God also.

Rewards (1). For many today the chief difficulty created by the Sermon on the Mount is its stress on rewards, which are mentioned nine times. But this is an element found throughout the NT, *e.g.* Mt. 10: 41 f.; Jn 4: 36; 1 C. 3: 8, 14; 9: 17 f.; Heb. 11: 6; 2 Jn 8; Rev. 11: 18; 22: 12. Some do respond to grace more readily than others, and 'God is not so unjust as to overlook your work and the love which you showed for his sake in serving the saints' (Heb. 6: 10). Even though Judaism had tended to work out a mathematical relationship between works and rewards, yet it realized that the latter were essentially an expression of God's grace (*SB* IV, pp. 487 ff.). For the nature of the reward see next section.

Alms (2 ff.). Almsgiving was considered by Judaism to be the foremost act of piety. The need was created by the large number of those physically and psychically incapable of work. There were also many landless men, who could not hope to maintain their families by their casual labour (cf. Mt. 20: 1-16, and also Jas 2: 14 ff.; 1 Jn 3: 17). In our modern setting it is our time rather than our money they need.

Most charity was exercised by the Synagogue as representing the community. This made begging less necessary and helped to preserve the anonymity of the poor. So the ostentation condemned is not in the giving to individuals but in the public proclamation of the amounts given to the community for the purpose (**trumpet** is vivid hyperbole). For **hypocrites** see additional note at end of the chapter; there is no suggestion that here (or vv. 5, 16; 7: 5) scribes and Pharisees are particularly under attack; the practices were not peculiar to them. **Their reward** was the praise of men, so God's reward, which they forfeited, is God's praise, His 'Well done'. **left hand . . . right hand:** a vivid expression implying absolute secrecy. Judaism insisted on charity being kept secret so as not to shame the poor; it should be so secret that we ourselves should forget we helped the poor man, when we meet him again.

Prayer (5-8). Neither community prayer, which Jesus never condemned, nor the secret outpourings of the heart, which need no guidance, is under consideration, but the then usual, though not compulsory, association of the individual, wherever he might be, with the national morning and evening prayer in the Temple (cf. Ac. 3: 1; 10: 3, 30). It was easy to arrange to be in a prominent place at the time. It was normal **to stand** for prayer. The use of **empty phrases** is noted as a Gentile weakness, though the Jewish Prayer Book provides some examples. Prayer is not intended as a memory-jogger for God (8), but as a means by which the Christian's desires are brought under God's scrutiny, and the one who prays is reminded of the character, will and purposes of God.

The Pattern Prayer (9-13). Cf. Lk. 11: 2-4. When the community, and the individual conscious of his unity with the community, are praying, some guidance as to the scope of their prayer is needed (completely private prayer is not under consideration). The shortened and slightly variant form of words in Lk. 11, the omission of any confession of sin beforehand and of any doxology at the end (the familiar one in AV is very early but indubitably not original) all suggest that we have a guide and framework for our petitions rather than a fixed formula.

I am a member of a community, so I say **our;** I have been made a son, so I say **Father. Who art in heaven** reminds me that there is neither inability to give nor folly in giving. I pray first that God may have His rightful place among men. The nearest approach to the meaning permitted by modern Eng. idiom is probably 'may your name be honoured' (Phillips), or 'may thy name be held in reverence' (Filson); **name** 'means God as he has made himself known' (Filson). The prayer for the coming of the **kingdom** (cf. note on 4: 17) is not merely for the Second Coming of Christ but also for subjection to His will in society and the individual. The **kingdom** implies submission, but God's **will** can be done even against their own will by those that rebel. **On earth as it is in heaven** applies to all three introductory petitions.

Daily (*epiousios*) has been found only once in non-Christian writings, so its meaning is uncertain; this is reflected in the varying early Christian interpretations. It may well mean 'daily ration' (cf. *Arndt*, pp. 296 f.), or 'bread for the immediate future' (Tasker). There is no justification for the Eng. Prayer Book rendering, 'our trespasses . . . those that trespass . . .', Trespass in the Bible has the connotation of rebellion, and any such sin would have to be confessed before a man could even think of normal prayer. At the most our falling short ('sin', Lk. 11: 4) and our failure to give God due honour are intended by **debts**, just as **we also have forgiven** (*aphēkamen*, an aorist and so a fact) those that have slighted our self-esteem. 'And do not bring us to the test' (NEB, cf. Jas 1: 2 f. and note on 4: 1-11): temptations are mainly our fault (Jas 1: 13 f.); testing is a divine necessity to reveal the reality of our faith and protestations. We should shrink from it, but when the time comes that we must pass through it, we ask for deliverance in it. **from evil:** So also Phillips; RSVmg., RV, NEB and most commentaries 'from the evil one'. The Gk. is ambiguous, but on the whole the personal rendering is better, for God uses Satan as the tester. It may well be that the original Aram. was equally ambiguous.

A Necessary Preliminary to Prayer (14, 15). Cf. 18: 23-35; Mk 11: 25. Some seared consciences unavailingly try to avoid the force of this warning by pleading that it does not apply to Christians. Others try to make out that their circumstances are so peculiar that they override Scripture. Should the regenerate man refuse to forgive the wrong done to him, he effectively cuts himself off from fellowship with God, who is the Forgiver, until he forgives. If the allegedly regenerate man is marked out by an unforgiving spirit, it is the truest sign that he has never been born again (1 Jn 3: 10, 14, 15).

Fasting (16-18). A person under strong emotional stress tends to shun normal food. Hence fasting, without any recorded command from God, became a natural way for the penitent, and for all who felt themselves under divine wrath, to approach God. In the Law fasting is commanded only for the Day of Atonement (Lev. 16: 29, 31; Num. 29: 7), where it is called *to afflict the soul* (RV), which suggests the essentially dual nature of true fasting; it must not be a matter of the body alone. Fasting is frequently mentioned elsewhere in OT, and indeed it is taken for granted. In NT it is nowhere commanded or even positively commended—the verses quoted in its support, *e.g.* Mt. 17: 21; Mk 9: 29; 1 C. 7: 5; Ac. 10: 30, are taken from inferior MSS corrupted by the Church's growing asceticism. Christ mentions fasting as something that will happen (*e.g.* 9: 15, cf. Ac. 13: 2 f.) and regulates its practice. In addition, by fasting in the wilderness (4: 2) He showed that it could have major spiritual importance.

Plainly Jesus is not calling the believer to disassociate himself from the fasts of the community, but is speaking of voluntary fasting (see note on 9: 14), whether regular or occasional (this is borne out by the Gk. syntax). Such a fast is the concern only of the faster and God. **17. anoint your head:** Self-anointing with olive oil was a regular custom, omitted only in times of mourning and fasting. Jesus did not tell His disciples that they should put on an appearance of joy, but that they should behave normally. The head is specially mentioned as the only part of the body where the anointing would be obvious. In addition the faster or mourner often put ashes on his head (cf. 2 Sam. 13: 19).

On Trust in God (6: 19-34)
In NT times, and indeed down to our own, the local Jewish community in measure fulfilled the functions of the modern welfare state, but its finances were normally precarious, and those helped by it had little status in it. This section is concerned with both the individual's security and status.

True Treasure (19-21). Cf. Lk. 12: 33 f. Oriental treasure normally consisted of silver and gold and also costly clothing (cf. Gen. 45: 22; 2 Kg. 5: 23). Here **on earth moth and** 'worm' (mg, lit. 'eating') would see to the latter and **thieves** to the former. That one could transfer one's treasure to **heaven** by charitable acts is often found in contemporary Jewish thought. With Jesus the motivation is

not reward in heaven as with the rabbis, though this is not denied, but the transference of the affections.

The Sound Eye (22, 23). Cf. Lk. 11: 34 ff. The Mishnah says, 'These are things whose fruit a man enjoys in this world while the capital is laid up for him in the world to come: honouring father and mother, deeds of loving-kindness, making peace between a man and his fellow; and the study of the Law is equal to them all' (*Peah* 1: 1). Jesus was speaking less to earth-bound men and more to those who thought in terms of 'both . . . and'. So He gives them the parable of the 'single eye' (RV). The exact meaning of *haplous* is hard to fix. From single we move to sincere, sound, and finally generous. The man who fixes his eyes on God (heaven), will give generously without second thought. The man who tries to look at God and the world at the same time will see neither clearly; in fact he will not see at all.

The Slave with Two Masters (24). Cf. Lk. 16: 13. *SB* and Schniewind stress that it was possible at the time for a slave to be shared by two owners. In spite of the Rabbinic evidence it seems clear that Jesus is speaking of the impossible in practice. 'Men can work for two employers, but no slave can be the property of two owners' (M'Neile). **Mammon,** a word of uncertain etymology, was used in the language of the time to mean property generally. It is not the name of a heathen god, but the Aram. word is probably kept to suggest that property can become a master and even a god.

Anxiety (25-34). Cf. Lk. 12: 22-31. Few of the numerous mistranslations in AV have been more unfortunate than its rendering 'take no thought' in this passage; it has provided both the fanatic and the sceptic with overmuch ammunition. *Merimnaō* means to be anxious, worried, careful; its use in Lk. 10: 41 illustrates its force. **25. Therefore:** vv. 19-24 have shown that there can be no satisfaction or profit from a 'both . . . and' attitude, therefore we must decide on an 'either . . . or'. **life** (*psychē*) . . . **body:** Jesus is here using OT words and is speaking, not of the fact of life, but of man's personality (generally and misleadingly rendered soul) and of the body by which it knows the world and makes itself known to it. The former needs food for its preservation, the latter clothing for its protection and honour (Schlatter). But personality (**life**) and **body** are God's gift, so will He not give the lesser as well? Commentators divide fairly evenly between the text and margin in v. 27, but both the context and the normal use of *hēlikia* favour **span of life.** In fact, few things shorten life more than worry.

Man is better than **birds** and 'wild flowers' (Phillips—whatever flower was meant by *krinon*, it would not be called a lily today) by the order of creation. The behaviour of bird and flower is that allotted them in creation. Man is not intended to imitate them, but to fulfil his role in creation (cf. v. 33); if he does this, he can be assured of God's care. The **Gentiles** (32) are mentioned not in condemnation but because they do not know God's order of creation. Those who know God's revelation behave unnaturally, if they do what those ignorant of it practise naturally; they then become **men of little faith** (30).

Up to this point Jesus has been speaking of the known problems that make men worry. In v. 34 He passes to those as yet unknown. When the morrow brings knowledge of them, it will also bring the answer to them.

Note on 'Hypocrite'. Hypocrite, which is merely a Gk. word written in English letters, is found in NT only in the Synoptic gospels and always on the lips of Jesus. We find it 13 times in Mt. (6: 2, 5, 16; 7: 5; 15: 7; 22: 18; 23: 13, 15, 23, 25, 27, 29; 24: 51), once only in Mk and three times in Lk. In Mt. it is used generally five times and in the remaining eight specifically of 'the scribes and Pharisees'.

In NT times the word had a wide range of meaning, but that of a bad man deliberately pretending to be good was not one of them. It is probable that the meaning 'actor' will satisfy all the NT passages; it certainly does in the Sermon on the Mount. Even when it is applied to the scribes and Pharisees we get the impression that they had so persuaded themselves of the rightness of their position and actions that they were oblivious of their wrongness.

The fact that the word is used only by Jesus, with His unique knowledge of human character and motivation, should make us reticent in judging those whom He so castigated. See further *NBD*, article 'Hypocrite', and the literature there mentioned.

On Criticism (7: 1-6)

Cf. Lk. 6: 37 f., 41 f. The chapter division coincides with a real break in thought. The obligation of judgment is laid on a limited number of people only. The context makes it clear that they are not under consideration but it is those who arrogate the right of judgment to themselves. Phillips' rendering 'Don't criticize people' would be idiomatically preferable, were it not clear that contemporary Jewish idiom implies that **you will be judged,** 'it shall be measured unto you' (RV) refers to God's action (*SB*, Schniewind, Filson, Schlatter).

5. You hypocrite: Less because a man,

whose vision was so impaired, could hardly see to remove **the speck,** and more because he was behaving as though he saw perfectly.

Schlatter is probably correct in linking v. 6 closely with vv. 1-5. The judgment Jesus is particularly condemning is our efforts to make all conform to our own standards of perfection. Quite apart from our own failure to conform, we are liable to find those we judge spiritually unprepared. We have to distinguish between our proclamation of Christ and our own understanding of His standards.

On Our Treatment of Others (7: 7-12)

Cf. Lk. 11: 9-13; 6: 31. The usual treatment of this passage makes vv. 7-11 an additional exhortation to prayer (but why does it not stand after 6: 15?) and regards v. 12 as an isolated saying, 'The Golden Rule'. It is quite possible that Mt. and Lk. are both dealing with a contextless passage on prayer. But Mt., by adding **so** in v. 12, indicates that we are to understand the whole passage in the context of this verse. God behaves to us, as we would expect an earthly father to behave, only better, for earthly fathers are **evil** (11). We would wish men to behave thus to us, so we should behave thus to them.

'The Golden Rule' is found in Tob. 4: 15, in its negative form which is also attributed to Hillel and Philo. It is unlikely that much difference of meaning should be read into the difference between the positive and negative forms, the more so as a number of Talmudic sayings virtually assume the former. So it should not be regarded as the mountain peak of Christian ethics.

It is very doubtful whether **ask . . . seek . . . knock** should be regarded as three stages in prayer. Rather we have the one separated from God who knocks, the one who has strayed who seeks, and the child at home who asks; all receive equally. **Evil** (*ponēroi*) stresses not men's positive wickedness, but their worthlessness when placed in God's light. Note Lk.'s 'Holy Spirit' in place of **good things. 12. the law and the prophets:** Here the whole OT, cf. 5: 17. Jesus means, 'This is what the OT teaches,' not 'this is the essence of the OT', as it is so often understood.

Three Contrasts (7: 13-27)

Jesus ends His address with a call to action and self-judgment.

The Two Ways (13, 14). Cf. Lk. 13: 23 f. The contrast between the two ways was common in Jewish thought (cf. Jer. 21: 8), but there are no real parallels in it to the two gates. Behind this is the teaching of both John the Baptist and Jesus, which demanded a step of decision, which for the moment left the man making it a single entity dealing with God purely as an individual. Judaism does not really know this position. Lk. 13: 23 f. shows that we have no right to interpret v. 13 except of Jesus' own time, though the consensus of Christian opinion is that it has been true of many other periods too.

True Fruit (15-23). Cf. 12: 33 ff.; Lk. 6: 43-46; 13: 26 f. **False prophets** are more likely, at the first at any rate, to be self-deceived than deceivers. It is its hunger, not its malignity, that gives the wolf its reputation. So it is with the man that would serve both God and mammon (6: 24). He serves God provided he can have mammon too. Only those actions that reveal character are a valid test with such men. Preaching and even miracles are no necessary indication of genuineness. Rev. 13: 3, 12 suggests (we are not entitled to say more) that even the resurrection of Christ may be counterfeited in the end time. The evidential character of all miracle is to be decided by the character of him who performs it.

The True Response (24-27). Cf. Lk. 6: 47 ff. **and does them:** The Gk. tense implies that not an isolated act but a lifetime of doing is implied. While the storm (25) undoubtedly refers to the final judgment, yet, as with the OT phrase *the day of the Lord*, any earlier catastrophe, which seriously foreshadows the final judgment, is included. Lk. 6: 49 shows that we are to understand light soil rather than literal **sand** (26). As the picture of any hill village in Galilee will show us, to build on **the sand** implies building in the valley bottom, where the flood waters are bound to come. It would be an act of extreme folly and improvidence.

The Effect of the Sermon (7: 28, 29)
Cf. Mk 1: 22; Lk. 4: 32. This astonishment is generally interpreted by the rabbinic custom, wherever possible, of citing an earlier teacher for the opinion or ruling given. This is inadequate, for frequently a rabbi had to give an independent judgment resting on no true precedent. The rabbis considered that they and the prophets before them were merely authoritative expounders of the Mosaic law. The authority was vested in this law and nowhere else. But Jesus repeatedly taught on His own authority. This explains the questions about authority (21: 23), the demands for signs (12: 38; 16: 1) and the controversy about tradition (9: 14; 12: 2; 15: 1 f.). This was bound to awaken the hostility of the religious leaders. The mass of the people **were astonished** but unprepared to abandon those who had been their guides for so long.

II. i. MIRACLES IN GALILEE (8: 1-9: 34)
The choice of incidents in this section is in every case to bring out Jesus' authority in action. It is difficult, however, to explain the order of events, where this differs from that in Mk. There are no grounds for suggesting that Mt. is trying to correct Mk's order.

The Healing of a Leper (8: 1-4)
See comments on Mk 1: 40-45 (Lk. 5: 12-16). Lk. 5: 12 makes it clear the healing was done in a town. In NT times the impurity caused by a leper was strongly insisted on but the regulations of Lev. 13 had been relaxed in one important detail. Except in walled towns the leper was allowed to live among his fellow-men, provided he had a house to himself (*SB* IV, pp. 751-7; Edersheim I, p. 492). Josephus is often quoted against this, but in *Ant.* III. xi. 3, *War* V. v. 6 he means Jerusalem by 'the city'; in *Contra Apion.* I. 31 he may be referring to the original enforcement of this command. R. G. Cochrane, *Biblical Leprosy*, has shown that Lev. 13 is not describing typical cases of leprosy (Hansen's disease), and it is not certain that leprosy in the modern sense was known in Palestine in OT times, though it was in NT. There is no evidence that the Messiah was expected to heal lepers (Edersheim I, p. 495).

The Healing of the Centurion's Servant (8: 5-13)
See comments on Lk. 7: 1-10. There seems to be no reason for trying to harmonize the two accounts. In dealing with the centurion's representatives Jesus was dealing with him. For mainly Gentile readers Lk. stresses the winning of Jews by a Gentile's love; for mainly Jewish readers Mt. stresses the acceptance of faith wherever found. There are no grounds for identifying the earlier healing of Jn 4: 46-54 with this miracle; it may, however, have given the centurion hope and boldness to approach Jesus.

The Healing of Peter's Mother-in-Law (8: 14, 15)
See comments on Mk 1: 29-31 (Lk. 4: 38 f.).

The Healing of the Crowds at Sunset (8: 16, 17)
See comments on Mk 1: 32-34 (Lk. 4: 40 f.). The quotation from Isa. 53: 4 is probably intended to make clear that Jesus' miracles of healing were not done merely by a word of power, but rather by an act of self-identification with the diseased. The passage, incidentally, is an answer to the claim that the Christian can demand physical healing of right as part of the work of Christ on the cross.

True Discipleship (8: 18-22)
Cf. Lk. 9: 57-60. This section is placed here to indicate that already early in Christ's ministry

there was little reality on the part of many who followed Him. **Foxes have holes . . . :** This does not imply that Jesus had to 'sleep rough' most nights (oriental hospitality would normally take care of that), but that He had nothing, however mean, to which He could retire at need. (This is not contradicted by Mk 2: 1; the house at Capernaum had doubtless been obtained for His mother.) The very fact that **another of the disciples** (21) was with Him is sufficient proof that his father was not yet dead. He did not want to be too far away when death came, perhaps because he wanted to make sure of the inheritance.

22. The dead means, as sometimes in rabbinic writings, the spiritually dead. For **the Son of Man** see additional note at the end of the chapter.

The Storm on the Lake (8: 23–27)
See the comments on Mk 4: 35–41 (Lk. 8: 22–25).

The Gadarene Demoniacs (8: 28–34)
See the comments on Mk 5: 1–20 (Lk. 8: 26–39). Mt. gives a much briefer account, but mentions a second demoniac (28), who is not mentioned in the other two gospels, since he played no major part in the story. There can be little doubt that the correct name of the district is 'the country of the Gergesenes', though it is not given by the best combination of MSS in any of the Synoptic Gospels. For a full discussion see Dalman, pp. 176–180.

Additional Note on The Son of Man. The title 'The Son of Man' (*ho hyios tou anthrōpou*) is found 31 times in Mt., 14 in Mk, 25 in Lk., 13 in Jn and once in Ac. 7: 56 (there are also three cases without the article, meaning a man). Except in the last case it is always used by Jesus Himself. This suggests that it was meant to veil the exact claims of Jesus, and that the apostles ceased to use it, once His death and resurrection made it no longer necessary.

It seems to have two main uses, both with some parallels in Jewish usage, though these are never brought together. Jesus is *the* man, the ideal heavenly man (1 C. 15: 45, 47), the Servant of Jehovah; cf. 8: 20; 9: 6; 20: 28; Mk 8: 31. Then He is the heavenly man who will come with the clouds of heaven as the judge (Dan. 7: 13; Enoch; 2 Esd.), cf. 16: 28; 19: 28; 24: 27, 37–44; 25: 31–46; 26: 64; Mk 8: 38; Lk. 17: 22 ff.; Jn 5: 27. The title was an obvious claim to special status, but it veiled its exact nature until the time had come for disclosure. In both its senses it stressed the links between Jesus and those He had come to save and rule.

The Healing of the Paralysed Man (9: 1–8)
See comments on Mk 2: 1–12 (Lk. 5: 17–26).

It is insufficiently realized that it is equally easy to say **Your sins are forgiven** and **Rise and walk,** but both are equally futile in the mouth of the ordinary man.

1. his own city: Obviously Capernaum. The phrase implies that He had had a home there for at least a year.

The Call of Matthew (9: 9–13)
See comments on Mk 2: 13–17 (Lk. 5: 27–32). There can be no doubt that Matthew and Levi (Mk 2: 14; Lk. 5: 27) are the same person. The idiom in v. 10 (*en tē oikia*) is the same as in Mk 2: 1, where it is translated 'at home'. But now we are in Matthew's house (Lk. 5: 29); hence it is argued (*NBC*, p. 771) that this must have been penned by Matthew. If the argument is valid, it proves no more than that the author used material from Matthew. **10. sinners:** This was used as a general term covering persons who were not allowed to act as judges or witnesses because of their moral unreliability. The Talmud enumerates them as dice players, pigeon racers, usurers, dealers in produce from the Sabbatical year, robbers and other violent criminals, herdsmen, customs officials and tax collectors.

The Discussion about Fasting (9: 14–17)
See comments on Mk 2: 18–22 (Lk. 5: 33–39). **your disciples do not fast:** See notes on 6: 16 ff. Fasting was prohibited to the bride and bridegroom and the wedding guests. Jewish fasts were (i) official, *viz.* the Day of Atonement, 9th of Ab (commemorating the destruction of the Temple by Nebuchadnezzar, and later also of the Second Temple by Titus) and on special occasions of drought, famine and pestilence; (ii) occasional private fasts due to special grief, etc. (cf. Tob. 12: 8; Jdt. 8: 6; Lk. 2: 37), which might become the normal feature of a person's life; (iii) regular private fasts. It is clear that some at least of the Pharisees had adopted the custom of fasting twice a week (Lk. 18: 12), *viz.* on Mondays and Thursdays, and John the Baptist had evidently taken over the custom. This seems to have been due to the prevalence of sin, *scil.* non-observance of the Law according to their standards. How attractive such a custom can become is seen in the *Didache* (early 2nd cent. A.D.), where Christians are exhorted, 'And you must not fast as the hypocrites do, for they fast on Monday and Thursday; you must observe your fast on Wednesday and Friday'!

The 'days of the Messiah' were compared to a marriage feast, so in v. 15 Jesus was not merely giving the first intimation of His death but also of His Messiahship.

Jairus' Daughter and the Woman with a Haemorrhage (9: 18–26)
See comments on Mk 5: 21–43 (Lk. 8: 40–56). In Jewish areas each synagogue was managed

by a committee of seven, in Gentile areas of three. In addition there was 'the ruler of the synagogue' (Lk. 8: 41), normally the most respected member of the community, who could but need not be a member of the committee of management. His chief task was the supervision of the services.

20. the fringe of his garment: See note on 23: 5. A special holiness was supposed to attach to the fringes because they were demanded in the Law (Num. 15: 38 ff.; Dt. 22: 12). The woman showed that faith and superstition can go hand in hand.

Acceptance and Rejection (9: 27–34)

We have here two miracles of healing peculiar to Mt. Though there are strong similarities between vv. 27–31 and 20: 29–34, they are probably accidental. The whole point of the story is the exceptional faith shown by the blind men. The fact that they received their sight proved that they believed (28 f.). This is the only case where healing is made entirely conditional on the faith of the person healed. **Son of David:** See 12: 23. It is quite possible that vv. 32–34 are a preview of 12: 22–24. Mt. ends the section of evidential miracles by an example of outstanding faith and equally outstanding rejection.

II. ii. THE MISSION OF THE TWELVE (9: 35–11: 1)

This section has no real parallel in the other Synoptic gospels. While there is little in it that is peculiar to Mt., much of it is found in other settings in Mk and Lk. Mt. has placed the choice of the Twelve somewhat later in Jesus' ministry in order to combine it with their being sent out in twos. To the instruction then given he has added other appropriate teaching. It seems that Mt. was not so much concerned with the Twelve as to give comprehensive teaching in Christ's words for those who should continue their work.

He had compassion for them (9: 35–36)

The need was not the motive for the choice of the Twelve, but for sending them out (9: 35–10: 1); this was true of the Seventy as well (Lk. 10: 1 f.).

The Choice of the Twelve (10: 2–4)

See comments on Mk 3: 13–19 (Lk. 6: 12–16). The language makes it clear that Mt. is recalling a choice which had been made earlier.

The Charge to the Twelve (10: 5–16)

Cf. Mk 6: 8–11; Lk. 9: 1–5; 10: 2–12. They were **disciples** (1), for they were learning, but when He sent them out they were **apostles** (2). This term meant that they were the valid representatives of Him who had sent them. As such they were given the same message as Jesus'

(7; cf. 4: 17) and His authority over disease and demons (1, 8). Since they were Jesus' representatives, they were under the same limitations as their Master. Hence they were not to go to **Gentiles** or **Samaritans** (5). This prohibition is the counterpart of the restriction laid on Jesus by the Father, 'I was sent only to the lost sheep of the house of Israel' (15: 24, *q.v.*). It is not mentioned in the parallel passages, for there is not the same stress on apostleship there.

It is likely that vv. 8–15 have been responsible for more fanaticism than any comparable passage of Scripture. That we are dealing with principles, not rules, is made clear by Paul's practice (though he was an apostle!). He took care to have a travelling companion of equal status (cf. Mk 6: 7), but, at least in Corinth, he made a point of not accepting the hospitality of any (1 C. 9: 12; 2 C. 11: 9; 12: 13) and of earning his own living. Again his taking first of Mark and later of Timothy is hardly to be explained by the disparity in age between him and the apostles at the first (cf. note on 17: 24–27). Quite simply, conditions varied so much between Palestine and the Gentile world, and even within the latter—contrast Ac. 16: 15 with the position in Corinth—that principles had to be differently applied. To this we must add that the apostles were coming as heralds of the king to His allegedly loyal subjects; the mission to the Gentiles was to men, who, if they knew their king at all, were in open rebellion against Him.

They were to go in haste and hence unburdened with baggage. As heralds they were to make no charge (8b), and they were to expect hospitality from the king's subjects (10). For most the **belt** served as a purse. **two tunics:** The tunic (*chitōn*) was the long wool or linen undergarment next to the skin; two could be worn (Mk 6: 9). Jesus was forbidding unnecessary comfort; a change of undergarment could be expected from those that received them. **nor sandals** (so Lk. 10: 4, but note 'carry'): But Mk 6: 9 expressly commands them. Since going barefoot on journeys was unknown, it is probable that we are to apply the **two** of **tunics** to the **sandals** as well and see a prohibition against a spare pair. There is a similar contradiction in **nor a staff** (so Lk. 9: 3), expressly permitted by Mk 6: 8. Since there is no suggestion that it was for defence (cf. Lk. 22: 36), it probably means that the next best stick would suffice.

The apparent haphazardness of Mk 6: 10; Lk. 9: 4 is corrected by v. 11. The king's heralds go to the king's subjects. The opinion of others is not always reliable, so vv. 12, 13 give the test of the suggested host. 'Will come . . . will return' (13, Phillips) is preferable. The shaking off of **the dust** (14) is probably explained by the mention of Sodom and Gomorrah; everything connected with the place carried a curse. Jesus knew that Israel's allegiance to God was in fact largely nominal (16a). The second half of the verse seems to have been a proverbial expression.

Predictions of Persecution (10: 17–25)
Cf. Mk 13: 9–13; Lk. 21: 12–17, 19. Since, apart from v. 16a, there is no suggestion of persecution in the ministry of this period, it seems wisest to see this section transferred from the eschatological discourse of ch. 24. The honour of apostleship includes suffering, even as the Master has suffered, but His spirit is with them. The promise of vv. 19 f. is not intended to be a lazy man's excuse for lack of thought and preparation in a position that has been foreknown and freely chosen. The disrupting influence of the unadulterated Christian message in society (21 f.), whether pagan, non-religious or nominally Christian, is one of the main charges those who proclaim it have to face. Western 'Christian' society has been created largely by the silencing of those who would not accept compromise (cf. also vv. 34–36).

17. Beware of men: 'Men' is frequently used in the Gospels of men without God. **22. he who endures to the end will be saved:** Cf. Rev. 2: 7, 11, 17, 26; 3: 5, 12, 21; 20: 4, etc. There are many passages in NT which stress the necessity of endurance and overcoming, and their theological interpretation is a matter of controversy. Their general setting and use suggest special status and honour in the kingdom rather than salvation from the second death. **23. you will not have gone through all the towns of Israel . . . :** It is purposeless to enumerate the many strange interpretations of this verse. Firstly it is a warning that the accomplishment of Christ's purposes will not be carried through by us, whether in the mission of the Twelve, or in the Church's mission to Israel (Rom. 9–11), or even in the wider field of missionary enterprise (though this is not directly envisaged). The apostle is his Master's representative, not His replacement. Secondly it is only the Master who must die; His representatives are not to court unneeded martyrdom. **25. Beelzebul:** See note on 12: 24.

The Apostles' Security (10: 26–33)
Cf. Lk. 12: 2–9. Our lack of fear is due to Christ's victory through death. The revelation of the **hidden** is God's work, to whom it is already **known.** A great deal of Jesus' teaching was given in private but was intended ultimately to be made public. There is no room for the

esoteric in Christianity. Verse 28 draws a contrast between men and God.

The Disunity Produced by the Gospel (10: 34–36)
Cf. Lk. 12: 51–53. See note on 10: 21. This passage is based on Mic. 7: 6. Very often in the Bible the inescapable result of an action is expressed as its purpose (34).

Conditions of Apostleship (10: 37–39)
Cf. 16: 24 f.; Mk 8: 34 f.; Lk. 9: 23 f.; 14: 26 f. The difference of expression here and in Lk. 14: 26 f. is explained by the hearers here already being disciples. **is not worthy of me:** The sense is given by Phillips, 'does not deserve to be mine'. **he who does not take his cross:** So far as is known the expression is one of Jesus' own coining. It means taking up the position of a condemned criminal.

Conclusion of Discourse (10: 40–11: 1)
Cf. 18: 5; Mk 9: 37, 41; Lk. 9: 48; 10: 16. We are finally reminded of the intimate relationship between the apostolic representative and the Master whom he represents. The rabbis repeatedly stressed, 'A man's representative is as the man himself'.

III. i. GROWING HOSTILITY (11: 2–12: 50)
This section runs from the doubts felt by John the Baptist to Jesus' turning from earthly relationships.

John and Jesus (11: 2–19)
Cf. Lk. 7: 18–35. It is most unlikely that John shared the popular views on the Messiah, but he had preached him as the Judge (3: 10–12); Jesus was apparently merely functioning as the agent of mercy. Jesus' answer was an oblique quotation of Isa. 29: 18 f.; 35: 5 f.; 61: 1—a direct one would have involved a public claim He was not yet ready to make. Lk. 7: 21 does not imply that all these miracles took place in the presence of the messengers; popular report will have guaranteed some of them.

3. he who is to come: This was not an official title of the Messiah. John knew that Jesus would understand its implications.

6. blessed is he who takes no offence at me: It is less what Jesus did and said that makes Him a stumbling block for many; it is rather that He does not conform to what we think He ought to have done and said. **7. A reed shaken by the wind:** There was nothing private about John's delegation. Though the crowd will not have been sure of John's meaning, they grasped that he was disappointed in some way in Jesus. Jesus defended him against the possible charge of fickleness. He was only being true to the message that had been entrusted to him. **10. This is he of whom it is written:** By applying Mal. 3: 1 to John Jesus confirmed the claims that John had made for himself. By calling him Elijah (14, cf. Mal. 4: 5) He implicitly denied the popular, literalistic interpretation of the passage—not dead in some Christian circles to this day—and thereby also the dominant messianic concepts of the time. **11. there has risen no one greater than John the Baptist:** Greatness may be the expression of greatness of spirit, but the Bible does not anticipate the judgment of God on a man, or it may be a greatness created by position. Of all who had heralded the king John was the greatest, for he was nearest to Him. But the least who would experience the full power of the king would be greater than he—in position, but not necessarily in character or final reward.

Schniewind's exegesis of the difficult v. 12 (cf. Lk. 16: 16) has much to commend it. The Pharisees spoke of bringing in the end of the age by force through fasting, study of the Law, etc. Jesus accepted the thought but transformed it. The **violence** is the whole-hearted acceptance of the preaching of John and Jesus (**until now**), which involved, as foreshadowed in John's baptism, a dying to self and to the past and the new life of the new age. This is more likely than 'God's power is at work through Jesus to establish his reign, but his kingdom is suffering violence; violent men are trying to seize or snatch away this blessing and keep men from accepting God's rule' (Filson).

Most of their contemporaries stood aloof from both John and Jesus, like children refusing to join either a mock marriage or a mock funeral in the market place. For them John was too mad, Jesus too vulgar. For **sinners** see note on 9: 10. **Yet wisdom is justified by her deeds:** Though the MSS support for this reading is superior, most think that the mg and Lk. 7: 35 are correct. In any case **wisdom** is Jesus (and John), 'children' are those who accept Him.
Rejection and Acceptance (11: 20-30)
Cf. Lk. 10: 13 ff., 21 f. The deliberate incompleteness of the Gospels is shown by there being no other mention of Chorazin, except in the parallel, Lk. 10: 13. The failure of the cities to repent was due to their being **wise and understanding** (25), thinking they knew how God should do His work. Contrary to M'Neile and Tasker we should see thanksgiving not merely for the revelation to **babes** but also for the hiding from **the wise and understanding.** An essential part of the gospel is that human advantages, including intelligence and knowledge, do not help a man to salvation (cf. 18: 3 f.).

Knowledge of God is by revelation, but there is no revelation that will enable us to grasp the inner mystery of the Son, the God-

man. There is nothing in Jn that goes beyond the saying of v. 27, a fact we should remember when the teaching of the Fourth Gospel is challenged as incompatible with the Synoptics.

The **babes** are those **who labour and are heavy laden.** While the evangelistic application to those under the weight of sin is not illegitimate, the call refers primarily to those who are not 'wise' enough to ease their way from under the burdens of life and of the Law (cf. 23: 4). **29. my yoke:** The yoke was a common symbol of submission and service. The Rabbis spoke of the yoke of the Law (cf. Ac. 15: 10) and of the Kingdom of Heaven. **rest** (*anapausis*): In LXX *anapausis* is used as a regular equivalent of *shabbat* (Sabbath). It was the true Sabbath-rest Jesus was offering, a desisting from their own work to do the work of God (Heb. 4: 9 f.—AV is inadequate here). That this is the meaning is borne out by the next two incidents, which deal with the true use of the Sabbath. **your souls:** Not merely the inner man but the whole man is intended.
The Plucking of the Ears of Corn (12: 1-8)
See comments on Mk 2: 23-28 (Lk. 6: 1-5). Mt. adds vv. 5 ff., in which Jesus mentions the temple-work of the priests on the sabbath. We can be as pedantic as the scribes in the question of Sunday observance. Jesus' argument is that those who are doing the work of **the lord of the sabbath** are not under sabbath laws. **something greater than the temple** (6, cf. 12: 41, 42): i.e. the Kingdom of God. The quotation of Hos. 6: 6 (7) is the denial of the right of judgment until the motives behind an act are known. It may be added that the hunger of the disciples shows that the customary sabbath hospitality had not been offered to Jesus and His disciples.
The Healing of the Man with the Withered Hand (12: 9-14)
See comments on Mk 3: 1-6 (Lk. 6: 6-11). **So it is lawful to do good on the sabbath:** To do the work of Christ is to do good; this is the principle that cuts through all human legalism and sophistry. It should be added that on the human plane the Pharisaic attitude towards using a doctor on the sabbath was eminently sensible. If life was in danger, all that was necessary should be done. If it was not, why trouble the doctor? It was this incident that showed the Pharisees that the point at issue between them and Jesus was not varying interpretations of the Law but a fundamentally different approach to it; hence the decision **to destroy him.**
The Healing of the Multitudes (12: 15-21)
See comments on Mk 3: 7-12 (Lk. 6: 17-19). Mt. by quoting Isa. 42: 1-4 wishes to make it clear that Jesus did not resist deliberate opposition. Once someone had made up his mind about Him,

he was left to it. It is not to be inferred, however, that there was an enthusiastic acceptance by the common people. They were drawn by His reputation as a healer, which had now reached its climax (15).

The Beelzebul Accusation (12: 22-37)

See comments on Mk 3: 22-30 (Lk. 11: 14-23) and note on Mt. 9: 32 ff. The very surprise of the people at the healing shows how little real faith there was. It was probably the man's instantaneous ability to speak and see that influenced them most. **23. the Son of David** (cf. 9: 27; 15: 22; 20: 30 f.; 21: 9, 15): We need not doubt that the title is used Messianically. If there were Roman spies around, it was a safer expression to use. **24. Beelzebul:** There is probably no connection with Beelzebub. It means 'lord of dung (*zebul*)', i.e. of heathen sacrifices. Others prefer 'lord of the high place'. **27. your sons:** Your fellow-Jews. Quite apart from the exceptional case in Ac. 19: 13-16, we know of a number of prominent rabbis who acted as exorcists. A baseless charge against Jesus would involve them equally. **31, 32. blasphemy against the Spirit:** Jesus does not imply that any sin is so great that it cannot be dealt with by the atonement. A man who deliberately calls good evil and evil good is so warped that he will not want forgiveness, a prerequisite for being forgiven. For v. 33 cf. 7: 16-20. **36. every careless word:** This is to be understood in the light of v. 35 (cf. 15: 11, 18, 19). A man's premeditated words are seldom a safe guide to character, the unpremeditated are.

The Demand for a Sign (12: 38-42)

See comments on Lk. 11: 29-32. For the Jewish religious leaders a request for a sign seemed reasonable. God had given Moses signs for his people (Exod. 3: 12; 4: 1-9); why should not Jesus, who came with a new authority, give them also? The signs given to Moses were of two types: (*a*) for unbelief (Exod. 4: 1-9)—these were adequately represented by His miracles of healing; (*b*) for faith (Exod. 3: 12)—this took place *after* the Exodus, even so **the sign of the prophet Jonah** would come at the end of His ministry.

40. three days and three nights: The period given in Jewish tradition. Problems raised by this phrase with regard to the day of the crucifixion are baseless (see Additional Note to ch. 27). In Biblical and Rabbinic time-reckoning part of a period is reckoned as a whole period. 'Rabbi Elazar (*c*. A.D. 100) said, "A day and a night make an *'onah* (i.e. 24 hour period) and the portion of an *'onah* is reckoned as an *'onah*".' **41, 42. something greater:** See note on 12: 6. They might be excused for not recog-

nizing His person, but not for their failure to accept His person and work.

The Peril of the Empty Man (12: 43-45)

See comments on Lk. 11: 24 ff. Though these verses are a literal statement of fact, they also form a parable. They are not a warning to the Jews in general (so M'Neile, Filson, Tasker, Schniewind) but are addressed to the scribes and Pharisees (Schlatter). Parabolically understood they refer to the work of the Law, which could prepare Israel for the Messiah but could not 'fill' it.

Jesus' True Relations (12: 46-50)

See comments on Mk 3: 19b-21, 31-35 (Lk. 8: 19-21). The interruption of Jesus' teaching was a personal insult and a rejection of its divine authority. On the other hand the incident makes 'it clear that not the whole of Jesus' generation was evil' (Tasker).

III. ii. THE KINGDOM OF HEAVEN (13: 1-52)

The Problem of the Parables. The rabbis often used parables, so the surprise of the disciples (10) cannot have been at the fact that Jesus used them. The rabbinic parable, when it went beyond a simile, was generally a brief semi-allegorical story, the meaning of which was normally obvious. Jesus' parables can be divided into two types. Some arise out of a stated background and effectively give God's answer to it. The majority, in spite of their variety, fall into this class, and we ignore their setting to our loss; it is not recorded that they caused any surprise. Then there are those grouped in this chapter, which are complete in themselves. No background is suggested beyond their general setting in Jesus' ministry. It is this purely parabolic teaching that caused the surprise. Modern efforts to supply them with suitable backgrounds as a basis for interpretation have carried little conviction.

The Interpretation of the Parables. The traditional exegesis of the Church saw in the parables masterpieces of allegory in which every detail had a meaning. Dodd (pp. 11 f.) reproduces Augustine's treatment of the parable of the Good Samaritan as an example. The method is far from dead but has been abandoned by almost all responsible expositors.

The dominant modern view, expressed especially by Dodd and Jeremias, swings to the other extreme. It has been described by Dodd (pp. 18 f.): 'The typical parable, whether it be a simple metaphor, or a more elaborate similitude, or a full-length story, presents one point of comparison. The details are not intended to have an independent significance. In an allegory, on the other hand, each detail is a separate metaphor, with a significance of its own . . . In the parable of the Sower the wayside and the birds, the thorns and the stony ground are not, as Mark supposed, cryptograms for persecution, the deceitfulness of riches, and so forth. They are there to conjure up a picture of the vast amount of wasted labour which the farmer must face, and so bring into relief the satisfaction that the harvest gives, in spite of all.'

In spite of valuable light thrown on the parables and the removal of much dead wood in exegesis, the method has often been singularly unsatisfying. It demands a seriously distorted picture of the apostolic Church and places the skill of the modern scholar in the place of the understanding of the first disciples and of the guidance of the Holy Spirit.

The truth seems to lie between the extremes. A parable has only one message, but many of the details are semi-allegorical contributions towards it. Where the setting indicates the meaning, it is comparatively simple to distinguish between the heart of the story and the necessary 'scenery' that has no bearing on the application. In the collection of ch. 13 there is no setting, and therefore interpretation becomes much more difficult; we have to be very careful what we dismiss as 'scenery'.

The Problem of Hardening (13: 10-17)
Cf. Mk 4: 10 ff. (Lk. 8: 9 f.). The outstanding simplicity of many of the parables, *when interpreted in their setting*, has made this explanation for parabolic teaching a major difficulty in exegesis. Once it is grasped that it refers to this collection of the Parables of the Kingdom, *and to them alone*, much of the difficulty vanishes.

It is illegitimate to concentrate on **because seeing they do not see** (13) and to ignore 'so that they may indeed see but not understand' (Mk 4: 12). The use of Isa. 6: 9 f. (cf. Jn 12: 39 f.; Ac. 28: 25 ff.; Rom. 11: 8) shows that we are concerned with something more than voluntary obtuseness. It is still more illegitimate to attribute this thought to the early Church and not to Jesus (Dodd, pp. 13 ff.). Far more acceptable is Jeremias's view. He separates Mk 4: 11 f. from these parables; on the basis of the presumed underlying Aramaic he renders Mk 4: 12 'unless they turn and God will forgive them'. But once again there is the driving of a wedge between Jesus and the early Church.

We cannot reasonably escape the conclusion that the teaching of this section of parables, but of them alone, was judicial in form, part of God's mysterious dealing with Israel. If the interpretation of these parables given below is accepted, it will be seen that every one to a

greater or less extent cuts across standard rabbinic teaching, and indeed many commonly accepted ideas in the Church. Therefore they will not have been understood by many of the hearers, just as they are often misunderstood today.

11. the secrets (*ta mystēria*) **of the kingdom of heaven:** This must be interpreted as an enlargement of Mk 4: 11, 'to you has been given the secret (*to mystērion*) of the kingdom of God'. This secret is Jesus Himself, so **the secrets** are the effects of His message and ministry. To say this is not to agree with the *Scofield Bible* that these seven parables 'taken together, describe the result of the presence of the Gospel in the world during the present age, that is, the time of seed-sowing which began with our Lord's personal ministry, and ends with the harvest'. As elaborated there this view demands a consistent and minute allegorization and implicitly assumes that we are dealing with a block of consecutive teaching, Mt. not having carried out its normal practice of grouping teaching.

The Parable of the Sower (13: 1-23)
See comments on Mk 4: 1-20 (Lk. 8: 4-15). The stress on the site of the parable (1 f.; Mk 4: 1) suggests that the parable was based on what Jesus could see from the boat. It also explains the use of the definite article with sower, rightly rendered in English idiom **a sower.** All this suggests it is unwise to lay heavy stress on sowing. The apparent wastefulness of the sower in sowing in unsuitable places is explained by the fact that he was followed by the ploughman (Jeremias); he had no means of judging what lay under the unbroken earth, or even where **the path** would run.

The explanation (18-23) shows that it is a parable of soils rather than of the sower. No suggestion is made why some soil is suitable, some not; there is not even a suggestion that the soil is to blame. It is really an affirmation of Isa. 6: 9 f. in practice. It has special relevance to Israel (Rom. 11: 25) but is true of all nations. Judaism has never had any understanding for the prophetic teaching of the remnant; the parable is a reaffirmation of it in equally ununderstood words.

The Parable of the Weeds (13: 24-30, 36-43) The kingdom of heaven may be compared to . . . : This and similar expressions (31, 33, 44, 45, 47) do not compare the exercise of God's sovereignty with some person or thing in the parable, but with the picture given by the parable as a whole. NEB renders well, 'The kingdom of Heaven is like this'. For **kingdom of heaven** see note on 4: 17. **weeds** (*zizania*): So also Phillips. The rendering 'darnel' (RVmg, NEB) is preferable, for *Arndt* and *SB* show a specific plant is intended (Heb. *zûn*), i.e. darnel, which the rabbis believed to be corrupt wheat. Schniewind throws cold water on interpretations that stress the similarity between wheat and darnel, at first at any rate, or the poisonous nature of ripe darnel seeds, because these points are not mentioned. Would it have been necessary for those who knew the properties of darnel or the use it could be put to?

29. lest you root up the wheat: Both the difficulty of distinction and the tendency of darnel to root itself more firmly than wheat are suggested.

38. the field is the world: Possibly 'mankind'; it is less the planting of men and more the implanting of divine or diabolical principles that is being stressed. In any case all possibility of exact allegory breaks down. It is not stated that at any given moment all men are either wheat or darnel, though we may perhaps infer that at the last they will be one or the other. It is generally taken as a 'church' allegory, but in fact it is the divine prohibition against any (including angels) making a final separation before the end. In addition we learn that the devil can transform men as effectively as the gospel. Considerable dissension has been caused by the allegorists who maintain that since the darnel is collected first, there must be a rapture of the wicked before that of the just.

The Parables of the Mustard Seed and Leaven (13: 31-33)
For the former see comments on Mk 4: 30 ff.; for the latter cf. Lk. 13: 20 f. Though the former tells of the exceptional and the latter of the commonplace, the two parables obviously belong together. While the mustard seldom exceeds four feet, under exceptionally suitable circumstances it can reach even 15 feet (*HDB* III, p. 463; *NBD*, p. 1,006). The **three measures** (*sata*) **of meal** represent the OT *ephah*, or about a bushel (56 lbs.). Passages like Gen. 18: 6; Jg. 6: 19, show that it was a not-uncommon quantity for a batch of baking. The **leaven** was generally a piece of dough from the previous batch of baking, which had been allowed to ferment.

The usual interpretation sees the rapid spread and all penetrating influence of the Kingdom through the Church for good in these parables. The consistent allegorist insists, 'Leaven is the principle of corruption working subtly; it is invariably used in a bad sense, and is defined by our Lord as evil doctrine (Mt. 16: 11 f.; Mk 8: 15)' (*Scofield Bible*). This forces him to give a bad sense to the parable of the Mustard Seed as well. Lev. 7: 13; 23: 17 cast doubt on the universally evil symbolic meaning of leaven

(the notes *ad loc.* in the *Scofield Bible* are not convincing). It seems more likely that leaven is symbolically neutral, referring to the hidden forces the human spirit can release. Since man by nature is evil, these forces are normally evil also, but as the symbolism of Lev. 7: 13; 23: 17 shows, they can be transformed to good by fellowship with God.

It seems wisest, therefore, to regard these parables as neutral. They proclaim the fact of growth and influence, but their quality is left in question. The mustard 'tree' is a most insecure growth that will in any case die down with the coming of winter; no Christian advance has of necessity any guarantee of permanence. Historically not every 'christian' influence has been spiritually welcome, and some are undoubtedly helping forward the coming of the final apostasy.

The Parables of the Hidden Treasure and the Pearl (13: 44-46)
Once again the two parables belong together. The difference between them is that in one case the action is the result of an accident (the man was probably a hired labourer), in the other it is the result of deliberate search. Both result in the finder's selling all, a term we have no right to water down. There is no suggestion of purchasing salvation, but that coming under the sovereignty of God means the complete denial of self (cf. 10: 38 f.; 16: 25; Jn 12: 25).

The Parable of the Net (13: 47-50)
The parable of the Weeds revealed that this world of men is the visible expression of invisible forces. Here it is rather the visible activity of the Kingdom through the Church that is under consideration; note that it is not the leaders of the Church but the angels that make the separation, as with the weeds. **the bad:** Probably, when used of the fish, the ritually impure, cf. Lev. 11: 9-12; Dt. 14: 9 f.

Conclusion of the Parables (13: 51, 52)
A **scribe,** in its NT sense, was one who so knew the OT that he could be trusted to copy and expound it—the normal connection with the Pharisees was in one way accidental; there were scribes of the Sadducees, and there were probably some linked with no party. Jesus wanted those who would undergo the discipline of knowing the Kingdom. They would be able to expound both the revelation of the OT (**what is old**) and that of the NT (**what is new**).

IV. i. THE SHADOW OF THE CROSS (13: 53-17: 23)
The Rejection of Jesus at Nazareth (13: 53-58)
See comments on Mk 6: 1-6; Lk. 4: 16-30.

It should be clear that the rejection here described (and in Mk) is a second one, subsequent to that in Lk. The details are quite different. If we take the tense of **he taught them** (*edidasken*, imperfect) strictly, it may mean that Jesus was there some little time—Mk 'he began to teach' is compatible with this. They had to show more respect to an established teacher with a number of disciples than they had at the beginning of His ministry.

The Death of John the Baptist (14: 1–12)

See comments on Mk 6: 14–29. Mt. saw in John's death a foreshadowing of the death of Jesus.

The Feeding of the Five Thousand (14: 13–21)

See comments on Mk 6: 31–44; Lk. 9: 10–17; Jn 6: 1–13. Dalman (pp. 172–176) makes it clear that the 'Bethsaida' of Lk. 9: 10 must be taken as an approximation, and that the miracle must have taken place much nearer the middle of the eastern shore, a little north of Hippos (the modern Ein Gev).

The Walking on the Water (14: 22–33)

See comments on Mk 6: 45–52 and Jn 6: 15–21 for vv. 22–27. The disciples' journey was to be to the other side in the general direction of (*pros*) Bethsaida, which was only just east of the Jordan (Mk 6: 45). There is no evidence for a Bethsaida west of Jordan (Dalman, pp. 161–166). That they landed further west (14: 34) will have been due to the storm.

Peter is often blamed for trying to walk on the water, but he had Jesus' permission. He walked a little distance with the wind in his back. **He saw the wind** by the spray whipped off the waves. He had virtually reached Jesus when he grew fearful, and he and Jesus will have walked back to the boat together in the teeth of the gale.

Healings at Gennesaret (14: 34–36)

See comments on Mk 6: 53–56.

36. the fringe of his garment: See note on 9: 20.

Washing of Hands and Defilement (15: 1–20)

See comments on Mk 7: 1–23. The washing of hands before and after a meal was a purely ritualistic action with little thought of bodily cleanliness. It was recognized that it was not based on the Law but on rabbinic authority. It may have been an old custom, but it had not yet been generally enforced in the time of Jesus. **5. What you would have gained from me is given to God** is usually interpreted to mean that the man refused to help his parents because he claimed his property had been dedicated to God, yet he continued using it for his own profit. Such an action would have been impossible then and probably at any time in Israel's history. *SB*, on the basis of Rabbinic sources, translate, 'As a sacrifice be what you might have gained from me'. No one could profit from a sacrifice, and this was a formula, not dedicating anything to God, but declaring that his parents must so look on it. It was putting under a solemn curse anything his parents might try to get from him. The Talmud makes it clear that this was not so uncommon, and that many rabbis were far from happy about the custom; they were probably influenced by Jesus' criticism.

Jesus was not advocating the abolition of the dietary laws (17, Mk 7: 19) but was stressing that they had nothing to do with pure and impure, but as Mk makes clear the abolition was the logical outcome.

The Syrophoenician Woman (15: 21–28)

See comments on Mk 7: 24–30. **22. Son of David:** See note on 12: 23. It is doubtful whether the woman knew the meaning of what she was saying; if she did, she was really under obligation to become a proselyte.

24. I was sent only to the lost sheep of the house of Israel: See note on 10: 5. This is less heartless than it sounds, for the way was always open for the woman to become an Israelite. As soon as the woman ceased to use empty words, which were perhaps intended to appeal to Jesus' vanity, and based herself on need she was heard.

Many Healings (15: 29–31)

See comments on Mk 7: 31–37. Mk concentrates on an individual, Mt. stresses the large numbers involved. As Mk makes clear, Jesus was moving in the region NE of the lake, largely Jewish but outside the jurisdiction both of Herod Antipas and of the religious authorities in Jerusalem. Since this area had seen little of Him, it explains the large number flocking to Him for healing.

The Feeding of the Four Thousand (15: 32–39)

See comments on Mk 8: 1–10. It is doubtful whether any positive distinction can be drawn between this miracle and that of the feeding of the five thousand (14: 13–21). Probably the site will have been much the same. We cannot even lay much stress on the different terms used for the baskets. 'The *spyris* (15: 37), cf. Ac. 9: 25, did not differ from the *kophinos* (14: 20) in size, but in material, and to a certain extent in use' (M'Neile). The power, which Jesus would not use for Himself (4: 3 f.), was freely available for the needs of others. Indeed, this section warns us against attributing any uniqueness to the feeding of the five thousand. Dalman (p. 128) considers that **Magadan** is a corruption of Magdal (=Magdala) and Dalmanutha (Mk 8: 10) of Magdal Nuna (=Magdal Nunaiya, i.e. Magdal of fish).

A Request for a Sign (16: 1-4)

See comments on Mk 8: 11-13 and Mt. 12: 38-42. NEB with the best MSS omits vv. 2b, 3, cf. Mk; for them cf. Lk. 12: 54 ff. Possibly the sign **from heaven** asked for was the voice from heaven (*bat qol*) met with occasionally in rabbinic stories.

The Disciples' Shortage of Bread (16: 5-12)

See comments on Mk 8: 14-21. The disciples took Jesus' saying literally, because they had just left Jewish territory (15: 39) for a semi-Gentile one (16: 13; Mk 8: 22), where they might find it hard to find a Jewish baker. Jesus used the term **leaven** (6) of the teaching of the religious leaders because, though very few Galileans were attracted by it (cf. Ac. 15: 10), they were being subconsciously won over to it, as the religious developments after the destruction of Jerusalem were to show.

The Confession at Caesarea Philippi (16: 13-20)

See comments on Mk 8: 27-33 (Lk. 9: 18-22) for vv. 13-16, 20. The fact that Mk and Lk. omit **the Son of the living God** suggests that Jesus pronounced His blessing on Peter because he had recognized Him as Messiah, not because he had realized His divine nature. The early acknowledgment of Jesus as Messiah (Jn 1: 41, 45, 49) had been an act of enthusiasm; Peter's confession expressed mature conviction created by divine revelation. **17. Bar-Jona**=son of Jona (*Yona*), which presumably is an unusual abbreviation of *Yochanan*, i.e. John (Jn 21: 15). **18. you are Peter** (*petros*) **and on this rock** (*petra*) **I will build my church:** Until it was demonstrated in the last decade of the 19th century that Jesus must normally have taught in Aramaic, the popular Protestant exegesis of this verse contrasted *petros*, a stone, with *petra*, a rock, thus seeking to rule out the thought that Peter was in any sense the foundation of the church. Already earlier, once the true nature of *koinē* Gk. began to be known, some were unhappy about a word play that suited classical Gk. better than *koinē*. Once it was grasped that the name bestowed was the Aram. *Kepha* (Gk. *Kēphas*, Eng. Cephas), it was clear that the alleged pun had to be abandoned, for it was impossible in Aram. That Kepha was the name given is shown by Paul's using it eight times to the twice he employs Peter (Gal. 2: 7 f.). It seems clear then that the much attacked rendering of NEB (and Phillips) is justified, 'You are Peter, the Rock, and on this rock . . .'

Fortunately the truth or falsity of Roman Catholic claims about the authority of the Papacy is not to be decided by the exposition of a doubtful pun. Unless, against the clear suggestion of the text, we picture Jesus as turning from Peter to the others, **this rock** cannot be Peter himself but is contrasted with him, i.e. it must be his confession. The greatness and leadership of Peter may be seen in Ac. 1: 15; 2: 14; 5: 3, 8, 15; 8: 14; 10: 46 f. On the other hand Mt. 18: 1; 19: 27; 20: 21; Lk. 22: 24; Ac. 11: 2; Gal. 2: 11, etc. show no sign that Peter or the others had any conception that an absolute primacy had been conferred on him. **my church** (*ekklēsia*): The word used by Jesus must have been *qahal* (Heb.), often rendered *ekklēsia* by LXX. In seeking to fix its meaning we must look away from connotations Paul's Gentile converts may have read into it. *Qahal* (Heb.) or *kenishta* (Aram.) was used for the whole congregation of Israel, i.e. Israel as a whole acting as the people of God; it was used also of the smaller local units, which ideally represented the whole. It is the wider sense that is used here, the narrower in 18: 17. **the powers of death:** A good rendering of 'the gates of Hades'. It is not a question of Satanic powers, but of death, which Jesus was to conquer in His resurrection. **19. the keys of the kingdom of heaven** are to be understood in the light of Isa. 22: 22; and the authority to bind and loose is not of admission and exclusion, but deciding what is and what is not the Lord's will. This latter promise is in 18: 18 extended not merely to the other disciples, but by inference to all spiritual Christians.

The First Prediction of the Passion (16: 21-23)

See comments on Mk 8: 31-33.

The Cost of Discipleship (16: 24-28)

See comments on Mk 8: 34-9: 1 (Lk. 9: 23-27). In reading the careful note on Mk 9: 1 we should bear three points in mind. (*a*) The usual modern view that Jesus was anticipating an early second coming is ruled out, quite apart from the attribution of fallibility to Him, by His emphatic statement, not so long afterwards, of His ignorance on the subject (24: 36, Mk 13: 32). (*b*) Interpretations involving the transfiguration, resurrection and the pouring out of the Holy Spirit all stumble over the time factor, for none of His hearers need have died by then. (*c*) The destruction of Jerusalem, though satisfying the time factor, does not possess the aura of glory implied, cf. Jesus' weeping over the city. The only interpretation that seems to do justice to all these factors sees no one incident foretold; rather the whole of the opening period of the Church's existence from the resurrection onwards is foreseen (the transfiguration was a foreshadowing of the resurrection). This in many ways found its close in the destruction of Jerusalem.

The Transfiguration (17: 1-8)
See comments on Mk 9: 2-8; Lk. 9: 28-36. Scripture does not interpret this incident, which was obviously a major happening in the Ministry (cf. 2 Pet. 1: 16 ff.; Jn 1: 14). Both Jn 17: 5 and 2 Pet. 1: 17 lead us to see in the transfiguration an act of the Father's. It seems more probable that it was the glory of the manhood rather than of the Deity of Christ that was revealed. By perfect obedience He had reached the goal that Adam should have attained, and death had no more claim on Him. Presumably He could have ascended to the Father then and there, but the conversation about His departure (Lk. 9: 31) marked His voluntary going forward to the cross. Was this perhaps the point suggested by Heb. 2: 10, 18; 5: 8, 9, which must have come before the perfected high priest offered up the perfect sacrifice? Note that it was the divine voice (17: 5 f.) and the cloud (Lk. 9: 34) that made the disciples afraid, not Jesus' glory.

The Discussion about Elijah (17: 9-13)
See comments on Mk 9: 9-13.

The Healing of the Demon-possessed Boy (17: 14-21)
See comments on Mk 9: 14-29. The evidence of MSS for omission of v. 21 cannot be questioned; cf. mg and Mk 9: 29.

20. you will say to this mountain: Rabbinic parallels suggest that moving mountains was a proverbial expression at the time for doing the impossible.

The Second Prediction of the Passion (17: 22, 23)
See comments on Mk 9: 30-32.

IV. ii. THE CHURCH (17: 24-18: 35)
The Temple Tax (17: 24-27)
In its setting this historical incident becomes virtually a parable of the disciple's relationship to other communities that claim his allegiance.

Exod. 30: 11-16 tells of a special half-shekel census tax given to the Tabernacle. After the exile a voluntary cultic tax of a third of a shekel was adopted (Neh. 10: 32 f.). Before the time of Jesus this had been changed to a compulsory half-shekel tax payable annually by every free male of twenty and over, whether he lived in Palestine or the diaspora. Refusal to pay would have been regarded as an act of apostasy. After the destruction of the Temple in A.D. 70 the tax had to be paid to the temple of Jupiter Capitolinus in Rome as a punishment for the rebellion.

25. From their sons: i.e. members of the royal family. Jesus claimed exemption in virtue of His sonship, and extended it through Peter to the other disciples. The miracle was not a gratuitous act of divine power, but a demonstration that those who do not insist on their religious rights can experience God's blessing in His provision. There is no suggestion that Jesus did not have the money available. The 'St. Peter's fish' found in the Lake of Galilee today is quite capable of holding a shekel coin in its mouth. Since there is no ground for disassociating Peter from the other disciples in the matter of temple-tax, it is hard to resist the conclusion that he was the only member of the Twelve over twenty (cf. note on 20: 20).

The Dispute about Greatness (18: 1-5)
See comments on Mk 9: 33-37 and 10: 15. From outside claims we turn to the church community itself. In a well-ordered society and family a little child, with all its faults, will not be concerned with any scale of greatness. God is so great, that any differences of rank in His kingdom must pale into insignificance, when seen in His light. In addition His scale of values is so different from man's that for Him the reception of a child can be ranked as the reception of Jesus (5).

4. Whoever humbles himself like this child: 'The sense is not humbles himself as this little child humbles himself but humbles himself until he is like this little child' (Tasker).

The Importance of the Little One (18: 6-14)
In this section vv. 8, 9 interrupt the connection between vv. 6, 7 and 10-14. They are a repetition of 5: 29 f., intended to point the reader back to that passage and would be best placed in brackets. They serve to underline the awfulness of sin and temptation. The change from 'child' to **little ones** suggests that we are dealing both with children and those that have become childlike (3 f.). **Causes one of these little ones . . . to sin** is not an adequate translation of the Gk. (see mg). Knox is better with, 'hurts the conscience of'. Modern psychology has demonstrated that failure to meet a child's standards can cause lasting psychic and spiritual damage; the same is true of many recent converts. There are those who have never come to faith because of the unfaithful conduct of the 'faithful', and there are many spiritual cripples thanks to their early impressions of a church. **7. Woe to the world for temptations to sin:** Knox, 'Woe to the world for the hurt done to consciences!'

The fact that we are repelled by sentimental pictures of children's guardian angels is no reason for rejecting the literal meaning of **in heaven their angels always behold the face of my Father . . .** It is, of course, true that 'The angel, therefore, symbolizes the believer's relation to God' (M'Neile), but in view of the almost universal, contemporary, Jewish belief in guardian angels, it seems impossible not to see a confirmation of the concept by Jesus, though not of many fanciful embroideries of it. So we have no ground for saying, 'Their angels are their counterparts, or their spiritual doubles, who have access at all times to the Father's presence' (Tasker). This seems to be an invalid deduction from some rabbinic sayings.

For vv. 12, 13 see comments on Lk. 15: 1–7. The use of the parable here shows that we are to include repentant 'tax collectors and sinners' among the little ones. The evidence of MSS is clearly against the insertion of v. 11 here (cf. Lk. 19: 10). **14. that one of these little ones should perish:** 'One' is neuter, looking back to the sheep, i.e. this is the conclusion of the parable, showing that it is the Father (MS evidence is about equally divided between **my** and **your**) who goes out after the lost, through the Son, of course. So long as there is hope He will do all that can be done without depriving a man of his personality.

The Church's Dealing with the Sinner (18: 15–20)

This section should always be read in the light of vv. 10–14. We are dealing with the human counterpart of divine love in action.

15. If your brother sins against you: The evidence of the MSS is unclear, but it is probably best to omit 'against you' (NEB). The words may well have been inserted to discourage the idea that Jesus was giving a charter to the busy-body. Should anyone enjoy carrying out this task, it is clear evidence that he is not suited to it. Since all sin damages, the Christian should not be indifferent to a brother's sin. A personal approach should rouse a minimum of ill-feeling and gives least publicity to the sin. The **two or three witnesses** (cf. Dt. 19: 15) are not merely to report on the offender's attitude, if he does not listen to them, but also to check on the validity of the accusation—the accuser is not always right. If he refuses to hear the local church, he is clearly a poisonous influence and must be excluded. In the mouth of Jesus **a Gentile and a tax collector** clearly imply that the one excluded is there to be won back. It would not avail the offender to appeal to the court of heaven, for if Jesus' teaching has been sincerely and lovingly followed, God will endorse the church's decision (18; cf. 16: 19).

In their original setting vv. 19, 20 show the two or three of v. 16 preparing for their task—only when they have been ignored, does the whole church come into consideration. **Agree** (*symphōneō*) implies a harmony that can be created only by much prayer and detailed study of the case. Those so engaged can be certain of Christ's presence with them. **20. gathered**

in my name: The rendering 'unto my name' (J. N. Darby) is more literal but hardly intelligible. *eis to onoma* in the papyri means 'to the account of', 'into the possession of', i.e. they meet as the conscious possession of Jesus. While v. 20 may be rightly used as a word of encouragement to those that meet in small companies for conscience' sake, it offers no support to those who think that by using a verbal formula they have become God's favourites.

Forgiveness (18: 21–35)

Peter evidently realized that if an erring disciple was to be reconciled to God, he had to be reconciled to his fellow-disciples as well. **As many as seven times:** The idea found in some older commentaries that the rabbis fixed the number of times a man had to be forgiven at three, is based on a misunderstanding of the rule that if the offender asked three times in the presence of witnesses for forgiveness, he had to receive it. Peter was probably choosing seven as the perfect but limited number. Jesus' answer reversed the proud boast of Lamech (Gen. 4: 24).

The parable that illustrates the point is placed at the court of some oriental potentate, where gold flows like water and the courtiers are called **servants** (*douloi*), i.e. slaves.

28. a hundred denarii: No trifle, for it represented a hundred days' wages for a labourer (cf. 20: 2). It is not the actual sums involved but the disparity between them that is the point of the parable. Tasker suggests two or three million pounds and two or three hundred pounds. M'Neile suggests a disparity of 600,000 to one. Jesus did not suggest that the debts owed us by men's sins might not be grievous—they often are—but compared with our debts to God they are virtually nothing. For v. 35 cf. 6: 15.

V. i. THE WAY TO JERUSALEM (19: 1–23: 39)

Most of this section is found in Mk and also very much in Lk.

Jesus' Teaching on Marriage and Divorce (19: 1–12)

See notes on 5: 31 f. and comments on Mk 10: 1–12. A frequent weakness in exposition springs from the idea that the Pharisees were a closely knit and unitary body. There are no grounds for thinking that the Pharisees involved in this incident were any more hostile than the one of 22: 35, or Lk. 10: 25. The question **Is it lawful to divorce one's wife for any cause?** shows that the questioners belonged to one of the rival groups of Hillel or Shammai and hoped to be able to quote Jesus in their favour.

The disciples felt, like so many moderns, that Jesus' answer was inhuman. He made it clear that He was not a new legislator but was holding up an ideal for the spiritual. For some men and women their physical make-up is such, that marriage is at best a social convenience for them. Others do not marry, because they have been castrated, or because they have been placed in circumstances, *e.g.* slavery, where marriage is impossible. Yet others will be lifted above the material and physical urge to marriage. Should they marry, they will not find Jesus' ideal impossible or even difficult. It is insufficiently realized by the Church that many, perhaps the majority of marriages between Christians are entered on a mainly physical level. For these the strict enforcement of Jesus' teaching may be very difficult.

Jesus' Blessing of the Children (19: 13-15)
See comments on Mk 10: 13-16; Lk. 18: 15-17. The story is so placed as to dispel any idea that in vv. 11 f. Jesus was attributing any special merit to celibacy. What motivated the parents (there is no suggestion that only mothers were involved) remains unknown, for there are no parallels in Jewish custom. The linking of the passage with infant baptism is a curiosity in Christian thought.

The Rich Young Ruler (19: 16-30)
See comments on Mk 10: 17-31; Lk. 18: 18-30. **Teacher, what good deed must I do to have eternal life:** In all legalistic systems there is the temptation to think that there must be some act so outstanding as to ensure eternal life (cf. Lk. 10: 25). In His answer Jesus said, **Keep the commandments;** the tense in Gk. implies not a single action but a continued process.

Mk and Lk. concentrate on the title 'good' given to Jesus and the rejection of it as unseemly, Mt. on the **good deed** and the rebuke that we are concerned with the Good One and not with a good principle. **If you would be perfect** is sufficiently explained by 'You lack one thing' (Mk and Lk.). The giving up of his possessions was not a universal law of perfection, as it was taken by Francis of Assisi to be, but the decisive challenge to a particular man. **24. a camel to go through the eye of a needle:** A rabbinic equivalent is an elephant to go through the eye of a needle. The popular interpretation in certain circles that the eye of a needle is a small door within a city gate is baseless. Salvation is obtained by complete trust in God; riches of any kind, including natural talents, make such trust virtually impossible. **26. with God** (*para theō*) **all things are possible:** This does not mean 'everything is possible for God' (NEB). It is hard to conceive of any Jewish teacher's making

such a trite remark. We should render, 'In God's presence all things are possible', i.e. the man who turns from men to God will find there the power to overcome the otherwise unovercomable. **28. in the new world** (*palingenesia*): Better 'in the world renewal' (Filson), which would be brought in by the Messiah. A transference of the concept from earth to heaven does violence to the sense. **The twelve tribes of Israel** in such a setting is equivalent to 'all Israel' (Rom. 11: 26).

Parable of the Labourers in the Vineyard (20: 1-16)
This parable was told to explain the warning of 19: 30. Being a parable it does not set out to give the whole truth, and it has to be supplemented by 25: 14-30. Its stress is that God owes no man anything (cf. Lk. 17: 7-10), and so every reward is essentially an act of grace. If the last are first, it is only in the eyes of those that expect more (the few minutes difference in order of payment is not under consideration). It is their disappointment that makes it seem that the others had preferential treatment. In a time of underemployment they should have been thankful that they had had a full day's work. Tob. 5: 14 and various rabbinic passages show that **a denarius a day** was a good day's wages; many earned less.

The Third Prediction of the Passion (20: 17-19)
See comments on Mk 10: 32-34.

The Request of James and John (20: 20-28)
See comments on Mk 10: 35-45; for vv. 25-28 cf. also Lk. 22: 24-27. The making of the request shows how little 16: 18 f. was looked on as giving a primacy to Peter. That James' and John's mother, Salome (cf. 27: 56 with Mk 15: 40), was involved is very strong support for the suggestion about their youth; cf. the note on 17: 24-27.

The Healing of Bartimaeus (20: 29-34)
See comments on Mk 10: 46-52; Lk. 18: 35-43. **30. two blind men:** See note on 8: 28-34. The exceptional fact that the name Bartimaeus (Mk 10: 46) has been preserved suggests that he became a well-known member of the Jerusalem church. Hence the other blind man recedes into the background in Mk and Lk. **Son of David:** See note on 12: 23.

The Entry into Jerusalem (21: 1-9)
See comments on Mk 11: 1-10; Lk. 19: 28-40; Jn 12: 12-19. **Bethphage:** Mk and Lk. have 'Bethphage and Bethany'. Since Dalman (pp. 252 ff.) has shown conclusively that Bethphage lay nearer Jerusalem than did Bethany, it seems likely that the donkey was fetched from the latter. In view of His links with the village, Jesus had probably made quiet advance preparations (cf.

note on 26: 18). **5. an ass . . . a colt:** 'Two animals in Mt. only. Probably "Matthew" or his source thought of two animals because of Zech. 9: 9. In this poetic verse the prophet speaks in parallel lines of the animal the king will ride; both lines refer to the same animal. But the double reference seems to have led to the prosaic assumption that there were two animals' (Filson). This is a typical example of modern statements on the passage; the facts are correct, the conclusions most doubtful. An unbroken donkey's colt would be steadied by the presence of its mother. **7. on them:** There is adequate MS evidence for reading 'on it' with Mk and Lk. (M'Neile, Tasker). Jn 12: 16 makes it highly improbable that it was the riding on the donkey that moved the crowd to enthusiasm. It was probably a prearranged demonstration by the Galileans who had formerly tried to make Jesus king (Jn 6: 15) and were now trying to force His hand. Many of them had already reached Jerusalem and came out to meet Him (Jn 12: 12 f.).

Jesus in the Temple (21: 10–17)
See comments on Mk 11: 15–19; Lk. 19: 45–48; for vv. 10, 11 cf. Jn. 12: 19. It is clear that Mt. places the cleansing of the Temple on the Sunday, Mk on the Monday; Lk. is too brief for us to draw any certain conclusions. The story of the fig tree makes much easier sense, if we accept Mk's order. We shall be wise, therefore, to see in Mt.'s order one of his deliberate inversions to bring out that the King of Israel is Lord of the Temple. The nearest picture we can get of what was happening is to imagine a cattle-market in a cathedral close. It had been permitted because those who sold had undoubtedly to pay space rent to the priests. **13. a den of robbers:** The sacred surroundings had doubtless no influence on the commercial morals of the dealers, and a pilgrim who had not brought his sacrificial animals with him was very much at their mercy. It is frequently urged that Jn 2: 13–20 must represent the same incident, having been misplaced by design or accident. There are, however, sufficient differences for us to take it as a separate incident. If it were not, it seems incredible that Mt. and Mk should not have recorded Jn 2: 19 as a preparation for 26: 61; Mk 14: 58. **16. Do you hear what these are saying:** The authorities could not discipline the mob of children excited by the arrival of the pilgrims and the events of the day, but they expected Jesus to disassociate Himself from them. In signifying His approval by quoting Ps. 8: 2 He implicitly claimed to be the Messiah.

The Cursing of the Fig Tree (21: 18–22)
See comments on Mk 11: 12–14, 20–24. The

view that Mt. has compressed incidents from two days into one has been given in the last section. We need not press **at once** (19 f.) to mean that the tree became visibly dead while they stood and watched it. The facts about the fig tree and its fruit can be best found in *HDB* II, pp. 5 f., or *NBD*, p. 422. 'To see if he could find anything on it' (Mk 11: 13) shows that in the ordinary affairs of life Jesus did not exercise a supernatural knowledge. What He hoped to find were a few figs left over from the autumn; at the height of Jerusalem, even under the most favourable circumstances, no fig tree could have had early ripe figs on it at Passover time. He did not find any left-overs on it, for which the tree was not blamed, but there was also no promise of any for the coming crop. The cursing of the fig tree was undoubtedly parabolic. Profession without fruit is an abomination. In spite of views to the contrary, the fig tree is not 'a picture of Israel', and so the parable is a general one, though applied in the first place to 'His own'. The fact that the acted parable is applied as a sign of the power of faith—for v. 21 see note on 17: 20—seems to support the general meaning suggested.

The Question concerning Jesus' Authority (21: 23–27)
See comments on Mk 11: 27–33; Lk. 20: 1–8. Jesus was not merely dodging a question by catching out His questioners. By confessing that they were not able to judge John the Baptist's authority, they confessed themselves incompetent, though representing the Sanhedrin, to judge the claims of one who was acclaimed by John as being so much greater than he (3: 11).

The Parable of the Two Sons (21: 28–32)
This is the first of three parables teaching the unworthiness of the religious leaders; they must not be transferred from them to the Jews generally. There are two difficulties in the text. There is good evidence for placing first the son who said 'Yes' and did not go. This puts the representative of the leaders where he belongs, i.e. first of all (NEB, Phillips, M'Neile, Schlatter, Nestle, B. & F. B. S. Diglot). Then, a small but significant group of MSS, which follow the RSV order, have in v. 31 'the second'. This is so absurd and cynical that it is probably correct (Schniewind). We can picture a man like Caiaphas giving such an answer as a refusal to be heckled by a Galilean artisan. When the authorities rejected John the Baptist, they confirmed an attitude taken up long before. For the outcasts John's invitation was the first indication that their rejection of God's will could be reversed.

The Parable of the Wicked Husbandmen (21: 33-46)

See comments on Mk 12: 1-12; Lk. 20: 9-19. The cynical response to the previous parable made Jesus turn to the people (Lk. 20: 9), though the representatives of the Sanhedrin continued to listen (45). Theological mountains have been built on v. 43. Without it British-Israel theory would lose one of its main foundation stones. It is also a main prop for the traditional view, whether in its Patristic or Calvinistic form, that the Church is Israel, or the new Israel, or true Israel, or has taken over the functions of Israel. If it were a momentous declaration of the end of Israel's rôle, one would expect that it would appear in the other Synoptics, at the very least. Such interpretations ignore the point of the parable and equate the husbandmen, instead of the vineyard (Isa. 5: 7), with Israel; they are the higher priesthood and other religious leaders. In fact, as Filson says, 'The Kingdom will be taken from the disobedient Jewish leaders; their rejection of the prophets and the Son makes them liable to judgment'. The destruction of Jerusalem meant the sweeping away of the whole ruling religious caste in Jewry. Even the *Nasi*, the representative recognized by the Romans after A.D. 70, was of the family of Hillel, a humble commoner, though of Davidic origin. Whatever the truth of the theological views mentioned, they must seek their justification elsewhere.

The Parable of the Marriage-Feast (22: 1-14)

Cf. Lk. 14: 16-24. The force of this, the third parable, is often lost by a wrong comparison with Lk.'s parable of a private banquet. Unlike the invitation of a private individual the royal one was virtually compulsory—hence Mt. gives no excuses. The refusal to attend the marriage of the king's son implied disloyalty to the royal house as well. Those envisaged in vv. 2-6 are the religious leaders of Jerusalem, and v. 7 foretells their destruction with that of Jerusalem (**their city,** singular). The arguments of M'Neile, Filson and Tasker that the verse is out of place forgets the unchronological element so often found in OT stories—obviously the destruction took place after the feast.

Jesus then turned to the crowd, which was enjoying the impotent fury of the representatives of the Sanhedrin, and stressed in vv. 11-14 that they had a responsibility as well. There are no grounds for thinking that Gentiles are here envisaged (Tasker), though in fact they were to reap the benefits of the rejection of the Jewish leaders (Rom. 11: 11, 12, 15).

A wrong use of Lk.'s parable has led to a misunderstanding of v. 9 in terms of Lk. 14: 21 ff. This has led to the question how a **wedding garment** could reasonably be expected from such people and how would they have had time to get one. Hence many, *e.g.* M'Neile, Filson, Tasker, Dodd, Jeremias, but not Schlatter or Schniewind, see in these verses another parable, the beginning of which has been lost. This criticism ignores the more leisured pace of the East and overlooks that the element of hurry is not present in Mt. Judging by similar rabbinic parables, the man had simply continued about his own business until it was too late to go home and change. The view often met with that the wedding garment is the king's gift (cf. *NBC ad loc.*), though at least as old as Augustine, has no evidence to support it. In other words, the wedding garment has no allegorical meaning such as Christ's righteousness. The earlier guests insulted the king by their refusal, this latter one by his unwillingness to turn from his own affairs to prepare himself. **12. Friend:** The king assumes that he has a good excuse. **13. outer darkness:** 'The dark outside' (Phillips); cf. note on 25: 30.

The Question about the Poll-tax (22: 15-22)

See comments on Mk 12: 13-17; Lk. 20: 20-26. **19. Show me the money for the tax:** For this tax and this tax alone the Romans had coined special silver coins with the emperor's figure and name, and only they might be used in payment (cf. *HDB* III, p. 428a; *NBD*, p. 841a).

The Question about the Resurrection (22: 23-33)

See comments on Mk 12: 18-27; Lk. 20: 27-40.

The Question about the Greatest Commandment (22: 34-40)

See comments on Mk 12: 28-34. Lk. 10: 27 shows clearly that we do not have original teaching by Jesus here. **Lawyer** (*nomikos*), though common in Lk., is found only here in Mt. It is probable that a scribe (Mk 12: 28) whose speciality was *halakah*, i.e. the detailed application of the Mosaic Law, is intended. There is no obvious reason why in the quotation of Dt. 6: 5 Mt. omits 'strength' (cf. Mk 12: 30, Lk. 10: 27). The NT does not really introduce a fourth element into Dt. 6: 5. MSS of LXX vary in their rendering of Heb. *lebab* between *kardia* (heart) and *dianoia* (mind). The former is more literal, the latter gives the sense better, because the intellect and will predominate over the emotions in Heb. *lebab*.

About David's Son (22: 41-46)

See comments on Mk 12: 35-37; Lk. 20: 41-44.

Woes against the Scribes and Pharisees (23: 1-36)

Cf. Mk 12: 38-40, Lk. 11: 39-52; 20: 45 ff. For **scribes** see note on 13: 52, for **Pharisees** see *The Religious Background*, p. 76, and articles *Judaism* and *Pharisees* in *NBD*, for **hypocrites** see note at end of ch. 6. The reader of this chapter must never forget that the bulk of the people approved of the Pharisees, even though they tried to avoid the more onerous points of their legislation, legislation they were not able to enforce in full until after A.D. 70. Hence Jesus must be speaking of the deeper things of the spirit, where only His eye could penetrate. We have in this section seven woes (13–31) with an introduction and conclusion.

Introduction (1–12). Jesus was not attacking their teaching in general but the way they applied it in their own lives (3). By saying they **sit on Moses' seat** (2) He acknowledged the general correctness of it. If one is to keep the Law of Moses, one is virtually compelled to accept the approach of the scribes. Sitting was the position of the teacher (cf. Lk. 4: 20). In the fourth century A.D. there were special synagogue chairs called Moses' seat for rabbis, but it is doubtful whether they existed in the first century; the sense is that they were official expounders of the Law.

The modern Jew considers vv. 3 f. a major insult, and so they are, if we take them purely at their face value. No Pharisee would have maintained his place in the brotherhood for long, if it had been obvious that he preached but did not practise. In the rabbinic expansion of the Law much was man-made commandment intended to guarantee the keeping of the divinely given laws. The learned man might be trusted to ignore or circumvent much of this man-made legislation in ways that the ordinary man knew nothing of. On a deeper level Jesus was condemning, not lawlessness on the part of those who preached law, but rather a strictness, especially among the disciples of Shammai, which was bearable for the richer and more leisured, but almost impossible for the poor. There has been all too much of this in the Church.

With vv. 5–7 cf. 6: 1–8, 16–18; it is the condemnation of all behaviour and ritual, even the anti-ritual of the extremer Protestant, which, professing to address itself to God, keeps one eye at least on man. **5. phylacteries:** See *NBD*, p. 995. In the first century A.D. their use had not yet become obligatory, so the pious were under very strong temptation to rebuke the non-observant by wearing them as large as possible. **fringes:** Better 'tassels' (Dt. 22: 12; Num. 15: 38 f. and cf. 9: 20; 14: 36): see *HDB* II, pp. 68 ff. They were almost universally worn at the time; they were intended as a reminder to the wearer (Num. 15: 39), not as a proclamation to others. Leading rabbis repeatedly insisted that the learned should not use their knowledge of the Law for personal

profit, but they took a very poor view of those who did not show them honour; they would have certainly subscribed to the modern adage that the soldier salutes not the man but his rank. This type of carnal honour is all too prevalent in the Church.

For vv. 8–12 cf. 20: 24–28. Titles which express a fact or are merely conventional often make communication easier and are normally unexceptional. Others are flattery and often worse. **rabbi . . . master:** Jn 13: 13 gives the usual titles of respect for the Jewish teacher, 'You call me Teacher (*rabbi*) and Lord (*mari*)'. Jesus was so uniquely Lord, that there was no room for a man to be so called in the Church. Teacher lived on (Ac. 13: 1; Jas 3: 1; 1 C. 12: 28; Eph. 4: 11) but there is no evidence for its being used as a title of respect. Even *kyrios* (lord), which to the Gk. speaker meant no more than Sir in secular contexts, is found after the resurrection in the NT only in Rev. 7: 14 as a title of address to others than Christ, on Christian lips that is to say. **9. call no man your father on earth:** Jesus is not suspending the fifth commandment. The rabbis disliked using the title 'father' except for the Patriarchs, but they were prepared to use it for an outstanding rabbi. We need a greater sensitivity to these things, not just criticism, in the Church today.

The First Woe (13). The meaning of this verse is sharply limited by v. 15. The fact that they had rejected both John the Baptist and Jesus showed that they had not submitted themselves to the sovereignty of God. Their teaching, if accepted in the sense it had for them, made it impossible for others to submit either. After the destruction of Jerusalem it was the greatest single human factor that made the Jews as a people reject Christ.

Widows' Houses (14) (cf. Mk 12: 40; Lk. 20: 47). The MSS are overwhelmingly in favour of the exclusion of this verse; Edersheim's argument (II, p. 410) that the eight Woes balance the eight Beatitudes seems a trifle far-fetched. Any interpretation involving deliberate knavery is grievously to misunderstand the Pharisees, even though they had their black sheep, some of whose acts are recorded in the Talmud. The insistence on fulfilment of vows and the encouragement of giving, where this was out of place, is a sufficient interpretation.

The Second Woe (15). Both Roman emperors and later a triumphant Church were to punish Jewish proselytizing by death, but the activity was wide-spread at this time. The Synagogue attracted many sympathizers, the *sebomenoi* or *phoboumenoi ton theon*, which RSV renders 'devout' (Ac. 10: 2; 13: 50), 'God-fearing' (Ac. 10: 22), 'you that fear God' (Ac. 13: 16), 'a worshipper of God' (Ac. 16: 14). The readiness of many of them to listen to Paul shows that the teaching they had received was very often for good. To become a full proselyte (*ger ṣedeq*) involved adopting all the legal minutiae of the Pharisees. It is noteworthy that only one, possibly two, of the latter class are expressly mentioned as becoming Christians, *viz.* Nicolaus of Antioch (Ac. 6: 5) and perhaps the Ethiopian eunuch (Ac. 8: 27). This principle holds also for the person more concerned to win a convert for a denomination than for Christ.

The Third Woe (16-22). See note on 5: 33-37. **blind guides:** It is their teaching rather than their practice which is here condemned. **You blind fools** (*mōroi*): Jesus the judge permits Himself language forbidden to His followers (5: 22). *Mōroi* here, as in the Sermon on the Mount, is a reproduction of the Aram. word.

The Fourth Woe (23, 24). It is one matter if I am very strict with myself because of the witness of the Spirit within me. If, on the other hand, I decide I must hold whatever I find in Scripture strictly, however small it is, experience shows that I shall become increasingly legalistic in my demands on others and increasingly blind to the real demands God is making on me.

The Fifth Woe (25, 26). This is a widening and intensification of the fourth woe. Had the Pharisees behaved literally in the way suggested by v. 25, they would never have been looked up to by the people. But their estimate of the character of others was normally based on the measure in which they observed externals. The acceptance of an invitation to a meal would depend mainly on the measure in which the laws of tithing and purity were observed there. Their attitude may be compared with our judgment of fellow-Christians by their outward orthodoxy. **26. You blind Pharisee:** The singular is probably due to the underlying Aram., which could be taken as singular or plural. 'Give for alms' (Lk. 11: 41): if my cup and plate are full of extortion and rapacity, I shall be too; my willingness to give up what I have includes the giving of myself. This seems to be the meaning of the extremely difficult sentence in Lk.

The Sixth Woe (27, 28). This is the culmination of the two previous woes. In Adar (March), after the heavy rains, graves were whitewashed to prevent those going to the Temple, especially priests, from being defiled by contact with the dead. The graves were made resplendent just because they were graves. The Pharisees marked themselves out by their

piousness and legalism just because they were sinners. Had they not been, they would not have felt compelled to act as they did. In their failure to realize this lay their play acting.

The Seventh Woe (29-31). Just as Christians are all too ready to make excuses for the many crimes committed down the centuries in the name of Christ (the Church's treatment of the Jews probably being the worst), so the rabbis could seldom bring themselves to a whole-hearted denunciation of the sins of their ancestors. They were virtually saying, 'It could not happen here'. The rejection of Jesus by the religious leaders shows the justice of His words.

Concluding Condemnation (32-36). The **prophets, wise men and scribes** are Christians (cf. Eph. 2: 20; Mt. 13: 52). The persecution of Jewish Christians here foretold (not many Gentile Christians were involved) fell into two parts, a lighter period before A.D. 70 and a more serious one culminating in the rebellion of Bar Cochba (132-135). Similarly, for Jewry the bloody defeat of Bar Cochba was probably a heavier blow than even the destruction of Jerusalem. We have no right to extend this woe beyond 135; it is also a warning against a too rigid interpretation of **generation. 35. Zechariah the son of Barachiah:** Jesus was giving the equivalent of our 'from Genesis to Revelation', for the Heb. Bible ends with 2 Chr. (not Mal.!), and the last righteous man mentioned by name in 2 Chr. to be murdered is Zechariah (2 Chr. 24: 20 f.). He was the son of Jehoiada, Berechiah being the father of the prophet Zechariah (Zech. 1: 1). Lk. 11: 51 does not contain 'the son of Barachiah'. It is possible that Mt. has added these words as a pointer to perhaps the worst of the judicial murders in the final days of Jerusalem (Jos. *War*, IV. v. 4). For a full discussion cf. Williams, II, pp. 45-48.

The Lament over Jerusalem (23: 37-39) Cf. Lk. 13: 34, 35. That these words fit magnificently in their present position is obvious. The condemnation of the scribes and Pharisees has shown that there is nothing more to hope for. Only the way to the cross remains. It could have been said twice; more likely Lk. moved it, for he does not have this context in his gospel. **Jerusalem:** From the time the ark was brought there by David and Solomon built his temple, Jerusalem became the expression of Israel in a unique way. **under her wings:** Cf. Ru. 2: 12. The fulfilment of v. 39 and also Lk. 13: 35 is at the Second Coming.

V. ii. ESCHATOLOGY (24: 1-25: 46)
The Eschatological Discourse (24: 1-36)
Cf. Mk 13: 1-32; Lk. 21: 5-33; 17: 23, 24, 37.
Owing to lack of space it is impossible to

deal with this section as it merits. The reader is therefore requested to read the careful contribution on Mk 13: 1-37 first—a somewhat less extreme presentation of the same view is given by Tasker. This will probably convince most readers that the view that would push the whole chapter to 'the Great Tribulation' and the Second Coming is unsatisfactory. After all a comparison of v. 3 with Mk 13: 4; Lk. 21: 7 shows that the destruction of the Temple was uppermost in the disciples' minds; any interpretation that makes it secondary must be mistaken.

Having read this we must go on to ask whether with all its correctness it has not exaggerated. For those who know Gk., Beasley-Murray will be specially useful.

This is an 'apocalyptic' discourse, and just as in Rev. we should hesitate to interpret the terms too sharply. **This generation** (34) undoubtedly normally refers to Jesus' contemporaries, but it can also mean 'this nation' (*Arndt*, Schniewind), and we cannot exclude Lang's explanation (pp. 70, 387) of the generation of the fulfilment. A reference to M'Neile *ad loc.* will make it clear that all three interpretations have had support in the past. In any case, even if we feel compelled with Filson and Beasley-Murray to accept the first interpretation, it does not force us to limit the scope of the prophecy. This tension between soon and not yet is found in much of the NT's teaching on the Second Coming.

Take Heed (4-8). Cf. Mk 13: 5-8; Lk. 21: 8-11: i.e. things would not develop as they expected. The period from A.D. 33 to 70 was not particularly marked out by wars and natural disasters, and the first serious claimant to be Messiah was Bar Cochba (132-135). **the sufferings:** The birth pangs of the Messiah, i.e. the sufferings that would precede the setting up of the Messianic kingdom. It was a technical term at the time. **the end is not yet:** 'Christ does not come with war' (Schlatter).

The Tribulation (9-14). Cf. 10: 17-23 and Mk 13: 9-13; Lk. 21: 12-19. Mk 13: 9-12; Lk. 21: 12 are represented by 10: 17-21, which was doubtlessly deliberately moved from here to its present place (see comment *ad loc.*). As already said on 23: 34 ff., it is difficult to restrict this to the period before A.D. 70. **You will be hated by all nations** (9) clearly looks beyond A.D. 70, unless we take the desperate step of making 'nations' an insertion by Mt. The same conclusion must be drawn from **this gospel of the kingdom will be preached throughout the whole world** (14). So it should be clear that the first two sections place the destruction of Jerusalem within a larger context (so also Tasker).

The Destruction of Jerusalem (15-22). Cf. Mk 13: 14-20; Lk. 21: 20-24. Some may allow themselves a double reference here both to A.D. 70 and the Antichrist. It is often forgotten that this is bound up with a questionable interpretation of a number of OT prophecies. Furthermore, if this double interpretation was intended, it is hard to see why Jesus did not give some hint of the fact. **the desolating sacrilege:** It would have been preferable to keep 'abomination of desolation' (so Phillips and NEB) as a conscious quotation of Dan. 9: 27; 11: 31; 12: 11, but 'the appalling abomination' (Beasley-Murray, Tasker) is better. This almost certainly means the Roman army; cf. the paraphrase in Lk. 21: 20.

The Climax (23-31). Cf. Mk 13: 21-27; Lk. 21: 25-28. Already in the previous section there were touches which surpassed reality, *e.g.* 'never will be' (21), 'no human being' (22). Tasker's exposition shows that this section can be pressed into the straitjacket of the fall of Jerusalem. It is easier to say that it includes the fall but looks on to a greater climax. **The coming** is world wide (27). In A.D. 70 the vultures of judgment (28) gathered at Jerusalem, now they will be everywhere (30). While v. 29, based on passages like Isa. 13: 10; 34: 4 suggests that the Coming has cosmic significance, it also points to the destruction of all earthly powers. We cannot interpret v. 29 merely of judgment; cf. Dan. 7: 13 f. For **the sign of the Son of man** (30) cf. Isa. 11: 10; probably it is the light of v. 27. The **loud trumpet call** (31) links with 1 Th. 4: 15 f. To see in v. 31 merely the Church liberated by the fall of Jerusalem for its true task of evangelism (Tasker) shows merely the extremes to which the straitjacket of a theory will bring one.

The Time of the Coming (32-36). Cf. Mk 13: 28-32; Lk. 21: 29-33. The time of the Coming is unknown, except to the Father, but there will be clear signs before it. It is not permissible to equate the fig tree with the Jews; it is never so used elsewhere. It is chosen because it stands out in the Palestinian winter more than other trees in its bareness, and the coming of leaves is a sure sign of spring. For the watcher the signs of the Coming will be equally clear, when they are given. There is no doubt of the textual authenticity of **nor the Son** in v. 36; Mk 13: 32. It is as irreverent to suggest that Jesus was making Himself temporarily ignorant for convenience as it is to deduce whatever other form of ignorance happens to suit the reader.

It is hard to avoid the conclusion that we are moving in the OT phenomenon of the Day of the Lord. There the Day is a final climax of judgment and blessing, yet there are repeated events which so foreshadow it, that they may be called the Day. So it would seem to be with the Coming. Ever and again it has seemed to be at the doors, and the greatest of these events was the fall of Jerusalem and the destruction of the Temple. It does not matter just how much of the discourse we apply to this event, so long as we realize that we must look beyond it. Even the events of A.D. 70 were means to a greater end.

Be Alert! (37–41). At this point the Synoptics go their separate ways, so it is wisest to see in 24: 36 the solemn end of the discourse and in 24: 37–25: 46 separate teaching intended to drive home its lessons. It may be possible to incorporate these sections into a complete outline of the Coming, but their original purpose was practical rather than theological and their hearers were not at the time able to give them a systematic interpretation. These comments confine themselves to Christ's original purpose. It should be considered also that though the actual 'apocalypse' has ended, 'apocalyptic' language continues; i.e. it is dangerous to make the picture language too literal.

The Coming is decisive and final. Neither people nor things can ever be the same again. One must decide one's attitude to it and to Christ before it happens, because afterwards it is too late. If the comparison above with the OT teaching on the Day of the Lord is correct, it means that men are constantly being faced with the possibility of minor events being equally decisive at the time. Jewish Christians for the most part did not grasp the decisiveness of the events of A.D. 70, and so the majority drifted into Ebionite heresy. The Gentile Christians did not understand the implications of the sack of Rome in 410, and so the Church became largely paganized. Those who did not accept the Reformation did not have another chance, and the religious boundaries drawn then have remained relatively fixed to this day. Each reader may wish to add other examples. The call to watch (*grēgoreō*), implying spiritual alertness, is not only in view of the Coming, but also of those judgments in the world, which by their decisiveness foreshadow the Coming.

There was ample warning of Noah's flood, but that did not make it any less sudden, when it came. Then the division was made by God's hand that shut to the Ark (Gen. 7: 16); at the Coming it is the action of the angels (31). There follow four parables illustrating various aspects of the Coming.

The Watchful Householder (24: 42–44)
Cf. Lk. 12: 39 f. The picture of Christ's coming as a thief in the night is found also in 1 Th. 5: 2; 2 Pet. 3: 10; Rev. 3: 3; 16: 15. The main stress is on the unpredictability of the time, but there is also a threat of loss, which is never expounded, the nearest being Rev. 16: 15.

The Faithful and Wise Steward (24: 45–51)
Cf. Lk. 12: 42–46. The Church is not a democratic assembly but 'the household of God' (Eph. 2: 19). To some of its members Christ delegates authority. Forgetfulness of the Coming, which is the present goal set for the Church, leads to the belief that they have inherent right to authority and that in turn to its abuse.

The Parable of the Ten Maidens (25: 1-13)
From the head servants Jesus turned to those of 'the household' of no particular standing. At a Jewish wedding the bridegroom, surrounded by his friends, went, generally after sunset, to the home of the bride to fetch her. The bride, dressed in her best, was carried in a litter to the bridegroom's house, a procession being formed by her and the bridegroom's friends. Light was provided by lamps on poles. When the bridegroom's home was reached the wedding supper was eaten.

Our interpretation of the parable must partly depend on whether we read **to meet the bridegroom** (Tasker) or 'the bridegroom and the bride' (Schniewind, M'Neile)—the MS evidence is fairly evenly balanced. Our decision should not be influenced by the non-mention of the bride in v. 6; etiquette would not permit it. The shutting of the door (10) strongly suggests the latter reading, for M'Neile is wrong in suggesting that the feast was at the bride's house. Tasker says, 'It is most probable that it is *this* (the bringing home of the bride) procession that the ten girls in the story are pictured as going to meet, though whether as official bridesmaids, servants of the bridegroom, or children of friends and neighbours we have no means of knowing.' Official bridesmaids are ruled out, for as honoured guests the bride's parents would be responsible for all they needed. Either or both the other explanations, including servants of the bride, are equally possible. They are persons who have received no invitation but who will be welcomed in, if they form part of the procession, the more so if they honour the bridal pair with lights. **Lamps** (*lampas*) is not the word used in contexts like 5: 15; 6: 22; Lk. 15: 8. It means a torch, which could be fed with oil. They kept their torches on because no Oriental likes to be in the dark. Seen from the angle of an everyday wedding, where the details in the story are fixed by what actually happened, it should be clear that the parable is refractory to any allegorical treatment (cf. introduction to ch. 13). The two features are that the girls had no claim to be guests, which is entirely secondary, and that their getting in depended on their being awake and ready at the right moment. **13. Watch therefore:** It is mental rather than physical alertness that is meant. This is no story of eternal destiny decided by the Coming. The foolish have lost something but need not be lost themselves.

The Parable of the Talents (25: 14-30)
Cf. Lk. 19: 12-27. It seems impossible to find any essential difference between the parable of the talents and that of the pounds (Lk. 19: 12-27). The difference in the size of the amounts entrusted—a talent was worth about fifty 'pounds'—is probably due to the latter's having been told to a wider audience, the former to the Twelve with their very much greater responsibilities, not this time in the Church but rather in the world. The difference between this and the previous parable is that there it was lack of serious thought that caused the trouble, here the lack of good will. There is no suggestion of the eternal fate of the third servant; like the foolish maidens he has lost something. **the worthless** (*achreios*) **servant:** 'useless' (NEB, Phillips). **the outer darkness** (*to skotos to exōteron*): 'the darkness outside' (Phillips), 'the darkness' (NEB); no special kind of darkness is meant—the reckoning takes place after nightfall. In Lk. it is not even mentioned. If we wish to continue the story, we shall find that the morning will come, and the slave is still his master's slave, only he has irreparably lost something. The often heard remark that no Christian could speak or think as the servant does in v. 24 comes from living in a monastery without walls.

The Judgment (25: 31-46)
This is not a parable but a description in apocalyptic language with a simile in v. 32. Since **them** (32) is masculine and **nations** (*ethnē*) is neuter, the correct translation is 'He will separate men into two groups' (NEB, similarly Phillips). We are witnessing the judgment of the individuals who make up the nations. The exact when and who is not important, for God's principles of judgment are immutable. **40. one of the least of these my brethren:** That 'the Jewish Remnant' is meant could never have suggested itself to the hearers, who had 12: 46-50 as a key to the interpretation. Anyone who befriends those whom Jesus is prepared to call **my brethren** in the hour of their need and persecution would do the same to their Master, if he had the chance. This passage is no complete answer to the problem of those who have never heard

the gospel, or have heard it inadequately. It does reveal, however, the type of criterion that will be used, and it is intended to be a warning to us. Since from His **brethren** He will expect more, not less, this can serve as a check on the reality of our profession.

EPILOGUE: PASSION, DEATH AND RESURRECTION (26: 1-28: 20)
The Plot to Arrest Jesus (26: 1-5)
See comments on Mk 14: 1, 2; Lk. 22: 1, 2; cf. Jn 11: 47-53.

The Anointing of Jesus' Head (26: 6-13)
See comments on Mk 14: 3-9. The differences between this incident and Jn 12: 1-8 make it difficult to believe that the same woman is involved. It was usual to offer a guest at a meal oil to anoint his head with, but there is no evidence from Palestine for such an anointing of an honoured guest's head. It was obviously a completely spontaneous action, though possibly prompted by Mary's action (Jn 12: 3).

The Betrayal Agreement (26: 14-16)
See comments on Mk 14: 10, 11; Lk. 22: 3-6. The complex character of Judas has always defied analysis. The NT does not try to motivate his action, but see 27: 3.

Preparation for the Passover (26: 17-19)
See comments on Mk 14: 12-16; Lk. 22: 7-13. The secrecy in the arrangements was to prevent Judas acting too early. If some prefer to see prior arrangement here and in 21: 2 f., it is not to depreciate Jesus' powers, but because the actions of the others involved suggest prearrangement. It would have been virtually impossible to find accommodation of the type described in Mk 14: 15 on 14 Nisan without prior arrangement, owing to the vast crowds of pilgrims that had to be accommodated in Jerusalem.

The Last Supper (26: 20-29)
See comments on Mk 14: 17-25; Lk. 22: 14-38; 1 C. 11: 23 ff. The supper demands the background of the Passover meal for its understanding. The rabbis distinguished between the Egyptian and the Palestinian Passover. One main difference was that the former had to be eaten standing and in haste (Exod. 12: 11), the latter reclining (Jn 13: 23, 25) and at leisure. **He sat at table** (20) is literally 'He reclined' (*anakeimai*). A necessary part of the meal was four cups of red wine. The second cup, that of Lk. 22: 17, was drunk after the 'proclamation' of the story of the Exodus. The 'morsel' given to Judas (Jn 13: 26) was during the meal that followed, i.e. Judas was at the Passover meal, but not at the institution of the Lord's Supper—following Jn 13: 30 rather than Lk. 22: 21; the former gives the impression of fixing the time. After the meal a half *matzah* (unleavened bread) that had been

hidden away was brought out and eaten. This will have been the **bread** of v. 26. Earlier Jesus will have said, as He showed the unleavened bread, 'This is the bread of affliction which our fathers ate in the land of Egypt'; His disciples must have understood **this is my body** in the same way. Though not so clearly, the red wine is used as a picture of the blood shed in Egypt. 'The cup of blessing' (1 C. 10: 16) was the third cup, which still bears this name. It precedes the second part of the Hallel (Pss. 115-118, possibly then 114-118), cf. **when they had sung a hymn** (30). The only part of the picture missing is the fourth cup, but this is explained by v. 29. Jesus deliberately did not close the ritual, because the fulness of the salvation He was bringing would not be realized until the fulness of His Father's rule (**kingdom**) was revealed at His Coming.

Owing to the constant liturgical use of the words of institution later MSS show considerable corruption and assimilation to one another. There is little doubt that **Take, (eat); this is my body** is the original wording for the bread; 'which is (given) for you' is a liturgical development—'broken for you' has no real claim to consideration. In fact the bread points to the life of Christ rather than to His death. Jeremias has made out a very strong case— some would call it absolutely convincing—when he argues for the authenticity of Lk. 22: 19b, 20 (see mg) against the majority of modern scholars. The omission of 'new' in v. 28 (Mk 14: 24) need not detain us. **The covenant** needed no explanation for the Twelve, but 'new' had to be added as a liturgical explanation for Gentile believers. Here too Mk 14: 24 gives the most primitive version. The form of the words in Lk. 22: 19 f.; 1 C. 11: 24 f. represents the liturgical form used *c.* A.D. 50. The fullest modern discussion may be found in Jeremias.

for many: This, as in 20: 28, represents a Heb. idiom meaning, 'All, who will be very many', cf. Isa. 53: 12.

This linking of the Lord's Supper with the Passover is not merely of antiquarian interest. The Passover lamb in the Palestinian Passover had no atoning or saving power. The service was merely a symbolic re-enactment of the Egyptian Passover. Similarly the Lord's Supper can be only a symbolic re-enactment of the all-saving sacrifice of the Cross. The first Supper looked forward to it, all others have looked back.

Additional Note on the Date of the Last Supper. The Passover lambs were always killed in the Temple on 14 Nisan, and they were eaten on 15 Nisan—the Jewish day began at sunset. The above exegesis was based on the assumption that the Last Supper was a Passover meal, it having been prepared on 14 Nisan (26: 17) and eaten soon after dark on 15 Nisan. No other view is possible, if we confine ourselves to the Synoptics. But Jn clearly identifies Christ as the antitype of the Passover lamb (19: 36) and implies, though it is not stated, that Jesus died at the time the lambs were being sacrificed. In addition he indicates that the priests on the Friday morning had not yet eaten the Passover (18: 28). It seems that for him the supper was on 14 Nisan as was the crucifixion. In addition superficial reading will find nothing in Jn 13-17 to suggest the Passover. To this basic fact have been added a number of further objections, which, so it is claimed, prove that the Supper cannot have been the Passover. The ten most important are listed and answered by Jeremias.

Earlier efforts at a solution of the problem either tried to minimize the impression created by Jn, interpreting 18: 28 to mean the *Chagigah*, or special festival offering (Num. 28: 18-22—cf. Edersheim II, pp. 566 ff.), or suggested that Jesus, knowing that He would die on 14 Nisan, anticipated the Passover, eating it twenty-four hours before others. The former is possible but runs counter to the general impression created by Jn; the latter is impossible, no priest would have sacrificed the lamb before the time, and it is contradicted by Mt. 26: 17; Mk 14: 12; Lk. 22: 7, all of which can refer only to 14 Nisan. Many scholars today reject the testimony either of the Synoptics or Jn, mainly of the former. Quite apart from inspiration, this is impossible; people's memories do not play them tricks in this kind of thing.

We must assume, therefore, that it was possible for the Passover to be eaten *officially* on two nights in that year. Two possible ways have been suggested. (i) *SB* II, pp. 812-853, argues from the known fact that the beginning of the month was fixed by visual observance of the new moon and that at least once there was deliberate fraud in the claim to have seen it. It maintains that in their ritual controversy with the Pharisees the Sadducean priests would have gained by 14 Nisan's falling on a Friday. The Pharisees, suspecting that in the year of the crucifixion Nisan had started a day late, insisted on keeping Passover on what they maintained was the evening of 15 Nisan, but the Sadducees 14 Nisan. Hence in this particular year it was possible for Jesus to eat the Passover with those that followed the Pharisees and yet die with the official Passover lambs on the official 14 Nisan. The theory is entirely possible but unprovable. (ii) More recently it has been claimed that according to the *Book of Jubilees* and the Essenes of Qumran the correct calendar was not a lunar but a solar one. According to this 14 Nisan would have been a Tuesday. Jesus ate the Passover at the same time as these people, was arrested on the Tuesday night, but was not crucified until the Friday. It has yet to be proved that the Sadducean priests were prepared to make concessions to a calendar they did not follow, something which is highly improbable. In addition, unless it is maintained that Jesus was crucified on a Wednesday (see Additional Note at end of ch. 27), it means that He was held under arrest for forty-eight hours, something contrary to the whole spirit of the Gospel account. Unless more evidence can be adduced, this view must be regarded with extreme suspicion, the more so as no Gentile reader would have guessed that two calendars existed among the Jews.

The Way to Gethsemane (26: 30–35)
See comments on Mk 14: 26–31; Lk. 22: 31–34, 39; Jn 13: 36–38; 18: 1.

The Agony in the Garden (26: 36–46)
See comments on Mk 14: 32–42; Lk. 22: 40–46. In our reconstruction of the scene we have to allow for a late hour of the night. The Passover never ends early, and we have to allow ample time for Jn 14–17. The failure of the Twelve to stop Judas shows that even then they had not really taken in what was to happen—was it due to a deep-rooted belief that when it came to the point Jesus would use His supernatural power to save Himself?—and so their sleep can easily be understood. The account of the agony must, at least in part, have come from Jesus after the resurrection. **39. cup:** Cf. 20: 22. It was a common OT term expressing the fate, good or bad but more often the latter, of a man or nation.

The Arrest (26: 47–56)
See comments on Mk 14: 43–52; Lk. 22: 47–53; Jn 18: 2–12. **49. he kissed him:** An act of insolence. There was not nearly as much kissing practised by the Jews as is often thought. A rabbi might kiss a pupil as a reward for special wisdom, but we do not find the pupils kissing their rabbis.

The Jewish Trial. Though the Jewish trial bears its unfairness on its face, we must not suggest that it broke the Jewish rules of jurisprudence. Older works, and some modern ones too, base themselves on the information contained in the *Mishna*. This took its present shape *c.* A.D. 200, and the Talmud itself bears witness that these rules were not in force at the time of Jesus' condemnation. He was tried according to Sadducean rules, of which we know nothing.

The trial before the Sanhedrin falls into three parts. (i) A preliminary investigation before Annas (Jn 18: 13, 19–24). This was presumably to save time, while Caiaphas was making arrangements with Pilate for a quick trial in the morning (see note on 27: 11). (ii) A hearing before as many of the Sanhedrin as could be collected in a hurry (26: 57–68). (iii) The confirmation of its verdict by a full Sanhedrin at dawn (Lk. 22: 66–71). Only the last was really official.

A very strong case has been made out recently that the Jews did in fact have the right to inflict the death penalty, especially in matters involving their religion. If this is correct, Jn 18: 31 must be interpreted to mean that once they had brought a political charge against Jesus (Lk. 23: 2), the case had passed out of their competence. The Sanhedrin was probably shirking the opprobrium they would have aroused by putting Him to death as a blasphemer.

The Second Stage of the Jewish Trial (26: 57–68)
See comments on Mk 14: 53–65; Lk. 22: 54, 63–65 (Jn 18: 13, 14, 19–24). **63. I adjure you by the living God:** Under the later legislation of the *Mishna* such an adjuration could be addressed only to a limited class of witnesses, who had to answer that justice might be done; it could not be addressed to the accused. It is improbable that it was legal under the Sadducees either.

64. You have said so: In some settings this could mean no more than a polite refusal to answer a question. Here, however, it must mean, 'I am' (Mk 14: 62). **hereafter** (*ap' arti*): We must render 'from now on' (NEB, *Arndt*). Jesus is not referring to the eschatological vision of Rev. 1: 7, but to the religious leaders' growing realization that all their efforts have been in vain, and that the prisoner is their King and Judge. **Power:** Another way of avoiding 'God' (see note on 4: 17). As in His use of 'heaven', Jesus conformed as far as possible to the practices of His time. **65. the high priest tore his robes:** An action expressive of grief that was obligatory on hearing blasphemy.

Peter's Denial (26: 69–75)
See comments on Mk 14: 66–72; Lk. 22: 55–62; Jn 18: 15–18, 25–27.

The Third Stage of the Jewish Trial (27: 1 f.)
See comments on Mk 15: 1; Lk. 22: 66–71. For legality's sake the verdict of the night council had to be rubber-stamped by the whole Sanhedrin. Time was saved by repeating the decisive question. When the same answer was given, the verdict of blasphemy was adopted.

It is often urged, especially in Jewish circles, that the whole story of the trial must be unhistorical, because none of the Twelve can have been present at it. (i) This is an implicit denial of the resurrection; otherwise the information could have come from Jesus Himself. (ii) It forgets that such trials were not held *in camera;* especially disciples of the rabbis were expected to attend to gain experience in legal matters. Some of them may well have been converted later (cf. Ac. 6: 7; 15: 5). (iii) Joseph of Arimathea (Lk. 23: 50 f.) was evidently present and could have given all the information needed.

The Death of Judas (27: 3-10)
Cf. Ac. 1: 18, 19. Judas had been admitted into the court room or was waiting in a nearby room. It seems that he had expected that Jesus would at the last use His miraculous power to save Himself and to confound His enemies, though it is hard to believe that this was the real motive of the betrayal. At any rate the reality caused a violent revulsion of feeling. **5. in the temple** (*eis ton naon*): There are no adequate reasons for doubting that Mt. is observing the usual distinction between *hieron*, the whole range of the temple area, usually rendered 'temple', and *naos*, the sanctuary itself and the court immediately around it, where only priests and Levites could go. Judas, in his desperation, seems to have hurled the coins into the court of the priests; some of the money could even have reached the temple porch. The perverse scrupulosity of the priests, for which there is also Talmudic evidence, forced them to regard the coins as 'holy' because they had landed in the sacred area, but they could not be put into one of the regular accounts. In vv. 9 f. we have a rather free quotation of Zech. 11: 12 f., apparently attributed to **the prophet Jeremiah.** The difference in the text of the quotation is not due, as so often in NT, to LXX, but may be a free citing from memory. Some have suggested, therefore, that Jeremiah is a slip. This is unlikely. The only explanation with some measure of probability is that at that time the 'Latter Prophets' were headed by Jeremiah, not Isaiah as now, so it would mean no more than 'in the prophetic books'. There is a full discussion in Williams II, pp. 50-55.

The Roman Trial. The Roman trial also fell into three parts. (i) The first hearing by Pilate is found in 27: 2, 11-14; Mk 15: 1-5; Lk. 23: 1-7; Jn 18: 28-19: 10—though some of the order here is different. The fullest account is in Jn, the Synoptics being less interested in what was essentially a preliminary hearing. (ii) The hearing by Herod. This is recorded only in Lk. 23: 8-12, because it was essentially an interlude. (iii) The second hearing by Pilate is found in 27: 15-26; Mk 15: 6-15; Lk. 23: 13-25; Jn 18: 39, 40; 19: 4-6, 12-16 (as said above, Jn's order cannot always be reconciled with that of the Synoptics). It should be noted

that with the exception of Lk. 23: 4 only the chief priests, the elders and the scribes are mentioned in the first two hearings. It was a desperate gamble by the Jewish authorities to get the case out of the way before there could be any public reaction. The multitude gathered in order to demand the release of a popular prisoner (Mk 15: 8), and it is doubtful whether they would have called for Jesus' death, had it not been presented to them as a choice between Jesus and Barabbas. Pilate really held the whip hand, until he virtually stepped down from his judgment seat and suggested that popular acclaim should settle the matter.

The First Hearing before Pilate (27: 11-14)
See comments on Mk 15: 2-5; Lk. 23: 2-5; Jn 18: 28-19: 10. **11. the governor asked him 'Are you the king of the Jews?'** This could not possibly be the beginning of the hearing, which had to start with a charge. The first step is given by Jn 18: 29 f. There was no love lost between Pilate and the Jewish leaders, so the insolence of v. 30 can only mean that some prior arrangement had been reached between Caiaphas and Pilate, which the latter chose to ignore. Then came the charge (Lk. 23: 2), which by its profuseness suggests that it was thought up on the spur of the moment. Pilate tried to push Jesus back on the Sanhedrin (Jn 18: 31). Only then did he turn to Jesus. In judging Pilate's attitude we must not forget that his spies must have brought him fairly full reports of the doings and teaching of Jesus, and especially since the triumphal entry a fairly full dossier must have been compiled. Pilate knew that he was dealing with an innocent man.

The Second Hearing before Pilate (27: 15-26)
See comments on Mk 15: 6-15; Lk. 23: 17-25; Jn 18: 39, 40; 19: 4-6, 12-16. There is no evidence outside the NT for Pilate's power to pardon a prisoner, and indeed it was an exceptional privilege, for pardon was normally a prerogative of the emperor.

16, 17. Barabbas: A small but influential group of MSS have 'Jesus Barabbas', which is accepted by NEB, B. & F. B. S. Diglot, Schniewind and considered probable by M'Neile, Filson and Tasker. It is difficult to explain its existence, if it were not original. Pilate's offer of the choice of Barabbas or Jesus seemed most shrewd. He knew of the tumultuous welcome of the triumphal entry and that the common people, especially the nationalists, loathed the Sadducean priests. He had no means of gauging how bitterly Jesus had disappointed the activists by His passivity since the Sunday of the Entry. In addition a Messiah who owed his life to Roman clemency would have been a blow to Jewish pride (Schlatter). **19. his wife sent word**

to him: Christian tradition knows much about Pilate's wife, but secular history knows nothing! So there is no point in speculating about her action. That she even knew of the trial may be some support for the suggestion that Caiaphas had gone round to Pilate's house the night before to arrange the trial. **22. Let him be crucified:** Jn 19: 6 shows that the horrid suggestion came first from the chief priests. They knew that this punishment would put Jesus' memory under a curse (cf. Gal. 3: 13; Dt. 21: 23). To many Jews He is still *talui*, the hanged one. **25. His blood be on us and on our children:** Few things in the Church's history are more shocking than its use of this cry. Just as little as Pilate could remove his guilt by washing his hands could the people pass on their guilt to their descendants for a hundred generations. At the most we could speak of the third and fourth generation, but surely the curse was outweighed by the prayer of Lk. 23: 34. **24. he took water and washed his hands:** A Jewish custom (Dt. 21: 6); Pilate had been long enough in the country to have seen it. **26. having scourged Jesus:** Scourging was part of the punishment of crucifixion; by weakening the victim, it probably accelerated death.

The Mockery of the Soldiers (27: 27-31)
See comments on Mk 15: 16-20; cf. Jn 19: 2 f. **29. Hail, King of the Jews:** In the insult to the people the penalty of rejection already begins to work itself out.

The Road to Golgotha (27: 32)
See comments on Mk 15: 21; Lk. 23: 26-32.

The Crucifixion (27: 33-44)
See comments on Mk 15: 22-32; Lk. 23: 33-43; Jn 19: 17-24. **Golgotha:** Those interested in the topography are referred to Dalman, ch. XXI, or Parrot. Miss Kenyon's recent excavations have shown that the traditional site will have been outside the city wall at the time. 'Calvary' is taken from the Latin. It means the same as Golgotha, but is, strictly speaking, not a Biblical name.

In the older MSS followed by RSV no reference is made to Ps. 22: 18 in v. 35. This was first done in Jn 19: 24. This helps to show the falsity of the sceptical view that the details of the passion were invented from alleged prophecies in the OT.

There is no real contradiction between v. 44 (Mk 15: 32) and Lk. 23: 39-43. Jesus' behaviour on the cross convinced one of the robbers, who had been mocking Him, that this was no false Messiah, who had broken down in the moment of crisis, but the true King.

The Death of Jesus (27: 45-56)
See comments on Mk 15: 33-41; Lk. 23: 44-49; Jn 19: 25-37. The evangelists, not being

scientists, make no suggestions about the cause of the darkness (45). All that can be profitably said is that it was not an eclipse; quite apart from its duration the moon was full. There is no reason to think that it extended beyond Judea.

46. Eli, Eli, lama sabachthani: Cf. Mk 15: 34. There are considerable variations in the older MSS due to Aram. being unknown to most Christian copyists. It seems clear, however, that Jesus was not quoting the Heb. of Ps. 22: 1 (*Eli, Eli, lamah 'azabtani*), which is the more remarkable as the Heb. Psalter was normally learnt off by heart by the pious. No explanation of this cry is offered in NT, and we do well not to try to explain the unexplained. The following points may, however, be worth consideration. The assumption that Jesus was associating Himself with Ps. 22 is made questionable by His use of the Aram. Then, while the Aram. (like the Heb.) is ambiguous, being translatable 'Why hast thou' or 'Why didst thou', the Gk. can only legitimately bear the meaning, 'Why didst thou forsake me?' (so RVmg). This combined with the loud voice suggests a forsaking ended and the shout of the victor rather than a cry of present dereliction. After all, the victor's shout of 'It is finished' (Jn 19: 30) shows that Jesus knew the victory won before he gave up His spirit.

Do we render **the son of God** (54) or 'a son of God' with mg and first edition of RSV? Lk's version, 'Certainly this man was innocent' clearly favours the latter.

51. from top to bottom: Stresses the supernatural nature of the event. The curtain could be either the one between the holy and most holy places, or the one that prevented the worshippers from seeing into the holy place when the temple doors were open. On theological grounds the former seems more likely.

52. many bodies of the saints who had fallen asleep were raised: This section of Mt. stands unique in the NT and we have no other Scripture to help us understand it. There are no references to it in Jewish tradition either. It was the earthquake that opened the tombs, Christ's resurrection that made the rising of the saints possible. Mt.'s own reticence suggests that he himself had no clear understanding of what happened.

Additional Note on the Seven Words from the Cross. We have not been given a four-fold gospel so that we should create a single gospel from it. Therefore there can never be certainty about our reconstructions. The fact that the scheme suggested contains an inner harmony does not guarantee its accuracy.

The most likely order of the seven words seems to be:—1. The prayer of Lk. 23: 34. 2. The promise to the penitent robber (Lk. 23: 43). 3. The words to Mary and John (Jn 19: 26 f.). 4. The cry of dereliction (Mt. 27: 46; Mk 15: 34). 5. 'I thirst' (Jn 19: 28). 6. 'It is finished' (Jn 19: 30; Mt. 27: 50). 7. The final prayer (Lk. 23: 46).

The Burial of Jesus (27: 57–61)
See comments on Mk 15: 42–47; Lk. 23: 50–56; Jn 19: 38–42. **60. he rolled a great stone to the door of the tomb:** This is usually taken as a description of the mill-stone type of tomb-closer sometimes used for Jewish graves (not as often as imagined). The language suggests, however, that the tomb was not entirely finished and that it was a large boulder that was rolled up; this would have been much more difficult for the women to tackle.

The Guarding of the Tomb (27: 62–66)
The day of Preparation (*paraskeuē*) was Friday (see Additional Note at end of ch.). The religious authorities would do no work on the sabbath, which was for them also 15 Nisan, but that did not prevent their having an interview with Pilate. They had to obtain permission for a guard, not because they had no soldiers of their own—there were the Temple police—but because the corpse of the crucified 'criminal' was Roman property entrusted to Joseph. Pilate's answer may be translated, **You have a guard** or 'Take a guard' (mg). The former permitted them to use the Temple police, the latter granted them a squad of Roman soldiers; most modern translations (except NEB) favour the former, most commentators the latter. But why should Pilate, feeling sore about the day before, grant them this favour of the use of Roman soldiers? In addition there were few more serious charges against a Roman soldier than to be asleep on duty. Is it credible that they would have put their heads in a noose by accepting the priests' proposal (28: 13 ff.)? Even a temple policeman on special duty was in some danger, but so long as the Captain of the Temple was satisfied the governor would hardly intervene.

It may well be that we should change the punctuation and end the chapter with the first words of the next, i.e. 'setting a guard after the sabbath' (*opse de sabbatōn*). The negotiation was carried out on the Sabbath, the work of sealing and setting the guard as soon as darkness had come.

Additional Note on the Day of the Crucifixion. Though the Church as a whole has shown remarkable unanimity in its acceptance of Friday as the day of the crucifixion, the view is too frequently met today that it must have been a Wednesday. The main

motivation is avowedly to allow a complete fulfilment in terms of three 24 hour days for Mt. 12: 40. One senses too a frequent anti-traditional note among some of its supporters. The great weakness of the view was that it involved a denial that the Last Supper was a Passover meal. It has now taken on new significance and possibility in the light of the suggestion that the Supper took place as a Passover on the Tuesday evening (see Additional Note on the Date of the Last Supper).

A crucifixion on a Wednesday would answer the objection that the gospels know nothing of a 48 hour imprisonment. There are, however, three passages that seem an insuperable barrier, to the acceptance of the theory, plus, of course, consistent Church tradition.

(i) Lk. 24: 21, 'it is now the third day' seems irreconcilable with it; cf. also Mt. 16: 21; 17: 23; 20: 19; Lk. 9: 22; 24: 7, though these latter passages would be easier to explain.

(ii) 'Next day, that is, after the day of Preparation (*paraskeuē*)' (Mt. 27: 62): *paraskeuē* without qualification had become a technical term for Friday, more especially Friday afternoon. Even if we could disassociate this from its context, it seems incredible that the priests would have waited until the Saturday after a Wednesday crucifixion before taking effective action to guard the tomb.

(iii) We have *paraskeuē* a number of times in Jn 19. In v. 14 it is qualified by 'of the Passover' and bears a non-technical sense; we would say 'Passover Eve'. In v. 31 we have 'Since it was the *paraskeuē* . . . on the sabbath (for that sabbath was a high day)'. Here we have the technical sense of Sabbath Eve again. Though 15 Nisan, along with similar feast days, was kept as a sabbath, the Jews use the term sabbath only for the Day of Atonement, in addition to the weekly sabbath. Obviously, if 15 Nisan and the sabbath coincided, it would be a 'high day'. Finally in v. 42 we have 'because of the *paraskeuē* of the Jews', where once more the meaning of Friday must be found.

In the light of all these passages it seems impossible to deny that the crucifixion took place on a Friday.

The Resurrection (28: 1–10)
Many efforts, none of them entirely convincing, have been made to bring together all the resurrection stories into one completely harmonious whole. It seems clear that, while the apostles soon realized the need for a fairly standardized account of the life and teaching of Christ, the impact of His death and above all resurrection was so immense that no attempt was made to weave the eye-witness accounts together.

It is clear enough that this passage corresponds to Mk 16: 1-8; Lk. 24: 1-11; Jn 20: 1, 11-18; an exact harmony eludes us. We are clearly intended to let Mt.'s story carry its own message without check and counter-check.

It has been urged that the two Marys in Mt. come only to look at the tomb, because the guard would prevent their doing more (*e.g.* Schniewind, Tasker). They were most unlikely to know about the guard, since it was set late the evening before—irrespective of whether the suggestion on 27: 66 (*q.v.*) is adopted. B. & F. B. S. Diglot is indubitably correct in translating v. 2, 'Now there had been a great earthquake' (so essentially Tasker)—there is good Hebrew-style story telling behind the narrative. We cannot otherwise imagine the women not sharing in the paralyzing terror of the guards. The rolling away of the stone was to let the women into the grave, not to let Jesus out. Resurrection life transcends grave-clothes, a sealed tomb and armed men.

Jesus did appear to the Eleven in and near Jerusalem, because He knew their need. Ideally, however, the meeting place was to be in Galilee (7, 10; 26: 32; Mk 14: 28), so Mt. omits all the Jerusalem appearances, except the one that attested His resurrection—even there Jesus probably appeared to the women because of their fear (8). The fact that the risen King was to show Himself in Galilee is a prophecy of the separation of His Church from the old symbolized by Jerusalem.

The opening words are a bit of clumsy writing. **after the sabbath** (*opse sabbatōn*) means after the sabbath had come to an end. **towards the dawn** (*epiphōskō*) **of the first day of the week:** *epiphōskō* means to dawn in a literal sense; Mt. is not speaking of the drawing on of the first day, i.e. nightfall on Saturday evening, but of the first signs of dawn on Sunday, cf. Mk 16: 2; Lk. 24: 1; Jn 20: 1. **9. Hail** (*chairete*): Lit. 'rejoice'. This had become a standard greeting with its original sense more or less lost and had been taken up as a loan-word in Aram. *Arndt* suggests 'good morning'; NEB is probably wise with its 'He gave them his greeting'. Phillips 'Peace be with you' has no justification.

The Bribing of the Guards (28: 11-15)
Filson remarks, 'The weakness of this story is, first, that it assumes that the Jewish leaders had advance notice of the resurrection, and second, that in it the guard consented to the circulation of a story which made them liable to the death-penalty.' The second difficulty, as pointed out earlier, has been created by the

expositor himself. There is no evidence that they were Roman soldiers. The former overlooks a common psychological phenomenon. The more I am personally committed in a matter, the less likely I am to notice anything that runs contrary to my preconceived notions. The thought of Jesus' death was impossible to the disciples, so the promises of resurrection passed almost unheard and entirely unheeded. The religious leaders had their minds fixed on Jesus' death, and so the rumour of resurrection—cf. the use of Jn 2: 19 at the trial—must have jarred horribly. While they will not have understood exactly what had happened, they never doubted that the empty tomb was a fact, and Mt. 26: 64 will have come ringing in the ears of those who had heard the words. One of the minor confirmations of the priestly fears is found in Ac. 6: 7.

The Commissioning of the Apostles (28: 16-20)
If, as we surely should, we take 'brethren' (10) in a wider sense than the Eleven, then there were more than the Apostles on the mountain, and we can identify the appearance with some probability with that of 1 C. 15: 6. Mt., however, ignores the others. Here was the consummation of the apostles' first appointment. Then He had given them a limited commission (10: 5 f.) because His own commission was limited (15: 24). Now His authority was world-wide and absolute, so their commission was also world-wide. The commission was given to the Eleven as the representatives of the Church to be. This is not a command to each individual (more are called to stay at home than to go) but to the Church as a whole. There may be good reasons why this individual or that should not go, but there are never good reasons for the Church's failing to reach out and go.

We need not be surprised at the first hesitant steps of the apostolic church. Far more important, as we learn from Ac., is that whenever it became clear that a new step forward was of God the leaders, at any rate, accepted it without hesitation.

19. baptizing them in (*eis*) **the name of the Father . . . :** More literally 'into the name', i.e. as the possession of, cf. note on 18: 20. There is no suggestion that men are made disciples by being baptized. NEB is nearer the sense with 'make all nations my disciples; baptize men everywhere in the name . . .'

The Ascension is not mentioned. Once the Commission had been given, it mattered not how the Lord of the Church moved to the right hand of the Father, where He waits until His enemies be made His footstool.

BIBLIOGRAPHY

Commentaries, etc.

B. & F. B. S. Diglot: Greek Text and English Translation of Matthew for Bible Translators (London, 1959).

BEASLEY-MURRAY, G. R., *A Commentary on Mark Thirteen* (London, 1957).

COLE, R. A., *The Gospel according to Mark. TNTC* (London, 1961).

FILSON, F. V., *The Gospel according to St. Matthew. BNTC* (London, 1960).

LANG, G. H., *The Revelation of Jesus Christ* (London, 1945).

M'NEILE, A. H., *The Gospel according to St. Matthew.* [On the Greek text.] (London, 1915).

SCHLATTER, A., *Das Evangelium nach Matthäus* (Stuttgart, 1929; 1963). Spiritual and scholarly.

SCHNIEWIND, J., *Das Evangelium nach Matthäus. Das Neue Testament Deutsch* (Göttingen, 1938).

TASKER, R. V. G., *The Gospel according to St. Matthew. TNTC* (London, 1961).

General

BORNKAMM, G., BARTH, G., and HELD, H. J., *Tradition and Interpretation in Matthew* (Eng. trans. London, 1963).

BUBER, M., *The Prophetic Faith* (London, 1949).

DALMAN, G., *Sacred Sites and Ways* (London, 1935).

DAVIES, W. D., *The Setting of the Sermon on the Mount* (Cambridge, 1964).

DODD, C. H., *The Parables of the Kingdom* (London, 1935).

EDERSHEIM, A., *The Life and Times of Jesus the Messiah* (4th edn. 2 vols. London, 1886).

GUTHRIE, D., *New Testament Introduction: Gospels and Acts* (London, 1965).

JEREMIAS, J., *The Parables of Jesus* (2nd edn. Eng. trans. London, 1963).

JEREMIAS, J., *The Eucharistic Words of Jesus* (2nd edn. Eng. trans. Oxford, 1955).

MACHEN, J. G., *The Virgin Birth of Christ* (2nd edn. New York, 1932).

PARROT, A., *Golgotha and the Church of the Holy Sepulchre* (Eng. trans. London, 1957).

STENDAHL, K., *The School of St. Matthew* (Uppsala, 1954).

STONEHOUSE, N. B., *Origins of the Synoptic Gospels* (Grand Rapids, 1963).

STRACK, H. L. and BILLERBECK, P., *Kommentar zum Neuen Testament aus Talmud und Midrasch* (6 vols. Munich, 1922-1961).

WILLIAMS, A. L., *Christian Evidences for Jewish People* (2 vols. Cambridge, 1911, London, 1919).

THE GOSPEL ACCORDING TO

MARK

STEPHEN S. SHORT

Authorship and Destination

This Gospel, like the other three in the New Testament Canon, is written anonymously. That its author was John Mark, however, is attested by such second-century church writers as Papias, Irenaeus, Clement of Alexandria, etc. John Mark lived in Jerusalem with Mary his mother during the early church period, his home being an early Christian meeting-place (Ac. 12: 12), and perhaps the main meeting-place of the church at Jerusalem. Possibly it was the venue of Jesus' 'Last Supper', and of the Easter Sunday evening resurrection-appearance. Mark accompanied Paul and Barnabas on the first stage of their first missionary journey (Ac. 13: 4-13). Later on he served with Barnabas in Cyprus (Ac. 15: 39), and later still he was at Rome (Col. 4: 10; Phm. 24; 2 Tim. 4: 11; also 1 Pet. 5: 13, where 'Babylon', as in Rev. 14: 8, seems to be used as a code-word for 'Rome').

That it was while Mark was at Rome that he wrote this Gospel is attested by Irenaeus, Clement of Alexandria, Origen, Eusebius and Jerome. Evidence of this adduced from the Gospel itself is to be found in the considerable number of Latin terms which Mark uses, preferring these to their Greek equivalents, e.g. his words for 'soldier of the guard' (6: 27), 'vessels' (7: 4), 'taxes' (12: 14), 'penny' (12: 42), 'scourged' (15: 15), 'praetorium' (15: 16), 'centurion' (15: 39). A further, though decidedly equivocal indication of Mark's Gospel having been written primarily for Christians in Rome, where he produced it, consists in the mention of 'Rufus' in 15: 21, with whom, inferentially, the original readers were well acquainted, and his possible identification with the Christian who lived at Rome named 'Rufus', mentioned in Rom. 16: 13 (assuming that Rom. 16 was addressed to Christians in Rome; see notes *ad loc.*). Further evidence in the same direction may be adduced from the phrase in 6: 48, 'the fourth watch of the night', on which see notes.

Whether or not Mark's Gospel was written for Christians in Rome, it was certainly written principally for Gentiles. This is indicated (a) by the way in which Jewish customs and terms are carefully explained (e.g. 7: 2 ff.; 12: 42; 14: 12; 15: 42); and (b) by the way in which the Aramaic words and sentences Mark introduces periodically are regularly translated thereupon into Greek (e.g. 3: 17; 5: 41; 7: 11, 34; 14: 36; 15: 22, 34).

Sources

There is no evidence of Mark's having been an eye-witness of most of the events in Jesus' life which he describes in this Gospel. Some have submitted, however, that the 'young man' mentioned in 14: 51-52 is the author's anonymous allusion to himself (for evidence regarding this, see notes *ad loc.*); in which event Mark would have been a witness of the sequel to Jesus' arrest.

There is no positive proof that the author used an earlier written narrative as a source of his Gospel, though some have claimed that he used such a narrative (now lost) of the Passion story. Augustine regarded Mark as having produced his Gospel by abridging the more extended record of Matthew, and this was the normal view till the nineteenth century. It is now held almost universally that Mark's was the earliest Gospel, and that it was used as a source for the writing of the Gospels according to Matthew and Luke. Evidence for this is found in the excision by Matthew and Luke of words and phrases from Mark's descriptions such as they seem to have regarded as superfluous, in order to make room for the large sections of additional material they were wishing to record. Further such evidence is that Matthew and Luke tend to improve on Mark's style when reporting the same incidents, and either to omit altogether statements by Mark which might offend or perplex, or else to present these in a less provocative form (e.g. 4: 38 b; 5: 26; 10: 17, 35-37; 14: 33, 37, 71; 15: 34). See also pp. 96 ff.

That Mark's main source for the writing of his Gospel was the preaching and instruction of the Apostle Peter is attested by Papias, Justin Martyr, the Anti-Marcionitic Prologue to Mark's Gospel, Irenaeus, and Clement of Alexandria, all of the second century. The testimony of Papias (bishop of Hierapolis *c.*

A.D. 140) reflects Christian opinion on the matter at the very start of the century, for his statement is in fact a quotation from an anonymous 'Elder', who was dead when Papias wrote. Evidence from the Gospel itself of Peter's having influenced Mark in his narration of events is as follows:—(*a*) The prominence of Peter in the story, including allusions to him which none but himself would probably have recalled (*e.g.* 16: 7); (*b*) The fact that at almost all the scenes described, Peter was present (N.B. 1 Pet. 5: 1 implies that he witnessed Jesus' crucifixion); and that at some of them (*e.g.* 5: 37; 9: 2; 14: 33, 66-72, etc.), he was one of the very few who were present; (*c*) The inclusion of such details in the record as suggest that the descriptions in question originated in an eyewitness (*e.g.* 1: 19; 4: 38; 6: 39; and such mentions of Jesus' acts and gestures as are related in 3: 5; 7: 33; 8: 23; 10: 16, etc.).

Date

Peter's martyrdom by crucifixion was predicted by Jesus (Jn 21: 18-19; 2 Pet. 1: 14). There are early Church writers who affirm that this occurred at Rome, in connection with the Neronian persecution of the Church in A.D. 64. But such writers express differing opinions as to whether Peter was alive or dead when Mark wrote this Gospel. Clement of Alexandria and Origen believed that Peter was still living, whereas Irenaeus and the writer of the anti-Marcionitic prologue to Mark's Gospel believed that he was dead. It could be inferred that such was also the belief of Papias, though he does not state this categorically. This is the most commonly held view today, with the consequence that Mark's Gospel is usually regarded as having been written *c*. A.D. 65. It was the opinion of Harnack, however, that this Gospel was written 'during the sixth decade of the first century, at the latest' (*Date of the Acts and of the Synoptic Gospels*, 1911, p. 133), for he did not regard it as incontestable that Peter was dead before Mark wrote. Harnack considered it self-evident that the book of Acts, in view of how it closes, was written prior to Paul's death, and in A.D. 62, or thereabouts, in which event, Luke's 'first book' (Ac. 1: 1), *viz.* his Gospel, would have

been written shortly before this, and the Gospel by Mark, consequently (fairly evidently, a source of Luke's Gospel), would have been written earlier still. It is difficult to see any really compelling reasons why Harnack's argument must be abandoned. Referring to Mark's record, T. W. Manson stated: 'The composition of the Gospel may be put several years earlier than the date commonly accepted' (*Studies in the Gospels and Epistles*, p. 45), suggesting between A.D. 58 and 65 (*ibid.*, p. 5).

Characteristics

Mark's Gospel is the shortest of those in the Canon. It is terse and full of action, a feature which would appeal to the practically minded Romans for whom, evidently, it was primarily written. The proportion of it which is devoted to recording Jesus' deeds, rather than His words, is greater in Mark's Gospel than in the others. Eighteen miracles are related, as against only four full-scale parables. An unusually large number of instances of Jesus' exorcizing of demons is noted (1: 23-27, 32-34; 3: 11, 22-27; 5: 1-20; 7: 25-30; 9: 17-29). Little is provided by way of comment on these happenings, the actions being left usually to speak for themselves.

Unlike standard biographies, Mark's Gospel states nothing about Jesus' birth, upbringing and appearance; and it specifies neither the length of His public ministry, nor His age at the time of His crucifixion. About a third of the record is devoted to a description of the eight days between Jesus' entry into Jerusalem on the colt, and His resurrection.

Theme

The thesis of this Gospel is that Jesus Christ is the Son of God. This is stated in the book's prologue (1: 1). As the story unfolds, Mark shows Jesus to have been proclaimed 'Son of God' by His heavenly Father (1: 11; 9: 7), by demons, who possessed supernatural knowledge (3: 11; 5: 7), and by Himself (12: 6; 14: 61 f.). The story's climax is that of a man of Roman nationality making this proclamation (15: 39), the author's intention, clearly, being that his action in this regard might be copied by those of Roman nationality for whom he wrote who read his book.

ANALYSIS

I. INTRODUCTORY EVENTS (1: 1-13)

The ministry of John the Baptist (1: 1-8).
(Parallels: Mt. 3: 1-12; Lk. 3: 1-20; Jn 1: 19-37.)
Mark informs his readers that the Old Testament had predicted that the arrival of the Messiah would be preceded by the coming of a fore-runner, quoting to this end Mal. 3: 1 and Isa. 40: 3. He identifies this fore-runner with John the Baptist, by indicating that John preached in the **wilderness** (4, cf. Isa. 40: 3), and by re-calling that John's clothing (6) was reminiscent of that of Elijah (2 Kg. 1: 8), who, in Mal. 4: 5, is equated with the **messenger** of Mal. 3: 1. John's message was twofold: (*a*) He called men to repentance, adding that if they did so, his cleansing of their bodies in baptism would symbolize God's cleansing of their souls from sin (4); (*b*) He announced his Successor, who would baptize people with the Spirit (7, 8). This Jesus did on the day of Pentecost (Ac. 1: 5).
The baptism of Jesus (1: 9-11). (Parallels: Mt. 3: 13-17; Lk. 3: 21-22.)
Jesus received baptism from John (9) by way of identifying Himself with sinners in anticipa-tion of His doing so to even greater purpose in His crucifixion. Both the Spirit (10) and the Father (11) bore witness to Jesus as being the Messianic Son of God, the Spirit in the form of a dove, and the Father in words echoing Ps. 2: 7 and Isa. 42: 1. Mark, in contrast to the later evangelists, only mentions the vision of the dove and the words from heaven as having been perceived by Jesus Himself.
The temptation of Jesus (1: 12-13). (Parallels: Mt. 4: 1-11; Lk. 4: 1-13.)
In Jesus' temptation, He was being urged by Satan to turn aside from His divinely appointed pathway of service and ultimate suffering. For a fuller treatment of this, see notes on Luke *ad loc.* Mark alone of the evangelists mentions the presence of the **wild beasts** during Jesus' temptation. It is more likely that their mention is to emphasize the awfulness of the experience than to depict them as friendly and subject to Jesus.

II. THE GALILEAN MINISTRY (1: 14-7: 23)

Christ's initial preaching in Galilee (1: 14-15). (Parallels: Mt. 4: 12-17; Lk. 4: 14-30; Jn 4: 43-45.)
Prior to Jesus' journey to Galilee (14), He had carried out His early Judaean ministry as described in Jn 1: 29—4: 43. The occasion of His pro-ceeding to Galilee was the arrest by Herod Antipas of John the Baptist (14), for the reason stated in 6: 17 f. The theme of Jesus' preaching in Galilee was to the effect that God's appointed period of waiting had now been completed, and

His kingdom was at hand; and that in view of this, men were to **repent** (i.e. turn from their sin to God), and **believe in** the good news (15). The implication of this announcement is that Jesus' conception of the divine kingdom was not the popular one of a cataclysmic outward triumph over all that was evil, but was the rule of God in people's hearts. Because of His advent and mission, Jesus showed this to be a present reality (Mt. 12: 28; Lk. 17: 21), though it would have a future consummation (Mt. 6: 10; Lk. 22: 18).
The calling of the first disciples (1: 16-20). (Parallel: Mt. 4: 18-22.)
The record assumes these fishermen to have had a previous knowledge of Jesus, which fact is confirmed in Jn 1: 35-42, where it is shown that they already believed Jesus to be Israel's Messiah. In asserting thus His right to people's whole-hearted allegiance to Him, Jesus displayed His consciousness of His personal authority. Jesus' command to them to **follow** Him (17) involved not only that they should accompany Him on His journeys, but that they should accept a disciple-Rabbi relationship in His regard. His promise to make them **fishers of men** related to their winning of others to His cause. Peter recalled to Jesus his sacrificing of his livelihood for His sake in 10: 28.
The exorcism in the synagogue (1: 21-28). (Parallel: Lk. 4: 31-37.)
In Capernaum, situated on the north-west shore on the sea of Galilee, as well as elsewhere in Galilee, Jesus was frequently given opportunities for teaching in the synagogue on the sabbath day. On the occasion here described, His presentation of His theme (15) was charac-terized by an authoritativeness which amazed the hearers, and forced them to contrast Him with the teachers to whom they were accustomed (22). This authoritativeness was also displayed in His exorcizing a demon from one of the congregation. The demon, in contrast to the onlookers, penetrated the mystery of Jesus' person, and so knew the explanation of Jesus' authority. The demon's cry: '**What have you to do with us?**' means 'Why are you inter-fering with us?' for the demons knew that the establishing by Jesus of the kingdom of God necessarily involved their own destruction (24). The effect of Jesus' words and deeds in the synagogue that day on the people as a whole was to excite wonder, but not to evoke faith; and thus it was throughout Galilee (28).
The healing of Peter's mother-in-law (1: 29-31). (Parallels: Mt. 8: 14-15; Lk. 4: 38-39.)
This story shows Jesus' power in the healing of a different type of malady, *viz.* fever. And His

method of healing was different, the grasp of His hand being here noted rather than some vocal utterance. The speed and completeness of the woman's cure is shown by her serving the company at table immediately afterwards. Although both this and the previous healing were performed on the sabbath day, no opposition to them is mentioned, since these cases were urgent, and the latter, additionally, was wrought in a private house.

The healing of the crowds at sunset (1: 32–34). (Parallels: Mt. 8: 16–17; Lk. 4: 40–41.)
The populace of Capernaum, aware now of Jesus' healing powers, desirous of securing from Him the restoration of their sick friends, **brought** (32) (lit. 'carried') them to Jesus at **the door** of Peter's house, awaiting **sundown** before so doing, when, with the sabbath over, this 'work' of carrying them was lawful. Jesus healed **many** (34), which, according to Semitic idiom, means 'all who were brought'. Although the demons discerned the nature of Jesus' person, Jesus deemed it unfitting that this should be announced by such minions of Satan (34).

Travelling and preaching throughout Galilee (1: 35–39). (Parallel: Lk. 4: 42–44.)
Jesus' praying during this retreat of His (34) (which, uncharacteristically, is not mentioned by Luke), reveals His communion with, and dependence on, His heavenly Father. It may have been occasioned, in part, by disappointment on the part of Christ that His miracles were only evoking a response of amazement, not of committal to Him. Determined not to be interrupted in His preaching ministry through having acquired fame as a healer, Jesus proceeded to other Galilean towns instead of returning to Capernaum.

The healing of the leper (1: 40–45). (Parallels: Mt. 8: 2–4; Lk. 5: 12–15.)
Though Jesus was resolved not deliberately to seek out sick people so as to heal them, He was prepared to cure such as this leper who happened to cross His path while He was engaged in more vital tasks. Leprosy, as described in the Bible, is probably not to be identified with the current disease of that name, though it was certainly a grave malady, and was regarded by the Rabbis as humanly incurable, a belief endorsed by Christ (Lk. 4: 27). Yet the Jews believed that the Messiah, when he came, would be able to cure lepers (Mt. 11: 5); and this leper was convinced Jesus could heal him (40). Having cleansed him, Jesus forbade the man to talk about his cure, for Jesus did not wish people to come to Him merely to receive physical benefits; but the man disobeyed, not being able to repress his joy. Jesus also told him to go to the priest at Jerusalem so as to comply with the regulations of Lev. 14, **for a testimony unto them,** meaning perhaps, 'so that they may appreciate that I do not disregard the ceremonial law wantonly, but only where this conflicts with the law of love'. An instance of the ceremonial law being over-ruled by the law of love had been furnished by Jesus' touching the leper.

The healing of the paralysed man (2: 1–12). (Parallels: Mt. 9: 1–8; Lk. 5: 17–26.)
Jesus' temporary withdrawal from Capernaum (1: 38) having now served its purpose, He returned there, and found people who would gather around Him to hear His preaching (2) rather than to be healed, though this story shows the latter category of folk still to be existing. The roof of the house where Jesus was teaching would probably have consisted in matting, covered with earth and twigs, suspended over rafters, and would be reached by an outside staircase. Dealing first with the greater need of the paralysed man whom his friends had let down through the roof, Jesus conferred on him the forgiveness of his sins, announcing this to him publicly. The scribes who were present were electrified at the proclamation, and drew the only conclusion which, to those failing to appreciate Jesus' Deity, is open, namely that He was blaspheming. Though they did not express this charge vocally, Jesus knew it to be in their minds. To prove, therefore, the reality of His possessing authority to confer forgiveness and of His having exercised it in this instance, Jesus provided a visible sign, healing the man's paralysis.

The calling of Levi (2: 13–14). (Parallels: Mt. 9: 9; Lk. 5: 27–28.)
Capernaum was a customs post. Levi, identified in Mt. 9: 9 with Matthew, a customs official in the service of Herod Antipas, immediately obeyed Jesus' call to him to become one of His disciples, from which it is to be inferred that Levi already knew of Jesus, and possibly already believed Him to be Israel's Messiah.

The feast in Levi's house (2: 15–17). (Parallels: Mt. 9: 10–13; Lk. 5: 29–32.)
Shortly after having become a follower of Jesus, Levi gave a reception in his home to some of his former business colleagues, and to other associates of his, for the purpose of giving them an opportunity to meet his new Master. It is probable that the **sinners** (15) whom Levi invited were so called, not on the ground of their being notoriously bad characters (though in verse 17 Jesus took up the word in a moral sense), but on the strength of their not being in the habit of studying and practising 'the tradition of the elders' (for which see notes on 7: 3), on which account they were despised by the

Pharisees (Jn 7: 49). Tax collectors also were despised, both because ultimately it was for the Romans that they were collecting money, and also because they commonly enriched themselves by making unjust and extortionate demands from people. To consort with such, and particularly to share meals with them, was regarded by the Pharisees as a mark of gross impiety. On Jesus being criticized for doing this, He replied that it was only by establishing contact with them that He could fulfil His mission of imparting to them salvation.

The discussion about fasting (2: 18-22). (Parallels: Mt. 9: 14-17; Lk. 5: 33-39.)
Jesus incurred further criticism on the grounds of His disciples not joining in with other pious Jews who were observing a fast (though not one prescribed in the law of Moses, which only ordained fasting on the Day of Atonement). Jesus' reply was that His presence among His people was as much an occasion for rejoicing as was that of a bridegroom among the guests at his wedding. The conduct appropriate to it, consequently, was as incompatible with the practices of contemporary Judaism (with their fasts, etc.), as was (i) a new patch on an old garment, which, as it shrank, would pull away the adjacent threads from the old garment, (ii) new wine in wineskins brittle with age, which, as it fermented, would cause the skins to burst. Jesus added, however, that the day would come when for His disciples to fast would be fitting indeed, namely when He died (Jn 16: 20), a statement proving that Jesus foresaw His death from this early stage of His public ministry.

The plucking of the ears of corn (2: 23-28). (Parallels: Mt. 12: 1-8; Lk. 6: 1-5.)
The Mosaic Law permitted a hungry traveller to pluck and eat corn from another person's field, so long as he only used his hands for the purpose, not a sickle (Dt. 23: 25). Since, however, the scribes, somewhat pedantically, regarded this as technically being 'reaping', they forbade the practice on the Sabbath, on which day reaping was divinely disallowed (Exod. 34: 21). On Jesus incurring criticism once again, this time on the grounds of His disciples having infringed this regulation, He referred His critics to the story 'in the passage about Abiathar the high priest', recounted in 1 Sam. 21: 1-6. This suggested rendering, which is parallel to the RSV's rendering of the equivalent Greek phrase in 12: 26 ('in the passage about the bush'), seems preferable to the rendering in the text here, **when Abiathar was high priest,** (feasible as that also is as a translation), in that it does not require that Abiathar was high priest when the event occurred, which was, actually, during the high priesthood of Abiathar's father

Abimelech. Jesus reminded the Pharisees that when, like the disciples, David on this occasion was hungry, what was a breach of the letter of the ceremonial law (Lev. 24: 9) was committed by himself; and the fact that Scripture does not condemn him for it shows that in cases where a human need existed, God allowed that regulations concerned merely with ritual matters might be waived. Since, furthermore, the Sabbath was ordained for the well-being of humanity, rather than as an end in itself (which was how the Pharisees tended to conceive of it), Jesus contended that humanity's Lord and Representative was authorized to be the official arbiter as to how the Sabbath should be observed (27, 28).

The healing of the man with the withered hand (3: 1-6). (Parallels: Mt. 12: 9-14; Lk. 6: 6-11.)
Jesus' statement of 2: 28 suggested to the Pharisees that His infringements of the Sabbath regulations which had been imposed by the elders on the Law of Moses were being undertaken deliberately, which inference they decided now to put to the test. The Pharisees in the synagogue fully recognized that Christ had the ability to heal the man with the withered hand; their solitary interest lay in whether He would do so (which, to their way of thinking, was to perform 'work'), on the Sabbath. Jesus bade them, therefore, consider thoughtfully what would be involved if He refrained from healing him. Indicating to them in His question of verse 4 the two alternative courses lying before Him, He claimed that to refuse to heal the man would technically be a 'work' just as much as to cure him, and an evil one at that, **to do harm,** in its essential nature, indeed, **to kill.** This, however, the Pharisees failed to appreciate, their great fault being **hardness of heart** (5), meaning not callousness, but unteachableness. So, on Jesus having healed the man, they resolved to have Jesus put to death, consorting to this end with the Herodians (6), the supporters of Herod Antipas, who feared that political unrest might result from Jesus' actions.

Jesus' acceptance with the common people (3: 7-12). (Parallel: Mt. 12: 14-21.)
The opposition to Jesus of the Jewish leaders was more than offset by His acclamation by the common people, who gathered to Him both from the south and from the north (8). Many of these were healed of their illnesses by simply touching Him, apart, apparently, from any direct action on His part (10). As in 1: 34, Jesus refused to accept testimony to the nature of His person from demons (12).

The choosing of the apostles (3: 13-19a). (Parallels: Mt. 10: 1, 2; Lk. 6: 12-16.)

Of the crowds who were flocking to Him, Jesus selected twelve men to be constantly with Him, so that they might receive from Him a more intensive spiritual training, and later (6: 7 ff.; 16: 15) be dispatched by Him to preach and heal. It is unlikely that James and John were called by Jesus **sons of thunder** because of their being quick-tempered, divinely given names always being bestowed with reference to some commendable characteristic. Perhaps the name related to their energy. A **Cananaean** (18), was a member of a strongly nationalistic Jewish group who was bitterly opposed to their Roman overlords. The group developed later into the Zealot party; hence in Lk. 6: 15 'the zealot'. **Iscariot** probably means 'from Kerioth'; Kerioth-hezron (Jos. 15: 25) was twelve miles south of Hebron. For comments on the variation in the apostles' names as given in the different lists, see notes on Mt. *ad loc.*

The protest by Jesus' family (3: 19b-21, 31-35). (Parallels: Mt. 12: 46-50; Lk. 8: 19-21). Jesus, having returned **home** to Capernaum (19), was hindered from taking proper meals through pressure of work (20). **His friends** (21), i.e. **his mother and his brothers** (31), regarded this as madness, and so set out from Nazareth to try to restrain Him from continuing His ministry. Jesus' brothers were unbelieving (Jn 7: 5) till after His resurrection (Ac. 1: 14), and even His mother misunderstood Him (Lk. 2: 49; Jn 2: 4). As to the identity of Jesus' brothers, see notes on 6: 3. The fact of Joseph not being mentioned here is presumptive evidence that he was now dead. This event gave Jesus an opportunity to teach that His closest affinities were with such as obeyed God's message through Him (cf. Lk. 11: 27 f.; Heb. 2: 11), rather than with such as were physically related to Him (35).

The Beelzebul accusation (3: 22-30). (Parallels: Mt. 12: 24-32; Lk. 11: 15-22; 12: 10.) It seems apparent that the religious authorities in Jerusalem, having heard of the stir created by Jesus' ministry, sent this deputation of scribes to Galilee to investigate the situation. They alleged that Jesus was possessed by **Beelzebul,** and that it was by Beelzebul's power that Jesus exorcized demons (22). **Beelzebul** means 'lord of the house' or 'lord of the high place'. 2 Kg. 1: 3 shows that a god of this name was worshipped at Ekron in the territory formerly occupied by Philistines. The styling of him as 'Beelzebub' ('lord of flies') was probably a mocking pun on his proper name. Beelzebul, being denoted here **the prince of demons,** is to be identified in this controversy with Satan. By way of reply, Jesus asked these scribes (23) as to why Satan,

who was the cause of demon-possession, should be concerned to terminate the condition. It would indicate that Satan's kingdom was involved in pursuing two opposite policies, in which event it would destroy itself through civil war (24-26). Jesus informed His critics thereupon of the correct explanation of His exorcisms, which was that He Himself, being endued with the power of God, was stronger than Satan, and that having bound Satan, He was able now to **plunder his house** (28). Jesus added that since the Holy Spirit was God's Agent in effecting these exorcisms, to attribute them to Satan was to **blaspheme against the Holy Spirit** (29), which was **an eternal sin,** in that it carried eternal consequences. By **blaspheme** here, is denoted not bad language, but defiant hostility.

The parable of the sower (4: 1-20). (Parallels: Mt. 13: 1-23; Lk. 8: 4-15.) This parable shows that the reason why Jesus was opposed by the religious leaders and others, and misunderstood even by His own relations (3: 19b-35), was the spiritual condition of their hearts. In addressing this parable to the crowds by the lakeside, Jesus wanted them to give careful consideration to the nature of their own hearts. Some hearers of His teaching, He pointed out, never grasped His message at all; others were discouraged through difficulties, and others again were seduced through prosperity, so that only a limited proportion became lastingly committed to it.

Prior to explaining the parable to His disciples, Jesus answered their question as to why He employed parables (10-12). The essence of His reply seems to be that He did so in order to test the spiritual responsiveness of His hearers. Those who were provoked by them into intensive reflection could proceed thereupon to obtain enlightenment concerning them (*e.g.* by asking Jesus their meaning, as did the disciples in this instance); whereas those who omitted to reflect on them would **see but not perceive** (quoting Isa. 6: 9 f.), i.e. understand the literal meaning of the words, but not the parables' deeper signification.

The aim of Jesus' parables, cntd (4: 21-25, 33-34). (Parallels: Mt. 5: 15; 10: 26; 11: 15; 7: 2; 13: 34; Lk. 8: 17 f.; 12: 2; 6: 38.) Just as a lamp is only useful when placed on a stand (21), the ultimate purpose of Jesus' parables was to reveal truth rather than to hide it (22), though they might express the truth in a somewhat mystifying manner initially. **Take heed what you hear,** said Jesus (24), i.e.: 'Do not regard these parables as being mere stories, but penetrate to the message which they are intended to impart'. **The measure you give** (of attention to the parables), **will be the measure you get** (of spiritual profit from the parables). **For to him who has** (by way of application of heart) **will more be given** (by way of divine blessing), whereas casual hearers will only land themselves in a state of ever-increasing confusion (25). By speaking in parables Jesus suited His teaching to the degree of receptivity of His hearers (33), hoping that through the parables His hearers might not only apprehend the truth, but be drawn to Himself, the discloser of the truth (34).

The parable of the seed growing secretly (4: 26-29).

In this brief parable, peculiar to Mark's Gospel, Jesus taught that the kingdom of God would certainly attain its consummation, even though initially nothing very dramatic was observable. By Jesus' ministry of preaching, the seed had been sown, and nothing could now prevent the harvest which would ultimately result from it. Rather than be fretful, therefore, one should show calm patience and confident expectation.

The parable of the mustard seed (4: 30-32). (Parallels: Mt. 13: 31-32; Lk. 13: 18-19.)

This further parable Jesus told testified to the mighty future destined for the kingdom of God despite the meagre company who up till then had been born into it. Mustard seed, proverbially the tiniest of seeds, within but a few weeks could develop into a shrub of over ten feet in height, furnishing an apt picture of the phenomenally rapid spread of Christianity during the apostolic era. **The birds of the air,** which rested in the shade of the shrub, were probably intended to depict the inclusion within God's kingdom of people from gentile nations (cf. Ezek. 17: 23; 31: 6; Dan. 4: 21 f.).

The storm on the lake (4: 35-41). (Parallels: Mt. 8: 23-27; Lk. 8: 22-25.)

From 4: 35 to 5: 43 are related three acts of divine power wrought by Jesus in a situation of human helplessness and despair (the last of these acts being a double one). The first of them was that of His stilling of one of the violent storms which not infrequently descended with great suddenness on the Galilean lake. Weary at the close of a day of teaching, Jesus was rowed eastwards across the lake by His disciples. Upon the boat's cushion (provided for the guest of honour, and placed at the stern, away from the splashing of the waves), Jesus rested His head, and fell asleep. On the storm arising, the disciples aroused Jesus, suggesting to Him that He was indifferent to their peril. His calming of the waters, however, caused them to be awestruck before Him (41).

The healing of the man with many demons (5: 1-20). (Parallels: Mt. 8: 28-34; Lk. 8: 26-39.)

Having given peace to people who were troubled by the world outside (4: 35-41), Jesus now gave peace to someone who was troubled by that which was within him. The probable location of the incident was at Kersa, a small town of that period on the east coast of the sea of Galilee. The name Kersa later became confused with Gerasa, a town over thirty miles south-east of the lake, which confusion explains how the corruption **the country of the Gerasenes** (1) has occurred. Most of the inhabitants of the area were Gentiles, which explains (*a*) why the farmers among them kept **swine** (11), which creatures were 'unclean' to the Jews (Lev. 11: 7); (*b*) why Jesus commanded the man, when healed, to proclaim his cure throughout the district (19). Contrast with this the injunction Jesus gave to the healed leper (1: 44), in view of the misunderstanding and dangerous enthusiasm Jesus foresaw resulting, had undue publicity been given to the leper's cure in Jewish circles. **The Decapolis** (20), however (meaning 'the ten cities'), where the cured demoniac promulgated his deliverance, was predominantly Gentile in population, being a group of towns, most of which were east of Jordan, and which were governed somewhat independently of the rest of Palestine.

The **tombs** (3) in which this demon-possessed man lived would have been caves. People's attempts to control him by binding him with chains had been in vain (4); yet the demons were exorcized by Jesus on the utterance of a single command (8). Jesus' purpose in asking the man his name (9) was probably so as to recall to his consciousness the awful plight in which he stood. As in 1: 24, the demons knew that their encounter with Jesus would result in their destruction (7). A likely reason for Jesus permitting the expelled demons to enter the swine (13) was so that the healed man, seeing the demon-occupied swine rushing madly into the lake, might be reassured as to the reality of his deliverance. The loss of the swine sustained by the local farmers, together with their fear of Jesus' miraculous powers (15), impelled them to request Jesus to leave their district (17). This He did; and there is no record that He ever returned to it.

The raising of the daughter of Jairus (5: 21-24, 35-43). (Parallels: Mt. 9: 1, 18-19, 23-26; Lk. 8: 40-42, 49-56.)

Although the Jewish religious leaders, for the most part, were hostile to Jesus, Jairus, the supervisor of the synagogue probably of Capernaum, to which city Jesus had just sailed from the east of the lake (21, Mt. 9: 1), was prepared to beg Jesus' help when his daughter was ill. Jesus responded to his entreaty, but the interruption that occurred, as recorded in 25-34, must have been most frustrating for Jairus, and meanwhile his daughter died. On reaching Jairus's home at length, Jesus announced that the child was merely **sleeping** (39), by which He meant that the period of her being dead was only going to be as short as a sleep. But the mourners (probably professional mourners, hired by the family, cf. Mt. 9: 23), understanding Jesus' words in a literal sense, ridiculed Him. Jesus only allowed His raising of the girl to be witnessed by such as truly believed in Him, besides the girl's parents (37, 40), so that the act might be rightly understood and reported; but to obviate His being thronged again (24) by the people, He did not wish the reporting of the miracle to be immediate (43), though, obviously, the deed could not have been kept secret for long.

The healing of the woman with the haemorrhage (5: 25-34). (Parallels: Mt. 9: 18-22; Lk. 8: 43-48.)
The continuous uterine bleeding from which, presumably, this woman suffered would have rendered her ceremonially unclean (Lev. 15: 25-30), with the consequence that law-abiding Jews would tend to shun her. This fact, together with her natural modesty, and the embarrassment she felt on account of the nature of her malady, made her anxious to secure the healing which she believed Jesus could impart to her without the publicity which was normally inevitable in the event of such healings. Such was her faith in Jesus that she believed He could cure her apart from a personal interview, and by her merely touching His clothes (28; cf. 3: 10; 6: 56), this, despite the failure to help her of the many physicians she had consulted (26). This faith of hers, on being put to the test, was fully vindicated (29), and on her being healed, she endeavoured to disappear unnoticed into the crowd. Jesus, however, conscious of a release from Him of supernatural power, and aware of how this had occurred, demanded that the person responsible should come forward. Though fearful of Jesus' anger, and dreading now being exposed, the woman presented herself before His face and explained to Him her action, whereupon Jesus commended her for her faith, and assured her of the completeness of her cure.

The rejection of Jesus at Nazareth (6: 1-6). (Parallel: Mt. 13: 53-58; cf. Lk. 4: 16-30.)
From Capernaum, Jesus proceeded twenty miles west-south-west to Nazareth, **his own country** (1), where previously He had been living, and He preached there in the synagogue (2; see note on 1: 21). His townsfolk admitted the wisdom displayed in His preaching, and also the power displayed in His miracles; but they were at a

loss to explain these things. Had He visibly descended on to this earth out of heaven (as many believed the Messiah would do), all would have been comprehensible. But He was merely the local **carpenter** (N.B. though the word *tektōn* could apply also to workers in stone or in metal, probably a worker in wood is here denoted); and His mother, brothers and sisters were all well known to them (3). The root of their perplexity about Jesus was their **unbelief** (6); and Jesus marvelled at it. Only at the unbelief of His townsfolk and, by contrast, at the faith of a foreigner (Lk. 7: 9), do the Gospels represent Jesus as marvelling. As in 3: 31, Joseph is not mentioned here in 6: 3, which suggests again that he was now dead. The 'brothers' of Jesus (3) were probably sons of Joseph and Mary subsequent to the birth from Mary of Jesus. The suggestions that they were either half-brothers of Jesus (i.e. children of Joseph by a former marriage), or else cousins of Jesus, are not natural interpretations of this passage, and arose when the state of virginity came to be regarded as 'holier' than that of marriage, and, as a consequence, belief in the idea of Mary's Perpetual Virginity was becoming popular. As to Jesus' being rejected by those among whom He had lived, He commented that this was what prophets generally had experienced (4). Because of the unbelief of the people of Nazareth, Jesus was unable, consistently with the principles on which He acted, to do miracles among them, apart from His healing **a few sick people,** who presumably, did display a modicum of faith in Him (5).

The mission of the twelve apostles (6: 7-13). (Parallels: Mt. 9: 36-11: 1; Lk. 9: 1-6.)
The purpose of this mission was twofold. It was partly to give the apostles some practical training in missionary work by way of preparing them for their later responsibilities as envoys to the world (see on 3: 14), and it was designed also to bring without delay to as many Galileans as possible the call to repentance. The reason for the urgency of the need for these to repent is not stated here in Mk, but Mt. 10: 7 shows this to have been in view of the near arrival of God's kingdom. Because of the haste with which the disciples would be required to act, they were to travel as light as possible. For the supply of their material needs they were to trust in God's care for them rather than in resources of their own providing (8). Should they discover, having been in some house for a day or two, a more congenial habitation near by, they were not to transfer themselves to it (10). On leaving villages which had proved unreceptive, they were to **shake off the dust** from their feet, as a token that their personal

responsibility to them had been discharged, and that the inhabitants would now have to answer for themselves (11; cf. Ac. 18: 6). Having received their commission, the disciples travelled throughout Galilee preaching and healing (12, 13), and thus proclaiming the kingdom in the way that Jesus did Himself.

The death of John the Baptist (6: 14-29).
(Parallels: Mt. 14: 1-12; Lk. 3: 19 f.; 9: 7-9).
Jesus, because of the miracles He wrought, was becoming regarded by many as a supernatural person, *e.g.* as a reappearance of **one of the prophets of old** (15), such as Elijah. The allusion here is not to the culminating Prophet foretold in Dt. 18: 15 f., and there is no mention at this point of Jesus being regarded as the promised Messiah. Another view which was prevalent, however, was that Jesus was the resurrected embodiment of John the Baptist (14), for though John wrought no miracles in his mortal life (Jn 10: 41), he would be quite expected to do so if he rose from the dead. This latter view was held by Herod Antipas (16), tetrarch of Galilee (Lk. 3: 1) and Perea from 4 B.C. till A.D. 39, who had been responsible for John's execution; and the circumstances of that execution are now related (17-29). John the Baptist had protested, presumably on the grounds of Lev. 18: 16 and 20: 21, against Herod's marriage to **Herodias, his brother Philip's wife** (17), Herodias having divorced Philip in order to marry Herod. 'Brother' here means 'half-brother'; and the 'Philip' here mentioned was not the tetrarch of Iturea and Trachonitis (Lk. 3: 1), but Herod Antipas' half-brother in Rome, so Josephus affirms (*Ant.* XVIII. v. 4). For making this protest Herod had imprisoned John (17), Josephus stating that the site of the imprisonment was Machaerus, a frontier fortress in the south of Perea, and east of the Dead Sea (*Ant.* XVIII. v. 2). Herodias, however, was not satisfied with John's merely being imprisoned, and schemed to have him killed (19). Her opportunity came on the occasion of Herod's birthday. Herod spread a banquet for his leading officials (21), at which, at the instigation, no doubt, of Herodias, her daughter performed a dance (22). This won Herod's favour, who promised her thereupon anything she cared to ask (23). Acting on her mother's instructions (24), she demanded the head of John the Baptist (25), who was incarcerated in the prison below; whereupon, with bitter regret (26), Herod ordered John to be executed and his head to be brought (27).

The feeding of the five thousand (6: 30-44).
(Parallels: Mt. 14: 13-21; Lk. 9: 11-17; Jn 6: 1-14.)

On the twelve apostles returning from their mission (30), the continual presence around them of the crowds (31; cf. 3: 20) induced Jesus to propose that they should journey with Him by boat to an isolated region on the lake's north-east shore in the vicinity of Bethsaida Julias (Lk. 9: 10). The fact that the crowds, who noticed their departure and proceeded to the apostles' destination by foot, arrived there first (33), suggests that the wind on the lake was unfavourable to the boat's quick progress. On disembarking Jesus' impression of the crowd was that they were **like sheep without a shepherd,** i.e. bewildered and helpless. He attended at once therefore to their primary need, and preached to them (34). When it was evening however, instead of agreeing to the apostles' perfectly reasonable suggestion of dismissing the crowds so that they could obtain food from the neighbouring villages (36), He Himself attended now to their physical need by multiplying and having distributed the five loaves and two fishes, which was all the food that was there available. The fact that twelve baskets of fragments were collected afterwards (43) suggests that each apostle carried one basket. This miracle was not only an expression of Jesus' compassion towards the hungry crowds, 6: 52 and 8: 16-19 showing that it was intended to teach the disciples some deeper truth. The state of the righteous in the life to come was pictured by the Jews as a great banquet presided over by their Messiah (cf. Isa. 25: 6 ff.; Lk. 13: 29; 14: 15; 22: 16, 30, etc.), and Jesus may perhaps have desired this 'feast' to be envisaged as an anticipation of that banquet. The significance attached to the miracle in John's Gospel, however, is that of Jesus Christ, depicted as the Bread of Life, offering Himself as 'food' to the famished world to which He had descended from heaven.

The walking by Jesus on the water (6: 45-52).
(Parallels: Mt. 14: 22-33; Jn 6: 15-21.) (On the section Mk 6: 45-8: 26 see p. 98.)
The urgency with which Jesus pressed His disciples to embark into the ship is shown by Jn 6: 15 to have been due to the intention of the crowd regarding Jesus, to 'take Him by force to make Him king'. While Jesus was departing by Himself to pray on the hills (46), His disciples crossed the lake, travelling probably from the region of Bethsaida Julias (see note on 31) to 'Bethsaida in Galilee' (45; Jn 12: 21), on the north-west shore of the lake. Their journey, however, proved difficult, though not on account of a sudden storm (as in 4: 37), but because of a strong headwind (48) (the wind during the previous few hours having changed direction, if the suggestion contained in the

G*

note on verse 33 is correct). From the hillside Jesus saw the disciples in distress, presumably by the light of the moon, and between 3.0 and 6.0 a.m. (**the fourth watch of the night,** adopting, as in 13: 35, the Roman reckoning; for in the Jewish reckoning the night was divided into three watches only), Jesus walked towards them across the surface of the water. **He meant to pass them** (48), probably in order that they might make a personal appeal to Him for help (cf. Lk. 24: 29). Though the cry (49) of the disciples on seeing Him was a shriek of fear rather than an appeal for help, Jesus responded to it and calmed their spirits (50), whereupon He entered the boat and the wind ceased (51). Their astonishment, though natural, is stated by Mark to have been blameworthy, in that having just previously witnessed Jesus' multiplication of the loaves (52), they should have been more conscious of the divine power with which He was endued.

The healings by Jesus at Gennesaret (6: 53-56). (Parallel: Mt. 14: 34-36.)

Gennesaret, where the disciples landed (53), was presumably a village on the small but heavily populated plain of Gennesaret just south of Capernaum. In this neighbourhood Jesus healed at this time many invalids. Like other male Jews who were loyal to the law, on each corner of Jesus' outer garment was a blue tassel (see Num. 15: 37 f.; Dt. 22: 12), and many obtained healing through expressing their faith in Him by the act of their touching such a tassel (56).

The discussion concerning purification (7: 1-23). (Parallel: Mt. 15: 1-20.)

The enthusiasm in relation to Jesus of those featuring in the story of 6: 54-56 stood in sharp contrast with the criticism of Him by most of the Jewish leaders. In 7: 1, as earlier in 3: 22, a deputation of scribes from Jerusalem journeyed northwards to Galilee to join issue with Him. Their objection to Him on this occasion had to do with the behaviour of His disciples (cf. 2: 18, 24), and was to the effect that they ate their meals without previously submitting their hands to a ritual cleansing (2), infringing thus one of the regulations contained in **the tradition of the elders** (5). The 'tradition of the elders' was a body of legislation which had been formulated by the rabbis, and to which the Pharisees attached great importance, in which were prescribed detailed applications of the Law, of Moses to particular situations. Jesus, however as also the Sadducees, rejected this supplementary legislation (though the Sadducees had their own tradition, which in many points coincided). He stressed to this end its human origin, styling it not 'the tradition of the elders'

as did these scribes, but **the tradition of men** (8), which stood in antithesis to **the commandment of God.** Quoting against those who upheld it Isa. 29: 13 (6, 7), He contended that although it may have been propounded with the aim of helping people to observe the Mosaic Law, in **many** cases (13b) it led people to disobey that law, and of this He provided an example. The Law of Moses enjoined that children had a responsibility to support their parents financially, and Jesus cited in this regard Exod. 20: 21 and 21: 17 (10). But some of the Jews evaded this obligation by taking upon themselves an oath to the effect that such resources of theirs which might otherwise have been available for the upkeep of their parents had been promised instead for the upkeep of the temple (11, 12). This sort of conduct constituted those practising it **hypocrites** (6), for despite the outward appearance of piety on their part to which it gave rise, in reality their behaviour was in complete variance with the will of God. Reverting thereupon to the subject of purification, Jesus urged that it was not consuming meals without a prior ritual cleansing that defiled a person, nor was it even the eating of particular kinds of food (18, 19), but that what did so was the state of that person's heart, which indeed was the root cause of every manifestation of moral evil (20-23).

III. THE NORTHERN JOURNEY (7: 24—8: 26).

The healing of the daughter of the Syrophoenician woman (7: 24-30). (Parallel: Mt. 15: 21-28.)

Apart from what is recorded in 8: 10-13 and 9: 30, Jesus' ministry in Galilee was now concluded. His declaration of His freedom from many of the regulations of Judaism with which that ministry terminated (7: 1-23) forms an appropriate prelude to this record of a second journey He undertook (cf. 5: 1) into Gentile territory. This time He proceeded not eastwards, but northwards, **to the region of Tyre** (24). (In view of verse 31, it is probably preferable here to omit **and Sidon,** as in the margin.) No reason for this journey is stated, but it may well have been undertaken with the aim of freeing Himself from the crowds so as to gain an opportunity of concentrating His attention more than had been possible previously on training and instructing His apostles.

Whilst in a certain house in this district, Jesus was approached by a **Greek** (i.e. Gentile) woman of **Syrophoenician** nationality (26) (i.e. a Phoenician who lived in Syria, as opposed to such Phoenicians as lived in Libya, Carthage, etc.), who begged Jesus to exorcize a demon from her daughter. This, however, Jesus declined at first to do, telling her that it was among the Jews, not among the Gentiles, that His appointed ministry lay. The figure of speech Jesus used in stating that fact was that in which the Jews were represented as **children,** the Gentiles as **dogs** (the diminutive Greek noun *kynarion* suggesting 'that the reference is to the little dogs that were kept as pets, and not to the dogs of the courtyard and the street'; Cranfield, *ad loc.*), and the benefits of Jesus' ministry as **the children's bread** (27). The woman accepted the truth Jesus here affirmed; but pressing somewhat further the analogy He had employed, she pointed out that when children were given their food, the dogs received some slight benefit through the crumbs which the children dropped on the ground (28). While thus she did not wish to diminish the Jews' privileges, she did nevertheless crave to obtain from Jesus, as it were, an incidental mercy. And she received it, Jesus healing her daughter (29) without even setting eyes on the child (as also in Mt. 8: 5 ff., and Jn 4: 46 ff.).

The healing of the man who was deaf and dumb (7: 31–37).
In **the Decapolis** (31; see notes on 5: 20), which was the area where the man who had been indwelt with many demons had witnessed to his cure, Jesus was requested to heal a deaf and dumb man who was brought to Him (32). The man in question, though living in a Gentile district, was probably Jewish, for Jesus addressed him when healing him in Aramaic. But it was not by a mere word that Jesus healed Him, though so to heal was His normal custom. As in the stories of Mk 8: 22 ff. and Jn 9: 1 ff., He used saliva (33) doing so, probably (and touching also his ears and tongue), in order to awaken in the man faith to expect healing. Because, being deaf, the man would not have been able to hear a vocal prayer on his behalf, Jesus indicated to him that He was praying by **looking up to heaven** (34). The fact that Jesus **sighed** demonstrated the spiritual wrestling in which He was engaged. Jesus then commanded the man's ears to **be opened.** He did not command also that his tongue be released, realizing that his difficulty in speaking was simply a secondary consequence of his inability to hear. The outcome therefore of Jesus' command to the man's ears to be opened was that both his auditory and vocal defects were remedied (35), Jesus fulfilling thus, in part, the prophecy of Isa. 35: 5, 6.

The feeding of the four thousand (8: 1–10).
(Parallel: Mt. 15: 32–39.)
Similar in many respects as is this narrative to that of Christ's feeding of the five thousand

(6: 30–44), there are, nevertheless, some arresting differences between the two accounts. This miracle was wrought in Gentile territory, *viz.* in 'the region of the Decapolis' (7: 31), southeast of the sea of Galilee; and it has been plausibly suggested therefore that whereas in His feeding of the five thousand, Jesus was symbolizing His ability to impart the bread of life to the Jews, in His feeding of the four thousand, He was symbolizing His ability to impart the bread of life to the Gentiles (see p. 98). The type of basket used for the gathering of the fragments seems to have been different in the case of the two miracles, for in the first of them this is denoted by the Greek noun *kophinos* (6: 43), whereas in the second of them this is denoted by the Greek noun *spyris* (8), this being (according to some authorities), a larger sort of basket than the former, and big enough for an adult human being to sit in (Ac. 9: 25). **The district of Dalmanutha** (10) to which Jesus departed after performing the miracle has not been identified, and Matthew has replaced this phrase by 'the region of Magadan' (Mt. 15: 39). See p. 158.

The request by the Pharisees for a sign (8: 11–13). (Parallel: Mt. 16: 1–4.)
Although Jesus, in His healings and exorcisms, had furnished many signs to the effect that the power of God's kingdom was being exercised at last in the overthrow of the domain of Satan (Mt. 12: 28), the Pharisees now demanded **a sign from heaven,** meaning probably some apocalyptic vision. Jesus refused their demand, however, realizing that were such a spectacle granted, men's allegiance to Him would virtually be compelled, and the need for the exercise of faith on their part, which He knew to be so vital, would be precluded.

The disciples' shortage of bread (8: 14–21).
(Parallel: Mt. 16: 5–12.)
While in the ship (13) crossing from Dalmanutha (10) to Bethsaida (22), Jesus warned His disciples against **the leaven of the Pharisees** (*viz.* false religion), and **the leaven of Herod** (*viz.* irreligion) (15). The disciples, supposing that Jesus was speaking about literal leaven, instead of using the word metaphorically to denote moral evil of a corrupting nature, assumed that Jesus was complaining at their not having brought with them sufficient bread for their communal needs on this journey they were making (16). Jesus was vexed with His disciples in consequence, but not so much for their having misunderstood His figure of speech, but for their having imagined that a shortage of food could be a worry to Him. Reminding them of how, with but the most paltry provision, He had twice fed great multitudes (19, 20), He

reprimanded them for having their **hearts hardened** (17; see note on 3: 5), and applied to them the words of Isa. 6: 9 ff., which in 4: 12 He had applied to 'those outside' the Kingdom of God.

The healing of the blind man at Bethsaida (8: 22-26).
As with the healing of the person who was deaf and dumb (7: 31-37), in order to awaken faith in this blind man, Jesus used saliva, and applied His hands to the functionless organ (23). But on account, perhaps, of the weakness of the man's faith, he did not at first attain full clarity of vision as a result of Jesus' dealings with him (24). Jesus would not, however, leave the man only half-cured, and the outcome of His placing His hands on the man's eyes a second time was that the restoration of his sight became complete (25). Desirous, probably, that the man's relations should know of his cure before other people, Jesus told him to go home, rather than to the near-by village (26).

IV. THE JOURNEY TO JERUSALEM (8: 27—10: 52)
Peter's acknowledgement of Jesus' Messiahship (8: 27-30). (Parallels: Mt. 16: 13-20; Lk. 9: 18-21.)
The main task Jesus had to undertake on the course of this journey of His from the north of Palestine to Jerusalem was to prepare His disciples for His ensuing crucifixion at the capital city. His initial need to this end was to ascertain whether the disciples, despite how He had been acting, remained as convinced that He was Israel's Messiah as they had been convinced of it when first they met Him (Jn 1: 41, 45, etc.), and when, a little later, they sacrificed their homes and livelihood so as to live in His company (Mk 1: 16-20; 2: 14). Resolved to enquire from them concerning this, Jesus conducted them to **the villages of Caesarea Philippi** (27), i.e. the countryside around this town which was situated on the lower slopes of Mount Hermon, near the source of the river Jordan. Paneas was its original name; but on its being rebuilt by Philip the tetrarch, it was re-named 'Caesarea', in honour of the Roman Emperor; but to distinguish it from the city of that name on the Mediterranean coastline, its full name became 'Caesarea Philippi', in recognition also of its founder. Jesus introduced this enquiry of His by asking the disciples as to what was the opinion of men generally concerning Himself. Their reply (28) was similar to that recorded in 6: 14, 15 (see notes *ad loc.*). On testing the disciples themselves regarding this, however, Peter, as the spokesman, no doubt, of the entire group, answered: **'You are the**

Christ' (29), meaning: 'You are the Messiah, God's appointed Saviour of His people, whose advent has been foretold in our sacred Scriptures'. The reason for Jesus enjoining them thereupon to refrain from promulgating this truth (30), was that He did not want people to integrate this identification into the 'political' concept of Messiahship which so many of them entertained, and imagine, in consequence, that Jesus was destined to expel the Roman legions from Palestine.

The first prediction of the Passion (8: 31-33). (Parallels: Mt. 16: 21-23; Lk. 9: 22.)
With the disciples unitedly convinced now that Jesus was the Messiah, He was able at last to give them explicit teaching about His forthcoming death (though incidental allusions to it had been made previously, *e.g.* 2: 20). **The Son of man must suffer,** He told them (31), the cause of the necessity being regarded by Him, doubtless, as the will of God, as that will was expressed in such Scriptures as Isa. 53. Peter, however, though convinced of Jesus' Messianic status, was appalled at the thought of its carrying such implications, and he contested Jesus' assertion concerning His future to His face (32). This protest of Peter's was seen by Jesus as a repetition of the devil's temptation of Him in the wilderness to seek popular acclaim rather than pursue the pathway of service and suffering to which His Father had appointed Him. He rejoined to Peter here therefore, as He had rejoined to the devil there (Mt. 4: 10), **'Get behind me, Satan'** (33).
Jesus' teaching on the cost of discipleship (8: 34—9: 1). (Parallels: Mt. 16: 24-28; Lk. 9: 23-27.)
Jesus, having indicated what Messiahship would mean for Him, proceeded to explain now what discipleship would mean for the apostles and His other hearers. The person who enlisted in His cause, He taught, would need to **deny himself** (34), i.e. abandon the attitude of self-centredness, **and take up his cross,** i.e. be prepared to face martyrdom, with the indignity of being made to carry the transverse beam of his cross to the place of execution, which was the practice under the Romans (Jn 19: 17). He would have thus to be willing to lose his mortal life; and all this, for Christ's sake **and the gospel's** (35), i.e. for the sake of spreading abroad the good news of the kingdom of God; for only in this way would he attain the **true** life, that of the age to come. He, by contrast, who aimed to **save his** (mortal) **life,** especially such as sought to enrich themselves, and **gain the whole world** (36), would be spiritually destitute in the eternal order, Christ Himself manifesting towards them then His utmost

displeasure (38). The coming of the kingdom of God **with power** (9: 1), moreover, would not be long delayed, for certain of those then listening to Him would still be alive when this occurred. That God's kingdom was a present reality in the ministry of Jesus, and yet would have a future consummation, is indicated in the notes on 1: 15. Various suggestions have been made as to what might be denoted here by **the kingdom of God come with power,** *e.g.* Jesus' transfiguration, His crucifixion and resurrection, the descent on the apostles of the Holy Spirit, 'a visible manifestation of the Rule of God displayed in the life of an elect community' (Vincent Taylor, *ad loc.*), the spread of Christianity throughout the Roman empire, etc. Since the natural implication of the words **there are some standing here,** etc. is that although most of those there standing would then be dead, a minority nevertheless would still be living (suggesting the elapsing of some thirty or forty years), the identification of the event with the destruction of Jerusalem by the Romans in A.D. 70 and its glorious sequel for the Christian Church has been proposed by some; and this suggestion is developed further in the notes on 13: 24-27.

The transfiguration of Jesus (9: 2-10). (Parallels: Mt. 17: 1-9; Lk. 9: 28-36.) According to ancient tradition the **high mountain** (2) on which Jesus was transfigured was Mount Tabor, ten miles south-west of the sea of Galilee. The objections to this identification are (*a*) that it is less than two thousand feet high; (*b*) that at this time a fortress stood on its summit; and (*c*) that since, in 8: 27, Jesus was near Caesarea Philippi, and in 9: 33 He was at Capernaum, a site north of Capernaum would have been more natural. Perhaps, therefore, the transfiguration occurred on a spur of Mount Hermon (9,000 ft.), though this was in Gentile territory, and it would therefore be somewhat remarkable to have found **scribes** at its foot (14); or perhaps it occurred on Jebel Jermaq (3,962 ft.), north of Merom, in the north of Palestine. To display to Peter, James and John yet further truth concerning Himself, Jesus re-assumed before them His pre-incarnate glory (Jn 17: 5). The appearance with Him of Moses and Elijah was doubtless so that the disciples might see the giver of the law and a representative of the prophets both testifying to Jesus as being the one to whom they had pointed forwards (4). Peter, however, misunderstood the sight, his proposal of making **booths** of inter-twined branches of trees for Jesus, Moses and Elijah (5), implying that he viewed them as all three being on an equality. God's answer to this suggestion was to remove

Moses and Elijah (8), and to proclaim concerning Jesus: **'This is my beloved Son; listen to him'** (7). The first part of this announcement had been made by the Father previously, at the time of Jesus' baptism, though as recorded in 1: 11 (on which see notes), it was addressed solely to Jesus Himself. The second part of the announcement identified Jesus with the Prophet whose coming was foretold in Dt. 18: 15-19. The reason why Jesus forbade Peter, James and John to disclose what they had seen to others till after His resurrection (9), was, presumably, that only as from then would they really have grasped its proper significance, and so be in a position rightly to propound it.

The discussion concerning Elijah (9: 11-13). (Parallel: Mt. 17: 10-13.) The beholding by Peter, James and John of Elijah, as it were, in vision, prompted them to enquire of Jesus as to how it was that His own coming had not been preceded, as the scribes had deduced and taught from Mal. 4: 5, by a coming of Elijah in person (11). Jesus replied, alluding to John the Baptist, who had exercised his ministry 'in the spirit and power of Elijah' (Lk. 1: 17), that already Elijah had come amongst them (13), adding that though indeed his coming was, in a certain sense, **to restore all things** (12), there were, nevertheless, definite limitations as to how such restoration was to be conceived; for the Scripture did not thereupon predict that so spiritually minded would the people then be that his successor the Messiah would be received by them with acclamation, but rather **that he should suffer many things and be treated with contempt.**

The healing of the demon-possessed boy (9: 14-29). (Parallels: Mt. 17: 14-20; Lk. 9: 37-43.) A distracted father, endeavouring to make contact with Jesus so as to obtain from Him healing for his demon-possessed son, had found nine of the disciples, but not Jesus Himself. He requested these, therefore to exorcize the demon. This they attempted to do, but without effect. Their failure gave rise to an argument between certain scribes in a crowd which had now assembled, and the disciples (14). Suddenly Jesus appeared on the scene, having descended from the mount of His glorious transfiguration to this scene of tragedy, frustration and helplessness. The amazement of the crowd on seeing Jesus (15) may have been due to His 'unexpected and opportune arrival' (so Cranfield), or possibly, as others have suggested, to some of the glory of His transfiguration still lingering on His face (cf. Exod. 34: 29, 30). On the boy's father having outlined to Jesus his predicament (17, 18), Jesus exclaimed: **'O faithless generation'** (19). It was probably the nine disciples, rather than the crowd or the scribes or the boy's father, to whom He was here referring, for the reason Jesus gave as to why the disciples could not exorcize the demon as stated in Mt. 17: 20 was: 'Because of your little faith'. The corresponding explanation as stated here in Mk 9 is: **'This kind cannot be driven out by anything but prayer'** (29). It is decidedly likely that this does not relate so much to the actual procedure of making requests from God, as to the attitude of moment-by-moment dependence on God which is the source and basis of prayer. Mk 6: 7 describes how Jesus gave His disciples 'authority over the unclean spirits', and 6: 13 relates how they exercised this. Their being castigated now as 'faithless', was not, as the word might have suggested, on account of any lack of expectation of success on their part, for their failure quite astonished them (28), but because their adequacy to cope with the situation now confronting them, was something which, in the light of their previous experiences, they were taking for granted. In contrast to the disciples who were 'faithless', the boy's father possessed faith, though a faith which he knew to be imperfect (24). Jesus informed him that a person who had faith should not say to Him: **'If you can'** (22), but should set no limit to His divine ability (23). This ability was displayed thereupon in the healing of the boy (25-27).

The second prediction of the Passion (9: 30-32). (Parallels: Mt. 17: 22, 23; Lk. 9: 43b-45.) The desire of Jesus that this journey of His through Galilee should be kept private (30) was due to His desire to forewarn His disciples regarding His forthcoming rejection without being interrupted (31). The piece of information additional to that mentioned in 8: 31 which Jesus disclosed here was that He would be **delivered into the hands of men,** conveying a hint of His being betrayed. The failure of the disciples to understand from Jesus' words here that He would shortly be put to death (32) was due to the infatuation of their minds with the popular notions as to the course which the Messiah was destined to follow. It was to avoid these conceptions of theirs being disturbed that **they were afraid to ask him** further concerning the matter.

The discussion concerning greatness (9: 33-37). (Parallels: Mt. 18: 1-5; Lk. 9: 46-48.) Jesus evidently had been walking in front of His disciples as they proceeded towards Capernaum (as in 10: 32); but He knew what they had been discussing among themselves on the journey (Lk. 9: 47), namely **who was the greatest** among them (34), and on their arrival at Capernaum, He asked them to confess it (33). On their refusal to do this, He told them that

the essence of greatness lay in performing acts of service for other people (35; also 10: 43, 44), even though the people concerned were as insignificant as the child He proceeded then to take up in His arms before them (36). His plea, thereupon, that they should receive such a child as that in His Name (37), meant that they were to act towards such children in kindly ways, because in a certain sense they represented Him. For their encouragement to that end He added that this service in their regard would be divinely evaluated as though done to Jesus Himself, even as service done to Jesus would be divinely evaluated as though done to God the Father.

The independent exorcist (9: 38-40). (Parallel: Lk. 9: 49-50.) It was not only Jesus and His followers who succeeded in casting out demons, as is shown by Mt. 12: 27. Ac. 19: 13 ff. confirms this, telling of certain non-Christian Jews who did so, though in the Name of Jesus. A Jewish exorcist who was engaged in casting out demons in Jesus' Name, though not himself a follower of Jesus, was seen by the apostle John, who, offended at the apparent inconsistency of such conduct, endeavoured to prevent him from continuing this practice of his (38). Jesus, however, criticized John's action in this matter, pointing out that the man in question was **not against** them (40), and that it was highly unlikely that he would follow up working a miracle in His name by publicly reviling Him (39).

Jesus' final teaching in Galilee (9: 41-50). Jesus taught that even a very small act of service done to another would be divinely rewarded (41), whereas inducing young believers in Him to sin was an outrage that incurred such a punishment, that it would be highly advantageous were a person who was contemplating such a course to be drowned in the sea prior to implementing his intention, so that the punishment attendant on that atrocity might be averted (42). Not only, however, was it wrong to cause sin in other people; it was wrong also to cause sin in oneself; and if temptation assailed one through such organs as one's hand, one's foot, or one's eye, precious as these organs were, it would be better, nevertheless, to remove them altogether, than, through retaining them, **to be thrown into hell** (43-47). The RSV margin mentions that Greek word translated here 'hell' is 'Gehenna'. 'Gehenna' is a transliteration into Greek of the Hebrew phrase 'valley of Hinnom', which lay to the west and south of Jerusalem. Here, at one time, children were consumed by fire in sacrifice to the heathen god Molech (Jer. 7: 31; 32: 35). After this practice had been stamped out by King Josiah (2 Kg. 23: 10), the valley became Jerusalem's refuse dump. Fires were always kept smouldering there so as to burn up the garbage, and maggots bred there in abundance, feeding themselves on the offal lying around. Because of the place's vile associations, the Jews, in due course, came to denote the place of future torment for the wicked by the name 'Gehenna', picturing that place in consequence as a domain **where their worm does not die, and the fire is not quenched** (48, echoing Isa. 66: 24). Developing further the thought of 'fire', Jesus then said: **For every one will be salted with fire** (49), meaning that every disciple of His, in order to be spiritually purified and made like salt, would need to undergo a fiery ordeal of suffering. Developing thereupon the thought of 'salt', Jesus said that the disciples were like salt, for they exercised the valuable functions of seasoning and purifying the world, and this was **good** (50). He cautioned them, however, against losing that which they had received from Him which was what had conferred on them their goodness. If, consequently, instead of arguing with each other as to which of them was the greatest (34), they were to **be at peace with one another**, what they would need for this purpose would be to have in themselves 'salt', i.e. love for their neighbours, and a readiness to serve them, and make sacrifices for their sakes.

Jesus' teaching on divorce (10: 1–12). (Parallel: Mt. 19: 1–12.)
Jesus, having now reached Perea, in the south of the country, and to the east of the river Jordan, resumed His ministry to the general public (1; and see notes on 7: 24). The question He was there asked by the Pharisees, **'Is it lawful for a man to divorce his wife?'** was put to Him **in order to test him** (2), i.e. to try to induce Him to incriminate Himself by contradicting the Mosaic Law. Jesus elicited from His questioners that Dt. 24: 1–4 allowed a man to divorce his wife, provided that the man safeguarded his wife's interests by writing out and giving to her **a certificate of divorce** (4), which would enable the woman to establish, as and when necessary, that her divorce had been formal and official, and that she was perfectly free, in consequence, to marry someone else. Jesus' comment on this Deuteronomic injunction, however, was that it did not represent God's absolute will, but something rather which, on account of the perversity of the human heart, He permitted, in order that the consequences of that perversity might be kept in restraint (5). He indicated, thereupon, that God's original intentions with regard to marriage were stated in Gen. 1: 27 (6), and in Gen. 2: 24 (7, 8a),

statements which depict the marriage bond as indissoluble. A married couple, Jesus therefore deduced, were **one** (8b). The margin states that the Greek here means 'one flesh', involving that the relationship between the pair was just as unbreakable as was a blood-relationship, such as that between a father and a son. His conclusion, consequently, was that **man** (i.e. the male member of the partnership, rather than some legal body), has no right to sever his matrimonial union (9). It is a fair assumption that divorce on the ground of adultery, being so obviously permissible, was not within the scope of what Jesus and the Pharisees were here discussing. Those committing adultery, indeed, were required to be put to death (Lev. 20: 10; Jn 8: 5), which would sunder the nuptial bond without the need of having recourse to divorce proceedings. Speaking privately to His disciples only (10), Jesus developed the teaching He had given to the Pharisees. Already He had shown that for a man to divorce his wife was a sin; but what He affirmed now was that if, additionally, that man married another woman, he made himself an adulterer (11). The adulterous union described in verse 12 was that which Herodias perpetrated, who, availing herself of the provisions of Roman law, had severed her union with Philip, and had married subsequently Herod Antipas (see notes on 6: 17).

Jesus' blessing of the children (10: 13–16). (Parallels: Mt. 19: 13–15; Lk. 18: 15–17.)
The disciples felt it to be an unwarrantable intrusion on their Master's time to have children brought to Him **that he might touch them** (13). Their rebuking those who conducted them to Jesus for this purpose earned a rebuke from Jesus for themselves; for He not only received the children, but went beyond that which was asked of Him, taking the children in His arms and blessing them (16). In saying: **'to such belongs the kingdom of God'** (14), Jesus' meaning, probably, was that the kingdom of God belonged to people who, though not literally children, were embued with such characteristics of children as trust and receptiveness. This truth is developed in verse 15. Children allow people to give them things apart from any thought of merit or desert on their part; and it is only by adopting such a childlike attitude that people can appropriate the blessedness of the kingdom of God.

The rich young ruler (10: 17–31). (Parallels: Mt. 19: 16–30; Lk. 18: 18–30.)
As a complementary emphasis to the truth of verse 15, where salvation is depicted as a free gift, the story narrated here indicates the immense costliness of salvation for certain people. A wealthy man (22b), despite his having

observed the Mosaic law as best he knew (20), was spiritually dissatisfied notwithstanding, and so asked Jesus what he needed to do **to inherit eternal life** (17). His approach to Jesus, however, was unbecomingly obsequious, for, in contravention of normal Jewish custom, he addressed Him as **'Good Teacher'**. Jesus rebuked him for this, reminding him that **'good'** was a designation which was normally reserved for God, only God being good without qualification (18). Jesus was not hereby disclaiming being either 'God' or 'good', but was merely criticizing His being addressed thus by someone who clearly was completely unaware of His divine nature. In reply to the man's enquiry Jesus tried to deepen in the man a consciousness of sin by quoting to him the commands of the so-called 'Second Table of the Decalogue' (19) (the injunction 'Do not covet' being interpreted here as **'Do not defraud'**). The implication to be derived from the man's retort that he had obeyed these laws from his youth (20), is that he had no understanding as to all that these requirements involved. There were qualities about this man, however, which caused Jesus greatly to love him (21a). But the way in which He expressed towards him that love was not by lowering His demands with regard to him in order the more easily to win him into the company of His followers, but by laying His finger with utter frankness on what it was that was impeding his quest for eternal life, namely his wealth. Telling him, therefore, that he lacked but a single thing (which, presumably, was an unreserved dedication to God's cause and kingdom), He bade him sell his possessions, giving the proceeds to the poor, and become then one of His disciples (21). But he could not bring himself to do this, and in contrast to the eagerness with which he **ran up** to Jesus (17), he went away sorrowful (22) (cf. Mt. 13: 45, 46). Commenting on the man's decision, Jesus told His disciples that by nature it was impossible for a rich man to receive salvation, as impossible indeed as for a camel, the largest animal in Palestine at that time, **to go through the eye of a needle** (25) (quoting here a current proverb which was memorable on account of its very grotesqueness). He hastened, however, to allay the disciples' amazement at this assertion of His by reminding them that **all things are possible with God** (27). To the rejoinder of Peter that what that rich man had failed to do had been performed by his companions and himself (28), Jesus answered that such would receive **a hundredfold now in this time,** though **persecutions** would constantly befall them, **and in the age to come, eternal life** (30).

But He warned them against being self-satisfied at what they had done, informing them that many disciples of His, prominent now because of their manifest piety, would find themselves in the life to come rated much less highly than certain far less conspicuous of His devotees, who nevertheless were of greater worth in the sight of God (31).

The third prediction of the Passion (10: 32-34). (Parallels: Mt. 20: 17-19; Lk. 18: 31-34.) The reason why the disciples were **amazed** as they walked behind Jesus on the road to Jerusalem (32), was probably because of the look of determination on their Master's face as He proceeded onwards (Lk. 9: 51). This third prediction of His approaching Passion which He thereupon made to them was fuller than the earlier ones, and included the additional facts that the Jewish leaders would cause His death to be at the hand of **the Gentiles** (33), who, prior to executing Him, would **mock him, and spit upon him, and scourge him** (34).

The request of James and John (10: 35-45). (Parallel: Mt. 20: 20-28.) That the disciples no more comprehended their Master's third prediction of His Passion than they did His earlier ones (8: 32; 9: 32), is proved, not only by the explicit statement of Lk. 18: 44, but also by this request to Him from James and John to be allowed to sit on His either side in His **glory** (37), meaning in the Messianic kingdom (Mt. 20: 21) He was about to set up, as they envisaged this. Jesus refused their request, explaining that the matter in question did not come within the scope of His personal jurisdiction (40). He indicated by implication, nevertheless, that the issue would be dependent, at least in part, on the willingness of His followers to suffer for His sake. Such suffering He described metaphorically as drinking from His cup and being baptized with His baptism, figures of speech which, although suggestive of suffering to the point of death, and involving this in the instance of Jesus Himself, did not involve this necessarily in the case of other people (cf. Isa. 51: 17; 43: 2). Jesus asked James and John, therefore, whether they were prepared to undergo this ordeal (38), and on their replying to Him in the affirmative, He told them that such in fact would be their experience (39), a prediction which was fulfilled in James being killed 'with the sword' (Ac. 12: 2), and in John being exiled to the island of Patmos (Rev. 1: 9). The sufferings of these, however, were comparable with those of Jesus only in a limited respect, for they were not, of course, atoning sufferings.

The disreputable request of James and John was succeeded by the equally disreputable reaction to it of their fellow-apostles (41). Addressing them all twelve, therefore, Jesus explained to them (as in 9: 35-37, on which see notes) wherein spiritual greatness really consisted. He showed them that whereas in the kingdoms of men the test of greatness lay in the number of people one could control (42), in His kingdom it lay in the number of people one could help (43, 44). He emphasized that the highest honour to which a man could aspire consisted not in occupying a kingdom's chief seats, but in serving other people. As an example of this attitude, He cited Himself, who came **to serve** (45). It is quite likely that He made the claim here, by inference, of fulfilling the rôle of God's 'Servant' foretold in Isa. 52: 13-53: 12, of whom the prophet declared: '*He poured out his soul to death*', and '*He bore the sin of many*' (Isa. 53: 12); for He depicted His supreme act of service on behalf of men as His giving **his life as a ransom for many**. The word 'ransom' implies deliverance from bondage by the payment of a price. The word 'for' (Gk. *anti*) normally bears a substitionary sense (as in Mt. 2: 22). With regard to the word 'many', see notes on 1: 34.

The healing of Bartimaeus (10: 46-52). (Parallels: Mt. 20: 30-34; Lk. 18: 35-43.) The **Jericho** of New Testament times which Jesus now entered (46) had been built by Herod the Great and his son Archelaus (Mt. 2: 22), and stood somewhat to the south of the OT city of that name, and to the west of the present one. Bartimaeus, the blind beggar who lived there, was among the first of those, outside the ranks of the apostles, who are recorded as having proclaimed Jesus to be the Messiah (though cf. Jn 4: 29, 42); for **'Son of David'** (47), the title by which he addressed Jesus, was one which was specifically Messianic, as is shown by its occurrence in the seventeenth of the pre-Christian 'Psalms of Solomon' (cf. also Mk 12: 35). The reason for Bartimaeus's conviction that Jesus could cure his blindness may have been his knowledge that Isa. 61: 1 (LXX) (cf. Mt. 11: 5) foretold that the Messiah would enable the blind to see (see notes on 1: 40). On his appealing for Jesus' help, he was rebuked by those around for making a nuisance of himself (48; cf. 10: 13). Jesus' cure of him (52) is the last healing miracle recorded in Mark's Gospel (cf. Lk. 22: 51). It is to be observed that Jesus did not command him to refrain from proclaiming His Messiahship, as He had done to the demons (cf. 1: 34, on which see notes).

V. THE JERUSALEM MINISTRY (11: 1-13: 37).

The entry into Jerusalem (11: 1-11). (Parallels:

Mt. 21: 1-11; Lk. 19: 28-44; Jn 13: 12-19.) Jesus, approaching Jerusalem from Jericho, reached **Bethany** (known now as El Azariyeh), on the east side of the **Mount of Olives** (1). Deeming that the time was now ripe for Him publicly to confess His Messiahship (cf. 10: 47, on which see notes), He decided to do so by an act which constituted a claim that the prophecy of Zech. 9: 9 related to Himself. Instead, therefore, of entering Jerusalem on foot, as was customary in the case of pilgrims, He resolved to enter it mounted on a **colt** (2), and one, furthermore, which had never previously been ridden, in accordance with the prophet's description of such a creature as 'a new colt' (LXX). Mt. 21: 2 and Jn 12: 14 indicate that the colt in question was that of an ass, and Jesus' use of this was a witness that, despite popular opinion, it was not as a warrior that He would fulfil His Messianic office (in which event a more appropriate beast on which to ride would have been a horse), but in great meekness and lowliness. Jesus told two of His disciples, accordingly, to fetch such a colt from the village opposite them, which perhaps was **Bethphage.** Whilst it is possible that Jesus' knowledge of the location of the colt, and of how people would respond to its being untethered (3), was due to an arrangement He had previously made with its owner, it is more likely that Jesus was exercising here His supernatural knowledge (cf. 1 Sam. 10: 2-7). On the colt being brought to Jesus, an improvised saddle was laid on it (7), on which Jesus sat. As a token of homage to Jesus, **garments** (cf. 2 Kg. 9: 13) and **leafy branches** were spread on the road before Him (8). The word **'Hosanna'** (9), which the crowds cried out, is derived from the Hebrew exclamation 'Save now', as recorded in Ps. 118: 25. It may have been an appeal to God to save the Israelite people now that the Messiah had appeared among them. **'Hosanna in the highest'** (10b) may mean: 'Save now (O Thou that dwellest) in the highest' (Cranfield). **'Blessed is he who comes in the name of the Lord'** (9b) (quoted from Ps. 118: 26) are probably best understood Messianically, for 'He who comes' was a standard title by which the Messiah was denoted (see Mt. 11: 3). The crowds, rightly, identified the coming of the promised **kingdom** with the coming of the promised King (10). It is probable that the lodging-place at **Bethany** to which Jesus retired for the night (11) was the home of Martha, Mary and Lazarus (Jn 12: 1, 2).

The cleansing of the temple (11: 15-19). (Parallels: Mt. 21: 12-17; Lk. 19: 45-46; and cf. Jn 2: 13-22.) One of the actions predicted of the Messiah in the OT was His cleansing of the temple worship (Mal. 3: 1–3), and to this He now attended. In the temple's outer court (the 'court of the Gentiles'), He found that the Jewish authorities had erected trading-booths, where wine, oil, salt, and various animals were being sold, all of which were needed for the sacrificial ritual. **Pigeons** (15) were used for such ceremonies as that described in Lk. 2: 22–24. It is implied that the merchants were guilty of profiteering in conducting these transactions (17b). The **money-changers** changed the Greek and Roman coinage of the Jewish pilgrims from the Dispersion into Tyrian currency, to enable them to pay the temple tax of half a shekel a year which was required from every male Jew (Exod. 30: 11 ff.; Mt. 17: 24), and which had to be paid in Tyrian currency. A further abuse to which the temple's outer court was put was that of people laden with baggage, instead of walking around the outside of these holy precincts, making a short cut by walking through them (16). All these activities Jesus stopped, quoting against those who engaged in them Isa. 56: 7 and Jer. 7: 11 (17). Mark alone, of the evangelists, relates Jesus to have continued the quotation from Isaiah so as to bring out the prophet's point that in the Messianic age the Gentiles equally with the Jews would be permitted to use the Jerusalem temple. The desire of Jesus, evidently, was to remove that which hindered the Gentiles being able quietly and reverently to worship God in what was intended as **a house of prayer for all the nations.**

The cursing of the fig-tree (11: 12–14, 20–25). (Parallel: Mt. 21: 18–22.)

The leaves of the fig-tree in Palestine appear in March, and are accompanied by a crop of small edible knobs called *taksh* which drop off before the true figs form, which ripen in June. An absence of *taksh* indicates that the tree in question will bear no figs. It was therefore, entirely reasonable for Jesus, shortly before Passover-time in mid-April, to go up to a fig-tree **to see if he could find anything on it** (13), and then to condemn the tree on discovering on it **nothing but leaves.** This action of His was a piece of prophetic symbolism of a type with which the Jews had been made familiar through such acts as those recorded in 2 Chr. 18: 10, and also Jer. 27: 2, together with 28: 10 ff. Jesus was proclaiming hereby that just as that fig-tree bore leaves but not fruit, the Jews, by means of their numerous ritual observances, made a fine show of religion, but had failed to produce those spiritual qualities which God most wanted from them, and for which indeed He had brought them into being. He was compelled,

therefore, to pronounce over them, as over the fig-tree, a sentence of doom (13: 2). On the fig-tree having, by the following morning, withered away (20), instead of Jesus impressing on His disciples, from this, the certainty of the doom which was to befall their nation, He used the incident as a practical demonstration of the power of faith (22), which could effect, so He informed them, not merely the withering of a tree, but the removal of a mountain (23), by which hyperbole He meant that by the exercise of faith in God, people can do what humanly appears utterly impossible. It follows from this, accordingly, that when engaged in the activity of prayer, given an attitude of faith in God (24), and forgiveness towards one's fellow men (25), the petitions which are made (assuming that these are not contrary to the will of God) will assuredly be granted.

The question concerning Jesus' authority (11: 27–33). (Parallels: Mt. 21: 23–27; Lk. 20: 1–8.)

It is to be presumed that **the chief priests and the scribes and the elders** (27) who now approached Jesus were a delegation from the Jewish Sanhedrin, to whom the temple police were ultimately responsible. They enquired from Him, accordingly, who had authorized Him to perform such deeds as His cleansing of the temple (28), desirous, no doubt, of forcing Him to admit that He had, in fact, no authority for so acting. In reply, Jesus recalled to their minds the case of John the Baptist, and He asked them whether John had ministered by divine appointment, or whether, by contrast, he had been commissioned for this by the Jewish authorities (30). This question they refused to face honestly on account of the perplexing consequences in which they saw they would, through facing it, become involved. To have admitted that John had been divinely authorized for his ministry would have been to have invited from Jesus the rejoinder as to what they made of the fact that He Himself had been identified by John as the One, greater than he, who was to succeed him (31), whereas to have alleged John to have acted purely from some private whim would have incurred for them the wrath of the people generally, who had always believed John to have been a prophet (32), and the more so latterly, now that he had been martyred. Impaled thus on the horns of a dilemma, they declined, through cowardice, to answer Jesus' question, whereupon Jesus declined to answer theirs (33), though He did so indirectly in the parable which He thereupon addressed to them.

The parable of the wicked husbandmen (12: 1–12). (Parallels: Mt. 21: 33–45; Lk. 20: 9–19.)

There were many estates at this time in Galilee which were owned by foreign landlords, and farmed by Galilean peasants, who, not un-naturally, felt highly disgruntled by the status they occupied. This situation may form the background to this parable which Jesus told, and which was designed not only to indicate that His authority, about which He was being questioned (11: 28), was even higher than that of the prophets (in that a prophet was a **servant** of God, whereas He Himself was God's **Son**), but additionally to warn those to whom He was speaking, and who were plotting His death, both of the heinousness of their proposed crime, and of the dreadfulness of its inevitable sequel. The parable's opening words '**A man planted a vineyard**' (1) must immediately have recalled to the hearers' memories the parable recorded in Isa. 5: 1–7 (with its provided interpretation), and indicated to them that it referred to the relationship of Almighty God to the nation of Israel. In accordance with con-temporary custom, the landlord is described as having leased the vineyard to certain **tenants** (representing here the Jewish leaders), in return for an agreed proportion of the vineyard's produce. The servants, however, whom the landlord sent to claim this rent which was owing to him, were abused and wounded (2–4), and some were even killed (5). On sending them finally his son, he too was killed (6–8). The consequence of this, as was hardly surprising, was the coming of the landlord, with govern-ment authorization no doubt, **to destroy the tenants and give the vineyard to others** (9), a clear prediction of the destruction of Jerus-alem in A.D. 70. Jesus reminded His audience, at that point, of the statement contained in Ps. 118: 22–23, deducing from it that although within but a few days the Jewish leaders would reject Him decisively and finally, He would subsequently be exalted, nevertheless, to the most honoured place of all.

The question about the poll-tax (12: 13–17). (Parallels: Mt. 22: 15–22; Lk. 20: 20–26.) Despite Jesus' warning to the Jewish religious leaders as given in the foregoing parable, they continued their campaign against Him. **Some of the Herodians** (13; see notes on 3: 6), who had come down from Galilee to celebrate the passover, joined with **some of the Pharisees** in asking Jesus a question out of **hypocrisy** (15), i.e. not to discover the truth, but **to entrap him in his talk.** The question was as to whether it was in accordance with the law of God to pay to Caesar the poll-tax (14), which had been demanded as from A.D. 6 from all provincial Jews. This particular tax was excep-tionally unpopular, being the token of the Jews'

subject status. The questioners felt that for Jesus to insist on its payment would alienate the people from Him, whereas for Him to deny the legitimacy of the tax would be something for which He could conveniently be reported to the Romans as a rebel against their authority. Jesus' reply was to the effect that since the money they possessed, having embossed on it the image of the Emperor Tiberius, was, according to the contemporary viewpoint, Caesar's property, it was implied hereby that they acknowledged their subservience to him, so that they should pay to him the poll-tax. What Jesus thereupon added, however, implied that should, at any time, Caesar demand some-thing which properly belonged to God, Caesar's demand then would need to be refused (17).

The question about the resurrection (12: 18–27). (Parallels: Mt. 22: 23–33; Lk. 20: 27–40.) Whereas the former question had been aimed to place Jesus in a political difficulty, this next one was aimed to place Him in a theological difficulty. It was addressed to Him by members of the priestly and aristocratic Sadducean party, who endeavoured now to make the doctrine of the resurrection, in which they disbelieved, look ridiculous. Their contention, ultimately, was that it was incompatible with the law of levirate marriage, as laid down in Dt. 25: 5–10, which they quoted loosely to Jesus (19). Jesus in effect denied that this was so, provided that the resurrection-life was correctly conceived; and He hinted that the reason why the Sadducees found difficulty with the doctrine of the resurrection was because of their prior rejection of the existence of angels (Ac. 23: 6–8); for just as angels, being immortal, did not need to marry, nor did human beings in their resurrection state (25). Turning His attention, thereupon, from the issue as to the manner of the resurrec-tion to that of its fact, Jesus demonstrated that belief in the resurrection was logically implied right back in the Pentateuch. He pointed out that in Exod. 3: 6, God described Himself as being, during the life-time of Moses, the God of men who, according to the flesh, were no longer alive (26), the inference being that God was still caring for them then, and that at the last, necessarily, He would raise up their bodies, so that they might become sharers together in the final blessedness. The fault, therefore, with the Sadducees was that they knew **neither the Scriptures** which taught the resurrection, **nor the power of God** which could effect the resurrection (24).

The question about the greatest command-ment (12: 28–34). (Parallel: Mt. 22: 34–40.) In the question submitted to Jesus now, as contrasted with those submitted earlier, there seems to have been no spirit of hostility, which, seeing that its propounder was **one of the scribes** (28), was unusual (cf. verses 38–40). On being asked as to which was the most important of all the commandments, Jesus replied by quoting the *Shema* (Dt. 6: 4, 5), which pious Jews recited daily, but He added, as did the lawyer in Lk. 10: 27, to what was stated in the Old Testament that God was to be loved with the **mind** as well as with the other human faculties (28, 29). Although Jesus had not been asked also as to which was the next most important of the commandments, so inseparable, in His eyes, were the first and the second (cf. 1 Jn 4: 21), that He expressed Himself further about that too, quoting, to this end, Lev. 19: 18 (31). It should be appreciated that there is a great deal more involved in 'loving God' and 'loving one's neighbour' than might super-ficially be imagined, the implications of the latter of these duties having been expanded by Jesus earlier, in His parable of the Good Samaritan (Lk. 10: 30–37). The scribe concurred with Jesus' answer (32), and, without in any way belittling the importance of offering sacrifices, commented that to love God was a higher duty still (33; cf. 1 Sam. 15: 22; Ps. 69: 30–31; Hos. 6: 6). While, however, the scribe had been appraising Jesus, Jesus had been appraising the scribe; and His final rejoinder to him was that he came quite near to possessing the necessary characteristics qualifying a man to enter **the kingdom of God** (34). Whether, by personal committal to Jesus, he was ever actually born into that kingdom is not stated.

Jesus' question about David's Son (12: 35–37). (Parallels: Mt. 22: 41–46; Lk. 20: 41–44.)

The initiative in the discussion was now claimed by Jesus, who asked those around Him a question, the purport of which was to show that the Messianic title **'Son of David'** (35; and see notes on 10: 47), used so commonly by **the scribes,** accurate though it was, did not how-ever convey the total truth regarding the Messiah's person. Proof of this fact, as Jesus pointed out, was that when David himself wrote concerning the Messiah in Ps. 110: 1, he characterized the Messiah, not, as might have been anticipated, as 'my son', but rather as **'my lord'** (36), with the implication that the Messiah possessed not only a human nature (as David's son), but a divine one too. Jesus raised this point, clearly, with the hope that His hearers might be induced to relate it to Himself.

Jesus' condemnation of the scribes (12: 38–40). (Parallels: Mt. 23: 1–39; Lk. 20: 45–47.)

Having criticized what the scribes said (35), Jesus criticized now what the scribes did. As to

their liking **to go about in long robes** (38a), these were the garments which characteristically were worn by men of learning. In a variety of situations they expected the utmost deference to be paid to them (38b, 39). From needy widows they extorted unreasonable sums of money; and they endeavoured to win the esteem of men by engaging themselves in prolonged acts of prayer (40a). The **greater condemnation** (40b) which Jesus said would ultimately befall them, was because the evil practices they committed were craftily carried out under the guise of religion.

The widow's gift (12: 41–44). (Parallel: Lk. 21: 1–4.)

Having spoken of the avarice of the scribes (40), Jesus spoke now about a woman whom He noticed who surrendered for the work of God **everything she had** (44). Next within the temple's 'court of the Gentiles' (see notes on 11: 15), was the 'court of the women', around the walls of which, according to the *Mishnah*, were placed thirteen trumpet-shaped offering-receptacles. In contrast with certain **rich people** whom Jesus saw deposit into them **large sums** (41), this widow, as unobtrusively as possible, no doubt, dropped into one of them **two copper coins,** the smallest coins in circulation (42). The reason why Jesus proclaimed this to have been a greater gift than the offerings of the rich (43), was that it was a sacrificial gift, and left her with nothing for herself, whereas the rich retained plenty for themselves.

The eschatological discourse (13: 1–37). (Parallels: Mt. 24: 1–50; Lk. 21: 5–36.)

'Mark 13 is the biggest problem in the Gospel' wrote A. M. Hunter; and he was right. The exposition of it presented hereunder, therefore, is submitted quite tentatively, and with due deference to the different way in which the discourse is treated in the notes on the parallel passages in the Gospels by Matthew and Luke.

(a) The circumstances of the discourse (1–4).

Having concluded a day of teaching in the temple (His entry into which is noted in 11: 27), Jesus emerged from it and, while so doing, had His attention directed **by one of his disciples** to the magnificence of its **stones** and **buildings** (1). Jesus' response was to predict the temple's complete destruction and devastation (2). Jesus spent the nights, at this time, on the Mount of Olives (Lk. 21: 37). When, therefore, He and His disciples had crossed the Kedron valley and had ascended this hill (from the slopes of which they would have obtained a magnificent view of the city and its temple), the four senior disciples asked Jesus when the temple's destruc-tion would occur, and what sign would indicate the imminence of this (3, 4). It is to be observed that the record here in Mark, as well as that in Luke (Lk. 21: 7), makes no mention of the disciples asking Jesus concerning any other matter than that. Necessarily, therefore, this was the dominant topic of which, in His reply to their enquiry, Jesus treated. Reference, however, to the record in Matthew's Gospel (Mt. 24: 3), shows that the disciples asked Jesus additionally: 'What will be the sign of your coming, and of the close of the age?' It is highly probable that the reason why they submitted to Jesus this supplementary question was because of the misapprehension under which they laboured to the effect that the return of Jesus and the close of the age were destined to coincide as regards time with the temple's destruction. Seeing, therefore, that some information about Jesus' second advent came, incidentally, within the scope of the disciples' enquiry, Jesus did, in His reply, say something about it, but only secondarily, and at the close of His answer to their basic question, as will be demonstrated in the notes which follow.

(b) *The discourse itself* (5–37).

It is here submitted that the key to the understanding of this discourse lies in Jesus' affirmation of verse 30: **'Truly, I say to you, this generation will not pass away before all these things take place',** which He thereupon endorsed by means of the intensely solemn assertion of verse 31, stating (with the use of a Hebraic idiom), that even though heaven and earth should pass away, His words (and this utterance, presumably, in particular), would never do so. Everything, therefore, which Jesus predicted up to that point in His discourse, He declared would be fulfilled within the ensuing forty years (understanding the word 'generation' in its normal and natural sense); and fulfilled it was. The teaching in this discourse on Jesus' second advent is confined to the statements of verses 32–37, and the change of topic is indicated by the word **'these'** in verses 29 and 30 being replaced in verse 32 by the adversative demonstrative adjective **'that'**. In verses 5–14, Jesus foretold the occurrence of various happenings which, despite how some might deign to interpret them, were not to be regarded as the immediate precursors of the destruction of the temple. All of them in fact took place during the succeeding forty years. The nature of the sign indicating the imminence of the temple's destruction (and which was that, consequently, concerning which the disciples had enquired in verse 4), Jesus described in verse 14a as **'the desolating sacrilege set up where it ought not to be',** which, in the corresponding statement in Luke's Gospel (Lk. 21: 20), is characterized as 'Jerusalem surrounded by armies'. When, therefore, the Christians in Jerusalem

saw the Roman legions investing their city, any notion that God might intervene miraculously to preserve it, as He did in the days of Hezekiah, was to be ejected from their minds, since precisely this was the divine sign of the proximity of the time when both city and temple would be razed to the ground. The Christians' resort, rather, on witnessing the commencement of this investment taking place, was, without delay, to **flee to the mountains** (14b); and this, in the event, the Christians at Jerusalem, because of Jesus' words here, did, hastening away just in time to the town of Pella, on the east side of the river Jordan. In verse 28, Jesus explained that just as one can foretell the approach of summer when one sees that **the fig tree puts forth its leaves,** the Christians in Jerusalem would be able to foretell the time of the sacking of their city, and the dawning of the glorious era beyond, when they saw **these things taking place** (29). That the statements in verses 24–27 could conceivably furnish an apocalyptic description of the Fall of Jerusalem and its sequel, will, of course, by very many, be hotly contested; but there is considerable evidence, nevertheless, that this is so. The apocalyptic language of verses 24 and 25 is remarkably similar to that used (i) in Isa. 13: 10, to describe the judgment of God upon Babylon, (ii) in Isa. 34: 4, to describe the judgment of God upon Edom, (iii) in Ezek. 32: 7, to describe the judgment of God upon Egypt, and (iv) in Jl 2: 10, to describe the judgment of God upon Israel. **'The Son of man coming in clouds'** (26), a description, so it is here maintained, of His acting in judgment against Jerusalem, is closely parallel to that provided in Isa. 19: 1 of God's acting in judgment against Egypt. It is to be recalled that Jesus had denoted the destruction of the Jewish State as a divine 'coming' earlier that same day, in His statement of Mk 12: 9. The assertion of verse 27 may relate to the increased impetus of world-wide evangelism which would follow the events of A.D. 70 (cf. the language of Ps. 22: 27 and Isa. 45: 22). This would harmonize with Jesus' affirmation of Mk 9: 1 (on which see notes). Verses 32 to 37 relate to Jesus' second advent. Because the date when this would occur was undisclosed (32), the paramount necessity for Christians with regard to it was to be watchful (35). To **watch,** therefore, was the injunction Jesus gave, not only to Peter, James, John and Andrew, but to Christians universally (37).

VI. THE PASSION (14: 1–15: 47)
The plot to arrest Jesus (14: 1–2). (Parallels: Mt. 26: 3–5; Lk. 22: 1–2.)
Previous attempts by the Jewish religious leaders to have Jesus arrested and killed have

been noted in this Gospel in 3: 6 and 12: 12. Now they made their final attempt (1), resolving nevertheless that this should not occur **during the feast** (2), lest this might provoke violent opposition on the part of supporters of Jesus who would be coming to Jerusalem from Galilee to observe the Passover.

The anointing of Jesus' head (14: 3–9). (Parallel: Mt. 26: 6–13; cf. Jn 12: 1–7.)

Simon the leper (3), who was entertaining Jesus on this occasion, must have been a healed leper, and quite probably it was Jesus who had healed Him. The woman who anointed Jesus' head did so as a spontaneous expression of her conception of the honour which was due to Jesus. **Nard** was a **costly** unguent made from a rare Indian plant; and the **jar** in which it was contained was probably a globular perfume-flask without handles. The woman snapped off the flask's neck, and poured, evidently, its whole contents over Jesus' head. On her being criticized for her action (4), Jesus replied that she was not to be blamed, for she had seized a unique opportunity of doing honour to Him (7), adding a cryptic remark (8), which may, possibly, have been to the effect that if it was not going to be wasteful for costly spices to be lavished on Him when, so shortly, He was to be buried, neither was it wasteful for this woman to have thus anointed Him now.

The betrayal agreement (14: 10–11). (Parallels: Mt. 26: 14–16; Lk. 22: 3–6.)

Judas's motive in betraying Jesus to the authorities was, in part, avarice (Mt. 26: 15), though it may also have been due to his having become embittered at the failure of Jesus to implement His consciousness of being the Messiah in a political manner. Ultimately, however, the act was inspired by Satan himself (Lk. 22: 3; Jn 13: 2, 27). The offer which Judas made to the chief priests (10) was that he would give them information as to when an opportunity would present itself for them to arrest Jesus in the absence of a crowd of people.

The preparation for the Last Supper (14: 12–16). (Parallels: Mt. 26: 17–19; Lk. 22: 7–13.)

It was more probably by means of Jesus' supernatural knowledge than on account of a prior arrangement that Jesus was able to tell His disciples that, on entering Jerusalem, **a man carrying a jar of water** would meet them (13; cf. 11: 2, on which see notes). The man would be readily identifiable because whilst men in the east carried wine-skins commonly, it was unusual for them to carry water-jars, this being regarded as a woman's work. Tradition has it that the room where the Last Supper was eaten was in the home of John Mark, in which event **the householder** (14) may well have been

Mark's father, who, nevertheless, seems to have died prior to the occurrence of the events of Ac. 12: 12. The two disciples, having **prepared the passover** (16) (i.e. the lamb, the wine, the bitter herbs, etc.), returned to Jesus.

The partaking of the Last Supper (14: 17–21). (Parallels: Mt. 26: 20–25; Lk. 22: 14–18; Jn 13: 21–30.)

As proof that Judas' treachery did not take Jesus by surprise, Jesus announced, during their participation of this meal, that one of the apostles would betray Him (18). Mark's record, however, does not describe Jesus' method of identifying the traitor to any of the others, but merely relates Jesus' statement to the effect that it was one of those who was dipping bread with Him into the common bowl placed centrally on the table, and containing a kind of fruit purée, known as the *harōseth* (20). Jesus added that although the traitor's treachery was foretold in the OT (verse 18 contains an echo of Ps. 41: 9, which in Jn 13: 18 is directly quoted), the traitor was not thereby absolved from personal responsibility for his deed (21).

The institution of the Lord's Supper (14: 22–25). (Parallels: Mt. 26: 26–29; Lk. 22: 19; 1 C. 11: 23–26.)

During the meal's course, Jesus gave thanks to God for a loaf of bread, and then broke off from it a piece for each of the disciples, and handed it to them, telling them that this represented the fact that, so shortly, His body would be broken (22). He then took a common cup containing wine, and passed it round the company, bidding them each drink from it (23), and telling them that it represented the blood which, on the morrow, He would shed in order to inaugurate the **covenant** of Jer. 31: 31–34, promising to those participating in it divine forgiveness and fellowship with God, just as the covenant of Exod. 24: 8 had been ratified by sacrificial blood (24). This, Jesus added, would be the last occasion of His drinking wine before doing so during the Messianic banquet of the future age (25; and see notes on 6: 30–44).

The walk to Gethsemane (14: 26–31). (Parallels: Mt. 26: 30–35; Lk. 22: 39; Jn 18: 1.)

After the company had sung a hymn (26) (i.e. the second part of the Hallel, consisting of Pss. 115–118), Jesus led out the disciples to the Mount of Olives where He had been spending the previous nights (Lk. 21: 37). Quoting to them on the way the words of Zech. 13: 7, He told them that they were about to become like a scattered flock of sheep, because of the slaughter of Himself their Shepherd (27), but that after His resurrection they would find Him in Galilee and would all be re-united (28). On

Peter protesting his fidelity to Jesus (29), Jesus predicted to him his threefold denial of Him (30).

The agony in the garden (14: 32–42). (Parallels: Mt. 26: 36–46; Lk. 22: 40–46.)
The 'Mount of Olives' was so called because of the groves of olive trees on its slopes. **Gethsemane** (32), which means 'an oil press', was evidently the site where the oil was crushed out of the olives. Jesus brought here His disciples, and in the hearing of Peter, James and John (33), He prayed that if it was consistent with the fulfilment of God's purposes, the suffering awaiting Him (denoted here symbolically as 'this cup'; cf. notes on 10: 38) might be averted (35, 36). But soon the disciples fell asleep (37), sleeping in the presence of Jesus' agony, as they had slept in the presence of His glory (Lk. 9: 32). Having found them sleeping three times (40, 41), waking them up finally, Jesus said to them: 'Enough of this!' (RSV: **'It is enough'**); and seeing then the approach of Judas and those who had hired him, He said: 'Let us advance to meet them' (42; RSV: **'Let us be going'**).

The arrest of Jesus (14: 43–52). (Parallels: Mt. 26: 47–56; Lk. 22: 47–53; Jn 18: 2–12.)
Judas, who had left the room of the Last Supper earlier than the rest (Jn 13: 30), and had established contact thereupon with the servants of the chief priests, in order now to guard against the possibility of their arresting the wrong man in the darkness, had told them that the person to be arrested was the one whom he would **kiss** (44). For a disciple to greet his teacher as 'Rabbi' (45, margin), and kiss him, was a common practice; but Judas, despicably, used these tokens of love as an instrument of betrayal. Further information as to what happened at this juncture is given in Jn 18: 4–9. On Jesus being **seized** (46), one of His disciples (*viz.* Peter, Jn 18: 10, who must have been bearing one of the 'two swords' mentioned in Lk. 22: 38), endeavouring with his sword to cleave the skull of one of Judas' rabble, merely succeeded in severing his ear (47) (which Luke alone records Jesus to have subsequently restored to him). Jesus drew His captors' attention to their failure to try to arrest Him while He was peaceably engaged in teaching people in the Temple (48, 49), desiring them to realize that it was their cowardice (verse 2) which had impelled them to act in this way. The disciples then fled (50; cf. verse 27). No hint is given of the identity of the **young man** mentioned in verses 51 and 52. Because of that, and of the fact that this appears on the surface such a trivial and pointless episode to relate in the middle of such a solemn story, it has been plausibly suggested that Mark is here placing on

record how he personally figured in this scene. If this was so, it may have been the case that when Jesus and His disciples had left his house (see notes on verse 14), Mark removed his outer garment and retired for sleep, but was aroused shortly afterwards by a messenger who acquainted him of the treachery of Judas. Without delaying to put on his outer garment Mark rushed to Gethsemane to try to warn Jesus of this situation, but arrived after the arrest had occurred. On catching up with Jesus and His captors he was himself assaulted, but escaped, though with the loss of his solitary piece of clothing.

The examination of Jesus by Caiaphas (14: 53–65). (Parallels: Mt. 26: 57–68; Lk. 22: 54, 63–71; Jn 18: 24.)
Jesus was led by His captors to the palace of the **high priest** (53), Caiaphas, who held office from A.D. 18 till A.D. 36. Here He was arraigned before the **council** (55), i.e. the Sanhedrin, which was the supreme judicial authority in Israel, and consisted of seventy-one members, and was presided over by the high priest, though it is possible that at this night session, only a proportion of them were present. Sorely as these men thirsted for Jesus' death, they were unwilling to assassinate Him, for such an action, inevitably, would have resulted in a riot, followed by repressive measures by the Romans. Their lust to have Jesus killed, therefore, they had to endeavour to gratify by means of the machinery of the law. But they could not, of themselves, inflict on Him capital punishment, having been deprived of this power by their Roman overlords (Jn 18: 31). They were allowed, nevertheless, to carry out a preliminary examination of those they detained by way of preparing the way for such to be formally tried before the Roman procurator. In this instance, however, the Sanhedrin found great difficulty in framing against their prisoner a valid charge, owing to the conflicting evidence presented by the witnesses (36). Even the recollection of Jesus' statement of Jn 2: 19 (58), proved unavailing (which assertion, clearly, was intended to be understood not literally, but as a prediction of His own death and resurrection). Ultimately the high priest, knowing of Jesus' claim to be the Messiah, asked Him outright: **'Are you the Christ?'** (61). Jesus replied in the affirmative, and, applying to Himself the words of Ps. 110: 1 and Dan. 7: 13, asserted in effect that though He was now being judged by them, the day would arrive when they would be judged by Him. Caiaphas was not concerned to test the truth of Jesus' claim to be the Messiah. Sufficient was it for him that a charge had now been established which could be represented to

the procurator in a political form, namely as a claim on Jesus' part to be the king (in opposition to Caesar) of the Jewish people (cf. 15: 2, 32; Lk. 23: 2). Jesus' affirmation, therefore, was pronounced 'blasphemy' (64), and He was unanimously deemed deserving of the death sentence. He was subjected thereupon to gross physical abuse and buffoonery (65).

Peter's denial of Jesus (14: 66-72). (Parallels: Mt. 26: 69-75; Lk. 22: 55-62; Jn 18: 15-18, 25-27.)

The high priest's palace was built around a **courtyard** (54, 66). The reason why Peter was enabled to enter it is stated in Jn 18: 15, 16. **One of the maids of the high priest** had previously seen Peter in Jesus' company; but Peter denied both to her and then twice to **the bystanders** (69, 70) that he had ever been associated with Jesus, deigning on the final occasion **to invoke a curse on himself** (71) should his statement be untrue. Peter's lapse was followed by his utmost penitence (72).

The trial of Jesus by Pilate (15: 1-15). (Parallels: Mt. 27: 1-2, 11-26; Lk. 23: 1-25; Jn 18: 28-19: 16.)

Early the following morning the Sanhedrin met a second time (1) to confirm their decision of the previous evening (14: 64). Thereupon they arraigned Jesus before Pilate, who was the fifth Roman procurator of Judea, and held office from A.D. 26 till A.D. 36. Pilate had come to Jerusalem from his normal residence in Caesarea, so as to endeavour to keep order during the Passover period. Knowing that Pilate would only concern himself with charges against people of a political nature (see notes on 14: 61), the Jewish authorities accused Jesus before him of claiming to be **'king of the Jews'** (2). Jesus' reply to this charge is given more fully in Jn 18: 34-37. When, furthermore, Jesus was accused **of many things** (3; Lk. 23: 2), He made no reply (5; Isa. 53: 7). But Pilate well knew that the real reason why the Jewish leaders had arraigned Jesus before him was their jealousy of His popularity and influence (10).

Barabbas, probably, was a Jewish nationalist who had been involved in a brush with the Romans in which fatalities had occurred (7). His supporters begged Pilate to release him (8) in accordance with his custom of releasing at Passover-time a prisoner of their own choice (6). The desire of Pilate was to release Jesus; but the priests inflamed the Jews who were present (who must have been the Jerusalem mob rather than the pilgrims from Galilee who were loyal to Jesus), to cry for Jesus' crucifixion (11). The consequence was that although Pilate believed Jesus to be innocent (14), in order to ingratiate himself with the Jews (15), he sentenced Jesus

to crucifixion, ordering this to be preceded, as was usual, by the punishment of scourging.

The mockery of Jesus by the soldiers (15: 16-20). (Parallels: Mt. 27: 27-31; Jn 19: 2, 3.) A cruel pastime in which the Roman soldiers would engage themselves periodically, was 'the game of the king'. The form which this took was that somebody would be chosen as 'king' (or should there be a condemned criminal available, he would be used for the purpose). He would be loaded with ludicrous honours—a mock crown, a mock sceptre, a mock robe of office, etc. and finally he would be put to death. This treatment was now accorded to Jesus **inside the palace (that is, the praetorium)** (16), i.e. on the courtyard around which the Antonia castle was built where the troops were stationed, which treatment must have seemed to the soldiers more apt than usual in the case of Jesus, seeing that it was for His alleged claim to be 'king of the Jews' that He had been condemned by Pilate.

The crucifixion of Jesus (15: 21-41). (Parallels: Mt. 27: 32-56; Lk. 23: 26-49; Jn 19: 17-37.) In the North African town of **Cyrene** (21) there was a considerable community of Jews (Ac. 2: 10), so many, indeed, that they had established in Jerusalem their own synagogue (Ac. 6: 9) where they could assemble together when attending the Jewish feasts. **Simon,** presumably, had come from his home-town of Cyrene to visit Jerusalem for the Passover. Because, evidently, the scourging Jesus had received had greatly weakened him, and had rendered Him unable, as was customary, to carry to the place of execution the transverse beam of the cross (see notes on 8: 34), the Romans conscripted Simon (in accordance with their law referred to in Mt. 5: 41), to carry the beam for Jesus. Jesus, together with **two robbers** (27), who had been sentenced previously, was brought to **Golgotha** (22). Here the victims were offered drugged wine, in order to dull their sensibilities, by the women of Jerusalem, who acted thus routinely out of regard for the words of Prov. 31: 6. Jesus, however, refused the opiate (23), both in view of His assertion of 14: 25, and also because of His determination to avoid nothing of the suffering His Father had assigned to Him. The victims would then be stripped, laid on the ground, nailed through their hands to the transverse beam, this being thereupon fastened to the upright stake which would be permanently in position, and to which the victims' feet would then be nailed. To each cross, an **inscription of the charge** against the victim was fastened, that which Pilate had ordered for Jesus reading: 'The king of the Jews' (26), a statement which, very naturally, much offended the Jewish leaders (Jn 19: 21-22). As Jesus suffered, He was taunted by those passing along the near-by road with two of the charges made against Him the previous night, that of threatening the existence of the temple (29; 14: 58), and that of claiming to be the Messiah (32; 14: 62). This mockery of the passers-by, as also Jesus' being stripped of His garments, the piercing of His hands and feet, and His association in His death with malefactors, all occurred in fulfilment of prophecy (Ps. 22: 6-8, 18, 16; Isa. 53: 12). Jesus had been crucified at 9.0 a.m. (25). From noon till 3.0 p.m., the sky became darkened (33), which portent symbolized God's displeasure at what men were doing to His Son. Jesus, aware that His Father had 'made Him to be sin' (2 C. 5: 21), and realizing that His Father, being holy, had been compelled on this account to withdraw from Him His presence while He suffered, cried to Him, in the words of Ps. 22: 1 '**My God, my God, why hast thou forsaken me?**' (34). Experiencing thirst, furthermore (Jn 19: 28), He was offered by the soldiers some of the **vinegar** ('sour wine' NEB) with which they commonly refreshed themselves (36). To the surprise, then, of all who were watching, Jesus, although seemingly so exhausted, **uttered a loud cry** (37), which Jn 19: 30 relates to have been 'It is finished', whereupon He expired. The tearing at that moment of **the curtain of the temple** (38; Exod. 26: 31-33), separating the holy place from the holy of holies, signified both that God had at last fully revealed Himself in the death of Christ, and also that the barrier of sin separating man from God had now been removed, and that the way, therefore, of man's entry into God's presence had been opened up (Heb. 10: 19-22). **The centurion** (39), who was the non-commissioned officer in charge of the execution squad, confessed that Jesus was **the Son of God,** and presumably became a Christian. As mentioned in the margin, there are some translations (such as the 1946 and 1952 editions of RSV, but not the 1962 edition) which prefer the *indefinite* article before **Son.** It is conceivable that a pagan, in order to express his feeling that Jesus was other than merely man, might refer to Him as 'a son of God', though the rendering in the text is much to be preferred, in that the confession of Jesus as **the Son of God** by a Roman was intended, no doubt, as the climax of this Gospel which was written, evidently, for the benefit of Romans in order to substantiate this very truth (1: 1). The women who beheld the crucifixion (40) were those who had accompanied Jesus and His disciples **in Galilee** (41), and had 'provided for them out of their means' (Lk. 8: 3). They included **Mary Magdalene,** who came from Magdala, on the west side of the Sea of Galilee, **Mary the mother of James the younger** (who may have been James the son of Alphaeus, 3: 18), **and Salome,** who, evidently, was 'the mother of the sons of Zebedee' (Mt. 27: 56).

The burial of Jesus (15: 42-47). (Parallels: Mt. 27: 57-66; Lk. 23: 50-56; Jn 19: 38-42.)

The normal custom among the Romans was that the dead bodies of those whom they crucified were left to hang on their crosses till they decayed. It **took courage** (43), therefore, on the part of Joseph of Arimathea to ask from Pilate **the body of Jesus.** This, however, he did that same **evening** (42), and indeed prior to sunset, for there was still time for him to purchase **a linen shroud** (46) before the sabbath began. Arimathea may perhaps be the same as Ramathaim-zophim (1 Sam. 1: 1), the birthplace of Samuel, the exact location of which is uncertain, though situated to the north of Jerusalem. Traditionally, however, it is identified with Ramleh, a town near the modern Tel Aviv. Joseph was **a respected member of the council** (i.e. the Sanhedrin), co-operating with whom in the burial of Jesus was another councillor, Nicodemus (Jn 3: 1; 19: 39). Joseph was **looking for the kingdom of God** (i.e. anticipating the fulfilment of Israel's Messianic hopes), and his being called in Jn 19: 38 'a disciple of Jesus' shows that he had been regarding Jesus as the Messiah. His effecting Jesus' burial, doubtless, was undertaken as much on account of his personal loyalty to Jesus, as out of consideration of the law of Dt. 21: 23, which required that those who had been hanged should be buried before nightfall, so as to prevent the defilement of the land. Joseph, who obviously had no inkling that Jesus would rise again, wrapped Jesus' body in the linen shroud, into the folds of which aromatic spices had been inserted (Jn 19: 39-40), and he placed it in a niche within an artificial cave which he had excavated for his own burial (Mt. 26: 60). A stone was rolled into position to form the tomb's door.

VII. THE RESURRECTION (16: 1-20)

The women's visit to the sepulchre (16: 1-8). (Parallels: Mt. 28: 1-8; Lk. 24: 1-12; Jn 20: 1-10.)

Despite the way in which womenfolk tended to be belittled in contemporary Jewish thought, in the story of Jesus' resurrection they figured very prominently. That Jesus' body had been anointed by Nicodemus immediately after His death is stated in Jn 19: 39-40. But **Mary Magdalene, and Mary the mother of James, and Salome** (1) desired to share in this anointing; and so **when the sabbath was past** (i.e. after sunset on the Saturday evening), they purchased the necessary spices, and then early on the Sunday morning they proceeded to the tomb (2). The purpose of their visit shows how completely they disbelieved that Jesus would rise again. Their question, furthermore, as to who would roll away the stone from the tomb's entrance (3) demonstrates their ignorance of the tomb having been sealed and guarded (Mt. 27: 62-66). The **young man** (5) whom, in the event, they saw in the tomb was clearly an angel, and he told the women to notify **the disciples and Peter** that, in accordance with the instructions given to them three days previously (14: 28), they were to proceed to Galilee, where the risen Jesus would meet them. Evidently Jesus wanted to show Himself as risen again to as many of those who had believed in Him as was possible, and since most of these were in Galilee where the major part of Jesus' ministry had been carried out, that was where He planned that the great manifestation of Himself should occur (see Mt. 28: 16-17; I C. 15: 6). Jesus' specific mention of Peter was in order to re-assure him that despite his denial of Him, he had not been cast off as a renegade. This encounter with the angel startled the women, and they **fled from the tomb,** and temporarily said nothing to anyone (8), though Mt. 28: 8 and Lk. 24: 9 indicate that they conveyed the message to the eleven subsequently.

Jesus' post-resurrection appearances and ascension (16: 9-20). (Parallels: Mt. 28: 9-20; Lk. 24: 13-53; Jn 20: 11-29; Ac. 1: 9.)
From the fact that verses 9-20 are relegated in the RSV to the margin, it is not to be deduced that they are no part of the inspired Word of God. The reason for their being relegated to the margin is that it is unlikely that they were written by Mark himself, the evidence for this inference being their considerable dissimilarity from the rest of this Gospel both as regards vocabulary and style, and especially their absence from the oldest and best extant manuscripts of the Gospel. It is unlikely, however, that Mark could have intended terminating his work with the banal anti-climax of the statement of verse 8. The likelihood, therefore, is either that Mark was prevented through death from consummating his story, or else that he finished it, but that the concluding column of his scroll (which would form the scroll's outer covering), was accidentally destroyed before ever it had been copied. It would not be unreasonable to suppose that such a final column contained (i) the story of an appearance of the risen Jesus to the frightened women mentioned in verse 8, which calmed their fears, and

enabled them to go with confidence to the disciples and proclaim to them the fact of Jesus' resurrection; (ii) such a story as that of Jn 21, in which, when the disciples were in Galilee (14: 28), Jesus appeared to them, restoring to Peter (16: 7) his faith and status among the apostles.

Taking the place of this, however, there has been attached to the end of Mark's record a brief account written by a Christian author, perhaps of the early second century, providing a brief summary of what took place subsequent to Jesus' resurrection. Another early Christian writer provided an even briefer summary still of these events, and this, included also in the RSV margin, was originally written as an appendix to the Gospel. The longer of these summaries describes (i) an appearance of Jesus to Mary Magdalene (9-11; cf. Jn 20: 11-16); (ii) an appearance of Jesus to the two travellers on the way to Emmaus (12, 13; cf. Lk. 24: 11-35); (iii) an appearance of Jesus to the apostles (14; cf. Lk. 24: 36-49; Jn 20: 19-29). Emphasis is laid on the disciples' disbelief in Jesus' resurrection despite repeated eye-witness testimony to its having occurred (11, 13, 14). Jesus commissioned the disciples to preach the gospel to people of all nations (15; contrast Mt. 10: 5, 6); and He ordained that such as had believed the gospel should be baptized (16). He listed a variety of signs by which the gospel would be attested (17, 18); but 'whether or no such evidential manifestations were intended to be continuous in the life of the Church must be considered in the light of the rest of the New Testament' (Cole).

Jesus' ascension to heaven is then described and His session thereupon at God's right hand (19; cf. Ps. 110: 1). But the final emphasis of the book is on the Lord Jesus still being spiritually present with His apostles, and confirming as authentic the message they preached by the effecting of such signs as those mentioned in verses 17 and 18 (20; cf. Heb. 2: 3, 4).

BIBLIOGRAPHY

On the Greek Text

CRANFIELD, C. E. B., *The Gospel according to St. Mark.* CGT (Cambridge, 1959; 2nd. edn. 1963).

TAYLOR, V., *The Gospel according to St. Mark.* Macmillan New Testament Commentaries (London, 1952).

On the English Text

COLE, R. A., *The Gospel according to St. Mark.* TNTC (London, 1961).

HUNTER, A. M., *The Gospel according to St. Mark.* Torch Commentaries (London, 1948).

NINEHAM, D. E., *St. Mark.* Pelican Gospel Commentaries (Harmondsworth, 1963).

THE GOSPEL ACCORDING TO
LUKE

LAURENCE E. PORTER

Authorship

All the Gospels are anonymous in the form we have, but ancient traditions have attributed authors to them. In the case of Luke this ascription goes back to the second century; and only a negligible minority of modern scholars would deny the common authorship of the third Gospel and Acts. The two prefaces to Theophilus state the fact, the general similarity of style and outlook supports it. From Eusebius in the early fourth century to the most recent writings of NT scholarship, identity of authorship and the unity of the work have been assumed as a settled matter. So C. K. Barrett (*Luke the Historian in Recent Study*, 1961, p. 8 n.), speaking of 'Luke-Acts', says: 'the term is inelegant, but I shall use it . . . because it emphasizes that the Gospel and Acts are together one book'.

Though there is perhaps not quite such unanimity as to the identity of the author of this double work, it seems reasonable to accept the evidence of the 'we-passages' in Acts. These are identical in style with the rest of Acts, whose author therefore must have been one of Paul's travelling companions, and a process of elimination among those mentioned in Acts and in the salutations of the Letters leaves a very small group of names, of whom Luke, designated by tradition, is the only one who will fit. Finally a strong point in favour of the Lucan tradition is that he was so unimportant a person in the early Church that it is difficult to see why his name should have become attached to it except for the reason that he actually wrote it.

If the ascription is correct, who was this Luke? He is the 'beloved physician' of Col. 4: 14; one of Paul's most faithful followers (2 Tim. 4: 11). Many doctors in his day were slaves who had succeeded in obtaining their liberty; one interesting suggestion is that were Luke one he might well have found it easier to earn a living as a ship's doctor than as the first-century equivalent of a general practitioner. (This view does not, however, find favour among scholars in general.) Further than this it is difficult to go, except that everything

points to his being a Gentile. Eusebius, following the second-century author of the anti-Marcionite prologue to this Gospel, says that he was a native of Antioch in Syria; the prologue also says that the Gospel was written in 'Achaea'. What is clear from the Acts record is that he had connections with Philippi. Sir William Ramsay (*St. Paul the Traveller and the Roman Citizen*) suggested that Luke was the 'man of Macedonia' of Ac. 16: 9; though he modified this view in the 14th edn. (1920), p. xxxviii.

Date

The date is much more difficult to determine. There are three main views. The one probably most widely held today is that Lk. was written about A.D. 80-85. The keystone of the argument in its support is that it must have been written after the Fall of Jerusalem in A.D. 70, since Luke changes Mark's prediction: 'when you see the desolating sacrilege (AV, the abomination of desolation) set up where it ought not to be' (Mk 13: 14) to 'when you see Jerusalem surrounded by armies' (Lk. 21: 20). The 'desolating sacrilege' is a vague term with little meaning except what it derives from the imagery of the book of Daniel. Armies are actually what was seen, therefore Luke must have written after the event. So B. H. Streeter says: 'Seeing that in A.D. 70 the appearance of Antichrist did *not* take place, but the things that Luke mentions *did*, the alteration is most reasonably explained as due to the author's knowledge of these facts' (*The Four Gospels*, 1924, p. 540).

But this takes no account of the possibility that Jesus did in fact refer to the coming Fall of Jerusalem in both these ways. If the Marcan version recalls Daniel, the Lucan echoes Zech. 14: 2, while the reference to armies is so vague and general that it is hardly necessary to see in it the description of an event that had occurred.

Others have tried to put the date as late as somewhere around A.D. 100, because of the mention of some events recorded also by Josephus in his *Antiquities* (A.D. 93-94). But Luke's historical data differ from Josephus's, a difficulty which Streeter (p. 557) meets by the suggestion that Luke had heard Josephus lecture, and was writing from lecture notes rather than from actual reading.

A third view is that the Gospel was actually written before A.D. 70. Acts ends with Paul still alive, and if this is because Luke stopped when he had brought the story up to date, Acts must have been written before about 65-66, and Luke (the 'first book' of Ac. 1: 1) earlier still. Furthermore there is little sign in Luke or Acts of the influence of the Pauline letters, a pointer to an early date before they had gained general currency.

It is clear that Luke knew and used Mark, which it must therefore postdate, but a date about A.D. 60 is quite possible for the third Gospel. In short, a date in the first half of the 60s of the first century would fit in with the evidence as well as the more generally accepted A.D. 80, and indeed with much of the evidence, better.

Sources and Structure

Twentieth-century NT scholarship has examined closely the sources of information on which the evangelists drew (see the article on *The Fourfold Gospel*). Both oral and written traditions lie behind the texts as we have them; of the latter suffice it here to say that there is general agreement that in the case of Lk. there are three main groups of sources:

1. The Gospel of Mark.
2. Certain material not included in Mk, which Lk. has in common with Mt., and called 'Q' by modern scholars.
3. Other material used by neither Mt. nor Mk; this group includes much of the oral teaching, as well as nativity and childhood stories.

There are various opinions as to how these three strands came to be woven together. Streeter, for instance, thought that the second and third had already been written up to form a Gospel ('Proto-Luke') before Luke came across Mk and incorporated it to give us the third Gospel. Not all scholars would agree with this interpretation of the evidence, but the subject, interesting as it is, lies outside the scope of this essay.

What is important for our purpose is that Mk provides for Lk. not merely a great deal of information, but also a *framework*. Beginning where Jesus' public ministry began, Mark devotes roughly the first half of his Gospel to His going about doing good and preaching the kingdom, and then in his second half shows Him under the shadow of the Cross, then dying and rising again. Luke prefaces to this two chapters of infancy stories, and adds a chapter of post-resurrection appearances and

the Ascension (mentioned neither by Mt., Jn, nor the 'short ending' of Mk). Luke's account of the Passion includes a considerable amount of matter used by him alone. Between the two halves of the Marcan narrative, he also places a long section of about ten chapters where he sets out in the form of a travel account (see below, pp. 224 f.) a great number of incidents, sayings and especially parables most of which neither Mt. nor Mk records. Included are such familiar parables as the Good Samaritan, the Prodigal Son, and the Pharisee and Tax collector.

Characteristics

The three synoptic Gospels tell substantially the same story, and yet each is quite distinguishable from the others by the way in which the author's own personality is seen in his telling of it. There are several characteristics which give the third Gospel especially an individuality of its own.

1. *It is the universal Gospel.* Says Balmforth (p. 17): 'What begins as a mission to Jews soon includes Samaritans and Gentiles as well'. Luke, a Gentile himself (he is expressly excluded from the 'men of the circumcision' in Col. 4: 11, 14), looks beyond the narrow limits of contemporary Jewish nationalism and prejudice. Christ's family tree is taken back beyond Abraham, the father of the nation, to Adam, the father of the race; and He is a 'light for revelation to the Gentiles' (Lk. 2: 32). A Gentile centurion is commended for faith unmatched in Israel itself (7: 9) and a Samaritan for thanksgiving when cured, alone of ten lepers, the others presumably Jews (17: 16). Most striking of all, a despised Samaritan is the hero of one of the noblest of all the parables (10: 30-35). Luke omits the story of the Syro-Phoenician (Mk 7: 24-30; Mt. 15: 21-28) possibly because it might give offence to Gentile readers (though it should be mentioned also that it is part of the block of 'omitted' material).

2. *It is the Gospel of rejoicing.* 'There is gladness at its beginning—"Behold I bring you good tidings of great joy"—there is gladness in its middle (chap. 15); and there is gladness at its ending when the disciples "returned to Jerusalem with great joy"' (A. M. Hunter, *Introducing the NT*, 1957, p. 53). There is sadness and sternness in plenty, but cheerfulness keeps breaking in.

3. *It is the Gospel for the 'down and out'.* 'Why do you eat and drink with tax-gatherers and sinners?' (5: 30) ask the Pharisees, and the whole Gospel might serve as the answer of the Son of Man who 'came to seek and to save the lost' (19: 10), fallen women, hated tax collectors and even a dying thief. The tax collectors were

not poor, of course, but socially they were despised and shunned. Jesus was born of poor parents, and it is the visit of humble shepherds rather than of oriental sages that captured Luke's imagination. The couplet from Mary's song:

He has filled the hungry with good things,
And the rich he has sent empty away,

finds its echo in numerous stories of Jesus' concern for the needy, and in parables like the rich fool and Lazarus and the rich man.

4. *It is the woman's Gospel.* One of the chief features of Luke's presentation of the Gospel is his respect and reverence for womanhood. The stories of the pregnancy of Elizabeth and of Mary, so difficult to tell, are related with a grace and delicacy that invest them with a singular atmosphere of purity. The glory of motherhood is here depicted with as much insight as is the tragedy of motherhood seen in the widow of Nain. Luke also delights to tell of the women who cared for Jesus (8: 1-3) and were faithful right to the end (23: 25).

5. *It is the Gospel of the supernatural.* It is true that all the Gospels have a large supernatural element; indeed they must have since their theme, the incarnation, is a supernatural event. But in two ways, Luke shows a particular interest. First, there is his interest in angels. Mt. and Mk record the appearance of angels after the temptations and accompanying the resurrection; Luke in addition has a series of such appearances in his first two chapters. Secondly he often shows a professional interest in the *details* of the miracles of healing. It is of interest that of the miracles recorded only in one of the Gospels, Lk. has more than any other.

6. *It is* par excellence *the Gospel of prayer.* As J. G. S. S. Thomson says (*The Praying Christ*, 1959, p. 11): 'of the four evangelists, Luke is the one who places greatest emphasis on prayer . . . the main lesson he is concerned to teach is the necessity for the soul's communion with God. He enforces that lesson by showing Christ as the believer's example in prayer. For instance, he shows how our Lord turned to the Father in prayer at all the great crises of His life—at His baptism, before the call of the Twelve, before Peter's confession, at the Transfiguration, and the Crucifixion. It is also Luke who supplies us with the parables of the importunate Friend and the Pharisee and the Publican, and with a treatise on prayer which accompanies them'.

Finally, in addition to these special interests of Luke it must be pointed out that he is a literary genius of the first order. He writes in language whose grace survives translation; he has the eye of the artist for detail and the gift of evoking in a few words a whole world of meaning. Ernest Renan was not a believer yet he judged the third Gospel 'the most beautiful book in the world'—*C'est le plus beau livre qu'il y ait.*

ANALYSIS

vii The crucifixion (23: 33-49)
viii The burial (23: 50-56)

IX RESURRECTION AND ASCENSION (24: 1-52)

i The empty tomb (24: 1-12)
ii The walk to Emmaus (24: 13-25)
iii In the upper room (24: 36-49)
iv The ascension (24: 50-52)

I. THE PREFACE (1: 1-4)

The third Gospel begins with a formal prefatory address, balanced in form and classical in idiom, to a certain Theophilus. It is composed of one continuous sentence with six main clauses, the first three balancing the second three: **many have undertaken** (1a) with **it seemed good to me** (3a); **to compile a narrative** (1b) with **to write an orderly account** (3b); **as they were delivered to us** (2) with **that you may know** (4). The vocabulary used is literary; *e.g.*, the Gk. word translated **Inasmuch as,** *epeidēper* (1) is found in the classics but nowhere else in either the NT or the LXX.

The four verses stand in marked contrast with the rest of the Gospel, whose Gk. has a strong Semitic flavour. There he is dependent on his sources, all Semitic in origin; here he is using no source, but probably a literary model; such prefaces are often found in Gk. literature, especially historical writing.

3. for some time past (EVV: 'from the very beginning'): *anōthen*, which in Gk. often means 'from above', is clearly used here in a temporal sense. **most excellent Theophilus:** Theophilus's identity is unknown; he may have been (*a*) an individual of this name; (*b*) a public official addressed pseudonymously; (*c*) a purely symbolic figure, 'Dear to God'. This third is the most unlikely of the three. The designation **most excellent** suggests a high official of perhaps equestrian status; it corresponds to our 'His Excellency'.

The contents of this epistle dedicatory furnish a clue to Luke's purpose in writing. Theophilus has a general knowledge of the faith, but Lk. wants him also to have **an orderly account,** a systematic knowledge, and a written account now that the day of eye-witnesses is passing. He claims that he has himself a sound knowledge of the events; that where his knowledge was limited he has done some research, and that what he is writing will serve as a corrective to some current traditions. His claim is moderate, but as Plummer (*ICC*, p. 2) points out, this is evidence for his honesty. 'A forger would have claimed to be an eye-witness, and would have made no apology for writing.'

II. PARENTAGE AND INFANCY (1: 5-2: 52)

Mt. and Lk. alone of the four Gospels record the infancy of our Lord. Mk and Jn introduce Him at the outset of His public ministry, Jn prefacing his story with a proclamation of His eternal deity and pre-existence. Mt. and Lk. narrate the events leading up to the nativity and the nativity itself, though with significant differences. Lk., for example, sets the birth of Jesus and the events preceding it in parallel with John the Baptist's; Mt. makes no mention of John until his mission begins (3: 1). The experiences and utterances of Mary are also given in considerable detail in Lk.; while Joseph is the main focus of interest from this point of view in Mt.

But perhaps the greatest difference between the two is that, as N. B. Stonehouse points out (*The Witness of Luke to Christ*, 1951, pp. 48 ff.), whereas Mt. relates the story to the OT prophets, 'the revelational message reported by Lk. is a *contemporary* prophetic message'. To herald Messiah's coming, the long silent voice of prophecy speaks again. Stonehouse lists no less than eleven prophetic utterances: (*a*) announcement of the birth of John, 1: 13-17, 19-20. (*b*) announcement of the birth of Jesus, 1: 28-35. (*c*) Elizabeth's salutation to Mary, 1: 42-45. (*d*) Mary's response, the *Magnificat*, 1: 46-55. (*e*) the prophecy of Zechariah, 1: 68-75. (*f*) the angel's proclamation to the shepherds, 2: 10-11. (*g*) the praise of the heavenly host, 2: 14. (*h*) the oracle to Simeon that he would **not see death before he had seen the Lord's Christ,** 2: 26. (*i*) Simeon's prophecy (*Nunc dimittis*), 2: 29-35. (*j*) Anna's prophecy (reported but not quoted), 2: 38. (*k*) our Lord's declaration that He **must be in my Father's house,** 2: 49.

i. The birth of John the Baptist announced (1: 5-25)

Zechariah, an aged priest, is ministering in the Temple when he is interrupted by the appearance of the angel Gabriel bringing the news that his wife, the elderly Elizabeth, will bear him a son. This son will be a prophet in the OT tradition; more, he will be Messiah's forerunner. So astonished is Zechariah that he cannot believe the news; for his incredulity he is stricken dumb until the promise is fulfilled.

5. in the days of Herod: An indication of date. Herod ('the Great') ruled Palestine and part of Transjordan as king of the Jews from 37 to 4 B.C. **Zechariah . . . Elizabeth.** Nothing is known about John's parents except what Lk. tells us. Both were of Aaronic lineage; Zechariah was a priest **of the division of Abijah:** These divisions dated from the division by David of the Aaronic families into twenty-four groups, the descendants of Abijah forming the eighth (1 Chr. 24: 10). Each division did duty in the Temple in rotation twice a year, each period of duty lasting one week.

In a godless age the couple lived lives of exemplary piety, yet were denied the blessing without which pious Jews were regarded as under the disapproval of God—they were childless (see Lev. 20: 20-21; Jer. 22: 30).

9. it fell to him by lot to . . . burn incense: The privilege of burning incense was permitted only once in the lifetime of any priest (cf. A. Edersheim, *The Temple: Its Ministry and Service,* 1874, p. 129); it was accorded, like all priestly activities, by lot. Zechariah was doubtless deeply impressed; at a given signal he had to offer the incense; as its smoke rose the whole concourse of worshippers prostrated themselves in private prayer. He now became conscious of the angelic presence standing **on the right side of the altar of incense** (11), i.e., in the place of authority. It was Gabriel, besides Michael the only named angel in the Bible (cf. Dan. 8: 16; 9: 21).

13-17. The angel's message: (a) Zechariah's prayer has been heard and will be answered. We are not told that he had been praying for a son; such a hope he may have given up long since. His prayer was probably more general, for 'the consolation of Israel' (in the accomplishment of which, had he but known it, his son would play a preparatory part). Plummer (*ICC*, p. 13) suggests that the Gk. *kai*, **and,** before **your wife** (13) implies that the son is an additional blessing. The child's name is to be **John:** 'Jehovah has been gracious'. (b) The promised son will be **great before the Lord,** and will be a perpetual Nazirite, set apart for the service of God. (c) He is moreover to be **filled with the Holy Spirit.** In Lk., apart from the nativity stories (John, 1: 15; Mary, 1: 35; Elizabeth, 1: 41; Zechariah, 1: 67; Simeon, 2: 25 f.), only our Lord Himself is so described (4: 1). (d) He will call men to repentance, as foretold in Mal. 4: 5 f. Messiah is not mentioned, so John's function as His forerunner is implied rather than explicit.

ii. The birth of Jesus announced (1: 26-38) Six months later Gabriel visits Mary, a young countrywoman of Nazareth, betrothed but not yet married to Joseph, an artisan of Davidic descent. She, he says, will conceive; her Son will be the long-awaited Messiah. To her puzzled enquiry, Gabriel replies that conception will be brought about by the supernatural operation of the Holy Spirit. Mary expresses her acceptance of this divine mission. The annunciations to Zechariah and to Mary are very similar. Gabriel greets both (1: 19, 26), both are distressed (1: 12, 29) and reassured by the words **'Do not be afraid'** and the promise of a son (1: 13, 30). Both ask questions (1: 18, 34) and receive answers (1: 19, 34 f.), but while Zechariah hesitates, Mary believes.

26. Nazareth 'lies high on a sharp slope in the Galilean hills. Its altitude is about 1,150 feet. From the summit above the village one looks south across the extensive plain of Esdraelon, west to Mount Carmel on the Mediterranean coast, east to nearby Mount Tabor, and north to snow-capped Mount Hermon (Ps. 89: 12)' (J. Finegan, *Light from the Ancient Past,* 1959, p. 298).

28-37. The angel's message: Mary's Son was to be infinitely greater than John. (a) His name was to be **Jesus,** 'Jehovah is salvation' (31). (b) He would be **great** (32), a title which, unqualified, is usually reserved for God Himself. (c) As heir to David's throne He will reign over God's people (33). (d) His kingdom will be eternal (33). (See 1 Sam. 7: 16; Dan. 2: 44; 7: 14; etc.)

34, 35. Note on the Virgin Birth. The validity of the tradition of the Virgin Birth is often assailed, mainly along three lines of attack:
(a) *Textual.* It is alleged that the NT references are later interpolations not found in the original text.
(b) *Historical.* It is denied that the belief was generally held in the Early Church, even if Mt. and Lk. *did* teach it.
(c) *Philosophical and scientific.* Such an event is held to be contrary to the laws of nature, and therefore impossible.

The subject is fully examined in most commentaries. Geldenhuys deals with it briefly from a conservative point of view (pp. 107 ff.). Balmforth (pp. 111-118) gives a careful and fair-minded exposition of the evidence. A fuller treatment is found in J. G. Machen, *The Virgin Birth of Christ* (New York, 1932).

There can be no doubt that the Virgin Birth is one of the cardinal doctrines of Christian theology, and these objections are completely answerable.

(a) *Textual*. This is not the place for detailed linguistic study, but it can be stated that claims that the text is unsound are not supported by a scrap of evidence. It is significant that a scholar like Dr. Vincent Taylor, who is no conservative in this matter, says that to explain away the difficulties by textual emendation raises more problems than it solves (see Balmforth, pp. 112 f.).

(b) *Historical*. While other NT writers do not mention the Virgin Birth, neither Mk nor Paul had any reasons for mentioning it. Then, as A. E. J. Rawlinson points out (*Christ in the Gospels*, 1944, p. 23), the considerable differences between Mt. and Lk. suggest that the belief 'must go back to a period earlier than that at which the traditions lying behind the two narratives diverged'. Thirdly, it has been suggested that the idea was borrowed from pagan mythology. Legends of virgin births do exist in antiquity, but the strong Jewish colouring of the NT accounts rules out the likelihood of such borrowing.

(c) *Philosophical and scientific*. Our attitude to the scientific possibility of such an event will depend on our general views on revelation, the NT, and the miraculous. If we believe in the deity of Christ and in scripture miracles, we shall no doubt agree with James Denney (*Studies in Theology*, 1910, p. 64): 'Jesus came from God, all the Apostles declare, in a sense in which no other came. Does it not follow that, as two of our evangelists declare, He came in a way in which no other came?'

iii. Mary's visit to Elizabeth (1: 39-56)
As soon as she hears that her elderly kinswoman is pregnant, Mary goes to stay at her home for three months. Elizabeth greets **the mother of my Lord** (43) with clear spiritual insight and complete lack of any jealousy—a trait that foreshadows her son (Jn 3: 30). Mary responds with the hymn of praise beloved in Christian devotion as the *Magnificat*.

A textual point first; some commentators give considerable weight to the reading 'Elizabeth said' for **Mary said** in v. 46, a reading mentioned by NEB in a footnote. The grounds for this support are mainly subjective; AV, RV and RSV do not even mention it in their margins. It is found only in a few Old Latin authorities.

The *Magnificat* is in form a beautiful lyrical poem uttered by a Jewish peasant girl whose cultural background was the OT writings, which supply the very expressions she uses. The main source on which she draws is the song of Hannah (1 Sam. 2: 1-10) to which her canticle corresponds in general outline as well as in various details, though there are echoes of other OT passages, as Leah's utterance (Gen. 30: 13; cf. v. 48) and some psalms (see the references in RSV, RV, etc.). The hymn falls into four stanzas:

(a) vv. 46-48. Mary praises God for His goodness to her.

(b) vv. 49-50. And to all those who fear Him.

(c) vv. 51-53. He succours the oppressed against the oppressor.

(d) vv. 54-55. In the final verses the song of praise ends in peaceful tranquillity.

'This beautiful lyric', says Plummer (p. 30), 'is neither a reply to Elizabeth nor an address to God. It is rather a meditation; an expression of personal emotions and experiences'. It is lyrical in tone not only because it is what Wordsworth declared all lyric poetry to be—the 'spontaneous overflow of powerful feeling' —but also because Mary knew the OT thoroughly, and many portions, especially the more lyrical ones, by heart. Their language became the natural vehicle of her praises.

Her emotion was evoked first of all because the unbelievable had come to pass: she was to be the mother of the Messiah, an honour which Jewesses longed for, but surely scarce dared to hope for. Mary could give no reason why she was chosen to be the recipient of such an honour, but the honour itself is the reason for her rejoicing: **my spirit rejoices in God my Saviour, for he has regarded the low estate of his handmaiden** (47, 48).

This great mercy bestowed on her is the manifestation of His might and His holiness not only to her, but **his mercy is on those who fear him from generation to generation** (50). The days of the oppressors are numbered: **he has scattered the proud in the imagination of their hearts, he has put down the mighty from their thrones** (51-52): This is especially true for His people Israel; what He has promised to Mary, in short, is a pattern of His purpose for His people. 'Perhaps Luke is . . . regarding Mary as the mouthpiece of Israel; through her the chosen people makes thanksgiving . . . God has looked on the humiliation of Mary (who is Sion) and now she is exalted' (Browning, pp. 41-42). Whether or not we agree with typology of this kind, it is clear that Mary saw in her experience the earnest of the fulfilment of God's promises also to His own whose land was in the occupation of alien overlords and who groaned as well under the burdens laid on them by religious leaders with their weight of tradition. Black as things might look, the great Light was about to appear bringing deliverance **to Abraham and to his posterity**, in that day and **for ever** (55).

iv. The birth and circumcision of John (1: 57-80)

Elizabeth's baby is born soon after Mary's departure. A week later he is circumcised amidst the rejoicing of neighbours and kinsfolk. Elizabeth announces that his name is to be John; the father, giving signs of assent, receives again the power of speech. Local interest is intense (65-66) and Zechariah gives utterance to his canticle, the *Benedictus* (67-79).

60, 63. 'His name is John': The name was common in NT days; the neighbours' surprise was due to pious parents choosing a name that was unknown in Zechariah's family.

67-69. The song of Zechariah. The spontaneous inspired utterance of the old man, like that of Mary, is full of the language of Scripture, no doubt the reflection of his long silent meditations on the words of Gabriel in the Temple months before. It is a gathering together of many OT strands, but whereas the *Magnificat* 'breathes a regal spirit . . . the Benedictus breathes a sacerdotal one' (Geldenhuys, p. 92). Many of the OT quotations are naturally from the Psalms, though there are also echoes of the prophets: v. 69, 'the house of His servant David'; v. 76 recalls the prophecy of the forerunner in Mal. 4: 5-6; vv. 78-79 evoke the prophetic picture (Isa. 9: 2; Mal. 4: 2) of the darkest hour before the Messianic dawn.

The last two verses of the *Benedictus*, in fact, set the scene for the advent of Messiah in the next chapter, as the last few verses in Mal. set the scene for His coming recorded in Mt.

80. he was in the wilderness: An ascetic life for John is already foretold in v. 15. It has been suggested that he was associated with the Qumran community of the Dead Sea Scrolls, but this is pure conjecture (see Leaney, *St. Luke*, p. 91; also F. F. Bruce, *Second Thoughts on the Dead Sea Scrolls*, 1956, pp. 128 f.).

v. The birth of Jesus Christ (2: 1-7)

An imperial order that all citizens should report at their own home town for census purposes brings Mary and Joseph from Nazareth to Bethlehem. Mary's Baby is almost due, and is actually born at Bethlehem itself. The impossibility of finding accommodation results in a feeding-trough having to do duty for a cot.

1-5. a decree went out from Caesar Augustus that all the world should be enrolled: This census raises historical difficulties. It is said to be impossible that a *Roman* census was held in the territory of Herod, an allied king, though it is admitted that there is evidence of a census some years later in Egypt, a similar case. **Quirinius was governor of Syria** in A.D. 6, when he held the census of Ac. 5: 37; whether he had already served in this capacity

several years earlier is debatable. But Luke probably means: 'This enrolment was held before Quirinius was governor of Syria'. Again the visit to Joseph's ancestral home town for registration is unusual, though attested for Egypt; Roman censuses were based on residence. Finally, the complete silence of the Roman records on this census is adduced by some as a ground for scepticism. But several authorities of weight (as Plummer, p. 48; Balmforth, p. 125; Finegan, *LAP*, pp. 258 ff.) are prepared to regard the account as historical, while conservative commentators like Geldenhuys (pp. 104-106) argue strongly in favour of it. (See also article, 'The Historical Background'.)

6-7. The details that Luke gives concerning the birth of Jesus build up an impression of poverty. Joseph and Mary appear to be in no position to secure suitable accommodation; they lack so everyday a necessity as a cradle. Later, Joseph will offer the poor man's offering at the Temple presentation (see note on 2: 24).

The date of the nativity. The time of year is not known; December 25 was chosen to establish a Christian festival as an alternative to a pagan festival of the sun at the winter solstice. Balmforth (p. 128) says that nothing as to the time of the year can be inferred from the narrative; Browning, however (p. 45), says that sheep were kept out in the Judaean pastures from March to November. As for the year, this too is uncertain: a *terminus ad quem* is provided by Herod's death in 4 B.C.

vi. The angels (2: 8-20)

Meanwhile, shepherds guarding their flocks in pastures not far away learn from an angelic visitor that Messiah has been born. They hasten to pay their respects, having heard the message confirmed by a great company of the angelic host. When they have seen the Baby, they broadcast the great news.

14. ' . . . and on earth peace among men with whom he is pleased!': The exact meaning of this verse has been much discussed. The AV (and RSVmg) 'good will among men' is based on a variant *eudokia* (nominative) which textually is not so strongly supported as *eudokias* (genitive), 'of good will'. So 'to men of good will' is preferable to 'good will among men'. But who are these 'men of good will'? The important point is that the NT usage indicates that the good will originates from God and not from men. It is 'men of His good pleasure', the objects and recipients of His good will; hence the RSV reading.

15, 17. Note the missionary interest of Luke in the spread of the gospel, **this thing . . . , which the Lord has made known to us** (15).

17. they made known the saying: To a group of simple men God's presence was manifested. They saw His glory shining around them, as Moses had seen His glory in the burning bush, and they were given, as he had been, a message to proclaim.

vii. The circumcision and presentation (2: 21–39)

Joseph and Mary are careful that the requirements of the law should be carried out; circumcision apparently in Bethlehem and purification for which they have to travel to the Temple at Jerusalem. Here they are greeted by two remarkable people, the aged and devout Simeon and Anna, who make prophetic utterance concerning the Child.

21. he was circumcised: The Mosaic law laid down (Lev. 12: 3) that boys should be circumcised at the age of eight days. Nothing is said by Luke of the doctrinal significance of the rite, but as in the case of John it was made the occasion of publicly obeying God in the bestowal of the name He had indicated. **22–24. when the time came for their purification:** In addition to circumcision, Lev. 12: 4-8 prescribed a service of purification 33 days after. The central feature was the offering of a lamb (see also Exod. 13: 2, here quoted in v. 23), or if this were beyond the means of the parents, a pair of turtledoves might be substituted. That this constituted Joseph's offering (v. 24) is further evidence of the family's reduced circumstances. **25. a man in Jerusalem, whose name was Simeon:** All we know of Simeon is what Luke tells here. He was righteous as to the Law, and devout as to his religion; his heart was set upon the Messianic hopes and **the Holy Spirit was upon him.** He had already received a promise that he personally would live to see Messiah's coming; here he is conscious that the hour of fulfilment has come. Simeon and Anna provide evidence that in the last decade B.C. there were still in the Jewish nation men and women in the highest OT tradition.

29–32. *Nunc dimittis.* The old man likens himself to a slave whose duty it has been to scan the horizon for a long-awaited visitor. Now he reports to the slave-master (the Gk. is our word 'despot') that his trust has been fulfilled, and he claims the privilege, his long watch being over, of going off duty.

This canticle, like those of Mary and of Zechariah, is full of OT associations. **thy salvation** (30) is personalized for Simeon in the little Child in his arms: 'The very presence in the world of this babe of Bethlehem, well before his public ministry could be discharged in terms of words and deeds, was acknowledged as the manifestation of the divine action of salvation' (Stonehouse, p. 54). This salvation, set within the context of OT prophetic expectation, was to be universal, **a light for revelation to the Gentiles** (32a; cf. Isa. 49: 6), as well as **for glory to thy people Israel** (32b).

34, 35. Simeon's words to Mary. The prophet then addresses the Babe's mother, telling her that the great honour which was hers would entail suffering also, a warning of whose truth she was already aware, and an indication of the way by which salvation would be accomplished.

36. there was a prophetess, Anna, the daughter of Phanuel: Anna occupies a position in the narrative corresponding to that of Simeon, but while his actual words are recorded, in her case only the fact that she prophesied is reported. **of the tribe of Asher:** Some members at least of the ten tribes are not lost! **she was of a great age:** The question of Anna's age is somewhat obscure. AV suggests that she had been 84 years a widow, RSV that she was 84 years old. The *BFBS Diglot* says: 'The Gk. may mean either 84 years old, or a widow for 84 years' (p. 9 n.).

39. they returned into Galilee, to their own city, Nazareth: It is not easy at first to harmonize Luke's account of the immediate post-infancy events with Mt.'s, but it is not impossible. A discussion of the problem will be found in the parallel section in Mt.

viii. Childhood and visit to Jerusalem (2: 40–50)

After the extraordinary events accompanying His infancy, our Lord's boyhood and young manhood are passed in obscurity. Only two things are recorded, His visit to the Temple at twelve, and His physical and spiritual growth (vv. 40, 52).

41. Now his parents went to Jerusalem every year at the feast of the Passover: The Jew was enjoined (Exod. 23: 17; Dt. 16: 16) to journey to Jerusalem for each of the great feasts (Passover, Pentecost, Tabernacles), but it seems clear that by the first century, even for Palestinian Jews, custom had often reduced the observance to one annual journey. **42. twelve years old:** The Jewish boy became a 'son of the commandment' at thirteen. According to Edersheim (*The Life and Times of Jesus the Messiah*, 1883, i. 235 and note) the legal age was customarily anticipated by one or even two years in the matter of going up to the Temple. Jesus simply accompanied Mary and Joseph. **46, 47.** Temporarily lost sight of, Jesus was found in the Temple, engaged in questioning the assembled rabbis about the law. At festival times rabbis found appreciative audiences for their instruction in the Temple courts, as at a later date Jesus Himself did (19: 47). On this occasion He was found sitting at the feet of such rabbis. **48–50.** When the boy was found, His mother with gentle reproof asked why He had caused them all this anxiety. His reply indicates that He was conscious already of the divine mission that lay before Him: **I must be in my Father's house.** 'He was the Son of the Father', comments J. N. Darby, 'though abiding God's time for showing it'.

ix. The silent years (2: 51-52)

After this remarkable revelation of intellectual alertness and spiritual awareness at so early an age, a veil is again drawn over the life of our Lord in His family at Nazareth until the beginning, eighteen years later, of His public ministry.

52. The general summary of v. 40 is repeated, with the additional information that other people recognized His character; in v. 40 **the favour of God was upon him;** in v. 52 He **increased . . . in favour with God and man.**

III. PREPARATORY ACTION (3: 1-4: 13)

With chapter 3 begins the narrative of the ministry of Jesus at the point where Mark begins his Gospel—the preaching of John the Baptist and the baptism of our Lord.

i. The Ministry of John (3: 1-20)

At a carefully specified point in history (3: 1-2), John startles his countrymen by his preaching, full of the fire and the faithfulness of the oracles of the OT prophets. He calls on them to repent and to make open acknowledgment of their repentance by being baptized, and he gives concrete examples of the sort of effect that should be visible in their manner of living.

1, 2. The six-fold synchronization dates, but only approximately, the ministry of the Baptist (see article, The Historical Background, p. 63).

3-20. Luke gives the fullest account of the ministry of John found in the Synoptics (see notes on Mk 1: 2-8). Mk quotes from Mal. 3: 1 and Isa. 40: 3, and then tells that John, clad in garb reminiscent of Elijah's (2 Kg. 1: 8), baptized in the wilderness, that he preached a 'baptism of repentance for the forgiveness of sins' and predicted the coming of One much greater than himself. Mt. (3: 3-12) omits the Mal. quotation (he includes it at a later point, Mt. 11: 10), but adds a note of urgency in John's preaching: 'the kingdom of heaven is at hand' (3: 2); he also records more than does Mk of John's warnings to his hearers: (a) Addressing them as the offspring of vipers, he urges them that if they wish to escape coming judgment, repentance evidenced by changed

conduct will avail more than the mere fact of their privileged position as sons of Abraham, members of God's chosen people. In Mt. 3: 7 it is the Pharisees and Sadducees who are so addressed.

(b) This prophetic message calling for personal righteousness is reinforced by an apocalyptic note of urgency. Time is short; 'the axe is laid to the root of the trees' (Mt. 3: 10; cf. Lk. 3: 9).

Luke, drawing, it would seem, on the source which he has in common with Mt., makes all these same additions except that he lengthens the quotation from Isa. 40 to include vv. 4-5 as well as v. 3, and that he omits the saying about the nearness of the kingdom and the fact (Mt. 3: 7) that scribes and Pharisees were among the crowd.

On the other hand he adds an interesting passage not found in Mt. or Mk, reporting John's practical suggestions for the implementation of genuine repentance. The people generally (**the multitudes,** 10) were told of the responsibility laid upon them to share with less fortunate neighbours their superfluity of food or clothing. Tax-collectors, universally despised and detested as unpatriotic tools, willingly placing themselves at the service of the Roman overlords or Jewish tetrarchs and as unscrupulous and dishonest extortioners lining their own pockets, were commanded to carry out their duties with scrupulous fairness and honesty. Swaggering and bullying soldiers were to refrain from summary appropriation of the goods of others, and from glib perjury to cover their tracks. It is interesting that there is nothing revolutionary in all this; even the tax-collectors are not ordered to give up their jobs. This is an 'interim ethic'—as it is sometimes called—a code of conduct whilst awaiting the day of the full revelation of the kingdom, when Roman taxes and much else beside will be swept away. A small point worthy of notice is that whereas we assume from the general tone of Mt.'s account (and Mk's also) that John's ministry was centred on one spot, Luke hints at a peripatetic ministry covering a wider area (3). The Fourth Gospel says that John was baptizing at Bethany beyond Jordan (1: 28) and represents him as active later in a district of Samaria (3: 23).

Baptism. The rite of baptism was no new thing. Water is often a symbol of cleansing in the OT, and by this time baptism may have become the mode whereby proselytes to Judaism were ceremonially admitted to their new faith. T. W. Manson (*The Servant-Messiah*, 1953, pp. 44 f.) suggests that John was inviting Jews to confess that by their sins they had forfeited the right to the status of sons of

Abraham, and must make a fresh start just like Gentile proselytes.

19, 20. Luke here records the arrest of John by Herod, not mentioned by Mt. or Mk until they record his execution (see note on 9: 7–9).

ii. The Baptism of Jesus (3: 21–22)
Jesus Himself joins the throng awaiting baptism, and is Himself baptized, whereupon the Holy Spirit comes down and rests upon Him **as a dove**, and a voice is heard from heaven. (See notes on Mk 1: 9–11.)

21. One of the places where Luke alone of the Synoptics records that Jesus **was praying** (see Introduction, Characteristics, 6, p. 205).

22. Luke adds the phrase **in bodily form** to describe the appearance of the dove. Plummer rightly comments: 'Nothing is gained by admitting something visible and rejecting the dove. Comp. the symbolical visions of Jehovah granted to Moses and other Prophets. We dare not assert that the Spirit cannot reveal Himself to human sight, or that in so doing He cannot employ the form of a dove or of tongues of fire' (p. 99). Further, it is intelligible that the Holy Spirit should be manifested in the form of a dove. It accords with the whole testimony of Scripture concerning Him.

iii. The genealogy of Jesus (3: 23–38)
The differences between the two genealogies of our Lord given in the gospels raise a number of important points. See notes on Mt. 1: 2–17.

iv. The Temptation (4: 1–13)
The experience of the Baptism, confirming the mission and Messiahship of Jesus, is followed immediately by the wilderness experience of the Temptation. Impelled into the deserts by the Holy Spirit for a considerable period He there fasts and wrestles with the suggestions of Satan: (*a*) to use His supernatural powers for the satisfaction of His purely material needs by turning stones into bread; (*b*) to attain the mastery of men's hearts by compromising, doing a deal with the Adversary; (*c*) to test the power and willingness of God to protect Him by engaging in a foolhardy escapade, plunging from a 'pinnacle of the Temple'. Resisted with words of Scripture, Satan gives up the contest for a time and withdraws.

Some scholars have seen in the three temptations a reference to contemporary political views. The first temptation is paralleled in the policy of the Herodians, who would keep the people quiescent by doles of food, *panem et circenses*. The aristocratic Sadducees were willing to co-operate with the Roman authorities in order to maintain their own position; the Pharisees pinned their hopes for the fulfilment of their nationalist aspirations on a miraculous intervention of God Himself.

Mk tells the story very briefly, and without specifying the three individual forms the temptations took. His introductory description of the ordeal is more forceful than either Mt.'s or Luke's: 'The Spirit immediately drove Him out into the wilderness'—Mt. and Luke both use the milder verb, **led.**

Mt. and Luke both give a detailed account of the actual temptations, but in a different order (Mt.'s second and third are Luke's third and second respectively). This need not be regarded as a contradiction. It is an intensely spiritual experience that is being described, lasting over a period of six weeks, and it seems reasonable to suggest that the three lines of attack were pursued by the enemy throughout the whole period. Furthermore, while Mt. 4: 2 suggests that the temptations followed the fasting, Mk and Luke both give the impression that fasting and temptation were simultaneous. What is important is to see how, when our Lord's physical resources had been taxed to the full by his fasting and His spiritual wrestling, Satan suggested easier ways to win men's hearts and to fulfil His mission than the way of the Cross that lay before Him.

Whence did the disciples and the evangelists derive their knowledge of this experience? Obviously, it would seem, from the Lord Himself. 'After the Baptism', says A. M. Hunter (*The Work and Words of Jesus*, 1950, p. 38), 'there follows, with psychological fitness, the Temptation . . . . How do we know anything about it? For "forty days"—an oriental round number—He was quite alone. Obviously, the story of the Temptation is a piece of spiritual autobiography told to the disciples by Jesus Himself, told with utter simplicity as a Jewish mother might have told it to a Jewish child. We may be sure that no later Christian would have invented such a story.'

2. for forty days: Maybe an 'oriental round number', as Hunter suggests, but it is interesting that the same expression is used in connection with Moses and Elijah, who both fasted 40 days (Dt. 9: 9; 1 Kg. 19: 8).

3. 'If you are the Son of God, command this stone to become bread': The devil's approach is very subtle. He challenges Jesus not only to satisfy His hunger but to substantiate also His claim to be God's Son. Wm. Manson (p. 37) shows further that to feed His people was one of the signs expected of the Messiah: in Isa. 49: 10 the promise 'they shall not hunger nor thirst' enters into the divine plan of salvation, while in Jn 6: 30 ff. He is challenged to prove His Messiahship by providing bread from heaven as Moses had done. **4. Man shall not live by bread alone:** Quoted from Dt. 8: 3. **5. all the kingdoms of the world . . . :** Although the ruler of this world (Jn 14: 30) may have been in temporary occupation, the **authority** and the **glory** that he offered had already been promised to Messiah and were His for the asking: *Ask of me, and I will make the nations your heritage, and the ends of the earth your possession* (Ps. 2: 8). This promise must have been much in the mind of Jesus since the baptismal Voice had quoted the preceding words: 'Thou art my beloved Son' (Lk. 3: 21; cf. Ps. 2: 7). That which was God's to give, He would not accept from another. **8. You shall worship the Lord your God, and him only shall you serve:** Quoted from Dt. 6: 13. No created being might demand or receive what belonged exclusively to God. AV includes the words, 'Get thee behind me, Satan', but these are omitted from the more recent versions because of lack of textual support in the MSS. It is not a question of whether Jesus actually uttered the words or not; we know from Mt. 4: 10 that He did. They are omitted from RV, RSV, etc., because the evidence that they formed part of Luke's original text is negligible. A later scribe inserted them to make the account harmonize with Mt.'s. **9. the pinnacle of the temple:** An interesting modern view says: 'Most probably at the S.-E. angle of the court of the Gentiles. This point overlooked the Kidron Valley some 100 yards below, and Josephus states that anyone standing there would become dizzy. Thus the words of Satan are particularly relevant: cast Thyself down, for it is written: "He will give His angels charge concerning Thee; they will hold Thee on their hands, for fear that Thy foot shall be crushed against a stone" ' (A. Parrot, *The Temple of Jerusalem*, E.T., 1957, p. 86). But this view involves difficulties: the only point of throwing Himself down would be to gain adherents, which He would not do by throwing Himself down *outside* the Temple area.

9-11. In his third attack, Satan not only returned to the taunt **if you are the Son of God** (cf. v. 3); but reinforced his suggestion also by an OT allusion (to Ps. 91: 11-12). But it is noticeable that he omits from his quotation the words 'in all your ways', thus changing a general rule of life to one particular expediency, and that quite clearly contrary to God's will. **12.** Again our Lord's reply is from Dt., here 6: 16. It is striking that all three of His replies to the tempter should be drawn from a context so much concerned with Israel's being tested by God (Dt. 8: 2) and putting God to the test (Dt. 6: 16) in the wilderness. The Father's

acknowledgment of Him as His Son was sufficient for this true Israelite: He would not **tempt** God by compelling Him to show by a miracle that He meant what He said.

IV. THE RETURN TO GALILEE (4: 14-8: 56)

The account of the Galilean ministry in general follows the framework of Mk, though there are a few non-Marcan passages. The following table shows how the two accounts compare with each other:

Luke	Mark, and other material
4: 14-30	Mk 6: 1-6a—omits the details of the synagogue service, and puts the rejection at Nazareth later than does Luke.
4: 31-6: 19	Mk 1: 21-3: 19—but Mk omits Luke's story of the miraculous draught of fish (Lk. 5: 1-11).
6: 20-49	Not in Mk, but in greater length in Mt.—the 'Sermon on the Mount'.
7: 1-8: 3	Not in Mk, but part in Mt. 8 and 11.
8: 4-18	Mk 4: 1-25.
8: 19-56	Mk 3: 31-35; 4: 35-5: 43.

In short, the contents of Lk. 4: 14-8: 56 fall into four parts:

Non-Marcan —(*a*) 4: 14-30.   (*c*) 6: 20-8: 3.
Mainly Marcan—(*b*) 4: 31-6: 19. (*d*) 8: 4-56.

Luke omits a lengthy passage from Mk after the Feeding of the Five Thousand (Mk 6: 45-8: 26), so the third Gospel does not include the walking on the water, the very important anti-Pharisee 'defilement' passage of Mk 7: 1-23, nor the story of the Syro-Phoenician woman. Scholars have discussed the omission at great length. Some have seen reasons why Luke should prefer not to include some or all of the passages; others (more improbably, perhaps) have thought that Luke's source was a mutilated copy of Mk from which this part was lacking. If, on the other hand, Streeter's view that the material from Mark was added to Proto-Luke (see article on The Four-fold Gospel, p. 98) is correct, Luke will have known how much of Mk he could use and still permit his gospel to fit into a standard papyrus roll.

i. The Arrival in Galilee (4: 14-15)
See notes on Mk 1: 14-15 *ad loc.*

ii. The Synagogue at Nazareth (4: 16-30)
Jesus comes to Nazareth and on the Sabbath attends the synagogue worship. In accordance with custom he is invited to read and comment on the day's lection from the Prophets. He announces that the Messianic promise has now become present fulfilment; it is clear that His hearers are deeply impressed. But when He goes on to say that the Gentiles are to share in

the blessing, as they in fact did even in OT times, mob violence broke out and an unsuccessful attempt was made to murder Him.

This episode, since the time of Augustine, has been assumed to be the same as that recorded in Mk 6: 1-6/Mt. 13: 53-58. If this be so, the question is asked, why did Luke put it at a different stage of the record from the other Synoptists? The whole problem is very carefully discussed by N. B. Stonehouse, *The Witness of Luke to Christ*, pp. 70-76, to which the student is referred. Suffice it here to point out that Luke does not suggest that this incident was the inauguration of the Galilee ministry; on the contrary he mentions (v. 23) that news has already come to Nazareth of what He had done at Capernaum. Stonehouse's summing-up is that 'the activity in Nazareth and in Capernaum are presented as *illustrative* of the preaching and healing ministry of Jesus as a whole'. Geldenhuys (p. 170) comments: 'Because it fits in so well with Luke's scheme, he placed it first, without pretending that it was also chronologically first'.

The scene in the synagogue: An interesting account of the synagogue and its worship is given in Edersheim, *The Life and Times of Jesus the Messiah*, i, pp. 430-450. After an introductory liturgy comprising a series of prayers and 'blessings' (eulogies), there followed a number of set readings from the OT according to a regular lectionary. Readers were designated for the various portions; if there were present a visiting Rabbi or person of distinction, courtesy required that he should be invited to read, perhaps from the *Haphtarah*, the reading from the Prophets, and to give a discourse traditionally ending at times with some reference to the Messianic hopes of Israel.

The Sermon in the Synagogue and its effect: The scene recorded in the Nazareth synagogue follows this pattern. Jesus had been brought up in the town (16) and was already being spoken of as a preacher in Capernaum (23). He was accordingly asked to read the *Haphtarah*. He turned to the opening verses of Isa. 61.

Expounding the passage, He proclaimed that the Messianic prophecy therein was even now being visibly fulfilled. His hearers were deeply impressed, and it seems not unfavourably; they **wondered at the gracious words which proceeded out of his mouth** (22), though there is a note also of incredulous astonishment: **'Is not this Joseph's son?'** (22). But His discourse developed in a way which they did not foresee; when they heard it they were resentful. He said that if they could not believe He was a prophet it was because **no prophet is**

acceptable in his own country (24), and that was why Elijah and Elisha had performed miracles for aliens, though many Jews of the day no doubt had the same needs as Naaman and the woman of Zarephath (25 ff.).

This turn of the message aroused their wrath; One whom they were prepared to listen to as their own equal was making out lepers and Gentiles as superior to them. In their fury the congregation tried to execute summary justice by lynch law. 'Jesus barely escaped with His life. Anyone else would probably have been killed then and there by this fierce and angry mob. But His hour was not yet come . . . . One day He won't "pass through the midst of them" any more. The angry crowds will press in upon Him to do Him to death' (Moorman, *The Path to Glory*, 1960, p. 47).

17, 20. the book: More correctly the scroll, or 'roll' (RVmg). **20. the attendant:** Or chazzan, 'a sort of verger in the Jewish synagogue, who had custody of the sacred books' (*NBD*). He also acted as schoolmaster to the younger children, and during actual worship had the responsibility of seeing that the scrolls were ready at the correct place for the readings. **22. gracious words:** Literally 'words of grace', as RV; not words of favour or mercy so much, but suggestive rather of an attractive and beautiful personality. **23. this proverb:** So also AV; RV has 'parable', Gk. *parabolē*, from a verb meaning to put things side by side, a comparison. In the NT it is used both for a short descriptive story or, as in this case, a simple proverb that 'enlightens the hearer by presenting him with interesting illustrations, from which he can draw out for himself moral and religious truth' (*NBD*). **what we have heard you did:** The allusion is clearly to miracles, of which reports were circulating. The Gospel miracles are regarded not merely as the compassionate acts of the Great Physician, but as the visible signs that the messianic age has dawned. The kingdom of God is not just a reformed moral order realized by human co-operation but a divine intervention. In the OT prophets, signs and miracles are to accompany the coming of the kingdom (*e.g.* Isa. 35: 5-6; Mal. 4: 2, etc.). 'The healing ministry of Jesus as well as the preaching of the kingdom of God', says A. Richardson, discussing this passage, 'is here set forth as the manifestation of the activity of the Spirit, which was to take place at the fulfilment of the time, in the acceptable year of the Lord' (*The Miracle-Stories of the Gospels*, 1941, p. 40). **25, 26.** For **Elijah** and the **widow** of **Zarephath** see 1 Kg. 17: 9 ff. **27.** For the cleansing of **Naaman the Syrian** from leprosy **in the time of the prophet Elisha** see 2 Kg. 5. **30. he**

went away: None of the Gospels records any subsequent visit by our Lord to Nazareth.

iii. A Day of Work (4: 31-41)

After the account of the scene at Nazareth, Luke, following Mk's framework, records our Lord's activity on one Sabbath day at Capernaum, which He appears now to have made His headquarters. In one single Sabbath He teaches in the synagogue, heals a demon-possessed man there, visits Peter's home and cures his mother-in-law, and then after sunset, the Sabbath being over and men entitled to rest after the worship and the necessary labours of the day, He devotes Himself to the healing of the sick and the demon-possessed of the neighbourhood. If His activity be such on the day of rest and even during the hours of rest, what will He not accomplish on a normal 'working' day?

Mk, who omits the Nazareth incident (though there is a possible reference to it later, Mk 6: 1-6), begins his account of the ministry with a series of five incidents where Jesus makes claims to authority which must bring down upon Him the wrath of the vested religious interests; not surprisingly these five stories are followed by five 'conflict' stories, where His authority is challenged. Mark's 'authority' stories are:

(a) 1: 16-20 *Discipleship:* Jesus claims authority to call men to give up their ordinary work to follow Him.

(b) 1: 21-22 *Teaching:* He teaches with His authority, not—like the scribes—with an authority derived from precedent. 'We see the final outcome of this servile secondhandedness in the dreary minutiae of the Talmud' (F. W. Farrar, *Luke*, CBSC, p. 107).

(c) 1: 23-28 *Unclean Spirits:* He uses the authority to exorcize demons.

(d) 1: 29-34 *Disease:* He exercises His authority over sickness and disease, both individual (Peter's mother-in-law) and the general healings after sunset.

(e) 1: 39-45 *Leprosy:* He reveals that His authority extends even to the dreaded leprosy, the seemingly incurable scourge of His day.

Luke omits the first of these episodes, presumably because he is going to deal with the call of the disciples more fully in connection with his story, unrecorded by Mk, of the miraculous draught of fishes (5: 1-11), but the others he relates in terms so similar to Mk's that it seems clear that here Mk was his source. Accordingly, the reader is referred to the notes on Mk 1 for more detailed commentary. The fifth of Mk's stories is found in Lk. 5; those in the present chapter are:

Teaching in the synagogue: Lk. 4: 31-32; Mk 1: 21-22.

Healing in the synagogue: Lk. 4: 33-37; Mk 1: 23-27.

Peter's mother-in-law: Lk. 4: 38-39; Mk 1: 29-31.

General healings after sunset: Lk. 4: 40-41; Mk 1: 32-34.

iv. Travelling and Preaching (4: 42-44)

A brief note tells us that despite an appeal from the inhabitants of Capernaum to stay (how different from the attitude of the people of Nazareth!) Jesus moves further afield and preaches in the synagogues of other towns. See notes on Mk 1: 35-38.

42. An interesting example of the impossibility of fitting the Gospels into schematic pigeon-holes! Luke, as has been already mentioned in the introductory notes, gives us more glimpses of the praying Christ than any of the others, yet here he omits Mk's emphatic point that He went to the wilderness to pray. **44. the synagogues of Judea:** The best MS evidence supports this reading, so also RVmg. But AV and RV following the *textus receptus* read 'of Galilee' which on the surface seems more reasonable. This looks like the attempt of a scribe to correct what he thought an error in what he was copying. In fact, 'Judea' was often used to mean the land of the Jews in a general way, and not merely the province of the name.

v. Miracles and Discourses (5: 1-6: 11)

The outstanding feature of this section is the growing hostility of the Pharisees, consequent upon Jesus' forthright assertions and the success attending His preaching. His authority over nature itself, seen in the miraculous draught of fish, seems to be the final factor that brings Simon and the sons of Zebedee to discipleship; the news of the healing of a leper brings great crowds to hear Him and to be healed. It is at this point that **Pharisees and teachers of the law** appear from **every village of Galilee and Judea and from Jerusalem** (5: 17), apparently to find out exactly what is going on. They find plenty of which to complain: He actually declares a man's sins forgiven, He consorts with tax-gatherers and harlots, He does not enjoin fasting upon His disciples nor does He rebuke them for plucking ears of corn on the Sabbath. He even Himself heals on the Sabbath. All these things constitute offences against the edifice of observances and regulations they have superimposed on the Law of God.

(a) **The miraculous draught of fish (5: 1-11)**
This story, as has already been noted, replaces Mark's simple account of the call of the disciples. It is quite clear that Simon was already a friend of Jesus, who visited his home (4: 38) and preached from his boat (5: 3); in fact Jn 1: 37-42

H*

tells of a meeting during the mission of the Baptist. The call to Simon is described in the Gospels in three successive stages: (i) the original meeting with Jesus (Jn 1: 41) where he received a new name: 'You shall be called Cephas (which means Peter)'; (ii) the call to forsake all and become a disciple (Mk 1: 16-18; Lk. 5: 11): **henceforth you will be catching men;** (iii) the call to apostleship (see below, on Lk. 6: 14).

1. the lake of Gennesaret: The Sea of Galilee (OT, Sea of Chinnereth, NT, Lake of Gennesaret or Sea of Tiberias). The small inland sea through which the Jordan passes in its northern reaches, a centre of the fishing industry in the first century, and surrounded in those times by an almost continuous series of villages and towns like Bethsaida and Capernaum. Today only Tiberias remains, and a few ruins marking the sites of some of the others. 'Changed patterns of commerce have robbed the lake of its focal importance in the life of the region' (*NBD*). **2, 3.** Peter, with the sons of Zebedee (10) were partners in a fishing business with two boats. Jesus sat in Peter's boat to teach the people. This is the first open-air preaching of our Lord that Luke records; hitherto He has preached in the synagogues. **4-7.** A very similar incident is described in Jn 21: 5-11; but the differences in detail are sufficiently noticeable to make it clear that there were two separate incidents. 'There is nothing improbable in two miracles of a similar kind, one granted to emphasize and illustrate the call, the other the recall, of the chief Apostle' (Plummer, p. 147). There is no need to see two differing traditions concerning the same incident. Here, Jesus is in the boat; in Jn He is on the shore; here He tells them to move out into deeper water, there they are simply to fish from the other side of the boat. In Luke's account the net was broken, in the fourth gospel we are specifically told the opposite. **8-10.** Like James and John, Peter was **astonished** at what had happened, but unlike them he was brought by the manifestation of divine power to an acute consciousness of his own unworthiness (cf. Isa. 6: 5; Job 40: 4; etc.). 'The story appears to presuppose a particular intensity in Peter's consciousness of sin' (O. Cullmann, *Peter*, E.T., 1953, p. 68). **10. 'Do not be afraid, henceforth you will be catching men':** Jesus speaks words of peace to the anguished Peter, words which re-echo Jer. 16: 16. **11. they left everything and followed him:** To gather around oneself a band of disciples was the prerogative of the great rabbis; this claim to authority to do the same must have further incensed the Pharisees.

(b) **A leper healed (5: 12-16)**
The last of the series of 'authority' stories: Jesus not only claims but exercises authority over the dreaded leprosy, to men of His day as widely-feared as is cancer in ours. See notes on Mk 1: 40-45 *ad loc.* Luke's account follows Mk's, but is briefer. Both tell how Jesus commanded the healed man to carry out the requirements of the Levitical law (esp. Lev. 13) reporting to the priest for a certificate of cleansing; but even this care to comply with the law did not lessen, in the eyes of our Lord's opponents, the enormity of His offence on the occasions when He healed on the Sabbath.

(c) **Stories of conflict (5: 17-6: 11)**
Luke, drawing on Mk, now records five episodes in each of which the Pharisees and scribes react violently to His claims:
(i) **Concerning the forgiveness of sins** (5: 17-26; cf. Mk 2: 1-12). Four men bring a paralytic friend for healing and, finding it impossible to get near to Jesus otherwise, they let him down through the roof. Recognizing the sick man's spiritual malaise as his most urgent problem, Jesus assures him of forgiveness, only to be accused of blasphemy for so doing. Luke makes two interesting changes of vocabulary: Mk uses the ordinary word for roof (Gk. *stegē*, from a verb meaning 'to cover'), Luke speaks of **tiles,** Gr. *keramos*, cognate with the word for a potter. Some see here a contradiction, but no doubt both words are used in a general sense for the roof. Then for the bed, Mk uses a word meaning a truckle bed usually of wickerwork or light wood carried by beggars, Luke's word simply implies something on which one lies down. Apart from these two words there is little difference between the Lucan account and the Marcan. In v. 24, Luke for the first time refers to Jesus as **Son of man.**

(ii) **Concerning social conventions** (5: 27-32; cf. Mk 2: 13-17). Jesus, having called Levi (=Matthew, see Mt. 9: 9) to be a disciple, accepted an invitation His new follower gave for his former colleagues. To the Pharisees' strictures concerning the company He kept He replies that as **a physician** sought the **sick** for his ministrations, so His place was with the sinners He had come to save, despite artificial conventions.

(iii) **Concerning fasting** (5: 33-39; cf. Mk 2: 18-22). Fasting, Jesus taught when challenged as to why His disciples did not fast, had its place, but not at the wedding breakfast when the bridegroom was present. Mt. (9: 14-17) and Mk follow this saying with two short parables, the patched garment and the new wine in old wineskins; Luke also adds a third: **no one after**

drinking old wine desires new, for he says, 'The old is good' (5: 39).

(*iv*) **Concerning the Law** (6: 1-5; cf. Mk 2: 23-28). Walking through a field on the Sabbath, the disciples pluck and eat ears of corn. To the objections of the Pharisees Jesus replies by quoting an OT case where the letter of the law had yielded place to the spirit of the law in an urgent necessity (1 Sam. 21: 1-6), and by asserting His own claim as Lord of the Sabbath to interpret its law afresh without reference to Talmudic tradition.

(*v*) **Concerning the Sabbath** (6: 6-11; cf. Mk 3: 1-6). In the story of the man with a withered hand Jesus shows again how the law of love must override ritual observances like the Sabbath, as indeed His opponents would override the law if it were a matter of saving a beast belonging to themselves.

Verse 11 summarizes the result of this series of conflicts: **They were filled with fury and discussed with one another what they might do to Jesus.**

For fuller comment on this section (5: 17-6: 11) see notes on Mk 2: 1-3: 6 *ad loc.*

vi. The Appointment of the Twelve (6: 12-16)

Events are now quite definitely leading to action by the scribes and Pharisees, and Jesus must now prepare His followers to continue His work when He is no longer with them. So from among those who have followed Him as disciples He selects and commissions twelve for the greater responsibility of apostleship. Mark gives at fuller length an account of Jesus' purpose in choosing this inner circle from among the number of His followers; Luke omits this, but characteristically prefaces a note that He spent a whole night in prayer before taking the step and making the choice.

13. apostles: From a Greek verb meaning 'to send'. Cf. the English word 'missionary', from a Latin verb with the same meaning. Apostles are men who are sent forth, i.e. commissioned for a particular errand. **14-16.** The list is interesting especially when compared with those given in Mk 3: 16-19; Mt. 10: 2-4; Ac. 1: 13. The order of the names differs slightly in the four lists, but each divides into three quartets, each beginning in all the lists with the same name. The names are:

(*a*) Peter, with Andrew, James and John.
(*b*) Philip, with Thomas, Bartholomew and Matthew.
(*c*) James the son of Alphaeus, with Simon the Zealot, Judas the brother of James, and Judas Iscariot (who is last in all the lists). **16. Judas the son** (RSVmg, 'brother') **of James** (cf.

'Judas not Iscariot' in Jn 14: 22) does not appear in Mt. or Mk; but Thaddaeus (Mk and Mt.) is usually presumed to be the same person. For an interesting study of what information we have on the Twelve, see Wm. Barclay, *The Master's Men* (1959).

vii. The Great Sermon (6: 17-49; cf. Mt. 5-7)

Having come down from the upland retreat where the Twelve have been chosen, Jesus is met in the plain by the customary large concourse of people, come from quite distant places, awaiting healing and relief. Again He graciously restores sick bodies and exorcizes evil spirits, and then expounds the laws of His kingdom, addressing primarily His disciples (6: 20; though 6: 17 ff. suggests that the crowds are still present). In Mt. 5: 1 the audience seems to be just the disciples up till 7: 12.

The relation between the Sermon on the Mount recorded in Mt. 5-7 and the 'Sermon on the Plain' given here has frequently occupied the attention of students. The similarities are clear enough to show that a common tradition lies behind the two accounts, yet there are significant differences which constitute a problem. Matthew's version is much fuller than Luke's, and there are considerable divergences also in actual detail. It is not, of course, impossible or even improbable that our Lord gave the Sermon to different audiences on different occasions, and that we have here independent accounts of two such discourses.

20-26. Both versions begin with a series of utterances, usually called the Beatitudes, definitions of true blessedness, which form as it were the text which the rest of the Sermon expounds. Matthew has a series of nine; of these Luke selects only the first, fourth, second and ninth; but adds to them four antithetical woes, which recall the prophetic language of the OT. Furthermore, whereas all Matthew's Beatitudes except the last are in the third person, Luke's are in the second.

27-31. The law of love, paralleled in Mt. 5: 44, 39, 40 and 42; and finishing with what is often called the 'Golden Rule' (31; cf. Mt. 7: 12).

32-36. The sayings of Mt. 5: 44-48, in a slightly different order.

37-38. An expanded form of Mt. 7: 1-2, a saying on the theme that whatsoever a man sows, the same shall he also reap. Luke adds a description of the reaping, suggesting in varying terms that it will be abundant.

39-49. A short collection of parables rounds off Luke's version as well as Matthew's. They are introduced by two sayings found also in Mt., but in different contexts. The relation between the two versions is as follows:

Lk. 6: 39. The blind led by the blind into a pit. Mt. 15: 14.

Lk. 6: 40. The disciple and his master. Mt. 10: 24-25.

Lk. 6: 41-42. The speck and the log (mote and beam). Mt. 7: 3-5.

6: 43-45. Trees and their fruit. Mt. 7: 16-20; also 12: 33-35.

6: 46-49. The two houses. Mt. 7: 21-27.

viii. Various Incidents (7: 1-8: 3)

The section 7: 1-8: 3 records four incidents not related by Mark; the healing of the centurion's servant, the raising of the widow's son, the answer to John the Baptist's perplexities and the anointing of Jesus. G. B. Caird gives them the felicitous titles of 'Love in action—the Gentile; the widow; the prisoner; the penitent'. The first and the third are found also in Mt., and so presumably came from Q; the second and fourth appear nowhere but in Luke.

(*a*) **The Centurion's servant (7: 1-10)**

A centurion sends a message by a number of responsible Jews, asking Jesus to come and heal his slave. The Jews speak highly of this Gentile and his generosity towards them; Jesus sets out to accede to his request. On the way He is met by a second deputation who bring the suggestion that He need not even visit the house; a word from Him, the centurion believes, will effect the desired cure even at a distance. The centurion expresses his consciousness of his unworthiness to trouble the Lord, for he knows his place as a Gentile, and has a keen sense of hierarchical propriety and of discipline. Jesus not only speaks the word of healing, but highly commends the petitioner also: **not even in Israel have I found such faith** (9).

This is the only narrative, absent from Mk, that Mt. and Luke have in common; the rest of the Q material contains exclusively teaching. In this incident, the dialogue in the two versions is practically identical, while the two narratives differ considerably, indicating, it is suggested, that the Q version contained dialogue only.

The miracle has several features in common with the healing of the Syro-Phoenician woman's daughter (Mk 7: 24-30; Mt: 15: 21-28) which Luke does not record. In both, the petitioner is a Gentile, parent or guardian of the patient, in both cases an apt saying procures a cure in the absence of the patient.

2. a centurion: A senior non-commissioned officer, probably in the forces of Herod Antipas. **a slave who was dear to him:** In Mt. 8: 5-13 the patient is called *pais*, which, like the English *boy*, could indicate a slave or a son. In Luke he is a slave, though in v. 7 he is again *pais*. John has a similar story, where the lad is **son** (Jn 4: 46) without qualification. The expression

dear to him means 'precious', either beloved like a son, or 'valuable' (RSVmg) like a slave. The evidence is not conclusive, but whether son or slave the picture is of one to whom the centurion was completely devoted. **5. he loves our nation, and he built us our synagogue:** Attempts have been made to identify this synagogue with that at Tell-Hum, the reputed site of Capernaum. Much archaeological work has been done on the site over the last hundred years, and the results have been fully described, *e.g.*, in the first of E. L. Sukenik's 1930 Schweich Lectures, *Ancient Synagogues in Palestine and Greece* (1934). Though it cannot be said with certainty that this particular synagogue was erected sufficiently early to be the one provided by the centurion, E. M. Blaiklock says, 'the synagogue excavated there [i.e., at Tell-Hum] by the Germans in 1905 [is] probably the meeting place mentioned by Luke' (*Out of the Earth*, 1957, p. 20). The more general view, however, is that it belongs to the second century, although it may well have been built on the site of the synagogue known to our Lord.

(*b*) **The Widow's Son (7: 11-17)**

Going on to Nain followed by a great crowd, our Lord is met at the gates of the town by a funeral procession. The grief of the widowed mother of the young man who had died arouses His compassion, as it has clearly awakened that of many of the townsfolk. He stops the procession and restores the son to her who mourns him. He is saluted as a great prophet: **God has visited his people!**

This is one of three miracles of resurrection effected by Jesus in the Gospels, the others being the raising of Jairus's daughter and that of Lazarus. It is remarkable that in works where the miraculous is so important an element the number of resurrections should be so small; this restraint is surely a very telling testimony to the reliability of the record. Raising the dead to life was one of the Messianic signs to which our Lord drew attention as having been accomplished (7: 22).

The story naturally recalls the restoration of sons to their mothers by Elijah (1 Kg. 17) and Elisha (2 Kg. 4). Indeed the language in which the story is told is in places actually quoted from the OT (*e.g.*, v. 15; cf. 1 Kg. 17: 23). When the people acclaimed Jesus as **a great prophet** (16), they no doubt meant that here was a new Elijah. W. R. F. Browning (p. 84) says: 'Jesus, meeting the cortege, is moved with compassion. There is no mention here of faith, but the incident recalls similar miracles recorded in the OT of Elisha and Elijah. Nain, in fact, was near the scene of one of them (Shunem)'.

13. Luke for the first time in his narrative speaks of Jesus as **the Lord,** particularly fitting in this context where He exercises power over death itself.

(c) **The enquiry of John the Baptist (7: 18–35)**
John the Baptist from the prison where he is incarcerated sends messengers to ask Jesus outright a question which perplexes him: is Jesus indeed the Messiah? In reply, Jesus makes no actual assertion but points to His miracles, which are Messianic signs foretold in the OT; He goes on to pay tribute to the greatness of John.

29–30. These two verses do not occur in Mt. at this point, though the sentiment they express is paralleled in Mt. 21: 31. In RSV, though not in AV or RV, they are placed in parenthesis. **all the people and the tax collectors justified God:** The only place in the Gospels where 'justify' is used thus. **the Pharisees and the lawyers rejected the purpose of God:** They 'frustrated' (AVmg) God's purpose. These contrasted attitudes are linked by Luke with John's baptism; in 3: 12 he records the concern and baptism of the tax collectors, but he makes no mention of Pharisees. Cf. Mt. 3: 7. For commentary on this very important section, see notes on Mt. 11: 2–19.

(d) **The anointing of Jesus (7: 36–50)**
Jesus accepts the invitation of one Simon, a Pharisee, to a meal, during which a woman of the streets comes in and demonstrates her gratitude to Jesus by wetting His feet with her tears and wiping them with her hair, and anointing them with the ointment from a costly flask she has brought. His host is rather surprised that Jesus should tolerate this show of emotion from so tainted a source; Jesus, by means of a parable concerning two debtors, shows that in the depths of her love and devotion she has shown herself considerably superior to Simon.

Attempts have often been made to identify this incident with the anointing by Mary of Bethany during the Passion week (Mt. 26: 6; Mk 14: 3; Jn 12: 3), but it is difficult to see in this unnamed penitent the Mary with whose character Luke was in fact well acquainted (Lk. 10: 39, 42). It seems quite clear that there were indeed two such incidents; there are many differences between the story of Luke on the one hand, and the other three Gospels on the other. Balmforth sets them out thus (*Clarendon Bible*, p. 173);

	Luke	*Mark/Matthew*	*John*
Person	a sinner	a woman	Mary of Bethany
Place	Capernaum (?) at the house of Simon the Pharisee	Bethany, at the house of Simon the Leper	Bethany, apparently at Lazarus' house
Time	during the Galilean ministry	Holy week	six days before the Passover
Objection	not a real prophet	waste of money	waste of money
Made by	Simon	some of those present	Judas Iscariot

It will be seen that the accounts of Matthew/Mark and of John agree in many details against Luke. In fact, the only important point where one of the others sides with Luke is in the name of the host; Luke and Matthew/Mark call him **Simon.** But Simon was such a very common name that nothing can really be made out of its double appearance here.

37. a woman of the city, who was a sinner: She is unnamed, either because of the tactful delicacy of Luke, or simply because he did not know her name. **39.** Simon is the typical Pharisee, absolutely sure what the Law demands of him, and completely incapable of discerning that there are circumstances where the law of love—'Thou shalt love thy neighbour as thyself' —transcends the minutiae of prescribed observances and regulations. So he attributes Jesus' failure to denounce the woman for what she is to a defect in His spiritual insight. The important point of the parable of the two debtors is that the woman's action does not earn forgiveness for her; it is rather the spontaneous devotion of one who is conscious of being forgiven already (47). As Geldenhuys (p. 236) says, the parable teaches that 'remission of debt produces great love, and not *vice versa*'.

(e) **Another preaching tour (8: 1–3)**
From now onward, Jesus is constantly on the move, preaching the gospel of the kingdom from village to village and from town to town. He is accompanied not only by the Twelve but also by a small group of women who show their gratitude for blessings received through Him by putting their means at His disposal for Him and His followers.

2. Mary called Magdalene: Mentioned again among the band of faithful women who stayed near Jesus to the end, and were found at His tomb on the first Easter morning; cf. Mk 15: 40, 47; 16: 1; Lk. 24: 10; Mt. 27: 56, 61; 28: 1. **3. Joanna** is mentioned also in Lk. 24: 10, but nowhere else; **Susanna** not at all. Guesses have been made as to the identity of **Chuza,** but they remain guesses; what is interesting is that Luke had some information regarding Herod's court (cf. also Manaen, Ac. 13: 1).

ix. **Parables (8: 4–18)**
The preaching tour begins with a new kind of teaching—teaching by parables. A great crowd of people gather together and He instructs them in spiritual truth by comparisons

with familiar everyday things, like the sower putting down his seed, and the ordinary household lamp. The picture of the sower makes its impression on all who hear it, but Jesus takes aside His disciples in order to explain to them its spiritual import.

It is true that Jesus had spoken in parables before this, but there are at least two points which mark a difference. First, the parable now becomes the main vehicle of instruction. The succeeding chapters of this Gospel contain the great parables which are the most characteristic and the most familiar feature of our Lord's teaching. Secondly, parables are found in various forms, ranging from the simplest of comparisons, short similitudes and even proverbs, to the full length narrative parable. Hitherto in Luke, the former have predominated, from now on it is the great parable stories that are given.

5–8. The parable of the sower. Luke's version is briefer than that of the other synoptics; for example, he omits the circumstance, recorded by both Matthew and Mark, that it was delivered from a boat to an audience on the shore. The parable itself also is shortened; *e.g.*, the rocky ground of Mt./Mk becomes **rock,** an expression that does not, of course, preclude the idea of some covering of earth for the seed to germinate. Matthew collects together with this parable a series of others all dealing with the kingdom of heaven; for notes on these parables of the kingdom, see commentary on Mt. 13. For commentary on the parable of the sower, see notes on Mk 4: 1–9.

9–15. The use of parables; The meaning of the parable of the Sower. Matthew and Mark tell us that the disciples asked a question about parables in general ('The disciples came and said to him, why do you speak to them in parables?' Mt. 13: 10; 'asked him concerning the parables', Mk 4: 10). Luke, on the other hand, says that they **asked him what this parable meant** (9). Jesus replied to both questions; first concerning the purpose of parabolic teaching, He linked His answer with Isa. 6: 9–10. Matthew gives this answer, which is far from easy to understand, at considerable length (Mt. 13: 10–15); Mark abbreviates it fairly drastically (Mk 4: 10–12); Luke even more so. Secondly, Jesus went on to explain the meaning of the parable of the Sower. The three synoptics all report the explanation, and their versions differ little from each other. It is sometimes suggested that because (among other things) the explanation is somewhat allegorical in method it must come from the early Church rather than from Jesus itself. But while agreeing

that the teaching of most of the parables is found in the story as a whole rather than in its details taken one by one, there are a few parables, like the wicked husbandmen in the vineyard (Lk. 20: 9–18) for instance, that clearly are allegorical. The sower seems just such a parable.

16–18. The parable of the lamp. A short similitude which Matthew places in the Sermon on the Mount (Mt. 5: 15) and which Luke himself repeats in 11: 33. The verses which follow the similitude are also repeated elsewhere by Luke; cf. 8: 17 with 12: 2, and 8: 18 with 19: 26. The light shines, and it is the Church's responsibility not to let it be hidden (16), but there is a responsibility also on the hearer as to how he hears (18).

x. The Protest of the Family (8: 19–21)
As the fame of Jesus grows, stories circulate concerning Him which give His relations the impression that He has become mentally unbalanced, and so they visit Him in the hope of persuading Him to return home. But He refuses to submit even to the dearest of earthly bonds, and speaks of the much greater circle of those who are His kinsfolk by faith and obedience. See notes on Mk 3: 31–35.

NOTE: The question of the identity of **his brothers** (19, 20) is often raised. Who were they? Roman Catholic theologians, in their desire to safeguard the (non-scriptural) doctrine of Mary's perpetual virginity, regard them either as offspring of a former marriage of Joseph, or as cousins of Jesus. But there seems to be no reason for not taking the words in their natural sense, as did Tertullian, and assuming that they were subsequently-born children of Joseph and Mary.

xi. Miracles (8: 22–56)
For detailed commentary on this section, see notes on Mk 4: 35–5: 43.

The next events that Luke records are four outstanding miracles: The stilling of the storm (22–25), the deliverance of the demoniac and the destruction of the swine (26–39), the raising of Jairus's daughter (40–42, 49–56) and the healing of the woman with a flow of blood (43–48).

The Lord and His disciples get into a boat to cross the sea of Galilee, and for the first and only time in the Gospels we see Jesus asleep. Exhausted by His labours, His sleep is too deep to be disturbed by a tremendous tempest which breaks out. The terrified disciples awaken Him, and to their amazement the storm is stilled at His word of command.

Arriving on the other shore in the **country of the Gerasenes,** Jesus has no sooner disembarked than He is met by the strange figure, naked and dishevelled, of a demoniac who lives among the tombs. The indwelling demon is exorcized and allowed by Jesus to go and possess a herd of grazing pigs, which immediately stampede into the sea. The herdmen see the wonderful sight of the demoniac now **clothed and in his right mind** but, partly through terror and partly because of loss of gain from their pigs, implore Jesus to go elsewhere. The cured man desires to follow Jesus as a disciple, but he is told that he can do a much more valuable service by remaining to testify in his own town.

The ungracious welcome to Jesus and unceremonious hustling out contrast strongly with the welcome He receives when He returns whence He came. Here another suppliant meets Him, not the patient this time, for she is but a young girl of twelve, but her father, Jairus, a ruler of the synagogue. He entreats Jesus to come and heal the child.

The Lord, however, interrupts His journey to the house of Jairus to heal a woman, twelve years a victim of haemorrhages, who has struggled through the crowd to touch the fringe of His robe, believing that she will thereby be healed.

The result of this delay is the arrival of fresh messengers from Jairus saying that the child is now dead. Jesus nevertheless continues on His journey, and finds the house of Jairus in the possession of the professional mourners, but since 'He does not desire to make a theatrical, spectacular business of the raising of the dead' (Geldenhuys, p. 262), He excludes all but the little girl's parents and His three own most intimate disciples, and entering the death chamber with them, He performs a second miracle of resurrection, restoring the daughter to her astonished parents.

V. A THIRD TOUR (9: 1-50)

The ministry of our Lord is now approaching one of its great crises. Mark's narrative, which hitherto Luke has followed fairly faithfully, seems to fall into two portions, the first telling of the Son of man who 'came not to be served but to serve' (Mk 10: 45a); the second telling of Him who came 'to give His life as a ransom for many' (Mk 10: 45b). So we have already seen how Jesus' claims to authority (chaps. 4–5) led to direct conflict with the Jews (chaps. 5–6); and how He prepared against His departure by appointing and training apostles (chap. 6) and by teaching the people in parables not easy to be forgotten (chap. 8).

Throughout the time He had been with them Jesus had been teaching His followers. Now Peter arrives at the point to which He has been leading them, and in a God-given moment of insight he realizes that Jesus is the Messiah. From now on the teaching becomes more sombre in tone, for they must learn what kind of Messiah He is to be, namely a suffering Messiah like the Servant of Jehovah in Isaiah chaps. 42–53, '*a man of sorrows and acquainted with grief*'. So from the moment of Peter's confession at Caesarea Philippi, Jesus began to impress upon the disciples what lay ahead of Him (v. 22). (For a different viewpoint on the Lord's challenge and Peter's confession, see notes on Mk 8: 27-30.)

The material in this section is for the most part paralleled in Mk, which was probably Luke's source. Apart from Peter's confession three important events are recorded, all bearing directly on 'the sufferings of Christ and the subsequent glory' (1 Pet. 1: 11):

(*a*) He mentions the death of John the Baptist. If the forerunner must die, this points to Him who must follow the same path.

(*b*) The feeding of the five thousand would remind the reader not only of manna in the wilderness, but also of the promised Messianic banquet to which he looked ahead.

(*c*) The Transfiguration links together the glory of the transfigured Christ and the Exodus which He must accomplish.

i. The Tour of the Twelve (9: 1-6, 10)

Jesus sends out the Twelve on a preaching tour. Mark's version is similar (6: 7-13); Mt. 10: 5-42 is longer and includes some material that Luke puts in the charge to the Seventy (see notes on Lk. 10: 1-20) and some from elsewhere. (See notes on Mt. 10: 5-42.)

ii. The death of John (9: 7-9)

The three Synoptics mention the death of John the Baptist at this point without committing themselves as to exactly when it occurred. Mt. and Mk describe the event at length, the Third Gospel merely mentions it, though its account of the Baptism is followed by a note (3: 19-20) that Herod had imprisoned John. (For detailed comment, see notes on Mk 6: 14-29.)

iii. The Feeding of the Five Thousand (9: 10-17)

This is the only miracle recorded in all four Gospels (Mk 6: 30-43; Mt. 14: 13-21; Jn 6: 1-13); Mk and Mt. have also a second miraculous feeding of four thousand (Mk 8: 1-10; Mt. 15: 32-39). Mark tells how Jesus takes the Twelve on their return to 'a lonely place' for a period of retreat (Mt. suggests that it followed receipt of news of John's death). But to 'rest awhile' proves impossible, for crowds gather and, seeing the group sailing across the lake, hasten round the shore to meet them on their arrival on the further shore (a detail that Luke omits). So Jesus preaches to them, and when the day has worn on, challenges the disciples as to what they are going to do about feeding them. John tells how Andrew and Philip, who are local men, make enquiries and report the presence of a boy with five loaves and two small fishes. The Synoptics mention this total of available food, but not the lad. Such as it is, the Lord takes it, gives thanks, and having seen that the multitude are seated in orderly fashion, feeds them all miraculously from it, and enough is left over to fill the twelve baskets or hampers that the disciples, as pious Jews, carry in order that they shall not need to depend on the generosity of Gentiles. (For notes on details, see section on Mk 6: 30–44.)

iv. The Revelation of His Person and first prediction of suffering (9: 18–27)

The great confession of Peter at Caesarea Philippi that Jesus is indeed the long awaited Messiah is the watershed of the Gospel narrative; henceforward the shadow of the Cross dominates the whole story. Jesus has set His face to go to Jerusalem, there to suffer. Detailed notes will be found in the commentary on Mk 8: 27–38 and Mt. 16: 13–27. Luke makes several interesting contributions of his own. He omits Peter's rebuke to Jesus after the prediction of the Passion, and Jesus' reply. 'The omission is no doubt deliberate to avoid an incident which might seem to reflect unfavourably on the Apostle' (Creed, p. 130). He omits also the reference to Caesarea Philippi, but on the other hand he characteristically begins his account with Jesus at prayer (18).

v. The Transfiguration (9: 28–36)

The Transfiguration (see Mk 9: 2–8; Mt. 17: 1–8) is the natural sequel to the previous incident, with its prediction of suffering. God speaks His approval from heaven as He did when at His baptism Jesus deliberately embraced His mission with all He knew it would entail. It was not until Jesus had told the disciples what He was facing that they saw His true glory.

Some days after the confession He takes Peter, James and John up a mountain for prayer. His appearance is transfigured with glory, and two celestial visitors, Moses and Elijah, converse with Him concerning His coming sufferings. Peter wants to make the experience permanent by building three tabernacles, thus offering equal honours to Moses and Elijah and to Jesus. God from heaven proclaims the uniqueness of His Son. Then Moses and Elijah are no longer seen; Jesus alone remains.

28. he . . . went up on the mountain: It was on a mountain that Moses had asked to see God's glory, and though this was not granted, his face so shone that he had to veil

himself for the protection of the people (Exod. 33: 12–23; 34: 29–35). On a mountain also Elijah, who was to see God's glory without dying, saw the manifestation of His power (1 Kg. 18). **29. as he was praying:** A peculiarly Lucan touch! **31. his departure:** The Gk. word is our 'exodus'. Moses, who had led the people to deliverance from Egypt in the first Exodus, speaks with Him whose own Exodus will bring deliverance from sin. **34. a cloud came and overshadowed them:** The overshadowing cloud is a familiar symbol of the divine Presence in the OT (cf. Exod. 40: 34; Lev. 16: 2; 2 Chr. 5: 13; etc.). **35.** To the message at the baptism quoted from Ps. 2: 7 and Isa. 42: 1 the voice adds a further clause, **listen to him** (Dt. 18: 15). **36. Jesus was found alone:** The Law and the Prophets have served their turn and pass away; He who is the fulfilment of both alone remains.

vi. The Healing of the demoniac (9: 37–43)

The mountain top experience is followed as so often is the case by a devastating return to everyday things. Down in the valley once more they are faced by the spectacle of the helplessness of their brother disciples to exorcize a demon. See notes on Mk 9: 14–29.

vii. Second prediction of suffering: last ministry in Galilee (9: 44–50)

The closing verses of the first section of Luke's account of the ministry of Christ include:

44–45. The second prediction of suffering (Luke's version is very short, not specifically mentioning either the crucifixion or the resurrection).

46–48. Calling a child to His side, Jesus rebukes the disciples for their desire for pre-eminence. For a fuller account of the incident, see Mt. 18: 1–5.

49–50. A warning against the uncharitableness of exclusiveness. More detailed comment on this last section will be found in the notes on Mark's fuller version (Mk 9: 31–41).

VI. THE LATER JUDAEAN MINISTRY (9: 51–19: 27)

The long section 9: 51–18: 14 is, together with the first two chapters and the last, Luke's most distinctive contribution to the Gospel tradition. It appears on the surface to be simply the account of the last great journey that our Lord made, after the final stages of His Galilean ministry, to Jerusalem and His Passion. Various names have been suggested for the section, but B. H. Streeter (*The Four Gospels*, ch. viii) said that most were unsatisfactory as taking something for granted. To call it the 'Peraean Section' overlooks the fact that part, at any rate, of the journey was west and not east of Jordan. The

'Travel Narrative' or the 'Travel Document' imply the existence of a document which Luke incorporated into his Gospel; of the existence of such a document no proof exists. Streeter himself proposes the 'Central Section', which begs no questions; others the 'Great Interpolation', seeing that it is interpolated whole into the Marcan framework. But whatever name be given to it, Reicke is not exaggerating when he calls it 'the central enigma of this Gospel' (*The Gospels Reconsidered*, ed. Aland, 1960, p. 107).

The question at issue is whether these chapters describe 'the great journey' from Galilee to Jerusalem as it actually took place, with the incidents recorded occurring just where Luke puts them; or whether on the other hand he uses the framework of the journey (which obviously must have taken place since the events of the last week in Jerusalem follow a ministry squarely placed in the north) as a convenient form for assembling various unrelated incidents and sayings.

It would be fair to say that the majority of academic critics favour the second view. 'The Lucan itinerary', says T. W. Manson, 'is difficult to follow . . . . Whatever else Lk. 9: 51-18: 14 may be, it does not appear to be a chronicle' (*The Sayings of Jesus*, 1949, pp. 255 f.). The essay by Reicke already mentioned is probably the most recent serious examination of the question. He suggests that, finding in his sources only the briefest references to the transition from Galilee to Judaea (cf. Mk 10: 1; Mt. 19: 1), Luke filled what he considered a gap in his information with '(1) instruction of the apostles regarded (*a*) as leaders and teachers of the Christians, i.e. as ministers, and (*b*) as missionaries; and (2) discussion with adversaries and opponents' (p. 111).

N. B. Stonehouse, on the other hand, while admitting that there are difficulties, argues that the section gives an intelligible account of a journey that actually took place. Jerusalem, he says, is always in view; it is never lost sight of as the ultimate destination (*The Witness of Luke to Christ*, pp. 114 ff.). His case is well argued, and will repay careful study. Moreover, though Stonehouse represents a minority view, he is by no means alone; Plummer (pp. 60 f.), while not arguing the historicity of the journey, appears to assume it.

i. The Journey to Jerusalem via Samaria (9: 51-12: 59)

(*a*) Samaritan unfriendliness and would-be disciples (9: 51-62)

Our Lord's final resolve is made; the time has now arrived for the accomplishment of that for which He had become flesh. His disciples do not understand; they want to call down fire from heaven upon the unmannerly Samaritans who have refused them hospitality. Meanwhile, other would-be disciples seek to attach themselves to Him, but they show no awareness of the totalitarian claims that discipleship makes upon men.

One of the strangest features of the Gospel story is the frequent insensitiveness of the disciples, especially at times of crisis. In Mk 10: 32-36, for instance, our Lord's third and clearest prediction of His sufferings elicits from John and James merely jockeying for personal position in the kingdom. Here, as He sets out on the final stage of the pathway to the Cross, the disciples are concerned only with spectacular vengeance on the churlish Samaritans who had outraged their feelings. That this obtuseness should be recorded is an impressive testimony to the trustworthiness of the record—it would surely never have been invented.

The **Samaritans** were a particular thorn in the flesh to the Jews. They were descended from the miscellaneous tribes with whom Sargon II of Assyria and his successors repeopled Samaria after the fall of the Kingdom of Israel in 722-1 B.C. (2 Kg. 17: 24-34, see also F. F. Bruce, *Israel and the Nations*, 1963, p. 66) and as such were not really Jews by race. But they adopted Jewish forms of worship and read the Jewish Torah, and when, on their return from exile, the Jews refused Samaritan help in the rebuilding of the ruins, the animosity was much increased. The ill-feeling persisted, Jewish disdain for these pseudo-Jews calling forth Samaritan resentment, which is very visible in the NT narrative. In this incident, Samaritan rudeness roused the anger of the sons of thunder, who wanted to be allowed to return it with interest.

51. he set his face: An echo perhaps of the third of the Servant Songs: '*therefore I have set my face like a flint*' (Isa. 50: 7). **53.** The **Samaritans** refused Him hospitality because He was going to **Jerusalem** to perform His religious obligations, by-passing their shrine on Gerizim which they judged in no way inferior to Jerusalem itself. **54.** The text of Luke has come down in various slightly differing forms; in this passage the readings supported by the main weight of textual evidence are shorter than the *textus receptus* of which the AV is a translation. Here the longer text (AV, RVmg, RSVmg) associates the desire for vengeance with an incident in the life of Elijah (2 Kg. 1: 9 ff.). This reference is omitted in RV and RSV. **55, 56.** The shorter version (RV, RSV) omits the words: 'You do not know what manner of spirit you are of, for the Son of man came not to destroy men's lives but to save them'. Despite the textual uncertainty the meaning of the incident is quite clear: evil is overcome not with evil but with good.

57, 58. The first would-be disciple. a man (Mt. says 'a scribe') wanted to join Jesus, who made His reply about the birds and the foxes. T. W. Manson, dismissing the suggestion that the saying was simply a current proverb, refers it to contemporary conditions in Palestine. Birds in the Bible are often an apocalyptic symbol of the Gentile nations (Dan. 4: 12; Mt. 13: 32; etc.); foxes in Jewish literature are those akin but hostile to God's people, in Lk. 13: 32 the fox being Herod. So everyone is at home in Israel's land, Roman overlords (birds) and Edomite interloper (Herod), except the true Israel. 'The true Israel is disinherited by them, and if you cast your lot with me and mine you join the ranks of the dispossessed' (*Sayings*, pp. 72 f.). See, however, the commentary on Mt. 8: 20.

59, 60. The second would-be disciple. Another candidate wishes to postpone taking up discipleship until he has performed the most sacred of filial duties, the burial of his father. Yet there is no hint that the father has already died. The claims of the kingdom are paramount: **Leave the dead to bury their own dead.** This saying, which has been much discussed, is followed in Luke by the command **go and proclaim the kingdom of God**; in Mt. (8: 22) it is simply Follow me.

61, 62. The third would-be disciple (Luke only). The excuse for delay is here less valid, being simply a matter of family farewells. The 'ploughman' answer of Jesus recalls that it was while ploughing that Elisha heard God's call (1 Kg. 19: 19 ff.).

(b) The Mission of the Seventy (10: 1–24) Seventy disciples, mentioned only by Luke, are sent out with a commission in very similar terms to that of the Twelve in 9: 1–10 (see note *ad loc.*). They return and report enthusiastically on the success of their mission; Jesus warns them against the danger of pride entering their hearts. There follows the record of a prayer of the Son to the Father, almost Johannine in its language.

1. seventy: Manuscript evidence is divided between 70 and 72. The latter would suggest six from each tribe, like the translators of the Septuagint. On the other hand, there were traditionally seventy nations (Gen. 10), seventy elders were appointed by Moses (Num. 11: 16 f.) and seventy members of the Sanhedrin. **two by two:** A. R. C. Leaney (p. 176) suggests that this may be an illustration of the witness principle of Dt. 19: 15. **2, 3. The harvest is plentiful . . . :** Two short similitudes introduce Jesus' charge to the Seventy; the plenteous harvest and the

lambs among wolves. In Mt., both are attached to the sending out of the Twelve (9: 37-38; 10: 16).

4-12. Instructions for the journey. Their marching orders resemble closely those given to the Twelve (9: 3 ff.; cf. Mk 6: 8-11; Mt. 10: 9-14), with the addition of (*a*) an injunction not to salute any man by the way (4); like Gehazi's (2 Kg. 4: 29), theirs is an errand of life and death, there is no time to waste on social exchanges. (*b*) a denunciation of the cities of Galilee, Chorazin, Bethsaida, and Capernaum, for their deafness to God's call to repent. **Chorazin** is not mentioned elsewhere in the Bible or in Josephus but its ruins are visible about $2\frac{1}{2}$ miles north of Capernaum; the denunciation of **Capernaum** is in terms reminiscent of the 'taunt song' against the King of Babylon in Isa. 14: 13-15.

16. They are given the authority which belongs to Him who sent them. A more forceful version of Mt. 10: 40.

17-20. The return of the Seventy. On their return they were full of enthusiasm at the wonderful things that they had been empowered to accomplish: **even the demons are subject to us in your name.** This was even more than they had anticipated, for they had been commissioned only to heal the sick and to proclaim the Kingdom (v. 9). In His reply the Lord warned them against pride: **I saw Satan fall like lightning from heaven** (18). The verb **I saw** is in the imperfect tense ('I was watching'); the participle **fall** is aorist ('fallen'). Because this saying recalls Isa. 14: 12—'*How you are fallen from heaven, O Day Star, son of Dawn!*', it has been interpreted throughout Christian history as a reference to a cosmic fall of Satan in the remote past; so, for instance, Gregory the Great as early as the sixth century. But Plummer (p. 278) says: 'The aorist indicates the coincidence between the success of the Seventy and Christ's vision of Satan's overthrow'. The kingdom has come, 'the success of the disciples is regarded as a symbol and earnest of the complete overthrow of Satan' (*ibid.*; see also note on Rev. 12: 9). Whichever of these two interpretations is accepted, it is quite evident that Jesus taught unambiguously that there is a personal power of evil.

The renewed promise of power (19) recalls Ps. 91: 13 and Dt. 8: 15; but the true ground for rejoicing is that their names are written in the register of God's kingdom (cf. Exod. 32: 32 f.; Ps. 87: 6; Heb. 12: 23; Rev. 3: 5; 17: 8; etc.).

21, 22. Cf. Mt. 11: 25-27. In these two verses we are transported from the Synoptic air right into the atmosphere of the Fourth Gospel;

they have been described as 'this thunderbolt from the Johannine sky'. And yet, as Plummer says (p. 282), 'it is impossible upon any principles of criticism to question its genuineness, or its right to be regarded as among the earliest materials made use of by the evangelists'.

Jesus **rejoiced in the Holy Spirit,** Luke's own phrase, which does not appear in Mt.'s version, but is reminiscent of the language of Luke's first two chapters. In v. 21, He delights that His Father has chosen babes; in v. 22 He rejoices in the perfect intimacy which He and the Father enjoy one with the other. The thought of v. 21 is developed by Paul in the opening chapter of 1 Corinthians.

23, 24. A beatitude given also by Mt. (13: 16–17), emphasizing that Jesus was speaking to the Twelve and not to His followers in general. To the apostles were given the gracious unfoldings of truth that marked the Lord's teaching to His intimates: they witnessed the fulfilment of things to which the prophets had looked forward with eager longing (cf. Heb. 11: 13; 1 Pet. 1: 12).

(c) **The Parable of the Good Samaritan** (10: 25–37)

The most remarkable feature of the Lucan account of the great journey is the series of parables, including several of the most memorable recorded in the NT, which are preserved in none of the other Gospels. Of these, the Good Samaritan stands first. A lawyer asks the Lord what are the great commandments, and is perhaps rather surprised to be told no new-fangled doctrine, but a restatement of the honoured laws of the Torah concerning love for God and one's neighbour. The lawyer asks who is his neighbour, a question that elicits this parable by way of reply, and the exhortation with it, **Go and do likewise** (37).

The introductory dialogue is often regarded as a parallel to Mk 12: 28–31, 34, but in reality the only connection is the linking together of Dt. 6: 5 and Lev. 19: 18, and, if Wm. Manson (p. 131) is right, it is possible that 'this synthesis of precepts accredited to the lawyer suggests that contemporary preachers, in attempting to summarize the Law in one or two brief sentences, had reached agreement upon this formula'. The two contexts are quite different, and the attitudes of the two questioners also. In Mk the scribe's question is purely academic; here there is at any rate a practical element.

25. a lawyer: The Gk. word *nomikos* is used by Luke alone of the Synoptics, except for Mt. 22: 35, where the word is omitted in several manuscripts. Luke probably uses the word in preference to 'scribe' (Gk. *grammateus*) as being more intelligible to his Gentile readers. **stood**

up and put him to the test: Was the lawyer's intention to enquire or to entrap? Leaney (p. 182) suggests 'trying Him out' to convey the exact meaning of the verb. The question, says Plummer (p. 284) was not 'calculated to place Jesus in a difficulty, but rather to test His ability as a teacher'; it 'does not imply a sinister attempt to entrap Him'. Moorman (p. 126), on the other hand, holds that 'by asking an awkward question, he wanted Jesus to stumble over it so that he could then turn to the crowd and point out that matters of this kind were much better left to lawyers and trained expositors'. Wm. Manson, Browning, and others, take a similar view. **29. desiring to justify himself:** I.e., wishing to regain some of the 'face' he had lost. **30. A man was going down from Jerusalem to Jericho:** The question is often asked whether the narrative parables are records of events that actually took place, or imaginative stories. Concerning the present story it has even been suggested that Jesus was recounting an otherwise unrecorded incident from His own experience; this is, of course, pure conjecture. But the story has the ring of the factual, robbers have infested the Jericho road from that day to this. H. V. Morton says that when he told a friend that he intended to run down to the Dead Sea for a day he was warned: 'Well, be careful to get back before dark' and was given grisly details of Abu Jildah, an armed gangster who even in 1934 was terrorizing travellers on that very road (*In the Steps of the Master*, 1934, p. 85). Another suggestion is that the parable is based on a historical event related in 2 Chr. 28: 15. **down . . . to Jericho:** Jericho had a long history in the OT; it lay about 900 feet below sea level; Jerusalem stands about 2,300 feet above sea level; hence **down. 31. a priest . . . when he saw him . . . passed by on the other side:** The priest was **going down that road;** he also had come from Jerusalem. If, as seems likely, he was coming from the exercise of his priestly duties, he would naturally wish to avoid contact with a possible corpse for fear of incurring ceremonial uncleanness (Num. 19: 11–19). But ordinary human compassion is a higher law than the observance of any ritual obligations (cf. 1 Sam. 15: 22; Isa. 1: 11–17; Am. 5: 21–24; Mk 2: 25–26, etc.). **32. So likewise a Levite . . . came to the place . . . and saw him:** A lesser official of the Temple, the Levite seems to have been as callous as his superior, for he also approached, saw, and passed on. It is possible of course that both were cowardly rather than callous: 'it was quite a common thing for bandits to use decoys. . . . When some unsuspecting traveller came by and stopped over the apparently wounded victim, the rest of the band would suddenly rush from their concealment and catch the traveller at every disadvantage' (W. Barclay, *And Jesus said*, 1953, p. 95). **33. a Samaritan:** A surprising *dénouement* to the story; 'the hearers would assume that the villain of the piece had arrived upon the scene' (*ibid.*). The priest and the Levite had neglected their plain duty to their neighbour; the despised Samaritan did what none could have reasonably expected him to do —a salutary lesson for John and James! **35. two denarii:** Mt. 20: 2 tells us that the denarius was the daily wage of an agricultural labourer, so the 'seventeen pence' of the RSVmg is not realistic as to the purchasing power of the coin, which nowadays would be at least 20 shillings.

36, 37. The meaning of the parable. Fanciful allegorizing interpretations like those of Origen and Augustine (see A. M. Hunter, *Interpreting the Parables*, 1960, pp. 24 f., and C. H. Dodd, *Parables of the Kingdom*, 1935, pp. 11 ff.) pay so much attention to the leaves that the tree itself is obscured. The important thing is not to identify each tiny detail in the story, but to see how Jesus, as well as drawing a superb picture of neighbourliness, or love, in action, brought home to the lawyer the challenge of the Law, in which he was an expert, to his own heart, to condition his thinking and to inspire and regulate his doing.

(d) **Mary and Martha (10: 38–42)**
The parable of the Good Samaritan emphasizes the need for practical application of God's word; the little scene in Martha's house shows that meditation has its place as well. While Martha attends to the household chores, her sister Mary sits as a learner at Jesus' feet. The overburdened Martha complains; Jesus gently suggests that she might have done the same instead of making such a labour of the house-work. This incident is particularly interesting in that Martha and Mary, well-known in the pages of John, appear here only in the Synoptics. **38. a village:** Luke does not name this village, which must have been Bethany, though some find that this view raises geographical difficulties. If the incident occurred during Jesus' visit to Jerusalem for the Feast of Tabernacles (Jn 7), it would explain His presence in Bethany at this time. **40. Martha was distracted:** So distracted indeed that not only did she resent her sister's apparent idleness, but even scolded Jesus for not sending Mary to help. **41, 42.** Jesus answers gently; the double vocative **Martha, Martha,** is a kindly mode of address. He points out that if she is overworked it is she herself who has created the toil.

one thing is needful: One simple dish would have sufficed, Martha has gone to endless unnecessary trouble to prepare a banquet, forgetting Prov. 15: 16-17! **Mary has chosen the good portion:** Notice with what tact the Lord, while commending Mary for her sense of values, does not condemn Martha by comparison; Mary has chosen the **good** portion, not the *better*.

(e) **The Lord's Prayer (11: 1-13)**
The sight of our Lord at prayer leads the disciples to ask Him to teach them to pray. He replies by teaching them what has come to be known as the Lord's Prayer, telling them the parable of the importunate friend at midnight, and by enunciating some general principles regarding prayer. This section is of outstanding interest since Luke, of all the evangelists, portrays most often the praying Christ (see Introductory notes, p. 205).

J. M. Creed (p. 155) says 'there is no close connection between this and the preceding paragraph'; yet it is noticeable that the encouragement to ask our heavenly Father for a day's rations at a time is the natural corrective to Martha's anxiety about many things. The Lord's Prayer is found here in a totally different setting from Mt.'s version, which comes much earlier as part of the Sermon on the Mount. Here the disciples seem to feel that they lack something. 'It was customary', says C. G. Montefiore, 'for a famous Rabbi to compose a special prayer': John the Baptist appears to have done so for his disciples (1).

The prayer that Jesus gave them on this occasion is much shorter than in Mt.; and Luke's version is much shorter still in the newer versions (RSV, NEB, etc.) than in the *textus receptus* and the AV. The main differences between Mt.'s and Luke's shorter versions are:
1. The address to God: 'Our Father which art in Heaven' becomes simply **Father** (Jesus' characteristic 'Abba'; cf. Mk 14: 36).
2. The third petition: 'Thy will be done', and the condition: 'as in heaven so on earth', are omitted.
3. Mt.'s 'Give us this day . . .' becomes **Give us each day** in Luke.
4. 'debts' in Mt. becomes **sins** in Luke; the completed fact recorded by Mt.: 'we have forgiven' is a continual performance in Luke.
5. 'Deliver us from the evil one', Mt.'s last petition, is omitted in Luke, as also is the concluding doxology (which is absent from the original text of Mt.).

For comments on the contents of the prayer, see notes on Mt. 6: 9-13.

5-8. The parable of the friend at midnight. The pattern prayer is followed by a parable teaching the importance of persistence in prayer. A man has nothing to set before an unexpected guest; the lateness of the hour precludes the possibility of purchasing bread. He therefore wakes a friend to beg him to lend. Not unnaturally, he is not received cordially, but he persists in his request and because of his very persistence (Gk. *anaideia* means 'shamelessness'; see NEB), the friend capitulates, gets up and gives him what he wants just to get rid of him.

It is clearly impossible to press the details in interpreting this parable; the point is that real prayer, effective prayer, must be in real earnest (cf. Jas 5: 16) and that if a human friend will even grudgingly satisfy the needs of one who is becoming a nuisance, how much more will a loving God answer the prayers which He delights to hear, and that not grudgingly.

9–13. A collection of sayings on prayer. This appendix corresponds roughly to the **Go and do likewise** of the previous parable, and is paralleled in Mt. 7: 7–11 (see notes *ad loc.*).

(*f*) Controversy with the Pharisees (11: 14–54)
An exorcism leads to the accusation that Jesus can do these things simply because He is in league with the prince of demons. He shows the absurdity of such a charge, for Satan is not divided against himself. The Jews want a sign, yet the signs are there clear enough in the OT, if they will but see them; they have the light but are wilfully obscuring it. A Pharisee invites Him to a meal; attacked by the Pharisees present for not observing social and ceremonial etiquette, He turns the tables by showing how far in their regard for the minutiae they have departed from the true law of God and even murdered God's servants. The result of this clash is, not unnaturally, a hardening of the determination of His enemies to accomplish His downfall.

14–26. The Beelzebul controversy. See also notes on Mk 3: 22–27; Mt. 12: 22–30. Mk omits the fact that it was an exorcism which started off this controversy; Mt. tells us that the dumb man was blind as well. Communication with the poor fellow must have been difficult; yet the cure was immediate and complete (Mt. 12: 22). The onlookers were amazed. Some attributed His power to demoniac powers; others wanted a sign, tangible evidence that He was not in league with the powers of darkness (14–16).

Jesus replied that if Satan were the source of His power then Satan's kingdom must be so divided that it would collapse (17–18). Taking the war into the enemy's camp He pointed out

that His hearers' **sons** (probably, their disciples) also exorcized demons; did they also do it by the powers of darkness? (19). No—His power was **the finger of God** (20), an expression used in Exod. 8: 19 (Mt. 12: 28 has 'the Spirit of God').

Then follow two short parables, the strong man spoiled (21, 22) and the unclean spirit returning to the empty house (24–26); and between them the assertion that in this warfare no man can be neutral: **He who is not with me is against me, and he who does not gather with me scatters** (23).

27, 28. Blessed is the womb that bore you. An incident recorded only by Luke, who was particularly interested in the place of women in the gospel tradition. Though this woman is rebuked for her flattery in words recalling 8: 21 and 10: 20, she stands in Luke's picture gallery with the women of 8: 1–3 and 23: 27.

29–32. See also under Mk 4: 21 ff.; Mt. 5: 15; 10: 26. Luke places at this point a saying which Mk and Mt. give in other contexts; Mk immediately after the parable of the sower, Mt. in the sermon on the mount. Here the spiritual blindness of Jesus' hearers leads naturally to the subject of **light** (33). A **bushel** was a measure of capacity, about a peck; a jar of this capacity would be found in the normal household.

37–44. Luke alone tells us that Jesus accepted the invitation of a Pharisee to dinner (probably a midday meal) and, apparently deliberately, refrained from using the water brought to each guest for handwashing before the meal. That in appropriate circumstances Jesus conformed in such matters is clear from 7: 44 and from Jn 13: 4–10; but here He has another lesson to teach. The ablution that was a welcome refreshment when offered as a courtesy became a burden when imposed as an inescapable obligation. At all events, His abstention caused astonishment and gave Him the opportunity of contrasting the care the Pharisees gave to the pots and pans with their lack of care about what was put into them (39 ff.). Then He uttered His three 'Woes' against the Pharisees (see notes on Mt. 23: 23–28). They are greedy—**full of extortion** (39); they are insincere—punctilious in little things while neglectful of larger obligations (42); they are arrogant—**you love the best seat in the synagogue and salutations in the market-place** (43). In fact they are unrecognized for what they are, dead men's graves without life towards God, but spreading uncleanness among men (Num. 19: 16).

45–52. See also Mt. 23: 4, 29–36, and notes *ad loc.* While the Pharisees withdrew to lick their wounds and to prepare further mischief, **one of the lawyers,** as ready to speak as his colleague in the previous chapter, complained: **Teacher, in saying this you reproach us also.** Three more 'Woes' follow, this time directed at the lawyers (in Mt. 23 all the woes are addressed to the 'scribes and Pharisees'). They are censured because they lay down rules for others that they do not obey themselves (46): because the only prophets they honour are dead prophets, for whose deaths they must share the responsibility (47–51); and because, ignorant themselves, they withhold knowledge from those who would learn God's law (52). **51. Zechariah** was probably the prophet whose death is recorded in 2 Chr. 24: 20–22. 2 Chr. was the last book in the Hebrew OT so **Abel to . . . Zechariah** would include all the martyrs of the OT.

53, 54. Their enmity all the stronger because of His words, they crowd round Him with question after question, hoping to trap Him into saying something for which He might be brought to trial or excommunicated.

(g) Public Teachings (12: 1–59)

The solemn note of the controversy with the Pharisees is continued throughout the twelfth chapter, where our Lord turns to His followers and utters a series of warnings they must heed. First He bids them be prepared for the persecution that surely lies ahead of them (1–12). Then He warns them against covetousness, a too high regard for material possessions, and reinforces the warning with the solemn parable of the Rich Fool (13–21). A section follows, placed in Mt. in the Sermon on the Mount, where the disciples are shown the needlessness and folly of anxiety about temporal necessities (22–34). Finally, almost the whole of the second half of the chapter (35–59) is eschatological in outlook, warning of the crisis which looms undoubtedly before them.

(i) Warning of coming persecution (12: 1–12)

The scene is vividly portrayed, one of Luke's masterpieces of simple yet telling narrative so often seen to advantage in his descriptions of the bustle and changing moods of a street crowd. Jesus left the Pharisees with whom He had been disputing, but they would not let Him go so easily; they **began to press him hard, and to provoke him to speak of many things, lying in wait for him, to catch at something he might say** (11: 53–54). But as on other occasions, especially at His crucifixion, it is He not they, the lonely figure and not the leaders of the establishment, who is clearly in command of events. Crowds gather, **many thousands of the multitude** (12: 1), to hear Him. Not a whit daunted by the forces hostile to Him, He returns to the attack: **'Beware of the leaven of the Pharisees, which is hypocrisy'.** This expression is interesting, since it occurs in Mk 8: 15 in another context, immediately before the Great Confession at Caesarea Philippi. Many, in fact, of the expressions in this chapter are paralleled, usually in different settings in Mt. or Mk; in Mt. mainly in the Sermon on the Mount (chaps. 5–7), the appointment of the Twelve (chap. 10) or the eschatological discourse of chap. 24.

1. His fearlessness has nothing in it of mere blind defiance. His eyes are wide open, and He knows full well that the Pharisees will return to the attack, and that if His disciples range themselves alongside Him, persecution will be their lot as it must assuredly be His. **2, 3.** One day, all will be revealed; but in the meantime, awaiting this Last Day, 'the halting and timid confessions of the disciples must become triumphant and public, even though they will bring persecution' (Browning, p. 119). **4, 5.** The only time in the Synoptics that Jesus calls His disciples **friends** (though see Jn 15: 14 f.). Human persecution is less to be feared than God's judgment on apostasy. **Gehenna** is the valley of the sons of Hinnom, running along outside a long stretch of the walls on the west and south of Jerusalem. Children had been sacrificed there to Moloch (Jer. 7: 31, 32); in our Lord's days it was the perpetually smouldering and vermin-infested incinerator for the refuse and sewage of the city. Its horrible associations and abominable condition made it an apt symbol of the sufferings of the lost. **6, 7.** But the Judge who is to be feared is also a Father to be trusted. He cares for the sparrows, nay, for each hair upon our heads; how much more will He not care for His own children? **8–12.** Loyalty to God can never remain an abstract idea: Jesus is Himself the object of it. From this follow three corollaries:

(a) A promise that if we confess Him now, He will confess us before His Father, and a warning that the converse is also true (this is given by Mk 8: 38 as a sort of pendant to the Caesarea-Philippi scene).

(b) The very difficult warning about blasphemy against the Holy Spirit: **And every one who speaks a word against the Son of man will be forgiven; but he who blasphemes against the Holy Spirit will not be forgiven** (10; cf. Mk 3: 28 f.; Mt. 12: 31 f.). Both Mt. and Mk place the saying in the context of the Beelzebul controversy (above, 11: 14–26). For comment, see note on parallels in Mt. and Mk.

(c) The promise that in persecution they will be sustained and empowered by the Holy Spirit Himself (11, 12; see Mt. 10: 19, 20; Mk 13: 11; also in the Lucan apocalyptic discourse,

21: 14, 15). Luke especially shows great interest in this promise, whose fulfilment he was later to describe in many incidents in Acts.

(ii) Warning against covetousness: the Parable of the Rich Fool (12: 13-21)
This discourse was brusquely interrupted by **one of the multitude** (13), who asked Jesus to intervene in a family dispute over the sharing out of an estate. The Greater than Solomon (11: 31) is asked to give judgment on the division, not of a baby but of an inheritance, and at that not even to act as an independent arbitrator, but to carry out the wishes of one party to the dispute: **Teacher, bid my brother divide the inheritance with me** (14). But He has not come to do that which Moses got into trouble for doing (14; cf. Exod. 2: 14); His mission was not to settle the differences which brothers, joint-heirs moreover of the covenant, ought easily to have composed themselves. Great rabbis were often asked so to act, but Jesus would not act as a great rabbi.

Instead of the reply he expected, the questioner heard the story of the Rich Fool (16-20). Jeremiah had said of the treasures of the rich that '*In the midst of his days they will leave him, and at the end he will be a fool*' (Jer. 17: 11); here is an eloquent comment on the text. A prosperous farmer is so well satisfied with the produce of his fields that he proposes to retire and lead an easier life, when he has dealt with his one outstanding problem, that of storage. But 'man proposes, God disposes', and that night not all his wealth can keep the angel of death from his door. He hears God Himself label him with Jeremiah's epithet: **Fool!** (20). He must leave his riches behind him; whose shall they be? These are questions that frequently occupied the thoughts of the OT writers; see, for instance, Job 27: 8; Ps. 39: 6; etc. Verse 21 provides the 'moral', the clue to understanding the parable.

(iii) Warning against anxiety and worldly care (12: 22-34)
Cf. Mt. 6: 25-34. These verses are almost entirely in close verbal agreement with Matthew's version in the Sermon on the Mount (see notes *ad loc.*) except for a few small additions:
32. The **little flock** are only lambs sent forth among wolves, but the good will of the Father who gives them the kingdom will surely not let them lack any protection of which they stand in need. **33. Sell your possessions and give alms:** Luke, ever practical, suggests how they can start to lay up treasure in heaven. **34.** If we know that we have treasure in heaven, the necessity to hoard earthly treasure disappears.
(iv) Warning of Crisis ahead (12: 35-59)
The rest of the chapter is taken up with Luke's

first great eschatological passage; men are warned to repent while there is still time. The emphasis is on the suddenness of the crisis and the consequent call for watchfulness. Furthermore, the present time is a time of crisis, overshadowing the disciples, the Lord Himself, and the nation of Israel.
(a) The Crisis and the disciples (12: 35-48)
35-40. They are slaves who must ever be alert, both for the unheralded return of their Lord, and for the possible intrusion of thieves. There is no exact parallel in Mt., though the Parable of the Maidens in Mt. 25: 1-13 elaborates a similar theme. The insistence is on watchfulness: **Let your loins be girded and your lamps burning, and be like men who are waiting for their master to come home from the marriage feast, so that they may open to him at once when he comes and knocks** (35, 36). The time their services will be called for is uncertain; they will not see their lord return. The first indication that he is back will be a knock on the door.
37. The idea of the master serving the slave is quite revolutionary; such an act would be quite unexpected (see 17: 7-10). But Jesus girded Himself to serve them (Jn 13: 4); some (*e.g.* Balmforth, p. 222) see a reference also to the Messianic Banquet. **39, 40.** Cf. Mt. 24: 43, 44.
41-48. These slaves, moreover, have each their appointed task to perform (cf. Mt. 24: 45-51). Verse 41 is missing from Mt.'s parallel which is otherwise very similar. Peter's question whether Jesus is speaking to the crowd or the disciples leads to special emphasis on the thought that superior privilege brings with it greater responsibility. Verses 47, 48 make a clear distinction between folly and rebellion. The slave who knows what is expected of him and fails to do it will be far more severely punished than the one who is merely careless in a general way. It is the Twelve whom Jesus has been carefully instructing since their call, and who therefore ought to know His will. The lesson of the parable of the Faithful Steward (42) is that **Every one to whom much is given, of him will much be required; and of him to whom men commit much they will demand the more** (48).
(b) The Crisis and our Lord (12: 49-53)
In these few verses of deep insight, the evangelist shows that the agony in Gethsemane was but the culmination of a long experience of facing the dark things that lay before Him; cf. Jn 12: 27.
51. The baptism here referred to is of course that which John and James so readily claimed they were capable of sharing (Mk 10: 38, 39). **52, 53.** The divisive effects of Christ's challenge

within the family, the misunderstandings and alienation of nearest and dearest, He Himself had been the first to suffer (8: 19-21, and even 2: 49), this having been predicted in the OT (Mic. 7: 6).

(c) The Crisis and Israel (12: 54-59)
Verses 54-56 have no parallel in Mt. George Adam Smith comments on the geographical exactness of the saying in vv. 54, 55 (*The Historical Geography of the Holy Land*, 1931, p. 66). Weather study is of vital importance to the farmer that he might be prepared for what is coming; why is this same perspicacity not also shown in spiritual matters?

56. hypocrites: A name used of the Pharisees in Luke only here and in 13: 15; but at least a dozen times in Mt. A hypocrite is originally a play-actor, someone pretending to be what he is not. At first, the word had no derogatory sense at all in Gk., though it had already come to have one in LXX. For the meaning of the word, see Wm. Barclay, *A New Testament Wordbook* (1955), pp. 56 ff.; for the Pharisees, H. L. Ellison, *art.* 'Pharisees' in *NBD*.

57-59. The Parable of the Lawsuit. In Mt. (5: 25, 26) this parable is found in the Sermon on the Mount. See note *ad loc.*

ii. The Peraean Ministry (13: 1-17: 10)
This title, commonly given to this section of the Gospel, is here used for the sake of convenience. It presupposes that the journey to Jerusalem took a longer route, east of the Jordan, presumably to avoid Samaritan unpleasantness. Mk 10: 1 says that Jesus 'went to the region of Judea and beyond the Jordan', and it is suggested that Luke is here giving details to fill in the summary. This reading of the geographical indications, however, is by no means universally accepted. N. B. Stonehouse (pp. 116 f.), discussing the problem, concludes: 'It appears then that it is plainly a misnomer to speak of this section as concerned with the "Peraean Ministry"'. He says that 17: 11 indicates that our Lord is still only as far on His journey as the Samaria-Judaea frontier, so that most of the events of 13: 1-17: 10 must be placed in Galilee. But whatever the location, our Lord's face is always towards Jerusalem (13: 22, 33).

(a) Warnings (13: 1-5)
Jesus takes two items of topical interest to point the moral of the urgent need for repentance.

1-3. News is brought to Him of a group of Galilean pilgrims, in Jerusalem for one of the feasts, who had run foul of the Roman procurator, Pontius Pilate. He ordered their execution and their blood flowed with that of their sacrificial beasts. His hearers seem to have regarded this as evidence of the exceptional wickedness of men on whom God allowed

such a catastrophe to fall, as did Job's friends and even Jesus' disciples (Jn 9: 2). But Jesus does not subscribe to this view; He does not even condemn Pilate's action, but warns His audience of their own need for repentance: **unless you repent, you will all likewise perish** (3). T. W. Manson (*Sayings*, p. 273) thinks that the messengers brought the news in the hope of tricking Jesus into some imprudent comment on Pilate; Plummer (p. 338) does not agree.

4, 5. A second catastrophe is mentioned, the collapse of the Siloam tower, unknown, like the previous incident, except in this passage. Eighteen persons lost their lives in an accident during building operations undertaken probably to strengthen Jerusalem's water-supply. Jesus draws the same lesson again.

(b) Parables and a Miracle (13: 6-21)
Jesus' stern note of warning that what has happened to others could happen to His hearers and that prudence therefore counselled repentance is followed in the Lucan account by the Parable of the Barren Fig Tree doomed to destruction, the miracle of the healing of the deformed woman, and the parables of the Mustard Seed and Leaven.

(i) The Parable of the Barren Fig Tree (13: 6-9)
The owner of a vineyard orders his gardener to cut down an unproductive fig tree growing there because it is occupying valuable space, but yields to the gardener's entreaties for one more chance.

This parable does not occur in Mt. or Mk, and since Luke makes no mention of the withering of the fig tree (Mt. 21: 19-22; Mk 11: 12-14, 20-22), many have assumed that Luke's parable is a 'softened-down' form of the act, others that it is the basis of Mark's story of the cursing. 'This is no more than a guess' says Balmforth (p. 225); Plummer (p. 339) says that the suggestion is arbitrary. At all events, the two passages are totally different in their emphasis. Luke's parable, following the teaching about the disasters, puts its stress on repentance, the other two synoptists on the inevitability of judgment.

6. his vineyard: Where the fig tree is growing; recalls the vineyard of Jehovah in Isa. 5. **7. these three years:** Long enough for a reasonable expectation of fruit when once the tree had reached maturity. The tree surely will bear after another year if it is ever going to. It is doubtful if we should see in the three years a reference to the duration of our Lord's ministry, or to the number of His visits to Jerusalem. **cut it down:** Cf. 3: 9.

(ii) The Sabbath Healing of an infirm woman (13: 10-17)
Having cured a badly crippled woman in the

synagogue on a Sabbath day, Jesus is rebuked by the ruler of the synagogue for having broken the Sabbath. He replies by defending the need to succour a neighbour in distress against mere traditionalist interpretations of the Law.

10. one of the synagogues: This is the last time Jesus is reported as teaching in a synagogue. **11. a spirit of infirmity:** Cf. 11: 14 where a dumb demon means 'a demon that causes dumbness'. **13.** This is the only exorcism in the Gospels accompanied by the laying on of hands. **14.** Plummer justly draws attention (p. 341) to the 'pomposity of the ruler of the synagogue, with his hard and fast rules about propriety', and sees in such lifelike details that 'all this is plainly drawn from life'. Rather than take on directly so redoubtable an opponent as Jesus, he addresses his observations to the congregation in general. That he should use his position of authority to condemn an act of mercy because it was done on the Sabbath gives point to our Lord's teaching on the urgent need for repentance. **15, 16.** Jesus answers, first (15) that they would all attend to their beasts on the Sabbath, so how much more important that human need should be succoured; secondly (16) that the Sabbath day of rest is eminently suitable for the crippled woman to obtain rest from Satan's 18 years of bondage. **17.** The adversaries retired crestfallen; the common people, as on other occasions, received Him gladly.

(iii) Two parables of the kingdom (13: 18–21)
Luke places here the parables of the grain of mustard seed (Mt. 13: 31, 32) and the leaven hidden in three measures of meal (Mt. 13: 33). Matthew puts both in his collection of parables of the kingdom in chap. 13.

For detailed comment, see notes on Mt. 13: 31-33.

(c) Further Warnings (13: 22-30)
On the move again with Jerusalem as the goal, Jesus is asked whether it is true that few only will be saved. He replies, not by satisfying curiosity, but by counselling effort to **enter by the narrow door,** otherwise there will be danger of being refused admission to the kingdom of God, the more galling as the Gentile nations will be seen entering in their place with the Patriarchs. Men's expectations will be turned upside down.

23. Nothing is known of the identity of the questioner nor of the motive for his question, if indeed it was prompted by anything more than mere curiosity. **24. strive:** The Gk. word is cognate with the English *agonize*, and is a favourite with Paul; e.g. 1 C. 9: 25; Col. 1: 29; 4: 12; also 1 Tim. 6: 11 and 2 Tim. 4: 7, in both of which it occurs both as verb and as noun,

'fight the fight'. It is connected with athletic contest, where the competitors go all out for victory. **the narrow door . . . many . . . will seek to enter and will not be able:** An echo of Mt. 7: 13 f., but not an actual parallel; there, there are two ways, here, one door only. **25.** The householder's refusal to open the door to admit those he professes not to know recalls the parable of the maidens in Mt. 25: 10-12. **26, 27.** These verses recall generally Mt. 7: 22 f. **28, 29.** Matthew appends a similar saying (8: 11, 12) to his account of the centurion at Capernaum (Mt. 8: 5-13; cf. Lk. 7: 1-10). Conditions are described on both sides of the closed door. Inside, patriarchs and prophets sit down with repentant Gentiles at the great messianic banquet; outside is despair for those who have depended on favouritism ('We have Abraham as our father', Lk. 3: 8) rather than on repentance for salvation. Their punishment is the worse for the realization of what might have been. **30.** A short summary of the section; the last day will reveal many reversals of human values.

(d) The Message to Herod and the Lament over Jerusalem (13: 31-35)
The progress of our Lord towards Jerusalem is interrupted by a message brought by Pharisee emissaries from Herod suggesting that He should get out of the way to avoid the death Herod intends for Him. He replies that He is not concerned with Herod's plans, but with the path laid down for Him towards Jerusalem. Fully aware of what awaits Him when He reaches the city, His concern is for her, and not for Himself.

The Herod referred to is Herod Antipas, tetrarch of Galilee (cf. 3: 1, 19; 9: 7 ff.), son of Herod the Great; he is the Herod of our Lord's trial (23: 7-12). It is debated whether Luke understands the Pharisees' warning as a friendly gesture or is rightly interpreted (e.g.) by N. B. Stonehouse as implying that 'they were virtually associated with Herod in wishing that He might be killed' (*The Witness of Luke to Christ*, p. 120).

32. Jesus replies first that He will go when it suits Him, not Herod; and secondly that Herod's word cannot be trusted; like the fox he is contemptible and crooked, not great nor even straight. **33.** Jesus knows that He will die, but He will die in the appointed place, Jerusalem; and at the appointed time, not today, nor even tomorrow, but the third day. This of course is not a literal indication of time, but 'since the period is measured in terms of days, Jesus appears to be intimating that the consummation is not far distant' (Stonehouse, p. 122). **34, 35.** Matthew places the lament after Palm Sunday, Jesus is already in Jerusalem (23: 27). In putting Him to death, Jerusalem is living up to her

233

ancient character of prophet-slayer (Jer. 26: 20-23; cf. Lk. 20: 10-12; Ac. 7: 52). **Jerusalem, Jerusalem:** The double vocative is a sign of affection and concern; cf. 10: 41; 22: 31. **as a hen gathers her brood:** A familiar figure in the OT, *e.g.*, Dt. 32: 11; Ps. 17: 8; 36: 7. **35.** The inevitable outcome of Jerusalem's ways will be utter ruin. When will they say **Blessed is he who comes in the name of the Lord?** To see Palm Sunday as its fulfilment is too limited; it is rather whenever, throughout time, a Jew repents and is converted (see Plummer, p. 353), and especially, perhaps, refers to Christ's welcome from the Jews at His second coming.

(e) Dinner with a Pharisee (14: 1-24)

Still moving on, Jesus has accepted an invitation to a Pharisee's house for a meal on the Sabbath day. After incurring the disapproval of His host by healing a man suffering from dropsy on the day of rest, He speaks of the principles of true hospitality and courtesy. His discourse includes the parables of the choice of places at table, and of the great supper.

(i) The man with dropsy (14: 1-6)

This is the last of the five Sabbath miracles of mercy recorded in the Synoptics—Luke records them all (4: 31; 4: 38; 6: 6; 13: 14 and the present incident). John adds two more (5: 10; 9: 14).

1. Jesus had previously accepted the invitations of Pharisees even though they were constantly engaging in controversy with Him; in fact, we never hear of His refusing such an invitation. **they were watching him:** This invitation appears to have had its ulterior motive. **2.** The man may have been brought in to trap Jesus, but it would not have been impossible, nor even unusual, for the uninvited to gain admittance to a private house (cf. 7: 37). In fact, the **let him go** of v. 4 rather suggests that he had come to be cured, not as a guest. **3.** Jesus answered their question before it was asked; cf. 18: 22 f. **5. Which of you, having an ass or an ox . . .** (of the word **ass,** RSVmg says 'other ancient authorities read *a son*'). Whichever is the correct reading, in both cases their act of mercy, unlike His on this occasion, would really be for their own benefit. Contrast this verse with 13: 15; there it is a matter of routine watering of stock; here it is a case of accident.

(ii) Places at table (14: 7-14)

See Prov. 25: 6, 7. The healing of the dropsical man seems to have taken place while the guests were assembling. When it is done and he has departed, the guests begin to take their places, some making for the seats of honour. Jesus proceeds to draw a lesson for the guests on the true humility that befits His followers, and then addresses to His host the counsel that he should invite to his feasts social inferiors in no position to return his hospitality rather than social equals who might.

11. This verse re-echoes the words of the *Magnificat* (1: 52), repeated again as a pendant to the parable of the Pharisee and the tax collector (18: 14) and in one of His disputes with the Pharisees (Mt. 23: 12).

(iii) The Parable of the Great Supper (14: 15-24)

The relation between this parable and that of the marriage of the King's son (Mt. 22: 1-10) is the subject of perennial discussion. The similarities are marked enough to invite comparison, the differences are sufficiently great to make it clear that the two parables are entirely distinct. Their contexts are totally different; the Lucan story is evoked by the comment of one of the guests: **Blessed is he who shall eat bread in the kingdom of God!** (15); the Matthaean follows the parable of the vineyard, and is in the setting of controversy with the Pharisees. In Luke **a man once gave a great banquet** (16); in Matthew a king sends invitations to a 'marriage feast for his son'. The guests in Luke's parable simply turn down the invitation (18-20); in Matthew's they ridicule the invitation and maltreat the servants. In both parables the invitations are amended and addressed to outcasts and the afflicted, but in Matthew's story this takes place only after a punitive military campaign against the murderers of the messengers.

15. The guest's ejaculation may have been insincere or merely superficial. 'Jesus questions, not the sentiment, which is unimpeachable, but the sincerity of the speaker, saying, in effect, "You talk beautifully about the kingdom of God but you do not mean a word of it. If you had the opportunity for which you profess to crave, you would unhesitatingly reject it"' (T. W. Manson, *Sayings*, p. 129). **16, 17. The second invitation.** 'It was a recognized custom to send a servant to repeat the invitation at the appointed time; cf. Est. 6: 14' (Creed, p. 191). Edersheim (ii, p. 427) quotes the Midrash (rabbinical commentary) on Lam. 4: 2 as authority for the Jerusalem custom of not going to a feast unless the invitation was repeated. **18-20.** The three excuses quoted all mean the same thing—'I've better things to do'. The discourtesy and the inadmissibility of the excuses lies in the fact that the men must have had these plans in mind at least when they received the original invitations, which they ought not to have accepted. A man's marriage, it is true, entitled him to a year's rest from social and military obligations (Dt. 24: 3); but courtesy should have prevented him from acceptance at the first. **21.** The original recipients of invitations, as well as the second group, lived in the city; this probably means that they are all Jews. The first group were the well-to-do, the elite of the nation, who were not interested, so now the outcasts and the despised, the publicans and sinners, are brought in. **23.** The highways and hedges could be outside the city, though, according to *Arndt* (under *phragmos*), 'Vagabonds and beggars frequent the hedges and fences around houses'. The Gentiles are now included in the invitation. **compel** (RSV, also AV; rather with RV, *constrain*): Force is not used, but the greatest efforts of persuasion. Creed suggests 'urge' or 'press'; NEB translates 'make them come in'; Ronald Knox: 'Give them no choice but to come in'. **24.** The punishment of those who had despised the invitation was complete exclusion from the feast. Matthew's parable ends much more sternly; those who have abused the messenger are destroyed and their city burned; while even at the wedding feast a guest who does not wear the robe provided is 'cast into outer darkness' (Mt. 22: 13). But then, in Mt. it is a king's invitation that is spurned, in Luke one from a private individual.

(*f*) Challenge to the Multitude (14: 25-35)
The scene now changes from the Pharisee's house; Jesus is walking along accompanied by a great multitude. He turns to them and discourses of discipleship, its cost and the disciple's need for intelligent thought and whole-hearted devotion.

(*i*) Discipleship calls for sacrifice (14: 26, 27)
Kinsfolk and life itself must yield to Him first place in the disciple's affections (26; cf. Mt. 10: 37, 38). **hate** must be considered in the light of OT usage: it frequently occurs together with 'love' in contexts where it clearly means to 'love less' (Gen. 29: 31 ff.; Dt. 21: 15 ff., etc.). It is not that a man must detest his family, but that they must take second place to the Lord in his affections.

27. Cf. Mk 8: 34. A criminal bearing his cross to the place of execution was no unfamiliar sight; what is really startling in this saying is the relation between this gibbet and the claims of the Messiah.

(*ii*) Discipleship may not be entered upon lightly (14: 28-33)
He who would follow Jesus must count the cost. 'The *parable of the "Tower"-builder, and of the king contemplating a Campaign*, is a call to self-testing. . . . By the lesser example of the farmer whose unfinished farm-buildings [alternative meaning of Gk. *pyrgos*, 'tower'] make him an object of ridicule, and the more important case of the king who, in planning a campaign,

has underestimated the strength of his enemy, and must therefore submit to his terms of peace, Jesus drives home the exhortation: Do not act without mature consideration' (J. Jeremias, *The Parables of Jesus*, E.T., 1963, p. 196).

(*iii*) Discipleship must be whole-hearted (14: 34, 35)
Half-hearted, it will be as insipid as stale salt. 'The true disciple is as salt; the half-hearted disciple, like tasteless salt, is useless' (Creed, p. 193). Matthew puts this similitude in the Sermon on the Mount. See note on Mt. 5: 13.

(*g*) Teaching Publicans and Sinners (15: 1-32)
The audience to whom these last sayings were addressed consisted of **great multitudes** (14: 25); tax-collectors and sinners join in with the throng, and for the third time Luke tells us that Jesus' willingness to consort with such people draws down upon Him the censure of the Pharisees (see 5: 30; 7: 39); the question will arise again when He accepts the hospitality of Zacchaeus (19: 7). It is this criticism which evokes from Jesus the three parables recorded in this chapter, of the lost sheep, of the lost coin and of the prodigal and his brother.

The three parables all concern lost things or creatures; each in its way presents God as seeking the lost, yet each has its own emphasis. The inanimate object in the second parable is simply lost. The animal in the first has gone astray through sheer stupidity. The son in the third has deliberately gone off by a headstrong act of self-will. So in turn the uselessness, the peril, and the misery of the lost life is demonstrated. Then again in each there is an element of repentance, in the first two in the refrain only; in the third underlying the whole parable.

The woman who has lost something of value makes a very thorough search; the shepherd tends the creature he has retrieved; the father extends to the son the whole gamut of forgiveness and reconciliation. In each case there is infinite trouble taken to find what is lost; and, as G. B. Caird (p. 181) points out: 'To call a man lost is to pay him a high compliment, for it means that he is precious in the sight of God'.

1, 2. The scribes and Pharisees see Jesus as debasing Himself by the company He keeps, even to the extent of engaging in the significant fellowship of a shared meal with them; they cannot accept His view that it is God Himself who wills that the outcasts should be gathered in.

(*i*) The Lost Sheep (15: 3-7)
Matthew records this parable (18: 12-14), but in a different setting, and with a different ending: 'So it is not the will of my Father who is in

heaven that one of these little ones should perish' (Mt. 18: 14).

A sheep has gone astray; normally the whole flock follows the wanderer, but here our creature has managed to detach himself from the main company. He wanders off through the wilderness (Gk. *erēmos*, a word that in the Bible includes not only the sand dunes or rocks that colour the popular imagination of a desert, but also scrub or rough pasture land; cf. Mk 6: 34 with 39; see *art.* 'Wilderness' in *NBD*); he nibbles on at what grass he finds. When he realizes he is alone he cannot, with his limited faculties, find his way back to the rest. If no one finds him he will stay where he is, or wander yet farther away, and starve. So the shepherd seeks until he finds him, and gently laying his burden across his shoulders, carries him back to the flock, **rejoicing,** and calls together his friends and neighbours to celebrate with him.

7. In the comparison between the shepherd's rejoicing and the joy in heaven over a repentant sinner, it is to be noticed that the emphasis is on the rejoicing rather than on the repentance, for the sheep clearly did not consciously repent. 'Neither the sheep nor the coin can repent; this may suggest that the sinner's repentance may be a gift of God, consequent on his being found, not the condition of his being found' (G. W. H. Lampe, in *Peake*[2], p. 836).

(ii) The Lost Coin (15: 8–10)
A woman has lost a silver coin, a drachma, the Greek equivalent of the Roman *denarius* of Mt. 20: 2, where it is the day's pay for an agricultural labourer. The total amount, ten drachmae, suggests a poor woman's savings rather than just the housekeeping money (T. W. Manson, *Sayings*, p. 284), or it may be, as Jeremias (pp. 134 f.) suggests, part of her headdress—and her dowry. Whichever it was, the small amount suggests poverty rather than opulence.

8. She **lights a lamp,** because the homes of the poor in Palestine are not well-lit, having but the smallest of windows. She turns the house upside-down, and takes no rest until the coin is found. **9.** Like the previous story, it ends in rejoicing with friends and neighbours. **10.** 'God, we are to understand, is not less persistent than men and women in seeking what he has lost, nor less jubilant when his search is successful' (G. B. Caird, p. 180).

(iii) The Prodigal Son (15: 11–32)
The third parable is probably the best known and loved of all our Lord uttered. Continuing the theme of the first two, it goes far beyond them in several ways: (*a*) The lost one on this occasion is a person, a wilful and rebellious son.

(*b*) It follows therefore that the part of the seeker is much larger; he not only seeks, but forgives and reconciles as well. (*c*) While there is rejoicing over the penitent scapegrace, there is also the churlish conduct of his elder brother. It is a parable with two main points.

11. There was a man who had two sons: The designation of the parable as the 'prodigal son' is hallowed by long usage, but it is really inadequate, for attention is drawn to all three of the main characters, not only the younger son. His arrant folly and his father's surpassing love and noble generosity make the first part of the story unforgettable, it is true; but it is the episode of the elder son that says to the listening Pharisees and scribes: 'Thou art the man'. **12. Father, give me the share of property that falls to me:** 'The younger son wanted an overdraft, the elder a current account'. There were two ways in which a Jewish father might pass on his property to his sons; by a will effective on his death; or by a deed of gift during his own lifetime. In the latter case, the property was legally vested in the son when the deed was executed, but the father enjoyed a life interest in the revenue (see, for instance, Jeremias, *Parables*, pp. 128 f.; T. W. Manson, *Sayings*, pp. 286 f.). Here it is clear that the father had gone well beyond his minimum legal obligations, placing capital at his younger son's disposal so that he might enjoy it forthwith instead of waiting for his father to die. **13. he gathered all he had:** I.e., he realized all his assets. **15.** His fair-weather friends having deserted him, he must now live by what means he can; he is forced to descend to the most degrading employment a Jew could imagine, tending swine. **16.** Hunger follows humiliation, he even envies his charges the carob pods on which they feed. Some have called carob pods 'St. John's bread', because they believed that John the Baptist ate these in the Jordan wilderness. 'To be compelled to eat St. John's bread was synonymous with the bitterest poverty and need' (Strack-Billerbeck, quoted by Geldenhuys, p. 411). **17–19.** Brought up with a jerk, the foolish young man comes to his senses and resolves to return to his father, to confess that he has abdicated any claim to sonship, but to beg for employment. **20. while he was yet at a distance, his father saw him . . . and ran and embraced him:** At first, the emphasis, as in the two preceding parables, is entirely on the father's joy. Scanning the distant horizon, he sees the object of so many prayers. Such is his delight that he runs, scarcely a dignified procedure for an elderly oriental, and cuts short the son's well rehearsed speech. So the request for a slave's employment remains unuttered, but the father divines what is in his son's heart. The son, indeed, ought to have known his father better; he is greeted as a beloved son. The servants are ordered to invest the son with the best robe, fitting for the guest of honour; to give to him the ring of authority and the shoes of freedom (slaves wore no shoes), and to slay the fatted calf that all may share in the father's gladness. **24.** So the son is restored to his former position. Some have said that this parable is not in line with the general teaching of Jesus in the NT, in that it has forgiveness without sacrifice, or even that we have here the Lord's original teaching before it became overlaid with theories of atonement (see Creed, p. 197). Such a view, however, assumes that each parable is a complete compendium of theology, a view that cannot be substantiated. Generally, a parable takes one point and drives it home, or very occasionally (as in this case) two points. The first part of this parable underlines the truth that genuine repentance must precede forgiveness; the father does not wait to listen to what his son has to say, for he can discern in his whole demeanour a changed attitude. The young man who had left home demanding 'give me' (12) comes back begging 'make me'.

25-32. With supreme artistry, Luke changes the whole atmosphere. **They began to make merry. Now his elder son was in the field:** The elder brother hears the sound of celebration, and frigidly stands outside while he enquires what it is all about. During his brother's absence he has lived under his father's roof, and yet has been in spirit as far away from the father as the prodigal himself. The contrast between the two sons is as great as that between the brothers in Mt. 21: 28-31.

The elder brother's hostility explodes; to the narrator's reproach that his brother has been culpably extravagant he adds, no doubt from his own jaundiced imagination, the accusation that he had frequented harlots (30). His ungracious manners contrast strikingly with his father's courtesy: **His father came out and entreated him** (28), and spoke to him of **this your brother;** the churlish reply says **this son of yours.**

By his whole attitude the elder son reveals his kinship with the Pharisee of Lk. 18: 11, 12. The whole parable points sternly at the Pharisees in Jesus' audience who, far from rejoicing that outcasts were finding blessing, **murmured, saying, 'This man receives sinners, and eats with them'** (v. 2).

(h) Teaching the Disciples (16: 1–17: 10)
The crowd appears to have been melting away, though the Pharisees were still listening (14);

Jesus now addresses His teachings to the disciples. His teaching ranges over various topics, and includes two of the major parables, the dishonest steward and Lazarus and the rich man.

(i) The parable of the dishonest steward (16: 1-9)
At first reading this parable comes with something of a shock since it appears to hold up a thorough scoundrel as a model to be imitated, which of course completely misses the point. Jeremias (p. 182) suggests that 'Jesus is apparently dealing with an actual case which had been indignantly related to Him'; but however that may be, the story bristles with difficulties, though many of these have arisen from treating the story as an allegory and attempting to see a meaning in each detail.

The central figure is called **the dishonest steward** (8), and there are varying views as to wherein he is dishonest. Some have suggested that his dishonesty had already been detected when the story opens and had led to his dismissal. According to this view the narrative tells of his efforts to put right the damage done. G. B. Caird (pp. 186 f.) gives an interesting account of this way of looking at the story, and suggests that the reduction of the outstanding debt may be simply the cancellation of the interest, bringing the steward's conduct more in line with OT teaching on usury; hence the commendation. There is little probability in J. N. Darby's dispensational interpretation: 'Israel was God's steward, put into God's Vineyard . . . but in all, Israel was found to have wasted His goods' (*The Gospel of Luke*, pp. 139 f.). Nor is the view too convincing that the steward's dishonesty lay in his cynical efforts to insure against the impending disaster by buying the protection of his master's debtors at the expense of the master himself. More probably the key to the parable is that a landowner on this scale will have given the stewardship to the man who promised him the highest income and whose payment would be the extra he could obtain. The steward's dishonesty consisted in **wasting his goods** by forcing too much out of the estate. What the steward deleted was the extra he hoped to get for himself. Only so can he be regarded as using his own money wisely; according to this view, only on the premise that he was giving away what was his can we make sense of it. Then, who was it that **commended the dishonest steward** (v. 8)? Was it the **master** within the parable, or the Lord who told the parable? That it was the rich man seems the natural view; but while it is generally accepted doubts are sometimes expressed as to why one who had suffered by his servant's dishonesty should praise him. The

237

solution surely is in the words of v. 8: **The master commended the dishonest steward for his prudence.** Faced by ruin, he took energetic action to ward it off; it is his foresight and resourcefulness which are commended, not his dishonesty. His planning and his efforts for his own personal ends put to shame the awareness and the perseverance of many of the sons of light who ought to recognize the things that lie ahead of them. 'It is all very well for you to be indignant', Jeremias (p. 182) paraphrases the words of Jesus: 'but you should apply the lesson to yourselves. You are in the same position as this steward who saw the imminent disaster threatening him with ruin, but the crisis which threatens you, in which, indeed, you are already involved, is incomparably more terrible'.

9. The parable ends with a piece of advice for His hearers: **Make friends for yourselves by means of unrighteous mammon, so that when it fails they may receive you into the eternal habitations:** Money, tainted as it is, should be used in such a way that **when it fails**—that is, at death, when it can no longer avail—spiritual enrichment will be ensured in contrast with that of this transitory life. The message is clear; in our stewardship for God let us be at least as whole-hearted and energetic as was the steward in prosecuting his own interests.

(*ii*) **Sayings about riches and pride (16: 10–15)**
Any doubts one might entertain about the meaning of the parable must be dispelled by the sayings that follow, underlining the paramount importance of integrity. Honesty must be seen in the minute details if it is to be manifested in the major affairs of life (10). If we are not faithful in material things, how can we be trusted in spiritual matters? (11) and if we cannot be trusted with what belongs to others, how can we be expected to be faithful in regard to our own? (12) To serve God is full-time employment; as with slaves, all our time and all our effort belongs to our Master (13). Finally, when the money-loving Pharisees scoff at Him (14), He warns them that though they may impress men, they cannot deceive God, who loathes their pride (15).

13. This verse is paralleled in Mt. 6: 24, in the setting of the Sermon on the Mount; the remainder is peculiar to Luke.

(*iii*) **Sayings concerning the new order (16: 16–18)**
Three short sayings concerning the kingdom, the law, and divorce. The first two occur in Mt. also, and so probably belong to Q, the third is found in all the Synoptics. For v. 16, see notes on Mt. 11: 12, 13; for v. 17, notes on Mt. 5: 18, and for v. 18, notes on Mk 10: 4, 11, 12 and Mt. 5: 31 f.

(*iv*) **The Parable of Lazarus and the Rich Man (16: 19–31)**
A rich man, enjoying every luxury of dress and of food, dies at about the same time as Lazarus, a poor wretch who sits at his door and begs, and whom he scarce deigns to notice. In the afterworld, their rôles are reversed; the beggar enjoys the felicity of **Abraham's bosom,** while the rich man is **in Hades, being in torment.** In this plight, he still wants to command menial service from Lazarus, but Abraham points out that he has already had more than his fair share of the good things; and apart from this, traffic between the two sides is quite impossible. Having failed to get some concession for himself, the rich man begs that Lazarus might be sent to his five brothers in order to warn them. But this request also is refused, since they have all the warning they need in the scriptures.

This parable is different from all the others in that the central character is named; some have, for this reason, held that it is to be regarded as historical narrative rather than parable. But this view, entirely apart from the fact that all the narrative parables probably tell of events that actually happened, ignores the element of symbolism that is quite apparent in the story. 'Abraham's bosom', the 'great chasm fixed', and 'this flame' obviously ought not to be pressed into too materialistically literal a meaning, and it would be rash to attempt a description of the after-life from the details given here. As Alan Richardson justly says, 'the aim of the parable is not to acquaint us with details of the life to come, but to confront us with our duty in this life' (*A Theological Word Book of the Bible*, 1950, p. 107).

Certain truths concerning the life to come are, however, inescapably insisted on in the parable. First, there is the finality of death as far as human destiny is concerned; the state of the individual soul after death is irrevocably settled during his lifetime. Secondly, whatever is figured by the symbolic language, the parable clearly teaches that the lot of the righteous is infinite happiness, and of the ungodly indescribable distress. Both the happiness and the distress are conscious, and what is more, the memory of this life with its lost opportunities subsists in the Beyond. Thirdly, in addition to this insistence on the reality of differing conditions after death, there is an equal insistence on the truth that there is for all men a sufficient guide to heaven in the scriptures.

19. There was a rich man: His name is not given; *Dives* is merely the Latin for a rich man. Whoever he was, he seems to fit the description of a Sadducee: he is wealthy, wearing dress befitting high rank. A thorough-going materialist whose philosophy seems to be 'let us eat and drink, for tomorrow we die', he is a rationalist also who does not believe in an after-life any more than do the brothers he wants, too late, to awaken to the truth. But this does not justify the assumption of T. W. Manson (*Sayings*, p. 295) and others that Luke is mistaken in mentioning Pharisees in v. 14, where he should have written 'Sadducees'; indeed, despite what has just been said, the parable has been regarded by some as an amplification of 16: 14 f., in which case the rich man would be a Pharisee after all. **20. Lazarus:** the only named character in a parable. It is the Gk. form of the OT name Eleazar, 'God is his help', and a sufficiently common name in NT days to make it unprofitable to speculate on the identity of this particular Lazarus. **22.** 'The image is derived from the custom of reclining on couches at meals. "The disciple whom Jesus loved" reclined in Jesus' bosom at the last supper (Jn 13: 23)' (Balmforth, p. 244). **23. Hades:** In general usage Gk. *Haidēs* was roughly equivalent to Heb. *She'ol*, the grave, the abode of the departed whether good or bad, but later it came to be used almost exclusively for the place of the wicked dead. **25.** A statement of a circumstance of the present narrative, not the enunciation of the doctrine that in the after-life there is a mere reversal of the fortunes of this life. **31. neither will they be convinced if someone should rise from the dead:** A saying abundantly fulfilled shortly afterwards. The majority of Jews refused to be convinced when Jesus Himself rose from the dead.

(v) Four more sayings (17: 1-10)
There now follows a short series of sayings, apparently quite miscellaneous, and yet, as Geldenhuys (p. 531) says: 'It appears to us that there is a unity between the various pronouncements and that (although Luke does not expressly say so) they were uttered on one and the same occasion'. Their general theme is the responsibility of the disciple towards others, warning them of the sinfulness of leading weaker ones astray, the need for a forgiving spirit and for real, practical faith, and the danger of trusting in the mere fulfilment of obligations to obtain merit.

1, 2. Occurs in Mt. 18: 6, 7 and Mk 9: 42. Who are the **little ones** in verse 2? There is no indication of children present on this occasion; most of the commentators take the phrase as referring to the weaker brethren among the disciples. Such a reading is suggested by the Marcan parallel; Mt. however puts the saying in the context of one of his child-passages (18: 1-5). There is, of course, no

reason why both should not be in view. **3, 4.** One of the marks of a disciple is willingness to forgive. Sin is not to be over-looked, nor lightly passed over; the wrongdoer must be rebuked, his sin must be discussed to his face and not behind his back. Repentance must precede forgiveness. But subject to these conditions there is no limit to the number of times forgiveness ought to be extended. In Mt. the passage is fuller and in the reply to a question of Peter's, it is followed by the parable of the unforgiving creditor (18: 15-35).

5, 6. The magnitude of the responsibility that these sayings impose awoke in the disciples a sense of their inadequacy; they **said to the Lord, 'Increase our faith!'** With oriental hyperbole Jesus gives them an insight into unsuspected possibilities. The sycamine is a tree of the mulberry family, its roots were regarded by the ancients as particularly strong. Strack-Billerbeck (quoted by Geldenhuys, p. 434) say: 'it was supposed that the tree could stand in the earth for 600 years'. To uproot it would be a virtual impossibility, to replant it in the ocean bed even more so, but faith in God surmounts impossibilities. Mk 11: 23/ Mt. 21: 21 has a similar saying in the context of the withering of the fig-tree; here it is a mountain that is to be cast into the sea.

7-10. A parable of service. From speaking of faith, Jesus goes on to talk of works, inadequate because the very best that we can do is nothing more than our duty (see note on 12: 37). **unworthy servants** does not suggest the servants have been remiss or done less than their duty, but that they had simply done what their master had a right to expect.

iii. The Last Journey to Jerusalem (17: 11-19: 27)
The last stage of the Journey has now arrived: **on the way to Jerusalem he was passing along between Samaria and Galilee.** Throughout this long journeying with which so much of Luke is concerned, Jerusalem, with the dark events that are to take place there, is constantly in view.

(a) Ministry in Samaria and Galilee (17: 11-18: 14)
(i) Ten lepers healed (17: 11-19)
At the entrance of a village, ten lepers stand at a respectful distance because of their disease and beg Jesus to have mercy on them. He sends them to the priest to certify the cleansing that He has bestowed. One only, and he a Samaritan, has the courtesy to return and thank his benefactor, who remarks on the fact that it should be a Samaritan who does so.

14. The actual healing is not described but assumed as a fact. In 5: 12-16 'he stretched out his hand and touched him', not fearing the contagion of the disease. **16.** The thanks of the Samaritan was evidence of fact for those who saw in the parable of the Good Samaritan a mere fable.

(ii) **The sudden coming of the kingdom (17: 20-37)**
Some Pharisees approach the Lord with questions about the time of the coming of the kingdom of God. He replies that though this question is on the minds of many, the important thing that they should know is that the coming will be unheralded, and that before the coming the Son of man will be rejected and suffer at the hands of sinners. In the days of Noah and Lot people lived entirely unconcerned, not suspecting that the Flood and the destruction of Sodom impended. It will be the same with the coming of the Son of man. The kingdom will be upon men before they know, its manifestation will be quite unmistakeable, and it will cut across all human relationship of class or kinship. No answer is vouchsafed to those who enquire about the details.

Luke has three main sections concerned with the last things: *(a)* 12: 34-59. The imminent crisis, about to fall, nay, upon them already; cf. Mt. 24: 43-51. *(b)* 17: 20-37. The unheralded coming of the 'day of the Son of man'; cf. Mt. 24: 23-28; 37-41. *(c)* 21: 5-36. The parousia of the Son of man, Luke's version in the main of Mark's apocalyptic chapter 13. The 'Little Apocalypse', as Mk 13 is sometimes called, appears almost complete in Mt. and Luke; the material in Lk. 17 appears woven by Mt. into his version of Mk 13.

20, 21. These verses have no parallel in Mt., and are not easy to understand, since the expression **in the midst of you** is rather ambiguous (RSVmg, with AV and RV, has 'within you'); the Gk. *entos* is not the usual word that Luke uses for 'in the midst of' (in fact it is found nowhere else in the Gospel). So the phrase is variously interpreted as 'among you', i.e. the King Himself is actually in your midst, or 'within you', the spiritual kingdom in the hearts of men. It is difficult to see how the latter can be the meaning here, since the words are addressed to Pharisees (20). Other possible renderings are 'within your possession' and 'within your reach'. **22, 23.** See notes on Mk 13: 21 (Mt. 24: 23). **24.** See note on Mt. 24: 27. **25.** A third prediction of the Passion (Luke only). **26-30.** See notes on Mt. 24: 37-39. **31.** See note on Mt. 24: 17, 18. **32.** A warning peculiar to Luke, evoked by the words **let him . . . not turn back** (31). **33.** Mk 8: 35 and Mt. 16: 25 have this saying in the context of the warnings of Jesus after Peter's confession.

34, 35. See notes on Mt. 24: 40, 41. **37.** Cf. Mt. 24: 28. In v. 20, the Pharisees ask 'When?' now they ask **Where?** but Jesus refuses to satisfy the curiosity of 'date-fixers' and the like.

(iii) **The parable of the Unjust Judge (18: 1-8)**
Jesus now tells another parable, whose purpose is clearly stated: **they ought always to pray and not lose heart.** It is the story of a cynical and unprincipled judge who is unmoved by a widow's plea for justice, but finally settles her case merely because her constant requests are becoming a nuisance to him.

This is an excellent example of the rule of interpretation that the lesson of a parable must be sought in its main point, and not in its details, for a judge who ignores the two great commandments and neither fears God nor regards man can surely hardly teach us anything about the character of God. The point of the parable is in an *a fortiori* argument; if an earthly judge, devoid of all sentiment of justice, yields to the importunity of the widow from sheer weariness, how much more will not God, who loves to hear His children's prayers, delight to answer them when, as in this case, the cause is just.

8-10. An apocalyptic note is introduced; the truths of the previous chapter seem still to be occupying His mind.

(iv) **The parable of the tax-collector and the Pharisee (18: 9-14)**
Again a parable is introduced by an indication of its interpretation; it is told to **some who trusted in themselves that they were righteous, and despised others.** A Pharisee at prayer is contrasted with one of the hated tax-collectors. The former takes up his position and gives thanks to God that unlike other men he performs all that the law demands and more besides. The tax-collector on the other hand, clearly distressed and agitated by his sense of his own unworthiness, pleads humbly with God for mercy. **This man,** says Jesus, **went down to his house justified more than the other.**

11. The Pharisee does not really pray at all. He asks God for nothing, and his thanksgiving is merely a form. 'He glances at God, but contemplates himself' (Plummer, p. 417). 'He thanks God for what *he is*, not for what God is' (J. N. Darby, p. 152). **12. I fast twice a week, I give tithes of all that I get:** Pious Jews made a point of fasting on Mondays and Thursdays; Pharisees gave tithes not only of their crops, as the law required (Dt. 24: 22 f.), but even of their garden herbs (Mt. 23: 23). **13.** The tax-collector's distress is seen in that he beats his breast; cf. 23: 48. His only plea is his great need; cf. Dan. 9: 19.

(b) Teaching on children (18: 15-17)
Cf. Mk 10: 13-16; Mt. 19: 13-15. These two parables occur only in Luke, but for the account of the rest of the journey Luke again follows Mk. In this episode the disciples, seeking no doubt to spare their Master from added strain, turn away children who have been brought to Him to be blessed. Jesus countermands their order and calls the children to Him, **for to such belongs the kingdom of God.**

For more detailed treatment, see notes on Mk 10: 13-16.

(c) The Rich Young Ruler (18: 18-30)
Cf. Mk 10: 17-31; Mt. 19: 16-30. A ruler asks Jesus about eternal life and how it may be obtained. Jesus' answer suggests that the question is superfluous, since the rules are there for all to read in the Ten Commandments. The man claims that he has always obeyed these, but still feels his need of something more. The Lord then says that possessions are the barrier in his case; he must dispose of them and distribute to the poor. The correctness of the diagnosis is proved by the attitude of the enquirer; he is saddened by the Lord's words, because he is **very rich** (23). There follow sayings on the barrier erected by riches between their possessor and true spiritual life, and on the reward of those who for God's sake make sacrifice of riches.

18. a ruler: All the synoptics say he was rich, Luke only calls him a ruler, Matthew only says that he was young. **22.** Mark adds that 'Jesus, looking on him, loved him'. His possessions must be disposed of not because wealth is evil in itself, but because in his case it keeps him from spiritual blessing. **25. a camel:** It is not necessary to read this as 'rope', nor to see the needle's eye as a postern gate. Hyperbole is a frequently used figure of speech in our Lord's teaching; cf. 17: 6; 6: 41; also Mt. 23: 24, etc. **28, 29.** In Jesus' reply to Peter's comment about what they, the disciples, have given up, Luke omits 'sisters' and 'lands', but adds **wife** to the Matthew/Mark account. Matthew follows the incident by the parable of the Workers in the Vineyard (20: 1-16). See also notes on Mk 10: 17-31.

(d) The third prediction of His death (18: 31-34)
The third of the three predictions of the passion recorded by all the Synoptics is uttered at this point (Luke himself has another: 17: 25). Luke omits the account of the ambition of James and John to occupy the highest places in the kingdom associated with the prediction in Mt. and Mk. This prediction is the first to link the suffering specifically with Jerusalem; Luke furthermore mentions that the sufferings

are in fulfilment of OT prophecy. For comments, see notes on Mk 10: 32-34.

(e) The Approach to Jerusalem (18: 35-19: 27)
(i) Healing a blind beggar (18: 35-43)
Cf. Mk 10: 46-52; Mt. 20: 29-34. At last the long journey is almost over and they come to Jericho. At the gates of the city our Lord performs a miracle of restoration of sight. A beggar calls on Him, crying for mercy. Mark identifies the beggar as Bartimaeus; Matthew says there were two beggars. He addresses Jesus by His messianic title **son of David,** Jesus stops and asks him what he wants. He asks that his sight might be restored; his prayer is answered with Jesus' comment, **your faith has made you well.** The result of this miracle is that not only the healed man but the onlookers also give praise to God.

(ii) Zacchaeus the Tax-collector entertains Jesus (19: 1-10)
The story of Zacchaeus, **a chief tax-collector, and rich,** is told only by Luke. He wanted to see this Jesus of whom he had heard so much, but he was so short that the crowd made it impossible for him to see anything. Accordingly, he climbed up into the branches of a tree on the route along which the party would pass. Jesus saw him in the tree and called him down, asking him for hospitality. The usual murmurs are heard that Jesus should eat with a tax-collector (cf. 5: 29, 30).

T. W. Manson calls the incident 'a fitting pendant to the parable of the Pharisee and the publican. In the parable He pillories the Pharisaic attitude towards these outcasts; in the case of Zacchaeus He shows by His own example a more excellent way' (*Sayings*, p. 312).

1. He . . . was passing through: They are now actually inside the city of Jericho. **2. a chief tax collector:** 'The title occurs nowhere else in extant Greek literature, so that its precise meaning is in doubt. He may have been a contractor who bought the local taxation rights from the Roman government' (Caird, p. 207). **3, 4.** There is no suggestion that he was trying to hide; he was quite open in his efforts to see Jesus. When Jesus spoke to him, he came down **joyfully** (6). **8.** The profession of Zacchaeus seems to have been evoked by the ungracious comments in v. 7. There is all the difference between him and the Pharisee in the parable who gave his catalogue of good deeds from motives of pure self-congratulation. With Zacchaeus it was not so, the almsgiving and restitution of which he speaks start now as a token of the change wrought in him by his meeting with Jesus; 'not to be regarded as in the parable in self-justification, but as a statement of what he intends to do henceforth. "I *hereby*

J

give to the poor"—it is an act done there and then' (Plummer, p. 435). **10. the Son of man came to seek and to save the lost:** The criterion in God's dealings with men is not man's merit but his need.

(iii) **The parable of the Pounds (19: 11–27)** Jerusalem is at last in sight, and because the general expectation is that the prophecies concerning the kingdom will be fulfilled once they arrive within the city, Jesus tells them another parable.

A nobleman, going to a distant capital to **receive kingly power,** leaves with various servants a pound each that they may trade until his return. He is not popular, and the citizens send a deputation in an unsuccessful attempt to secure the rejection of his claim. On his return with the desired royal dignity he calls the servants to give account of their stewardship; the successful ones are rewarded according to their success. One who confesses he has made no effort is rebuked and his pound taken from him; the rebels who have tried to throw off their master's rule are slain.

Matthew has a parable (the talents, 25: 14–30) which has striking similarities, but the differences are so marked that there is no possibility that the two are records of the same parable.

It is sometimes said that Luke's story is so mixed up that it cannot be genuine, that into Matthew's straightforward story he has worked the 'sub-plot' of the rebellious citizens. This, it is alleged, makes the story unbalanced and inconsequential. But these criticisms are without validity if, as seems likely, Jesus was relating an actual event, for real life is not always symmetrical! Josephus tells how Herod's will divided his territories after his death among his family, and how, before its bequests became valid, they had to be confirmed by the Roman Emperor. Herod's son Archelaus went to Rome for confirmation in his post, and was in fact followed by an embassy of protesting Jews. In the event, Augustus sided with Archelaus.

12. The nobleman going to receive kingly power becomes in Mt. 25: 14 'a man going on a journey'. **13.** Each servant receives a **pound** or **mina,** worth, according to RSVmg, about $20 or £8. In Mt. 25: 15 different amounts—5, 2 or 1 talent—are given according to the recipient's ability. The talent was worth about $1,000 or £400, but its purchasing power was much more than that. **16, 18.** The successful servants have made profits of 1,000% and 500%; in Mt. 25: 16 f. each has made just 100%. **17–19** shows different rewards from those in Mt. 25: 22 f.

VII. THE PASSION WEEK (19: 28–22: 13)
i. The Triumphal Entry (19: 28–40)
Cf. Mk 11: 1–10; Mt. 21: 1–9. Now they enter the city, as the prophet Zechariah (9: 9) had long ago foretold, with their King welcomed by the plaudits of the people as He comes not as a military conqueror on a charger, but meek and lowly, seated on an ass, as befits the Ambassador of peace. With true majesty the Son of David moves on towards His passion. He had made arrangements for the ass that Zechariah's prophecy might be fulfilled; He will be equally careful to see that all the other prophecies are fulfilled, even though it be His own death that is prophesied.

39, 40. It is Luke only who records the request of the Pharisees to Jesus to silence the crowds who acclaim Him as the Messiah; and His reply that if they were silenced the very stones would cry out.

For notes on details, see comments on Mk 11: 1–10.

ii. Jesus' view of the City (19: 41–44)
Cf. Mk 11: 11; Mt. 21: 10, 11. Jesus sees before Him now what earlier was but the distant goal (13: 34–38). His heart is saddened again, and He weeps over the city. Had His followers not sung His praises, the stones would have cried out. Those very stones are now witnesses to the people's blindness and obstinacy; soon their enemies **will not leave one stone upon another in you.** Zechariah the priest (1: 67) had praised God who had visited His people; **you,** says Jesus to the people of Jerusalem, **did not know the time of your visitation.**

iii. The Cleansing of the Temple (19: 45–48)
(Cf. Mk 11: 15–19; Mt. 21: 12, 13. For the relation of the Synoptic record of the Temple cleansing, dated early in Holy Week, to John's, which is placed at the outset of the ministry, see notes on Jn 2: 13–17.) Jesus expels from the Temple those who are turning God's house into a mere place of self-enrichment; who like robbers on the Jericho road have a sanctuary into which they can withdraw with their spoils after an attack. The Temple cleansed, Jesus spends the last few days of His freedom teaching the people there. See notes on Mk 11: 15–19.

iv. Controversy (20: 1–44)
Cf. Mk 11: 27–12: 37; Mt. 21: 23–22: 46. **he was teaching daily in the temple (19: 47)** describes His activity during the opening days of the week which is to see His crucifixion. **1. he was teaching the people in the temple and preaching the gospel:** Proclaiming the good news under the very shadow of the Cross. The Jewish leaders would love to silence Him, but various reasons make it unwise from their point of view. First, it is clear that the

upsurge of popularity which greeted His arrival on Palm Sunday is not yet spent: **all the people hung upon his words** (19: 48). Then, His action in protesting against the commercialization of the Temple worship is no doubt approved by many who could by no means be reckoned amongst His followers. Thirdly, while He is in the Temple He is under their eyes, and might possibly be caught out in something He says.

They have certainly not given up. The wheel has come full circle; our Lord's public ministry which began with conflict with the Pharisees because of His claims to unique authority closes in a further series of conflicts on the same subject.

1-8. So the attack begins. They come with an apparently guileless request for a statement from Him on the source of His authority for what He does. Instead of a direct reply He puts a question to them: **Was the baptism of John from heaven or from men?** (5). Caught in the dilemma between admitting that they have refused the messenger of heaven or provoking popular anger by denigrating John, who by now has become a popular hero, they retire temporarily from the fray.

9-19. Jesus pursues His attack in His parable of the wicked husbandmen. The scene is the vineyard of Isa. 5: 1-7; the tenants refuse to pay their dues to the owner, and maltreat his messengers. Finally he sends his son and heir, whom the tenants murder in order themselves to seize the inheritance. The owner of the vineyard exacts retribution upon the murderers; the prophecy of Ps. 118: 22, 23 is fulfilled when the stone regarded by the builders as unfit for use becomes the chief cornerstone of the building. This stone, furthermore, brings disaster on every adversary. There is no difficulty in interpreting the parable; Isaiah tells the identity of the vineyard, its owner and its husbandmen; the Pharisees **perceived that he had told this parable against them** (19). Their determination to silence Him increases.

20-26. Spies and *agents-provocateurs* are set to watch Him, and if possible trap Him into compromising words. Luke does not mention the co-operation of the Herodians which, Mark and Matthew tell us, the Pharisees have enlisted, but he rewrites this introductory verse to make their intentions crystal clear. They open the question of tribute to Caesar, inviting Jesus to say either that it was unlawful, which would embroil Him with the Romans; or lawful, which might alienate His own followers. Replying, He shows that by using coins bearing the effigy of Caesar they are tacitly admitting the Roman claims; and, as J. M. Creed says: 'The answer of Jesus carries the implications (1)

that man's relationship to God is established in its own right, and (2) that this relationship does not justify a repudiation of Caesar in his own sphere'.

27-40. This assault having failed, the Sadducees take a hand. For details of the Sadducees and their beliefs, see *NBD*. Their outlook was quite different from that of the Pharisees, whose oral tradition they rejected; they accepted nothing but the books of Moses, rejecting the existence of angels and the truth of life after death which had to be proved from the Prophets or the Writings. They pose a question which will, they hope, show that personal survival in after-life is at variance with the Mosaic teaching. According to Dt. 25: 5-10, if a man dies without an heir, any unmarried brother of his has an obligation to marry his brother's widow. The Sadducees propound the case of a woman who under this law in turn weds seven brothers; of which is she the wife in the life to come? Jesus replies, first that there is no marriage in heaven, since immortal beings have no need of procreation; and secondly that the very Pentateuch from which they have quoted bears strong testimony to the truth of life after death, for He who says (Exod. 3: 6) **I am the God of Abraham, the God of Isaac, and the God of Jacob** is the God not of the dead, but of the living! So another attempt to score a debating point has not only failed but recoiled on them to show the hollowness of their teaching. **37. in the passage about the bush:** the Hebrew way of referring to Exod. 3.

41-44. In Mt. and Mk, the victory over the Sadducees is followed by a question concerning the great commandment which Luke places not here but as a preface to the parable of the Good Samaritan (10: 25-28). Jesus now puts His own question to His adversaries; it is reported by all three Synoptics: How can Messiah be David's Son if in Ps. 110: 1 David calls Messiah **Lord?** Luke, eloquently silent, records no reaction to this question. Mt. 22: 46 tells us that the Jews are completely silenced; Mk 12: 37 says that 'the common people heard Him gladly'. For detailed comments on Lk. 20: 1-44, see notes on Mk 11: 27-12: 37.

v. Condemnation of the Scribes and Pharisees (20: 45-47)
Recorded also by Mark, and by Matthew at greater length (Mt. 23: 1-10). The long conflict of words is over; Jesus now utters a final scathing denunciation of the scribes (and Pharisees, Mt. 23: 2). See notes on Mk 12: 38-40, which Luke has almost verbatim.

vi. Jesus' observation of the widow (21: 1-4)
Cf. Mk 12: 41-44. With the spurious piety of

the Pharisees and scribes, Jesus contrasts the sacrificial giving of a poor widow who casts into the treasury a mere two mites, while the rich make their lordlier donations. But it is not the amount given that is the measure of the sacrifice; it is the amount the giver has left when he has given. This widow has kept nothing back for herself. See notes on Mk 12: 41–44.

vii. The Apocalyptic Discourse (21: 5–38)

Cf. Mk 13: 1–37; Mt. 24; 25. The three Synoptics all place between the close of Jesus' public ministry and the events of the last few hours a long apocalyptic discourse, frequently referred to as the 'Little Apocalypse'. This discourse has been the subject of much discussion.

First, many who do not take kindly to the idea of predictive prophecy at all claim that Jesus did not foretell future events, and that passages which claim that He did are merely the early Church's ideas on the Last Things or her *ex post facto* 'prophecies' concerning incidents like the Fall of Jerusalem which had already taken place at the time of writing. In reply to such criticism it can confidently be said that for many years now there has been an increasing recognition of the essential part that apocalyptic and eschatology have in the teaching of Jesus; He *did* speak of things which had not yet come to pass.

Others accept this view, but see in the discourse a composite sermon composed of sayings of Jesus cognate to the subject, some or all of them authentic, but uttered at varying times and different occasions during His ministry.

Thirdly, the discourse according to Mt. 24: 3 was occasioned by two questions the disciples asked: when would the fall of Jerusalem be? and what would be the sign of His coming and of the close of the age? The result is that the two events, the impending and the remote, are in view, and it is not always easy to distinguish between them in the chapter.

Fourthly, there is the question of the relationship of the accounts of the discourse to each other. T. W. Manson (*Sayings*, p. 323) analyses Luke's version and finds that about half of its contents derives from Mk, another fifth is definitely non-Marcan (i.e. from Luke's own source), the remainder cannot be assigned with certainty to either. He interprets this as giving two possible alternatives: either that Luke had Mark's account before him and rewrote it freely (which for various reasons Manson deems unlikely) or that what we have is Luke's own source supplemented by passages from Mk. The discussion is interesting, but perhaps insufficient weight is given to the

possibility that Mark and Luke each had an accurate summary of a discourse actually given on this specific occasion. Such summaries might have been independent of each other, and yet have verbal coincidences especially at important points. Even identical wording need not demand the explanation that one was dependent on the other.

Matthew, as has already been noted (see notes on Lk. 17: 30–37) includes in his version not only the material from Mk 13, but also that from Lk. 17; he also follows the discourse with a series of apocalyptic parables (chap. 25) which neither Luke nor Mark records. Notes on Mk 13 should be consulted for detailed commentary, the present notes will particularize only when Luke and Mk differ.

5–7. Cf. Mk 13: 1–4. In the opening verses Luke omits indications of place and people that Mk and Mt. give. The saying of vv. 5, 6 Mark places 'as he came out of the temple'. His companion are 'disciples'. Luke omits the place altogether and says merely that **some** spoke of the temple. V. 7 is placed by Mark 'on the mount of Olives, opposite the temple', and Peter, James, John and Andrew are with Jesus; here simply **and they asked him.** The discourse starts with reference to the stones of the Temple, a recurrence of the *motif* of 19: 40 and 20: 17, 18.

8–11. The signs of the coming judgment are going to be the rise of false Messiahs and the break-up of both the social and the natural orders with wars, disturbances, earthquakes, famines and pestilences. **8.** Luke adds to Mark's verse: **Do not go after them.**

12–19. The disciples themselves will know severe persecution from the authorities and even from their kinsfolk and friends. **12.** Here there is no reference to floggings, which Mk foretells (13: 9); Luke was later to describe in Acts some of the floggings the disciples endured. **14, 15.** This passage diverges from Mk 13: 11, to which however a close parallel is found in Lk. 12: 11, 12. **18.** The promise that **not a hair of your head will perish** is lacking in Mk. It is the experience of Daniel's three companions in the fiery furnace (Dan 3: 27). Cf. Ac. 27: 34.

20–24. Cf. Mk 13: 14–20. This passage, which tells of the catastrophes attending the fall of Jerusalem, differs at two important points from Mk's parallel: (*a*) The reference in Mk 13: 14 and Mt. 24: 15 to 'the desolating sacrilege set up where it ought not to be' (Dan. 9: 27; 11: 31; 12: 11) becomes in Luke **Jerusalem surrounded by armies.** Many critics adduce this fact as evidence to date Luke after the fall of Jerusalem, but this very general reference to armies surrounding the city does not imply detailed knowledge of the events of A.D. 70. More likely is the suggestion of Geldenhuys (p. 532) that 'Luke is writing for Greek readers who would not understand what Jesus meant by the Jewish expression, and so paraphrases it'. (*b*) Luke omits the saying in Mt. and Mk (13: 20) about 'shortening the days for the elect's sake', replacing it by the statement that **Jerusalem will be trodden down by the Gentiles until the times of the Gentiles are fulfilled** (24). This refers probably to the end of the present world order.

25-28. The Great Consummation (Mk 13: 24-27). Before this section, Mk and Mt. introduce a passage which Luke has at 17: 20-23; Mt. also inserts the Lucan saying (Lk. 17: 24) about the day of the Son of man. Luke's description of the actual consummation shows two differences from Mk's: (*a*) after the prediction of signs in sun, moon and stars, he says there will be parallel calamities on earth: **distress of nations in perplexity at the roaring of the sea and the waves, men fainting with fear and with foreboding of what is coming on the world** (25, 26); the sea is frequently a figure for the troubled world in the OT (cf. Ps. 107: 26-28; Isa. 57: 20, etc.); and (*b*) Mk, followed by Mt., places immediately after the actual appearing of the Son of man in glory the sending of the angel to gather in the elect from the four winds. Luke says instead: **look up and raise your heads, because your redemption is drawing near.**

29-31. The parable of the fig-tree (Mk 13: 28, 29). A short parable on discerning the signs of the times; very similar in all three Synoptics except that to Mk's fig-tree Luke adds **all the trees** (29).

32-36. Closing sayings. All three Gospels tell how these things (presumably those associated with the fall of Jerusalem) will take place in the present generation. Mk, however, gives no fixed time limit for the final parousia. God's word is surer, outlasting heaven and earth, but He has not revealed the precise date at which these events will occur, neither to the angels nor even to the Son (Mk 13: 32). Instead of this forthright declaration, Luke has a warning against a life of pleasure and indulgence blinding the eyes to the coming crisis, and a general exhortation to watchfulness. It is in this final section that Mt. inserts the warnings of Lk. 17: 26-30.

37, 38. Luke adds as a sort of footnote to the discourse a statement similar to that of 19: 47, 48 that Jesus preached daily in the Temple to large congregations, adding that he spent His nights on the mount of Olives.

viii. The conspiracy of the priests and of Judas (22: 1-6)
Luke follows Mk 14 closely, but omits the story of the anointing at Bethany, probably because he has already described the similar scene of 7: 36-50.

The **scribes** have not been idle since they dropped the conflicts of words in the Temple, and in Judas's approach to **the chief priests and captains** (the officers commanding the Temple police) they have had, from their point of view, a stroke of rare good fortune. As one of the Twelve, he is in a position to enable them to arrest Jesus in some quiet place without publicity and possible demonstrations. The crowds who saluted His triumphal entry, and those who have thronged daily to hear Him in the Temple, show that He enjoys a considerable measure of public support.

The betrayal by Judas is the definite act of Satan himself (3). But how is it possible that one who has enjoyed the daily companionship of Jesus can commit such an outrage? Did he see things going wrong, and turn 'king's evidence' to save his own skin? Was he disillusioned when Jesus did not seize the lead of some nationalistic rising, like the Messiahs of popular imagination? Was it just that he was a bad character? (John implies that he was certainly that, 12: 6.) Whatever it be, the ultimate reason for so black a deed remains an insoluble and horrible mystery.

ix. Preparations for the Passover (22: 7-13)
As with His mount for His entry into the city a few days before, Jesus has made secret arrangements for the use of an upper room where, before He suffers, He may enjoy the last hour of intimate fellowship with His disciples. Peter and John are sent on ahead to make necessary preparations for the celebration of the Passover; their guide will be easily identifiable by the water jar he is carrying. Few men care to be seen in public doing woman's work such as this!

VIII. THE LAST HOURS (22: 14-23: 56)
i. The Last Supper (22: 14-38)
I have earnestly desired to eat this passover with you before I suffer: Like one leaving his family and first desiring a farewell meeting. 'When we see the divine glory in the person of Christ, we find the human affections shining out' (J. N. Darby, p. 171). The preparations have been made, **the hour came,** not only for the feast but also 'his hour . . . to depart out of this world' (Jn 13: 1); Jesus sits down with the Twelve and tells them clearly that it is the last time before He suffers. He gives them wine and bread, warning them that one of their

company is the betrayer. Even such solemn circumstances do not prevent them from squabbling about their relative importance, perhaps with an eye to the succession when their Leader is gone. He recalls them to reality by reminding them of the glorious future ahead, but before that, severe testing, especially for Peter.

Two problems arising from this passage call for mention: (*a*) the differences between Luke's account and the others, and (*b*) the question whether the Passover itself was actually eaten or not.

(*a*) Luke's account of the Supper is extant in two versions, the longer one as in AV and RV, and the shorter as in RSV, omitting vv. 19b, 20. There is good textual support for both readings, perhaps slightly more for the shorter. Taking the shorter text as a basis of comparison, there are outstanding differences between Mk and Luke:
(i) In Luke the cup precedes the bread (in the longer reading a second cup follows the bread), and there is no mention of the 'blood of the covenant'. (ii) The prophecy of Judas's treachery follows the institution, instead of preceding it as in Mk. (iii) Luke adds a number of sayings not recorded at the Supper by Mark.

Theologically, the most important of these differences is certainly the omission of the reference to the 'blood of the covenant', more remarkable still when linked with the fact that Luke does not include the 'ransom passage' of Mk 10: 45/Mt. 20: 28. Some claim this as evidence that Luke has no doctrine of a substitutionary atonement. It should not be overlooked however that even in the shorter version the covenant is not entirely absent, for in v. 29 the verb twice translated **appoint** is etymologically cognate with 'covenant'. The longer text (19b) adds to the Mt./Mk version the injunction to perpetuate the rite: 'Do this in remembrance of me' (cf. 1 C. 11: 24).

(*b*) In v. 7 Luke specifies that it was the day **on which the passover lamb had to be sacrificed.** In v. 15 Jesus says **I have earnestly desired to eat this passover with you.**

Some argue that the second statement implies that the meal to which they sat down was actually the Passover; others that the first statement means that they met together on the Passover eve in preparation for the feast-day itself, and that they ate a fellowship meal; for such gatherings there were set rituals, some of which have survived. There is probably insufficient evidence to make a final decision. G. Dix, in *The Shape of the Liturgy* (1945), gives an interesting account of the ritual of the fellowship meal, and argues that the supper

followed this. J. Jeremias puts the case cogently for regarding the meal as the Passover in *The Eucharistic Words of Jesus* (1955), pp. 14 ff. Balmforth also discusses the question exhaustively (pp. 261-265).

It is worthy of note that in none of the accounts in the NT (Synoptics, Jn, 1 C. 11) is there any mention of a lamb being slain. If the crucifixion itself took place on the Passover eve (see Jn 19: 14), then Jesus was on the cross at the very time the Passover lambs were being slaughtered, giving thus rich meaning to 1 C. 5: 7, 'for Christ, our paschal lamb, has been sacrificed'. There is some evidence for the observance of different religious calendars in Judea at this time: any group that chose to keep Passover by another calendar from that followed in the Temple would have to dispense with the lamb. (The reader should also note the discussion of the parallel passage in Mt.)

17. If, as has been suggested, this cup is the final cup of the preceding meal, it does not help to decide the point, since both Passover and fellowship rituals included several cups. **24-26.** Mk has a similar passage (10: 35-45), rather longer, and associated with the third prediction of the Passion. **25. benefactors** (Gk. *euergetēs*): A favourite title adopted by Hellenistic kings. **27.** A parabolic saying that recalls Mk 10: 45. **31-33.** Peter is exhorted to stand fast, for Satan has made a similar application concerning him to that he made concerning Job (Job 1: 9-12). **35-38.** When He first sent them out to preach they were welcome everywhere. He now ironically suggests they should sell their cloaks to buy swords—they will need them! They do not detect the irony; Peter takes Him literally to the extent of using his sword.

ii. In the Garden (22: 39-46)
The scene changes from the upper room to the garden; at the supreme crisis of His life Luke once more shows us our Lord at prayer. He makes no reference to the special position of Peter, James and John, the attention being centred on Jesus Himself; and though only one prayer and not three is mentioned, the intensity of His agony is seen in the blood-like sweat and the sustaining angel, peculiar to the Lucan account.

39. The name Gethsemane does not occur here. As on the preceding days, Jesus goes to the mount of Olives (cf. 21: 37), though this means that Judas will know where to find Him. **43, 44.** Omitted in some ancient MSS, but retained in RSV.

iii. Betrayal and Arrest (22: 47-53)
Events move swiftly. Judas arrives with his new-found allies, and makes to salute the Lord with the traitor's kiss. Jesus reminds him that

it is the Son of man whom he thus betrays. Peter, itching to do something, smites off with his sword the ear of the high priest's slave; Jesus' last miracle of healing is the curing of this wound. Unresisting and majestic, Jesus asks why they bring this armed rabble, when at any time they could have arrested Him in the Temple. Luke knew the answer to this question; he has already given it in 22: 2, 'they feared the people'.

48. Luke does not record the fact that the kiss was a pre-arranged sign, as do Mt. and Mk. **52.** Luke only mentions that the rulers were present in person.

iv. Jesus in custody (22: 54-65)
(a) **Peter's denial (22: 54-62)**
Jesus is unceremoniously bundled along to the high priest's house to await His trial. Peter follows, **at a distance** it is true, but he has at least the courage to follow. Arrived at the palace he sits down among a crowd warming themselves at the fire. In this atmosphere his resolution weakens, and almost without realizing he thrice denies any knowledge of Jesus. The cock-crow reminds him of Jesus' warning. The act is done; too late he repents with bitter tears.
(b) **The soldiers' horseplay (22: 63-65)**
The boasted fairness of Roman justice and Jewish law is reduced to farce by the coarse buffoonery of the soldiers as they while away the hours of their guard-room duty.

v. The Trials (22: 66-23: 25)
Luke gives the completest account of the trials in the Synoptics; he alone tells of the hearing before Herod and of the fact that there were two sessions before Pilate.
(a) **The Trial before Caiaphas and the Sanhedrin (22: 66-71)**
As soon as morning breaks, Jesus is interrogated by the Sanhedrin, and they seek to extract from Him a claim to Messiahship. He gives them the answer they desire, and says also that He is Son of God (an answer they think they have cleverly tricked Him into giving, vv. 69, 70), but He warns them that they will have dealings with Messiah again, on a very different footing.

Matthew and Mark place the denial after this preliminary trial, Luke before. There is probably no contradiction. A trial at night, and before the comparatively small number of members of the Sanhedrin who could be mustered at once, could claim no shred of legality. An informal examination as soon as he had the prisoner in his hands was most likely made by Caiaphas and the rulers available, to be confirmed by a formal trial in full session when daybreak made the proceedings legal. Note that Luke does not refer to the suborned and yet inconsistent witnesses mentioned by Matthew and Mark.

(b) **The first trial before Pilate (23: 1-7)**
Having no power themselves to carry out the capital sentence, the Sanhedrin commit the accused to the court of Pontius Pilate, the Procurator, senior representative of the Roman power in Judea. They know that blasphemy will not be regarded by the occupying power as sufficient ground for the death sentence; so three trumped-up charges are formulated: (i) perverting the people by stirring up disaffection and rebellion, (ii) forbidding the people to pay tribute to Caesar, and (iii) Himself claiming to be a king. It is clear that Pilate is not impressed, yet he is loth to anger the Jews by acquitting Jesus. A very convenient way out appears to present itself when Pilate discovers that Jesus is a Galilean and therefore subject to the jurisdiction of Herod, who happens to be in Jerusalem (see article *The Historical Background*, p. 59).
(c) **The trial before Herod (23: 8-12)**
The personality of our Lord seems to have exercised a curious fascination over Herod Antipas (see notes on 13: 31-33); now he **was very glad, for he had long desired to see him . . . hoping to see some sign done by him.** But it is at once clear that Jesus has no intention of satisfying his curiosity, and the 'trial' degenerates into mere horseplay. The prisoner is returned to Pilate, and the only positive result of the incident is the reconciliation of Pilate and Herod (cf. Ac. 4: 27).
(d) **The second trial before Pilate (23: 13-25)**
The final decision now rests squarely with Pilate, and even in Luke's brief account can be perceived the weak and vacillating character that John in his longer account portrays so clearly. 'Pilate', says Helmut Gollwitzer (pp. 46, 49), 'has power, but not freedom . . . . Pilate represents those people who *would like* to act rightly, but do not decide to do so'.

In his desire to evade his responsibilities, Pilate clutches at two straws. First he suggests to the Jews that Jesus does not deserve the death penalty, but a flogging might teach Him not to stir up the people. This does not satisfy His pursuers, so Pilate brings out his second suggestion. An annual custom permits an amnesty for one prisoner. Let Jesus be the one set free. No, say the Jewish leaders, **release to us Barabbas**—a man lying under sentence of death for acts of the very kind of which Jesus was falsely accused.

Pilate capitulates: **And their voices prevailed** (23) **. . . Jesus he delivered up to their will** (25).
vi. The Way to Calvary (23: 26-32)
In accordance with Roman custom the execution is carried out without delay. Mark (15: 15)

tells us that Jesus was first flogged, a most brutal treatment as inflicted by the Romans. This, together with all He has gone through since He left the upper room, has weakened Him to such an extent that His custodians, fearing that His premature collapse might rob the gallows of its victim and them of their sport, press into service Simon of Cyrene (either a Cyrenian on a visit to the city for the feast perhaps, or a member of the Jerusalem synagogue of the Cyrenians) to relieve Him of the load of the heavy burden of the cross-bar of the gibbet which is proving too much for Him.

27–31. An incident recorded by Luke alone. A sympathetic group of women follow Him with the death wail of funeral mourners. He tells them that it will soon be they who will need comfort, for Jerusalem's doom is at hand (cf. 13: 34, 35; 19: 41-44, etc.). **29.** What dreadful calamities our Lord describes, that Jewish women should count barrenness a blessing! **30.** Quoted from Hos. 10: 8. **31.** A proverb: green wood does not normally burn, nor are innocent men executed. But if these things *do* happen now, how much worse will it be for dry wood and evil men?

vii. The Crucifixion (23: 33-49)
With two condemned criminals, Jesus is taken to a place called **The Skull,** and there the three are crucified, with Jesus on the middle cross. He prays for His murderers, and this prayer evokes curiously different reactions in His hearers. The execution squad are too intent on their gambling to heed what was taking place. The rulers scoff at such an inglorious end to one who claimed to be a king. The soldiers, parrot-wise, repeat the sneers of the rulers. A placard mocking His claims is nailed above His head. One of the criminals hanging at His side vents all his bitterness on the one who claims to be the Messiah. One person, and one alone, seems to see any further, the other criminal, who begs and receives forgiveness and peace from the dying Lord Jesus. Then, committing Himself to His Father, Jesus dies, and the manner of His dying opens many eyes. The centurion in charge of the execution exclaims **'Certainly this man was innocent!'** The multitudes depart beating their breasts.

In all four Gospels two things above all impress in the account of the actual crucifixion. First, there is the amazing restraint with which the most brutal and dastardly crime of all history is described. To cite but one instance, none of the four tells of the nails driven through hands and feet; we know of them only through the mention of the wounds (cf. Jn 20: 25). The full horror of the scene stands out more

clearly because there is no attempt to harrow the feelings, no detailed insistence on the physical sufferings. Secondly there is the unmistakable impression that throughout the dreadful scenes it is in reality He who controls the course of events.

'Luke's picture of the crucifixion of Jesus', says Creed (p. 284), 'is based upon Mark, but his treatment, which is highly characteristic, has given a different tone to the scene. Jesus' love for the sinner, powerful in death as during life, and His unconquered trust in the Father's providential care, lighten the unrelieved gloom of the Marcan narrative'. Certain it is that Luke's picture is coloured by the three 'words from the cross' that he, and he alone, records. The general prayer for forgiveness for His persecutors, together with the personal assurance of forgiveness for the repentant malefactor reveal especially clearly that He who is God Himself is also perfect Man, still showing in the hours of bitter agony the same compassion and loving kindness as in the days of His active ministry. And the last word that Luke records as falling from His lips is the culmination of His life of constant communion with the Father in prayer, so frequently insisted on in the third Gospel: **Father, into thy hands I commit my spirit!** 'He says: Father', says Gollwitzer (p. 81). 'This one word "Father", uttered by His Son in the extreme torture and agony of death, expresses more than any other word could convey of willing consent, of the inmost, heartfelt union of His will with the will of Him who permits Him to be put to death'.

33. The Skull: So-called because of the shape of the ground. Mt., Mk and Jn give the Aramaic form Golgotha, but Luke contents himself with its Gk. equivalent. In this verse, AV, following the Latin Vulgate, translates 'Calvary', the only occurrence of this Latin form in our English Bible. **34.** The prayer for His enemies is omitted in some MSS (see RSVmg), but the textual evidence for its retention is extremely strong. For the prayer itself, see Lk. 6: 20, 35, etc. **they cast lots to divide his garments:** Cf. Ps. 22: 18. **35. the rulers scoffed at him:** Cf. Ps. 22: 7. Mt. 27: 46 and Mk 15: 34 quote also Ps. 22: 1 as a saying of Jesus from the Cross. **36. offering him vinegar:** Cf. Ps. 69: 21. **38.** AV includes a note that the superscription was in Hebrew, Greek and Latin (cf. Jn 19: 20), omitted on textual grounds by RV as by RSV. **43. Paradise:** A word of Persian origin meaning an enclosed park or garden; used in LXX for the Garden of Eden. Notice how the prayer for mercy **when you come in your kingly power** is answered by the assurance of blessing **today. 45. the curtain of the temple was torn in two:**

This was the veil which separated the holy place from the holy of holies. It kept sinful man at a distance from the presence of God's glory, for only the high priest, on the annual Day of Atonement and bearing the blood of sacrifice, might enter (Lev. 16; Heb. 9: 7; 10: 19 f.). Now that the perfect sacrifice has been slain, the barrier is removed: God is fully revealed to man, and man has unimpeded access to God. **46. Into thy hands . . . :** Quoted from Ps. 31: 5. **47. 'Certainly this man was innocent!':** Luke rightly interprets the intention of the centurion's exclamation in Mk 15: 39, 'Truly this man was the Son of God!' (so RSV of 1962 and subsequent editions, in agreement with AV and RV, as against 'a son of God', RSV of 1946 and 1952). Mark discerns in the exclamation a more profound significance, confirming his own emphasis (Mk 1: 1). **48. beating their breasts:** In token of deep grief (cf. 18: 13).

viii. The burial (23: 50–56)
Joseph of Arimathaea 'was a disciple of Jesus but secretly, for fear of the Jews' (Jn 19: 38). Now he comes out openly and requests Pilate's permission to inter the body of Jesus in his own tomb, newly rock-hewn. Hereby he not only fulfils the requirements of Dt. 21: 22, 23, but he also dissociates himself from the deed of the Sanhedrin to which he belongs. The request is granted, the women take note where the tomb is, so that they can return later to embalm the precious remains.

IX. RESURRECTION AND ASCENSION (24: 1–52)
i. The Empty Tomb (24: 1–12)
(For comparison with notes on this chapter, read notes on Ac. 1: 1–14, a summary of this chapter.)

The enforced rest of the Sabbath over, the women return **at early dawn** next day to the tomb, only to find that the great stone which sealed its mouth is **rolled away** and the tomb empty. As they are wondering what has happened, angelic visitors tell them that Jesus has risen from the dead as He has said He would. The women go back to the apostles to report what has happened, but their story is received with incredulous scepticism.

Luke's story is in general outline very much like Mark's, but there are considerable differences in detail.
(a) Mark has one young man at the sepulchre, Luke has **two men.** (Matthew incidentally has an angel, John has two angels.) These are not necessarily contradictions. The **dazzling apparel** of Luke suggests supernatural beings (cf. 9: 29). The difference between one angel or two may

be due to nothing more than the fact that two were present, but that one only engaged in speech. At all events, the descriptions that we have are expressions in human words of a phenomenon that far transcended human experience.

But the truth of the story of the empty tomb does not depend on our ability to devise a satisfactory scheme of harmonization, but in the tremendous effect that the event had on the disciples, and on subsequent history.
(b) The lists of women's names in the two Gospels are slightly different. But neither of them is necessarily complete.
(c) Luke omits the message reported by Mark that Peter and the disciples are to meet Jesus in Galilee. The post-resurrection appearances recorded by Luke are all in Judea, but the disciples are reminded of teaching He gave them in Galilee.
(d) In Mark, the women were so startled by the events at the tomb that they found themselves unable to give the message to the disciples. In Luke, on the other hand, they go and report to the disciples all that has happened, though of course there is no message of a rendezvous in Galilee for them to convey.

The fact of the resurrection is one of the best historically attested facts of ancient history. For a clear and concise survey of the evidence, see J. N. D. Anderson, *The Evidence for the Resurrection* (London, 1950).
4. behold, two men: Cf. the Transfiguration (Lk. 9: 30) and the Ascension (Ac. 1: 10).
ii. The Walk to Emmaus (24: 13–25)
Later the same day two disciples are walking towards Emmaus, talking sadly over the events of the last few days when an unrecognized stranger overtakes them and joins in their conversation. He begins by seeking information, but before long they are hearing from His lips a thorough exposition of the messianic prophecies, with special emphasis on the theme of the necessity of Christ's sufferings. Arriving at their journey's end they invite Him to accept their hospitality. Soon again the rôles are reversed, their Guest seems to become their Host, for, presiding at their table, He breaks bread as they have seen Him do it before, perhaps when He fed the five thousand. A flash of recognition, and He is gone. They return at once to Jerusalem and there the disciples tell them that Peter also has seen Him.

The Emmaus discourse is one of the most important in the NT, for in it our Lord taught how His life and mission, His death and resurrection had to be viewed in the context of God's self-revelation in the OT scriptures. It thus forms the vital connecting link between the OT promises and the apostolic exposition of their fulfilment in Jesus of Nazareth.

The OT is a book of unsatisfied longings and unfulfilled promises, which found their fulfilment when Christ came. The tragedy of the Jews was that their own presuppositions blinded them to much of what the Scriptures teach concerning the Messiah. Various strains of prophecy and promise blend in the figure of the Messiah, God's Anointed, whom He will send into the world. At times, He is the Shepherd of Israel, gently leading His sheep and caring for them. At others He is the coming King of glory and King of righteousness, who will rule the nations with a rod of iron and scatter the enemies of His people.

But there is another character, the Suffering Servant of Jehovah, the Man of sorrows, acquainted with grief, despised and rejected of men, nay even, in the hour of dereliction, forsaken by God Himself. To the Jews He was the personification of their own suffering nation, or perhaps one of the great martyr-heroes of their history. But Jesus leads the Emmaus couple to the truth that the Messiah and the Suffering Servant were one: **Was it not necessary that the Christ should suffer these things . . . ?** It was only when the Scriptures had been opened to them thus (32), that their eyes could be opened also (31).

13. two of them: The masculine pronouns used of the couple and even the **foolish men** (25) of EVV do not preclude the idea of man and wife, sometimes suggested to have been the case here. **Emmaus:** About 7 miles from Jerusalem. Its direction and actual location are not definitely known. **18. Cleopas** may be the same one mentioned in Jn 19: 25, but the name was quite common and there can be no certainty. Indeed Cleopas and Clopas may be quite different names, Clopas being perhaps a graecized form of the Aramaic name otherwise graecized as Alphaeus.

iii. In the Upper Room (24: 36-49)

While they are exchanging these wonderful experiences, He again appears. Despite these wonderful things they are paralysed with fear, for it seems they have been taken off their guard: **they were startled and frightened, and supposed that they saw a spirit.** He invites them to touch Him, He eats in their presence of the very food they are eating. He repeats briefly the lesson of the Emmaus road, and commissions them to preach **repentance and remission of sins . . . in his name to all nations.**

iv. The Ascension (24: 50-52)

The story has reached its conclusion. Six weeks after the resurrection (it is Luke himself who gives us the length of the interval, Ac. 1: 3), Jesus takes His disciples out to Bethany, where, lifting His hands in blessing, He is parted from them. The mode of departure does not seem to be recorded in Luke; the words **and was carried up into heaven** (RSVmg) have not very strong textual support. Again, for the details we must go to Luke's other book: Ac. 1: 9 tells us 'a cloud took Him out of their sight', the cloud that is the symbol of God's presence, the cloud out of which God had spoken in the mount of transfiguration.

What Luke does insist on is that, robbed again of their beloved Master within a few short weeks of His reappearance in resurrection life, this time they are neither depressed nor dispirited, but superlatively happy: **they returned to Jerusalem with great joy, and were continually in the temple blessing God.**

BIBLIOGRAPHY

BALMFORTH, H., *St. Luke.* Clarendon Bible (Oxford, 1930; school edition, 1935).

BARRETT, C. K., *Luke the Historian in Recent Study* (London, 1961).

BROWNING, W. R. F., *St. Luke.* Torch Commentaries (London, 1960).

CAIRD, G. B., *St. Luke.* Pelican Gospel Commentaries (Harmondsworth, 1963).

CREED, J. M., *The Gospel according to St. Luke* (London, 1930). [On the Greek text.]

DARBY, J. N., *The Gospel of Luke* (London, 1859).

ELLIS, E. E., *The Gospel of Luke.* Century Bible (London, 1966).

GELDENHUYS, J. N., *Commentary on the Gospel of Luke.* NLC (London, 1950).

GODET, F., *The Gospel according to St. Luke* (Edinburgh, 1879).

GOLLWITZER, H., *The Dying and Living Lord* (London, 1860).

LAMPE, G. W. H., 'Luke', in *Peake's Commentary on the Bible*2 (London, 1962), pp. 820–843.

LEANEY, A. R. C., *The Gospel according to St. Luke.* BNTC (London, 1958).

LUCE, H. K., *St. Luke.* CGT (Cambridge, 1933). [On the Greek text.]

MANSON, T. W., *The Sayings of Jesus* (London, 1949).

MANSON, W., *The Gospel of Luke.* MNT (London, 1930).

McNICOL, J., 'The Gospel according to Luke', in *NBC* (London, 1953), pp. 840–864.

MOORMAN, J. R. H., *The Path to Glory* (London, 1960).

PLUMMER, A., *The Gospel according to St. Luke.* ICC (Edinburgh, 1896). [On the Greek text.]

STONEHOUSE, N. B., *The Witness of Luke to Christ* (London, 1951).

THE GOSPEL ACCORDING TO
JOHN

DAVID J. ELLIS

The late Archbishop William Temple wrote: '. . . the point of vital importance is the utterance of the Divine Word to the soul, the self-communication of the Father to His children. The Fourth Gospel is written with full consciousness of that truth . . .' Here, indeed, is the distinctiveness of the Fourth Gospel. For here the Word of God is living and active. It is Jesus Christ.

It Is possible, however mistaken, to come away from the Synoptic Gospels with the impression that the essence of Christianity lies in trying to obey Christ's moral commands and in emulating His unselfish life. In the same way one may read Paul blinded to the definite personality of the Christ he worshipped. But no one dare come away from the Fourth Gospel without having seen that the writer utterly believed in the possibility of daily communion with the exalted Lord since He is the selfsame Person as the actual Man of flesh and blood who worked and taught in Palestine.

It is certain that the Gospel of John was regarded by its earliest readers as an authoritative exposition of the Church's life, in so far as this is represented by the union of every member with the risen Christ. The universality of its membership may well be pictured in Jesus' preaching to the Samaritans and the presence of Greeks at the Feast of the Passover. Its teaching on the spiritual nature of worship is reflected in the conversation between the Saviour and the woman of Samaria, and perhaps in Jesus' acted parable in the purging of the Temple. The Christian ordinances are symbolized in the Lord's discourse on 'water and spirit', and their effectual working in the life of the believer by His teaching on the Bread of Life. Here especially, John sees the dangers which attend any inordinate emphasis upon the outward sign above the inward grace which it symbolizes. John does not record the institution of the Lord's Supper. Instead he dramatically records the lesson in humility which Jesus taught His 'friends', showing them the necessity of being knit into one by their mutual love and warning them of the fatal possibility of eating 'his bread' whilst acting in treachery towards His kingdom. The allegory of the real vine in John is possibly the fullest expression in Jesus' teaching of what it means to be a disciple—a member of the Church, of Him.

There is in John a remarkable underlying agreement with distinctive Pauline teaching. Both John and Paul show that Christ is the express image of God, that creation subsists in Him, and that by adoption through Christ men are made the sons of God. Yet none of these doctrines is explicit in the recorded apostolic preaching in the Book of Acts. In that, emphasis was laid upon the Messiahship of Jesus, His death, resurrection and exaltation, with the added hope of His return to consummate the kingdom of God. Meanwhile God had provided the presence and guidance of the Holy Ghost for all those who repented and were baptized. Yet, John's experience is complementary to that of Paul. The latter constantly rejoiced in freedom from sin and the yoke of the law through the death and resurrection of Christ. This he enjoyed as a prelude to the ultimate manifestation of all the sons of God in glory. John, however, does not ignore sin. But he sees the tabernacle of God with men in Jesus Christ as the means by which men may enjoy positive communion with God here and now. Eternal life is already a fact. 'He that abides in love abides in God, and God abides in him' (1 Jn 4: 16).

John is markedly distinct from the first three Gospels. In a number of instances, however, the writer may have fallen back upon the Synoptic narratives. The feeding of the five thousand, and his references to 'the Twelve' seem to assume that the reader is familiar with the Synoptic record. There is no simple parabolic method in Jesus' teaching as recorded here. Rather is there a collection of discourses in which the relation of the Father to the Son is worked out with theological precision. In the Synoptics there is no formal recognition of Jesus' Messiahship—apart from those uttered when Jesus afterward enjoined silence upon some who would have confessed Him openly—until late in the ministry (cf. Mk 8: 29). But in John there are those, who with the Baptist recognize early on that Jesus is the Messiah at the moment of their first meeting with Him.

Yet this is only what we should expect from the nature of those special manifestations which, as John records, Jesus made to the Baptist and his disciples.

The distinctiveness of John's presentation of Jesus' teaching is compared with W. F. Howard and others with the Targumic principle of translating the Hebrew scriptures with a running commentary. Here and there in the Fourth Gospel it is clear that we have the inspired comment of the Evangelist alongside the words or actions of Jesus Himself. The Gospel is the work of reflection as well as recollection. No clearer statement concerning its purpose could be made than in the closing words of the penultimate chapter: '. . . these are written that you may believe that Jesus is the Christ, the Son of God, and that believing you may have life in His name' (20: 31). The miracles of Jesus here, then, are signposts (Gk. *sēmeia*) towards the grounds for belief in Jesus. This is just why the Jews have special mention in the Gospel. John regards the unbelief of the Jews as one of the prominent tragedies of the earliest Christian years.

More positive reactions to the Christian message, however, came from Docetics, whose name comes from the Greek verb *dokein* 'to appear' or 'to seem'. These were semi-Christian teachers, who, in slightly varying ways according to a variety of different schools of thought, taught that if Christ were God then He could not be truly human. A later development of Docetism emphasized that God is impassible, that is, He is incapable of change such as human flesh permits in mankind, or as human emotions display in human beings. To them deity was by necessity totally removed from any kind of human contact, and therefore, as one of their leading exponents declared, when commenting on the Passion of Christ, 'he only seemed to suffer'. John combated these ideas by special emphasis upon the humanity of Jesus (cf. 2: 24; 4: 6 f.; 6: 51; 11: 35), which reaches its climax in the Gospel with the solemn declaration by Pilate, 'Here is the man!' (19: 5) and the physical details surroundings Jesus' final moments of suffering on the cross (cf. 19: 28, 34 f.).

' "Jesus", writes F. F. Bruce, "came by water *and* the blood"; that is to say, Jesus was manifested as Messiah and Son of God not at His baptism only but on the cross as well; the one who died was as truly the Incarnate Word as the one who was baptized' (*The Spreading Flame*, 1958, p. 246).

F. von Hügel pointed out that this Gospel is history from the eternal point of view (*EB*, 1962, vol. 13, p. 99). So the facts so often plainly elaborated in the Synoptics are interpreted in John. Some scholars have even seen the relation of John to the Synoptics as a juxtaposition of history and theology. The Synoptics, they claim, are presenting theology from a historical point of view, whilst John writes history from a theological standpoint. When we read of Jesus' word to the disciples, '. . . I call you friends . . .' (15: 15) we know He is the supreme Friend who drew the children to Him (cf. Mt. 19: 13 ff.) and who spoke of them as they played at weddings (and funerals!) in the market-place (Mt. 11: 16 f.). He is the Friend who told of the compassionate Samaritan and the long-suffering Father (Lk. 10: 29-37; 15: 11-32). And conversely when we read in the Synoptics of Jesus' authority to forgive sins, it is in John that we learn whence such authority is derived in eternity and how it is exercised in full co-operation with the Father.

No arguments regarding the authorship of this Gospel can be concluded without all the facts, external and internal, in mind. It is generally held that the writer was a Jew, living in Ephesus towards the end of the first century, though some scholars have advanced a date somewhat later than this. It has been held by some that three minds have contributed to the final result—the witness (cf. 19: 35; 21: 24), the Evangelist, and a redactor. In spite of this view, however, there has been little agreement by the main proponents of this theoretical trio as to the part played by each member in the composition of the finished Gospel. Some argue that the special chronological arrangement of John is due to the redactor, while others, notably Bernard, believe that he was responsible for the placing of a few minor notes.

It has been cogently argued that the Gospel was first written in Aramaic, and that though the writer was widely influenced by Greek thought he was more interested in the background of Jewish thought as a prelude to the message of Christ. Indeed, it is probable that the supposed influence of Greek ideas in John is an idea which has been taken too far by some modern commentators. Any special usage of Greek words and ideas in the Gospel may merely reflect that there were terms in current use at the time when the Gospel was written which were specially valuable for depicting the Person and Work of Christ in the way which is germane to the Fourth Gospel.

A distinction has been made between the Elder John, and the Apostle of the same name. Eusebius assigned Revelation to the Elder and the Gospel to John the Apostle. Modern scholars have, from time to time, reversed this order and assigned the Gospel to the Elder and the

Revelation to the Apostle. Whatever may be the difficulties regarding the author of the Apocalypse, he was certainly identified as the Apostle John by Justin Martyr (*c.* A.D. 140). It is clear that the theological outlook of the two books is strikingly similar, so that we can say with certainty at least that the *milieu* of the two works seems to be identical. None of the usual arguments set forth in order to distinguish 'the beloved disciple' from John the Apostle is finally convincing. That he should have been known in this manner is quite in keeping with the various ways in which this disciple is portrayed in the Gospel. Indeed, the statement of

Papias recorded by Eusebius (*HE* III. xxxix 4), which has been widely used to keep John the Apostle distinct from 'the elder John' can be read to mean that the Elder and the Apostle are one and the same.

The Letters of John are almost certainly from the Evangelist. The First Letter applies the Gospel to the problems of the primitive Church. It is less concerned with the hostility of the Jews, however, and more with the dangers of Gnosticism. Westcott has said that the burden of the Gospel is 'Jesus is the Christ', of the Letter that 'the Christ is Jesus' (p. lxxxviii). (See pp. 606 ff.).

ANALYSIS

PART ONE—INTRODUCTORY (1: 1-2: 11)

I   THE WORD MADE FLESH AND MANIFESTED (1: 1-2: 11)

   i Prologue (1: 1-18)
   ii The witness of John (1: 19-34)
   iii Jesus' first followers (1: 35-2: 11)

PART TWO—THE PUBLIC MINISTRY (2: 12-12: 50)

I   CHRIST'S PREACHING OF HIS MESSAGE (2: 12-4: 42)

   i The cleansing of the Temple (2: 12-25)
   ii Jesus and Nicodemus (3: 1-21)
   iii The Baptist's final testimony (3: 22-36)
   iv The Samaritan woman (4: 1-42)

II   REVELATION BY DEEDS AND WORDS (4: 43-6: 71)

   i The official's son (4: 43-54)
   ii The cripple of Bethesda (5: 1-47)
   iii Feeding the masses (6: 1-15)
   iv A storm at sea (6: 16-21)
   v Living Bread (6: 22-59)
   vi Disciples' faith and unbelief (6: 60-71)

III   JESUS, THE SOURCE OF ALL TRUE BLESSING (7: 1-10: 39)

   i Controversy at the Feast of Tabernacles (7: 1-52)
   ii The true Light and its implications (8: 12-59)
   iii The man blind from birth (9: 1-41)
   iv The Good Shepherd (10: 1-21)
   v Final encounter with the Jews (10: 22-42)
   vi Lazarus' resurrection and its sequel (11: 1-57)

IV   THE LAST SCENE OF CONFLICT (12: 1-50)

   i The supper at Bethany (12: 1-11)
   ii The Messianic Entry (12: 12-19)
   iii The Greeks' request and Jews' rejection (12: 20-43)
   iv Christ's summary of His message (12: 44-50)

PART ONE—INTRODUCTORY

(1: 1-2: 11)

I. THE WORD MADE FLESH AND MANIFESTED (1: 1-2: 11)

i. Prologue (1: 1-18)

There is probably no other place in the NT where so much is said, as here, with such economy of words. Here is set forth the uniqueness of Christ and the great consequences which follow from His self-sacrifice embodied in the Incarnation. In this Prologue John announces his main theme, which is the glory of Jesus Christ shown by all which He both said and did. **1. In the beginning was the Word:** Unlike the Synoptic writers, the fourth Evangelist begins the story in eternity; and it is from here that he understands the significance of the work of Christ. **In the beginning** (cf. Gen. 1: 1) pushes back our conception of the purpose of God beyond even Creation so that the Word, as the second Person of the Trinity, existed in His own right. The **Word** (Gk. *ho logos*) was supposedly employed by the writer for reasons of making the Gospel relevant to his first readers. Yet the conception of *ho logos* is of supreme importance for the Evangelist's doctrine of Christ apart from any other special reason for which he used the term. [See Additional Note 1. see p. 287]. **and the Word was with God** (Gk. *kai ho logos ēn pros ton theon*): That is, from eternity there has ever been a distinction within the Godhead. It does not help us much to understand this as the Word existing 'over against' the Absolute God. The simpler sense suggested here seems to be endorsed elsewhere where prepositions are similarly used (cf. Mk 6: 3;

cf. also Mk 10: 27). **and the Word was God** (Gk. *kai theos ēn ho logos*): The fulness of the Godhead and the Word are identified. The active Word immanent in the world is no less God than the transcendent God beyond all time and space. The absence of the definite article in front of 'God', taken by some to mean that the Word possessed something less than full deity, implies, however, that other persons exist outside the second Person of the Trinity. **2. He was in the beginning with God:** Both the Word and His relationship to the Eternal are eternal. There was never part of His pre-existence which found Him to be separated in any sense from the Godhead. So the deity of Christ is set forth without yet any specific personal qualities being ascribed to Him as the second Person of the Trinity. C. K. Barrett aptly comments: 'The deeds and words of Jesus are the deeds and words of God; if this be not true the book is blasphemous' (p. 130). **3. all things were made through him** (Gk. *di' autou*): The Word, coming forth from God, was the Agent in Creation, which, unlike Him, is not eternal, and yet, **without him was not anything made that was made** (cf. Prov. 8: 30). There is not, as some Gnostic thinkers were disposed to believe, any other means of creation than God Himself. There is a possible alternative reading here, *viz.*, 'without him was not anything made. That which has been made was life in Him.' The usual reading is preferable, however. John tells his readers that in Christ there is a visible link between God and the material world. This world rightly belongs to God, who made it (cf. Heb. 1: 2; 11: 3). It is generally agreed that Gnosticism was never far from the mind of the writer of the Gospel.

The Gnostics taught that only spirit can be good and matter is essentially evil. But John, in common with Paul (cf. Col. 1: 16) maintains by his doctrine of creation by the Word of God, and the Incarnation of that Word, that this world of matter is indeed the handiwork of the Almighty, who has entered into it in Jesus Christ. It is not *essentially* evil, though man by sin has wrought misery within it (cf. Gen. 1: 10, 12, 18, 21, 25). **4. In him was life:** The universe, made by the Word of God, and immersed in His living active will, shows in itself the organic, active property of life. And this principle in the created world shows itself again in Christ, who has come to bestow life by the Incarnation (cf. 10: 10). This life becomes the **light of men.** It is the living, developing element in the universe that shows God to man (cf. Rom. 1: 20); it is the basis and truth of revealed religion. **5. The light shines . . .:** This is the burden of the Fourth Gospel, namely, that God is revealed absolutely in Jesus Christ. All that men may expect by way of revelation and salvation is to be seen in Him. Yet God has provided man with continuous revelation, for the light shines **in the darkness,** which describes man's distance from God, and showing that God has always revealed Himself to man in some way. The Incarnation, however, has revealed God with unique clarity, such that, in the nature of the case, **the darkness has not overcome it.**

'Life' and 'light' are two words especially associated with John in the NT. Later in the Gospel Jesus asserts that He is both the Life (cf. 11: 25; 14: 6) and the Light (cf. 8: 12; 9: 5). In the Prologue, however, these claims are put into their essential setting. What Jesus claims to be *in* the world He is *always*. This is characteristic of God in the OT. Divine activity has created life and sustains it. God is, thereby, the source of man's illumination (cf. Ps. 36: 9 f.). In the Gospel, moreover, 'life' carries distinct overtones of salvation, deliverance. In so far as it is brought into the world by Christ (cf. 2 Tim. 1: 10), it denotes His particular work on behalf of mankind, the most responsible section of the created world. 'Light' in John implies revelation which leads men towards 'life', which places men under solemn responsibility, and by this brings them into judgment if they refuse it (cf. 3: 19). The presence of darkness is usually taken for granted where 'light' is mentioned. And when there is no response to the true Light, then, whatever 'light' men may profess to have, in reality they have no light at all (cf. 9: 41).

6. There was a man . . .: Now the theme distinctively breaks in upon human history. John the Baptist is mentioned here first since he acted as a **witness to the light** by being a 'burning and shining lamp' (cf. 5: 35) so that through his work **all might believe. 9.** The meaning here has been obscured by the AV. It is best preserved by rendering (as RSV) **coming into the world** and attaching the phrase to **the true light,** not to **every man.** He, distinct from John, is **the true light,** Gk. *to phōs to alēthinon,* meaning real or genuine light (not true as distinct from false, which would be expressed by *alēthēs*). In what sense can He be said to enlighten every man? Only in the sense that 'light' brings judgment (cf. v. 5 and 3: 19-21). Christ's coming has shed light on the darkness of the human situation and continues to do so in the life of every man. **10. the world was made through him . . .:** This applies to that part of creation (cf. v. 3) which is capable of making sensible response. The **world** (Gk. *kosmos*) is the world of people, especially those who, in this Gospel, are confronted with the truth in Christ. (Often in the Gospel, however, it is described as 'this world', which refers to *our* world over against the world above from which Christ came; cf. 8: 23.) Both uses of the term imply the antagonism which was shown to Christ. **the world knew him not:** This use of the verb 'to know' (Gk. *ginōskō*) means 'to recognize'. It is noteworthy that the Evangelist never uses the corresponding noun 'knowledge' (Gk. *gnōsis*); he is at pains to avoid that form of Gnosticism which taught salvation by knowledge for an intelligent élite. Since 'knowing' in John implies observation, obedience and trust, it is not surprising that 'knowing' and 'believing' are almost synonymous (cf. 17: 3; 6: 69). **11. He came to his own home: his own home** is a paraphrastic translation of Gk. *ta idia,* though it aptly expresses what the writer intended in referring to that particular area—Palestine—which within the world occupied a special position in God's favour (cf. 19: 27). But **his own people** (*hoi idioi*) **received him not,** though from 13: 1 onwards the title *hoi idioi* is restricted to those who did receive him. This at once summarizes the rejection of Christ and the reasons, humanly speaking, for His suffering. To such, however, who received Him by faith in His name **he gave** (Gk. *edōken*) **power to become children of God.** This is God's gift. Men have no natural claim to be the children of God. Only Christ gives men the power (Gk. *exousia*—'right') to become such. These **were born** since life in Christ commences by birth, i.e., by the distinct activity of God as the Source of all. This birth contains no human element at all; nor does it lie within the scope of human achievement, or **the will of the flesh,** nor is it mediated by reason of maturit

—**the will of man** (Gk. *ek thelēmatos andros*). **14. And the Word became flesh:** There is no suggestion in these words that at the Incarnation the Word became a Person. Personality had always been His possession. 'Flesh' (Gk. *sarx*) denotes the human realm compared with the heavenly (cf. 3: 6; 6: 63). Here, then, is the great inexplicable part of the doctrine of Christ, that the Eternal Word entered into human life. Nor did He surrender His identity in flesh, for while He dwelt among men—a fact to which the Gospel essentially turns—there were those who **beheld his glory,** i.e., the visible manifestation of God, whose nature was, as men had understood in the past, **full of grace,** denoting the initiative taken by God when He bestows favours upon men, **and truth** as the final and perfect embodiment of divine revelation. The grace of God and the truth of God are alike enshrined in the Christian message. God in Christ calls men to trust Him and adore Him. And the perfect balance of grace and truth, demonstrated in the unfailing equanimity exercised by Jesus on earth, is shown in the succeeding chapters. Often He took the initiative in coming to men when they needed Him; and He embodied the truth in His own Person (cf. Exod. 34: 6; Jn 14: 6), as **the only Son from the Father,** that is, uniquely Son of God. His eternity precludes any notion that His being was derived from the Father, but, as the words suggest, His existence and work were never independent of the Father—a fact to which Jesus Himself bore testimony (cf. 10: 25, 30). John leaves the doctrine of the Logos at this point, and now concentrates upon the relationship between the Father and the Son. **16. from his fulness have we all received:** The doctrine of Christ and of God which opens this Gospel is never to be regarded as a mere credal affirmation. The fulness of grace and truth is something which is mediated to men via experience. And the Evangelist is not alone in this. 'We have received it', he writes, perhaps linking the testimony of other believers at Ephesus in his day, or joining in spirit with all who subsequently to his own testimony would have faith in Christ. Moreover, the combined testimony of the people of God concluded that the Christian life was **grace upon grace,** as every experience of His loving help led on to a fuller experience of God's goodness. **17. For the law was given through Moses:** God's gift of salvation to His ancient people was through the external compulsive power of law. Now, in Christ, men are constrained to love God by the compelling power shown in Jesus Christ. **18. No one has ever seen God:** This is a basic assumption of the OT. Even where it might be suggested that

something of God had been seen by men (*e.g.* Exod. 33: 22 f.; Isa. 6: 1; Ezek. 1: 1), the Aramaic Targums, which were paraphrases of certain parts of the OT, tended to use circumlocutions for the divine name, and would have rendered it by some such term as *memra*, i.e. 'the word'. But the importance of this for understanding the background of John has been over-emphasized by some commentators. God is now seen in the incarnate Word, **the only Son.** There is a variant reading here, *viz.*, 'God only-begotten', which is supported by a number of important MSS, and by some of the earliest patristic commentaries. It would be quite in accordance with what John elsewhere records concerning the deity of Christ (cf. 20: 28; 1 Jn 5: 20). Yet acceptance of the usual reading seems preferable since this also accords well with John's writing (cf. 3: 16, 18; 1 Jn 4: 9). Christ dwells **in the bosom of the Father,** an expression denoting a relationship of love and perfect understanding.

ii. The witness of John (1: 19–34)
The Evangelist now turns to John the Baptist in order to spotlight the person of Jesus through his ministry. The philosophical language of the Prologue is dropped and we pass to a chronological record of some six days (not seven as some infer from v. 41) taking us eventually to 2: 11.

19. the Jews have special mention throughout the Gospel. Here they seem to be the leaders of the people in Judaea, and are the strongest opponents of the Lord. Possibly John wishes to portray the tragedy of those who fail to recognize Jesus as the Messiah, or His coming as the advent of the kingdom. **Levites** were members of the Temple staff who attended to its material care and acted as its guards. **20. I am not the Christ:** John's answer to the first question shows how dramatic must have been his appearance in Judaea as the Baptizer. Few could escape noticing him. **21. Are you Elijah:** John disclaims any connection whatever with Messianic fulfilment (cf. Mk 9: 13; Mal. 4: 5 f.). **Are you the prophet:** The prophet like Moses (Dt. 18: 15 ff.) who in these days was widely expected to arise on the eve of the messianic age (cf. 6: 14; 7: 40). **No:** So John's threefold denial in self-abnegation is complete. The three answers which he gives ring true as those which would naturally succeed each other in heated conversation. When pressed, however, the Baptist admits that he is **the voice . . . .** (23). He claims no dignity save that which is conferred upon him as a preacher of the Word (cf. Isa. 40: 3). **the way of the Lord:** Stauffer has shown that this conception lies at the heart of the earliest records of the ministry of Jesus (*NTT*, pp. 25–29). **24. the Pharisees**

(cf. *NBD*, pp. 981 f.) apparently had a special interest in the authority which lay behind John's baptismal practice. **26. I baptize with water . . .:** John makes no reference here to Christ's baptism with the Holy Spirit. This was not understood, we may presume, until he had seen that Spirit descending upon Jesus at His baptism. But he does point out that there is someone close to hand who is unexpected. Their acquaintance with baptismal practice is clear (cf. v. 25). But Christ will exceed their understanding of what forms true religion. For John this is based on pure faith; he will not even be presumptuous enough to call himself His slave (27). **28. Bethany** is not the Bethany of Mary and Martha (cf. 11: 1; Mk 14: 3-9). Some texts read 'Bethabara'. But though its precise location is uncertain by the third century, ch. 11 indicates a careful distinction between two such places known by the same name (cf. 10: 40 with 11: 18), and the reference there to 'the place where John at first baptized' is significant. **29. Behold, the Lamb of God:** Here an amalgamation of OT metaphors seems to present itself. We may recall the Paschal lamb (Exod. 12) or the divinely given offering of Abraham (Gen. 22: 8), where the force of the Heb. text might be that 'God will *see* . . . a lamb . . .' Or we may think of the expiatory sacrifices in general Jewish liturgical practice (cf. Lev. 23: 12 ff.). There appears to be an obvious link with Isa. 53: 7, where, in the LXX, Gk. *amnos* 'lamb' renders Heb. *raḥel* (cf. Ac. 8: 32). Here the sin-bearing function is implicit more than explicit. Yet it is not unlikely that the daily Jewish offerings were in John's mind. The greatest OT passage is that which depicts the goat for Azazel which carried away Israel's sin (cf. Lev. 16: 21) into a solitary land. Barrett sees John's reference as twofold: the Paschal lamb of Exod. 12, together with the victim who vicariously bears away Israel's sin in Lev. 16. It is altogether unlikely, as Dodd suggests, that the title is purely Messianic, and synonymous with the titles of 1: 49, and the lamb (Gk. *arnion*) of the Apocalypse (cf. Rev. 14: 1), who leads His people in victory. Yet it is significant that it *is* only here and in Revelation that Christ is described as the Lamb of God (cf. note on 19: 36). Burney has suggested that some confusion has arisen here between Aramaic 'servant' and 'lamb' (*talya;* cf. *AOFG*, pp. 104-109), but this rests entirely on the validity of Burney's general thesis that John was originally an Aramaic work. **the sin of the world:** John saw by faith that Christ was able to bear away the totality of sin, which idea, indeed, will have been close to his mind if he were thinking of the Isaianic prophecy (cf. Isa. 53: 11). This then is the principle upon which life in the new age begins, that Christ is the universal Saviour. **32. I saw the Spirit descend . . .:** John's work was to show men the way to Christ. So, too, from the beginning, the Spirit singles out Christ. He descends upon Him, and in so doing makes His unique witness that Jesus is Son of God (cf. v. 34). And the imparting of the Spirit which the Lord Himself makes is likewise for a witness to Himself (cf. 16: 14). Note the fact that in the Synoptics (cf. Mt. 3: 16) it is Jesus who sees the Spirit coming down, whilst here He is observed by the Baptist. This makes the whole incident clearly one which was shared by Christ and His forerunner, and not a private experience known only to the one or the other. **34. . . . the Son of God** (cf. Mk. 1: 11): The close connection between John's recognition and the manifestation of the Spirit must be noted. Only by the Spirit can a true confession of Christ be made (cf. 16: 8-11; 1 C. 12: 3). Some early authorities read here 'the chosen One of God'. But this reading is probably an assimilation to Lk. 9: 35 (cf. Ps. 2: 7; Isa. 42: 1).

iii. Jesus' first followers (1: 35-2: 11)
John's renewed confession now induces two of his disciples to go after Jesus (cf. Mt. 11: 2-6; Lk. 7: 18-23). **37. followed:** No doubt lay in the minds of those who understood John's message. **38. Rabbi:** The term occurs frequently in John (cf. 1: 49; 3: 2; 4: 31; 6: 25, *et alia*). It is a title given to a teacher. There were many in NT times (cf. *NBD*, p. 1072). **39. about the tenth hour:** i.e., about 4 p.m. The following verses, 40-42, are an appendix to the event just described in vv. 35-39. **40. Simon Peter** is the double name usually employed in John. **41. the Messiah:** Only John uses this transliteration of the Heb. *māshiāḥ.* The mention of the title here in no way conflicts with the 'messianic secret' of Mark. Here it is a personal and private testimony, and in its context it accords well with the apostolic preaching (cf. Ac. 10: 38). Moreover the sequence of events just enacted would be such that would inevitably lead some to recognize in Jesus the embodiment of OT ideals and expectation (cf. Dan. 9: 25; on the term in OT generally see *NBD*, pp. 811-818). **42. Cephas** (cf. Mk 3: 16): The word is Aramaic. There is no suggestion at present regarding the purpose for which Simon was given this name. **45. We have found him of whom Moses . . . wrote . . .:** Barrett suggests that this refers to Rabbinic interpretation of a number of Pentateuchal passages. (But cf. 3: 14; see also Gen. 49: 10; Dt. 18: 15; Ac. 3: 22; 7: 37.) Yet Philip makes Jesus known by terms which would have been commonly understood— **. . . the son of Joseph. 46. Come and see:**

Nathanael reflects the general wariness of the Jews in NT times, and retorts that no recognition of the Messiah could be expected until he were seen. So Philip's answer invites Nathanael to see for himself. **47. Behold, an Israelite indeed, in whom is no guile:** Unlike Simon, Nathanael is given no second name. Jesus' omniscience is seen by his reference to **the fig tree** (48). There is no allegorical significance here. **49. the Son of God:** On Nathanael's lips this may mean little more than 'Messiah' (cf. Ps. 2: 7); to the Evangelist it means much more. **the King of Israel:** The definite article is omitted in the Greek text. Nathanael's confession was spontaneous and all-embracing. This is a messianic confession. The true Israelite acknowledges his true King. **50. do you believe:** Perhaps Nathanael's acclamation, however, was restricted to this messianic and nationalistic sense (cf. 2 Sam. 7; 13 f.). If this is so, Nathanael will indeed see **greater things. 51. You will see the heavens opened** (Gk. *aneōgota*): Perhaps this is an eschatological picture (cf. Mt. 26: 64; but see also Mk 1: 10, where the verb used means 'torn apart', echoing Isa. 64: 1). **the angels of God ascending and descending:** An undoubted reference to Jacob again (cf. Gen. 28: 10-17). Westcott understands this of prayers taken to God through Christ, and the answers sent in Him, seeing that He is ever present (cf. Mt. 28: 20). But Jesus' words are more likely to have been coloured by Jewish theology and apocalyptic (cf. Dt. 33: 2 f.; Zech. 14: 5 f.; Dan. 7: 13 f.). **upon the Son of man:** The Heb. text of Gen. 28: 12 is grammatically ambiguous. Some rabbis interpreted 'on it' (Heb. *bō*) to refer actually to Jacob himself, and saw in the event an interaction of the heavenly and earthly man. More probably we should understand this picture as denoting the embodiment, in Jesus, of a heavenly fellowship between God and man, brought about by the death of Jesus, which John sees as one with His glorification, and which would be underlined by his usage of 'Son of man'. In the Synoptics the idea is founded not on Ps. 8, but on Dan. 7. The Son of man is a heavenly figure who enters the earthly realm, yet whose real abode is ever in heaven (cf. 3: 13; 6: 62; Mk 13: 26; 14: 62). His appearance on earth is but part of a journey which ultimately will take him back into heaven (cf. 6: 27; 8: 28; Rev. 1: 14). Probably Jesus' teaching was not static on this matter, but comprehended a wide range of connotation. Whatever the disciples understood by the term as it was used by Him it needed some re-interpretation (cf. Mk 8: 31). T. W. Manson suggested that the idea of *corporate personality* was used by our Lord, based upon the remnant interpretation of passages in Isaiah

referring to the Servant of the Lord, but with Himself as the starting point and centre, 'the Proper Man, whom God Himself hath bidden'. Whatever else may be thought, Jesus used the term whilst speaking of Himself as the pre-existent, heavenly Man, who had entered the world to achieve the purpose of God (cf. S. Mowinckel, *He That Cometh*, 1956; J. Klausner, *The Messianic Idea in Israel*, 1956). **2: 1. Cana in Galilee:** Not definitely located, though Dalman, (*Sacred Sites and Ways*, 1935) would identify it at Kefr Kenna. (Cf. also J. A. Thompson, *The Bible and Archaeology*, 1962, p. 359.) It is interesting to note that Nathanael belonged here (cf. 21: 2). The link with Nathanael seems to be implied by **on the third day,** i.e. after Jesus' interview with him formerly. **the mother of Jesus was there:** She is never named in John, presumably because of the special care which the beloved disciple had for her (cf. 19: 25 ff.; also 2: 12; 6: 42). **his disciples** probably means the Twelve, though no 'call' is recorded in this Gospel, apart from the 'Come and see' and 'Follow me' of 1:39, 43. **3. When the wine failed** (Gk. *hysterēsantos oinou*): There are a couple of later glosses to the first half of this verse, both attempts to clarify the situation. The mother of Jesus reported the matter to Him presumably knowing that He could save the situation. **4. O woman, what have you to do with me** (Gk. *ti emoi kai soi*): This is a translation of an idiom, both in classical Greek and Hebrew, meaning 'leave me to follow my own course'. No one has any *right* of access to the Lord in this manner (cf. Mk 1: 24; Mt. 8: 29). **My hour has not yet come:** Some commentators would restrict the meaning of 'the hour' to the moment of the death or exaltation of Jesus. The term, however, must include some thought which connects His passion and exaltation with the general pattern of works which He is already performing, as here (cf. v. 11). There is divine constraint upon the Person of Jesus so He performs His works only as He receives direction from the Father (cf. Mk 14: 41; Mt. 26: 18; see also Lk. 13: 31 f.; 22: 53; Jn 7: 30). But our Lord's mother is a woman of faith, and she understands enough to prepare the servants at the wedding for Jesus' intervention. **6. Jewish rites of purification:** Ritual purification was usually observed by Jews before and after meals. John, however, seems to make the reference capable of spiritual interpretation also. We may summarily reject any significance in the fact that there were six jars. The inadequacy of the old covenant was to be superseded by the cleansing and satisfying new covenant. **8. Now draw some out** (Gk. *antlēsate*): This verb often denotes the drawing of water from a well (cf. *antlēma*, something to draw with, in 4: 11). When the jars were filled, more water was drawn from the well and taken to the feast. Others, notably Hoskyns and Davey, suggest that the saying teaches that Christ is the well of living water. **9. the steward of the feast** was the person to whom the running of such festivities was entrusted. **10.** The serving of a poorer wine at the end of the banquet was not necessarily to be expected. The emphasis is all upon the excellence of what the Lord provided. So, to take the former spiritual lesson a stage further, the sign points to the superiority of the new order over the old. **11. signs** (Gk. *semēia*): The miracles of Jesus in John are so called to draw attention away from the miracles *per se* and point to their significance. 'Signs and wonders' alone provide no basis for true faith (cf. 4: 48). The whole life of Jesus is, indeed, an acted sign (cf. 12: 33; 18: 32), but each of His signs in particular shows that they are the 'works of God' (cf. 10: 37; 14: 10, and especially 6: 25-30) and faith is the only faculty which can rightly apprehend them (cf. 4: 54; 6: 14; 12: 18). The overall importance in John's use of this term, therefore, lies in the visible representation of invisible and eternal reality which Jesus' miracles make. Their purpose is to encourage belief; and Jesus' disciples did in fact believe at this point (cf. 20: 31).

PART TWO—THE PUBLIC MINISTRY (2: 12–12: 50)

I. CHRIST'S PREACHING OF HIS MESSAGE (2: 12-4: 42)

i. The Cleansing of the Temple (2: 12-25)

This incident, coming where it does in John, raises the question of the relationship between the Fourth Gospel and the Synoptics (see Introduction). The event is placed near the end of the ministry in the first three Gospels (cf. Mk 11: 15-19; Mt. 21: 12-17; Lk. 19: 45-47). Scholars are divided as to whether there was only one cleansing of the temple or two; while those who consider only one to have taken place are again not agreed as to whether this was at the beginning of the Lord's ministry (as in John's Gospel) or during Passion Week (as recorded by the other three Gospels). C. K. Barrett maintains in his commentary (pp. 162 f.) that there was only one such incident in the life of the Lord. William Temple gives reasons for accepting 'the Johannine narrative as correct' so far as chronological order is concerned (*Readings*, p. 170); while R. H. Lightfoot thinks that the cleansing during Passion Week 'is more

likely to be historically correct' (*St. John's Gospel*, p. 112).

It should be said, however, that the older view of there being two cleansings has much to support it. Westcott says, 'a comparison of the two narratives is against the identification' (*The Gospel according to St. John*. Greek Text, Vol. 1, p. 96), and he gives various reasons to support his view. The *Commentary on the Gospel of St. John*, by W. Milligan and W. F. Moulton (1898), old but still valuable, asks: 'But is it really at all improbable that two cleansings should have taken place, separated by such an interval of time as the Gospel narrative presupposes?' (p. 27), and lends further support to this view. Among recent writers, R. V. G. Tasker holds to the view of two cleansings (*The Gospel according to St. John*, TNTC, p. 61).

Whatever may be the case, what seems uppermost in the mind of John is, as R. H. Lightfoot observes: 'to represent the judgment or discrimination effected by the presence and work of the Lord among men as in operation from the outset of His activity'. The temple incident calls attention to this aspect of His work (p. 112, *op. cit.*). That its significance is fundamental to John may perhaps be attested by the fact that he records that the animals were driven out of the temple. In Christ sacrificing Judaism is brought to an end. Here, notes Barrett, John 'begins to develop the main theme, that in Jesus the eternal purposes of God find their fulfilment' (p. 163). (See note on v. 21. For *Passover*, see article 'The Religious Background of the NT'.) **14. those who were selling:** That is, for the purpose of sacrifice. This was a service provided especially for worshippers who travelled long distances to Jerusalem. The **money changers** sat in the Temple precincts mainly on business of exchanging currency for the payment of Temple tax which was exacted from all adult male Jews, including those from the Dispersion. This exchange was used as a commercial enterprise, and profits were made, mainly because the high priests had insisted that all such dues should be paid in Tyrian currency. **15. he drove them all . . . out:** The wording of this verse would imply that the main object of Jesus' anger were the moneychangers. But the **sheep and oxen** were driven out *with them*. This may lead us to suppose that the marketing of the animals here was not altogether objectionable, though this, too, may have been abused (cf. next verse), since the normal place for this cattle market was on the Mount of Olives. **16. . . . a house of trade** (cf. Zech. 14: 21, *'there shall no longer be a trader . . .'*): John does not record the stronger language reminiscent of Jer. 7: 11 as do the Synoptists. This is probably because his emphasis is different. John sees deeper implications in Jesus' action, which involve (cf. vv. 18-22) the end of the temple cultus. **17. Zeal for thy house will consume me:** Cf. Ps. 69: 9 (the words immediately following are applied to Christ in Rom. 15: 3). The future tense seems to provide the more acceptable reading. This gives the psalm a messianic flavour. **18. What sign have you to show us:** Here is an example of a wrongful request for a sign. The parallels in the Synoptics (cf. Mk 11: 28) show that it was proof of Christ's authority which the Jews sought. Jesus does not explicity answer their request, but for such an answer see on 7: 17. Yet in His answer here, Jesus provides a sign for those who will heed what He says. Even the disciples, however, failed to understand what He meant until after the resurrection. **19. Destroy this temple:** As, indeed, the Jews would virtually do in their folly not many years hence. **20. It has taken forty-six years to build:** The Temple was begun in 20 B.C. by Herod the Great. This saying, then, might seem to imply that the structure was complete in A.D. 27, that is, just within the span of the Lord's ministry. But we know that the Temple was by no means completed until A.D. 64. There is, however, no problem. The clue to the seeming difficulty may lie in John's use of Gk. *naos* for 'temple' which is normally distinguished from Gk. *hieron* (also translated 'temple'; cf. v. 14). In this case, the meaning is either (*a*) 'the inner sanctuary has taken forty-six years to build . . .' or (*b*) 'the whole work has taken forty-six years, *so far*'. The latter is probably the better explanation of the words. **21. the temple of his body:** The body of Christ is a regular Pauline metaphor for the Church (cf. Eph. 2: 21 f.). Further, just as in a parallel passage (Mk 11: 17) the true house of God is a 'house of prayer for all nations' so through the Holy Spirit the same will be true in Christ's Body—the Church. **24. Jesus did not trust himself to them** (Gk. *ouk episteuen hauton autois*): Jesus' knowledge of men was absolute and sympathetic by virtue of the Incarnation. He knew men, indeed, with the knowledge of God. Presumably He saw the imperfections of their belief (v. 23).

ii. Jesus and Nicodemus (3: 1-21)
The link here with what has preceded seems to be that our Lord now demonstrates that divine understanding of men by His interview with Nicodemus. But the message which Jesus brings to him, though spoken for his personal good, has a universal application. The Evangelist's comments (vv. 16-21), which set the work of Christ in its universal setting, are intended as a sequel to that challenge presented

to the individual. **1. a man of the Pharisees** (see article 'Religious Background of the NT', and *NBD*, pp. 549b; 981f.): Pharisees were represented on the Sanhedrin. They were not as a whole so hypocritical as people think, since many of them had preserved much that was best in Judaism from Maccabean times onwards. **2. by night:** That this was for reasons of secrecy is almost beyond doubt. This is recalled later (cf. 19: 39) when Nicodemus embalms the Lord's body. And his cautious remarks in the Sanhedrin (cf. 7: 50 ff.) are worthy of note. **Rabbi:** Cf. 1: 49. **we know** seems to refer to those who had seen Jesus' 'signs' (cf. 2: 23). Nicodemus, therefore, represents Jews who are confronted by the inescapable uniqueness of Jesus' ministry. **a teacher come from God:** Nicodemus at least believes that Jesus' preaching is of divine origin. **unless God is with him:** Though true, this is inadequate as an expression of faith (cf. Ac. 10: 38; Exod. 3: 12). 3. **Truly, truly:** This formula, often repeated by Jesus (cf. 1: 51; 3: 5, 11; 5: 19, 24, 25; 6: 26, 32, 47, 53; 8: 34, 51, 58; 10: 1, 7; 12: 24; 13: 16, 20, 21, 38; 14: 12; 16: 20, 23; 21: 18) is a form of the Heb. *amēn, amēn*, from a verb root meaning 'to be sure, or founded'. The *double* Amen on the lips of Jesus is peculiar to John. It therefore adds some poignancy to the words which follow in each case; though it should also be noted that Jesus uses these words in reference to something which has gone before, suggesting, 'In truth there is a much deeper meaning in this than you think'. **born anew** or, 'born from above' (Gk. *gennēthē anōthen*): Christian experience commences with birth, for it is a *new* existence—a new creation (cf. 2 C. 5: 17; 1 Pet. 2: 2). But the act of begetting belongs to God. It is, says R. V. G. Tasker, to be 'likened to physical birth, for it is an emergence from darkness to light, when the restricted and confined is at last set free' (p. 67). The word *anōthen* can be rendered 'again' or 'from above', though 'anew' is better since it makes clearer that second birth is, indeed, *new* birth in quality as well as essence. **he cannot see:** No very clear distinction should be made between this statement and the similar one **he cannot enter** (v. 5). To 'see' might imply enjoyment, and 'enter' possibly denotes becoming a citizen. The Lord's statement, however, corrects the idea in Judaism that national ties alone were sufficient for entry into the kingdom, and that this **kingdom of God,** mentioned here only by John, though it is one of the leading ideas in the Synoptics, is concerned with the material world, *viz.*, for the Jews primarily the overthrow of the Roman army of occupation. The kingdom of God is the reign of God, where His will is supreme, whether in the individual heart or in the community of His people in this life or in the life hereafter. Only God's children understand what His will is—and there is the connection between the 'new life' and the kingdom of God. **4. Can he enter . . . and be born:** Nicodemus presumably understood only one side of the Lord's reference to new birth (cf. v. 3). **5. water and the Spirit:** This is linked immediately with new birth. There is not much to commend the view that 'water' refers to physical birth, and 'the Spirit' to spiritual regeneration, though John's baptism and/or proselyte baptism might well have provided a background of thought, particularly John's prediction concerning the relation between water and the Spirit in 1: 33 f. It seems best to apply the primary meaning of Ezek. 36: 25 ff., where water and Spirit denote cleansing and regeneration respectively. One application of 'water' may, indeed, be the act of John's baptism to repentance; though the idea of Christian baptism is not entirely unconnected, since in the NT it is closely linked with the imparting of the Spirit to the individual (cf. Ac. 2: 38). **6. flesh . . . spirit:** There is a gulf between what is basic to all human nature, flesh, and what is specifically divine in its origin, spirit. Both flesh and spirit bring about their respective fruits (cf. 6: 52-55). **7. You must be born anew:** Jesus' reply, addressed now not to one but to many, embraces all who need new birth. **8. The wind** (Gk. *pneuma*) **blows where it wills:** Jesus intends to refer to both wind and spirit. Just as the wind is unpredictable, so in the spiritual realm man cannot foresee the working of the Spirit. **the sound** might also refer both to 'noise' and 'voice', thus pressing the analogy further. **11. we speak of what we know:** Nicodemus, although a representative of the learned and pious in Israel, had failed to grasp the meaning of the work of God. Jesus now identifies Himself with all those (whether Jews at large, or His disciples) who had in some way comprehended the working of the Spirit. They had *seen* it, that is, had by experience mediated through faith. And the plural again reflects Jesus' kindliness as He spoke, through Nicodemus, to all those Jews, who, for whatever reason so far, had rejected His ministry. **12. earthly things . . . heavenly things:** The former (Gk. *ta epigeia*) means Christ's teaching on earth about the new birth. Earthly things are therefore those which, in fact, originate in God yet have their place on the earth, sometimes understood by human analogy. 'Heavenly things' (Gk. *ta epourania*) have no earthly analogy which will help us to understand them. They concern the supreme revelation of God in Christ, and in this the

mystery of the Son's relationship to the Father. This is expanded in the following verse. **13. No one has ascended . . . but he who descended:** The Son of man (cf. 1: 51) is the link between heaven and earth. By the Incarnation are shown heavenly things. This, however, in only part of the story. He has yet to ascend in exaltation and power, though this (cf. next verse) will be by way of suffering. [**who is in heaven** (margin) though omitted by a number of early MSS should probably be left in the text. Jesus revealed the life of God, which exists in heaven, whilst He was upon earth. His permanent dwelling-place is there; He only 'dwelt among us . . .' (cf. 1: 14).] **14. And as Moses lifted up the serpent:** Cf. 8: 28; 12: 32, 34. In these references to 'lifting up', with the possible exception of 8: 28, two ideas are combined: first is the Lord's death on the Cross uplifted; but then in John, the Son of Man returns to the Father to be uplifted in exaltation when He will attract all men to Himself (cf. next verse). The lifting up is all one great drama; it is the work of the Father when from the moment of the lifting up on the Cross He receives the Son back to Himself. **15. eternal life:** Cf. 3: 16, 36; 4: 14, 36; 5: 24, 39; 6: 27, 40, 47, 54, 68; 10: 28; 12: 25, 50; 17: 2 f. This life bears the quality of the new age of God (cf. Dan. 12: 2); but it is a present gift from God. Duration is not the main idea though that is present. Christ is Himself both the personification and guarantee of this life (cf. 1 Jn 5: 12), and the Father, by raising the Son, bestows upon Him the authority to grant this life to others (cf. 5: 26 f.; 17: 2 f.). **16. For God so loved the world:** We now pass to the inspired comment of the writer of the Gospel (so RSV punctuates, rightly, although NEB continues our Lord's words to v. 21). The work of Christ finds its origin in the Father's love; this is the only 'reason' behind His self-revelation. Love is not merely a continuous attitude of God. He has acted. In Christ He gave His unique Son, the very image of Himself. His love is reciprocal. Only those may enjoy it who respond by receiving God's gift in Christ. And when they receive Him, their response is inevitably one of giving back their love to God (cf. 14: 21, 24 f.). This is new in Jewish ears. Their particularistic ideas of God's special favour for Israel now give way to His revealed love for all mankind. **his only Son:** Cf. 1: 18. **should not perish** (Gk. *mē apolētai*): Another characteristic word in John (cf. 6: 12, 27, 39; 10: 28; 11: 50). Here the verb is used intransitively, in the middle voice, to mean 'to be lost' or 'to suffer destruction'. This is the only alternative to life eternal, for it is separation from Christ and God. There is no active sense of judgment yet (cf. next verse). That follows *ipso facto*, for condemnation passes upon all who refuse life in Christ (cf. v. 18). **17. God sent the Son . . . not to condemn:** Cf. 5: 27; 9: 39 ff. Our text wisely renders Gk. *krinō* as 'condemn' (cf. 12: 47 f.). **19.** Christ as the world's true Light shows men what they essentially are. **21. he who does what is true** knows that there can be no goodness apart from the Source of all good. Faith must be accompanied by a new quality in living which only can give credence to belief (cf. Jas 2: 14, 17, 24). **iii. The Baptist's final testimony (3: 22-36)** **22. The land of Judea:** We should probably understand the words to mean 'into the Judean countryside'. The words occur nowhere else in the NT. **23. John also was baptizing** might appear to conflict with the Synoptic tradition (cf. Mk 1: 14). But John makes it clear (v. 24) that the Baptist was not yet in prison, whereas Mark (1: 14) shows that Jesus did not begin His *Galilean* ministry until after John's arrest. The Evangelist is here recording an earlier, Judaean and Samaritan ministry of Jesus, between His baptism and appearance in Galilee, of which the Synoptists have nothing to say. **Aenon** and **Salim** were in Samaritan territory (cf. W. F. Albright, *Archaeology of Palestine*, 1960, p. 247; *NBD* p. 1125). At this stage John and Jesus work together. The setting serves to bring out the force of v. 30. **25. a discussion . . . over purifying:** This is (intentionally) unspecified. The passage leads up to the displacement of John as the forerunner of Jesus and as the last representative of expectant Judaism. **27. No one can receive . . . except what is given:** There is not a trace of bitterness at the news of Jesus' success. That such authority is divinely given, John believes is self-evident. **29. the friend of the bridegroom:** A graphic parable showing the central place to be occupied by Christ, and yet the unique position afforded to John the Baptist as 'best man', as His close friend. 'The bride' may refer to Israel (cf. Isa. 62: 4; Ezek. 16: 8; Hos. 2: 19 f.) and to the Church as the new Israel (2 C. 11: 2; Eph. 5: 25 ff.; Rev. 21: 2; 22: 17), but this should not be pressed. There could be some allusion here to the marriage at Cana (cf. v. 25; 2: 1-11). **this joy of mine is now full:** Fulfilment is linked with joy several times in John (cf. 15: 11; 16: 24; 17: 13). The Baptist's joy is that which comes at the completion of one's task. **30. He must increase, but I must decrease:** The significance of John's ministry lasts only in so far as he opened up the way for the fuller and eternal work of Christ. Vv. 31-36 were almost certainly not uttered by the Baptist (see RSV

quotation-marks). The theme of the Nicodemus interview and the Baptist's confession are welded into one by the Evangelist to sum up the truth manifested so far in Jesus. **31. He who comes from above** (Gk. *anōthen*) is a designation of Christ which confirms the nature of His work (cf. 13: 1). In the Synoptics, 'he who comes' (cf. Mk 11: 9; Mt. 11: 3, etc.) is a messianic title. **34. not by measure:** The fulness of the Spirit marked the Lord's ministry on earth, whereas the prophets of OT times were given the Spirit by measure. **36. the wrath of God:** In the NT for the most part the wrath of God is spoken of in eschatological terms. Here only in John, like eternal life, it is set in the present as men stand to be judged here and now according to their relationship with Christ, and so, as in Rom. 1: 18, are placed in an eschatological position.

iv. The Samaritan woman (4: 1-42)
Samaritans are not infrequently mentioned in the Gospels (cf. Lk. 9: 51-56; 10: 29-37; 17: 15 f.; and *NBD*, pp. 1131 f.). **1. the Lord:** Some MSS read 'Jesus' here, presumably because the former title is rarely used synonymously with Jesus in the Gospel (cf. 6: 23; 11: 2). V. 2 is an editorial comment correcting false rumours. **4. He had to pass through Samaria:** In John, Jesus is shown as working in close association with His Father, even in the events leading up to the final 'hour'. But here it is probably no more than a geographical necessity which is meant. **5. Sychar:** Usually identified with the modern Askar, not far distant from the traditional 'Jacob's Well' to be seen today, though W. F. Albright (*Archaeol. Pal.*, p. 247) favours the Old Syriac reading 'Sychem', that is, Shechem (cf. Ac. 7: 16). **near the field that Jacob gave to . . . Joseph:** That this was near to Shechem is fairly clear (cf. Gen. 48: 22 'mountain slope', Heb. *shechem*, also Gen. 33: 19; Jos. 24: 32). **6. wearied as he was** (Gk. *kekopiakōs*) is one of a number of intentional emphases in the Gospel (cf. Introduction) to underline the humanity of our Lord. **the sixth hour:** i.e. twelve noon. **9. Jews have no dealings with Samaritans:** This antagonism goes back to the late sixth and fifth centuries B.C. when exiled Jews returned to Judah from Babylon, who regarded this mixed populace as unclean. The rift was widened by the erection of the rival Temple on Mt. Gerizim. In rabbinical literature specific prohibitions exclude virtually all contact between the two parties. Such regulations may lie behind John's statement here (Gk. *synchraomai* means 'use together with', *e.g.* pots and pans). Accordingly NEB renders: 'Jews and Samaritans, it should be noted, do not use vessels in common'. **10. If you knew**

the gift of God: Only this gift of God can ever close such breaches between man and man, as they learn to share everything given by the Father through Christ. But the Son is Himself also the Gift (cf. 3: 16). **living water:** Primarily flowing water. In the OT, however, the picture was used for divine activity in giving life to men (cf. Jer. 2: 13; Zech. 14: 8; Ezek. 47: 9, etc.). **14. whoever drinks** (Gk. *hos d'an piē*): Barrett rightly would translate 'whoever shall drink', i.e. once for all, contrasted with the day-to-day necessity for water. **a spring of water** (Gk. *pēgē hydatos*): Jacob's well is described by the same word (v. 6). It was supplied by running water. But the RSV wisely makes the distinction between v. 6 and v. 14. (The Gk. word *phrear* is used in v. 11 f.) Both words are employed because this *phrear* is also fed by an underground *pēgē*. The spring of which Jesus speaks comes from outside the man, thus ensuring an unfailing supply. **15.** The woman, however, does not see that Jesus is speaking of a spiritual counterpart to the well which she used continually. **16. call your husband:** This is a startling approach in the light of eastern social reserve with such matters. **17. I have no husband:** Her reply was both a pitiful defence and a truthful confession. And Jesus observes the honesty of the statement though it may not have been seen by the woman who made it. But He will go further than accept what is right in order to expose the whole truth. Tasker comments: 'because she has spoken the truth, the truth makes her free—free to receive the gift that Jesus can give her' (p. 76). **19. a prophet:** There is alarm in these words. The Samaritans however, did not accept the authority of the prophets after Moses. But if Jesus is a prophet He must be *the* prophet of Dt. 18: 15 ff., the prophet like Moses, the *Taheb* of Samaritan expectation. **20. Our fathers worshipped on this mountain:** i.e. Gerizim, which was sacred to the Samaritans. This was the place where, according to the Samaritan text of Dt. 12: 5, God 'has chosen', not 'will choose' to put His name. Surely someone with prophetic insight can now solve the age-old problem? But the question is irrelevant here. Worship will, henceforward, be offered to God in every place (Mal. 1: 11) through Christ. **22. salvation is from the Jews:** In spite of the evidence of this woman's unsatisfactory life, Samaritans tended to be stricter than the Jews. But the election of the latter was for the spreading of the saving power of God to the 'uttermost part of the earth' (cf. Isa. 49: 5 f.). **23. in spirit and truth:** That is, in virtue of new birth, and in the light of the revelation of truth in Christ. 'Spirit' is vague enough here to denote both

that supernatural essence of Christian life, and the means, *viz.*, the Holy Spirit, through whom it is imparted. There can be no separation of the two; the former follows acceptance of the latter. **24. God is spirit** (Gk. *pneuma ho theos*) is more a question of describing sovereign freedom which God has in contrast to men, enclosed in a material world, than it is a definition of His nature. Men must therefore worship Him in spirit by which alone they can commune with Him. **25. Messiah is coming:** The Lord's words concerning the essential mode of worship cause her to respond. She believes at least that God will ultimately reveal His purpose. **26. I who speak to you am he:** Lit. 'I am (he) who speaks to you'. This self-disclosure makes the Lord's immediate purpose complete (cf. v. 19). 'I am' occurs many times in John (cf. 6: 35, 51; 8: 12, 18; 10: 7, 9, 11, 14; 11: 25; 14: 6; 15: 1, 5). Its strong resemblance to the OT Yahweh ('I will be what I will be') has been often noted. But the idea is not necessarily inherent in all these references as they stand, though certain implications may have suggested themselves to John and his earliest readers. This is the first self-confession of Jesus in the Gospel. **28. the woman left her water jar:** This is no allegorical reference. At this poignant moment the woman may, indeed, have set down her jar for Jesus' use. She tentatively asks: **Can this be the Christ?** **32. I have food to eat:** Just as the woman did not perceive the meaning of Jesus' references to living water, so the disciples apparently misunderstand Jesus' saying here about food (cf. Ps. 119: 103) by which He refers to His mission in life, **to do the will of Him who sent me** (34) in His works and words (cf. 9: 4; 10: 25, 37 f.; 14: 10 f.; 17: 4; also 7: 17; Dt. 8: 3). **and to accomplish his work:** Jesus' obedience to the Father was full and perfect (cf. 17: 4). **35. Do you not say:** i.e. 'is it not a common fact?' There is probably no proverb here. Barrett links this with the supposedly seasonal accuracy by which first fruits were offered to God on 16 Nisan (cf. *art.* 'Environmental Background to the NT'). **the fields are already white:** That is evidenced by the dealings with Nicodemus and the woman of Samaria. **36. sower and reaper . . . rejoice together:** Jesus has both sown the seed and reaped an early harvest. **38. I sent you to reap:** Probably a reference to the baptismal activity of the disciples in which they had truly entered into the labours of others, like John the Baptist (cf. 3: 23; 4: 2). **42. the Saviour of the world:** What ultimately transpired during Jesus' two days' stay in Samaria we shall probably never know; they may provide a background to Philip's Samaritan mission of Ac. 8: 5 ff.

But we do know that certain Samaritans were convinced beyond all doubt that Jesus was God's provision for universal salvation.

II. REVELATION BY DEEDS AND WORDS (4: 43–6: 71)

i. The official's son (4: 43–54)
There is one similarity between this miracle and that of the healing of the centurion's slave (cf. Mt. 8: 5–13; Lk. 7: 1–10). It lies in the fact that both cures were effected from some distance. **44. his own country** (*patris*) must mean here not Nazareth in Galilee, as it usually does in the Synoptics (cf. Mk 6: 4, etc.), but, in view of the messianic context, Jerusalem in Judaea, regarded by all Jews as their proper home. **48.** The signs which Jesus performs are only intended as sign-posts to the compassion of God. To use them alone as a basis for belief is not enough. **50. The man believed the word:** Even so, his faith was not yet *saving* faith. It was only as yet assurance that Jesus was genuine (cf. v. 53). **52. the seventh hour:** i.e. about 1 p.m. **53. he himself believed and all his household:** This was now absolute faith which gave value to his earlier belief without seeing (cf. 20: 29). **54. the second sign:** Cf. 2: 11.

ii. The cripple of Bethesda (5: 1–47)
This has some similarities with a cure recorded by the Synoptists (cf. Mk 2: 1–12; Mt. 9: 2–8; Lk. 5: 18–26). Both incidents give rise to controversy. In Mark the connection between the man's condition and Jesus' power to forgive sins is emphasized, whereas here the man's sins are mentioned almost in passing (cf. v. 14). It is interesting to note how at festival times Jesus severely indicted the unbelief of the Jews (cf. v. 29; 11: 55 ff.; 7: 2–9) in a way which finally hastened the climax of His ministry. **1. a feast:** The absence of a definite article leaves this unspecified, though some (among them R. H. Lightfoot and J. Rendel Harris) have suggested that this may have been New Year. **2. Beth-zatha:** Both the MS evidence for the name and its precise meanings are uncertain. 'Beth-zatha' (or perhaps 'Bezatha') has much to commend it, being known to Josephus. On the other hand many scholars still prefer the AV rendering 'Bethesda' (lit. 'house of mercy') possibly because of its suitability as a place where Jesus performed a miracle. Beth-'eshda ('house of outpouring'), preferred by Calvin, seems to be confirmed by the copper scroll from Qumran Cave 3. [Vv. 3b and 4 are rightly omitted from the text. They are clearly a later addition to the story, and find no strong manuscript support. They probably preserve some tradition which accounted for the moving of the water. The narrative reads perfectly well without them.] **6. Do you want to be healed:** Not a superfluous question. It seems that our Lord addressed the most needy case there and accordingly wished to evoke some faith from this man. **7. when the water is troubled:** The phenomenon is interpreted in the verses omitted as an angelic intervention. Westcott comments: 'The healing properties of the pool may have been due to its mineral elements'. Excavations at the Pool of St. Anna have revealed five porticos (cf. *NBD*, pp. 143 f.). **9. the sabbath:** In a terse statement the Evangelist prepares for the discourse which now follows. **10. it is not lawful:** The Jews treat what they see in terms of law. Rabbinic writings made careful distinctions regarding the removal of furniture on the sabbath. A bed may not be carried, though to carry a patient lying on a bed was permissible. **13. the man . . . did not know who it was:** This seems strange to us, but the oriental mind learned to accept the supernatural, often forgetting to trouble itself with the means of its operation. In any case, **Jesus had withdrawn** to avoid the curiosity of the crowd. **14. sin no more:** This implies that Jesus saw some connection, however indirect, between this case of suffering and some sin of which the man was guilty (cf. 9: 23). Forgiveness has not been mentioned, though 'no more' suggests that sin so far in the man's life was forgiven. **17. My Father is working still, and I am working:** The rest of the discourse flows from this statement. God rested on the seventh day, according to the scriptures (cf. Gen. 2: 2 f.). Yet sabbath observance was not intended as a rest of inactivity, but rest which comes from spiritual communion with God, who is ceaselessly active as Creator and Sustainer of the universe. **18. he . . . called God his Father** (Gk. *patera idion*): This, above all else so far, incited the Jews to murderous hatred of Jesus, together with His avowal that He acted in direct communion with the Father, saying, **'the Son can do nothing of his own accord'** (19). Jesus' relationship with the Father is unique, so that He does not work independently of the Father. **the Son does likewise:** Jesus' range of activity is coextensive with the Father's. **20. greater works than these:** That is, greater than the healing of this cripple. These will compel the attention of the Jews, *e.g.* the raising of Lazarus (cf. 11: 45). **21. as the Father raises the dead:** Most Jews believed that the raising of the dead was reserved for a coming age (cf. Ezek. 37: 13) and would be realized in the Messiah. V. 22 is a statement later explained in v. 27. Meanwhile one clear purpose for this delegation of auth-

ority to Christ is **that all may honour the Son** (23), recognizing His equality in authority and action. **24. he who hears . . . and believes:** The construction here shows that both hearing and believing are to be taken together. Hearing is not a passive activity only. The great *Shema'* ('Hear, O Israel . . .') of the OT (Dt. 6: 4–9) presupposed faith by works. So here the word of Christ evokes a response (cf. 6: 63, 68; 15: 3), and he who makes it **has eternal life: he does not come into judgment**—by faith he now anticipates and enjoys final acquittal and the life of the resurrection age. **25. the hour is coming and now is:** Cf. 4: 23. The 'dead' here are the spiritually dead. The Son of man has already awakened them by His word. That those who hear will live is based upon OT expectation (cf. Isa. 55: 11). So Christ's word bringing life separates man from man, thereby bringing some into judgment (cf. v. 27). **26. he has granted the Son . . . to have life:** It is part of the Son's essential nature, shared with the Father, that He is capable of being a source of life to others (cf. 1: 4). **27. because he is the Son of man** (Gk. *hoti hyios anthrōpou esti*): The Danielic Son of man (cf. Dan. 7: 13 f.) is never far from the minds of the Evangelists. Here, clearly, His humanity is uppermost in thought. Because He fully shares humanity, and in virtue of the supreme authority conferred on Him by the Father, He can dispense judgment. **28. all who are in the tombs:** Cf. v. 25. Both good and bad are included (cf. next verse). The resurrection of those physically dead is something to come later in the divine programme. Jesus' voice will be heard in final judgment, though there is no embroidering of the details (cf. Dan. 12: 2). **30. I seek not my own will:** This puts the judgment spoken of by Christ beyond all question. In Him there is no suggestion of self-aggrandisement (cf. vv. 41–44). **31.** Jesus' saying here might seem to contradict what He says later (cf. 8: 13 f.). But there is no contradiction. Here, He is referring to those claims which He might have made by self-assertion. But His testimony is at one with the Father's, so He trusts Him (cf. v. 32). **34. I say this that you may be saved:** So great is Jesus' concern for the Jews that He will draw their attention to the work of John the Baptist if that will lead them to Him. **35. He was a burning and shining lamp** (Gk. *lychnos*): John's testimony, at the best, was secondary (cf. 1: 8, 33; 8: 14). He bore witness as a *lamp* through which the true light shone in the measure of the oil given him. **you were willing to rejoice:** Religious fervour, perhaps, led many Jews to interest themselves in John's preaching, since it was concerned with the

proclamation of the kingdom. **37. the Father . . . has himself borne witness:** This presumably refers to the baptism of Jesus. They did not hear His voice (cf. Mk 1: 11) nor did they see His form (Gk. *eidos*, external form; cf. Lk. 3: 22) —in the dove which descended (1: 32)? **38. you do not have his word abiding in you:** Here Jesus' charge against the Jews comes to its climax. If the Word of God had a real place in them they would have recognized both the authority of Christ and the Baptist. **39. You search the scriptures:** The verb may be either imperative or indicative. The latter gives the better sense. Jews believed the scriptures to be life-giving, but they failed to understand them as a witness to Christ (cf. v. 21; Lk. 24: 25 ff., 44 ff.) in that they did not find their way to Him. **42. you have not the love of God within you:** Their devotion to God was not genuine, else they would have received Christ's testimony. Yet they are further condemned in that they are ready to receive some self-styled teacher (v. 43). **45. it is Moses who accuses you:** They need not think that Moses is their advocate; he is their prosecutor, and judgment lies in the authority of the Word (12: 47). **47. how will you believe my words:** Belief in the OT sees it as incomplete, ever pointing forward to fulfilment (cf. Dt. 18: 15 f.). This argument addresses the Jewish religious mind. If they do not believe the scriptures it is hardly likely that they will accept the teaching of this Rabbi upon them.

iii. Feeding the masses (6: 1–15)
1. After this: Some feel that this chapter should precede chap. 5 in chronological sequence, on the ground that 7: 1 follows more naturally on chap. 5 (see especially 5: 18). But the idea is insufficiently grounded to make it satisfactory (see note on 7: 15). **the Sea of Tiberias:** So named after the city, founded by Herod Antipas in A.D. 26 in honour of Tiberius Caesar. John may have used the up-to-date name for the benefit of non-Jews (cf. 21: 1). **4. the Passover . . . was at hand:** This Passover is probably a year later than that of chap. 2 because on the earlier occasion the Baptist had not yet been imprisoned; and according to Mark he was not only imprisoned but executed by the time of feeding of the 5,000. The Passover was near enough, perhaps, to allow John to insert a chronological note, which gives point to the later discourse (vv. 22–59) in the light of the Paschal feast (cf. 1 C. 5: 7; Mt. 15: 29–39). **5. a multitude was coming to him:** Having walked round to the NE corner of the Lake, Jesus is moved with pity upon them (cf. Mk 6: 33 f.). **Philip:** In the Synoptics it is the disciples who express concern for the crowd.

Here, complementarily, Jesus puts one of them to the test. **9. what are they among so many:** Andrew's problem is recorded to show how meagre are man's resources in proportion to his needs. **11. when he had given thanks** (Gk. *eucharistēsas*): That John records this at length, whilst he does not record the Last Supper in detail, is surely significant. Thanksgiving is, however, only what we should have expected Jesus to make, and John's word for this may carry a technical meaning which would *immediately* associate this event with the Holy Communion. The primary lesson here seems to be that Jesus was acting in dependence upon the Father, so that eucharistic associations should not, in any case, be pressed too far. **12. Gather up the fragments:** Any thought-projection on the part of the Evangelist here to the completeness of the Body of Christ symbolized at the Communion table is quite unlikely. Rather is it plain evidence of the fact that Jesus cared about wastage, and intended to bring back the disciples to the reality of human need far from the world of the miraculous. **14. This is indeed the prophet:** The recent murder of John the Baptist had increased the desire to find a popular Messiah. Their acclamation hailed Jesus as the prophet like Moses (Dt. 18: 15 ff.) who had formerly fed his people in like manner (cf. 1 C. 10: 1-5). **15. they were about to make him king:** The multitude 'like sheep without a shepherd' (Mk 6: 34) was an army looking for a captain to lead them against the Romans. **Jesus withdrew:** Mark tells us that it was for prayer (cf. Mk 6: 46). This was a critical moment. Worldly kingship was far from the mind of Jesus (cf. 18: 33 f.) as the temptations had already shown (cf. Mt. 4: 1-11).

iv. A storm at sea (6: 16-21)
The disciples now return to the western side of the sea of Galilee. **19. they had rowed about three or four miles:** The Gk. *stadion* was equal to about 606 feet or 185 metres, rather less than an English furlong so 'five and twenty or thirty furlongs' (AV). **Jesus walking on the sea** (Gk. *epi tēs thalassēs*): The precise meaning of the Gk. phrase has been disputed. Some claim that it means 'by the sea' (i.e., 'on the shore'), as in 21: 1, so withdrawing miraculous meaning from the words, and supporting their claim with the contention that the gladness of the disciples to receive Jesus into the boat did not lead to their *actually* receiving Him thus, because **immediately the boat was at the land.** But their arrival at the shore need not be so speedy as these words suggest, for their distance (v. 19) would suggest that, when they saw the Lord, they were about half way across. And

the text is difficult to understand unless they did actually take Jesus with them into the boat.

v. Living Bread (6: 22-59)
25. Rabbi, when did you come here: The question of the crowd opens up the whole discourse. Their question was one involving both time and manner, for their curiosity in the miraculous was not easily lost. So Jesus says, **you seek me . . . because you ate your fill** (26). But what kind of interest was it? They only came to Him for the satisfaction of the moment, and not for **the food which endures** and which, here and now, nourishes eternal life in those who take it. **27. on him has God . . . set his seal:** The sign of the loaves and fish are the divine authentication of the words of Jesus. **29. This is the work of God, that you believe:** Their grasp of the main idea of Jesus' words is still limited. But Jesus says that faith in Him will bear fruit naturally, not as a labour of duty. The tense denotes continuation rather than a single act. **30. Then what sign do you do:** Their unbelief is scarcely credible. The miraculous feeding has apparently produced no inward effect. Jesus refuses their allusion to Moses because their understanding of that miracle (cf. Exod. 16: 15; Neh. 9: 5) was defective. **32. my Father gives you the true bread:** The manna of Moses was not 'the real bread', and in any case, it was not given by Moses but God. The real bread **gives life to the world** (33). The people begin to appreciate the distinction which Jesus is making between the manna and the spiritual sustenance of which the manna is a type, so they answer with more respect but still with incomplete understanding, **Lord, give us this bread always** (34), like the Samaritan women's 'give me this water' (4: 15). Therefore Jesus makes the nature of the true bread plainer still. **35. I am the bread of life:** Hitherto in the discourse this bread is given by the Son of man (v. 27) as the Father's agent (v. 32); now He identifies it with Himself, thus calling forth the sharpest criticism yet. **he who comes to me shall not hunger:** Total commitment to Him will result in total salvation. Just as there is nothing partial in God's giving of life, so there can be no partiality in receiving Christ. **37. All that the Father gives me will come to me:** Is this *so* arbitrary? Temple adds, 'To realise that my not "coming" is itself due to the will of the Father, who has not yet drawn me, and to accept this, is one beginning of trust in Him, one sign that in fact He is really drawing me to come' (Vol. i, p. 88). **38. the will of him who sent me:** Cf. vv. 39 f. The will of God is the kernel of the work of Christ in salvation. And Christ's doing of that

will is perfect so that He should **lose nothing** (39). Eternal life is the gift which God wills to give to men. **40. I will raise him up:** Westcott has aptly commented that the doctrine of eternal life makes the necessity of resurrection obvious. John always thinks of eternal life as a possession here and now, though **the last day** shows he does also include the idea of judgment. **42. Is not this Jesus, the son of Joseph:** Jesus' elaboration of the Bread of Life sayings undoubtedly led some of His hearers to accept what He was saying as true (cf. v. 34). Now, however, it is not so much the Bread of Life which they query, but that these claims should be made by One of such humble origins. **44. No one can come to me unless the Father . . . draws him:** The Jews' incredulity does not help the matter. The initiative in saving men always is taken by the Father, so the solving of theological riddles will bring no ultimate advantage, for **they shall all be taught by God** (45; cf. Isa. 54: 12 f.). God teaches men in that He alone can utter His word. All who hear and respond worthily to that word inevitably will turn to Christ. The test is plain (cf. vv. 45 f.). **51. the bread which I shall give . . . is my flesh:** In summing up, Jesus again reminds the hearers that the manna was only a type of the real bread of God (cf. vv. 49 f.). *He* is the true Bread of Life. It is *His* life which will be given. This is Jesus' sacrifice of Himself, for he could hardly give His flesh and blood (cf. v. 56) apart from death. **53. unless you eat the flesh . . . and drink his blood:** The question concerning the relationship of this saying to the Lord's Supper, in which those who partake do so by faith (1 C. 10: 16) is inescapable. In the Synoptics the Lord's Supper is recorded primarily as that which the Lord Himself instituted. Here, however, we may see the teaching of the Lord Jesus which can only be fully understood in the light of the feast which He inaugurated, and which, without referring directly to that Supper, conveys truth which should give the Lord's Supper deep meaning for the believer. The language is vividly metaphorical, denoting the appropriation of Christ by faith. 'It is a figure', says Augustine, 'bidding us communicate in our Lord's passion, and secretly and profitably store up in our memories that for our sakes He was crucified and slain' (*On Christian Doctrine* 3. 16). Bernard explains the words **he who eats my flesh and drinks my blood** (54) to mean: 'He who reflects upon my death, and after my example mortifies his members which are upon earth, has eternal life—in other words, "If you suffer with me, you will also reign with me" ' (*On Loving God* 4. 11). It should be noted that 'flesh' here corresponds to

'body' in the Synoptics and in 1 Cor. 10: 16; 11: 24, 27, 29. If there is any distinction to be made between the two it would be that 'flesh' stresses the utter humanity of Christ, whilst 'body' would signify His person as an organic entity, and the fact that John had docetic teachers very much in his mind should not be overlooked in this connection. 'My body' and 'my flesh' would alike represent Aram. *bisri*. **58. This is the bread which came down from heaven:** The contrast between Christ and the Law, between the living Bread and the manna, is now complete. As the Lord Jesus is fully identified with the Bread of God, so only he who partakes of Him will know what life from God really means.

vi. Disciples' faith and unbelief (6: 60–71)
Jesus now concentrates upon the disciples when opposition hardens elsewhere. **60. This is a hard saying:** It is hardly surprising that the disciples should be filled with consternation, knowing so little about the future for Jesus as they did. **62. Then what if you were to see the Son of man ascending:** He came down to give life. The time is coming when He will return to the Father in power and glory. If they have seen Him in the flesh, which He is to give for the world, and are amazed, what then will be their reaction when He goes away in a blaze of glory? **63. It is the spirit that gives life, the flesh is of no avail:** Cf. vv. 53, 55. The words of Jesus must be understood in a spiritual, not a carnal sense. His flesh is the vehicle of the Spirit, and therefore can impart life. But, as He said to Nicodemus, nothing basic in human nature can help man in his need. **64. some of you . . . do not believe:** Jesus has accepted the Passion, and knows already who they are who will not believe. Further, this is His first reference to the traitor, and coincides exactly with the Synoptics' first references to the Passion. Jesus insists (v. 65) that some will inevitably turn back, and turn back they did (v. 66) at that precise moment. **68. You have the words of eternal life:** Cf. Mk 8: 29. The first impulsive faith of the disciples now gives way to rational conviction based on experience. Jesus' words may be hard to understand, yet their claims and genuineness are all too clear. They believe now, but they were chosen already (v. 70), though one of them, instead of going back, remains within the Twelve, a disloyal member, perhaps seeking to distort the kingdom to his own pattern. He was the son of **Simon Iscariot** (71; cf. 13: 2, 26). His name indicates that he came either from Kerioth Hezron, or (less probably) that he was linked with the *sicarii* (cf. Ac. 21: 37 f. and *NBD*, pp. 673 f.).

III. JESUS, THE SOURCE OF ALL TRUE BLESSING (7: 1-10: 39)
i. Controversy at the Feast of Tabernacles (7: 1-52)

2. feast of Tabernacles: Otherwise known as 'Booths', an autumnal festival, lasting eight days from 15th to 22nd Tishri inclusive (Lev. 23: 33-36), the last day of which was sabbatical. Jerusalem would be thronged with pilgrims celebrating harvest-home, and God's historic care in the wilderness wandering; and many erected their own shelters near the Holy City for the occasion (cf. Lev. 23: 42). **3. his brothers:** There is no good reason to suppose that they were not the children of Mary and Joseph. They urged our Lord to make an open show of His power, and in v. 5 the Evangelist indicates that their request grew out of their unbelief. Some MSS insert 'then', presumably to reconcile this with other passages such as Ac. 1: 14. But the fact that they were unbelievers *as yet* enables us to see partly why Jesus committed the care of His Mother to another disciple (cf. 19: 25 ff.). **6. My time** (Gk. *ho kairos ho emos*): Not the Johannine 'hour' (Gk *hōra*). There may be some little distinction. 'Time' here speaks of opportunity, whereas 'hour' elsewhere (cf. 7: 30; 8: 20; 12: 23; 13: 1; 17: 1) speaks of His appointed death and exaltation. **7.** For most pilgrims one visit to Jerusalem for Tabernacles might have little to distinguish it from others. But for Jesus it means that His presence, awakening sin in others, stands to evoke their hatred. **8. I am not going up:** Jesus' movement towards Jerusalem will only be, as Stauffer puts it, when 'The Father had given the sign!' (p. 27). **10. then he also went up . . . in private:** John records a number of visits by Jesus to Jerusalem (cf. 2: 13; 5: 1; 12: 12), but this one accords clearly with the Synoptic writers (cf. Mk 9: 30), where Jesus' secrecy is a prelude to the final drama which leads to the Arrest, Trial and Crucifixion. And because of His private entry, Jews in the city were asking where He was (v. 11). They were not kept waiting long (v. 14). This is John's first notice of public preaching by Jesus in Jerusalem as distinct from answering questions. **15. learning** (Gk. *grammata*, lit. 'letters'): Those who contend that chap. 6 is displaced refer, among other things, to the fact that this question seems to follow on from the saying about Moses' 'writings' (*grammata*) in 5: 47. This cannot be pressed. The words **he has never studied** mean that Jesus was not trained in the rabbinical schools. With the present question we may compare the Jewish leaders' later observation that Peter and John were 'uneducated (*agrammatoi*), common men' (Ac. 4: 13); their ability to expound scripture was

explained by their having 'been with Jesus'. **17. if any man's will is to do his will, he shall know:** There can be no greater authority than this which can be put to the test. Elsewhere, our Lord was similarly questioned (cf. Mt. 21: 23; Jn 6: 30) and He gave always the same answer in principle. **19. none of you keeps the law:** If these men really sought to do the will of God (v. 17), then the law of Moses would be their supreme guide in all matters. But they deny Jesus' authority, and their threat to kill Him enabled Jesus to turn round the argument. They had accused Him of openly breaking the Sabbath (cf. 5: 1-9). **22. Moses gave you circumcision:** Although this was practised by the patriarchs, Moses regularized it within the Law (cf. Lev. 12: 3). And it is certain that Rabbinic interpretation of the Leviticus passage made circumcision on the Sabbath supreme over the Sabbath itself. **24. judge with right judgment:** Jesus' teaching here on circumcision adds to the general Sabbath controversy as we have it recorded in the Synoptics. Jesus is concerned with making men whole, and not merely with bringing a more liberal interpretation to bear upon Levitical regulations. **28. you know where I come from:** Jesus' openness was a source of astonishment. Surely the authorities had not capitulated? But no; the Christ will have no known origin, that is, the time and manner of His appearing were expected to be a mystery. **29. I know him . . . he sent me:** Jesus claims both divine knowledge and authority. It seems that John almost suggests (v. 30) that the Jews were physically incapable of laying hands on Him before 'the hour' struck. **33. I go to him who sent me:** The verb 'I go' (Gk. *hypagō*) in John denotes particularly our Lord's return to where He belongs (cf. 8: 14; 13: 33, 36; 14: 4 f., 28; 16: 5, 17, etc.). His death would not be the end of His work. It would be, as Luke puts it, only an 'exodus' (Lk. 9: 31) to the Father. **34. where I am:** Cf. 14: 3; 17: 24; also 8: 21; 13: 33. Christ is essentially with the Father always, in spirit. But shortly He will return there bodily. In some of these passages a more precise historical separation is in view. 'Where I am' could be accentuated to mean 'where I am about to be'. But in all separation remains a hard fact—**you cannot come.** The Jews sought Him now in anger. The time is coming when they will seek Him in anguish. **35. the Dispersion:** This was a collective name for Jews in foreign lands (cf. Jas 1: 1; 1 Pet. 1: 1). To go to them was bad enough, but they ironically add **and teach the Greeks?** The real irony, of course, lay in the fact that they were speaking the truth and did not foresee Christ's mission to the Gentiles in the Body of His

Church. So now Christ openly makes a universal invitation on the eighth and **last day of the feast** (37). **let him come to me and drink:** Probably the ritual libations of water offered on certain days during the Feast of Tabernacles were fresh in the Lord's mind. These reminded Jews of the seasonal faithfulness of God (cf. Zech. 14: 7 f.). The idea of spiritual nourishment has, however, been elaborated already (cf. 4: 14; 5: 26; 6: 53 ff.). Here we are explicitly told that **Out of his heart shall flow rivers** (38), meaning that others may slake their thirst at the overflowing bounty of life in the believer. A general collocation of references is in mind (cf. Isa. 44: 3; 55: 1; 58: 11; Zech. 13: 1; 14: 8). The reference is to the Spirit who would come in all His cleansing and refreshing power after Jesus was glorified through death and exaltation (1 C. 12: 13). **40. This is really the prophet:** As Moses had drawn water from the rock, so now Jesus promises His people water to drink (cf. 6: 14; 1 C. 10: 4). **43. there was a division:** The people seem to have adopted a three-fold standpoint. Some remained convinced that Jesus was an impostor, probably linking His Galilean origin with their doubts. Others believed that He could be the prophetic forerunner of the Messiah. And others accepted His claims in their entirety. **47. Are you led astray . . . also:** The officers who returned helpless to the chief priests need make no specific confession. Their amazement eloquently testified to their reaction to Jesus. But the Pharisees retort, 'none of the *spiritual* leaders have been so misled'. If the others had been beguiled by this Jesus, so much the worse for them. But were they *all* adamant? No, one of them, Nicodemus, showed tactful impartiality, for he had, indeed, given Him a hearing (v. 51). **no prophet is to rise from Galilee:** Lit., 'out of Galilee a prophet does not arise'; but Papyrus 66, the oldest extant manuscript of Jn, has the singular reading 'the prophet' (cf. v. 40) for 'a prophet' of our other authorities. (The reading with the article had been conjectured by Rudolf Bultmann before it turned up in P 66.) [**The woman taken in adultery** (**7: 53–8: 11**) is treated in Additional Note 2; see p. 287.]

ii. The true Light and its implications (8: 12–59)
In this section we come to the second great self-disclosure of the Lord which is brought to a climax by the ensuing discussion. **12. I am the light of the world:** The division among the Jews (cf. 7: 43) was due to blindness. Jesus declares that He is the Light of which Life is the source and which shines on the way to a fuller experience of God. In the beginning God manifested Himself by the bringing of Light

(cf. Gen. 1: 2). The feast of Tabernacles, moreover, brought to remembrance God's heavenly guidance of Israel by the fiery pillar and a ceremony of lights was performed which provided illumination throughout the Temple. Darkness is where God is unknown. He who follows Jesus emerges from chaotic darkness like the world at the beginning. **15. I judge no one:** Though He has authority to execute judgment as Son of man (cf. 5: 27), Jesus withholds it (cf. 17: 2). The statement probably accounted for the insertion of the adultery passage preceding this. Significantly too, that deals with a capital offence which was only chargeable on the testimony of several witnesses (cf. Dt. 17: 6; also v. 13 above). **16. even if I do judge . . . it is not I alone:** Jewish law required evidence from at least two witnesses (Dt. 19: 15). But though Jesus' witness is irrefutable, they answer that God's evidence cannot be asked for corroboration as if He were an earthly witness (cf. v. 19). **20. the treasury:** The area containing offering-chests, probably in the Court of Women (cf. Mk 12: 41) close by the Sanhedrin chamber. **his hour:** Cf. 7: 30. **21. I go away:** Cf. 7: 33. Now Jesus explains that His departure to the Father will have dire consequences for some (cf. 16: 8–11). **22. Will he kill himself:** A gross misunderstanding of Jesus' words. Yet they are unconsciously ironical for He would, indeed, lay down His life (cf. 10: 17). **23. You are from below:** Both realms, 'above' and 'below', meet on earth, the scene, indeed, of their conflict. The terminology may be that of a three-decker universe, but it is used in an ethical sense to distinguish the realms of good and evil. **25. Even what I have told you from the beginning:** Gk. *ho ti kai lalō hymin* could be rendered with the opening words 'Why do I speak to you at all'? (SO NEB) which would fit in with the general sense of the passage. **26. When you have lifted up the Son of man:** Though the 'lifting up' idea is usually fraught with theological implications (see note on 3: 14), here it is less so. Jesus refers to the act of the crucifixion by men, which would, nevertheless, bring about His exaltation. His death will demonstrate His obedience. His exaltation will endorse His messianic claims. So forthright were Jesus' words here that **many believed in him** (30). **31. If you continue in my word:** Some Jews had believed in Him (Gk. *pepisteukotas autō*) in a manner which formally accepted His teaching. Others (cf. v. 30, Gk. *episteusan eis auton*) had exercised dynamic faith in Him. **32. the truth will make you free:** Only by setting aside all preconceptions, tradition and self-will can a man see the whole truth, especially the truth about himself. **33.**

We . . . have never been in bondage: These Jews were not denying the plain facts of their history. Rather they were asserting that religious freedom had always been granted to them in some way. **35. The slave does not continue in the house:** Jesus speaks, however, of serfdom under sin (cf. Rom. 6: 17). A son is always free; a slave cannot free himself (cf. Gen. 21: 9-14). Isaac remained in his father's house, whereas Ishmael, son of Hagar, was put out. **36. So if the Son makes you free:** John reserves the noun *hyios* in relation to God for Christ alone. **39. If you were Abraham's children:** There are several variant readings suggested for this. The main alternative reads, 'If you *are* Abraham's children, then do Abraham's works.' (But cf. v. 42 which would suit the former reading better.) 'Children' implies blood relationship (cf. 1: 12), though John uses the plural *tekna* rather than *hyioi* regardless of finer implications. **40. this is not what Abraham did:** Perhaps Jesus is thinking of the welcome given by Abraham to God's messengers (cf. Gen. 18). **42. If God were your Father:** Cf. v. 39. Jesus denies the Jews' ultimate right to claim descent from Abraham spiritually. Yet more, if any nation could claim the right to address God as Father, it was Israel (cf. Hos. 11: 1; Mal. 2: 10). But Jesus refuses to acknowledge even this right, since these Jews have rejected the unique Son of God. Now follow two sharp unanswerable questions. **43. Why do you not understand:** It is because they cannot listen to His message. Their difficulty is a moral one, not intellectual. So the Jews' silence evokes some of the sternest ever of Jesus' rebukes (v. 44). **46. Which of you convicts** (Gk. *elenchei*) **me of sin:** None! Then He *does* speak the truth, and the burden of guilt lies hard on their side by what He has said. Indeed, the Spirit will later convict *them* of sin (cf. 16: 8). But their ears are dull because they are **not of God** (47). **48. you are a Samaritan:** Their hot repudiation of Jesus' words led them to suggest that His denial of their kinship with Abraham was founded on Samaritan prejudice, and it may well be that Jesus' words had reminded them of the terminology of Samaritan theologians. The term 'Samaritan', however, is more probably a simple means of abuse (cf. v. 41). **51. he will never see death:** Here is madness indeed! for **Abraham died** (52). Jesus, however, speaks of death as the final and irrevocable separation from God. **56. Abraham rejoiced that** (Gk. *ēgalliasato hina*) **he was to see my day:** Abraham anticipated the fulfilment of the initial promise of God (cf. Gen. 12: 3), especially at times of trial (cf. Gen. 22: 18). **he saw it and was glad:** Some ancient commentators believed this to be Abraham's vision

(cf. Gen. 15: 17-21) of the extent of his posterity. Philo interpreted the laughter of Abraham (cf. Gen. 17: 17) as rejoicing rather than incredulity. Others have suggested that Abraham saw Christ's work from Paradise. Surely it rather refers to that penetration into the purpose of God, by which Abraham rejoiced in the Word of God, who was now made flesh for men to see. But how, ask the Jews, can He know so much about Abraham? **58. before Abraham was, I am:** This is a clear claim to eternity of being. What correspondence with the Ineffable Name was intended in Jesus' use of the expression **I am** must be open to question. It must be remembered that Jesus is primarily answering the Jews' cavil concerning the length of His life. But that they saw blasphemous implications in what He said is clear (v. 59); perhaps they discerned an echo of 'I am he' in Isa. 41: 4, etc. So the conclusion to which the argument has led is that the time of special privileges for the physical descendants of Abraham has passed away (cf. Mt. 3: 9). The eternal Word has come in flesh to found a new community. The chosen people is now made up of Christ's followers, and the prerogatives of Abraham's seed have passed to them.

iii. The man blind from birth (9: 1-41)

In this section there is a perfect illustration of the fact that what Jesus does is inseparable from what He says. The next note of time occurs in 10: 22. There the passage follows on closely from chap. 9. So possibly the controversies in chap. 8 should be regarded as summing up discussions between Tabernacles and Dedication. **2. who sinned, this man or his parents:** They assume the old explanation of suffering so hotly challenged by Job. Moreover, the suggestion that the man himself might have been at fault seems to rest on Jewish speculation with regard to transmission of guilt or something carried over from Rabbinic Judaism, where, for example, in Midrash Rabbah on Dt. 31: 14, a pregnant woman who sins makes her unborn child to sin (cf. N. P. Williams, *Ideas of the Fall and Original Sin*, 1927, p. 98). Jesus repudiates any notion that there is a direct causal connection between his blindness and some sin. **3. but that the works of God might be made manifest in him:** The right attitude is to see in suffering not a reason for imputing guilt, but an occasion for the revealing of God's glory in the way it is dealt with. [There is a further possible rendering by an alteration of punctuation, *viz.*, 'It was not that this man sinned, nor his parents. But that God's work may be shown in him, I must do His works who sent me while it is day'.] **5. As long as I am in the world, I am the light of the**

world: So long as Jesus remains, performing the work for which He was sent, there remains the inescapable revelation of the character of God. **7. Go, wash in the pool of Siloam** (modern Silwan): Cf. Isa. 8: 6. This pool lies at the southern end of the Tunnel of Hezekiah from the Virgin's Fountain, at the southern extremity of the Tyropoeon valley. John explains its meaning, doubtless seeing a significance in the light of Jesus as **sent** from God. **14. it was a sabbath day when Jesus made the clay:** Here is the strongest reason for the Pharisees' rejection of the sign. Mishnaic rules for healing and the use of saliva on the Sabbath were complicated; but Jesus had made clay, and so had done work. So they triumphantly claim that Jesus **is not from God** (16) if He can openly break the Sabbath. **17. He is a prophet:** There is no theological significance in this. The man simply realized that Jesus possessed extraordinary powers. **18. The Jews did not believe:** Either the whole story is a fabrication, they say, or else the man has confused the day on which he received his sight. His parents are dumbfounded, too, and they **feared the Jews** (22). The fear of excommunication held them. This could operate in two ways. The less severe, meant here, involved separation from the privileges of the synagogue for a period up to thirty days, though actual attendance at the synagogue was required as a disciplinary measure. This could virtually be enforced by anyone—even a woman. The more severe form involved flogging and exclusion from all social contact, except within the family, though it was seldom enforced. In Jesus' days the severe ban could only be inflicted by the Sanhedrin, but by the time of John's writing local synagogues could enforce both forms—and did so against the Christians. **24. Give God the praise:** A colloquialism meaning 'admit the truth' (cf. Jos. 7: 19). **we know that this man is a sinner:** This is where they condemn themselves (cf. 3: 18). **25. one thing I know:** Stubbornly, the man refuses to be coerced away from the plain fact. They may know their theology; he knows his cure. Which is ultimately more acceptable? The coming of sight has not solved all his problems, but his new life is beyond question. So their cross-examination cannot shake him. **27. Do you** (of all people) **. . . want to become his disciples:** No, indeed they do not. **28. we are disciples of Moses:** Their taunt against the man as **his disciple** and themselves as those who adhered to the law foreshadows the inevitable cleavage which was to take place between Christians and Jews in early NT times. **33. If this man were not from God he could do nothing:** Now the man comes towards the climax of his faith. Jesus, he believes, must be sent from God. And the Pharisees' rejection of so open a sign astonishes him. **34. You were born in utter sin:** Their insinuation of the man's moral legacy, and their anger at his resistance, causes them to cast him out, and in principle cast out the Saviour with him. **35. Do you believe in the Son of man:** [Some MSS, followed by AV and RV text, read 'Son of God' here.] Barrett is probably right in saying that, as yet, the man's faith was imperfect. Perhaps the question should be phrased, 'You believe in the Son of man, do you not?' In the light of ch. 10, we may see Jesus, the Shepherd, taking care (v. 35) of a sheep lately sent away from the fold of Jewish legalism. **37. You have seen him:** The primary meaning is that the man, with his eyesight restored, had seen the Son of Man without realizing who He was. Elsewhere in the Gospels seeing the Son of Man is reserved for the future (cf. Mk 14: 62). But by the eye of faith the future sight of Him can be enjoyed here and now. **39. For judgment I came . . . that those who see may become blind:** Cf. Isa. 29: 18; 35: 5; 42: 7, 18. Here there is an interchange between physical and spiritual sight. Jesus is more concerned with the latter, though the man just cured had received both. Those Jews who rejected Jesus had become wilfully blind to the truth (12: 40; cf. Isa. 6: 9 f.). Jesus had come to give spiritual sight to those who knew they were blind, but also to correct the defect of those who were satisfied with the 'sight' which they already possessed, so that they could now move forward on a new basis of faith. **41.** The Pharisees understand that Jesus is speaking of spiritual sight, and take their stand on their knowledge of the scriptures. Jesus now shows them that their sin lies nevertheless in their possession of the truth without understanding it, whereas ignorance from blindness is teachable. And the fact that they insist that they can 'see' makes their sin wilful.

iv. The Good Shepherd (10: 1–21)

This section is an elaboration of matters raised in ch. 9. The shepherds in Israel had failed; now the Good Shepherd takes over. The passage is a lengthy parable (Gk. *paroimia*, v. 6) and the alternation between symbolism and reality has to be followed carefully by the reader. **2. he who enters by the door is the shepherd:** Here is a straightforward reference to what most Jews would have seen day by day; but later both the door (v. 7) and the shepherd (vv. 10, 14, etc.) symbolize different aspects of Jesus Himself. The wording suggests that the gatekeeper was someone paid by a number of shepherds collectively to keep their sheep in one fold since Jesus refers to several shepherds by inference (v. 16) and repeats **his own sheep** on a number of occasions (vv. 3, 4, 12, 14). **6. figure** (Gk. *paroimia*) is used alone by John among the Gospel writers (cf. 2 Pet. 2: 22 and Prov. 1: 1, LXX) and seems to mean 'a veiled utterance' as distinct from forthright speech (cf. 16: 25, 29). **7. I am the door of the sheep:** He does not say 'of the fold' for it is the sheep who concern Him, so perhaps, 'I am the door *for* the sheep'. **8. All who came before me:** Jesus does not refer here to the OT prophets. He means self-appointed leaders in Israel. **9. and will go in and out:** The emphasis here is different from that in v. 7. Christ is the only Way into the security of the fold of God. But once entered the sheep enjoy complete freedom. **11. I am the good Shepherd:** God is depicted as the Shepherd of Israel in the OT (cf. Ps. 23: 1; Isa. 40: 11; Jer. 31: 9; Ezek. 34; *et alia*). Gk. *kalos* here suggests the beauty of perfect competence as well as of moral goodness. True care of the sheep comes about through ownership. Those who have no right over the sheep flee when there is danger, but Jesus, in virtue of that relationship He has with the Father (cf. v. 15) lays down His life for the sheep. **16. other sheep:** These are the Gentiles. They are already His sheep, though He has yet to bring them to join the others; thus they will constitute **one flock**—not 'one fold' (AV)—in virtue of their attachment to the **one shepherd**. These verses have an obvious bearing on the methods of seeking Christian unity (cf. Eph. 2: 11-22; Ezek. 34: 23); as in 11: 52, it is Christ Himself who 'gathers into one the children of God who are scattered abroad'. **17. For this reason the Father loves me:** The perfect conformity of will between Son and Father is shown, says Jesus, by His laying down of His life. **that I may take it again:** The resurrection of Christ in the NT is consistently spoken of as an act of God. Here, however, Jesus shows that it is something in which He will participate in action (Gk. *labō*), receiving it again. **18. I have power . . . I have power:** That is, supreme freedom is the prerogative of Jesus in His Incarnation. But He lays down His life by virtue of the command of the Father, which speaks as much of the Father's authority as it does of the Son's ability to know what the will of the Father is. Vv. 19-21 follow very suitably after 9: 41, and some scholars transfer them to that position, but as there is no textual evidence for this the justification for it is insufficient.

v. Final Encounter with the Jews (10: 22-42) 22. the feast of Dedication (Heb. *ḥanukkah*): This feast celebrated the re-dedication of the Temple in 164 B.C. by Judas Maccabeus after its defilement by Antiochus Epiphanes. A prominent feature of the feast was the illuminations provided by the lighting of lamps in the Temple, and in houses round about. **24. If you are the Christ, tell us plainly:** This was no desire really to know, but a question asked in annoyance by the Jews who had so far been incapable of catching Jesus in His own argument. But Jesus cannot tell them plainly, for with their wrong views either 'yes' or 'no' would have been equally misleading. Either He must show messianic signs according to the scriptures, or else He must make Himself the kind of Messiah that they wanted. **26. you do not believe, because you do not belong:** The sheep recognize their shepherd for what He does. But the very fact that these Jews had asked such a question put them well and truly outside the flock of God. **27. Indeed,** their following Him and His knowing them are mutual. **30. I and the Father are one** (Gk. *hen*): The neuter gender rules out any thought of meaning 'one Person'. This is not a comment on the nature of the Godhead. Rather, having spoken of the sheep's security in both Himself and the Father, Jesus underlines what He has said by indicating that in action the Father and He can be regarded as a single entity, because their wills are one. **33. We stone you . . . for blasphemy:** Jewish legal tradition, supported by the Mishnah and other Rabbinic literature, made blasphemous any statement in which a man uttered the Ineffable Name. But their charge is a tragic consequence of their blindness. Jesus is indeed both Man and God. **34. Is it not written . . . 'I said, you are gods':** This answer, with its appeal to Ps. 82: 6, is a typical Rabbinic argument. It seems to imply 'I have given you the truth in allegorical form. You cannot accept that. Very well, I will now meet you with the kind of argument you do appreciate' (cf. 7: 15-24; Mk 12: 35 ff.). The psalm refers to Israel's judges—sometimes called 'princes'—who, even though they failed, were designated 'gods' because they administered justice as part of their divine commission. How then can they charge Jesus with blasphemy if He is evidently sent from God (36)? **38. the Father is in me and I am in the Father:** These words will occur once more in the Lord's great prayer (cf. 17: 21) and will be considered there. **40.** Jesus returns to the place where His ministry began. Associations with John the Baptist are strong here, and as Temple suggests, Jesus may have gone over the whole story of His emergence into public again. John, indeed, spoke the truth. That is evident. And upon this evidence many believe in Him (42).

vi. Lazarus' resurrection and its sequel (11: 1–57)
Jesus' earlier self-disclosure (cf. 5: 18) had incited the Jews to murderous hatred. But Jesus had added to that the claim that His was the power to bestow life (cf. 5: 21). The subsequent story shows how a demonstration of this power set the Jews in their final determination to put Him to death (cf. vv. 46, 53). The sign has a number of counterparts in the Synoptics (cf. Mk 5: 21-43; Lk. 7: 11-16 and parallels). **1. Lazarus of Bethany:** This was close to Jerusalem (cf. v. 18) and is carefully distinguished by the Evangelist from Bethany of Transjordan (cf. 1: 28) where, most probably, Jesus was when the news of Lazarus' sickness reached him. **2. Mary who anointed the Lord:** This identification precedes the incident recorded later (cf. 12: 1-8). There is no persuasive reason, apart from verbal resemblance, to identify her with the woman of Lk. 7: 36-50. **4. This illness . . . is for the glory of God:** At once Jesus suggests that He intends doing something, as well as implying that He knew how near to death Lazarus was, in fact. And John assures us that Jesus loved the family (5). **6. he stayed two days longer . . . where he was:** Jesus so moved in perfect accordance with the divine plan that not even His love for Lazarus' sisters moved him to go to Bethany a moment early. Indeed, the messenger must have reached Jesus about the time that Lazarus died. Jesus waited because He knew it was better, although He knew that it would add to the temporary grief of the sisters. His tears of sympathy (cf. v. 35) were perfectly natural. Nor is it true to say that Jesus waited in order to perform a greater miracle, and thereby evoke greater wonder from the bystanders, by adding to the restoring of breath to the body the greater wonder of restoring the already decomposing flesh (cf. v. 39). This is inconsistent with all that we know about Him. The extra hours of sorrow were more than compensated for the sisters; and who can measure the effect upon Lazarus himself? **9. Are there not twelve hours in the day:** So long as time remains for Him to work, Jesus is assured that no harm will befall Him. 'Hour' here is not used in the Johannine technical sense. **11. Lazarus has fallen asleep:** Jesus' knowledge of the circumstances is clearly supernatural. Yet to Him physical death is like sleep (cf. Mk 5: 39) and He will awaken Lazarus again. 'Sleep' became the favourite metaphor to denote the state of death in which early Christians awaited the parousia (cf. Ac. 7: 60; 1 Th. 4: 13 f.; 1 C. 15: 20, 51 *et alia*). **15. I am glad that I was not there:** Here is the perfect sympathy of the Lord. He

knows that greater *faith* will be aroused both in the sisters and the disciples than if He had been there to prevent Lazarus from dying. Yet the desire to comfort the sisters is not far from Jesus' mind. He says, **Let us go to him. 16. Thomas** is one of the most consistent characters in the NT. Though only mentioned by name four times in John (cf. 14: 5; 20: 24 ff.; 21: 2) he is most clearly depicted. He asks for hard facts, and, however unpalatable they may be, he will accept them for he is loyal to what he believes. **25. I am the resurrection and the life:** Martha cannot think much beyond the traditional belief concerning resurrection, taught by the Pharisees and indeed endorsed, so far as it went, by the Lord Himself (cf. 5: 28 f.; 6: 39 f., 44, 54). But Jesus shows that in Him eschatological hope becomes actual and present. Death is only the moment when eternal life passes from activity and experience in the material world. The life which Jesus promises is immortal. So in response to this revelation Martha heaps up all the messianic terms she can muster to express her faith in Christ. **28. The Teacher is here:** Jesus' friends will habitually have referred to Him as 'the Rabbi' (Gk. *ho didaskalos*); cf. 13: 13 f.; 20: 16; Mk 14: 14. **33. Jesus . . . was deeply moved** (Gk. *enebrimēsato*) **in spirit and troubled** (Gk. *etaraxen heauton*): These two Greek phrases speak of indignation and sorrow respectively. Temple aptly renders the second as 'shuddered'. It is certain that Jesus was moved with sorrow for Lazarus—so close a friend. But the sight of the professional mourners may account for the first expression. It is likely, also, that Jesus already contemplated the violent reaction which this miracle would ultimately produce. *Enebrimēsato* also occurs in the Synoptics (cf. Mt. 9: 30; Mk 1: 43), and probably suggests there the physical and spiritual energy involved in working wonders. **35. Jesus wept** (Gk. *edakrysen*): The Jews' weeping was not unlike the loud organized mourning of the East. Jesus shed tears. He groans again as He contemplates the great encounter with the arch-enemy of man—death. **40. Did I not tell you that . . . you would see** (Gk. *opsei*) **the glory of God:** Perhaps we are meant to understand by this that Jesus promised Martha that she would have a vision (suggested by the word for 'see') of the glory of God over and above the physical event to be witnessed by the others. (For *opsei* as used by John in this sense, cf. 1: 51; 3: 36; 11: 40.) **41.** So, as the stone is removed, Jesus faces the challenge of all challenges so far in His ministry. But He meets it with prayer, given moreover to help others to see that He is acting in communion with the Father. **43. Lazarus, come out:** In this momentous event others are allowed to share. They lift the stone, but only Jesus can bring the dead man out. They free him from the grave cloths, but only after Jesus has imparted life to him. The astounding facts are recorded in rapid succession.

Some of the bystanders believed. Others **went to the Pharisees** (46). This is a turning point in the Saviour's ministry. In the Synoptics the same crucial moment seems to come at the cleansing of the Temple. **48. the Romans will come and destroy both our holy place and our nation:** This is a typical Sadducean reaction. So far the priestly party have shown little interest. Now they are alarmed for their privileged position. ('Holy' is added to make the sense here. It is not in the Greek text.) So Caiaphas now takes the lead. He was high-priest that fateful year. (The expression **that year** does not imply that John regarded the Jewish high priesthood as an annual office; Caiaphas in fact occupied it from A.D. 18 to 36.) It is, he says, **expedient that one man should die** (50), so that all Jews do not otherwise perish. His pronouncement was prophetic. As John shows, he could not have spoken more eloquently of the vicarious death of the Lord Jesus. But his words are tinged with bitter irony as well. Not many years hence the Jewish nation will suffer bitterly under Rome. **54. Ephraim** was some fifteen miles NE of Jerusalem. Jesus remained there until Passover. The final paragraph shows how many there must have been who were watching the mounting tide of events with intense interest.

IV. THE LAST SCENE OF CONFLICT (12: 1–50)
i. The supper at Bethany (12: 1–11)
1. Six days before the Passover: A chronological difficulty arises here from the uncertainty with regard to the day of the Crucifixion. Westcott suggests that this took place on 14 Nisan, and that therefore, the visit to Bethany was made on 8 Nisan. If the Crucifixion took place on a Friday then this visit was made the preceding Friday, the intervening Sabbath being left out of the reckoning as a *dies non*. **3. costly ointment** (Gk. *nardos pistiké*) was probably liquid perfume. This anointing may be compared with other accounts (cf. Mk 14: 3–9; Mt. 26: 6–13), where the mention of the house of Simon may be explained by the fact that Jesus stayed in and near Bethany for a time (cf. 'two days', Mk 14: 1). (It has even been suggested that Simon was the father of Martha, Mary and Lazarus.) The reference to Mary's wiping Jesus' feet with her hair is the only parallel with another Synoptic story (cf. Lk. 7:

36–50), where, however, the situation is quite different. **6. he was a thief:** This is the only clear reference to Judas's tendencies apart from the blood-money which he gained from the chief priests (cf. Lk. 22: 5). **7. let her keep it for the day of my burial:** The sense here is not absolutely clear without reference to the Markan account (cf. Mk. 14: 8). The ointment could hardly be kept if it were used at that moment. But Jesus seems to say that Mary has anticipated His burial, even though she may have reserved the perfume for some charitable purpose elsewhere. **10. the chief priests planned to put Lazarus also to death:** In endeavouring to suppress the news of Lazarus' resurrection they are already finding that their policy of expedient death must be extended further than one person.

ii. The Messianic Entry (12: 12–19)
John alone records the reason for the glad acclamation of the crowd at this juncture (cf. Mk 11: 7–10; Mt. 21: 4–9; Lk. 19: 35–38). **13. Hosanna:** They took up the antiphonal chant of the last of the Hallel psalms (Heb. *hoshi‘a nā*, lit. 'save us now'; cf. Ps. 118: 25). Jesus' action was designed to stir the faith of the onlookers, which, at least among the disciples, was not understood until later (v. 16) as a fulfilment of scripture (cf. Zech. 9: 9). The act was intended as a sign of peace; Zechariah goes on to say (cf. Zech. 9: 10), 'he shall command peace to the nations'. And Jesus clearly intended *that* significance to underlie His announcement of the kingdom (cf. F. F. Bruce: 'The Book of Zechariah and the Passion Narrative'; *Bulletin of the John Rylands Library, Manchester*, 43, 1960–61, pp. 336–353). **19. the world has gone after him:** An idiom simply meaning 'everyone'. But to the Evangelist this may well have suggested the universal appeal of the gospel (cf. v. 32).

iii. The Greeks' request and the Jews' rejection (12: 20–43)
The presence of these 'God-fearing' *Hellenes, viz.*, Greek-speaking foreigners who had adopted Jewish worship, but not the law in its entirety, is mentioned only by John. Yet the discourse which follows seems to echo a number of Synoptic passages (cf. Mk 4: 1–9; 8: 34; 9: 1, etc.). They may have come to Philip being attracted by his name. Philip's possible hesitancy suggested by his consulting Andrew before they both tell Jesus about the visitors, is possibly to be accounted for by the remembrance of Jesus' former words about Gentiles (cf. Mt. 10: 15; 15: 24). **23. The hour has come:** Jesus sees that events now point directly to His approaching Passion. Yet He will be glorified as the Heavenly Man since the Incarnation spells out His hum-

iliation. **24. unless a grain of wheat falls . . . and dies:** The Synoptic parable of the seed depicts the kingdom (cf. Mk 4: 1-20; Mt. 13: 1-9; 18-25; Lk. 8: 4-15); in John a similar metaphor is used to denote the King. He teaches that what becomes true of Himself is a principle in all nature. So Paul (cf. 1 C. 15: 36 ff.). **25. He who loves his life loses it:** The saying about life through death (v. 24) is capable of general application, and Jesus here applies it to His followers (cf. Mk 8: 35; Mt. 10: 39; Lk. 17: 33) in their sufferings with Him. To hate (Gk. *miseō*) one's life means to turn one's back on it as of secondary importance compared with the cause that matters most. **26. where I am, there shall my servant be also:** Jesus is not promising some happy issue out of suffering, *viz.*, in future glory. He is saying that the experience which is about to befall Him may be expected by His faithful disciple. But just as that servant may expect to share Christ's suffering, so also, of course, he can expect to enter into glory with Him (Ac. 14: 22; Rom. 8: 17; 1 Tim. 2: 11 ff.). **27. Now is my soul troubled:** Jesus now faces the call to His personal endurance. He expresses the same feelings in the Garden of Gethsemane later (cf. Mk 14: 32-42; Mt. 26: 36-46; Lk. 22: 40-46), so we learn from this that He felt this agony of spirit at other times than the Thursday night before His death. **what shall I say? 'Father, save me from** (Gk. *ek*) **this hour':** Did these words form an actual prayer, or were the words only contemplated? Jesus was certainly not thinking of avoiding the Cross. The preposition *ek* ('out of') implies that He committed Himself into the Father's hands as death drew near. In any case it is clear (v. 28) that He came to this moment for the Father's glory. **30. This voice has come for your sake:** Yet the sound was unintelligible to some, and misunderstood by others. God had glorified His name once (cf. 11: 40) and now in the Passion He would glorify it again. **31. Now is the judgment of this world:** The world stands judged before the prospect of the Cross, both for its part in crucifying the Prince of Life, and for the fact that its moment of victory will, by the resurrection, come to be the moment of its utter defeat. **32. I, when I am lifted up . . . will draw all men:** Until then He was subject to restriction in the range of His mission (cf. Lk. 12: 50); after that, His saving grace would be equally available to Greeks (like the present inquirers) and Jews. Whatever broad meaning may attach to 'lifting up' (see note on 3: 14), the crowd is shrewd enough to detect what Jesus has in mind at this moment, and they can connect it with Jesus' earlier words

(cf. vv. 34, 23). No special passage suits what they say they **have heard from the law** (34), though we may think of Isa. 9: 6 f.; Ps. 110: 4, etc. **34. Who is this Son of man:** But Jesus cannot explain by word only (cf. 8: 25). Their only hope of understanding is to **believe in the light** (36), that is, to try to understand Him as He is. For a few hours yet the Light is still shining in the world, and with this the special privilege given them of becoming 'enlightened men' by believing what they see (cf. 20: 29).

With these words Jesus departs. His last utterances (cf. Mk 13: 35 f.) urged His hearers to take that final opportunity of putting faith in Him, yet, **they did not believe in him** (37), thus bringing to pass a prophecy of Isaiah. This prophecy did not become meaningful only through the event; the event fulfilled the prophecy in so far as the word of Isaiah declared the will of God (cf. Isa. 53: 1). Neither Jesus' words, the 'report', nor His works, the 'arm of the Lord', had convinced them. **39. they could not believe:** The consequence of unbelief was bound to follow. As Temple has aptly put it: 'God does not cause sin, but He does cause its appropriate consequence to result from it by the law of the order of creation' (*Readings*, p. 202). **40. He has blinded their eyes:** Cf. Isa. 6: 10. The blindness of the Jews is part of the divine plan, therefore; though they are not thereby absolved from guilt, for they 'hated the light' (cf. 3: 20) and so brought into bondage the freedom of their wills. But out of their unbelief arises the mystery of that Sacrifice which is to redeem the world. (Isa. 6: 10 is similarly applied in Mk 4: 12 and parallels and in Ac. 28: 26 f.) **41. Isaiah . . . saw his glory:** Cf. Isa. 6: 1. John seems to base his reference on a Targumic paraphrase of the prophet's words, which originally omitted any personal description of the Almighty. His glory was manifested in the Incarnation, and was thus seen again by mortal men (cf. 1: 14). **42. many even of the authorities believed in him** (Gk. *episteusan eis auton*): It is surprising that John uses this phrase meaning full belief when they obviously, because of their position on the Sanhedrin, avoided embarrassment by remaining secret disciples (but cf. the use of the phrase in 2: 23). Nicodemus and Joseph of Arimathea were examples among them.

iv. Christ's summary of His message (12: 44-50)

In view of the finality of Jesus' words in v. 36a amd His subsequent departure from the Jews (36b), coupled with the decisive nature of the quotations of v. 37, some scholars have suggested that vv. 44-50 are displaced, and should probably follow v. 36a. Whether this is so or not, we may reasonably conclude that the Evangelist chose to end the present section of the Gospel by bringing together some of the Saviour's most pregnant sayings containing the leading ideas in His self-revelation, i.e. on Light, His authority from the Father, the nature of judgment, the Father's command to the Son in His preaching, and the Life which issues from His words (cf. comments on 5: 24-29; 7: 17; 8: 12). **46. I have come as light into the world:** Jesus sheds light on the way to God. The man who believes in Him in fact puts his trust in God. His trust is not based on the limited temporal life of Jesus 'in the days of his flesh', but in the eternal Life of God which was made known in Christ. And because God wills the salvation of men He gave Christ the commandment for His message.

PART THREE—FINAL DISCOURSES AND EVENTS (13: 1–21: 25)

1. THE UPPER ROOM MINISTRY (13: 1-17: 26)

i. Practice and precept in humility (13: 1-17) John does not record the details of the supper itself. But he does preserve certain actions and words which were lasting symbols of Christ's nature, and which He wished the disciples ever to remember. **1. before the feast of the Passover:** It is held by some that John's chronology differs from that of the Synoptics in placing the Last Supper earlier in Passion Week, **before** the Passover, whereas the Synoptists represent it as a Passover meal (cf. Mk 14: 1-26). The apparent discrepancy of one day could, however, be overcome if it could be clearly shown that the Pharisees and other groups in Israel commemorated Passover a day earlier than the Sadducees. Some support for two distinct calendars has been provided by the Dead Sea Scrolls. R. V. G. Tasker has suggested that this whole verse might be separated from the adjoining passage and understood as an introduction to it. (For further indications of time, cf. 18: 28; 19: 14, 31, 42.) **2. during supper** (Gk. *deipnou ginomenou*): For *ginomenou* (present) there is a well-attested variant *genomenou* (aorist), whence AV, 'supper being ended'. C. H. Dodd (*Interpretation of the Fourth Gospel*, 1953, p. 401) points out the significance of this phrase, indicating that the following action has its setting within the Lord's Supper with its theme of remembrance. If this were the Passover meal we should have expected John to be much more explicit. Further, the **already**

of this verse, referring to Judas, implies that the moment of his defection during Passover had not actually arrived. **4. laid aside his garments:** By this act Jesus pictures the humiliation which, in its fullest expression, meant for Him the laying down of His life. There can be no further allegorical significance than this, and to look for it is to overlook v. 15 which plainly states that the act was primarily an exemplary one. Jesus took the slave's posture, when He took the towel, which indeed He adopted supremely as the Servant of the Lord. **8. If I do not wash you, you have no part in me:** Both AV and RV render 'with me' which is, in fact, much nearer to what Jesus actually said. Jesus' words again enforce the point that what He is doing is an enacted parable. If Peter, therefore, will be associated with his Lord he must let Him do what He wishes. Men must not only have the desire to serve Christ, but to accept His service for them. And that some cleansing is typified here seems reasonable, though we should not press the picture further. **10. except for his feet:** C. K. Barrett rightly suggests that the textual problem of these words, whether or not they should be omitted (as some MSS), cannot be decided on textual grounds alone but also on interpretation, for the shorter reading makes it impossible to suppose that what Jesus had done was not of supreme importance. **14. you also ought to wash one another's feet:** Jesus has spoken of that fundamental cleansing which He brings by way of His life and death. Now those who are cleansed by Him must work out their cleansing by loving and humble service each for the other. **17. blessed are you if you do them:** The lesson must appeal to our wills as well as to our intellects. And he who puts into practice what he knows finds true happiness.

ii. The Traitor (13: 18-35)
18. I know whom I have chosen: In spite of Judas, Jesus can say that his knowledge of them all has been full from the beginning. But Judas's action only shows how fully the scriptures (*e.g.* Ps. 41: 9) are fulfilled in Him (cf. 17: 12). **lifted his heel against me:** It is in compassion that Jesus does not disclose the details of the traitor's act. 'Heel' (Gk. *pterna*) is a NT *hapax legomenon* (occurring once only in the NT). E. F. F. Bishop tells how this saying, especially among Arabs (and the Heb. 'heel' *'aqeb* [cf. Jacob], is cognate with the Arabic term), implies a dastardly insult on the part of a close friend. **23. One of his disciples, whom Jesus loved:** Some have thought that this was the 'ideal' disciple who did not figure in real life, who perfectly responds to Jesus' teaching. This, however, may be dismissed.

According to 21: 24 he was 'the witness' on whose evidence this Gospel is founded, and by whom it was written (cf. also 19: 26; 20: 2). This witness was known to the Jerusalem authorities and provided first-hand testimony of the Crucifixion (cf. 18: 15; 19: 35). For a fuller discussion see *Introduction*. **25. Lord, who is it:** This question, put by John, accords well with the general impression which we have of him throughout the NT. Elsewhere (cf. Mk 14: 17 ff.; Mt. 26: 20 ff.) each of the disciples asks in astonishment if he himself is the traitor. But this man, with clearer conscience, asks Jesus for direct nomination. **26. he to whom I shall give this morsel:** At Eastern meals it was a common gesture of special friendship for the host to offer a morsel to one of the diners. Jesus' action, then, seems to say to Judas that in spite of his intention, the Saviour's love remains unchanged. **30. he immediately went out:** Judas' intention now becomes a settled purpose. He goes out from the light and companionship of Jesus' and His friends into the night (cf. 6: 64). The lesson here for all time is surely that even with the love of God upon him, man is free to choose evil rather than good. **31. Now is the Son of man glorified:** Cf. 17: 1. Jesus, in the perfection of human character, accepts Judas's decision. But this does not go unnoticed. **34. God will also glorify him in himself:** The dignity with which Jesus as Man accepts the desperate resolve of Judas is counterpart to the dignity with which God will invest Him through the work upon which He now embarks. **34. love one another:** With what emotion these words were uttered at this moment we cannot tell. Judas had displayed the evil born of self-centredness. Jesus was about to show to them His undiluted love for the Father in obedience to His will. He is to leave them physically—they cannot follow— and the only bond which will keep them together is love, fostered within them by the Spirit (cf. 14: 15 ff.).

iii. Comfort for the disciples in distress (13: 36–14: 31)
36. you shall follow afterward: It is here that the stark truth of what Jesus says begins to dawn upon Peter. But he is undaunted. He thinks more of Christ's companionship than of his own life, whatever failure he may have suffered later in the story. But he does not yet understand that Jesus promises him that he will follow, indeed. It will be to death, and after death to vindication. The thought of separation is hard enough. But the thought of failure at the moment of separation is far worse. So Jesus comforts the disciples by urging them to look into the future joy of re-union.

14: 1. believe in God, believe also in me: Currency in English has undoubtedly weakened the force of this statement. The words are capable of three renderings: (*a*) 'you believe in God, (so) believe also in me'; (*b*) 'you believe in God and you believe in me'; and (*c*) 'believe in God and believe in me' (as above). On the whole, the last of the three is preferable. Jesus is concerned to strengthen their faith in the face of the trials soon to begin. As Jews they profess to have faith in God. Now they must learn what it is to renew that faith in Christ. **2. many rooms:** Jesus has been rejected by the stewards of the house of God on earth (cf. 2: 16), so He returns to the eternal counterpart in heaven. But these disciples must not think that they are left behind because of any lack of the Father's hospitality. **3. I will come again:** The final thought here is certainly an eschatological one—the second advent of Christ. But that by no means exhausts what Jesus is saying. Jesus will come again in the Spirit (cf. vv. 18, 21, 23). There is no vacuum between the days of His flesh and the final arrival in the Father's house, even for these (cf. 20: 22, where see note), however much arresting delay there is before the completion of the work. **6. I am the way, and the truth, and the life:** Not, 'I *show* the way . . .'. Christ is *Himself* the vital link between heaven and earth (cf. 1: 51) so apart from His teaching (the truth) and His work (to bring life) there is no salvation. What Jesus *is* cannot be separated from what He *does*. **7. If you had known me:** The pluperfect tense here (Gk. *egnōkeite*) is puzzling. The readings of other MSS, notably Sinaiticus, D (*Codex Bezae*, Cambridge) and P 66, seem to imply 'if you have known me, you will come to know the Father as well'. The second half of the verse would support this. So, the verse seems to tell us that when these men come to find that Jesus is indeed the Way, they will date their vision of the Father from that revelation. **8.** The instances in which Philip appears in the Gospel are noteworthy (cf. 1: 45 f.; 6: 5 ff.; 12: 21 ff.; 14: 8). His question here is evidence to the slowness with which he had developed spiritually. **9.** But there is nothing in the ministry of Jesus which should not lead men to the Father, for He is uniquely the image of God (cf. Col. 1: 15; Heb. 1: 3). And as Jesus has already indicated (cf. 10: 25), the evidence of His works is a lower path to faith in God (cf. 20: 29). **12. greater works than these:** The works performed by the Christian are done in communion with the living Saviour. But they are greater in their sphere of influence. Jesus' works were limited to the days of His flesh and the land in which He lived. But the Church which is His body has a worldwide influence in winning men for Him. **16. another Counsellor** (Gk. *paraklētos*): The word is borrowed from legal usage. There it denotes an advocate or defending counsel, although this specifically seems to be secondary in John—except perhaps 16: 8–11 where He is the *prosecuting* Counsel! It is derived from Gk. *parakaleō*, 'to call alongside', thus 'a helper'. Elsewhere in the NT *parakaleō* frequently denotes a memorable utterance encouraging or hortatory in character (cf. Ac. 2: 40). Barrett shows that it is just a combination of these two functions which seems to lie behind the statement here. The Holy Spirit speaks of 'things to come' (cf. 16: 13) and thereby, whilst bringing conviction to the consciences of men, strengthens the believers (here, and cf. 16: 7–15; 1 C. 14: 3 ff.). For His intercessory ministry, another essential aspect of His work as Paraclete, cf. Rom. 8: 26. **17. the Spirit of truth:** This qualification is always employed in conjunction with the Paraclete in John (cf. 15: 26; 16: 13; 1 Jn 4: 6). **whom the world cannot receive:** By very definition the world and the Spirit are contrasted. The world is materialistic and thereby basically hostile to anything which does not conform to the nature of matter. In 14: 16 f. we have the first of five 'Paraclete Sayings' in the upper room discourse, the other four being 14: 25 f.; 15: 26 f.; 16: 5–11 and 16: 12–15. Together, these five sayings present a doctrine of the Holy Spirit in advance of any references to Him elsewhere in the Gospels, but bearing a remarkable affinity with the portrayal of His presence and ministry in Acts. **18. I will come to you:** Cf. v. 3. Jesus probably refers to the post-resurrection appearances and the Spirit's advent as well as to the great day of His coming. **19. because I live, you will live also:** A fresh thought appears to enter the narrative at this point. But it is probably preferable to link these words with the previous clause, i.e., 'but you will see me because I live; and you will live!' **20. you will know that I am in my Father:** The resurrection appearances would be unearthly visitations of Jesus after His resurrection, tangibly demonstrating to them His divine incursion into their affairs. The real basis of their union with Him will not be His appearances to them, but their love for Him by which their vision will constantly keep Him in view. And the verification of their love must ever be in their keeping of His commands. **21. I will . . . manifest myself to Him:** That Jesus combines the beatific vision and His eschatological appearance seems evident from Judas's question (cf. v. 22). The very word (Gk. *emphanizō*) seems to carry overtones of OT theophany (cf. Exod. 33: 18). But Jesus

assures Judas that this will be no mere passing visitation. The Father and He together will **make our home with him** (23). **27. Peace I leave with you:** This is more than the conventional greeting or farewell. It is *His* peace, not like the world's estimate of tranquillity, but bringing comfort and strength in the midst of distress. **28. the Father is greater than I:** These words need lend no support to a lowered doctrine of Christ. The Father is 'greater' in that the Incarnate Son derives His being from Him. And Christ could especially utter this as the *Word* Incarnate. Moreover, the 'greatness' of the Father means that the revelation of Him manifested in Jesus is full so far as was possible in a human person. The world of creation and history, in which the Word is immanent, is what it is because God is what He is. But His nature is not dependent upon its manifestation. **31. Rise, let us go hence** (Gk. *egeiresthe agōmen enteuthen*): Did Jesus leave the room at this precise moment? Were the discourses of chaps. 15–16 spoken *en route* to Gethsemane? C. H. Dodd (*Historical Tradition in the Fourth Gospel*, p. 72) has shed some helpful light upon this point: *egeiresthe* can be taken to mean 'bestir yourselves'; similarly *agōmen enteuthen* may be taken as 'Let us encounter the enemy' in which case the link with the preceding verse would be exceptionally strong. As R. V. G. Tasker puts it: 'Jesus is here giving expression to his *spiritual* determination to meet the prince of this world' (p. 170). No physical movement from the upper room need therefore be understood at this point. And, as Dr. Dodd has pointed out, 'rise', though referring to sleep in Mk 14: 42, is frequently used of stirring oneself from a state of lethargy. Westcott aptly comments that though similar words occur in Mark, they are 'such as would naturally be repeated under like circumstances' (p. 211).

iv. Union with Christ and its consequences (15: 1–27)

1. I am the true vine: Some would place the following discourse in the Temple precincts by the door to the Holy Place where was a golden vine, symbol of the life of Israel (cf. Isa. 5: 1–7; Jer. 2: 21; Ps. 80: 8–16). But it has already been suggested that there are grounds also for supposing that Jesus was continuing His ministry in the upper room (cf. 14: 31). All that Israel was destined to be, but failed to be, Jesus was—the true (ideal) vine, producing acceptable fruit for God in His personal life and in the lives of His disciples, united to Him by faith. There may be a connection between these words and those spoken by the Lord during the Last Supper concerning the fruit of the vine with its implications concerning

His blood by which all disciples are made sharers with Him in the new Israel (cf. Mk 14: 25). **my Father is the vinedresser:** He has charge of the whole (cf. Mk 12: 1-12). **2. Every branch . . . that bears no fruit, he takes away:** The absence of fruit in the branch of the vine casts grave doubt upon its real union with the central stem, however otherwise it may appear. Such useless members must be cut off; perhaps Judas is the outstanding example. **every branch that does bear fruit he prunes** (Gk. *kathairei*): The word means literally to cleanse, the inference being the cutting away of dead wood which is a complete antithesis of the life evidenced by fruit. **3. You are already made clean:** By the total effect of the Lord's teaching the disciples had been cleansed and prepared for the continuance of His work. **4. Abide in me, and I in you:** The two parts of this statement must be taken as they stand without understanding their inter-dependence in any conditional sense. The revelation of which Jesus has just spoken cannot sustain life. Life in Christ must be identified with union with Him. **5. I am the vine, you are the branches:** Each member of Christ enjoys equality of status with all others. Yet Christ does not describe Himself as the central stem. He *is* the vine. Every branch is incorporate. **7. ask whatever you will and it shall be done for you:** Union with Christ is the basis of prayer. This prayer, moreover, will be effective. What the member wills will be one with His will since their union is complete. Yet the branch, in the nature of the case, depends upon the vine, for its prayer is a sign of that dependence. **8. so prove to be my disciples:** This saying is no anti-climax. It rather describes all that is involved in full discipleship. **9. so have I loved you:** The aorist here (Gk. *ēgapēsa*) denotes a completed action. There is no restraint with Christ's love. In the reality of the Incarnation lies the totality of His love which He has lavished freely upon these men. **16. I chose you and appointed** (Gk. *ethēka*) **you:** He chose them to be His friends. That is, His choice was first motivated by the desire to *have* them (cf. Mk 3: 14), and then to send them out as His missionaries. His sending them forth is grounded in His confidence in them as His friends, and this conversely (same verse) is their ground of confidence in prayer. **18. the world . . . hated me before it hated you:** There are no middle feelings which may make the disciple's lot bearable in this world. Jesus warns them that the love within the Church will find a strong contrast outside. **20. Remember . . . I said . . . 'A servant is not greater than his master':** Cf. 13: 16; there it was

a lesson in humble service; here it becomes a lesson in endurance. But their work, like His, will reap positive fruits as well as negative. If there were those who kept Christ's word, so they may expect to find similar sympathy with their message here and there. But the basis of the world's hostility (v. 21) will be lack of the knowledge of God. **22. now they have no excuse for their sin:** Jesus' work constituted evidence of God's intervention in the world. Here, as in 14: 11, is the appeal to a lower form of evidence. But, nevertheless, true righteousness has been manifested in Christ. Men have seen the right way to live in Him. But they still do not believe (cf. 20: 29). **25. They hated me without a cause:** Cf. Ps. 35: 19; 69: 4. This is the witness of *their* law, says Jesus pointedly. But though they may reject Him, and remain blind to the witness of their scriptures, the Holy Spirit will yet bear witness. **27. you also are witnesses:** Their insight into the truth which communion with Christ brings arises out of the divine nature of that truth itself. But it is the Incarnation that gives it its impetus. And when it is received it carries with it the conviction of the deity of Christ. So the witness of the Incarnation becomes united with the testimony of Christ's disciples. With the conjoining of the witness of the Spirit and the disciples in vv. 26 f. cf. Ac. 5: 32, 'we are witnesses . . . and so is the Holy Spirit'.

v. The disciples, the world, and the Advocate (16: 1-33)
1. to keep you from falling away: The treatment which the infant Church was to receive was destined to provide the strongest cause of apostasy, as the early history of the Church showed. **2. They will put you out of the synagogues:** Cf. comment on 9: 22. The plural here seems to imply that each case of excommunication will be a direct act of antagonism, in their experience, against Christ, (cf. 9: 22). **4. their hour:** Cf. Lk. 22: 53. The hour of the world will be when men wreak their vengeance upon the Church unrestrainedly. **5. none of you asks me, 'Where are you going?':** Both Peter (cf. 13: 36) and Thomas (cf. 14: 5) had in fact asked this question verbally already. But then it was because of their dismay rather than because of a real desire to know Jesus' destiny (cf. 14: 6). **7. it is to your advantage that I go away:** There is a twofold point in these words. First, the departure of Christ in the body is both the necessary condition and cause of future individual union. Then each member of His spiritual Body will become a veritable shrine of deity (cf. 1 C. 3: 16; 6: 19). Second, it will be to the disciples' advantage that the Spirit, when He is imparted,

will empower the Church's ministry, convicting the world (cf. v. 8) in respect of its state before God. **8. of sin, and of righteousness, and of judgment:** The supreme sin lies in unbelief (v. 9). Jesus' return to the Father will mark the vindication of His righteous life here below, and since His return to the Father is by way of death and resurrection, He pronounces judgment over the prince of the world whose domain is clearest of all in death. In this sentence is prophesied the Church's spiritual power within and over the world. **13. he will guide you into all the truth:** There will not be one permanent or fundamental principle which is overlooked in the Spirit's ministry to the Church. **whatever he hears** signifies that His ministry will ever be direct from the Father. **the things that are to come:** Prophecy is one function of the Spirit. This is not merely prediction of the future, near or far (cf. Rev. 1: 1, 19), but an aspect of the Spirit's ministry as the earnest of what is yet to be. There are three functions of the Spirit mentioned in this discourse (cf. 14: 26; 16: 13) in which the three phases of the NT message seem to be summarized, *viz.*, history, doctrine, and eschatology. **14. He will glorify me:** The Spirit does not usurp the authority of the Son. But since the Son shares the authority of the Father in revelation, the triune God is here depicted in perfect harmony of operation. **16. again a little while, and you will see me:** Both the 'little while's' of this verse may be understood as one and the same. There is less justification for understanding the second as referring to the parousia of Jesus. If anything were to distinguish the two phrases (Gk. *mikron*) it would be that John uses a different verb 'to see' in each half of the verse. The first is his normal Gk. *theorein*, whilst the second is his more suggestive Gk. *opsesthai* with its inference of beatific vision (cf. 1: 51; 3: 36 and esp. 11: 40). The whole statement makes better sense when understood as a reference to the passing of Jesus from physical sight, and His subsequent resurrection appearances. We are certainly right in omitting the first occasion of the words 'because I go to the Father', found in AV (cf. v. 17). In v. 17 the disciples are remembering the statement of vv. 5 and 10. But when Christ reappears their sorrow will indeed **turn into joy** (20; cf. 20: 20). **22. no one will take your joy from you:** Just as the new life given in childbirth fills the mother with mystical joy, overcoming all the former anguish, so the joy of the resurrection, for all the world's persecution, will become the dominant factor in Christian experience. **23. In that day you will ask nothing of me:** 'Ask' here seems to be used synonymously with 'ask'

in v. 24, in which case the statement refers to the direct approach to God which believers may make in the light of the exaltation of the Son. If, on the other hand, there be some subtle difference of meaning, the former statement will refer to the anxious questions which were heaped up in chaps. 13-16, as distinct from prayerful supplication which they will make henceforth in Jesus' name. The second half of the next verse could be used to endorse either interpretation of v. 23. **25. in figures** (Gk. *en paroimiais*): The RSV text would suggest that Jesus is making reference to the discourses of the immediate past. But the wording might well mean that He speaks of the parabolic method which He employed as a whole. Their understanding of the same message will, in a day to come, be enlarged by the richness of experience. **27. the Father himself loves you:** Cf. 15: 12-17. No greater impetus for prayer could be given than in these words. In this unique way, the Father makes Himself known. **28. I came from the Father and have come into the world; again, I am leaving the world:** The repeated **I came from the Father** suggests that v. 28a should be linked closely with v. 27b, continuing to state what the disciples **have believed.** This would then mean that the disciples had accepted the divine mission of Jesus in all its implications. If, however, v. 28 be taken quite separately from v. 27, it becomes a crystallization of the Christian message. In either case the words show just how plainly Jesus was now speaking to the disciples. **33. I have said this to you, that in me you may have peace:** Jesus is not only concerned to prevent their distress when they see the tragic events a few hours hence. Rather the whole Paschal discourse, and especially that of the present chapter (cf. 16: 1), has been specifically designed to calm these timorous disciples in the face of provocation. The world, as the great outer ring of human experience, will move this way and that; but at the centre **—in me—** is the stable compass directing their way into the peace of God. And because the will of the world had already exposed itself, Jesus could consider it defeated in principle already. There only remains His love which He will pour out in prayer for His friends and the world which He came to redeem.

vi. The great prayer of Jesus (17: 1–26)
This prayer, as the text shows, covers three distinct matters. Jesus consecrates Himself for the work which He is about to undertake (vv. 1-5). He then prays specifically for the disciples (vv. 6-19), and finally for the whole Church (vv. 20-26). Consecration, indeed, is the key

thought which pervades the whole. In attempting to analyse the meaning of individual phrases we inevitably lose the majesty of the prayer as it stands, and the spontaneity with which the Saviour passes from one phase to the next. After a study of the details it should be read without interruption.

1. **these words:** From chapter 13 to 16 Jesus has unfolded the meaning of His departure. His teaching ends with the words, 'I have overcome the world' (cf. 16: 33), meaning that ultimately it could be said that, in Him, the purpose of God had been, and will be achieved. So with His eyes lifted towards heaven, Jesus terminates His work as a prophet on earth, and contemplates His work as a Priest, entering, in spirit, the Holy Place. This prayer, accordingly, has often been called His 'high-priestly' prayer—first, apparently, by David Chytraeus (16th century). **glorify thy Son:** The departure of Judas had signified the arrival of the 'hour' in which Jesus committed Himself to His death (cf. 13: 31), yet the glorification of the Son has already been manifested by His words and works (cf. 1: 14; 2: 11). **2. thou hast given him power:** Already Jesus claimed to have power in the exercise of judgment (cf. 5: 27) and forgiveness (cf. Mk 2: 10). Already He has said that He judges no man (cf. 8: 15) and now He sees His power to be in the authority to 'give eternal life.' (cf. 1: 4, 12). **3. And this is eternal life, that they know thee:** The knowledge of the Father must be linked now with the apprehension of the Son, since the revelation of God in Christ cannot be transcended. This is not intellectual understanding, but the perfection of personal, moral trust. **Jesus Christ whom thou has sent:** Literally, as in RV, 'him whom thou didst send, *even* Jesus Christ'; it may be that '*even* Jesus Christ' is an explanatory addition by the Evangelist (cf. 1: 17). **4. I glorified thee on earth:** The glory of God was paramount in the life of Jesus. He could only pray with this fact established by a life of submission to the Father. The tense denotes a completed action in the past. **5. glorify thou me in thy own presence:** This is no selfish request *for* recognition. Rather it is a prayer which already recognizes that the historic life-giving work of Christ may truly reveal the eternal nature of the Godhead, and the relation of the Word, immanent and active in creation and salvation, to the eternal and unchanging transcendent God. **6. thine they were:** Jesus ever recognizes the priority of the purpose of God. But His part in that purpose was to reveal the name of God, i.e. His nature. The divine revelation was by words. Jesus imparted these to the disciples (cf. v. 8). Now they have

received them and know in truth (8), an intellectual conviction borne of the evidence they have seen in Jesus, that He had come forth from the Father, **and believed,** that is, put their moral trust in the fact that Jesus was *sent*, coming not on His own authority alone, but with the full authority of the Godhead. **11. Holy Father, keep** (Gk. *tēreson*) **them:** That is, separate from the profanity of the world, **in thy name.** Their holiness will be achieved only by relationship with the Father (cf. Lev. 11: 44 f.), whose name has, in principle, already been given to the Son (cf. Phil. 2: 9), **that they may be one.** Union can be perfectly expressed by a loving relationship (cf. 5: 42 f.; 14: 9-15) and is a reflection of that eternal union enjoyed by the three Persons within one substance, the Trinity. **12. none of them is lost but the son of perdition:** The defection of Judas was the one tragic exception which proved the rule. The fulfilment of scripture in his case (cf. Ps. 41: 9; Jn 13: 18, 31) indicates that Judas was destroyed only by his own qualities, which might have been turned to good account but were perverted to an evil end. **16. the evil one:** Whilst it is clear that Jesus believed in and taught the personality of Satan, the words here might convey the sense that He wished the disciples to be guarded from that personal *power* of evil which had shown itself in Judas (cf. 1 Jn 5: 18 f.). **17. Sanctify them in the truth:** This is not a prayer for purification. They are already clean (cf. 15: 3). But it is the truth, the revelation of eternal values, that can both keep them unstained in the world, and provide the burden of their message. This truth is the Word of God (cf. Ps. 119: 142), which can bring deliverance (cf. 8: 32). **19. I consecrate myself:** He is to become a 'high priest for ever' in virtue of His vicarious death. And the truth is related to Christ's death, so far as disciples are concerned, in that their ministry will only be relevant if it is coloured by the implications of that death (cf. Heb. 7: 26 ff.; 1 C. 1: 23).

Now the Lord turns to pray for the entire Church. Because His prayer is effectual the work of evangelism will go forward. So unity must be worldwide. **21. that they may all be one . . . that the world may believe:** That first miracle of unity which was to mark the earliest disciples Christ sees as the vital character of the Church in all ages. Nothing less than organic unity will satisfy the prayer of the Saviour. It is **as thou, Father, art in me:** and this unity is for a specific purpose that the world may learn that He is, indeed, the Word Incarnate, bringing to men the knowledge and love of God (cf. v. 23). **24. I desire that they . . . may be with me:** That companionship which had begun a few years earlier the Lord wishes to take into eternity. Historically they would not follow Him immediately (cf. 13: 33); yet Peter would eventually follow Him through suffering (cf. 13: 36). But now with His work finished, with His will perfectly expressed as being one with the Father, Jesus makes this one personal request. Yet he will derive the greatest joy from knowing that they will behold His glory, so completing their apprehension of Him. Their vision of the Father will also be satisfied. **25. the world has not known thee:** This clause is essentially, if not grammatically, subordinate to what follows: 'although **the world has not known thee, yet I have known thee and these** (the disciples) **know that thou hast sent me**'. The Saviour thus declares this intention to manifest the name of God again in the crucial act of the Cross. But this is the darkness before dawn, after which the Saviour will reveal the love of God realistically and effectively within each of His own. Thus, in His exaltation He will continue to teach them.

II. THE BETRAYAL, ARREST AND EXECUTION (18: 1 — 19: 42)

i. The arrest. Peter's denial (18: 1–27)

1. the Kidron valley: This lies between the Temple hill and the Mount of Olives. On the further side Jesus entered Gethsemane. John does not record the agony of the Garden (cf. Mk 14: 32–42; Mt. 26: 36–46; Lk. 22: 40–48) but He does record a similar agony to which the Saviour gave expression (cf. 12: 27–33). Jesus clearly understood all that was to happen as being part of the divine plan. **5. I am he** (Gk. *egō eimi*): With this majestic answer (cf. 8: 58), Jesus forestalled the plan arranged between Judas and the armed officers (cf. 8: 24, 28; 13: 19). The Synoptists tell us of the deadly kiss. Here, however, we have a picture of the Saviour taking the initiative at every stage (cf. v. 11 below). The falling to the ground of His captors was not necessarily miraculous, but possibly their falling over each other in confusion at Jesus' calm. **9. This was to fulfil the word which he had spoken:** Here is an inspired commentary which takes the words of Jesus' prayer (cf. 17: 12) quite literally. Jesus was therefore willing and able to enter into the implications of His prayer life. **10. a sword:** The meaning of this dramatic act is that Simon Peter was not going to accept such a tame release as was suggested by Jesus' appeal to the officers. **Malchus:** Only John names the injured officer, as only Luke records his being healed again (cf. Lk. 22: 51). **11. shall I not drink the cup:** This is John's counterpart to the Gethse-

mane utterance 'not what I will, but what thou wilt' recorded by the other evangelists (cf. Mk 14: 36–40; Mt. 26: 39–42; Lk. 22: 42). He announces that His desire is to take the cup, for that, indeed, is the Father's will for Him. **13. Annas:** Matthew alone (cf. Mt. 26: 57) mentions Caiaphas's house; the other evangelists simply refer to the chief priests (cf. Mk 14: 53; Lk. 22: 54) and Luke gives no account of the Jewish hearing. Annas was former high priest (A.D. 6–15). In Hebrew law, the high-priesthood was an office held for life. But under the Romans it was frequently changed. Annas had been deposed in A.D. 15, but was succeeded by other members of the family, besides Caiaphas, who was high priest from A.D. 18 to A.D. 36. Yet even after his deposition, Annas remained an elder statesman of Judaism. **15. another disciple:** He is probably, though not certainly, the beloved disciple (cf. 13: 23; 19: 26; 20: 2; 21: 20). He was known to the high priest, and apparently knew the Sanhedrin members and their households fairly well (cf. Malchus's name, v. 10). His entry into the audience chamber illustrates the truth that he who remains close to Christ is the more likely to resist temptation to deny Him. **17. Are not you also** (Gk. *mē kai sy*) **one of this man's disciples:** The form of the question would normally expect a negative answer, though 'Yes' may have been the reply expected. This question favourably reflects the position of the other disciple. **19. The high priest then questioned Jesus:** This is almost certainly Annas. Attempts have been made to prove that it was Caiaphas by placing v. 24 after v. 13, *e.g.*, by the Sinaitic Syriac, by the minuscule 225, and by Luther. But most commentators adopt the usual order of the text to whichever of the two men they believe this reference to apply; the suggestion that an early copyist placed v. 24 where we have it, after accidentally dropping it out after v. 13, while possible, is unconvincing. Annas continued to be known as high priest long after his deposition (cf. Ac. 4: 6). **22. one of the officers . . . struck Jesus:** This blow may well have been an indication of the loyalty which many of the Jews continued to feel towards Annas, whom they regarded as the rightful high priest, though he was forcibly living in retirement. Jesus' reply makes it clear that nothing hurts more than the truth in the ears of those who have already made up their minds against it. **24. Annas then sent him bound to Caiaphas the high priest:** Caiaphas's name here seems to support earlier comments on v. 19. Caiaphas has not yet figured in the trial (cf. Mk 14: 53–65; Mt. 26; 57 f.; Lk. 22: 63–71), although AV attempts to represent him as having done so by the mistranslation: 'Now Annas had sent him bound unto Caiaphas...'.

The scene now returns to Simon Peter. **26. Did I not see you in the garden:** The final question may well have been put out of fellow-feeling for Malchus, the injured officer. John omits any reference to the oaths and curses with which Peter consummated his denial. Nor does he explain, as does Mark (cf. Mk 14: 72), how remorse swept into the man's heart. It was presumably on the way to Caiaphas that Jesus turned to look upon Peter (cf. Lk. 22: 61).

ii. Pilate's judgment (18: 28–19: 16)

This part of the proceedings was enacted in order to get the death sentence confirmed (cf. Mk 15: 2-20; Mt. 27: 11-31; Lk. 23: 1-25). **28. the praetorium** was the official residence of a procurator. He would have normally resided at Caesarea, on the coast, and come to Jerusalem at festival times to preside over law and order. The Jews did not enter here in accordance with custom that no Jew should enter Gentile houses where there was always the possibility of defilement; to incur such defilement at present would make them unfit to eat the passover (see note on 13: 1). **31. It is not lawful for us:** Power of life and death had apparently not been exercised by the Sanhedrin since the time of Herod the Great, though opinions differ on this point. **32. the word which Jesus had spoken:** How far Jesus' earlier words about being 'lifted up' (cf. 3: 14; 12: 32) had been understood is difficult to say. But the evangelist clearly sees their fulfilment in the Passion. **33. Are you the King of the Jews:** The English text misses what might possibly have been a note of scorn here: 'You! Are you king of the Jews?' Pilate implies that the prisoner did not look much like a revolutionary leader who had caused so much disturbance by calling himself king (cf. Lk. 23: 2). The religious charge had been replaced by a political one to carry more weight with Pilate. Jesus' answer challenges Pilate's conscience (v. 35), but he brushes it aside. Nevertheless, Pilate is puzzled that such a claim should have evoked the Jews' hostility (v. 35b). **36. My kingship:** Jesus refers to His place in the divine purpose. If that kingship were earthly His servants would resist Pilate and his men (cf. Mt. 26: 53). **37. Every one who is of the truth hears my voice:** Jesus' reply to Pilate's question is again non-committal, in so far as He refuses Pilate's terms of reference. But He *is* king, though not in the sense in which Pilate would understand the word. **38. What is truth:** At the best this was a quasi-philosophical question. Yet by asking it Pilate is demonstrably not 'of the truth'. **39.** Pilate's fears are now twofold.

He is aware of the pressure of Jewish custom at Passover, and he is further moved by his wife's fears (Mt. 27: 19). **40. Barabbas** was an insurgent (cf. Mk 15: 7) and therefore, like Jesus, a 'political' prisoner. Their renewed cries show that the Jews' former outburst began with Jesus' earlier appearance (cf. Mt. 27: 13 f.). **19: 1. Pilate took Jesus and scourged him:** Elsewhere (cf. Mk 15: 15) Jesus is scourged after sentence is passed (though John does not say expressly when the sentence was passed, its passing is implied in 19: 13-16). The implication of John's account is that Pilate hoped either to satisfy the Jews short of capital punishment, or else to obtain direct evidence from Jesus under torture. **3. they came up to him** (Gk. *ērchonto pros auton*): The words seem to tell us that the soldiers did some mocking obeisance. That this was all part of a 'game of the king' is evidenced in Jerusalem today where a tableau is marked on stones close to Gabbatha (cf. v. 13). Their mockery is possibly directed as much against the Jews generally as against Jesus personally. Whether these Roman soldiers understood the implications of the trial is hard to say. **5. Here is the man:** The most poignant moment so far. Pilate's appeal to the Jews' finer feelings goes unheeded. John, moreover, records this as part of the Christian message; here in Jesus is the perfection of humanity tragically portrayed at the point of His self-sacrifice. Perhaps, also, the Evangelist's anti-Docetic purpose is in mind. **6. Take him yourselves:** Pilate is determined to exasperate the Jews as far as possible. He knows that they have no authority to crucify; yet by demanding crucifixion they have handed Jesus over to the Romans for their decision. **7. We have a law . . . he ought to die:** Cf. Lev. 24: 16. The Jews now return to the religious charge on the seeming failure of the political charge. **9. Where are you from:** Pilate is afraid. His question is interpreted on two levels by John. Jesus gives no reply (cf. Mk 15: 5; 14: 60 f.; Lk. 23: 9), since Pilate is not now likely to be moved by any answer He gives him, even if he understood anything about the divine origin of Jesus' mission. **11. You would have no power . . . unless . . . from above:** Jesus means that Pilate is an instrument under divine control (cf. Rom. 13: 1 ff.). So, too, was Caiaphas. But Caiaphas's failure brought the whole drama into operation, so he **has the greater sin. 12.** The Jews' answer to Pilate now virtually forces his hand. So he brings Jesus before the seat of judgment (Gk. *bēma*, 'tribunal', v. 13; cf. Rom. 14: 10; 2 C. 5: 10), from which alone sentence could be pronounced. **13. sat down . . . at a place called . . . Gabbatha:** The precise location is not certain, though we have reason to believe that part of the Pavement (Gk. *lithostrōtos*) is still visible beneath the Ecce Homo Arch (cf. *NBD*, p. 445). In spite of suggestions to the contrary, we must understand that Pilate himself sat down here, though the verb (Gk. *ekathisen*), used transitively, might mean 'he caused (Jesus) to sit down'. The Docetic 'Gospel of Peter' (late 2nd century) takes it in this latter sense. The procurator's action at this moment is not likely to have been in a light-hearted vein, but the idea that the verb is ambiguously used to suggest that, in fact, Jesus *was* sitting in judgment on His accusers, is worthy of attention. **14. Preparation of the Passover:** Cf. 18: 28; 19: 31; i.e., Passover Eve, Friday of Passover Week. **15. We have no king but Caesar** are words which form the greatest Jewish apostasy of all time. Thus 'Israel abdicated its own unique position under the immediate sovereignty of God' (C. K. Barrett, p. 454; cf. 1 Sam. 8: 7). **16. Then he handed him over** (Gk. *paredōken auton*): Put in this way, Pilate's action, in the eyes of the Evangelist, carries the overtones of the divine plan: though Jesus died at the hands of Roman soldiers, the Jews were primarily responsible for His death.

iii. The Crucifixion and Burial of Jesus (19: 17–42)

17. bearing his own cross: Cf. Mk 15: 21. The Evangelist may be drawing some special attention to the fact that, in contrast to others, Jesus bore His own cross. M. Black has pointed out that the Greek (literally rendered in RV, 'bearing the cross for himself') may be the translation of the ethic dative in Aramaic (pp. 75 f.), the reference being to that part of the gallows (the *patibulum*) which was carried by Jesus. **Golgotha** has not been identified with certainty. There are two sites which make claims to be the place of the skull (cf. A. Parrot, *Golgotha*, 1957). According to an early tradition the place was so named because Adam's skull lay buried here. This tradition is preserved inside the Church of the Holy Sepulchre. **19. a title** (Gk. *titlos*): This was usually a statement of the charge placed over the criminal's head. The Jews at once disputed the wording, but Pilate was determined to have the final word. To the Jews the title, as it stood, was a blasphemous insult (cf. Dt. 21: 23; Gal. 3: 13). **23. the tunic was without seam:** There is no reason to suppose that Jesus wore this garment with intended significance; but John's seeing some connection with the high priest's robe may be another matter (cf. Exod. 38: 31 f.). The soldiers' dividing of His clothing was customary, though John saw the scriptures fulfilled here (cf. Ps. 22: 18). In the psalm the two clauses represent the parallel structure of

the Hebrew poetry. **26 f. Woman, behold, your son . . . Behold, your mother:** Such was the love of Jesus that He should make provision for His mother at the last moment. Jesus hands her into the care of the 'beloved disciple' until such time as His brothers will accept their responsibility toward her as true followers of Him. And it may be added that the brothers did, quite soon, accept this responsibility, for Mary is later seen in their company, whereas John seems to be grouped quite distinctly from them (cf. Ac. 1: 14). The two passages might suggest that deeper fellowship which begins at the foot of the Cross and is maintained in prayer. **28. I thirst:** Jesus prepares to utter the final words from the Cross, bringing scriptures to fulfilment as He does so (cf. Ps. 69: 21). And that the Evangelist sees anti-Docetic material in this detail is certain. NEB has suggested that instead of 'hyssop' here we might read 'javelin'. The reading in the text could be accounted for by accidental dittography—Gk. *hyssōpos* for *hyssos;* though G. D. Kilpatrick has notably maintained 'hyssop' in the text in his edition of the Greek Testament and his Gk.-Eng. Diglot (BFBS). See also his 'The Transmission of the NT and its Reliability' in *Journ. Trans. Vict. Inst.* 89 (1957), p. 99. **30. It is finished** (Gk. *tetelestai*): This is the moment at which Jesus has fully entered into every phase of human existence from birth to death. So His work is completed—the work which the Father gave Him to do. More than this, He dismisses His spirit through which He consciously and willingly offered Himself spotless to God (cf. Heb. 9: 14). **31. Preparation:** Cf. notes on vv. 14, 41; 18: 28. **that sabbath was a high day:** Because it coincided with Passover in the Temple calendar. **34. blood and water:** In view of the Evangelist's comments upon this (cf. next verse), we may take his record of these details as part of his scheme to set forth the absolute humanity of the Saviour. Jesus' speedy death was remarkable (cf. Mk 15: 44). Various commentators have shown how medically accurate this tradition is. Yet physical details can never outweigh the theological implications here. The blood is clearly a symbol of the means of salvation offered to all through the death of Christ, for apart from this there is no means for removing sin (cf. Heb. 9: 22). The water may be understood in an equally symbolic manner with other allusions in the Gospel (cf. 4: 14; 7: 38 f.; 1 Jn 5: 6). By the death of Jesus sinners may be forgiven and receive the life of God imparted through the Spirit. These things, writes John (v. 35), are themselves sufficient to bring men into conscious communion with the living God. And for Jews particularly, the ideal Lamb of God perfectly accorded with the ancient sacrificial regulations of the Passover (cf. Exod. 12: 45; Num. 9: 12; Dt. 21: 23; see also Ps. 34: 20). **37. They shall look on him whom they have pierced:** Cf. Zech. 12: 10. The conditions which obtain in Zechariah appear to be very different from those at the crucifixion, in so far as there was no apparent grief among the Jews (see, however, the further application of the oracle in Mt. 24: 30; Rev. 1: 7). But, as F. F. Bruce puts it: 'it is the event that has suggested the *testimonium*, and not the other way about' though there are clear links with the later oracle of Zech. 13: 7 concerning the stricken shepherd of Israel (cf. F. F. Bruce, 'The Book of Zechariah and the Passion Narrative', *BJRL* 43, 1960–61, pp. 350 f.). **38. Joseph of Arimathea:** Like Nicodemus, he was a member of the Sanhedrin (cf. Mk 15: 43). Joseph may well have been one of the secret disciples mentioned earlier (cf. 12: 42). Together with Nicodemus he brought **a hundred pounds' weight** (i.e. about 70 lbs *avoirdupois*) of spices, and gave the Lord's body a royal burial (39, 40). Their action not only showed their devotion to Jesus, but prevented possible mutilation after burial. **41. a new tomb:** Here, because also of the difficulty of moving the body far on Sabbath Eve (cf. Lk. 23: 54), they laid Jesus.

III. RESURRECTION APPEARANCES
20: 1–31)

1. Mary Magdalene came to the tomb early: Cf. 19: 25; Lk. 23: 56. I.e., on Sunday morning. **2. They have taken the Lord:** Her fears were aroused since body-snatchers might have been at work. The **we** is reminiscent of the Synoptic narrative (cf. Mk 16: 1–8; Mt. 28: 1–8; Lk. 24: 1–12), where we are told that several women visitors came to the tomb. **4. the other disciple outran Peter:** Cf. v. 2; 13: 23; 19: 26; 21: 20. This is a natural touch, showing how vividly the beloved disciple, probably the younger of the two men, recalled the event. **6. Simon Peter . . . went into the tomb:** That impulsiveness which marked Simon through the years of Jesus' ministry is still there. And what he saw (cf. next verse) seems to describe what the burial cloths would look like if Jesus had left the tomb without disturbing them. **8. Then the other disciple . . . saw and believed:** The appearance of the cloths was enough for him. Yet he needed this much evidence for as yet neither of the two men understood the scriptures with regard to the resurrection (cf. Ps. 16: 10; Ac. 2: 29–32), that the same divine necessity which determined Jesus' death also

determined His rising from the dead. **10.** Apparently the faith of the beloved disciple was enough to kindle faith in Peter, so that they both left the tomb.

Mary, however, had followed the others to the tomb and now arrived, waiting outside weeping (v. 11). **16. Mary:** Hearing her name was sufficient to tell her who it was who spoke to her. It was the same powerful voice which had lifted this woman from her earlier demon-possessed life (Lk. 8: 2). **She turned and said to him in Hebrew, 'Rabboni':** There is some evidence, especially from a consideration of the possible Aramaic background to the Gospel, that **turned** here means 'recognized'; this is supported by the Sinaitic Syriac, and suggested also by M. Black. (**Hebrew** here is not classical Hebrew but Aramaic—a closely related language which employs the same script; cf. *NBD*, pp. 712 f.) **17. Do not hold me:** The 'touch me not' of the AV is weak. The attitude expressed in Mary's emotion would be such as would prevent Jesus, if not from entering into His glory, at least from imparting that vital manifestation of which He had spoken to His disciples (cf. 14: 15 ff.). Says Jesus rather: **I am ascending.** Jesus' appearance to Mary now is to assure her that He is returning to the Father. John does not present the ascension as a physical event which happened after forty days' interval from the resurrection, but as something which was already taking place. In John Christ's death is His exaltation—His 'lifting up'. Never before has Jesus spoken of **my brethren:** yet even now He distinguishes His sonship from theirs by saying **to my Father and your Father.**

19. fear of the Jews: Each of the resurrection appearances of Jesus fulfilled a special purpose. For Peter and the beloved disciple it was the proclamation of victory; for Mary it was the satisfaction of love; now for the rest of the disciples it is the calming of fear. **20. he showed them his hands and his side:** No substitution had taken place; He was the same Jesus. How He could pass through closed doors is a mystery to us, though in the light of what is known about the nature of matter such 'unnatural' phenomena are by no means so inconceivable as they once were. **22. Receive the Holy Spirit:** The breath of God is a regular metaphor in the scriptures for the Holy Spirit (cf. Gen. 2: 7; Ezek. 37: 9 f.). The first effusion of the breath of God made man a living being. Here, the breath of the risen Christ makes the timorous disciples into new men. There is no reason for assuming that the Holy Spirit was not fully imparted at this moment. A comparison with the Lukan account (cf. Lk. 24: 33) would suggest that others besides the ten disciples were present here. What is later described in the Acts (cf. Ac. 2: 1-4) was an outpouring of the Spirit especially understood in the light of the apostles' international ministry on the Day of Pentecost. That they were quickened here is beyond question. (But see H. B. Swete, *The Holy Spirit in the NT* [London, 1909], pp. 164-168.) **23. If you forgive the sins of any:** These words, properly understood, refer to the disciples as the first nucleus of the Spirit-filled society. Its ministry in the gospel will be effectual. Some will be forgiven; others will reject its message and be hardened. If we are inclined to doubt the power of the Church to fulfil such a responsibility, it is because we know (as the apostles knew) that the 'spirit of the world' still plays its part in the lives of its members. But when the Church functions as the true Body of Christ she can pronounce on sin with the same assurance as Jesus when He gave this command. **25. Unless I see . . . I will not believe:** Thomas (cf. 11: 6) in fact demanded the basic evidence for resurrection, i.e., the identity of that Body which he had known before Jesus died, and with it the evidence of continuity. The production of that evidence here is therefore fundamental to the cumulative nature of the resurrection passages, and Thomas can do little else than cry, **My Lord and my God!** (28). So to that disciple who most firmly demanded factual evidence was given the honour of making the first confession of faith in the completeness of the revelation summed up in the resurrection of Jesus Christ. **29. Blessed are those who have not seen and yet believe:** We are probably mistaken if we understand these words as a rebuke. Others may count themselves happy (though not happier) to believe with less palpable evidence. The Lord embraces all those who had come to faith prior to His death without any such compelling evidence of His deity with all those who subsequently would believe on the evidence of the Word written and spoken. But the faith of all will be equal in status. **31. these are written that you may believe:** Our textual authorities vary between the aorist tense (implying the dawn of faith) and the present (implying the persistence of faith). Not all the facts of the life of Jesus are recorded. The Gospels are not biographies. They are *Gospels*, which, writes C. H. Dodd, 'declare the glory of God by revealing what He has done'. To comment on this last sentence would mean re-reading or re-expounding the Gospel. To give ground for faith and the possession of **life** has been the Evangelist's object throughout. **that Jesus is the Christ, the Son of God:** Christ is not restricted to the Jewish conception of the Messiah, but is to be understood in the sense of **the Son of God** presented in this Gospel as the Revealer of the Father.

IV. APPENDIX (21: 1-25)

The last two verses of chap. 20 probably constituted the original ending of the Gospel. The present chapter was probably added as an appendix, to clear up a misunderstanding that had arisen regarding Jesus' words concerning the future of the beloved disciple (vv. 20-23), and to record the restoration of Simon Peter to a position of unique responsibility within the Church (vv. 15-19).

3. I am going fishing (Gk. *hypagō alyein*): The construction would imply a return to one's former occupation. Since each of the resurrection appearances conveyed some spiritual truth (cf. note on 20: 19), so here the risen Lord makes His power known in daily occupations. That the men had no catch is not surprising since they had been away from fishing for years! **5. Children** (Gk. *paidia*): A colloquialism perhaps meaning 'friends' (so NEB). **6. Cast the net on the right side:** Whatever may be the further implications of this command, the primary lesson is one of complete obedience to the Master. **7. It is the Lord:** This alone would suggest that the event occurred after the earlier appearances, and would further imply that the resurrection appearances of 20: 19 ff. are not necessarily to be placed before the ascension of 20: 17. **Peter . . . sprang into the sea:** This distinguishes the incident from the miraculous catch of Lk. 5: 1-11. There Peter is painfully conscious of his sin; here, with impetuous joy, perhaps tinged with remorse, he rushes to the Saviour. The quick intuition of the one disciple and the quick action of the other are typical. **11. a hundred and fifty-three:** The number is significant enough to have been recorded. It was a large catch, and would therefore naturally have been counted. That 153 symbolizes one of each kind (Jerome) or refers to the sum of the numerals in 10 and 7 —the commandments and the gifts of the Spirit (Augustine)—is highly conjectural, involves an unnecessary allegorizing of other details in the chapter, and is therefore clearly unwarranted. **15. do you love me:** In these verses two different words are used for 'to love' (Gk. *agapaō* and *phileō* respectively) but John probably uses them quite synonymously (compare 3: 35, *agapaō*, with 5: 20, *phileō*). **more than these** (Gk. *pleion toutōn*): Either masculine or neuter may be understood. Masculine is clearly intended, however; Peter had readily assumed that his loyalty could be counted on. Now Jesus asks:

'Do you love me more than these (disciples)?' **18. you will stretch out your hands:** Cf. 13: 36 f. This ultimately points to death, though it may speak of Peter's lot in the meanwhile of being at the mercy of others as a messenger of the gospel. But then another will gird him, carrying him to his martyrdom. **19. Follow me:** It is to loyalty true enough to suffer death that Jesus bids His followers. **23.** That the question of the Lord's second advent was much in the minds of people at the time is evidently true from the fact that they imagined it possible that one of His disciples should remain alive until He came again. But Jesus discountenances such a thought. **24. This is the disciple who is bearing witness:** The beloved disciple remains to bear out the truth of Jesus' words, whether we understand **these things** to refer only to the last few verses or to the whole Gospel. **we know** is either an undefined collective (cf. 1:14) or possibly a joint statement from the elders of the church from which John originally wrote (cf. 3 Jn 12). **25. I suppose:** The use of 'I' seems strange after the former 'we'. But there is a little evidence that this verse was added some time after the writing of the Gospel (the first scribe who copied *Codex Sinaiticus* originally omitted it, but added it later); it could be an inspired comment by one of the earliest collectors of the four Gospels into a single volume. The words are a common enough hyperbole, but behind them lies the truth that, as T. R. Glover whimsically suggested, there are not four Gospels but 'ten thousand times ten thousand, and thousands of thousands, and the end of every one says, "Lo, I am with you always even unto the end of the world".'

ADDITIONAL NOTE I.
The Word (Gk. *ho logos*). John's doctrine of the Word has been shaped by two influences. The Word is conceived as distinctly related to the Word of the OT. And the conception here is also coloured by contemporary Greek thought as it was preserved in the late first century.

Christianity was cradled in Judaism. But the Evangelist recognizes that Gentile missions necessitated a presentation of Christ in terms which would be understood by both Jew and Greek. The 'word' for the Jew *did* things. He conceived language as something vitally active. How much more so this would then be true of the Word of God! It was by the Word that God brought the earth and heavens into being (cf. Ps. 33: 6–9) so that the earliest writers of the OT could unhesitatingly speak of the utterance of God in the act of bringing forth (cf. Gen. 1: 3,

9, 11, 14, 20, 24, 26). Moreover, the Word of God never returned to Him as an unfaithful echo, but ever fulfilled that purpose for which it had been spoken (Isa. 55: 11), pre-eminently as a life-giving power (Isa. 55: 3) and as a constraint upon His messengers (Jer. 23: 29). This is a basic assumption of the OT. Where, however, certain passages of the OT implied that something of God could be seen by men (*e.g.*, Exod. 33: 22 f.; Isa. 6: 1; Ezek. 1: 1; Isa. 48: 13, etc.), or that He possessed human parts, the later Aramaic Targums removed such references, inserting circumlocutions instead, usually *memra*, 'the word', which may lie behind John's employment of *logos*. God has now been seen in the Word made flesh. It should be remembered, too, that the Book of Proverbs, with other Wisdom Literature, personifies Wisdom and represents her as associated with God in the creation of the world (cf. Prov. 8: 22–31).

To the Greek mind *logos* was similarly a significant term. From Heraclitus onwards, when thinkers began to formulate a doctrine of the creative control inherent in the universe, the *logos* came to be a technical term among philosophers, particularly the Stoics (as well as Philo).

This authority, writes John, revealing the very nature of the Godhead and His wisdom in creation and salvation is made known in Christ. He wields eternal power by reason of His deity. But His acts are rational and therefore revelatory. He is God. He is Christ. He is Lord. Therefore He can alike make unparalleled claims and give unequalled promises (cf. Heb. 1: 1; Col. 1: 16 ff.). It is mainly this idea of God, active and immanent in the created world and revealed in the events of history, that is implied in John's use of 'the Word'. But no doubt he recognizes the Greek conception as conveying rationality of the universe which implies a thinking purposive mind. John adds distinct personality to the two ideas, even though there may be hints at personality in the Proverbs passage. Though the Word is not specifically mentioned in the Gospel after the Prologue, the fact that Jesus is the Eternal Word Incarnate should never be lost sight of wherever He speaks or acts. And with the testimony of Revelation (cf. Rev. 19: 13) to this Word, John would have his readers remember that his is no theological treatise alone, but a testimony to Christ as the One who alone is worthy to receive glory and honour. '"Worship God"! The testimony of Jesus is the Spirit of prophecy' (Rev. 19: 10).

ADDITIONAL NOTE II.
The Woman Taken in Adultery (7: 53—8: 11). It is certain that these verses are a later

insertion into the original work. They are omitted by the best authorities for the text, though one group of MSS places them after Lk. 21: 38. They completely break the thread of chapters 7 and 8, and the adjoining verses read perfectly well without the passage in question. They may well have been inserted to give an illustration of Jesus' words, 'You judge according to the flesh, I judge no one' (8: 15). But the story has an authentic air about it, and adequately describes the perfect balance which Jesus ever kept between truth on the one side, by which He condemns the woman's sin, and grace on the other, with which He withholds condemnation from the woman herself.

The dilemma of the situation in which the scribes and Pharisees brought this woman to Jesus lay in the fact that if Jesus said she should not be stoned, He then would be open to a charge of withstanding the authority of the Jewish Law; but if He said she could be, He could be accused under Roman law of incitement to murder, since capital jurisdiction was withheld from the Jewish authorities. Jesus' action in writing on the ground with His finger was intended to take their callous eyes off the woman, and to give them an opportunity to withdraw. His reply, **'Let him who is without sin among you be the first to throw a stone at her'**, raises the whole issue from a legal plane to a moral level.

Jesus then turns to the woman, and refuses to pass judgment on her, even though He has the right to do so. For an essential condition of His treatment of this woman is the certainty of His own sinlessness.

BIBLIOGRAPHY

BARRETT, C. K., *The Gospel According to St. John* [on the Greek text] (London, 1962).

BERNARD, J. H., *A Critical and Exegetical Commentary on the Gospel According to St. John* [on the Greek text], *ICC* (London, 1928).

BERNARD, T. D., *The Central Teaching of Jesus Christ* (London, 1900).

BLACK, M., *An Aramaic Approach to the Gospels and Acts* 3 (Oxford, 1967).

BURNEY, C. F., *The Aramaic Origin of the Fourth Gospel* (Oxford, 1922).

DODD, C. H., *The Interpretation of the Fourth Gospel* (Cambridge, 1953).

DODD, C. H., *Historical Tradition in the Fourth Gospel* (Cambridge, 1963).

HOSKYNS, E. C. (ed. F. N. Davey), *The Fourth Gospel* (London, 1947).

HOWARD, W. F., *The Fourth Gospel in Recent Criticism and Interpretation* (London, 1935).

HOWARD, W. F., *Christianity According to St. John* (London, 1943).

HUNTER, A. M., *According to John* (London, 1968).

LIGHTFOOT, J. B., *Biblical Essays* (ed. J. R. Harmer) (London, 1893).

LIGHTFOOT, R. H., *St. John's Gospel* (Oxford, 1961).

NUNN, H. P. V., *The Authorship of the Fourth Gospel* (Eton, 1952).

STRACHAN, R. H., *The Fourth Gospel, its Significance and Environment* (London, 1941).

TASKER, R. V. G., *The Gospel According to St. John. TNTC* (London, 1960).

TEMPLE, W., *Readings in St. John's Gospel*, 1st and 2nd series (London, 1959).

WESTCOTT, B. F., *The Gospel According to St. John* [on the Greek text] (London, 1908).

WESTCOTT, B. F., *The Gospel According to St. John*. Speaker's Commentary (London, 1880, reprinted 1958).

Other main references:—

The Gospels Reconsidered (Oxford 1960).

DODD, C. H., *The Bible and the Greeks* (London, 1954).

EDERSHEIM, A., *The Life and Times of Jesus the Messiah* (London, reprinted, 1959).

KLAUSNER, J., *Jesus of Nazareth*, E.T. (London, 1950).

RAWLINSON, A. E. J., *The New Testament Doctrine of the Christ* (London, 1949).

STAUFFER, E., *New Testament Theology*, E.T. (London, 1955).

THE ACTS
OF THE APOSTLES

E. H. TRENCHARD

Authorship and Date

That Luke is the author of the dual documents Luke-Acts is a fact so well established that a brief summary of the evidence is sufficient here. (1) The Anti-Marcionite Prologue (c. 160), names Luke as the author and all other external evidence is consistent with this statement. (2) Luke is named as a companion and fellow-worker of Paul's in Col. 4: 14; Phm. 24: 2; Tim. 4: 11. (3) The link between the two documents is found in the address to Theophilus (Lk. 1: 3; Ac. 1: 1), in a style common to both, in an approach to persons and incidents which is consistent with a common authorship. (4) The author of the Acts reveals his presence as a participant in Paul's labours by using the pronoun 'we' in 16: 10-18; 20: 6-21: 17; 27: 1-28: 16. If the ascription of the Anti-Marcionite Prologue is correct, then the modest author is Luke, and he is the 'beloved physician' who was with Paul in Rome.

Luke's purpose. Luke's stately introduction to the Gospel (1: 1-4), important from many points of view, clearly defines his purpose of presenting the 'most excellent Theophilus' with a carefully compiled account of the facts of the beginnings of Christianity. The reference to 'the first book' in Ac. 1: 1 has the effect of including the dual work under the same introduction and general purpose, though the second work has naturally to continue the ministry begun by Christ in the Gospel, describing how He effects it through the power of the Holy Spirit in the apostles as the gospel is preached first in Jerusalem, and then world-wide.

Behind Theophilus we may imagine a group of interested readers of some culture and position who are beginning to take an interest in the strange happenings which took place in Palestine and the Near East from A.D. 27 onward. God chose a man of culture, with a wide interest in contemporary history, master of an excellent Hellenistic Greek, a fine story-teller and an exact historian, to write a wonderfully selective account of the great happening from the birth of John the Baptist until Paul's first imprisonment in Rome (c. 62).

Luke's methods. Luke makes no idle claim when he states that he 'followed all things closely (or accurately)' (Lk. 1: 3) with a view to compiling an orderly account of what had taken place. For parts of Paul's ministry he had his own memory and notes. For the rest, he sought out reliable eyewitnesses and previous documents (Lk. 1: 1, 2), using them conscientiously. He is so sensitive to atmosphere, and so faithful to his sources, that the early chapters of both Gospel and Acts are Hebraic in setting and style, despite the fact that he is a Greek, writing in Hellenistic Greek. Sir William Ramsay's classic researches, which found expression in works such as The Church in the Roman Empire and St. Paul, the Traveller and the Roman Citizen, showed once and for all the accuracy of Luke as an historian. The extensive journeys through a variety of provinces described in Acts necessitated numerous references to provinces, cities, institutions, native and Roman officers of different grades, customs, etc., in relation to which a careless story-teller would be bound to fall into endless traps. Luke, however, falls into none and his work is taken as reliable evidence in all matters he touches on.

The date of writing. Some critics have attempted to prove a late date for Acts, quoting mainly the author's supposed dependence on Josephus for the account of the death of Herod Agrippa I. As Josephus wrote his Antiquities in 93, this would give a date near the end of the first century. Actually Luke's account, while consistent with that of Josephus, is independent of it and we are more impressed by the fact that the story closes abruptly when Paul had spent two years as a prisoner in Rome (probably in 62), without giving a clear account of the result of the appeal to Caesar, noting also that the emphasis on the general protection afforded to Christians by Roman officials would have been out of place and anachronistic after the Neronian persecution of A.D. 64/5.

It is very probable indeed that Luke used the two years of Paul's Caesarean captivity to gather his material for Luke and early Acts from eye-witnesses and documents in Palestine. Adding this to his own notes and information from Paul himself he could have had all his material at hand during the two years in Rome and could then have given shape, in two stages, to his great work. Writing is one thing and circulation another, but Luke intended his work to be read in times when it seemed possible that Christianity might attain official recognition, i.e. before A.D. 64.

The place of Acts in the NT. If Luke wrote a two-part account of the beginnings of Christianity for the benefit of Theophilus and his friends—as well as for all men everywhere in the course of the centuries—why is Luke separated from Acts in the NT? The answer is found in God's providential care of the canon of the NT, working through the spiritual perception of discerning Christians during the early years of the second century, when four presentations of the Gospel were recognized as especially authoritative and gathered together as 'The Gospel', subdivided into the sections 'according to Matthew', etc. John was seen to be the spiritual consummation of the series, and Luke was given the third place. About the same time the Letters of Paul were gathered together under the title of 'The Apostle', and before long it was seen that Acts was the divinely provided link between 'The Gospel' and 'The Apostle', welding two fundamental series into a library already comprising the greater part of our NT. The importance of this history of the beginnings of the Church and the spread of the gospel from Jerusalem to Rome was further appreciated during the anti-Marcionite debate which straddled the middle of the second century.

God's providence thus provided the ideal bridge between the ministry of our Lord and that of the apostles contained in the Letters, which answers numberless questions arising from the study of the Letters which would have presented insoluble problems apart from the second section of Luke's masterpiece.

Purpose and Plan

The need of a history of the early years. We have already seen that Luke wished to give an accurate selection of the facts of the origins of Christianity to Theophilus and the 'reading' class he represented. All other purposes must be subordinated to this primary one, remembering that he was inspired thereto by the Holy Spirit. Luke saw the Lord's mission, the descent of the Holy Spirit which gave birth to the Church, and the apostolic labours which extended the

gospel world-wide, as one great happening. The 'first book' (1: 1) therefore demanded the writing of its supplement and complement, which is the book we are studying.

The plan of 1: 8. Our Lord's command in 1: 8 has been rightly considered to be the ground plan of Acts: (*a*) a Jerusalem ministry, chs. 1-7; (*b*) a Palestine ministry—reaching out to Syria in the end, chs. 8-12; (*c*) a world-wide ministry, chs. 13-28. Luke is obviously very much concerned with establishing for his readers Paul's apostolic call and special ministry, but this did not and could not be seen in perspective apart from a clear account of the early years of the church, during which Peter's apostolic ministry is especially prominent. Hence the parallelism between the 'Acts of Peter' (chs. 1-12) and the 'Acts of Paul' (chs. 13-28), in which many analogous features have been discerned.

Luke's writing is 'apologetic'. In the real sense of the word it was so in various ways. (*a*) He presents the origins of Christianity to cultured readers of the Graeco-Roman world, showing that the disturbances associated therewith as a rule owed nothing to its essential nature, but were stirred up by Jews who rejected their Messiah. (*b*) Many of the speeches of Acts present the Christian message to Jewish audiences, showing the historic foundations and prophetic predictions which manifested Jesus of Nazareth as the Messiah. (*c*) In Paul's Jerusalem and Caesarean speeches the Christian message of hope and resurrection is shown to be the heart of the OT revelation. It is not therefore a heresy, but the true continuation and fulfilment of the former revelation. (*d*) Before both ignorant and cultured Gentiles, Christ the Lord is shown to be God's messenger over against the multiplicity of the 'lords many' of the contemporary pagan scene (14: 14-18; 17: 22-31). (*e*) Luke establishes Paul's apostleship by the threefold account of his conversion and the gradual manifestation of the signs of his special ministry, until God's works through him were recognized by all except the Judaizers. The opposition of the latter, though a diminishing force within the Church, explains Luke's insistence, which links naturally and closely with Paul's own defence of his apostleship in Galatians, 2 Corinthians, etc.

The developments of a transitional period. Much confused comment has been made on Acts because writers have failed to take into account that the story covers thirty years of development during which God's special witness on earth passed from the hands of the godly remnant of Israel—representing the ideal nation—to those of the church, composed at first entirely of Jewish believers, but latterly of believers who were probably mainly Gentile in origin. It was essential that the risen Messiah should be first presented to Israel in Jerusalem, according to the well-established principle 'to the Jew first'. It is also clear that the universal nature of the church, as superseding Israel's witness, was not forced upon the understanding of the apostles until they were able to bear it. Hence the descent of the Holy Spirit on Gentile believers—extending to them the blessings of Pentecost—did not take place until some years had passed, when it was also plain that official Israel had rejected the risen Messiah as finally as it had rejected the Palestine ministry of Jesus of Nazareth. The instruments who received light in order to guide the church through these stages were themselves Jews by birth and not bound to throw over their national and religious 'customs'. To this must be added the transition seen in Paul's ministry, who was first called as it were in secret. Afterwards he worked alone in Cilicia—in silence as far as the record is concerned—before becoming Barnabas's helper in Antioch. Luke denotes this period by the use of the terms 'Barnabas and Saul', but eventually he was revealed as God's apostle to the Gentiles in the course of the first journey. The phrase 'Paul and his company' in 13: 13 marks the moment of public acknowledgment. In the writer's view the discussions and the strong claims—then and there acknowledged—of Gal. 2: 1-10 cannot be fitted into the period of subordinate ministry indicated by the term 'Barnabas and Saul' without overriding this principle of historic development. It belongs to the moment of Paul's apostolic plenitude, both in the revelation of doctrine and in the working out of missionary strategy. Notes in the Commentary will indicate points in which the factor of constant growth from Jewish

beginnings to the fulness of the apostolic presentation of 'the faith which was once for all delivered to the saints' must be borne in mind in order to avoid doubtful exegesis. The movement is not wholly contained within the historical period of Acts, but closes with the Letter to the Hebrews in the Canon, and with the verdict of history when the Temple was destroyed by Titus. After that distinctively Jewish elements are gradually eliminated from the testimony of the church.

Chronological Table

Luke is vague in recording the passage of time, and extra-biblical data only help on three occasions: the death of Herod Agrippa I (A.D. 44), the proconsulship of Gallio in Achaia (A.D. 51-52), and the beginning of the procuratorship of Festus in A.D. 59. Other dates are necessarily approximate and the suggestions of scholars differ considerably. This tentative scheme is meant only as a general guide.

A.D.	
30	Pentecost.
33 or 34	Conversion of Saul.
42 or 43	Barnabas co-opts Saul in his labours in Antioch.
44 (fixed)	Herodian persecution and visit of Barnabas and Saul to Jerusalem.
45-47	First journey.
47-48	Period in Antioch and visit to Jerusalem on circumcision question (chap. 15) (14 years after Saul's conversion).
48-52	Second missionary journey (end fixed by Gallio's proconsulship).
52-57	Third missionary journey.
57	Paul arrested in Jerusalem.
57-59	Paul a prisoner in Caesarea.
60-62	Paul a prisoner in Rome.
62	Probably freed.
65 (?)	Martyrdom in Rome.

ANALYSIS

I. THE LINK WITH THE GOSPEL
(1: 1-26)
i. Theophilus and the 'First Book' (1: 1)
Theophilus: The title 'most excellent' given to Theophilus (='friend of God') in Lk. 1: 3 marks him out as a high official in the service of Rome, or a member of the equestrian order. It also confirms our impression that he was a real person, already a believer, maybe, or at least greatly interested in Christ and His message. Luke doubtless hoped to reach a wide circle through his correspondent. The absence of the title in 1: 1 may indicate that the relations were less formal and more brotherly than when the 'first book' was written, although dates are probably close (see Introduction, pp. 289 f.). The dedication to Theophilus indicates that the gospel was beginning to spread among cultured persons of the Graeco-Roman world.

The continuance of a divine work (1: 1). Luke would have been in hearty sympathy with the brief *résumé* of apostolic ministry in Mk 16: 20: 'They went forth and preached everywhere, the Lord working with them . . .'. The same Lord who **began to do and teach** as recorded in the Gospel, continued His mighty works by the Spirit through the apostles in the period following the consummation of the cross and the resurrection. The whole process is continuous throughout all the historical phases and the centre is the great Servant who declares: 'My Father works hitherto and I work'. The work takes priority over the teaching which is based on it.

ii. The commandment given to the Apostles (1: 2–5)
The need of teaching. The Lord's redemptive work was consummated, so that nothing divided His person from heavenly spheres. He nevertheless spent a clear, historical period of forty days with the apostles before **the day when he was taken up.** Phrases here and in the epilogues of the Gospels indicate that the period was of the greatest importance to apostolic witness for His servants needed a continuance of their training *after* the tremendous fact of the crucifixion, in the light of the resurrection and under the personal guidance of the same Master. The mention of the Holy Spirit in relation to these commandments does not, of course, weaken the authority of the Master, but stresses once more that the whole work was a 'combined operation' of the Triune God. 'The Spirit of the Lord is upon me because He has anointed me to preach . . .' (Lk. 4: 18; cf. Isa. 61: 1, 2) was as true after the resurrection as before.

The apostles. The Twelve were the accredited and commissioned witnesses both to the person and work of Christ, the depositories of the truth related to the great event of God's intervention in history, in the person of His Son, for the redemption of men. So much depended on the accuracy of their ministry that the risen Lord continued to instruct them until His ascension. In 1: 21, 22 we shall return to the characteristics of the ministry of the Twelve in contrast to that of Paul, but note here the importance of the joint witness of the Holy Spirit and the apostles (Jn 14: 26; 15: 26, 27; Ac. 5: 32). These men were not self-appointed babblers, but **the apostles whom he had chosen** speaking in words which were inspired and confirmed by the Holy Spirit.

The substance of the commandment (1: 3, 4, 8). The 'commandment' mentioned perhaps included the various aspects of the Great Commission detailed in Mt. 28: 19, 20; Lk. 24: 44–49; Jn 20: 21; 21: 15–17. In our context the Lord speaks of the **kingdom of God,** by which we may understand all the spheres which acknowledge God's sovereignty, with special reference here to believers who should enter the kingdom through the world-wide preaching of the gospel. The 'kingdom' and the 'church' should not be set in opposition, but the latter should be understood as the central province of the kingdom because of its most intimate relation with the King. (For a balanced presentation of this great theme, see G. E. Ladd, *The Gospel of the Kingdom*, Loudon, 1959.) The command to await **the promise of the Father** in Jerusalem (4) links back to John the Baptist's prophecy (5; cf. Mt. 3: 11) and further back still to the promises of the out-pouring of the Holy Spirit by OT prophets (Jl 2: 28, 29; Isa. 32: 15; etc.). The Father's counsels direct the different phases of the work of redemption, so that **the promise of the Father** is a phrase which aptly describes the gift of the Holy Spirit, the necessary complement of the Incarnation and Atonement.

iii. The Times and Seasons (1: 6, 7)
The disciples' question (1: 6). Is this question yet another proof of the slowness of the apostles in comprehending the spiritual nature of the kingdom, or can it be understood with reference to the particular point at which they had arrived in their instruction by the Master? Let us note the following factors: (*a*) The apostles were steeped in OT prophecies in which the constantly repeated theme is the restoration of Israel to the heart of a universal kingdom on earth. All pious Israelites meditated on this theme (Lk. 1: 33, 55, 68–75). The fierce and unspiritual nationalism of the majority of Jews did not annul these prophecies, though it did distort them. (*b*) The risen Christ taught His disciples that it behoved the Messiah to suffer and then 'to enter into his glory' (Lk. 24: 26, 27), opening their minds to understand prophetic Scripture concerning His sufferings and resurrection (Lk. 24: 44–46). (*c*) The disciples, having understood the meaning of Isa. 53, naturally meditated on the possibility of the manifestation of the kingdom, as nothing had been revealed which would annul the predictions,

The answer (1: 7). There is no rebuke expressed or implied in the Master's answer, which reiterates that there are 'times and seasons' but remits the order of their manifestation to the Father's authority (cf. 1 Th. 5: 1). In the meantime they had a task to perform in the power of the Holy Spirit and must await further light on the time of the messianic kingdom (1: 7, 8). The 'times' are *chronoi* and the 'seasons' *kairoi;* although the meaning of these terms overlaps, *chronoi* lays more stress on the duration of the period and *kairoi* on the crises which mark their consummation.

iv. The Apostolic Witness (1: 8)
Its power. You shall receive power when the Holy Spirit has come upon you, for the new

age was to be that of the Holy Spirit who alone could empower the witness and complement the external and historic work of the Son by those internal and subjective energies which would regenerate and sanctify all true believers (cf. I C. 2: 4, 5).

The witnesses. In the first place we must understand the apostolic witnesses who were to speak of Christ and His work as the chosen depositories of the truth (cf. note on I: 2), declaring what they had seen and heard as good eye-witnesses should do (I Jn I: 1-3). But while, in that sense, the apostles could have no successors, all true Christians feel—or should feel—the personal obligation placed on them by the command: **you shall be my witnesses.**

The sphere. In Jerusalem and in all Judea and Samaria and to the end of the earth denotes a universal sphere of witness to be reached by stages. It seemed impossible to begin **in Jerusalem,** where the Lord Himself had been rejected and crucified, but such was the command and chs. 2-7 reveal the means by which it was implemented. The next stage was **all Judea,** which, with Samaria mentioned and Galilee implied, coincided with Palestine. Chs. 8-12 narrate the fulfilment of this commission. Peter was to open the door of the world-wide Gentile sphere, and Paul was to be its apostle. Luke tells the story of this last stage in chs. 13-28. We have here, therefore, the programme of the early stages of world evangelism and the main structure of Luke's history.

v. The Ascension (I: 9-II)
The fact and the purpose. It was the Lord's good pleasure to provide a definite and visible end to His ministry on earth in fulfilment of Jn 16: 28: 'I came from the Father and have come into the world; again, I am leaving the world and going to the Father'. Lk. 24: 50 and Ac. I: 12 fix the place as being the Mount of Olives, 'over against Bethany'—a place hallowed by many memories. Our Lord's resurrection body was visibly **lifted up** before the disciples until a cloud—presumably a celestial phenomenon, the cloud which enfolds the divine presence (cf. Lk. 9: 34 f.)—received Him out of their sight. Besides marking the end of Christ's earthly ministry, the ascension inaugurated His session at God's right hand (Ac. 2: 36; 5: 31; Rom. 8: 34; Heb. I: 3; I Pet. 3: 22, etc.), and coincides with the 'glorification' without which the Holy Spirit could not be given (Jn 7: 39; cf. Jn 15: 26; Lk. 24: 49). Both Father and Son are spoken of as sending the Holy Spirit.

The Ascension and the Coming (I: 10, II). The **men . . . in white robes** were certainly angelic messengers sent to warn the disciples against a sentimental longing for the wonderful days of fellowship with the Master on earth and to cheer them by the prediction of our Lord's personal and visible return **in the same way as you saw him go into heaven.** The period of witness led to a definite goal.

The return to Jerusalem (I: 12). Lk. 24: 52, 53 speaks of the disciples' 'great joy' on returning to the upper room, which indicates a complete understanding of their Lord's last instructions and of the angelic message. They awaited the coming of the **power** with eager expectation, expressed in prayer and supplication. **A sabbath day's journey** was about six furlongs and was the distance a pious Jew might travel without breaking the rest of the seventh day. The term does not indicate that the ascension took place on the sabbath.

vi. Waiting for the Promise (I: 12-14)
Zahn and others suggest the probability that the disciples returned to that same upper room which had been placed at the Lord's disposal for the celebration of the Passover (Lk. 22: 7-13).

The Eleven (I: 13). It is natural that there should be a 'roll-call' of the apostles before the new stage of the work was inaugurated. The names are given as in Lk. 6: 14 ff. For considerations on the differences between this list and that of Matthew and Mark, see F. F. Bruce, *The Acts of the Apostles*, p. 43. The important fact to be noted in this context is that one member of the original apostolic body, Judas Iscariot, was missing, which leads directly to the appointment of Matthias.

The waiting company (I: 14, 15). As many as 120 persons could be accommodated in a large upper room. Eleven were apostles, and the rest faithful disciples. Mary's presence is noted before she disappears from the pages of Holy Writ, and it is fitting that she should have shared in the experience of the birth of the spiritual body of Christ. The phrase **with his brothers** reveals the secret of the conversion of these formerly antagonistic men (Jn 7: 5). Every line prepares us in some way for the great event, and expectancy was naturally expressed by a spirit of prayer which identified the yearnings of the company with God's declared purpose.

vii. The Appointment of Matthias (I: 15-26)
The twelfth apostle. The oft repeated idea that the Eleven should have waited for the Lord to make it clear that Paul was to be the twelfth apostle fails to take into account the following considerations: (*a*) The election of Matthias is given by Luke as a part of the introduction to Pentecost; twelve witnesses, representatives

of the true Israel, were to stand together that day (2: 14). (*b*) Peter could not be wrong in his understanding of the situation and yet inspired in the quotations from the Psalms and in his estimate of Judas. (*c*) The Twelve were apostolic witnesses to the ministry, death and resurrection of Christ (1: 21, 22), and that Paul could never be. He underlines their specific ministry in 13: 31. His ministry was to the risen Lord as Head of the Church (Eph. 3: 1-12; Col. 1: 24-29, etc.).

Peter's speech (1: 16-22). We must note that 1: 18, 19 constitutes an explanatory parenthesis given by Luke for the benefit of his readers, which sums up the recollection of the end of Judas in Jerusalem when the author gathered up his evidence in (say) A.D. 57-59. For the rest, the speech has two movements: (*a*) Peter sees in Ahithophel the type of the arch-traitor, Judas, and applies the 'traitor' psalms to the latter (2 Sam. 17: 23; Ps. 69: 25; 109: 8). Judas had really been **numbered among us**, great though the mystery is, and his vacant office must be filled. (*b*) The remaining movement (21, 22) is of great importance since it shows that the Twelve had necessarily to be eye-witnesses of the whole of Christ's earthly ministry so as to be reliable witnesses to the great fact of the resurrection.

The election. The Eleven could discern no difference in eligibility according to the given conditions between Joseph Barsabbas and Matthias, and so had recourse to the system of lots (as between two alternatives) sanctioned in the OT. The Urim and Thummim seem to have been used in similar circumstances. The moment was unique for the Master was not there in person to appoint His witness, and the Holy Spirit was not yet given in the special way of Pentecost. The Eleven would remember Prov. 16: 33 and acted accordingly. The silence of Scripture as to the future ministry of Matthias is no more significant than that which surrounds the work of the majority of the apostles.

II. PENTECOST AND THE PREACHING (2: 1-47)

i. The Descent of the Holy Spirit (2: 1-13)
The Event (2: 1-4). The company was gathered in normal assembly (*epi to auto*), in the **house** previously referred to (2: 2; cf. 1: 14, 15). The **rush of a mighty wind** revealed the event and an appearance of **tongues of fire** was seen on each Spirit-filled disciple. It is probable that the company speedily left the house and proceeded to the Temple, where the **sound** (perhaps a 'solemn declaration') drew the crowds together. The **wind** as a symbol of the Spirit was known through Ezekiel's prophecy (Ezek.

37: 9-14) and was used by the Lord (Jn 3: 8). The **fire** represents the outworking of divine energies.

The meaning of the Descent. (*a*) The coming of the Spirit closes the series of happenings which together constitute God's intervention in human history for the salvation of man, and cannot be separated from the incarnation and earthly ministry of Christ, His atoning death and triumphant resurrection. His exaltation made possible the outpouring (1: 33; Jn 7: 39). (*b*) John the Baptist's prophecy and Christ's reference back to it in 1: 5 show that this baptism was the culmination of the work of the Messiah. The cross removed the obstacle of sin so that believers could again live in full communion with God. (*c*) The baptism with the Spirit is thus a 'once for all' event with continuous results, its benefits being extended to Gentile believers in Caesarea (10: 44-48; 1 C. 12: 13). (*d*) Everything indicates the tremendous novelty of the great event, and fulfils the Lord's purpose (future when He spoke): 'on this rock I will build my church' (Mt. 16: 18).

Speaking with tongues (2: 4-13). This is a 'sign', a happening outside the usual course of nature and the workings of human intelligence, which gave evidence of the presence and power of the Holy Spirit. There are further cases as the benefits of Pentecost are extended in 10: 46 and 19: 6, but apart from these references tongues are mentioned only in Mk 16: 17 (in the longer appendix to Mk) and in 1 C. 14: 13, where 'speaking with tongues' becomes an internal matter for the local church, ecstatic and unintelligible unless interpreted. On the day of Pentecost the tongues were intelligible to a number of hearers from different countries, and it is impossible to say how these two manifestations are related.

The reactions of the multitude (2: 5-13). The many devout Jews of the Dispersion who had gone to Jerusalem for the feast are selected for special mention—perhaps an early emphasis on universality. Many of them had lost the use of Aramaic and would normally depend on Greek as a *lingua franca*. The proclamation of **the mighty works of God** (11) in the languages of the countries of their adoption would naturally excite their keen interest, followed by amazement as it was found that *all* understood what was being said—presumably by one or other of the speakers. It was a *teras* (a wonder) which became a *sēmeion* (a sign) that God desired to make Himself known despite the Babel-confusion of human tongues. Here was a remarkable story to take back to countries spreading from Persia to Rome and over the

North of Africa (8-11)! We must remember, however, that all the hearers belonged to the commonwealth of Israel.

Apart from the amazement and perplexity of the pilgrims, we know nothing of other immediate reactions except that of the 'smart' people who produced the easy formula: 'These men are drunk'! Their theory was soon deflated by Peter.

ii. Peter's Speech (2: 14-36)

The kerygma for Jews. Now filled with the Spirit, Peter could begin to 'proclaim as a herald' the great fact of redemption, lifting up his voice, as he stood **with the eleven,** to give solemn utterance to the inspired message (2: 14). Before Jews, the 'herald's message' (Gk. *kerygma*) generally includes the following features: (*a*) the guilt of the people who crucified their Messiah; (*b*) God's reversal of their verdict in the resurrection and exaltation of Jesus; (*c*) the evidence of Christ's well-known ministry of grace and power; (*d*) appeals to OT texts; (*e*) the continuing possibility of blessing for Israelites who would repent and believe.

Introduction (2: 14, 15). The **third hour** was 9 a.m., when Jews would not normally have had a meal, much less have taken wine. 'This is not drunkenness', says Peter, in effect, 'but inspiration.'

Joel's prophecy (2: 16-21). NT writers quote from the OT in a variety of ways, more often on the basis of analogy of principle than on that of direct fulfilment. In the writer's view, a special use made of an OT prophecy does not annul its meaning as fixed by the original context. In Jl 2: 28-32 the prophet speaks of the outpouring of the Spirit on *everybody* as the climax of the blessings God will bestow on restored Israel. This is preceded by the usual portents of judgment in the last days and by a promise of salvation to all who call on the name of the Lord. The terrible portents of 2: 19, 20 were not fulfilled by the darkening of the sun on the day of the crucifixion and are constantly associated with the Day of Jehovah (Isa. 13: 9-11; Ezek. 32: 5-8; Jl 2: 10; 3: 15; Hab. 3: 11; Mt. 24: 29 and parallels; Rev. 6: 12; 8: 12). The Holy Spirit descended on a limited company, and has still not filled all persons, old and young, of all social categories. The conditions for quotations from the OT in the NT are fulfilled if we understand that elements of Joel's prophecy were seen in the happening of Pentecost, and that the cross and resurrection had opened a new age which would culminate in universal spiritual blessing. (See article 'The New Testament Use of the Old Testament', pp. 132 ff.)

Christ and Israel (2: 22-24). Peter appealed to the personal knowledge of the Palestinian Jews when he spoke of the ministry of Jesus of Nazareth, whose mighty works showed that he was attested by God as His messenger to Israel (22). The terrible responsibility for the rejection of such a Man fell squarely on the shoulders of the inhabitants of Jerusalem: **this Jesus . . . you crucified and killed by the hands of lawless men.** But their unreasoning hatred became the instrument for the fulfilment of the divine plan established in the foreknowledge of God.

The Resurrection (2: 24-32). The apostles were above all 'witnesses to the resurrection' (1: 22) and Peter states: **God raised him up,** for the Prince of life could not be held down by the pangs of death (24). The shameful verdict of the Sanhedrin was reversed by Omnipotence.

Both Peter and Paul (13: 35) appeal to Ps. 16 as a prophecy of the Resurrection. Much of the psalm expressed David's own experiences, but certain elements—as in all the messianic psalms—could only be fulfilled in his greater Son. Note especially the phrase: **For thou wilt not . . . let thy Holy One see corruption** (27, 29). As a prophet David saw that the resurrection life of his descendant would be the means of fulfilling the covenant (29-31; cf. 2 Sam. 7: 12-17; Ps. 89: 3, 4, 26-37; 132: 11-18).

The exaltation of Christ (2: 33-35). The verb **raised up** of 2: 32 refers to the resurrection to which the apostles bore witness, but it leads directly to the exaltation of the Messiah as prophesied in Ps. 110: 1. Peter has not forgotten the original theme, and relates the outpouring of power witnessed by the multitude that day to the fact of Christ's exaltation. David did not rise from the dead, nor did he ascend into heaven to be exalted to a throne of glory, so that Ps. 110: 1 must refer to another. **Sit at my right hand, till I make thy enemies a stool for thy feet** presupposed a completed task and then a period of waiting—not divorced from activity—until the final triumph over the enemy is achieved.

The appeal (2: 36). Prophecy and contemporary facts had been welded into a strong argument which was the basis of a direct appeal to **all the house of Israel.** God had constituted Jesus, the crucified one, both Lord and Messiah for His people, despite their tragic rebellion.

iii. The First Christian Church (2: 37-47)

Repentance and baptism (2: 37-41). They (37) refers to those who received the word, crying, **what shall we do?** Peter's answer is cogent and clear in the light of other Scriptures, for repentance, 'a change of mind and attitude', is the negative aspect of that faith in Christ which is clearly implied. Baptism in itself could not procure the forgiveness of sins and the reception of the Holy Spirit, but was the outward sign of a new attitude which abjured the crime of the great rejection and placed the confessors on the side of the Messiah. **In the name of Jesus Christ** (38) shows that the converts confessed Jesus as Messiah and participated in the fulness of their Lord and Saviour.

By the phrase **to all that are far off** (39) Peter understood the dispersed as well as Palestinian Jews, and the promise was for the humble-minded who escaped from the **crooked generation** of rebellious Israel, forming a faithful remnant of witnesses.

The foundation of the church (2: 41). Peter could have used Paul's description of his church building: 'like a skilled master builder I laid the foundation . . . for no other can anyone lay than that is laid, which is Jesus Christ' (1 C. 3: 10, 11). The word was faithfully preached and received by a large number of believers who were then baptized and added to the church. It has been objected that 3,000 people could not have been baptized by immersion in Jerusalem. Nothing, however, is said about the time taken or the number of persons employed in the task. Around the city there were plenty of places for ceremonial ablutions, and there were also many irrigation pools.

The practices of the church (2: 42). This verse sums up succinctly the main elements of the life and activity of the Jerusalem church: (*a*) **Perseverance in the apostles' teaching.** The apostles were called upon not only to witness to the world but also to teach the Christian family. At this stage the teaching would be mainly the reiteration of the facts of the ministry, death and resurrection of Christ seen in the light of OT prophecy. We must think of the large company divided into groups for such instruction by the apostles and their helpers. This 'oral tradition'—in the right sense—was to give rise to the written material we find in the Gospels and opened the way for the further revelations of the Letters. (*b*) **Fellowship** (*koinōnia*) indicates an openhearted sharing in which each believer gave to others what he had himself received, whether of spiritual or material blessings (see its basis in 1 Jn 1: 1-4). (*c*) **The breaking of bread** in this context is equivalent to the Lord's Supper (taken as part of a common meal), as only a fundamental activity of the church would be put alongside **teaching** and **prayers.** The solemnity of our Lord's charge, 'Do this in memory of me', in the shadow of the cross would lead to speedy obedience once the church was formed. (*d*) **The prayers.** The emphasis is on collective prayer, for in times of the plenitude of the Spirit there

is always a glad recognition of the spiritual profit and blessing flowing from joint praises and petitions. A church lacking these features is in danger of spiritual decay.

Outward influence and spiritual unity (2: 43-47). The outward influence of the church was seen in a widespread awe, in the performance of miracles and in the addition to the company of those whom God was saving (43, 47). The great features of the inner life of the church were joy in the Lord, the community of goods, fellowship, and meetings in the temple courts (44-46). Believers were so near the cross and the resurrection and so filled with the Spirit, that for a while selfishness was swallowed up in love. It was thus easy to sell possessions and think of the good of all. In this way arose the 'church-community' of Jerusalem, which, considered as an experiment, was of a temporary nature; it lent itself only to a peculiar set of circumstances which did not persist and were not reproduced elsewhere. In later years the church in Jerusalem was chronically poor, and the difficulties of distribution are illustrated in 6: 1. Considered as an example of love, however, the community has much to teach us. The increase (47) was the natural result of the spiritual state of the church.

III. THE NAME OF THE LORD JESUS IN JERUSALEM (3: 1-5: 42)
i. The Power of the Name (3: 1-10)
The first stage of the plan—the evangelization of Jerusalem—was quite hopeless if the Twelve had to measure themselves against the Sanhedrin and the dominant high-priestly party, backed in a last resort by Rome. But their Master had promised that they should do 'greater works' in His name because He went to the throne of God to administer a completed mission, and His name is His own authority manifested through His servants (Jn 14: 12-26). They spoke and prayed in the name, but in this section it is very important to note that they performed miracles in the name, as this power provided them with both credentials and protection until the rebellious capital had been filled with the message of the crucified and risen Messiah. Over against the carnal power of the Jewish rulers, God appointed another 'power' through the name which turned the weakness of the apostles into spiritual strength and dignity.

The healing of the lame man (3: 1-10). The **ninth hour** (3 p.m.) was that of national prayer associated with the evening sacrifice. Peter and John worshipped as Israelites with no sense of a need to break away from the temple.

The details of the healing stress the hopeless lameness of the temple beggar and the material poverty of the apostles. But the name was there, and by its power the man's feet and ankles were strengthened so that he could enter the Temple courtyard leaping and praising God. (For details of the setting see *NBD, art.* 'Temple'.)

Despite the fact that Palestinian Jews had been very familiar with our Lord's healing work, the worshippers in the temple were **filled with wonder and amazement** (10). The wonder-worker had been crucified, but a similar power to his was still working in Jerusalem!

ii. Peter's Second Speech (3: 11-26)

The setting. The audience was entirely Jewish and was found in the temple courts—the visible centre of their religious life. The Christology is messianic, with close links with the OT, as is natural at this stage.

The source of the power (3: 12, 13). Peter passes at once from the people's astonishment to the beginnings of the race—Abraham's call and God's covenant with him—for power through the name of Jesus was directly related to the purposes of the God of Abraham.

The titles of the Messiah. The Christology of the period is especially revealed by the names applied to the Saviour in this speech and in the following verses. **Servant** (or 'Child') in 3: 13, 26; 4: 27, translates *pais* and links with the 'Servant Songs' of Isa. 42-53. The **Holy One** (14) links with 4: 27 and was known even to demons (Mk 1: 24). The **Righteous One** (14) is used by Stephen (7: 52), by Ananias (22: 14) and by John (1 Jn 2: 1), expressing one important aspect of the person and work of the Messiah. **The Author of life** (15) is in striking contrast with the Jerusalemites' choice of **a murderer** (see also Heb. 2: 10; 12: 2). **That prophet** (23) fulfils Moses' prophecy in Dt. 18: 15, 16. A little later the apostles were to speak of 'the Lord's Anointed' (4: 26). Each title focused messianic prophecy fully on the person of Jesus of Nazareth. At this stage there is no reference to the pre-incarnation Son and Creator as in Phil. 2: 6-11; Col. 1: 15-20; Jn 1: 1-3; Heb. 1: 1-3.

The Jews' verdict and God's verdict (3: 13-15). The glorious titles of the Messiah emphasize the guilt of those who rejected Him. God's work in resurrection, witnessed to by the Twelve, reversed the shameful verdict of the Sanhedrin.

Healing by 'faith in the name' (3: 16). However awkwardly the best Greek text reads here, it certainly emphasizes the saving inter-relations between the name and the faith of the healed man who was the 'living text' of this discourse.

Repent! (3: 17-21). Although Peter seems to allow some excuse for ignorance, yet only sincere repentance could blot out the crime of rejecting the Messiah and make possible His return in blessing. The phrases of 19-21 must be interpreted in the light of the many prophecies of blessings on Israel and the nations in the coming kingdom. It would be absurdly anachronistic to suppose that Peter was applying them to the church by a spiritualizing method!

The prophets and the Prophet (3: 22-26). Moses' prophecy of Dt. 18: 15, 16 may be interpreted as God's raising up of true prophets in general, but some Jews (especially the Qumran community) certainly considered it as in some sense messianic (cf. Jn 1: 21b; 6: 14) and the same concept is underlined in Heb. 1: 1. **Samuel** is important as inaugurating a prophetic period in which 'schools' of the prophets maintained a witness in Israel. The Jews were **the sons of the prophets and of the covenant** (25) in the Hebrew sense of having a close participation in the covenant and prophecy leading to messianic blessings (26). But their portion might either be lost by incredulity or confirmed if they received the Servant God had raised up—as He had previously raised up Moses. **God . . . sent him to you first, to bless you in turning every one of you from your wickedness.** It was a national question, for Christ was sent to the chosen people. It was a moral question, needing repentance. It was a personal question for each one needed to receive the personal Saviour.

iii. The First Collision with Official Judaism (4: 1-22)

Peter and John arrested (4: 1-4). The temple area was controlled by the priests, and the dignity of the captain of the temple (the *sagan*) was second only to that of the high priest. Pending trial, those who **were . . . proclaiming in Jesus the resurrection from the dead** were put into custody in the lock-up under the control of the *sagan*. The dominant party was Sadducean in doctrine, hating the idea of resurrection. In the meantime two thousand more souls had been added to the church, making a total of 5,000 (4).

The trial (4: 5-22). Here we have the first post-pentecostal collision of the two 'powers': that of the Jewish 'establishment' and that of the name of the risen Lord. (For the constitution of the Sanhedrin see *NBD, art.* 'Sanhedrin'.) Peter and John stood where their Master had stood, being accused—presumably on the basis of Dt. 13: 1-5—of having employed unauthorized methods of healing, invoking the name of one recently convicted of 'blasphemy'. The accusation gave Peter a wonderful opening for witness before the authorities, which he used to the full in the power of the Holy Spirit.

The healed man was present as a living text proclaiming the essential goodness of the work performed (9, 21, 22). The power was well known, for it was that of Jesus of Nazareth, crucified by those judges but raised by God's power. The judges were the foolish builders of Ps. 118: 22 and all salvation was through **the name** (8–12).

Men from the school of Jesus (4: 13). The rulers' estimate of Peter and John as 'uneducated laymen' reflects the spiritual pride of the professionals in theology, but does not mean what many readers of the AV suppose. The skill and power of Peter's defence were admitted, but as the apostles had not been trained in rabbinical schools, their obvious capacity was due to their training in the 'unofficial school' of Jesus.

The Sanhedrin's decree (4: 14–18, 21, 22). The hands of the rulers were tied by the 'evidence' of the healed man and by the enthusiasm of the multitude. In secret session they decided that it was unwise to condemn the apostles to flogging or death, but they did decide that speaking and teaching in the name of Jesus was to be prohibited. The seriousness of the decree must not be underestimated, as any future preaching became an act of defiance against the supreme Jewish tribunal. War was declared between the earthly authority of the Sanhedrin and the divine authority of the Name.

Peter declares a basic principle (4: 19–22). The rabbis themselves justified civil disobedience in certain circumstances if a superior divine command could be proved. Peter appealed to such a command to justify the declaration of what they had seen and heard.

iv. God's Plan and the Disciples' Prayer (4: 23–31)
The apostles and the Christian family (4: 23). The apostles returned to the Christian family and their information, seen in the light of the prophetic word, became the basis of intelligent and powerful prayer (cf. 1: 14).

Characteristics and results of the prayer (4: 24–31). This is a wonderful model for prayer in times of persecution, being unanimous and empowered by the Spirit. It was appropriately addressed to the **Sovereign Lord** for He was able to suppress the wrath of the Jerusalem rulers and carry out His plan until final triumph was achieved. Ps. 2 is a 'key' portion of prophecy showing that God will establish the kingdom in the hands of His Anointed despite the confederated wrath of peoples and rulers. The disciples saw the crisis of the cross as a 'sample' both of the great rebellion against God's **holy servant Jesus**

and of the way in which God caused the rebels **to do whatever thy hand and thy plan had predestined to take place** (28). With such confidence in God's providence they only needed to present the threats of the Sanhedrin before their Sovereign Lord to make a twofold plea: (*a*) for boldness in witness; (*b*) for renewed manifestations of power **through the name** (29, 30).

The experience of v. 31 was not another 'baptism of the Spirit', but a renewed manifestation of His power among believers entirely surrendered to God's will. The prayer was answered, as is noted here and in the succeeding passages.

v. Unanimity and Grace (4: 32–37)
The Christian community described in these verses would appear to the Jews as a special sect of Judaism, rather like that of Qumran, except that it had its centre in the heart of Jerusalem and gave an aggressive testimony, in marked contrast to the passive separation of the Essenes. For the 'church-community' see notes on 2: 43–47. In 4: 32 Luke underlines the inwardness of the fellowship which sprang from **one heart and soul**—that of the closely knit spiritual body in Jerusalem.

Barnabas. While great grace was upon them all, and no one laid claim to his own possessions (4: 32, 33), every general movement is better understood by a concrete example, so Barnabas is mentioned. He also stands out in dramatic contrast to Ananias and Sapphira and his name prepares the way for further developments in the future (11: 22 ff.). The apostolic testimony was especially to the fact of the resurrection (4: 33).

vi. Power for Judgment: Ananias and Sapphira (5: 1–11)
The historic moment. Very many Christians, nominal or otherwise, have committed Ananias's sin and have not fallen down dead, but let us remember: (*a*) That he and his wife sinned against the bright light of the almost perfect testimony of the early Church; (*b*) that God often shows His disapproval openly when sins besmirch the beginnings of a new stage of His witness in the world, so that all who follow may, at least, know His mind on the matter (see Achan, Jos. 7; Nadab and Abihu, Lev. 10: 1–7).

The voluntary nature of giving. Peter's statement in 5: 4 shows clearly that no pressure was brought to bear on believers to induce them to sell their properties or to bring the sale price to the common fund. Presumably the couple could have stated that they wished to keep back a part of the price, when the other part would have been accepted.

The nature of the sin. Whether Ananias and Sapphira were carnal Christians or 'mere professors' cannot be determined and does not affect the case. They wanted to stand before the church as equal to Barnabas in faith and generosity, and such seekers after human glory fall under the Lord's strong condemnation (Jn 5: 44). Not only so, but they were prepared deliberately to plan means whereby they could keep their financial reserves in secret and still acquire the reputation they craved. This meant an acted lie, which Sapphira, at least, was prepared to back up by a deliberate untruth (5: 8). Let no one marvel that divine disapproval should have been manifested by immediate judgment in days of the plenitude of the Spirit of holiness. The lie was to God (and to the Holy Spirit, who is God) although they wished to act their part before men. The 'agreeing together' to tempt the Spirit of the Lord was especially heinous, as the sin links back to that of rebellious Israel in the wilderness—the sin of 'seeing how far a man can go' with his cravings and desires in opposition to God and in His very presence (Mt. 4: 7; Exod. 17: 2; Dt. 6: 16).

The judgment and its effects (5: 5, 6, 10, 11). From the point of view of the Christian company the death of Ananias and Sapphira was a drastic example of 1 C. 5: 7—an act of discipline in order that the 'fresh dough' of the early church might yet continue unleavened. It must not be deduced that sickness and death among the Lord's people are always directly related to some special sin, as discipline through trials may be the special experience of those who follow the way of holiness (Heb. 12: 4-11). In exceptional cases there are such visitations for the health of the local church (1 C. 11: 30).

The name was shown to be powerful, not only for witness and healing, but also for judgment, and the fear which came upon the church and others was entirely salutary.

vii. A Climax of Blessing Through the Name (5: 12-16)

A period of many miracles (5: 12, 15, 16). The prayer of 4: 30 was abundantly answered, and the scenes in Jerusalem in this climax of apostolic witness remind us of the heyday of our Lord's ministry in Galilee and of Paul's ministry by works and word in Ephesus, at a later date (19: 11). Peter's shadow and Paul's handkerchiefs were unimportant in themselves, but served as a medium for faith, analogous to the mud with which Jesus anointed the eyes of the blind man (Jn 9: 6, 7). The blessing was shared by neighbouring towns (16).

None of the rest dared join them (13). This difficult phrase may well be understood in relation to the normal meetings of the believers in Solomon's Portico. Read as NEB: 'They used to meet by common consent in Solomon's cloister, no one from outside their number venturing to join them.' That is, worshippers passing by kept away from the Nazarene throng unless they were of those being added to the church.

viii. The Second Clash with the Sanhedrin (5: 17-42)

An impossible situation (17, 18, 22). The power of the name, manifested in many works of healing, preserved the apostles and gave them tremendous popularity and prestige in Jerusalem. The situation was similar to that following the resuscitation of Lazarus (Jn 11: 47-53) when the rulers had either to believe—which they would not do—or decide on desperate measures of violence, despite the danger from the mob. All the apostles seem to have been thrown into **the common prison**—presumably by the *sagan* (see 4: 1).

Deliverance for witness (19-26). The deliverance effected by the angel was for further witness, not for escape to safety, as is made clear by the command of v. 20—the message of life must be proclaimed, and in the temple itself, centre of the enemies' territory! This surprising intervention adds greatly to the guilt of the judges who were **much perplexed** but continued to sin against so clear a light (21-26).

The accusation (27, 28). The apostles were accused of rebellious defiance of an official decree (4: 18), with the addendum—clearly reflecting the uneasy consciences and hidden fears of those who dared sentence Jesus Christ—that they were plotting to avenge the death of their Master. Notice how the high priest—with mingled scorn and fear—speaks of **this man's blood.**

The defence and witness of the apostles (29-32). Peter speaks with and for the Twelve, and his brief discourse is a marvel of cogency and clarity. '**We must obey God rather than men**' links back to Peter's words at the end of the former trial (4: 19, 20). Then, as in all trials before that tribunal, the accused became the accusers of the guilty judges. Two great facts were first asserted: God **raised** up **Jesus** in fulfilment of His promises, but the rulers had hanged Him upon the shameful **tree** (*xylon*). Two sublime titles, **Leader and Saviour,** belong to Jesus in this messianic exaltation (31) (cf. Dan. 7: 13, 14; Ps. 110: 1). A double gift comes from the hands of the exalted Messiah for Israel—**repentance . . . and forgiveness of sins.** Naturally, what was given potentially needed to be received subjectively. Two witnesses guaranteed the historic facts of God's work through Jesus whom He had raised up, for the **Holy Spirit** confirmed the witness of the apostles (32). The speech concludes with a reference to Pentecost—God **has given** the Holy Spirit **to those who obey him** by submitting to His Son.

Luke probably gives only the main points of Peter's witness, but even so it is a model for public utterance. Its very cogency aroused the homicidal rage of the Sanhedrin judges in general (33) but God willed a gracious extension of opportunity to Jerusalem.

Gamaliel's counsel (34-39). Gamaliel, the teacher of Saul of Tarsus, was the leader of the more liberal sector of the Pharisees, and his learning was so appreciated that he received the honourable appellation of the 'Rabban', 'our teacher'. In private session he makes a plea for moderation in typically Pharisaic terms. In support of this he adduces two examples of self-appointed 'messiahs' whose factions were destroyed by the Romans (not mentioned by name) and who were slain. The **Theudas** of 5: 36 cannot be the false messiah of the same name mentioned by Josephus as his rising took place at a date later than that of this trial. The name was common, and there must have been a former rebel called Theudas. **Judas the Galilean** led a dangerous revolt in A.D. 6 opposing a census ordered by Quirinius, governor of Syria. (This is not the census mentioned in Lk. 2: 1.) The Zealot movement, ready to oppose Rome by violence, sprang from Judas's rebellion. In 5: 38, 39, Gamaliel draws the moral from these incidents: leave the Nazarenes alone, for if the movement is of man **it will fail;** should it be of God the Sanhedrin could not overthrow it, and might be found 'fighting against God'.

The moderation of Gamaliel stands out pleasantly against the unreasoning hate of his colleagues, but his arguments are weak and his position untenable. How much more evidence did the leaders of the nation need in order to determine if Christ and His work were of God or the devil? We are reminded of the Lord's challenge to the Pharisees in Mt. 21: 23-27. It was no moment for halting between two opinions, and blindness is evidenced not only by aggressive opposition to the truth, but also by failure to act on it when it is revealed.

Suffering and witness (5: 40-42). With tremendous inconsistency the Sanhedrin accepted Gamaliel's advice but proceeded to have the apostles beaten, reiterating the prohibition to speak in the name. The beating would be the Jewish 'forty strokes save one' (Dt. 25: 3).

The disciples did not resign themselves to suffering, but rejoiced **to suffer dishonour for the name** in the place where their Lord had been condemned (cf. Phil. 1: 29). At the same time they continued to obey the higher authority, and **did not cease teaching and preaching Jesus as the Christ.**

IV. TIMES OF TRANSITION AND STEPHEN'S WITNESS (6: 1-8: 1a)

i. An Administrative Problem Solved (6:1-7)
General considerations. The appointment of the Seven has been traditionally understood as the establishment of a permanent 'order of deacons' in the church, devoted to its material needs. Doubtless the incident before us coloured popular ideas about the diaconate at a later date, but we must remember: (*a*) the need arose in the Jerusalem church-community which was not to be the model for future local churches; (*b*) although the verb *diakoneō* appears, the Seven are not called deacons; (*c*) the only two administrators of whom we read anything apart from their names and functions in this section— Stephen and Philip—became known for ministries different from their function here. We get the impression of a situation arising from the temporary communal life of the Jerusalem church, the problem of the Hellenistic widows being dealt with in a practical and spiritual fashion. General lessons of corporate living and service stand out clearly, but no fixed model is imposed on future local churches. The atmosphere is Jewish, and this must modify deductions based on this passage as to the election of church officers; the modern democratic principle of 'one man, one vote' would be entirely anachronistic in this setting. In the OT, apart from the priestly function, determined by descent, God Himself chose His servants, often by the means of others already tried and proved. Elders were men of experience and judgment and no decisions were cast back on a mere number of 'members'. The **brethren** addressed in v. 3 were perhaps outstanding men who could discern the spirituality and capacity of their companions, presenting suitable men to the apostles. The **multitude** could approve, but not direct (5). The second **they** of v. 6 refers to the apostles who took the final responsibility and identified themselves with the Seven by the laying on of hands.

The **Hellenists** (Greek-speaking Jews) in the church come into prominence here, as they will be God's instruments for initiating the second and third stages of the programme of evangelization.

Differing ministries (6: 1-6). The language difficulty—some of the disciples were Aramaic-speaking and some Greek-speaking—must have caused real difficulties of administration and the needs of the Hellenistic widows had been overlooked. Up to that time the Twelve had received all the voluntary offerings and had been responsible for their distribution among thousands of believers. The complaint showed that a devolution of ministries was necessary. It was not right that the specific ministry of the Twelve should be subordinated to administrative work (2, 4) and so help was needed. But administration was a delicate matter affecting the well-being of the whole church, so that this humble service required a good reputation, wisdom, and, above all, a manifestation of spiritual power (3). The brethren who helped in the selection of suitable men (3, 5) would naturally bear these conditions in mind, and also, very wisely, thought of presenting Hellenistic helpers, as is shown by the names of the Seven. There could thus be no further thought of favouritism in favour of the **Hebrews** (Aramaic-speaking believers). Stephen is especially noted as a **man full of faith and of the Holy Spirit** (5) and the wise and practical proceedings were accompanied by prayer (6).

The climax of testimony in Jerusalem (6: 7). Luke again interrupts his story for a moment to sum up the results of past witness; indeed, v. 7 denotes both the zenith and the end of the 'prosperous' period of the evangelization of Jerusalem and we may suppose that everyone in the city had had an opportunity of hearing and believing the message. The word increased, the number of disciples was multiplied and even **a great many of the priests were obedient to the faith.** The future testimony of these priests is not revealed, and it must be remembered that no one had been taught that Christians must give up their Jewish customs.

ii. Stephen's Witness Determines a Crisis (6: 8-7: 1)
Transition and crisis. As the implications of the Christian *kerygma* became increasingly apparent, and as the multitude grew accustomed to miracles, a reaction against the disciples was bound to come. It actually centred round Stephen and originated among the Hellenistic Jews who had returned to Jerusalem, meeting in their own synagogues.

Stephen and his message (6: 8-15). Stephen was full of the Spirit, of wisdom, **grace and power,** being empowered by God to work miracles among the people (3, 5, 8). As a Hellenist, he found his sphere of witness in the Greek-speaking synagogues, with special mention of that **of the Freedmen.** This may have included the Cyrenians, Alexandrians and Cilicians (9). Saul of Tarsus would possibly

attend the same synagogue, although indeed he was no Hellenist but a 'Hebrew born of Hebrews' (Phil. 3: 5).

Stephen's ministry was so powerful that his opponents despaired of victory in discussion and resorted to plots and violence. What was his message? It doubtless included the elements common to the *kerygma* presented to Jews but the accusations levelled against him, with the terms of his own defence (6: 11, 13 with ch. 7), make it probable that his preaching emphasized the new life of the gospel in a way which clashed with official Judaism. The accusations, as such, were false, yet the instigators would take care that they bore some resemblance to the truth. The similarity of these charges to those adduced in the trial of Jesus is striking. Stephen was said to have used **blasphemous words against Moses and God;** before the Sanhedrin he was alleged to have stated that Jesus of Nazareth would **destroy** the temple and **change the customs** attributed to Moses (11, 14). We may gather that he stressed the tremendous 'novelty' of the new creation founded on the death and resurrection of Christ, with the relative unimportance of the material types which foreshadowed the great reality.

Stephen's trial (6: 12 ff.). The Hellenistic fanatics were successful in getting the high priest to convoke the Sanhedrin once more. Whether the Roman governor was absent from his province (as some have thought) or not, the political position was favourable to the high-priestly caste, who would note a change of attitude in the multitude. Perhaps Caiaphas saw in the incident the possibility of a flanking attack against the Nazarene sect which did not directly involve the redoubtable apostles. Stephen went much farther than they did in emphasizing the clean break with the old order implied by the work of Christ. The official accusation would reflect the false witness already noted, and then Stephen, his face shining with celestial light (15), was allowed to speak in his own defence (7: 1).

iii. Stephen's Defence (7: 2-53)
Stephen's method. At first sight a long extract from Israel's history seems a strange means of 'defence' against the charges noted in 6: 11, 14, but (a) it assured a hearing for the message, as the judges could not cut short a summary of their sacred history; (b) it appealed to the valid Hebrew concept that God reveals Himself by what He does in history and not only by what He proclaims through the prophets. Stephen's hearers were to understand the diversity of God's self-revelation as **the God of glory** (2) and to see their own crime prefigured in the behaviour of national leaders who had

repeatedly rejected both divine revelation and the men God had raised up to further His purposes.

The experience of Abraham (2-8). The title **the God of glory** links on to the vision granted to Stephen before his martyrdom (55, 56). It is significant that Abraham knew God and submitted to His commands in distant lands, first in Ur and afterwards in Haran. The land was promised, but God's providential purposes were variously fulfilled before it was occupied by the Israelites.

The experience of Joseph (9-16). God revealed some of His purposes to faithful Joseph, but the patriarchs, moved by jealousy, resisted them, though God turned their evil into good. The point is that Joseph, rejected by his brethren and exalted by pagan Pharaoh, became the means of his family's salvation in time of famine. As a result the nation was multiplied outside Palestine. The parallel with the rejected Messiah is complete. The reference to **seventy-five souls** (14) differs from the computation of Gen. 46: 27 and Exod. 1: 5, but agrees with the LXX, the reading of which appears in an early Hebrew manuscript of Exodus from Qumran. The exact number would depend on the inclusion or exclusion of Joseph's family and on the number of his children. The reference to the burial place of the Hebrew fathers (16) presents a difficulty, as Jacob was buried at Hebron, in the cave of Machpelah which Abraham bought from Ephron the Hittite (Gen. 23: 16 with 49: 29 ff.), while Joseph was buried in Shechem, in the property bought by Jacob **from the sons of Hamor. They were carried back** generalizes the situation and we have an obvious conflation of the two purchases, one carried out by Abraham directly and the other mediately through his descendant Jacob. We must remember the strong sense of racial solidarity among the Hebrews, and that Stephen is speaking extempore.

The experience of Moses in Egypt (17-29). The theme is still God's purposes and the blindness of Israel. Despite the apparent failure of the promises during the Egyptian captivity, God saved Moses from death and had him trained in the Egyptian court. Moses' spiritual experiences are summed up in Heb. 11: 24-26, but here we glimpse his plan for delivering his people, perhaps by using his position and influence. His overtures were scornfully rejected by the Hebrews. The man who thrust him aside represents the many rejectors, down to the time of Caiaphas himself.

The experience of Moses as the leader of the people (30-41). The theme of the self-revelation of the God of glory is very clear in the reference to the **flame of fire in a bush** (30), which turned Horeb into **holy ground** (33). The Israelites had said: **Who made you a ruler . . . ?** but after forty years God said to Moses: **now come, I will send you.** The **angel** is practically identified with Jehovah, as in Exod. 3: 2 ff.

The whole of the Exodus is summed up in v. 36, and a further criminal rejection of God's instrument is noted in 39-41 when the people set up the golden calf at the foot of the mount where God manifested His presence.

The 'Prophet' prediction of Dt. 18: 15-18 (cf. Ac. 3: 22 f.) throws the consummation of God's purpose forward, beyond Moses and the system he was led to establish, and is a partial answer to the accusation of 6: 11. Moses, as God's mouthpiece, proclaimed the **living oracles,** which were broken by the sinning people. Were their descendants any more obedient to the witness of Moses? Was it Stephen who spoke blasphemous words against him, or did the Sanhedrin deny him by their acts as their fathers had done?

The temple theme (42-50). Amos's strong denunciation of apostates went back to the seemingly ideal conditions of the tabernacle worship in the wilderness (Am. 5: 25-27). The **tent of witness** (44) was made according to the pattern, but what was the internal spiritual condition of the people? **The book of the prophets** (42) means the Twelve Minor Prophets; Stephen quotes from the LXX, except that 'beyond Damascus' becomes **beyond Babylon,** in the light of the Babylonian exile.

The 'sanctuary' story is summed up in 44-50, and is related to the accusation of 'speaking words against this holy place' (6: 13). Stephen recognizes the divine origin of the tabernacle and of the temple which replaced it, but in line with the highest OT revelation, he sees the material 'dwelling' as a figure and promise of a final spiritual reality. The witness of the throne and temple in the reigns of David and Solomon was effective and widespread according to the terms of Solomon's inaugural prayer, which evidences a clear vision both of the infinitude of the Creator and of the universal significance of the house (2 Chr. 6: 12-33). But the generation which rejected the Christ had become carnally proud of its privileges and particularist in its outlook. For them the quotation from Isa. 66: 1, 2 was especially fitting.

Stephen accuses his judges (51-53). Perhaps Stephen had something more to say about the revelation of the glory 'in the face of Jesus Christ', but signs of impatience among the judges may have warned him to get quickly to his peroration. Realizing that he would not be granted a fair trial, he was led by the Spirit to pronounce a solemn 'woe' on the leaders who had rejected both the Christ Himself and the loving invitation to repentance given by the risen Christ through the apostles. Their 'circumcision' was meaningless, for it did not affect heart or ear (cf. Dt. 10: 16; Jer. 4: 4; etc.); they had resisted the strivings of the Holy Spirit even more persistently than their fathers, for their predecessors had martyred the prophets, and they had betrayed and murdered **the Righteous One** (cf. 3: 14; 22: 14), theme of prophetic promises. Claiming to be the guardians of the law, they were really chief among its transgressors. On this note the widespread testimony in Jerusalem was brought to a close, and the lament over the city was heard once more (Lk. 13: 34, 35; 19: 41-44).

iv. Stephen's Martyrdom (7: 54-8: 1a)
The rage of the judges (54). RV 'they were cut to the heart' is more expressive than RSV **they were enraged** and preserves the metaphor behind *diapriō*. Stephen's words had revealed their fanaticism, rebellion and hypocrisy, and as they would not repent they raged against him with a vehemence more suited to a lynching than to proceedings before a court of law (57, 58). Some remnants of respect for procedure are seen in that the witnesses throw the first stones (cf. Lev. 24: 14) and Saul seems to have presided over the lapidation (58).

Stephen's vision (55, 56). The glory had departed from Jerusalem and was centred **at the right hand of God** where Stephen saw **the Son of man standing** to receive him (cf. Lk. 12: 8). The relation between the vision and the theme of the speech must not be missed. Cf. Christ's own testimony before the same tribunal based on Dan. 7: 13, 14 (Mt. 26: 64-66).

Stephen's prayers and death (59, 60). Pilate was probably in Caesarea and faced with so many problems that Caiaphas and his associates felt it safe to take matters into their own hands, having Stephen stoned with no appeal for Rome's confirmation. Death by stoning was a dreadful proceeding, but less shameful than crucifixion. Stephen's first prayer was analogous to his Master's last: **Lord Jesus, receive my spirit,** with obvious reference to the vision, which may have persisted to the end. His final prayer was like Christ's first petition from the cross: **Lord, do not hold this sin against them.** The leaders were perpetrating one more heinous crime, but Stephen longed for the blessing of the nation, despite this (cf. Rom. 9: 1-5).

Luke's simple and telling phrases stress the dramatic contrast between the cruel violence of the stoning and the inner peace and joy of the martyr and intercessor who **fell asleep** on earth in order to join his Lord in heaven.

Saul of Tarsus is named (7: 58; 8: 1a). The mention of Saul as presiding over the lapidation links the martyrdom to the first general persecution of the church, and, indirectly, to the subsequent phase of evangelization led by the former persecutor. He appears as an enemy, but 'the kicking against the goads' of conscience doubtless began as he listened to Stephen's testimony and saw his triumphal end. Saul was already a leader of Pharisaic Judaism (8: 1; 9: 1, 2; 22: 5; 26: 10; Gal. 1: 14), and, as he voted death sentences against the Nazarenes, he may have been a member of the Sanhedrin, despite his relative youth.

V. PERSECUTION AND EXPANSION (8: 1b-9: 43)
i. The Second Stage of Christian Witness (8: 1b-25)
The anonymous evangelists (8: 1b-4). Jerusalem had been thoroughly evangelized under the protection of the name, but Palestine was to hear the word by the lips of those who were scattered throughout its area by the fierce persecution raging in Jerusalem. Thus 'God fulfils Himself in many ways' and brings His purposes to pass through the wrath of men. We reach the second stage of the programme of 1: 8—'all Judea and Samaria'.

It is impossible to overstate the importance of individual witness in the spread of the gospel. Philip is mentioned later as God's messenger to Samaria, but **those who were scattered went about preaching the word** (4). Hundreds of anonymous evangelists were preaching the gospel to thousands of souls, and the message became known over the whole area. When the preaching of the word is 'professionalized', a large part of the vitality of Christian witness is lost.

A severe persecution (8: 1-4). The persecution probably affected the Hellenistic Christians much more than the Aramaic-speaking disciples, faithful to all the 'customs'. The apostles were respected, probably because some of their aura of popularity as workers of miracles persisted. The sweeping statement **they were all scattered** (1b) would probably be modified if one could see the picture in the writer's mind. The Twelve would scarcely have remained had there been no flock at all to care for, and many Hebrew Christians were found in Jerusalem later on.

Saul **laid waste the church** (3) with the fierce energy of a devastating army. The

L

details of 8: 1, 3 should be supplemented by Paul's future statements which revealed a conscience for his crimes which his future service never entirely stilled: 22: 4; 26: 9-11; 1 C. 15: 9; Gal. 1: 13; Eph. 3: 8; 1 Tim. 1: 13.

The **devout men** (2) who buried Stephen's body were probably pious Jews who could appreciate the power of the martyr's life and witness.

Philip in Samaria (8: 5-8, 12, 13). Different Greek texts give 'the city of Samaria' (AV, RV) or **a city of Samaria** (RSV; cf. NEB, 'a city in Samaria'). A smaller city and its surrounding area fits the picture better than the busy, Hellenized capital, then called Sebaste. Good seed had been sown thereabouts by the Master Himself, and some must have flourished (Jn 4: 39-42). Although a Jew, Philip was well received, being helped by the 'credentials' of his miracles (6-8). His message is beautifully described (12) as **the good news about the kingdom of God and the name of Jesus,** which links the saving work of Christ with God's overall purpose in the kingdom. Believers were baptized, but no manifest evidence of the Spirit's power was granted them at first. This does not mean that they were not regenerate.

Simon Magus (9-11, 13). Simon seems to have had special knowledge and maybe demon help, which enabled him to work certain wonders and claim to be **that power of God which is called Great.** The Samaritans worshipped Jehovah, but probably thought of Simon as a special agent of Deity: 'God's grand vizier' as someone has suggested. He was impressed by Philip's spontaneous miracles, recognizing powers superior to his own, and so **believed.** Peter's stern denunciation in 20-23 shows that he never was regenerate. His baptism is the classic example of the outward sign wrongly applied to one whose profession of faith was not genuine.

The visit of Peter and John (14-25). Why did the Spirit not 'fall upon' the Samaritan believers as He did later on the Gentiles who received the word in Caesarea (10: 44-48)? It must be remembered that the Samaritans had maintained a Jehovistic worship for centuries, divorced from Jewish witness, God's channel of salvation (Jn 4: 22). The believers 'in the name' might have desired to run their own show, carrying the schism over to the church. For that reason Peter and John—who came from the hated Jerusalem, but were Christ's commissioned apostles—arrived to inspect the work in Samaria, and, recognizing the hand of the Lord, became the means of conveying the fulness of the Spirit by prayer and an act of identification, the 'laying on of hands'. The church was thus seen to be one, and Samaritans were blessed through the only channel of Christian testimony. The normative experience was clearly the reception of the Holy Spirit when men and women believed (10: 44; 19: 2; Eph. 1: 13; 1 C. 12: 13) and nothing is elsewhere known of any apostolic 'gift' by which the Spirit was bestowed. This is the exception, and must be explained as such. (We may note, also, that it must have been just as hard for the church in Jerusalem to recognize the Samaritans, and vice versa; cf. also Peter, Ac. 10: 14.)

Simon's errors (14-24). To Simon's unregenerate eyes, the manifestation of a new power in the believers sprang from a 'magic touch'. If he had *that* in his repertory it would produce a wonderful effect on the multitudes. According to his standards, everything had its price, so that he offered to buy **the gift!** Hence the word 'simony' to describe the purchase of ecclesiastical offices. As Peter clearly saw, such a fundamental error meant that Simon was entirely foreign to the way of life. **Repent . . . pray . . . ,** said Peter, but Simon replies in effect: 'You pray for me to save me from the punishment!' (22-24), which shows that he still thought in terms of magic power and of 'influence', having no desire to draw near to God personally as a repentant sinner. An anti-Christian sect called the Simonians existed in the second century, but the traditions which connect it with this Simon are unreliable.

ii. Philip Preaches to the Ethiopian (8: 26-40) The minister of state (26-28). Ancient Ethiopia is not Abyssinia but ancient Nubia, south of Aswan, which was a highly developed area in antiquity. The king was considered as a god and retired from public view, so that active government devolved on the queen mother, who always bore the title of **Candace** (27). Her ministers would be eunuchs and among them the Chancellor of the Exchequer would be one of the most important. Jews penetrated into all lands which offered possibilities for commerce, so that the official may have heard of Jehovah, the God of Israel, through them. The long and arduous journey to Jerusalem was undertaken for **worship,** which indicates that the eunuch was at least a God-fearer. The story illustrates the great principle: 'He that seeketh findeth'. We imagine that the Ethiopian may have been disappointed in the temple ritual but the only certain thing is that he acquired a roll of the prophet Isaiah which he eagerly read as he returned home (27, 28). The reading, the Spirit's command to Philip, the meeting between the seeker and the Lord's servant illustrate very clearly God's providential workings (28, 29).

Reading and understanding (29-35). The meaning of Scripture is not always self-evident, even to the earnest seeker, and God provides those, who, having been taught themselves, are able to guide others (30, 31). The portion could not have been more suited to the Ethiopian's needs, but he echoed an ancient enquiry (34)—who was the Sufferer who overcame? The Jewish rabbis (especially of later date) sometimes thought in terms of suffering Israel; the eunuch wondered if it could be Isaiah. The sublime prediction goes far beyond the experiences of a nation or a prophet, and the Lord Himself emphatically declared that the Suffering Servant of Jehovah of Isa. 42-53 was also the triumphant Messiah (Lk. 24: 25-27, 44-47). The apostles repeatedly underscored the lesson they had learnt from the Master (2 C. 5: 21; 1 Pet. 2: 21-23; Phil. 2: 6-11). The quotation in vv. 32, 33 is from the LXX and the passage presents textual problems even in the *MT*. We can be sure that Philip included Isa. 53: 4-6 when he preached **the good news of Jesus** from this scripture. The lesson may have lasted for hours as the chariot was driven slowly on, and brought full conviction to the heart of the Nubian potentate. Jesus Christ was the Messiah, the Lamb of God, the Sinbearer!

The baptism of the Ethiopian (36-39). The sight of water—the road to Gaza crosses several river beds or wadis—suggested baptism to the new convert (37), for Philip had been faithful to the commission of Mt. 28: 19. The Ethiopian says in effect: 'Is there any requisite other than faith for baptism?' V. 37 of the AV is not in any good Greek text, but according to F. F. Bruce, the early insertion in the Western text 'certainly reflects primitive Christian practice' and constitutes the earliest known baptismal creed: 'I believe that Jesus Christ is the Son of God.' This baptism followed profession of faith. The joint descent into the water (38, 39) certainly suggests immersion.

Separation, joy and service (39, 40). This important case of conversion did not deflect Philip from his work as an evangelist which seems to have centred thenceforth on Caesarea, with special reference to the coastal area (40; cf. 21: 8). The new convert did not mourn the loss of his teacher, but rejoiced in his Saviour (39). The story is parenthetical in that it does not advance the story of the spread of the gospel westward, but shows how the good news was spread in all kinds of unlikely places during the early years. We can take it for granted that the eunuch witnessed in Nubia.

iii. Saul's Conversion and Call (9: 1-30)
Saul and his call. The Christian message was spreading over all Palestine, and before long Peter was to preach the gospel to a Gentile household, opening the door of the Kingdom to the uncircumcised. At this moment the Lord lays His hand on the Chief Inquisitor, who, in God's counsels, was to be the apostle to the Gentiles. Years were to pass before Barnabas and Saul set out on what is called the 'first missionary journey', but God commissioned his servant betimes so that he might be trained in secret before being recognized as the apostle who would complement the work of the Twelve in the Gentile world.

Long afterwards Paul spoke of God's providential workings in him from his very birth (Gal. 1: 15) for, born a Hebrew, son of Hebrew parents, trained in the best tradition of Judaism and yet a citizen of Tarsus and of the Empire, thoroughly conversant also with Hellenistic culture, he was ideally fitted to bridge East and West, bearing the message prepared and nurtured in Israel to the ends of the earth. His rare intellectual endowment was energized by a strong temperament which knew nothing of half-measures. As persecutor he was terrible, but once he had yielded obedience to Jesus the Christ, his loyalty was absolute and his service unstinting. This was God's chosen vessel, the great teaching apostle, commissioned by the glorified Lord to mark out the lines of missionary strategy and to be the principal 'steward of the mystery' of Christ and His church (Eph. 2; 3; Col. 1: 24-2: 7; 1 Tim. 1: 12-17; 2 Tim. 1: 8-12; Ac. 26: 16-20).

The conversion narratives. Luke emphasizes Paul's apostleship by giving the story of his conversion and commission three times in Acts: here, as a part of the general history; in 22: 3-16 as Paul's testimony before the Jews; in 26: 9-19 as the main element in his defence before Agrippa II. Differing purposes determine the slight differences of detail, mainly due to the degree of condensation.

A proposed extension of the persecution (1, 2). Saul breathed out threatenings against the Nazarenes after the supposed manner of fire-breathing dragons (1) and saw the danger of the spread of the 'disease' among the Jews of the Dispersion, where the Sanhedrin's influence was weaker. This body had certain extra-territorial powers over synagogues abroad, and the extradition of Jews for trial was not unknown. In Damascus some ten thousand Jews met in several synagogues, and news of the presence of Nazarenes among them had been received in Jerusalem.

Saul's rage was the more deeply inflamed by the thrusts of an uneasy conscience, which is the only explanation of his 'kicking against the goads' (26: 14). Conversions such as this are not produced in a psychological vacuum. For other references to the Christian faith as **the Way** see 18: 26; 19: 9; 22: 4; 24: 14, 22.

The encounter (3–6). The lightning-swift light (so the verb), brighter than Syria's noon-day sun, could only be the *shekinah* glory, indicative of the divine presence. From this glory came the amazing question: **Saul, Saul, why do you persecute me?** Who was the person who spoke thus? The voice from the glory could only be the voice of God; hence **Lord** in Paul's question, **Who are you, Lord?** (5), is meant as a divine title, not as a mere courtesy 'Sir'. **I am Jesus, whom you are persecuting** was the answer—a revelation which meant that, in one tremendous moment of time, Saul had to identify the Lord Jehovah of the OT whom he zealously sought to serve, with Jesus of Nazareth whom he ferociously persecuted in the person of His saints. The shock to his innermost soul was tremendous and showed itself physically in the loss of sight; but once the identification had been made Saul had no doubts or reserves, and from that time forward could truthfully say: 'For me, to live is Christ' (Phil. 1: 4). RSV preserves the true text of this narrative, but the added details of the later narratives should be noted. Paul's companions 'felt' the celestial presence but did not see the Lord; they heard Saul's voice, but not that of the Lord (7; 22: 9).

Ananias and Saul (7–19). Perhaps the three days' rest was necessary so that Saul might recover from the shock and meditate on the meaning of the celestial encounter before receiving further messages. The fact that Saul really *saw* the Lord (cf. 26: 16) is important from the point of view of his special apostleship (1 C. 9: 1; 15: 8).

Why was Ananias of Damascus chosen to convey Saul's commission (cf. 22: 14-16) instead of the apostles in Jerusalem? (a) As a Jewish Christian, who adhered to the 'customs' of Judaism, Ananias was an unimpeachable witness to the truth of Saul's call and apostleship. (b) It was fitting that Saul, the leading persecutor of the disciples, should be received into the fellowship by one of the despised Nazarenes in Damascus whom he had meant to seize. (c) An ecclesiastical reason becomes clear as we read Gal. 1: 15-2: 10, for it had to be made quite clear that Paul's apostleship was not received from men, but directly from the Lord. The intervention of Ananias supports the view that, in NT times, there was no idea of any special succession of grace flowing from the apostles. Ananias acted in a prophetic capacity, and his remonstrance (13) is not that of a stubborn servant, but is rather a sign of holy familiarity

with his Lord. The directions were clear, and he learnt that the ex-persecutor was praying, having received a further preparatory vision.

Once his doubts were removed, Ananias thoroughly identified himself with the Lord's purpose: **Brother Saul,** he said, **the Lord Jesus who appeared to you on the road . . . has sent me.** Again the 'laying on of hands' meant identification, for Saul now belonged to the people he had formerly persecuted. The scales fell from his eyes—something of symbolic import—and he received the fulness of the Spirit and was baptized (see note on 22: 16).

The terms of the commission (15, 16). For fuller detail of the commission see 26: 16-18. Even in this abbreviated account the following fundamental points stand out clearly: (a) Saul was a 'chosen vessel' especially set aside by the Lord Himself (15). (b) He was to be the Lord's standard-bearer among **the Gentiles** (cf. Rom. 11: 13)—a special 'grace' finally recognized by all (Gal. 2: 7-9). (c) He was to witness before **kings** (men in high places) which is the theme of chs. 21-28. (d) A ministry to **the sons of Israel** was not excluded, though it was to be largely rejected (22: 18). (e) He who had caused many to suffer for Christ's sake was to be made an example of suffering for Christ's sake (16).

Witness in Damascus (19-25). Damascus was the scene of Saul's first fellowship with Christians and of his first service for the Lord, and Christological depth marked his earliest messages for he heralded Jesus as **Christ** and **Son of God** (20, 22). The Jews soon perceived the danger of the witness of an outstanding theologian turned renegade, and persecution was the natural result.

The visit to Arabia (Gal. 1: 17). Paul's own story of these days (Gal. 1: 13-20) is important, and he stressed the fact that he did not receive his authority from those who were apostles before him. The visit to Arabia is mentioned in relation to that theme, and its significance is limited by it. 'Arabia' (the Nabatean kingdom) was a large, ill-defined area east of Syria and Palestine, reaching northwards from the Gulf of Akaba nearly to Damascus itself; any quiet spot where meditation was possible and revelations could continue would have suited his purpose, although the hostility of the Nabatean authorities (2 C. 11: 32) suggests that he also engaged in more active witness there. See pp. 438 f, 446.

The first visit to Jerusalem (26-30; cf. Gal. 1: 18, 19). Paul refers to this visit for the purpose already noted, while Luke is interested in it from the point of view of the spread of the gospel. Hence the difference in detail and emphasis. Saul's escape from Damascus was dramatic and humiliating (cf. 2 C. 11: 32 f.) and his reception by the saints in Jerusalem more than cool. Was the conversion story true, or was Saul's approach the action of an *agent provocateur*? Fortunately Barnabas had full knowledge of the facts, and was able to present Saul as one who had seen the Lord and witnessed in Damascus (27). Saul's hope that his witness to his old companions of the Hellenistic synagogues would be effective was not realized (cf. 22: 17-21) and a plot was soon laid to take his life. The journey to Tarsus initiates the hidden period of Saul's life during which he was probably disowned by his family and suffered the 'loss of all things' (Phil. 3: 8). It may be highly probable that he witnessed in the synagogues of Cilicia and that certain sufferings listed in 2 C. 11: 21-28 belong to this period. We do not meet him again until Barnabas sought him as a co-worker in Antioch (11: 25, 26).

iv. Peter's Apostolic Labours (9: 31-43)
Peace and prosperity (31). This *résumé* sums up the situation following Saul's conversion, when the saints in Palestine enjoyed a period of peace and prosperity. The mainspring of the persecution had been broken, while the Jews had other matters to think about, especially when Caligula insisted that his image should be set up in the temple. The danger of rebellion was only averted by the assassination of the emperor in A.D. 41. Believers, however, walking in the fear of the Lord, were multiplied. The expression **the church throughout all Judea . . .** is quite special, for everywhere else in the NT 'church' in the singular is either the whole company of the redeemed, or else a certain local church—never a federation of local churches. The exception is due to Luke's sensitiveness to historical development, for, at that moment, believers throughout Palestine still felt themselves to be members of the original Jerusalem community.

Peter's journey (32). This verse emphasizes the wide range of Peter's apostolic labours. The groups formed by anonymous witness were not left to fend for themselves but received pastoral and teaching visits from Peter, and, most probably, from other apostles and missionaries as well.

The healing of Aeneas (33-35). Lydda was on the route from Jerusalem to Joppa, where the foothills merge into the Plain of Sharon—a likely place to have received early Christian witness. Once again a miracle was God's megaphone, directing attention to a powerful and saving word. The form of address from the apostle to the sick man is very direct: **Aeneas, Jesus Christ heals you.** Peter spoke, but the Lord was present in healing power, and the

man gave proof of his faith as he arose and rolled up his pallet. **All the residents of Lydda** may be a relative term—all whose hearts were opened by the sign to receive the saving word. Quite probably, however, we are intended to envisage a mass-movement.

The raising of Tabitha (36-43). This story takes us back in spirit to the simplicity and power of the Gospel narratives of healing. We do not know exactly what the brethren of Joppa hoped for when they sent for Peter, but they knew that his presence would be a help in a moment of deep sorrow and distress. Tabitha ('Gazelle') had beautified herself by good works and her departure was much lamented (39). On his arrival Peter needed to be alone with the 'God who raises the dead', in the presence of the corpse, in order to discern His will. His prayer as he knelt reminds us of the spiritual struggles of Elijah and Elisha in similar circumstances. Peter received the assurance he sought and turned to the body with the simple command: **Tabitha, rise.** What a moment when the greathearted sister was presented again to the believers—alive! (41). The high value of Tabitha's previous testimony underlined the powerful message of the miracle and **many believed in the Lord.** By these means Peter had been led of God to the place where he was to receive new and strange marching orders, constituting one of the greatest landmarks in the history of redemption (43).

VI. GENTILES ENTER THE KINGDOM (10: 1-11: 18)
i. The Meaning of Caesarea
A crucial moment. The commission of Mt. 28: 19 includes all nations but the ultimate goal was reached by the stages we have noted already. The apostle to the Gentiles was converted and commissioned while the gospel was preached in the whole of Palestine. Peter, prepared by various experiences for the great new lesson he was to learn and teach, was now to open the door of the kingdom to the Gentiles by the only possible 'key'—the Word preached in the power of the Holy Spirit (Mt. 16: 19).

Caesarea, an extension of Pentecost. Peter expressly associates the event in Cornelius's house with that of Pentecost and with the Lord's purpose to baptize His own by the Holy Spirit, so that in Caesarea the one fundamental provision was made available to Gentile believers, as it is to each believer united by faith to the one body (1 C. 12: 12, 13).

No Jew imagined that Gentiles could not be saved, but—quite logically as far as God had then revealed His thoughts—all were convinced that Gentiles must become Jewish proselytes if they were to share in messianic blessings. God's working and revelation in this crisis made it clear to submissive hearts that the cross opened the door of salvation to all mankind on equal terms, for *all* must repent and believe in order to be saved. Jews were thus put on a level with the 'sinners of the Gentiles' (Gal. 2: 14-17).

ii. **Divine Messages and an Encounter (10: 1-33)**

Cornelius and his vision (1-8). An **Italian Cohort** is known to have served in Syria in A.D. 69. Cornelius was in command of 100 men, part of the Caesarean garrison. Centurions had the responsibilities of captains but were non-commissioned officers. Cornelius must have had some private fortune as he maintained a large establishment and gave alms generously. He was obviously a 'God-fearer', a Gentile who attended the synagogue services and modified his way of life so as not to scandalize the Jews. Above all, he is a classic example of the type of Gentile, who, in patient well-doing, sought 'for glory, honour, incorruption and eternal life' (Rom. 2: 7, 10). His prayers and alms did not gain him salvation, but were the outward signs of an attitude of soul which God could bless.

A **vision** is 'something seen' not normal to human sight, and one was granted to Cornelius as he gave himself to prayer at **the ninth hour** (cf. 3: 1). His fright was natural but he accepted the situation at once and listened carefully to the good news given by the angel. There is no sensationalism in the narrative; the exact instruction of the angel reads like an address on an envelope: Mr. Simon Peter, c/o Mr. Simon, The Tannery, Sea Road, Joppa. With military promptness Cornelius obeyed the instructions received from heaven (3-8).

Peter's vision and its confirmation (9-23). By special providences God prepared his servant Peter for the visit of Cornelius' emissaries. Peter's hunger was an element of revelation, and one may imagine that he was gazing at the elongated lateen sail of a boat entering the harbour as he waited for his food. In his trance the unclean animals he was commanded to kill and eat were gathered up in a sail-like object lowered from the sky. The command seemed all wrong, for a Jew had not only to reject the unclean animals listed in Lev. 11, but also to refuse all meat not prepared in the *kosher* manner. His protest was very 'Peter-like', but the voice repeated the command three times, with the epoch-making explanation: **'What God has cleansed, you must not call common'** (15; cf. Mk 7: 19). Voices in the street below were enquiring for Peter and at that very moment the message of the vision was confirmed

by a command given by the Lord the Spirit: 'Go with these men; **I have sent them.**' Further resistance would have been rebellion. The pieces of the jig-saw puzzle were falling into place as the apostle learnt that God had made possible the cleansing of all men (cf. 28).

The journey and the reception (24-33). Next day Peter set out northward with witnesses from Joppa and the messengers from Cornelius. The distance was about 30 miles. The reception was warm, for a company of hungry souls were waiting for God's messenger. The verb for 'worship' (25) is *proskyneō*, which can mean a man's reverence for a superior, and the sight of a Roman centurion at the feet of a Galilean fisherman was remarkable evidence of the revolutionary changes wrought within the sphere of the kingdom. The mutual explanations (27-33) are quite clear and the well-known v. 33 shows that never did a preacher have before him a better prepared audience.

iii. **Peter's Message to Gentiles (10: 34-43)**
Introduction (34, 35). The general features of the early *kerygma* are all present, but adapted to a company of Gentiles. As many were God-fearers, some reference to the prophets was possible (43), but the emphasis falls mainly on the life, death and resurrection of Jesus Christ as a historical reality witnessed to by the Twelve. In his introduction Peter shows that he had learnt the lesson of the house-top vision (34, 35).

Phases of the main message (36-43). *God's word to Israel in Christ Jesus (36-38).* The partially known facts of our Lord's earthly ministry were authoritatively interpreted for these Gentiles. Jesus Christ was **Lord of all,** the Preacher of **peace,** God's Anointed for a ministry of healing, restoration and spiritual liberty.

The apostolic witness (39-42). The apostles were **witnesses to all that he did** in Jerusalem and Palestine (=**the country of the Jews**). The tremendous significance of the death and resurrection of Christ demanded the best of proofs of the fact itself, and these were supplied by men chosen to accompany the risen Lord. The mention of the central fact of the cross is brief and undoctrinal (39), but the typical *kerygma* declaration follows: **but God raised him on the third day and made him manifest**—not publicly, but to the body of **witnesses** to which Peter belonged.

The prophetic and apostolic messages (42, 43). Peter joined the prophetic witness of the OT with the historic witness of the Twelve in order to show that Christ was ordained by God not only as final Judge of all, but also as the Saviour who gives **forgiveness of sins** to all believers. There was much more to say, but the saving facts had been announced, and were immediately received by faith.

iv. The Holy Spirit Falls on Gentile Believers (10: 44-48)

The gift of the Holy Spirit (44-46). The 'hearing' was the submission of faith which united these souls to the Lord in whom they believed. The power of the Holy Spirit fell on the believers at once, investing them with celestial energies and gifts by which they spoke with tongues and glorified God (45, 46; cf. 2: 3, 4, 11). The Pentecostal baptism was extended to Gentile believers on the sole ground of repentance and faith in Christ.

Baptism in the Name (47, 48). Peter's question (47) is a kind of challenge, addressed especially to the Jewish Christians brought from Joppa. Despite the absence of circumcision, the Gentile believers had received the Holy Spirit just as the Jewish believers had received Him in the upper room. Who could **forbid** the **water** of baptism? By that symbolic act they passed visibly to the sphere of the name, having been transferred from the realm of darkness to the kingdom of God's beloved Son (Col. 1: 13), apart from any prior link with Israel. The repercussions from Peter's decision would be felt throughout the world and for all time.

v. Reactions in Jerusalem (11: 1-18)

An inevitable question (1-3). It was natural that the **apostles and brethren who were in Judea** would want to know the meaning of the extraordinary happenings in Caesarea. 'They that were of the circumcision' (RV) is better than **the circumcision party** as such a party was formed only following these discussions. These men asked why Peter had broken the rules of ordinary Jewish living (2, 3).

Peter's defence (4-17). Peter, backed by the witnesses from Joppa, defended his action in the only way possible—by telling the story of God's dealings with him and Cornelius. The connection between Caesarea and Pentecost comes out clearly (15): **the Holy Spirit fell on them just as on us at the beginning,** and this is linked with the Master's promise based on the Baptist's prophecy (16; 1: 4, 5). All must submit to what God had clearly revealed, strange though the lesson might be.

The consequences (18). The spiritual leaders of the churches in Judea accepted the new revelation and glorified God. Many Jewish Christians, however, might hear only partial accounts of the event, which seemed to them quite insufficient to demolish the apparently inexpugnable position of Israel as presented in the OT. 'Let the message be preached to the Gentiles', they said, 'but on believing they must be circumcised and placed on the basis of the Jewish covenant.' These conservative Jewish Christians became known as the Judaizers. We shall meet them again in ch. 15 and the Letter to the Galatians is the inspired answer to their pleas, which would have reduced Christianity to the dimensions of a Jewish sect.

VII. ANTIOCH, A NEW CENTRE OF MISSIONARY ACTIVITY (11: 19-30)

An extended witness (19-21). Years had passed since the dispersion noted in 8: 1, 4, but waves of blessing still resulted from the original impetus. Jews had been reached by Hellenistic Christians in Phoenicia, Cyprus and Antioch—the great Syrian capital which bridged East and West. It may be assumed that Jewish Christians in Antioch soon heard of the great happening in Caesarea, and would thus be emboldened to preach Jesus as Lord to the Gentiles, many of whom were heartily sick of the 'gods many and lords many' of paganism. Using a Hebrew idiom, Luke tells us that **the hand of the Lord was with** the anonymous witnesses so that **a great number** of Gentiles turned to the Lord (20, 21).

Barnabas in Antioch (22-24). On hearing the news of a mass movement among the Gentiles, the Jerusalem Church neither sought to impose the authority of the 'mother church' nor did it wash its hands of an important happening. Instead the brethren sent Barnabas, the man of grace and wisdom, to see if the work was of God, and to act accordingly. He greatly helped this new church, composed of believers from Jews and Gentiles, contributing what was needed in line with the Spirit's operations.

Barnabas and Saul in Antioch (25, 26). Barnabas was humble enough to recognize his need of help in teaching, so sought and found Saul in Tarsus. A wonderful partnership in service was established, by which the church was built up. The emphasis during a year's labour was on the teaching of the word (26). So many people were now talking about Christ in Antioch that their presence was felt by the populace, who coined the nick-name 'Christians', i.e. 'Christ's men'. In early times this name was mainly used by outsiders or by enemies (26: 28; 1 Pet. 4: 16).

Barnabas and Saul in Jerusalem (27-30). Extra-biblical history mentions periods of scarcity during the reign of Claudius (A.D. 41-54), one of which especially affected Judea (28). The prophecy of Agabus stirred up loving generosity among the saints in Antioch, who knew that the Judean brethren would be the chief sufferers, so that each gave according to his ability—a principle afterwards to be established on a wider scale in 2 C. 8; 9. Barnabas and Saul were the bearers of the gift to the elders in Jerusalem.

The date of Saul's second visit to Jerusalem as a Christian is fixed in general terms as being that of the Herodian persecution (12: 1, 25) and in the writer's view cannot be made to coincide with that of Gal. 2: 1-10. The following factors should be considered: (*a*) Dates may not be changed in order to fit an *a priori* hypothesis, and that of this visit is A.D. 44. (*b*) The circumcision question did not become acute until after the great blessings of the first missionary journey (15: 1, 2). (*c*) Luke still uses the term **Barnabas and Saul** which marks the period prior to the general recognition of Paul's apostolic 'grace', which was manifested by the Spirit's working through him during the first journey. As a helper of Barnabas, he could not have defended his apostleship in the terms of Gal. 2: 1-10. The turning point is found in 13: 13. (*d*) The recommendation to 'remember the poor' of Gal. 2: 10 would sound strangely when Barnabas and Saul were in Jerusalem for the express purpose of passing on the Antiochene gift to the Judean poor. (For another view than that propounded here see notes on Gal. 2: 1-10, pp. 447 ff.)

VIII. HEROD'S ATTACK ON THE CHURCH (12: 1-25)
i. Herod, the Apostles and the Church (12: 1-17)
Herod Agrippa I. This monarch was the son of Aristobulus, fruit of Herod the Great's marriage with the Hasmonean princess, Mariamne. He was clever, charming, ambitious and unscrupulous. He was utterly loyal to Rome, having been helped by both Caligula and Claudius to wide authority in Palestine, but knew the importance of gaining the sympathy of the Jewish leaders in order to consolidate a kingdom practically co-terminous with that of Herod the Great, over which he ruled from A.D. 41 to 44. A persecution of the Nazarene sect was an easy way to ingratiate himself with the Jews, and he saw the importance of striking down the leaders (1, 2).

The Lord and His servants (1-5). Why did the Lord allow James to be beheaded while He intervened miraculously to deliver Peter? The answer is found in the mystery itself, for we cannot possibly investigate the reasons which determine the lifespan of God's servants on earth, but we can be sure that God was glorified both in the martyrdom of James—the first martyr among the apostles—and in the deliverance of Peter (cf. Mt. 20: 20-23).

The praying church (5, 12). Many foolish remarks have been made about the Church which prayed and was surprised at the answer. This church was a company of potential martyrs, skilled in the ways of the Lord, and assured that any one of them might glorify God either by life or by death (cf. Phil. 1: 19-24). As real, human people, they *were* surprised at the *manner* of Peter's deliverance—should not we have been?—but the Jerusalem church is a model of constant prayer and faith on a sublime level.

The deliverance (6-11). Agrippa wanted to make quite sure that his important prisoner should not escape (6)! Peter had denied his Lord at that very time of the year, but in this case he slept soundly on what seemed to be his last night on earth (cf. 1 Pet. 5: 7). God had His plan for Peter, the need was urgent, and man could do nothing about the problem, which explains angelic intervention. All the phrases and circumstances indicate a *heavenly* messenger who limited his help to what Peter could not do for himself (7, 8, 10). As soon as the apostle was free, he had to 'come to' and think for himself (11).

Peter and the Christian company (12-17). Peter supposed that believers would be gathered for prayer in Mary's house, so presented himself there. The story of his knocking at the outside door, of Rhoda's surprise and confusion, with the reactions of the believers, stands out clearly in Luke's graphic style. The psychological reasonableness of every point convinces us of its truth—an invention in the style of later martyrologies would have been very different! The disciples' supposition that it was **his angel** must be read with Mt. 18: 10. 'The angel is here conceived of as a man's spiritual counterpart, capable of assuming his appearance and being mistaken for him' (F. F. Bruce). The good news was to be given **to James and to the brethren**, which indicates that James, the brother of our Lord, was in Jerusalem at the time, but not any other apostle. The **brethren** would include the elders of the church (17, cf. 15: 4, 22). Peter **went to another place**—probably one of the many convenient hiding places in the Judean hills. The regular meeting-places of the church would be the first to be raided when Herod's search-parties set to work. There was no bravado, and no assumption that miraculous deliverances would be repeated.

ii. The End of Herod Agrippa I (12: 18-25)
The dramatic contrast between the apostle's deliverance by an angel and the end of the proud, persecuting monarch, smitten by an angel in the moment of being acclaimed as a god, is obvious to all. Josephus speaks of a

feast in honour of the emperor in Caesarea, while Luke notes the end of a crisis between Herod and Phoenicia, but this information is complementary and not contradictory. It must be remembered that Herod was a professing Israelite and as a monotheist, claiming to sit on David's throne, could not accept the king-god concept so common in the East. The crowd's adulation: 'The voice of a god and not of man!' (22) was the climax of a life of tortured ambitions changed by the God he defied into a death sentence. Herod's dream was thwarted for ever. But the word of God grew and multiplied (24).

IX. THE SYSTEMATIC EVANGELIZA-TION OF THE GENTILES: PAUL'S FIRST MISSIONARY JOURNEY (13: 1-14: 28)

i. Paul's Missionary Strategy

The first missionary journey is the beginning of a systematic apostolic work among the nations, which determines the fulfilment of the last stage of the over-all plan. The outstanding figure is Paul, for during this journey Barnabas's colleague was shown to be God's chosen vessel as apostle to the Gentiles. Not only did Paul receive revelations regarding the nature and constitution of the church (Eph. 2: 11-3: 11; Col. 1: 25, 26) but he was also the great missionary strategist, to whom God commended His plan for heralding the kerygma to the Gentiles. He saw the need of establishing centres of witness in busy ports and other centres of communication, counting on the gifts that the Holy Spirit would raise up in the new churches—not only for the edification of the believers, but also for the extension of the gospel in surrounding areas. The early visits to local synagogues did more than comply with the established order 'to the Jew first', for they also provided a nucleus of pious converts in each place, already instructed in the OT scriptures. The help of various colleagues made it possible to confirm new churches by visits, and Paul's Letters were also written with this end in view. But Paul never settled permanently in any one area, understanding that God had commissioned him as a spiritual pioneer. By such means a vast area was evangelized, stretching from Palestine to the Adriatic, in little more than a decade, c. A.D. 45-57. See Rom. 15: 17-21.

ii. Barnabas and Saul Separated for Special Service (13: 1-4a)

The prophets and teachers in Antioch (1, 2). It is important to note that God's purpose was made known to certain prophets and teachers, experienced in the ways of God, and willing to wait on Him by worship, prayer and fasting.

It was such men—and not the Antiochene church as such—who received the message providing for the systematic evangelization of the Gentiles, and we may believe that they were praying under the sense of this very need. The command Set apart for me Barnabas and Saul . . . probably came by means of a prophetic message.

The separation (2-4). This is no ordination, for Saul was an apostle with long years of service behind him, and Barnabas was a spiritual father to the Antiochene church, devoted to the Lord's work for many years. When the Holy Spirit indicated that these two outstanding workers were to lead the next forward movement, their colleagues bowed to the Lord's will and identified themselves with Barnabas and Saul by the act of laying on of hands. The church was doubtless present at the final act (14: 26). The sending by the brethren was merely an act of fellowship, for being sent out by the Holy Spirit, they went down to Seleucia (4).

iii. Witness in Cyprus (13: 4b-13)

The route (4-6). Seleucia was Antioch's port, and the missionaries sailed from there to Cyprus, Barnabas's native island, taking with them John Mark, cousin to Barnabas. Personal links would be helpful, but the first steps of this stage of the journey look rather like a 'family concern'. The typical work of evangelizing the Gentiles did not really get under way until the party arrived at the mainland under Paul's leadership. In Salamis they proclaimed the word of God in the synagogues of the Jews (5) and then seem to have passed rapidly through the island westward until they reached the capital, Paphos.

Sergius Paulus (6-12). The missionaries presumably preached to Jews and Gentiles in Paphos, but Luke focuses our attention on an incident which brought Paul into prominence as the God-appointed leader of the expedition. Sergius Paulus was senatorial proconsul of Cyprus, and, like many thoughtful men of his day, interested in the mysticism of the East. Hence Elymas ('the learned one') attracted his attention. Probably Bar-Jesus was the man's Jewish name and 'Elymas' his professional title. When Sergius Paulus heard of Barnabas and Saul and summoned them to his presence, the jealous ire of the false prophet was roused, and he probably denounced the Nazarene 'heresy' (8). Then Saul, who is also called Paul (9) filled with the Holy Spirit, openly declared the deceit and villainy of Elymas, pronouncing a doom of temporary blindness upon him—a punishment fitted to the crime of making a living by deepening the spiritual blindness of his dupes (9-11). There is every

L*

reason to think that the proconsul really believed, being interested in the word rather than the sign (see phrases in 7, 8, 12); Sir William Ramsay found indications that some members of the family later became prominent in Christian circles in Asia Minor (*The Bearing of Recent Discovery on the Trustworthiness of the NT*, 1915, pp. 150 ff.).

The name Paul. Saul was the apostle's Jewish name, and **Paul** would be his cognomen as a Roman citizen. The latter was more fitted for the leader of an evangelistic mission to the Gentiles, and Luke does not drop into using it casually, but notes thereby that the Paphos incident brought to a head the wide recognition of the 'signs' of Paul's apostleship, which publicly confirmed the secret call on the Damascus road. The expression 'Barnabas and Saul' is dropped as belonging to a transitional stage which had now been superseded, and it was **Paul and his company** who set sail to Pamphylia (13). (As a Roman citizen Paul was in a special class, but for the custom—at least as early as the second century B.C.—of Jews' having a Gentile as well as a Jewish name cf. Ac. 12: 12, 'John whose other name was Mark'.)

On to Pisidian Antioch (13: 13–16). John Mark's defection in Perga may have been due to his dislike of the change of leadership by which Paul seemed to displace his revered cousin. Tragic indirect results would follow later. There is not the slightest hint in Luke's story that Paul fell sick in Perga and decided to get to the healthier climate of the interior, which is Ramsay's supposition in support of the 'South Galatian' theory of the destination of the Letter to the Galatians, according to which the 'churches' of Gal. 1: 2 were those planted during the present journey (*St. Paul the Traveller*, pp. 95 ff.). The crossing of the Taurus mountains would have been a difficult undertaking for a sick man. Gal. 4: 13 attributes the evangelization of the Galatians to a sudden change of plan due to serious illness, whereas it is precisely at this point in the Acts narrative that Paul comes to the fore as leader and decides to get to Pisidian Antioch because it was an important road junction. Luke details the synagogue message and general procedure in Pisidian Antioch as typical of Paul's strategy, and as a model for future operations. Pisidian Antioch was not actually in Pisidia, but in Phrygia, part of which was temporarily included in the Roman province of Galatia—a fact which did not affect ethnic and linguistic factors. (A judicious statement of the cases for and against the 'South Galatian' and 'North Galatian' views respectively is given by D. Guthrie in his *NT Introduction: The Pauline Epistles*, 1961, pp. 72 ff.)

iv. Paul's Kerygma to the Jews (13: 14–41) Paul and Barnabas in the synagogue (14–16). The importance of beginning the witness in new territory in the local synagogue has already been noted. Division and persecution were bound to follow the preaching, but meanwhile the Messiah had been presented to the Jews, according to God's plan, and the first converts were either Jews or God-fearers—i.e. men nurtured in the Scriptures, of a high moral standing and completely free from the degrading influences of paganism. The importance of such a nucleus in the local churches can scarcely be overestimated and accounts for the stability of the witness in the early years. The order of service in the synagogue, and the function of the rulers are sufficiently indicated in v. 15. (See also *NBD, art.* Synagogue.)

The general theme. Paul's presentation of the *kerygma* to the Jews of the Dispersion should be compared with Peter's when he faced the Jews in Jerusalem (2: 14–36; 3: 12–26; etc.). The main points will be seen to be identical, but adapted to an audience far from the scene of the cross and resurrection. Paul, like Stephen, reviews Israel's history, but his purpose is to show God at work until the promises are fulfilled in Jesus the Messiah, rejected by the Jerusalem leaders, but divinely approved by the mighty act of resurrection. The pivotal point is the raising up of David, who links on to the Son of David.

God's dealings with Israel until the time of David (17–21). Israel was chosen by God, and therefore delivered from Egypt and introduced into Canaan. The times of the judges and of Saul were of relative failure, but God had prepared His king who would do all His will. The **four hundred and fifty years** (19) may extend from the patriarchs to the beginning of the judges, as the period in which God ordered the giving of the land.

David's Son and John's witness (23–25). David was a man who fulfilled God's will **in his own generation** (36, 37) but whose Son was to be the Messiah. This would strike a sympathetic chord in the hearts of Jewish hearers, but they would be amazed when they heard: **Of this man's posterity God has brought to Israel a Saviour, Jesus, as he promised** (23). The introduction of John the Baptist's testimony before an audience of the Dispersion was telling, as he was widely believed to have been a prophet (24, 25).

The happenings in Jerusalem (26–31). The Jews of Antioch, would, of course, have heard garbled reports about the crucifixion and it was a delicate matter to report on the great rejection. Paul insists on the message of salvation in Jesus (26) and attributes the rejection to (*a*) the leaders' lack of recognition of their Messiah; and (*b*) their lack of a true understanding of the messianic prophecies relating to the sufferings of Jehovah's Servant (27-29). As in Peter's preachings, there is a strong emphasis here on the resurrection as God's act which negated the leaders' verdict and made possible the preaching of the good news; the incredible is made credible by the reliable witness of the early apostles (30, 31).

Paul's message (32-41). On the basis of God's manifest work of salvation Paul can say: **we bring you the good news . . .** (32). The basic fact of the resurrection of Jesus is proved, as with Peter, by references to the Psalms and Isaiah (see also 30, 31). God's purposes of blessing through the Son (linked with David) were announced in Ps. 2: 7 and Isa. 55: 3, and the Messiah who saw no corruption was prophesied in Ps. 16: 10 (cf. 2: 25-31). **Let it be known to you therefore, brethren . . .** introduces Paul's application of God's great saving work to the needs of the Jews of Antioch; vv. 38 and 39 are characteristically Pauline. Paul's great verb *dikaioō* is obscured in RSV. Read as in RV: 'Through this man is proclaimed unto you remission of sins; and by him everyone that believeth is justified from all things, from which ye could not be justified by the law of Moses.' (See also vv. 38, 39 in NEB.) Both the context here and the sum of Paul's teaching in Romans and Galatians give the meaning that the law cannot justify the 'worker' from anything, since all his works are stained with sin, so that only the believer who establishes vital contact with the Saviour who died and rose again is 'justified' from all things. The remission of sins had often been stressed in Peter's *kerygma*, but here we have a preview of Paul's doctrine of justification by faith. The warning (41) is taken from Hab. 1: 5. In the prophecy wilful sinners would be overwhelmed by the judgments which were to fall on Judah during the Babylonian invasion. Here the **scoffers** (perhaps Paul saw some already in the congregation) were in danger of a final judgment on unbelief.

v. Typical Reactions to the Message (13: 42-52)
First converts (42, 43). Paul's message had an immediate effect on a number of Jews and pious Gentile God-fearers whose new-found faith caused them to follow the missionaries for further instruction.

Opposition and division (44-48). The news that a powerful new message was being preached in the synagogue by visitors from Palestine brought a great crowd together on the following Sabbath, but this widespread interest had the effect of stirring up the jealous opposition of unbelieving Jewish leaders. Obviously they created such tensions in the synagogue that Paul and Barnabas had to withdraw with their converts, but not before they had pointed out the necessity of a first message to Israelites, the rejection of which opened the way for a full testimony to the Gentiles. The Christ-rejectors showed by their attitude that they were **unworthy of eternal life** and Isa. 49: 6 was quoted as evidence that the Messiah-Servant, proclaimed by His messengers, was to be a means of **salvation to the uttermost parts of the earth** (46, 47). We must not deduce any change of policy from v. 46, for Paul returned again and again to the Jews of the synagogues after this date. We can well imagine the joy of the Gentiles as they entered the kingdom through faith in Christ, knowing that they, too, as believers, showed that they were on heaven's list of citizens (**ordained** is *tetagmenoi*, appointed, enrolled or inscribed, 48).

Extension and expulsion (49-52). Hundreds of converts became God's witnesses to the surrounding area, and this factor will be assumed in future instances. In the meantime hostile Jews succeeded in enlisting the help of God-fearing women of social standing who could influence their relatives in high places. Thus the resulting persecution and mob pressure was directed from above; or, at least, was carried through with the connivance of the authorities. As the missionaries' commission was to preach everywhere, and contacts in Antioch were being made difficult or impossible, their purpose was better forwarded by flight to Iconium, but not before they had pronounced a typical symbolic judgment on the Christ-rejectors (51; cf. Mt. 10: 14 and parallels). The disciples left in Antioch depended on the Lord, and so **were filled with joy and with the Holy Spirit** despite their tribulations and the loss of their spiritual leaders (52).

vi. Witness in Phrygia and Lycaonia (14: 1-20)
Work in Iconium (1-5). This city lay to the east of Antioch, and was also a centre of communications and a garrison town. The missionaries' experiences in Antioch · were repeated in large measure in their next centre of witness. Undeterred by former sufferings, they went together to the synagogue and **a great company believed, both of Jews and of Greeks.** There soon came a first reaction against the message and the messengers (2) which did not hinder a prolonged stay in the town, during which Paul and Barnabas exhibited their apostolic credentials of **signs and wonders.**

The good effect produced by the miracles doubtless enabled them to resist pressure longer than in Antioch, but possible outside influences (cf. 19) finally provoked a violent persecution supported by the rulers. Stoning was talked of, and the Lord's servants once more followed the divinely indicated strategy in such cases (6; cf. Mt. 10: 14, 23). We may suppose the same joy and power in the newly formed church, as was evident in Antioch. Iconium was on the borders of Phrygia and Lycaonia, and the escape route led to Lystra, due south, in the heart of Lycaonia.

Ministry and a miracle (8-13). The healing of the lame man was not the first happening in Lystra. The missionaries had preached in the surrounding country, and doubtless had given their usual testimony in the synagogue, and we may deduce that Timothy was converted at that time (6, 7; cf. 16: 1, 2). Luke has no need to detail a type of work already well known, and goes on to something which reveals Paul's methods in an area on the margin of the Hellenistic world. The story of the miracle is similar to that of the healing of the lame man at the temple gate by Peter (3: 1-8), although the reactions of a Gentile crowd are very different. Paul had doubtless preached in the open air in such a way that the lame man was attracted to the message and **had faith to be made well.** The command is forthright, and the leaping up and walking instantaneous (9, 10). The ignorant crowd was impressed, but Paul could not speak to them of the power of the God of Abraham, as Peter had done to the Jews. The excited shouting went on in the Lycaonian speech, not in Greek, so that the apostles seem not to have been aware that the priest of Zeus was taking advantage of the miracle to prepare sacrifices and garlands. That gods should have come down to perform works of mercy seemed the more probable in Lystra as a local legend preserved the story of the hospitality which a pious couple dispensed to Zeus and Hermes, unaware of the quality of their guests. That a miracle can be a godsend to a local shrine has been obvious throughout the history of world religions.

The message proclaimed to ignorant pagans (17, 18). The great interest of this section lies in the way Paul sought to gain entrance for at least a minimum of light in the understandings of uncultured pagans; his fundamental approach is analogous to the one he used to the learned pagans of the Areopagus, though the terms are so different. The missionaries first used 'sign language' by avoiding any raised dais and rushing among the people, tearing their clothes in token of their horror.

Paul was probably the speaker and proclaimed that they were merely men, albeit 'men with a message', which was aimed precisely at turning deceived human beings from the worship of hollow vanities to that of the living Creator God, whose handiwork all could see. Generations had passed with no special revelation in pagan lands, though God's goodness in providing for **fruitful seasons** for the satisfaction and gladness of men had been a constant witness to His being and to His providence (15-17). This was doubtless intended as an introduction to a more concrete presentation of Christ and His saving work, and we suppose that some doubtless were led to seek fuller light. The rest, however, were disappointed with the 'gods' who refused to function, and their disillusionment made them the more ready to receive a very different impression when the Jews from Antioch arrived.

'Given up to death for Jesus' sake' (19, 20: cf. 2 C. 4: 11). There is no need for Luke to stress the fickleness, cruelty and violence of men living under demon-controlled systems of idolatry. The simple statements of two verses reveal both the hatred of religious enemies of the gospel and the crazy reactions of the Lystra mob, who stoned the 'god' of yesterday and **dragged him out of the city,** leaving him for dead. But Paul considered himself as under constant sentence of death, and trusted God who raises the dead (Rom. 4: 17; 2 C. 1: 9, 10; 4: 7-14). He was not dead, as many supposed, but was miraculously helped to overcome utter prostration and dangerous wounds so as to continue his journey to Derbe next day. Timothy was a witness of what it cost to serve the living God in spheres under the sway of heathendom (2 Tim. 3: 10-13).

vii. The Return Journey to Syrian Antioch (14: 21-28)

Derbe, end of the outward journey (20, 21). In Derbe, south-east of Lystra, near the border of the Galatian province, a strong church was founded. Over the other side of the Taurus range was Paul's native town of Tarsus, but he and his company turned back from Derbe along the route of their triumphs and sufferings.

Confirming the churches (22, 23). The dangerous return journey well illustrates Paul's set purpose of strengthening the churches he left so quickly after their foundation. Although the Lycaonian and Phrygian churches showed no sign of spiritual fluctuation, Paul exhorted them to constancy in the inevitable tribulation. He was also able to discern what the Holy Spirit had done in his absence, for a number of brethren in each church had given proof of having received the pastoral gift, and these were appointed as elders. The special prayer and fasting of v. 23 seems to be related to the act of committing these leaders to the Lord, for much would depend on their faithfulness and zeal. Ac. 20: 17-35 beautifully illustrates the relationship which existed between the apostles and the elders of the different churches, as also between the latter and the flocks they shepherded. It is widely agreed that during the apostolic age, elder=bishop (overseer)=pastor (cf. 20: 17, 28), and that there was a plurality of these in each local church, forming the 'presbytery' (1 Tim. 4: 14).

A welcome in Syrian Antioch (24-28). After preaching the word in Perga, Paul and his company sailed to Syrian Antioch from Attalia. The whole church of the home base is more in evidence in the return of the missionaries than in their departure, and they were able to report on a work fulfilled, since God had widely opened the door of faith to the Gentiles. The chronology of the first journey and of the subsequent stay in Syrian Antioch is complicated by Luke's vague phrases: 'a long time', 'no little time', etc. Some two years would be a reasonable guess for the first journey, from 45/46 to 47/48.

X. AGREEMENT ON THE POSITION OF THE GENTILE BELIEVERS (15: 1-35)
i. The Circumcision Question (15: 1-5)
Discussions in Antioch (1, 2). As more and more uncircumcised believers entered the church, the fears of Judaizing Christians increased, for the kingdom, rejected by the majority of the Jews, was fast being peopled by converted Gentiles. This seemed contrary to the special promises and covenants of the OT and Judaizers believed that the only remedy was to campaign for the circumcision of all Gentile converts, so that they might belong to the assembly of Israel. On the other hand, Paul and Barnabas were assured by God's revelations in a new age that the church was universal and spiritual and in no wise to be subjected to the legalistic requirements of Judaism. Men from Judea were teaching in Syrian Antioch that circumcision was necessary to salvation and the resultant distress was acute. The leaders thought it necessary to act quickly in order to avoid a division which would cut the church into two branches.

The embassy sent to Jerusalem (1-5). The name 'council of Jerusalem' is quite inappropriate to the discussions between the Antiochene leaders and the apostles and elders in Jerusalem on the position of Gentile believers. Leaders of the two large churches involved discussed the matter fully and made recommendations for their area, which is rather different from the modern concept of an ecumenical council. The Antiochene embassy was formed by Paul, Barnabas 'and some others', doubtless leading brethren in the church.

Private discussions (6). Luke describes the public occasion for he is interested in the advance of the history of the kingdom, although v. 6 allows a place for private discussions. These probably included the recognition of the apostolic 'grace' granted to Paul and of the evangelistic mission of Paul and Barnabas. This is the aspect of the talks which Paul is keen to put on record in Gal. 2: 1-10. We have put forward reasons for thinking that the brief visit of 11: 30; 12: 25 could not coincide with the tremendous occasion detailed here, but find the following reasons for a coincidence between Gal. 2 and this passage: (a) The question of circumcision is the same; (b) the place is the same; (c) the *dramatis personae* are the same; (d) following the marvels of the first journey, the time is ripe for the full recognition of Paul's apostleship; (e) time is allowed for the 'fourteen years' of Gal. 2: 1. We shall see later that there was no reason why the letter of 15: 23-29 should have been produced in the Galatian controversy. The smooth flow of discussion and resolution in 15: 7-29 would have been very difficult apart from a prior understanding between Peter, James, John on the one hand and Paul and Barnabas on the other, which is precisely what is indicated in Gal. 2. (For another interpretation see notes on Gal. 2: 1-10, pp. 447 ff.)

ii. Public Discussion (15: 6-21)
Persons involved (6, 12, 22). The people most concerned with this matter are the apostles present in Jerusalem, the elders of the church, and the visiting embassy, but vv. 12 and 22 seem to indicate the presence of the whole church. Full debate was permitted, and then Peter, Paul and Barnabas brought the discussion to a head so that James (who seems to have presided) might propose a solution.

Peter's speech (7-11). Peter's remarks are a marvel of simplicity, humility and of spiritual logic. Never has 'freedom from the law' been better expressed. The Caesarea experience showed clearly that God gave the Holy Spirit to uncircumcised Gentile believers just as he had done to the 120 disciples on the day of Pentecost. Why put such people under the yoke of the law that Israelites had never been able to bear? In his final phrase he places both Jew and Gentile on an equality, saying: **'we believe that we** (Jews) **shall be saved through the grace of the Lord Jesus, just as they** (Gentiles) **will.'**

The witness of Barnabas and Paul (12). The principle God had established in Cornelius's house, had been confirmed by the abundant and victorious experiences of the first journey. The church must recognize the further revelations God was giving through inspired messages confirmed by mighty works.

James' summing up and proposal (13-21). Symeon's (i.e. Peter's) experience, says James, shows that God's purpose in this age is **to take out** (of the Gentiles) **a people for his name.** The divine purpose is supported, in the usual way, by a quotation from the OT (Am. 9: 11-12). The point was that God had announced universal blessings for the Gentiles in the end times, so that the calling out of a people to His name in this age finds its place in the general perspective of prophecy. Fulfilment of the prophecy is partial and analogical rather than literal, as in the case of 2: 16-21. Unless the promises given through the prophets to Israel are interpreted with reference to the same people and in the same sense in which they were originally given, the exegesis of prophecy becomes a guessing game controlled only by the predilections of the expositors.

The main conclusion is the confirmation of the liberty of the Gentiles already revealed: **'Therefore my judgment is that we should not trouble those of the Gentiles who turn to God'** (19). The question of principle was clear, but practical difficulties remained: (*a*) How were converts from Judaism and the nations to live together? (*b*) What would be the effect of Gentile Christian liberties on the progress of the gospel where there were synagogues? James's mention of the Jews of the Dispersion in v. 21 is very important to a correct exegesis. The answer is that Gentile believers in the area most affected (Cilicia and Syria) were to be asked to abstain from practices which were repugnant and scandalous to the Jews because of the constant reading of such legal prohibitions as those of Lev. 11 and 17. Such wise restraint would go far to diminish friction between brethren and would remove obstacles to the spread of the gospel. The exegetical difficulty is to explain why the fundamental sin of fornication should have been included in this list of stumbling blocks to the Jews. The Gk. word is *porneia*, normal for fornication, and it is difficult to see why it should be confined here to 'marriage within the prohibited degrees' (cf. 1 C. 5: 1). We must remember that sexual purity was extraordinarily rare among pagans, but at the same time abstinence from sexual sin could never have been treated as voluntary or optional as the other restraints later were

(cf. 1 C. 5; 6: 12 ff.). The debate on this problem is still open.

iii. The Letter (15: 22-29)

Its value and limitations. The letter expresses in writing the agreement reached. It is important to note the following points: (*a*) It was written in the name of **the brethren, both the apostles and the elders** (23). (*b*) It was not a rescript binding on the whole church for ever, but a communication from the persons named **to the brethren who are of the Gentiles in Antioch, Syria and Cilicia** (23). It constituted a strong recommendation, but must not be considered an obstacle to future normal revelations through the apostles, with special reference to the authority of Paul as apostle to the Gentiles. For spheres further afield the production of the letter would not be helpful for Paul's apostolic authority had to be defended against any idea of a subordinated authority derived from Jerusalem or from earlier apostles (Gal. 1 and 2). (*c*) The collaboration of the witness of the Holy Spirit and the apostles was normal to the epoch and refers to the recommendation about **necessary** or 'convenient' things at that time of transition. When the church spread widely over Gentile lands and the Jewish element became a small minority, the question ceased to have validity. In regard to 'doubtful things' we can learn all that is necessary from Paul's writings, especially 1 C. 8 and 10, with Rom. 14.

iv. Rejoicing and Ministry in Antioch (15: 30-35)

When Barsabbas and Silas read the letter and confirmed it personally a great cloud was lifted from the minds and hearts of the believers in Antioch, and this relief opened the way for renewed labours in which many gifted brethren taught and preached the word (35). The risen Lord was conferring abundant and varied gifts on His church (Eph. 4: 7-13).

XI. THE GOSPEL REACHES MACEDONIA: THE SECOND MISSIONARY JOURNEY (15: 36-18: 23a)

i. A Tragic Separation (15: 36-39)

The purpose of the journey (15: 36). The second journey, under the guidance of the Holy Spirit, was to open vast new areas to the gospel, mainly in Macedonia and Greece; but the original purpose was that of revisiting the churches already formed so that they might be strengthened in the faith (cf. notes on 14: 21-23).

A sharp conflict of opinions (15: 37-39). We can only guess at possible deep psychological motives behind the sharp discussion between Paul and Barnabas, arising from the change which led to Paul's acknowledged leadership.

The blood-relationship between Mark and Barnabas may have played its part. In the matter at issue both distinguished leaders were right from different points of view. Barnabas had a shepherd's heart, and probably had personal reasons for knowing better than Paul the depth and sincerity of John Mark's repentance. On the other hand, Paul—also a spiritual shepherd—was concerned with the spiritual success of the second journey in which much depended on the help they might receive from younger men. These must be tried and proved in a public fashion, and it could not be said that John Mark had been so tested since his defection. It is a kind of sad consolation to know that outstanding and spiritually minded leaders can hold irreconcilable opinions at times, when the wise thing is for each to get on with the work in different spheres. The passages showing that Mark 'made good', later on, even in the eyes of Paul, are well known: Col. 4: 10; Phm. 23; 2 Tim. 4: 11.

ii. New Companions (15: 40–16: 5)
Silas had been one of the bearers of the Jerusalem letter, and we must understand that he had first returned to Jerusalem and then been led again to Antioch (33, 40). Silas is identical with Silvanus (2 C. 1: 19; 1 Th. 1: 1; 2 Th. 1: 1; 1 Pet. 5: 12), and seems to have been a cultured Roman citizen. He replaces Barnabas as an intimate companion of Paul, while Timothy was soon to be the junior helper. The Antioch church gave the two men an official send-off on their important mission, the first stage of which consisted in the confirmation of churches in the united province of Syria and Cilicia (40, 41).

Timothy chosen as a younger helper (1–5). Paul and Silas must have crossed the Taurus range by the Cilician Gates and struck the end of the former route in Derbe. Lystra linked Derbe and Iconium, and there Paul found that his convert, Timothy, had grown in spiritual stature, being well reported of by the churches in the district. Paul took the initiative in choosing the new helper, but Timothy's own sense of a call to a new kind of labour must be understood, and the Pastoral Letters throw light on the part played by the presbytery and prophets in the call and preparation of the young worker. This is an occasion in apostolic missionary history in which the mind of the Spirit is manifested not only to the candidate, but also to the spiritual leader on the field and to the elders of the local churches (1 Tim. 1: 18; 4: 14; 2 Tim. 1: 6; 2: 2).

Timothy's circumcision (16: 3). Paul would on no account allow the Gentile Titus to be circumcised, even in Jerusalem (Gal. 2: 3–5), but he himself caused Timothy to be circumcised.

The seeming inconsistency arises from the fact that Timothy was **the son of a Jewish woman who was a believer,** brought up in Hebrew piety. He could exercise a ministry among Jews and Gentiles so long as his racial position was clear and his circumcision would facilitate such a service. Titus was a Gentile born, converted and active in the gospel before visiting Jerusalem, so that his circumcision would have indicated that something was lacking in his spiritual life which could be supplied by the Jewish rite. In this case Paul's arguments in Galatians apply in their entirety.

A note on progress in the area of the first journey (4, 5). The churches of the Lycaonian and Phrygian portions of the Galatian province were near enough to the centre of the dispute on circumcision (Syrian Antioch) to make it advisable for them to receive the Jerusalem letter (4). In v. 5 we have one of Luke's summaries of progress which follows the confirmation of the churches founded during the first journey and settlement in the East of the circumcision dispute. From this optimistic summary onwards he deals with new ground opened during the second journey.

iii. New Ground (16: 6–10)
The region of Phrygia and Galatia (6). As the Lycaonian and Phrygian churches in the province of Galatia have already been visited, the area called **Phrygia** here must be the ethnic region of that name attached to Asia. **Galatia** would then be the real ethnic 'Galatia' of the north, the former kingdom of the Galatians (Celts). Numerous details in the Letters show that Luke passed rapidly over considerable periods of Paul's ministry when a full story would not forward his general purpose, so that there is nothing impossible in J. B. Lightfoot's theory that the period of uncertainty noted in v. 6 saw the founding of the North Galatian churches because Paul was held up by an illness (Gal. 4: 13), which, as has been said, fits badly into the story at the point noted in 13: 13, 14. (For a defence of the 'South Galatian' destination of the Letter to the Galatians see pp. 443 f. Since 1897 it has been widely accepted in Britain, although the 'North Galatian' view is held by probably the majority of scholars in the United States and the continent of Europe.)

Negative and positive guidance (6–10). Maps must be consulted in order to trace Paul's probable movements at this time. His labours in Asian Phrygia and Galatia (we may think of Pessinus) left him on the N.W. borders of the province of Asia (another ethnic amalgam). He naturally thought of the great possibilities of Asia, and could easily have descended from the highlands to the coast. The time was not yet ripe, however, and the missionaries were forbidden by the Spirit to evangelize Asia then. Should they turn N. and N.W. to the prosperous provinces of Bithynia and Pontus? Again the attempt was vetoed by **the Spirit of Jesus,** presumably by means of a prophetic message or a vision. **Opposite Mysia** would be the high land at the junction of the three great provinces of Galatia, Bithynia and Asia, Mysia being included in the last of these. From whichever part of Galatia they came, the fact that they were forbidden to evangelize Asia or Bithynia meant that they were compelled to come out at the coast in the direction of the port of Troas, at some distance from the ancient city of Troy. There Paul, in a night vision, saw the Macedonian who appealed for help. This positive guidance cast light on the past vetoes, and they rightly concluded that they were to cross the northern part of the Aegean Sea to Macedonia. Luke had his share in the decision, and the beginning of a **we** passage (10) shows that he joined the apostolic band at that point as a fellow-labourer.

iv. Peaceful Advance in Philippi (16: 11-15) The journey and the city (11, 12). After a quick voyage the missionaries landed in Neapolis, a port at the eastern end of the Egnatian Way, but proceeded at once to Philippi, converted into a Roman colony following the defeat of Brutus and Cassius in that area in 42 B.C. Why a declining city, peopled mainly by Roman citizens and without a synagogue, should have been chosen as the first base for missionary work on the continent subsequently to be known as Europe, has puzzled scholars, and must be attributed to direct guidance.

The place of prayer (13-15). Jews had not been attracted to Philippi, so that no synagogue had been established. But the apostles found a meeting place for prayer, used by Jewish (or proselyte) women, on the banks of the river Gangites. The beginnings in Macedonia could not have been humbler, but as the missionaries told their story to the women, Lydia at least was converted and placed herself and her house at the disposal of the Lord's servants. V. 40 seems to indicate that the church met in her house, which was likely to be commodious as her business was important (14). Before the interruption (16), we must suppose a period of successful witness both at the place of prayer, in Lydia's house and perhaps by public preachings, as a church had been founded and brethren could be visited after the release of Paul and Silas.

v. Progress Through Persecution (16: 16-24) The healing of the slave girl (16-18). The slave had a 'Python spirit'; F. F. Bruce remarks:

' "Pythons" were inspired by Apollo, the Pythian god, who was regarded as embodied in a snake (the Python) at Delphi (also called Pytho).' Why an evil spirit should have given the testimony to the apostles (17) is a mystery, but is analogous to expressions used in the presence of the Master (Mk 5: 7) with the same use of **the Most High God.** We should correct **the way of salvation** in RSV to '*a* way of salvation' (RVmg, NEB), so that the testimony is really a subtle distortion of the truth of the *one* way identified with the Lord Jesus Christ. In any case, demonic witness was never accepted either by the Lord or by His servants so that, despite obvious dangers, Paul exorcized the pythonic spirit in the name of Jesus Christ.

Roman justice goes wrong (19-24). The slave girl would no longer bring revenues to her owners by her divinations, so that these, quite foreign to the spiritual issues involved, turned on the men responsible for changing a valuable medium into a mere working girl. The account is abridged, for the accusation presented to the two collegiate chief magistrates was so cleverly worded that it could not have been drawn up in the midst of turmoil. The citizens of Philippi were Romans, but the leaders of the apostolic band were Jews, so that the accusation questioned the legitimacy of the proclamation of new teachings and practices in a Roman colony, as there was nothing to show that the new religion was a *religio licita*, one authorized by imperial law. According to the accusation, such teachings had produced the present disturbances. The magistrates would have been justified in examining such an accusation, appealing, perhaps, to the proconsul of Macedonia for a ruling; but, instead of such a judicial and judicious procedure, they yielded at once to mob pressure, ordering Paul and Silas to be beaten violently in their presence, giving them no chance to speak in self-defence or to allege their Roman citizenship. On their strict charge (23) the governor of the prison took all possible measures against the escape of the accused (23, 24).

vi. God Speaks by the Earthquake and by His Word (16: 25-40) God's intervention (25, 26). God's voice was first heard in Philippi in quiet conversations by a flowing stream. Afterwards the city had been filled with the word of apostolic witness. Then God's powerful word effected a miraculous healing, and was afterwards heard through the triumphant songs and prayers of the suffering prisoners (25). Now, exceptionally, God spoke through an earthquake (cf. 1 Kg. 19: 11, 12) which shook the foundations of the prison, opened all doors, and broke the bonds of all the prisoners. The atmosphere is tense with mystery and emotion, but the Lord's servant is in absolute control of the situation, even to the point of seeing that the prisoners should not take advantage of the opportunity to escape (cf. 25). The governor of the prison might have been an old army officer, for whom suicide would be the only honourable solution to the problem of the loss of his prisoners. Paul could probably see the man silhouetted against the opening of the door, and cried out in time to save his life (27, 28). How could the officer get to the point of asking about spiritual salvation in such a brief space of time (30, 32)? Or was he only anxious about his professional standing? If the latter, why did he fall down in supplication before Paul and Silas, or why did Paul advance a spiritual answer? We should remember the following factors: (a) The governor of the prison may have known a good deal about the apostles' witness prior to this event. (b) He would certainly have noted the remarkable demeanour of the prisoners, and may have heard their songs and prayers. (c) The moment is one charged with intense emotion, as God is working by extraordinary means, so that the personal danger of the officer and the sense of a spiritual crisis might well have coalesced in his thoughts and reactions. (d) The conversion of the officer and of the members of his household was not only due to the great declaration, **Believe in the Lord Jesus, and you will be saved,** but also to **the word** which was fully preached both to the man and his household (32). Measures would have been taken to restore the security of the prison, as the Western text says explicitly, but Luke concentrates on the joy with which the officer and his household received the word, showing their faith by their kindly care of the Lord's servants whom they had treated so brutally before (33, 34). The officer's household would probably be composed of his wife and family, servants and attendants. It is mere surmise that small children were present and were therefore baptized, as the whole household rejoiced in their new-found faith (34).

Paul's stand before the magistrates (35–40). The magistrates (*stratēgoi*='praetors' because Philippi was a Roman colony) considered that the two unwelcome visitors had been taught a lesson, so better get them out of the city now without more ado. To their surprise, the men returned a message claiming their rights as Roman citizens, and demanding that the magistrates themselves should lead them out of the prison as an acknowledgment of illegal violence. Was it arrogance and lack of faith? Was Paul deeply attached to his Roman citizen-

ship and Greek culture as Ramsay thought? The fact seems to be that Paul never claimed his rights unless he found himself in an extremity (22: 25–29) or when such a claim might help in the spread of the gospel (see notes on 25: 10–12). His stand in this case would be a definite help to the Christian flock which he had to leave at a moment when popular feeling had been stirred up against it. Wrong had been done, but as it was publicly acknowledged some measure of protection was assured to the budding work. The Macedonian Christians in general were a great cheer to Paul's heart, and the letter to the Philippians makes it clear that a well-ordered, zealous and self-sacrificing community was born, first in peace and then in affliction.

vii. The Foundation of the Thessalonian Church (17: 1–9)
Thessalonica (Salonika) is still an important port, but was relatively more important during the first century as it handled much of the east-west trade passing from the East through Macedonia, and so to Rome along the Egnatian Way. It is typical of the kind of city Paul sought for as a centre for his message, and in this case the word rapidly spread from the Christian church to all the surrounding area (1 Th. 1: 8). Luke rightly calls the civic authorities 'politarchs' (6), a designation attested on inscriptions for the chief magistrates of several Macedonian cities.

Beginnings in the synagogue (1–4). Testimony in the synagogue often took the form of discussions, and vv. 2, 3 give an admirable summary of Paul's arguments when dealing with Jews: (a) Prophetic scriptures showed that the Messiah was to suffer and rise from the dead. (b) Those scriptures had been fulfilled in Jesus, whom Paul presented to his fellow-countrymen as their Messiah. A full example of his presentation of the *kerygma* in such cases has already been given in 13: 16–41. Paul's cogent reasoning convinced some Jews and many God-fearers and highly-placed ladies (4). The **three weeks** (2) must refer to the first three sabbaths of unhindered testimony in the synagogue, which were followed by an indefinite period of preaching in the house of Jason, his host, before the riot and Paul's flight. A sufficient time for the founding of a church fully acquainted with the main Christian doctrines is demanded by the contents of the two letters to the Thessalonians.

Opposition and flight (5–9). Perhaps the strange methods adopted by the jealous and antagonistic Jews were due to the fact that believing ladies in high places would influence authority in favour of the Christian church rather than against it. It seems as if the Jews could only get a hearing by producing a riot, of which the politarchs had to take cognizance (6, 7). The accusation is different from that of the Philippian citizens, but is equally subtle: (a) the missionaries were notorious disturbers of the peace (6); (b) their propaganda was contrary to the decrees of Caesar; (c) they proclaimed 'another king, Jesus' (7). It was well that Paul had been hidden and was not there to answer in person for even the breath of suspicion of any subversive propaganda against the Emperor could be fatal. It was such an accusation which affected Pilate so strongly (Lk. 23: 2; Jn 19: 12). Jason would probably be a well-known Jewish citizen who could not be tried on the grounds of Paul's message, but could be made responsible for public order, and the security would be bail to a considerable amount. He may have had to promise that Paul would keep away from Thessalonica, which would explain the persistent obstacle to his revisiting the city during the following months (1 Th. 2: 17, 18).

viii. A Church in Beroea (17: 10-15)
Flight and encouragement. Again we note the method of leaving the continuance of the work to less conspicuous brethren while Paul repeated his methods in another city. Beroea was about 60 miles from Thessalonica, but somewhat off the main routes, which might have been an advantage at the moment. The 'nobility' of the Beroean Jews consisted in their open-mindedness, for as the visiting preachers appealed to the OT scriptures, they were very willing to examine them again in the light of the message to see if these things were so. It is thus easy to understand that many soon believed, and that the blessing rapidly spread to the Greeks, among whom were more ladies of high society (11, 12). The Thessalonian Jews, who were such bitter enemies of the Gospel (see their character in 1 Th. 2: 14-16), were not long in getting wind of the work and repeated their technique of stirring up the mob (13). After an uncertain period, the brethren hurried Paul away in the direction of Athens by the sea-route (14) while Silas and Timothy stayed to strengthen the nascent church. Paul, meditating on the possibilities of Achaia, sent back the urgent message of v. 15. Besides the churches founded in Philippi, Thessalonica and Beroea, we must suppose the up-surge of a number of satellite churches in the Macedonian area, due to the labour of various workers and the testimony of a host of anonymous witnesses (Rom. 15: 19; 1 Th. 1: 8; 2 C. 8: 1).

ix. Paul in Athens (17: 16-34)
A varied witness (16-21). Perhaps Paul thought of Athens as a place in which he could pray about future strategy, remote from the usual conflicts; but he could not see the noble city—the 'mother' of western civilization—full of foolish idols without being passionately stirred to immediate witness in the synagogue, and in the market place, speaking to all who would listen in a city notorious for its liking for 'intellectual chat' (21). What a change from the days of Socrates and Plato! The Epicureans formed a philosophical school which thought of pleasure as the greatest good, though their pleasure might be presented as refined and tranquil; the rival school of the Stoics was pantheistic, but especially stressed the superiority of a reasoning will over the passions of men, putting a high value on human self-sufficiency. Paul's preaching of Jesus and the resurrection (anastasis) was thought to be the presentation of foreign divinities and as questions of religion and morals were the province of the learned body, the Court of the Areopagus (so called because it had formerly met on the Areopagus, the 'Mars' hill' of AV), an opportunity was unexpectedly provided for a Christian witness before the intellectual élite of the day.

The speech (22-31). This first encounter between the Christian message and Greek philosophy has always aroused an almost excited interest. On the surface the results do not seem very striking (33, 34), but there is no ground for imagining, on the basis of a superficial interpretation of 1 C. 2: 1-5, that Paul was mistaken in his methods, correcting them when he went to Corinth. Luke was divinely led to give a summary of the speech for our learning and we must think of it as an introduction to Christian doctrine which would have led to the full message of the cross had the learned men of Athens been prepared to listen. Scores of interesting questions arise from the speech, which has been analysed in many learned writings (see, e.g. N. B. Stonehouse, The Areopagus Address, 1951), but our space only allows us to note the main movements: (a) A striking introduction was provided by the altar dedicated 'To an unknown god'—one which might have been overlooked, despite the crowd of 'divinities' honoured by so many temples and altars. The Athenians, then, were very religious, since they feared such an omission. Paul changes the stress, underlining their ignorance of the true God (22, 23). (b) God the Creator is proclaimed, who is Lord of heaven and earth, not needing men's poor temples for a dwelling place. This is the language of Isaiah and of all the OT prophets. The Creator is also the Lifegiver (24, 25; cf. Isa. 66: 1, 2). Many of the scholarly hearers would assent to the strong monotheism of these phrases. (*c*) God's dealings with His creatures, or God in His providence, is the next step in the argument. Instead of the 'gods many' who help their favourites and devotees within narrow territorial limits, Paul proclaims the God who caused the race to spring from one man, providentially ordering man's boundaries of space and time so that they might seek and find God within a relatively ordered life (cf. the Noachian covenant, Gen. 9: 1-17). Paul quotes lines from Epimenides and Aratus in which Zeus is considered as the source of all life, and these quotations would help to maintain the interest of the councillors (26-28). (*d*) Humanity's great crisis is emphasized (29-31), for a true understanding of man's relationship with a Creator God would obviate the folly of idolatry, which tries to represent divinity by means of material and man-made objects. Centuries of **ignorance** had gone by, **overlooked** by God—which does not annul human responsibility during the period—but times had changed, and God had intervened by fixing a day of judgment and by appointing the Judge who had been approved in the sight of men by the fact of his resurrection **from the dead.** Now men must **repent** and turn to God.

Paul had prepared his hearers as well as he could by stressing the highest moral and spiritual levels their thoughts could rise to, and at least **some** were impressed by the proclamation of human responsibility before their Creator God. But the concepts of v. 31 were strongly opposed to their ideas about the 'soul of the universe' moving in endless cycles, as also to the reabsorption of the human soul into that of the universe. A kind of future existence might well have been admitted, but **the resurrection of the dead** required a complete change of outlook, only possible if hungry and submissive souls turned to the Lord for light and salvation. The mockers made it impossible for Paul to continue, but a wonderful body of truth had been expressed, essential to our thinking about God and His providence.

Reactions and results (32-34). Luke certainly shows that the world of Hellenistic culture was not likely to receive the gospel with open arms, but there is no 'failure' as far as the proclamation is concerned, since **some . . . believed,** among them distinguished figures like Dionysius and Damaris, so that a church was founded which was a temple to the only true God amid the many shrines of Athens. The mockers would reap what they sowed; the procrastinators never heard Paul again as far as we know; but the vital nucleus of believers would continue to preach the wonders of divine wisdom in the centre of Greek civilization.

x. Corinth (18: 1-18a)

The city. While Athens was the cultural capital of Greece—as also of the whole area of Hellenistic civilization—Corinth was the commercial centre. Destroyed in Rome's wars of conquest, it had been rebuilt as a Roman colony by Julius Caesar in 46 B.C. on the narrow isthmus which separates the Greek mainland from the large peninsula of Peloponnesus, having Cenchreae and Lechaeum as its ports on the East and West respectively. The great temple of Aphrodite made it a centre of idolatrous worship on the lowest possible moral level. This low level of sexual morality must be borne in mind when reading the Corinthian Letters. Politically, Corinth was the capital of the Roman province of Achaia.

Paul's arrival (1-4). Paul's state of mind when he arrived at Corinth is revealed in 1 C. 2: 1-5. There may have been other preoccupations as well as the relatively meagre result of the great witness in Athens. He was comforted by meeting Aquila and Priscilla, lately expelled from Rome by the Claudian edict against the Jews (2), who were probably Christians already. Their common trade helped to cement a wonderful friendship and fellowship in service which was to last for many years. See especially Rom. 16: 3, 4. Work in the synagogue seems to have begun on a minor key until the arrival of Silas and Timothy (4).

A mighty work (5-11). Paul was cheered by the good news that the Macedonian churches were constant, faithful and generous in the midst of persecution. During the following months the Thessalonian Letters were written. A stronger testimony in the synagogue accelerated the inevitable reaction of the Jews who refused the message of Jesus the Messiah, but not before **Crispus, the ruler of the synagogue,** had been converted, with **Titius Justus,** a godfearing Gentile, whose house became the centre of the work. He may be 'Gaius, mine host' of Rom. 16: 23, in which case his full name would be Gaius Titius Justus. For reminiscences of these early days in Corinth, see 1 C. 1: 14-16. The **many** Corinthians converted (8) would have been won mainly from paganism, so that the proportion of well-taught and disciplined converts from the synagogue would be less than elsewhere; a fact which accounts for a certain instability of the work in Corinth. A tremendous attack by influential Jews was to be expected, but Paul was prepared for it by the vision of vv. 9, 10, in which the Lord encouraged His servant to continue to speak in Corinth in view of the **many people** to be won. Paul was assured that he would not be forced to leave the work hastily to begin again elsewhere as in so many other cities.

Gallio ignores the Jews (12–17). Gallio was brother to Nero's tutor, Seneca, the Stoic philosopher, and as his proconsulship most probably began in July 51, we have here an approximate date for the Corinthian ministry. The Jews were not so clever in formulating their accusation as in Thessalonica for they wished to prove that Paul's doctrines were not genuinely Jewish, and therefore not protected by the concessions made by Rome to Israel. To Gallio, however, that looked like an internal squabble between Jewish sects, so he scornfully referred the matter back to their own religious tribunals. Jews were not popular, so that he did not interfere when his sentence gave rise to some Jew-baiting. The victim, Sosthenes, must have been the ruler of the synagogue who replaced Crispus. This ruling was probably of considerable importance for the spread of the gospel during the following years, for Achaia was a major province, and Gallio an outstanding figure, so that his ruling, implying that Christians were covered by the special authorization given to the Jews, would influence minor authorities in the whole of the Aegean area. Thus was the Lord's promise (10) fulfilled and Paul himself was able to guide the early stages of a difficult work.

xi. The Journey to Syria (18: 18b–23)
Paul's vow (18b). Paul was to visit Jerusalem and Antioch again before entering new fields. The discussion about his vow can be simplified by the consideration that, during this period of transition, Jewish believers did not generally forsake the customs of their people, so that Paul was completely free to take a vow, shave his head, or to offer sacrifices, according to his own leading, fulfilling also the principle of 1 C. 9: 20. Let us remember that his plan of service still led him to the synagogues where these were found. Gentile colleagues were entirely and necessarily exempt from all such things, and one day the transition period would end. See note below on 21: 23–26.

Ephesus (19–21). Paul was received in a friendly fashion when he visited the synagogue in Ephesus, but he had not planned for a long stay then. Aquila and Priscilla remained as able witnesses, while Paul promised to return.

The end of the second journey (22, 23a). It is implied that the **church** visited following the landing at Caesarea was Jerusalem, after which the apostle spent some time in the well-loved church of Antioch in Syria. The new territories which had been evangelized since he was last in Antioch were Macedonia and Achaia (practically the whole of modern Greece), and probably an area in ethnic Galatia; the approximate dates were A.D. 48–53.

XII. THE EVANGELIZATION OF ASIA: THE THIRD MISSIONARY JOURNEY (18: 23b–21: 16)
i. A Ministry of Confirmation (18: 23b)
In a few words Luke sums up many months of confirmatory labours in which Paul goes **from place to place** where churches had been founded in Phrygia and Galatia. If he employs the ethnic terms for the areas visited, **Phrygia** would mean Galatian and Asian Phrygia and **Galatia** the ethnic Galatia in the north. A second visit to the Galatians in which he 'told them the truth' is implied in Gal. 4: 16 (see p. 452).

ii. Apollos Appears (18: 24–28)
Apollos the man (24, 25). Alexandria was famous for its school of philosophy, literature and rhetoric, which influenced the large Jewish minority. Apollos was obviously the product of Alexandrian Judaism, but in some way he had heard of Jesus apart from the main apostolic stream of witness. Christian witnesses may well have preached in Alexandria before the great consummation of Pentecost. Apollos's courage was equal to his eloquence, for he at once preached in the synagogue in Ephesus on his arrival there.

Instruction and blessing (26–28). Paul's friends, Aquila and Priscilla, realized that Apollos's message was incomplete, so they invited him home for further instruction. Thus God raised up an outstanding witness to the truth in those years, who was to be made a special blessing in Corinth. The fact that **the brethren . . . wrote** an introductory letter on Apollos's behalf to the Christians in Achaia (mainly Corinth) shows that a Christian church already functioned in Ephesus, though it seems to have been Jewish in composition. For Apollos, see 1 C. 1: 12; 3: 5, 6; 4: 6; 16: 12.

iii. The Twelve Disciples (19: 1–7)
Paul in the 'upper country' (1). See notes on 18: 23 and 16: 6–8. The term fits in well with the assumption that churches had been founded in the highlands of Galatia. How much we should like to know of these busy months which Luke dismisses in a few words!

The group in Ephesus (1–7). The twelve disciples could not have been in contact with Aquila, Priscilla and the 'brethren' in Ephesus, or the conditions described would not have obtained. As in the case of Apollos, the men had heard of Jesus, had been baptized with John's **baptism of repentance,** but had not been informed of the 'consummation' in Jerusalem. A separate and early stream of witness probably stemmed from Galilee. Paul's question: **'Did you receive the Holy Spirit when you believed?'** (properly translated in RSV), shows that he expected disciples to receive the Spirit as soon as they believed. The reply (2) does not indicate that the disciples knew nothing about the Holy Spirit (clearly presented in the OT and in the Baptist's teaching), but that they had not heard of the giving of the Holy Spirit through the Messiah as promised by John. The significance of the 'laying on of hands' corresponds closely to that of 8: 17 and, according to its fundamental meaning of identification, denotes the closing of the breach between an incomplete position, bringing it into line with apostolic authority.

iv. The Evangelization of Asia (19: 8-20)
The province. Asia was one of the major Roman provinces, including the whole of the prosperous and thickly populated Ionian coast from the Hellespont to Lycia, with a deep spread inland to the heart of Asia Minor. During its evangelization **all the residents of Asia heard the word of the Lord, both Jews and Greeks** (10). The great centre was Ephesus, situated at the mouth of the Cayster River. Later on its importance declined because of the silting up of the harbour, but in the first century it was the metropolis of a vast area, important both for its commercial links and its religious significance. The temple of Ephesian Artemis—'Diana of the Ephesians' in AV—was counted as one of the seven wonders of the world, and brought worshippers from all over the world. Originally a nature cult, the worship of the 'mother goddess' had been assimilated to that of the Greek Artemis.

The hall of Tyrannus (8-10). Paul made his usual beginning in the synagogue, stressing the theme of the kingdom of God (8), and he was soon beset by the stubborn unbelievers among the Jews who reviled **the Way.** He withdrew the disciples when further testimony in the synagogue became impossible, and found a preaching centre in the **hall of Tyrannus.** It has been deduced from the habits of the Ephesians that Paul worked at his trade in the mornings (cf. 20: 34) while the normal activities were carried on by Tyrannus in his **hall** (which might be compared to a lecture hall with a gymnasium, where leisure was spent); Paul then gave his 'lectures' during the siesta time after 11.00 a.m. He afterwards reminded the Ephesian elders of this public ministry which was complemented by visits 'from house to house' (20: 20). Distinguished visitors seem to have listened to the preaching in Tyrannus's hall, since Paul won friends even among **the Asiarchs** (the principal citizens, 31). Despite the many plots of the Jews, and the sharp suffering of that period, Paul was enabled to continue in Ephesus for a period covering from two to three years (10, 20, 31 with 20: 19; 1 C. 15: 32), and his ministry provides the

most perfect example of the strategy which selected important centres from which the gospel could be widely spread throughout the whole area by his colleagues and converts. During this time Epaphras evangelized the towns of the Lycus valley (Col. 1: 7). At some point during Paul's Ephesian ministry he paid his 'painful visit' to Corinth (2 C. 2: 1; see p. 416).

The 'Name' in Ephesus (11-20). In chs. 4-6 Luke described the power of the name over against the strength of Judaism. Here the same name is shown to have prevailed against both the superstitious worship of Artemis of the Ephesians and the false 'names' of the prevalent magic. Once more a servant of Christ was accredited by means of miracles which drew attention to the word. The hellenistic world respected the occult powers associated with the East, so that it would not be difficult for the Sceva family to 'work up a connection', claiming, perhaps to know the sacred name of the God of Israel. F. F. Bruce suggests that we should read **high priest** 'in inverted commas', as something which the head of the house claimed to be in Gentile lands, where little was known of the priestly hierarchy in Jerusalem. The misguided exorcists thought that they could put the names of **Jesus** and **Paul** into their bag of tricks (cf. 8: 19) and use them for casting out demons. The first attempt was so disastrous that their ridiculous failure was widely commented on, creating a wave of interest in **the name of the Lord Jesus** as preached by Paul and his associates (13-17). The significance of the event was especially clear to the professionals of magic arts, who burnt their satanic literature, despite the high market price at that time (19). But again and again the emphasis is placed not on the miracles, but on the name and the **word** which spread and **prevailed mightily** (20).

v. Future Plans (19: 21, 22)
Paul and the future (21, 22). These verses are important as they open up perspectives leading to a wider and different ministry which was to follow the three missionary journeys. RSV is doubtless right in printing **Spirit** with a capital in v. 21, as Paul was divinely led to plan a tour of confirmation in Macedonia and Greece, and then to go to Jerusalem (it is the period of the collection for the poor saints in Judea) after which he understood that his mission as apostle to the Gentiles must take him to Rome. His thoughts are clearly expressed in Rom. 15: 15-29, written a few months later, when his vision already included Spain.

vi. The Riot in Ephesus (19: 23-41)
The reason for the narrative. We have seen how Luke sometimes condenses the description

of months of important ministry into a few words, but here we have a long section on an event which does not advance the annals of world evangelization. It seems that he was led to select typical incidents which illustrate the impact of the *kerygma* on different sectors of the hellenistic world. Here superstition—as is always the case—is entwined with material interests resulting from local cults. The number of converts was so considerable that Demetrius (president of the silversmiths' guild) realized that the business of the shrine-makers was on the decline. At the same time, it was still possible to inflame the masses into violent opposition to the men who were thought to have brought discredit to their goddess, of whose shrine the city of Ephesus prided itself on being the **temple keeper** (35).

Demetrius and the guild (23-28). Demetrius's speech is a marvel of carnal ingenuity, for he plays alternately on the theme of possible financial loss and on that of despite done to the goddess. He could thus excite the company but could not lead his men to any practical suggestion or conclusion, though maybe the enraged shouts (28) were designed to arouse the masses.

The gathering in the theatre (28-41). This theatre has been excavated by archaeologists who calculate that there was seating capacity for more than 25,000 people. It was a natural gathering place, but the meeting was extraordinary, unofficial, uncontrolled and confused (32). Paul's Macedonian colleagues were dragged there, but escaped with their lives. Paul himself was persuaded by Christians, and by friendly Asiarchs, not to present an 'apologia' in the theatre, as the temper of the mob was dangerous, and he might well have been lynched. We do not know what Alexander the Jew was supposed to do (33), but, in any case, he could not get a hearing. The senseless reiteration of the cry **Great is Artemis of the Ephesians**—especially in its AV form with 'Diana' instead of **Artemis**—has become proverbial as an illustration of frenzied and ignorant local fanaticism.

The town clerk's speech (35-41). The **town clerk** was the principal local official, directly responsible to the proconsul for public order. He probably waited for the mob to shout itself hoarse before attempting to control it. Then he made his masterly speech: (*a*) The honoured position of Ephesus as 'doorkeeper' or warden to the goddess was universally known and indisputable—a wise sop to their exacerbated local pride and superstition (35, 36). (*b*) They had brought Gaius and Aristarchus there, but these men could not be accused of

sacrilege or of blasphemy. This shows that Paul did not attack local superstitions directly, but outflanked them by a clear preaching of the gospel (37). (*c*) Concrete complaints could be dealt with by the usual procedure before the **proconsuls** of Asia (the generalizing plural is perhaps used because at the moment the proconsulship was vacant). (*d*) Larger issues could be decided in lawful assembly. (*e*) The commotion was dangerous in view of Roman concern in all matters relating to public order (40). The speech was like a cold shower on a feverish head, and the official **dismissed the assembly** (41).

vii. From Ephesus to Achaia (20: 1, 2)
Departure from Ephesus (1). Paul's work in Ephesus was done, and the Asiarchs would probably advise his leaving the city. Luke's account of the evangelization of Asia is very brief, and should be supplemented by studying Paul's address to the Ephesian elders (17-35), as well as the passing references to this ministry in the Letters to the Corinthians, written from Ephesus. The apostle was often in danger from Jewish plots, and under a constant strain. Could some of the imprisonments mentioned in 2 C. 11: 23 be fitted into the Ephesian ministry? Some scholars have thought so, but this cannot be roundly affirmed. Besides this suffering, he carried the tremendous burden of the attitude of an anti-Pauline party in the Corinthian church which caused him much anguish of spirit, while he felt the constant pressure of anxiety for all the churches he had been led to found (2 C. 11: 28, 29). The Ephesian period is a great success story, but the hero was also a martyr (2 C. 1: 8-11).

Macedonia and Greece (2, 3). Paul's aim was to encourage the believers, but behind the vague phrase **when he had gone through these parts** may lie a journey to Illyricum, on the Adriatic coast (Rom. 15: 19). **Greece** here means Achaia, and the background of the journey is supplied by 2 C. 1: 15-2: 16. We gather that the three months' visit to Corinth (implicit in vv. 2, 3) was a happy one, thanks to Titus's good work and the effect of the letters. In Gaius's hospitable home Paul was able to dictate his great letter to the Romans, inspired by his plans for proceeding thither after his proposed visit to Jerusalem (Rom. 15; 16). At the same time he completed his plans for conveying the help of the Gentile churches to the poor 'saints' in Jerusalem (1 C. 16: 1-3; 2 C. 8; 9; Rom. 15: 25-28).

viii. From Corinth to Miletus (20: 3-16)
A plot and a change of plan (3-6). Paul had thought to embark in Corinth for Syria, but, on learning of a plot against him, he changed his

route, undertaking the long détour around the Aegean Sea. He was thus in Macedonia again, and celebrated the Passover in his beloved Philippi (3, 6). We can better understand the list of the names of his companions, with a mention of the districts they came from, if we remember that the main purpose of the journey was to convey a considerable sum to Jerusalem, and that these men were not only colleagues, but representatives of the churches in their districts (4; with 1 C. 16: 3 f.; 2 C. 8: 16-23). The meeting place was to be Troas, and the pronoun **we** (6) shows that Luke joined the apostle again in Philippi (where the previous 'we' section ended in ch. 16).

Events in Troas (7-12). We understand v. 7 to indicate that the Breaking of Bread on the first day of the week was customary during the apostolic period. Pliny the Younger's communication to Trajan (*c.* A.D. 112) indicates that 'a sacred meeting' was held early on a fixed day, doubtless Sunday, among the Christians in Bithynia. Luke seems to be 'seeing' the crowded upper room with its many lights as he pens v. 8 (he was there at the time). The lesson to be deduced from the story of Paul's extended ministry and of the accident to Eutychus, is not that preachers should not go on too long, but that in days of the plenitude of the Spirit everything was subordinated to the word. Paul embraced the corpse and recalled back the departed spirit, returning to the upper room, not to comment on the accident or the miracle, but to continue the ministry of the word until the day dawned. It might be the last opportunity to build up the believers in Troas, and that was the overriding consideration. At the same time the Christians were not dead to natural affection, and the members of the family who took Eutychus home alive **were not a little comforted** (12).

Paul's lonely walk (13-17). While the ship slowly coasted the S.W. promontory of Mysia, Paul walked across the headland to Assos, doubtless seeking solitude and communion with his Master. The names which Luke lovingly transcribes—Assos, Mitylene, Chios, Miletus—are redolent of mythical and historical lore, prized by a classical scholar such as he was. At Miletus, birthplace of western philosophy, Paul had summoned the elders of the Ephesian church to meet him, avoiding the delay which would have been inevitable had he made a halt in Ephesus.

ix. The Address to the Ephesian Elders (20: 17-38)

The leaders of the church (17, 18). This section throws clear light on church government and ministry in the orbit of Paul's labours, and demands a more thorough analysis than we can give here. When Paul wished to counsel the leaders of the church, a definite number of men set out to meet him. Not one, nor the whole church, but a group obviously recognized by all as the **elders** were invited. In v. 28 these men are called *episkopoi*, translated **guardians** in RSV, but usually 'bishops' or 'overseers'. That they were also the 'shepherds' or 'pastors' is clear from the same v. 28. Here, as elsewhere (cf. 14: 23) the identity of 'elders'='overseers' ('bishops')='pastors' is established, each term defining a particular aspect of the qualifications and mission of the leaders of the local church. The message is not so much an exhortation from an apostle to elders, but rather the presentation of a great example of pastoral service, and Paul might have said with Peter: 'So I exhort the elders among you, as a fellow elder' (1 Pet. 5: 1).

The first movement of the address: an example of service (18-21). Paul can confidently appeal to his own example of service **from the first day**. (*a*) Personal experiences predominate in v. 19, such as humble service, **tears** and **trials**. (*b*) Varied ministry is stressed in vv. 20, 21, for nothing **profitable** was withheld, either in public or private teaching and preaching, while the 'proclamation' to Jew and Gentile called for **repentance to God and . . . faith in our Lord Jesus Christ.**

Second movement: the future course (22-27). Paul goes on to speak of his future course, which provides both example and warning. (*a*) The journey to Jerusalem (22-24). This journey was not a 'mistake', since a Spirit-empowered apostle had received instructions from his Lord about the matter, while the messages through the prophets rightly stressed the danger involved. This is what **bound in the Spirit** must mean so that the **imprisonments and afflictions** predicted could not turn him from his course which must be accomplished, irrespective of personal considerations, since his life was not precious to himself but only as a means of serving the Lord (23, 24). (*b*) The **ministry** is defined as testifying to **the gospel of the grace of God** which is identified with the proclamation of **the kingdom** (24, 25). (*c*) **the whole counsel of God:** Paul's conscience was clear with regard to his service in Ephesus, for he had proclaimed, not a part of a divine message, but **the whole counsel of God** revealed in the OT and completed by the NT revelations (25-27).

Third movement: warnings for the elders (28-31). (*a*) The **Holy Spirit** had fitted the overseers for their labours in relation to the flock for which Christ died, so that their responsibility was very great. (*b*) First they must take care of their own testimony, so as to be able worthily to care for the flock. The strange phrase **which he obtained with his own blood** may indicate the oneness of essence between Father and Son manifested even in the work of redemption (cf. 2 C. 5: 19), but another translation is possible: 'with the blood of His own', with 'Son' or 'Servant' understood. (*c*) Perils would arise from within and without, and v. 30 reminds us of the many warnings of the Pastoral Letters. (*d*) The warning was emphasized by memories of Paul's own constant admonitions (31).

Fourth movement: commendation to the Lord and the Word (32). Paul will no longer be with them, but he commends them into the mighty hand of his Lord and to the enlightenment and power of the word, which is able to build them up with a view to the great **inheritance** of the **sanctified**.

Fifth movement: the example of generous giving (33-35). The epilogue underlines the fact that love delights to give, and is thus fully blessed. Paul was especially careful that he should not be classified with religious leaders who turned their sacred mission into a motive of personal aggrandisement or material profit. The elders must follow this example. The quotation at the end of v. 35 shows that collections of 'Sayings of Jesus' circulated which have not been incorporated into the canonical Gospels.

The farewell (36-38). We are thankful for this glimpse of the 'family relations' of the believers, and for the manifestation of love and gratitude from the taught to the teacher.

x. From Miletus to Jerusalem (21: 1-16)
The Christian family in Tyre. From Patara the apostle and his company were on the route of the wheat trade from Egypt to Rome. Tyre was the great merchant city of the Phoenicians in ancient times, but lost a good deal of its importance after its savage destruction by Alexander the Great in 332 B.C. The existence of a Christian church in the city shows how the gospel had spread throughout Palestine and neighbouring countries by the year 57. The command (doubtless through a prophet) that Paul should not go up to Jerusalem has puzzled many, but in view of 20: 22-24 must be considered as a prediction of trouble ahead, which was overridden by a revelation given to Paul himself. The idea that Paul obstinately pressed on against the prohibitions of the Holy Spirit must be rejected. The farewell and prayer meeting on the beach is especially revealing, and more so as these believers—unlike the elders of Ephesus—had had but little personal contact with the apostle (5, 6).

If circles of local churches lose the sense of their oneness as a spiritual family, the mere preservation of sound doctrines and right practices will mean but little.

Paul in Caesarea (7-14). There were **brethren** to be **greeted** in **Ptolemais** on the way to Caesarea, the natural port for Jerusalem. We should like to know more about the constitution of the church into which Gentile believers were first introduced on equal terms with the Jews (ch. 10), but we are only given a glimpse of **Philip the evangelist, who was one of the seven** (cf. 6: 5), and his **daughters**, hosts of the apostolic company. Philip had continued to exercise the special gift of an **evangelist** from the dispersion onward (ch. 8). The fact that his daughters **prophesied** throws interesting light on the ministry of gifted women, as prophecy is, by definition, a public ministry. 1 C. 11: 5 supports the view that such gifted women had more than a merely domestic ministry in apostolic times.

The symbolic and vocal prophecy of Agabus (11) is very much in the style of OT prophetic ministry, and gave rise to renewed appeals that Paul should spare himself bonds and imprisonment. But his witness before governors and kings must needs be fulfilled, and when Paul persisted in his willingness to suffer all things **for the name of the Lord Jesus,** all submitted to what was recognized as **the will of the Lord** (12-14).

The important third journey had lasted from approximately A.D. 53 to 57; the three great expeditions had together opened up vast areas to the gospel, stretching from Antioch to Illyricum. Apart from our Lord's own ministry on earth, no such period of time has had anything like the significance of the twelve years A.D. 45-57. From now until the end of Luke's story, Paul will be Christ's 'ambassador in bonds' (Eph. 6: 20).

XIII. THE AMBASSADOR IN BONDS: PART ONE: IN JERUSALEM (21: 17-23: 35)
i. Contact with the Jerusalem Church (21: 17-26)
Difficulties real and imaginary. The description of Paul's arrival at Jerusalem, his contacts with the brethren, and their advice calculated to conjure the perils which might arise from the opposition of the Jewish-Christian multitude, certainly involve exegetical difficulties, but these have been exaggerated by the failure to take into account the transitional nature of the period. This failure in perspective leads expositors to judge the situation as if the Jerusalem church were a local church in Gentile lands after the

testimony had passed to the great majority of Christians of Gentile birth. When the Jerusalem elders said to Paul: **you yourself live in observance of the law** (24; cf. 1 C. 9: 20) they recalled the well-known fact that Paul, in Jewish circles, observed the customs so as to be able to continue his ministry among Jews to the end. When this is understood, there is no need for excuses on one hand or for condemning a compromise on the other. It is of interest to note that, apart from a passing reference in 24: 17, Luke does not mention the primary purpose of the visit to Jerusalem: the handing over of the funds resulting from the offerings of the Gentiles, which occupied so much of Paul's thoughts at that time (see note on 20: 3–6; Rom. 15: 25–28; 2 C. 8; 9). What he does record is that Paul and his company were well received by James and the elders, and given ample opportunity to detail what God had done among the Gentiles, which motivated sincere praise.

The problem and a proposed solution (20–26). Obviously the great majority of believers in Jerusalem (after the dispersion of 8: 4) accepted Jesus as their Messiah, thinking of themselves as the 'faithful remnant', without understanding the universal nature of the church and its freedom from the shadows of the old regime. They were pious Jews confessing Christ (20) and still practising the customs they had received. The enemy Jews had taken care to represent Paul's labours among the Gentiles as the sabotage of an apostate who taught Jews **to forsake Moses, telling them not to circumcise their children or observe the customs.** This was not true, but the elders of Jerusalem were concerned with the fact that it was largely believed in their own community. They did not go back on their letter of 15: 23–29 (25) but suggested that Paul should show by something visible and concrete that he, as a Jew among Jews, observed the customs. Previously he had purified himself after a vow of his own (18: 18b); now he is to undertake the expenses for four men, who, at the end of the period of a Nazirite vow, had to offer the prescribed sacrifices. This was a recognized act of piety among the Jews. It is not often noted that the solution was probably successful with reference to the multitude of Jewish Christians, and the generous offerings of Gentile believers would have helped towards mutual understanding and fellowship. The danger arose unexpectedly, not from the legalistic section of the Jerusalem church, but from unbelieving **Jews from Asia**, who, visiting Jerusalem, recognized Paul and Trophimus. (For a Nazirite vow see 18: 18b with Num. 6: 2 ff. In NT times the vow usually lasted 30 days.)

ii. The Riot in the Temple Area (21: 27–40) Paul in danger of a violent death (27–31). The prophecies as to perils in Jerusalem were fulfilled, but Paul was delivered from the hands of fanatical Jews in order to fulfil his ministry as an ambassador of Christ in bonds. The plan proposed by the elders went forward normally, with Paul's full co-operation (26). Despite the RSV translation of v. 27, the time reference in 24: 11 makes it probable that the violent interruption took place early in the proceedings: 'when the seven days were going to be fulfilled' (F. F. Bruce, *Acts, Gk. text*, p. 394). The Asian Jews had seen the Gentile, Trophimus, with Paul in the city, and then, finding the apostle with the Nazirites within the sacred precincts, near the chambers assigned to the purification rites in question, supposed—no proof was ever forthcoming—that he had introduced a Gentile beyond the outer court: an offence punishable by death and one which would have defiled the temple (27–29). The Asian Jews denounced the supposed crime to the worshippers in the temple, and the news spread like a train of gunpowder to the multitudes in the city. Paul was seized and dragged out to the Court of the Gentiles, while the temple attendants shut the gates of the inner court. This picture of the excitable mob, so easily induced to an act of lynching by a false report, is in entire agreement with the atmosphere of the times—the years preceding the great rebellion.

The intervention of the Romans (31–42). The Roman garrison had its barracks in the tower of Antonia, a fortress overlooking the Temple area at its NW angle, which accounts for the rapid appearance of troops under the leadership of the military tribune (colonel in charge of a cohort and senior Roman official in Jerusalem at the time) who would be fearful of riots on feast days. The officer could get no clear charge from the mob and formed his own conclusion that this was a renewal of trouble by the *sicarii* or **Assassins** (38), chaining Paul and having him borne towards the fortress steps.

Paul managed to get the ear of the tribune, who, struck by his good Greek and citizenship of Tarsus, rather surprisingly admitted his request to address the multitude (37–40). Josephus mentions an Egyptian who claimed to be a prophet and led a multitude into the desert in A.D. 54, where his followers were either killed or dispersed. Lysias confuses them with the *sicarii*, the dagger men employed by fanatical anti-Roman Jews.

iii. Paul's Defence before the Multitude (22: 1–30) Paul and his fellow countrymen (1, 2). Luke is concerned to present the apostle over

329

against representative persons or companies, typical of his age. The speech from the steps of the tower of Antonia underlines the Jewish rejection of his person and message in the very heart of Judaism. Miraculously the seething mob quietened at the sound of a polite address in Aramaic, here called **the Hebrew language,** and thus received one more opportunity to respond to the Christian message.

Paul's history as a Jewish leader (3-5). A younger generation of Palestine Jews would know little or nothing of Saul of Tarsus, though Paul could appeal to the memories of the high priest and the Sanhedrin (5). There is an obvious fitness in stressing his former complete identification with zealous and fanatical Judaism, his training in Gamaliel's school, and his leadership of the persecution of the Christian **Way.** No one could understand better than he the religious passions now aroused in opposition to himself and his message.

The renewed story of his conversion (6-16: cf. 9: 1-19; 26: 12-20). If Paul was formerly what the Jews continued to be, they could become as he was now if only they could understand the significance of Christ's appearance on the Damascus road. Hence the story of his conversion, which tallies with Luke's account in ch. 9, with the addition of Saul's question: **What shall I do, Lord?** (10). The bystanders may have heard Saul's voice, but not the Lord's (9). It is natural that Ananias's intervention should be stressed here and not in 26: 12-20, as the witness of a pious Jew would be valuable as a means of gaining the ear of the Jerusalem crowd, but useless before Agrippa and an audience of Palestinian and Roman officials. Ananias's message is here couched in OT terms, with the use of **the Just One** (14) as a messianic title (cf. 3: 14; 7: 52). Emphasis falls on the reception of a messianic message to be delivered **to all men** (15).

The middle voice imperative of v. 16 means: 'Get yourself baptized and your sins washed away', and must be understood in the light of NT teaching on forgiveness of sins and baptism (see notes on 2: 38; 8: 12 ff.; 8: 36 ff.; 10: 47). Saul had been closely associated with crimes against Christ and His church, and his baptism was a public dissociation from those sins, and thus a 'cleansing'.

The vision in the Temple (17-21). The vision in the temple must belong to Paul's first visit to Jerusalem following his conversion (9: 26-30). It is difficult to understand why Paul introduced an incident, which, although it explains his mission to the Gentiles, was bound to raise the ire of the mob by the very mention of a command to leave Jerusalem to go far away

to the nations (18-21). The point is to be found presumably in his own intercession (19, 20), which reveals Paul's long-held conviction that his former record as a persecutor would serve to convince the Jews that some special and divine communication had caused him to preach the message he had formerly so violently rejected. In this he was mistaken and was so informed by his Master from the beginning, for Jerusalem was to reject him as it had the Lord Himself, the Twelve and Stephen.

Reactions to the witness (22, 23). The spell was broken, and frantic protests followed the story of the vision in the temple. The Jews again pronounced their sentence against the followers of the Crucified: **'Away with such a fellow . . . he ought not to live!'**

Paul claims his Roman citizenship and Lysias convokes the Sanhedrin (24-30). In commenting on 16: 35-40 we have already expressed the opinion that Paul, as a Hebrew descended from Hebrews, took no natural pride in Hellenistic culture or in Roman citizenship. If he had wished to boast in fleshly matters they would have related entirely to his race and religion (Phil. 3: 4-7; cf. Rom. 9: 1-5). He knew the Graeco-Roman world well, and would use his knowledge of it and his Roman citizenship if thereby he could further the kingdom of God. There was no further attachment. The terrible Roman scourging, so lightly proposed by Lysias, would have killed him or maimed him for life. Such a crisis elicited the fact of his Roman citizenship— how proved we do not know—which exempted him from scourging (24, 25). The attitude of Lysias changed at once. He himself had bought the precious privilege, but his prisoner had been born to it (28) and as a privileged Roman must be protected and given the opportunity of a fair trial. Paul's future witness to governors and kings hinges on the privileges of Roman citizenship, with the probability that he was able, at that time, to bear the financial burdens of the trials and the eventual appeal to Caesar. Unable to get information by torture, Lysias decided to convoke the Sanhedrin and place Paul before this supreme council. This blood-guilty tribunal thus heard a renewed witness, though in circumstances not of its own choosing.

iv. Paul before the Sanhedrin (23: 1-11)
The circumstances. Paul's presence in this session of the Sanhedrin completed his witness in Jerusalem. His attitude and his statements have been criticized, but we must remember that it would have been fatal if the session convoked by Lysias for the investigation of charges against Paul had been converted into

trial by a court invested with full authority
ver Jews in religious matters. The situation was
elicate and the atmosphere tense, and Paul
wed his life—under God's providences—to the
rotection afforded by Rome to a citizen as
et uncondemned by its tribunals. The Sanhedrin
vas the continuation of the tribunal guilty of
he blood of Christ, of Stephen and of other
Christian witnesses. Internal dissensions, as
vell as methods both corrupt and violent, had
obbed it of much of its ancient prestige, and it
vas soon to reap the utter ruin it had sown.
he president was the vile Ananias, whose
nscrupulous intrigues maintained him in
ower from A.D. 47 to 58, despite many
ccusations against him. He was assassinated by
Zealots in A.D. 66. Paul's methods must be
idged against this background, and we must
lso remember that Luke's account is necessarily
bbreviated. Unlike Peter and John (4: 5-20),
'aul was a recognized rabbi who 'spoke the
anguage' of his judges, being utterly familiar
vith the machinery and proceedings of the
anhedrin.

Paul and Ananias (1-5). The session had
robably been opened in the normal way, so
hat Paul's declaration of having **lived before
5od in all good conscience** (1) would be the
pening phrase of his defence. For his concern
n doing nothing against his conscience, see 1 C.
: 4; 1 Tim. 1: 5, 19; 3: 9; 2 Tim. 1: 3.

Ananias broke the law in spirit and in letter
vhen he ordered his underlings to smite Paul
n the mouth and the apostle's angry retort
lad in it something of the old prophetic witness
gainst iniquity in high places, and may even
e taken as a prediction of Ananias's violent end
3). Our Lord 'opened not His mouth' in
imilar circumstances, but different times
lemand different types of witness within the
ramework of divine truth. The stern denuncia-
ions of Mt. 23 exemplify Christ's condemnation
f religious iniquity. However, though apt and
prophetic, Paul's stern rebuke was contrary to
he letter of Exod. 22: 28, and he at once
dmitted it. The president was a criminal, but
he 'seat' was sacred. **I did not know . . . that
ne was the high priest** possibly means: 'I did
not recognize his high priesthood (in my
ebuke).' (Cf. 1 Th. 5: 12 for this use of the
ame verb.)

The Hope and the Resurrection (6-9).
Paul's declaration (6) looks like a tactical move
n order to divide the council and thwart any
possibility of an adverse sentence. Such a move
ust then was legitimate and necessary, but could
Paul, in good conscience, at that stage, declare:
I am a Pharisee, a son of Pharisees'? The
erm has an unpleasant sound in many ears

because of the opposition of the sect to the
Master's person and ministry, but before
judging Paul we must bear in mind: (a) The
Pharisees held fundamental doctrines based on
the OT, which the Sadducees utterly refused.
The faithful remnant, who looked for the
hope of Israel, were all Pharisees doctrinally,
and did not have to unlearn the Biblical truths
they possessed, but only to apply them to
Jesus as the Christ and to reject legalism. A
Sadducee would have to cease to be one on
becoming a Christian, but not a Pharisee.
(b) The **hope and the resurrection of the
dead** was not a theological sophism but the
essence of the gospel. Paul stirred into life
something real in some of his old companions
when he reminded them that their most
treasured possession was the messianic hope and
the doctrine of the resurrection. This was true
OT succession, and not the sterile formalism
of the Sadducees and the legalists (cf. 26: 5-7, 23).
The effect was striking as some scribes of the
Pharisees were, momentarily at least, prepared
to advocate an absolutory sentence and admit
the possibility of a special revelation given to
Paul—with reference, presumably, to his
encounter with the risen Christ near Damascus
(9). We can hope for blessing in the hearts of
some of these—the Nicodemuses and the
Josephs of Arimathea of their day.

The sequel (10, 11). The strife between
Sadducees and Pharisees in the council was such
that the pagan Lysias had to rescue his prisoner
by armed force (10). Paul must have felt both
physically and spiritually battered and worn
that night, and so received special cheer from
his Lord (11). Notice there is not a whisper of
reproach but: (a) encouragement from the
Lord of all comfort; (b) the ratification of the
witness in Jerusalem, despite all the turbulence;
(c) the confirmation of the purpose that Paul
should witness in Rome, with equal fidelity
and efficacy.

v. From Jerusalem to Caesarea (23: 12-35)
A renewed deliverance (12-24). Illegal and
violent solutions of inter-party problems were
becoming frequent in Jerusalem, as the time of
the 'dry tree' approached (Lk. 23: 31), and the
plot of the forty fanatical assassins is typical
of the times. They could count on the
co-operation of at least a 'rump' of the
Sanhedrin (12-15). This time God's deliverance
was effected, not by angel intervention as in
12: 6-10, but by means of Paul's nephew. The
apostle's witness had been blessed to some of
his relatives (Rom. 16: 7), despite the probable
rupture with the family (Phil. 3: 8) and we
would like to think that his sister was a Christian
(16). The puzzle is how the young man could

have got to know of the plot were he suspected of Christian sympathies, or why he should have taken the risk of warning his uncle if he was associated with fanatical Jews. The secret is not revealed and God ordered the circumstances in His providence. The story of vv. 16–22 is detailed and graphic, revealing Luke's presence and observation, although he does not name himself. The nephew's witness confirmed Lysias's conviction that the presence of Paul in Jerusalem would be a source of continued disturbance and that it would be difficult to preserve the life of this Roman citizen outside the fortress. His decision was to transfer him to Caesarea to be tried by the procurator, Felix. His estimate of the violent courage of the Jews is revealed by the size of the escort as far as Antipatris: 200 heavily armed soldiers, 200 light armed men and 70 horsemen (23)! The **mounts** (in the plural) for Paul suggest the presence of friends; perhaps Luke was one (24).

Lysias's letter (25–30). The clever way in which the events referring to Paul's arrest are summarized—with a twist of the facts in favour of the tribune (27)—is obvious. The psychological fitness of the communication is evidence that the historian had first-hand knowledge of it, though how, we do not know. Luke had a good eye for relevant documents!

Caesarea (31–35). Caesarea was the capital of the province and owed much to Herod the Great's planning and building. Antipatris was 25 miles from Caesarea, and beyond the sphere of action of the fanatical mob in Jerusalem so that the foot soldiers returned, leaving the cavalry to escort the prisoner to the capital. Felix took cognizance of Lysias's letter and of the arrival of Paul, ordering his accommodation in Herod's praetorium until the accusers could come down from Jerusalem. Paul's status as a Roman citizen was respected.

Antonius Felix was not a good example of a Roman procurator; he owed his position to the influence of his brother Pallas, a favourite of Claudius and a freedman of the emperor's mother, Antonia. He had dealt severely with bandits, but had stirred up widespread opposition by his violence and venality. Tacitus remarks that he 'exercised the power of a prince with the mentality of a slave'. His third wife, Drusilla, was a daughter of Herod Agrippa I.

XIV. THE AMBASSADOR IN BONDS: PART TWO: IN CAESAREA (24: 1–26: 32)
i. Paul before Felix (24: 1–27)
A time of testimony before rulers. During the two years spent as a prisoner in Caesarea, Paul was to witness before Felix, Drusilla, Festus, Herod Agrippa II, Bernice, and also

before a varying number of high officials, thus fulfilling the Lord's purpose announced in 9: 15.

The accusation (1–9). In order to exercise the maximum pressure on the governor, the high priest, Ananias, attended the trial in person, accompanied by some councillors. Tertullus was perhaps a Hellenistic Jew, trained in Roman legal procedure, and to him was committed the presentation of the accusation. (a) The exordium (2–4) was hypocritically flattering, for Felix's record was bad and the Jews hated him. (b) To call Paul **a pestilent fellow** was insulting and the description of his activities too vague for legal purposes (5). (c) Tertullus could bring no evidence to prove that the main charge—that of profaning the temple—was a fact (6). (d) Verses 6b–8a (RSVmg; cf. also AV) are from the Western Text, and though lacking in support in the best texts, seem to reflect an attempt to twist Lysias's action in arresting Paul—compare Lysias's own manipulation of the evidence in the opposite direction (23: 27). **The Jews** made Tertullus's unsatisfactory accusation their own (9).

The defence (10–21). (a) The necessary exordium (10) was brief, but courteous, with a mention of the only true fact in Felix' favour—the length of his governorship made him well acquainted with Jewish matters. (b) In the second phase Paul shows the absence of proof of any particular offence against public order or Jewish customs during the few days he was in Jerusalem (11–13). (c) The third phase turns one point of the accusation into a testimony: he did follow **the Way**, but this was in perfect accord with the law and the prophets. The resurrection hope was also that of many of the Jews, so that Paul, in his activities, maintained a good **conscience toward God** and man (14–16). (d) The fourth phase marks a return to the accusation, noting the pious and patriotic purpose of his visit, stressing his worship according to the laws of purification, and putting his finger on the weakest point of a weak case—why were the Asian Jews, who accused him of defiling the temple, not there to substantiate the charge which gave rise to the riot? (17–19). (e) The closing phase made it clear that the Sanhedrin had been unable to formulate any charge against him, as the belief in the resurrection would also condemn the Pharisees (21).

Paul was not so much concerned with clearing himself—although his defence was a very able one—as with proving the Christian faith to be a legitimate interpretation of the OT, the sacred book of the Jews, and indeed its due fulfilment. Christians, therefore, should share in the privileges of the *religio licita* granted to the Jews. The wise and effective testimony is apparent to all.

Felix' decision (22). The high priest's charges had collapsed through lack of proof, and Felix should have set his prisoner at liberty. The delay—the excuses were paltry—means that he wished to use Paul as a pawn in the game of his intrigues with the Jews, thinking also that the prisoner might be a possible source of illegal income (22, 26).

The two years' imprisonment (23-27). Felix was interested in his unusual prisoner and heard him speak of his faith in Christ Jesus when his wife Drusilla was in Caesarea. Paul emphasized the great principles of justice and self-control—so obviously lacking in his judge—showing that there was a future crisis of judgment. Felix was terrified, but put off the day of consideration and decision—which never arrived. Tradition has it that Drusilla influenced him against the truth, and this is psychologically probable as Felix had induced her to leave her husband Azizus, king of Emesa, in order to 'marry' him. The acceptance of the stern and wholesome teaching of v. 25 would have meant breaking with the life personified by Drusilla. Paul was in *custodia libera*, chained by one wrist to a soldier, but otherwise able to order his own life (23), so that prayers, letters, counsels to visitors continued. Luke probably used this time for gathering up material for both Luke and Acts.

ii. Paul before Festus (25: 1-12)
Festus and the Sanhedrin (1-5). We can only judge Festus's character by brief references in the writings of Luke and Josephus, and he strikes us as a worthy but limited official of the equestrian class, out of his depth when confronted with the complicated and explosive situation in Judea, rendered even more dangerous by the impact of nascent Christianity. He could not avoid an official visit to Jerusalem almost immediately after taking up his governorship, and was at once beset by Jewish leaders who claimed Paul as a 'religious' prisoner, though behind the façade of legality they planned to have him ambushed and killed (2, 3). Festus, who would know of Paul's Roman citizenship, insisted on a trial in Caesarea.

The trial before Festus (6-9). After the period noted in v. 6, Festus sat on the **tribunal** (Gk. *bēma*)—symbol of Roman judicial authority —and heard the confused and malicious **shouting** of the Jewish plaintiffs (v. 24). The substance of the charges can be gathered from Paul's brief defence: he had neither committed an offence against **the law** (the OT Scriptures)

nor against **the temple,** nor against **Caesar** (8; cf. 24: 10-21). As in the trial before Felix, the vague charges were not substantiated by any evidence valid before a Roman tribunal (cf. 17-19). Festus was concerned not to provoke the fierce Jewish leaders and asked Paul if he would agree to be referred back to the Sanhedrin, certainly unaware of the plot to kill him.

The appeal to Caesar (10-12). Paul found himself in a worse position than when Lysias had remitted him to Caesarea, and realized that the strong and persistent pressure of the Jewish leaders would hinder his release from any Palestinian prison. Hence his dramatic **appeal to Caesar** (11) in which he reaffirmed his rights as a Roman citizen. As the Jews had urged a political offence, Paul could quite firmly declare that he ought to be tried by Roman justice. He may have been moved by two other considerations pondered over during his imprisonment: (*a*) He was assured that he must minister in Rome, and his appeal would take him thither (19: 21; 23: 11). (*b*) A favourable verdict before Caesar's tribunal would establish a precedent, practically equivalent to declaring Christianity a *religio licita*, which was greatly to be desired, since the gap between Judaism and Christianity was becoming increasingly apparent. An appeal to Caesar was a long and expensive matter, but the die was cast.

iii. Agrippa and Bernice in Caesarea (25: 13-26: 1)
The king and his sister (13). Herod Agrippa II of our portion was the son of Herod Agrippa I of ch. 12 but had not been able to obtain from Rome the wide domains of his father and had to be content with Chalcis, a small kingdom in the Lebanon mountains, later exchanged for Trachonitis and associated territories to the NE of Galilee. He was granted the privilege of appointing the high priests in Jerusalem. He was, of course, subordinate to Rome, but represented a house which had frequently served the Empire well and was useful to Rome in dealing with the Jews. Bernice, a younger sister, was the widow of another Herod (her father's brother) who had also been king of Chalcis! Her close association with her brother was suspect. Both strove unsuccessfully to ward off the great rebellion, and both were finally driven by Jewish fanaticism to throw in their lot with Rome. These were the last members of the Herod family to influence Jewish history or to cross the triumphant path of Christian testimony. Herod Agrippa II does not seem to have inherited the anti-Christian policy of his father. It was convenient both for the king and the governor to maintain good relations, which

explains the early and prolonged diplomatic visit to Caesarea (13, 14).

Festus's problem (14-21). Festus could make no sense of the Jewish charges against Paul, yet had not released him and had admitted his appeal to Rome. Hence his problem —how was he to word the official charge (26)? The wording was also, of course, of great importance to the prisoner as a favourable report would give a good start to the proceedings in Rome. Festus realized that his royal visitor—Jew by religion and thoroughly versed in Palestinian politics—was the man to solve his problem. At the same time the audience for the investigation could be turned into an act of homage to his guests, and into a convenient display of his own authority and resources as Rome's representative.

In general the private explanation given by Festus in 14-21 is a fair summary of the situation, with some trimming in his own favour (16, 17), but the main interest centres on v. 19 where the reaction of a reasonably honest and cultured Roman to the Christian message is revealed. The phrase **their own superstition** (of the Jews) is not necessarily derogatory, for the meanings of 'superstition' and 'religion' meet in *deisidaimonia*, the word used. But all that Festus had perceived in Paul's witness was that it was about **one Jesus, who was dead, but whom Paul asserted to be alive.** The tremendous meaning of the resurrection was lost on this well-meaning pagan.

The public explanation given to the distinguished gathering (24-27) was naturally more formal, and stressed the need for Agrippa's examination in order to formulate a charge on remitting the prisoner to the Emperor. Agrippa would already know a good deal about the Christian 'Way' and was probably familiar with the name of Paul. Hence his interest in conducting the examination (22). Providentially, therefore, the cream of Palestinian aristocracy, with high-ranking Roman officials, were arrayed to hear the witness of the 'ambassador in bonds', and, owing to the special circumstances, no one was in a hurry (23). We reach the zenith of this special ministry as far as Palestine is concerned. After the introduction by Festus, Agrippa took charge, and at once gave Paul permission to speak in his own defence (26: 1).

iv. Paul's Defence before Agrippa and Festus (26: 2-23)
The substance and style of the defence. This speech is not an improvised defence and testimony as was his message to the multitude in ch. 22, for Paul had had ample time for preparation and realized the importance of the occasion. For this reason the speech is so rich in doctrinal, historical and apologetic interest, and therefore very difficult to summarize in limited space. Some scholars inform us that Paul remembered his lessons in rhetoric learnt in the schools of Tarsus, as he gives unusual attention to style on this occasion, though the language is, of course, hellenistic and not classical Greek. Others, however, regard it as extremely doubtful that Paul ever attended Greek school in Tarsus, interpreting Ac. 22: 3 to mean that Jerusalem was the city of his boyhood.

The exordium (2, 3). The exordium was obligatory in such 'apologies' before distinguished judges, and again Paul knew how to combine courtesy and truth, being indeed **fortunate** to be able to marshal his arguments before a potentate thoroughly versed in Jewish questions, and not ignorant of the beginnings of Christianity.

Saul the Pharisee (4, 5). Paul is desirous that his conversion and Christian ministry should be seen against the background of his early history as an orthodox Jew, adherent of the strictest party, that of the Pharisees. Although he was a native of Gentile Tarsus, his life was lived among those of his own nation, though this does not exclude Greek influences.

Paul adhered to the Hope of Israel (6-8). He was no dangerous deviationist, but held firmly to the hope which sprang from the fundamental promises given to the nation (Gen. 12-15) and which found their consummation in the resurrection; for from the beginning Abraham had learnt to trust in the God who gives life to the dead (Rom. 4: 16-25). The ideal nation of the twelve tribes (actually represented by the faithful remnant) had never given up this hope in the course of their divine worship, and the resurrection of the dead is incredible only to those who do not know God.

Saul the persecutor (9-11). Paul goes back to his history and shows that not only was he a Pharisee, but also the outstanding leader of the first general persecution of the church in Jerusalem. We may note the graphic details of that tragic period and Saul's **raging fury** against the **saints.** It is difficult to understand the reluctance of some scholars to admit that the statement **when they were put to death cast my vote against them** means that Saul, despite his youth, was a member of the Sanhedrin, for lesser courts could not bring in death sentences.

Saul's conversion (12-15). For the third time we are presented with this vital narrative (cf. 9: 1-19; 22: 6-16). Its importance as an explanation of Paul's ministry is obvious, and Agrippa would see the force of an experience analogous to that of prophets in the OT when called to divine service, noting the *shekinah* glory (the **light from heaven, brighter than the sun**), the prostration, the command: **rise and stand upon your feet.** (Cf. Exod. 3: 1-15; Isa. 6: 1-9; Ezek. 1: 1-3: 4; Dan. 10: 7-11.) Ananias's part in the event is naturally omitted here, and the terms of the commission are given as if they were fully announced on the road to Damascus. In the best texts the important reference to Saul's 'kicking **against the goads**' is given only here (14). Saul the Pharisee became Paul the apostle because he saw Jesus as the Lord of glory and could not be disobedient to the heavenly vision (19).

Paul's commission (16-18). The messages from the Lord to His apostle were to be continuous (16) and he thus received the deposit of divine truth—also called the 'mystery'—which he was so careful to administer (1 C. 4: 1-6; Eph. 3: 1-13; Col. 1: 26-2: 6; 1 Tim. 1: 12-14; 2 Tim. 1: 11-14; etc.). In his labours he was promised deliverance (17; cf. Jer. 1: 18) and his summary of our Lord's communication includes such vital themes as spiritual illumination, the conversion of believers **from darkness to light,** their translation from Satan's **power** to God's, the **forgiveness of** their **sins** and their standing among the **sanctified** (17, 18; cf. Col. 1: 12-14 for an almost identical summary). How strangely such terms would fall on the ears of the distinguished audience in the hall of Herod's palace!

Paul's preaching (19-23). Paul has described his commission and now passes on to the way in which he fulfilled it, as obedient **to the heavenly vision.** (*a*) The sphere of service (20) includes Damascus, Jerusalem, the country of Judea and the vast Gentile lands. The third item offers some difficulty as we have no other mention of labours in Judea as a province. Perhaps Palestine in general is meant, and Paul would not cease to preach wherever possible as he travelled to and from Jerusalem. (*b*) The main themes were repentance from sin, conversion **to God** and **works** which would prove the reality of conversion (20). (*c*) The link with the OT is provided in vv. 22, 23. The Jews tried to kill him, not because he had abandoned the OT revelation, but because he proclaimed **to small and great** the prophetic content of the OT as fulfilled in the sufferings and resurrection of Jesus the Messiah, who would, through His servants, spread spiritual **light both to the people** (Israel) **and to the Gentiles** (cf. 13: 47). This emphasis links back

to the preliminary mention of the resurrection theme in vv. 6-8.

v. The Effects of the Message (26: 24-32)
Festus's exclamation (24, 25). The blasé audience expected to be mildly interested in the defence of a man so well known because of his effective propaganda and so well hated by the Jews; but as Paul developed his thesis and told his thrilling story in refined and skilful language, the interest must have increased and the tension mounted. Some must have come to the unexpected conclusion that the message of the Jewish rabbi had something to do with them! The tension is clear from Festus's loud exclamation when Paul came to a pause—perhaps before a final peroration which he was not permitted to give. Festus, sensing the tension but unable to follow the meaning, abbreviated the proceedings by his shout, which admitted Paul's learning, but put his testimony down to a divine madness—the expression was not necessarily insulting. Paul rejects all idea of 'madness'—even of the oracular sort—and insists on his **sober truth,** turning at once to Agrippa who could recognize the terms of his address.

Paul and Agrippa (26-29). Paul's appeal to Agrippa takes for granted, not only his knowledge of the OT scriptures, but also his acquaintance with the origins of Christianity which held the attention of Palestinians over many vital years (26). The challenge to Agrippa's belief in the prophets (27) suggested a belief also in their fulfilment in Jesus Christ—hence the king's reply: 'In short you are trying to make me act the Christian!' (trans. F. F. Bruce). The 'almost thou persuadest me' of the AV must be abandoned on textual and exegetical grounds. Paul took up the king's slightly cynical evasion, with a word play on *en oligō* ('in short') and turned it into a most telling testimony: **Whether short or long, I would to God that not only you but also all that hear me this day might become such as I am—except for these chains.** How much wealthier was he, in Christ, than the wealthiest listener! How much happier than the happiest! Luke tells us nothing of spiritual fruit, but by such means the gospel was introduced into the highest spheres of the Empire in these and in succeeding years.

Drafting the report for Caesar (30-32). The king, the procurator and their advisors withdrew for consultation, and the general opinion was that Paul was innocent, but that Festus must needs send him to Rome since he had appealed. It was not mentioned that on those same grounds, Felix and Festus should have released him long ago! It is a natural deduction from vv. 31, 32 that the report drawn up for Caesar's tribunal was favourable to the prisoner.

XV. THE AMBASSADOR IN BONDS: PART THREE: ON THE JOURNEY TO ROME (27: 1–28: 15)
i. A Detailed Report
At first sight Luke's narrative of the hazardous journey to Rome seems disproportionately long when compared with his brief summaries of periods and circumstances which would throw much more light on apostolic ministry and on the function and testimony of local churches. Perhaps Paul's Master would have us know what His servant was like when he shared the vicissitudes and dangers of life with his fellow men, and that the work of service and ministry must not be estimated merely by sermons and writings. Paul, as God's man (23), became the real leader of a heterogeneous company of people on board a ship drifting toward wreckage, and was the means of their temporal salvation. Luke's narration is acclaimed as one of the masterpieces of 'shipwreck' literature—it reads well in NEB—but we are concerned, not so much with the dramatic incidents, as with the witness of an apostle who was in the counsels of God just as much in the perils of the sea as when he received those special revelations which did so much to complete the NT scriptures.
ii. From Caesarea to Fair Havens (27: 1–12)
Paul and his companions (1, 2). Julius, a **centurion of the Augustan Cohort,** and possibly an officer-courier in the Emperor's service, was about to leave Caesarea with soldiers and prisoners, so that Paul was handed over to his custody. He was accompanied by Aristarchus of Thessalonica, who afterwards laboured with the apostle in Rome (Col. 4: 10; Phm. 24), it being probable therefore that he volunteered to serve him (cf. 20: 4). Luke's presence is indicated by the pronoun **we.** A coasting vessel en route to Asian ports served for the first stage of the journey, until Julius could transfer his company to a wheat vessel going to Rome.

From Caesarea to Myra (3–6). In Sidon there were **friends** (doubtless a local church) to care for Paul, who was treated with courtesy and kindness by the centurion. The journey was slow from the start, and the ship from Adramyttium worked with difficulty round the east end of Cyprus, coasting Cilicia and Pamphylia before getting to the harbour of Myra in Lycia. There Julius transferred his company to an Alexandrian wheat ship bound for Rome. It was probably under government

contract, and Julius would be senior officer on board.

Myra to Fair Havens (7–12). Large sailing vessels of the period could tack to a certain extent, but persistent head winds made progress difficult as they left Cnidus (extreme SW of Asia Minor) and sought the shelter of the eastern and southern coasts of Crete. The delays were a serious matter as the period 15th October to 10th November was considered dangerous for navigation and ships were then laid up until after February. The **fast** (9) was that of the day of Atonement which fell late in the year 59—an indirect confirmation of the estimated date of this journey.

It was now clear to the owner, to the captain and to Julius that it would be impossible to get to Rome before winter, so that the consultations (9–12) were to decide whether to winter in Fair Havens, or to try to push on to Phoenix, further along the south coast of Crete, which was thought to provide a better harbour for their purpose. Modern Phineka is largely silted up, but there is no reason to suppose another port, and it does face SW and NW (follow RSVmg here). Paul could proffer advice as a respected Roman citizen, brought up in the area, although he was a prisoner on a vague, non-criminal charge; but the centurion naturally followed the advice of the experts.
iii. Paul's Witness in the Storm and Wreck (27: 13–44)
The storm (13–20). A south wind seemed to promise an easy passage to Phoenix, less than 100 miles to the west, but Paul's prediction of disaster found early fulfilment when a violent NE wind from off Crete struck the ship with such force that the only solution was to run before the gale with a minimum of sail. The **boat** (16) was the dinghy, normally towed behind. The undergirding (17) of the hull with ropes, to brace the timbers against the impact of the waves, was a well-known operation. As no land or sky was visible, navigation was impossible, though the westward course (when driven by a NE wind) seems to indicate some steering to avoid the dreaded Syrtis shoals off the North African coast. The operation noted in verses 18–20 tended to relieve strain by throwing overboard all unnecessary rigging and to lighten the ship. The situation was desperate and the conditions for the 276 people aboard distressing in the extreme (20).

Paul's moral leadership (21–26). No maritime skill was of any avail, but God's servant received a message not only for himself but also for the frightened crowd on board. Addressing them, he reminded them of his rejected advice in Fair Havens. There was nothing wrong in this according to Paul's straightforward thinking and it enhanced his authority as he gave them a message full of cheer. There was a supreme God, whom he worshipped and served, and to whom he belonged. His God had sent an angel to confirm His purposes for His servant, saying: **Do not be afraid, Paul; you must stand before Caesar; and lo, God has granted you all those who sail with you** (24). Paul accepted God's message with unreserved faith, knowing that things would turn out exactly as he had been informed. As something clear to his own prophetic spirit, he added that they would **run on some island.** Being perfectly confident himself, he was doubtless able to instil some cheer into men and women who had hitherto felt that pagan Fate had doomed them to perish in the raging sea. We deduce that Paul had interceded for his fellow passengers, for it is said that God granted them to him as a gift (*kecharistai*, v. 24).

Approaching Malta (27-38). Fourteen days from Fair Havens to Malta seems a long time, but experts calculate a drift of only 26 miles a day in such circumstances (F. F. Bruce, *The Book of the Acts, ad loc.*). Perhaps the noise of breakers on the Malta coast warned the mariners of the proximity of land and led them to check the situation by soundings (27, 28). The anchors were cast from the stern and not from the bow, as the vessel needed to be held—by a minimum of sail—in the direction of the wind and ready for beaching when morning came. These precautions taken, they **prayed for day to come.** How long the hours must have seemed from midnight to dawn! Paul again intervened for the general good when he perceived that the sailors intended to steal a march on the rest by getting to shore in the dinghy. Their skilled help was needed for the dangerous manoeuvre of beaching, so, on Paul's warning, the soldiers cut the ropes and let the dinghy drift—a swift Roman reaction which lost them the boat! Before daybreak Paul nerved the company for their forthcoming ordeal by very practical advice and example. He renewed his divinely-given assurance of protection for their lives, but reminded them of the need of food after the prolonged fast, for physical energies would be necessary. He himself took bread, and ate it, but not without the striking testimony of giving thanks to God before them all (33-35). The rest plucked up courage and 'took food themselves' (NEB) before throwing the rest of the wheat into the sea in order to lighten the ship as much as possible for beaching.

The wreck (39-44). The light of day revealed an unknown coast, but a bay and beach offered them the possibility of running the ship ashore. Anchors were cast off, the oars which served as rudders loosed, and the foresail carried the ship forward. Verse 41 seems to indicate that, before striking the beach, they were caught in a cross current caused by the island of Salmonetta and that the bow of the ship got fixed on a shoal. The waves were breaking up the stern, but the bow served as a diving board for swimmers, while the rest helped themselves over the remaining distance by planks. According to Paul's prediction, no life was lost. It is strange that Paul's own life should have been endangered by the rigidity of Roman discipline at the very moment when others were saved thanks to his prayers and counsels. Prisoners—who might or might not be guilty—must not be allowed to escape (we remember the Philippian jailer's reactions, 16: 27) and so should be killed. Julius, however, intervened against his subordinates' advice in order to save Paul, in whom he now had a personal interest. Despite the absence of a beach, it seems to be sufficiently established that St. Paul's Bay, as it is now called, was the opening on the N. coast of Malta where the wreck took place.

iv. Blessing in Malta (28: 1-10)

Malta and its inhabitants (1, 2). The island of Malta had been used as a trading centre by the Phoenicians and Carthaginians, and had been visited by a variety of peoples; the harbour of Valletta was well known. The **natives** were 'barbarians', not because they were uncivilized, but because they did not speak Greek. They spoke a language derived from Phoenician, and were little affected by the Graeco-Roman culture. Their kind reception of the victims of the wreck contrasts well with practices on the Cornish coast as late as the eighteenth century.

Was Paul a criminal or a god (3-6)? Paul's practical and humble helpfulness is spotlighted in v. 3, but seemed badly rewarded by the viper's bite. His shaking the torpid creature **into the fire** and remaining unharmed may be reflected in Mk 16: 18 (in the later appendix to the Gospel). The reactions of the natives were natural in the circumstances—here is a prisoner who escapes death in a shipwreck, but is bitten by a serpent. The Fates got the criminal after all! But when Paul continued his homely tasks unharmed, they decided **that he was a god.** Better that way round than in the contrasting case in Lystra (14: 8-20).

A ministry of healing (7-10). The chief magistrate, called Publius, possessed lands near

M

the site of the wreck and shared in the hospitality. In that way Paul learned that Publius's father was suffering from dysentery and was led to pray for him, laying his hands on the sick man who was healed. The laying-on of hands is only rarely associated with healings in the NT, but see Lk. 4: 40 and Ac. 9: 17 (with Mk 16: 18). Others were naturally desirous of receiving similar blessings and brought their sick to be healed. Luke does not mention preachings and conversions, but the analogy of the Ephesian ministry—and all Biblical precedents—suggests that miracles always open the way for the word. We should like to think of a number of disciples among the grateful people who brought their gifts to the apostolic party as they boarded the 'Castor and Pollux'.

v. Paul reaches Rome (28: 11-15)

The journey renewed (11-14). Suitable weather about mid-February encouraged Julius to embark his company on another Alexandrian ship (probably belonging to the wheat fleet) and to continue the journey so dramatically interrupted. Syracuse, the great Sicilian harbour, and Rhegium on the Italian side of the Straits of Messina, had figured largely in Greek and Roman history. Of greater interest to us is the fact that brethren were found in Puteoli— another evidence of the wide spread of the Gospel by A.D. 60. As Paul was invited to stay with them, his ministry in Italy began there. It seems as if Julius decided to travel by road from Puteoli, so that a seven days' stay there would enable him to equip himself and his men—after the loss of nearly everything in the wreck — before entering Rome. The believers would have helped Paul and his company.

An official welcome to Rome (15). Luke anticipates the longed-for goal: **And so we came to Rome** (14), but adds an important note with reference to welcoming companies of brethren from the church in Rome, some of whom got as far as **Three Taverns,** 33 miles along the Appian Way, and others 10 miles further on to **the Forum of Appius** (15). The wait in Puteoli would allow time for messengers to announce the coming of the apostle. Paul had prepared the church for his coming years before by writing his Letter to the Romans, and had perhaps received favourable news by letter. But now brethren—including elders, doubtless—press along the Appian Way to give him an official reception (*ēlthon eis apantēsin hēmin*). This was the long-awaited sign of a friendly reception. **On seeing them, Paul thanked God and took courage.**

XVI. THE AMBASSADOR IN BONDS: PART FOUR: PAUL'S MINISTRY IN ROME (28: 16-31)

i. Paul's Witness to the Jews in Rome (28: 16-28)

Paul in 'free custody' in Rome (16). The best Greek texts make no reference to the way in which Paul was handed over to Roman authorities, but the relative comfort of his captivity is emphasized (16). He was able to provide for his own lodging, but was fastened to his soldier guard by a light chain. He had to be available when his case was tried, but was quite free to receive visits, to preach and to write in the meantime. Finance did not seem to be a problem at that time.

Paul's explanations to local Jewish leaders (17-22). The first three days in Rome were probably devoted to contacts with Christian leaders, but Paul was not likely to forget his 'debt' to the 'Jew first' (Rom. 1: 14-16). Not only must he fulfil his mission to 'the people', but it was necessary to find out whether local Jews were to act as his accusers at the instance of the Sanhedrin. Paul could not go to the synagogues, but the Jewish elders responded to his invitation and met him in his lodging. The explanation of the appeal to Rome (17-20) is brief but exact, and Paul is careful to show that there was no hostility on his part to the Jewish nation. The **hope of Israel** was the messianic hope, incarnate in Christ Jesus and brought to a climax by the resurrection (cf. notes on 23: 6; 24: 15; 26: 6-8, 22, 23).

Strangely enough, the Jewish leaders in Rome had received no specific information from Jerusalem about Paul and therefore no instructions to present the case for the accusers. The high priest and his colleagues must have realized the hopelessness of seeking an adverse sentence in Rome when they had failed in Caesarea. The elders, however, were desirous of hearing the truth about the Nazarene sect, **everywhere . . . spoken against,** from the lips of such a well-known leader. Because of the slow growth of the Christian church in Rome over the years, and the frequent decrees of expulsion against the Jews, there was probably little contact either way between the two communities in Rome.

Discussions with the Jews and a last warning (23-28). Great numbers of Jews came for information and discussion to Paul's lodging, which was obviously commodious. Paul's presentation of the gospel to the Jews has been considered in notes on 13: 16 ff.; 17: 2, 3; etc., and his method is unchanged in Rome, for the exposition would necessarily be based on OT scriptures fulfilled in the ministry, death and resurrection of Jesus, proclaimed as the Messiah. This constituted a solemn testimony to the kingdom of God which depended on the recognition of the rightful King (23). The long session **from morning till evening** would include the discussions common to Jewish debate. As always, the word divided the company into those who were persuaded of its truth, and the rest who were incredulous. Before the guests departed, arguing now among themselves, Paul couched his last recorded warning to his own people in the well-known words associated with Isaiah's call (Isa. 6: 9, 10). The heart of Israel—seat of desires, affections and will in Scripture—had grown dull, or gross, and this inner evil of wrongly directed desire closed the people's ear to the message and shut their eyes to the glory of God in the face of Jesus Christ (26, 27).

ii. Paul's wide Ministry in Rome (28: 30, 31)
Luke's abrupt ending (30, 31). It seems extraordinary that Luke should not give us clear information about the result of the appeal to Caesar, so dramatically presented in chs. 25 and 26. It can be deduced from the tendencies noted above, and from these verses, that the case went by default because the accusation was not followed up. The **two whole years** (the aorist tense of **lived** denotes something completed) would give time to wind up the legal proceedings. Believing Paul to be the direct author of the Pastoral Letters, we follow conservative scholars in thinking that from 62 to 65 Paul was a free man, visiting Crete and points round the Aegean Sea (Tit. 1: 5; 2 Tim. 4: 13, 20) and *possibly* fulfilling his desire to visit Spain. When Nero turned against the Christians he was arrested again and wrote 2 Timothy as a farewell message to his younger colleague. Paul is the hero of the Acts from ch. 13 onwards, but we must remember that Luke's purpose was to trace the spread of the gospel from Jerusalem to the ends of the earth (1: 8). This vast movement reached its climax when Paul, the apostle to the Gentiles, exercised a wide ministry in the metropolis of the Empire, so that the abrupt end is far from being an anti-climax, for the author's task was completed.

The nature of Paul's ministry (30, 31). In the first place, Paul received all who came to him. These would be men like Epaphras, who linked the apostle with the churches of the Lycus valley in the province of Asia, and gave occasion for the Letter to the Colossians (Col. 1: 7, 8). Other visitors would share his vision for the evangelization of the West (Rom. 15: 17-29) and would go from his lodging to Gaul and Spain. His intercessions, teachings and counsels linked him with the whole westward

movement of the kingdom. As for Rome, he proclaimed **the kingdom of God** to varying companies of people, with results such as those mentioned in Phil. 1: 12-18. By his **teaching about the Lord Jesus Christ** he handed on his deposit of Christian doctrine according to his own principle expressed in 2 Tim. 2: 2.

It is still much more probable that Philippians, Colossians and Ephesians were written during the two years in Rome than during a supposed, but unrecorded, imprisonment in Ephesus, in which case we owe the deep and full Christology of these sublime writings—the climax and crown of his special revelation—to his meditations and inspiration during the time when he could not travel, but was therefore freer to receive and express the truth of Christ and His church, the centre of God's plan throughout the ages. God's 'ambassador in bonds' fulfilled his ministry both before the highest tribunal of the Empire (cf. 2 Tim. 4: 17) and in the deepest recesses of the sanctuary, giving glory to 'Him who by the power at work within us, is able to do far more abundantly than all that we ask or think. To Him be glory in the church and in Christ Jesus unto all the generations of the age of the ages' (Eph. 3: 20, 21).

BIBLIOGRAPHY

Commentaries

BLAIKLOCK, E. M., *The Acts of the Apostles: An Historical Commentary*. TNTC (London, 1959).

BRUCE, F. F., *The Acts of the Apostles*2 [On the Greek text] (London, 1952).

BRUCE, F. F., *The Book of the Acts*. NIC (Grand Rapids, 1954).

HANSON, R. P. C., *The Acts of the Apostles*. NCB (Oxford, 1967).

KELLY, W., *The Acts of the Apostles*2 (London, 1914).

KNOWLING, R. J., *The Acts of the Apostles*. EGT [On the Greek text] (London, 1900).

LAKE, K., and CADBURY, H. J., *The Acts of the Apostles* [Vol. IV of *The Beginnings of Christianity*] (London, 1933).

MUNCK, J., *The Acts of the Apostles*. Anchor Bible (New York, 1967).

PACKER, J. W., *The Acts of the Apostles*. CBSC (Cambridge, 1966).

PAGE, T. E., *The Acts of the Apostles* [On the Greek text] (London, 1886).

RACKHAM, R. B., *The Acts of the Apostles*6. WC (London, 1912).

WILLIAMS, C. S. C., *The Acts of the Apostles*. BNTC (London, 1957).

WILLIAMS, R. R., *The Acts of the Apostles*. Torch Commentaries (London, 1953).

General Works

CADBURY, H. J., *The Book of Acts in History* (New York, 1955).

Acts

CADBURY, H. J., *The Making of Luke–Acts* (New York, 1927).

DIBELIUS, M., *Studies in the Acts of the Apostles*, E.T. (London, 1956).

DUPONT, J., *Études sur les Actes des Apôtres* (Paris, 1967).

DUPONT, J., *The Sources of Acts*, E.T. (London, 1964).

JACKSON, F. J. F., and LAKE, K. (editors), *The Beginnings of Christianity*, Part I: *The Acts of the Apostles*. Vols. I–V (London, 1920–33).

KNOX, W. L., *The Acts of the Apostles* (Cambridge, 1948).

O'NEILL, J. C., *The Theology of Acts* (London, 1961).

RAMSAY, W. M., *The Church in the Roman Empire*4 (London, 1895).

RAMSAY, W. M., *St. Paul the Traveller and the Roman Citizen*14 (London, 1920).

SIMON, M., *St. Stephen and the Hellenists in the Jerusalem Church* (London, 1958).

SMITH, J., *The Voyage and Shipwreck of St. Paul*4 (London, 1880).

WILCOX, M., *The Semitisms of Acts* (Oxford, 1965).

THE LETTER TO THE ROMANS

LESLIE C. ALLEN

It was probably during the winter of A.D. 56-7 that the apostle Paul in a house in Corinth wrote his letter to the Romans. His third missionary journey was drawing to a close, and for three months he was the guest of Gaius (cf. Ac. 20: 3). He could look back upon twenty years of Christian life and service. He had toured the chief cities of most of the eastern provinces of the Roman Empire, preaching Christ, establishing young communities of Christians and building them up into holiness and harmony. His previous letters had all been concerned with the problems and needs of local churches; now out of his missionary experience he dictates to Tertius his mature thoughts about God's gospel for the world and its place in history and in society.

This is the end of an epoch for Paul. He has canvassed the eastern Mediterranean for Christ's sake, and now he looks further afield. From Corinth he will go back to Jerusalem; from Jerusalem he, the apostle to the Gentiles, hopes to cross the sea to Rome, the capital of the Gentile world. But it is to be only a stepping stone. He intends to set out from there and lead a Spanish campaign. For this new venture he will need the backing of the household churches at Rome for prayer, personnel, finance and initial contacts. He had not founded the Christian community at Rome, and has never been there. This letter is to be his letter of introduction to people who for the most part had only heard about him, and heard perhaps conflicting reports. He writes ahead, informing of his visit and mentioning his plans. To help win their support he carefully explains the content of his missionary preaching and its relation both to God's past and future plans for the world and to contemporary society. The first eight chapters, after an opening greeting, expound the doctrinal basis of the gospel. 'The righteous-by-faith shall live' is its theme-text. It serves as a pointer both to the sin and death that characterize the religious and pagan world, and to God's universal offer of justification and eternal life in Christ through His Spirit. In chapters 9 to 11 Paul reasons out from Scripture and his missionary experience God's present and future plans for Jew and Gentile. In the rest of the letter he discusses the outworking and implications of the gospel in the Christian community and in pagan society.

ANALYSIS

Romans 1: 1-8

IV THE GOSPEL FOR THE WORLD IN GOD'S PLAN (9: 1-11: 36)

 i The Jews' tragic rejection of Christ (9: 1-5)
 ii God's present plan for Jew and Gentile (9: 6-10: 21)
 iii God's future plan for Jew and Gentile (11: 1-32)
 iv Praise of God's wisdom (11: 33-36)

V THE GOSPEL IN ACTION (12: 1-15: 13)

 i Behaviour in the church and in the world (12: 1-21)
 ii Church and state (13: 1-7)
 iii Motives for Christian behaviour (13: 8-14)
 iv Corporate harmony and personal convictions (14: 1-15: 13)

VI PAUL'S MISSIONARY PLANS (15: 14-33)

VII CLOSING MESSAGES (16: 1-27)

I. GREETINGS AND PRAYER (1: 1-15)

1-7. Paul formally introduces himself to the churches at Rome, for this is the first direct contact he has had with them. He gives his credentials and shows the centrality of Jesus Christ in God's gospel for the world. 1. He works not in his own right but as a **servant** at the disposal of his King and Lord. **Servant** (literally 'slave') has OT associations of a royal minister of state (*e.g.* 2 Kg. 22: 12) and of devotion to the worship and service of God (*e.g.* Ps. 113: 1). Paul's apostolic task is not a career of his own choosing but his response to the summons of God, who has singled him out like Jeremiah to be His herald (cf. Gal. 1: 15; Jer. 1: 5). 2-4. That **the gospel** is **of God** is proved in that it was no new-fangled human idea but His own OT promises come true. God's 'mighty act' (NEB for **power**) in raising Jesus from the dead also authenticated the gospel. These verses echo an early confession of faith to which Paul also referred in his sermon at Pisidian Antioch (Ac. 13: 23, 32 f.). The subject of the gospel is God's eternal **Son, Jesus Christ our Lord,** the incarnate Saviour and promised King who binds His subjects to Himself and to each other. He is the properly accredited Messiah, 'born' (RV) of David's line in His earthly life (**according to the flesh**) and so qualified to be King of God's people. As great David's greater Son He had inherited the coronation promise of Ps. 2: 7: *Thou art my son, this day have I begotten thee.* By the resurrection —by the imparting of new life—God had officially 'installed' (Moffatt) Him as His Messianic King (cf. Ac. 13: 33). The Gk. word underlying **designated** most probably means 'appointed', as in Ac. 17: 31. **Son of God** may partly be used as a title of the Messiah (cf. Ac. 9: 20 with Ac. 9: 22). Christ fulfilled His sonship in officially taking up His kingship.

According to the Spirit of holiness means 'in the realm of the Holy Spirit', denoting Christ's post-resurrection life (cf. 1 Pet. 3: 18). In Rabbinic thought the age to come was to be the era of the Spirit: for the Church it had dawned with the resurrection of Christ. 5. Ps. 2 had promised the Messiah not only royal honours but royal dominion to the ends of the earth (cf. 10: 12 n.). Accordingly God had commissioned Paul (**we** is like the editorial 'we') to work throughout the world to win allegiance to Christ's name, and had equipped him with enabling **grace** that fitted him for his task (cf. Eph. 4: 7 f.). The object was the **obedience** that flows from **faith**, to make Gentiles first trust, then obey (cf. NEB). 6. This world-wide commission explains Paul's interest in and authority over the Romans themselves. RSV interprets correctly AV's literal 'the called of Jesus Christ'; it is God the Father who calls (8: 30). When God issues His summons He claims a man as Christ's possession and appoints him to a destiny of salvation (cf. Isa. 42: 6; 43: 1). 7. Like God's people in the OT they have been set inside the intimate circle of God's love. **Called to be saints** (Gk. *klētois hagiois*) or 'saints by calling' (J. N. Darby) echoes a term used of Israel—'*holy convocation*' (Gk. *klētē hagia*: Exod. 12: 16; Lev. 23; Num. 28: 25). An ordinary letter in the 1st century A.D. began 'A. to B. greetings' (Gk. *chairein*). Christians gave this conventional opening a subtle spiritual turn by substituting **grace** (Gk. *charis*). To this Gentile-based greeting Paul adds the Jewish salutation of **peace** (Heb. *shālōm*). This beautiful invocation of divine blessing may be an echo of the Aaronic benediction of Num. 6: 24 ff. 'Note how this born-and-bred monotheist can set Jesus unequivocally on that side of reality which we call divine' (A. M. Hunter).

8-15. After that official introduction Paul, on

342

a more personal note, confides his prayers. It was usual in a letter to follow the opening greeting with a prayer to a god (cf. C. H. Dodd's commentary for examples). In a Christian letter the true God, reached through Jesus Christ, took over where other gods generally held sway. Paul's praying was marked by thanksgiving, persistence, acknowledgment of God's sovereignty and a desire to be a channel of grace to others. **8.** News of the existence of believers at Rome had spread to every church in the Roman Empire. **9f.** As part of the Christian work which expressed Paul's spiritual worship of God (**serve** is Gk. *latreuō*: cf. Gk. *latreiā*, 'worship', in 12: 1), he longed to visit them (cf. 15: 23 n.), but so far God had kept him elsewhere (Ac. 19: 21). Arrest, trial, two years' languishing in prison and shipwreck were to intervene before his prayer was answered. **12.** 'In the same breath he takes the low place with them' (Darby) in gracious humility. Paul tactfully corrects himself to make it clear that he will not come to lord it over them but to receive as well as give (cf. 2 C. 1: 24). This verse came true for Paul: see Ac. 28: 15. **14f.** At Rome Paul hoped to engage in evangelism as well as in ministry to the churches. His apostolic commission had endowed him with a sense of world-wide missionary **obligation** (cf. 1 C. 9: 16 f.; Ac. 9: 15) which, as it transcended all types of civilization and degrees of culture, naturally extended to cosmopolitan **Rome,** where representatives of all these types could be found. **Greeks** are those who had adopted the international Hellenistic civilization, as distinct from **barbarians,** who kept up their national language and culture. On the other hand, **Greek** in v. 16 is a religious term meaning 'Gentile'. **Wise** and **foolish** are educated and uneducated people.

II. THEME AND TEXT OF THE GOSPEL (1: 16–18a)

16. Paul must have paused here and pondered. Rome—what thoughts of grandeur, power and even pride the word must have evoked in Paul the Roman citizen! But **the gospel** of Christ not only equalled but eclipsed the achievements of Rome. It too was something to be proud of, for it was God's own means—as dynamic as the resurrection (cf. v. 4)—of saving any one in the world who entrusts himself to Him (for **faith** see 3: 22 n.), an offer made **first** in time to **the Jew,** then to the Gentile. The gospel knows no frontiers save the frontier of faith. **17. The righteousness of God . . . revealed** continuously in gospel-preaching, is a complex term (see note below). In brief it is God's righteous way of putting men right with

Himself. On man's side it is 'based on faith and addressed to faith' (NEBmg. Lit. 'from faith to faith': cf. 3: 22). Paul takes Hab. 2: 4 as his theme-text: 'The righteous-by-faith shall live' (cf. RSV, NEB). In its primary meaning the text was an assurance that despite threat of invasion and upheaval the man whose life was in line with God's will would be preserved and prosper under God's good hand on account of his firm loyalty to God. In the new fulfilment in the era of Christ the issues are lifted to another plane. There is a divine warfare against sin. Faithfulness is stripped to its core of faith and linked closely with 'righteous'. The promised life is the very life of the risen Christ. **18.** The gospel not only reveals God's **righteousness.** Also 'the death of Jesus Christ on the Cross is the revelation of God's wrath from heaven' (Karl Barth). The **wrath** of God is generally taken as the outworking of God's judgment in human history. But the parallelism of **is revealed** in vv. 17 f. suggests a double reference to the contents of the gospel, and accordingly some have explained **wrath** in terms of the proclamation of judgment to come in the apostolic gospel. But 3: 25 and 8: 3 demonstrate a close connection between the Cross and God's **wrath** or condemnation of sin. In the OT 'righteousness' and 'wrath' are found as two sides of one coin. When 'righteousness' is God's intervention on behalf of His oppressed people, 'wrath' is a complementary aspect of the same process, the same intervention as experienced by the enemy oppressors (Isa. 59: 16-18; 63: 1-6). If righteousness is directed towards the restoration of man, it is directed against sin (see note at end of ch. 5)—**all ungodliness and wickedness**—and takes the form of **wrath.** In so far as sin is a force that controls a man's life, **wrath** must be directed against that man until he is rescued from its power. At the Cross God intervened **from heaven** and 'condemned' or defeated 'sin' by the death of His incarnate Son (8: 3). Apart from Christ **men** are doomed to meet God's **wrath** at the judgment day (2: 5), for it is their own **wickedness** that sets them in opposition to God and prevents His spiritual and moral **truth** from influencing their lives. But in advance 'the fire of wrath was kindled on Golgotha' (Barth). The last judgment was anticipated at Calvary. Sin was judged and deliverance was made available for the believer. He is shielded from God's **wrath** by the propitiatory power of the Crucified (3: 25).

NOTE ON RIGHTEOUSNESS

Righteousness has been defined by William Manson as 'a way of salvation which does justice to the moral reality of God's relations with men, while at the same time enabling men's restoration to right relations with God'. This definition of the word is far from what would be found in an English dictionary. This is because its roots lie deep in the Hebrew Scriptures, the seed-bed of the NT revelation. In the OT 'righteous' is primarily a term used in a court of law meaning 'in the clear', 'in the right'. It refers to the verdict of a judge upon a man on trial. Jer. 3: 11 reports God's verdict: 'Israel hath justified herself more than Judah' (AV) means that Israel 'has shown herself less guilty' (RSV). 'Righteousness' could also be applied to a judge. The rôle of a judge in Hebrew lawsuits was often to champion the oppressed against their oppressors, to protect and vindicate against wrong treatment. He was 'righteous' in so far as he came to the aid of the victimized. In Lk. 18: 6 it is the judge's reluctance to try the case of the wronged widow that earns him the epithet 'unrighteous'.

The term 'righteous' came in due course to have a wider range of application than the law court. It developed also a moral significance: presumably the acquitted man helped by the judge against his adversaries received this verdict because he had previously acted in a morally right way. But the legal and moral uses of the word are not synonymous. When a judge acquitted a man and made him legally 'righteous' he did not thereby make him morally righteous.

As the reference to Jer. 3: 11 has shown, the idea of 'righteousness' came to be applied to the relations between God and man. God has as it were a law court to condemn wrongdoing and a court of appeal to reverse the verdict of corrupt judges of His people. God's righteousness is both His moral holiness and His saving activity on behalf of Israel. 'Righteous' became part of the vocabulary of the covenant between God and His people. In Gen. 15: 6 'righteousness' is Abraham's right relationship to God based upon his approval. The patriarch was not only 'in the right' before God his Judge but also 'right with' his covenant-God. He had a favourable standing of acceptance with God. The covenant relationship meant that Israelites could appeal to God for help, just as in an ancient treaty a vassal-king could appeal to his overlord if he was attacked. When foreigners invaded, Israel could appeal to the supreme Judge for aid. This appeal was made even when Israel had broken her side of the covenant and was strictly no longer eligible to claim God's 'righteousness'—but God did intervene to champion His unworthy people! The way was being paved for the NT where God reveals 'righteousness' to those completely outside a covenant-relationship in fulfilment of His own gracious promises. In Jg. 5: 11 God's activity in defending Israel against the Canaanites is called His 'righteousnesses' or 'righteous acts' (AV; RSV 'triumphs'). His 'righteousness' in this sense is His intervention in warfare. The Judge executes His judgment as a Warrior; the law court is the very field of battle. In Romans 'righteousness' is God's saving victory over sin, man's enemy, as well as a moral attribute of God and man, and man's acceptance by God. In the Cross and resurrection of Jesus Christ God has acted in moral and saving righteousness; He has offered to man the gift of the righteousness of acceptance with the intent that man may go on to live a life of moral righteousness.

III. THE GOSPEL FOR THE WORLD: 'The righteous-by-faith shall live' (1: 18b-8: 39)

Paul explains the doctrine of his gospel in terms of Hab. 2: 4, unfolding its relevance for the new Christian era. God by the death of Christ has set men right with Himself, if they will but put themselves by faith into His hands. The faith-righteous man shares the life of the risen and exalted Christ now in part and hereafter fully.

i. 'The righteous-by-faith . . .' (1: 18b-5: 11)
The apostle brings out the Christian significance of the first half of the text. Words associated with righteousness occur 36 times in this section and words associated with faith occur 29 times. The passage is pervaded with a law-court atmosphere. Men are guilty in God's court but by the good offices of God in Christ a favourable verdict is secured. The force of the forensic language is that men who were estranged from God, victims of their own sin, are reconciled to God by God in Christ and liberated from sin's fatal consequences.

(a) The failure of the world (1: 18b-3: 20)
God's salvation is enhanced by first erecting a dark backcloth of human failure and then setting against it the splendour of divine grace. Paul proves why at the day of judgment God's wrath must fall upon the world of Jew and Gentile before he presents the alternative of faith-righteousness in Christ.

The failure of the pagan world (1: 18b-32)
Paul is first speaking of mankind in general in v. 18, but as he goes on he has Gentiles specifically in view. He weighs up the Hellenistic society of his day and finds it wanting. Everywhere is chaos. Animals have become gods, man has become woman, wrong has become right. Nature without the true God has become unnatural. The Creator has been rejected and creation is in chaos: for the apostle these two facts are cause and effect. **19f.** The absence of truth is not God's fault: it has been deliberately

suppressed. 'There is no possible defence' (NEB) for the non-Jew. God has shown enough of Himself in the natural world for men to be unable to plead ignorance. The natural world is a window through which God has shown part of Himself to man, through which thinking man may 'see' His unseen **power** and 'divineness' (Knox. The NEB brings out the paradoxical play on words).

The rest of the chapter is made up of three parallel sections grouped round the phrase **God gave them up,** which is solemnly hammered out in vv. 24, 26, 28. **21-24.** Because they did not **honour** Him, their fate was the sexual **dishonouring** of their bodies. Rejecting the evidence before them (cf. Ac. 14: 17), men substituted irrational ideas about God for a right use of reason (cf. v. 20). Paul is echoing the LXX of Jer. 2: 5; 10: 14, where **futile** and **fools** are applied to idolaters. They degraded God to the level of created things. Ps. 106: 20 is in the apostle's mind at the beginning of v. 23. This is Israel all over again. The Gentile world too did not consider His works (Ps. 106: 7, 13). They too lapsed into idolatry, worshipping a lot of dummies. As God *gave* Israel *into the hand of the nations* (Ps. 106: 41, LXX *paredōken*), so **God gave up** (Gk. *paredōken*) the Gentiles to their fate. Israel's experience had been mirrored and magnified in the Gentile world. Wrong behaviour was not merely the consequence of wrong worship, but a divine chastisement for it, although it was not the full punishment for their sin (cf. 3: 25), the final separation from God which is 'death' (v. 32, cf. 6: 23) or God's wrath at the judgment day (2: 5, 8). God made them harvest the crops they themselves had sown. **25-27.** Because they **exchanged** the real God for false gods, by way of temporary punishment they **exchanged natural** sexual intercourse for homosexuality. **25.** Paul breaks out of the foul atmosphere of vice and idolatry into the fresh air of a doxology. **27. Error** is their idolatry: Gk. *planē* (lit. 'wandering') is often so used in the LXX. **Penalty** is more literally 'corresponding penalty' or 'fitting wage' (NEB): the punishment fitted the crime. **28.** Because they did not **see fit** (Gk. *edokimasan*) to acknowledge God, their fate was an unfit (Gk. *adokimon*) mind. The price they paid for rejecting God was to become moral rejects. **29-31.** A haphazard catalogue of sins of personality and of personal relationships. **32.** This is the climax of sin. To assent coldly and objectively to others' sins is worse than to succumb to temptation oneself in the heat of the moment. Gentiles had inexcusably stifled their conscience (cf. 2: 15) so that evil was accepted as if it were good. All such must

expect sentence of death at the judgment day.

The failure of the Jews (2: 1–3: 20)
Paul subtly turns to prove the Jews defenceless too, first in veiled language, later openly with 'a "Thou art the man", somewhat after the manner of Nathan's parable to David' (Sanday and Headlam). **1f.** The Jew 'stood in his own estimate on a higher elevation than that of mankind at large. But the words "O man" were intended to disallow that claim' (B. W. Newton). The would-be judge is himself put in the dock—and condemned—on the same charge as the Gentiles. There is the same pattern of experience: knowledge and wilful ignoring. The Jews, including Paul who has previously felt this shock of failure himself, **know** of God's judgment of wrongdoers from the law, 'the embodiment of knowledge' (v. 20). **3.** The Jew's attempt to cover up his own sin with tut-tutting will not avert his punishment. At the end of the verse **you** is emphatic: 'you, any more than they' (NEB). **4f.** God's **kindness** in deferring judgment has been abused: it has not coaxed the Jew into **repentance,** but served to provoke blatant presumption. Wealth of grace, when thus slighted, turns into wealth of **wrath** ('treasure up' is better with AV, RV), which will be paid out at the **day** of **judgment. 6.** The Jew cannot escape the evidence of his own Scriptures. That the verdict will be based upon actual behaviour and not upon high ideals or theoretical superiority God's Word has already made clear (Ps. 62: 12; Prov. 24: 12 are echoed). **7. Eternal life**—life in the age to come which follows the day of judgment (5: 9 f., cf. Gal. 6: 8)—will be given only to those who prepare for it with consistent good living which aims at **glory,** or enjoying the radiant presence of God (cf. 5: 2), and **honour,** God's 'well done' (cf. Jn 12: 26; 1 Pet. 1: 7) and **immortality,** which Christ makes possible (2 Tim. 1: 10; 1 C. 15: 53). Paul's usage of this vocabulary elsewhere makes it clear that this blessing is for the faith-righteous man. 'Oh, it is a living, creative, active, mighty thing this faith! So it is impossible for it to fail to produce good works steadily' (Luther). 'It is faith alone which justifies, but the faith which justifies can never be alone' (Calvin). The Christian is not exempt from a trial of works (14: 10 ff.; 2 C. 5: 10; Jn 5: 29). 'The righteous will be rewarded not on account of but according to their works. Good works are to them the evidence of their belonging to that class to whom for Christ's sake eternal life is graciously awarded' (C. Hodge). Cf. 8: 13 n. **8.** Those who 'by their wickedness suppress the truth' (1: 18) will encounter God's **wrath.** NEB has 'governed by selfish ambition' for **factious:** Gk. *eritheia* is 'the ambition which has no

conception of service and whose only aims are profit and power' (W. Barclay, *A NT Wordbook*, p. 40). **9–11.** It is perhaps significant that the Gk. words for **tribulation** and **distress** occur three times in the LXX of Dt. 28: 53 ff. in a curse on those who break the covenant-law. Paul is reminding **the Jew** of what he already knew but liked to forget. If the Jews' ancient priority of privilege counted for anything, it meant priority of responsibility (cf. Am. 3: 2). The principles of God's judgment are the same for all. Ultimately, 'God has no favourites' (NEB). Gk. *prosōpolēmpsiā* (**partiality**) is only found in Christian writings. It is based on the LXX translation of a Hebrew phrase 'lift up the face'. Originally it was used of accepting with favour a prostrate suppliant by raising his chin with the hand. Later the expression for favour became an idiom for favouritism. **12–16.** V. 11 is expanded: Jew and Gentile stand on an equal footing. The **law** is not a charm which can guarantee the Jew immunity but the very plumbline of his own judgment. Paul is attacking his fellow-Jews on their own ground, countering one popular tenet of Judaism with another. The principle of doing the works of the law, carried to its logical conclusion, cancels out the privilege derived from possessing the law. It also amounts to a criterion by which both Jew and Gentile will be judged together. For the Jew merely to listen to the law being read out in the synagogue Sabbath by Sabbath does him no good. And although Gentiles were not blessed with a revelation of the law, like Israel at Sinai, yet they do at times show a natural awareness of its standards. 'When the heathen honours his parents, he does something that is good and in keeping with the law. At another time he violates the law, but that is not Paul's point' (Anders Nygren). **15. Conscience** is here a man's moral consciousness by which after a deed is done he pronounces it right or wrong. It is 'a juridical faculty after action, not a legislative faculty before' (R. H. Fuller). Thus besides the Gentile's instinctive behaviour there is another witness to the fact that he knows God's standards, albeit imperfectly. The last clause is apparently a further definition of the activity of **conscience**. Man

> *ever bears about*
> *A silent court of justice in his breast*
> *Himself the judge and jury, and himself*
> *The prisoner at the bar.* (Tennyson, *Sea Dreams*)

16. On the **day** of judgment God will bring **secrets** out into the open, both the mental accusations of Gentile consciences and the reality behind Jewish claims. Part of Paul's gospel was that judgment to come would be in the hands of Jesus Christ acting as judge for God (Ac. 17:

31). The verse does not dovetail smoothly into the preceding one; probably it goes with v. 13, and vv. 14 f. are in parenthesis.

17–24. The law, their boast, has been broken. The so-called Jew had a superior air about him, which Paul could describe easily because it had once been his own. **17.** He complacently wallowed in the possession of the **law**. His **relation to God** made him cocksure. **18–20.** He knew it all. He expected the rest of the world to kowtow to him. They had to come to him to get the benefit of his moral discernment and learning. They were **blind,** 'benighted' (NEB), **foolish, children,** but not he, because he had the law. The phrases in vv. 19 f. 'may have been phrases used by the "Foreign Mission Committee" of Pharisaic Judaism' (A. M. Hunter). **21f.** A deliberate anticlimax. Paul cites the Jews' flagrant breaches of the law, which were obviously well known. They did not live up to their own ideals, and therefore had no cause for smug self-satisfaction. **23.** The very people who shook their heads over the Gentiles' dishonouring God were doing the same. **24.** Isa. 52: 5, as it appears in the LXX, sums up the situation.

25–29. Circumcision is no security. To the average Jew the sign of circumcision, his distinguishing mark, exempted from judgment as surely as the sign of the rainbow. But Paul points out its uselessness unless the covenantal obligations inherent in the rite are kept. 'If you flout the law, you are to all intents and purposes uncircumcising yourself' (J. B. Phillips). 'The heroes of God without God may be compared to a traveller who remains standing under the signpost instead of moving in the direction to which it directs him. The signpost has become meaningless' (Barth). **26.** Reversing the argument, Paul contends that an **uncircumcised** Gentile who does keep these obligations is virtually circumcised, a member of the Israel of God (Gal. 6: 16), and will be treated as such at the day of judgment. The apostle has Gentile Christians in mind, as comparison with 8: 4 shows (see RV). **27.** Cf. Mt. 12: 41 for the thought. **28, 29.** Being a 'Jew' depends not upon rite, race or **written code,** but upon an attitude of **heart.** Paul is reiterating a lesson the OT itself often taught (*e.g.* Dt. 10: 16; Jer. 4: 4). Was this also Stephen's words (Ac. 7: 51) still ringing in Paul's ears? A true Jew is one who lives up to the meaning of his name by pleasing God and winning His **praise,** not his neighbour's (cf. Mt. 6: 1; Jn 12: 43). **Jew** (Gk. *Ioudaios*) comes from 'Judah', which is linked with *hōdāh* 'praise' in Gen. 29: 35; 49: 8.

3: 1–8. Jewish protests are silenced. On his missionary travels Paul must have met many

Jewish hecklers in synagogue and market-square. From his experiences he here replies to some Jewish reactions to his gospel. **1.** Does not this condemnation of the Jews deny that they have any racial privileges? **2.** Indeed not: in a non-saving sense they have many, such as being trustees of God's OT promises. Paul intended to go on to mention other privileges, such as the ones listed in 9: 4 f., but the first diverts him to another objection. **3.** According to Paul some of the Jews (most in fact, but Paul is being charitable; cf. 11: 17) have been bad trustees and have let God down. Does not this mean that there is no future for God's people and that He will be forced to abandon them and let them down? **4.** Paul shudders at the blasphemy. God will ultimately keep His promises to them, he will argue in ch. 11. Instead of God's faithfulness being nullified, may the opposite happen: may God make His word come true and at the same time may the statement wrung out of the Psalmist by bitter experience (Ps. 116: 11) be verified—may **every man** break his word (cf. AV, RV), because God's faithfulness would thereby be enhanced. Paul quotes Ps. 51: 4 in support. He has the whole verse in mind (cf. 11: 26 n.): *Against thee, thee only, have I sinned . . ., in order that thou mayest be justified. . . .* God used David's murder and adultery to glorify Himself. By divine intent 'man's sin brings out into a clearer light the justice and holiness of God' (A. F. Kirkpatrick, *The Psalms, ad loc.*). **5.** But, it may be objected, if human wrong shows up the rightness of God in greater relief (Gk. *synistēsin:* cf. 5: 8 n.), if the worst in man brings out the best in God, man's sin surely serves a useful purpose in God's plan. Then what room is there for human responsibility and liability? Ought not God in fairness to recognize this service and give man credit for it instead of condemning him in **wrath** at the day of judgment (2: 5, 8)? Gk. *epipherōn* should probably be translated not **inflict** but 'pronounce': cf. its forensic use in Jude 9. Paul apologizes for even quoting this implication that God is unfair and fallible. **In a human way** means 'as if God were a man.' **6.** That God would **judge the world** was common ground for Paul and his Jewish critic. Paul tries to checkmate his opponent with a clear implication of that fact: such a God must give 'righteous judgment' (2: 5). *Shall not the Judge of all the earth do right?* (Gen. 18: 25) may have been at the back of Paul's mind. **7.** The objector—and perhaps Paul himself—is not satisfied, and presses his point. What right has God to judge him **as a sinner** if he lies? For the logical conclusion of Paul's contention is that a man can lie to the **glory** of God, seeing that

God uses his lie to throw His own truth into sharper relief. **8.** He goes on, 'since the end— God's glory—is good, does not that justify the means, which in this case is my sin?' (F. F. Bruce). Paul has been accused of implying this by his teaching about God's grace. Does he not say 'Where sin abounded, grace abounded all the more' (5: 20)? And did he not suppose a crucifixion to be the means of salvation? Paul faces up to this objection that his gospel breeds immorality in ch. 6, a more appropriate point in his train of argument. At the moment he merely snaps a retort in disgust.

9–20. The OT confirms Jewish failure. Paul's accusations have been universal in scope. Jew and Gentile alike are **under** the thumb of **sin.** Despite their historic privileges the Jews cannot claim exemption from the workings of God's moral law. **10–18.** This indictment has the authority of Scripture behind it. The OT affirms the sin of God's people as well as promises of their salvation (2). Paul may be using an existing collection of OT texts originally compiled to show that the whole being of man has shared in evil (**throat, tongues, lips, mouth, feet, eyes**). A string of verses from the Psalms and Isaiah show not merely what man can be like but what a Jew can be like, since the Jew who is meant to read the OT cannot with a good conscience shrug off these verses as referring only to 'Gentile sinners'. **19. The law** in its first occurrence means the OT, as in 1 C. 14: 21. A longer title is used in v. 21. Now not only the Gentiles but the Jews also have been put on trial in God's court and shown to be defenceless. This condemnation was in line with God's purposes of ultimate grace (cf. 11: 32). **20.** Ps. 143: 2, here quoted, is a permanent principle. No one will be able to pass God's scrutiny on the day of judgment who supposes that his behaviour conforms to God's standards revealed in **the law.** On the contrary, in Paul's experience, as he will explain in 7: 7–25, to know God's standards is to realize one's own hopeless inadequacy. 'It is the straight edge of the law that shows us how crooked we are' (Phillips).

(*b*) **Faith-righteousness (3: 21–4: 25)**
God's gift of faith-righteousness (3: 21–31)
The analysis of mankind has revealed signs of desperate failure. The verdict of the day of judgment is a foregone conclusion. Is there then no hope? David in Ps. 143 knew the only possibility: to throw himself, unrighteous as he was, upon God's promises of salvation. Before pleading with God not to enter into judgment with him he had appealed: *In thy faithfulness answer me, in thy righteousness.* To this hope Paul now turns in v. 21, after quoting Ps. 143: 2 in v. 20. The appeal has been answered for

mankind. **The righteousness of God has been manifested.** He has personally undertaken to set men right with Him (see 1: 17 n.). It has happened **now,** wiping out the past and inaugurating a new age with new prospects. For Paul and for every believer all the preceding exposure of failure and of coming wrath is only a 'then', something that lies behind him. In the rest of this paragraph Paul goes on to define the new **righteousness** as to its channel, warrant, scope, cost, basis, divine consequences and human implications. As to its *channel,* saving **righteousness** comes to man **apart from law.** It does not depend on doing one's best to keep up to the standards of God's moral law, as Judaism taught. The *warrant* for it is in the OT (see v. 19 n.). Although it cuts across the tenets of Judaism, the contemporary heir of the OT, yet there is clear evidence in the Scriptures that this is really and solely how God works, as ch. 4 will show. **22f.** Its only *channel* is **faith in Jesus Christ.** Faith is the opposite of self-reliance. It is 'an act which is the negation of all activity' (C. H. Dodd), an act of life-committal, entrusting oneself to **Jesus Christ,** the spearhead of God's saving work. The *scope* is universal, impartially embracing any Jew or Gentile who commits himself in trust. A universal offer of salvation matches the already proved universality of sin. The **glory of God** here refers to the reflection of God's radiant being in man, the moral and spiritual kinship to Him with which Adam was created as the image of God. The image is sadly disfigured in fallen man. It is only in Christ, the Second Man and the greater Image of God, that the work of restoring the image can begin (2 C. 3: 18; cf. 5: 2 n.; 8: 30 n.). **24.** As to the *cost,* getting right with God costs man nothing but was very costly to God. God Himself in His **grace** or generous, undeserved love has by Christ's work of 'ransom' (Moffatt) bought the believer out of sin's slave-market (cf. 6: 6, 17; 7: 14). **Redemption** also hints at the Exodus of God's people in Christ (cf. 9: 17 n.; Dt. 7: 8; Isa. 51: 11). The logical subject of **they are justified** is 'all who believe' in v. 22; the intervening words are best taken as a parenthesis. **25f.** The divine *basis* of setting men right is the sacrifice of Christ. God proffered Him as the antidote to human sin. But He was more: He became not only **an expiation** but 'the means of propitiation' (Moffatt; cf. AV, RV) or 'place of propitiation'. While **expiation** deals with human sin, propitiation deals also with wrath, the divine reaction to sin. Up to now the threat of God's wrath has been hanging over men's heads, ready to fall like the sword of Damocles. In Christ the threat vanishes, for it descended upon Him

(1: 18). Here is 'a theological comment on the meaning of the Markan cry from the cross: "My God, my God, why has thou forsaken me?" (R. H. Fuller). In Christ the God of love (5: 8) Himself provided the means of inflicting His wrath upon man's sin in such a way that man is saved. The underlying Gk. word *hilastērion* means 'mercy seat', the cover of the ark and the place of propitiation, in Heb. 9: 5. Probably here too a ceremonial reference is intended and Paul has in mind the rites of the Day of Atonement (Lev. 16), which culminated in the sprinkling of the mercy-seat with the blood of sacrifice. Christ is our mercy-seat and Christ the sacrificial victim. Subjectively propitiation is brought about through the medium of **faith** (cf. RV), whereby the individual claims it for himself. Objectively it is achieved by virtue of Christ's **blood** poured out in a sacrificial death. The *divine consequence* of God's setting men right in this way is that He upholds His **righteousness.** Paul is now highlighting a specific facet of **righteousness,** God's moral justice. He must often have heard his gospel criticized in Jewish circles on the ground that it made a mockery of God's **righteousness.** Some of this criticism that the Christian view of God is immoral has been reflected earlier in this chapter. The notions of Christians that a moral God (*a*) had made an accursed execution the means of blessed life (Gal. 3: 13) and (*b*) accepted sinners, were clearly preposterous, argued the Jew. Paul replies that (*a*) the OT and Judaism do not go far enough. Taken as the full and final revelation of God they, and not the Cross, are a scandal. It is only the God of the Cross who clarifies His **righteousness.** In seeming complacency God had leniently **passed over** the **former sins** of Jew (2: 4) and Gentile (1: 24 n.; Ac. 17: 30), but He had only done so because His eye was on the Cross. Now He had acted according to character and rent the heavens (1: 18) in a display of His abhorrence to, and punishment of, sin. It is only the Christian view of God and sin that makes sense. (*b*) God may now for the first time receive back the repentant sinner without prejudice to His moral justice because acceptance depends on **faith in Jesus.** Translate: 'He is righteous *even while justifying ...*' (H. C. G. Moule. The Gk. *kai*—and—is here adverbial). 'By appropriating to himself the homage rendered to the majesty of God by the Crucified One, the believer is himself crucified as it were in the eyes of God: moral order is established and judgment can take end by an act of absolution' (F. Godet). **27-31.** The *human implications* of God's justifying activity are threefold. (*a*) Self-sufficient claims are invalidated by the principle of self-effacing **faith.** 'The whole matter is now on a different plane—believing instead of achieving' (Phillips). 'Self-contained, self-sufficient, self-justifying goodness cannot be real goodness because its effect is to set up man's moral independence of God; it is thus the expression of man's egoism, and is in its very nature a rebellion against the source of all good' (G. O. Griffith). (*b*) Now therefore the human race is put on a common level: Jew and Gentile meet at the Cross (cf. Eph. 2: 11 ff.). **God is one** is part of the *Shema* or Jewish creed, based upon Dt. 6: 4 ff. From an article of the Jewish faith Paul deduces that as God of all He will treat all on the same principle on the day of judgment. **On the ground of** (Gk. *ek* as in v. 26 and 1: 17) and **through** (Gk. *dia* as in vv. 22, 25) are variations due to style. (*c*) **The law** is placed 'on a firmer footing' (NEB). Despite Paul's attitude to the law in vv. 21, 28 its moral obligations are ultimately met in the Christian life, as chs. 6, 8 explain.

Faith-righteousness a divine principle (4: 1-25)
This chapter enlarges the claim made in 3: 21 that faith-righteousness has Scriptural warrant, and explains the assertions made in 3: 29 ff. that God accepts both Jew and Gentile, but only on the ground of faith. Paul took it for granted that God would never be false to the basic principles of His OT revelation. God stays the same and His Word is ever contemporary (cf. v. 23 f.). There must be an essential unity between the old and the new revelations of God. Faith-righteousness is in fact nothing new, but the ground on which God met with the very founder of Israel. The apostle is incidentally striking at the roots of Judaism's national and spiritual pride. He takes as his text Gen. 15: 6, which puts in a nutshell the relationship between God and Abraham in the Genesis stories. This whole chapter is a careful analysis of that text and its implications. In the light of it Paul gives four answers to the question of v. 1. (*a*) Abraham became right with God by faith, not by works. That the text itself makes clear (2-8). (*b*) He became right with God by faith, not by circumcision. So teaches the position of the text, coming as it does before Gen. 17 (9-12). (*c*) He became right with God by faith, not by the law. This again is evident from the position of the text, which comes much earlier in the Pentateuch than the account in Exodus of the giving of the law (13-17a). (*d*) The context of Gen. 15: 6 defines Abraham's faith as confidence in God's promise of life (17b-25). In the course of each answer Paul shows that there is a principle at stake which is relevant to the gospel.

1-8. Abraham had faith-righteousness. In his mind Paul is arguing with fellow-Jews. As later Jews did, they probably cited Gen. 26: 5 to support their claim that it was Abraham's obedience to the law that made him acceptable to God. **3.** But Scripture gives a different answer. **Righteousness** here and in Gen. 15: 6 is 'a right relationship to God conferred by a divine sense of approval' (J. Skinner, *Genesis*). Isa. 41: 8 sums it up in the word *friend*, as James saw when he connected the two verses (Jas 2: 23). **Reckoned** has other OT roots apart from the text quoted. It is used to describe the judgment or estimate of the priests as representatives of God whereby they approved or rejected an Israelite's offering (*e.g.* Lev. 8: 18; 17: 4). Thus here and in Genesis it refers to a divine evaluation, which although it may conflict with a human assessment is in no way fictitious (cf. 2: 26). 'Reckon' was also a current commercial term for crediting something to one's account. It is not out of generosity that an employer credits his staff with their salaries: they have a claim to remuneration. **5.** But the relationship between man and God does not fall into the category of **work** and wage-claims. Empty hands outstretched in **faith** are all that man has to show to God. A right relationship based on grace is paid into the believer's account, as it were: he is accepted, **ungodly** though he has been. **6-8.** God accepts the ungodly? Yes, Paul can prove it. Using a Rabbinic comparative principle of interpretation, he defines Gen. 15: 6 in terms of Ps. 32: 1 f., where 'reckon' occurs again: reckoning-righteousness means not-reckoning-sin. 'The only thing of my very own which I can contribute to my redemption is the sin from which I need to be redeemed' (William Temple).

9-12. Faith justifies, not circumcision. Having established that disregarding sin in forgiveness is the same as regarding as righteous, Paul can now apply *blessed* of Ps. 32 to the man regarded as righteous. But is the Gentile excluded from this category? In reply Paul again takes Abraham's experience as the pattern of God's dealings with man. Gen. 15 comes before Gen. 17: his acceptance on the basis of faith preceded his **circumcision.** The order is important: it implies that **circumcision** was never meant to be exploited as an automatic rite which could predispose God to accept a man. In **circumcision** God was merely confirming and adding His signature to His earlier pronouncement, which was based on Abraham's personal confidence in Himself. Abraham was a virtual Gentile in Gen. 15. His spiritual successors are therefore (*a*) Gentiles who trust as Abraham did and (*b*) only those Jews who **follow** in the footsteps (cf. AV, RV) of Abraham's **faith.**

13–17a. Faith justifies, not the law. The **promise** of Gen. 17: 4 ff. to the faith-righteous Abraham, that his posterity would be found the world over significantly antedated the giving of the law. **Law** is a shorthand expression loaded with deep psychological content. Here as often one must know the man before one can know the meaning of his words. Paul's attitude towards the law is coloured by his own experience inside Judaism. What had originally been founded upon God's gracious act of redemption (Exod. 20: 2) had eventually become by and large the basis of human claims upon God. Added 'explanations' turned it into a burden that crippled a conscientious Jew like Paul, a burden made all the heavier by loss of spontaneity, of joy and of a sense of God's gracious initiative. Paul attacks the law for the legalism with which it had become synonymous. The Jews had dragged it down and perverted it into an organ of human achievement. To such God's **promise** could not come. The law is 'a heap of clinkers marking a fiery miracle which has taken place, a burnt-out crater disclosing the place where God has spoken, . . . a dry canal which in a past generation and under different conditions had been filled with the living water of faith and of clear perception' (Barth). **15.** The law cannot bless, only condemn: see 3: 20 n.; 5: 13 n. **16.** The **promise** was a matter of **grace** on God's side and of **faith** on man's. It was thus independent of the law. God was in advance making it clear that his heirs would not be confined to Jews (cf. Gal. 3: 8). **17.** Indeed, God **made** him **father of many** Gentiles, as Gen. 17: 5 declares (Gk. *ethnē* means 'Gentiles' as well as **nations**). Abraham was 'assigned the rôle of a mediator of blessing in God's saving plan for *all the families of the earth*' (G. von Rad, *Genesis*, on Gen. 12: 3).

17b–25. Abraham's faith is compared with Christian faith. The promise of v. 17a was given to Abraham as he stood **in the presence** of God. The context of Gen. 15: 6 links Abraham's faith with God's promise of Isaac. His wife's and his own sexual deadness (19; Gen. 18: 11 ff.) ruled out confidence in himself and directed him to God, who can both renew life and issue His creative call (cf. Isa. 41: 4 and *Let . . .* in Gen. 1). **18.** His **hope** based upon believing God's promise cut right across the grain of natural expectation. 'We are able to hear his "Yes", whilst above him cries out to him "No"' (Barth). **So** directed Abraham's gaze up to the stars studding the night sky. **19.** RSV rightly follows RV in omitting AV's 'not', which some ancient MSS added to the text. 'Faith does not mean to close one's eyes to the facts. Faith has no kinship

with optimistic self-deception' (Nygren). There was a Rabbinic saying that a centenarian is 'as though he were dead and gone'. **20.** Paul disregards Abraham's temporary lapses from faith in Gen. 16: 2; 17: 17 either because his thoughts are centred upon Gen. 15 or because Abraham's doubts were short-lived. **21f.** It was Abraham's throwing himself upon God's promise and His power to keep it that underlay God's accepting him as right with Himself. **23f.** And it is the same today! Christian faith is Abraham's faith all over again, faith in the same Giver of miraculous life, who has now demonstrated His power in the miracle of the resurrection. **25.** The verse reads like a line of Semitic poetry. **Jesus our Lord who . . .** is probably a quotation from a confession of faith used in the worship of the Palestinian churches. The first half echoes Isa. 53. Paul uses the quotation to round off and support his comparison of Abraham's and the Christian's faith because it links **justification** with Jesus' risen life. His resurrection is the basis of the believer's justification. The resurrection justified Christ (1 Tim. 3: 16; cf. Rom. 1: 4 n.), proving Him not personally subject to God's wrath, and this condition is shared by those who are in Him.

(c) **The joys of faith-righteousness (5: 1–11)**
The righteous-by-faith . . . has been expounded. Before going on to the Christian force of *. . . Shall live*, and in the process of transition to it, Paul lifts up his heart in an outburst of joy and thanksgiving for the implications of faith-righteousness (cf. 8: 31 ff.; 11: 33 ff.). Justification is for him not merely a doctrine to define and defend: he has found it a cup of blessing that runs over into his whole life. **1.** There is strong support for 'let us have' in manuscripts and versions. But a statement of assured fact reads more naturally here than an appeal. The fact that the two verbal forms were pronounced in the same way in Hellenistic and later Greek explains the textual variation. **Peace** is here not an inward feeling but the relationship of reconciliation with God. The Christian is no longer in the enemy camp. Through Christ's atoning death God now deals with him as a friend (cf. vv. 10 f.). **2.** Christ has put us on a new footing with God, setting our feet firmly on the rock of **grace**. There is the prospect of one day enjoying the fullness of God's presence. **Glory** is the radiant brightness of God's presence, His Shekinah-glory. Christians are already privileged to share the restoration (cf. 3: 23) of this radiant glow in standing (8: 30) and in progressive growth (2 C. 3: 18), but the consummation of the process is yet to come (Phil. 3: 21; 1 Jn 3: 2). **3f.** These blessings are realities which do not belong

merely to a detached spiritual world, but are relevant to the concrete world of human affairs. The joy of being right with God enables a man to take in his stride **suffering** borne for Christ's sake (cf. Hab. 3: 17 f.). Indeed he finds it helps him on his way. God has designed it to produce by a chain reaction the qualities of constancy, sterling **character** (Gk. *dokimē*— something tested) and convinced **hope**. 'We are weaned from the world, and become better able to perceive and appreciate what is heavenly. So the hope which is already in us becomes clearer and brighter' (J. N. Darby). **5.** Scripture attests the certain fruition of hope in God: allusion is made to the LXX of Ps. 22: 5. The ultimate basis of the Christian's hope lies not in his reaction to persecution, although that may strengthen it, but in God Himself as a God who has proved His **love**. The chief blessing **poured** out with His Spirit (an echo of Jl 2: 28) is a sense of His love (cf. 15: 30). When once the Spirit has made His Calvary-love overwhelmingly real to a man in inward experience, he is bound to think evermore: if God loves me as much as that, He will love me to the end. **6-8.** The extent of God's **love** is shown in that there was nothing admirable or lovely about man which could have evoked it. Human self-sacrifice demands intrinsic worth in its object, whether scrupulous fairness or kindly goodness. God's love, revealed in Christ's death, wonderfully makes no prior demands at all. God has proved how well He loves us, His love is confirmed and enhanced (Gk. *synistēsin:* cf. 3: 5 n.) in that it was shown to weaklings, to impious **sinners,** when He broke into history at the crucial moment, His appointed **time** for inaugurating a new era of grace. **9f.** Since God has already done so much, He can be trusted to put the finishing touches to His work (cf. Phil. 1: 6). The past guarantees the future. Acceptance through Christ's death (cf. 3: 25) carries with it an assurance that He will finally save from the **wrath** of the day of judgment when sinners are punished (cf. 2: 5 ff.; 1 Th. 5: 9). Reconciliation assures us of the future bliss of eternal life. Christ's risen and exalted life is an extra guarantee: 'His life is a pledge and security for the life of all His people' (C. Hodge). Cf. 6: 8; Jn 14: 19. ' "Jesus died, and Jesus lives"—these are the truths that contain everything for us. All that a dying and a living Saviour can do is ours' (A. Bonar). **11.** Paul again brings his readers back to earth (cf. v. 3 AV, RV). The fruits of justification do not all lie in the future by any means. Christ in establishing friendly relations with God has given something which makes us **rejoice** here and now **in God** Himself.

ii. ' . . . Shall live' (5: 12-8: 39)
Paul now turns to the second half of his theme-text. The promise of life is shown to find its fulfilment in Christ and in the Spirit. 'Life' and 'live' occur 25 times in this section and only three times in the preceding one. 'Die', 'death', etc. occur 37 times here and only six times before (five in 5: 6 ff.).

(a) Life in Christ (5: 12-7: 6)
First Paul expounds the principle of life in Christ and then he makes a threefold demand for the practical outworking of what it implies.

Solidarity in Christ (5: 12-21)
Just as the first main section contrasted the hopelessness of man with God's gift of faith-righteousness, so now life in Christ is set over against death in Adam. Adam was a **type,** fore-shadowing his future Counterpart: both are heads and inclusive representatives of the human creation, Adam of the old and Christ of the new (1 C. 15: 45 ff., 2 C. 5: 17). But Christ is viewed not only as the Second Man, but also as the Servant. V. 19 is a direct allusion to Isa. 53: 11. The whole section can be regarded as a linking up of Gen. 3 and Isa. 53: 11 with Hab. 2: 4. The ideas of **righteousness, justification, many** and **obedience** come from Isa. 53: 11 (see v. 19 n.). The thought of **life** comes from Hab. 2: 4. The opposite themes of **sin, trespass, condemnation, disobedience** and **death** are suggested not only by contrast with the positive concepts, but also by the story in Gen. 3 of Adam's eating the forbidden fruit in spite of God's threat of death. These are the key ideas of this section. Paul has reflected upon his OT sources and woven them together with the unifying thread of the work of Christ. The work of the Servant-Man who by His obedience brought righteousness and life to the new humanity in Him is enhanced by setting it against the dark background of Adam's failure and its fatal results for Adam's race.

> *When all was sin and shame,*
> *A second Adam to the fight*
> *And to the rescue came.*

One must therefore not expect to find in these verses a clear-cut comprehensive doctrine of original sin. The purpose is to stress God's work of renewal in Christ, and all else is sub-ordinate to that purpose. There is much mystery concerning the nature and extent of our cor-porate relationship with Adam, which systematic theologians have variously attempted to explain. G. O. Griffith has helpfully compared 'the psychological notion of a general "racial unconscious mind" which each individual coming into life inherits, with its race-memories, urges, inhibitions and sense of guilt. From this inheritance he cannot dissociate himself—cannot achieve a self-contained self-hood; he is bound up with the race and the race with him.' Since the entry of sin 'each man who is born into the world . . . finds a compromised situation confronting him. . . . Each generation and each individual act in such a way that the inner strength of rising individuals and generations is enfeebled, deflected and at times destroyed' (F. J. Leenhardt). **12.** The sentence is left unfinished. It should logically have continued 'so through one Man righteousness came into the world and through righteousness life'. But Paul breaks off the comparative construction and does not return to his main thought till vv. 18 f. Adam opened the door to sin and let it loose in the world of men. His sin marked the invasion from outside of an evil force. Once it had ignited a fatal spark in **one man** it **spread** like wildfire through the human race. **Sinned** refers to actual sins (cf. 3: 23) viewed as an individual expression and endorsement of Adam's representative act. 'The individual sins are, as it were, only the eruptions of this sin for ever bubbling in the deep' (Emil Brunner). **Death** is not merely physical but the sign of the extinction of man's spiritual life. In order to make the main thought clear vv. 18 f. will be considered before the parenthetical vv. 13–17. **18.** The verse is a summarized formula without verbs in the Greek (notice AV's italics). God's two-part plan for the old era in Adam and for the new era in Christ had means, scope and result in both cases. The *means* was (*a*) **one man's trespass**—almost 'fall' since Gk. *paraptōma* is literally a 'fall sideways'—and (*b*) **one man's act of righteousness.** Over against Adam's wrong act towers the Cross where Christ fully accomplished the will of God. The *scope* was and is **all men.** The limiting phrase in v. 17 suggests that in the second case it is restricted to those who actually accept God's offer of salvation. To suppose that Paul taught the universal salvation of all individuals is to ignore the realism which years of missionary experience must have inculcated in him. 'All in Adam', 'all in Christ' is meant. The *result* of God's double plan, was (*a*) **condemnation** and (*b*) 'justification of life' (AV), a favourable verdict which leads to eternal life. **19.** The second half is a quotation of Isa. 53: 11 with the verb put into the passive because underlying the whole passage is the thought of God's execution of His plan rather than of the Son's accomplishments by themselves. The future tense refers to the day of judgment which heralds the consummation of the new era in Christ (cf. 6: 5 n.). The new humanity in Christ will be constituted **righteous,** in the right, 'acceptable to God' (Knox). **Many** is literally 'the many' (so

NEB, Gk. *hoi polloi*). It is a Hebrew idiom for the mass of men. Paul had in v. 18 translated it into Greek idiom as **all. Obedience** is probably a paraphrase of the Hebrew word underlying *knowledge* in Isa. 53: 11. Modern Hebrew study suggests that it really meant 'humiliation', 'submission'. Phil. 2: 8 also stresses Christ's obedience in His rôle of Servant. **13f.** Paul is side-tracked by **all men sinned.** To speak of sin after Adam and before Moses raises a problem. If sin is defined as the conscious breaking of God's moral standard, how could what God regards as sin qualify for the death-penalty when that standard was not known in the period between Adam and Moses? Paul is using the OT representation of mankind's history. He leaves his theological difficulty unanswered (cf. 2: 12 ff. where he answers it in terms of natural law). The fact is that men did die before the Mosaic law was given, although their sins were not like Adam's, who deliberately broke a known rule. **15–17. Type** implies likeness, and Paul must carefully point out that there is contrast in the character and result of Adam's and Christ's influence. Christ's work is a glorious power for good, the opposite of the wretched mass-murder which arose from Adam's sin. God has intervened to check the expanding process of sin. In Adam **one trespass** had a condemning effect; in Christ **many trespasses** are forgiven. Instead of being subjects of King Death, men's prospect is to live like kings. They may share in the Messianic Kingdom, if only they accept God's **gift of righteousness. 20.** Paul is speaking from personal experience (cf. 4: 13 n.). He had found that the law, introduced in the old era of Adam, had an effect in keeping with its era; it made one realize one's sin and actually triggered off a reaction of sin, as 7: 7 ff. explains. 'The law is not simply a reagent by which the presence of sin may be detected; it is a catalyst which aids or even initiates the action of sin upon man' (C. K. Barrett). It 'came in on the side' (Gk. *pareisēlthen*) with the subordinate rôle of an accessory working on fallen Adam's side. The law was God's way of bringing sin to a head (1 C. 15: 56) before He broke its virulence with strong grace. **21.** King Sin has been deposed along with **death,** the instrument of his tyranny. Grace is now on the throne and will dispense the life of the age to come to those made right with God by Christ's work.

NOTE ON SIN

Paul did not conceive of sin merely as an action or attitude contrary to God's will. A study of the vocabulary used in association with it clearly shows that he personified it. Sin is a king (5: 21; 6: 12), a slave-owner (*e.g.* 6: 6), is dead or alive (7: 8 f.). Sin is an external power alien to man's true nature as God intended it. It is an enemy that has invaded man, has occupied his 'flesh', and holds him captive (7: 23). The world apart from Christ is under sin's control (3: 9). Christ's work was to attack sin on its own ground and defeat it (8: 3). The man in Christ enters into this victory and is delivered from sin's tyranny (6: 18; 7: 24). But it is obvious from Paul's arguments in chs. 6-8 that the Christian is not made morally perfect at conversion. Christ's work of personal deliverance is a reality for the Christian, but it is on a different plane of reality from the moral issues of every-day living. Yet it must find its counterpart in the Christian's life. Paul argues that because sin *has been* once and for all deposed on one plane of reality, it *should* not reign on the moral plane of human thought and behaviour. In this life sin is ever trying to re-assert its old authority, but Christians are urged to shut their doors against it, for it has no right to come in again.

Living out life in Christ (6: 1-7: 6)
The faith-righteous man has been brought within the circle of the new humanity headed by, and summed up in, Jesus Christ. Union with Christ is for Paul 'the sheet-anchor of his ethics' (J. S. Stewart). For the move is no mere formality, but implicitly demands a corres-ponding moral change. Paul explains why as he counter-attacks a mistaken conclusion from his teaching on divine grace (cf. 3: 8), drawn both by Jewish legalists and by antinomian Christians. God is certainly magnanimous in His grace (5: 20), but to conclude from this that sin no longer matters and that His grace may be exploited for evil ends is a travesty of the truth. Union with Christ calls for a new moral life. Paul hammers this home with three heavy blows. (*a*) The Christian is one with Christ—in death to sin (6: 1-14). (*b*) In Christ Christians are God's righteous servants (6: 15-23). (*c*) The Church is committed to Christ in a new marriage-union (7: 1-6).

1-14. Christians have become one with Christ in His relation to sin. So Paul argues in a series of deductive and inductive arguments which now overlap, now attack the problem from a new angle and now reveal earlier presuppositions. It will be easier to consider the passage as a whole rather than verse by verse. As ever, the starting point is the Cross. Christ **died** in relation **to sin**: He passed out of sin's environment. His death removed the possibility of His ever meeting it again, for it was **once for all,** a clean break. His resurrection by His Father's majestic power (4, **glory**: cf. Dt. 5: 24) marks His permanent freedom from sin's

instrument of tyranny (cf. 5: 21 n.). All this is personally relevant to the Christian, for he is **in Christ Jesus,** who has represented His people and included them within Himself (cf. the concept of the body of Christ). For a man to be in Christ implies that he was there at Golgotha and in the garden-tomb. What is true of Christ is true of the Christian. For him personally Christ's death marked the end of the old era, and His resurrection the inauguration of the new era. God transcends time and at conversion takes a man back to A.D. 33. When he is incorporated into Christ on profession of faith, he is given a personal share in the great events of Christ's work and transferred from his old existence to a new plane of life. In the early Church when baptism generally followed hard on the heels of a man's accepting the gospel, baptism and the divine renewal behind faith could naturally be regarded as the outside and inside of the same thing. Baptism by immersion is a dramatic mime of what God has done with a man. It is to this enacted parable of salvation that Paul appeals. Let us look back, he says, and see what God has done in our lives. Our baptism was the outward evidence that He incorporated us believers into Christ. Our being plunged into water means that He associated us with Him in His **death.** Therefore we too **died** as far as sin is concerned, moving out of and beyond the old era. How then can we—dead and buried men—go back to the old life—'breathe its air again' (Knox, v. 2) by carrying on sinning? It would be a contradiction in terms. God made to share in Christ's crucifixion our Adam, our-selves as we were in Adam (6, **old self,** lit. 'old man'): from our new standpoint 'the man we once were' (NEB) is relegated to a bygone age. In Christ's death we were 'justified' (7, **freed**), from sin, released from its prosecu-tion. God's intention was to change our behaviour (v. 6: cf. v. 4; 8: 4 for other practical clauses of purpose), to put out of action our **sinful body,** lit. 'body of sin', the body in so far as it has become enemy-occupied territory. The body at work expresses the personality, and so it comes to mean the personality in action (there are close links with Heb. psychology here). Paul might have gone on to say that we were raised with Christ in baptism (Col. 2: 12; cf. Eph. 2: 6), but he deliberately breaks the parallelism in order to stress that the new life is not merely a *fait accompli* but a continual endeavour. Instead he speaks about the future. Just as Christ's death and burial were the precursors of His resurrec-tion, so our vital share in the former events guarantees our coming resurrection (cf. 2 C. 4: 14; Phil. 3: 21). The new era in its fulness lies in the future, and the old is still running its course; on another plane the new era has been projected forward and the old already finished. For the Christian the two eras overlap. His past participation in the end of the old era, and his future participation in the beginning of the new are both pointers to his present obligation to behave in keeping with the new era and not the old (4, **walk** is a Biblical idiom for behaviour). **11.** The man **in Christ** must take account of the fact that he has shared in His clear-cut break with sin in His death and God-directed risen life, and conduct himself accordingly. **12f.** The Christian's behaviour must not be characteristic of sin's old régime (5: 21). His personality had for long been enemy-occupied territory, and indeed is not only doomed to suffer the fatal consequences of its occupation before resurrection (8: 11), but continues to have in it subversive elements which urge rebellion. But God has set His flag flying over the body and claimed it as His own territory. Let not then the Christian fight to keep sin in power. Let him not go on as of old (Gk. *paristanete:* present imperative) making his faculties available to sin as weapons (so the Gk. *hopla* signifies elsewhere, not **instruments**) of wickedness. Rather let him turn them into weapons of right living and make a fresh start (Gk. *parastēsate:* an ingressive aorist) by putting himself and them at God's disposal. **14.** Sin's mastery is broken for good because the era in which law was in active control promoting sin (5: 20) is over, and now **grace** is in control (5: 21).

15-23. A new Master has replaced sin. Union with Christ has made the Church God's righteous servant. Paul still has in his mind the thought of Christ as the righteous and obedient Servant of God. Men in Christ move in a new atmosphere of obedience and righteousness (5: 18 f.) and are themselves God's servants. Accordingly 'servants' is better than **slaves** throughout this passage (Gk. *douloi:* cf. *doulos* of Christ as the suffering Servant, Phil. 2: 7). It is these concepts that belong to grace in the new era (cf. 5: 15 ff.) and are safeguards against its being interpreted in terms of indifference to moral laxity, as its contrast with the law might at first suggest. Sin was a master in the old era of Adam and demanded shameful living which it promised to repay with death. The righteousness of Christ that leads to eternal life (cf. 5: 19, 21) calls forth from Christians right living as its corollary. The whole passage is the application of 5: 12 ff. to the Christian's moral life. **15.** Paul is going to tackle the same question (cf. v. 1) from a different angle. **16.** Man's freedom is limited. Either he puts himself at sin's disposal and becomes its servant,

and eventually dies; or else he devotes himself to Christ-like **obedience** to God with the result that he—not only enters into life but also —does what is morally right. **17f.** For Christians the first possibility has been ruled out, ever since their voluntary submission to a new authority, the **standard** or 'pattern' (Gk. *typos*) of obedience, Christian moral teaching (cf. Tit. 2: 1 ff.). Paul will give details of that teaching in chs. 12 ff. There has been a change of ownership. **19.** An apology for describing the relationship between God and a Christian in such crude, human terms (cf. 8: 15). Lack of moral sensitiveness demands that its moral implications be shown to be so compelling and inexorable. The time is past when their faculties could be put at the disposal of dirty and uncontrolled habits which lead to 'moral anarchy' (NEB). Now, in the new era of Christ, they are to be devoted to right living that is the basis of saintliness. **20f.** The readers' consciences support the writer's argument, for now they blush at the immorality of their old lives when **righteousness** had no jurisdiction over them. And how unprofitable it was, leading only to **death. 22.** Christians' lives are to reflect the change of ownership. They are to produce moral behaviour that makes for saintliness and prepares for life in the age to come. **23.** Sinners can only expect to die—that is the fair **wages** which sin pays its servants. God's servants have the sure prospect of **life** because they are **in Christ;** yet they cannot earn it but only receive it as a gratuity.

7: 1-6. A new Husband has replaced the law. The Church has been united to Christ in marriage. The third appeal to Christians to become what they are in Christ revolves around a new metaphor, that of a fruitful marriage-union. Christians constitute a widow who has married again. The first, unhappy marriage, with its offspring of bad living, has been brought to an end. The new marriage demands suitable progeny—good living. Marriage, in which two become 'one flesh', is a natural illustration of incorporation into Christ and is used elsewhere in the NT (*e.g.* 1 C. 6: 16; Eph. 5: 29 f.). It has its roots in the OT where God's people, bound to their Lord by covenant, are represented as His wife (*e.g.* Hos. 2: Jer. 2). Marriage is regarded as the wife's subjection to the husband as master. The first husband was the law—a picture drawn from the state of being 'under (the control of) the law' in the old era (6: 14). In Christ Paul had escaped his involvement with the law and so with sin, whose unwitting accomplice the law was. The fact carries with it strong moral obligations. **1. The law** is probably not the general concept of law but the moral and social law revealed in the OT which the Church had taken over. **2f.** Death releases from the marriage-law: a widow is perfectly free to re-marry. **4.** In a new sense death has released Christians from the law. The illustration of the marriage-law is a parable (not a detailed allegory) of their relationship to the law. A death has taken place, and so the ties which bind men in subjection to the law have been broken. The death is that of the crucified **body of Christ** in which they were represented. Their consequent oneness with their risen Lord is a figurative new marriage-union with Him which calls for offspring dedicated **to God.** **5.** In the era of **the flesh** the law had been the means of evoking sinful feelings and impulses which operated in human faculties and produced deadly offspring. **Flesh** in the OT is often man in his weakness over against the omnipotent God; in the NT it is often human nature whose weakness is shown in its constant and inevitable succumbing to sin. Here it refers to the pre-Christian life (cf. 8: 9 n.). **6. Dead** to the tyranny of the law, Christians have a new sphere of service—**the new life of the Spirit.** The last two phrases are virtually a heading to the next section.

(b) Life in the Spirit (7: 7-8: 30)
With the headline at the end of 7: 6 Paul reaches the second application of . . . *Shall live* (Hab. 2: 4) to the Christian life. As in the section on *The righteous-by-faith*, he first discusses the opposite of his intended point in order to highlight the necessity and the glory of God's gift of the Holy Spirit.

The letter kills (7: 7-25)
Paul analyses from a Christian standpoint his own past experience of the law, as an objective standard which he knew to be right but which he could not reach, however hard he tried. Intention went one way, action went another. Some have found difficulty in squaring this account of failure with Phil. 3: 6. But there Paul is testing his life against certain prescribed standards of outward conduct held by his Judaizing critics and challenges them to point out any failure of his to carry them out. Here he probes into the inner failures of which only God and he were aware, failures that were now heightened by his present Christian knowledge. 'The true meaning of sin was not discovered at the feet of Gamaliel but at the foot of the Cross' (E. K. Lee). **7.** Having made disparaging references to the law, Paul now makes clear that it is not on a par with sin. But it had introduced him to sin by provoking him to taste the sweetness of forbidden fruit. 'Law says, *Don't* walk on the grass: sin says at once, *Shall* walk on the grass, if I like' (G. T. Thomson). **Known** in its first occurrence refers to involve-

ment and experience rather than awareness. Significantly the one commandment that defeated Paul was the tenth, the one that concerns an inner attitude and not externals with which it is by comparison easy to conform. **Covet** in Greek is a wide word covering all kinds of wrong desire. **8.** Sin used **the commandment** as a starting-point from which to launch its attack upon him. The law brought responsibility for wrong-doing and gave sin an active power (cf. 4: 15; 5: 13). **9.** Paul had enjoyed a blissful, carefree childhood, unrestricted by the law and so by sin. Relatively speaking, this was life. 'But all of a sudden I met Moses, carrying in his hand the law of God'—Spurgeon's boyhood experience was apparently Paul's too. At the age of thirteen he followed Jewish practice and became a *bar mitswāh*, lit. 'son of commandment'. He was received into the community and regarded from then on as morally responsible. Then it was that sin sprang to life, inactive no longer. A sensitive teenager, Paul found that the inner tensions of growing manhood and the new responsibilities which the law laid upon him from without tragically combined. He was filled with misery and felt estranged from God. **10.** In his experience the intended guide to **life** (Lev. 18: 5) led him fatally astray (cf. NEB). **11. Deceived** is an allusion to Gen. 3: sin had the same rôle as the tempter in Eden (cf. 2 C. 11: 3) and tricked him by using for its own ends the law, of all things. The law did not prove the remedy for evil, as the Rabbis taught, but an irritant from which a fatal allergy developed. **12f.** Paul must again insist that the law is of divine origin and the revealed standard of morality. It was not this good thing that Paul found fatal, but sin, which the law exposed in its true colours. **14.** From here to the end of the chapter Paul uses the present tense, emotionally re-living his life as Saul the Pharisee. There is no need to assume that the crisis of conversion has intervened between 13 and 14. The verse begins with 'for' (AV, RV), giving the reason for the good law's bad effect upon him. The reason lay within: he had been **sold** like a slave into sin's control (cf. 6: 17 f.) because he was made of weak 'flesh' (**carnal**: Gk. *sarkinos*) which had succumbed to sin (see v. 5 n.; 8: 3). **15-20.** He lived a Jekyll and Hyde existence, with Mr. Hyde as the dominant self. He gave full theoretical assent to the law, but was forced to act against his better judgment by sin which was 'squatting' (Hunter) in his flesh. In his case it was not merely that he knew God's will and approved what is excellent, yet did not do it (2: 17 ff.). He knew and approved and intended to do it, but *could* not. In so far as he regards himself as his better self, he had since adolescence (**no longer**: cf. 9 n.) become mere putty in the hands of sin which controlled him completely. In so far as his identity was that of his lower self, he was bad through and through. **21–23.** Paul had known the distress of bitter conflict which racked him and tore him apart. In his unintegrated life there were two laws or governing principles at war. His faculties and powers were enemy-occupied territory. Sin had invaded them and was fighting to stamp out every attempt at resistance—and succeeding again and again. **24.** Vividly recalling his emotions, as in a nightmare, Paul desperately shrieks for help from any source. His sin-dominated personality (cf. 6: 6) is enduring a living death (cf. vv. 9 ff.). **25.** Another cry from the heart, this time of relief and triumph. He knows that his appeal has been answered, and thanks the One who came to his rescue, **God** who has given the victory through **Jesus Christ** (cf. 1 C. 15: 57). Then, his emotions exhausted, Paul dispassionately sums up his divided life under the law. Without the aid of Christ (**of myself**, Moffatt 'left to myself'), his better self made sincere efforts to comply with the law, but his **flesh** dragged him down to surrender to sin. 8: 1 will give a corresponding counterpart to his cry of relief.

The Spirit makes alive (8: 1–30)
Judaism taught that the Holy Spirit had been withdrawn and would only be restored when the age to come began: then Jl 2: 28 would be fulfilled. The Church knew that it had been fulfilled: the awaited age to come had been inaugurated. It is true that in its full splendour it still lies in the future, but in the outpoured Spirit the power and life of the full age to come are anticipated. He is pledge and foretaste of the future and puts within the Church's grasp a new potential of which they not only may but must avail themselves.

1–4. The basis of the Spirit's work is the Cross. There is not so clear-cut a break as the chapter division and our own section heading suggest. The calm contrast of 7: 25 b and 8: 1 is a double deduction from the emotional contrast of 7: 24 and 7: 25 a. Both 7: 25 b and 8: 1 begin with Gk. *ara* (**so, therefore**); then in 7: 25 (Gk. *oun*) indicates a transition (see Arndt and Gingrich, *Greek Lexicon, s.v., ara*). **I of myself** is matched by **those who are in Christ Jesus.** God took it upon Himself to end in principle the constant mastery of sin over man. God in Christ subdued sin, doing what the law was powerless to do because it had such poor material to work on—**the flesh.** Human nature had let the law down by falling under sin's spell. The pre-existent (so **sending** implies) Son became man and con-

quered man's enemy on its own ground. **The likeness of sinful flesh** does not deny the real humanity of Christ; it affirms His personal sinlessness. 'Flesh' could not be used here by itself (contrast 1: 3) because it had been used in the context in an immoral sense. God made Him a 'sin-offering' (margin). There may well be a reference to Isa. 53: 10, where the same phrase is used in the LXX: He was the suffering Servant who became an atoning sacrifice. On the Cross Jesus absorbed the worst that sin could do and drained it of its power. God thereby executed a sentence of condemnation against the enemy and overcame sin (see note appended to 1: 17). Now, in the new era inaugurated by God's mighty act, sin has lost its control over the man in Christ (cf. 6: 7 n.; 7: 25 b). Slavery to **sin and death** was a mark of the old era of Adam to which he belonged before. **In Christ** he finds himself released and put under a new authority, that of **the Spirit of life** (see note on sin at the end of ch. 5). God's aim was the meeting of the law's **just requirement** in behaviour that fits the new realm of **the Spirit** and not the old régime of **the flesh.** Paul's quarrel was not with the law as morality (cf. 7: 12, 14) but with its degraded form as legality. 'Paul as a Jew had thought that men should keep the law in order that they might be saved. As a Christian he saw that men must be saved in order that they might keep the law' (C. A. Anderson Scott).

5–13. The Spirit is contrasted with the flesh. (See Gal. 5: 19–23 for further exposition of this contrast.) Men in the new era must live differently from those in the old. **5–8. To set the mind** and **the mind that is set** both represent Gk. *phronēma* (RV 'mind'), which, far from being contrasted with action, is an underlying attitude to life that determines behaviour. The outlook dictated by **the flesh** separates from God in a living **death** because it fights against the God of life in inevitable disobedience to His law, as ch. 7 has described. The Spirit prompts to new interests and aims, which are the secret of true **life** and harmony with God. **9f.** Christians must not fall in with the suggestions of **the flesh** because they have left its era behind and are now in the era of **the Spirit.** The decisive test of belonging to Christ is possession of the Spirit which is demonstrable (cf. Ac. 10: 45 f.), being outwardly verified by evidence of His gifts (cf. 1 C. 12: 4–11) and/or of His fruit. **Spirit of God, Spirit of Christ** and **Christ** are used interchangeably: the Spirit is the Father's agent in making the Son real to the Christian. The Spirit (read 'the Spirit is life' in 10) gives **life** to the justified (cf. 5: 21), although sin has made it inevitable that the bodies which express their personalities will one day die. **Dead** is a vivid expression for 'doomed to die'. **11.** But Jesus' resurrection is a guarantee of the future resurrection of the Christian's body. The Spirit will then bring His reviving process to completion. **12f.** The Christian is obliged to resist the tendencies of **the flesh,** which lead to ultimate death. If any man accepted in good faith into a church persists in a low level of living, Paul categorically denies that such a man really belongs to Christ or will attain to eternal life (cf. v. 9 n.; 2: 7 n.). Life in the consummated age to come is a prospect only for those who kill off the (immoral) actions of their personalities which are so used to the bad old ways (cf. 6: 6 n.).

14-17. The Spirit assures of sonship. Cf. Gal. 4: 4-7. **14.** Practical God-likeness, which comes of willing response to the control of His Spirit, is proof of being **sons of God.** 'Like Father, like son' is the thought, as in Mt. 5: 45. **15f.** The Spirit (so read twice for **spirit**) **of sonship** is the Spirit of the Son (Gal. 4: 6) transferred to the Christian: He enables him to look at God with Christ's eyes and makes in him the Son's own filial response to the Father (cf. Mk 14: 36). **Abba** is 'Father' in Aramaic; **Father** represents the Gk. equivalent. The cry passed bilingually into the worshipping vocabulary of the Church, and it is here regarded as evidence that the Spirit is at work. The Christian's own conviction of sonship is supported by the Spirit's evoking this cry in the worship of the church (cf. Gal. 4: 6; 1 C. 12: 3). The Spirit is not one who maintains the frightening, servile conditions of the old era, but gives the confidence that God is a personal Father. In referring to **sonship** Paul is not alluding only to the Hellenistic custom of adoption, but no doubt has OT parallels in mind (cf. 9: 4; Gen. 15: 2 f.; Exod. 2: 10; 1 Chr. 28: 6; Isa. 1: 2). 'Son' or 'sons' was a title of the OT people of God; it passed to Christ who summed up their destiny in Himself (Hos. 11: 1; Mt. 2: 15), and thus it passed to the Church in Him. **17. Children** have the prospect of an inheritance: so it is with Christians. They, like Christ and with Christ, are **heirs of God** (cf. Mt. 21: 38; 25: 34). But before sharing His glory they must be prepared first to live out His sufferings (cf. 2 Tim. 2: 11 f.). Identification with the crucified Christ by faith (6: 3) is no substitute for identification on the level of practical experience (cf. 2 C. 1: 5; 4: 10; Phil. 3: 10 f.). Viewed in this light, the adversities of the present life do not contradict but rather confirm the prospect of glory in the consummated age to come.

18-25. The Spirit assures of future glory. **18.** Cf. 2 C. 4: 17. Present adversity did not make Paul stumble but faded into comparative insignificance—so real to him was the unseen age to come. **19-23.** It was possession of the Spirit that made it real, for He is its **first fruits,** a specimen sheaf cut and brought as sure evidence that a whole field of such sheaves is waiting to be harvested. When the new age fully comes it will reveal the Church in their true light as **sons of God,** in all respects like the exalted Son (cf. Col. 3: 4; 1 Jn 3: 2). It will also transform the world of nature, fulfilling the OT Messianic promises of a renewed earth (e.g. Isa. 35). At the Fall God enslaved nature to **futility** and **decay** (**futility** echoes the refrain of *Ecclesiastes*), but such was not to be its permanent state, for God even then envisaged its emancipation. As willy-nilly the rest of creation was dragged down with man (Gen. 3: 17), its leader (Ps. 8: 6), so it will rise with him. Nature is dependent upon God's glorification of the Church. In poetic idiom it cranes its neck (**earnest longing:** Gk. *apokaradokiā*, Phillips 'is on tiptoe'), waiting for this signal of its own restoration; it is in labour for the birth of the new creation. 'It is nothing short of a universal law that suffering marks the road to glory' (Sanday and Headlam). The Church in so far as they are physically part of the material world share nature's many pains, but they too look forward to release from infirmity, to the renewing of their bodies so that they are like that of the risen and exalted Son (cf. Phil. 3: 21). **24f.** 'We were saved with this hope in view' (Moffatt). The salvation given at conversion had implicit in it promises which have yet to be fulfilled. Contrary experience may now bombard the believer's senses, but it cannot reasonably invalidate his glorious **hope** because its fulfilment essentially lies in the future (cf. 2 C. 4: 18). We must bide God's time.

26-27. The Spirit intercedes. **26. Likewise** links 'groan' (Gk. *stenazomen*) of v. 23 with **sighs** (Gk. *stenagmois*). The Spirit does not despise such expressions of frailty, but makes them the means of His pleading the Church's interests before God; thus He turns the **sighs** to good account. Inarticulate feelings of inadequacy and vaguely conceived yearnings may at times be the nearest one can get to expressing oneself aright to God because 'we cannot tell what is really best for us' (Hodge) and the needs we do express in prayer are often lesser needs. But the **sighs** become the very voice of the Spirit in intercession (cf. v. 15 f.). **27.** God, scrutinizing the whole conscious and unconscious make-up of every man (an OT thought: cf. 1 Sam. 16: 7; 1 Kg. 8: 39; Ps. 139: 1 f.; Jer. 17: 10), understands what the Spirit means by His dumb sighs deep within because it is His own purpose for His own people that the Spirit is pleading to be realized.

357

28–30. The Spirit carries out God's plan. The Spirit is active not only via the unconscious or semi-conscious mind but throughout the whole range of life's experiences. He is co-operating with the Christian **in everything** to bring about a **good** end. V. 29 explains the good end (**to be conformed . . .**) and 5: 3 f. the general thought. Read the first alternative in the margin. The text has followed some ancient authorities which add **God** as the subject of the verb, but in the Greek *ho theos* (**God**) reads unnaturally after *ton theon*, the same noun in another case. But the addition is evidence that the verb was regarded as having a personal subject. The theme of the section suggests that the Spirit is the implicit subject (so NEB). **Those who love him** is an OT expression for God's followers who throw themselves whole-heartedly into His service and identify themselves with His aims (*e.g.* Exod. 20: 6; Jg. 5: 31; Dan. 9: 4). The Spirit co-operates with such because they have been summoned by God and assigned a rôle in His redemptive purposes (cf. 1: 6 n.). God's eternal plan was to create for Himself a family modelled upon His unique Son. Before the world began (Eph. 1: 4) He intended this destiny for those whom He had made the objects of His personal care and concern (**foreknew:** cf. Gen. 18: 19; Jer. 1: 5; Am. 3: 2). The Spirit is responsible for the gradual moral transformation which they are now undergoing on earth. **30.** All the steps in God's purposes that are now accomplished have been leading up to the end expressed in v. 29. Having decided long ago whom He would appoint for this destiny, He summoned them, made them right with Himself and illumined them with His glory (cf. 2 C. 3: 18; 4: 6). Paul may be echoing the LXX of Isa. 45: 25, where 'justify' and 'glory' occur together describing a single activity.

(c) Triumphant life (8: 31–39)
In a grand climax inspired by God's outworking of His purposes Paul lifts up his heart in a lyrical assertion of security and triumph. The passage is parallel with 5: 1–11. Both are encouraging deductions from earlier doctrinal truth. Both stress the love of God in allowing His Son to die, the death and risen and exalted life of Christ, God's being on our side, the Christian attitude to adversity, and the past being a guarantee of the future. **31.** The Christian's reaction to all the foregoing truths is first a sense of complete security. *With the Lord on my side I do not fear* (Ps. 118: 6) is in Paul's mind. **32.** An allusion to the LXX of Gen. 22: 16. The apostle regards Abraham's un-hesitating but painful surrender of Isaac as an illustration of what it meant to God to give up

his own Son to death. The greatest gift carries a promise of all smaller gifts: He is 'all other gifts in one'. **32f.** Does not sin threaten? No, God's chosen need have no fear of any accusing finger at the judgment day, since God has dealt with their sin. Isa. 50: 7–9 is a promise that Paul claims for the Church. The Judge Himself, **Christ Jesus** (cf. 2: 16), will not **condemn**, seeing that it is He who carried through the mighty saving acts of death and resurrection, who now sits triumphant as His people's King (Ps. 110: 1). The exalted Servant there continues His work of intercession (Isa. 53: 12). **35.** Is not adversity a threat? No, His **love** will never let go of His own, whatever strains and pressures are brought to bear on them. Paul writes out of experience as one who has himself known the firm, unyielding grip of Christ's love in these very crises (2 C. 11: 23 ff.). **36.** Indeed, they are not obstacles to God's purposes, but His appointed way for His people, as Scripture makes clear in Ps. 44: 22. Note the contrast between the original context of despairing complaint and the apostle's tones of exultant triumph: Christ and hope of heaven transformed the attitude of God's servants towards a hostile environment. **37.** Far from being victims of circumstances, Paul and all who stand with him are given 'overwhelming victory' (Phillips, NEB) **through** Christ whose love was 'strong as death' (Gk. *agapēsantos*—an aorist—points to the Cross). **38. Death** cannot **separate** because it is 'swallowed up in victory' (1 C. 15: 54) nor **life** because, for all its infirmity and decay, it is yet the scene of Christian service (Phil. 1: 20 ff.). The loving Lord guards and guides through all the unknown contingencies of the present and future. **Angels** and **principalities,** and **powers** too, the hostile or potentially hostile forces behind the material universe, have been stripped of their power to harm by Christ's victory (Col. 2: 14; 1 Pet. 3: 22). **Height** and **depth** in Hellenistic Greek were astrological terms for the highest and lowest points reached by a star. It was a widespread contemporary belief that men's lives were fated by the positions of the stars as spirit-powers. Paul asserts that all such fears are groundless for the Christian. **Creation** has implicit in it the comfort that there is no factor or force in the universe that is not under the control of the God who made it—and He is for us. The truth that God is creator of all gives added assurance to the redeemed (cf. Isa. 40: 28 ff.; 42: 6 f.; 44: 24).

IV. THE GOSPEL FOR THE WORLD IN GOD'S PLAN (9: 1–11: 36)
The cry of triumph of 8: 31 ff. has died away and in the ensuing silence another shadow falls

across Paul's mind, requiring like the rest to be dispelled by the light of God in Christ. Why had the Jews not come flocking into His kingdom? Why had Christ's own people not welcomed Him when He came home (Jn 1: 11)? Why had the Christian mission to the Jews sagged so miserably? In the OT it appeared that Israel was to be the missionary body evangelizing the world. In present experience the Jewish response to their Messiah was a miserable parody of what had been promised. It was a bitter disappointment, but it was more: it opened the door to all sorts of doubts. 'Does their faithlessness nullify the faithfulness of God?' (3: 3). If God let Israel down like that. . . . 'By no means' (3: 4): Paul could not admit that premise, let alone draw the conclusion that He might let the Church down. But it was a problem that had been burning deep in Paul's mind for years, especially as it sprang directly out of his missionary experience. He had seen the synagogue reject the gospel time and time again. But the problem was larger than that: since all was under God's control, Paul himself had been personally involved in bringing about God's rejection of the Jews. What was the strategy behind God's tactics? After enquiring into the OT where God had revealed some of His plans, Paul arrives at the convictions of chs. 9-11, convictions based both on reflections upon his missionary experience and on his knowledge of the OT. These chapters are the product not of a systematic theologian but of a mature missionary thinking aloud and interpreting the facts by Biblical principles. Paul meant 11: 33 f. to be taken seriously. He did not claim to know the complete answer from A to Z. But he did claim to have found important clues which were enough for man to know of God's unfathomable designs. It is important to understand the angle from which Paul was writing. He had no intention of answering those who queried, or were curious about, the truths of divine sovereignty and election and human responsibility and their compatibility. Rather, he is interpreting the first-century missionary situation in terms which he shared with both his Christian and Jewish contemporaries. He with them had taken over the viewpoint of the OT and it did not occur to him to question it. His Jewish critics demurred only at his application of OT doctrines, and not at the doctrines themselves.

Paul found three different clues that helped to solve his problem. The first is a number of OT precedents and promises of divine control over the history of God's people for His appointed ends. He stressed God's sovereignty in order to hit out at the cocksure Jewish notion that God *had* to save them, bound by the bonds of the law, circumcision and good works. Paul insists strongly that God is free and gracious. Side by side with the first clue he places a second one without attempting to square the two. The Jews have refused to go God's way, and, as long as they do not believe, put themselves out of God's saving reach. The third clue, again unco-ordinated with the earlier ones, is God's faithfulness. The One who never breaks a promise can be trusted to bring Israel to salvation. God's present tactics may be pro-Gentile and anti-Jew, but His overall strategy is for the ultimate benefit of the Jews and the enrichment of the Church.

i. The Jews' tragic rejection of Christ (9: 1-5)

1f. Paul is heart-broken that the bulk of his fellow-Jews still stand outside God's kingdom. He solemnly expresses the sincerity of his sorrow. **3.** His words here are 'white-hot with love and wild with all regret' (J. S. Stewart). So strong are his feelings that, were it feasible, he would become *anathema* (Gk. for **accursed**; cf. Dt. 7: 26) and have his union with Christ severed if his beloved people could take his place. The servant here reveals how deeply he has imbibed the self-sacrificing spirit of his Servant-Lord (cf. 1 Jn 3: 16). **4f.** What an anticlimax to so glorious a heritage is the Jews' present hostile reaction to God's purposes! With **sonship** compare 8: 15 n.; Exod. 4: 22. **Glory** is the Shekinah-glory, God's localizing His presence in a unique way within Israel (cf. Exod. 24: 16; 29: 43). **The covenants** (cf. Eph. 2: 12) are the basic covenant made with Abraham and its later amplifications and confirmations in Israel's history. **The worship** is the elaborate ritual of tabernacle and temple. With **the promises** cf. 1: 2; 3: 2; 4: 13. At the end of 5 the margin is the more natural rendering of the Gk. from the point of view of syntax. In face of the general Jewish denial that Jesus was the Messiah, Paul is driven in reaction to avow his own recognition of Him in terms stronger than he tends to use elsewhere. See further A. W. Wainwright, *The Trinity in the New Testament*, 1962, pp. 54 ff.

ii. God's present plan for Jew and Gentile (9: 6-10: 21)

God's purposes have been revealed (9: 6-29)

6-13. The OT gives evidence of a preliminary narrowing process in God's purposes, and it is in this light that the present situation is to be explained. The rejection of Christ by most of the Jews does not come as a surprise to God, and on second thoughts need not to the Church, since it is in line with a divine principle. God is indeed *fulfilling* His **word.** As in the early history of Israel His habit was to select only one branch of the family tree for His special purposes, so it has been designed that at first the Church should contain only a certain number of Jews. Neither blood nor behaviour qualifies a Jew for divine acceptance. **6-9.** Paul argues again (cf. 2: 25 ff.) that the Jews' view of themselves as automatically a chosen nation is a fallacy. Their slogan of assurance 'We have Abraham as our father' (Lk. 3: 8; Jn 8: 33, 39) is historically unsound, since the chosen line by-passed his son Ishmael according to Gen. 21: 12. God's choice depends not upon a hereditary process but upon His personal **promise,** as Gen. 18: 10 proves. In Paul's mind **promise** is antithetic to adhering to the law (4: 13 ff.). **10-13.** Nor on the other hand can God's choice rest upon works, upon any supposed claim with which man may arrogantly demand a place in God's redemptive purposes. God did not wait to see how Jacob and Essau would turn out before He selected one of them (Gen. 25: 23; Mal. 1: 2 f.). His own call was the decisive issue, irrespective of individual merit or demerit. Paul is returning to his attack on Judaism's justification by works (chs. 2, 3).

14-29. The non-Christian Jew cannot dictate to God on this issue. Paul vetoes the possibility that one may accuse God of unfairness and think to compel Him to do otherwise. He gives three reasons. (*a*) Scripture reveals the principle of God's free will (15-18). (*b*) It would be tantamount to claiming to be God's equal instead of God's creature (19-24). (*c*) Scripture reveals the promise of the very things which have taken place—God's limitation of His people to a Jewish remnant and the extension of His people to include Gentiles (25-29). (*a*) **15-18.** God is free. **15 f.** Exod. 33: 19 implies that God's grace cannot be forced into a groove of man's making. When God condescended to reveal Himself to Moses it was not because even Moses had any claim upon God by his service. This was meant as a principle for the future (**will**) as well as for Moses. **17.** Exod. 9: 16 shows that God is free too to employ instruments which apparently oppose His purposes but whose use will lead to His ultimate glory and to world-wide blessing. As Paul later makes clear (vv. 22 f.; 11: 7), he sees contemporary Jewry in the rôle of Pharaoh. The Exodus has been re-enacted in Christian history with Israel playing Pharaoh's part. Their opposition and persecution have only served to promote God's ends (cf. 11: 12; Ac. 8: 1, 4). **18.** The Jews may not glibly hold Gentiles to be outside the pale and themselves to have an incontrovertible claim upon God's grace. Just as God had permitted Pharaoh to be hardened against His word (cf.

Exod. 8: 32; 9: 12), so He had the Jews. (*b*) **19-24.** Man is God's creature. **19-21.** Paul has ringing in his ears a conclusion drawn in actual discussion by a Jewish objector, as by Job in Job 9, 10: God's ways are then simply immoral fatalism (cf. 3: 5, 7). This conclusion Paul rejects, but he waits until ch. 10 to answer it (cf. 3: 8 n.). But, like Zophar in Job 11: 7 ff., he is shocked at his opponent's thus shrugging his shoulders at the transcendent God and attempting to 'bandy words' (Knox) with Him. Paul protests in OT language: man is nothing but the product of the Potter's hands. So the OT stresses again and again, *e.g.* in Gen. 2: 7 where *formed* (Heb. *yātsur*) is the activity of a potter (Heb. *yōtsēr*). There is a clear echo of Isa. 29: 16 in 20 and of Jer. 18: 6 in 21. The divine Craftsman could put His **lump** of humanity to any providential use for which there is a need, without first asking man's permission. **22-24.** God had demonstrated His **power** by cutting off the unbelieving Jews from their inheritance, and He had declared a sentence of condemnation against them (cf. Mt. 10: 14 f.; Ac. 13: 46, 51). **Desiring** must mean 'because He desired' not 'although . . .' in view of the comparison with Pharaoh (cf. v. 17). They had shown themselves 'fit only for destruction' (Knox), 'ripe and ready to be destroyed' (Moffatt), yet God had not destroyed them but put up with their hardness of heart so that they might be object-lessons of His **wrath** (contrast 2: 4 f., where His patience is attributed to His kindness: the two ideas are complementary). Alongside this severe judgment, and enhanced by it, was God's glorious dealings of grace with the Church. 10: 1 and ch. 11 show that latent in Paul's mind is the hope that **the vessels of wrath** (a phrase borrowed from the LXX of Jer. 50: 25) would eventually be re-shaped when God's present purposes were fulfilled (cf. Jer. 18: 4, 8; 2 Tim. 2: 20 f.). (*c*) **25-29.** This is prophecy come true. **25f.** Paul cites Hos. 2: 23; 1: 10 as adumbrations that the Church, the elect instrument of God's purposes, would largely be made up of Gentiles. The OT reveals God's plan that the Gentiles were to become His **people,** His **beloved,** His **sons.** Cf. Ps. 87; Isa. 19: 25. **Place** means for Paul the whole Gentile world. **27-29.** Secondly, Isaiah's teaching on **the remnant** in Isa. 10: 22 f.; 1: 9 pointed forward to the present situation, when a Jewish minority formed the nucleus of the Church. It was not that anything had gone amiss in the execution of God's plan: of that the OT gives assurance.

The Jewish and Gentile reactions to the gospel (9: 30-10: 21)
God's plan is centred in a universal gospel of

faith-righteousness (cf. 1: 16 f., 3: 21 ff.). Gentiles are in the Church simply because they have accepted that gospel. The bulk of the Jews are at the moment outside the Church simply because they have refused it. Reference to the OT proves the validity of this assessment. Earlier Paul has been analysing the contemporary situation in terms of God's overall control. Now he paradoxically but unhesitatingly affirms the responsibility of man's choice when confronted with the gospel. 'If we are dealing with two measurable categorical contraries, both of them on the same plane, we must reject the contradiction, since a definitive assertion and its definitive negation cannot both be true; but the case stands otherwise when we are dealing with the interspheriing mysteries of the human and the divine. Conscience affirms the freedom of man, and faith the freedom of God: the Scriptures affirm both; and Paul rests his case on the Scriptures' (G. O. Griffith). First Paul briefly gives the human explanation of the situation in 30–33; then in ch. 10 he develops his thesis at greater length.

30–33. The Jews' position is their own fault. It is sadly ironic that the goal which the Jews missed the **Gentiles** have reached without trying. The Jews had been going the wrong way about it. They sought to get right with God by their **works,** basing their hope of salvation upon the **law,** which they could not keep. The Gentiles now in the Church had made no such attempt but accepted the ready-made faith-righteousness offered by God through the work of the Cross. To the Jews a crucified Messiah was a stumbling-block (1 C. 1: 23), but to those who read the OT with Christian eyes this comes as no surprise since Isa. 8: 14 envisages this very situation. Christ is the Stone, as He Himself claimed (Mt. 21: 42; cf. Ac. 4: 11). Isa. 28: 16, quoted from the LXX, presents positive teaching about the Stone: God will certainly save the man who makes Him the object of his faith. Paul is quoting from a collection of OT quotations current in the early Church (cf. 1 Pet. 2: 6 ff.).

10: 1–4. The Jewish rejection of faith-righteousness is a tragedy. Paul reaffirms (cf. 9: 1 ff.) his longing that not ruin (9: 22) but salvation may be the Jews' lot. Their obvious sincerity is misguided. ('Behind these verses it is not hard to discern Paul's own struggle to find salvation'—A. M. Hunter.) They cannot grasp that Christ has inaugurated faith-righteousness, which spells the termination of attempting to get right with God via the law (Gal. 3: 23 ff.).

5–13. The gospel of faith-righteousness is easily attained and universally available. **5.** Law-righteousness demands life-long success in the moral struggle as its prerequisite for eternal life (Lev. 18: 5: Paul implicitly contrasts with it Hab. 2: 4, as Gal. 3: 11 f. shows). **6–8.** But the OT also witnesses to the gospel of faith-righteousness. Dt. 30: 12 ff., with its emphasis upon the initiative of divine grace and upon humble reception of God's proffered word, may be applied to the gospel. The change to **descend into the abyss** is influenced by Ps. 107: 26: Gk. *abyssos* can refer to both the sea and Hades. The gospel of faith-righteousness is not something to strive and strain after with superhuman efforts, but is **near** at hand, ready for a man to take on his **lips** and into his **heart.** It is news of something already done by Christ: He has taken the initiative and come to man; He has conquered sin and death, and risen triumphant. **9f.** Man has only to **believe** and **confess** to be saved. **Confess** comes before **believe** to conform to the order **lips ... heart** in the quotation. The next verse has the logical order. Salvation depends upon outward profession matched by inner conviction. **Jesus is Lord** was the earliest confession of faith (cf. v. 13 n.; 1 C. 12: 3); this may well refer to its use in baptism. To believe in the resurrection (cf. 4: 24) is no mere intellectual assent, but involves the shattering realization that God has miraculously intervened and inaugurated the Messianic reign (cf. 1: 4 n.; 6: 11 n.). After such a realization no man can ever be the same as he was before. **11–13.** Isa. 28: 16 is quoted again to confirm that the believer's salvation is guaranteed. Paul now borrows 'all' (Gk. *pās*) from Jl 3: 5 (quoted in 13) and adds it here (cf. AV, RV 'whosoever') to bring out the implications. If keeping the law were the condition for salvation, salvation would be merely a Jewish concern; since faith is the criterion it is available to any, Jew or Gentile (cf. 3: 22). The risen **Lord** has been given universal dominion, and 'he has enough and to spare' (Knox) for any who appeal to Him for salvation (cf. Eph. 4: 8). Now that the Spirit has inaugurated Christ's kingdom upon earth (cf. Jl 2: 28 ff.) the universal offer of Jl 2: 32 is operative. In the OT text **the Lord** represents Yahweh or Jehovah, the Heb. name for God. Here as often in the NT it is re-interpreted of Christ (cf. 1 C. 1: 2; Ac. 3: 21, 36) since God had conferred upon Him His own name, 'the name which is above every name' (Phil. 2: 9).

14–21. God has given the Jews every opportunity. He has done everything possible to get the gospel across to them, but they have not responded with faith. **14f.** The gap between God's gospel and a man's appropriation of it must be covered by a chain whose four links are the apostles, preaching, hearing and faith.

God **sent** (Gk. *apostalōsin*) the apostles to them. Isa. 52: 7 is quoted as the divine authorization of their mission. **16.** An adjacent verse, Isa. 53: 1, is put on the apostles' lips as their report that their making the message heard—about the suffering Servant—has met with little response of faith from their fellow-Jews who heard it. The Jews broke the last link in the chain. **18.** But if they did not believe, that is not because they did not have the opportunity to hear it. It is underlined that the fault is not on God's side: He has let the Jews hear the gospel. Ps. 19: 4 is true of the apostolic testimony: it has penetrated every corner of the earth (Paul is thinking of the then known world). **19–21.** Moses and Isaiah have the answer why the Jews did not accept the gospel. Dt. 32: 21 revealed that **foolish** Gentiles (cf. 2: 20), a non-nation (cf. 9: 25), would understand. So difficulty in understanding was not the problem. Isa. 65: 1 f. discloses the real obstacle to be the Jews' obstinate disobedience in the face of God's repeated appeals, so that God had to turn to the Gentiles instead (cf. Lk. 14: 16–24).

iii. God's future plan for Jew and Gentile (11: 1–32)

The present state of affairs was not to be permanent. Paul took seriously God's election of the Jews and His OT promises to them and could not entertain the idea that they were to be by and large excluded from attaining those promises. When the 'full number' of the Gentiles had been incorporated into the Church, then, and only then, it would be the turn of the Jews as a whole—not a mere handful as now—to acknowledge Jesus as Lord and thus reveal their now hidden character as God's elect. Their prejudiced, closed minds would be opened to the truth of the gospel, just as once his own had been, and then the final outworking of the 'one new man' in Christ (Eph. 2: 15) would be realized. This hope was the driving force behind Paul's world-wide evangelism, for ultimately it would redound to the Jews' advantage. The full evangelism of the Gentiles would usher in the salvation of Israel. It is significant that Paul did not assert, as the manner of some is, that the OT promises to Israel had automatically passed *en bloc* to the largely Gentile Church, because such a view would make mockery of God's election. Nor, however, did he dissociate the Church from Israel's promises: that would deny the unity of the 'olive tree' and ignore the continuity of the OT people of God with the Church, which for Paul was ultimately to comprise the 'full number' of the Gentiles *plus* the bulk of the Jews. Until then the Church would be lop-sided and incomplete and the purposes of God among men not yet fulfilled.

To prove that God has not abandoned Israel, Paul argues that their rejection is both partial and provisional. For the time being a remnant is being saved (1-10). Eventually God will save the rest when He has finished gathering Gentile Christians (11-32).

1-10. Now a remnant of Israel is being saved. **1-5.** Scripture echoes and re-echoes with the sure principle which Paul is quoting: **God has not rejected his people** after having lavished such care and concern upon them (Ps. 94: 14; 1 Sam. 12: 22; Jer. 31: 37; 33: 24 ff.). 10: 20f. cannot be God's last word, for He is not fickle. His faithfulness to covenant-promises may not be exploited by arrogant presumption, but it is a dependable source of security to the humble believer. Paul regards himself as a token of God's faithfulness to His people. If Israel were rejected, he himself would not have been saved. But Paul is not a lone survivor. He finds a historical parallel in 1 Kg. 19 where Elijah was reassured that he was not left alone despite the opposition of so many Israelites to the true faith. As then God had preserved 7,000 followers, a fraction of the nation, so now there is a Jewish-Christian **remnant, chosen by grace** (cf. 9: 6, 27-29). **6. Grace** by its very definition is the opposite of **works**: the self-made Jew is automatically debarred from the faithful few. **7. Israel** as a whole has not achieved salvation, but out of it has been saved the **elect** minority, while the majority have been made insensitive to the gospel for the time being (cf. 9: 18 n.). **8.** Scripture is finding a fresh application. God has sent most of the Jews into a paralysing **stupor**, according to Isa. 29: 10. Their present state is that of blind, deaf men, as Israel of old were described in Dt. 29: 4. **9f.** The Psalmist's curse has come true (Ps. 69: 23 f. LXX). Their very religious observances, as a substitute for Christ, only lead the Jews astray. 'The picture of a blind, decrepit old man, bowed down in age and infirmity . . . is a very pathetic representation of a people in a state of religious senility' (E. K. Lee).

11-32. Eventually Israel as a whole will be saved after the full quota of Gentile Christians has been made up. **11-15.** Israel has only **stumbled** over the Stone (9: 32 f.), not collapsed altogether. God has not dropped them. The unbelief of most of the Jews has been God's temporary means to the end that the gospel should come to the Gentiles. The Gk. for **trespass** may be translated 'lapse' (Weymouth, Moffatt) or 'false step' (Knox). The Gentiles' acceptance of the gospel made the Jews **jealous** (cf. Ac. 13: 44 ff.)—and designedly so. The reason why Paul made much of his Gentile **ministry** was that it fulfilled God's revealed purpose (Dt. 32: 21 quoted in 10: 19), which was to provoke his **fellow Jews** not merely to jealous indignation, but in the case of **some** to emulation, to a positive desire to share the blessings accruing to Gentile Christians. His Gentile missionary work was not only for the Gentiles' sake, Paul assures them in anticipation of his later attack on their cocksureness and contempt for Jews. His Gentile apostleship was but a round-about way of reaching the Jews. Arguing from the greater to the less as in 5: 9 f., Paul contends that if Israel's falling away has resulted in so much good, **how much more** can be expected when they are restored! Their return to God's favour will mean the influx of new, blue blood into the Church and so re-invigoration and revival. **16.** What guarantee is there that the Jews will play so glorious a rôle? The answer lies in Israel's ancient religious history. There is a natural sanctity in Israel, endowed by God. In so signally revealing Himself to their forefathers (cf. v. 28) in His mighty acts and promises, God had set a pattern to which Israel would again conform in due course. 'When the first loaf is consecrated, the whole batch is consecrated with it' (Knox), and Israel's patriarchs were like the first loaf. Paul has Num. 15: 20 f. in mind. Israel's ancestors have left to their descendants a legacy of spiritual wealth which they will one day claim and use. In a sense the Rabbis were right about Israel's election: they went wrong in also holding a vigorous doctrine of works which denied God's grace and in failing to submit to God's will by recognizing Jesus as the Messiah, the only avenue of God's blessing.

17–24. The illustration of root and branches in v. 16 is developed into a horticultural allegory describing God's plan for present and future. The idea comes from Jer. 11: 16 where Israel is compared with an *olive tree*, once *fair with goodly fruit*, but now spoilt by sin and due for punishment: *its branches will be broken* (AV, RV). Paul finds the current situation explained in his verse. The tree is the people of God. Its branches are living Jews. Now **some of the branches,** unbelieving Jews, have been pruned away and the only natural branches left are the believing remnant of Israel. But the divine Gardener has replenished the tree with a **wild olive shoot.** Gentile converts to Christianity comprise a cutting from an oleaster shrub inserted into the stock of the cultivated olive tree. There is evidence in ancient horticultural books that occasionally this strange practice was followed in the belief that an oleaster scion would invigorate an old tree (see Leenhardt's commentary; W. M. Ramsay, *Pauline and Other Studies*, pp. 219 ff.). But the normal

practice was to use a good quality olive scion. The very unusualness is no doubt an intended part of the allegory. God has acted in grace that transcends human custom and expectation. But the Gardener has not finished His work yet. The **natural branches** that have been removed will one day be **grafted back,** as soon as they cease to **persist in their unbelief.** Now there are only a few Jewish branches left (cf. v. 17) in company with a large wild shoot taken from the Gentile world: they are all there because of their common faith, faith in God who has revealed Himself through Jesus Christ. One day the Jewish and Gentile Christians will be joined on the tree by the mass of renegade Jews, who will come to share their faith and be restored as active members of the people of God.

Paul gives this explanation in the context of a warning, at which he has already hinted in vv. 13 f. There was evidently an anti-Jewish bias among Gentile converts. Gentiles were learning to shout down Judaism's proud claims with even louder counter-claims of their own privileges and the Jews' deprivation. In their eyes it was no doubt a shameful thing to be a Jew, a member of the race that had rejected their Messiah. They deserved all the kicks they got. God had had to come to the Gentiles before He could get any satisfaction (cf. 10: 20 f. n.). Paul deplores this unhealthy attitude of contempt: it was the mentality of the worst type of Jew all over again. He reminds them of their debt to the Jewish heritage. 'In a sense the converted Jew is the only normal human being in the world. To him, in the first instance, the promises were made, and he has availed himself of them. He calls Abraham his father by hereditary right as well as by divine courtesy. He has taken the whole syllabus in order, as it was set. . . . Every one else is, from one point of view, a special case, dealt with under emergency conditions' (C. S. Lewis). Paul warns the Gentile Christians that the Jews' fate could be theirs unless they **continue in** God's **kindness** (cf. 2: 4 ff.; 8: 13 n.; 1 C. 10: 12). God can thin out the branches again. The Jews' fate should arouse in Gentile Christians not arrogance but humble faith and respect for a God who is not to be trifled with. Woe to the Christian 'for whom grace is no longer grace on the hundredth or the thousandth day as it was on the first' (Godet).

25–32. God's plan is in two stages. **25.** The first stage is the rejection of most of the Jews in order that God may make up the **full number,** which only He knows, of Gentile Christians. **26.** The second stage, which He will put into operation as soon as the first is completed, is a

mystery, a secret design of God which human minds would not have hit upon apart from revelation. **All Israel will be saved,** brought into the Christian blessings into which now only a remnant of the Jews have entered. **All Israel** means the Jews as a collective whole, not the arithmetical sum of all individual Jews. The phrase is obviously contrasted with **part of Israel,** and **Israel** consistently refers to the Jews in chs. 9–11. **So** signifies 'by such means' described in v. 25 b. **Saved** is to be taken in the same spiritual sense as in vv. 11, 14. (The question of a political future for converted Israel does not arise here, but hangs upon the interpretation of other Scriptures.) In Scriptural support of this astounding statement, Paul cites Isa. 59: 20 f., mainly from the LXX. 'To Zion' of the Heb. text become 'for Zion's sake' in the LXX; here it is changed to **from Zion** under the influence of Ps. 14: 7. God had pledged Himself to Israel for ever (the unquoted continuation of the OT passage is no doubt also in Paul's mind: cf. 3: 4 n.). His plan was that Jesus, the **Deliverer** (cf. 1 Th. 1: 10), would first set out with His witnesses from Jerusalem to the end of the earth (cf. Ac. 1: 8; Mt. 28: 19 f.) and then eventually go back to His own people and turn their unbelief to faith. The concluding words are from Isa. 27: 9: God had promised so to do. He would freely forgive the Jews' rejection of Christ. **28f.** At present the mass of unbelieving Jews have a dual character in God's eyes. They are the temporary objects of His displeasure, having opposed and rejected **the gospel.** This was intended for the benefit of the Gentiles so that they might have the opportunity of receiving it (cf. v. 11). But simultaneously they are the objects of His election-love as heirs of the glorious Israel of old (cf. v. 16 n.), since the never-changing God does not take back a gift or cancel a summons. **30f.** Now the Gentile Christian had passed from rebellion to pardon; so would the Jew one day. As for the Gentile the present is a reversal of the past, so for the Jew the future will be a reversal of the present. Now the Jew is serving the Gentile as the means of God's pardoning the latter; the Gentile is to serve the Jew as the means of pardoning the Jew. **32.** God gave up one class of man, the Gentiles, to rebellion as a preliminary to pardoning him now; so God is now treating the other class, the Jews, in preparation for granting them pardon later on.

iv. Praise of God's wisdom (11: 33–36)
Paul's discussion dissolves into worship, for 'theology is doxology or it is nothing at all' (E. Stauffer). The interpreter of God's purposes to man is forced to break out in spontaneous praise

to God: 'How great Thou art!' He has seen God's purposes of lavish grace (**riches**) and **wisdom** stretching from horizon to horizon, but clearly there is yet a vast universe of the divine will beneath and beyond, out of human sight. Isa. 40: 13 and Job 41: 11 are testimonies to God's transcendence and gracious initiative. How futile is any attempt on the part of little man, Jew or even Gentile, to think that He regards men as His consultants to tell Him what to do, or that they can ever earn acceptance with God by merit. For God is 'Source, Guide and Goal of all that is' (NEB).

V. THE GOSPEL IN ACTION (12: 1–15: 13)
'The gospel has two sides—a believing side and a behaving side', as A. M. Hunter quotes. It is to the second side that Paul now turns. Previously in chs. 6–8 he had laid down the general principle of the 'newness of life' required of the Christian. Here he analyses God's requirement into a series of duties that range over most of life and also present by analogy principles to cover every situation.

i. Behaviour in the church and in the world (12: 1–21)
A new life of self-dedication (12: 1–2)
1. The worship of 11: 33 ff. turns into an appeal for worship in the widest sense as a response to God's **mercies.** Divine initiative and human response is the pattern in both OT and NT. The OT ritual laid down as the medium of part of Israel's obedience to the God who had redeemed them must find a counterpart in the Church. Their personalities in all their manifestations (cf. 6: 6 n.) must be sacrificed alive as a whole-offering which satisfies God's moral requirements. **Living** has all the associations of the resurrection life that is life indeed, which was expounded in chs. 5–8. **Spiritual** (Gk. *logikēn*) is derived from 'word' (Gk. *logos*) and so here means 'figurative, metaphorical' as distinct from the material **worship** of OT ritual. NEB has 'the worship offered by mind and heart'. **2.** The old 'age' (margin) is still running its course in one sense, but in another sense it has already passed away (cf. 6: 4, 5, 8 n.). The Rabbis used to contrast 'this age' with the 'coming age'. For the Christian who has entered the age to come the old conventions and habits in vogue around him are out of date. Instead his whole attitude to life must be renewed (cf. 6: 4), re-modelled on the lines of his new status, and orientated towards God. His aim must be to exercise sound spiritual judgment at every turn, in every situation to find out God's **will.** This rather high-sounding phrase resolves itself in practice into what is good for God and for one's neighbour, what is personally pleasing to God, and

what is the ideal response to a situation (cf. Eph. 5: 9 f.).

Co-ordination in the church (3-8)

Paul ventures by virtue of his apostolic authority to develop co-operation and harmony in the local church. A this-worldly spirit of self-seeking and competition must not rear its ugly head. An exaggerated view of one's own importance must give way to a sensible estimate of one's position. Christians' **faith,** or the gospel which they believe (cf. v. 6) is the standard by which to measure themselves. 'They then and only then achieve a sober and sensible estimate of themselves as, equally with their fellows, both sinners revealed in their true colours by the judgment of the Cross and also the objects of God's undeserved and triumphant mercy in Jesus Christ' (C. E. B. Cranfield). From that source the Christian learns too that he is **in Christ,** a phrase which implies corporate solidarity: he is in the **body** of Christ. Consequently, like a limb he is responsible for making a specific contribution to the well-being of the whole church, and must neither neglect his own function, as if he was superfluous, nor usurp others' functions, as if he was meant to do everything (cf. 1 C. 12: 12 ff.). God has allocated different functions to different spiritual limbs in Christ's body, and Paul stresses that the credit belongs to the Giver and not to the gifted. He proceeds to enumerate some of those functions (cf. a different list in 1 C. 12: 4 ff.) and the way in which they are to be carried out. The wide range of the list 'shows clearly that Paul made no such hard and fast distinction between clerical and lay ministries as later emerged in the Church' (C. H. Dodd). The prophet, 'the eye of the Church to receive new revelations' (F. Godet), must check what he says against the Christian **faith** to see that they agree (cf. 1 C. 14: 29; 1 Jn 4: 1). A man equipped for practical **service** (cf. 1 Pet. 4: 11) or a teacher or a preacher must each confine himself to his own work and not think he can do another's task and/or neglect his own. When one gives to Christian funds, that is a spiritual work to be done whole-heartedly, not reluctantly or in a niggardly way. A supporter of a Christian project (**he who gives aid:** Gk. *proistamenos,* which Arndt and Gingrich define here as 'be concerned about, care for, give aid'; 'helper' in 16: 2 is Gk. *prostatis,* a cognate noun) should not tail off into indifference. The 'sick visitor' (Moffatt) must make himself affable or his visit will be wasted. In fine Paul's advice is: do your own job, and mean what you do.

Love in action (9-21)

Turning to broader questions of personal attitudes and relationships in the church and outside, the apostle counsels **genuine love** that takes its cue from God's love in Christ and is out for the very best for other people. It is to be guided not by sentiment or indulgence but by the highest moral standards. Its manifold implications include touches of affectionate tenderness and mutual rivalry in showing respect. **11.** The Christian's consistent attitude must be one of enthusiasm, a warm fervour which the Spirit promotes (cf. Ac. 18: 25; Rev. 3: 15), and the dedication of every activity to Christ as **Lord** (cf. Col. 3: 23 f.). **12.** The church must be marked by a confident tone inspired not by wishful thinking but by the solid reality of the Christian hope. This will result in a dogged refusal to give in to adverse pressures. But how is it maintained? By persistent praying that keeps regularly in touch with God. **13.** Further outworkings of love towards other Christians are the relief of material **needs** and the opening of the home to Christian visitors to the locality (cf. Ac. 16: 15; 1 Pet. 4: 9). **14.** The early Church obviously treasured the Sermon on the Mount: Paul here echoes his Master's words (Mt. 5: 44; Lk. 6: 28). A natural reaction to persecutors is to be transcended by invoking a blessing upon them: this is the new way of love. **15.** One's natural mood must give way to a ready sympathy with the experiences of others. **16.** Read with NEB: 'Have equal regard for one another'. This being 'actuated by a common and well-understood feeling of mutual allowance and kindness' (Alford) rules out any caste system and calls for a willingness to mix unselfconsciously with slaves and others low on the social ladder (cf. Phm. 16). Prov. 3: 7, here quoted, warns against the vanity that is the basis of snobbery. **17-21.** Paul uses an adjacent precept (Prov. 3: 4, quoted from the LXX) to urge Christians not to provide their pagan neighbours with just cause for criticism. One way is non-retaliation, and this principle the apostle now elaborates. The early Church, set as they were in naturally suspicious or hostile communities, needed wise and cool heads. It takes two to keep the peace, but the Christian must not be responsible for breaking it. It is the natural reaction to retaliate, a reaction based partly at least on an instinct for fair play. But it can safely be left to God eventually to get justice done, on the day of judgment (cf. 2: 5, 8). Dt. 32: 35 claims **vengeance** as God's right and so not man's. But there is one positive way in which the Christian may react. Scripture lays it down with vivid irony (Prov. 25: 21 f.). Tit-for-tat would only aggravate the situation and set up a vicious circle, but there is a real possibility that repaying the other party's hostility with unexpected kindness and 'treating him as someone in need' (Barth) will make him burn with pangs of guilt and remorse and realize the error of his ways; and so the breach will be healed and 'vengeance be transformed into the victory of love' (H. C. G. Moule).

ii. Church and state (13: 1–7)

As part of the 'living sacrifice' which the Christian is to offer (12: 1) Paul lays down what his general attitude should be towards the state. The apostle 'shares to a certain extent the thankful attitude of the provinces which recognized in the empire the guardian of peace, the principle of order versus chaos, the bulwark of order and justice' (J. Weiss). **1f.** The Christian view is conditioned by the relationship between God and the state. God is no merely 'religious' God: in His providential care are included the control of nations and the maintenance of civil order within them. The OT had taught Paul that it is God who sets up civil rulers and that their authority is delegated from Him (*e.g.* Jer. 27: 5 f.; Dan. 2: 21, 37 f.; 4: 17). God is as much the God of Nero as He was the power behind Cyrus (Isa. 45: 1 ff.). From this truth of divine sovereignty stems the individual Christian's obligation of civil obedience. Generally speaking, to subject oneself to the civil authorities is but an indirect way of obeying God Himself. At bottom the issue is in a sense not 'either God or state' nor 'both God and state' but 'God via the state'. This is a general and basic principle; it is not lightly to be laid aside, but it may be complicated by specific circumstances which create a conflict of loyalties, as Ac. 4: 19 f.; 5: 29; Rev. 13 acknowledge. Over every man hangs the sobering prospect that he will be answerable to God for his civil behaviour and will be punished by Him for civil misdemeanours. **3f.** A second reason for civil obedience (**for** is parallel with **for** in v. 1) is the general axiom that the state upholds moral standards (to a certain level at least). In that respect the Christian should instinctively view the government not as an enemy but as an ally and helper towards his own moral endeavours. In fact the civil power is God's **servant,** doing God's work positively and negatively by encouraging virtue and discouraging vice. With **for your good** cf. 8: 28 f.: this is one of the providential ways by which God accomplishes His purpose for the Christian. The civil ruler is empowered to inflict retribution upon **the wrongdoer,** as is shown by his right to use **the sword** for the maintenance of civil order. It is implied that the state has a God-given power, albeit capable of abuse, of life and death over its subjects. 'Through the state there takes place a partial, anticipatory, provisional manifestation of God's wrath against sin' (C. E. B. Cranfield). **5.** The motive for civil obedience comes **not only** from a desire to **avoid God's wrath,** either in its provisional (v. 4) or final (cf. v. 2) form, **but also** from the consciousness the Christian has of the subordination of the state to God. **6f.** Moreover it is this consciousness that justifies the Christian's paying taxes to the authorities: 'it is as God's servants (and therefore as those whose claim must not be rejected or evaded) that they busy themselves earnestly with this very thing, namely the matter of tribute' (Cranfield). There is no doubt a reference here to the saying of our Lord (Mk 12: 17). 'The Christian is under obligation to pay his dues to the state because, as a beneficiary of it, he owes it some payment in return for the protection and amenities it provides, and because no state can function without resources and therefore a fundamental refusal to pay taxes would be a fundamental "No" to the state as such' (Cranfield). **Taxes** are direct taxes, the 'tribute' of the Gospels, while **revenue** is an indirect tax on goods. It should be remembered that Paul is here laying down the political obligations of the Christian in an authoritarian state. His obligations in a democracy, where every citizen has a responsible, albeit small share in government, are not necessarily confined to the obligations enumerated in this passage.

iii. Motives for Christian behaviour (13: 8–14)

Paul adduces two motives for goodness. The first is love, and the second is the consummation of the new age. The two are implicitly linked. Love for Paul is the supreme blessing of the Spirit who is poured out in the last days in anticipation of the Messianic age in its fulness (cf. 5: 5 n.). **8–10.** The Christian's political, economic dues (v. 7: Gk. *opheilas*) lead on to his social dues (**owe** is Gk. *opheilete*). He has one such obligation—**love.** 'The debt of love is permanent, and we never get out of it; for we pay it daily and yet always owe it' (Origen). Paul echoes his Master's approval of Lev. 19: 18 as the summary of the law (Lk. 10: 26 ff.; cf. Mt. 22: 40) as far as human duties are concerned. Love aims at the very best for others. He who loves another will shrink from harming him in any way, and thus from breaking those of the ten commandments that refer to treatment of one's **neighbour.** It is love that keeps the law; and the law is the yardstick of love. This love is no feigned emotion but an active, continual attitude fostered by the Spirit, by which the love of God in Christ, having once been poured out in the Christian's heart, proceeds through his whole life and beyond him to every man he meets. **11–14.** The age to come begins with 'the day of the Lord' (1 Th. 5: 2); accordingly this age (cf. 12: 2 n.) may be regarded as the preceding **night.** Day and night are also natural picture-words for right and wrong. Paul alludes to the baptismal hymn he quotes in Eph. 5: 14 and urges Christians to rub the sleep out of their eyes, to live now in the light of the coming day, to be up and doing—good works (cf. Jn 3: 19 ff.; 1 Jn 1: 7; 2: 8 ff.). **Salvation** is the fulfilment of the promise implicit in initial salvation (8: 24 n.). The attitude of the early Church was to expect Christ's return in their lifetime; indeed, only thus can the Christian hope exert any moral stimulus (cf. Lk. 12: 3b). Light and darkness also carried associations of war in the contemporary Jewish world. One of the scrolls of the Dead Sea sect describes the war between 'the sons of light' and 'the sons of darkness'. Paul here makes use of this mixed imagery that was 'in the air', as he did also in 1 Th. 5: 8. **Night** is the time for **revelling,** etc. and is a cover for any shameful act; but now the night is over for the Christian who lives in the **day** of Christ's resurrection (cf. Eph. 5: 8: 'Lord' is a resurrection title) which sets a new pattern of moral propriety. The thought of putting on Christ is a baptismal one (cf. Gal. 3: 27). Indeed, these verses ring out as loudly as 6: 1 ff. with the call to live out the implications of baptism. The new convert who strips off his clothes before baptism and dresses himself again afterwards is enacting a symbolic demand upon himself to don new habits that express Christ: 'Put on the character of the Lord Jesus Christ' (Moffatt). The OT had prepared the way in likening a new status and a new kind of life to a new garment (Isa. 59: 17; 61: 10; Zech. 3: 4). Gal. 5: 16–24 is Paul's own commentary on the last two clauses.

iv. Corporate harmony and personal convictions (14: 1–15: 13)

Paul turns from general moral exhortation to advice in handling specific situations that arise from human diversity. Nowhere is his level-headed insight into problems of personal relationships displayed more than here. Every individual carries within him a set of convictions born of past experience and the influence of other personalities upon his own. He is apt to consider his opinions sacrosanct and rationalize principles out of them. A desire for self-justification may prompt him to regard with scorn those who do not conform to his views, and write them off as unreasonable and intolerable. Even a group of individuals with similar backgrounds and interests is liable to be broken up by this kind of reaction. The danger lurks constantly at the door of a church: there the basis of union is not similarity of interests nor

mutual attraction but an individual response to God's offer of salvation made to men of all types (1: 14). Petty differences can soon be blown up into major issues under these circumstances. To prevent such a situation developing the apostle here gives advice both to critics and criticized. He appears not to have in mind problems besetting the Roman churches, but to write from earlier experience of trouble in other fellowships, in order to warn the Romans of dangers that are likely to arise. First, when a Christian thinks another at fault in a practice not covered clearly by the moral traditions passed on to the Church by the apostles (1 Th. 4: 1 ff.) he must stifle his impulse to interfere, and be tolerant (14: 1–12). Secondly, when a Christian is considered by others to be thus at fault, his desire must be not to injure them; he should be prepared to make concessions rather than be the cause of trouble in the church (14: 13–15: 6). Thirdly, Paul adduces broader incentives to unity (15: 7–13).

1–12. An individual Christian is responsible to the Lord alone. In Corinth, where Paul was writing from, he had had to deal with the issue of eating meat, and it is to this very situation that he most probably refers here to illustrate his teaching. Read 1 C. 8–11 for the background of the problem and a fuller discussion. The problem arose from the fact that the slaughter of animals in the Hellenistic world was connected closely with religious ritualism, as it was in Judaism (cf. Lev. 17). The chances were that a joint bought in the market had been consecrated to pagan gods. Some Christians with tender consciences preferred to be vegetarians; others reasoned the matter out and concluded that there was nothing wrong in eating meat. Paul himself shared fully the conclusions of the latter group (cf. Col. 2: 20 ff.; Paul is there condemning not an individual's right to follow his conscience but an attempt to compel a company of Christians to conform—or else). But his heart went out to the others in sympathetic understanding. The mixture of Jews and Gentiles in a church provided another problem. It was one which the apostle had met in Galatia (Gal. 4: 10), but in the much more acute form of an attempt to secure a human claim upon salvation. The Christian Jew or proselyte had been in the habit of regarding certain days as holy, such as the weekly Sabbath and the annual Day of Atonement. It was ingrained in his conscience that not to observe them was wrong. On the other hand, an ex-pagan could make out a foolproof case to prove that such practices were no longer necessary (cf. Col. 2: 16 ff.).

In all such differences of opinion the natural

reaction is to seek to bring about uniformity—to one's own opinion! Paul condemns this attitude and lays down directions for the Christian who thinks another is in the wrong. In the scrupulous man, background and psychological make-up have combined to produce a reaction of emotional abhorrence to behaviour that other Christians find unobjectionable. Such a man is certainly **weak** and has not grasped the full implications of his **faith.** But any quick forceful attempt to 'educate' him would end in disaster, Paul wisely realized. Accordingly, he does not take the logical step of ordering conformity. Instead he counsels: let the other man be. The principle he adduces is the Christian's personal responsibility to his Lord and Master. He is God's, for it is God who **has welcomed** him into fellowship with Him; and so others are obliged to **welcome** him too, not give him the cold shoulder. He is Christ's **servant** (cf. v. 9) and responsible to Him. It is nothing less than usurping Christ's sovereign authority over a fellow-Christian for one to criticize him over a difference of opinion: for the less scrupulous to **despise** the more scrupulous, and for the more scrupulous to **pass judgment** on the less scrupulous. Christian fellowship does not imply a right to run other people's lives for them: only Christ can—and will—discharge such a right. The temptation to criticize some one else must be resisted. Instead one must re-examine one's own views, in case they are based upon selfish expediency and personal profit, and in an exercise of spiritual judgment come to as informed and responsible a conviction as one is psychologically capable of. Whichever conclusion one comes to, one must consecrate it and its outworking to the Lord, for the whole of life is to be devoted to Him as 'a living sacrifice' (12: 1). Whatever a Christian does is to be his personal act of worship to Christ and of thanksgiving to God. 'You are not your own' (1 C. 6: 19). The doctrine that the risen Christ is Lord and Judge of all (Ac. 17: 31) finds an application here. Christ confronts the Christian at every turn, in life and also in death; he is His for good and all. Accordingly, the Christian's duty is not to find fault with his neighbour's behaviour where a difference of opinion is concerned—such a judgment unconsciously has the effect of approving his own behaviour as praiseworthy—but to leave the verdict to God who will judge all men at His 'tribunal' (Moffatt) and receive all the **praise** Himself. Cf. 2 C. 5: 10 where the **judgment seat** is Christ's. In 2:16 God is said to judge through Christ or to delegate judgment to Him. Paul oscillates easily between God and Christ: there are several instances in this very passage. In the free quotation from the LXX of Isa. 45: 23 the apostle may well be interpreting **Lord** as referring to Christ (cf. Phil. 2: 10; compare **live** with **lived** in v. 9 and the contrast of **Lord** and **God** in v. 6).

14: 13-15: 6. Paul now changes sides, and advises not the critics, but the criticized. Before, he was addressing both the 'strong' and the 'weak', but now he singles out the non-scrupulous person with whom the scrupulous Christian finds fault. Two points are made: (a) the sanctity of conscience and (b) the responsibility not to impede another's Christian progress. The apostle's considered standpoint 'as a Christian' (NEB) is that of the non-scrupulous, in line with Christ's own teaching in Mk 7: 14 ff., but he can appreciate the problem the other side has and urges sympathy for them. If the scrupulous are wrong from an objective, absolute point of view, they are subjectively right—and that is more important than the 'strong' realize. The 'weak' have a conscience about whatever it is, and one's duty is always to obey one's conscience even if others regard it a superstitious qualm over a trifle. **Faith** in 22 f. is subjective: a strong 'conviction' (NEB) of what is right and God's will for oneself. One must respect one's own personal convictions; to act despite a troubled conscience amounts to sinning against God. 'If in doubt, don't' is not merely a safe principle to follow, but a vital principle in matters of conscience. C. H. Dodd helpfully compares the saying attributed to our Lord in one MS of Lk. 6: 4: 'On the same day, seeing some one working on the Sabbath, He said to him "Man, if you know what you are doing, blessed are you; but if you do not know, cursed are you and a breaker of the law".' The second point for the 'strong' to bear in mind when they feel inclined to resent and ignore the criticisms of the 'weak' is the consequences of their enlightened behaviour. Love takes precedence over knowledge. If the 'strong' do not care about the sensitivities of the 'weak' but openly fly in the face of them, what will the result be? Will the 'weak' be **injured,** ruined, for example by their being led to act against their consciences? Will they be put off and made to backslide as a result of the example of the 'strong', which to them is sin? If so, the overall loss is surely far, far greater than the net gain. It is not worth division and disharmony in the church. Paul urges: consider the long-term results of thoughtlessly pursuing what is good to you. On occasions (C. K. Barrett points out that **eat, drink** are aorist infinitives referring to particular occasions) a policy of vegetarianism, teetotalism and any other abstention one may personally think unnecessary is better than causing some one else in the fellowship a spiritual set-back. Such callousness is far from the spirit of Christ's dying love. 'Those who meet at the foot of the Cross find that they are spiritual blood brothers and must act as such' (A. M. Hunter). It is a question of priorities: the things of value in **the kingdom of God** are spiritual things, and the 'strong' are exalting **food and drink** above them if they eat and drink to the spiritual detriment of some of their fellow-Christians and so ultimately of the Christian community as a whole. Paul is most probably alluding once more (cf. 12: 14 n.) to the Sermon on the Mount (Mt. 6: 31 ff.) **15: 1f.** The Christian is no self-contained unit: his actions may well have repercussions on his **neighbour.** He must therefore be motivated by **his good** so that he may grow and progress. 'To please my neighbour is not weakly to comply with his desires but to act with a view to his lasting benefit' (W. E. Vine). The **weak** are psychologically incapable of making concessions, but the **strong** can and ought. **3.** 'Why should I?'—Paul anticipates the question by pointing to the example of Christ. He fulfilled Ps. 69: 9 in its deepest possible sense as the epitome of the righteous sufferer. The text is as it were His voice speaking to His Father. If making God's enemies His own enemies took Him to the Cross, should not the Christian put himself out a little for his spiritual kith and kin by helping them carry their burdens? **4.** Paul breaks off to urge his readers ever to be alert to the personal message of the OT, since it is expressly meant for them. Reading it will keep the Christian's hope undimmed and bright, and confirm the reality of the divine unseen. It is from the Scriptures that he will derive **encouragement** and remain true. **5.** A closing prayer for **harmony** in the church. The OT encourages and sustains because behind it is God, the source of these very qualities. May the self-denying example of Christ be followed so that, secondary matters not obtruding, a harmonious setting may be procured for the church's concerted worship of God.

15: 7–13. Paul puts his appeal for unity on a broader basis. Underlying much of the friction in the early churches must have been the presence of both Jews and Gentiles together. The Jewish Christian would have to fight hard against the temptation of religious snobbery. The Gentile Christians would tend to regard the Jew and his traditions as a hangover from the obsolete past (cf. 11: 18, 25 n.). Over against these natural reactions Paul again makes Christ's example the Christian criterion. To spurn a fellow-Christian is to be out of step with Christ,

who has **welcomed** him as well as oneself. The Gentile in the Church who looks down upon the Jew as a back-number must remember that Christ Himself submitted to becoming a Jew (Gal. 4: 4) and received the Jewish heritage of the Messianic promises (cf. 9: 4). The Jew in the church who despises his Gentile fellow-believer as an interloper and a second-rate Christian must remember that Christ came also for the very purpose of bringing Gentiles into the Church. In both these purposes God was showing His **truthfulness** in making His word come true. Lest doubts linger in the Jew's mind, Paul reminds him that the admission of the Gentiles is in line with his own traditions and was envisaged in the OT, the source-book of God's plans. Ps. 18: 49 is taken as the words of the pre-incarnate Christ to His Father (cf. Heb. 2: 11 ff.), promising that He will lead Gentiles' praises to God. The invitations of Dt. 32: 43 (LXX) and of Ps. 117: 1 and the Messianic promise of Isa. 11: 10 (LXX) all look forward to the Gentiles' participation in the worship of the Church (cf. v. 6) and in possessing the Christian hope as validly as Jewish Christians. Behind this **hope** is the one God who inspires it equally in Jew and Gentile. Paul's prayer is for right perspectives; he harks back to the vocabulary of 14: 17. May spiritual qualities be exalted in the Christian community in place of discord over material and human matters. If **hope, joy, peace,** a continual attitude of faith and **the power of the Holy Spirit** fill the vision of God's people and direct their judgment, then secondary matters will fall into their proper place and be viewed aright.

VI. PAUL'S MISSIONARY PLANS (15: 14–33)

14–16. Paul first tactfully apologizes for his letter (cf. 1: 12 n.) and then justifies it. He regrets if he has appeared to be taking liberties **on some points** (*e.g.* 6: 19; 11: 25; 14: 4). He is fully aware of the mature balance—the firm grasp of doctrinal truth and its warm-hearted outworking—to be found in the Roman churches. But he has written to refresh their memory. And he claims the right to instruct them by virtue of his apostleship (cf. 1: 6 f.; 12: 3). He is nothing less than Christ's agent to the Gentile world, and even God's priest to offer to Him a sacrifice consisting of Gentile converts won to the gospel and nurtured in the faith (cf. Phil. 2: 17). This is a specific application of the priesthood of all believers, whereby all Christian work is viewed as a sacrifice. **17–21.** Paul reviews his past missionary work and policy. The phrases he has used may be high-sounding, but they are fully justified by the results. He does not want to take any credit for other people's work, like some 'superlative apostles' he has come across (2 C. 10: 13 ff.; 11: 4 ff.). The past record of his own work is the testimonial of his apostolic commission. But it is not his personal achievement but Christ's work **through** him. His preaching and teaching, his travelling and feats of endurance (cf. 2 C. 11: 23 ff.), his miracles (cf. Ac. 14: 8 ff.; 2 C. 12: 12), his effectiveness brought about by the Holy Spirit—all these confirm his apostolic claims, should the Romans have any qualms or reservations about him. His area of missionary work has been vast: the eastern provinces of the Roman Empire from **Jerusalem** to the province of **Illyricum,** on the east coast of the Adriatic. The latter limit refers to his most recent journey recorded in Ac. 20: 2: behind Luke's vague description apparently lies work done further west than Macedonia. Paul had evangelized half the Roman world by his method of visiting the main centres and leaving converts to preach the gospel in the surrounding regions. There were areas he had not visited but this was because they were already covered by other pioneer missionaries. Isa. 52: 15 (LXX) represents a principle in the proclamation of the gospel of the Servant which governs Paul's policy (2 C. 10: 13 ff.): his task is to open up virgin territory.

22–32. The apostle outlines his future plans. Now he is free to visit Rome, an ambition he has had **for many years.** Ac. 19: 21 and 2 C. 10: 16 are evidence that he already had a western mission in mind two years or so before. It may well have been Priscilla and Aquila who had suggested it to him about seven years previously (Ac. 18: 2). His idea was to do pioneer work in Spain, as there were already Christians in Italy. But he would call at Rome on the way, and indeed sought their commendation and backing in the Spanish mission. Such is the force of **to be sped on my journey:** cf. the use of the verb in Ac. 15: 3; Tit. 3: 13; 3 Jn 6. Rome was to be his base of operations. He apparently hoped that the Roman churches would contribute to expenses, provide assistants and generally support his western campaign. This may partly explain why Paul so carefully defines his missionary preaching in this letter, as C. H. Dodd suggests. Before setting out for the west the apostle had an errand: he must first take to Jerusalem the proceeds of a collection for the poor in the church there. James, Peter and John had asked Paul to 'remember the poor' in this way in return for their recognizing his missionary work among the Gentiles (Gal. 2: 10). Since then Paul's relations with the churches of Judaea had deteriorated, but nevertheless he had encouraged the churches of Greece, which was divided into the two Roman provinces of **Macedonia** and **Achaia,** to contribute to a relief fund. Actually the churches of Asia and Galatia also contributed, as Ac. 20: 4; 1 C. 16: 1 make clear. They had willingly complied with his fervent appeals (1 C. 16: 1 ff.; 2 C. 8: 9). Indeed, it was only fair that they should repay with **material** aid those who had given them **spiritual blessings.** When the business of the fund had been signed and settled (so perhaps 'sealed' means), Paul was intending to visit Rome on his way to Spain. He is sure that he will bring to Rome a special **blessing** from Christ (cf. 1: 11). But Paul cannot get his coming visit to Jerusalem off his mind, and he must return to it. The strong terms in which he craves the Romans' prayers show how worried he is about it. **The love of the Spirit** is 'the love which the Spirit inspires' (Moffatt, cf. Weymouth). This uncovering of Paul's inner thoughts casts much light upon the narrative of Ac. 20 f. Even before the journey he is very conscious that he is walking into a den of lions. Stephen's fate was printed indelibly on Paul's mind. He knew, no doubt, that distressed synagogue officials had reported the harm the cause of Judaism had suffered at Paul's hands (Ac. 21: 28). Now Paul was to visit the headquarters and the Jews would have a unique chance to get their hands on him. But he had another worry: would the Jerusalem church accept his gesture of unity and fellowship? In their eyes Paul had let down the Christian cause badly by unscriptural policies (Ac. 21: 20 ff.). Could they have fellowship with such a brother? Was not the money he brought a bribe to get them to condone his misdemeanours? Poor as they were, ought they not to stand firm for the truth and avoid the temptation? Such might be their reactions. In fact they accepted the money, but demanded proof of Paul's orthodoxy. James in embarrassment had to give way to the pressure of 'myriads' (so literally Ac. 21: 20) and make Paul submit to a test of soundness. Amid all these thoughts of danger and disunity Paul turns to the God of peace and as he commits his readers to Him no doubt he also casts himself upon Him in a silent prayer.

VII. CLOSING MESSAGES (16: 1–27)

1–2. Paul introduces a lady who was presumably the bearer of the letter, and commends her to the Romans' Christian care. **Phoebe** belonged to the church at the port of Corinth, **Cenchreae.** It is uncertain whether Gk. *diakonos* is an official term, **deaconess,** or a more general one, 'servant'. Too little is known of the constitution of the early churches for a final decision (cf. Phil. 1: 1 n.; 1 Tim. 3: 11 n.).

3–16. The apostle sends his affectionate greetings to those he knows in Rome. Most of them are not mentioned elsewhere in the NT, but behind the mention of the names obviously lies a wealth of personality, service and warm fellowship. **3. Prisca** (a more formal variant of Priscilla) **and Aquila** were partners not only in marriage but also in the leather business (see Ac. 18: 3 n.). After Claudius's edict had expelled the Jews from Rome in A.D. 49, they had come to Corinth (Ac. 18: 2). From there they had moved to Ephesus (Ac. 18: 18 ff.) and in fact toured extensively combining business with Christian service (cf. **all the churches**). Now, the edict apparently having become a dead-letter, they had returned to the imperial capital. **4.** No details are known of this occasion: it may have been that of Ac. 19: 23 ff. **5.** They opened their **house** for Christian meetings. The **church** here mentioned was obviously only a part of the total number of Christians in Rome. Vv. 14 f. seem to refer to two other household churches in Rome. Apparently there were at least three churches there, and probably more. **7. Andronicus** and **Junias** (or perhaps **Junia**, a lady, as in AV) must have belonged to the same group of Hellenistic Jews in the Jerusalem church as Stephen (Ac. 6: 1 ff.). They had done distinguished work as commissioned missionaries: **apostles** is used in a wider sense than the Twelve, as in Ac. 14: 4, 14; 1 C. 15: 5 ff. **8. Ampliatus** was a common Roman slave name. In the Catacombs there is a tomb ornately inscribed with this name in the cemetery of Domitilla, the cousin of Domitian, a later emperor. If it refers to the person here mentioned, it probably reflects the high esteem in which he was held by his fellow-Christians. **10, 11.** For **family** read 'household' with AV, RV: the reference is to a staff of slaves or ex-slaves. **Narcissus** may well be the famous freedman who was a counsellor of the Emperor Claudius and played a large part in the political intrigues of his day. He had committed suicide shortly before this letter was written, and his household of slaves would pass to the emperor, probably with the distinguishing name of *Narcissiani*. Lightfoot suggested that these *Narcissiani* were among the 'saints of Caesar's household' in Phil. 4: 22. **12. Tryphaena and Tryphosa** are generally supposed to have been sisters. Is there subtle wit here? Both names are connected with the Gk. word *tryphaō* 'live luxuriously, live a life of ease'. Paul is perhaps playing on the derivation: these certainly did not live up to their names! **13. Rufus** was very likely a son of Simon of Cyrene who carried the cross (Mk 15: 21), especially if Mark's Gospel was written from Rome as tradition

strongly suggests. Was it at the difficult time of Ac. 9: 28 that Paul was made welcome at Rufus' home and looked after by **his mother,** before the family moved to Rome? **16.** Paul may have been authorized to pass on the greetings of **all the churches** by their representatives, if they were now at Corinth waiting to set off to Jerusalem with the fund (cf. Ac. 20: 4). The **holy kiss** was apparently a feature of Christian communal fellowship; in this case it would be given partly in Paul's name.

17–20. Paul rather jerkily inserts into his greetings a warning against disturbers of the peace (cf. Gal. 6: 11–16; 1 C. 16: 22). Are they antinomians or Judaizers? The terms Paul uses suit either, but more probably he had Judaizers in his mind. He was very likely still brooding over his forthcoming visit to the Jerusalem church and his mind passed on to the havoc that their ilk had already caused in his circles. He complains not of Hellenistic Jews found in churches in company with Gentiles, but of outsiders from Judaea who had followed him around to Antioch (Ac. 15: 1), Galatia and Corinth (2 C. 11) in an attempt to counteract his 'looseness' (cf. Gal. 2: 4). They might well turn up in Rome. Phil. 1: 17 probably means that they were there a few years later. **18.** 'Their own belly' (margin) may refer either to their obsession with clean and unclean food or to their working for their own ends (**appetites**). They presented an attractive, plausible case which might well convince the unwary. **19.** Paul urges the Romans to live up to their reputation of **obedience** by developing their moral judgment so as to be able to cope with this new attack. He appears to be deliberately quoting our Lord's own warning (Mt. 10: 16). **20.** If they are diligent in this way, the trouble will soon be settled. The Judaizers are working for Satan (2 C. 11: 15). But God Himself will work through the Romans' efforts and quickly restore the **peace** which characterizes Him and which He imparts to His own. There appears to be an allusion to Gen. 3: 15.

21–23. After the closing verses at the end of v. 20 the remaining verses are a postscript. **21.** Was **Jason** Paul's host in Thessalonica (Ac. 17: 5 ff.)? **Sosipater** looks like a longer form of Sopater, the Berean who was about to travel to Jerusalem with Paul (Ac. 20: 4). **22.** Paul must courteously have said to his amanuensis: 'Add your own greetings, Tertius.' **23. Gaius** is presumably the Gaius of 1 C. 1: 14, whom Paul had baptized. Paul was staying with him, and indeed his door was ever open to any Christian traveller. **Erastus** had an influential post as an important municipal official. His name has been found on a pavement which he donated to

Corinth. V. 24 is rightly omitted as not original.

25–27. Paul closes with a long doxology, summing up the main thoughts of the letter. God had long kept to Himself His plan of salvation, but now He had acted at last, and disclosed it in the work of **Jesus Christ.** Paul had been commissioned with this **gospel** by God Himself and instructed to make the divine plan known throughout the world, commanding men to trust and obey (cf. 1: 5 n.) the one and only God. Supporting him in this work were the OT Scriptures (cf. 3: 21), now unlocked by the key of Jesus Christ and seen to be the manifesto of the **wise** God's plan. For the Church the present is the point upon which all eternity impinges. The planning of *eternal* ages past (**long**: Gk. *aiōniois*) has burst out into time, the present time. The **eternal** God (Gk. *aiōnion*) reveals Himself to men through the living Christ. It is the Church's privilege to share in God's *eternal* praise (Gk. *eis tous aiōnas tōn aiōnōn:* 'for ages and ages').

[Note: This doxology appears in the Byzantine text after ch. 14 and in papyrus 46 after ch. 15; this probably points to the early circulation of shorter editions of the Letter. On this subject, as also on the question whether the greetings of ch. 16 belonged to a copy intended for the church of Ephesus (which has been inferred from verses 3–5 in particular), see F. F. Bruce, *The Epistle of Paul to the Romans*, pp. 25 ff., 266 ff.]

BIBLIOGRAPHY

Commentaries:

BARRETT, C. K., *The Epistle to the Romans*. BNTC (London, 1957).

BARTH, K., *The Epistle to the Romans*, E.T. (Oxford, 1933).

BRUCE, F. F., *The Epistle of Paul to the Romans*. TNTC (London, 1963).

DODD, C. H., *The Epistle of Paul to the Romans*. MNT (London, 1932).

GODET, F., *The Epistle to the Romans* (Edinburgh, 1880).

HODGE, C., *The Epistle to the Romans* (Edinburgh, 1835).

HUNTER, A. M., *The Epistle to the Romans*. TC (London, 1955).

LEENHARDT, F. J., *The Epistle to the Romans* (London, 1961).

MOULE, H. C. G., *The Epistle to the Romans*. EB (London, 1893).

MURRAY, J., *The Epistle to the Romans*, NIC (Grand Rapids, 1959–65).

NYGREN, A., *A Commentary on Romans*, E.T. (London, 1952).

SANDAY, W. and HEADLAM, A. C., *Romans*. ICC [on the Greek Text] (Edinburgh, 1902).

Books on Paul important for Romans:

HUNTER, A. M., *Interpreting Paul's Gospel* (London, 1954).

SCOTT, C. A. A., *Christianity according to St. Paul* (Cambridge, 1927).

STEWART, J. S., *A Man in Christ* (London, 1935).

THE FIRST LETTER TO THE CORINTHIANS

PAUL W. MARSH

Corinth

Situated in southern Greece on an isthmus dividing the Corinthian Gulf from the Saronic Gulf, Corinth became a natural centre for trade and a convenient halting-place for travellers moving east and west.

Although destroyed by the Romans in 146 B.C., it was reformed as a Roman colony under Julius Caesar a century later. The new city was at first peopled by Caesar's veterans and freedmen, but gradually Greeks returned, hellenizing the Italians and giving their language to the colony. However, its geographical position on the trade routes of the Middle East transformed it into the most cosmopolitan of cities, influenced by the life and habits of all the nations of the Mediterranean seaboard. From 27 B.C. onwards it was the seat of administration of the Roman province of Achaia.

Corinth was depraved. Going beyond the licentiousness of other trading cities and ports it lent its own name as the symbol of debauchery and corruption. As Robertson and Plummer state, 'The name of Corinth had been a byword for the grossest profligacy, especially in connection with the worship of Aphrodite Pandemos (1 *Corinthians*, *ICC*, p. xii). This monstrosity—sexual perversion in the name of religion—overshadowed the life of the city as a mushroom cloud of moral destruction.

Paul and Corinth

It was not, however, the great evil of this city which probably urged Paul to work there, but rather the strategic position it occupied. Its trading community ensured that anything preached in Corinth would soon reach far beyond the province of Achaia.

Paul first came to Corinth during his second missionary journey (Ac. 18: 1-18), and remained for eighteen months. Initially alone, he was subsequently joined by Silas and Timothy. Discouragement experienced during his earlier activities in Greece expressed itself in his 'much fear and trembling', as he walked the streets of Corinth and argued in the synagogue (1 C. 2: 3). Threatened and reviled by the Jewish community, Paul received God's personal promise

in a much needed vision of preservation from the mob and of fruitful service (Ac. 18: 10). The Jews, further inflamed by the conversion of Crispus and his household, launched a united attack on Paul before Gallio, the proconsul of Achaia. This hostility may well have continued unabated, for it would seem from the subject matter of the Corinthian letters that by far the majority of the converts came from the pagan community of that city.

After eighteen months Paul moved from Corinth together with Priscilla and Aquila. Leaving them in Ephesus he continued his travels in Syria. At the same time, Apollos, contacted in Ephesus by Priscilla and Aquila and brought to a full knowledge of Christ, went on to Corinth to consolidate and extend the activities of the church.

Paul's Letters and Subsequent Visits to Corinth

From the Acts and Paul's letters to Corinth we understand that three visits were paid and four letters written.

The first visit resulted in the founding of the church and is recorded in Ac. 18, to which Paul refers in 1 C. 2: 1-5.

Then came the first letter, which Paul mentions in 1 C. 5: 9. He had written telling the believers 'not to associate with immoral men', meaning not the 'immoral of this world', but the immoral who bore 'the name of brother'. Because they had misconstrued his meaning, Paul explains the issues involved more fully when writing for the second time, i.e. in 1 Corinthians as it appears in our NT.

Nothing more is known of this 'first letter'. Some scholars suggest that part of it might be identified with 2 C. 6: 14-7: 1. This seems improbable but is widely accepted. For a fuller discussion of the subject, consult D. Guthrie, *NT Introduction: The Pauline Epistles*. We assume therefore that this first letter has not survived. As Dr. Leon Morris states, 'This need cause no surprise. Paul's reference to it in 1 C. 5: 9 shows that it had been misunderstood. He mentioned it only to clear up a misconception as to what it meant. Thus the newer

373

letter superseded the older, and accordingly there was no point in preserving it' (1 *Corinthians*, *TNTC*, p. 21).

Now to the second letter, 1 Corinthians. The situation in Corinth had deteriorated. Dissensions and factions developed. The rhetoric of Apollos, coupled possibly with an allegorical method of preaching, contrasted sharply with the lack of eloquence and studied simplicity of Paul. Comparisons made by the congregation hardened into cliques.

Paul, now living in Ephesus, undoubtedly received frequent reports, for except during the winter months regular contact between the two cities was maintained. Knowledge of one such report has been preserved, that of 'Chloe's people' (1 C. 1: 11). So disturbing was this news that Paul despatched Timothy (1 C. 4: 17) and wrote immediately, dealing at the same time with a letter received from the Corinthian converts themselves concerning problems about which they required guidance (1 C. 7: 1).

For the purpose of this introduction it is assumed that Paul's second visit to Corinth now took place. This is the 'painful visit' referred to in 2 C. 2: 1. For a full discussion of this visit the reader should consult Robertson and Plummer's Commentary on 1 *Corinthians* (*ICC*). It is sufficient to record here that Paul's words, 'For the second time I am ready to come to you' (2 C. 12: 14), 'This is the second time I am coming to you' (2 C. 13: 1), and 'As I did when present on my second visit' (2 C. 13: 2), indicate very clearly a second visit before the writing of 2 Corinthians. (See pp. 416, 420.)

It is therefore suggested that Paul's second letter (1 Corinthians) failed in its attempt to correct and conciliate the warring factions, but that the situation deteriorated still further. A personal visit from Ephesus, painful in the extreme, therefore became necessary. This second visit is nowhere recorded in the Acts, possibly because of its brevity—a brief absence from Ephesus during Paul's three years' ministry —and its painful character.

Returning to Ephesus Paul wrote again. References to the third letter in 2 C. 2: 4 and 7: 8 indicate its extremely serious and censuring tone, so much so that Paul temporarily regretted its despatch. Had this letter failed in its purpose the situation might have deteriorated far beyond Paul's power to retrieve it. As it is, 2 C. 7: 9 records the measure of his joy at their repentance —'I rejoice, not because you were grieved, but because you were grieved into repenting'.

Did this third letter, like the first, fail to survive? While further discussion of this problem belongs properly to the introduction to 2 Corinthians, it may be observed for the sake of completeness, that not a few scholars, and notably Strachan, argue strongly that the 'severe letter' is preserved in part in 2 C. 10-13. The change in tone from commendation (chapters 1-9), to censure (10-13) is explained by this hypothesis. Upholders of the unity of 2 Corinthians explain this abrupt change by suggesting that in 1-9 Paul is addressing the reconciled majority, while in 10-13 he returns to the recalcitrant minority (see pp. 416 f., 433 f.).

Worried as to the effect of the 'severe letter', Paul proceeded to Troas hoping to find Titus who had presumably taken it to Corinth. Great was his relief and joy on finally locating his colleague in Macedonia, to find that his fears were groundless and that the church was restored (2 C. 2: 12 ff.; 7: 6 ff.).

To express his thankfulness to God Paul's fourth letter (2 Corinthians) was written, to be followed shortly afterwards by his third visit.

Paul's three visits and four letters may therefore be set out as follows in their chronological order:

1. The church founded; first visit.
2. The first letter (referred to in 1 C. 5: 9).
3. The second letter: 1 Corinthians.
4. The painful visit.
5. The third letter: severe in tone (2 C. 2: 4; 7: 8).
6. The fourth letter: 2 Corinthians.
7. The third visit.

Authenticity

Robertson and Plummer remark 'that those who attempt to show that the Apostle was not the writer succeed chiefly in proving their own incompetence as critics' (1 *Corinthians*, *ICC*, p. xvi). Internal and external evidence for the Pauline authorship is exceedingly strong.

It is the first letter in the NT to be referred to in early Christian literature. Clement of Rome writing to Corinth about A.D. 95 quoted it by name and called it the 'letter of the blessed Paul, the Apostle'. The writings of Ignatius echo the epistle as do those of Polycarp. No NT book is more quoted by the early church Fathers; among them, Justin Martyr, Irenaeus and Tertullian. It heads the list of Paul's letters in the Muratorian Fragment and is included in Marcion's Canon.

Internally, the character, style and language of the letter are all consistent with what we know of the apostle and his writings, while historically it conforms with the demands of the Acts narrative.

Occasion of Writing

Two factors prompted Paul to write 1 Corinthians: (i) reports of dissensions received from Chloe's people and (ii) a letter received from the believers in Corinth seeking guidance on a variety of questions. While seeking in this letter to restore the unity these factions threatened to destroy and to answer the problems which concerned them, Paul took the opportunity of introducing detailed teaching on the resurrection.

Date

While it is impossible to date the letter with certainty, it was clearly written from Ephesus (1 C. 16: 8) on Paul's third missionary journey, probably around A.D. 55.

1 C. 16: 8 indicates that Paul planned to remain in Ephesus until Pentecost and then leave. This could not refer to his very brief visit to Ephesus immediately after leaving Corinth for the first time (Ac. 18: 19). Allowing time for the ministry of Apollos, the writing of the first letter (1 C. 5: 9), and the development of party rivalries, we find Paul back in Ephesus

toward the end of his three years' ministry there.

Ac. 18: 12 reveals that Gallio, the proconsul of Achaia, was in Corinth during Paul's stay. An inscription found at Delphi, recording certain privileges granted to the city by the Emperor Claudius, mentions the name of Gallio and is also dated. From this we therefore learn that Gallio was proconsul of Achaia in early A.D. 52. From the Acts narrative it is reasonable to deduce that Paul left Corinth during that year. Ac. 18: 18 indicates that while he did not leave immediately, no great time elapsed before his departure. The NEB rendering of this verse is good; 'Paul stayed on for some time, and then took leave . . .' Allowing for the completion of the second missionary journey and of most of Paul's three years in Ephesus, we are brought to the mid-fifties before 1 Corinthians could be written.

ANALYSIS

I. INTRODUCTION (1: 1-9)

i. Salutation (1: 1-3)

Paul's salutation follows the pattern of most first-century Greek letters, having three parts; the writer's name (1), the addressee (2), and a greeting (3).

1. called . . . an apostle: Two facts concerning himself. The situation in Corinth demands the full use of his God-given office and authority. **Sosthenes** is unknown unless he be identified with the Corinthian Jew of Ac. 18: 17, although this would pre-suppose his conversion and removal from Corinth to Ephesus. **2. the church of God:** One church in spite of its divisions; God's church, not Apollos's, or Cephas's, or Paul's. **sanctified . . . saints:** Two words derived from the same root, emphasizing the high moral standard which is to characterize God's church. They are set apart (*hēgiasmenois;* a perf. part. implying a fixed state) in spite of their blatant imperfections. **call on the name:** A phrase by which Christians were identified in the early church; cf. Ac. 9: 14, 21; 22: 16; Rom. 10: 12. **3. grace . . . peace:** A characteristically Pauline greeting, bringing together both Greek and Hebrew salutations.

ii. Thanksgiving (1: 4-9)

Dissensions there may be, not to mention gross immorality and a host of other evils flowing from the carnality that had captured the church; yet Paul gives thanks! Assailed by Satan as they are, their spiritual life is evident. They are Christ's, and in a missionary situation surrounded by pagan depravity, this is abundant cause for praise.

4. The **grace of God . . . was given,** they **were enriched in him** (5), Christ's testimony **was confirmed among** them (6). The three verbs are aorists, a tense demonstrating the historical finality of their position. **grace . . . given:** God's loving favour, which frequently expresses His empowering for life and service. For its use with this verb see 3: 10; Rom. 12: 3, 6; 2 C. 6: 1; Eph. 4: 7. **5. enriched:** Cf. 2 C. 6: 10; 9: 11 and the cognate verb in 1 C. 4: 8. **all**

speech and **all knowledge:** The high-lights of their spiritual enrichment, stressing their grasp of truth and their ability to express it; qualities particularly prized by Corinthians and indeed by Greeks in general. Paul deals with the carnal abuse of these very qualities in the first three chapters of this letter. **6. confirmed:** To establish durably, make real with the deepest conviction; a technical term in Greek commercial law, meaning to warrant, guarantee a title to. Their gifts were adequate evidence of Christ's work in them. See NEB; cf. Rom. 15: 8; Heb. 2: 3, 4. **7, 8. spiritual gift** (*charisma*): The church was deficient in none; evidence that gifts can co-exist with the grossest evil. The matter is dealt with fully in 12: 1-14: 40. **as you wait:** The expectation of the coming of Christ is constantly with the apostle; it is the one hope which characterizes every local church in a persecuting pagan society; cf. 16: 22; 1 Th. 1: 10. **the revealing** (cf. Rom. 8: 19; 1 Pet. 1: 7, 13; 1 Jn 3: 2) and **the day** are synonymous for that one great cataclysmic event, **the end,** the second coming of Jesus Christ, until which He Himself will **sustain** them. **guiltless:** Unimpeachable—although not sinless, no charge can be preferred against them (cf. Rom. 8: 33; Col. 1: 22, 28). **9. God is faithful:** What He has begun He will complete (Phil. 1: 6), for He has **called** them just as He called Paul (1: 1), and that **into the fellowship of his Son,** the very antithesis of division. The nine verses of this introduction record nine occurrences of the name of the Lord Jesus Christ. In all Paul's thinking, He is of cardinal importance and whether it be the problem of division, moral failure, or doctrinal error, Christ is the answer and Paul has cause to give thanks.

II. DIVISIONS IN THE CHURCH (1: 10-4: 21)

i. The fact of division (1: 10-17)

In flagrant disregard for the fellowship of Christ into which they had been called (10), dissensions abound. The facts are painfully obvious, for through Chloe's people the petty, yet bitter quarrelling has been reported (11). Personalities, methods of preaching and, probably, aspects of doctrinal emphasis become rallying points for division. That this is not the will of Paul, or Christ, the apostle makes abundantly clear (13-17).

10. I appeal . . . brethren: No matter how deep the divisions, he insists on the unity of the family of God; his **brethren.** Note the frequent use of this word. The instrument of appeal is **the name of the Lord Jesus Christ,** one who cannot be divided; cf. v. 13. **that you all agree:** Literally, speak the same thing; an expression taken from Greek political life which might be paraphrased, 'Drop party cries'. **dissensions** (*schismata*—cliques, not schisms) can result only in **quarrelling** (11), an expression of the works of the flesh, and evidence of the carnality of the Corinthian church, cf. *eris* in Gal. 5: 20, 'strife'; also Rom. 1: 29-31; 2 C. 12: 20; 1 Tim. 6: 4. **Quarrelling** is never right and is nowhere condoned or excused. **12. I belong to Paul:** A loyal clinging to their father in Christ, which overlooked his limitations of speech and appearance. **to Apollos:** Drawn by the rhetoric and possibly, the more allegorical approach of Paul's successor. **to Cephas:** The man who walked with Christ, the leader of the Twelve; an appeal to the traditionalist. **to Christ:** Possibly the ultra-libertarians, who stressed their complete liberty in Christ, formed the Christ party and either coined for themselves the watchword 'All things are lawful', or else perverted Paul's use of it to excuse their own excesses (see 6: 12 ff.; traces of the same attitude are found in chapter 8). All are wrong, and each alike receives Paul's condemnation. **13. Is Christ divided:** Or, 'Is Christ parcelled out among you?': the property of one small section of the church. Westcott and Hort, with Lightfoot, make the phrase affirmative, but this breaks up the homogeneity of the three-fold interrogative. Paul reduces the situation to basic principles; other leaders cannot take the place of Christ. **Was Paul crucified . . . :** The thought is ludicrous. His persistent teaching must demonstrate irrefutably the fallacy of factions; cf. 1: 23; 2: 2. **baptized in the name of Paul:** The Son, with Father and Holy Spirit, was the **name** designated by Christ, according to Mt. 28: 19. That the trinitarian formula was used at this stage by Paul or his associates is not clear. The Acts record rather suggests that the name of Christ alone was used. However, Paul's point is clear; none could accuse him of making personal proselytes. **14-16. I baptized none . . . except:** Almost certainly to avoid making personal disciples (15). Those whom he did baptize were the very first converts. For **Stephanas,** see 16: 15; **Crispus,** Ac. 18: 8; and

Gaius, possibly Rom. 16: 23 (perhaps also to be identified with the Titius Justus of Ac. 18: 7). The administration of ordinances then passed into the hands of local leaders; a most important missionary principle. **17. not . . . to baptize but . . . :** The apostle is not speaking in absolute terms, but is underlining the priority of his calling, **to preach the gospel. eloquent wisdom:** Such wisdom, *sophia logou*—cultivating expression at the expense of matter (17) —is the gift of the mere rhetorician, courting the applause of the ordinary Greek audience' (Robertson and Plummer). Paul determined that such 'language of worldly wisdom' (NEB) should not empty the **cross of Christ of its power.** For other uses of *kenoō* (**emptied,** vain, fruitless) see 9: 15; Rom. 4: 14; 2 C. 9: 3; Gal. 2: 2; Phil. 2: 7, 16.

ii. False wisdom and the gospel (1: 18-2: 5)
(a) The message of the cross (1: 18-25)
Worldly wisdom, that expression of carnality among the Corinthian believers, is the very antithesis of the wisdom of God revealed in the cross of Christ. This section abounds in contrasts as Paul demonstrates the total alienation of thought between that worldly wisdom so prized by the Corinthians and the wisdom of God. The gospel, the word of the cross, is folly to the wise man of this age, but God will reveal their falsity, showing His foolishness as superior to their wisdom! **18.** Men react differently to the one message—**the word of the cross**—according to their condition. To **those who are perishing,** in the process of, or on the way to perish (*apollymenois* is a pres. part.), it is 'sheer folly' (NEB); whereas to those 'on the way to salvation' (NEB) it is **the power of God.** Again the pres. part. is used, implying not uncertainty but the final issue. It is not just the wisdom of God, but **power,** God's wisdom in action.

19. Paul maintains and elaborates this contrast. The worldly man with his wisdom will be destroyed in all his scepticism of God's ways. **it is written:** A very free rendering of the LXX translation of Isa. 29: 14, where 'the prophet, referring to the failure of worldly statesmanship in Judah in the face of the judgment of the Assyrian invasion, states a principle that the wisdom of man is no match for the power of God. Paul seizes the principle and applies it' (Robertson and Plummer).

20. Where . . . where . . . where: The challenge to produce the **wise man, scribe,** or **debater** who can stand before God reflects the scene of Isa. 33: 18 when all sign of the apparently invincible Assyrian conqueror has been swept away by the power of Jehovah. The exact designation of **wise, scribe, debater** (perhaps Gentile, Jew, Greek) is not clear. Most probably,

N*

Paul is making no specific reference to Jew or Greek, but his terms refer to all those champions of worldly wisdom, whom God is determined not merely to outclass, but to prove utterly foolish. **21. it pleased God:** Indicating the sovereignty of His choice, to save men through faith in the message of the cross and through no other means. **those who believe:** A pres. part. indicating habitual faith. See v. 18 for the same usage. **22, 23. Jews . . . signs . . . Greeks . . . wisdom:** The national characteristics of Jews and Greeks only increase their difficulties in accepting what is preached—**Christ crucified.** Jewish demands of Christ for a **sign** indicated the pattern of their thought; cf. Mt. 12: 38; 16: 1, 4; Mk 8: 11 ff.; Jn 6: 30. The sign of Jonah proved the greatest stumbling block of all. Greek speculation could not accept a doctrine of salvation based on the **folly** of the crucified Nazarene. The acceptance of **Christ crucified,** 'Christ nailed to a cross' (NEB), called for the abandonment of all their cherished concepts. As in 2: 2 (see note) the perfect tense indicates that the Christ cannot be separated from the cross. **24. Christ the power of God:** As demonstrated in the miracles of incarnation, death and resurrection; cf. Rom. 1: 4. **the wisdom of God:** True wisdom, for it brings salvation, the point at which Greek thinking failed. Christ Himself is the personification of wisdom (30). **called:** Having an effectual calling, as in Rom. 8: 30; 9: 11, 24, etc. **25. foolishness of God:** The cross in all its **weakness** and **foolishness** when measured by human standards is presented by God as His power and wisdom, both infinitely greater in saving capacity than all man's mightiest efforts can produce.

(b) **The messengers of the cross (1: 26–31)**
Further, not only is the message of the cross folly (18–25), but to present that message, God takes men commonly considered to be foolish, weak and of no consequence and through them vindicates the superiority of His own wisdom as seen in the gospel of Jesus Christ (26–31). **26. For consider . . . :** The circumstances of the Corinthian church illustrate Paul's point. **your call:** A reference to their conversion, not vocation, which came to them for the most part as people not **wise, powerful,** or **noble** by worldly standards. **not many:** Some were in fact gifted, influential and cultured. Crispus was ruler of the synagogue (Ac. 18: 8) and Erastus, the city treasurer (Rom. 16: 23). **27. God chose:** Poor and weak, but objects of God's sovereign choice through whom He has purposed to shame the **wise** and **strong.** Repeated three times, this verb points ahead with unerring certainty to the accomplishment of His purpose, not only **to bring to nothing the things that**

are (the wise, etc.), so excluding all human boasting, but to His complete and absolute exaltation in Christ as the fount of all true wisdom and salvation (30, 31). To this end, as media of the revelation of His power and wisdom, He uses **what is low and despised . . . even things that are not**—the nonentities of this life—'mere nothings' (NEB). **to bring to nothing** (*katargeō*): To reduce to ineffectiveness, render inoperative. The verb has considerable breadth of meaning (cf. 2: 6; 6: 13; 13: 8, 10, 11; 15: 24, 26). **30, 31. He is the source . . . :** From the meanness of man Paul turns to the greatness of the Godhead. 'You are in Christ Jesus by God's act' (NEB). Christ is revealed as the embodiment of God's **wisdom . . . righteousness and sanctification and redemption.** While AV, RV, and RSV translate these last three qualities as co-ordinates, it is possible, with RVmg, to regard them as definitive of wisdom. In either case, Christ is all of these, which eliminates the possibility of all human boasting—except **in the Lord.** The quotation is from Jer. 9: 23, an example of a passage which in the OT refers to Jehovah, being applied to Christ; cf. 2: 16.

(c) **The preaching of the cross (2: 1–5)**
So convinced was Paul of the superiority of the word of the cross over the wisdom of the world and of God's purpose to use human nonentities for the revelation of His wisdom in Christ, that he resolved when preaching in Corinth to do so with all the simplicity and weakness of ungarnished, trembling speech, that the dynamic of the cross of Christ alone might be experienced. This was to achieve the one objective, that their faith should rest not in the wisdom of men, but in the power of God.

1. the testimony (*martyrion*) **of God:** As a mere witness himself Paul had no need of lofty speech. He was concerned with relating facts. **2. Christ crucified:** A perf. part., signifying the enduring efficacy and effects of the death of Christ; cf. 1: 23.

3. in weakness: 'weak . . . nervous and shaking with fear' (NEB); a reference perhaps to his unimpressive bodily presence (cf. 2 C. 10: 10); his initial loneliness and discouragement after his experience in Athens (cf. Ac. 17); anxiety for the Thessalonian Christians; the overwhelming wickedness of Corinth; and possibly, sickness (cf. Gal. 4: 13). **4. in demonstration of the Spirit:** As opposed to the plausible, persuasive words of wisdom, which Paul so strictly avoids. **demonstration** (*apodeixis*): Found only here in NT; it indicates stringent proof leading to absolute certainty. The power of **the Spirit,** not worldly wisdom, demonstrated Paul's message to be true, and on this their faith could rest (5).

iii. True wisdom and the Spirit (2: 6-16)
(a) The impartation of wisdom (2: 6-13)
In showing the total inadequacy of the wisdom of the world and the complete sufficiency of God's wisdom in accomplishing man's salvation, Paul has aimed blow after blow at the cause of dissension in Corinth. Worldly wisdom will devastate a church.

Yet the church is not without wisdom. To those who are called, Christ the wisdom of God (1: 24) is made our wisdom (1: 30) and is increasingly comprehended as maturity develops. This true wisdom, hidden in past ages and unrecognized by men of worldly power and intellect, has now been revealed through the Spirit. Just as a man alone knows his own thoughts, so the Spirit comes from the being of God himself to give understanding of His mind to those who have received Him. This is the wisdom Paul himself imparts as taught by the Spirit of God.

6. among the mature (*teleioi*): Does not here mean 'perfect'. While the word was common in the mystery religions, this in no way coloured Paul's usage. As a pioneer, in common with modern missionaries, he took the language of his day and invested it with Christian content. Note the terminology which Paul consistently employs: *teleioi* are the mature Christians; cf. 14: 20; Phil. 3: 15; Eph. 4: 13. In the same class are the *pneumatikoi*—'the spiritual' (used synonymously in 2: 13-3: 1). In contrast to these are the *nēpioi*, 'the babes' (cf. 3: 1), who are identified as *sarkinoi*, 'men of the flesh', 'fleshy', or 'those made of flesh' (3: 1); also *psychikoi*, 'unspiritual', 'natural' (2: 14), and at an even lower level, *sarkikoi*, 'of the flesh', 'fleshly', or 'characterized by flesh' (3: 3, 4, see note). *Teleioi* and *pneumatikoi* signify ideal Christians, those dominated by the Spirit. A growth to this maturity is envisaged, when they will be able to understand the wisdom Paul imparts. **rulers of this age:** Possibly spiritual world-rulers (cf. Lk. 22: 53; Eph. 2: 2; Col. 2: 15) who have usurped control of the world, but who are **doomed to pass away** (cf. 15: 25), also, possibly, those who crucified Christ: Pilate, representing the ruling world power, in league with the rulers of the Jews, especially in view of v. 8. See also Ac. 3: 17. The 'power of darkness' (Lk. 22: 53) operates through human agencies.

7. secret and hidden wisdom (*mystērion*, 'secret'): Not unintelligible, or difficult to understand, but a secret hidden in the counsels of God, now made known by His Spirit; here, that age-long purpose of redemption, reconciliation and restoration through Christ, kept secret, but now revealed (cf. Rom. 16: 25, 26; Eph. 3: 3-10).

However, this wisdom of God still remains hidden in a very real sense to those who are perishing (1: 18). **decreed before the ages:** God's redemptive plan is no afterthought (cf. Eph. 1: 4). **for our glory:** I.e., for the attainment of our complete salvation; cf. Rom. 8: 18-23. **8. Lord of glory:** Perhaps the most exalted title given to Christ; cf. Jas 2: 1. It associates Him in dignity and majesty with the Father; cf. Eph. 1: 17; Ac. 7: 2; Ps. 24: 7. **9. as it is written:** Paul regularly uses this phrase when quoting from canonical Scriptures, yet this question agrees exactly with not one OT text. Origen and others suggest a quotation from the Apocalypse of Elias, or the Ascension of Isaiah, but it may well be that they were quoting Paul. Possibly the saying was in circulation as a floating logion in Paul's day; the Gospel of Thomas includes it as one of the 'secret' sayings of Jesus. Alternatively, we may assume that Paul is 'quoting' very freely and from memory, and probably from the LXX translation of Isa. 64: 4 with reminiscences of Isa. 65: 17. Clement of Rome in the earliest extant quotation of 1 C. 2: 9 goes back to the LXX of Isa. 64: 4, indicating his opinion as to its original source. The verse itself clinches Paul's argument that the natural man through his physical senses is not able to understand God's wisdom in the cross of Christ. **10. God has revealed:** Demonstrates the superiority of the divine disclosure to man (**to us**, i.e. to things that are not) over the strugglings of human wisdom. The verb is aorist, indicating a definite time for the revelation; the secret now made known. **the Spirit searches:** God's medium of revelation, the Spirit, fathoms the depth of God's being. The activity is not indicative of ignorance, but of accurate knowledge. The depths are plumbed. **the depths of God** (*ta bathē*): Some Gnostics recognized a divine essence as 'the deep', 'the unknowable', but the Spirit knows all. **11.** Two Greek words are commonly translated 'to know'. Both occur in this verse; **what man knows . . .** (*oida*) and **no one comprehends . . .** (*ginōskō*). *oida* is to know by reflection based on intuition or information supplied (rendered 'understand' in v. 12). *ginōskō* is to know by observation and experience; to know, recognize, comprehend. *ginōskō* here seems to put the things of God a degree more out of reach than does *oida* the things of man. **12. received:** Aorist, indicating a definite time. **The spirit of the world** may mean Satan (cf. Jn 12: 31; 2 C. 4: 4; Eph. 2: 2; 6: 11, 12; 1 Jn 4: 3; 5: 19), although in the NT **world** (*kosmos*) is not regarded as inherently evil. More probably it means 'the temper of the world', the spirit of human wisdom, as alienated from God, and would be equivalent to human wisdom in v. 13. **the gifts bestowed:** 'all that God of his own grace gives us' (NEB), the content of Christian revelation and experience, made comprehensible by the Spirit. **13. interpreting spiritual truths . . . to those who possess the Spirit:** The Greek is ambiguous and is capable of the alternative translations shown in the RSV footnote. The problem arises from (i) the different meanings which *synkrinontes* may have, i.e., **interpreting** (LXX usage); combining (classical usage); comparing (the obvious meaning in 2 C. 10: 12), and (ii) the gender of *pneumatikois* **(spiritual),** which may be masculine or neuter. Modern translations, as Phillips and NEB, support RSV text, which makes good sense in that at the end of this paragraph Paul returns full circle to v. 6 ('among the mature we impart wisdom', i.e., to those who possess the Spirit). In addition, the transition of thought is achieved in the new paragraph, from v. 14, where by comparison, the unspiritual man is brought under discussion. For a detailed study of v. 13, see Robertson and Plummer.

(*b*) **The recipients of wisdom (2: 14–16)**
The unspiritual, natural man lacks spiritual discernment. To him the things of the Spirit just do not make sense. By contrast, the spiritual man, without fear of refutation, can make mature judgments in everything, knowing that he has the mind of Christ.

14. unspiritual (*psychikos*): The unrenewed natural man, as distinct from one who is actuated by the Spirit; cf. Jas 3: 15; Jude 19, 'worldly people'. **does not receive:** Does not accept, i.e., rejects, 'refuses' (NEB). **15. The spiritual man judges . . . :** The verb, *anakrinō*, is used three times in vv. 14, 15, and is translated, **discerned, judges,** and **judged.** Basically the word means to examine well, search out, sift. The spiritual man can therefore scrutinize and sift since he has the faculty to do it, but the unspiritual man finds the spiritual man and spiritual truths beyond his scrutiny; cf. v. 14. **to be judged by no one:** Presumably by no unspiritual person. **16.** A quotation from the LXX of Isa. 40: 13, which uses '*mind*' for spirit, which in God are identical, and seals Paul's argument concerning the inscrutability of spiritual things except to those who **have the mind of Christ. we have the mind of Christ:** Because we have His Spirit; cf. 2 Pet. 1: 4.

iv. Carnal misunderstanding concerning God's servants (3: 1–9)
(*a*) **Carnality and its effects (3: 1–4)**
Paul's exposition of the spiritual and unspiritual brings him to another fundamental cause of the dissensions which threaten to wreck the Corinthian church: gross carnality. Yet even as he

prepares to castigate his readers, the rebuke is softened by that recurring term of affection, **brethren.** The Corinthians at conversion had been babes in Christ, and for that there is no censure. However, the passage of time had seen no growth, but rather, a fleshly attitude dominated the believers, expressing itself in jealousy and strife, as they lived on the 'purely human level of your lower nature' (NEB).

1. I . . . could not address you: Refers to Paul's initial visit when the church was founded. Then they were not **spiritual,** i.e., the mature of 2: 6, but understandably **babes** (*nēpioi*), **men of the flesh** (*sarkinoi*), and therefore received **milk.** See note on 2: 6. **2. even yet:** Describes a wholly inexcusable condition. By now they should have grown up. **3. still of the flesh:** Not *sarkinoi* of v. 1, which was excusable at that stage of their development, but *sarkikoi* (used twice in this verse), indicative not just of their state, but of their attitude, fleshly, and wholly inexcusable; cf. Heb. 5: 11–14. Here, **flesh** for Paul has a moral and ethical significance; cf. Rom. 7: 5, 14; 13: 14; Gal. 5: 13. Its usage in the NT is varied; (i) material flesh (15: 39); (ii) the body itself (1 Pet. 4: 1); (iii) medium of relationship (Mk 10: 8); (iv) human nature, with special relation to its frailty (Jn 1: 14); (v) seat of sin; Paul's characteristic usage for man's evil nature, as opposed to the higher one. Sin is not inherent in flesh, as the Gnostics held, but its power is manifest in the flesh. **jealousy and strife:** Both works of the flesh (cf. Gal. 5: 20); and the latter, flowing from the former, creates the parties to which Paul again refers. **like ordinary men** (*anthrōpoi*): Repeated in v. 4, **merely men,** and is used as the equivalent of *sarkinoi*.

(*b*) **The true function of the apostles (3: 5–9)**
Carnality has obscured entirely their understanding of the true function of God's servants, so Paul explains the real relation between himself and Apollos. Far from establishing varying schools of thought and conflicting loyalties, they as God's servants, insignificant fellow-workers, were called so to labour according to His direction that their complementary activities might result in a divinely given growth. They are nothing, God is all.

5. What then is Apollos . . . Paul: The neuter **what,** instead of 'who' focuses attention on their activities rather than their personalities. **servants** (*diakonoi*): A word denoting active service. **as the Lord assigned to each:** May refer to the faith granted to each believer, or the ministry granted to each of His servants. The context suggests the latter. **6. I planted, Apollos watered, but God gave the growth:** The first two verbs are aorists summing up the specific tasks which Paul and Apollos completed (cf. Ac. 18: 1–18 and 18: 24–19: 1 respectively), but an imperfect expresses the continuous God-given **growth** through it all.

8. are equal: Literally, are one thing (neuter), 'on the same level' (Moffatt); this gives the lie to any accusation of opposing factions that Paul and Apollos were at variance. It is well expressed by NEB, 'they work as a team.' Yet, each is individually answerable to God (cf. vv. 10 ff.). **9. fellow workers for God:** A phrase occurring only here. Literally, 'God's fellow workers', RSV footnote. Two meanings are possible; 'fellow workers with one another in God's service', or 'fellow workers with God', as AV. While the force of the Greek may favour the latter, the context suggests the former, i.e., the unity of Paul and Apollos in the work for God. **God's field, God's building:** The emphasis is on the process which results in the tilled field and final edifice. The former looks back to vv. 6–9, and the latter ahead to vv. 10 ff.

v. True conception of the local church (3: 10–23)

(a) **The builders: their responsibility and reward (3: 10–15)**
It is about the building process that Paul is concerned. While he has laid a good foundation —'Jesus Christ and him crucified'—the local believers in Corinth have the responsibility for raising the structure. For good or bad they will incorporate the equivalents of gold, silver, etc., according to the lives they individually live. The final Day of reckoning will come, involving not the salvation of those who built, but the gain or loss of wages as the work is tested.

10. commission: A rather weak rendering of *charis* (grace), which here involves an enduement of divine power (cf. 15: 10). **skilled master builder** (*sophos*): Literally 'wise': used of skilled craftsmen who built the tabernacle; cf. LXX of Exod. 35: 10; 36: 1, 4, 8. **I laid a foundation:** The aorist refers to his eighteen months' stay, as do 2: 1; 3: 1, 6. **another man is building:** Not a reference to Apollos, but indicates the termination of Paul's contribution. **Let each man:** Stresses the personal responsibility of **each** one taking part. It is not merely the doctrinal structure of the church that is here in view, but all aspects of its corporate life. **12. gold, silver,** etc. cannot be pressed into representing specific details in the building. Rather, that which is valuable, true and enduring is contrasted with the worthless, shallow and inferior qualities of Christian conduct and service. **13. the Day will disclose it:** The day of judgment; cf. 1 Th. 5: 4; Heb. 10: 25. **it will be revealed with fire:** The Day itself will be so revealed; cf. 2 Th.

1: 7, 8; 2: 8; Dan. 7: 9 ff.; Mal. 4: 1. **sort of work:** Quality, not quantity, is signified. **14, 15. a reward:** Might be translated 'wage', as in v. 8. As Paul and Apollos will receive wages according to their work, so will the one who builds, according to what survives the testing fire. Similarly, he whose work is burned suffers the **loss** of wages, though not of salvation. **as through fire:** 'The imagery is that of a man who has to dash through the flames to escape to safety' (Leon Morris). It is the fire of judgment (13), not purgatory.

(b) **God's concern for His church (3: 16, 17)**
The imagery changes as Paul moves from the builders and their process of building, to the picture of God's temple, the sanctuary of His presence; the church at Corinth. If anyone through dissension and strife would mar this holy shrine, God will mar him.

16. God's temple (*naos*): Comprising the holy place and holy of holies, rather than *hieron*, which comprised the whole temple area. Here the local church is referred to, but see 6: 19 for its application to the individual believer.

17. If anyone destroys . . . destroy him: The verb has two meanings: (i) to defile, corrupt, (ii) to destroy. To rend a church with division is to reduce it to ruin and in exactly the same terms God will deal with those responsible. This verb (*phtheirō*), chosen no doubt for its double meaning, does not convey the thought of annihilation or eternal torment, but leaves one in doubt as to the exact nature of the divine retribution. The enormity of the sin of dissension in God's sight is clear.

(c) **The need for true wisdom (3: 18–23)**
The situation is urgent and in the face of impending judgment Paul appeals again to those who cling so foolishly to the wisdom of this world, which, as he has already shown and the Scriptures themselves declare, God will bring to nothing. From the vain boasting of men he turns them to the immeasurable greatness of their possessions in Christ. They are not to be gripped within the narrow confines of a party, for all teachers are theirs, the world itself with all its contrary currents; and they are Christ's and He is God's. All culminates in that unity of the being of God in which they are all partakers. To understand this is true wisdom.

18. let him become a fool: By accepting God's wisdom which the world calls folly, already expounded in 1: 18–20; 2: 14. **19. it is written:** A quotation from Job 5: 13, not from the LXX, but possibly Paul's own rendering of the Hebrew. **He catches:** In Greek a participle, indicating the strong grip God has on the slippery cleverness of the wicked (cf. 1: 20). **20.** is typical of the freedom with which Paul quotes from the LXX (Ps. 94: 11). However, **wise,** which he introduces in the place of 'man', is found in the context which is contrasting the designs of men with those of God. **21, 22. For all things are yours . . . :** Paul and the 'party leaders' do not possess the Corinthians, rather, the Corinthians possess these servants of God and not only so, but **all things** (neuter)—all God's creatures without limit (cf. Rom. 8: 32). **the world** (*kosmos*): The universe we inhabit. **life or death:** Viewed physically, but over which Christ has given victory (cf. Phil. 1: 21; 1 C. 15: 55-57), involving all circumstances whether in **the present** or **the future. 23. you are Christ's:** Possessing 'all things' they do not possess themselves (6: 20; 7: 23). Yet no one can say that his possession of, or in, Christ is greater than another's (1: 13). All individually and equally are members of Christ's body (12: 27; see also 12: 14-26). **Christ is God's:** A statement of the relation of Christ to God which in no way detracts from His deity. His essential nature and equality (Phil. 2: 6) with God are not under discussion, but His sub-ordination for man's salvation; cf. 11: 3; 15: 24 ff.; Jn 14: 28; 20: 17.

vi. Correct attitude to the servants of God (4: 1-21)

(*a*) **Do not sit in judgment (4: 1-5)**
Paul returns to the question of 3: 5. Whereas in 3: 5-8 he had demonstrated that, far from being party leaders, he and Apollos were mere servants accountable to God, as they were themselves (3: 10-17), now he outlines the correct attitude they should adopt toward the apostles. It is not for the believers in Corinth to sit in judgment on the respective merits of Paul, Apollos and Cephas. Paul is not concerned that he should receive a favourable report or party backing from Corinth, or any other human court. His judge is his Master, Christ, and his hope, divine commendation. Therefore, abandon party preferences, for Christ at His coming will deal with true values, not the estimates of carnal Corinthian minds.

1. as servants (*hypēretēs*): A word used only once by Paul (it originally denoted an under-rower in a trireme) and used by Luke for those who minister the word (cf. Lk. 1: 2; 4: 20). **stewards:** The *oikonomos* was a house manager with responsibility for the stores; a slave in relation to his master, but an overseer in relation to the other servants (cf. Lk. 12: 42; 16: 1). For Paul's 'stores', the mysteries of God, see 2: 7. **3. be judged by you:** The same verb as in 2: 14, 15 (see note), used 3 times in vv. 3, 4. The verb implies nothing as to the verdict; only the process of sifting evidence. **human court:** Literally, 'human day', in contrast to the Lord's day of judgment; cf. 3: 13. **I do not even judge myself:** That the use of conscience and self-criticism are essential is not denied, for Paul has a clear conscience (cf. v. 4), yet in the context of stewardship, Paul is no more competent than the Corinthians to pass judgment on his life and service. His assessment can only be subjective. **5. do not pronounce judgment:** The negative *mē* with the present imper. could be rendered, 'stop pronouncing judgment'. **before the Lord comes:** Or until . . . ; *heōs an* with the subjunctive, giving a sense of uncertainty, not of the coming, but of the time. **things now hidden in darkness:** Darkness may have an ethical significance as 'things morally bad', or perhaps, things either good or bad of which one is ignorant. **commendation from God:** Has an undoubted connection with the wages, or reward, of 3: 8, 14. **from** (*apo*) indicates the finality of the award from which there is no appeal.

(*b*) **Learn from the example of Paul and Apollos (4: 6, 7)**
Using Apollos and himself as an example, or illustration, Paul has endeavoured to teach the Corinthians the true function and character of God's servants, both toward each other as equals (3: 8), in relation to the church and before God Himself. And for this one purpose only: that they might learn **to live according to scripture.** For them, it is the necessity of learning the subordinate place of man and the exalted position of God; human wisdom abandoned for God's, human leaders abandoned for Christ. This is the cure for factions—the puffed up pride that would 'patronize one and flout the other' (NEB)—and for their conceited boasting, which mistook God's gifts for their own achievements.

6. applied all this to myself and Apollos: The verb *metaschēmatizō* means literally, 'to change the form of', 'alter the arrangement of'. Therefore, 'Paul implies that while speaking of himself and of Apollos he had others in view. If the congregation understands that it is forbidden to judge Paul and Apollos, she will more easily concede that all judging is forbidden' (Grosheide, 1 *Cor.*, p. 102). **all this:** The preceding 5 verses. **to live according to scripture:** An excellent rendering of an obscure phrase which may be a quotation, or one of Paul's well-known expressions. Literally, 'not beyond what is written'. **puffed up:** Used by Paul 6 times in this letter (4: 6, 18, 19; 5: 2; 8: 1; 13: 4) and only once outside it (Col. 2: 18), indicating the extent to which the sin of pride had gripped the Corinthian church. **7. who sees anything different in you:** The verb *diakrinō* has various meanings, but here suggests, 'to distinguish favourably from others', and is well rendered by NEB, 'Who makes you, my friend, so important?' Pride's bubble is pricked.

(c) Corinthian pride and the apostles' trials (4: 8–13)

So pernicious is their pride, Paul can no longer restrain his pent-up passion. With biting irony he assails their carnal conceit, contrasting their imagined exaltation and attainments with the utter degradation, poverty and distress which were the apostles' daily lot. If they should learn from the illustration of Paul and Apollos in vv. 1–5, how much more from the selfless conduct of these apostles who for Christ's sake (10) are reckoned fools, dishonoured and destitute—yet toiling with their hands lest they be a burden to the church—suffering every indignity, considered 'the scum of the earth' (NEB). While Corinthians cavort as kings, rending the church they wish to rule, the apostles turn the other cheek, try to conciliate and teach the lesson of true humility.

8. filled: Used of food, 'to be satiated', 'fed full'. **become rich . . . become kings:** Both verbs are aorists and the latter might well be translated, 'you have begun to reign!' All three verbs are suggestive of the fulfilling of all the blessings of the Messianic kingdom; cf. Lk. 22: 29–30; 1 Th. 2: 12; 2 Tim. 2: 12. Their own little millennium was already launched! **without us:** The 'without' of exclusion; 'and left us out' (NEB). **9.** bears the stamp of the arena; doomed men on show. **spectacle** (*theatron*): From which we derive 'theatre'. The verb is used in Heb. 10: 33. **to the world, to angels and to men: angels** and **men** are probably descriptive of **world.** Concerning the presence of angels in the world, see 11: 10; Gal. 3: 19; Heb. 1: 14. **10. wise:** Not the word Paul has used in previous chapters. *phronimoi* may be translated, 'sensible', 'prudent'; 'sensible Christians' (NEB). Paul's irony is continued. **11.** Note the contrast with v. 8. It is as **servants** (slaves) of Christ and God that Paul and the apostles suffer; cf. 4: 1. See also 2 C. 6: 4–10; 11: 23–29. Their experiences were Christ's; **hunger** (Lk. 4: 2), **thirst** (Jn 19: 28), **buffeted** (Mk 14: 65), **homeless** (Lk. 9: 58), **reviled** (1 Pet. 2: 23), **persecuted** (Jn 15: 20). **12. we labour** (*kopiōmen*): Indicates toil involving weariness and fatigue, an attitude he inculcated in others; cf. 1 Th. 1: 3. He spent himself that he might not be a burden (cf. 9: 6; 2 C. 11: 7; 1 Th. 2: 9; 2 Th. 3: 8; Ac. 18: 3; 20: 34), but note his reaction to gifts from Philippi (Phil. 4: 10–18). **we bless:** Their action conformed with Christ's command; cf. Lk. 6: 28. **13. refuse of the world:** While the word has two meanings, 'rubbish' or 'sweepings from a thorough cleaning', and

'scapegoat', it is more probable that the former is intended here. **offscouring:** Approximates to the previous noun in both its meanings and signifies the scrapings of a plate.

(d) A personal appeal for reconciliation (4: 14–21)

With a change of tone so characteristic in Paul's letters, the apostle moves to conciliation in his final appeal to the divided church. To induce a sense of **shame** on the level of human comparison would not be difficult, but he would rather plead from the uniqueness of his position as their **father in Christ,** that they copy him. **Timothy,** his own child in Christ (as they themselves were), had already been sent to remedy if possible the deteriorating situation. Paul himself would shortly arrive to deal with those whose haughty, arrogant speech served only to reveal their poverty of power. Yet while the **rod** is ready, how much better that he should come in **gentleness,** the situation already resolved.

14. to admonish: Used only by Paul in the NT, reflecting the duty of a parent; cf. Eph. 6: 4. It carries a note of sternness and can be translated, 'to warn'. **my beloved children:** No matter how dire the distress, Paul will not disown his relationship. At the point of sharpest censure, he uses the term of deepest endearment. **15. countless guides:** Tutors or guardians, servants who escorted the children to school (*paidagōgos*, as in Gal. 3: 24). A position of great responsibility and trust, but not of father-hood. As there was one planting, one foundation, so one spiritual father. **16. be imitators of me:** On the basis of his special relationship, Paul calls for a family likeness, particularly in the terms of vv. 10–13; cf. 11: 1; Phil. 3: 17; 1 Th. 1: 6. **17. I sent you Timothy:** The verb may be translated as an epistolary aorist, 'I am sending . .'. **Timothy** had probably already left Ephesus, although the letter may well have arrived before him; cf. 16: 10, 11; Ac. 19: 22. **18. Some are arrogant:** A conspicuous failing in the Corinthian church; a concomitant of the stress on worldly wisdom (vv. 6, 19; 5: 2; 8: 1), leading them to suppose that Timothy's arrival indicates Paul's fear to come himself. **19. if the Lord wills:** Paul is not his own master; cf. 16: 7; Jas 4: 15. **not the talk . . . but their power:** These two—*logos* and *dynamis*—are contrasted. Paul has no time for the former. Note the contrast in 1: 17 and 1: 24; 2: 1 and 2: 4. **20. kingdom of God:** Characterized by spiritual power. In this context the phrase signifies the inward reign of Christ over the hearts and lives of the believers (Rom. 14: 17; see also 1 C. 15: 24 note), and is in contrast to the shallowness of the church's experience, cf. v. 8. **21. with a**

rod (i.e., to chastise and rebuke) **. . . or with love . . .:** Yet the two attitudes are not mutually exclusive, for as a father Paul knows the significance of the lesson taught in Heb. 12: 4–11.

III. MORAL DISORDERS IN THE CHURCH (5: 1–6: 20)

Carnality continued to take its devastating toll of spiritual life in Corinth. Whether it was their emphasis on worldly wisdom, resulting in division, or the conceit of self-satisfaction which expressed itself in a blatant disregard for the basic concepts of Christian morality (chapters 5, 6) all stemmed from the fact that although 'in Christ', they were still very much 'of the flesh, and behaving like ordinary men'.

i. The case of immorality (5:1–13)

(*a*) The offence and its implications in the church (5: 1–8)

Corinth was a by-word for immorality, yet with all the debased, licentious habits of the Greeks, there was no relationship commonly known among them to compare with the depravity to which one of the Christians had sunk, **living with his father's wife.** Condemning their continued arrogance Paul calls for the immediate excommunication of the offender, for the purity of the whole church is in peril; an evil which if discreetly concealed can only lead to the utter pollution of the whole body. The sacrifice of Christ, the Passover **lamb,** demands conformity with those standards of purity typified in the diligent rooting out of all **leaven** in the ancient Jewish festival.

1. not found even among pagans: Although such cases of immorality can actually be quoted, they were most uncommon and certainly not countenanced, as in the Corinthian church. **is living with:** Literally 'to have', which, while not necessarily suggesting formal marriage, most certainly indicates a permanent relationship. **his father's wife:** Not the offender's mother, but a stepmother, probably divorced from the father. The latter may even have been dead. **2. you are arrogant: you** is emphatic, stressing the incongruity of their attitude. **mourn:** Often used of mourning for the dead (cf. Mk 16: 10); it may reflect Paul's attitude to the loss of this church member. See Moffatt. **Let him . . .** ('that he . . .' AV): RSV, with Moffatt, translates *hina* (that) as giving the verb the force of an imperative. Mourning should result in the offender's removal. **3. I am present in spirit: I** is emphatic; Paul does what they should have done. He maintains spiritual contact although physically removed (cf. Col. 2: 5). **I have already pronounced judgment:** The verb is perfect and indicates finality. Note Paul's disciplinary authority, a reflection of 4: 21.

See also 2 C. 13: 2, 10. The construction of vv. 3–5 is not easy. There are several possibilities:
- (i) Take **in the name** with **assembled** and **with the power** with **deliver,** as AV, or
- (ii) Take **in the name** and **with the power** with **assembled,** as NEB and many Greek commentators, or
- (iii) Take **in the name** and **with the power** with **deliver,** or
- (iv) Take **in the name** with **deliver** and **with the power** with **gathered,** as Robertson and Plummer and Leon Morris, or
- (v) Take **in the name** with **I have already pronounced judgment,** as RSV, Moffatt and *CGT.* The sense of this last construction is good, for here Paul's solemn judgment bears the authority of the name of Christ as will the assembled church bear the stamp of His power.

5. to deliver this man to Satan: The expression occurs elsewhere only in 1 Tim. 1: 20. It implies formal excommunication where one is removed from the sphere of the church to that of Satan, the world, a 'dominion of darkness'; cf. Eph. 2: 11, 12; Col. 1: 13; 1 Jn 5: 19. **destruction of the flesh:** Two views are possible and both may be true: (i) **flesh** may be understood as the seat of sin, man's evil nature. He is to be handed over for the mortification of the flesh—the destruction of sinful lusts—to learn again the terror of Satan's power. For Paul's characteristic usage, see 3: 3 note; Rom. 8: 6–9, 12, 13; Col. 3: 5. (ii) **flesh** may be physical. **destruction** (*olethros*) is a strong word implying physical suffering and destruction. Such is involved in God's punishments and in Satan's attacks; cf. 11: 30; Ac. 5: 1 ff.; Lk. 13: 16; Heb. 2: 14; 2 C. 12: 7. **that his spirit may be saved:** Punishment is plainly remedial. At the judgment day, **the day of the Lord Jesus,** he will be with the Lord's people (cf. 1: 8; 3: 13; 4: 5). **6. boasting:** The outcome of their arrogance (2), and wholly out of place. **a little leaven . . .:** A common illustration carries home the point. One such immoral man could utterly corrupt the church. Paul had seen the principle at work among the Judaizers in Galatia; cf. Gal. 5: 9. **7. Cleanse out the old leaven:** Symbolized the removal of moral impurity and recalled the practice of Israel in preparation for the Jewish Passover (Exod. 12: 15 ff.) A custom developed when with candles the smallest crumbs of leavened bread were searched out in every corner of the house (cf. Zeph. 1: 12). **you really are unleavened:** So they were in Christ. Paul urges them to be in character—'bread of a new baking' (NEB)—what they were in theory. **For . . .** (*kai gar*): Introduces an additional urgent reason for purging: **Christ, our paschal lamb** is already slain and the house is not yet cleansed (cf.

Dt. 16: 4-6). **8. Let us . . . celebrate the festival:** The verb is present subjunctive, suggesting continuity. Godet remarks, 'Our festival is not for a week, but for a life-time'. **malice and evil:** In direct contrast with **sincerity and truth.** The old and new life are mutually exclusive. Note Paul's contrast in this letter between worldly wisdom and divine wisdom, the fleshly and the spiritual, the old and the new. The Christian is not a patched up pagan, but **a new** person (cf. Eph. 2: 1-5). **sincerity** (*eilikrinia*): Probably derived from *eilē*—the sun's rays, or heat—suggesting transparent purity of purpose and character.

(b) A misunderstanding rectified (5: 9-13)
There follows in vv. 9-13 what appears to be a digression from the immediate subject, although connected with the theme of immorality. Paul is perhaps reminded by the unmixedness of *eilikrinia* (8) of what he had written in a previous letter, and so proceeds to clarify the issue about mixing with fornicators. The Corinthians had misunderstood Paul, thinking he had forbidden them to associate with immoral pagans. Concerning such Paul has no brief; to avoid them is impossible. His concern is with Christians, and with those who return to the immoral and sinful practices of pagan society, no association is possible.

9. I wrote: Not an epistolary aorist, but a letter, apparently well known to the Corinthians, now lost. See Introduction, p. 373. **not to associate:** Literally, 'not to mix yourselves up together with'. The verb occurs elsewhere in the NT only in 2 Th. 3: 14. It implies a close relationship. **10.** summarizes the three vices characteristic of the non-Christian world; moral laxity, greed (**greedy** and **robbers** are brought into one class by a single def. art. coupling both nouns) and superstition. **11. rather I wrote:** May be epistolary aorist and could be rendered, 'Now I write . . .', as in RSVmg. **one who bears the name of brother:** A profession denied by conduct, but not necessarily implying an unregenerate state. A pagan environment continues to exert tremendous power over those newly born again. **idolator:** Note the ease with which a man might be influenced by previous practices; cf. 8: 10; 10: 7, 8, 14 ff. **reviler** and **drunkard:** Added to the list of v. 10, reflecting again the social background from which the converts were drawn. **not even to eat with such:** Mirrors the life of Asia throughout the centuries; the shared meal demonstrates friendship, its prohibition, utter separation; cf. Lk. 15: 2; Gal. 2: 12. Its secondary result was to bar the offender from the Lord's Table. **13. God judges those outside:** The church must set its own house in order; God deals with the world. The tense of the verb is best regarded as present, indicating the normal attribute of God. **Drive out:** Possibly a quotation from Dt. 17: 7.

ii. Lawsuits and heathen courts (6: 1-11)
The mention of judgment in 5: 12, 13 brings the apostle to another matter for censure. Grievances between Christians had apparently been taken to the civil courts for settlement. If believers are destined to **judge the world** and **angels,** the settlement of trivial temporal disagreements should surely not be beyond the capabilities of the local church (1-6). **Lawsuits** between Christians are wrong; better by far to suffer injustice than to fight (7, 8). Let them reflect (9-11). They were **washed, sanctified, justified,** and yet have begun to act with that unrighteousness so characteristic of those destined to be excluded from the kingdom of God. Such conduct is blatantly wrong.

1. grievance (*pragma*): In its legal sense, a cause for trial, a case. **go to law:** The verb is in the middle voice, i.e., they were seeking judgment in their own interests. **the unrighteous:** Does not suggest that the court judges were unjust, but indicates their relationship to God in contrast to that of the saints. Rabbis taught the Jews never to take a case before the Gentiles. **2. the saints will judge the world:** Anticipates Christ's return and the final judgment. This goes beyond our Lord's teaching to the Twelve in Mt. 19: 28; Lk. 22: 28 ff. (see also Dan. 7: 22), in terms of both the judges and the judged. It is possible to understand **judge** in the Hebraic sense of 'reign', a function incorporating judgment, and basic to NT eschatology; cf. Rom. 8: 17; 2 Tim. 2: 12; Rev. 2: 26, 27; 3: 21; 20: 4. **cases** (*kritērion*): Has various uses—means or rules of judging; the place of trial, the tribunal (RVmg and Robertson and Plummer); persons that judicate; the cases before the court (AV, RV, RSV, NEB). **3. judge angels:** Some angels are reserved for judgment; cf. Mt. 25: 41; 2 Pet. 2: 4; Jude 6. **4. why do you lay** (*kathizete*) **them . . . :** Three renderings are possible; *kathizete* may be imperative, as rendered by AV, or indicative and affirmative, or indicative and interrogative as in RV, RSV, and NEB. The third rendering is generally preferred. **those who are least esteemed:** A strong expression, rendered 'despised' in 1: 28. Identified in the terms of RSV text, such judges, whatever status they may have in the world, have as such no status in the church. Pagan judges are of little significance compared with those who will judge the world. Settling differences between Christians before heathen courts is utterly shameful.

5. no man among you wise enough: Illustrates the poverty of true wisdom in Corinth in contrast to their apparent regard for worldly wisdom. Note the progression of thought in vv. 4-6; to have cases is bad, that they should be between brethren is worse, but that they should be brought before unbelievers is scandalous. **7. defeat for you:** A default, defect and so in this context, a defeat. It refers not to the legal outcome, but to the spiritual issues involved. Origen notes that a legal victory may be a spiritual defeat. Nowhere in this section does Paul seek to discredit civil justice. **With one another** is the key to his thinking and the basis of his censure. Lawsuits may be forced on a believer, or become inescapable in his dealings with unbelievers. Paul's teaching and conduct revealed his respect for the law as appointed by God; cf. Rom. 13: 1-7; Ac. 18: 12 ff.; 25: 16. **Why not . . . suffer wrong . . . be defrauded:** Reflects the law of Christ; cf. Mt. 5: 39-41. **8. you . . . wrong and defraud:** Their cases against each other were not based even on just grievances. Rather than **suffer wrong,** they would inflict it. **9.** No English version conveys the significant connection between vv. 8 and 9: **you wrong** (*adikeite*) (8), but wrong doers, **unrighteous** (*adikoi*) **will not inherit** (9). Such Corinthians must re-examine their standing in Christ. Paul thus moves from the particular to the principle involved; cf. Eph. 5: 5, 6. It is a warning against antinomianism. **idolators:** Grouped with those guilty of sexual sins, illustrating the immoral character of Greek religion with its temple prostitutes. **10. kingdom of God:** Referred to in its future aspect, while in 4: 20 it has a present significance; cf. 15: 24. **11. But** (*alla*): Preceding each of the three verbs in the Greek text, it serves to contrast forcefully their present state with that from which they came. **you were washed:** The middle voice—you had yourselves washed, emphasizing the voluntary character of their action. Nothing in the context identifies this act with baptism, although the same word has this association in Ac. 22: 16. Washing is indicative of regeneration (Eph. 5: 26; Tit. 3: 5) of which baptism is the visible confession. The use of the aorist as in **sanctified** and **justified** is suggestive of one definite act. **justified** coming last (*edikaiōthēte*, declared righteous) brings Paul's thought to a climax, contrasting their present condition with the **unrighteous** (*adikoi*) of v. 9. **in the name:** Qualifies all three verbs and emphasizes the divine origin and execution of salvation.

iii. Fornication and purity (6: 12-20)
Paul returns to the subject of immorality, now to deal with it not as a particular issue, as in chapter 5, but as a general principle. Fornication, condoned by the average Greek and Roman alike, and indeed being an almost integral part of pagan religion in Corinth, became a snare to test the moral discipline of the local church to the hilt. To those 'declared righteous' (11) came the temptation born of past licentious living to substitute licence for liberty. Paul's doctrines were easily perverted (Rom. 5: 20; 6: 14) and the seed of antinomianism sown. The lesson, **All things are lawful for me, but not all things are helpful** (12) had yet to be learned. Vv. 12-14 demonstrate the true use of Christian liberty in fulfilling God's purpose for the **body,** while the remaining verses (15-20) apply this to the problem of the **prostitute** and the consequent desecration of the **temple of the Holy Spirit.** The lesson is summarized in the final verse, a principle to govern all conduct: **glorify God in your body.**

12. All things are lawful for me . . . : Possibly a phrase previously used by the apostle now misused by the Corinthian Christians to excuse their excesses. However, see note on 1: 12 where it is suggested that the phrase may have been a watchword of the libertarian party. In either case, this twice repeated maxim is now qualified (**but . . . but . . .**) to prove that **all things** is not an unrestricted absolute. There are moral bounds; **not all things are helpful,** some things enslave. **13, 14. Food is meant for the stomach . . . :** Probably another current saying, suggesting to the Corinthians that as one indulges an appetite for food, that being the function of the stomach, so should the physical urge for sexual indulgence be gratified. Paul refutes the argument: **stomach** and **food** are purely temporal. Not so the body; cf. 15: 35-50. **The body is not meant for immorality . . . :** If **stomach** answers to **food,** the **body** answers, not to **immorality,** but to **the Lord.** Each is fitted for the other; cf. vv. 15a, 17, 19; Eph. 3: 16, 17; 2 C. 6: 16. **14. God raised . . . :** The body is meant for immortality; cf. 15: 20; Rom. 8: 11. Note the contrast; the **stomach** and **food** God destroys, the **Lord** and the **body** God raises. **15. members of Christ:** In the sense of limbs, as NEB, 'limbs and organs of Christ'. His possession of us is physical as well as spiritual. Hence the horror of using parts of His body for fornication. **16. Do you not know . . . :** Paul appeals to the obvious, to common knowledge, as whenever he uses this phrase (3: 16; 5: 6; 6: 2, 3, 9, 15, 16, 19). It is the choice of being **one body with her** (16), or **one spirit** with Him (17).

17. united: Literally 'to glue', signifying the closest of ties, which here results in complete union, or fusion. The one verb expresses union with Christ and union with a prostitute (see 'joins himself . . .' in v. 16). **18. Shun immorality:** Literally, 'Flee'. Some things are too powerful to be opposed and safety comes only in flight. See 10: 14; 1 Tim. 6: 10, 11; 2 Tim. 2: 22. **Every other sin . . . is outside the body:** Literally, 'All sin . . .' Every sin has an outward aspect and effect, including immorality (16), but the unique difference for the fornicator, who **sins against his own body,** is that his sin is against the very nature and purpose of the human body. Other sins too which Paul has mentioned affect the body, *e.g.*, drunkenness, but fornication uniquely so. Its appetite stems wholly from within and demands the gratification of personal lust, the acme of self-violation. **19. your body is a temple:** Brings into sharp contrast the Christian concept of holiness with that of pagan Corinth, where in the temple of Aphrodite prostitutes were priestesses, intercourse with whom counted as consecration. **temple** (*naos*): See note on 3: 16. There the reference is to the church, here to the individual Christian. **of the Holy Spirit:** Cf. Rom. 8: 11; 2 C. 6: 16; 2 Tim. 1: 14. **20. bought with a price:** Carrying the seal of God's purchase; the Holy Spirit (Eph. 1: 13, 14). **bought:** Suggestive of the whole redemptive act, having the imagery of the slave-market and the consequent change of ownership. See 1 Pet. 1: 18, 19. **So glorify God in your body:** A positive injunction balancing the negative of v. 18. **So** (*dē*): Strengthens the imperative; 'Be sure to . . .'

IV. DIFFICULTIES IN SOCIAL LIFE (7: 1–11: 1)

i. Marriage (7: 1–40)

(*a*) General background (7: 1–7)

Paul now deals with a variety of subjects mentioned by the Corinthians in their letter to him, the first of which is marriage. That Paul favoured celibacy is clear (1, 7, 8, 9, 27b, 38b) and for this he presents his reasons: the prevailing circumstances (26, 29), undivided devotion to Christ (32, 34, 35), and freedom from physical necessity (37). Recognizing its practical necessity, Paul countenances marriage (2), stipulating the mutual responsibilities of husband and wife and the relation of these to their spiritual lives (5). To understand Paul's teaching, two facts must be remembered: (i) Ascetic practices were highly esteemed, demanding among other things a celibate life. This probably prompted some such question in their letter to the apostle as, 'Is marriage to be permitted?' Paul replies, recognizing many advantages of celibacy, but maintaining too the virtue of marriage (2, 9, 28, 36, 38a). (ii) Conditions at that particular time suggested that marriage might be unwise (26, 29). Paul is therefore not writing a treatise on marriage, but is answering their question within the context of current attitudes and the cir-

cumstances of the day. A balanced picture of the Christian concept of marriage is therefore to be gained from a study of the NT teaching as a whole; cf. Jn 2: 1–11; Eph. 5: 21–33; 1 Tim. 5: 14; Heb. 13: 4; 1 Pet. 3: 1–7.

1. It is well for a man not to touch a woman is probably quoted from the Corinthians' letter; an ascetic party in the church may have taken this stand by way of reaction from the laxity of the environment. 'So far as I am concerned', Paul comments in effect, 'that would suit me very well, *but . . .*' Note his repeated use of **it is well** (commendable, but not *morally*, or intrinsically, better), in this connection in vv. 8, 26, 38. **2. Because of the temptation to immorality:** Reflects not a low view of marriage, but the moral conditions of Corinth. Paul is a realist, not a mere theorist. His attitude is defined in Eph. 5: 21–33. **each man . . . each woman . . . :** A clear statement of monogamy. **3. conjugal rights:** Literally 'debt' (*opheilē*). These are jointly shared by husband and wife. **give** (*apodidotō*): A present imperative, indicating the normal condition, the mutual paying of a debt. A wife is no mere chattel. The relationship is clarified further in v. 4, where the same statement is predicated separately of both husband and wife, demonstrating their equality. **4. does not rule** (*ouk exousiazei*): They have not the right to use their own bodies just as they will. **5. Do not refuse one another:** May be translated, 'Stop defrauding one another', to bring out the force of the pres. imper. with the neg. *mē*. It suggests that married couples in Corinth were refraining from intercourse on the grounds of mistaken asceticism. Only a limited period of abstinence by agreement, for special devotions, is permissible. Clearly then, procreation is not the sole purpose of intercourse. **Come together again** is suggestive of something far more frequent, regular and intimate. **6. I say this:** Refers back to the preceding 5 verses. Marriage is permitted by concession, but is not a command for all. **7. each has his own special gift** (*charisma*): Marriage, just as celibacy, is a special gift from God. The same word is used for gifts of the Spirit in 12: 4–11.

(*b*) The unmarried and widows (7: 8, 9)

Specific classes are now dealt with; here those without marriage ties. The guidance is a restatement of vv. 1 and 2.

8. the unmarried (*tois agamois*): Probably refers to men—bachelors and widowers. The case of virgins is discussed in vv. 25–38. However, Leon Morris maintains that the term includes all not bound by the married state. **remain single as I do:** The verb, an aorist, suggests a permanent and final decision. The suggestion that Paul was a member of the Sanhedrin and therefore must have been married, is hard to substantiate. It is by no means certain that he was a member, nor is it certain that every member of the Sanhedrin in the period before A.D. 70 had to be married. But if Paul had once been married, he could now have been a widower, or his wife may have left him at his conversion (she would then be included in the 'all things' of Phil. 3: 8). **9. aflame with passion:** A verb in the present tense (as is **cannot exercise self-control**) and indicative of a continual struggle such as would make spiritual growth impossible. Such a man has not the gift of celibacy.

(*c*) **The married (7: 10, 11)**
Here both partners are Christians (the case of mixed marriages comes next), and for such divorce is not permitted. If, however, it does take place another marriage is out of the question. The mention of the woman first and the note in parenthesis referring only to her leaving her husband, suggests that Paul had an actual case in mind.

10. I give charge: A military word, 'I command'. There is now no question of concession (6). **not I but the Lord:** Not merely Paul's command, but Christ's; cf. Mk 10: 9; Lk. 16: 18. Christ's allowance for fornication is not mentioned (cf. Mt. 5: 32; 19: 9).

(*d*) **Mixed marriages (7: 12–16)**
Some had married before their conversion and Paul now speaks to them. The Christian partner should not divorce the unbeliever who consents to continue the marriage relationship. The union is **consecrated** and the children undefiled. If however, the unconverted partner desires a divorce, the Christian is free to permit it.

12. I say, not the Lord: That is, in this instance Paul cannot refer to any direct command of Christ, as he could for the previous case (10, 11). Yet his words carry the full weight of inspiration and apostolic authority. **14. the unbelieving husband is consecrated through the wife:** This meets the fear of the Christian partner that the believer is going to be defiled in terms of 6: 15. But there is nothing unholy in such a marriage where the unbeliever elects to stay with the Christian partner. Such consecration has nothing to do with personal consecration as understood in terms of conversion and salvation, but of **consecration** of the unbeliever for the purpose of the marriage union. On the analogy of *whatever touches the altar shall be holy* (Exod. 29: 37; Lev. 6: 18), so the unbelieving husband, in becoming one flesh with his believing partner, is sanctified in the wife for the purpose of marriage. On this basis the **children** of such a marriage are not **unclean** (*akatharta*), a word used for ceremonial impurity, but the

very reverse; as far as the marriage is concerned, **they are holy,** that is, clean. Therefore the believer is required to separate from neither the unbelieving partner nor the children. **is not bound:** Seems to imply freedom to remarry. The unbeliever having 'taken himself off', which is the force of the middle voice of **separate,** no further compulsion to preserve the marriage remains on the believer. **God has called us to peace:** This encompasses the whole problem of mixed marriages. The believer is to become involved neither in the turmoil of seeking to terminate such a partnership, nor in the conflict of seeking to preserve it against the will of the unbeliever. Here submission issues in **peace** (Rom. 8: 28).

16. how do you know: Expresses the uncertainty of the believing partner being able to save the other by clinging to the marriage in spite of the partner's determination to end it. An exactly opposite view is, however, taken by Lightfoot and Findlay, expressing the hope of salvation, 'How do you know that you will not save your husband?' (so also NEB). The RSV rendering is probably to be preferred.

(*e*) **The life the Lord assigns (7: 17–24)**
V. 17 sums up the apostle's teaching on mixed marriages and at the same time introduces a general principle which must govern the actions of those converted to the Christian faith. This is defined in v. 20, **Everyone should remain in the state in which he was called,** and restated in v. 24. Just as a believing partner in a mixed marriage is not to seek dissolution of the union, so with Jewish and Gentile converts, and indeed with the slave. While their conversion to Christ will produce a fundamental moral and spiritual change, yet their social status will not be altered. In that environment they are to live for Christ. Undoubtedly exceptions will be found, as when a pagan partner contracts out of marriage, or a slave is offered his freedom. Nevertheless, the principle is valid, **in whatever state each was called, there let him remain with God** (24).

17. lead the life (*peripateitō*): A pres. imper. with the force of 'continue walking'. There is a social continuity with the past. Christianity is not intended to bring a violent revolution from without, but to be a sanctifying influence within society. The position in life when **called,** is the one **the Lord assigned. This is my rule:** Strong apostolic authority. For the same usage see 11: 34; Tit. 1: 5; Ac. 24: 23. **all** is emphatic. **18, 19. to . . . remove the marks of circumcision** was not required. They should remain within Jewish society. To remove such a sign as a Jew, or to seek it as a converted Gentile was pointless; the rite 'counts for nothing' (Moffatt) in the Christian code; cf. Gal. 5: 2, 3; Ac. 15: 1, 5, 19, 24, 28. Converted Jews and Gentiles were both needed within their social groups. Paul never ceased to be a Jew; cf. 9: 20. **the commandments of God:** The moral law, understood in terms of Gal. 5: 6; 6: 15. **20. remain:** A pres. imper. with the same force as **lead the life** in v. 17. **21** is capable of two interpretations: **avail yourself,** literally 'rather use', refers either to the opportunity to become free, or to the opportunity to use one's vocation as a slave, i.e., to continue as a slave and so fulfil the general principle to remain in the state in which one was called. RSV, Moffatt, Phillips and NEB take the former view, which is the more probable from the use of the aorist imper. which is suggestive of availing oneself of a new opportunity as opposed to the pres. imper. of vv. 17, 20, 24. **22. a freedman of the Lord . . . a slave of Christ:** What matters is not one's temporal state, but one's spiritual standing and relationship. This was Paul's boast; cf. Rom. 1: 1; Phil. 1: 1; Tit. 1: 1. **23. You were bought:** See note on 6: 20. **do not become slaves of men:** Refers not to physical slavery—no such injunction would be needed—but probably to the temptation of yielding to social and religious pressures, which would be incompatible with their being slaves of Christ.

24. each: As in vv. 17, 20 it is emphatic, stressing the duty of the individual.

(f) The advantages of remaining single (7: 25-38)

Having dealt with marriage in relation to widows, unmarried men and those already married, Paul now turns to the **unmarried women**—virgins. What he writes is in response to questions on the subject from Corinth and without the knowledge of those questions and the identity of the virgins, the exact translation of this passage, especially vv. 36-38, must remain a matter of conjecture. Paul's opinion concerning these young women is influenced considerably by **the impending distress** (26), which he further defines by saying that **the appointed time has grown very short** (29). See also v. 31. Of this situation we have no precise knowledge, although to some extent it seems in Paul's mind to be associated with events leading up to the Second Coming. So critical and precarious are the circumstances, that before dealing with the particular case of the virgins, the apostle urges that marriage and all aspects of life be conducted with the utmost caution and solemnity (26-31).

In these circumstances the advantages of remaining single are obvious. The man or woman without other responsibilities is able to be concerned wholly in the **affairs of the Lord,** while those who are married become engrossed in each other. **Undivided devotion to Christ** is the apostle's aim (32-35).

Having established the principle involved, Paul returns to the particular case of the young woman he has in mind (36-38). The problems of interpretation are considerable. While the translators of AV and RV had a father and daughter in mind, RSV views them as an engaged couple (see note on v. 36). Although the precise identity of the individuals must remain in doubt, Paul's conclusion is clear. If the young woman marries she **does well,** but to remain single is to **do better.** So the principle enunciated in 7: 1, 2 is carried through; in the present circumstances it is better not to marry, although for most marriage must be the norm.

25. concerning the unmarried (*parthenoi*): The word means virgin, normally applying to women only, although in Rev. 14: 4 it refers to men (see p 654). Thus RSV translates it loosely to cover unmarried men and women, and NEB renders it 'celibacy'. Most translations and commentators restrict the meaning here to unmarried women. **I have no command of the Lord:** Indicates as in v. 12 that Christ gave no specific instruction. **I give my opinion:** Not that Paul is not sure of his facts (cf. v. 40). The situation does not call for a command, as opposed to v. 10, for the individuals involved must decide for themselves between the possible alternatives; cf. vv. 27, 28, 35, 36-38. Paul presents principles for guidance. **26. the impending distress:** May be rendered 'present distress', or 'necessity'. The word is a strong one and is used in Lk. 21: 23. Paul's usage has been variously interpreted as (i) a reference to events preceding the Second Coming (and so vv. 29, 31), (ii) general opposition to Christian profession, although the language is too strong for this, (iii) particularly difficult circumstances through which the Christians in Corinth were then passing. Combined influences of all three might be involved. **28. you do not sin:** Marriage may be unwise because of the **impending distress,** but not sinful (cf. v. 36). **worldly troubles:** Literally, 'affliction in the flesh', an experience normally balanced by compensating blessings and joys. Yet the worry and distress resulting from family responsibilities in times of violence and persecution are immeasurably increased. **29. the appointed time . . . :** As with vv. 26 and 31 it may be understood in terms of the Second Advent, although the apostle nowhere else suggests that its anticipation should lead to the abandonment of basic human relationships. Rather, he uses it as a stimulus to holiness (1 Th. 5: 1-10). A local crisis of extreme gravity more probably existed and Paul's allusions to it were readily understood in Corinth. See Phillips's translation. **from now on:** I.e., during the emergency, not merely the unmarried, but all in the church, the married, the mourners, the joyous, the traders, all must live in measure as detached from their experiences. **31. as though they had no dealings with it:** The compound form of the verb intensifies its meaning, i.e., 'not using to the full'. Phillips is excellent, 'Every contact with the world should be as light as possible'. **the form of this world . . .** (*schēma*): Literally, 'the outward appearance'. All is transitory, explaining why contact with it should be light. **32. free from anxieties:** I.e., the **worldly troubles** of v. 28. Note their effect in Mk 4: 19; Lk. 21: 34. Yet there is a proper anxiety which Paul proceeds to employ, to demonstrate the advantage of remaining single; **the unmarried man is anxious . . . to please the Lord.** This was Paul's own great desire; cf. 2 C. 5: 9; Gal. 1: 10; 1 Th. 2: 4; 4: 1; 2 Tim. 2: 4. However, the equally right anxiety in the realm of family life—**worldly affairs**—to please one's partner, introduces a potential conflict of loyalties which becomes apparent under conditions of stress and crisis (33)—**interests are divided** (34). A case in point: single men and women invariably remain in missionary work, while married men and women frequently abandon the task for 'family reasons'.

34. his interests are divided (*memeristai*): This clause involves a problem of punctuation and therefore translation. Should *memeristai* (**divided**) be taken with v. 33, or with v. 34? While AV and RV take it with v. 34, RSV, together with Moffatt and NEB, link *memeristai* with the preceding sentence. There are also a number of textual variations which complicate the issue. A decision is difficult, but Paul's general sense is clear. **holy in body and spirit:** Refers to consecration, not ethical attainment. The single woman is unhindered by such responsibilities as characterize a married woman. **35. restraint:** Literally 'halter' or 'lasso'. See NEB: 'keep you on a tight rein'.

36. Yet even in the present circumstances Paul sees the possible necessity for some to marry. The verse obviously answers a question raised by the Corinthian believers. **his betrothed** (*parthenos*): Literally, his 'virgin', has been interpreted in three ways; (i) the father and his virgin daughter (AV, RV), (ii) a couple involved in a 'spiritual marriage' while remaining celibate (Moffatt and NEB), (iii) a young man and his fiancée (RSV) According to (i), the father was responsible for his daughter's marriage. Yet if he felt that 'he behaveth himself unseemly' (RV), i.e., was treating her unjustly in failing to arrange a

marriage, and 'if she be past the flower of her age' (so RV renders *hyperakmos*), i.e., of marriageable age with the bloom of youth commencing to fade, then he may arrange a marriage. **it is no sin:** She has not the gift of continence (cf. v. 7). On the other hand, if he is aware of no such 'necessity' (RV) then he may keep her as his own virgin daughter. If (ii) the 'spiritual marriage' is correct, vv. 36, 37 are translated as in RSV except that *parthenos* becomes 'spiritual', or celibate 'bride'. This practice existed in the 2nd century and was condemned by Cyprian in the 3rd century, but there is no evidence that it existed in Paul's day. The third suggestion (RSV) translates *parthenos* as **betrothed** and *hyperakmos* as **if his passions are too strong.** This interpretation is probably the most attractive. In the lower social classes from which most of the members of the Corinthian church were drawn the contracting of marriages would often be left to the young people concerned and would not be viewed as the responsibility of the parents.

(*g*) **Widows** (7: 39, 40)

Remarriage is only permissible **in the Lord**, i.e. if she marries a Christian, but, as in v. 8, the apostle considers **she is happier** if she remains single.

39. A wife is bound: Christian marriage is indissoluble till death.

40. I have the Spirit of God: Cf. v. 25. Paul's **judgment** is Spirit-led. Robertson and Plummer conclude, 'The preference given to celibacy is tentative and exceptional, to meet exceptional conditions.'

ii. Food offered to idols (8: 1–11: 1)

(*a*) **Idols are nothing** (8: 1–6)

Food and **idols:** The problem loomed large in Corinth for the two were inextricably linked. Undoubtedly much of the meat available to the shops had been originally offered in pagan rites and later disposed of by the priests as surplus to their needs. But that was not all; normal social functions involving a meal were often held in temples, creating situations where Christians would almost inevitably be present and participate. On such occasions sacrifices to the idols would be made. What should the Christian do? That was their problem and the substance of the question to Paul. While one scorns the very existence of idols and eats with impunity, another, weak in the faith, is stumbled and destroyed; for him the idol is a living reality. The conclusion? Avoid anything that would cause your brother to fall (13). In vv. 1–6 Paul states the principle that our **knowledge** of the absolute nonentity of idols must be balanced by **love.**

1. Now concerning: Paul's phrase for introducing the subjects on which the Corinthians have sought guidance; cf. 7: 1, 25; 12: 1; 16: 1. **'All of us possess knowledge':** Possibly a statement from their own letter, and on this assumption RSV adds quotation marks. As with wisdom, the Corinthians had a typically Greek regard for **knowledge.** Alone, it engenders pride; **puffs up** (see note on 4: 6). **Love builds up:** A word used of building construction, cf. v. 10; 10: 23; 14: 4, 17 for *oikodomeō* in this letter. Note the contrast; hollowness and solidity. **2. imagines:** 'thinks'—is used with similar effect concerning wisdom in 3: 18. True knowledge should lead to humility, the recognition of ignorance. Love aids this attitude (cf. 13: 12b). **3. one is known by him:** The divine response to human **love.** To obtain His recognition is all important. One who truly loves is better equipped to solve the problem of food offered to idols than one who merely knows. **4. we know:** Appears to introduce more quotations from the Corinthian inquiry. Note the RSV quotation marks. Paul accepts their assertions, **'an idol has no real existence'** and **'there is no God but one',** but reserves his treatment of the underlying implications of idolatry to 10: 14-22 (cf. Gal. 4: 8). **5. in heaven or on earth:** The abode of the gods of Greek mythology. **many 'gods' and many 'lords':** Pagan terms of address. **lord** (*kyrios*) is a title frequently given to gods in Greek inscriptions. **6. one God . . . one Lord:** As opposed to many, affirms strongly the positive Christian position. The prepositions are instructive; of **God: from whom** (*ek*—out of), the source of creation; **for whom** (*eis*—into), the flow-back of redeemed creation, suggesting the direction of our lives—we live for Him (cf. Rom. 11: 36; Eph. 4: 6); of **Christ: through whom** (*dia*—by means of), the medium of creation; **through whom we . . .,** the medium of the new creation (cf. 2 C. 5: 17; Col. 1: 15-20).

(b) The weak brother (8: 7-13)
While one scorned the very existence of idols and ate freely, another weak in the faith is encouraged to do what he feels to be wrong. He eats and for him the idol once again becomes a living reality. He stumbles, wounded, a spiritual wreck. For Paul his duty is clear; **I will never eat meat, lest I cause my brother to fall.**
7. not all possess this knowledge: Literally, 'this knowledge is not in all'. There is a difference between knowing theoretically (*oida*, vv. 1, 4) and having that knowledge in one as an activating reality. **accustomed to idols:** Suggests force of habit (note that the AV is based on an incorrect variant). Even though they are now Christian, habits formed over years of idol worship reawaken in their conscience old associations and sensations of the idol's power. **8, 9. Food will not commend us . . . :** The future tense

looks to the judgment. Food is amoral and of itself will bring neither approbation nor condemnation. What will be of consequence will be the misuse of their **liberty** (*exousia*, 'authority', 'right'). See Rom. 14: 13-20.
10. in an idol's temple: May refer to the occasion of some official function or festival. **encouraged:** Literally, 'built up', i.e., the weak man's conscience is built up to participate, to its own downfall. Note the ironical contrast with v. 1. They sought to build up with *knowledge; love* would build differently. **11. is destroyed** (*apollytai*): The present tense; his ultimate condition is not being discussed. 'spiritual disaster' (Phillips), 'ruined' (Moffatt), give the sense. Goudge comments, 'Every word helps to bring out the heinousness of the enlightened Christian's conduct. The weakness of the person injured, the greatness of the injury . . . his relation to the injured, the love of Christ for him, the means by which the injury is inflicted, all make the guilt greater.' Cf. Mt. 18: 6, 7. Many a Muslim and Hindu has trod this path. **12. sinning . . . wounding . . . sin against Christ:** The enormity of the sin is revealed. His brother was Christ's (cf. Mt. 25: 40, 45). **wounding:** The only metaphorical use of the verb in the NT. Note the three metaphors used concerning the **weak conscience: defiled** (7), **stumbling-block** (9), **wounding** (12). **13.** Paul's principle—avoid the cause of stumbling—is based on love, not knowledge. The two words stressed in this passage, **weak** (5 times) and **brother** (4 times), reveal a condition and relationship which should have evoked tenderness and love, but which received only the callous disregard of a misguided knowledge. See Rom. 14 for a fuller treatment of the subject.

(c) Paul's example (9: 1-27)
This chapter is not a digression written in self-defence, nor as some conclude, an insertion from some other letter. It is an illustration of the apostle's privileges as a freedman in Christ; privileges he did not use. The typical man of knowledge in Corinth insists on the full exercise of these rights (liberty—8: 9), riding rough-shod over the susceptibilities of the weak. Paul shows a better way, and the principle he enunciates in 8: 13 he demonstrates in daily conduct, a life which shows by its refusal to claim its rights, the exercise of the highest right of all—to **become all things to all men . . . to save some** (22).
(i) Paul's rights as an apostle (9: 1-14)
These rights were all the more reasonable in connection with the Corinthian church because of his special relationship with them (1, 2). He had a **right** to be supported by the local churches among whom he worked; the **right** to **food and drink** (4), the **right** to take around **a wife**

(5), the right to refrain from secular work (6). These are rights based not on mere expediency or personal desire, but on the practice of **other apostles** (5); on the analogies of human experience—the soldier, the farmer, the shepherd (7, 10); on the clear commands of the Mosaic Law (8, 9); on the recognized rights of the Levites in the Temple (13), and finally, on the explicit decree of Christ himself (14). God's servants called to full-time service, whoever or wherever they may be, are therefore the direct responsibility of God's churches. Every apostle was not called to be a Paul.

1. Am I not free: 'Not here as in Rom. 6: 18, 22, but from all external law of all kinds as in Gal. 4: 22-31; 5: 1; 1 Pet. 2: 16' (Parry). The thought is resumed in v. 19. **Have I not seen Jesus . . . :** A claim made all the more emphatic by the use of *ouchi* (**not**) in preference to the ordinary negative (*ouk*) of the preceding questions. The reference is primarily to the Damascus road experience (Ac. 9: 3, 17, 27; 22: 14), but see also Ac. 22: 17, 18 and Ac. 18: 9, where 'vision' is the same word as is used of the transfiguration in Mt. 17: 9. His ability to testify to the resurrection of Christ fulfilled in part the requirements for apostleship laid down in Ac. 1: 21, 22. **my workmanship** refers back to 3: 5-7, but it was **in the Lord,** for God gave the grace and the growth (3: 7b-9). **2. the seal of my apostleship:** Among other things the seal was the mark of authenticity. Their existence as a living church vindicated Paul's claim. **3.** may be taken with either the preceding or the following verses. If **defence** (*apologia*—a legal word as is **examine**) refers to the authenticity of his apostleship, it should be taken with vv. 1, 2. Most commentators take this view, as also Phillips and NEB. If however **defence** has to do with his contention concerning rights and freedom—the theme of the chapter— then it may legitimately commence a new paragraph as in the RSV. **4. the right to our food and drink:** Maintenance from those he serves. In using the plural Paul may be associating Barnabas with himself, cf. v. 6.

5. a wife: Undoubtedly the correct translation of *adelphēn gynaika;* cf. NEB. The churches would be responsible for the support of the woman as well as the man. **the brothers of the Lord:** Most probably the sons of Mary and Joseph (cf. Jn 7: 5; Ac. 1: 14; Gal. 1: 19), although the phrase could include a wider circle of relatives. The view that they were first cousins has been held by some Protestant expositors on grounds other than the Roman Catholic dogma of Mary's perpetual virginity. **6. only Barnabas and I: only** is singular (*monos*) referring to Paul, while **Barnabas** seems to be added as an

afterthought; 'I only—and Barnabas . . .' The inference is that all other apostles refrained from working for a living. Paul's practice of working with his hands would offend the Greek mind; cf. 4: 12; Ac. 18: 3; 1 Th. 4: 11; 2 Th. 3: 8-12. **7.** Each with his different status, the soldier— a wage-earner, the vine planter—an owner, the shepherd—probably a slave, had one thing in common: they derived their living from their occupation, a right Paul relinquished. **8. human authority:** Refers to v. 7, which Paul has argued from human analogies, but **the law** vindicates his claim. The quotation is from Dt. 25: 4. **9. Is it for oxen that God is concerned:** Calls for a negative answer (10). The suggestion that God is not concerned for the welfare of oxen is more apparent than real. God in His general providence cares for all creation, cattle, birds and even the grass of the field (cf. Ps. 145: 9; Mt. 6: 26, 30), yet the animal creation exists for man's benefit (cf. Gen. 1: 28). Paul considers that the allegorical significance of the text in Dt. 25: 4 completely outweighs its literal meaning. The verse is similarly applied in 1 Tim. 5: 18. **10. entirely** (*pantōs*) **for our sake:** May be rendered, 'doubtless, or clearly for our sake' (so RVmg, Knox and NEB). God's care for the oxen is not altogether excluded. **12. others:** May refer to Apollos, or Peter (5), or even suggest that there were resident teachers in Corinth supported by the church. Their claim was rightful and his even more so, cf. v. 2. **we have not made use of this right:** Anticipates Paul's arguments of vv. 15-23. **we endure** (*stegomen*): A verb expressive of Paul's character and used only by him in the NT. He would bear up under all pressures for the sake of others, cf. 13: 7 note; 1 Th. 3: 1, 5. **obstacle** (*enkopē*): Literally 'an incision', a word, notes Findlay, which became a military term in later Greek for breaking up a road to hinder the advance of an army. There must be no such obstacle in the way of the gospel. **13. Do you not know . . . :** Cf. 6: 15 note. The provision for **those who serve at the altar** is outlined in Lev. 7: 6, 8-10, 14, 28-36; Num. 18: 8-20; Dt. 18: 1-4. The Levite was supported by the things of the altar. He had his rights through which he lived. By the tithes of the people the work of God was supported— and when these were withheld the Levites were forced to till their fields (Neh. 13: 10). In response to Malachi's call to the people, the tithes were brought and the Temple service resumed, with consequent blessing for all. **14. In the same way:** Reveals the continuity which exists between OT and NT orders. **the Lord commanded:** Paul's final authority; cf. Mt. 10: 10; Lk. 10: 7. The case is proved; the care of God's servants is His people's concern.

(ii) Paul's rights assessed in relation to the needs of others (9: 15-23)

Having justified his claims, the apostle forthwith abandons them! All his carefully planned arguments in vv. 3-14 lead to the final declaration, **But I have made no use of any of these rights** (15). The underlying reason for Paul's statements must be borne in mind, that the Corinthians should learn through his example to be prepared to surrender their right to eat food offered to idols, in order that weaker brethren might not be stumbled. His abandonment of personal rights is for one purpose only; that the gospel may be presented freely (18). This is a right to claim and one of which to boast, the right to refuse all remuneration lest it blunt the edge of his message, causing misunderstandings among those he sought to reach (15-18).

That Paul was not paid for his work gave him independence, freedom of thought and action. Yet it was not a liberty to be selfishly employed, but rather a means to **win the more** (19). Whatever the condition of men, wherever he might find them, whether Jew or Gentile, he was free to identify himself with them in their need and so win them for Christ (19-23). Throughout these two paragraphs the overriding consideration with the apostle is: How can I best preach the gospel? How can I best bring others to Christ? He had learned the true relation of personal rights to Christian responsibility.

15. I would rather: Weakens the Greek. Paul is saying it were good (*kalon*), i.e., better for him to die than accept remuneration. **boasting:** In making the gospel free of charge (18), not in his personal ability to do so, for he received support from other churches in order to make it free in Corinth; cf. 2 C. 11: 7-10. There is no contradiction with Gal. 6: 13, 14 where Paul is refusing to boast of circumcision. See Rom. 5: 3; 1 C. 1: 31; 2 C. 11: 30; 12: 5, 9; 2 Th. 1: 4 for subjects in which Paul boasts. He never boasts on his own behalf; cf. 2 C. 12: 5. **16. necessity is laid upon me:** Paul *had* to preach; cf. Rom. 1: 14; Ac. 9: 15, 16; 26: 19. That was nothing to boast of. He was called to do so (2 Tim. 1: 11). He was a slave to obey (Gal. 1: 10—written in connection with preaching the gospel). **Woe to me:** The impulse of a quickened conscience, the knowledge of future judgment and the constraint of the love of Christ.

17 is rather obscure. **if I do this of my own will:** Could refer to ordinary teachers, not conscious of a particular call, but preaching because they wished to. Such would receive wages (*misthos*—reward). **if not of my own**

will would then refer to one such as Paul who acted, not on the basis of his own volition, but as **entrusted with a commission.** As such, his **reward** (wages) was not in the form of money, but the privilege of presenting the gospel freely (18). Perhaps it is better to understand both parts of the verse as referring to the slave under **necessity** to serve (16); he may preach willingly and receive the **reward** of v. 18, or even if unwilling, he is still not excused from his duty. Willing or unwilling, Paul could not escape his responsibility. **commission** (*oikonomia*): Stewardship. See 4: 1-4 in connection with stewards (*oikonomoi*). **18. make the gospel free of charge:** Paul's regular practice to which he frequently refers; cf. 1 Th. 2: 9; 2 Th. 3: 8; Ac. 20: 33-35; 2 C. 11: 7-12. This last reference explains **not making full use,** for he had accepted support, though not from Corinth. See also Phil. 4: 14-16.

19. that I might win the more: Paul's guiding principle, motivated by love. Nothing less could enable one who was **free** (see v. 1—not only in matters of support, but in all aspects of Christian experience) to make himself a **slave to all.** Here Paul returns in thought to 8: 1-3. His love which surrendered all rights would save, where their knowledge tenaciously defended would destroy. **20. I became as a Jew:** Illustrated by his circumcision of Timothy to avoid needless offence (cf. Ac. 16: 3; also 18: 18; 21: 18-26), but where Judaism conflicted with Christian revelation Paul was adamant (cf. Gal. 2: 4, 5). **those under the law:** As distinguished from the Jews, all who had accepted the Jewish religion, even Judaizing Christians who considered themselves bound by the Mosaic law. **not being myself under the law:** Although conformity is permitted where principles are not compromised, Paul is careful to emphasize his freedom from the law (*nomos*), which here undoubtedly means the Mosaic law as a whole; cf. Rom. 7: 4; Gal. 2: 19; 5: 18; Eph. 2: 15; Col. 2: 14. **21. to those outside the law:** The heathen. Peter similarly accommodated himself; cf. Gal. 2: 11-14. See also Ac. 17: 22-28 where Paul uses illustrations readily understood by the heathen mind. Yet Paul is **not without law to God.** He is not lawless. The **law of Christ** governs his conduct; cf. Rom. 8: 2-8; Gal. 6: 2; see also Jas 1: 25; 2: 12; Gal. 5: 13, 14.

22. To the weak I became weak: Reveals the extent of Paul's identification; he drops the **as** used of the other groups. The **weak** are undoubtedly included as a separate group in view of the theme of Paul's argument (8: 7-13). **all things to all men:** Never involved the abandonment of principle, but demonstrated the ability to enter the lives of others with the acutest understanding and sympathy. **have become:** Perfect tense, an accomplished fact still continuing to govern his life. **23. that I may share** (*synkoinōnos*): The noun expresses the experience of being a co-partner, the emphasis being not on getting, but *sharing* with others in the **blessings** of the gospel.

(iii) **The result (9: 24–27)**
To share in blessings is one thing, but to receive a **prize** is quite another. If the abandonment of personal rights and the identification of oneself with others for their spiritual blessing were desirable, then the Corinthians were sadly lacking. Not only would they fail to share with others in the blessing of the gospel to the extent that the apostle desired, but in the Christian race they were lagging far behind. As a stimulus to renewed consecration and effort, Paul gives yet another illustration. He makes two points; the motive for competing—to gain the prize, and the means employed—self control.

24. in a race: Paul draws on the Corinthians' knowledge of the Isthmian Games which were held every fifth year close by their city. He frequently has this metaphor of the athlete in mind; cf. Ac. 20: 24; Phil. 3: 12–14. **So run:** Run to win; why be an also-ran? Note Paul's example in 2 Tim. 4: 7. **25. self-control:** A basic requirement. Ten months of rigorous training preceded the Games. A thorough knowledge of the rules was demanded (2 Tim. 2: 5). If such discipline at best could yield a **perishable wreath,** how much more worthy of discipline is the **imperishable**? Cf. 2 Tim. 4: 8; Jas 1: 12; 1 Pet. 5: 4; Rev. 2: 10; 3: 11. **26. I do not run aimlessly . . . beating the air:** The athlete keeps his eye on the track, the boxer on his opponent. Every stride must be purposeful, every blow must count; cf. Phil. 3: 14; Heb. 12: 1, 2. **27. I pommel my body . . . :** Paul's greatest problem in the contest is himself. Distractions and hindrances arise chiefly from within. **body** (*sōma*): Here synonymous with bodily desires, the flesh, through which Satan so easily strikes; cf. Rom. 6: 6; 8: 3. Paul overcomes this, not through asceticism (Col. 2: 23), but by utter dedication in training, the constant employment of himself in the service of Christ. His approach is positive; cf. Gal. 5: 16; Phil. 1: 20–22. **disqualified** (*adokimos*): Paul's concern is lest he should lose, not his salvation, but the victor's wreath, the prize for which he has exhorted others to run.

(*d*) **Dangers of indulgence (10: 1–22)**
In using himself as an example Paul has demonstrated to the Corinthians the superiority of love over knowledge, the better course of relinquishing one's rights in order to help those in spiritual need. On these grounds alone it is better to refrain from eating meat offered to idols and so save the weak from stumbling. Yet a further and most cogent reason exists for abstaining from the meat of heathen sacrifices. The situation is such that eating food in idols' temples constitutes an unjustifiable temptation to become deeply involved in all the implications of pagan worship, which is the very antithesis of the Lord's Supper.

(i) **The example of Israel (10: 1–13)**
In spite of the great redemption of the Exodus and the miraculous deliverances and provisions of the wilderness wanderings, many Israelites perished (5). Lacking in self-control they fell into sin, of which Paul enumerates four instances: they became **idolators** (7), indulged in **immorality** (8), tested the Lord (9), grumbled and **were destroyed** (10). From this solemn lesson Corinth must learn (6, 11). Scornfully to reject the existence of idols and on the basis of this superior knowledge to eat sacrificial meat in the very temples where evil, corruption and immorality reign, is to court disaster (12). Undoubtedly, they will be invited and tempted to attend. Better by far to refuse, and see God make a way of escape for them (13).

1. RSV ignores 'for' (*gar*) with which the chapter commences, linking it with 9: 27. What the athlete won by discipline, the Israelites lost by indulgence. **our fathers:** The spiritual ancestors of all Christians, whether Jews or Gentiles. Note the emphasis on **all:** it occurs five times in these verses. Although the privileges extended to all, the majority abused them. **the cloud:** Cf. Exod. 13: 21, 22; 14: 19, 20; 40: 34–38; Num. 9: 15–23; 14: 14; Dt. 1: 33; Ps. 78: 14; 105: 39. **the sea:** Associated with the cloud in Exod. 13: 21; 14: 20. **2. baptized into Moses:** Passing through the cloud and sea they were united with their human leader and deliverer, Moses. This becomes a type of Christian baptism, figurative of our union with Christ; cf. Rom. 6: 3; Gal. 3: 27. The aorist middle may suggest the voluntary character of that baptism (cf. Ac. 22: 16). **3. supernatural food:** Literally 'spiritual food', i.e., manna (Exod. 16: 4, 16 ff.), of heavenly origin. **supernatural drink:** The water from the rock. **4. supernatural Rock:** Cf. Exod. 17: 6; Num. 20: 7 ff., identified as Christ. The whole history is spiritualized. The manna, the water and the rock, truly material, become subjects of divine miraculous provision. Paul's usage goes beyond a mere typological reference—**the Rock was Christ,** not 'is', or, 'is a type of'—and is a clear statement of the pre-existence of Christ. **followed:** Christ the Rock was constantly with His people, the true source of every provision. Note the use of 'Rock' as a divine name in the OT (Dt. 32: 4, 15, 18, 30, 31, 37; Ps. 18: 2, 31; Isa. 30: 29, etc.). **5. with most of them:** Contrasts strongly with the repeated 'all'. Only two who saw the Exodus survived. 'What a spectacle for the eyes of the self-satisfied Corinthians; all these bodies full-fed with miraculous nourishment, strewing the soil of the desert!' (Godet). **6. warnings for us:** Paul applies the lessons of history. *typoi* (**warnings**) is capable of various meanings; the mark of a blow (Jn 20: 25); the stamp of a die; a standard (Rom. 6: 17); a type (Rom. 5: 14); as here, an example for imitation or warning (Phil. 3: 17; 1 Th. 1: 7).

7. Do not be idolaters: A quotation from Exod. 32: 6 in connection with the worship of the golden calf. Such idolatrous festivals commonly included dancing and singing. In view of the trouble at Corinth (chapter 8), the warning is of primary importance. **8. immorality:** A temptation already assailing the church, associated as it was with Corinthian temple worship (chapters 5 and 6). Israel succumbed in similar conditions to idolatrous fornication; cf. Num. 25: 1–9. The tone of Paul's warning is softened by the use of the first person: **We must not indulge. 9. We must not put the Lord to the test:** Could fit a variety of circumstances, *e.g.*, the misuse of the Christian liberty in attending pagan feasts (14–22). **test** (*ekpeirazein*): Has a primary and secondary meaning; (i) to prove, as Abraham was tested (Heb. 11: 17); (ii) to test with the purpose of causing failure, hence to tempt. In the incident referred to (Num. 21: 5 ff.), God was put to the test, tried beyond measure, by the persistent ingratitude of His rebellious people.

10. nor grumble: Almost certainly refers to the incident of Korah (Num. 16: 41 ff.), where violent retribution ensued. **the Destroyer,** though not mentioned in the Numbers passage, is viewed by Paul as the agent of God's wrath, as in Exod. 12: 23. Findlay suggests that Paul had in mind the murmurings of jealous partisans and unworthy teachers in Corinth (cf. 1: 11, 12; 4: 6, 18 ff.). **11. upon whom the end of the ages has come:** Paul probably means that the end of 'this age' and the inauguration of 'the age to come' are being experienced by their generation; between the saving work of Christ and His parousia the two ages overlap (cf. Heb. 9: 26; Mt. 13: 39, 40, 49; 28: 20).

12. Therefore: The application is plain: **anyone who thinks that he stands**—the wise (3: 18), the rich (4: 8), the man of knowledge (8: 10)—**take heed. 13. no temptation** (*peirasmos*): Consolation after warning. It can be understood in the more general sense of 'trial' as

in NEB. The trials besetting the Corinthian church were indeed temptations to sin. Paul may have in mind the plea of some that they were forced to attend the temple feasts. Nevertheless, whatever the temptation—to idolatry, fornication, or any other—it is **common to man.** Theirs is no special case; the Israelites had it long before them. **God is faithful:** He can be trusted; cf. 1: 9; 1 Th. 5: 24; 2 Th. 3: 3; 2 Tim. 2: 13; 1 Pet. 4: 19. **beyond your strength:** As Christians; cf. 2 C. 12: 9, 10. **the way of escape** (*ekbasis*): Note the def. art.—every trial has its own particular God-given way of escape. **able to endure it:** Ability to endure is given **with the temptation,** not apart from it. The word is characteristic of the apostle's attitude to all forms of trial; cf. 2 Tim. 3: 10, 11.

(ii) **The implications of the Lord's Supper (10: 14–22)**

Paul has already conceded the point, at least academically, that an idol as such has no existence (8: 4). Idols as deities do not exist. He agrees with the Corinthians that indeed **there is no God but one.** This position he still maintains (10: 19), but clarifies the issue; sacrifices offered by pagans are not to deity, but **to demons.** Therefore, stipulates the apostle, it is better to keep away from pagan temple festivals. Think of the meal in which you share there and recall too the remembrance meal of the Lord's Supper. Just as we, by partaking of the bread and wine, identify ourselves with all that the death of Christ means, so by partaking in a temple meal you become partners with demons. The implication of eating meat at a heathen feast is analogous with the practice of Israel. They, eating the sacrifices, communed with God. To share in an idol sacrifice is to commune with demons. The two are incompatible. Is not this the very sin of putting God to the test (22)? Keep away from idols.

14. Therefore: Links the verse closely with v. 13 and suggests that idol feasts are the primary temptation Paul has in mind. **my beloved:** Cf. 4: 14; 15: 58; 2 C. 7: 1. His commands flow from deep affection. **shun the worship of idols:** As with immorality (6: 18), flight is the only sure way of escape. The phrase clearly refers to idol feasts. **15. sensible men** is void of all sarcasm. They could well appreciate Paul's arguments and understand the validity of his conclusion. **16. The cup of blessing:** A Hebraism, the name given to the third cup of the Passover feast over which a prayer of thanksgiving was pronounced. **blessing** (*eulogia*) therefore refers not to the cup but to the prayer over it. This is made clear by **which we bless** (*eulogoumen*), i.e., for which we give thanks; cf. Mt. 26: 26, 27; Mk 14: 22, 23; 1 C. 11: 23 ff.

participation (*koinōnia*): Variously rendered, 'communion', 'partnership', or 'fellowship'. It is used to express our relationships on a human level (cf. 2 C. 1: 7; 8: 4; Heb. 10: 33; 1 Jn 1: 7), as well as the divine (cf. 1: 9; Phil. 3: 10; 2 Pet. 1: 4; 1 Jn 1: 3). Participation on both levels may be expressed in terms of identification, or association of oneself with the object defined. Their very act of participation in the cup declared their association with the sacrificial death of Christ.

17. Because there is one bread . . . : Earlier RSV editions used 'loaf' in common with the RVmg and NEB. **Bread,** while a literal translation of the Greek, fails to express Paul's meaning as adequately as the idiomatic rendering 'loaf', which immediately conveys the impression of a single unit. Paul's concept of the unity of the body of Christ is clearly expressed through the analogy of the one loaf, a symbol preserved by many churches at the Lord's Supper. **many:** In diversity there is unity. This is developed in 12: 12-31; Eph. 4: 1-16; cf. Jn 1. 7.

18. Israel: Literally, 'Israel after the flesh'. The Israel of history is distinguished from the spiritual Israel of God; cf. Gal. 6: 16, also Phil. 3: 3. **partners in the altar:** The Jews in eating sacrifices from the altar associate themselves with all that the altar signifies. Eating at pagan sacrificial feasts was analogous with this (20, 21). **20. to demons and not to God:** Possibly a quotation from Dt. 32: 17. Robertson and Plummer and also Grosheide suggest that as in Dt. 32: 17 **God** should be rendered 'god', *ou theō* having the force of 'to a no-god'; cf; Dt. 32: 21. This improves the sense. **demons:** The real force behind all pagan religion; attested not only by the OT and NT, but by missionary experience. Idolatry is a medium through which satanic power is particularly manifest; cf. 1 Jn 5: 19, 21. **21. You cannot drink:** Not the physical impossibility, but the moral and spiritual incompatibility of participation in the **table of the Lord** and the **table of demons.** The respective hosts are clearly demonstrated by these genitives. To partake of both the Lord's Supper and heathen feasts (21) must inevitably **provoke the Lord to jealousy.** This phrase is reminiscent of Dt. 32: 21, referred to in v. 20. **the Lord:** Almost certainly a reference to Christ, to preserve the continuity of thought from the previous verse—another instance of the freedom with which the apostle applies to the Lord Jesus OT references to Jehovah; cf. 1: 31; 2: 16. **Are we stronger than he:** Israel could not stand before the might of Jehovah (6-10). The Corinthians have still to learn their essential weakness; cf. v. 12.

396

(*e*) **Practical guidance (10: 23-11: 1)**
Paul brings together the threads of his arguments on the subject of eating meat offered to idols. Three canons of conduct emerge, each applicable to differing circumstances. (i) Eating at heathen festivals involves idolatry and is unconditionally condemned (14-22). (ii) Eating whatever is sold in the market, regardless of its origin, is unreservedly permitted (25). (iii) Eating in a pagan friend's house is similarly sanctioned, except when the sacrificial origin of the meat is pointed out. This conditional prohibition is not on the grounds of involvement in idolatry, but merely out of consideration for the informant (27-29). The controlling motive is twofold; a desire for the glory of God, and the blessing of men (31-33).

23. All things are lawful: See 6: 12 note. **not all things build up:** Recalls the basic principle enunciated at the commencement of this section; cf. 8: 1. **24. the good of his neighbour:** Recalls the command of Christ; cf. Mt. 22: 39; Lk. 10: 27-37. It is the fundamental guide for social conduct in both the OT and NT. **25-27** are directed against over-scrupulousness. When shopping in the **meat market,** or eating in the home of **one of the unbelievers,** no question should be asked. **For 'the earth is the Lord's . . .':** A quotation from Ps. 24: 1 and Paul's justification for the advice just given, agreeing with our Lord's pronouncement in Mk 7: 14-19; cf. Ac. 10: 15; 1 Tim. 4: 4. **28. But if some one:** Possibly the heathen host, but more probably a fellow-guest—a weaker brother, as it is his conscience which is the more likely to suffer. The informant uses the regular pagan word for **offered in sacrifice** (*hierothyton*), either out of respect for the host, or as one recently converted, who still thinks in terms of his old life.

29. I mean his conscience . . . do not eat: Exemplifies the principle of v. 24. Vv. 29b and 30 seem to be out of sympathy with Paul's preceding statement. To avoid this RSV has placed vv. 28, 29a in brackets, making 29b refer to v. 27. Little is gained by such a reconstruction. The meaning of Paul's statement depends on the translation of *hina ti gar*, **For why . . . ?** *hina ti* never means 'by what right' but 'for what purpose'. Accordingly, Findlay translates, 'For what purpose is my liberty judged by another conscience?' i.e., 'What good end will be served by my eating under these circumstances, and exposing my freedom to the censure of an unsympathetic conscience?' Similarly, the second rhetorical question, **If I partake . . .** (30), is rendered, 'Why incur blame for food for which I give thanks . . . ?' (Robertson and Plummer). In asking these two questions Paul puts himself in the place of the strong brother who must recognize the futility of insisting on his liberty and giving thanks, when his action can only result in offence and denunciation by the weaker brother. NEB and Phillips treat the two questions as objections raised by the strong Christian, the answer to these objections being supplied in vv. 31 ff. Undoubtedly, Rom. 14: 16 is the key to the correct understanding of these verses. **with thankfulness:** Literally, by grace. If the AV and RV reading is followed, it suggests that the strong partake only by the enabling grace of God. Modern versions follow the RSV. Both translations are legitimate and make good sense. **31. the glory of God:** The overriding consideration. This extends beyond the immediate subject to **whatever you do;** cf. 6: 20. **32. Give no offence:** Literally, cause of stumbling; cf. 8: 9. It summarizes Paul's attitude to unconverted Jews and Greeks; cf. 9: 19-22. **the church of God:** The sing. noun may refer to those in the local congregation at Corinth (1: 2), but is probably used in its widest significance, as in 11: 22; 15: 9. **33. to please all men:** Not to be understood as currying favour (cf. Gal. 1: 10) but in terms of his sympathetic understanding of others' needs as in 9: 19-22, with the consequent abandoning of his own rights and privileges, i.e., **not seeking my own advantage. 11: 1. Be imitators:** In that attitude of self-sacrifice for the salvation of others (10: 33) which characterized Paul and Christ. **of me:** Cf. 4: 16; Phil. 3: 17; 1 Th. 1: 6. **of Christ:** The supreme example; cf. Rom. 15: 2, 3; 2 C. 8: 7-9; Eph. 5: 2; Phil. 2: 4-7.

V. DISORDERS IN PUBLIC WORSHIP (11: 2-34)

i. Veiling of women (11: 2-16)

Paul now deals with the subject of public worship. The first matter requiring attention, that of the veiling of women, reflects a situation commonly misunderstood in western culture. Underlying Paul's reasoning is the principle of subjection. Woman's subjection to man is understood not in the sense of inequality, or inferiority, but in terms of Christ's relation to God. This position of subjection was expressed by the **veil** and the **long hair** worn by women; a custom consistently followed in much of Asia and the Middle East from the dawn of history to the present day. To break with such a convention is deemed **disgraceful,** being a revolt against the dictates of nature and accepted conduct. The problem which exists for those who seek to interpret the text lies in determining to what extent the apostle is teaching conformity with local concepts of subordination and pro-

priety and the degree to which Christians today should conform to the letter of these instructions. One thing is certain; within the context of our contemporary culture, the modern western hat—decorative, attractive and often obstructive—cannot be said to compare with the veil, either in appearance, function, or purpose. At best it is a token veil. Its significance when taught in the church is valuable, but in common thought the hat is no longer the local means of expressing subordination. To what extent must local churches modify their traditional modes of worship in the light of a changing culture? That western culture has no means of expressing woman's subordination—having abandoned the concept—is perhaps the strongest argument for the retention of the 'token' veil, signifying a divinely appointed status. To be quietly, though not dowdily, dressed in all aspects of one's person is perhaps the most effective way in our western culture of fulfilling the injunctions and principles of this section.

2. I commend you: There is no contradiction with v. 17. In general, the traditions—the delivered instructions (cf. 11: 23; 15: 3; 2 Th. 2: 15; 3: 6)—had been faithfully kept. That they wrote to Paul concerning their problems indicates their desire to conform with his instructions. **3. head:** Symbolic of authority, supremacy. **man:** Male, not mankind. **the head of every man is Christ:** Cf. Eph. 1: 22; 4: 15; 5: 21-33; Col. 1: 18; 2: 19. **the head of every woman is her husband:** Cf. Col. 3: 18; 1 Pet. 3: 1. **the head of Christ is God:** Cf. Jn 14: 28; 1 C. 3: 23; 15: 27, 28. These three statements express partnership as clearly as subordination (cf. v. 11). NEB legitimately translates, 'While every man has Christ for his Head, woman's head is man as Christ's Head is God.' It is subordination among partners; man is to woman as God is to Christ, but not as Christ is to man. **4. with his head covered:** In corporate worship the male has no visible superior. Therefore a head covering would be improper. It is not suggested that men were acting in this way; the statement gives point to the censure on women who were acting like men. **dishonours his head:** Almost certainly a reference to his own physical head, but an allusion to Christ cannot altogether be excluded. The uncovered head was contrary to Jewish custom, although, in fact, it was an optional matter at the time. For Paul, the head covering of the Jewish male possibly symbolized his continuance in spiritual darkness from which the Christian had been liberated. Now in worship he need not be veiled (the woman remains veiled only as a sign of her subordination to man). Logically therefore, a Jew or Muslim attending Christian worship should not be required to remove his headwear for 'the veil remains unlifted' (2 C. 3: 13 f.). **prophesies:** Cf. 12: 10. **5. any woman who prays and prophesies . . . :** Suggests that women took part in public worship in Corinth. Paul makes no comment concerning the practice; he is dealing with the veil, not the ministry of women (cf. 14: 34; 1 Tim. 2: 12). There is nothing in the text to indicate that they took part only in informal meetings, in sisters' meetings, or in family prayers and not in the general meetings of the church. Feeling the compulsion to pray or prophesy, the women would find it easier to take part without the encumbrance of a veil and might be tempted to throw it aside. **dishonours her head:** Either shames her own head, or dishonours her husband. In either case she abandons that expression of subjection which contemporary custom demands of her. Ordinarily, in any public place a woman was veiled. In an immoral society like Corinth any act of impropriety must be sternly checked. **shaven:** Literally, *the* shaven. The def. art. denotes the class to which such a woman would belong. This may refer to her putting herself in the same category as a male, or, as David Smith renders it, being 'the same thing as the shaved adulteress'.

6. she should cut off her hair (middle voice): If she discards her veil like a man, she should crop her head like one too! Paul makes his point in the strongest terms. **7. man ought not** (*ouk opheilei*) **to cover his head:** He is under moral obligation to be bare-headed, as is the woman to be veiled (*opheilei*, v. 10). **glory:** Man as the crown of God's creation honours and magnifies Him (cf. Ps. 8: 5, 6; Gen. 1: 26, 28). In the OT the reference is to mankind, i.e., men and women (*Heb. 'adam*, Gk *anthrōpos*), that is, the crown of God's creation. Here, Paul using *anēr* refers only to the male, not with the intention of degrading the woman, but with the purpose of defining her relationship to man—she is **the glory of man.** This he further clarifies in vv. 8 and 9. **woman is the glory of man:** Being formed from him (cf. v. 8; Gen. 2: 22, 23). **9.** vv. 8 and 9 are parenthetical, as indicated by RSV. The creation of **woman for man** is clearly stated in Gen. 2: 18. God's purpose, not only in Christ (3), and social custom (5b, 6), but also in creation itself is to give woman a position of subjection.

10 presents two major problems of translation and interpretation: (i) the meaning of **veil.** The word here is *exousia*, authority. While the context might suggest that this be interpreted as 'a sign of being under authority',

i.e., 'a veil', the word itself suggests that it is rather 'a sign of her own authority'. A study of life among veiled women in Asia reveals that both aspects of the word are true and that in experience no contradiction exists. The concept fundamental to all cultures utilizing the veil, is the subjection of woman to man. Yet within the realm of subjection, the woman has a place of authority, dignity, respect and security. This is provided by the veil itself which preserves her dignity in contrast to the unveiled woman whose bare face is the evidence of loose morals, or the general shamelessness of western habits. Many Muslim women confess to a feeling of utter nakedness and shame on being seen without a veil; the veil is their greatest right and security. Paul argues from a somewhat similar background. For a Corinthian woman to throw off her veil in church was not only to deny her subjection, but to abandon her dignity. (ii) **because of the angels:** A phrase variously interpreted—(*a*) that the angels are present in worship and will observe their conduct and be offended. That they do observe human conduct, see Lk. 15: 7, 10. (*b*) because they might tempt the angels (cf. Gen. 6: 1, 2). (*c*) because the angels do so, i.e. veil themselves, as in Isa. 6: 2. This is an attractive interpretation. **11, 12** are parenthetical, but preserve the balance of Paul's argument, proving that woman is not inferior to man. Throughout, the apostle is reasoning not on the basis of her inferiority, but of her partnership with man. Neither is **independent** of the other and as Christians—**in the Lord**—this relationship is enhanced. In Christ the submissive wife is not despicable. **all things are from God:** Woman was made from man, but now he is born of her—and God makes both. **13, 14. Judge for yourselves:** A final appeal based on humanity's sense of propriety instilled by **nature itself. is it proper:** I.e., becoming, natural. **long hair is degrading to him:** Paul argues within the limits of his location and period. Differing cultures have had differing concepts as to what is fitting, but as a generalization the statement is still true. Most men, whether eastern or western, wear their hair short in contrast to their womenfolk. **15. if a woman has long hair, it is her pride:** Still true in general. Asian women usually regard the length of their hair with pride. Even within a western culture a woman's hair is kept longer than a man's. Yet the limitation too of such generalizations must be recognized. The average African woman is singularly bereft of this source of pride; this is neither the physical nor cultural pattern by which she can demonstrate, through this natural **covering,** the principle of subjection.

16. we recognize no other practice: Adds finality to the argument. Any deviation from the apostle's ruling could only be interpreted as an exhibition of brazen disregard for the accepted codes of conduct by the women of his day. The principle endures; women should show clearly their subjection. The means of expression will vary according to the race and culture in which the church is planted.

ii. The Lord's Supper (11: 17-34)

(a) Its abuse (11: 17-22)

However well the traditions had been maintained in other aspects of their corporate life, their assembling as a church for the Lord's Supper had been sadly marred by their deep-seated factions which revealed themselves in the formation of cliques or parties. The fellowship meal, itself designed to be a demonstration of unity in Christ (10: 16, 17), degenerated into an unholy free-for-all, in which the memory of their Lord became blurred beyond all recollection before the poverty of one and the gluttony of another. The prosperous ignored the poor; the practice of fellowship was forgotten. Such humiliation of the needy could only increase their divisions, while their despicable disregard for the church of God inevitably earned divine retribution. The love feast was dead.

17. I do not commend you: In v. 2 they could be praised, but here where basic Christian instincts should have sufficed, Paul could not commend. **when you come together:** Their corporate worship is marred. The verb is used three times; see vv. 18, 20. **for the worse:** Defined in vv. 18-21 by the terms **divisions, factions, each one goes ahead,** etc.: the very antithesis of corporate fellowship. **18. there are divisions** (*schismata*): They had developed (see 1: 10-13) far beyond cliques confined to private homes, a mere undercurrent of unrest. The church was visibly rent (21). Note Robertson and Plummer's rendering, 'I continually hear (present tense) that dissensions among you prevail' (*hyparchein*, not simply the verb 'to be'). **19. there must be** (*dei*): '*dei* affirms a necessity lying in the moral conditions of the case' (Findlay). Corinth being what it was, Paul acknowledges the inevitability of this. See NEB. **factions** (*haireseis*): Basically, a wilful choosing of one's own line independent of other authorities; cf. Tit. 3: 10. *hairesis* differs little from *schisma*, but perhaps signifies the attitude of mind which produces it. The self-willed by their **factions** reveal those who are **genuine** (*dokimoi*—those who have been tried and have stood the test). Compare *adokimos*, 9: 27—'disqualified'. **20. not the Lord's supper:** Rather, their own. The disorders make it a travesty of the true. **21. one**

goes ahead . . .: Indicates clearly that an actual meal was envisaged. The early church observed this practice of the common meal, known as the *agapē*, or 'love-feast'; cf. 2 Pet. 2: 13, RSVmg; Jude 12. **one is hungry and another is drunk:** The division of poor and rich. There was no sharing of food, contrary to the custom of the common meal. **drunk:** Must be given its usual meaning of intoxication; cf. Mt. 24: 49; Jn 2: 10; Ac. 2: 15; 1 Th. 5: 7. **22. Do you not have houses . . .:** I.e., if the purposes of the love-feast are abandoned—the expression of mutual love through the shared out food, culminating in the remembrance of Christ's great act of love—then it is better to eat at home.

(b) Its institution (11: 23-26)

In marked contrast to the deplorable display of personal greed and humiliation at the common meal, Paul reminds his readers of the solemn simplicity with which the Lord Jesus had ordained this act of remembrance. This record is the earliest extant written account of our Lord's institution of the ordinance.

23. I received from the Lord . . . I . . . delivered . . .: A direct revelation to Paul is not implied. The two verbs *paralambanō* and *paradidōmi* are not words used for receiving and communicating a direct revelation, but for transmission in a chain from one to another. The tradition stems from the words of Jesus Christ himself in the upper room; that is what is meant by **from the Lord.** Leon Morris seeks to demonstrate the possibility of a direct revelation from the use of the preposition *apo* (**from**), citing Col. 1: 7; 3: 24 and 1 Jn 1: 5. It is, however, the particular verbs used, rather than the preposition, which determine the interpretation. There was no need for a supernatural communication; the facts were readily available to Paul. More important, Paul had already **delivered** this communication to the Corinthians. They had no excuse. **24. given thanks:** Used by Luke, while Matthew and Mark have 'blessed'. Both words refer to the same prayer of thanksgiving. **'This is my body'** has become the main support for Roman and Lutheran views of transubstantiation and consubstantiation, views rendered vulnerable by the fact that the Supper preceded the Passion. Christ himself was physically present. His words were symbolical and a similar usage of **is** may be found in Jn 8: 12; 10: 9, etc. See the note on Mt. 26: 26. **Do this:** A present imperative conveying the idea of continuity. Just as the Passover had been a memorial of Israel's deliverance from Egypt, so the Supper is to be an act of remembrance. **25. the new covenant** (*hē kainē diathēkē*): Found only once in the LXX in Jer. 31: 31; Christ probably had this reference in mind. While *diathēkē* is used regularly in Greek for a will (cf. Heb. 9: 15-18, RSV), LXX uses it consistently for 'covenant.' The choice of *diathēkē* rather than *synthēkē* is significant. The latter is a covenant in which the parties contract on equal terms, whereas in the former one party only lays down all the conditions (hence its use also for a will). This is the relation between God and man. There is no **new covenant** without the **blood.** Hebrews expounds the association; cf. Heb. 9 and 10. (Consult the exposition of Heb. 9: 15 ff. for a fuller treatment of the subject.) **my:** Emphatic. **26. as often as:** Gives no directive as to how often, though a frequent remembrance is implied. In Ac. 20: 7 it was arranged for Sunday evening. The first day of the week may well have been the convenient and regular time for its observance. **you proclaim** (pres. indic.): The breaking of bread is a continual proclamation of the Lord's death; not an act of mourning, but an occasion of living hope **until he comes.**

(c) **Warnings and instructions (11: 27-34)**
The apostle warns his readers. While the Supper may be a fitting climax to the spiritual fellowship of the *agapē*, it is not to be the culmination of a carousal. Neither may its celebration be marred by divisions, whether expressed in the contempt of the rich for the poor, or in party spirit. **As often** may be too often for the man or woman who with that contempt born of undue familiarity ceases to **examine** his own spiritual condition. Such conduct can only court **judgment** and to some in Corinth retribution has already come. Sober self-examination preserves from condemnation.

27. an unworthy manner: Caused through the lack of love, factious spirit, greed and contempt which Paul has been rebuking so strongly. **guilty of profaning . . . :** The guilt is not primarily against fellow-believers, great as that is, but against the person of Christ symbolized in the elements (cf. Ps. 51: 4). **28. examine:** I.e., let a man test himself. It calls for a minute scrutiny of heart and motives to ascertain one's moral and spiritual condition before partaking. Note its usage in 2 C. 13: 5; Gal. 6: 4. **29. without discerning the body: the body** is held by some commentators to refer to the church (so also Moffatt and NEB). Others understand it in terms of the Lord's Supper as in v. 27. Both interpretations make good sense. *diakrinein* (to discern) is rendered **judge truly,** rightly, in v. 31. It seems to carry this basic idea in v. 29. One who judges rightly will distinguish, discriminate. Therefore, depending on the significance given to **the body,** one who participates without due self-examination does not distinguish between the Lord's Supper (the

body) and an ordinary meal, or alternatively, does not discern the true character of the Body, the Church. **judgment:** Not final condemnation (cf. v. 32), but a very definite punishment according to the measure of guilt (30). **30. That is why . . . :** A direct connection exists between their sickness and death, and the judgment of the previous verse. **31. if we judged ourselves truly:** An unfulfilled condition. The verb is used almost synonymously with **examine** in v. 28. Absence of self-judgment necessitates divine judgment. **ourselves:** Emphatic. **32. we are chastened:** Implies discipline for the purpose of improvement. God's judgment of His children is remedial (cf. Ps. 94: 12; Prov. 3: 11, 12; Heb. 12: 5-11; see also 1 C. 5: 3-5), even though it involved sickness and death. **the world** (*kosmos*): Here, all that is at enmity with God, destined to be condemned; cf. 1 Jn 5: 19. **33, 34.** The practical remedy lies with them. **wait for one another:** Satisfy your hunger **at home:** these are correctives to vv. 21, 22, which, together with the self-examination already demanded, will create a proper atmosphere for the Lord's Supper. **About the other things:** Probably questions from the Corinthians' letter which were still outstanding, in addition to less important details concerning love-feasts and the remembrance service.

VI. SPIRITUAL GIFTS (12: 1-14: 40)
The background of rivalry, envy and division in Corinth must be constantly borne in mind. In conditions where the base qualities of party spirit were apparent, where moral standards were disregarded, where women emulated men and the rich despised the poor, the apostle could write, **you are not lacking in any spiritual gift** (1: 7). In this also their rivalry and envy were evident. The possession of spiritual gifts and the attainment of moral stature were not yet related in experience. To remedy this inconsistency is Paul's main purpose in these three chapters. In chapters 12 and 13 he lays down the general principles involved—the place of gifts and the power of love—while in chapter 14 he deals with specific details.

i. Varieties of gifts (12: 1-11)
Moving forward from his introductory statement that genuine expressions of spiritual gifts may be discerned by the loyalty of the utterance to Jesus Christ (1-3), the apostle establishes that the gifts in all their variety emanate from the one **Spirit of God.** He overrules, and in granting these experiences individually to whomsoever He wishes, removes the ground for envying and aping another's experience.

1. Now concerning: Probably another matter raised in the Corinthians' letter; cf.

7: 1, 25; 8: 1; 16: 1. **I do not want you to be uninformed:** A phrase regularly introducing an important subject in Paul's writings; cf. 10: 1; Rom. 1: 13; 11: 25; 2 C. 1: 8; 1 Th. 4: 13. **2. led astray** (*apagomenoi*): Has the sense of leading away by force; cf. Mt. 26: 57; 27: 2, 31. The agent is not specified. As with **however you may have been moved,** the suggestion is that of the domination of the power of evil. **3.** In sharp contrast to v. 2, the motivating influence here is the **Spirit of God. 'Jesus be cursed!'** (*anathema*): The word itself was the equivalent of the Hebrew *ḥerem*, signifying anything that was devoted to God for destruction as under His curse (as Achan in Joshua's camp). The expression would most likely come from a Jew and in all probability had been frequently used by Paul himself in his unregenerate state (cf. 1 Tim. 1: 13). Possibly, he and other Jews had sought to give scriptural authority to these words by appealing to Dt. 21: 23. The blasphemy he tried to make believers utter (Ac. 26: 11) may have been 'Jesus is anathema'. It is not necessary to assume that someone at Corinth in ecstatic utterance had spoken these words, although the matter is put forward so specifically that this might well have occurred. In either case, Paul is assuring the believers that the controlling **Spirit** will not lead men into blasphemy. Similarly, **'Jesus is Lord'** is a real confession, clearly distinguishing the Christian from the Jews and pagans around him. As a confession this is frequently used in the NT; cf. Rom. 10: 9; 2 C. 4: 5; Phil. 2: 11. **4. varieties** (*diaireseis*): Occurs nowhere else in the NT. Here it is possibly used in the sense of apportionings, or distributions, as suggested by the use of the verb in v. 11. In the LXX it is regularly used for the 'courses' of the priests. **gifts** (*charismata*): A typically Pauline word (used only once by any other NT writer, 1 Pet. 4: 10), signifying special endowments of the Spirit to men. A 'grace-gift', it is taken from the same root as *charis*—grace. For a full discussion, see Sanday and Headlam, *Romans, ICC*, pp. 358 f. **5. service** (*diakonia*): The use of the gift. The word, cognate with *diakonos*, 'servant', is used frequently of the work of the apostles and other believers; cf. Eph. 4: 12; Rom. 11: 13; Col. 4: 17; 2 C. 4: 1; Rom. 15: 31; 1 C. 16: 15. Note the strong trinitarian emphasis in connection with the distribution of spiritual gifts in the church: **the same Spirit** (4) . . . **Lord** (5) . . . **God** (6). Distinctions between the functions of the Godhead, in **gifts, service** and **working,** must not be pressed. Just as these are complementary ideas expressing one complete experience, so **Spirit, Lord** and **God** emphasize unity of function; cf. 2 C. 13: 14; Eph. 4: 3-6.

6. working (*energēmatōn*): The energizing of the gift, it conveys the idea of power, cf. v. 10. **7. To each:** Spiritual gifts are not to the select few. **the manifestation of the Spirit:** May mean, 'that which the Spirit makes manifest', or 'that which manifests the Spirit' (as NEB), depending on whether the genitive is taken as objective or subjective. Both refer to the spiritual gift; one as producing it, the other revealing Him through it. The **common good** is in view, not the advantage or self-glorification of the gifted individual. Vv. 8-11 enumerate the gifts for the **common good. 8. utterance of wisdom:** Not easily distinguished from **utterance of knowledge.** While the latter indicates an intelligent grasp of Christian principles and facts, the former expresses an understanding of their application, a spiritual insight into the principles. **9. to another faith:** Not a reference to saving faith possessed by all Christians, but to the special gift of 'mountain-moving' faith that defies the 'impossible'; cf. 13: 2; Mt. 17: 20; 21: 21. As in one sense all have knowledge (8: 1), so all have faith, but not of the order of *charismata*. **gifts of healing:** Frequently evident in the NT period and used by Paul himself; cf. Ac. 19: 11, 12; 20: 9-12. Both nouns are plural, suggesting possibly gifts for a variety of healings demanded by different diseases. **10. working of miracles:** See note on **working** (6). Accordingly, **miracles** were most evidently acts of power. Such instances are recorded in Ac. 5: 1-11; 13: 11. **prophecy:** Primarily not foretelling, but telling forth the Word of God with power to meet a specific need (cf. 14: 1; Rom. 12: 6; 1 Th. 5: 20; 1 Tim. 1: 18; 4: 14). This was the function of both OT and NT prophets. However, the element of prediction must not be excluded. **to distinguish between spirits:** An attitude demanded of all believers (1 Th. 5: 20, 21; 1 Jn 4: 1), but a gift granted only to some. **various kinds of tongues** and **the interpretation of tongues:** These come at the end of Paul's list although their use was probably the most prized in the Corinthian church. As one of the *charismata* the gift of tongues was supernatural and therefore does not refer to human languages, which could be learned and interpreted without divine aid, but rather to an ecstatic experience granted to some, not all. This is a miraculous spiritual language for communion with God. The plural **kinds** points to considerable variation within this experience. While some speakers could also interpret (14: 5, 13), to others it was a separate gift (14: 27, 28). The subject is also dealt with in chapter 14. **11. one and the same Spirit:** Responsible for all these gifts. Paul's constant repetition in vv. 4, 5, 6, 8, 9 of their single divine source suggests that their attainment should not be the subject of rivalry or jealousy, for the divine distribution is **as he wills.** Note that the personality of the Spirit is implied here.

ii. Unity in diversity (12: 12–31)
Just as the gifts are many, but the Giver one, so the recipients, varied and dissimilar in quality and function, form one organic whole. This Paul states briefly (12, 13), and demonstrates through the illustration of the human body (14–26). The apostle argues (i) no one can opt out of the body on the ground of dissatisfaction, or jealousy for a 'higher' gift. The body's constitution demands their God-given function (14–20), (ii) there is mutual dependence through-out the body (21, 22), (iii) there must be mutual respect and care. Sympathetic understanding produces true harmony (23–26). The remaining verses (27–31) apply the illustration to the church, the varieties of gift being restated, with a series of rhetorical questions indicating the chaotic condition which would result from all the believers exercising the same gift. Unity in diversity creates a balanced body. This analogy is used frequently by the apostle (cf. Rom. 12: 4, 5; Eph. 4: 16; 5: 30; Col. 2: 19).

12. so it is with Christ: As in the human body, members of Christ are indissolubly associated with Him. They are a new creation (2 C. 5: 17; Eph. 4: 22–24), His life is theirs (Gal. 2: 20), they constitute His body (Eph. 1: 23). The same truth was taught by Christ in the figure of the vine (Jn 15: 1–8). **13. by one Spirit we were all baptized . . .: by** (*en*) is rendered in the RV and NEB as 'in', indicating the sphere in which baptism takes place (the same prep. *en* is similarly used in Mt. 3: 11 and is translated 'with water' and 'with the Holy Spirit', i.e., they are to be immersed in the Spirit as in water). **baptized:** May refer not to the rite, but to the act of regeneration in the Spirit to which the ordinance bears witness. **made to drink of one Spirit:** A parallel statement, in purely figurative language, symbolic of the indwelling of the Spirit at the new birth; cf. 3: 16; Eph. 1: 13. **made to drink:** Conveys the idea of being saturated or imbued with one Spirit; an 'irrigation' of one's inner life by the Spirit of God. **all:** Constantly contrasted with **one**; the extreme diversity of background, character and gift at Corinth find absolute unity in the Church—the body. **14.** In the body diversity is not a problem to be overcome, but is essential for its existence. **15, 16.** The **foot** envying the **hand** and the **ear** the **eye,** probably reflect the condition of the weaker members in the Corinthian church envying the apparently higher and more responsible members with

their spectacular gifts. **17.** A **body** all **eye** or **ear** not only eliminates other necessary functions, but ceases to be a body: the conclusion arrived at in v. 19. **18. God arranged the organs . . . as he chose:** The aorists are preserved in RSV, pointing to God's design of the human frame in creation. The believer's particular function in the church is the result of divine planning. Discontent can only result in deformity. **each one:** No believer, however lowly, lacks a God-given gift. **21. 'I have no need of you':** The attitude of those possessing the apparently superior or more spectacular gifts, in contrast to the lowly members of vv. 15–20. The **head** cannot afford to look down on the **feet,** for without them she is rapidly reduced to the same lowly level; the body crippled. Independence cannot exist in the body of Christ. **22. weaker parts:** Only **seem to be** so. Their intrinsic worth, purely as part of the body, makes them **indispensable.** This applies with even greater force to **which we think** in v. 23. These members are not specified and indeed would vary in different cultures. **23. we invest with the greater honour:** Probably refers to clothing, with which parts considered **less honourable** and **unpresentable** were covered. The verb **invest** is used of clothing in Mt. 27: 28. **24. presentable:** Literally, well-formed, not needing the adornment of clothes. **God has so adjusted the body:** His sovereign choice (18) is matched by His tender care, an attitude to be emulated in Corinth. **25. that:** Introduces a *hina* clause denoting the purpose for which God has balanced the body, giving **greater honour to the inferior part.** It is to eliminate **discord** and to inculcate mutual **care:** the two great needs of the believers in Corinth. **discord** (*schisma*): Immediately recalls the primary problem broached in 1: 10 (see also 11: 18), there translated 'dissensions'. A humble acceptance of God's appointments in the body (27–31) will restore harmony. **the same care for one another:** Might be rendered more strongly 'anxiety', 'thoughtful trouble'. **26** expresses an organic necessity. Pain cannot be isolated; sensations transmitted to the brain affect in measure the whole being. Whether expressed in terms of suffering or rejoicing, this is the Christian law of sympathy—to 'feel with' another. **27. you are the body of Christ: you** is emphatic. The divided Corinthians in spite of their shortcomings are undeniably 'Christ's body' (NEB), for they were 'all baptized into' it (13), and are **individually members of it.** The objective now is a balanced body (28–31) and its attainment depends on their individual response to the Spirit's choice for them (11). **28. God has appointed:** Note the divine sovereignty (18,

24). The verb is middle, indicating His own purpose. **the church:** Clearly the Church Universal. **first . . . second . . . third:** The ranking of gifts in order of honour, an order maintained in Eph. 4: 11; see also Rom. 12: 6-8; Eph. 2: 20; 3: 5. **apostles:** Not restricted to the Twelve, but including Barnabas, James the Lord's brother (Gal. 1: 19), Paul and lesser known figures (Rom. 16: 7); cf. 1 C. 15: 5, 7 indicating a wider group than the Twelve. While **prophets** and **teachers** were not necessarily apostles, apostles were both prophets and teachers, cf. 4: 17; 14: 6; Col. 1: 28; 1 Tim. 1: 11. **teachers:** Closely linked with pastors (Eph. 4: 11) and would bear considerable responsibility on the local level for building up the church through the exposition of the Word of God. **workers of miracles . . . healers:** See note on vv. 9, 10. **helpers:** The noun is found nowhere else in the NT, but occurrences of the verb (Ac. 20: 35; Rom. 8: 26) suggest helping particularly the weak and needy. Deacons may also have had a part in this responsibility. **administrators:** Derived from the idea of piloting a boat. Steersmanship in the local church was a gift demanded of elders. Note that these verses deal with gifts, not offices. The officer in the church officiated by reason of his gifts. **tongues:** See v. 10 and chapter 14. **29, 30** enforce the argument in typically Pauline style, stressing the necessity for diversity. All the questions demand negative replies. **31. earnestly desire the higher gifts:** Not in the evil sense of the verb ('envy', 13: 4). This they had done (cf. 3: 3). Rather, they were to desire the higher gifts from higher motives, being anxiously careful for one another (25). **a still more excellent way:** Either the way in which to seek the higher gifts—through the controlling influence of love—or love viewed as an end in itself, surpassing all *charismata*, which invests life with a moral quality without which spiritual gifts in themselves become objects for dissension. 13: 1-3 and 14: 1 underline this latter view.

iii. The supremacy of love (13: 1-13)
It is hardly correct to refer to this chapter as a digression, providing as it does that cardinal Christian quality without which all the *charismata* are worthless. Moreover, the theme of 'gifts' as it is continued in chapter 14 proceeds to unravel its many practical problems under the all prevailing plea, **Make love your aim.** It is the essential link between the principle expounded in chapter 12 and the practice explained in chapter 14.
Love is a specifically Christian revelation. The Greek language with all its richness, incapable of expressing this deep reality, provided an obscure word to be invested with an entirely new connotation by the NT writers. While Greeks praise wisdom and Romans power, Paul pens a psalm in praise of love which stands alone, by-passed or ignored in a world of hate.
The three paragraphs of this chapter are its natural divisions: (i) the absence of love can be compensated by no other quality however spectacular, be it spiritual gifts or religious zeal (1-3), (ii) its characteristics, reminiscent of the character of Christ and the fruit of the Spirit (4-7), demand (iii) an eternal continuance when the earth-bound qualities of the church have forever ceased (8-13).
The apostle's sensitivity to the nature of love is perhaps most adequately perceived when, by the substitution of the name of Jesus for love, a simple, yet perfect picture of the incarnate Christ stands out.

1. tongues of men and of angels: While including the gift of tongues (12: 30), it extends beyond this to include all ecstatic utterance, in languages known and unknown, earthly or heavenly. None can compensate for a lack of love. **love** (*agapē*): Found in LXX, Philo, and other Jewish Greek literature, but thus far attested only once unambiguously in pagan Greek. In classical Greek its verbal and adjectival forms are used of contentment or affection, but to the exclusion of all sense of sexual passion (although both noun and verb are capable of such a meaning in LXX, *e.g.* 2 Sam. 13: 15). Taken up and invested in NT Greek with a new meaning and spiritual fervour it gained an exclusively Christian connotation. **noisy gong** (literally, copper or bronze) is preferable to trumpet as suggested by some commentators (as Phillips). The **gong** and **cymbal** were associated with pagan worship. **2. prophetic powers . . . all mysteries . . . all knowledge:** Paul moves from the ecstatic gifts to those of instruction. **mysteries:** The revelation of God's deep purposes by the Spirit; cf. Mt. 13: 11; Eph. 3: 3 ff. **knowledge:** Cf. 12: 8. **faith:** As in 12: 9. **to remove mountains:** A common proverbial phrase used of great difficulties; cf. Mk 11: 22, 23. **3. give away all . . .:** Literally, to feed with small mouthfuls. The verb is aorist; in one act all is given away, doled out to the poor. **deliver my body to be burned:** The ultimate self-sacrifice in a most painful form. There may be an echo here of Dan. 3: 28, or possibly a reference to an Indian who burned himself alive in Athens (Lightfoot). Such burnings are not uncommon in pagan religion today. Westcott and Hort argue strongly for the variant 'that I may glory' (see RSVmg), which only differs by one letter in the Greek. However, most commentators support the RSV reading. Paul has cited all four classes of spiritual gifts:

the ecstatic (tongues), the instructive (prophecy), the wonder-working (faith), the helps (giving). Without love three results ensue: I convey nothing (1), **I am nothing** (2), **I gain nothing** (3). **4. patient and kind:** Cf. 2 C. 6: 6; Gal. 5: 22; Col. 3: 12. **patient** (*makrothymeō*): Not a limp, unresisting acquiescence, rather patient perseverance in the face of injury received. It is a divine quality; cf. Rom. 2: 4; 1 Pet. 3: 20; 2 Pet. 3: 9; 1 Tim. 1: 16. **kind:** The active complement of patience. **not jealous** (*zēloō*): Here used in its bad sense in contrast to 12: 31, 'earnestly desire'; cf. Ac. 7: 9; 17: 5; Jas 4: 2. **boastful:** Nowhere else in the NT, but used by later Greek writers for intellectual pride and rhetorical display—a Corinthian failing. **5. not arrogant:** The basic constituent of pride. Used only by Paul in the NT; cf. 4: 6 note, 18, 19; 5: 2; 8: 1; Col. 2: 18. **rude:** Used in 7: 36 and seems to suggest unseemly or unmannerly conduct, such as the behaviour of the women in 11: 5, 6, or the rich at the Lord's Supper in 11: 21. **its own way:** Cf. 10: 24, 33. The principle applies to lawsuits in 6: 1 ff. **not irritable:** 'not quick to take offence' (NEB). In Ac. 15: 39 the noun is rendered 'sharp contention'. **resentful:** Love does not bear a grudge. Literally, 'does not reckon up', a word from accountancy. See NEB and Phillips. Cf. Rom. 4: 8; 2 C. 5: 19; 2 Tim. 4: 16. **6. wrong:** I.e., others' wrongdoing; cf. Rom. 1: 32; 2 Th. 2: 12. **rejoices in the right:** Literally, 'with the truth'. Love and truth unite to rejoice in its triumph over wrong; cf. 2 C. 13: 7, 8; Jas 3: 14. Christ is the truth (Jn 14: 6); the Spirit also (1 Jn 5: 7). **7. Love bears all things** (*stegō*): From the basic meaning, to cover, or roof over, two usages emerge, (i) to protect that which is covered and in so doing (ii) to bear or endure what descends upon it. The latter meaning is the more usual as in 9: 12; 1 Th. 3: 1, 5. **believes all things:** While love learns spiritual discernment, it maintains its faith in others. Far better to be deceived in a doubtful case and suffer hurt, than as a sceptic to hurt another who should have been believed. In this spirit it **hopes** looking for the ultimate triumph of truth and **endures,** steadfast in all things; cf. Rom. 8: 25; 2 Tim. 2: 10. Endurance is more active than patience. **8. prophecies . . . tongues . . . knowledge . . . will pass away:** The contrast is with unending love. These three principal gifts are taken as illustrative of all the *charismata* which are purely temporary and transitory, given for building up the body of Christ (Eph. 4: 11-16), a process to be completed at the consummation **when the perfect comes** (10). In God's immediate presence, prophets, ecstatic speech and limited understanding are alike rendered redundant. Note the force of

katargēthēsontai, 'will pass away'—to render useless, inoperative (cf. 1: 28 note). **9. imperfect:** Present **knowledge** and **prophecy** are only 'fragmentary'. **10. when the perfect comes:** Anticipates the Parousia, the culmination of this age. To suggest that **the perfect** refers to the completion of the Canon of Scripture fails to find any support in the biblical usage of **perfect,** or in any of its cognate forms. Such an interpretation exists only by virtue of the need to explain the absence of certain *charismata* in many churches today. **11, 12** are an illustration of the ultimate condition of **the perfect** (*to teleion*) in contrast to the present **imperfect.** The tenses employed give force to the illustration; three imperfects—**spoke, thought, reasoned**—denoting habitual action in the past, followed by a perfect—**when I became a man** ('now that I am become a man', as in RV, is better), giving the sense of completeness. **gave up** (*katērgēka*): Is the fourth occurrence of the verb *katargeō* in vv. 8-11, previously rendered by the passive **will pass away,** underlining again the transitory nature of all the gifts, and by implication, the enduring character of love which will crown the final Day. **12. in a mirror dimly:** Corinthian mirrors of polished metal were famous, yet at best they reflected a somewhat blurred and distorted image. **dimly:** Literally, in a riddle, or enigma, and rendered by Moffatt, 'baffling reflections'. The sense is clear. Our knowledge only fragmentary, our reasoning sometimes faulty, deduces often a distorted image of divine reality. At His coming we shall see and know with an immediacy as yet unknown. **face to face:** Cf. Num. 12: 8; Job 19: 26, 27; 1 Jn 3: 3; Rev. 22: 4. **I know in part; then I shall understand fully:** The knowledge common to all believers and not the *charisma* of v. 8, which will pass away. **13. So:** Renders accurately the Greek *nyni de* ('but now', AV) in its logical rather than temporal sense. **Faith, hope** and **love** in contrast to the transitory gifts **abide,** even at the coming of the Lord. **abide:** The Greek verb is singular, although the subject is plural, indicating the indissoluble unity of these virtues. **the greatest of these is love:** 'Love is the root of the other two; "Love believeth all things, hopeth all things." Faith and hope are purely human; Love is Divine' (Robertson and Plummer).

iv. Prophesying and tongues (14: 1-40)

The apostle now proceeds to apply the principles which he has so clearly laid down. The variety of spiritual gifts within the fundamental oneness of the body of Christ (chapter 12) may be kept in perfect balance only by the exercise of love, in whose light the true value and function of all *charismata* are readily assessed (chapter 13).

There are higher gifts, earnestly to be sought (12: 31), not with the greed and envy so characteristic of Corinth, but in the spirit of love. Chapter 14 deals with this discernment. The gift of prophecy is to be desired more than tongues (1–25), yet the exercise of each has its proper place and both must be carefully controlled to avoid abuse (26–33a). Any participation by women in the church must be similarly regulated, that their subordination may be evident (33b–36). In summarizing his instructions, the apostle presents them as divine directives (37–40).

(a) **Prophecy is superior to tongues (14: 1–25)** The Corinthian believers, carried away by the mysteriousness and extreme ecstasy associated with tongues, gave to this experience an importance in relation to the other *charismata* which was quite out of keeping with its God-given function. While recognizing the place of tongues in personal worship (2), Paul sees the great need of the church for inspired preaching, the prophetic word, through which it may be built up (3, 5). Illustrations strengthen his argument; (i) their own experience of Paul as a teacher (6), (ii) the meaningful sounds of inanimate instruments (7, 8), (iii) the sounds of human language (10, 11). Just as the well known bugle call galvanizes the army into action, so a language understood by the hearer will produce positive results. Conversely, while one may worship in deepest harmony with the spirit in a tongue, the uninitiated in the church, bereft of gifts, is in no position to endorse what is said (13–19). Finally, while tongues may be a sign to the unbeliever of impending doom, it is through the gift of prophecy that he will be led to salvation (20–25).

1. Make love your aim: Literally, pursue love—a characteristic Pauline verb for spiritual endeavour; cf. Rom. 9: 30, 31; 12: 13; Phil. 3: 12 ff.; 1 Th. 5: 15; 1 Tim. 6: 11; 2 Tim. 2: 22. The verse summarizes chapters 12 and 13, and sets the tone for what follows. Note the repeated phrase, **earnestly desire . . . prophesy** (12: 31; 14: 39). **2. a tongue:** One of the *charismata*, understood only by God unless accompanied by the gift of interpretation. It is not merely a foreign language, for no one understands it, and it is addressed to God. **in the Spirit:** While interpreted by the RSV (also Moffatt, and NEB, 'inspired') as a reference to the Holy Spirit, it could equally refer to the spirit of man, as distinct from his mind. **mysteries:** See note on 13: 2. **3. he who prophesies:** The gift of inspired preaching, perceiving the will of God and speaking to the specific needs of the congregation. See note on 12: 10. **upbuilding:** Paul's dominant desire for the

Corinthian church. It lies behind chapter 3: cf. 8: 1; 10: 23; 14: 4, 5, 12, 17, 26. See also 2 C. 12: 19; Eph. 4: 29; Rom. 14: 19; 15: 2. This metaphorical usage is peculiar to Paul in the NT. **4.** The contrast is between the edification of one individual through a tongue and of the whole congregation through prophesying. **5. even more to prophesy:** Places the balance where it ought to be without deprecating the gift of tongues. **unless some one interprets:** Reintroduces the possibility of tongues being used in meetings of the church; cf. vv. 13, 26, 27. **6. if I come . . . how shall I benefit you . . . :** The criterion is still their edification, profit. Uninterpreted tongues give nothing. **revelation . . . knowledge . . . prophecy . . . teaching:** These demand intelligent speech and build up. The former pair imply an inward endowment, the latter their outward expression. **Revelation** precedes **prophecy** as does **knowledge** the **teaching**. **7, 8. lifeless instruments . . . flute . . . harp . . . bugle:** Each has its particular function, the first two being associated with feasts, funerals and religious functions, the last with fighting. Yet the instrument's tune and rhythm, its call must be clear, interpreting the occasion of festivity or mourning, the need to charge or retreat. **9. So with yourselves:** What is achieved by the inanimate is demanded of the human tongue. For edification the word must be intelligently expressed. **10, 11. many different languages . . . and none is without meaning:** But all are valueless if ignorance of the language prevents communication. **12. So with yourselves:** Be articulate in the language that builds up the church. **eager for manifestations of the Spirit:** Commendable, but the motive is crucial; not puffing up the self, but by love building up the church. Paul's words may be tinged with irony. **13. the power to interpret:** May be granted to the man who already has the gift of tongues. That gifts are given in answer to prayer clearly demonstrates the possibility of a developing ministry in keeping with spiritual growth and the needs of the local situation. The *charismata* are not given in a 'package deal'. **14. my mind is unfruitful:** May mean, 'my mind is not profited'—it gains no fruit, as NEB, or 'my mind produces nothing for the benefit of others', as Moffatt. **15. I will pray with the spirit and . . . with the mind also:** For Paul **mind** is intelligence. He therefore uses a means of communication intelligible to mind and spirit, both his and the congregation's. Here Moffatt translates *pneuma* as 'Spirit'. **16. if you bless with the spirit:** I.e., in a tongue. As an expression of ecstatic utterance Paul uses a variety of terms; **speaks** (13), **pray** (14), **sing** (15), **bless, thanksgiving** (16)—all aspects of a corporate act of worship in which the believers took part as they were led; cf. v. 26. Yet the presence of **one in the position of an outsider** demands that every part of the worship be intelligible to him, either in the language of the worshippers, or if a tongue, through interpretation. **outsider** (*idiōtēs*) suggests not laity, for no such distinction then existed, but rather, the unlearned, or inexperienced believer, or as RVmg suggests, one that is without gifts. The word occurs in Ac. 4: 13 and 2 C. 11: 6. **the 'Amen':** A colloquial expression for associating oneself with the prayers, etc., offered in congregational worship. The practice of the synagogue was adopted in Christian churches. Cf. Ps. 106: 48; Neh. 5: 13; 8: 6. **17. you may give thanks well enough:** The tongue itself is not despised, but the ungifted is not edified. Hence it fails to meet the test. **18, 19. I speak in tongues more than you all; nevertheless in church . . . :** The gift in which Paul excelled was not paraded in church to impress, but in private, personal worship expressed in untrammelled joy the deep devotion of his ransomed spirit. **20. do not be children in thinking . . . be mature:** A preference for tongues over intelligent speech was childish, immature. Yet **in malice**—comprehensive of all evil dispositions—a child-like innocence was commendable. Mature thinking, intelligibly expressed, is essential if unbelievers are to be converted; cf. vv. 23–25. **21, 22. In the law it is written . . . :** Isa. 28: 11 ff. is quoted. God speaks to the rebellious, unbelieving, in an unintelligible tongue, as He spoke to the scoffing Israelites through the Assyrian foes. The illustration shows nothing more than that, spectacular as tongues may be, they are ineffective in bringing unbelievers to salvation. They are however **a sign for unbelievers** of their own impending doom, as was the Assyrian tongue to the unbelieving Jews of Isaiah's day; not a saving sign, but a judicial sign of condemnation: a sign to be rejected confirming them in their unbelief; cf. v. 23. It seems that on occasion our Lord's use of parables was somewhat similar; cf. Mt. 13: 10–15. On the other hand, **prophecy is not for unbelievers but for believers,** in that it creates those who believe, bringing them to faith. **23. the whole church:** Suggests a general gathering for worship as opposed to the more limited and informal groups which might meet in various parts of the city. **all speak in tongues:** I.e. all who take part, as in v. 24. For the sake of his argument Paul is probably stating an extreme case. Undoubtedly some would normally take part in an intelligible tongue. **you are mad:** A conclusion drawn not only by **unbelievers**

(*apistoi*) but by those who as yet are unlearned—**the outsiders.** See v. 16 note. **24. by all:** Suggestive of the cumulative effect of the inspired word presented by speaker after speaker. The gender may be neuter or masculine; by everything, or everyone. **convicted:** Has considerable breadth of meaning; cf. 'convince', Jn 16: 8; 'expose', Eph. 5: 11; 'rebuke', 1 Tim. 5: 20. **called to account** (*anakrinetai*): Used of judicial examination. See note on 2: 14, 15; also 4: 3; 9: 3. **25. the secrets of his heart are disclosed:** Being the direct result of the examination. This verb and the preceding two in v. 24 reveal varying aspects of the one experience, involving convincing, convicting, exposing, sifting, revealing; the product of prophecy, the invasion of man's soul by the Spirit of God. The inward rebuke of the Spirit results in the outward response of the sinner; **falling . . . he will worship . . . and declare that God is really among you.** If to him tongues suggest that the church is mad, prophecy proves that God is present.

(*b*) **Tongues and prophesying in the local church** (14: 26–33a)
The apostle having concluded his arguments on the respective merits of tongues and prophesying, issues directives. His conclusions summarize the previous 25 verses. (i) Of first importance, all must be for **edification** (26). The church must be built up; cf. vv. 3, 4, 5, 6, 12, 17, 19. (ii) If there are tongues, they must be accompanied by interpretation (27, 28); cf. vv. 2, 5. (iii) The **prophets** are to participate (29). (iv) Decorum and order must be maintained (30–33).
26 presents graphically the composition and manner of worship of a congregation in the early church. **each one:** Not that everyone present would of necessity take part; rather it indicates the general distribution of gifts throughout the local church. **has a hymn, a lesson . . . :** The verb 'to have' is repeated with each gift in the Greek text and is possibly suggestive of the individual possession of specific gifts. Each comes prepared to contribute, yet equally ready to remain silent as the need becomes evident; cf. v. 32. **27. If any speak in a tongue:** If implies the possibility of no such individual being present. This is the more significant in view of Paul's grammar where, in this particular construction, *eite* ('if') should normally be followed by another *eite*, so completing a distributive sentence. This second part could have commenced at v. 29, but the idea of the presence of prophets being in doubt is so unacceptable to Paul that he abandons the construction and inserts an imperative: **Let two or three prophets speak . . .** It matters little if tongues are

not present, but prophets there must be. **each in turn:** Ensured the preservation of order, as did **let one interpret,** rendering it impossible for several to break out in ecstatic utterance together. **28. let each of them keep silence:** As with all other *charismata*, the exercise of tongues must be under the immediate control of the speaker. **29. two or three prophets:** As with tongues, the number that could profitably be heard in one meeting. **let the others weigh what is said:** While it could refer to the whole congregation, **others** were most probably the remaining prophets, or others in the church who had the gift of discernment; cf. 12: 10, 'the ability to distinguish . . .' The advice was sound, for false prophets early infiltrated the churches; cf. 2 Pet. 2: 1; 1 Jn 4: 1. **30. If a revelation is made to another:** The guidance of the Holy Spirit throughout is clearly anticipated. **31. you can all prophesy one by one:** Not all in one meeting, for the limit of two or three is set, but an opportunity will eventually come to all so gifted. **so that all may learn:** Suggests that the varying needs of all the believers will be met through a variety of speakers; some by one, some by another. This in no way invalidates a sustained Bible-teaching ministry such as Paul, Apollos, Timothy and others undoubtedly pursued. **32. the spirits of prophets . . . :** Reads almost as a maxim and makes explicit the statements of vv. 28 and 30, that under the superintendence of the Spirit the recipients of gifts are in full control and are responsible for their use. **33. For God . . . :** The order so achieved reflects the character of the Giver of gifts. **not of confusion but of peace:** The very antithesis of the chaos and commotion that currently reigned in the church at Corinth; see 11: 17–22.

(c) Women in church (14: 33b–36)

The guiding principle in Paul's teaching concerning the place of women in the life of the church is subordination, submission. What constitutes subordination? Here again the principles of Scripture must be worked out within the framework of contemporary society. That the problem is complex is clear, not only from the reference to their participation in 11: 5, but also from what was obviously known to the apostle: the ministry of women in the OT and also within his own life-time in the Church (cf. Ac. 21: 9). While on the one hand one must recognize that almost all the heretical sects of Christendom number women among their leaders, yet it is also beyond dispute that God has vindicated the ministry of women, consecrated, holy women, whose lives have been humbly sacrificed in the service of Christ in the missionary world. Understood within the context of

the NT it is hard to accept that all spoken ministry is denied to women.

33b. As in all the churches . . . : Taken by RSV and NEB with the following verses and is probably the reading to be preferred. Following RSV, the basis of Paul's appeal is the general conduct of the churches. This accords with v. 36. **34. the women should keep silence:** This is the third call to **silence.** See v. 28 for tongues without interpretation and v. 30 for one prophet giving way to another. As tongues and prophecy are subject to limitations, so is the speaking of women. This may be understood in two ways: (i) if 11: 5 is taken as giving permission to women to pray and prophesy, then this prohibition must refer to the abuses of such freedom; a departure from the subordinate attitude which the law and society demand, the calling out, and asking of questions which disrupts the orderly state of the meeting on which Paul is insisting (see vv. 33, 40); (ii) the limitation may refer to the occasion: **in the churches.** It may be held, although it is nowhere suggested in the text, that the apostle is referring to the more informal meetings of Christians in 11: 5, in contrast to the formal gatherings of the whole church which he undoubtedly has in mind in 14: 1–40, cf. especially v. 23. The phrase **they are not permitted to speak** does not clarify the issue. The verb *lalein* (to speak) is too general to refer to any particular kind of speaking. It is used of tongues (27) and also prophecy (29) and refers equally to the questions with which the women might interrupt a discourse. So general is the word that the suggestion that Paul is merely referring here to irregular talking, be it chattering, calling to children, soothing or more often rebuking babies, or interjecting a remark or query, cannot be ruled out. At church services in Asia the rebuke is frequently heard, 'Sisters, be silent; don't talk in church'. And the verb used is the general equivalent of *lalein*. Few things are so conducive to confusion and disruptive of peace as the noise which emanates from the women's section of the congregation—the sexes are segregated—in an Asian worship service. They **should be subordinate:** this is the crux of the matter; not only to their husbands (11: 3–9; 14: 35), but in questions of conduct, submitting in all things for the good order and decent arrangement of the service (40). It is on the same grounds of submissiveness that Paul states categorically that a woman shall not teach (cf. 1 Tim. 2: 11, 12). **as even the law says:** A reference to Gen. 3: 16. **35. let them ask their husbands at home:** To have asked one's husband in church would have involved calling across the room, creating disorder. Paul has, as in chapter 11, married women in mind. The unmarried could ask through their own families. **shameful:** Scandalous; a strong word, found elsewhere in the NT only in 11: 6; Eph. 5: 12; Tit. 1: 11. Such is Paul's estimate of one who ignores the limits of subordination and disrupts the order of holy worship. **36. Did the word of God originate with you . . . :** Is Corinth the fount of revelation, the sole repository of truth? Corinth was obviously at variance with **all the churches;** gross disorder reigned (chapter 11), the reflection of their arrogant self-esteem (4: 8, 19).

(d) **Conclusion (14: 37–40)**
The verses are reminiscent of 11: 16, but now his source of authority transcends the ruling of the apostles and the practice of the churches; it is the command of Christ. The test of their spirituality is their acceptance of his claim. The balance assiduously sought throughout is finally summarized; the priority of prophecy, the legitimacy of tongues, and well-ordered worship.

37. a prophet, or spiritual: The second is the wider term including all who have spiritual gifts, although here it could refer specifically to one who spoke with tongues, the gift Corinthians considered to carry the hallmark of spirituality. **he should acknowledge:** The pres. imperative, literally, let him *ever* acknowledge, or recognize. The same verb is used in 16: 18; 2 C. 1: 13. **a command of the Lord:** The stamp of apostleship, the conviction of inspiration. The point is, those who have spiritual gifts are not to act as a law to themselves, but are to conform to the law of Christ revealed through the directives of the apostle. **38. If anyone does not recognize this:** Sometimes, as here, the verb (*agnoei*) implies wilful ignorance or disregard. **he is not recognized:** The whole verse is cryptically and concisely expressed in five Greek words. Such opposition is dismissed with suitable brevity. This implication of wilful ignorance in *agnoei* perhaps gives force to the variant reading 'let him be ignorant' (RV), especially as it is supported by papyrus 46, our oldest Pauline manuscript. **39. earnestly desire:** Cf. 12: 31; 14: 1. Prophecy is of paramount importance in edifying the church. Nevertheless, tongues have a God-given function (5). **do not forbid:** No spiritual gift is to be despised. **40** expands the thought of v. 33. **decently** (*euschēmonōs*): Cognate forms are found in 7: 35; 12: 23, 24 with the underlying concept of comeliness and beauty. Worship should be attractive. **in order** (*kata taxin*): 'Everything in its proper place and sequence', expressing the precision with which a well-ordered army moves.

VII. THE RESURRECTION (15: 1–58)
Although there is no suggestion that the Corinthians had written about the subject, the apostle had undoubtedly heard reports of misconceptions gaining ground in the church. By some even the possibility of a resurrection was being denied (12). It is not altogether surprising that such a problem should exist, for nothing in the Greek background of the Gentile converts suggested the plausibility of a physical resurrection (cf. Ac. 17: 18, 32). The Jewish minority in the congregation, while probably accepting the doctrine in view of their OT background, would be in no position to influence the Gentile majority. Paul's answer, the product of uncompromising conviction and lucid reasoning, demonstrates the position of fundamental importance that this doctrine holds in the Christian faith. Based on the historical resurrection of Christ (3–11), its denial not only relegates the Messiah to a martyr's grave, but renders faith futile, sin triumphant and the hope of glory a pitiful myth (12–19). In terms of positive truth, Christ risen from the dead gives assurance of human resurrection, the conquest of death, the subjugation of evil and daily empowering for Christian service (20–34). Yet how are the dead raised? Anticipating inevitable queries, the apostle, from nature, OT history and Christian revelation, describes the body that is yet to be (35–58).

i. The resurrection of Christ (15: 1–11)
A risen Christ was fundamental to Paul's gospel (1–4); it was historically attested (5–8) and uniformly preached by all the apostles (9–11).

1, 2. I would remind you: So also NEB. However, many commentators prefer the 'declare', or 'make known' of AV and RV, suggesting that this is not a mere reminder, but an emphatic declaration of the message originally given. Note the usage in Gal. 1: 11, 'I would have you know'. **preached . . . received:** Both aorists recalling the specific time of their belief. **you stand:** A perfect, signifying their stand already taken, the results of which continue into the present. **you are saved:** A continuous present tense, stresses the progressive nature of their salvation; cf. 1: 18; 2 C. 2: 15. **if you hold fast:** To deny the resurrection was to relinquish their hold on what Paul had taught, for without the resurrection, they would have believed in vain. **in vain** (*eikē*): Without grounds. If their understanding of the gospel did not commit them to belief in the resurrection, theirs was no saving faith. **3. delivered . . . received:** See notes on 11: 23. The essential point is that the message was not of Paul's creation; he merely transmitted the truth, facts committed to him. **Christ died:** An atoning death, **for our sins:** cf. 2 C. 5: 21; Gal. 1: 4; Heb. 9: 28; 10: 12; 1 Pet. 2: 24; 3: 18, etc. **in accordance with the scriptures:** A fact the disciples originally found hard to accept; cf. Lk. 24: 26 ff.; see Ac. 3: 18; Isa. 53. **4. he was buried:** The evidence of His death. Outside the Gospels, Paul is the only NT writer to refer to it; cf. Ac. 13: 29; Rom. 6: 4; Col. 2: 12. **he was raised:** Literally, 'has been raised'. Paul changes from the aorists to the perfect, signifying the continued life after the resurrection; cf. Rom. 6: 9. For similar uses of the perfect in this chapter see vv. 12, 13, 14, 16, 17, 20. **in accordance with the scriptures:** Isa. 53: 10–12; Ps. 16: 10. See also Lk. 24: 46. **5–7** give a limited list of the resurrection appearances. **Cephas:** Lk. 24: 34. **the twelve:** A general term for the apostles, Judas excepted. **five hundred brethren:** Not recorded in the Gospels, but that most were still alive at the time of writing provided incontrovertible proof. **James:** Probably the brother of our Lord. **all the apostles:** As a reference to the twelve follows Cephas, so the **apostles** following **James** (assuming him to be the brother of the Lord) refers to a somewhat wider circle of Christ's followers. Paul's use of 'apostle' is of wide application; cf. 12: 28 note. So far as Cephas and James are concerned, Paul's information was probably acquired during his visit to Jerusalem described in Gal. 1: 18 f. **8. Last of all . . . also to me:** 'even to me' (NEB); a reference to his Damascus road experience, the vividness of which never faded in his memory; cf. Ac. 22: 6–11; 26: 12–18. **one untimely born:** Literally, an abortion. It could point to the dramatic suddenness of his spiritual birth and the extraordinary manner in which he joined the apostolic group, or, in keeping with v. 9, be a term of abuse hurled by his enemies—a miscarriage of an apostle—a charge he did not endeavour to deny. Yet another suggestion is that Paul's conversion (from violent opposition to Christ) is an anticipation of the day when Israel shall see him, but happening before the due time. **9. least of the apostles, unfit . . .:** **least,** not in the character of his apostleship (cf. 9: 1, 2; 2 C. 11: 5; 12: 11, 12), but because he **persecuted the church:** cf. 1 Tim. 1: 15; Eph. 3: 8. This too he never forgot; cf. Gal. 1: 13; 1 Tim. 1: 12–14; Ac. 26: 9–11. **10. But by the grace of God:** Paul's unworthiness serves only to enhance sovereign grace. **not in vain** (*kenos*): Empty, fruitless. **I worked harder than any . . . :** Signifies the character of the grace given; a divine enduement of power; cf. 3: 10; 2 C. 9: 8; 12: 9; Eph. 3: 7; 2 Tim. 2: 1 for examples of this usage in Paul's letters. It was not Paul but **grace** that **worked. 11. I or they:** Whatever their comparative importance, or intensity of activity, all the apostles **preach** (continuous present) the same gospel of which the resurrection is an inalienable part. This the Corinthians had **believed** (aorist). Not only the resurrection of Christ, but their belief in it was an historical fact.

ii. The consequences of denying the resurrection (15: 12–19)
The denial of a resurrection of the dead must inevitably involve a denial of Christ's resurrection, which in turn demands an admission that the preachers are false, faith is vain, sin remains and the Christian dead have perished. There is no hope.

12. some of you: Probably Gentile believers who while accepting the Greek concept of the immortality of the soul could not accept a physical resurrection. If the resurrection of Christ is a proven fact, which none of them denied, it is illogical to say **there is no resurrection of the dead. 13. Christ has not been raised:** Since they had never questioned the resurrection of Christ, Paul's reasoning reveals the inconsistency of their assertion. **14. our preaching** (*kērygma*) **is vain:** *kērygma* refers not to the act of preaching, but to the content; cf. 1: 21; 2: 4. The message is **vain** (*kenos*, as in v. 10): without meaning, and inevitably, their **faith** in that message. **15. We are . . . found** (*heuriskometha*): Often used in moral judgments when detecting the true character of an individual or matter; so 'we are even discovered to be' (Amplified Bible). **testified of God:** Here *kata tou theou* (of God) could be translated, 'against God' (its more usual meaning), i.e. accusing God of doing something that He did not do. However, it is probably better to render it simply as 'concerning God', in keeping with the previous phrase, 'false witnesses of God' (RV). **17. faith is futile:** Surely so if sin remains unatoned. *mataios* (**futile**) differs little from *kenos* (v. 14), except that it is concerned more with lack of result, and *kenos* with lack of reality. **in your sins:** Deliverance depends on Christ being raised from the dead; cf. Rom. 4: 24, 25; 6: 1–11; Eph. 2: 1, 5. **18.** While denying the possibility of a resurrection for humanity, the Corinthians fully expected those who were **asleep in Christ** to be saved, being united with Him in an after-life state. The apostle therefore demonstrates that no salvation is possible if there is no resurrection. **have perished** (*apōlonto*): Experiencing total ruin, not extinction, but total loss of the salvation for which they hoped **in Christ,** for it is those who are not **in Christ** and die who perish; cf. 1: 18; 2 C. 2: 15; 4: 3. **19. only:** Emphatic and qualifies either **hope** (as RSV, RVmg), or **in this life** (as AV, RV, NEB), or the whole clause, i.e., 'If in this life we are hopers in Christ and have nothing beyond.' This last is favoured by many commentators. **have hope:** The perf. part. with the

O*

verb 'to be', expresses not what we do, but what we are: we are hopers. Hope seeks fulfilment (cf. Rom. 5: 1–5; 8: 24, 25; 1 Th. 4: 13, 14), yet if the resurrection is denied and nothing lies beyond, **we are of all men most to be pitied** (pitiable).

iii. The consequences of Christ's resurrection (15: 20–28)

Turning from the terrible conclusions which must accompany any doctrine of no resurrection, the apostle now enumerates the glorious consequences of Christ's being risen from the dead. Man will surely rise, as surely as all must die. It is a matter of order, Christ first, then when He comes again, those who are His. As first fruits He had vanquished death; but now as Sovereign He subdues every evil beneath His feet and death the last great foe can terrify no more. Paul contemplates the last majestic scene; earth's history ends as the Son delivers up the kingdom to the Father, and God is all in all.

20. But in fact . . .: The argument of the previous paragraph, based on a false premise (13, 14), ended in tragedy. Paul now reasons from **fact,** a fact the Corinthians accept. **first fruits:** Reminiscent of the first sheaf from the field brought to the Temple in thanksgiving and offered to the Lord (cf. Lev. 23: 10 ff.), a promise of the full harvest yet to be. Others had been raised from the dead, only to die again. Christ is uniquely the first fruits in that He died, rose and is alive for evermore (Rev. 1: 18; Rom. 6: 9) in anticipation of believers who have fallen asleep, but will be raised to be with Him for ever; cf. 1 Th. 4: 16, 17. **21. For as by a man . . . by a man:** Developing from the concept of first fruits the thought implies unity of species. This theme of the last Adam is worked out more fully in Rom. 5: 12–21. **death:** The penalty of sin resulting from Adam's rebellion. **22. all die . . . all be made alive:** The implication of **all** is governed by the context. It is often argued that since **all** who are **in Adam,** i.e., all humanity, **die,** so **all** who are **in Christ,** i.e., all the redeemed, are **made alive.** However, in this passage Paul is thinking primarily of those who **have** fallen asleep in Christ (18), to which also v. 20 probably refers. The unbelieving dead are not under review. Therefore **all** may refer to believers in both clauses: **all** believers **die** because they are **in Adam,** and **all** such will **be made alive** because they are **in Christ.** This is further supported by v. 23 where the **order** of resurrection is stated; first Christ, then those who are His. The apostle would not deny the resurrection of the lost, but they are not mentioned in the **order** here, for they just do not form part of Paul's present subject.

23. order (*tagma*): A cognate form of *taxis* (14: 40), a military metaphor, suggesting companies appearing in their proper order and position. **at his coming** (*parousia*): The second advent. The word itself is of general application to any individual's arrival or presence as in 16: 17; Phil. 2: 12; 2 Pet. 1: 16. Used of Christ's second coming it often suggests not merely arrival, but His continued presence; cf. Mt. 24: 3, 37; 1 Th. 4: 15 ff.; 5: 23; 2 Th. 2: 1, 8; Jas 5: 7, 8; 2 Pet. 3: 4. **24. Then comes the end** (*telos*): The absolute end—the termination of world history—rather than a third order implying the resurrection of the lost; cf. Mt. 24: 6, 14; Mk 13: 7; Lk. 21: 9; 1 Pet. 4: 7. **Then** permits an interval between Christ's coming and the final consummation; a period for **destroying** all opposing powers; a period which culminates in His delivering the kingdom to God; cf. 2 Th. 1: 7–10. **when** (*hotan*): Denotes indefiniteness of time. **the kingdom** (*basileia*): Note the initial preaching of Jesus and His purpose to establish that reign, or sovereignty; a spiritual realm (Col. 1: 13) not merely in the lives of His people (Lk. 17: 21) but also visible, a kingdom yet future; cf. Lk. 19: 11 ff.; 21: 10 ff., espec. v. 31. See also 2 Tim. 4: 1. This sovereignty, a commission granted to the Son, will when fulfilled be **delivered** to the Father. **destroying** (*katargeō*): See 1: 28; 13: 8—render inoperative—opposition is liquidated. **rule, authority and power:** Words not evil in themselves; their content is determined by the context. They are declared **enemies** in v. 25. **25. he must reign until . . .:** Strong necessity, both the prophetic word (Ps. 110: 1) and the divine commission of the kingdom demand it. **until he . . .:** Until God has put all Christ's enemies beneath Christ's feet, in accordance with Ps. 110: 1. **26. The last enemy . . . death:** Resurrection terminates death's power for those who are Christ's; cf. Lk. 20: 35, 36. The state of the unbelieving dead is not mentioned as Paul is concerned only with conditions as they affect believers. **27. 'For God . . .':** A reference to Ps. 8: 6, which refers to man's position of dominion over all creation. Christ as the last Adam, the perfect man, fulfils God's purpose in the highest possible sense. Heb. 2: 5–9 makes a similar exposition. **it says** (as also NEB— 'Scripture says') probably gives the best rendering. Others render, 'he says', meaning either the psalmist speaking to God, or Christ speaking in the psalmist, i.e., announcing the subjugation of all things. **28. the Son himself will also be subjected . . .:** The question here is one of function. Just as the incarnate Son was subject, or subordinate to the Father to effect eternal redemption at His first advent (cf. Jn 5: 19;

8: 42; 14: 28), and to that extent owned Him as greater, so coming again the second time for the final accomplishment of that commission the same relationship continues. The task completed, the Redeemer, man's Mediator, surrenders the kingdom to Him who sent Him. Their essential equality and unity remain; cf. 3: 23 note. **God . . . everything to every one:** The Son's mediatorial function completed, God now reigns not through Christ, but as 'immediate sovereign of the universe' (Hodge). **iv. Arguments from Christian activities (15: 29-34)** Paul with typical abruptness terminates his reasoned arguments and turns with obvious passion to the reality of daily experience, as if frustrated by the Corinthians' failure to comprehend the resurrection hope that lay behind his every word of witness and mode of life. To risk one's life for Christ were utter folly if the dead are never to be raised. Their rejection of the truth is a sin which threatens to undermine their whole Christian experience.

29. baptized on behalf of the dead: One of the most difficult phrases in Scripture. Of the many interpretations offered the most plausible is perhaps that which views the practice as an irregular type of baptism, possibly by proxy (so Moffatt) for those who died unbaptized. This is what the text appears to say, for **on behalf of** is the natural translation of *hyper*. However, no such baptisms are recorded before Tertullian's time. The obvious futility of such a practice, if the dead are not raised, would greatly strengthen Paul's argument. Would he reason from so heretical a practice without condemning it? He might. That he does not identify himself with the practice is clear from the pronoun **they,** whereas in the next verse he reverts to 'we' (RSV **I**). Others view it as regular Christian baptism and translate as, 'with an interest in the resurrection of the dead', i.e., expecting to be raised. The Greek text does not mean this. Still others suggest a baptism of suffering or death, as in Lk. 12: 50. Apart from the difficulty of making the Greek mean such a thing, Corinth was not a persecuted church. Grosheide offers an interpretation which renders *hyper* as 'above', suggesting that Christians in Corinth were baptized over the graves of the dead believers, thus expressing their unity in Christ with them. While it is an historical phenomenon, there is nothing to connect the practice with Corinth. Chrysostom's view that baptism was in any case for the dead, i.e., for oneself as dead in sin, illustrates how from the earliest centuries of the Church this verse has posed a constant problem. **30. Why am I** (literally, 'we') **in peril:** An appeal to the manner

of life of Paul and his colleagues. If there is no resurrection their conduct is senseless. Why throw one's life away? Cf. Rom. 8: 36; 2 C. 4: 11; 11: 23 ff. **31. by my pride in you:** An assurance that he is speaking the absolute truth, i.e., 'As surely as I am proud of you, I die daily'. See Moffatt and NEB. In spite of their failings in vile Corinth, Paul saw much in them for which to give thanks; cf. 1: 4-9; also 2 C. 7: 14. **I die daily:** Cf. 2 C. 1: 8-10; 4: 7-12; 11: 23b. **32. beasts at Ephesus:** Refers almost certainly, not to any encounter in the arena—such would surely have been recorded in the Acts, or 2 C. 11—but to the fierce struggles with Jews and Gentiles in that city when his life was gravely threatened. 2 C. 1: 8, 9 may refer to this. **'Let us eat . . .':** A quotation from Isa. 22: 13 and a reasonable philosophy if there is no resurrection. Man is then no better than the beasts that perish (cf. Ec. 2: 24; 3: 21). **33. Do not be deceived:** The negative *mē* with the pres. imper. probably suggests, 'Stop being deceived . . .', i.e., by this pernicious doctrine. **'Bad company . . .':** Keeping company with men who reject the resurrection will corrupt Christian character. The quotation is a line from Menander's *Thais*, *c.* 320 B.C., although it may by Paul's time have been a common Greek proverb. **34. sin no more:** The category in which their attitude really belongs. Their doctrinal error has moral implications; they had missed the mark. **no knowledge** (*agnōsia*): The emphatic position of the noun is expressed by Robertson and Plummer, 'For utter ignorance of God is what some have got'. *agnōsia* denotes failure to take knowledge, not merely that lack of it.

v. The nature of the resurrection (15: 35-49) Paul is in no mood for foolish questions, yet accepting their anticipated queries, he turns them to the world in which they live, to things that they can see and understand. The resurrection body? It is like the seed which dies before it sprouts and grows. Then it appears in another form, a different form for every kind of seed (35-38). This differentiation is discernible throughout the entire animal kingdom (39) and is perceived in the infinite variety of the stars (40, 41). The principle, obvious in nature, is illustrative of the resurrection body. Man, the seed, is sown perishable, inglorious, weak, physical, but is raised a transformed being. The earthy likeness will be transformed into a heavenly one (42-49). **35. 'How . . . what kind of body . . .':** Paul deals with the latter question first and in detail, while the former is only answered by implication, for it is an act of God to be accepted by faith. **36. You foolish man** (*aphrōn*): Implies lack of understanding. 'A senseless question!' (NEB). They should know better; the resurrection is well illustrated in the things with which they are most familiar. This is emphasized by the emphatic **you** in **you sow. come to life:** A passive verb. The quickening, germinating process is of God and is contingent on the death of the grain—**it dies.** Both are fundamental to the resurrection. **37, 38. the body which is to be:** While in appearance different, it is in essence the same, for **wheat** yields **wheat**—**to each kind of seed its own body**—suggesting continuity of essential character or identity. **God gives** this body. Note the implicit answer to the **how** of v. 35. **39, 40, 41** explain **each . . . its own body.** Diversity abounds in God's creation, not haphazard, but God-given. Further, while there is a differentiation of species—**men, animals, birds, fish, stars**—yet within each class there are multitudinous differences distinguishing one individual creation from another, **for star differs from star in glory.** If therefore in the present universe these personal characteristics are evident within the various categories of creation, God is well able at Christ's coming to invest each individual believer with a new resurrection body which will be in perfect harmony with his own essential being (see 42a). **celestial bodies:** While some suggest that this refers to heavenly beings, as opposed to earthly beings (**terrestrial bodies**), the weight of opinion seems to favour interpreting the phrase in terms of v. 41—the **sun, moon** and **stars.** This involves a dual meaning of **bodies** (*sōmata*), for **terrestrial bodies** undoubtedly denotes the living organisms on earth. **glory:** In the sense of splendour and beauty (as Moffatt). **42, 43, 44. So it is:** On the basis of the preceding principle, the nature of the resurrection body is now more clearly defined. **the dead:** Believers, as throughout the chapter. Using again the figure of the seed, the concepts of the **perishable, dishonour, weakness** are introduced, all characteristics of the **physical** (*psychikos*), the body fitted for this present transient life. **perishable:** Cf. Rom. 8: 21; Gal. 6: 8; 2 Pet. 1: 4; 2: 12, 19. **dishonour:** Rendered 'degrading' in 11: 14 and 'menial' in Rom. 9: 21; 'humiliation' (NEB) gives this sense (cf. Phil. 3: 21). In sharp antithesis **imperishable, glory, power** portray the **spiritual body** that is to be; qualities that make it perfectly adapted to the new life to be lived. Two facts emerge; (i) God can bring life out of death, and (ii) the new body, while identical in essence with the first, is as different from it as the plant from the seed. **physical** (*psychikos*): Natural, signifies that which pertains to the soul or life of man, i.e., what he is in Adam. See 2: 14 note. **spiritual** (*pneumatikos*): Denotes that

which pertains to the spirit, generated and controlled by the Spirit of God. See 2: 13, 15; 3: 1; 14: 37. **45. Thus it is written:** Only the first clause refers to Gen. 2: 7 (note RSV quotation marks). The second part is Paul's comment. **first** and **Adam** are the apostle's insertion, to give the correct sense in this context. The contrast is between the first and the last Adam. The first Adam became a life-possessing soul; the last Adam a life-imparting spirit. Adam and therefore humanity are on the natural level, subject to decay; Christ on the spiritual level— **life-giving. the last Adam:** In the first, man finds his genesis; in the last, he gains his goal. **46. the physical . . . then the spiritual:** A general law—seedtime precedes harvest, the physical is preparatory to the spiritual. **47, 48, 49.** As the physical and spiritual bodies were contrasted (42-44), so now Adam and those in him are compared with Christ. On the one hand are the **man of dust** and all humanity in his **image,** on the other the **man of heaven** and we in His **image** at the resurrection. **from the earth** defines man's origin, as **from heaven** denotes Christ's. The **first man** stands at the head of the old creation, the **second man** at the head of the new. **we have borne:** An aorist, probably viewing this in its entirety. Literally, 'we did put on', the verb is commonly used of wearing clothes. **we shall also bear:** The weight of textual evidence supports the subjunctive *phoresōmen* ('let us bear'), but the context demands the future *phoresomen* ('we shall bear'). There would be hardly any distinction in pronunciation between these two forms by the first century A.D. It refers to the day of resurrection. Note the similar thought in v. 53. We shall have **the image** or likeness of Christ; cf. Rom. 8: 29; 2 C. 3: 18; Phil. 3: 21; Col. 3: 10; 1 Jn 3: 2.

vi. The result of the resurrection (15: 50–58) Whether we are living or dead at the coming of Christ, this wonderful transformation will take place; the resurrection day will have come and the final victory of Christ will be proclaimed.

50 serves better as an introduction to the new (as in RV, NEB), than as a conclusion to the preceding argument. **the perishable:** That is, the physical man (**flesh and blood**) as he is in this world needs a transformation; without it he inherits nothing. It is not this present physical body that will find its possession in **the kingdom. inherit:** Here understood in the broader sense of taking final possession at the coming of Christ. **51. a mystery:** Cf. 2: 7; 4: 1; 13: 2; 14: 2; here, the fact that the living as well as the dead will experience immediate physical transformation at Christ's advent, to possess **the kingdom** and all that the **imperishable**

conveys; cf. vv. 50 and 53. **We shall not all sleep:** Paul was prepared for an imminent return of Christ, but equally so for death; cf. 2 C. 4: 14; 5: 1-10; Phil. 1: 21-24. One should be in a constant state of readiness; cf. Mk 13: 32, 33, 37; Ac. 1: 7; 1 Th. 4: 13 ff.; Phil. 4: 5; Rom. 13: 11, 12; 1 C. 7: 29-31; 16: 22. **52. the last trumpet:** The final manifestation of God to man in his earthly condition. It heralded the Lord's descent at Sinai; cf. Exod. 19: 16; Heb. 12: 19. See also Mt. 24: 31; 1 Th. 4: 16; Rev. 11: 15. **53** applies the principle of v. 50. **perishable** and **mortal nature** are used synonymously, although the latter is a more comprehensive word. **put on:** An aorist indicating the momentary character of the change, cf. v. 52. The verb (*endyō*) 'implies that there is a permanent element continuing under the new conditions' (Robertson and Plummer). See 2 C. 5: 4. **54.** The reference is to Isa. 25: 8. **'Death is swallowed up . . .':** The moment of Christ's appearing, when death is utterly destroyed (cf. v. 26). **'. . . in victory':** Paul's own rendering of the Hebrew expression ('for ever' in English versions), differing from that of LXX—although LXX repeatedly renders the expression thus elsewhere, and Paul's choice of the rendering here provides a link with **victory** in Hos. 13: 14, quoted in the next verse. **55. 'O death . . .':** From Hos. 13: 14. **thy victory:** It reigned from Adam; cf. Rom. 5: 14. **thy sting:** Portrays death as venomous. Satan's fangs are drawn. (AV 'O grave' in place of the second **O death** reflects the inferior reading (*hadēs*) of the 'Received Text'.) **56. The sting of death is sin:** Sin causes death; cf. Rom. 5: 12, 13, 21, etc. **the power of sin is the law:** Paul expounds this in Rom. 7: 4-20. **57. victory through . . . Christ:** He is the end of the law (Rom. 10: 4); free from sin (1 Pet. 2: 22); conqueror of death (Ac. 2: 24); redeemer of His people (Heb. 9: 28). **gives:** The pres. part. not only signifies that it is characteristic of God to give **the victory**, but that victory may be continually experienced. **58. be:** Literally, 'become' what they had not fully been before. **steadfast, immoveable:** Cf. 7: 37; 16: 13; Col. 1: 23; a firm grip of the fact of the resurrection will strengthen their stand and give added incentive for service; cf. 3: 13 ff.; 15: 10; 2 C. 9: 8.

VIII. CONCLUSION (16: 1-24)
Paul brings his letter to a close, dealing briefly with a variety of matters which still require his attention.
i. The collection (16: 1-4)
Believers in the church at Jerusalem were in need; it was the Corinthians' privilege to help them. Instructions are given concerning the

proper procedure for collecting the offerings, which in due course the apostle will send, or himself take to their destination.

1. the contribution for the saints: Cf. Rom. 15: 26; 2 C. 8: 1 ff.; 9: 1 ff. Presumably the Corinthians already knew of the proposed contribution (there is no mention of Jerusalem until v. 3) and may have asked for further instructions in their letter. **2. the first day of every week:** Suggests that Christians regularly met on Sundays, the first indication of the practice; cf. Jn 20: 19, 26; Ac. 20: 7; Rev. 1: 10. Note the guidance given; it should be regular and systematic, involving every member, each giving according to his means. **store it up:** The inference being that the gifts are to be put by at home week by week. **3. accredit by letter:** The money was theirs, not Paul's, and he carefully avoided personal contact with it. Baseless allegations could too easily be made; cf. 2 C. 8: 20-22; also 2 C. 12: 14-18. RSV follows the RV reading, but most translators (Moffatt, Phillips, NEB) adopt the RVmg alternative, that Paul would write a letter of commendation to be taken by those men whom they themselves should select. **4. If . . . I should go:** Then no letter would be necessary.
ii. Personal matters (16: 5-18)
Paul's plans are fluid. He would like to spend time with them, not merely to call while passing through. However, the opportunities in Ephesus prevent him from cutting short his ministry there. Timothy will see them on his way back to Ephesus; they are to look after him well. Apollos may come later. In the meantime there are local men to whom they do well to listen.

5. Ac. 20: 1, 2 suggests that Paul finally carried through this plan, although 2 C. 1: 15, 16 indicates that alternatives were later suggested. See also 2 C. 1: 23. In addition a brief 'painful visit' probably took place from Ephesus, preceding that of Ac. 20. See Introduction, p. 374. **6. I will stay with you: you** is emphatic and is repeated three times in vv. 6, 7, emphasizing that it was particularly with them that he wanted to spend time. A passing visit would not permit him to accomplish all that he hoped to do. This letter left several matters still unresolved; cf. 11: 34. He finally spent three months in Greece (cf. Ac. 20: 3). **wherever I go** and **if the Lord permits** reveal the uncertainty of his plans. Either this was written before the occasion of Ac. 19: 21, 22, or Paul was not yet in a position to confirm his intentions. **8. Ephesus:** The place from which Paul writes. **Pentecost:** Gives a general guide as to time, for by then the ships would again be sailing. **10, 11. When Timothy comes:** Cf. 4: 17; Ac. 19: 22. **put him at ease** (literally, 'without fear') and **let no one despise**

him, recall phrases in Paul's letters to him long after; cf. 1 Tim. 4: 12; 2 Tim. 1: 7. His temperament and, at this time, extreme youth, made it easy for people to underestimate his true worth. **doing the work of the Lord as I am:** Cf. 1 Th. 3: 2; Phil. 2: 20-22. **12. As for . . .:** The same usage as in 7: 1, 25; 8: 1; 12: 1; 16: 1, which suggests that they had written asking about **Apollos,** hoping he would come to them. **the other brethren:** Probably those of v. 11 who may have taken Paul's letter to Corinth. **not at all God's will:** Most commentators and versions prefer 'his will', i.e., Apollos himself was adamantly opposed to going. He may well have felt that the situation in Corinth was too critical for him to handle. However, there is sufficient evidence for the absolute use of *thelēma* ('will') in Jewish Greek to mean 'God's will' to lend support to the RSV rendering here. **13, 14.** The apostle inserts his final brief exhortation. The first four imperatives call for militant action, the last for **love.** The first pair are defensive, the second offensive. **watchful:** A call to alertness, often associated with the second coming; cf. Mk 13: 35, 37; 1 Th. 5: 6; Col. 4: 2. **stand firm:** Be stable, a quality hitherto lacking; cf. Rom. 11: 20; Gal. 5: 1; Phil. 4: 1; 2 Th. 2: 15. **be courageous:** Literally, 'act like men'. LXX usage suggests courage for the fight as in Jos. 1: 6, 7, etc. **be strong:** Cf. Eph. 3: 16; sometimes linked with **courage** in the LXX as in Ps. 27: 14. **love:** Recalls chapter 13, a quality which must dominate even in the fight. **15, 16. household of Stephanas:** Cf. 1: 16. **first converts:** Literally, first fruits. See note on 15: 20. As there were conversions in Athens (also in the Roman province of Achaia) before Paul's Corinthian visit this refers either to their being the first *family* to be converted, or indicates that they came to Christ elsewhere before Paul arrived in the city. **be subject to such:** The service of others characterized such men as Stephanas, and now the others were to be subject to them, so creating an endless circle of mutual care and esteem; a certain remedy for division (cf. Phil. 2: 3). Those who serve, work and labour gain Paul's respect. The last verb (*kopiaō*) suggests toil involving fatigue; those who spent themselves for Christ and His people; cf. 4: 12 note; 1 Th. 1: 3. **17, 18. Stephanas, Fortunatus and Achaicus** possibly brought the Corinthians' letter to Paul and would return with his reply. Their presence had a twofold effect; **they have made up . . .:** brought Paul a breath of Corinth; **they refreshed my spirit . . .:** their presence alone proved to the apostle that such men of sterling character, as servants of the Corinthian church, were God's own guarantee of its ultimate stability and growth.

iii. Final greetings (16: 19-24)

19. The churches of Asia: The Roman province of Asia—Ephesus and its neighbouring cities. **Aquila and Prisca** had intimate associations with Corinth, where their home had been the base for Paul's activities (Ac. 18: 2 f.). Now in Ephesus the church met **in their house,** as it was later to do in Rome (cf. Rom. 16: 5). **20. a holy kiss:** The customary greeting of Paul's day; cf. Rom. 16: 16; 2 C. 13: 12; 1 Th. 5: 26. **21. with my own hand:** Having dictated the letter up to this point the apostle pens the concluding sentences himself as a token of its genuineness; cf. 2 Th. 3: 17; Col. 4: 18. **22. accursed** (*anathema*): Absence of **love for the Lord** could have but one result; cf. 12: 3; Gal. 1: 8, 9. **love:** The use of *phileō* instead of *agapaō* may suggest, 'If one does not have even affection for the Lord'. Note John's use in Jn 21: 15-18. **Our Lord come** (*Marana tha*): A transliteration of the Aramaic. While the verb has been rendered by past, present and future tenses, it is probably best to understand it as an imperative; a prayer not only characteristic of the time (see Rev. 22: 20), but well fitted to the context. According to the *Didachē* (10: 6), an early second-century manual of church order, it was used as an invocation at the Lord's Supper. **23. The grace . . .:** A phrase with which all Paul's letters begin and end, not as a mere convention, but in the conviction of its sure supply and all sufficient power. **24. My love** embracing **all in Christ,** it ties into one the diverse strands of Paul's deeply stirred emotions. Rebuke, exhort, praise, counsel, scourge, encourage; do what he must—or they their worst —he will **love** them to the end.

BIBLIOGRAPHY

FINDLAY, G. G., *The First Epistle of Paul to the Corinthians*. EGT (London, 1900).

GODET, F., *The First Epistle to the Corinthians* (2 vols. Edinburgh, 1886; reprinted Grand Rapids, 1957).

GOUDGE, H. L., *The First Epistle to the Corinthians.* WC (London, 1903).

GROSHEIDE, F. W., *Commentary on the First Epistle to the Corinthians.* NIC (Grand Rapids and London, 1953).

GUTHRIE, D., *NT Introduction: The Pauline Epistles.* (London, 1961).

HÉRING, J., *The First Epistle of Saint Paul to the Corinthians* (London, 1962).

HODGE, C., *An Exposition of the First Epistle to the Corinthians* (Edinburgh, 1957; reprinted, London, 1958).

KELLY, W., *Notes on the First Epistle to the Corinthians* (London, 1878).

MOFFATT, J., *The First Epistle of Paul to the Corinthians.* MNT (London, 1938).

MORRIS, L., *The First Epistle of Paul to the Corinthians.* TNTC (London, 1958).

PARRY, R. St. J., *The First Epistle of Paul the Apostle to the Corinthians*. CGT (Cambridge, 1916).

ROBERTSON, A. and PLUMMER, A., *A Critical and Exegetical Commentary on the First Epistle to the Corinthians*. ICC (Edinburgh, 1911).

SMITH, D., *The Life and Letters of St. Paul* (London, 1919).

THRALL, M. E., *I and II Corinthians*. Cambridge Bible Commentary on NEB (Cambridge, 1965).

VINE, W. E., *First Corinthians* (London, 1951).

THE SECOND
LETTER TO THE CORINTHIANS

DAVID J. A. CLINES

Historical Background

The following is a suggested outline of events between the writing of First and Second Corinthians.

(i) About the time of his dispatching 1 Corinthians, Paul sent Timothy to Corinth (1 C. 4: 17; 16: 10). He was to travel via Macedonia with Erastus (Ac. 19: 22). We know nothing of the specific purpose of his visit, nor indeed can we be sure that he ever reached Corinth; we next hear of him with Paul in Macedonia (2 C. 1: 1).

(ii) Paul made a hurried visit from Ephesus to Corinth. The purpose of this visit is not known (perhaps it was because 1 Corinthians had not been well received, or else because Paul had heard that his apostolic authority was being challenged); it is clear, however, that it ended disastrously and with great humiliation for Paul (cf. on 2 C. 12: 21). He refers to it later as a 'painful' visit (2: 1).

(iii) In order to rectify the situation he wrote a letter 'out of much affliction and anguish' (2 C. 2: 4), known as the 'severe' letter (7: 8). It was taken to Corinth by Titus, who was to return to Ephesus via Macedonia and Troas.

(iv) Impatient for news of how his letter had been received, Paul travelled to Troas to meet Titus (2 C. 2: 12; Ac. 20: 1). When he did not find him there, he was too anxious to settle down to preaching, so he crossed to Macedonia (2 C. 2: 13).

(v) In Macedonia he met Titus, who brought good news from Corinth. In his joy and relief, Paul wrote 2 Corinthians (the fourth of his letters to Corinth known to us). It is clear from the letter that he now commanded the general support of the church, but there was apparently still a dissentient minority as well as glaring moral errors in the lives of church members.

The 'Previous' Letter

It is sometimes argued that the previous letter referred to in 1 C. 5: 9 is to be found embedded in 2 C. 6: 14-7: 1. There is no doubt that the passage in question breaks the train of thought very sharply, and also that it could easily have been misunderstood in the way the 'previous'

letter had been. If the passage is omitted from its present position in 2 Corinthians, 7: 2 appears to read very naturally directly after 6: 13.

The main objection to this theory is that it is extremely difficult to imagine how this fragment of the 'previous' letter (it is surely not the whole letter) became interpolated at this point in 2 Corinthians. It is improbable that part of another manuscript was accidentally copied into 2 Corinthians, and even more improbable that an editor of Paul's letters inserted this section in what appears to be a most unsuitable place. It is more likely that Paul himself digressed from his theme (a habit in which he indulges quite frequently); in 7: 3 ('I said before that you are in our hearts') he resumes the subject from which he knows he has digressed.

The 'Severe' Letter

The 'severe' letter referred to in 2 C. 2: 3 f. and 7: 8 ff. has been traditionally understood to be 1 Corinthians, but it is recognized by most modern interpreters that the terms in which Paul speaks of the letter are inapplicable to 1 Corinthians.

A suggestion which has been accepted by many scholars is that the 'severe' letter has been partly preserved in 2 C. 10-13. Several features in these chapters correspond to what we know of the 'severe' letter, although the principal subject of that letter, the 'offender' of 2 C. 2: 5-11, does not find a place there.

The marked *change of tone* at the beginning of 2 C. 10 from expressions of joy and confidence to indignant self-defence and condemnation of his opponents is easily explained by the hypothesis that the final portion of the 'severe' letter begins here. If 2 Corinthians is a unity it may well seem rather tactless of Paul to append these harsh and sarcastic words to his delicate appeal for contributions to the collection (ch. 8, 9). On the other hand, it has appeared even from ch. 1-9 that there is still some resentment against Paul at Corinth (cf. 1: 13, 17; 5: 12 f.; 6: 12 f.); it would not be unlike Paul to begin his letter with praise of his converts and thanksgiving to God for their progress in the faith (cf. 1 C. 1: 4-9; Phil. 1: 3-11; 1 Th. 1: 2-10), and to leave to the end his criticisms and his vindication of himself (cf. Gal. 6: 12-17; Phil. 3: 2-4: 3; 2 Tim. 4: 14-18). There is some truth also in R. A. Knox's view that the severity of ch. 10-13 is less out of keeping with the rest of the letter than the confidence and approval of ch. 7-9.

Certain *references to a visit* are intelligible if 2 C. 10-13 is part of the 'severe' letter and therefore earlier than 2 C. 1-9. Thus 1: 23 'It was to spare you that I refrained from coming to Corinth' may be understood in the light of 13: 2 'If I come again I will not spare'; 2: 3 'I wrote as I did, so that when I came I might not be pained' could refer to 13: 10 'I write these things while absent, in order that when I come I may not have to be severe'. But these references are equally explicable if 2 Corinthians is a unity: 1: 23 explains why he has not come when he said he would, 13: 2 points out that he cannot postpone his visit indefinitely; 2: 3 explains why he wrote the 'severe' letter, 13: 10 why he writes the severe parts of this letter.

It is also argued that between the 'severe' letter and 2 Corinthians Paul's *attitude to self-commendation* has changed: in ch. 10-13 Paul commends himself (11: 5, 18, 22-29; 12: 1, 12),

but in the later letter, ch. 1-9, he says that he will not commend himself 'again' (3: 1; 5: 12). It becomes apparent, however, when all his references to self-commendation are taken into account, that his attitude is this: he will not commend himself as the false apostles do, with words unsubstantiated by actions (3: 1 ff.), nor according to worldly standards (5: 12, 16) (though he feels compelled at one point to prove that he can outstrip his opponents even if he is judged by such standards [11: 18-29]), nor beyond the bounds of truth (10: 13), but by his honest life (1: 12 ff.), his faithful preaching of the gospel (4: 2), and the testimony of his converts (3: 2). These credentials are not his own achievements, but are due to the grace of God (1: 12; 4: 1), so that it is the Lord, not he himself, who gives him his commendation (cf. 10: 18).

Thus, although the hypothesis that 2 C. 10-13 is part of the 'severe' letter cannot be disproved, it does not appear necessary; its greatest weakness is the absence of any reference in 2 C. 10-13 to the person who was the occasion of the 'severe' letter (cf. on 7: 12), and it is 'better to assume that the whole of the "sorrowful letter" is now lost than to assume that its most important part is no longer extant' (D. Guthrie).

ANALYSIS

I. GREETINGS (1: 1-2)

1. an apostle of Christ Jesus by the will of God: Cf. 1 C. 1: 1. The presence of **Timothy** in the superscription does not mean that he is co-author of the letter, but only that he was present when it was written. **Achaia:** The Roman province comprising all Greece south of Macedonia. The most important church in Achaia appears to have been that in Corinth, the capital of the province, though we know of others, in Cenchreae (Rom. 16: 1) and Athens (Ac. 17: 34). It is the greeting, presumably, rather than the letter itself, which is addressed to **all the saints who are in the whole of Achaia. 2. Grace to you and peace:** Cf. Rom. 1: 1.

II. THANKSGIVING FOR GOD'S COMFORTING (1: 3-11)

i. His Comforting in all Afflictions (1: 3-7)
3-7. 'I thank God that He strengthens me in my trials—not for my sake alone, but so that I may share my strength with others (3, 4). (This is all through Christ, in whose sufferings and strength I have a share [5].) Thus *my* trials and *my* strengthening bring *you* strength in your affliction (6), and so I have every hope that you will be strengthened too (7).'

3. Father of mercies: A Semitic turn of phrase for 'merciful Father'. **comfort:** I.e. 'encouragement' and 'consolation', with the overtone of 'strengthening' (present by derivation also in the English 'comfort'). **4.** God's comforting is more than enough for Paul himself, and overflows into comfort for others. **us:** 'We', 'us', and 'our' in 2 Corinthians is often to be understood of Paul alone, as is shown clearly by *e.g.* 7: 5 ff. But sometimes of course it includes his fellow-missionaries (*e.g.* 4: 6) or the Corinthian church (*e.g.* 2: 11). **5. share . . . in Christ's sufferings:** Because he is a follower of Christ, he suffers affliction and persecution as Christ did, and so shares in the 'fellowship of his sufferings' (Phil. 3: 10 RV; cf. 2 C. 4: 10 f.; Col. 1: 24). **6. for your comfort and salvation:** His afflictions, like all the rest of his life, are for their sake (cf. on 4: 15 'all for your sake'). The close bonds between Paul and the Corinthians mean that they suffer when he suffers, and likewise share in his strengthening. This at least is the ideal, and though lately they have not enjoyed this reciprocity, Paul has every confidence that when they hear of God's strengthening of him in his recent affliction (8 ff.) they will find it to be to their strengthening also.

ii. His Comforting in a Recent Trial (1: 8–11)
8. That he does not speak more precisely of his **affliction** suggests that the Corinthians must have known the nature of it, though they were apparently unaware of its intensity. A severe illness would suit his language (and would explain why he felt he had the 'sentence of death *within*' himself [9 RVmg]), as would also an outbreak of persecution or mob violence, or a flogging such as he refers to in 11: 23 ff. The riot in Ephesus (Ac. 19: 23-41) might well be thought to be the occasion referred to, except that Luke does not hint that Paul was in any personal danger at that time. **Asia** is the Roman province of that name; Ephesus was its most important city. He **despaired of life,** but he never despairs of God's ultimate deliverance of him (4: 8).

9. He was so close to death (he felt God's **sentence of death** had been passed on him) that he could turn only to the **God who raises the dead** (cf. Rom. 4: 17; 2 C. 4: 14), a title of God with which he was familiar from the Jewish prayer, the Eighteen Benedictions: 'Blessed art thou, O Lord, for thou makest the dead to live.' **to make us rely not on ourselves:** Cf. 2: 16b; 3: 5 f.; 4: 1, 7; 13: 4. **10. he will deliver us again:** Cf. 2 Tim. 4: 17 f. **11.** They must **help** him by their **many prayers** in his future trials, so that when God has answered their prayers by delivering Paul, **many,** not only Paul, may **give thanks** to God on his behalf.

III. EXPLANATION OF HIS ALTERA-TION OF PLANS (1: 12-2: 13)
i. His Conduct has Always been Honest (1: 12-14)
12-14. 'I dare to ask for your prayers because my conscience assures me that I have always acted honestly, especially where you are concerned (12). I am sincere in all I write; I hope you will give me credit for this (13)—you have to a certain extent done so already—and realize that there is nothing in my conduct you need be ashamed of. By God's grace I will be able to be just as proud of you at Christ's judgment seat' (14).

12. holiness and godly sincerity: He had been accused of dishonesty (cf. on 12: 16; 8: 20 f.) and equivocation (1: 17; cf. 2: 17; 4: 2). **earthly wisdom** (cf. 1 C. 1: 17; 2: 4, 13): His detractors had said he lived like a worldly man (1: 17; 10: 2; cf. 5: 16). **the grace of God,** expressed in the love of Christ (5: 14), is the dominant ethical force in his life. **13, 14.**

It had apparently been said in Corinth that he was insincere and lacking in candour in his letters, writing one thing and meaning another. His critics had fastened on his failure to carry out his expressed intention of visiting Corinth, and Paul deals with their criticism in the following verses. He is thinking also of a more general complaint, that the Paul of the letters is a different person from the Paul they know in the flesh (cf. 10: 1, 10). His reply is that his letters mean just what their recipients read and understand by them; he hopes that they will not only understand his letters but also fully understand or realize that they can be proud of his integrity. They have already shown their partial understanding of this by their punishment of the offender (2: 9) and their reception of Titus (7: 7, 11, 15). But he is concerned not only to justify himself (cf. 13: 7), but also to be able to reciprocate their pride in him (**as we can be of you on the day of the Lord Jesus** [cf. 1 C. 1: 8]). On that **day** of Christ's appearing and of His judgment seat (cf. 5: 10), the value of the Corinthians' lives and of Paul's work as an apostle will be tested (cf. also 1 C. 3: 12 f.; Phil. 2: 16; 1 Th. 2: 19 f.).

ii. He is not Fickle in Changing his Plans (1: 15-22)
15-22. 'I was so sure of your approval of me that I wanted to revise my plans and visit you twice, once going to Macedonia, and a second time returning from Macedonia (15, 16). This change of plan, however, has been dubbed by my opponents "vacillation", and worse, "unspirituality" (17). I have my reasons for changing my plans (15b, 23), but let me first assure you that I am no will-o'-the-wisp, neither in my plans (17) nor in my preaching (18). Nor is Jesus Christ, the subject of our preaching (19); so far from being unreliable, He is the very fulfilment of all God's promises (20). It is His reliability that we acknowledge whenever we say the Amen in His name. This confession also honours God's faithfulness (20b), and it is this faithful God who gives us the gift of steadfastness (21), and has certified me and my fellow-workers as reliable (22).'

15. Paul's *first* plan (in his mind when he wrote 1 Corinthians) was to visit Corinth after Macedonia and continue to Jerusalem if he judged it opportune (1 C. 16: 4-7). His *second* plan (presumably intimated to the Corinthians by Titus) was to travel Ephesus—Corinth—Macedonia—Corinth—Jerusalem (16). The change of plan brought against him a charge of fickleness, which he is at pains to refute (1: 17-2: 3). His opponents will have even more ground for criticism when they read this letter, for he has changed his mind again, and his *third* itinerary is in fact Ephesus—Troas—Macedonia —Corinth. Nevertheless, there was never any question of a total change of plan; he would still be coming to Corinth in order to receive their contribution for Jerusalem. His revised plan would have given them the **double** (lit. 'second') **pleasure** of two visits of the apostle. **16. send me on my way:** The word (*propempō*) may mean that they would not only make travel arrangements for him and accompany him to the ship, but also provide from their number travelling-companions (cf. 1 C. 16: 3). **17. vacillating:** The use of the article before the noun 'vacillation' suggests that he is replying to a charge ('*the* fickleness of which I am accused'). **like a worldly man:** Lit. 'according to the flesh' (cf. 5: 16; 10: 2 f.). **ready to say Yes and No at once:** I.e. 'changeable' rather than 'double-tongued'. There is no connection with the similar phrases in Mt. 5: 37 and Jas 5: 12. **18. Our word** probably means 'all communication of mine to you', preaching as well as announcement of travel plans. **As surely as God is faithful:** An oath, like 'God is witness' (Rom. 1: 9, etc.), elliptical for 'As God is faithful to His promises that He will punish the deceiver, I swear . . .'. Less probably, the phrase means that God's providential faithfulness will ensure that His apostle is free of duplicity. **19. in him it is always Yes:** This is not a strictly logical development of his argument. There is no objection to being yes *or* no, only to being yes *and* no. But Paul seizes on the word 'Yes', and says Christ is 'Yes *and not* No'. This striking phrase is elucidated by the next verse. **20. all the promises:** Phrased emphatically, 'How many soever be the promises of God' (RV). Specifically, they are the OT promises of a Saviour, *e.g.* Ac. 13: 23; Gal. 3: 14; Ac. 2: 39. **their Yes:** I.e. their execution and fulfilment, which proves God to be reliable. **Amen:** 'Truly, surely', is a Heb. equivalent for Gk. *nai* 'yes' (they occur together in Rev. 1: 7). The train of thought is: 'Christ is God's Yes; that is why it is in Christ's name that we say Amen (=Yes) at the end of our prayers'. **21. Establishes** continues the word-play on 'Amen' with another reference to the meaning of the Heb. verb *'āmēn* 'to establish' (a similar play on the words 'sustain' and 'faithful' in 1 C. 1: 8 f.). **commissioned:** Lit. 'anointed' with the Holy Spirit for service. **us:** He is not thinking of the anointing common to all Christians (cf. 1 Jn 2: 20), but of the appointment of Silas, Timothy, and himself (probably himself primarily) to the Christian ministry. **21, 22. commissioned . . . put his seal . . . given:** These three terms refer to the same event, Paul's conversion and calling to apostleship. **Put his seal upon us** virtually

means 'endued us with power from heaven' (cf. Jn 6: 27). Perhaps, however, the metaphor of the seal is from the commercial world, where a seal attests or validates a document. **Spirit . . . as a guarantee:** The Spirit *is* the guarantee, or better, the 'deposit', or 'first instalment' of salvation (so also in Rom. 8: 23; Eph. 1: 14). Paul's argument is: 'If God has put His mark of approval upon me, how can I be an unreliable, fickle kind of person?'

iii. Why he has Not Visited Them (1: 23–2: 4)

1: 23–2: 4. 'No, it was not from fickleness that I changed my plans, but out of consideration for you, to avoid the pain and mutual embarrassment of another visit like the last (2: 1). My "severe" letter likewise was for this purpose, to clear up our differences before I arrived' (3, 4). **23. to spare you:** Cf. on 13:2. **I refrained from coming:** More accurately, 'I did not come any more' after the two previous visits. **24.** On reflection, he realizes that the word 'spare' has unfortunate connotations. If he can *spare*, he could also have been overbearing, so he hastens to add, 'Not that we lord it . . .'. The verse is better punctuated: 'Not that we lord it over your faith (we work *with* you for your joy), for you stand firm in your faith'. He does not tyrannize over their Christian life, for first, he is merely a *fellow*-worker, and secondly, they are strong enough to stand on their own feet. **2: 1. another painful visit:** Lit. 'not come again to you with sorrow'. The Gk. could mean 'that my second visit should not be a painful one', but this is not his second visit (12: 14). **2.** 'If I hurt you, who will be left to gladden me but sad people? A great comfort that will be!' Cf. Knox: 'Was I to make you sorry? It meant bringing sorrow on those who are my own best source of comfort'. **3. I wrote:** The 'sorrowful' or 'severe' letter, his third letter to the Corinthians (cf. 7: 8; 10: 10; Introduction). **as I did:** Reprovingly, as parts of this letter also are written (13: 10). Better a severe letter than a visit which would hurt everyone. **4. not to cause you pain:** He did hurt, and knew he would, but his intention was not to produce pain, but repentance leading to joy (cf. 7: 8-12).

iv. Punishment and Forgiveness of the Offender (2: 5-11)

5-11. The 'severe' letter has had at least one salutary effect: the leader of the opposition to Paul has been punished by the church, and has repented of his rebellion. Paul therefore forgives him, and asks the church also to forgive him.

The person in question here has been traditionally identified with the incestuous man of 1 C. 5; this view is necessary only so long as the existence of an intermediate letter is not recognized, and is now generally abandoned for the following reasons. (i) The Corinthians' attitude to this offender is a matter of obedience to Paul (9); the case of the incestuous man was a matter of ethics. (ii) Here, the church discipline has been sufficient punishment, and the offender is to be restored (6, 7); in 1 C. 5 the wrong-doer has been delivered to Satan for the destruction of the flesh (5). (iii) It puts it too mildly to say that the incestuous man caused pain to the church only 'in some measure' (2 C. 2: 5).

5. any one: Tactfully, he speaks indefinitely, but he refers to a definite individual ('him' [7, 8]). **Not to me** only, or mainly (cf. 7: 12). The fact that one man has opposed Paul is far less important than that he has carried the church with him into rebellion against Paul's God-given authority. **6. The majority** need not imply any minority but the offender himself; it would be better translated 'community, church'. The nature of **this punishment** is unknown. **8. Reaffirm** means 'decide in favour of' love, or 'confirm, validate' your love for him by public announcement of his forgiveness.

9. I wrote: Cf. on v. 3. They have proved themselves **obedient** in this matter, but they have yet to prove that they unanimously accept Paul's authority (cf. 10: 6). **11.** 'Some Satan destroys through sin, others through the unmeasured sorrow following on repentance for it. To take by sin is his proper work; by repentance, however, is more than his due, for that weapon is ours, not his' (Chrysostom). **Over us** probably means 'over you and me'; Satan would have gained the advantage over them if he had been able to keep Paul and his converts estranged.

v. How he Met Titus in Macedonia (2: 12–13)
12–13. Paul reverts to the account of his travels (1: 15 f.), only to embark almost immediately on a digression which lasts until 7: 4.

13. His **mind could not rest** because of anxiety over how his severe letter had been received in Corinth (cf. 7: 5 'fear within'). **them:** His converts, later mentioned as a church (Ac. 20: 6 ff.).

IV. THE APOSTOLIC MINISTRY (2: 14–5: 21)
i. His Apostolic Travels Ordained by God (2: 14–17)
14–17. 'I thank God that all my travels are steps in the triumphant progress of the gospel (14); in fact, through my preaching I am God's travelling dispenser of life and death (16). This task has immense responsibilities, but I am able to discharge them because I am no mere travel-ling salesman, but a man commissioned by God' (17).

14. thanks: The mention of 'Macedonia' brings the sudden memory of his joyful reunion with Titus there (7: 6 f.), and he interrupts the account of his travels with gratitude for God's guidance of his affairs. **leads us in triumph:** The picture is of a victorious Roman general leading his captives in triumphal procession. Paul thinks of himself as one of Christ's captives: if he stays in Troas or leaves for Macedonia, if he goes to Corinth or remains in Ephesus, it is not according to his own desire, but at the direction of Christ. For the picture of the triumph, cf. Col. 2: 15 where the captives are the defeated evil powers, and 1 C. 4: 9 where the apostles form the rear of the procession, the position assigned to those who were to die in the arena. **fragrance of the knowledge:** It is possible that the metaphor of the Roman triumph is here continued by reference to a custom of burning incense along the route of the procession; to the victors it would be a 'fragrance of life', but to the defeated a reminder of their imminent execution, a 'fragrance of death' (16). **15. aroma of Christ:** In v. 14 the fragrance (Gk. *osmē*) is the knowledge of God, in v. 15 the aroma (Gk. *euōdia*) is Paul, who spreads that knowledge. It is not necessary to attempt to harmonize the two uses of the metaphor; having taken up a metaphor, Paul often uses it in more than one sense (cf. 'letter' [3: 2 f.], and 'veil' [3: 13 ff.]). **16. a fragrance from death to death:** Perhaps a reminiscence of the Jewish doctrine concerning the Torah, that if a man uses it in the right way it becomes for him a medicine of life; if not, a deadly poison (TB, *Yoma*, 72b). **from death to death:** Probably 'more and more deadly' (cf. *'from strength to strength'* [Ps. 84: 7]). Paul's view of the 'deadly' effect of the gospel has the Lord's authority (cf. Mt. 18: 18; Jn 9: 39), yet 'it is always necessary to make a distinction between the proper and natural office of the gospel, and that which it has by accident, which is to be imputed to the perversity of men' (Calvin). **Who is sufficient:** I.e. capable of bearing such responsibility, as a dispenser of life and death, unless qualified by God? (cf. 3: 6). **17.** Paul's reply is that he is 'sufficient', but only because he has been **commissioned by God** (cf. 3: 5; 1: 9). **Peddlers** are hucksters or retail tradesmen (ill-famed in antiquity), especially wine-merchants, who sell shoddy goods, adulterate good wine by mixing it with water, or have an eye to their own profit rather than the customer's benefit. Which of these malpractices Paul ascribes to the 'many' (cf. 11: 13, 20) is hard to tell (probably the last);

they are all eschewed by **men of sincerity** (cf. on 1: 12).

ii. **This is not Self-praise, for he Needs None (3: 1–3)**

1–3. 'My remarks about myself (2: 17) might sound like self-praise, but I really need none (1), for you Corinthians are sufficient letter of recommendation to commend me both to yourselves and to the world (2). You prove, by the work of the Spirit in your lives, that I indeed brought Christ to you—and that not in word only' (3). The metaphor of letter is exploited in several ways, which cannot be completely harmonized.

1. Self-advertisement is one of Paul's failings, according to his opponents. Their criticism doubtless stemmed from expressions of his authority in the 'severe' letter, and such passages as 1 C. 2: 16; 4: 16; 11: 1; 14: 18; Paul is at pains to deny this misrepresentation (cf. 2 C. 4: 5; 5: 12; 10: 13). He had nothing against **letters of recommendation** in themselves. What else was 8: 16–24 or the letter to Philemon? (Cf. also Rom. 16: 1; 1 C. 16: 10.) But self-commendatory letters and 'spiritual bills of clearance' (Hughes) are alike unnecessary for Paul, though *de rigueur* for **some** (a favourite term of his for his opponents [cf. 10: 2; Gal. 1: 7; 1 Tim. 1: 3]). **2.** Because Paul has played such an intimate part in the conversion and the Christian life of the Corinthians, his credentials are **written on** their **hearts,** a more permanent and more convincing commendation than those written merely with ink on paper. But what is written on their hearts must be expressed in their lives (cf. Mt. 12: 34), and so Paul's commendation is **known and read by all men. Your,** though weakly supported by MSS, is probably preferable to 'our' (RSVmg, NEB); the two words are frequently confused in MSS of the NT because they were coming to be pronounced identically. **3.** Paul uses his metaphor somewhat differently: the Corinthians are not only his letter of recommendation, but also a **letter from Christ** (their lives bear the mark of His authorship), **delivered** or perhaps 'written at dictation' by Paul. This last word (lit. 'ministered') is chosen because Paul is already thinking of the law/gospel contrast (6 ff.), where 'ministration' figures prominently. **tablets of human hearts:** Lit. 'tablets of flesh, that is, hearts'. **With the Spirit of God** and 'tablets of flesh' are characteristics of the nature of the New Covenant (Jer. 31: 33; Ezek. 11: 19; 36: 26).

iii. **All his Ability is from God (3: 4–6)**

4–6. His reflections on the contrast 'tablets of stone'/'hearts of flesh' lead (by way of Jer. 31: 33) to a profound and moving study of the contrast Old/New Covenants. But first he will answer his question of 2: 16; what sufficiency he has does not come from himself, but from God.

4. His **confidence** is in his own integrity, corroborated by what the Corinthians know of him (1–3), and guaranteed to him **through Christ. 5.** He does not depend upon the qualification of himself or other Christians (cf. 10: 12), but on that of **God**; so he had learned in Asia (1: 9b). **6. ministers of a new covenant:** Paul (together with all preachers of the gospel, of course) plays a similar rôle in the New Covenant to that of Moses in the Old: just as the law was given 'through Moses' (Jn 1: 14), so the knowledge of Christ is spread abroad 'through us' (2 C. 2: 14). (For the law as given by the mediation of *angels*, cf. Heb. 2: 2; and for *Christ* as Moses' counterpart, cf. Heb. 8: 6; 12: 24.) **written code . . . Spirit:** The contrast is between the Old and New Covenants (Jer. 31: 33 is still very much in Paul's mind; and cf. Rom. 7: 6). There is no suggestion here of 'the letter of the law' versus 'the spirit of the law'; this distinction is proper elsewhere, though it is noteworthy that Christ (contrary to modern use of the phrase) regards the 'spirit' as more stringent than the 'letter' (Mt. 6: 20 ff.). **the Spirit:** It is not certain that there is a direct reference to the Holy Spirit; the contrast may be that between the external and the internal (cf. Rom. 2: 29; 'outwardly'/'inwardly'='in the letter'/'in the spirit').

iv. **The Superiority of the New Covenant (3: 7–18)**

(a) **Its Superior Glory (3: 7–11)**

7–11. The New Covenant is more glorious than the Old because (i) it comes from the Spirit, and does not lead to death (7, 8); (ii) it brings acquittal, not condemnation (9, 10); (iii) it is permanent, not transitory (11).

Though 2: 14–3: 6 is inspired by a polemical motive, Paul seems now, in turning to the superiority of Christianity over Judaism, not to be assailing hypothetical judaizers at Corinth (cf. introduction to ch. 10), but merely developing the high point of 2: 14 and 'magnifying his office' (Rom. 11: 13).

7. dispensation: 'A dispensation is not a period or epoch (a common, but erroneous, use of the word), but a mode of dealing, an arrangement or administration of affairs' (W. E. Vine). **of death:** In effect, not intention. Cf. Rom. 7: 10 and Midrash Rabba, *Exodus*, 41: 1: 'While Israel were standing below engraving idols to provoke their Creator to anger . . . God sat on high engraving for them tablets which would give them life'. **splendour:** Paul fastens on the fact that Moses' face shone (Gk. *dedoxastai*, Exod. 34: 29, 35 LXX) as symbolizing the glory (Gk. *doxa*) of the Old

Covenant. *Doxa* does duty both in an abstract sense ('splendour, majesty, glory') and in a physical one ('brightness, rays of light'); for Paul, the spiritual can be well expressed by the physical. **could not look at Moses' face:** Rather, 'look steadfastly' (RV). Exod. 34: 30 says merely that because of the brightness *they were afraid to come near him.* Paul here apparently reproduces a current Jewish view (*e.g.* Philo, *Life of Moses,* 2: 70), which is not incompatible with the Exodus narrative. **Fading as this was** is to be elaborated in v. 11. Here it means 'for all its impermanence the splendour was none the less bright'. **8. the dispensation of the Spirit:** 'The administration of the New Covenant which is symbolized by the Spirit (or, by spirit)'. **9.** 'If splendour accompanied the dispensation under which we are condemned, how much richer in splendour must be that one under which we are acquitted!' (NEB). **10.** In comparison with the New, the splendour of the Old Covenant hardly seems to be splendour at all, like the light of the moon and stars before the brightness of the sun (Calvin).

(*b*) **Its Superior 'Openness' (3: 12–18)**

12–18. The New Covenant is moreover 'open'; Paul's ministry of the New Covenant has the same 'openness' or frankness as the Covenant itself (cf. 2: 17; 4: 2 ff.).

12. Since he has **such a hope** that the New Covenant will prove to be glorious (7 f.), justificatory (9 f.), and permanent (11), he can speak frankly in the most exalted terms of his vocation, even though to his opponents this reeks of self-commendation (1). **very bold:** Better, 'frank and open' (Moffatt). RSV fails to bring out the contrast between Paul's openness and Moses' veil. **13.** It is not said in Exod. 34 that the glory on Moses' face was fading, but Paul deduces reasonably enough from *the skin of his face shone because he had been talking with God* (Exod. 34: 30) and *when*(ever) *he came out the skin of Moses' face shone* (34: 34 f.) that when he was *not* talking to God, the glory was fading. To conceal **the fading splendour** was not necessarily Moses' own motive for covering his face; Paul is probably thinking that it was God's providence that the Israelites never saw that the glory was fading. **the end:** Older commentators, translating 'could not steadfastly look to the end of that which is abolished' (AV), thought of Christ as the End (cf. Rom. 10: 4, 'the End of the law'); but why should Moses have desired to hide Christ from them? Paul's meaning probably is: If the Israelites had ever seen the glory on Moses' face altogether faded, they might have thought that the glorious law was abrogated. **14. hardened:** More appropriately, 'blinded'. **The old covenant** in v. 6

meant 'the old régime', here 'the *terms* of the old covenant', i.e. the Pentateuch or the whole OT. Paul rings the changes on **that same veil** (as he does on 'letter' [1 ff.], and 'limit' [10: 13 ff.]): in v. 13 it is the veil over Moses' face; in v. 14 the (metaphorical) veil over the Jews' hearts. It **remains unlifted** so long as they find permanence in the Old Covenant. (A less likely punctuation gives the sense: 'The same veil remains, it not being revealed that in Christ it is taken away'). **16. when a man turns:** The Gk. is ambiguous: 'when he (Moses)/it (Israel)/one (anyone) turns'. Certainly Paul is thinking of Moses and Exod. 34: 34, and most probably is saying that any Israelite can, like Moses, have the veil removed if he **turns** (i.e. is converted) **to the Lord** (in this case, Christ). There is a play on the literal and spiritual meaning of the word 'turn'. **17. the Lord is the Spirit:** Either he means that the Lord (Christ) is the 'spirit' which is characteristic of the New Covenant (6) (cf. 1 C. 15: 45, 'The last Adam became a life-giving *spirit*'); or that He is *one with* the Spirit (for Christ and the Spirit as identical *in experience,* cf. Rom. 8: 9 ff.). Whichever interpretation is adopted, it is clear that Paul's thought has come full-circle again to v. 6. The spiritual **freedom** is freedom from the 'law of sin and death' (Rom. 8: 2; cf. Gal. 5: 1). **18. we all:** All Christians, not just one man, Moses. **unveiled:** Once for all (perfect participle), unlike Moses' repeated veilings and unveilings. The **beholding** (present participle) is constant, not temporary and occasional, like Moses'. **beholding:** The word meant in classical Gk. 'to look at oneself in a mirror', but that requires steady looking when mirrors are metal, and so the word has probably come to mean simply 'to gaze steadily'. 'Beholding as in a (dull) mirror' (RVmg, cf. AV) is out of place here (it is the excellence of Christian vision that occupies Paul, not its present imperfection as in 1 C. 13: 12). More tempting is 'reflecting' (RSVmg, NEB): 'every Christian has become a Moses' (J. Héring), and Num. 11: 29 is fulfilled! But it seems rather that Paul is contrasting Christians with Moses in the presence of God, not Moses before the people. **into his likeness:** Man is already created in the likeness of God (Gen. 1: 27; 1 C. 11: 7; Jas 3: 9), but this is not incompatible with the Christian's growth in likeness to Christ (cf. Rom. 8: 29; Eph. 4: 24; Col. 3: 10) and his eventual perfect similarity to Him (1 Jn 3: 2). **from one degree of glory to another:** Cf. on 2: 16 'from death to death'.

v. His Ministry of Light Against Darkness (4: 1–6)

1–6. Paul returns (1) to the subject of his apostolic ministry (cf. 3: 6), expanding his theme of the 'openness' of his gospel (2). 'It is true that to unbelievers it is not "open" (3), but that is because they (like the Jews, 3: 14) are blinded by Satan to the glory of Christ (4), who is the theme of my preaching, now that God Himself has enlightened me' (6).

1. This ministry is that of the New Covenant (3: 6), which he says he has received **by the mercy of God,** thus excluding self-esteem (cf. 3: 1) and self-sufficiency (cf. 3: 4). **we do not lose heart:** The responsibilities are God-given; so is the energy for their fulfilment. **2.** Denney's warning is sound, that we must not read Paul 'as if he had been expressly accused of everything which he says he does not do, and as if he deliberately retorted on his opponents every charge he denied'. But 12: 16 shows he had been accused of craftiness, and 2: 17 refers undoubtedly to his opponents' insincerity. **2. open statement of the truth:** He is accused not so much of obscurity as of lack of candour (cf. 2: 17 f.). **3.** 'But how do you explain the fact that the gospel is not equally plain to all?', someone might ask. This is due, replies Paul, not to obscurity in the gospel, but to the blindness of unbelievers. **4. the god of this world:** A unique expression for Satan, though reminiscent of Christ's 'the prince of this world (*kosmos*)' (Jn 12: 31). **this world** (*aiōn*): I.e. the present age, which is in process of being superseded (and in some senses has been superseded [5: 17; Gal. 1: 4; Heb. 6: 5]) by the age to come, otherwise called the last days, the kingdom of God, etc. (1 C. 2: 6; Ac. 2: 17; Mt. 12: 28; 1 Jn 2: 8). Satan's authority, even over this age, is usurped, and only partial, for God Himself is king of the ages (1 Tim. 1: 17). **The likeness of God** describes Christ not only as 'very God' (cf. Heb. 1: 3), but also as 'the proper man', fulfilling the purposes for which man was created in God's image (cf. on 3: 18). **5.** Paul underlines 'Christ' in v. 4, and exclaims, 'It is not myself I preach! No, it is Christ as Lord. I am no lord (1: 24); I am your slave! (cf. 1 C. 3: 5).' **for Jesus' sake:** He deliberately uses the name that recalls Christ as servant (cf. 10, 11; Phil. 2: 10). **6.** The connection with what precedes is unclear. Either, **for** introduces a reason why Paul cannot preach himself: because he knows he owes everything to God. Or, v. 5 is a parenthesis and the sense is: 'In *their* case, the god of this world has blinded their minds. (It is not so with me) for the God who created light has shone in my heart'. **the God who said, 'Let light shine':** 'Then indeed He said, Let it be, and it was; but now He said nothing, but Himself became our light' (Chrysostom). **has shone in our**

hearts: Paul is thinking probably of his own conversion in particular (cf. the great light from heaven, Ac. 26: 13), but he associates his fellow-missionaries with himself.

vi. Paul the Unlikely Apostle (4: 7–12)

7–12. Paul is recalled from his reflections on the the glory of his ministry by the sobering thought of his own natural insufficiency. But this paradox of a frail mortal as God's spokesman is in fact designed by God to instil in him an aversion to 'confidence in the flesh' (cf. 1: 9; 12: 9). Possibly Paul's apparent unsuitability as God's messenger had been ridiculed by his opponents; if so, he is making capital out of their criticism.

7. this treasure: The light of the knowledge of Christ, or possibly, what springs from that, 'this ministry' (1). It is entrusted to **earthen vessels,** the bodies of His apostles. The inappropriateness of the vessel to the treasure it contained did not prompt Paul to doubt his vocation; rather, it illustrated the truth that *salvation is of the Lord* (Jon. 2: 9; cf. 2 C. 4: 13) (Denney). **8. afflicted . . . not crushed:** More accurately 'harried . . . not hemmed in' (Moffatt). There is a play on the words **perplexed . . . not driven to despair,** which Hughes reproduces with some success as 'confused but not confounded'. **10, 11.** He compares his own constant experience of persecution and suffering with that of **Jesus,** the name reminiscent of the suffering servant (as in v. 5). Vv. 10, 11 are equivalent, except that in v. 10 his life is a dying life, *like* Jesus', in v. 11 a dying life **for Jesus' sake. carrying:** Lit. 'carrying about' in his missionary travels. The **life of Jesus** is the life that Jesus lives now, His resurrection life (cf. Rom. 6: 4; Phil. 3: 10 f.). **12.** His physical sufferings (little dyings which will eventually lead to death, 1: 8 f.) are the means by which spiritual life becomes operative in the Corinthians.

vii. The Christian Hope is his Encouragement (4: 13–18)

13–18. 'But my life is not unrelieved gloomy suffering. I share with you a hope of future bliss (14, 17), and so I speak out with assurance (13). The present suffering is but temporary, and will be swallowed up in eternal glory' (17, 18).

13. he . . . who wrote: The author of Ps. 116, a hymn of thanksgiving for deliverance from death. Not just this verse (10), but the whole psalm fits the experience of Paul admirably, and was doubtless in his mind. Ps. 116: 6 is reminiscent of the theme of 2 C. 1: 9 and 4: 7; v. 5 is magnificently illustrated by 4: 10–12; v. 9 has its Christian counterpart in 4: 16–5: 5. (The Heb. of Ps. 116: 10 is obscure [cf. RSV], but Paul quotes LXX). **we too believe:** I.e. have our trust in God. **we speak:** The sense is, 'We speak out confidently' (cf. 3: 12). **14.** Though in 1 Th. 4: 17 and 1 C. 15: 51 he has spoken of the Second Coming as imminent, here he contemplates, for the moment, his own death. His views on the Coming have not changed (as some maintain), but his life-expectation has diminished because of recent experiences (1: 9; 4: 8 ff.); and in any case he has not abandoned hope of being alive at the Coming (5: 2 f.). **With Jesus** does not mean 'to be with Jesus', but expresses the Christian's togetherness with Christ in His resurrection: just as *without* Christ there is no resurrection (1 C. 15: 14), so the believer's resurrection is *with* Christ. **15. all:** I.e. all my sufferings, are for your sake. They are 'for Jesus' sake' in that he suffers because he preaches Christ's gospel (4: 11), they are for his converts' sake in that they benefit (1: 6), and ultimately they are for God's sake in that He is more greatly glorified. 'All for your sake' is a minor theme of the letter (cf. 1: 6; 5: 13-15). **16. So we do not lose heart** looks back to v. 1, and sums up the chapter. In turning his attention, in what follows, from the present to the future, the same conviction remains unshaken. **our outward nature** (AV: 'outward man'):=Earthen vessels (7), bodies (10), mortal flesh (11). His **inner nature** is his whole personality, which is undismayed and undespairing (8); his body is beaten and decaying, but his spirit is daily reinvigorated. **17. slight momentary affliction:** It is only by comparison with the eternal glory that it seems insignificant (Hodge). **weight of glory:** In Heb. the same root means 'to be heavy' and 'to be glorious'; hence the striking image of glory 'outweighing' affliction (usually we think of affliction, not glory, as heavy). **Glory** is the *leit-motiv* of the world of the resurrection (Héring).

viii. But will Death Intervene before the Advent? (5: 1-10)

1-10. The prospect of death is exceedingly unpleasant, because it involves a bodiless 'nakedness' (3). But he is not afraid, for his attention is concentrated on the resurrection body that awaits him (1). Better, of course, than being clothed with this new body *after* death would be to put it on while still living, i.e. at the Parousia (2-4). Yet death, mitigated as it is by hope of immediate reunion with Christ (8), is preferable to this bodily life of 'absence' from Him (6-8). Whether he will be dead or alive at the Parousia, however, he cannot tell; the fixed point on his horizon is the judgment seat of Christ, and his present concern must be to fit himself for that by pleasing Christ (9, 10).

1. we know: He deduces from the familiar saying of Jesus (Mk 14: 58) that by virtue of his union with Christ the Christian too will have a new body **not made with hands.** The contrast between the **tent** (the mortal body) and the **building** recalls that between temporary tabernacle and the permanent temple. **destroyed:** I.e. dismantled. **We have** need not imply that our resurrection bodies are already prepared, but that we are assured of them (cf. 1 Jn 5: 15). **2. Here:** 'In this tent' or 'meanwhile'. Changing the metaphor for the resurrection body from 'house' to 'garment' (though retaining the word **dwelling**), Paul expresses his longing to **put on** the new body over the old, as one puts one garment on over another, i.e. to be 'further clothed' (4) at the Parousia with the new body while he is still alive. **3.** If this occurs, he will not even momentarily be **naked,** divested of a body. **4.** He would willingly be out of this body, not because disembodiment is desirable, but because of the resurrection body which will inevitably follow death. He expressly disassociates himself from Platonists, Pythagoreans, and Gnostics, who thought of the body as a prison for the soul, and were only too glad to be free of it. **Anxiety** introduces a false note here; the sense is rather '*When we are burdened* (by the cares of life) we sigh, not to be rid of the body, but to have the new one superimposed'. **5.** God is the one source of **this very thing,** the clothing with the new body. **has prepared:** The Christian hope is already partly actualized by the work of Christ; God has **given us the Spirit as a guarantee** of its complete realization (cf. 1: 21 f.). **6. So** refers back to 5: 1 and 4: 16, but perhaps also to the Spirit as guarantee (5). **of good courage:** In the face of death. But courage to face death is for him a courage to face life. Death is the worst that life can bring, so all other hazards and afflictions he can take in his stride. **7.** The sense in which we are away from the Lord (6) is here clarified: the presence of Christ by **faith** is known (cf. Eph. 3: 17), but not the 'face to face' **sight** of Him (cf. 1 C. 13: 12). **8.** Paul must indeed be **of good courage** to be able to say he would **rather be away from the body** or 'unclothed'; this is an evil, but a lesser evil than being absent from the Lord. 'Do you see how, concealing what was painful, the words "death" and "the end", he has employed instead of them such as provoke great longing, calling them presence with God; and leaving aside those things that are accounted to be sweet, the things of life, he has expressed them with painful names, calling the life here an absence from the Lord?' (Chrysostom). **9.** It is not for him to make the decision whether he will be **at home** in the body or **away** from it when the Lord returns, but he can decide to make his life pleasing to Christ. It is possible that **at home** means 'at home with the Lord', and **away** 'in the body'. Paul's endeavour then is to please Him, whether called before His judgment seat (10), or preaching the gospel (11). **10. we . . . all:** All Christians, not all men (as in Rom. 2: 6 ff.). The judgment seat of God (Rom. 14: 10) is here called **the judgment seat** (Gk. *bēma*, lit. 'tribunal' or 'platform' on which the seat is placed) **of Christ,** who is the judge (cf. 2 Tim. 4: 1; Ac. 17: 31). The judgments dispensed are evaluations of the worth of individual Christian lives, varying from 'Well done, good and faithful servant' (Mt. 25: 23) to a total rejection of a life as worthless (**evil,** Gk. *phaulos*, strictly 'mean, worthless') (cf. 1 C. 3: 12-15). In accordance with this assessment the good or evil character of a Christian's life is recompensed by reward or loss of reward (the word for **receive** [Gk. *komizomai*] means 'to receive what is one's own or one's due', and thus emphasizes the strict impartiality and ustice of the judgment). The believer's salvation is of course not called in question here; it is **what he has done in the body** that is judged.

ix. His Motives in his Ministry (5: 11-15)

11-15. 'It is in the light of the judgment seat of Christ that I conduct my ministry. God is witness to my integrity, and so you may be too (11, 12). There is no self-interest in my ministry—it is all for your sakes (13). And that is because my life is shaped by the self-giving love of Christ, who died for the sake of others (14), that their lives in turn might be free of self-interest' (15).

11. Paul's critics had very possibly claimed that he used dishonest methods of persuasion (cf. Gal. 1: 10; 1 Th. 2: 3 ff.). He replies by acknowledging that he **persuades** men, but he does so with a good conscience, **in the fear of God,** for his motives are **known to God,** and will be revealed at the judgment seat. He does not mean that it is because he knows how terrifying the judgments of God upon un-believers are that he persuades men to accept the gospel. **12.** Again, as in 3: 1, Paul realizes that protestations of his integrity will be read as self-commendation. Far from commending himself, he says, he is simply giving the church weapons to employ in his defence, in which he hints, perhaps with gentle irony, they are already eager to engage themselves. **13.** They may well defend him, for he has never lived for himself, but only for God and his converts. If he was ever beside himself, lost in spiritual ecstasy (had his critics also said that he was quite crazy? cf. 11: 16), that was for God's sake; if he was in his **right mind,** that was for the Corinthians'

sake. **14. The love of Christ,** expressed pre-eminently by His giving Himself for others, **controls** Paul, i.e. dictates Paul's motives in life, restraining him from a life of self-interest. The love of Christ, however, has this effect not only on Paul, but also on all those for whom Christ died. In the death of Christ, **all** who are 'in Christ' also died to the old life of self-interest (cf. Rom. 6: 3 ff.). (Note that it is not 'then were all dead' [AV], but 'all [believers] died' in union with Christ.) **15.** And further, His death was in order to create in those who died with Him a life-for-others, that they **might live no longer for themselves.** The idea of life-for-others runs like a ground bass through-out the paragraph (cf. 4: 15; 10: 8).

x. The Theme of his Ministry (5: 16-21)

16-21. 'Because what motivates me now is Christ's love for others, external appearance and distinctions do not enter into my estimate of others, not even of Christ (16). This radically altered view of people is a revolution the New Order brings about (17), this New Order which is both God's doing and characteristic of God Himself. He is the one who in His love for others was reconciling the world to Himself (18a, 19a), and who has ordained the proclama-tion of this reconciliation through us His messengers (18b, 19b, 20). He Himself has put an end to the estrangement caused by sin by giving Christ as an atonement for sin'.

16. From now on: Ever since he discovered the meaning of Christ's death as self-giving love for others. To 'know no man after the flesh' (AV) is rightly understood by RSV as to **regard no one from a human point of view.** He does not mean that he once knew the earthly Jesus, and now knows Him no longer as such; still less is he making a distinction between the Jesus of history and the Christ of faith, or declaring that knowledge of the historical Jesus is valueless. **17. he is a new creation:** Better, 'there is (an instance of) the New Creation'; in his case at least **the old** order **has passed away** and **the new** order **has come,** i.e. there is a partial realization of the hope of new heavens and new earth ('there is a new world' [NEB]; cf. 2 Pet. 3: 13; Isa. 65: 17; Rev. 21: 1, 4 f.). In this context, **the new** is specifically seen in the changed outlook on people (16), and the change from self-interest to life-for-others (15). **18.** As in the old creation, every-thing was created by God through His word, so in the new **all . . . is from God** through Christ. God Himself brings about the recon-ciliation; the idea of a loving Jesus winning over a stubborn and wrathful God is foreign to Paul's gospel.

19. God was in Christ reconciling may

mean 'God was in Christ, reconciling' (AV), or 'in (=by, through) Christ God was reconciling' (RSVmg). The context does not call for a special emphasis on the fact that God was in Christ, and indeed the phrase sounds Johannine (cf. Jn 10: 38) rather than Pauline, so the latter translation (parallel to v. 18) is to be preferred. **God was . . . reconciling:** Paul's use of the imperfect instead of the simple past tense (as in v. 18) perhaps indicates his hesitation to say that the world has been reconciled in the same sense as 'we' have; in the case of the believer, the reconciliation is effective in both parties, while in the case of the world the reconciliation means that 'He was disposing of everything that on His part made peace impossible' (Denney). But the reconciliation is of cosmic effect; it is not merely the church, but the world, the universe (cf. Col. 1: 20), that is the object of God's reconciliation. His reconciliation is evidenced, first, by His **not counting their trespasses against them,** but by putting them to the account of their substitute (21), and secondly, by His entrusting to His apostles **the message of reconciliation,** that God has made peace with the world. 'At bottom, the Gospel is not good advice, but good news. All the good advice it gives is summed up in this— Receive the good news' (Denney).

20. Paul emphasizes the dignity of his office by calling himself an **ambassador,** the technical term for a legate of Caesar, who speaks not only 'on behalf of' but also 'in the place of' (AV) his master. Cf. the plenipotentiary status of Paul in 2: 14-16. But he does not simply stand on his dignity; he beseeches men. **We beseech you:** 'You' is lacking in the Gk. He is not addressing his converts who have already been reconciled (18), but giving the substance of his message: 'We beseech (men), saying, Be reconciled to God, accept His offered friendship'.

21. V. 20 expands 'entrusting to us the ministry of reconciliation' (19), v. 21 develops 'not counting their trespasses against them'. **Made** is devoid of any idea of compulsion; Christ's sacrifice was freely willed (Jn 10: 8). **made him to be sin:** The Heb. word for 'sin' (*ḥaṭṭā't*) and consequently the LXX *hamartia* 'sin', Paul's word here, are occasionally used for 'sin-offering' (*e.g.* Lev. 4: 24), and it is probable that this is Paul's meaning here. Christ's death is frequently spoken of as a sin-offering (*e.g.* Rom. 8: 3 [RV, NEB]; Heb. 7: 27; 9: 12; Jn 1: 29; Isa. 53: 6, 10), and all legitimate inferences from other interpretations of 'made him to be sin' (*e.g.* He stood in the place of sinners, He accepted the penalty of sin) are embraced by the concept of Him as a sin-offering. Paul is careful to avoid any suggestion

that Christ became sinful or a sinner (though a too strict parallelism with 'we become righteousness' as an equivalent of 'we become righteous' might suggest this), and explicitly asserts that He **knew no sin. We . . . become the righteousness of God** means 'we become righteous before God', with the added nuance that it is *God's* righteousness that is imparted to us.

V. RENEWAL OF BONDS BETWEEN PAUL AND THE CORINTHIANS (6: 1– 7: 16)

i. An Appeal for the Corinthians to be Reconciled to Paul (6: 1-10)

1-10. 'Do not let God's gift of reconciliation lie idle in your lives (1)—for this is the Day of Salvation when old hostilities are broken down (2). I for my part have gone out of my way not to provoke opposition (3), but have rather striven to prove my good faith by enduring hardships for the sake of the gospel (4, 5), and by manifesting the fruits of the Spirit (6, 7), no matter what my reputation or outward appearance might be' (8-10).

1. Paul is **working together** with God in that God's work is the reconciliation, Paul's the proclamation of it. Although the words **with God** are not in the text, they are supplied more naturally than references to other Christian workers (cf. 1 C. 3: 9), or the Corinthians themselves as collaborators. **We** throughout chaps. 6 and 7 plainly means Paul himself. **The grace of God** appears to be in particular the gift of reconciliation. The Corinthians will **accept** it **in vain** if they do not allow it to operate in their lives, i.e. if they will not be reconciled to Paul. Thus it is likely that 6: 1 begins his plea for full restoration of friendly relations, a plea which becomes explicit in 6: 11-13 and 7: 2. **2.** He quotes Isa. 49: 8 in order to show that the promised age of salvation has now arrived and that therefore it is for Christians to live in accord with its principles. **now is the acceptable time:** He does not primarily mean, 'Today is the acceptable time, tomorrow may be too late', but 'Today we are living in the new age, when salvation and reconciliation are present realities'.

3-10. The theme of the apostolic ministry, first introduced in 2: 14, is now briefly recapitulated, with the reappearance of many motifs from his earlier treatment (*e.g.* endurance in affliction [4: 16]; sincerity [2: 17; 4: 2]; outward appearance and inward reality [4: 7 ff.]). His intention is to remove all grounds of suspicion and criticism, which have only made for strained relations. **4, 5.** His hardships ('a blizzard of troubles' [Chrysostom]) are arranged in

427

three groups of three, preceded by the keyword **endurance,** his attitude in them all. The first group, **afflictions** (pressure of a physical and mental kind), **hardships** (inescapable difficulties, 'necessities', AV), **calamities** (frustrating situations) are general trials imposed on him by circumstances or his opponents. The second group are particular sufferings inflicted on him by men: for **beatings,** cf. on 11: 24, for **imprisonments,** cf. on 11: 23, and for **tumults,** see Ac. 13: 50; 14: 19; 16: 19; 19: 29; 21: 30. The third group of hardships are those he imposed on himself for the sake of the gospel: **labours** as an evangelist and a leather-worker (1 C. 4: 12), **watching,** i.e. sleepless nights (Ac. 20: 31; 1 Th. 3: 10; 2 Th. 3: 8), **hunger,** 'fastings' (RV), probably through poverty (Phil. 4: 12), and imprisonment. **6.** A different kind of proof of his integrity commences here, his God-given qualities of character (the first of which is perhaps endurance, v. 4). **Knowledge** may seem out of place here, but spiritual wisdom is a gift of God (1 C. 2: 6 f., 12 f.). **7.** The first two items, **truthful speech** and **the power of God** are probably to be taken as continuing the list of personal qualities. **Weapons . . . for the right hand** are offensive weapons (*e.g.* sword) and **for the left** are defensive (shield). Cf. Eph. 6: 16 f. By **weapons of righteousness** (a phrase from Isa. 59: 17) he means that he uses only upright methods of self-defence and attack on his critics. **8–10.** The contrasts here are not only between his reputation and his real character (*e.g.* impostor/true), but also between his 'outer' and 'inner' nature (4: 16) (*e.g.* having nothing/possessing everything); in the latter case he would regard both aspects as true, though from different viewpoints. **9.** It is not clear whether he means that he is unjustly **treated** as **unknown,** a nobody, or that he really is **unknown** to men, yet **well-known** to God (cf. 1 C. 13: 12, where the same verb 'to know fully' is used). Better than **punished** is 'chastened' (RV) or, 'disciplined by suffering' (NEB); he agrees that he is chastised by **God's** affliction, but has not been given over to death (cf. Ps. 118: 18). **10. sorrowful:** I.e. full of pains, griefs. His experiences bear a striking resemblance to those of the Servant of Isa. 53. **poor, yet making many rich:** Cf. 8: 9.

ii. They Should Return Paul's Affection (6: 11–13)

11–13. 'I have spoken without reserve to you, my friends, and my love for you is equally unreserved (11). It is you, not I, who are holding something back in your affection (12). Play fair (if I may use a children's phrase), and return my love!' (13). **11.** His address of them by name, **Corinthians,** is a mark of affection (elsewhere only Gal. 3: 1; Phil. 4: 15). **our heart is wide** ('enlarged', RV): 'Just as what is heated expands, so the work of love is to enlarge' (Chrysostom). The phrase is reminiscent of Ps. 119: 32 (AV), 'Thou hast enlarged my heart', but there the meaning is 'Thou hast increased my understanding' (cf. RSV). **12. you are restricted in your own affections:** 'Any stiffness between us must be on your side' (J. B. Phillips). **13. In return:** For the moment he uses playground language, 'fair's fair', appealing to them as to children, who have a strong sense of fair-play. Perhaps, however, he means, 'I address you as (my) children'.

iii. A Warning against Association with Pagans (6: 14–7: 1)

6: 14–7: 1. In his first letter to the Corinthians, the 'previous' letter (cf. on 1 C. 5: 9), Paul had warned them not to associate with 'immoral men'. Some misunderstanding of his meaning had prompted him to write in 1 C. 5: 9 that he had referred only to such within the church, and he went on, in chaps. 8–10, to deal with the legitimacy of a Christian's occasional participation in social activities with pagans. Perhaps because of further misunderstanding he now insists that *permanent* association with unbelievers is to be eschewed.

For the hypothesis that this section was originally part of the 'previous' letter, see Introduction. There can be little doubt that the passage is logically connected neither with what precedes nor with what follows; the view that the Corinthians' association with unbelievers was an obstacle to the full restoration of friendly relations between them and Paul, and thus follows 6: 11–13 appropriately (A. Menzies), has not met with general acceptance. Perhaps some connection may be discerned thus: having assured the Corinthians of his unconditional love for them, Paul is emboldened to admonish them, yet with love (7: 1), not censoriously. **14. Do not be mismated** (RV 'unequally yoked') **with unbelievers:** A spiritual application of the law *You shall not plough with an ox and an ass together* (Dt. 22: 10). He is speaking generally of permanent association with unbelievers; but not all associations are yokes. He does not exhort them to abandon any such ties they may have contracted (cf. his instructions to the Christian husband of an unbelieving wife [1 C. 7: 12 ff.]), but warns them not to continue forming them. **15. Belial:** Originally 'the place of swallowing up', the underworld (cf. Ps. 18: 4), from Heb. *bala'* 'to swallow up', but later re-interpreted as a compound noun from *b li* 'without' and *ya'al* 'profit', i.e. 'worthlessness'. Hence 'sons of Belial' (*e.g.* Dt. 13: 13) are 'worthless fellows', and Belial comes to be a proper name meaning 'worthless one'. It is first used as a term for Satan in intertestamental literature, and appears only here in NT.

16-18. These verses are a catena of OT quotations (cited from LXX), the applicability of which is founded on the assumption of the fundamental similarity, if not identity, of the old Israel and the new.

16. The temple of God is not the individual believer (as in 1 C. 6: 19), but the whole body of believers (as in Eph. 2: 21). **I will . . . move** (lit. 'walk') **among them . . . my people** is from Lev. 26: 12. **I will live in them** is suggested by Ezek. 37: 27, *My tabernacle shall be among them*; perhaps Paul deliberately substitutes 'live' or 'dwell' to emphasize the permanence of God's dwelling among His people under the new covenant.

17. The first three lines of this verse were originally a call to the exiles to leave Babylon (Isa. 52: 11). The return from exile, constantly compared with the exodus (*e.g.* Isa. 43: 16-19), is here contrasted with it: the Egyptians were spoiled (Exod. 12: 35 f.), the Babylonians left with their 'unclean' possessions (but cf. Ezr. 1: 4). **Come out from them** must be understood with the qualification of 1 C. 5: 10. **Then I will welcome you** is from Ezek. 20: 34, also in reference to the return from exile as a new exodus (cf. v. 36). **18.** 2 Sam. 7: 14, *I will be his father, and he* (Solomon) *shall be my son* is conflated with Isa. 43: 6, *Bring my sons from afar and my daughters from the end of the earth* (at the return from exile). **7: 1. These** is emphasized: 'Since these are the promises we have'. **let us cleanse ourselves:** By including himself with them, and call them **beloved** (a word of which he is not prodigal), he softens the severity of his warning.

iv. His Confidence in Them (7: 2-4)
2-4. 'Take me back into your hearts. I have done nothing to cause you to keep me out (2). But I am not saying "Welcome me back" in order to complain that you haven't done so already; that kind of meanness finds no place in the undying affection I have for you (3). Yes, I have the greatest confidence and pride in you now that you have responded to me so loyally' (4).

2. Open your hearts means not 'tell me everything', but 'make room for me in your hearts' (cf. 6: 12). He resumes the appeal begun in 6: 11-13. **we have corrupted no one, etc.:** Probably a denial of charges made against him. **taken advantage:** Cf. 12: 17 f. Alternatively, he implies that these are the practices of his opponents. **3.** The tone changes from

exhortation to rejoicing as he recalls his meeting with Titus (6 ff.; cf. 2: 13 f.). **I do not say this to condemn you:** Exhortations contain implicit reproofs, but he does not say this by way of reproof, but in order to complete the reconciliation, that he may be as much in their hearts as they are in his. **I said before** probably refers to 6: 11-13, and so indicates he is aware that he has digressed in 6: 14-7: 1 (see Introduction). But he did not use precisely these words in 6: 11-13 (though 'widen your hearts also' [13] implies them), so some think he is referring to 3: 2 (RV), 'Ye are . . . written in our hearts' (but see on 3: 2). **To die together and to live together** simply means that they have a sure place in his heart no matter what happens to him, 'come death, come life' (F. F. Bruce). **Live** follows **die** not because he is thinking of the after-life, but because life seems a less likely possibility to him than death (cf. 4: 11).

v. Reflections on the Severe Letter and its Consequences (7: 5-13a)
5-13a. Paul resumes from 2: 14 his narrative of his journey to Macedonia, and describes first his relief at the arrival of Titus with good news from Corinth (5-7), and secondly, his reflections on the severe letter and its salutary consequences (8-13a). **5. came into Macedonia:** Ac. 20: 1. **our bodies:** Rather, 'my body'. The Gk. is singular (lit. 'our flesh'), and he is plainly speaking of himself alone. Both mind (cf. 2: 13) and body must have been affected by nervous tension. What the **fighting without** was we do not know (perhaps persecution; the Macedonian Jews would not have welcomed him back); the **fear within** was doubtless over the situation at Corinth. **6. the coming of Titus:** From Corinth with news of the church's acceptance of the severe letter. **who comforts the downcast:** A reminiscence of Isa. 49: 13. **7. Longing** to see Paul again, or to be reconciled to him, **mourning** for their past behaviour to him, **zeal** for him revealed by their obedience in punishing the evil-doer, and in defending him against his critics. 'Previously the longing, lamentation, and eagerness had been St. Paul's, and it was a delight to his emissary to find similar feelings in the Corinthians' (Plummer). Hence the repeated emphasized **your. I rejoiced still more:** I.e. his joy at their response was doubled when he saw how glad they had made Titus.

8. if I made you sorry: I.e. 'If I hurt you', not 'If I caused you to repent'. **my letter:** The 'severe' letter (cf. 2: 3 f.). **For I see that that letter grieved you** is explanatory of **I made you sorry with my letter,** not of course of **I do not regret it.** Knox's version is clearer than RSV: 'Yes, even if I caused you pain by my letter, I am not sorry for it. Perhaps I was tempted to feel sorry, when I saw how my letter had caused you even momentary pain, but now I am glad; not glad of the pain, but glad of the repentance the pain brought with it'. **9.** He would not like them to think that he is rejoicing over their humiliation, so he carefully explains why he felt such joy: it was not their sorrow but the fruit of their sorrow that gave him joy. They did not receive the letter with natural human irritation or self-justification but with **godly grief,** in this case sorrow for sin. **10. Worldly grief** is not only a regret for sin in which there is no place for repentance (cf. Heb. 12: 17), for 'all sorrow, whether it be due to disappointment, affliction, bereavement, or sin, is deadly in its operation so long as it remains unsanctified' (Tasker). It is the repentance, not the salvation (RVmg), that **brings no regret.** Paul is perhaps quoting an aphorism found in fuller form in the Jewish *Testament of Gad* (late 2nd or 1st cent. B.C.), 5: 7, 'True repentance after a godly sort driveth away the darkness, and enlighteneth the eyes, and giveth knowledge to the soul, and leadeth the mind to salvation'. **11.** The Corinthians themselves are the proof of this statement. See how their repentance has led to salvation, i.e. to salutary results. It has produced **earnestness** to set matters right, **eagerness to clear** themselves of Paul's accusations by correcting their behaviour, **indignation** at the shame brought on the church, or at the trouble-maker (2: 3) or the false apostles (11: 13), **alarm** (lit. 'fear') at God's wrath, or perhaps at Paul's anger (cf. 13; 1 C. 4: 21), **longing** for his favour and his return, **zeal** for Paul and against his opponents, **punishment** upon the offender(s). In **every point** they have **proved** themselves **guiltless,** or 'clear', now (not that they *were* guiltless, but Paul does not want to cloud his joy by thinking of their rebellion), by disassociating themselves from, and punishing, those who had defied Paul's authority. **the matter:** He uses this neutral term to avoid specifying the unpleasant subject (cf. 'any one', 2: 5). **12.** By saying that he wrote the severe letter **not on account of the one who did the wrong** (2: 5 ff.) nor **on account of the one who suffered the wrong** (himself) he cannot mean that the contention between his opponent and himself was not the occasion of the letter, but 'it was not so much for his sake and mine as for the sake of us all. My main object was to bring you to realize your real attitude to me, and to realize that the bonds between us are too strong to be quickly shaken off'. **vi. The Joy of Titus (7: 13b–16)** **13b.** Paul now returns to the thought of v. 7,

and describes in detail the joy of Titus. The fact that he speaks of Titus' mind being **set at rest by you all,** together with 'the obedience of you all' (15), and 'perfect confidence' (16), has been used by some as evidence that the church was now completely reconciled to Paul, and that therefore chaps. 10–13, which plainly depict a hostile minority, cannot be part of this letter (cf. Introduction). But we may surely allow Paul, in the relief and enthusiasm of the moment, now that the offender has been punished and the church has expressed its loyalty to him, more optimistic expressions than later reflection will warrant; moreover there are indications even within chaps. 1–9 that all was not well at Corinth (cf. 5: 12; 6: 12). **14. if I have expressed to him some pride in you:** The 'if' is not hypothetical, but= 'since' (cf. 9: 4). It is plain that Paul had spoken proudly to Titus of the Corinthians' loyalty (hoping against hope, it may be), and Titus was no doubt anxious for Paul lest his confidence in them should be rudely disappointed. **Some pride** does not mean that his praise was hedged by qualifications, but rather has the nuance 'considerable pride'. 'His love had enabled him to see deeper than the rebellious attitude of the moment' (F. V. Filson). **I was not put to shame:** By being proved wrong. **just as everything we said** (i.e. have ever said) **to you was true:** A passing reference to his truthfulness (cf. 1: 15 ff.).

15. fear and trembling: Not panic, but 'an anxious scrupulous desire not . . . to do less than one ought to do' (Denney). **16.** His **perfect confidence** is not simply 'perfect reconciliation', but also confidence for the future. So these words pave the way for the next topic, the collection for the Jerusalem poor (chs. 8, 9).

VI. THE COLLECTION FOR THE JERUSALEM POOR (8: 1–9: 15)
Paul was organizing a collection from his Gentile churches for the poor in the Jerusalem church, and he had already broached the subject with the Corinthians (1 C. 16: 1–4). The breakdown in relations between Paul and the Corinthian church had very probably brought about also an interruption of preparations in Corinth for making a contribution, and Paul must naturally have felt unable to continue his exhortations to them on this subject so long as the breach between them remained unhealed. The loyalty to himself which the Corinthians had evinced by their reception of Titus encouraged him now to re-open the subject; a reference to the collection a few months later (Rom. 15: 26 f.) indicates that the Corinthians

had responded well to the exhortations of these chapters.

The motive for this collection was doubtless originally Paul's undertaking to 'remember the poor' (Gal. 2: 10), given upon a previous occasion when he had been involved in a famine relief fund (Ac. 11: 27-30; Gal. 2: 1-10). But he saw also spiritual significance in the 'offering for the saints': it was a way for Gentile Christians to express their gratitude to the Jews for the spiritual blessings they had received through them (Rom. 15: 27; cf. Rom. 11: 11; Jn 4: 22). He regarded it as the visible token of his 'offering up of the Gentiles' (Rom. 15: 16), and as such set great value on it, even endangering his liberty and life (Ac. 21: 10 ff.) in order to deliver the gift personally (Ac. 24: 17).

Although he does not say so specifically, it is more than likely that he also looked upon the gift as a bond that would draw Jewish and Gentile Christians closer together, and would prove, by removing Jewish suspicions of his Gentile mission, that the 'middle wall of partition' (Eph. 2: 14) had indeed been broken down. Hence his request for the Roman Christians' prayers that the gift might prove acceptable to the Jerusalem saints (Rom. 15: 30 f.), that is, that they might accept not only the money, but also the spiritual implications of the gift.

He encourages the Corinthians to give by appealing to the example of the Macedonian churches (8: 1-7), to the example of Christ Himself (8: 9), and to the eagerness they themselves had previously shown (8: 10 f.; 9: 1-5); he further makes arrangements for the visit of Titus (8: 16-24), and expounds the principles of Christian giving (8: 12-15; 9: 6-15).

i. The Example of the Macedonians (8: 1-7)
1-7. 'Let me tell you of the great liberality of the Macedonian churches (1, 2). Though they were so poor, they gave to the fund more than could have been expected (3) (as though I was doing them a favour to allow them to contribute! [4]), for they gave more than their money to the Lord's work—they gave themselves! (5). Encouraged by *their* response, I have asked Titus to visit *you* and make final arrangements for your contribution (6). May Corinthian generosity match Corinthian excellence in other spiritual gifts!' (7).

1. The generosity of the Macedonians and their joy amid afflictions are the **grace of God . . . shown.** The **churches of Macedonia** known to us by name are Philippi, Thessalonica, and Beroea. The Philippians are praised for their generosity in Phil. 4: 15. **2.** Their **joy** combined with their **poverty** has **overflowed in a wealth of liberality,** not perhaps a great

amount of money (the amount is never mentioned), for it is their spirit of generosity that Paul is urging the Corinthians to emulate. For the Macedonians' joy in affliction, cf. 1 Th. 1: 6; 5: 16; and for Paul's, 2 C. 7: 4. The **extreme** (lit. 'abysmal') **poverty** of the Macedonians is illustrated by the fact that Paul never finds it necessary in his letters to Thessalonica and Philippi to warn these Christians against the dangers of wealth or to address an exhortation to the rich (cf. 1 Tim. 6: 9 f., 17 ff.). **3. beyond their means:** More literally, 'contrary to'; their gift was so generous that it was almost in contradiction to their poverty. **4.** 'It was they, not Paul, who did the begging' (Chrysostom); perhaps Paul had been reticent about asking them because of their poverty. The **saints** here are the church at Jerusalem (so also 9: 1; 1 C. 16: 1). Rom. 15: 26 speaks of the collection more specifically as for 'the poor among the saints at Jerusalem'. **5. not as we expected:** I.e. 'They have done more than I expected' (Moffatt), in that **first** and foremost they **gave themselves** (not just their money) **to the Lord and to us,** i.e. put themselves at the Lord's disposal and so at Paul's, by offering to send some of their number to accompany him (8: 18 f., 9: 4). Reflection on their action may well have inspired Rom. 12: 1 f., written a few months later.

6. Titus had **already made a beginning** of organizing the collection, perhaps when he carried 1 Corinthians to Corinth (if indeed he was the bearer), or more probably even earlier, for the abrupt introduction of 'the collection for the saints' in 1 C. 16: 1 suggests that the Corinthians already knew about it (cf. 12: 18).

ii. The Example of Christ, and Principles of Christian Giving (8: 8-15)
8-15. 'I do not mention the Macedonians in order to put pressure on you to equal them, but just to show you how genuine self-giving love acts (8). (And of this the greatest example is, as you know, the Lord Himself [9].) So I am not commanding, but I do advise you to complete the collection you began so enthusiastically last year (10, 11). The enthusiasm is the important thing—not the amount, for that is dictated by your income (12). I am not asking you to enable the Jerusalem Christians to live in luxury at your expense (13), but to ensure an equitable distribution of goods (it may prove beneficial to you one day!) (14), which after all is a biblical principle' (15).

8. He is not commanding them, for love and liberality, which is an expression of love, must be spontaneous, but he is giving them the example of **the earnestness of others** (the Macedonians) as a touchstone to test their **love**

to him; if their expressions of love are as **genuine** as the Macedonians', they will give as generously as they. **9.** This sentence, though formally a parenthesis, provides the finest example of self-giving love (he says **grace,** the same word [*charis*] as is translated 'gracious work' in vv. 6 f.)—that of **our Lord Jesus Christ,** the full title adding to the impressiveness of the appeal (Plummer). **For your sake** is placed in an emphatic position (cf. 5: 15). **He became poor** by becoming man (cf. Phil. 2: 5 ff.). His earthly poverty is not directly in view here. In what way Christ became poor Paul does not specify, for he is interested here not in the theology but in the ethics of the incarnation. **10.** 'I do not command (8), but I give my advice, which is the suitable way of approaching people like you (**best for you** is more literally 'suitable for you'), who have already proved that you need no commanding.' **a year ago:** Rather, 'last year' (as in 9: 2), i.e. any time between 9 and 21 months ago (Hughes). **not only to do but to desire:** Desire is in the climactic position because the desire to give (the spirit of liberality) is greater than the gift itself. This does not commit Paul to the doctrine that the only thing necessary is a good will. A more prosaic interpretation is: 'since it was you who led the way, not only in giving, but in proposing to act, as early as last year' (Knox), i.e. 'you began the preparations for the collection earlier than the Macedonians'. **11. out of what you have:** I.e. 'in proportion to your means', 'according to what a man has' (12) (cf. 1 C. 16: 2). He does not oblige them to match the Macedonians' giving 'beyond their means' (3). **14. As a matter of equality** does not mean a doctrinaire equalization of property. Scripture avoids 'on the one hand the injustice and destructive evils of agrarian communism, by recognizing the right of property and making all almsgiving optional; and on the other the heartless disregard of the poor by inculcating the universal brotherhood of believers' (A. P. Stanley). **your abundance:** Though mainly from the lower classes (1 C. 1: 26-28), the Corinthian Christians appear to have been better off than the Macedonians, even though these numbered among themselves (at least in Thessalonica) 'not a few' of the upper classes (Ac. 17: 4). **that their abundance may supply your want:** If necessary in the future. **15.** Paul quotes Exod. 16: 18 to illustrate God's intention that *all* His people should have enough for their needs. The OT narrative appears to indicate that no matter how much manna anyone had gathered, when it was measured it was found to be (miraculously) the exact amount sufficient for his needs, an omer per day.

iii. Forthcoming Visit of Titus (8: 16-24)
16. Paul is sending Titus, as he began to say in v. 6, to supervise the final stages of the collection. He is not coming himself, partly to avoid any criticism that some of the collection will go into his pocket (cf. 20 f.), and partly because he wants the collection to be ready when he arrives with friends from Macedonia (9: 3-5). **The same earnest care for you:** The enthusiasm of Paul and Titus is not simply for the Jerusalem Christians, but **for you,** the Corinthians. **17. our appeal:** The 'urging' of v. 6. **he is going:** With this letter. **18. the brother who is famous for his preaching of the gospel:** Possibly Luke. Several pieces of evidence connect Luke with Philippi (*e.g.* Ac. 16: 11 f. 'we' and 17: 1 'they'; 20: 3 'he' and 20: 6 'we'), and make it possible that he was the representative of the Philippian church who accompanied Paul to Jerusalem (no Philippian is mentioned in Ac. 20: 4, but Luke was certainly with them [5]). So he could be the one 'appointed by the churches (of Macedonia) to travel with us' (19). **20. We (='I') intend** by sending not only my own colleague Titus, but also a man of repute, chosen by the Macedonian churches independently of me, and another trusted brother (22), to give no occasion for any to **blame us about this liberal gift.** It is bound to be a large sum; all the more reason why the handling of it should be above suspicion **21.** He quotes Prov. 3: 4 (LXX), *Provide things honest in the sight of the Lord and men.* Justice has to *appear* to be done. **22. Our brother** is unidentifiable. **23.** 'In short, to forestall any criticism, let me set down their qualifications'. Titus is Paul's own representative, his 'minister for Corinthian affairs' (**fellow-worker in your service**); the other two are **messengers** (Gk. 'apostles', i.e. officially appointed delegates) **of the churches** of Macedonia. They are **the glory of Christ,** i.e. they bring credit on Christ by their life. Less likely is the interpretation that they reflect to others something of the splendour of Christ. **24. before the churches:** What the representatives of the churches see and hear will be reported to their home churches.

iv. Why Titus is being Sent (9: 1-5)
1-5. He explains why, instead of coming himself, he is sending Titus and the two other brethren: to make sure that the collection is finalized by the time he himself arrives.

1. It is unnecessary for him to go on writing, partly because his envoys will be arriving, and partly because he has already given instructions (1 C. 16: 1-4). **2.** Their **readiness** is their 'desire' of 8: 10 f. They are not fully ready (4), i.e. the collection is not completed. **Achaia** primarily means Corinth (cf. on 1: 1). **most of them:** He does not mean that some are still unwilling to give, but that it is the Corinthians' zeal that has been for most of them the greatest incentive to contribute. **3.** His **boasting** about them would **prove vain**, if, after boasting to the Macedonians that the Corinthians were more than keen, he should find that this zeal had not been directed into finishing the collection. **4.** If, as seems likely, Titus' two companions were Macedonians, then two Macedonians at least would know very soon that the Corinthians were not quite ready. This would not be so serious because the deadline had not yet been reached, but if Paul were to arrive in Corinth on his way to Jerusalem, accompanied by Macedonian delegates, and were to find the collection still incomplete, it would be a humiliation both to him and the Corinthians. **If some Macedonians come** is not hypothetical, but = 'when' (cf. 13: 2). **lest . . . we be humiliated:** The disgrace would really be the Corinthians', but Paul so much identifies himself with his converts that he feels the disgrace to be his. **5.** If he arrives while the collection is still incomplete, the contributions which will be made then will be more like an **exaction** (the Corinthians would feel under an obligation to give) than a **willing gift;** the time for spontaneous giving will have passed.

v. The Nature of Christian Giving (9: 6–15)
6–15. 'Giving is like sowing: you reap in proportion to what you sow (6). Giving must be methodical and cheerful (7). If you give in that way, God will make sure you have enough for your own needs and enough to give away (8), as the psalmist says (9). Yes, if you sow benevolence, God will keep on increasing the amount you have to sow (10). And your enrichment, spiritual as well as material, will result in greater generosity, and also in much thanksgiving to God from those who receive your gift (11), for giving does not only bring help to the saints, but causes God to be glorified by them (12). And it is not only they who will glorify God—you too, by your giving, will prove your obedience to Christ, and so glorify God (13). What an expression of fellowship, with giver and getter joined by their prayers for one another! (14). But what is the origin of giving? God, who put giving into our hearts by the gift of His Son. Thanks be to Him!' (15).

6. Prov. 11: 24 f. and 19: 17 are echoed here (cf. also Lk. 6: 38). In itself, this is not a very exalted motive for giving, but it is Paul's purpose to expound the whole nature of giving, and in any case 'it is right to present to men the divinely ordained consequences of their actions as motives to control their conduct' (Hodge).

7. as he has made up his mind: The giving is not to be casual, but planned. There will be a certain moral **compulsion** to give if Paul arrives before the collection is complete. **God loves a cheerful giver:** More exactly 'It is the cheerful giver that God loves', a quotation from Prov. 22: 8 (LXX). **8.** There is no risk in generous giving, for God will always recompense the giver with **enough of everything** for his own needs and enough to give to **every good work. 9.** He reinforces the thought of v. 8 by quoting Ps. 112: 9, which says of the liberal man who **scatters abroad** (i.e. does not sow sparingly) that his almsgiving **endures for ever,** i.e. he will never run short of money for giving. **Righteousness** is used here in the sense of 'almsgiving' (RSVmg, NEB; cf. Mt. 6: 1). **10. seed to the sower and bread for food:** A quotation from Isa. 55: 10 (LXX). **Your resources** are 'what you have to sow with', and the **harvest** (lit. 'the fruits') **of your righteousness** (the wording borrowed from Hos. 10: 12 [LXX]) is the reward for benevolence. **11.** The reward of their benevolence will be that they **will be enriched in every way,** spiritually as well as materially, and this will have two results: first, they will be able to give with **great**(er) (lit. 'all' or 'every kind of') **generosity,** and secondly, **through us** (Paul) and our delivery of the collection for the saints, a great volume of **thanksgiving to God** will be produced. **12. supplies:** More literally, 'helps to supply'; the Corinthians were not the only contributors. **the saints:** Cf. 8: 4. **13.** Benevolence is to be the **test** of the Corinthians' sincerity, as affliction was that of the Macedonians (8: 2). **you will glorify God:** Many commentators prefer the translation 'they (the Jerusalem Christians) will glorify God' for this proof of Gentile loyalty and obedience to Christ, of which they had been highly suspicious. **and for all others:** A gift to a part of the Church is a gift to the whole Church (1 C. 12: 26); or perhaps Paul is expressing a hope that this will not be the last gift the Corinthians will make to needy Christians. **14. they long for you:** Better, 'they are drawn to you' (Moffatt), or 'their hearts will go out to you' (NEB). The Jerusalem Christians will recognize that this generous gift owes its origin to the surpassing grace of God in the Corinthians, just as in the Macedonians (8: 1). **15.** In reflecting on the grace of generosity to be given by God to the Corinthians, Paul is led to think of Christ, God's inexpressibly generous gift.

VII. PAUL'S SELF-DEFENCE AGAINST THE 'FALSE APOSTLES' (10: 1–13: 10)
In spite of Paul's general satisfaction with the

church at Corinth, there was apparently still a group which disputed his apostolic authority, and professed themselves followers of certain leaders whom Paul refers to as 'false apostles' (11: 13). Their activities and teaching are to us far from clear, though this is not of course due to any intention on Paul's part to make only obscure references to them, but to the fact that they were only too well known both to the Corinthians and to Paul.

Certain facts about the 'false apostles', however, are plain. They were Jewish Christians (11: 22 f.), visitors from outside Corinth (cf. 11: 4), who came armed with letters of commendation (3: 1) claiming for them a higher authority than Paul's (10: 7). Their method of gaining adherents was to assert their own authority, no doubt with some eloquence (cf. 10: 10; 11: 6) and a great deal of mutual admiration (10: 12), and to denigrate Paul before his converts (10: 1 f., 10; 11: 7, etc.). They were evidently not averse to receiving financial support from the church (11: 12, 20), yet behaved in a high-handed and insolent way toward it (11: 20), and boasted of the Corinthians as though they were their own converts (cf. 10: 5). It is attractive to suppose, in view of their claim to be 'Christ's' (10: 7), that they based their authority on their having seen Christ in the flesh (could not, for example, the Seventy [Lk. 10: 1 ff.] have regarded their commissioning from Christ as of a higher order than Paul's, who presumably had never seen Christ in the flesh?). Support for this view from 5: 16, however, where Paul says he knows no man any longer after the flesh, can only be gained by an erroneous interpretation of that statement.

Virtually nothing is known of their teaching. Many have seen them as judaizers, but Jewish Christians do not necessarily judaize, and if they were in fact requiring the Corinthians to keep the law, it would be very strange that Paul does not attack their doctrine (as he does in Galatians). It is not likely that Paul's exposition of the superiority of the New Covenant to the Old (3: 7-18) is dictated by polemical motives, nor should we see in 'servants of righteousness' (11: 15) an allusion to judaizers who insisted on law-works.

Yet Paul calls them 'false apostles' (11: 13). He enters into no dispute about their authority or about their teaching, but on the ground of their unchristian behaviour both to the Corinthians (e.g. 11: 20) and to himself (cf. e.g. 10: 13-15), he feels justified in saying that they are doing the devil's work.

i. Paul, 'Humble' by Preference, 'Bold' if Necessary (10: 1-6)

1-6. 'I am accused of being inconfident when

I am in Corinth, and overbearing when I am away. I prefer the gentle approach (1), and I hope I shall not have to be "bold" against my opponents when I come. But I will if they continue to accuse me of unspirituality (2); my activities are not worldly—nor are my weapons; they are spiritual, and therefore strong enough to crush all opposition and disobedience (3-5), and I am prepared to use them against my critics if necessary' (6).

1. 'In the very sentence in which he puts himself and his dignity forward with uncompromising firmness, he recalls to his own and his readers' hearts the characteristic temper of the Lord' (Denney). **Meekness** is an inward virtue, the acceptance of God's discipline and will, **gentleness** is 'consideration' (Moffatt) for others. These are the qualities of Christ Paul would prefer to imitate. **I who am humble . . .** reproduces his critics' charge that he displayed cowardice when present, bravado when absent (cf. v. 10). Probably they referred to the failure of his 'painful' visit (cf. on 2: 1) and the subsequent severe letter (cf. on 2: 3). **humble:** 'A Uriah Heep, very humble and cringing and artful' (Plummer). **2. count on, suspect:** The same verb in both cases. **Suspect** is too weak; better, 'who have made up their minds that I move on the low level of the flesh' (Moffatt). **Some,** the false apostles and their partisans (cf. on 3: 1), have by their remarks about Paul implied (they may not have spoken so plainly themselves) that he was acting **in worldly fashion.** The criticism is too general for us to infer the particular charges, but cf. 1: 17; 2: 17; 4: 2; 5: 11, 16; 7: 2; 8: 20 f. **3.** A more literal translation: ' . . . who reckon that we walk according to the flesh (2). For though we walk *in* the flesh, we carry on a war not *according to* the flesh (3)'. To live *in the flesh* is to be a human being (cf. Gal. 2: 20; a different meaning in Rom. 8: 9); to live *according to the flesh* is to be at the mercy of the impulses of the sinful nature. His humility (1) is not worldly cowardice or craftiness, nor is his boldness self-assertion. Cowardice is the last thing to accuse him of; his whole life is a **war** against opposition to the truth of the gospel (cf. 6: 7; 1 Th. 5: 8; Eph. 6: 11-17). **4.** Because his **weapons** are not **worldly** but spiritual, they **have divine power.** For the concept of spirit as powerful, and stronger than flesh, cf. e.g. Zech. 4: 6; Isa. 31: 3. **5.** There is a destructive element in his apostolic work (cf. v. 8), directed against the **arguments** or sophistries of men, and, to use the widest terms of reference, **every proud obstacle,** lit. 'high thing' or 'rampart' (Moffatt); the military metaphor is continued. **take every thought captive:** 'Thought' probably means 'plot, design'. An alternative interpretation is that his goal is not simply outward submission, but inward obedience (in **thought** or 'mind') to Christ. But there is no suggestion of an assault on reason or a 'sacrifice of the intellect'. **6. ready to punish:** As Christ's apostle, he has the authority to pass sentence (Mt. 16: 19). **every disobedience:** I.e. anyone who is still recalcitrant when the church as a whole re-affirms its allegiance to Christ and to Paul. Moffatt suggests that the military metaphor is still being used: 'I am prepared to court-martial anyone who remains insubordinate, when your submission is complete'.

ii. Paul's Authority not Inferior to the False Apostles' (10: 7–11)

7–11. 'Face the facts! Are my opponents sent by Christ? so am I (7). I could say more, but forbear for the moment (8)—any expression of my authority would only give fresh grounds for complaint about my severe letters (9). Bold as brass his letters are, they say, but he has no strength of character (10). Such critics had better realize that I am capable of acting in the spirit of my letters' (11).

7. Look at what is before your eyes: Other possible translations are: 'You look only at what lies before your eyes' (cf. RV), i.e. only at externals; 'Do you look . . .?' (AV, RVmg). RSV means: 'Face the facts! I belong to Christ as much as they do'. The claim to be **Christ's** does not appear to have any connection with the 'Christ-party' of 1 C. 1: 12, but is a claim to special authority given by Christ (see introduction to this chapter). The mere assertion of superior authority by Paul will not settle the issue, so he simply says that his commissioning is at least not inferior to theirs. **8.** 'Though were I to claim higher authority than theirs, I would not be exaggerating'. He takes the word **boast** from his opponents' mouths; they doubtless labelled all his claims to apostolic authority as 'boasting'. **A little too much** perhaps gives the wrong nuance to a word which may also mean 'a little more' than he has done (in v. 7, perhaps in vv. 3–6), or than he usually does. The proper work of **authority** is to build up (so also 12: 19; 13: 10), and this has been the effect of Paul's work in Corinth. It is only the rebellious (not **you,** he hopes) who suffer its destructive work (cf. v. 5). Perhaps he also alludes to the 'false apostles', whose authority has been used only for destruction. **shall not be put to shame:** By being proved to have exaggerated. **9.** 'But I will say no more about my *authority*, for that would be "frightening" you!' **10. His letters are weighty and strong:** A valuable contemporary estimate of his writings by witnesses not prejudiced in

his favour! **his bodily presence:** Not only his physical appearance, but also the way he acts when present. **speech of no account:** Devoid of rhetorical artifice (cf. 1 C. 1: 17; 2: 1–5). He appears to admit the charge (11: 6). **11.** He does not retort that when he comes he will *speak* well, but he will *act*. **what we say by letter:** Particularly about being severe (cf. vv. 2, 6).

iii. His Motto is 'Nothing beyond the Limit' (10: 12–18)

12–18. 'Of course, I would not dare to class myself with these men who boast without limit (How foolish self-commendation is! It has no external standards of reference) (12). I will keep within my limits—and my 'limits' include you (13), for I was the first to preach the gospel in Corinth, and so I have staked out a claim to you (14). I do not boast beyond my 'limits'—of work done in territory other than my own; and I hope this will remain my policy when I move on to other countries (15, 16). But all this talk about boasting in work done or not done is beside the point; we should glory in the Lord, not our work (17). And it is His commendation we need, not our own' (18).

12. In v. 11 he has affirmed his readiness to use his strength against his opponents, but now in mock humility and cowardice he says that of course he would not **venture** to put himself in the same **class** or even to **compare** himself with these authoritarian 'apostles' (cf. 11: 20). By their commendation of one another, they show themselves to be **without understanding** because they do not see that their judgments are purely relative. **13.** He plays on the word **limit.** If he is to boast at all, he **will not boast beyond limit,** i.e. he will limit himself to the truth (unlike the false apostles, whose conceit knew no bounds). But the **limits** within which he will keep will be, in another sense, *geographical* limits, the provinces which **God has apportioned** to him as apostle to the Gentiles (Gal. 2: 9). Unlike his opponents, he will not encroach on other men's territory (cf. Rom. 15: 20) and steal their converts. **14.** 'It is not **we** (=Paul) **who are over-extending ourselves,** stepping outside the agreed boundaries, **as though we did not reach you,** "as if you lay beyond my sphere" (Moffatt). No, I was **the first to come all the way to you with the gospel** (cf. 1 C. 3: 6–10; 4: 15), and so you are within my province.' **15. Beyond limit** does not mean 'excessively' (as in v. 13), but 'beyond the limit of my commission' (cf. NEB), and thus is equivalent to **in other men's labours.** When the Corinthians' **faith increases** and makes his presence there no longer necessary, he will be able to turn his attention to lands beyond them (cf. Rom. 15: 23-29). Instead of **our field among you** we should translate: 'that . . . our field may be greatly enlarged *by* you', i.e. they can open up new fields for him if they will acknowledge his authority at Corinth and so let him get on with his work elsewhere. **16. without boasting of work already done:** His personal principle of not building on another man's foundation (Rom. 15: 20) both avoided friction with other missionaries and ensured the rapid spread of the gospel over a wide area. He did not object to others doing 'follow-up' work, provided they built in accordance with the foundation already laid (1 C. 3: 10 ff.), and did not take the credit for another's work to themselves. **17.** A Christian worker should not boast of work he has not done, nor even of work he *has* done, but only **of the Lord.** Paul here condenses Jer. 9: 24.

iv. Paul Expresses his Intention to Boast (11: 1–21a)

(a) Why he must boast (11: 1-6)

1-6. 'If I go on to boast about myself, do be patient with me! (1). (It is only because I am driven to it by my concern for you [2] and my fear that unless I boast of my credentials you will lose, together with your respect for me, your respect for the gospel I preach [3]. Yes, I do believe that if some one were to come with an utterly different gospel, you would accept him [4]). I am entitled to boast, I think, because I am in no way inferior to these "apostles" (5); perhaps I am ineloquent, but I do at least know what I am talking about, as you can bear witness' (6).

1. The **little foolishness** is the boasting of vv. 21 ff. He knows it is foolish (cf. 10: 17), but he feels it is necessary for the sake of the Corinthians. They have accepted the false apostles on the strength of their credentials, and since higher appeals have not been totally successful, Paul must appeal on this low level also. **Do bear with me** may alternatively be taken as an indicative, 'I know you do bear with me', or ironically, 'Yes, I know, you have to do a lot of "putting up" with me!' **2.** He feels the **jealousy** for the Corinthian church that a father feels for his daughter (cf. 1 C. 4: 15), that is, for her honour. It is a **divine** jealousy (lit. 'the jealousy of God') because God too feels it. Paul has **betrothed** the church **to Christ, to present** it **as a pure bride** to Him, at the Parousia. (For the universal Church as Christ's bride, cf. Eph. 5: 27 ff.; Rev. 19: 7 f.) **3.** But he fears that the bride-to-be, instead of being a pure bride presented to her one husband, will be seduced by the false apostles. **4.** Paul is so fearful for the stability of the Corinthians that

he can even imagine them being carried away by some utterly different gospel. The whole sentence must be regarded as hypothetical: 'If some one were to come . . . you would submit' (an alternative MS reading makes this interpretation explicit). It is improbable that he refers to the false apostles; if they had preached another Jesus, would he have simply defended his own authority and not said one word in refutation of their heresy?

5. these superlative apostles (or 'super-apostles'): A sarcastic reference to the Jewish Christians who had come to Corinth (see Introduction to chap. 10). The original twelve apostles are not in mind (as in AV, RV).

6. unskilled in speaking: Without formal rhetorical training. His **knowledge** of the truth has been given him by God (4: 6). It is either this knowledge of the truth that he has always **made plain** (cf. 4: 2), or else the fact that he possesses it.

(b) Has he wronged the Corinthians? (11: 7-11)

7-11. 'Why then do you regard me as inferior to these "apostles"? Have I wronged you in some way? Was my sin to have preached to you without demanding wages? (7). It was at the expense of other churches that you heard the gospel (8), and why? because I would not impose on you by taking money (9a). And this will always be my policy (9b, 10). Does this prove I don't love you? Of course not!' (11).

7. The false apostles, in their campaign of vilification against Paul, had apparently claimed that his financial independence of the Corinthians (cf. 1 C. 9) betokened a lack of intimacy with them; perhaps also that it was most undignified for the apostle to the Corinthians to support himself by manual labour, it being the custom in Greece for orators and preachers to be paid by their adherents. The earlier insinuation of some that his refusal to accept maintenance betrayed a bad conscience about his apostolic claims (1 C. 9: 1-15) does not appear to have been revived. It is arguable that these extremely perverse criticisms were not actually made, but are ironically imagined by Paul in order to introduce the contrast between his and the false apostles' attitudes to financial support (12 ff.). **8.** He **robbed other churches** (he is thinking especially of the Macedonians, cf. v. 9) by accepting their gifts which they could ill afford. It was not fair (therefore 'robbery') that they should have had to support Paul when the Corinthians could have done so. **9. did not burden:** More exactly, 'did not put pressure on anyone', or 'sponged on no one' (NEB). **my needs were supplied by the brethren** (Silas and Timothy) **from Mace-**

donia (Ac. 18: 5): Previously he had had to
spend some of his time in manual labour, but
now with the Macedonian gift he could 'devote
himself entirely to preaching' (Ac. 18: 5 NEB).
10. We do not know whether the Corinthians
had ever offered him support, but in any case
he has now spoken to them so plainly about
their failure to provide for him that it would be
too embarrassing on both sides for him ever to
receive anything from them. **As the truth of
Christ is in me:** An oath (cf. 1: 18). **this
boast of mine shall never be silenced in the
regions of Achaia:** I.e. 'I will never accept
money from the church of Corinth' (cf. 1 C. 9:
15). **Achaia:** Cf. on 9: 2.

(c) **The false apostles (11: 12–15)**
12–15. 'My policy of not accepting support will
be one way at least of showing my superiority
to these "apostles" (12)—false apostles they
really are, doing Satan's work (13). No wonder
that his servants disguise themselves as true
apostles (15), seeing that he himself disguises
himself as an angel of light' (14).

12. what I do: I.e. his policy on not accepting support (10). Though the false apostles
sneer at Paul's refusal of maintenance, they
admit to themselves that it is a powerful proof
of his integrity, and they would gladly drag
him down to their own level and boast that
in all respects they **work on the same terms**
as he. **13.** They are **false apostles** (not so much
'false teachers'), for they claim Christ's authority
when they have none but their own; and
deceitful workmen because they are serving
not Christ but themselves (perhaps also because
they are doing destructive work [cf. 10: 8]).
14. The belief that **Satan disguises himself as
an angel of light** is not explicit in OT (though
he appears among the 'sons of God' in Job 1: 6,
but not in disguise), and it is suggested that
Paul may be alluding to a Jewish legend that
Satan appeared to Eve in the form of an angel
and sang hymns like the angels (*Life of Adam
and Eve* [2nd–4th cent. A.D.], 9: 1 [R.H.Charles,
*The Apocrypha and Pseudepigrapha of the Old
Testament*, vol. ii., p. 136]). But it is equally
possible that Paul is referring to the habitual
conduct of the devil as the deceiver (cf. 2: 11;
Eph. 6: 11; 1 Tim. 3: 7), rather than to a particular incident. **15.** They are **servants** of Satan
in that the work of destruction and vilification
they are doing is Satan's work. But in v. 23
Paul seems to admit that they are servants of
Christ. Similarly, Peter, a servant of Christ,
could do Satan's work (Mk 8: 33). **Their end
will correspond to their deeds:** A Biblical
principle applicable to all men, whether Christian or not (Prov. 24: 12; Rom. 2: 6; 2 C. 5: 10;
1 Pet. 1: 17).

(d) **The folly of boasting (11: 16–21a)**
16–21a. 'Before I begin to boast according to
the flesh (21b–29), I repeat (cf. 1) that I recognize
that it is a foolish thing to do (16), and sub-
Christian (17), but I am driven to it (18). You
tolerate fools so easily that you should have
no difficulty in putting up with me! (19). Oh,
yes, you can tolerate far worse things than folly
—even personal injury and abuse (20). I must
confess, I have been too weak to inflict that on
you!' (21a).

16. 'I repeat (cf. v. 1), I know boasting is a fool's
game, and I would not like anyone to **think
me foolish,** for, to be honest, it goes very
much against the grain for me to play the fool.
But even if you will not pay me the compliment
of realizing that I speak with tongue in cheek,
pay me the attention you would a fool (**accept
me as a fool**), so that I too (remember, I
didn't start it!) **may boast a little** for the sake
of the record'. **17.** He cannot claim **the Lord's
authority** for boasting, for to boast is not in
accord with the character of Christ. Yet boasting,
i.e. producing his credentials, seems to be the
only way of re-establishing his authority. 'By
itself indeed it is not "after the Lord", but by its
intention it becomes so. And therefore he said,
"that which I speak", not accusing the motive,
but the words; since his aim is so admirable as
to dignify the words also' (Chrysostom).
18. of worldly things: Lit. 'according to the
flesh'. Paul will for a time boast on the same
low level (21b–29), but his true boast is in
his weakness (30) and the power of Christ
(12: 9).
19. The Corinthians are so sure of their own
wisdom (cf. 1 C. 4: 8–10) that it gives them a
certain pleasure to indulge **fools. 20.** They can
easily bear with *folly*, for they put up with far
worse things than that, tyranny, oppression,
violence, insult (all of which, he implies, have
been practised by the false apostles). **makes
slaves:** Contrast Paul's attitude (1: 24; 4: 5).
preys upon you: Lit. 'devours' by exacting
money (cf. Mk 12: 40). **takes advantage**
(cf. 12: 17): Or possibly, 'catches you, like birds
in a trap'. **21a.** Paul ironically reproaches himself for having proved weaker than the domineering false apostles, and implicitly rebukes
the Corinthians for preferring their tyranny to
his gentleness.

**v. Boasting 'According to the Flesh' (11:
21b–29)**
21b–29. 'Here are my credentials. I am a pure-
blooded Jew (22), and a servant of Christ, as is
proved by all I have suffered for the gospel's
sake (23), at the hands of officials (24, 25a) and
mobs, and through natural calamities (25b);
often in danger on my frequent journeys (26),

437

suffering bodily privations (27) and mental distress' (28, 29). **22.** There is little difference between the terms **Hebrews, Israelites,** and **descendants of Abraham. Hebrews** perhaps refers to the fact that they spoke Aramaic as well as Greek (cf. Ac. 6: 1), though 'a Hebrew of the Hebrews' (Phil. 3: 5) refers to pure descent, 'a Hebrew born of Hebrew parents'. **23. Servants of Christ** is their own description of themselves, and Paul will not argue about their standing before God, plain though it is that they are doing Satan's work in Corinth (13). His reply to their claim to superiority as apostles of Christ is that for him the signs of a true apostle are his sufferings in the service of Christ. He is a **better** servant of Christ because he has suffered, while they have not. He does not mean, by speaking of his **far greater labours** and **far more imprisonments** to contrast the number of his sufferings with theirs, but simply to contrast his real sufferings with their mere claims. **I am talking like a madman:** He winces at the thought of where this self-praise is leading. **imprisonments:** Luke informs us of only one before this time, at Philippi (Ac. 16: 23), but we know of four later: in Jerusalem and Caesarea, and two in Rome. Very probably he had been imprisoned in Ephesus during the two-year visit of Ac. 19. Clement of Rome (*Epistle to the Corinthians* [A.D. 96], 5: 6) says that Paul was imprisoned seven times. **often near death:** Cf. 'I die daily' (1 C. 15: 31) and 2 C. 1: 9; 4: 10 f. **24.** Only two of the thirteen incidents in vv. 24, 25 are recorded elsewhere in the NT, and even this list must be selective (cf. 'apart from other things', v. 28). **forty lashes less one:** The law (Dt. 25: 1 ff.) allowed 40 stripes, but to prevent an infringement of the law through miscalculation, Jewish custom had 'built a hedge around the Torah' by limiting the number to 39. The punishment, to which half a tractate of the Mishnah is devoted (*Makkoth*), was inflicted in the synagogue (cf. Mt. 10: 17) by the minister (or servant), who gave 13 stripes on the chest and 26 on the shoulders (*Makkoth*, 3: 12). **25. beaten with rods:** By Roman lictors. Only one instance of this punishment is recorded in Acts (16: 22 f., 37; cf. 1 Th. 2: 2; for an attempt to beat him, cf. Ac. 22: 24 ff.). It was contrary to Roman law that a Roman citizen (as Paul was) should be beaten, but cases were not unknown. **stoned:** At Lystra (Ac. 14: 19). Being **shipwrecked** is not mentioned by Luke. A later one is described in Ac. 27. **27.** Privations he has suffered (cf. on 6: 4 f.). **toil and hardship:** The same phrase as in 1 Th. 2: 9; 2 Th. 3: 8. **28. all the churches:** Perhaps he means 'not only those founded by me'. **29. weak:**

Not only weak in conscience (1 C. 8: 7) (cf. Knox: 'Does anyone feel a scruple? I share it'), but weak in all other ways too. **Who is made to fall:** He is no doubt thinking particularly of the Corinthians, who have been 'made to fall' by the false apostles.

vi. Boasting in Weakness (11: 30–12: 10)

The word 'weak' (29) has led him to reflect on the subject of weakness. I would far rather boast of my weaknesses, he thinks, than of my strengths, because it is in my weaknesses that *God's* power has been evidenced. He illustrates the theme of his weakness by the story of his escape from Damascus (11: 32-33), and by the account of his vision of the third heaven and the subsequent thorn in his flesh (12: 1-10).

(a) **His escape from Damascus (11: 30-33)**
30-33. 'No, I will boast no more "according to the flesh". If I must boast, it will be of unheroic things, my weaknesses (30). God knows I would rather boast of them (31). One such inglorious episode, in which I glory nevertheless, was my escape from Damascus' (32, 33). **30.** 'The true apostle, . . . far from being able to boast of honour and power . . . is, like Jesus, a suffering and dying figure, whose work and power and victory arise from his weakness and infirmity and defeat' (J. Munck). **31.** A solemn asseveration of his preference for reflection on God's strength in his weakness, rather than on what *he* has achieved. Some think, less probably, that he is binding himself with an oath that all the details of vv. 32 f. (or 24-27) are correct. **32, 33.** This rather humiliating incident (Ac. 9: 23 ff.), which a boaster 'according to the flesh' would keep well hidden (and perhaps Paul had been called a coward because of this escape), is Paul's first illustration of 'strength made perfect in weakness' (12: 9); it is an admirable foil to the episode of the third heaven (though the contrast between 'let down' [11: 33] and 'caught up' [12: 2] may be only fortuitous). Many, however, feel these verses to be strangely placed here, and regard them, since they describe a 'suffering' of Paul's, as an afterthought (cf. 1 C. 1: 16) to the catalogue of vv. 24-27. Opinions differ on the function of the **governor** (lit. 'ethnarch') under **King Aretas** IV of the Nabataeans (his capital was Petra); he may have been the viceroy of Aretas, or (if the Romans were at this period in possession of Damascus) merely head of the Nabataean colony there, or a (Jewish) ethnarch responsible for the Jewish community in the city. Paul's stay of three years in (Nabataean) Arabia (Gal. 1: 17) and Damascus (Ac. 9: 22) had apparently provoked both Nabataeans and Jews against him; it seems to have been at the instigation of

the Jews that the ethnarch had the city gates watched in order to seize Paul.

(b) The third heaven and the 'thorn in the flesh' (12: 1–10)

1–10. The visionary experience is not related for its own sake, but as a preface to the lesson of the 'thorn in the flesh'. His physical weakness, which gives an opportunity for the power of Christ to be displayed, is a more agreeable subject of boasting than his experiences of the sublime, about which he is noticeably reticent. **1. I must boast:** He is impelled by the situation (cf. 11: 1, 16 ff., 21, 23), but he knows that **there is nothing to be gained** from it—it is not edifying (cf. 10: 8). **2.** He refers to himself as **a man in Christ** because the man who underwent such experiences seems to be almost a different person from the Paul of everyday life. His specification of the date, **fourteen years ago,** is reminiscent of the dating of their visions by OT prophets (*e.g.* Am. 1: 1; Hag. 1: 1; 2: 1, 10, 20). If A.D. 56 is accepted as the date of 2 Corinthians, Paul would have had the vision while he was in Tarsus (cf. Ac. 11: 25); others reckon it a couple of years later, while he was in Antioch (cf. Ac. 11: 26). **The third heaven** was apparently regarded by Paul as the highest heaven; the concept of three heavens may have been deduced from the expression 'heaven and the heaven of heavens' (1 Kg. 8: 27). Later the view that there were seven heavens became dominant in Judaism (cf. TB, *Hagigah*, 12b). **whether in the body or out of it I do not know:** Paul recognized the possibility of a corporeal ascension (like Elijah's or Christ's; cf. 1 Th. 4: 15 ff.) as well as of an incorporeal rapture, in which the soul was separated from the body (cf. 5: 1 ff.). During his vision he was not conscious of his body, and so now he cannot say whether it was a corporeal ascension or not. **3. Paradise** (originally a Persian word meaning 'park, pleasure-garden') was used in LXX of the garden of Eden, and hence in later Jewish literature and NT (Lk. 23: 43; Rev. 2: 7) of the abode of the blessed after death. V. 2 and v. 3 refer to the same vision, and 'paradise' merely describes the character of the third heaven. **4. things that cannot be told:** Either because they cannot be expressed in words (cf. Rom. 8: 26), or because they are specially sacred (cf. NEB). **5.** He continues to speak of **this man** (lit. 'such a man') as if he were not himself. Such experiences may well be boasted of, but because they are *given*, and are not his own achievement, they reveal nothing of his own character. **6.** He could go on to boast of his experiences without exaggerating (cf. 10: 8), but he wants no one to judge him on his unverifiable statements about himself, only on the

evidence before their eyes. **7. The abundance of revelations:** Either means 'the abundance of things revealed' during the one rapture of vv. 2 f., or should be translated 'the excellence of the revelations'. **a thorn . . . in the flesh:** The word for 'thorn' (*skolops*) meant in classical Gk. a 'stake', but the meaning 'thorn' was apparently more common in Hellenistic times. In spite of views that the thorn in the flesh was suffering in persecution (was this a thorn only for Paul?), or doubts or temptations to evil (if so, why should the Lord tell him not to pray for its removal?), the most natural interpretation is that it is a physical ailment. If it is the same thing as the 'weakness in the flesh' of Gal. 4: 13 f. (as seems probable, but cannot be proved), we can define the malady as being of a repulsive nature (cf. 'you did not despise me', lit. 'did not spit me out'), as well as acute ('thorn') and recurrent ('three times', 'harass'). The most probable conjectures are ophthalmia (cf. Gal. 4: 15; 6: 11; Ac. 23: 5) and malarial fever (perhaps contracted at Perga [Ac. 13: 13], and the cause of his journey to the healthier climate of Galatia [Gal. 4: 13]). The **messenger of Satan** is the thorn in the flesh, not a personal enemy. Like Job's calamities, the thorn was inflicted by Satan, though permitted by God. **harass:** Lit. 'buffet', a frequently recurring action. **9. he said:** The perfect tense is used with its proper significance, 'He *has* said (and His answer still holds good)'. **My grace is sufficient:** The 'summit of the epistle' (Hughes). Christ's promise has had a marked effect on Paul's attitude to life (cf. 3: 5; 4: 7, etc.). **Grace** is not just a vague benignity, but indicates 'power' as well as 'favour' (Strachan). **my power is made perfect in weakness:** 'My strength finds its full scope in thy weakness' (Knox). It is the **power of Christ,** not freedom from the pain, that is indispensable to him. **may rest upon me:** Lit. 'may tabernacle upon me', the word (*skēnoō*) being reminiscent of the shekinah glory which filled the tabernacle (Exod. 40: 34). **10.** He is **content,** or rather, 'well content' (NEB), with weaknesses, not because they are desirable in themselves, but because it is in them that the power of Christ becomes conspicuous. 'Weakness' means more to Paul than physical weakness; whenever the proud natural man that is in him sees his dignity, reputation, finances, comfort, or liberty suffer, he feels his own weakness, and Christ's strength.

vii. Paul not Inferior to the False Apostles (12: 11–13)

11–13. 'There now, I have been a fool and done my boasting! But it is your fault that it was necessary; had you been loyal you would have sprung to my defence unbidden. With good reason you could have commended me, for though I am nothing in my own right, I am not all inferior to your precious "apostles" (11); all the signs of a true apostle I performed among you (12). Are you thinking that I made *you* inferior, because I didn't sponge on you? I'm so sorry!' (13). **11. I am not at all inferior:** Better, 'I was not inferior', when in Corinth. **these superlative apostles:** Cf. on 11: 5. **12. The signs of a true apostle:** A comprehensive term for all the proofs that he has been sent by God (cf. 1: 12; 4: 2; 6: 4; 1 Th. 1: 5). **Patience,** or 'endurance', may be intended as one of these signs (it has a wide range; cf. on 6: 4); or perhaps he means that despite all opposition he patiently and consistently exhibited the marks of a true apostle. **Signs, wonders,** and **mighty works** are three terms for miracles, expressing three aspects of the nature of miracle (the same phrase in Ac. 2: 22; Heb. 2: 4; cf. 2 Th. 2: 9). They are another instance of the signs (marks) of a true apostle. **13.** His meaning appears to be: '*I* was not inferior, so that could not have been why you would not defend me. Did I make *you* inferior, by favouring you less than the other churches?' **burden:** Cf. on 11: 9. **viii. In Anticipation of his Third Visit (12: 14–13: 10)** *(a)* **Why he will not 'burden' them (12: 14–18)** **14–18.** 'On my forthcoming visit I will continue my policy of financial independence; I claim a bigger salary than your money—yourselves! It is I who should be supporting you, not you me (14). I will gladly spend all I have for you; and will you let your love diminish as mine increases? (15) Is there a suggestion abroad that some of the collection for Jerusalem will go into my pocket? (16) Answer me this: have I ever taken advantage of you through my delegates (17), Titus or the other brother? The honesty of Titus is beyond suspicion; am I not one with him in character and action?' (18) **14. the third time:** His first visit was on his second missionary journey (Ac. 18: 1 ff.), his second the 'painful' visit (2 C. 2: 1; see Introduction), the third will be to collect the gift for Jerusalem (Ac. 20: 2). **children ought not to lay up for their parents:** An appeal to an obvious fact of human life. One does not expect little children to save up for their parents' future; rather the other way around. **15.** He will not only put by a little something for his children in the faith; he will gladly **spend** all he has and have his energies utterly **spent** for their sake. **16.** His opponents

are bound to grant that Paul himself never received money from Corinth, but they insinuate (Paul probably speaks more plainly than they did) that Paul will take his own share out of the collection for the Jerusalem poor. **You say,** or better, 'they say', is not in the Gk., but is rightly supplied to indicate that this is a charge brought against Paul—not an admission he makes! **got the better of you:** Lit. 'trapped' (cf. 11: 20).

18. I urged Titus to go: This probably refers to Titus' original visit (cf. on 8: 6), not his visit with the severe letter (2: 13; 7: 13 ff.). It is just possible that 'I urged Titus' and 'sent the brother' are epistolary aorists, and should be translated 'I am urging Titus and sending the brother' (= 8: 17 f.), in which case Paul's meaning is: 'Are you going to complain because I am sending my fellow-workers? Have they ever wronged you in the past?' **Did we (=I) not act in the same spirit:** Titus is above reproach (cf. 7: 13 ff.). Could Paul, therefore, being in such harmony of spirit with Titus, be guilty of duplicity?

(b) **Fears for what he will find in Corinth (12: 19–21)** **19–21.** 'You must not think that I have been speaking simply in order to defend myself. It has really been for your upbuilding (19). I am afraid that when I come I will find disharmony and opposition (20), and the morals of pagans among members of the church (21). I want to prevent this by dealing with the critical and the disobedient now.'

19. Since 10: 1 he has not just been defending himself, but clearing away misconceptions and negative attitudes for the sake of the **upbuilding** of the church (cf. 10: 18; 13: 10). And it has not simply been a defence **before you,** but **in the sight of God,** to whom alone he is answerable. **20. For:** I.e. 'there is *need* of upbuilding for . . .'. **you may find me not what you wish,** but stern and ready to punish (13: 1 ff.). Paul's fears for the state of the church have been thought incompatible with his satisfaction expressed in chap. 7. But here it is a question of order and morality (21) within the church, in chap. 7 a question of their submission to his authority. There was still much room for improvement within the church, but Paul could not begin to restore order and impose punishments on offenders until his apostolic authority was generally upheld in Corinth. **21. God may humble me before you:** He will be humiliated if he finds his converts still living like pagans. **Again** is to be taken with **humble,** a reference to his previous humiliation on the 'painful' visit. **Mourn** perhaps means 'mourn as over the dead', with the implication that the offenders will have to be excluded from the church.

(c) He can be severe if necessary (13: 1–4)
1–4. 'If you have accusations to bring against your brethren, make sure that they are fully substantiated when I arrive (1), and I will punish all wrong-doers with appropriate severity (2); that should convince you all that I have Christ's authority (3). Weak I may be in myself, but when I come to judging evil you will find that Christ has given me enough vigour for that' (4).

   1. This is the third time: Cf. on 12: 14. He introduces the prescription of Dt. 19: 15, *any charge must be sustained by the evidence of two or three witnesses*, apparently meaning that if on his *third* visit he finds them still in sin, his three visits will be *three* sets of evidence (**witnesses**) against them, and so he will be quite entitled to punish. (This view explains why he emphasizes 'here for the *third* time I am coming'; the number of his visits is otherwise unimportant.) An alternative interpretation is that when he comes, he will set up a full judicial enquiry, if it is necessary, and all discipline will be imposed after a just trial with sufficient witnesses. **Any charge:** Of Corinthian against Corinthian, not, apparently, against Paul. **2. those who sinned before:** Cf. 12: 21. **the others:** Either those who may have fallen into sin since his second visit, or the rest of the church who have tolerated the sinners. **if I come again:** Not hypothetical, but = 'when' (cf. 9: 4). **I will not spare:** He has delayed visiting them in order to spare them (1: 23) by giving them time to rearrange their affairs, but he cannot put off his visit indefinitely, for the gift for Jerusalem is a pressing matter; so he warns them to be prepared. **3.** He will demonstrate his apostolic authority, which they have doubted, by exercizing his power, given him by Christ, who is **powerful in** (better, 'among') **you** (cf. *e.g.* the 'signs and wonders and mighty works' [12: 12]). **4.** To be sure, Christ was **crucified in weakness,** and sceptics might think that that is all that can be said of Him (cf. 1 C. 1: 23), but believers know that He **lives by the power of God** evidenced in His resurrection (Rom. 1: 4; 6: 4; 1 C. 6: 14; 15: 43). And as Christ, so His apostle: Paul is **weak,** lacking in self-assertion and self-assurance, **in him,** i.e. by virtue of his union with the Christ who did not His own will; but like Christ, he will display the power of a resurrection life (**we [=I] shall live with him**) when it comes to dealing with the Corinthians.

(d) Punishment can be avoided if they will examine themselves (13: 5–10)
5–10. 'It is yourselves, not me, you should be

testing for marks of genuineness. Can you say that Christ is living in you? You should be able to, unless perhaps you were never converted (5). What I hope is that you will discover by yourselves, without needing me to inflict punishment, that I do indeed have Christ's authority (6). I would prefer that, even though it may mean that I will have no opportunity to prove my apostleship (7), for my own good name is secondary to the interests of the gospel (8). Yes, when you are living the life of faith and are "strong" so that I do not need to assert my authority (and so am "weak"), I am glad (9). All these warnings I give now so that when I come I may be able to use my apostolic authority not for punishment, but for its proper work, your edification' (10).

   5. Examine yourselves: 'Yourselves' is emphatic and implies 'Don't examine me'. **holding to your faith:** Not fidelity to doctrine, but the vitality of the faith which works (Allo). 'Are you living the life of faith?' (NEB). **6. We have not failed** the test of genuineness. **7.** 'I could prove to you *my* genuineness (as an apostle of Christ) by meeting your sin with the severity of my authority. But I would far rather you did not sin (**not do wrong**) than that I should be proved a true apostle; yes, I would rather you did **what is right,** even though that may mean that I appear not to be a true apostle (through lack of opportunity to assert myself)'. **8. the truth:** Roughly equivalent to 'what is right' (7). He means that 'he cannot desire that they should be found to be doing wrong, in order that he may be proved to be right' (Plummer). Some interpret **the truth** as 'the gospel', which gives a similar sense: He cannot allow himself to further his own interests (even to clear his name), if this would hinder the work of the gospel in men's lives. The verse should not be taken as a general principle, that no one can successfully oppose the truth (however valid this principle may be). **9. improvement:** Better, 'perfecting' (RV), i.e. full restoration to health. He is not content only that they should do no evil (7) but desires that they should be perfected in holiness (cf. 1 Th. 3: 11 ff.). **10.** At the conclusion of the section 10: 1–13: 10 he admits the charge he refers to in 10: 1, that he is severe while absent and humble when present, for he has now explained why he behaves thus. **authority . . . for building up:** Cf. 10: 8; 12: 19.

VIII. FINAL EXHORTATIONS AND BENEDICTION (13: 11–14)
11. farewell: Or perhaps 'rejoice' (as Phil. 4: 4). **Mend your ways:** More literally 'be perfected' (the same word as in v. 9). **12. a holy**

P*

441

kiss: Paul encourages them to put Christian significance (a *holy* kiss) into a customary mode of greeting. Judaism knew of a 'kiss of reconciliation'; there was also the customary kiss of greeting exchanged before or after a synagogue service. The Christian 'holy kiss' apparently soon became incorporated into the liturgy (cf. Justin Martyr, *First Apology*, 65). **14.** This benediction, the fullest in Paul's letters, is couched in trinitarian form; as a witness to the primitive Christian belief in the trinity it is all more impressive because it is a spontaneous and not a consciously formulated expression of it. **The fellowship of the Holy Spirit** seems to mean the sense of unity within the church which the Holy Spirit bestows.

BIBLIOGRAPHY

Commentaries on the English Text:

DENNEY, J., *The Second Epistle to the Corinthians. EB* (London, 1894).

HODGE, C., *An Exposition of the Second Epistle to the Corinthians* (New York, 1860; reprinted Grand Rapids, 1950).

HUGHES, P. E., *Paul's Second Epistle to the Corinthians. NLC* (London, 1962).

KELLY, W., *Notes on the Second Epistle to the Corinthians* (London, 1882).

STRACHAN, R. H., *The Second Epistle of Paul to the Corinthians. MNT* (London, 1935).

TASKER, R. V. G., *The Second Epistle of Paul to the Corinthians. TNTC* (London, 1958).

Commentaries on the Greek Text:

HÉRING, J., *The Second Epistle of Saint Paul to the Corinthians*, E.T. (London, 1967).

MENZIES, A., *The Second Epistle of the Apostle Paul to the Corinthians* (London, 1912).

PLUMMER, A., *A Critical and Exegetical Commentary on the Second Epistle of St. Paul to the Corinthians. ICC* (Edinburgh, 1915).

THE LETTER TO THE GALATIANS

F. ROY COAD

The letter to the Galatians is happily free from critical problems concerning authorship, scholars having been virtually unanimous in endorsing it as a genuine work of the apostle Paul. The problems which do exist relate to the date of composition of the letter, and to the location of the churches to which it was addressed.

In the middle of the first century, the Roman province of Galatia covered a great tract of central Asia Minor. The north-eastern part of the province, centred upon the three tribal capitals of Pessinus, Ancyra and Tavium, was controlled by a people of Celtic or Gallic descent (hence the name *Galatia*—cf. *Gaul* and *Galicia*), who had entered the land some three hundred years before and established dominance over the earlier inhabitants. Their lands lay away from the main trade and travel routes of that time, although they were to come brilliantly into their own in later centuries, after Constantinople had become the centre of imperial rule, and the main highways passed through Ancyra (modern Ankara).

In contrast, the south western part of the province was based on the Roman *coloniae* of Pisidian Antioch and Lystra (a third of its cities, Iconium, also became a *colonia* at a later date). Through it ran the highly important roads to Syria and the East from the Greek towns of the western seaboard of Asia Minor, and the native inhabitants (Phrygian around Antioch and Lycaonian around Lystra) had come strongly under the influence of foreign manners: of the Greeks who had followed Alexander, of the Jews who had been settled there by the Seleucid kings, and then of the Roman conquerors.

Debates concerning the destination and the date of the letter are closely involved with this division of the country. We may distinguish three main views.

i. That it was written to churches supposedly founded by Paul in the northern part of Galatia. This is the oldest view, but it has lost much ground since the researches of Sir W. M. Ramsay, in the late years of the nineteenth century, into the history and peoples of Asia Minor in classical times (see pp. 314, 319).

ii. That it was written to the churches which were undeniably founded by Paul in Southern Galatia during his first missionary journey, but that the letter was written at some time after one of his later visits to those churches.

iii. That it was written to those same churches, but immediately after the first missionary journey, and before the apostolic council of Acts 15.

The third view is that adopted in this commentary, and an explanation of this view is desirable at this point.

The destination of the letter

Acts names *Galatia* (or, more accurately, *Galatic territory*) twice in its accounts of Paul's journeys: once in 16: 6, on the outward stage of the second missionary journey, and again in 18: 23, on the outward stage of the third missionary journey. Until the end of the nineteenth century this *Galatia* was commonly held to be the northern region of the Roman province of that name, the only part in which dwelt persons strictly by race *Galatian*. The southern part of the province had later been severed from Galatia, and thus the fact that it was part of Galatia in the apostle's day tended to be overlooked. Thus, on each of these journeys, Paul was held to have deviated from the direct westerly and north westerly route across Asia Minor to visit this region. He certainly did not visit North Galatia on his first journey. The churches which he established in this northern part of Galatia, it was held, were those to whom this letter was written.

This view presented three major difficulties. *First*, there are no other known indications that Paul established churches in North Galatia, which lay well away from the Aegean centres of his work, and from the roads to them. Such foundations also seem out of keeping with what we know of Paul's missionary strategy. *Second*, if the letter was not written until the later journeys of the apostle, it must have been written considerably after the council of Ac. 15,

443

when the very question at issue in the letter was deliberated upon in Jerusalem. On that occasion an agreed and authoritative statement had been issued by that church, under the authority of James, the apostles and the elders. In such circumstances, it is inconceivable that this letter should make no reference to that decision, even while it is arguing the whole issue out afresh. (It is no answer to point out that no reference is made to the council's decisions in 1 C. 8 or 10. The question there discussed, that of food sacrificed to idols, was indeed covered in the findings of the Jerusalem council, but it was peripheral to the debate: nor were the Jerusalem findings on the whole relevant to the issues at Corinth. On the other hand, the letter to the Galatians deals with the whole issue of the Jewish obedience, which was precisely the crux of the Jerusalem council).

Third, this view is normally associated with the identification of the visit of Paul to Jerusalem described in Gal. 2 with that of Ac. 15: a view which leads almost inevitably to the conclusion that one or other of the accounts is inaccurate (see commentary on Gal. 2: 1-10 below).

As against this view, then, many commentators look for the destination of this letter to the churches established by Paul on his first missionary journey in the southern part of the Roman province of Galatia. Although Luke does not use the term in his account of that journey in Ac. 13 and 14, they lay within *Galatic territory*. The work of Sir W. M. Ramsay at the end of last century established convincing reasons, based on a profound knowledge of the political and social conditions in Asia Minor in the first century, for believing that the letter was addressed to those churches. Such a view accords convincingly with other Biblical data and has been widely adopted by British and American scholars.

The date of the letter

Even if this second view as to the recipients of the letter is accepted, its date must still be determined. Many commentators, impressed by the similarity of the thought and style of the letter to that to the Romans, consider that it must have been written at much the same time, probably during the third missionary journey. Others see it as written just before that journey (this was Ramsay's original view, but he later dated it before the Council of Ac. 15). (See also Hogg and Vine, p. 7.) But this view still leaves us with the second of the difficulties referred to above, and normally with the third as well.

An attempt to explain the second difficulty, the lack of reference to the Jerusalem decrees of Ac. 15, is made by suggesting that Paul's own actions relating to those decrees, described in Ac. 16, had themselves lent colour to the allegations of his opponents. He had taken care to deliver the decrees to the South Galatian churches, thus causing the churches to conclude that his apostolic authority was subject to that of the Jerusalem leaders. He had also circumcised Timothy, and thus strengthened the circumcision party. Thus, on this view, we account for the expression 'even if we' in Gal. 1: 8, and for the allegation that he himself preached circumcision (referred to in Gal. 5: 11). These two matters, Paul's authority and the teachings of the circumcision party, are the two main themes of the letter.

Yet such a view surely renders the lack of direct reference to the very decrees which had given rise to the misunderstanding, still more inexplicable: particularly when the non-circumcision of Titus is specifically discussed (2: 3 ff.). A reference to the incident concerning Timothy would have been inevitable, on this hypothesis.

Both difficulties are removed by the belief that the letter was written before the events of Ac. 15 had taken place. It is of interest that Calvin came to this conclusion purely on the internal evidences (see his commentary on 2: 1-5), although he did not follow through the implications as to the destination of the letter.

The situation then becomes plain. Paul, returning from his first missionary journey to Antioch, finds himself in controversy with the Judaizing teachers from Jerusalem who, we know from Ac. 15: 1, visited the city at that time (see also Gal. 2: 12). While he is engaged in this very controversy, news reaches him that similar teachers, following hot-foot in his steps, have visited the newly founded churches of his first journey (Ac. 13 and 14), and are succeeding in betraying his work. The result is this letter written white-hot with urgency, and under great emotional stress. The issues which it raises were, a few weeks later, to produce the Council of Jerusalem.

If this third view is adopted, it has important results for NT chronology, and for the understanding of the progress of doctrine within the Testament. Galatians becomes the first of the writings of the NT, written in A.D. 48 or 49, less than twenty years after the crucifixion. Following the data in the letter itself, we must then place Paul's conversion in approximately A.D. 33. The view has other far-reaching results, which cannot be discussed here: one notable difficulty, concerning Paul's Damascus visit, is referred to in the commentary on 1: 18-24.

ANALYSIS

I. INTRODUCTION (1: 1-5)

1, 2a. From the profound mystery of Deity, the Word had spoken. Such was the certainty which had gripped and inspired the soul of Saul of Tarsus. Within that wonder, lay another: the knowledge that he himself was an instrument of that divine Word. In Jesus, God had appeared: the resurrection had established that fact beyond doubt. Now Saul of Tarsus was the bond-servant and the deputed legate of the Lord Jesus Christ: **Paul an apostle,** by direct divine appointment.

There were men who did not understand it so. They, too, professed the name of Christ—but to them the message which Paul was preaching was a betrayal of the ancient ways of God. Nurtured in the tradition of the ancient covenants, and gripped by the Jewish Law, as the divinely appointed way of life, they could not easily adapt themselves to the thought that these things were now to be laid aside. Moreover, they could claim proud, if strictly unsanctioned, authority: the credentials of Jerusalem, the church of the apostles and of James the brother of the Lord. To them Paul was but an upstart from Antioch of Syria, and they did not hesitate to emphasise it.

So Paul takes pains, as he opens his letter, to assert the basis of his authority. Did his opponents claim the authority of men of note? His authority needed no such mediation, but came directly from the God who had spoken decisively in Christ, raising Him from the dead. Yet, even among men, he was not alone. With him were the devoted companions the Galatians knew.

[Note: **from men** and **through man:** the prepositions imply respectively the primary source and the intermediary source of authority.]

2b. Who, then, were these **churches of Galatia**?

The answer to that question has been discussed in the introduction: this commentary takes them to be the churches founded in South Galatia by Paul on his first missionary journey (Ac. 13 and 14).

3-5. In challenging Paul's authority the Jewish teachers had an ulterior motive: to discredit the gospel which he preached. So, in his salutation, Paul re-affirms the essentials of the gospel. It was a self-giving for our sins and a deliberate movement of the will of God: a free act of divine grace, unquestionable by man, to which it is an impious presumption to add any further requirement. To emphasize this the transcendence of God is stressed. The will of Him whose glory extends to the aeons of the aeons (**for ever and ever**) has moved to deliver us from this single evil aeon (**the present evil age**). The deliverance is His act in which He delighted; a deliverance, as it were, for Himself (on the significance of the use of the middle voice see Vine, *Expository Dictionary of NT Words,* 'Deliver' 8). If Christ **gave Himself,** dare we add a further requirement?

We must not overlook the importance of this passage at this extremely early stage of Christian teaching. The name of **our Lord Jesus Christ** is already coupled in equality with that of **God the Father:** a fact the more striking in view of the intense Jewish feeling which surrounded the whole subject matter of this letter. Moreover, His self-giving is **for our sins:** the redemptive purpose of the death of Christ is already established as the basis of the Gospel in this its earliest surviving formulation. Here, then, we have the earliest and most essential elements of Christian preaching.

II. THE OCCASION OF THE LETTER (1: 6-9)

Something of the teaching which was brought by the Judaizing teachers to Galatia can be learned from later references in the letter. It accepted the Messiahship of Jesus, but added another requirement to that of faith in Christ: acceptance of the Jewish obedience, particularly as symbolized in circumcision and the keeping of the ethical and ceremonial law (Ac. 15: 1; Gal. 3: 2, 10; 4: 10, 21; 5: 2; 6: 12, 13).

To Paul also it was axiomatic that faith in

Christ exercised a radical effect upon conduct (5: 19-24). But the place which the Judaizers gave to the law was not, for him, only a different emphasis. It perverted his message, was **a different gospel,** and **contrary to that which we preached to you:** a reversal (*metastrepsai*, v. 7) of the gospel.

The reasons for that antagonism are worked out in detail in the letter. The new teaching was retrograde, a return to bondage (5: 1; see Ac. 15: 10). Behind it all lay yet a deeper reason. To surrender to the Judaizers was to reduce the way of Christ to merely another of the quarrelling Jewish sects, and inevitably to throttle at birth the universal message of Christ. Paul himself must have realized this: but it was a vision far beyond the horizons of the narrow sectaries of Jerusalem, concerned as they were with the minutiae of observance and with the fear of the only persecution which the Church had yet known (6: 12). The apostle keeps his counsel, but his realization burns in the passion of his words. Here, if ever, was an issue where to hasten slowly, to be insufficiently radical, was to defeat the purposes of God: was to **desert Him who called you.**

[Notes: i. **8. accursed:** *anathema.*

ii. **6, 7. a different gospel—not that there is another:** There are different views on the precise sense here, which are reflected in different versions. Was Paul implying that the Judaizers' message was no gospel at all; or that it was not a different message, but merely a perversion of the true? The difference arises from contrary views of the force of the Greek words *heteros* and *allos* taken *e.g.*, by Lightfoot and Ramsay.

iii. **8. even if we:** Paul's own divine authority is valid only while his message remains authentic. Cf. Peter (Gal. 2: 11).

iv. Notice the change from a remote possibility, **if we . . . should preach** (8) to a contingency only too really present, **if any one is preaching** (9).]

III. THE AUTHORITY OF PAUL AND OF THE GOSPEL HE PREACHED (1: 10-2: 21)

1: 10. The AV translated the first question literally: 'For do I now persuade men, or God?' By the sheer incongruity of any other reply, this demands the answer 'men': but it is felt that this does not conform with the context, and most other translations follow the course of the RSV and translate the Greek word *peithō* (persuade) by **seek the favour of** or a similar expression (see Ac. 12: 20). The question is thus parallel to that which follows: **am I trying to please men?** The whole verse takes

a side-glance at the charge that Paul was watering down his message to win men over—the very charge which he later brings against his opponents (6: 12). This rendering of *peithō* is accurate and well attested.

Yet the AV rendering may express a deliberate ambiguity in the original. Paul, reared an ardent Pharisee, had bowed before the unanswerable act of God. What was his opponents' case? Faced with God's unquestionable act, they were virtually insisting that God could work in their way, and in no other. So, ironically, Paul may be asking—does he, like his opponents, seek to persuade God to bow to his ideas, or men to bow to God's? The obvious answer is that suggested by the AV—'men'. The renderings of most other translations, of course, require the answer 'God'. See 2 C. 5: 11; cf. Ac. 17: 4. The emphatic 'now' would suit this interpretation. Paul, the persecutor, had now bowed to the irresistible act of God (notice also the 'still' in the latter part of the verse).

[Note: The Gk. places an article ('the') before 'God', but not before 'men'. On this Lightfoot draws attention to a similar construction in 4: 31 ('not of *a* bondwoman', i.e. of *any* bondwoman, 'but of *the* freewoman', i.e. of the *only* lawful spouse), suggesting a similar sense in this passage.]

11-17. Paul now commences the first section of his argument, and develops it until the end of ch. 2. It concerns the basis of his own authority, and therefore that of his message. He sets out to demonstrate his direct dependence upon God for the gospel which he preached: an approach which requires him to avoid both horns of a dilemma. On the one hand, he must show that his teaching was not derived from any human agency: on the other, that it was no idiosyncrasy, but had been acknowledged and recognized by his fellow-apostles.

His conversion was the first and most telling evidence in his favour. He can offer the only convincing explanation for that dramatic reversal of the whole tenor of his life: an unveiling (*apokalypsis*) of Jesus Christ. He emphasises that there was no question of human influence at the sensitive stage immediately following this revelation: he **did not confer with flesh and blood,** but retired (into solitude?) to Arabia. This information adds to the knowledge we derive from Ac. 9. The precise time that he was in Arabia is not known, for the three years of v. 18 include the considerable activity in Damascus of which Ac. 9 informs us.

What was the revelation by which Paul received the gospel (12)? The other revelation, of v. 16, was centred upon the dramatic experience on the Damascus road (see note ii), but the growth of understanding of the gospel was not necessarily of a supernatural nature. Paul's own concern is to avoid the allegation of mere human speculation. The careful argument of this letter is evidence enough of the source of the revelation in Paul's meditations upon the OT. We can deduce some of the passages which were most formative: the story of Abraham, Habakkuk, and the latter part of Isaiah were obviously prominent. Behind and confirming his convictions lay the consciousness of a divine overruling and shaping of his life (15; cf. Jer. 1: 5 and Isa. 49: 1).

[Notes: i. With v. 12 cf. 1 C. 11: 23; Eph. 3: 2–12; Col. 1: 25–29. Contrast 1 C. 15: 3 and see Gal. 1: 18. There is no contradiction. See Cullmann *The Early Church*, 1956, art. *The Tradition*, pp. 59 ff.

ii. **16. to reveal his Son to me** (*en emoi*): This implies the Damascus road experience, but other renderings prefer 'through me' (i.e. by Paul's preaching; as Lightfoot), or 'in my case' (i.e. in distinction from others; as Hogg and Vine).]

18–24. The visit to Jerusalem referred to here is also recorded in Ac. 9: 23–30. From there we learn that Paul's introduction to Peter was not easily accomplished, until Barnabas befriended him. Paul adds the following information to that which we gather from Ac.:—

i. At Jerusalem 'the apostles' to whom Barnabas introduced him (Ac. 9: 27) were two in number only (James, although not one of the twelve, fulfilled the requirements of apostleship) (v. 19).

ii. Paul indicates that a meeting and consultation (*historēsai*) with Peter was a definite purpose of his visit to Jerusalem; a purpose on the part of the disciple of Gamaliel which pays eloquent tribute to the intellectual and spiritual capacity of the Galilean fisherman (v. 18).

iii. Although Paul 'went in and out among them at Jerusalem' (Ac. 9: 28), he had not been able to visit the Judean churches (v. 22).

iv. Some allege a discrepancy between the **fifteen days** of v. 18 and the apparently longer period implied by Ac.: but the former period relates explicitly only to the duration of Paul's actual residence with Peter.

In 2 C. 11: 32 Paul tells us that his escape from Damascus took place while that city was guarded by a governor of Aretas, king of the Nabateans. On the chronology discussed above, the date of Paul's escape would be A.D. 35 or 36 (the inclusive mode of reckoning must be borne in mind). For the problems associated

with this see the *NBD* articles *Aretas*, *Chronology of the NT* and *Paul*.

Ac. also refers to the retirement to **the regions of Syria and Cilicia,** with the more specific information that Paul returned to his native Tarsus (Ac. 9: 29, 30). The name Syria and Cilicia is that of the combined Roman political division, and does not necessarily imply that Paul visited Syria itself, although that is possible. Compare also Ac. 22: 17–21, where we learn that the urgency of Paul's brethren was confirmed in a personal vision.

Paul then disappears from the account in Ac. for a period of some ten years, until Barnabas brought him from Tarsus in Cilicia to Antioch in Syria (Ac. 11: 25, 26). That they were not years of idleness is shown by references in the other letters. Many of the experiences which Paul describes in 2 C. 11: 23–27 may be dated to this period, including the beatific vision of 2 C. 12: 2–4. Paul's evangelization of his home district during this period, clearly implied in Gal. 2: 2, would also account for his avoidance of Cilicia on his first missionary journey, when the missionaries travelled to the mainland by way of Barnabas's native island of Cyprus.

Paul's anxiety to affirm the accuracy of his account (v. 20), indicates how important these facts are to his argument. He is still laying stress on his isolation from influence, other than that of Peter and James. The tacitly suggested unity with those two leaders, on the other hand, could only add strength to his case.

[Note: **23. the faith:** The use of 'faith' as a synonym for the gospel is of course in line with the whole exposition contained in this letter. See Lightfoot *in loco*.]

2: 1–10. With this section we reach a question which is crucial to the understanding of the place of this letter in the NT story. On which of Paul's visits to Jerusalem did these incidents take place?

The second visit recorded in Ac. appears at Ac. 11: 30 and 12: 25. The story of Paul's contacts with Jerusalem and his fellow-apostles is essential to his argument, and we should not therefore expect him to omit any of his visits to Jerusalem. On the face of it, therefore, we have described here incidents of the famine visit of Ac. 11: 30 and 12: 25. Calvin, indeed, says in his commentary on these verses that 'on any other supposition, the statements of Paul and Luke cannot be reconciled'.

Two difficulties, however, appear.

i. First and foremost is the difficulty of chronology. A casual reading of Ac. 12 suggests that the famine visit took place before the death of Herod Agrippa I in A.D. 44. A casual reading of Gal. 2: 1 suggests that fourteen years elapsed from the first visit of Gal. 1: 18: and that was three years after Paul's conversion. No probable system of chronology could justify this, as Lightfoot saw (*Commentary*, p. 124) (although it has been suggested that 'fourteen' could be a copyist's error for 'four').

ii. There are certain apparent similarities between Ac. 15 and this chapter, which have led to a traditional identification of the visit of Gal. 2 with that of Ac. 15 (see p. 317).

Is this dilemma as serious as it appears? Further study suggests that the dilemma does not in fact exist, and that the visit of Gal. 2 is after all the famine visit of Ac. 11: 30 and 12: 25.

i. It is known from Josephus (*Antiquities* xx. 5. 2) that the famine recorded in Ac. 11: 28-30 took place during Roman governorships later than the death of Herod, and the most probable date for the famine visit is A.D. 46. The account of the persecution and of Herod's death in Ac. 12 is in fact a flashback, picking up the account of what had been happening in Jerusalem while the events of Ac. 11: 19-26 were taking place. (See F. F. Bruce, *The Book of the Acts*, pp. 257 f.) Moreover, the fourteen years of Gal. 2: 1 are not necessarily dated from the previous visit at all—it is just as likely that both periods (the three years of 1: 18 and the fourteen of 2: 1) are dated from the same starting point—Paul's conversion.

Now fourteen years back from A.D. 46 on the old inclusive reckoning would bring us to A.D. 33, a date for Paul's conversion which is not at all out of the question.

ii. The apparent similarities between this account and Ac. 15 tend to disappear on closer examination, and it is the discrepancies which become more obvious. Calvin's suggestion of irreconcilability was not frivolous.

Further support for the identification with the earlier famine visit is afforded by such hint as the passage contains of the situation within the Jerusalem church. By Ac. 15 the eldership had assumed a much more prominent position in the councils of the church than is implied here—a development accounted for by Peter's (and possibly John's) travels from Jerusalem in the interval (see v. 11 below).

If Gal. 2 does in fact describe events during the visit of Ac. 15 we could not of course maintain that the letter was written before that visit, and the difficulties already described on any other hypothesis would again arise (see introduction). If, on the other hand, we identify Gal. 2: 1-10 with the famine visit, all the pieces of the puzzle fall convincingly into place. Indeed, the **revelation** of v. 2 could be Agabus's prophecy of Ac. 11: 28, although this is not

altogether in harmony with the tone of the passage in Gal. It is easier to assume that a personal revelation to Paul, coinciding with Agabus's prophecy, led him to accept a delegation to a city which he had every reason to avoid. (See a similar combination of events in Ac. 9: 30 and 22: 18.)

We can now return to the main theme of the letter. On this visit two events important to Paul's argument occurred. First, he laid before the leaders of the church the gospel which he was preaching, **lest somehow I should be running or had run in vain.** It is uncertain whether this phrase implies a desire to ensure himself at length of the full fellowship of the Jerusalem leaders in the message committed to him, now that it had been thoroughly tested in practical evangelism in his native province (see Lightfoot *in loco*); or whether he wished to forestall the undoing of his work by a faction from Jerusalem. In either event, the result for his present argument was similar. Hitherto he had been dealing with one horn of the dilemma, and had emphasized his freedom from human influence. Now he was able to show that his gospel had been acknowledged and recognized by his fellow-apostles.

The second event of the visit was unplanned. One of Paul's companions on his visit was Titus, a Greek, who thus appears as one of the earliest, as he was to be one of the latest, of Paul's fellow-workers. The question of Titus's circumcision had been raised, apparently by a group described as **false brethren** (4). It would seem that the leaders, 'the men of repute' (6) (F. F. Bruce—there is nothing necessarily derogatory in the phrase) may have wavered. Paul, who was ready on appropriate occasion to become as a Jew in order to win Jews (1 C. 9: 20), and who would himself later circumcise Timothy, son of a Jewish mother and therefore, in Jewish eyes, himself Jewish (Ac. 16: 3), and would himself submit to requirements of Jewish ritual (Ac. 21: 20-26), realized that in this demand applied to a Gentile lay the crucial question of the future of the gospel (see commentary on 1: 6-9). Adamantly he had stood his ground, and with the indisputable facts of his own work to support him (7, 8), he had won his point. The very confusion, almost incoherence, of his language in this passage (a phenonemon which recurs in the letter) is evidence of what that struggle had cost him, and of how deeply it stirred him to find himself fighting the same battle yet again. Today, looking back at the long history of the Church, we can realize something of the immensity of the issues for which he contended, and can admire again the largeness and penetration of his vision.

For the purpose of his present argument, Paul has said enough. One unanswerable fact faced any doubters: **the grace that was given to me.** With that evidence of God's approval Paul, directly authorized by God, had also received **the right hand of fellowship** from the Jerusalem leaders. From that freedom given by the Jerusalem leaders what great things were to spring!

How carefully Paul fulfilled the other part of the agreement, to **remember the poor,** is apparent from his other letters: was it not indeed the very purpose of this visit to Jerusalem (Ac. 11: 29, 30)?

[Note: The poorly attested variant reading of v. 5, which omits the negative, is surely incredible. It would require the emphasis in v. 3 to be placed on 'compelled': suggesting that Titus *was* circumcised, but voluntarily as a concession to the weaker consciences.]

11-21. Into the claims of the Judaizers the name of Peter was entering: Peter, who had himself suffered from the antagonism of **the circumcision party,** and whose experiences at Joppa and Cæsarea had made him a natural sympathiser with Paul. What lay behind this?

That the incident described in these verses took place some two or three years after the meeting of the preceding verses is probable. Peter had visited Antioch, apparently about the time of the return of Paul and Barnabas from their first missionary journey, only to be followed there by the circumcision party, suspicious of him as ever (see Ac. 15: 1). These Judaizers claimed the authority of James (Gal. 2: 12), but apparently without justification (Ac. 15: 24). The brief unhappy incident which followed rings true to the experience of all who have seen the fruits of the jealous carping scrutiny of men warped by party spirit. Both Peter and Barnabas evoke our sympathy, for an excessive attachment to dogmatic strife on the part of lesser men will always batten upon the more honourable. If malice could drive such as these into prevarication, it behoves us to recognize the spirit of the heresy hunter and to shun it for the plague it is, however orthodox its trimmings. Ac. 15: 2 indicates that Barnabas was soon rallied by his stronger companion, while Peter himself took well to heart the comments which Paul had made, taking them up and applying them decisively in Jerusalem soon after (cf. v. 14 with Ac. 15: 10).

The tenor of Paul's reference to Barnabas indicates that the latter was known to the Galatian churches—a further indication that they were the churches of the first missionary journey.

The historical survey is over, and Paul is able to turn to more congenial matter. Whether the closing verses of the chapter represent the gist of his discussion with Peter, or whether they are added for the purposes of the letter, is of little importance. In them Paul is able to restate the basic gospel, not in terms of the theological exposition which is to follow, but in terms of personal experience.

It is clear that Paul's opponents shared the common position of justification by faith, but the force of the repetition in v. 16 suggests that **works of the law** (not merely its ceremonial aspects) were added as an additional agent of justification. So Paul repeats his own experience. **16. we have believed in Christ Jesus, in order . . . :** The Greek aorist corresponds to that in 3: 6. It was a deliberate and permanent act, arising consciously and from reasoned knowledge: a personal committal to Christ, *eis Christon Iēsoun*, not a mere mental assent (and can therefore exist in company with a great deal of mental bewilderment or doubt). The third repetition, which closes v. 16, glances back to Ps. 143: 2. The expression **Gentile sinners** in v. 15 ironically picks up the standard Jewish terminology.

The verses which follow are confused and have been treated in very different manner by different versions. **Sinners** (17) appears to refer back to the same word in v. 15. If the gospel made empty the Jews' privilege of the law, reducing them to the status of Gentiles without the law, was not Christ the agent of their reduction to the status of sinners? Paul was to answer this question in Rom. 3, at a later date, with the bold assertion that 'there is no distinction'. Here he answers in a manner similar to that in which he will answer the charge of antinomianism (see commentary on 5: 1). To attempt to justify myself by the law is to rebuild the very standard of judgment which I by my sin have destroyed, and which itself condemns me (18). In fact, I have received the sentence of death from the law itself: and by that very sentence the law has removed me from its jurisdiction (19). For the sentence of death has been executed—but executed in the body of Christ on the cross (cf. Rom. 7: 4). Therefore, if I live now, it can only be by right of Christ, and in freedom from the condemnation of the law. My life can now be nothing but the life of Christ, maintained by the continuation of that once-for-all act of faith in Him (20).

Have we here the beginning of that development of Paul's thought on identification with the body of Christ which later leads to the doctrine of the Church as the body of Christ?

Compare the link with the death of Christ as it is expressed in the Lord's Supper (1 C. 10: 15-17).

To close the section, Paul turns his opponents' argument against themselves. They had suggested that his gospel emptied the law of meaning. He shows that their doctrine, retaining the law but adding to it faith in Christ, simply emptied the cross of meaning. Wherein had the death of Christ changed the situation? On this basis the cross was a pointless excrescence on the scheme of salvation (21).

[Note: Calvin's commentary on vv. 17-20 is of particular importance and should be consulted.]

IV. THE GOSPEL EXPLAINED AND EXEMPLIFIED (3: 1-4: 31)

3: 1-5. The proof of his authority and that of his message is complete, and Paul turns to the positive task of expounding the gospel. The exposition proceeds by the following stages.

3: 1-5.   An appeal to the Galatians' experience.
3: 6-14. An appeal to Scripture.
3: 15-24. The relationship of law and the promise worked out.
3: 25-29. The full achievement of the gospel.
4: 1-7.   Recapitulating with a history of redemption.

The argument from experience is simple and effective. The gospel had *worked:* their own senses saw its evidence (hence the 'senseless' Galatians and the 'bewitchment' of v. 1). The Holy Spirit was an obvious possession of the new converts, without the outward tokens of the law. It is the same argument that had carried the day for Peter after Cornelius's conversion (Ac. 11: 17), and which he was to use as effectively at Jerusalem (Ac. 15: 8, 9). In passing, we might acknowledge the insight which this argument gives into the life of those churches, and ask ourselves whether it would be as effective in our own churches today.

The **miracles** (5) would probably have included those supernatural evidences of the Spirit which were common in the early churches (see Ac. 14 in relation to the S. Galatian churches). Yet no stress is laid upon such manifestations elsewhere in this letter: rather the working of the Spirit is seen in moral qualities (5: 16-24), and the word here undoubtedly includes the patent moral transformation of many of the converts. Calvin applies it to 'the grace of regeneration, which is common to all believers'.

The gift of the Spirit is the continuous work of the Head of the Church: the Greek implies liberality (v. 5).

[Note: **1. publicly portrayed:** The sense is 'placarded up, as on a public poster'.]

6-9. For his argument from Scripture, Paul goes directly to a verse which had unlocked for him a new understanding of the OT. In following the apostle's exposition here and in Rom., a sympathetic mind can picture the OT blazing with a new light to him: there is little wonder that he spoke of that vision as a revelation from God, or that it has brought to birth a similar light in many a later soul.

Yet the quotation in v. 6 was not unfamiliar in current Jewish exegesis. It is taken from a passage in Genesis (15: 6) where, interestingly enough, Abraham's faith was at a low ebb (Gen. 15: 2, 3). At such a moment, God had seen the movement of faith in Abraham's soul, and treasured it the more for the weakness from which it sprang. Abraham, in his weakness, became 'the model man of justification by faith' (Principal D. Brown): heir to a promise embracing all nations.

The promise to Abraham had been threefold: a promise of descendants, of blessing to all nations, and of the land for an inheritance. In the second aspect, germane to the apostle's immediate purpose, he sees the essence of the gospel (8). The blessing carried within it the promise of the Christ; but its scope made baseless the Judaizers' attempt to limit it. The aspect of the seed is taken up in startling manner later in this same chapter, as in the parallel passage in Rom. 4: 16-25, and the promise of the Christ is found yet more explicitly in that aspect. The aspect of the land is merely hinted at in v. 18 of this chapter, but appears in Rom. 4: 13. To Paul and his Christian contemporaries its meaning could only be spiritual, a point made explicit by the writer to the Hebrews (Heb. 11: 8-10, 16). The land was the temporal and material background to the mighty acts of redemption of which the whole promise spoke: but in Rom. 4: 13 it becomes 'the world', while in the vision of the Apocalypse 'a new heaven and a new earth' is seen as an essential part of the ultimate state (Rev. 21: 1). For, in man's redemption, the redemption of man's environment also is comprised (Rom. 8: 19-23): while even in his redemption, man remains man, not aspiring to godhead, but limited still to appointed bounds (cf. Ac. 17: 26) and maintained by the free grace of God.

10-14. The previous section contained the positive testimony of scripture to faith: this section contains the negative testimony to the law. First, the law on its principle of strict recompense cannot in the nature of things bless, but only curse. Second, Habakkuk had spoken of living on the principle of faith (Hab.

2: 4—the original Hebrew had the sense of faithful endurance, but the context includes the Pauline sense, cf. Hab. 3: 17-19): a principle which clearly excluded the legal principle of strict recompense.

Then, by a daring use of the Deuteronomic curse on the hanged man (Dt. 21: 23)—a curse much quoted by those Jews who rejected Christ—Paul reverts again to the thought of 2: 20. There, the capital condemnation of the law on the sinner had been executed, but executed in the body of Christ. Here it is the curse on the sinner which is taken and absorbed on the cross. There the sinner, dead to the law, was alive to God: here, free from the curse, he is open to the promised blessing. That blessing is identified with the experience of the Spirit to which Paul has already appealed.

[Note: It is of interest to notice that Paul also quoted from Habakkuk in his address at Pisidian Antioch, Ac. 13: 41.]

15-18. At the next stage of his exposition, Paul turns to consider the true relationship between law and the promise. In an argument similar to that of Rom. 4, but with a significant difference, he argues from the priority of the promise. It is unthinkable that God should qualify a free promise by a condition imposed unilaterally, centuries later: still less is it possible that the condition should be such as virtually to nullify the promise, changing a free gift into something to be 'earned' by conformity to a law beyond man's capacity. The reference to the **inheritance** (18) picks up the fact that the solemn ratification of the promise (see v. 17) in Gen. 15 related particularly to that aspect of the promise which concerned the land.

The reference to a **will** (15) causes an unnecessary difficulty by importing inappropriate associations with death (as Heb. 9: 16, 17). The most helpful modern equivalent is that suggested by F. F. Bruce; a settlement of property (the purist would prefer *an irrevocable settlement*). Ramsay explains the passage by reference to Greek law by which members of a family only might inherit: to benefit a stranger in blood it was therefore necessary to adopt him into the family, the act of adoption itself being both irrevocable and constituting the title to the inheritance.

Verse 16 is a parenthesis, but contains an important thought. The AV 'seed' obscures the force of the original, for the original was a collective noun which would have been inappropriate in the plural. The argument is directed not so much to the distinction between singular and plural, as to emphasizing that a collective noun might equally have a purely singular meaning: in effect, that God deliberately

used a word not normally used in the plural. Hence the word, apparently comprising the whole nation, is seen to have a deeper meaning referring to the single seed—Christ. The NEB reproduces the sense ingeniously by using the word 'issue' (RSV **offspring**). There also lies behind the verse the thought of the one seed chosen out of many as the true seed: Calvin pointing out the narrowing of the line of promise from the first generation of Abraham's descendants. We have here, then, another pointer to that corporate capacity of our Lord which was implicit in His own use of the title *Son of Man*, and is related so closely to the doctrine of the Church as the body of Christ.

[Note: **17. four hundred and thirty years:** From the LXX of Exod. 12: 40.]

19-22. The argument from priority was particularly powerful to the Jewish mind (cf. Jn 1: 30), but it raised an important question. **Why then the law:** The answer given is that the fulfilment of the promise would be dangerous until man has learned his own sinnership, and is prepared thus to welcome the Saviour-seed, in whom alone the promise is secure and mankind can find wholeness and unity (Col. 2: 10); the offspring in whom the whole offspring would be one. **because of transgressions** thus has the sense of 'to reveal' rather than 'to curb' transgressions (see 1. Tim. 1: 8-11).

Verse 20 has attracted a vast number of interpretations: it is probable that the meaning is that the law, needing a mediator (which implies the existence of two parties), cannot be stronger than the weaker of those two parties, namely man. The promise, however, rests upon God alone and is unbreakable.

It may be possible, however, that Paul is answering an objection unknown to us, so that the full significance of the words is lost. V. 21 reads as if intended to be a part of the argument, while the interpretation just given reads it as a fresh start in the argument. The opposition might have argued on these lines: the law was the product of mediation, implying a conflict. God was one; a gift implies no conflict. Was the conflict then between the promise on the one hand and the law, the righteousness of God, on the other? For then it was the law which was manifestly triumphant, and Paul's argument from priority is turned back on himself.

Whatever lies behind vv. 20 and 21, Paul's reply is the same. If the law had been triumphant, then the cross of Christ would have been unnecessary: **righteousness would indeed be by the law** (21). As this was manifestly not so, then the law was a stage in God's purposes, preparatory to the full promise through **faith in**

Jesus Christ (22). (For **the scripture** see Rom. 3: 10–18.)

23–29. So Paul triumphantly sums up the full achievement of the gospel. The law was the essential forerunner to faith: now, in Christ, the full freedom of the gospel's achievement stands revealed. Here is a new relationship to God and man, transforming every possible social relationship.

Verse 27 is important (and cf. Rom. 13: 14). Baptism is a 'putting on' of Christ, a 'clothing oneself' with Christ (the middle voice implying a conscious and responsible act). The sign is spoken of as comprising the underlying reality which it symbolizes (cf. Gal. 2: 20 with Rom. 6: 3–11). Because it is a self-clothing with the one Christ, it is also a becoming-one-in-Christ on the part of all who share the experience. Thus it is a symbol of the miracle by which the single offspring can resume its collective sense. **If you are Christ's, then you are Abraham's offspring, heirs according to promise.**

[Note: **24, 25. custodian** (*paidagōgos*): Not 'teacher' ('schoolmaster' as AV), but rather 'supervisor and moral trainer'.]

4: 1–7. In this section the story of the gospel is recapitulated in terms of simple soul-experience, and thus the eyes of the Galatians are turned (in preparation for the appeals which follow) from doctrinal disputation to their fulness in Christ. We may prefer to see the individual's experience in this description; or (with Calvin) the generic experience under the old and new covenants. Both are valid applications.

Verse 3 presents a difficulty. The RSV translation **the elemental spirits of the universe** introduces a Colossian nuance which is foreign to the atmosphere of this letter. The argument has previously remained entirely within a Jewish and OT context, and it is startling to assume that Paul equates these with the demonic powers of the stars which were then prominent in popular superstition, and are implied in the RSV rendering. The same problem arises in v. 9. Possibly the expression is deliberately ambiguous, hinting at the bondage of a materialistic Jewish rite, at current superstitions, and also at the persistent survivals of the ancient Anatolian religion, corruptly harnessing the most elemental instincts of life, which the Galatians would know so well. In contrast, see the grace of God in Christ!—**born of woman** (but what a contrast to the corrupt religion of the goddess-mother), **born under the law** (but He who came to deliver us from the slavery of the law). Here the Son of God comes to stand where we stand, that He might shoulder our curse, and raise us from out of it to **adoption as sons.**

[Notes: i. **4. sent forth** (*exapesteilen*): 'Sent forth from out of'. Precisely the same word is used in v. 6 of the Spirit.

ii. **5. adoption:** See commentary on 3: 15 above.

iii. Note the transition: v. 5 'we', v. 6 'you' (plural), v. 7 'you' (singular).]

8–11. The doctrinal explanation of the gospel is now followed by a number of appeals to the Galatians. The first appeal is to the contrast between their old standing and their new. The passage again hints at the mixed Jewish and Gentile background of the Galatians (see commentary on v. 3), and harmonizes well with the account in Ac. 13 and 14 of the S. Galatian churches. That account also demonstrates that the detailed argument of the letter from the OT scriptures would not be unfamiliar ground even to the Gentile converts among them: it was precisely that familiarity which had smoothed the path of the Judaizers.

Notice the careful correction in v. 9, pointing again to Paul's intense consciousness of the sovereign act of God in the Gospel, and illuminating his sense of the impious nature of the Judaizers' rejection of that act.

[Note: **9. once more:** *Anōthen* (as Jn 3: 3).]

12–20. The second appeal is personal, and presents us with an insight into the warm heart of the apostle, and his intense self-identification with those whom he sought (cf. 1 C. 9: 19–23).

Ac. does not mention the ailment which had led to Paul's first visit to Galatia (vv. 13–15): v. 15 might suggest a disfiguring ailment of the eyes, but this is mere speculation, and not a necessary meaning of the verse. Why should this incident have so impressed the Galatians? Did Paul make for the Roman *colonia* of Antioch to seek medical attention for his complaint? It is tempting to allow speculation to run on. There was one of Paul's later companions whose knowledge of that district was so intimate as to suggest a resident's acquaintance, and that companion was Luke, 'the beloved physician' (Col. 4: 14) (see Ramsay, *Historical Commentary on the Galatians*, pp. 205 f., 209, 215 ff., *Bearing of Recent Discovery on the Trustworthiness of the NT*, ch. 3). It was Luke who could give such a detailed account of Paul's first visit to Pisidian Antioch (Ac. 13), and who joined Paul's party on the second missionary journey at Troas, not long after he had passed through the same district (see the 'we' in Ac. 16: 6–11). The self-effacing spirit of the author of Acts would then be sufficient explanation for the absence of reference to the illness in that narrative. But fancy is an unprofitable guide: moreover, tradition makes Luke a citizen of the Syrian Antioch, and Ramsay had yet another theory.

Verses 17 and 18 are obscure, but suggest that the Judaizers had used both flattery and threats of excommunication in their discussions with the Galatians (but see F. F. Bruce 'they simply want to cut you off from any contact with me . . .').

The closing verses of the paragraph are remarkable for the expression **until Christ be formed in you,** carrying still further the intense sense of the union of the risen Christ with His own which we have already remarked in the letter. What an indication they also give of Paul's personal involvement with the spiritual struggles of his converts!

[Notes: i. **13. at first:** The Gk. might suggest that there had been two visits to the Galatians (see Ac. 14: 21). This is not essential in *koinē* usage (see NEB text and footnote).

ii. **14.** Lit. 'your affliction in my flesh'.]

21–31. The third appeal is made by way of allegory. This type of argument is uncongenial to the modern mind, but Paul is meeting on its own ground the method of debate which was urged against him by his opponents. Lest any might be tempted to slip too easily into this mode of *eisegesis*, it is well to observe that the apostle makes use of allegory only in relation to doctrine which he has already established by careful *exegesis*! 'Imagination and ingenuity are poor substitutes for apostolic authority' (Hogg and Vine, p. 220).

The passage contains two points of importance, in addition to its obvious teaching. First, the apparently incidental quotation from Isa. 54: 1 (v. 27) is another sign of the influence exercised upon the formation of Paul's understanding of the gospel by the latter part of that prophecy. This type of quotation is often of more significance in establishing such influence than the quotation of an obvious 'proof text'.

Second, this allegory marks a transition in the thought of the letter. Hitherto the contrast has been between law on the one hand and faith and the promise on the other. The letter now passes over into the contrast which had been hinted at in 3: 2, 3, between flesh and the Spirit.

Lightfoot remarked that Paul's confident application of Scripture in v. 30 is a striking tribute to his prophetic insight: at that time it was, to human eyes, far from certain that the old Jewish system would be cast out from its inheritance.

V. THE OUTWORKING OF THE GOSPEL (5: 1–6: 10)

5: 1. This verse stands equally as the conclusion of what has gone before (some in fact attach part of it to the previous sentence), or as the commence-

ment of the practical application which follows. It strikes the keynote of the letter. 'The controversy relates to the liberty of conscience, when placed before the tribunal of God' (Calvin).

As Paul turns to the practical outworking of the doctrine he has expounded, he faces the worst misunderstanding of all: that of antinomianism, the idea that freedom from the law was freedom to disregard its precepts, and therefore to sin at will.

Paul's answer is bound up with two important features of his previous teaching.

First, the new life of the believer is not his own life at all, but rather the life of Christ in him. So Paul had earlier replied to those who accused him of making Christ the **agent of sin** (2: 17): far from reducing Jews to the status of **Gentile sinners,** Christ had lifted both Jew and Gentile alike to an entirely new plane. Both alike had died with Him and now lived in his new life (see 2: 20 and 4: 19). Developing this thought, he now shows that the freedom of Christ is not freedom for wilful thoughts and desires: paradoxically, that is the worst bondage of all, bondage to the flesh. Rather, it is the holy freedom of Christ Himself becoming my own freedom. **For freedom Christ has set us free.** (It is noticeable that the verse contains no definite article before **yoke:** it is **a** yoke of slavery, and thus as applicable to the slavery of the flesh as to the bondage of Mount Sinai).

Second, the result of faith is the enduement of the Spirit and the Spirit is the antithesis of the flesh (3: 2, 3). The result of faith is not a theoretical or forensic change in its subject, but rather the practical and continuing ministration of the Spirit from the Source of all life (3: 5). Where the Spirit reigns, the flesh cannot have the pre-eminence. This is developed in vv. 16–25 below.

2–12. First, there must be a warning. There could, at this point in history, be no compromise with those who would strangle the gospel of Christ in its cradle: nor, for its part, could the law demand other than total obedience. In evaluating vv. 2–5 we must remember this, and also that Paul himself circumcised Timothy (Ac. 16: 3). It is not circumcision as an act which is in view (as v. 6 shows), but rather circumcision entered into as a deliberate commitment to the Jewish rite, or as relying on its efficacy for salvation.

Verse 6 contains an equation which is of profound importance. It is the reality which matters, not the form; and faith, when worked out into practical and tangible reality, equals love. The parallel passage in 1 C. 7: 18, 19 substitutes for **faith working through love** the words 'keeping the commandments of God'. Is this to contradict the teaching of Galatians, and to reinstate the law upon its throne? Far from it, for Paul is to claim in v. 14 of this chapter also that the whole law is fulfilled in love (see commentary below). Rather, it is the first sign of a remarkable turn in the argument, which we will find made explicit in the next section of this chapter, and which finds the law and faith ranged on the same side in this new battle against the flesh and the antinomian heresy which is its fruit. Both passages must be read in the light of Rom. 13: 8–10 and of 1 C. 13 (where the trinity of faith, hope and love which is contained in vv. 5, 6 of this chapter is developed in classic form).

The confused and staccato conclusion to the paragraph, from v. 7, betrays the intense emotion under which the apostle wrote: small wonder, when even his own words were twisted against him (11)! Yet his touching confidence in his converts (10), and his sense of tragedy in their lapse (7), both reveal the warmth of his heart and explain the roughness of his denunciation of the false teacher or teachers. The passage ends with a mocking reference to circumcision (cf. Phil. 3: 2) (but a reference to excommunication might be implied—see F. F. Bruce and W. M. Ramsay *in loco*) and there may be a play on words between the Gk. for **hindered you** (*enkoptō*) (7) and **mutilate** (*apokoptō*) (12). Hogg and Vine link the verse with 4: 17 'they want to shut you out', but a different Gk. word (*ekkleiō*) is used there.

[Note: **11. the stumbling block of the cross:** The Gk. for 'stumbling block' is *skandalon*, as 1 C. 1: 23, and hence the phrase 'the scandal of the cross'.]

13–15. Paul now turns to the first part of his reply to the antinomians (see commentary on 5: 1). Paradox as that first reply was, it finds its expression in two further paradoxes, both products of the alchemy of love. True freedom finds its fulfilment in slavery—the slavery of love (13). **Servants** (slaves) **of one another** stands in emphatic contrast to the **yoke of slavery** of v. 1: cf. Mt. 20: 26–28. Second, the equation of faith with love is further developed, as we anticipated in v. 6; and in love, the outworking of faith, the law finds its complete fulfilment (14). So, by a turn in the argument which is the achievement of inspired genius, faith and the law are seen no longer as antagonists, but as allies. It is a turn of thought for which the transition from the opposition of faith and law to that of flesh and Spirit had cleared the way (see commentary on 4: 21–31).

Something of a calmer frame asserts itself in

the mind of the apostle, evidenced by the hint of wry humour in v. 15.

[Note: **13. opportunity:** *Aphormē*, a base of operations in war.]

16–25. The second part of the answer to the antinomian perversion of Paul's teaching is now developed. The answer lies in the place of the Spirit in justification by faith. The reception of the Spirit had been seen in 3: 1–5 as the proof of the truth of Paul's teaching. Now it is seen as its ultimate justification in experience.

Hence there is a leap in his thought. **The flesh** appears in an altogether grosser sense than hitherto, while the conflict between faith and the law which has been resolved in the preceding section can be dismissed with a side glance (18). 'Works' are now seen as an essential part of the gospel of faith, but they are works expressing themselves as the inevitable fruit of salvation and of the reception of the Spirit, not works as forming a painful pathway to a salvation which it is beyond man's power to win. Hence the apostle does not in fact use the word 'works' specifically: there are evil **works** of the flesh (19), but the virtues are **fruit** of the Spirit (22). Where such works exist, the Law is irrelevant: **against such there is no law.**

Thus there appears in embryo a theme which is later to be developed in the Roman letter: the conflict between flesh and the Spirit (Rom. 7). In this letter there is no scope for argument as to whether the conflict exists in pre- or post-conversion experience, and debate over the passage in Rom. would have been avoided if more attention had been paid to its germ in this letter. It may be theologically inconvenient to be told that the convert is still liable to fulfil the desires of the flesh (v. 16 and 6: 1), and in the same context that **those who do such things shall not inherit the kingdom of God,** but it happens to accord with experience. (For **the kingdom of God** see also Rom. 14: 17.)

It is noteworthy that the essential fruits and signs of the Spirit recorded in vv. 22, 23 include none of the ecstatic *charismata* with which they are so often identified (see commentary on 3: 5). Beyond this, comment on these verses is superfluous. They stand with their peers in Christian ideal: Phil. 4: 8; Jas 3: 17; 2 Pet. 1: 5–7; Rom. 5: 3–5. (The evil list of vv. 19–21 also has its parallels: Rom. 1: 29–31; 3: 10–18; 1 C. 6: 9–10; 2 C. 12: 20.)

Verses 24, 25 indicate respectively profession and practice.

[Notes: i. **17. to prevent you from doing what you would:** This could be read in two ways:—

(a) 'to prevent you from doing the evil things which you would otherwise wish to do', or (*b*) 'to prevent you from doing the good things which your conscience prompts you to do'. Hogg and Vine prefer the former, placing the words **for these are opposed to each other** in parentheses. The majority of opinion is, however, against them, as surely is the context.

ii. **18. not under the law:** Calvin distinguishes between the *directing capacity* of the law and the *penalty* of the law. Its directing capacity remains, but grace frees us from the penalty.

iii. **24. crucified the flesh:** Compare and contrast the similar metaphors in 2: 20 ('I have been crucified with Christ') and 6: 14 ('the world has been crucified to me').]

5: 26–6: 10. These verses are their own commentary, in their essential simplicity and practicality. We might be in a different world from the stormy atmosphere of conflict which had provoked the letter. As in all his letters, Paul the pastor asserts himself over every other capacity.

Here are the gentle and humane rules which are to regulate inter-personal relations. The absence of self-centredness, of pre-occupation with my own dignity and standing, is to be balanced by that true concern which places myself in the position of another, and acts to that other as I would then wish others to act towards myself (5: 26–6: 2). Yet this forgetfulness of self, this unselfconscious thought for others, can be expected only of one who has learned to live with himself; to accept his own abilities and calling, and the niche in which his own inherent gifts must place him. Only in this way can a man attain the quiet assurance and confidence of a responsibility taken and conscientiously fulfilled (6: 3–5).

Finally, there is the emphasis on generosity and unselfish stewardship of material possessions. Ranging from the needs of teachers (6) (not only visiting teachers, such as the apostles, but where necessary and appropriate the needs of local teachers such as the elders of Ac. 14: 23 in these same churches), Christian concern is to reach to the whole **household of faith,** and then to **all men** (10). It is significant that the exhortation on sowing and reaping appears in the centre of this passage, flanked on both sides by instructions of practical kindness and well doing towards our needy fellows. We cannot limit its significance to this one aspect of Christian living, but, set as it is, it binds the 'sowing to the Spirit' inseparably and for ever with the practical expression of Christian mercy and kindliness. In this context, then, the expression **his own flesh** (8) is doubly significant: this is not merely 'flesh' in the general sense, but also

in the specific sense of self-indulgence in the face of others' needs.

[Notes: i. The warmth of the **brethren** in v. 1 is particularly pertinent to the letter. Cf. 4: 12–20; 5: 7–12.

ii. **1. you who are spiritual** (*hymeis hoi pneumatikoi*) refers not to any special order of 'spiritual men' ('pneumatics'), but potentially to any believer who is fulfilling 5: 25.

iii. **2. the law of Christ:** See commentary on 5: 13–15, and cf. Jas 2: 8.

iv. The AV introduces an unnecessary difficulty in vv. 2, 5, by translating two different Gk. words by **burden** (the RSV has **burden** and **load** respectively). The verses have in mind, respectively, oppressive trials or difficulties (v. 2), and due responsibilities (v. 5).

v. **7. mocked:** A striking word meaning 'to turn up the nose at': vividly, 'to cock a snook'.]

VI. CONCLUSION (6: 11–18)

The argument is over, and the apostle takes the pen from his amanuensis to add a few final paragraphs in his own **large letters** (were these for emphasis, or because of impaired eyesight, see 4: 12–15, or is it simply a humorous reference to an idiosyncrasy?). Something of the pain of the conflict creeps back into his mind (12–13) only to provoke an inspired outburst of loyalty which will live for ever in Christian hymn (14). Paul closes by reverting again to that irresistible and sovereign act of God which had transformed his life, and the life of a world beside: **neither circumcision counts for anything, nor uncircumcision, but a new creation.**

What is **the Israel of God** (16)? That it is only a faithful remnant of the natural Israel is surely out of harmony with the letter: although it might be a generalized and non-exclusive reference to those Hebrews who, like Paul himself, had obeyed the truth in Christ. Is it, then, the Church? Potentially, perhaps. Yet the concept of the universal Church, however it arose in the churches at large, is as yet future in Paul's own thought, to be developed from germs of thought such as those which we have traced in this letter, and not to reach full maturity until the Ephesian and Colossian letters of the closing years of his life (see Hort, *The Christian Ecclesia*, chs. 7–9, esp. p. 148). Nor does Paul use the term elsewhere of the Church.

Who, then, constitute the Israel of God? The apostle himself supplies the answer—**all who walk by this rule:** those who, by sharing the faith of Abraham, have become the sons of Abraham. We can have no closer definition.

So we leave the apostle with the only glory he desired: on his body the *stigmata* (brand-marks) of Jesus. The debt which, under God, we and human history owe to him for his almost solitary vision we can only begin to understand.

BIBLIOGRAPHY

BRUCE, F. F., *The Epistle to the Galatians: an Expanded Paraphrase*, in *An Expanded Paraphrase of the Epistles of Paul* (Exeter, 1965).

CALVIN, J., *Commentary on the Epistle of Paul to the Galatians* (Pringle's translation, Edinburgh, 1854).

COLE, R. A., *The Epistle of Paul to the Galatians*. TNTC (London, 1965).

DUNCAN, G. S., *The Epistle of Paul to the Galatians*. MNT (London, 1934).

HOGG, C. F., and VINE, W. E., *The Epistle of Paul the Apostle to the Galatians* (London, 1922).

HUNTER, A. M., *Galatians*. Laymen's Bible Commentaries (London, 1959).

LAKE, K., *The Earlier Epistles of St. Paul* (London, 1911).

LIGHTFOOT, J. B., *Saint Paul's Epistle to the Galatians* (London, 1865; 1896 edn. quoted).

LUTHER, M., *Commentary on Saint Paul's Epistle to the Galatians* (Middleton's edition, repr. London, 1953).

RAMSAY, W. M., *A Historical Commentary on St. Paul's Epistle to the Galatians* (London, 1899).

RIDDERBOS, H., *St. Paul's Epistle to the Churches of Galatia. NIC* (Grand Rapids, 1953).

ROPES, J. H., *The Singular Problem of the Epistle to the Galatians* (Cambridge, Mass., 1929).

STOTT, J. R. W., *The Message of Galatians* (London, 1968).

THE LETTER TO THE EPHESIANS

GEORGE E. HARPUR

This letter forms a fitting crown to the extant writings of Paul the apostle of the Gentiles. In it his teaching is brought to an integrated wholeness and finality. Doctrines which are presented piecemeal elsewhere are here gathered in impressive harmony, each in its place in the whole concept of salvation. Doctrines which are given extensive exposition in earlier letters, such as justification in Romans, are here condensed and embedded in the outline of the eternal purpose, in proportion to the rest of the faith. The unity pressed in 1 Corinthians to combat their divisions is now found in its dispensational and cosmic settings (1: 10; 4: 13). The second advent is disentangled from the emotional comfort and intellectual curiosity which surround it in Thessalonians and given its brief but important place as the ripening of the eternal plan at a strategic time (4: 13, 30). The Jew-Gentile relationship which tormented the Galatian area appears as part of a cosmic unifying process (2: 15). Paul himself no longer needs to press his claims to apostleship, but can show the significance of the office in revealing the plan of God at the right moment (3: 1-5). The Christology set out in Colossians against Gnostic belittlement is assumed now as beyond question, and crucially connected with the purpose of God for men (1: 22, 23; 2: 6). The Ephesian letter is a fitting climax and *raison d'être* for all Paul's activities and doctrine. It is a statement of what God is doing in the whole business of creation and salvation.

Authorship

The letter presents such a perfect co-ordination of Paul's teaching that it is not surprising that its authorship did not come into question from Marcion's time, if not Ignatius's (Ign. *Eph.* 12: 2) until comparatively recent years, and this very fittingness is a factor in the attack upon its Pauline origin. The suggestion of E. J. Goodspeed is that the letter was written as an introduction to the issue of a collection of Paul's letters, made by a sympathetic follower in the latter part of the first century. He maintains that it bears the marks of literary dependence upon the other letters rather than originality (*The Meaning of Ephesians*, 1933, and *The Key*

to Ephesians, 1956). As to the first point, there is no documentary evidence for supposing the letter was ever placed in any introductory, or even final position in the collection. Even if there were, such a covering letter could as well be Paul's as anyone else's. On the other score the issue is brought down to earth by the examination of the facts of the case. This has been carried out exhaustively by C. L. Mitton (*The Epistle to the Ephesians*, 1951) in a comparison of Ephesians with admittedly Pauline letters (he excludes the Pastorals) but chiefly with Colossians. The difficulties are set out by E. J. Goodspeed in his book, *The Key to Ephesians*, in twenty-one points. His first point is that 'Ephesians reflects no definite, localized, historical situation which it is intended to meet' but this would be a valid objection only if it could be shown that Paul was unable or unwilling to write a circular letter. See under 'Destination and Occasion' (below). Next he thinks that the high value put upon Paul's activities (3: 2-4), could not have come from his own pen. But we find in Gal. 1: 11-2: 11 and 2 C. 11: 23-12: 11 that Paul could assess his position and worth as an apostle in the highest of terms. The statement here in Eph. 3: 2-4 is qualified straight away in 5 where he brackets other apostles and even prophets with himself; and in 8 he sets his own value down as the least of all the saints. Many other of the points are inconclusive, open to other interpretations, or hardly count in this matter. For example: number four, that 'Church' in Ephesians is always universal— but does he have to mention the local church in a letter which is agreed to be a circular, partly on the ground that it does not deal with any local matters? The use of *ekklēsia* in its local sense would be out of place in the theme of the letter. Number nine is that the principalities and powers which the Colossians were tempted to worship have in Ephesians become enemies to be fought. But why not? Paul would fight anything that displaced the worship of Christ. Did he not attack these powers of darkness in 1 C. 10: 20 f.? Number seventeen is that Eph. 6: 4 is hardly like Paul when all he had to say in Col. was 'do not irritate your children'. Paul was far too clever, and too much a Jew, to fail to see the value of home training in religion. Can we really believe that such an idea never occurred to him? It is certainly granted that there are minor discrepancies of word usage and viewpoint but such things can never be conclusive. Paul, of all people, had the least stereotyped kind of mind, and his adaptability of conception and fluidity of language can be seen in all his letters. Development of thought and variation of expression merely underline Pauline authorship or at the very least are as valuable in support as in opposition. The concept and teaching of Ephesians as a whole forbid the view that it is a mere patchwork of words and phrases culled from his other writings, its coherence too complete and individual. It raises considerable difficulties if we take 'Paul' to be a pseudonym, or view the personal references (1: 1, 15; 3: 1-4, 7, 8, 13; 4: 1; 6: 19-22) as manufactured and artificial. First, the alleged follower must have been a spiritual giant to be capable of co-ordinating the various doctrines of Paul's letters into what is admittedly a work of magnificent unity, from which the apostle himself could have learned a great deal. How could such a man be hidden, or why should he try to hide himself? Anonymous documents could find acceptance, *e.g.* Hebrews. Second, if he were an opponent of Paul, and therefore afraid to use his own name, why did he issue an edition of Paul's letters? And how would he evade the many still alive who knew what Paul had written, and who would certainly dispute a letter emerging years after Paul had died? Third, Paul's own warnings about letters purporting to come from him, would have raised suspicions in such circumstances, and of such suspicions there is no evidence whatever. There is a brief summary of the pros and cons of Pauline authorship in articles included in the *Studies in Ephesians* edited by F. L. Cross in 1956; cf. also the article on 'Ephesians' by F. Foulkes in *NBD*.

Ephesians and Colossians

A comparison of vocabularies shows clearly what has always been known, that these two letters have much in common. Indeed they have, though they have some fundamental differences also.

(a) Words

The evidence of word-lists shows that the letters are close together as to date, and that there is an overlapping of related themes. The result is that one often throws light upon the other. It is instructive to compare Eph. 1: 4 with Col. 1: 22, 23, 28; 1: 17 with 1: 9; 1: 20 ff. with 2: 10; 2: 5 f. with 3: 3; 3: 1-5 with 1: 26; 3: 16-19 with 1: 27; 4: 13-16 with 2: 19; 4: 20-24 with 3: 10; 5: 3-7 with 3: 5-8; 5: 5-17 with 4: 5; 5: 18 f. with 3: 16; 5: 22-24 with 3: 18; 5: 25-27 with 1: 28; 6: 21 f. with 4: 7 f. For almost identical phraseology compare Eph. 1: 7 with Col. 1: 14; 2: 5 with 2: 13; 3: 2 with 1: 25; 4: 16 with 2: 19; 4: 22-24 with 3: 8-10; 4: 32 with 3: 13; 5: 19 f. with 3: 16 f. Three words common to these letters will repay closer study, i.e. *oikonomia*, plan or stewardship: *plērōma*, fulness; and *mystērion*, mystery. That they are used with different meanings is hard to substantiate satisfactorily, for context determines precise meanings, and many words in any case have a degree of ambiguity and some range of meaning.

(b) Style

There are slight differences of style. For example, a fulness of expression in Eph. which is unusual: 3: 5 'his holy apostles and prophets'; and a tendency to hyperbole: 1: 19; 3: 8, 20. A softer, heavier style which may be attributed to the fact that in Col. Paul is in battle with opponents whilst in Eph. he is not dealing with any pressing situation and he may well have relaxed his rule to eschew any 'excellency of speech' (1 C. 2: 1, 4). Mixing of metaphors, abrupt transitions and large parentheses are typical of Paul's style, and can scarcely be hidden, nor indeed convincingly copied.

(c) Contents

Col. is aimed at a particular local need and therefore contains what is absent from Eph.: personal greetings (4: 9-17); doctrinal warnings (2: 6-9); arguments against error (2: 16-23); a developed Christology (1: 15-20), Eph. being concerned with ecclesiology. Col. 4: 18 is something which would necessarily be omitted from a circular.

(d) Viewpoint

The only important question of divergence in a matter common to both letters concerns the headship of Christ. It is pointed out that this is ecclesiastical in Eph. 5: 23, but cosmic in Col. 2: 10. But Eph. contains 1: 22; and Col. contains 1: 18 and 2: 19. The headship of Our Lord is in fact universal, and within this is His headship of the Church which is organic rather than organizational.

Destination and Occasion

The following things have to be taken into account in any satisfactory explanation of this. i. Early MSS and writers witness to the omission of 'at Ephesus' at 1: 1. ii. All MSS nevertheless refer to the letter as *To Ephesians*. iii. Marcion calls it the epistle to the Laodiceans. iv. There are no personal greetings. v. The letter does not deal with any local questions, nor is it polemic in character. vi. Tychicus, of the province of Asia (Ac. 20: 4), accompanied the letter to a definite circle of brethren. vii. Paul wrote from prison (3: 1; 4: 1), probably from Rome (6: 20). viii. Eph. 3: 2 might be considered rhetorical, but not 1: 15. Paul envisaged a circle large enough to include some with whom he was unacquainted.

Epaphras had brought somewhat disturbing news about the churches in the area of Colossae (Col. 1: 7, 8; 4: 12, 13), necessitating a letter attacking error. Having dealt with that Paul might well consider the time opportune for a positive constructive summary of his teaching without having to turn aside to deal with controverted points. The Gnostics were developing their doctrines into a philosophical scheme. While Tychicus waited for some turning point in events at court to carry news to Asia (Eph. 6: 21; Col. 4: 7, 8) Paul would have time to lay out with precision an encyclical letter, which would inevitably be coloured by the recent composition of Colossians, and also have connections with all his other letters of any importance. With the issue of his trial soon to be reached a clear statement of the inspired basis and significance of the believing Jews' and Gentiles' union in the Church was now needed for the Church at large, together with a clarification of this in the light of the divine purpose in history. Ephesians is just such a letter. It would certainly be sent to an important and strategic centre whence a truly Pauline church could circulate it widely. Either the original had a blank space for the destination to be filled in, and the different handwriting then set the contemporary textual critics questioning it, or, perhaps more likely, the address to Ephesus was deleted from the circulated copies. Marcion probably saw one with Laodicea entered therein. Local matters and personal greetings would obviously be

omitted, and the verbal instructions to Tychicus could cover all that Paul wanted to say to churches he knew personally. See 6: 21 where the 'you also' perhaps envisages a larger circle of recipient churches. The date and the identification of the imprisonment are dealt with in the article on The Pauline Letters.

Ephesus

This famous city was not only a strategic place in the missionary plans of Paul (for three years it was his centre of operations; see *St. Paul's Ephesian Ministry*, by G. S. Duncan, 1929), it also figures largely in the literary scene of early Christianity. It is traditionally viewed as the place in which John wrote his contributions to the NT, and it takes first place in the seven letters of the Apocalypse. The letters to Timothy are connected with the city, and later on Ignatius wrote to the church there from Smyrna. The city was a first-class trading centre ranking with Alexandria and Antioch. A religious metropolis of great importance in the world-famous cult of Artemis, its downfall was due to the silting up of the Cayster. Its remains were recovered to modern readers by J. T. Wood in his *Modern Discoveries on the site of Ancient Ephesus* (1890).

Theme

The great spiritual blessings brought to individuals now by the promised Spirit (1: 3-2: 10), and the inclusion of the Gentiles with the Jews (2: 11-3: 13), the movement of spiritual growth of these as Christ's body (3: 14-4: 16), in manifesting the new moral standards (4: 17-6: 9) are all unfolded as having been eternally planned, and now in this age in actual achievement through the living union forged in Christ. Though this presently entails a spiritual conflict (6: 10-20), it will reach its perfect culmination in the age to come.

ANALYSIS

I GREETINGS (1: 1 f.)

II THANKSGIVING AND PRAYER (1: 3-19)

    i The blessings bestowed in Christ (1: 3-10)

    ii Shared by Jew and Gentile (1: 11-14)

    iii Prayer for spiritual enlightenment (1: 15-19)

III THE NEW LIFE IN CHRIST (1: 20–3: 21)

IV UNITY AND DIVERSITY (4: 1–16)

V MARKS OF THE NEW LIFE (4: 17–6: 20)

VI FINAL GREETINGS (6: 21–24)

I. GREETINGS (1: 1 f.)

The greetings follow the normal contemporary letter formula of writer, recipients and greeting. **apostle . . . by the will of God** marks the authority of the document. Many printed editions of the Greek text insert 'in Ephesus' in brackets, a reading which the RSV relegates to the margin, but which gives a better rendering. See above under the paragraph 'Destination'. The phrase **in Christ Jesus** and its equivalents occurs over thirty times in Eph., a watermark of Paul's style. It implies not only personal identification with Him, but in some contexts it indicates relationship in the 'corporate' Christ. See 1 C. 12: 12. Grace and peace are regular elements in benedictions traceable back to the oldest in Num. 6: 25, 26.

II. THANKSGIVING AND PRAYER (1: 3–19)

i. The blessings bestowed in Christ (1: 3–10)

The unlimited blessings which prompt this doxology are those spiritual benefits first promised to Abraham and later confirmed by prophets (Jl 2: 28) and the Baptist (Mk 1: 8), and finally bestowed by the baptism of the Spirit at Pentecost as indicated by our Lord (Jn 7: 39; Ac. 1: 5), hence verse 13 **the promised**

Holy Spirit. They reach from eternity past to the fulness of time. The cross section of them which occupies verses 4–11 traces them from before the foundation of the world, through the experience of salvation and apostolic enlightenment on to the consummation in the fulness of time. The whole complicated sentence (3–14, RV) is perhaps over-simplified in the RSV which breaks it up into several sentences. The four periods of blessing referred to above, each rounded off with a clause which begins with the words 'according to' (5, 7, 9, 11) should be read in the RV too. **3.** Paul plays on the word 'bless' which basically means to speak well of. We bless God by declaring Him to be blessed; He blesses us by actual enrichment. **heavenly places:** The realm of heavenly things; the word occurs only in Eph., five times in all. **4–5.** God's election antedates creation, and the selection is made in Christ. The objection to taking this to mean 'chosen to be in Christ' is that the purpose of the election is clearly stated—**that we should be holy and blameless.** Positive sanctification and negative blamelessness begin now, but are not fully achieved until we are **before him.** The twin ideas of being holy and blameless should be consulted in the parallel in Col. 1: 22, 23, and in 1 Th. 3: 13; 5: 23. **in love** usually connects with the preceding words but is here probably best taken with 5 (see 3: 17; 4: 2, 15, 16; 5: 2). The destination fixed for the believer is sonship, a purpose of divine love so great it could not have been foreseen (1 C. 2: 9 f.). The full meaning of this lies ahead (Rom. 8: 23, 29) but the earnest is already given (14; Rom. 8: 15; Gal. 4: 4 f.). **through Jesus Christ:** As in Jn 1: 12. **6-8. Beloved:** A messianic title which emphasizes the love already referred to in the previous verse. Redemption concerns the person; pardon has to do with our offensive activities. By such brevity does the Apostle condense the great doctrines of atonement and justification. **9-10.** Parts of the text of both 8 and 10 are taken into the scope of 9. The RV should be carefully compared. *Mystērion* is a secret which is now revealed, 'his hidden purpose', NEB. It is a pagan word, used for secret rites. It occurs often in the NT and in contemporary Jewish literature, and is found in the LXX of Dan. 2 for secret things. It does not necessarily imply anything very difficult; see the article in *NBD*. Here it is the hitherto hidden purpose of God, now made known by inspired men (Eph. 3: 5). The **wisdom and insight** is ours, not God's; compare the prayer in Col. 1: 9. **a plan for the fulness of time:** An arrangement or administration to be carried out when the appointed period has been completed and the time is ripe. God's purpose is not limited to man's salvation, it is a cosmic intention **to unite all things** in heaven and earth under the control of Christ (cf. Heb. 2: 5-8).

ii. Shared by Jew and Gentile (1: 11-14)
who accomplishes all things: The omnipotence and wisdom of God will secure His sovereign will whatever militates against it. Part of the Gk. of 11 is translated in 12, **have been destined,** an abbreviated version expanded in the NEB to 'we have been given our share in the heritage, as was decreed'. Note the parallel in Col. 1: 12. **appointed to live** emphasizes the present way in which we should cause His glory to be praised. Paul returns to this demand for consecration in 2: 10. **we who first hoped** and **you also who have heard** can be taken to indicate older Christians through whom the gospel came to Asia and the newer ones, but the reference to **the praise of his glory** (12, repeated in 14), together with the sections from 2: 11 to 3: 13, in which he deals with the union of Jew and Gentile in one body in Christ, show that the reference is to those in Israel whose hope in the Messiah anteceded that of the Gentiles. This would appear to demand that all the previous section, with its first person plural pronouns, speaks of Jewish believers. This is no real difficulty, for, if so,

Paul only states the Jewish remnant's inheritance of blessing in order to bracket with them in the next sentence all the Gentile believers. Paul is not suggesting that the churches he was addressing contained only Gentiles. His pronouns move from **we** (Jews) to **you** (Gentiles) and on to a larger **our** (14) which includes both Jews and Gentiles. When the Gospel broke out of the swaddling clothes of Judaism the Gentiles also came to trust in Christ, so 13 AV, but the construction is better if we understand that they too 'were made a heritage', the verb being supplied from the Gk. of 11. The clause **in whom also** occurs a second time in the text but only once in this translation. The second occurrence makes clear that the Gentiles also shared the sealing of the Holy Spirit. The baptism of the Spirit came upon the first Gentile converts exactly as it did on the Jews at Pentecost (Ac. 11: 15-18). With this they inevitably received all the spiritual blessings in Christ. The argument is set out in Galatians. This teaching of the equal status of the Jew and Gentile in Christ is prominent throughout the whole doctrinal section of Eph. Though Paul was still in prison on this account (it was the root of the Judaizers' opposition) the battle for it was virtually over. He can calmly state the doctrinal position which he envisaged as apostle of the nations, and for which he fought and suffered so much. The participle rendered **have believed** makes the time of sealing coincident with the time of believing, a point left doubtful in the AV both in this verse and in Ac. 19: 2. The seal of the New Covenant is spiritual and inward (Jer. 31: 33); the reality, of which the circumcision was the outward sign, wrought by the Spirit in the heart. The guarantee points back in authenticating, and forward promising completion, as a part payment made in advance. **until we acquire possession:** There is a time fixed for the redemption of the pledge (4: 30, and 1 Th. 4: 16 f.). The **praise of His glory** is a thought frequently expressed from 4 onwards, stressing the intention never far from Paul's mind, that everything about the saint should bring glory to God.

iii. Prayer for spiritual enlightenment (1: 15-19)
Their personal faith in Christ and their attitude to other believers gave evidence that they were in fact endowed with the afore-mentioned blessings, and therefore he prays that they may have an insight into three things: (*a*) the hope, the eternally planned consummation of all this blessing; (*b*) the value of the contents from God's standpoint; (*c*) the power by which it is to be achieved. **17. the Father of glory**

(cf. 1 C. 2: 8; Ac. 7: 2) is something more than just 'the glorious Father'; He intends to endow His people with a share in His glory (Rom. 8: 17; 2 Th. 1: 10). **a spirit of wisdom:** No article, therefore perhaps a manifestation or work of the Spirit whom they had already received. What they needed was His active illumination in their hearts, wisdom to grasp, and revelation, the unveiling of the secrets involved. Mere intellectual information is not enough, it is the enlightening of the eyes of the heart, the inner man's vision of Christ. **19.** The power is at work **in us who believe** as in 3: 20 and Phil. 2: 13. To convince them of the immensity of this dynamic power Paul uses a battery of words: surpassing, greatness, power, energy, strength and might. The three things which Paul wants them to grasp are dealt with, in reverse order, in the following sections. When he has shown them what the power is and what it does, he works his way to the riches of the glory (3: 16), and finally to the first point of his prayer, the hope of the calling, in 4: 1, 4. The way in which his thought and exposition develop without any big grammatical break from his prayer can also be seen in Col. 1: 9 ff.

III. THE NEW LIFE IN CHRIST (1: 20–3: 21)

i. The resurrection life of Christ (1: 20–23)

The power which the Christian is to get from acquaintance with Christ is the force which has accomplished the most tremendous event in history, even exceeding that of the act of the original creation. Out **from** among **the dead,** the phraseology which first confused the disciples in Mk 9: 9, 10, and refers to the bodily resurrection of Christ, the firstborn from the dead (Col. 1: 18). Other men had been raised only to die again, but Christ is in an order of His own, He could not die any more. **at His right hand:** One of many NT echoes of this most-quoted OT verse, Ps. 110: 1. The four terms used in 21 are from the terminology of Jewish and Gnostic speculation, but Paul is not necessarily endorsing this analysis of the heavenly hierarchies, but see 6: 12. Whatever rule there is, Christ is far above it in authority, whether named as in opposition now or as reigning with Him in the age to come (Zech. 14: 9; Dan. 7: 27). Then will Ps. 8: 6 here quoted be seen to be fulfilled (cf. 1 C. 15: 24–28; Heb. 2: 5–10). The destiny of the Church is linked with Christ as He fulfils the destiny of man. He holds two headships, one over the universe achieved by His death and exaltation (Phil. 2: 9–10), and the other over the Church by its

formation into a body at Pentecost (1 C. 12: 13). The Church is related to Christ in an organic way, as the body is to its head. Paul has previously used the body as a figure for the Church, without considering Christ to be its head (1 C. 12: 21), but here the figure is developed and the head is viewed as distinct from the members. Paul has extended the view of the Church functioning in a coherent fashion to that of its functioning as an expression of its head, i.e. Christ **23. fulness:** *Plērōma* could be referred to Christ, in which case the whole expression is equivalent to Col. 2: 9, but more likely it refers to the Church, in which case the Church is seen as either (*a*) *that without which He is incomplete*—not personally incomplete, but that He cannot reach His destiny alone, He must have His partner (5: 32)—or (*b*) *that in which He completely expresses Himself*—that is, He fills it, which is the teaching of 3: 17–19 and 4: 13–16. The NEB renders 'and as such holds within it the fulness of him who himself receives the entire fulness of God', cf. NEB marginal alternatives. The last clause in the chapter adds to the grammatical problem. The English versions construe the verb as middle voice, so denoting Christ's omnipresence, but some older versions take it as passive—*Him who all in all is being fulfilled.* This is an awkward phrase, indicating the progressive way in which Christ is being fulfilled in the Church (4: 13), or that the fulness of the Godhead is permanently resident in Christ (Col. 1: 19). This is the first mention of the Church in this letter, and it is immediately defined as that which is His body: not any group of Christians, or of churches, nor even Christendom, but the aggregate of those who are in Christ by the baptism of the Spirit (1 C. 12: 13).

ii. The resurrection life of believers (2: 1–10)

The power by which God's eternal purpose will be carried out has already delivered them from their old life, and lifted them into the heavenly realm in identification with Christ, and set them on the road to fulfilment. **1, 2. he made alive** is supplied from 5, because the construction is broken. Paul is continuing his theme from 1: 20 and the flow of his mind will be caught if we read 'raising Him from the dead . . . and you who were dead'. Their spiritual death is described on three planes: (*a*) The personal level. Their condition was due to breaches of the will of God, but also to sins in the more general sense, including omissions and inward failures. (*b*) The racial level. They followed the men of this age, as opposed to the standards of the world to come. (*c*) The supernatural level. Satan was at work in them. His realm is what might be called the lower heavenlies (6: 12). 'Of the spirit' (RV) is better; Satan is the fount of the spirit of the age. **sons of disobedience:** A Hebraism for 'disobedient people'. **3-6.** A transition from the second to the first person to show that the Jews are in the same position of need as the Gentiles. **we lived:** We conducted ourselves, as in 1 Tim. 3: 15, caring only for wishes that were carnal, led away by the commands that spring from the nature and thoughts of an unregenerated life. We were in ourselves objects of wrath, divine wrath (5: 6), as all men are. **4-6.** God is exact in judgment but **rich in mercy.** His love springs from Himself, not being called forth by anything in us, for He loved us in our spiritual ruin. The new life He gives us is not a thing apart, it is a participation in Christ's life. **alive together:** See Col. 3: 4. The parenthesis in 5 is expanded in 8-9. The believer's new life is a share in Christ's risen life and also in His reign in the heavenlies. (Rom. 5: 17). **7-10. the coming ages:** Both the millennial period and the eternal state will exhibit the infinite kindness of God demonstrated to redeemed sinners, especially in their manifestation as sons, and in their glory. By 'the grace', the article indicates the grace mentioned before at 5, and bracketed with mercy, love and kindness. **you have been saved:** The perfect tense, you have been and you are now saved. Grace is bestowed upon those who accept it. This is done by faith, but faith does not possess salvation meritoriously as if faith were any credit. **this** is neuter, not referring to either grace or faith, which are feminine, but to the scheme of salvation itself, and therefore translated **this is not your own doing.** No human activity can result in salvation, it is God's gift. The Christian glories in nothing but Christ. **workmanship** means a creative product. In Christ a new creation begins (2 C. 5: 17), one with a moral intention, not for levitical ritual, or mere outward ceremonies, but a manner of life laid out in advance (1 Pet. 2: 21).

iii. Jew and Gentile united in the Church (2: 11-22)

In passing from the effect of the resurrection on individuals to its collective effect, he proceeds in each case in the same fashion: from the past (1-3; 11-12) to the present (4-6; 13-20) and on to the future (7-10; 21-22). The alienated Jew and Gentile are now reconciled in Christ and formed into a home for God. **11-12.** Their deficiencies as Gentiles are marked in three pairs of statements. *Physically* they lacked the ancient sign of the covenant, and family links with the promised Messiah. *Politically* they had

no part in Israel's national or religious life. *Spiritually* they had no prospect or knowledge of the true God.

13-18. But all that had been changed by the death of Christ, which was for all men without distinction. Through this new way God is as accessible to the Gentile as to the Jew. The two parties had become one, not only by Christ, but in Christ. The wall of hostility alludes to the balustrade which surrounded the Temple proper in Jerusalem, barring the entrance of Gentiles (Ac. 21: 28 f.). The blood of Christ also abolished (made null and void) the law of Moses, its moral intentions having been otherwise secured (Rom. 8: 4). **the law of commandments and ordinances** (the latter meaning decrees—Lk. 2: 1 etc.— not ceremonies as such): The code of law embodied in decrees or enactments, i.e. the whole Jewish legal system. The **new man** is in place of the two; new in status, privilege and relationship, but its core was the elect remnant of Israel at that time. The death of Christ not only took away the barrier between Jew and Gentile, but also the barrier between them both and God. Isa. 52: 7 and 57: 19 are brought in to show from the prophetic scriptures that this was indeed planned. The reconciliation does not take place on Jewish ground, for He rent the veil as He broke down the fence. Both are elevated to God by a real, not ritualistic access. **19-22. So then** summarizes 13-18 and goes on to show what has taken the place of the situation in 11 f. **sojourners:** Resident foreigners who though physically present have no actual citizen rights. Gentile believers now share citizen rights in the heavenly Jerusalem, being householders with family rights. From the metaphor of a body Paul has passed quickly through that of a city and a family and now presents that of a building. In 1 C. 3: 10, 11 where the same metaphor is used the Lord is the foundation, but here He is the corner-stone, the primary foundation stone which sets the bearings for the entire building. **the apostles and prophets,** the NT ones, constitute the first layer, in which Peter was the first stone, *Petros.* Being keyed into Christ as they are added, the many stones are added to each other, to complete the shrine. A parallel picture of the growth of a body can be seen in 4: 13-16. **joined together** denotes a process of compaction and is used again at 4: 16. By **you also** Paul reiterates the Gentiles' place in all this. The concept of God taking men for an abode was not new, and no doubt ultimately derived from Lev. 26: 11 f. See 2 C. 6: 16.

iv. This mystery was formerly a secret (3: 1-6)

Having shown what is the greatness of God's power in raising Christ, and in constituting the Church His body, he now begins to expound something of the riches of the glory of this inheritance. He starts to express it in prayer, but in typical fashion is deflected by his own words . . . **prisoner on behalf of you Gentiles** and only returns to his prayer in 15.

Paul was not Caesar's prisoner, it was the will of Christ which held him captive (4: 1). It was because of his battle for Gentile liberty from the law that he got enmeshed with Rome. This was his stewardship (cf. Col. 1: 24, 25); to reveal and explain God's arrangements for the incorporation of the Gentiles in the Church, without law or circumcision. This had brought him into conflict with the Judaizers (who were 'zealous for the law') and ultimately with Rome (2 Tim. 2: 9; 4: 16 f.). For if Gentile believers were stated to be non-Jewish then they came under Roman laws about illegal religions. So long as they were regarded as a Jewish sect (Ac. 28: 22) they were immune from this law and its death penalty. What he had **written briefly**, summarily (in 1: 9 or 1: 3-14), showed his comprehensive insight into the secret purpose of God, hidden from previous dispensations, but now made known to a group of inspired men. V. 6 is a restatement in threefold form of that part of the secret which concerns the Gentiles. That the Gentiles should be blessed was clearly revealed in the OT but that they should be blessed without having to become Jews was unforeseen, as also was the fact that God would introduce a new thing, the body of Christ. They now share the inheritance, are equally members of Christ's body the Church, and the promise is now extended to them also (Gal. 3: 29).

v. The significance of Paul's apostleship (3: 7-13)
Of the good news which announces this unveiled secret Paul was a special messenger, sent to make God's purpose clear to the Gentiles, to demonstrate it before all men and the entire cosmos.

Paul traces the gift which enabled him to be a minister to the same resurrection power mentioned previously, 1: 19; and see Gal. 2: 8. He uses a comparative-superlative, **the very least,** to express his utter unfitness for the work. He (*a*) evangelizes the Gentiles, (*b*) enlightens all men, (*c*) in order to inform the whole supernatural world. The evangel he describes as the untrackable wealth of the Christ. The enlightenment is the plan, secret in all previous ages (Col. 1: 25-27), but inherent in the creation of the universe. The information is laid out in the Church, where all heavenly intelligences may view the many-hued wisdom of God. Angels baffled by the amazing liberties allowed to Satan and men can now justify God, as they behold the clear deliberate purpose of God in the ages now unfolded in the Messiah, both Himself personally and His members corporately. **12.** Faith in Christ gives us free and confident **access** to God, because of sonship (1: 5) based on redemption. In view of all this (2-12, Paul's privilege, the wonderful plan, and the nearness to God Himself) they should not lose heart over Paul's trial and imprisonment. These were a joy (Col. 1: 24) to him and should be considered by them as something to glory in. Many thought otherwise, because they did not see the situation as he did, or else, like the Judaizers, they saw it all too clearly.

vi. Prayer for spiritual enduement (3: 14-21)
Resuming from 3: 1 he prays that the power (1: 19) which has altered their whole status before God (2: 1-22) might now work increasingly in them until God's full intention is realized.

In deepest reverence Paul offers this particular prayer to **the Father,** *patēr*, from whom every *patria*—group descended from a common ancestor—is derived. The Church is a family in a unique sense, as sharing His very life and nature. He uses the phraseology of his original prayer, 1: 18, 19, both as to the riches and to the power, and now applies these to the inner man (2 C. 4: 16), by the work of the Spirit. The alteration to their status had been instantaneous, but their moral change is progressive, in five ways: (*a*) by the strengthening of their inward spiritual life. (*b*) by the dwelling of Christ in their hearts. K. S. Wuest expands the word to 'settle down and feel completely at home in.' Cf. Gal. 4: 19. (*c*) by this firm foundation in love which provides power for comprehension. 'To lay hold of', not mere mental apprehension but the actual acquiring. It is the grasping of that fulness which is the goal for the Church (1: 23; 3: 19; 4: 13). This is only attained communally, **with all the saints,** for each individual has only his own finite measure. (*d*) by experiencing the love of Christ. Knowing what is beyond knowledge is a paradox that envisages an ever-expanding experience. (*e*) by being **filled with all the fulness of God,** a conclusion expounding Jn 17: 20-23, i.e. the Church revealing Christ in all His divine fulness. If the sea were filled with empty containers, the containers would be filled with the fulness of the sea. That God should have such an incredible purpose for man calls for a doxology indeed (20 f.). In it Paul stresses again the limitless power at work in the saints to achieve this goal, which is infinitely more than man could ask for himself or even imagine. There will then be endless glory for God through the Church, inasmuch as it will be a vehicle for the display of all the glories of Christ.

IV. UNITY AND DIVERSITY (4: 1-16)
i. Maintenance and basis of Christian unity (4: 1-6)
The high ecclesiastical doctrine of the previous sections calls for a manner of life which exhibits the transformation envisaged in it, and because of its nature this must be shown in the Christian community (4: 1-16), amongst men in general (4: 17-5: 20) and in the particular relationships of Christian men and women (5: 21-6: 9).

2. with denotes the frame of mind which accompanies the actions of the walk, being the new spirit of 23. Twin virtues of the renewed mind are lowliness (now for the first time presented as a virtue) and meekness (being not weakness but the eliminating of self-assertion). The next pair shows how they receive others' actions directed against them. By all these four tempers they are to show an eagerness to forge a bond made of peace by which spiritual unity is safeguarded. The seven unities are a list, being introduced without a verb. Every expression of unity is based on these. **one body:** The new body of 2: 15, 16. **one Spirit:** Given alike to Jew and Gentile, 1: 13. **one hope:** As previously expounded there are no second-class Christians in God's plan. **one Lord:** Even Christ the source of all unity. **one faith:** Either the common faith given to all the saints (Jude 3), or, possibly, the subjective faith each believer puts in Christ. **one baptism:** Usually taken to refer to baptism in water, but it may reasonably refer to the baptism of the Spirit. These seven unities can be compared with the four unities which Paul sets out in 1 C. 12: 4-13, where he deals at length with the unity produced by the baptism of the Spirit. The four unities there shown are one Spirit (4, 9, 11), one Lord (5), one God working in all (6) and one body (12 f.). It would be strange to omit all reference to the Lord's supper, which is so clearly connected with the unity of the body (1 C. 10: 17), and insert baptism in water which is an unsafe basis of unity (Ac. 8: 13, 20-23). In the other items in this list, 'one' seems to mean 'one only' not 'one sort of' ('one faith' is doubtful), and is best so taken here. The seven items are so arranged that the first is set against the last, the second against the sixth, the third against the fifth, so connecting hope with faith, and Spirit with baptism. The 'one Lord' stands appropriately central to all. **one God:** He is the Father of all in Christ in the most real

sense. He is over all the members, and manifested through all because working in all. Paul uses the abstract word for unity, strictly 'oneness', both here in 3, and later in 13. He is dealing with something spiritual, not a concrete, organized entity, for the NT churches were self-governing, and devoid of any central ecclesiastical bureau of control.

ii. The gifts that develop this corporate life (4: 7-16)
The unity is accompanied by diversity, like the unity of the natural body; and using this figure Paul shows that the various members each contribute to the whole until the organism reaches maturity. In the case of Christ's body, this maturity is His fulness, as outlined in 3: 18, 19.

Here again Paul is elaborating a conception found in 1 C. 12, this time from vv. 24 f. Each several member has received a gift and the proportionate grace for its exercise. He takes his illustration from Ps. 68: 18, which he loosely quotes, using a text found partly in the LXX but mainly in the Targum and Syriac Peshitta. The triumphant warrior is elevated to his throne as he returns with hosts of prisoners, receiving gifts from the conquered peoples, and issuing gifts to his followers. Of the three things found in his text Paul ignores the host of captives, and substitutes instead a Descent. (a) The Ascension is the elevation of Christ far above all the heavens, where He is to fill all in all, as dealt with in 1: 20-23. (b) The implied Descent may well be more than the incarnation, the descent to Hades is the real parallel to His being lifted up **far above all the heavens.** (c) He does not explain the captivity, but from this context of the descent to Hades it has been taken to refer to the deliverance thence of those who had in previous ages believed; but the idea is certainly wider than that, spiritual powers being included as His captives (Col. 2: 15; 1 Pet. 3: 22) and of course, all the redeemed (2 C. 2: 14 f.). An early hymn, probably Gnostic, runs:

'*and to lead captive a good captivity for freedom.*
'*I was strengthened and made mighty and took the world captive . . .*
'*and the Gentiles were gathered together who had been scattered abroad.*'
(Odes of Solomon 10: 3-5).

Consult also the additional note on the Odes of Solomon by F. F. Bruce in 'The Fourfold Gospel' (pp. 99 f.). (d) The **gifts** (11) come from the ascended Christ, and are part of the promise of the Spirit. Paul ignores some gifts he has elsewhere listed, and gives those most directly related to the building up of the

Q

Church. First **apostles,** in the narrower sense
of 2: 20, the permanent authority. **prophets:**
Inspired men who revealed the truth of God.
evangelists: Preaching missionaries, through
whom men became followers of Christ. **pastors
and teachers:** Elsewhere called elders or
bishops, who cared for the converts and their
growth. All pastors in a local church should be
able to teach (some privately and others publicly)
as well as to shepherd (see 1 Tim. 5: 17); but
there were also teachers in the Church who
had a more roving commission than administrators (Rom. 12: 7; 1 C. 12: 27). The three
purposes of 12 are set out as co-ordinate in the
RSV, but the RV accords more with the Gk.:
the clauses can be variously construed. The
third and ultimate intention is a recurrent
theme of the letter (1: 23; 2: 21; 3: 19; 4: 13-16;
5: 27). All this activity is to go on until the
Church reaches the measure of the fulness of
Christ. It is an attained unity, whilst the unity
of 4: 3-6 is a unity already existent. The integrated oneness of the baby is real enough, but
it is not the conscious oneness of the mature
man. The unity towards which the Church
moves is one of personal knowledge of the
Son of God. The faith is more what we usually
mean by knowledge, i.e. full acquaintance
with the mind of Christ. **14. so that:** The
final clause—as the Church moves towards
this final maturity it graduates from infancy
and the instability that is due to inadequate
doctrine and inadequate experience of Christ.
The spiritual novice is wide open to false
doctrine and to false men. **cunning** suggests
the clever handling of dice. **wiles** recurs in
6: 11, traced to their ultimate source. **15.
speaking the truth in love:** Maintaining the
true doctrine in a compatible spirit and manner
of life, not as a weapon for fighting but to secure
a balanced growth in Christ (Col. 3: 16). This
will produce a mature expression of the Head
in every member of the body. **16. joined:**
An architectural metaphor indicating harmony.
knit: As a body is by ligaments and joints,
indicates solidity. When the parts are each
working properly the head will see by its
overall control that the whole body develops
aright.

V. MARKS OF THE NEW LIFE (4: 17-6: 20)
i. In personal character (4: 17-24)
17-19. As always, Paul proceeds from the
dogmatic to the pragmatic, for the fulness
of Christ can only at present be seen to operate
in the Church in the spheres of character and
service. These latter are actuated by the operation
of the mind, and the moral breakdown of the

Gentile world is rooted **in the futility of their
minds.** They are empty of the real values of
God and eternity. This vanity, Paul teaches,
originates in an inner cause, a darkened intellect:
and in an outer cause, separation from God.
Man is in the dark without God, for God is
man's true sunlight. Both these causes spring
from the **ignorance** of God **that is in,** or
among, **them,** and this ignorance in turn
arises from the hardness or obduracy of heart
by which men repel God's revelation of Himself.
Rom. 1: 18-21 unfolds this further, and both
sections should be studied, together with
Eph. 2: 2, 3, for a true understanding of the
unbeliever's condition. **19. become callous:**
I.e. ceased to care. The soul, when deprived of
spiritual resources, turns for satisfaction to the
body, and even the high tides of philosophical
culture break eventually on this barren shore.
20-24. To **learn Christ** is both to hear Him
(hear about Him is inadequate) and to be
taught in Him. The latter is initiated by the
oral instruction of the new convert. This
consisted of that outline of Our Lord's life
and teaching which is the core of the synoptic
Gospels (Lk. 1: 3, 4), and was enjoined upon
all (Mt. 28: 19 f.); teaching which it is perilous
to ignore (1 Tim. 6: 3 f.). **the truth is in
Jesus:** Absolute truth, not an aspect of it, as if
He were to be compared with Confucius.
Christ is the truth (Jn 14: 6), therefore to learn
Christ is to learn truth. The discarding of the
old man and the wearing of the new are two
halves of one action. The moment by moment
repetition of this decision is the secret of the
Christian's changed life (Rom. 6: 13 f.). Note
the contrast between **deceitful** and **true.**
Human nature cannot be reformed (Rom. 8: 7),
it must be regenerated. The new (*kainos,* new
in kind) creation, which replaces the old of
Gen. 1: 27, restores the likeness of God, and the
renewal takes place in the innermost being,
in the spirit of the mind. **righteousness** is
right conduct towards God, and **holiness,**
here, is right conduct towards men.

ii. In the Christian community (4: 25-5: 2)
In this section and the following one Paul
deals with eight evils and the virtues which
are their opposite numbers, so contrasting the
walk of the Gentiles and the walk of the
Christian. It is an early exposition of the theme
of the Two Ways, prominent in the *Didache*
and the *Epistle of Barnabas.* The sections that
follow are Paul's application of 22-24.

(a)	4: 25	falsehood	v. truth
(b)	4: 26, 27	resentment	v. self-control
(c)	4: 28	stealing	v. generosity
(d)	4: 29, 30	evil speech	v. edification
(e)	4: 31-5: 2	malice	v. love

(*f*) 5: 3-14 impurity v. chastity
(*g*) 5: 15-17 imprudence v. wisdom
(*h*) 5: 18-20 debauchery v. joy

25. putting away: Remove, the same word as put off in 22. The command is quoted from Zech. 8: 16, and the next verse is from Ps. 4: 4 LXX. It is interesting to see how Paul interprets the second half of the verse from the Psalm, and to compare Mt. 5: 22-24 with the following clause in 27. Quick action takes opportunity out of the hands of the devil (*diabolos* could indicate slanderer). The anger in 26 is the feeling of provocation not just the expression of it. **29. as fits the occasion:** Grasping the appropriate chance of imparting grace. **30.** For **the day of redemption** see Rom. 8: 23: the believer looks forward to a resurrection body in a liberated creation at the return of Christ. Bitterness, wrath and malice are three emotional states, the other three items are the outward manifestations of these. The Christian emotions of kindness and tenderness reveal themselves in forgiveness and self-sacrifice (5: 2). Given the nature of children, God's loved children have the ability and the opportunity of imitating their Father. All virtue is fully revealed in Christ crucified (see 1 Pet. 2: 21-24). The levitical language (reproducing Ps. 40: 6, as does Heb. 10: 5) indicates the typology of the OT sacrifices.

iii. A challenge to pagan evil (5: 3-20)
The sixth of his points, regarding impurity, is greatly extended because of the pressing ubiquity of the problem in contemporary society. **But** and **not even be named** both stress the seriousness of this kind of evil, which prevents a church from treating such people as Christians, as in vv. 5 ff. where the same three things are specifically mentioned. The same viewpoint is taken in 1 C. 5: 11-13. Covetousness is placed in very disreputable company; it is the antithesis of Christianity (Ac. 20: 35). Paul urges (4) that even in word they should refrain from smut, from speech on the level of morons, and from double-meaning jokes. Some people's lives make it clear that they are not in the kingdom of God at all, but that does not mean that they are beyond salvation (see 1 C. 6: 9-11). What to do with professing Christians who behave like this is made clear in 1 C. 5: 4-5. Paul's teaching on separation should be carefully examined in 1 C. 5: 9-13. By walking in the light they would be able to apply a test and so discover the will of God (9 is a parenthesis). Verses 13 f. should be set against the background of Jn 3: 19-21: that which comes to, responds to, the light becomes light itself. The quotation is not from the OT, but probably from a Christian hymn based on

the language of Isa. 60: 1. **15-17.** By so coming to understand the will of the Lord they can step out of the imprudent and short-sighted policies of most men. Wisdom can turn evil days to good account. **18.** The stimulus for effective living does not come from wine, but from allowing the Holy Spirit full possession of the heart, an echo of the prayer of 3: 16, 17. **be filled with the Spirit:** The fulness of the Spirit is the subject of a command, in contrast with the baptism of the Spirit. The latter is not something to be sought for, it is part of that initial experience of every Christian (even weak ones like the Corinthians, 1 C. 12: 12, 13) by which they are incorporated into Christ. The fulness of the Spirit describes an experience or condition which could be lost or repeated (Ac. 4: 31; 6: 5; 7: 55; 9: 17; 11: 24). Being filled with the Spirit is here, as in Acts, connected with joy, courage, spirituality and character. Miraculous gifts do not necessarily prove that those who possess them are even Christians (Mt. 7: 21-23). **19-20.** 'The music that flows' is in contrast with that which follows drunkenness. **psalms** are those of the OT, or suchlike (1 C. 14: 26 Gk.). **hymns and spiritual songs** are not easy to distinguish, but praise is prominent in the former word, while the latter is general.

iv. Between wives and husbands (5: 21-33)
21. The injunctions that follow are particular examples of the command concerning subjection. The division into marital, filial and occupational categories, though temporary (Gal. 3: 28), is to be accepted as the present providence of God. 5: 22-6: 9 should be compared with the condensed equivalent in Col. 3: 18-4: 1, and with 1 Pet. 2: 18-3: 7. The apostles seem to have used formally-arranged instruction in dealing with these matters, judging from the pattern observable in these cases. The threefold division of society is, however, a natural one, and universally applicable, and apart from the close parallels of Eph. 6: 5-9 and Col. 3: 22-4: 1 the treatment is independent in each case. The submission of the wife is to be matched by the Christ-like love and consideration of the husband, and similarly in the other groups. Failure on the part of one does not justify it on the part of the other, though it necessarily makes success more difficult. Paul intermingles three different facts, each of which he transfers in a figure to Christ and His Church. (*a*) The husband-wife relationship itself. The Church is a bride espoused to Christ. (*b*) A man's headship makes his wife to be his body. The Church is Christ's body. (*c*) Physical union makes man and wife one flesh. Christ and His Church are one (cf.

1 C. 6: 15-17). As to the first, the relationship springs (25) from the love and sacrifice of Christ. He uses the figure of the bride's preparation in 26 and her presentation in marriage in 27. **the washing of water** is figurative, like the wedding (Rev. 19: 7, 8). The laver, like other equipment in the Tabernacle, was typical, and spoke of that renewal brought about by regeneration (Tit. 3: 5). **sanctify her, having cleansed:** That is, the sanctification is the result of the cleansing. Both words are used by the Lord when He deals with the matter in Jn 15: 3; 17: 17 (there are quite a few points of contact between this letter and the Gospel of John). It is, as He indicates, the spoken word that does the cleansing. Our 'presentation' is a frequent thought in Paul's writings, *e.g.* 2 C. 11: 2; Col. 1: 22; and in Jude 24 similarly. As to the second (23), the head of a body is its preserver, ruling and protecting it. So is Christ the Saviour of His body. The third point is illustrated from the creation of man. Eve was one with Adam both in her origin and in her union (Gen. 2: 21-24). In this way the creation of man carried a secret mystery, a hint of the purpose of God which no one would have guessed (3: 9). The AV text seems to have picked up a gloss from the context of the quotation in v. 31. The final words of the chapter echo the LXX of Est. 1: 20, a book not otherwise quoted in the NT.

v. Between children and parents (6: 1-4)
Obedience to parents is to be **in the Lord**, not limiting it to Christian parents, but making it a religious obligation to Christ. **2.** It is objected that the second commandment, Exod. 20: 4, contains a promise and therefore the fifth cannot be described as the first **with a promise.** But it is the first in the table of duty towards our neighbours. The promise is generally true, notwithstanding that in some cases God's providence orders otherwise. It is easier to be severe or indulgent, but children need discipline and admonition when combined with a gentle understanding of their needs and limitations.

vi. Between servants and masters (6: 5-9)
The apostles did not consider it to be any part of their mission to alter the structure of human society (on the contrary, 1 Pet. 2: 13, 14; Rom. 13: 1, 2) by any direct activity. Christian standards of behaviour would, and do, profoundly affect society in the course of time. Paul did not imply that slaves should for ever remain slaves any more than that children should remain minors for ever (1 C. 7: 21). **servants** in 6 rather masks the fact that Paul uses the same word as he uses to open the paragraph, so teaching them to regard their slavery as he regarded his imprisonment (3: 1). **from the heart** might be better attached to the

following verse, as in Col. 3: 23. The master was not to treat his slaves on the ground of his legal rights but on the basis of his own treatment by his Master, Christ. V. 9 echoes Deut. 10: 17.

vii. The heavenly warfare (6: 10-20)
The command of 10 is derived from 1: 19; 3: 16. **Put on the whole armour:** The Christian's new wardrobe (4: 24) includes a warsuit! The cosmic purpose of God embroils the believers with the spiritual hierarchy of the unseen world organized under the power of Satan. It is an obscure world, hinted at in Job 1 and Dan. 10, but the saint's defence and attack are not obscure. He fights in no worldly fashion (1 C. 10: 2 ff.). His armoury is figuratively described; a notion based on Isa. 59: 17, and also used by Paul in 1 Th. 5: 8, though the detailed treatment varies throughout. The use of the whole outfit enables the Christian to overcome the enemy in a day of fierce conflict, whereupon he is **to stand,** taking up his position in readiness for the renewing of the battle with a relentless foe. The instructions for such preparation are explicit. He is to tighten his belt with sincerity, truth in the objective sense being used below in 17 for the sword. He cannot afford to be slack in his dealings with God or with himself. Personal integrity will be linked with that moral rectitude, **righteousness,** Rom. 6: 13, which guards the heart as a breastplate, for vital parts are exposed by sin. God's soldier is equipped with the gospel of peace for sandals, suggesting that his movements are dictated by the needs of gospel witness. With all this a shield is required and this is provided by personal trust, 1 Jn 5: 4 f. Salvation, the helmet, is a gift provided by the Lord; 'take' here meaning receive, a different word from that in 16. His offensive weapon is the spoken word of God (see on 5: 26, and also at Heb. 4: 12). But he has an auxiliary weapon, not in the allegorical picture, viz, prayer, his vital communication with headquarters (18, 19). The need for it is plain, if adverse pressure might close even the mouth of an apostle (19). The ambassador of Christ's kingdom was at earth's highest court, but ignominiously treated to chains, contrary to international usage, but his ultimatum must be boldly delivered.

VI. FINAL GREETINGS (6: 21-24)
That Tychicus was a messenger of Paul's is clear from Tit. 3: 12. He was from the province of Asia (Ac. 20: 4), and certainly visited Ephesus later on (2 Tim. 4: 12), and appears to have taken this letter and the Colossian one with him on this journey, accompanying the distribution of the circular with verbal information.

The closing greeting is, quite appropriately in a circular, couched in the third person. The unusual qualification appended to the end may reflect his awareness of the fact that there were in the Church those whose teaching and influence were inimical to the glory of Christ. But it also notes that devotion to the Lord which will endure imperishably for ever.

BIBLIOGRAPHY

ABBOTT, T. K., *The Epistles to the Ephesians and to the Colossians. ICC* (Edinburgh, 1897).

BARTH, M., *The Broken Wall* (London, 1960).

BRUCE, F. F., *The Epistle to the Ephesians* (Glasgow, 1961).

CROSS, F. L., (ed.), *Studies in Ephesians* (London, 1956).

DUNCAN, G. S., *St. Paul's Ephesian Ministry* (London, 1929).

GOODSPEED, E. J., *The Meaning of Ephesians* (Chicago, 1933).

GOODSPEED, E. J., *The Key to Ephesians* (Chicago, 1956).

HODGE, C., *The Epistle to the Ephesians* (London, 1856).

MITTON, C. L., *Epistle to the Ephesians* (London, 1951).

ROBINSON, J. A., *The Epistle to the Ephesians* (London, 1904).

WESTCOTT, B. F., *St. Paul's Epistle to the Ephesians* (London, 1906).

WOOD, J. T., *Modern Discoveries on the site of Ancient Ephesus* (London, 1890).

THE LETTER TO THE PHILIPPIANS

H. C. HEWLETT

Philippi and the Church

The obedience of Paul to the Macedonian vision (Ac. 16: 9 f.) provided not only a notable landmark in his own travels and service but a turning point of apostolic history. Departing from Roman Asia, and entering Macedonia with the gospel of Christ, he planted in Philippi the first church in that province. That others were converted there besides the few expressly referred to is obvious from the reference to 'the brethren' in Ac. 16: 40. On two later occasions Paul revisited Philippi (Ac. 20: 2, 6), and the letter itself bears witness to his happy bond with the Philippian Christians.

Philippi itself was a city about ten miles inland from Neapolis, and was strategically placed on the Egnatian Way, the great Roman road running some five hundred miles from the Adriatic Sea through Thrace to the Bosphorus, and one of those roads which in the overruling of God were of the utmost use of the messengers of the gospel. Named after Philip, father of Alexander the Great, the city was refounded in 42 B.C. by Antony and Octavian (later the emperor Augustus) as a Roman colony. Its life and constitution were accordingly patterned on those of Rome, and its citizens enjoyed Roman citizenship.

The Purpose of the Letter

The apostle has been greatly cheered by the coming of Epaphroditus from Philippi bearing the gifts of the church. Grateful for the further fellowship from them and yet concerned both by the severe illness of their messenger, and by a divisive tendency among the Philippians themselves, he decides to send Epaphroditus back to them, and with him the letter. He takes occasion to express his thanks for the gift, and to give them fresh tidings of his circumstances, especially in regard to his imprisonment. He seeks for Epaphroditus the honourable welcome due to him, and thereby ensures that it is free from any misunderstanding of that good man's position. Grieved by their lack of harmony, he pleads with the Philippians to be marked by the mind of Christ and thus to be brought to a new and happy oneness of interest and character. This pleading begins early in the letter, and

skilfully prepares the way for the direct, personal entreaty to two believers named in 4: 2. Finally, his long experience of the perils besetting the churches moves him to warn trenchantly against any Judaizers on the one hand or libertines on the other who may appear on the scene.

The Place and Time of Writing

It was believed anciently that the letter was written from Rome during the years mentioned in Ac. 28: 30, but this has been challenged in modern times in favour of Caesarea or Ephesus. Against Caesarea is the weighty fact that, far from expecting release there, Paul appealed to Caesar, and hence awaited the long journey to Rome. Against Ephesus is the fact that there is no express record in Scripture of an Ephesian imprisonment of Paul—although one if not more of the frequent imprisonments of 2 C. 11: 23 might be assigned to the period of his Ephesian ministry, during which, as we know from 1 C. 15: 32 and 2 C. 1: 8, he was exposed to grave dangers of which nothing is said in Ac. 19. On the whole, however, the arguments for Rome appear strongly to confirm the traditional belief. We note (a) that there is no mention of an appeal from his present situation to Caesar, and hence it is likely that Caesar was trying the case, (b) that the terms 'praetorium' and 'Caesar's household', while of use in the provinces, apply more naturally to Rome, (c) that the time needed for the happenings of 2: 25-30 is not incompatible with the Roman imprisonment. J. B. Lightfoot has shown that the Roman dating was feasible even if the letter were written in the early part of Paul's time in Rome, especially as the Egnatian Way would greatly facilitate travel between Philippi and Rome. This would be even more true if the letter were dated toward the end of the imprisonment. (d) It has been objected in favour of Ephesus that when Paul wrote to the Romans he regarded his work in the east as completed (Rom. 15: 25). But the intervening years would give ample opportunity for the modification of his plan for the west, particularly as the overruling of God had permitted lengthy imprisonment in Caesarea and in Rome. It was just such an overruling of his purposes that had brought him to Philippi in the first place.

The following considerations point to a date late in Paul's detention in Rome: (*a*) Paul expected an early decision on his case. (*b*) This would permit the widespread appreciation of the reason of his bonds mentioned in 1: 13, and the reaction of the brethren in more active witness in 1: 14-17.

The Unity of the Letter

This has been disputed by some because of the sudden change of tone in 3: 2, but the long autobiographical passage that follows is entirely in keeping with the compact statement of Paul's outlook in 1: 21, 'To me to live is Christ'. Concerning the change of tone, Lightfoot has suggested that Paul was interrupted, and resumed his writing with a new burden on his heart. But it is to be noted that Paul's review of his life in ch. 3 follows naturally on ch. 2. As to the Judaizers, they had been so inveterate in their antagonism to Paul's preaching, and so persistent in seeking to subvert the churches he had planted, that they must have been very often in his thoughts, so that in giving his counsels to the Philippians he might well turn quickly to words of warning against these enemies. The sharpness of 3: 2 accords with the fact that the tactics of the Judaizers were not new, and the years had fully exposed the evil of their ways.

It is ever to be remembered that Paul is writing not a formal treatise, but a warm and loving letter, and that a rapid change of topic is in accord with the nature of a letter. Paul himself was a 'chosen vessel', suited to such a task spiritually, intellectually and emotionally, and the quick changes in emphasis and tone in his letters find their source, on the human side, in the wealth and power of his thinking and feeling. It may be concluded therefore that the letter is a single document, given from the eager heart of a man with many burdens for the churches he so truly loved.

Special Features

The phrases 'in Christ' or 'in Christ Jesus' and 'in the Lord' or 'in the Lord Jesus' are frequently used by Paul in relation to the believers' life and activities. In this letter they point not only to their standing before God in view of union with the Risen One as fellow-members of His body, but also to their finding in Christ the very sphere of their spiritual life, and that a life vigorous and joyous. Thus, though the issue of his imprisonment is still undecided, Paul writes with a joy triumphant over all his circumstances and bids his readers rejoice in the Lord and thus share his joy as they share his conflict. In the first pair of phrases the emphasis is on the wonder of such a personal relationship with Him, and hence the personal name is used; in the second pair, the use of the title 'Lord' emphasizes His authority and power, and therefore the believers' responsibility of submission and of dignity, behaviour and service.

The majestic passage in 2: 6-11 reminds one of 2 C. 8: 9 in that in both the self-humbling of Christ is presented as supreme stimulus to that self-abnegation, that spending of oneself for others which must ever be the distinctive glory of Christian character. That the Son of God has loved him and given Himself for him is an ever-present and ever-dominant note in the apostle's consciousness.

ANALYSIS

V ENCOURAGEMENT, GRATITUDE AND FINAL GREETINGS (4: 1-23)

   i The secret of harmony (4: 1-5)
   ii The secret of peace (4: 6-9)
   iii The secret of contentment (4: 10-20)
   iv Farewell (4: 21-23)

I. GREETINGS (1: 1-2)

1. Paul and Timothy: Paul links Timothy with himself both as a dear colleague and as one who shares his burden of love for them, and whom he will therefore send to them (2: 1-9). They are **servants** (*douloi*, 'slaves') **of Christ Jesus,** those who freely acknowledge His dominion over them, with its twofold right of complete ownership and of disposal of them at His pleasure. Here, as often in Paul's writings, the order is 'Christ Jesus'. This sets Him forth as pre-existent yet condescending to humiliation on earth. 'Jesus Christ' views Him as despised and yet subsequently glorified (see 2: 11; Ac. 2: 36). The former is peculiarly fitting in this letter where Paul presses the example of the mind of Christ in His self-humbling. See also 2: 5. (Cf. W. E. Vine, *Expository Dictionary*, p. 275.)

Paul addresses three classes, **saints** (*hagioi*), **bishops** (*episkopoi*, 'overseers'), and **deacons** (*diakonoi*, 'ministers', those who attend to the well-being of others). Here in very simple form is the constitution of a local church. **Saints** refers to the whole body of Christians as the holy people of God, set apart for Him in Christ. The **bishops** (identified with elders in Ac. 20: 17, 28 and Tit. 1: 5, 7) are a recognizable group within the church. This is not surprising, for as early as Ac. 14: 23 we find Paul and Barnabas appointing elders in the churches of Asia Minor. The **deacons** are likewise a recognizable group, and according to NT usage include those who minister in spiritual things (cf. 1 C. 3: 5) and in temporal things (cf. Ac. 6: 3). The order is striking, in that **the saints** are addressed first. The **bishops and deacons** exist for **the saints,** not the saints for them. (See article on 'The Apostolic Church' pp. 102 ff.) The expression **grace . . . and peace** (2) brings together well known Greek and Hebrew greetings; their treasure is for all believers.

II. PAUL AND THE PHILIPPIAN CHURCH (1: 3-26)

i. Thanksgiving, Confidence and Prayer 1: (3-11)

So glad is Paul at every mark of the work of God in His people that thanksgiving characterizes all his letters save that to Galatia. Here he thanks God **in all** his **remembrance** of them,

and even in memory of stripes and prison (Ac. 16: 23). He makes with joy every prayer of his for them, for from his first dealings with them their fellowship has been a cheer to him. The words **you all** (4) occur nine times in the letter: he recognizes no factions, actual or threatening: all the people of God are dear to him. Their fellowship, their partnership, has been marked by their special interest in him (4: 15, 'you only'), by their gifts, by their prayer (1: 19), by their conflict (1: 30), and all has been a **partnership in the gospel** (5), a partnership of **grace** (7).

6. I am sure: His confidence is strong that God will bring to completion His good work in them, to be seen in the day of Christ, at His return, for he knows that his yearning over them is borne of Christ's yearning: **I yearn for you all with the affection of Christ Jesus** (8). Moreover they have shared with him **in the defence and confirmation of the gospel** (7), in that courageous witness in the court of law or before men generally which confirms that the gospel is true. How pure is Paul's motive is shown by his claim, **God is my witness** (8). Loving, he prays that their love **may abound more and more,** not irresponsibly but guarded and guided **with knowledge and all discernment** (9). Thus sensitive in appreciation of moral issues, they **may approve what is excellent** (10), distinguishing wherein one thing differs from another and so able to choose what is of superior quality. Their love will then be keen-sighted for each other's good. Moreover they will be **pure and blameless** (10), in singleness of motive before God, and without cause of stumbling to themselves or to others unto the day of Christ. Finally, they will be **filled with the fruits** (*karpos*, singular) **of righteousness** (11). Does this mean that righteousness bears the fruit, or that righteousness itself is the fruit? Both thoughts seem to be present here. Only that 'righteousness from God that depends on faith' (3: 9) can be adequate to produce rectitude of conduct. We are made righteous that we may become righteous. But this fruit is **through Jesus Christ.** In Him alone we are righteous, and by Him alone can the life be beautiful. All this is **to the glory and praise of God,** that the life of the Philippians may serve that supreme purpose which is the goal of Christ Himself (see 2: 11).

ii. Paul's immediate circumstances (1: 12–20)

A note of triumph pervades this section. Paul rejoices in the overruling of God that turns to good things that might well discourage. He seeks that the cheer he has received may be shared by them in their conflict. All his mingled experience **has really served to advance the gospel** (12). Remembering that Paul's hours in the dungeon at Philippi had led to the conversion of the jailor, the Philippians would readily appreciate this. The gospel has made progress both in his testimony amongst his guards, and in the stimulus given to other Christians to more zeal in preaching Christ: **it has become known throughout the whole praetorian guard** (13). The praetorians were the imperial bodyguard, those powerful and sometimes turbulent troops of whom the emperor was praetor, or commander-in-chief. What a mission field Paul has had among these guards! And his testimony has gone beyond them **to all the rest,** to all others who have heard of this prisoner. (If Paul is writing from some other place than Rome, then Gk. *praitōrion* here means 'Government House', as in Mk 15: 16; Jn 18: 28; Ac. 23: 35; the NEB rendering, 'to all at headquarters here', covers all the possibilities.)

The impact of Paul's witness has been wide-spread among the Christians of Rome; **most of the brethren** (14) have been emboldened **in the Lord,** in their witness to Christ. Yet the apostle notes two classes among them. Some are moved by **envy and rivalry** (15); their preaching is **out of partisanship . . . thinking to afflict me** (17). Jealousy of Paul impels them to attempt to steal a march upon him, and thus to distress him. Others are moved by their love for him and their appreciation of his lonely stand as one set by God **for the defence of the gospel** (16). In both cases he finds cause for rejoicing in that **Christ is proclaimed** (18).

19. I know that . . . this will turn out for my deliverance: On the lips of such a man as Paul this means far more than deliverance from bonds. The latter are incidental; his **deliverance** is related to the great purpose of his life, and consists in being preserved from any failure to honour Christ. This will be achieved **through your prayers and the help of the Spirit of Jesus Christ.** In answer to their prayer the supply (*epichorēgia*, 'rich provision', 'support') of the Spirit, His abundant blessing, will be poured by God into Paul's life. His **eager expectation and hope** (20) picture to us this battle-scarred veteran with head outstretched with longing that now as always **Christ will be honoured in my body** (20). His concern is not whether it means life or death, but only

that through him Christ may be glorified before men and seen in His true greatness.

iii. Paul and his prospects (1: 21–26)

As for himself, the outlook is only bright. Life for Paul finds all its meaning and coherence in **Christ** (21). This is life indeed. Death **is gain,** for then the momentary, the vision of the Damascus road, will become the abiding. If he lives on, he says, **that means fruitful labour,** literally 'fruit of work', i.e., the more work the more fruit. His dilemma is between two good things. He is **hard pressed between the two** (23). His joy, his heart's longing, is to **depart** (*analyō*, to break camp, to set out on his last journey) **and be with Christ, for that is far better** than the richest experience on earth. Death, for the Christian, is to be 'away from the body and at home with the Lord' (2 C. 5: 8). In this disembodied state, his condition is one of consciousness, of freedom from sin and of completeness in holiness, and moreover of the joy to which earth has no equal, that of beholding Christ directly and of dwelling in His presence. For Paul death has no fear, but only gladness. On the other hand their joy, their good, lies in his remaining for their help. His joy, or their joy? This is the issue, and to state it is to know the answer. He will remain. The result on their part will be **ample cause to glory in Christ Jesus** (26) for His goodness in sparing Paul to them.

III. EXHORTATION AND EXAMPLES (1: 27–2: 30)

i. Exhortation to courage (1: 27–30)

His unselfish choice seeks from them a fitting response: **Let your manner of life be** (*politeuomai*, lit. 'to behave as a citizen', hence 'to conduct oneself publicly') **worthy of the gospel of Christ** (27). The gospel is radiant with the dignity of its heavenliness; so must be the lives of those possessing citizenship of heaven (3: 20). Nor is this in any sense unpractical, for it will manifest itself in their courageous oneness in witness in the gospel and in their constancy amid persecution. **27. that you stand firm in one spirit, with one mind striving side by side:** One in spirit and one in soul, united in their perception of the right as even in their choice of it. As he later points out, their tendency is to strive among themselves; they must strive **for the faith of the gospel.** According to Lightfoot and others, the **faith** is here objective, that which is believed, the content of the gospel message, as in Jude 3, 'to contend for the faith': if so, it may be the earliest NT instance of this use of the word.

28. not frightened . . . by your opponents: The persecutors ranged against them and their message. To these adversaries the believers' fearlessness is **a clear omen** (*endeixis*, 'sign', 'evidence', 'demonstration') **of their destruction** (*apōleia*, perdition, as in 3: 19). On the other hand it will be an evidence of the believers' possession of salvation, here again spiritual and eternal, and not merely deliverance from foes. This evidence is God-given; He alone can impart such reality.

29. it has been granted (*charizomai*, to give as a favour, or mark of approval, as in 2: 9) **to you** (emphatic by position) as a boon, that which from heaven's viewpoint is an added privilege. Their belief in Christ is consummated in suffering for His sake. Their conflict is akin to Paul's. His deep encouragement in Christ is therefore to be their experience also (30).

ii. Plea for unity (2: 1-4)
The oneness which Paul craves to see in the life and service of the Philippians demands a true humility and a setting aside of all self-interest. To move their hearts, he alludes to their spiritual wealth, and to their warm regard for him personally. **1, 2. If there is any encouragement in Christ,** including His responsive joy in their sufferings, **any incentive of love,** their love inciting them to grant Paul's desire, **any participation in the Spirit,** any sharing with each other of which the Spirit is both secret and power (cf. 2 C. 13: 14), **any affection and sympathy,** and well he knew the Philippians had such for him, **complete my joy.** In 1: 4 he has spoken of his joy in them. Now he pleads that only one ingredient is needed to fill his cup. This they will grant by being one in thought, one in love, one in desire, and one in singleness of thought.

3. Selfishness or conceit will only feed their incipient dissension. Their positive steps to unity are first, **in humility count others better than yourselves.** Humility is the recognition of our true littleness as those dependent utterly on God. Counting others better than ourselves is vividly illustrated in 1: 25 in Paul's preference of their joy to his joy. Secondly, **let each of you look not only to his own interests, but also to the interests of others** (4). Looking to the interests of others rather than to one's own is entirely opposed to the spirit of the world, so truly described in Ps. 49: 18, *a man gets praise when he does well for himself.*

iii. The mind of Christ: humiliation and exaltation (2: 5-11)
The apostle now shows that the supreme example of this mind, this looking on the interests of others, is the self-humbling of Christ. In doing so he gives a sublime unfolding of the tremendous fact of the incarnation, and does

so in what has come to be widely recognized as an early Christian hymn on the humiliation and exaltation of Christ (6-11). This interpretation of the passage is based, among other considerations, on its poetical structure and Semitic linguistic substratum; it may have existed in Aramaic before it became current in a Greek version. This does not exclude the possibility that Paul was its author; if so, he has, for purposes of his present argument, incorporated an earlier composition of his own at this point. In any case, the hymn may well be the earliest extant statement of the threefold division of Christ's career: pre-existence, life on earth, subsequent exaltation. So far as the second and third phases are concerned, the hymn appears to be based on the fourth Isaianic Servant Song (Isa. 52: 13–53: 12), where the Servant's exaltation following his humiliation is most clearly celebrated. The very wording of the Song is echoed here and there throughout the hymn.

There are in vv. 6-8 three main actions:

(*a*) **though he was in the form of God:** The participle *hyparchōn* ('subsisting', *though he was*) indicates that He was already in existence. 'Its tense (imperfect) contrasted with the following aorists points to indefinite continuance of being' (Gwynn). **the form of God** (*morphē*, the essential form) is the very way in which Deity necessarily exists. Hence 'it includes the whole nature and essence of Deity, and is inseparable from them, since they could have no actual existence without it . . . The Son of God could not possibly divest Himself of the form of God at His incarnation without thereby ceasing to be God' (E. H. Gifford, *The Incarnation*, p. 35). **did not count equality with God a thing to be grasped:** This **equality with God** (*to einai isa theō*, the neuter plural *isa* being adverbial) was not that of nature but of 'state and circumstances' (Gifford). 'The expression refers to rights which it was an act of condescension to waive' (Lightfoot). **a thing to be grasped:** Gk. *harpagmos*. The passive sense (cf. RV 'prize') is more appropriate to the context than the active 'robbery' of AV. 'He did not regard His being on equal conditions of glory and majesty with God as a prize and treasure to be held fast' (Gifford, *The Incarnation*, p. 71); or as a dignity to be coveted and seized, as did the first Adam (Gen. 3: 5 ff.) and Lucifer (Isa. 14: 13 f.); or (better still) as something to be exploited to His own advantage.

(*b*) **but emptied himself:** This use of *kenoō* with the reflexive object indicates a true and complete self-surrender, variously interpreted by commentators: He 'stripped Himself of the insignia of majesty' (Lightfoot); it was 'a laying aside of the mode of divine existence' (B. F.

Westcott on Jn 1: 14); He divested Himself of this equality of state and thus 'made himself of no reputation' (AV); 'emptied himself of all but love' (C. Wesley). These and other attempts have been made to paraphrase Paul's concise affirmation, but it is best illuminated when we recognize that **emptied himself . . . unto death** (7, 8) is a literal rendering of the statement in Isa. 53: 12, that the Servant *poured out his soul to death*. Utter self-denial is indicated, not any such metaphysical relinquishment of divine attributes as the once popular 'kenosis' theory, based on this passage, envisaged. (This 'kenosis' theory was invoked to explain how Christ on earth could make statements, *e.g.* with regard to OT authors or events, which were thought to imply on His part ignorance if not downright error. Paul's language gives no countenance to such a theory, and is in fact incompatible with it. Rather, in H. C. G. Moule's words *ad loc.*, 'a perfect Bondservice . . . will mean . . . a perfect conveyance of the Supreme Master's mind in the delivery of His message'.) Christ's possession of the fulness of the Godhead was not impaired by His self-emptying. Nor, when He emptied Himself by **taking the form** (*morphē* again) **of a servant**, did He exist any the less 'in the form of God', although the divine glory was veiled except to those who had eyes to discern it (Jn 1: 14). Never was 'the form of God' more fully manifested on earth than in Him who wore the servant's form. Jn 13: 4 f. (cf. Lk. 22: 27) is a graphic commentary on these words, especially in the light of Jn 13: 3. For the general attitude of Christ see Mk 10: 45; though there *diakoneō* ('serve') is used as against *doulos* ('slave') here, both words reflect the Heb. *'ebed* of Isa. 42: 1; 52: 13; etc. 'The form of a servant, man by nature; therefore the form of God, God by nature' (Chrysostom in Gifford). He took the servant's form by **being born in the likeness of men.** The expression does not detract from His true manhood, but guards the essential fact that He was thenceforth not only man but God. The plural 'men' relates Him to the race. Both this phrase and that immediately following echo Daniel's description of *one like a son of man* (Dan. 7: 13) to whom universal and everlasting dominion is given.

(*c*) **being found in human form: Form** (*schēma*) refers to the outward appearance, that which strikes the senses. In appearance, dress, toil, and kindred matters, as well as in the essential inwardness of His incarnation, He shared sinless human experience. **he humbled himself:** Again a voluntary act. This He did in that he **became obedient unto death, even death on a cross.** His obedience to God, like that of the Isaianic Servant, extended to death itself, and that the death of supremest shame, of 'being made a curse' (Gal. 3: 13).

The three actions set forth above found full response on the part of God. In vv. 6-8, all is of Christ; in vv. 9-11, all is of God. In the symmetry of the passage—

(*a*) 'He humbled himself' finds its response in **God has highly exalted him** (cf. Lk. 18: 14). He was taken from the fathomless depths of Calvary's woe up to the right hand of God, to be 'higher than the heavens', and this in His holy manhood. The language here echoes the announcement of the Servant's high exaltation in Isa. 52: 13.

(*b*) 'He emptied himself' finds its response in **God . . . bestowed on him the name which is above every name.** For 'bestowed' (*charizomai*) cf. 1: 29. Here is reputation indeed for the one who was made 'of no reputation' (AV). The name is the ineffable name of the God of Israel, spelt with the consonants *YHWH*. He who once said, *I am the LORD (YHWH), that is my name; my glory I give to no other* (Isa. 43: 8), now bestows that name on His Servant, and enhances His own glory thereby.

(*c*) 'He did not count equality with God a thing to be grasped' finds its response in **that at the name of Jesus** (or the name Jesus, since Gk. *Iēsou* may be either genitive or appositional dative) **every knee should bow . . . and every tongue confess . . .** Here is honour that may be paid to God alone (Isa. 45: 23); here is homage rendered by those **in heaven** (*epouranioi*, all intelligences in heaven whence He descended), **on earth** (*epigeioi*, all intelligences on earth where He suffered), **and under the earth** (*katachthonioi*, all intelligences in the realm of death which He conquered). To Him every creature shall confess, either by choice or by compulsion, **that Jesus Christ is Lord,** making full acknowledgment of His divine supremacy, **to the glory of God the Father,** whose pleasure it is 'that all may honour the Son, even as they honour the Father' (Jn 5: 23). God's glory is the goal of the work of Christ.

iv. Manifesting the mind of Christ (2: 12-30) This section of the letter begins with Paul's urging the Philippians to obedience to his plea that the mind of Christ be in them, and then we may see (but this undesigned by Paul!) three men in whom that mind has been made manifest: himself, Timothy and Epaphroditus. In vv. 12-16 is a two-fold bidding, the first referring to deliverance from the dishonour of dissension, and the second to beauty of life and witness. The apostle reminds them of their past obedience, itself a trait of the mind of Christ, and seeks it still. **12. work out your own**

salvation (cf. 'my deliverance' in 1: 19): This salvation is a present one, and not so much individual as collective. The church at Philippi is in peril from inward strife, and the marring of the unity in which alone the true purpose of the church will be realized. **Work out** (*katergazomai*, the compound verb indicating achievement or bringing to a conclusion) **. . . with fear and trembling** lest they fail in this and so dishonour Christ. The phrase **with fear and trembling** occurs three times elsewhere in Paul's letters, *viz*., 1 C. 2: 5; 2 C. 7: 15; Eph. 6: 5, and is charged with distrust of self and its resources and abilities. This achievement he seeks will be possible because God is working in them **both to will and to work** (13), touching both desire and activity, and moulding their will in order to mould their ways, **for his good pleasure,** the purpose of His heart for the honour of His Son, in Him and in His people.

As to life and witness their actions must be **without grumbling or questioning** (14). Lightfoot comments that the one is 'the moral and the other the intellectual rebellion against God'. They are the fruit of pride concerning oneself and of resentment concerning others. Free from these stains they will be **blameless and innocent** (*akeraios*, 'unmixed', 'unadulterated', and therefore free from guile), **children of God,** displaying a character befitting the family of God. Thus even though they live in an age with a moral bias against God, they will bring no reproach on Christ and will shine as lights in the world. **Lights** (*phōstēres*, 'luminaries', used of stars in Gen. 1: 14-16, LXX, and only elsewhere in the NT in Rev. 21: 11) suggests the heavenly radiance of their witness in a world of spiritual darkness (15). This witness is a **holding fast the word of life** (RV 'holding forth'). As a result Paul himself will exult when Christ comes that his toil has not been in vain (16). They will be his rejoicing then (cf. 4: 1; 1 Th. 2: 19 f.).

Vv. 17-18 provide an impressive glimpse of the mind of Christ in Paul. Very humbly, he compares his own possible death to a drink-offering, in which he will be **poured as a libation** (as in 2 Tim. 4: 6) **upon the sacrificial offering of your faith,** upon their presentation of themselves to God as a burnt-offering, as in Rom. 12: 1. As the drink-offering was complementary to the burnt-offering (see Num. 15: 10; 28: 7), so Paul accords the greater honour to them, willing to have his supreme sacrifice reckoned to their credit, not his own. To him this will be only joy, and he bids them accept it with like joy.

In Timothy is afforded a second example of the mind of Christ (19-24). In revealing his purpose to send him to them, that he may be **cheered** and encouraged by the news Timothy will bring back, Paul pays warm tribute to his colleague. **20. I have no one like him:** Other possible interpretations of *isopsychos* (lit. 'equal-souled') are that Paul has no one else so like-minded with himself, or (in the light of the following words, **who will be genuinely anxious for your welfare**) like-minded with the Philippians. The RSV rendering implies that in the limited circle of those available at the time there is no one else who has Timothy's outlook of genuine concern for their welfare. Instead, they **all look after their own interests, not those of Jesus Christ** and hence of His people. Timothy has proved his **worth,** as the Philippians already **know,** in serving with Paul in moral and spiritual kinship. But, while sending Timothy, Paul longs to follow later himself. His confidence is strong that he will be set free, and that for their sakes.

The third of these noble characters is Epaphroditus. He has been the bearer of gifts sent by the Philippian church to Paul, and this service has almost cost him his life. Whether his illness was contracted on the journey or after arrival at Rome, it has been so severe that tidings of it have caused concern at Philippi. Then when Epaphroditus has learned in Rome of their knowledge of his sickness, far from being comforted, not to say elated, by the attention drawn to him, he is distressed all the more that they have this care. So for their sakes Paul sends him back to them, the bearer of this priceless letter. He calls him **my brother,** of the one family of God, **and fellow worker,** in toil for the one Lord, **and fellow soldier,** in the one conflict for the faith, **and your messenger and minister** (*leitourgos*, primarily a public servant, but used of service Godward and manward, and here as conveying the thought of a task not so much personal as representative). In these titles for Epaphroditus Paul expresses his real appreciation of his coming and of his ministry to him, and also commends him to them on his return. Paul's longing for them in 1: 8 (*epipotheō*, as in 2: 26, to yearn, especially for one who is absent) is matched by that of Epaphroditus. Again, the latter **has been distressed** (*adēmoneō*, to be in great distress or anguish, cf. Mt. 26: 37). The mercy of God in sparing Epaphroditus has been a mercy to Paul also, lest he should be over-tried in seeing the Philippians deprived by death of the messenger they have sent for his sake. They are to accord Epaphroditus a glad welcome, as befits his bond with them and his sufferings, and to value highly such men, because for the apostle's sake and theirs he risked **his life** (*paraboleuomai,* 'playing the gambler with his life', H. C. G. Moule). The length of his absence from home and the fact that he carries a letter dealing, *inter alia*, with dissension in the church both add to the wisdom of this commendation.

IV. WARNING DIGRESSION (3: 1-21)

This chapter is of special importance because of its revealing of the motives which have dominated Paul's life. While warning trenchantly against false teachers who lead their followers astray, he pictures himself in the figure of an athlete in a race, running with his eyes fixed on the goal. A comparison of chapters 2 and 3 provides confirmation of the integrity of the letter as being one document and that Pauline. The one deals with Christ's downward descent, and the other with the upward call; the one shows how Christ laid aside heavenly glory to win such as Paul, and the other how Paul has laid aside earthly glory to win Christ; the one shows Christ taking the form of a servant, being made in the likeness of men, and the other how the believer's body will be conformed to the body of His glory.

i. Warning against Judaizers (3: 1-3)

1. Finally, my brethren, rejoice in the Lord: As to all other matters (*to loipon*), he bids them meet such in the strength which only the joy of the Lord can give (see Neh. 8: 10). This prepares for the stern counsel of v. 2. ' "Rejoice in the Lord" is evidently put here emphatically, with direct reference to the warning that follows' (Alford, *Gk. Test.*, *in loc.*). **To write the same things,** to keep pressing the same lesson of joy in the Lord, so basic to this letter, finds no reluctance in Paul, and is for their safety, again a preparation for v. 2. The three terms of contempt, **dogs . . . evil-workers . . . those who mutilate the flesh** (2) refer to one and the same class of person, the Judaizers, who have so relentlessly followed where Paul has been, and sought to pervert the gospel of Christ (Gal. 1: 7). **Dogs,** the epithet for Gentiles, is turned back on these false teachers, as indeed being scavengers. They are **evil-workers,** in motive, in doctrine and in results, for all is evil which denies the entire sufficiency of the work of Christ. They are the concision (*katatomē*, 'mutilation', i.e., the mutilators, in scornful contrast to *peritomē*, the true circumcision as in v. 3), for they know nothing of that circumcision which is of the heart (Rom. 2: 29). For the strength of the terms used, cf. Mt. 3: 7; 23: 27. Far from dishonouring circumcision, they alone fulfil its true meaning who **worship God in spirit** (RV, following a variant reading has 'worship by the Spirit of God'), **and glory in Christ Jesus** (cf. 1: 26; Rom. 5: 11; 1 C. 1:

31; 2 C. 10: 17; Gal. 6: 14), **and put no confidence in the flesh,** the self-life. They do indeed have confidence, but only in Christ.

ii. Paul: past and present (3: 4-17)

But Paul does not write as one who despises what he has never known. On the contrary, he could excel all his critics both in privileges of birth and upbringing, and in behaviour. **Circumcised on the eighth day,** therefore no proselyte; **of the people of Israel,** the covenant people; **of the tribe of Benjamin** (cf. Rom. 11: 2), whence perhaps his name Saul (cf. Ac. 13: 21), of a tribe which remained true to David's line when ten tribes seceded; **a Hebrew born of Hebrews,** the Aramaic-speaking son of Aramaic-speaking parents, and no Hellenist (cf. 2 C. 11: 22); **as to the law a Pharisee,** member of a strictly observant sect (cf. Ac. 26: 5); **as to zeal a persecutor of the church,** showing zeal of God though mistaken (Rom. 10: 2; Gal. 1: 13 f.); **as to righteousness under the law blameless,** without reproach from men (cf. Ac. 23: 1; Mk 10: 20). All these gains (7, note plural, as if in those early days he had feasted his eyes on each in turn) he had counted **loss** (*zēmia*, singular, all being massed together, not just valueless, but actual damage), seeing their true nature in the fact that with such a past he had been a hater of Christ. **I counted . . . indeed I count,** i.e. I still count, after all the experience of the years, **everything as loss** (8). This has been for Christ's sake, **because of the surpassing worth of knowing Christ Jesus my Lord,** henceforth Paul's dearest ambition (cf. v. 10).

Indeed, these past gains he now counts as **refuse** (*skybalon*, 'dung', 'rubbish'). **8. that I may gain Christ:** It was his choice at his conversion; it is his choice still. Christ is his true gain here and hereafter (cf. 1: 21). **9. and be found in him:** In his faith-union with Christ, in his constant experience and enjoyment of this union, and (finally and especially) in the day of Christ. This means having no self-righteousness from law-keeping, but **the righteousness from God that depends on faith. 10. that I may know him:** Personally, in constantly enriched experience, until the day when he knows as he himself is known (1 C. 13: 12; cf. Exod. 33: 13, *that I may know thee*). Christ is Paul's supreme attraction, and to know Him he must know also **the power of his resurrection,** 'the power of the risen life of the Saviour realized in Paul's daily life and service' (F. Davidson, *NBC*, p. 1,034), **and may share his sufferings,** that sacred fellowship which Paul in his own afflictions for the gospel's sake experienced with the suffering Christ cf. Col. 1: 24), **becoming like him in his**

death, in an identification with Him in His death that adjusts all things to its claims (cf. 2 C. 4: 10 f.). Moreover, as this conformity (*symmorphizomenos*) concerns the *morphē*, the essential form as in 2: 6, he counts it not strange but true to his life and standing in Christ. **11. that if possible I may attain the resurrection from the dead:** This relates not simply to Christ's coming again, and the physical resurrection, for Paul's share in the blessedness of that is a matter not of attainment but of grace. The coming again and its consequences for the body are alluded to in 3: 21. V. 11 brings to a climax the longings of v. 10, all of which relate to present experience. As the logical and only satisfying consequence of partnership with Christ's sufferings and conformity to His death, he seeks now, even in the present body, to live as a victorious, risen man. The thought is like to that of 2 C. 4: 10, 'that the life of Jesus may also be manifested in our bodies'.

Such is his desire, but he humbly owns that he has not reached the goal in present experience, much less in consummation in glory. **12. Not that I . . . am already perfect,** or 'perfected', the result in his character of obtaining what he aims at: he presses on to lay hold of that for which he was laid hold of by Christ Jesus. At his conversion Christ had placed him in the heavenward race for the very purpose of winning its prize. This is not yet in his grasp. **13. one thing I do,** with utter singleness of purpose, **forgetting what lies behind,** not elated by victory or cast down by failure, **and straining forward to what lies ahead,** as the athlete urges every energy into the one task, **I press on** (*diōkō*, as in v. 6, the zeal once given to persecution now transformed and moving him to nobler deed) **toward the goal,** the end of the race where Christ waits to reward, **for the prize of the upward call** (14). In the light of the context, it is difficult to suppose that this prize can be anything less than Christ Himself (cf. v. 8). **15. those . . . who are mature** in appreciation of Christ's purposes are to be **thus minded,** in striving still onward. If any do not realize the need for still pressing on he is confident that God will show it to them. **16. Let us hold true,** or, let us walk in the same path (*stoicheō*, to be drawn up in line, i.e. shoulder to shoulder). In this race there is no selfish individualism. No one wins at another's expense, to another's loss. Paul's love urges his readers to run with him, and with him to receive the garland of victory.

iii. Warning against libertines (3: 18, 19)
It will be well for the Philippians to keep their eye on the example of such as Paul, for tearfully he warns that **many . . . live as enemies of the cross of Christ** (18). Here it is not false teaching, as in v. 2, but evil living; libertines, not Judaizers, are now in view. These enemies claim the benefits of the cross, but deny its power in their life. **Their end is destruction,** eternal doom, as in 1: 28. They worship their sensual appetites and glory in the gross indulgence which they deem liberty but which is actually a thing of shame (cf. Rom. 16: 18). Far from having the mind of Christ, their **minds** are **set on earthly things.** Pretending to the skies they grovel in earth's corruption.

iv. The Christian's true home and hope (3: 20, 21)
In sharp contrast the believer looks to the unseen and eternal, and sets his mind on things that are above, not on things which are on earth (Col. 3: 2). **20. But our commonwealth** (*politeuma*, the sphere of our citizenship, our 'city home', H. C. G. Moule) **is in heaven:** A form of words which would be specially appreciated by the Philippians in view of their city's status as a Roman colony (cf. Moffatt's rendering, 'we are a colony of heaven'). From heaven **we await a Saviour,** or, we expect as Saviour, whose coming again is our continuing hope, to bring us the final phase of salvation, **the Lord Jesus Christ.** Far from indulging or even despising the body, we are to respect it, even in its present humiliation, for He **will change our lowly body to be like** (*symmorphos*, conformed to, as in v. 10, and no mere outward fashion) **his glorious body:** RV, 'the body of his glory' (cf. the Hebrew idiom 'the body of his flesh', rendered literally into Greek with reference to Christ in Col. 1: 27), here in contrast to 'the body of our humiliation' (RV). This is the very climax of all Paul's desire, and it will be realized through Christ's power **to subject all things to himself,** and thus to bring the universe into complete harmony with His holy and loving purposes. Then all limitation and all failure will be past, and in the glorified body Paul will rejoice in the liberty of a capacity to know Christ surpassing the highest yearnings of the path here.

V. ENCOURAGEMENT, GRATITUDE AND FINAL GREETINGS (4: 1-23)
i. The secret of harmony (4: 1-5)
1. Therefore . . . stand firm thus in the Lord: The words look back to the prospect unfolded in 3: 20-21, and in the certainty of that final triumph encourage to an unfaltering perseverance; **in the Lord,** as encompassed by His power and controlled by His authority. Most affectionately Paul repeats the longing and the

love of 1: 8 and 2: 12, and tells of what the Philippians will be to him at the coming again of the Lord. They are his **joy** now, especially if they heed his plea in 2: 2, but will be so then in full measure, and his very **crown** (*stephanos*, the wreath of victory in the games, of worth or of festal gladness, cf. 1 Th. 2: 19, 'crown of boasting'). Then before touching a sore spot in their affairs, he assures by repeating the word **beloved** that their well-being is vital to him. Euodia and Syntyche, both ladies, **these women** in the following verse, are entreated **to agree in the Lord** (2). That each is separately entreated indicates that both require such counsel. That they have been outstanding in their labours makes their disagreement the more sad and hurtful to others. Each is reminded of her true sphere **in the Lord,** and that all strife ends in submission to His will. This is the secret of harmony. It is well for others to help and not hinder the coming together of the erring ones. The identity of the **true yokefellow** (3) is not revealed. Of conjectures made that to be preferred as being the most obvious is that it alludes to Epaphroditus (so Lightfoot), in which case the term **true yokefellow** will aptly sum up the titles of 2: 25. If the Ephesian provenance of the letter could be sustained, the **yokefellow** (*syzygos*) might well be Luke; another possibility is that *Syzygos* is a personal name. **they have laboured side by side with me** (*synathleō*, as in 1: 27): They have shared the toil and trial of Paul's work in the gospel. As he looks back over this he thinks of one Clement and of others who have likewise shared his work with him, but he cannot stop to recount their names but rests on the fact that all are recorded in the **book of life** (cf. Isa. 4: 3; Mal. 3: 16; Lk. 10: 20; Ac. 13: 48). In that family register of heaven they are known and valued (see note on Rev. 3: 5). Three things will help to maintain harmony, *viz.*, rejoicing in the Lord, showing **forbearance** to all, and remembering the Lord's presence (4 f.). **forbearance:** Gk. *epieikes*, 'yieldingness', 'gentleness' or 'sweet reasonableness' (so Matthew Arnold). **5. The Lord is at hand:** This could refer to His coming again, but seems here to indicate His present nearness, as calming and encouraging.

ii. The secret of peace (4: 6-9)

The way of peace is to **have no anxiety about anything** (6), not being careless but free from the strain which turns so easily to distrust, and to bring every request to God, **by prayer** (*proseuchē*, prayer in its devotion) **and supplication** (*deēsis*, prayer in its personal detail) **with thanksgiving,** for appreciation of past mercies stimulates to trust for future ones. Paul's own prayer life alluded to in 1: 3-5 is excellent

example here. *The garrison of peace* is afforded by **the peace of God,** which He gives to us and which **passes all understanding,** transcending all our mental capacity to grasp and to appreciate (7). This **will keep** (*phroureō*, to stand guard, to protect) **your hearts and your minds in Christ Jesus,** as in the very abode of peace. *The discipline of peace* follows naturally from the thought of the garrison. **Finally,** concerning every occupation of the mind comes the reminder that inward peace is not preserved by feeding the thoughts upon the unwholesome. **Whatever is true, . . . honourable** (worthy of respect) **. . . just . . . pure . . . lovely** (winsome) **. . . gracious** (in good repute), and in the widest range, whatever is of **excellence** (morally) and **worthy of praise,** this and this alone is suited to their minds (8). Disciplined minds will find the path of daily life set forth in the teaching and practice of Paul himself, and in this path they will prove the reality of the presence of the God from whom all peace comes. Thus both the first and second sections of this chapter close with the wonder of the divine companionship.

iii. The secret of contentment (4: 10-20)

Having poured out his heart concerning their spiritual need, particularly with regard to their lack of oneness, he is free at last to express his unfeigned gratitude for the gifts brought by Epaphroditus. He has reserved this to the end so that the closing part of his letter may deal with the bond between them which has been confirmed so truly by their generosity. **10. I rejoice in the Lord greatly,** not for selfish interests, but tracing His goodness in that **you have revived your concern for me. Revived** (*anathallō*, to sprout or flourish again as a tree): Their thought for him had been unchanging but it required suitable opportunity, as the tree the coming of spring. He makes no complaint of financial want. Indeed, there is no instance in the Scripture records of apostolic days of any servant of Christ making known his own material needs to any but his Lord. **I** (emphatic, speaking from the schooling of long experience) **have learned, in whatever state I am, to be content** (*autarkēs*, independent of external circumstances, used, *e.g.*, of a city needing no imports and therefore self-sufficient). This is no stoical indifference to prosperity or adversity, but the confidence given by the secret of contentment he is now to disclose. He knows **how to be abased,** to be brought low in the humiliation of want, and **how to abound,** having more than present requirements (12). The repeated **I know** indicates that the years have been ample in their lessons in both directions, and more, he not only knows

479

these experiences but how to triumph in them, as is evident in respect of want in the words of 2 C. 6: 10. **12. I have learned the secret:** *myeō*, here only in the NT, is the technical term for initiation into the Greek mysteries, hence more generally to let into a secret. What is hidden, a mystery, to the natural man lies open to faith in the power of Christ. He is ready for **any and all circumstances,** not being their victim but their victor. And the secret is just this: **I can do all things in him who strengthens me** (13). Dwelling in Christ, whose enabling power put forth in transforming His own at His coming again has been seen in 3: 21, he finds in Him the enabling for triumph in all present circumstances. Even if it be in abasement, in being brought low, he is strengthened by One who has known abasement, having humbled Himself (cf. *tapeinoō* in 2: 8 and 4: 12). His sufficiency in Christ in no wise detracts from their kindness, and he speaks of their gifts as a sharing of his trouble (14). This is the true viewpoint which should characterize all such giving, not a meeting of need, but a partnership of service, and here actually in his sufferings. Very gratefully he reminds them that **in the beginning of the gospel,** when first they had heard and been blessed by it, and he had left their province, they alone of the churches had shown him such response (15). Indeed, before he left their province, while he was still in Thessalonica (cf. Ac. 17: 1-9), they had twice sent him much help (16). And the value he sees in the gift is far more than its benefit to him. It is **fruit which increases to your credit** (17), 'the harvest of blessing which is accumulating to your account' (A. S. Way, *The Letters of St. Paul, in loc.*). On his side his account is settled, for he says, **I have received full payment** (*apechō*, in constant use in the papyri in the sense of 'I have received' as a technical expression in the drawing up of a receipt). But the greatest value of their gifts has been that which they have meant to God, **a fragrant offering, a sacrifice acceptable and pleasing** (18), true response to the love of Christ in giving Himself for them 'a fragrant offering and sacrifice to God' (Eph. 5: 2). Because they have honoured God in meeting His servant's need God will honour them by meeting all their need.

19. my God: A phrase seven times used by Paul, see 1: 3, the God whose faithfulness and power he has proved so truly, **will supply every need of yours,** and this on magnificent scale, **according to his riches in glory in Christ Jesus.** Thus not to them, not to him, but to their **God and Father** the **glory** must be eternally (20).

iv. Farewell (4: 21–23)

And now their faces rise before him, dear because of their fellowship, but dearer still because they are all **in Christ Jesus,** and he sends to everyone his greetings and those of the brethren with him (21). These latter are unnamed, but with full heart Epaphroditus will be able to speak of them all. Then he passes on the greetings of all the believers, i.e. in Rome, and **especially those of Caesar's household** (22)—a term including members of the imperial civil service whether in Rome or in the provinces. One last word follows, seeking for them **the grace of the Lord Jesus Christ** (23), the grace manifested so wonderfully in 2: 5-8, the grace of the One who though He was rich for their sakes became poor.

BIBLIOGRAPHY

LIGHTFOOT, J. B., *Saint Paul's Epistle to the Philippians* (London, 1881).

GWYNN, J., *The Epistle to the Philippians.* Speaker's Commentary (London, 1881).

MOULE, H. C. G., *Philippian Studies* (London, 1897).

VINCENT, M. R., *The Epistles to the Philippians and Philemon.* ICC (Edinburgh, 1897).

KENNEDY, H. A. A., *The Epistle to the Philippians.* EGT (London, 1903).

MICHAEL, J. H., *The Epistle of Paul to the Philippians.* MNT (London, 1928).

MÜLLER, J. J., *The Epistles of Paul to the Philippians and to Philemon.* NIC (Grand Rapids, 1955).

SCOTT, E. F., *The Epistle to the Philippians.* IB (New York, 1955).

BEARE, F. W., *A Commentary on the Epistle to the Philippians.* BNTC (London, 1959).

MARTIN, R. P., *The Epistle of Paul to the Philippians.* TNTC (London, 1959).

HENDRIKSEN, W., *A Commentary on the Epistle to the Philippians* (Grand Rapids, 1962).

BARTH, K., *The Epistle to the Philippians* (London, 1962, translation of German edition of 1927).

Monographs on Phil. 2: 6-11

GIFFORD, E. H., *The Incarnation* (London, 1911, reprinted from *The Expositor*, 1896).

ROBINSON, H. W., *The Cross of the Servant* (London, 1926), reprinted in *The Cross in the Old Testament* (London, 1955), pp. 55-114.

MARTIN, R. P., *An Early Christian Confession* (London 1960).

MARTIN, R. P., *Carmen Christi* (Cambridge, 1967).

THE LETTER TO THE COLOSSIANS

ERNEST G. ASHBY

Colossae, set in beautiful surroundings in the valley of the Lycus, a tributary of the Maeander, was in Paul's day a city of little importance. Herodotus (c. 484-425 B.C.) and Xenophon (c. 430-354 B.C.) in their accounts of Xerxes and Cyrus respectively testified to its past greatness, but even by Strabo's time (c. 60 B.C.-A.D. 20) it had declined, being overshadowed by the neighbouring cities of Laodicea and Hierapolis.

It seems clear (1: 4; 2: 1) that Paul was personally unknown to the Colossians, having approached Ephesus from the upper country and not by the regular trade route down the Lycus valley. Epaphras had been their evangelist, acting on Paul's behalf (1: 7) and doubtless the other churches in the vicinity, and perhaps all the churches in Asia mentioned in the Revelation were the result of the Ephesian mission (cf. Ac. 19: 10).

It is assumed that Paul is writing from Rome, both in his letter to the Colossians and to Philemon. Few now favour Caesarea as an alternative, and the reasons once quoted to support this view are now used in favour of the Ephesian theory. Certainly Paul's expectation of a speedy release, followed by a visit to Colossae does not fit Caesarea, and it is strange that amongst his companions he does not mention Philip the evangelist. Much more can be said for Ephesus. 2 C. 11: 23 implies numerous imprisonments and Paul suffered some great affliction in Asia (2 C. 1: 8) which some explain by a literal interpretation of 1 C. 15: 32 and think this the occasion when Paul's friends risked their lives for him (Rom. 16: 3, 4). But such an interpretation is by no means certain, and later traditions also employed to point to the same conclusion are of doubtful value. But even granting an Ephesian imprisonment, which is quite possible, it still does not fit the facts so well. Distant Rome seems a safer hiding place for a runaway slave than local Ephesus. Acts does confirm the presence of Luke at Rome, but does not suggest that he was at Ephesus. Aristarchus was seized, but not necessarily officially imprisoned at Ephesus, and as he accompanied Paul to Rome he may well have shared his imprisonment there. Ephesus rather suggests a short, sharp crisis, whereas the contents of Colossians seem to require an imprisonment of some duration to provide for leisured thought, and the development of doctrine in this letter might imply a later rather than an earlier date. But Paul's request to Philemon for a lodging does favour an Ephesian rather than a Roman origin, for after Rome Paul hoped to go westwards, though there is considerable uncertainty concerning his later movements. In *St. Paul's Ephesian Ministry* G. S. Duncan argues in favour of Ephesus, for he thinks that Paul is writing to a church of comparatively recent origin, and that he would almost certainly visit it before leaving the province of Asia. An adequate discussion of the whole subject may be found in D. Guthrie's *New Testament Introduction: The Pauline Epistles* pp. 92-98 and 171-174.

Such discussion is interesting but has little bearing upon the exegesis of the letter save to affect its date.

Far more important is the purpose of the letter. It demonstrates the apostle's sense of responsibility towards all Christians everywhere, even those he had not met, and lays tremendous emphasis upon the need of correct doctrine and right belief. The Colossians had been well taught but were now assailed by false teaching stigmatized as 'empty deceit', which he regarded as dangerous. It is difficult to identify the heresy in the absence of precise formulation, but certain ideas are refuted. References to circumcision, food regulations, the Sabbath and other legal enactments indicate that fundamentally it was Jewish, but not the Judaism which had troubled the Galatians. This was a syncretistic doctrine, fused with some elementary form of gnosticism, not surprising in a country where cosmological speculations and mysterious theosophy so readily found a home and where Jewish orthodoxy was suspect. Gnosticism, later to develop into a variety of forms, was a false intellectualism strongly tinged with mysticism. One of its fundamental tenets was the inherent evil of matter, thus denying any direct agency of God in the work of creation, and interposing a whole series of emanations and intermediary powers who must be placated and worshipped, and also destroying any true belief in the Incarnation. The material body, they taught, was evil, man's prison, and the way of release was by superior knowledge (*gnōsis*) granted to the initiated, leading to perfection (*teleiōsis*).

There were two ways of approach: either to suppress the body by rigid asceticism (as here) or to ignore it as unimportant, thus leading to grave licence (a thought not found in this letter, but it may explain 1 C. 5, 6). Here Paul has only to deal with the initial stages, but there was the danger that Christians seeking a deeper experience might try to accommodate themselves to current religious or philosophical ideas. As Paul confronted this error he doubtless meditated deeply under the guidance of the Spirit, and the result is one of his greatest christological passages. Here we see not merely the individual but cosmic significance of Christ: He is not only personal Saviour but Lord of creation and Head of the Church. Hence all such intermediaries are unnecessary; in fact any such attempt to worship these serves but to detract from the unique glory of Christ and is thus a false theosophy. The great glory of the letter is that it points to the sole sufficiency of Christ. Far from being progressive, the Jewish elements in this teaching were retrogressive, a return to the mere shadow, while the Gnostic elements were in direct opposition to the very fundamentals of the Christian faith. Certainly there *is* progress in the Christian experience, a maturity which Paul seeks for *all* these converts, and the fullness (*plērōma*) is to be found in

Christ alone. Through Him deliverance comes, not by asceticism and suppression but by identification with Him in His death and risen life, and this is worked out in a number of personal relationships.

Critics have put forward two main arguments against Pauline authorship. The first is that the Gnostic heresy which Paul attacked belonged to the second century A.D., but as he was dealing with a tendency and not with the fully developed system, as was later true of Irenaeus, the criticism is largely irrelevant. The second argument that the development of thought or change of vocabulary and style apparent in the letter militates against Pauline authorship is an unwarrantable criticism of his ability or versatility, to say nothing of the fact that such stylistic criteria are no very firm grounds of critical proof in any circumstances. Here Paul merely develops his earlier thought (cf. 1 C. 8: 6; 2: 8, 10) and changes in vocabulary are explained partly by change of topic and also by the fact that at times he is adopting the very catch-words of his opponents. The letter to Philemon is clearly Pauline, and this has so many close ties with Colossians that it helps to confirm the traditional view of the authenticity of this also. A fuller discussion of its authenticity may be found in Guthrie *op. cit.* pp. 167-171. Some comment on its affinities with Ephesians will be found in the Introduction to that letter. To Paul was granted some vision of the ultimate purposes of God: here the emphasis is on the glory of Christ in relation to His Church, His resources being at their disposal; in the Ephesian letter the emphasis is on the destiny of the Church which is to be for the praise of His glory.

ANALYSIS

III SAFEGUARDS AGAINST ERROR (2: 8–3: 4)
    i The Fullness of Christ (2: 8-10)
    ii Spiritual Circumcision (2: 11, 12)
    iii Christ's Victory (2: 13-15)
    iv Christian Freedom (2: 16-19)
    v Our Death with Christ (2: 20-23)
    vi Our Life with Christ (3: 1-4)

IV CHRISTIAN LIFE IN ACTION (3: 5-4: 6)
    i Discard the Old (3: 5-11)
    ii Put on the New (3: 12-17)
    iii Social Relationships (3: 18-4: 1)
    iv Prayer and Wisdom (4: 2-6)

V CONCLUSION: PERSONAL GREETINGS AND CHARGES (4: 7-18)

I. INTRODUCTION: SALUTATION
(1: 1, 2)

In his opening greeting Paul links Timothy with himself, an association too frequent to be of use in identifying the provenance of the letter. Introducing himself as an apostle **by the will of God** he acknowledges his call as an act of unmerited divine grace. If he does stress his authority here it is not because it has been challenged as in Galatia, but because he is presenting his credentials to Christians unknown to him personally, and he is endorsing the message of Epaphras. **Timothy,** lacking the direct commission of the risen Christ, is described as **our brother** (but cf. 1 Th. 2: 6). While earlier letters are addressed to churches, later ones, as here, are addressed rather to the individual members. It is to the **saints** or dedicated men in pagan Colossae that he writes, saints as set apart for God, brethren in their mutual love and fellowship. In view of the wording of Eph. 1: 1 it is unlikely that any stress is to be laid on the title **faithful** as indicating those not carried away by false teaching. He employs his usual greeting, the Hebrew and Greek salutation adapted to a Christian message.

2. The rsv following the reading of many of the best MSS omits 'and from Christ Jesus our Lord' which renders this form of greeting unique and somewhat surprising in view of the emphasis in this letter on the position of Christ. But its very uniqueness suggests that it may well be the correct reading.

II. CHRIST'S PERSON AND WORK
(1: 3-2: 7)
i. Thanksgiving (1: 3-8)

Though Paul's rendering of thanks to God, here described as **the Father of our Lord**

Jesus Christ, does follow the pattern of contemporary non-Christian letters giving thanks to their deities, it was no merely conventional opening. Its omission from Galatians and 2 Corinthians indicates that it was included only when the progress of converts was a real cause for thanksgiving, as in every prayer for the Colossians. Such rejoicing sprang from no first hand knowledge but from the report of Epaphras on their faith, hope and love. This trilogy appears also in 1 Th. 1 in the order of practical experience and in 1 C. 13 in the order of spiritual value. Here faith in Christ, the heavenly relationship, and love to the saints its earthly manifestation are made dependent upon hope. Christ is the sphere in which this faith works rather than its object; in other words faith derives its significance from their position 'in Christ', and being not self-centred it opens out into a wider perspective embracing all those who share this common faith. The hope which maintains this faith and love is not so much the hopeful attitude as the object hoped for, even Christ Himself (cf. 1: 27). But hope of necessity involves some future element, and while 'realized eschatology' rightly stresses the present enjoyment of spiritual experience, the creation still waits with eager longing for the consummation at the parousia (Rom. 8: 19). If, as A. M. Hunter thinks [*Paul and his Predecessors*, pp. 33-35 and *Exp T.* xlix p. 428 f.], this idea of a triad of graces was pre-Pauline, this could be Paul's interpretation of it. This hope had reached them through the gospel (cf. Eph. 1: 13) and quite unlike the false philosophies of which Paul is soon to speak, which are but local, this message demonstrates its truth by its universal character and its capacity for fruitfulness and development wherever it has gone. At Colossae it had been received not merely with intellectual assent but thoroughly grasped and appreciated 'in its genuine simplicity, without adulteration' as Lightfoot happily renders it. As the better MSS in v. 7 show, reading **on our behalf** instead of 'for you', Epaphras their preacher was Paul's representative, a beloved colleague, and at some time perhaps a sharer in Paul's imprisonment (Phm. 23), discharging his Christian service with faithfulness. Through him Paul received a favourable report of their love engendered by the Holy Spirit, as well as other less pleasing details tactfully omitted from his thanksgiving.

6. in the whole world is not to be taken as hyperbole: he had visited many provinces and worked in large representative centres from which the message could spread, and as Johannes Munck shows, Paul thought in terms of nations [J. Munck: *Paul and the Salvation of Mankind*, p. 52. The reference here is to his work in the East].

8. This is the only explicit reference to the Holy Spirit in the letter, but there is abundant evidence of His power at work.

ii. Prayer (1: 9–14)

Paul employs this report as the occasion for continued prayer for their further progress in the spiritual realm. As C. F. D. Moule states, 'the whole Christian vocabulary of knowledge is very closely connected with obedience', so different from the outcome of what was falsely brought before them as 'deeper knowledge'. True knowledge is practical, growing out of the fear of the Lord (Prov. 1: 7), and right conduct is both the aim and hallmark of right knowledge. Clearly the apostle has no desire for elementary standards nor time for superficial knowledge. To him a knowledge of the will of God is the indispensable prerequisite of a life pleasing to Him. In the divine therapy a mental transformation is the means used to achieve an ethical renewal (Rom. 12: 1, 2). Using some of the catchwords of those seeking to lead them astray, he prays for their full development in knowledge and apprehension of the will of God, **in all spiritual wisdom and understanding:** that is to say, he prays for a mind instructed in spiritual truth which also grasps the application of principles to the problems of life, with a view to worthy daily conduct which shall please the Lord in every way. Thus after evangelization comes pastoral care and he prays for the deepening of their character, to take effect in fruitful activity, in good works of every kind as they grow by (or in) the knowledge of God. But this is no human wisdom to inflate their pride as had been the Corinthian danger. This deepened character and increased strength of achievement is by the power of God's **glorious might,**

not calculated to exalt the flesh but to promote humility. The aim is not the stolid impassivity of the Stoic but patient endurance in a spirit of joy.

There is progressive thought here: knowledge promotes service (9, 10), service is repaid by strength (11), and all is crowned by thanksgiving (12). Thanksgiving is due to the Father for making men, Gentiles such as were some of these Colossians, competent to share the inheritance of the saints in the realm of light, this no doubt after the analogy of the allotment of territory to Israel in Canaan. Not only is there deliverance from the authority and jurisdiction of darkness, those powers under whom the Lord suffered when it was their 'hour' (Lk. 22: 53), but He has transported believers, a thought reminiscent of OT captivity, not into the kingdom of angels or principalities, to whom the false teachers would urge them to pay homage, but into **the kingdom of his beloved Son.** Here the picture is varied slightly: it is deliverance, not now by the exercise of might and power (13) but by a gracious payment of the ransom, resulting in **the forgiveness of sins.** Eph. 1: 7 states the price paid, the shedding of His blood, which is not explicitly mentioned in the best MSS here. This **redemption,** the apostle makes clear, is a present experience, for His kingdom is in operation having broken into the world of time, though its fullness is still in the future reserved for hope.

12, 13. Light and **darkness** are terms used in various religions, and in the Dead Sea Scrolls. Christ's kingdom is contrasted with this present evil age.

13. Deliverance once for all effected by Christ on the Cross is received by individuals as they come into union with him.

iii. Christ and Creation (1: 15–17)

The thought of the kingdom naturally leads on to the king, and this great Christological passage is comparable with Jn 1: 1–4 and Heb. 1: 2–4, and in line with the Lord's own teaching in John's Gospel and with the Wisdom literature of the OT. Christ is the visible likeness of God the invisible, for while no man has seen God, the Son not merely set Him forth but could claim, 'He who has seen Me has seen the Father'. He is, in fact, the effulgence of the glory of God, the very stamp of His nature, the light which shines into men's hearts (Heb. 1: 3; 2 C. 4: 6). He is **the first-born of all creation,** a phrase which the Arians made to mean that Christ was a created being and not co-eternal with the Father, but the context rules this out completely. The title here given emphasizes the thoughts of priority and superiority, declaring, as Lightfoot states, 'the absolute pre-existence of the Son'. The reference here is to His deity rather than His humanity, to the Son in His eternal being rather than the incarnate Son.

Three significant phrases are employed, **in him . . . through him and for him** (16): 'In Him' conveys a wealth of meaning far deeper than Philo's Logos which was virtually the Idea or the Ideal. Here is no abstraction but a divine person: Christ is the source of life as He is also the agent of all creation including the heavenly and invisible, and those very powers whom they were being urged to placate. Christ is outside creation, prior to it, distinct from it, and He is sovereign to it all, for it was created through Him and indeed for Him. In Him the purpose of the universe is found, in Him is its principle of coherence, and it is He that 'impresses upon creation that unity and solidarity which makes it a cosmos instead of a chaos' (Lightfoot).

16. The NT seems to mention five types of angel-ruler: four of them here (also 'powers' in Eph. 1: 21 and Rom. 8: 38), but no definite hierarchy can be deduced from these.

iv. Christ and the Church (1: 18)

After dealing with the cosmic significance of the Son in His eternal being, Paul now passes to the subject of the incarnate Son in His historical mission and revelation. The Church is described not as the body of Christians but as the Body of Christ, so vital a union that to persecute the members on earth is to persecute the Head in heaven. Here Paul seems to go further than the metaphor of earlier letters (1 C. 12: 12 ff.; Rom. 12: 4, 5), dealing with the functions of individual members, and this is distinctively a Pauline revelation. As in Ephesians, Christ alone is the Head. The Sovereign of the universe is also Head of the Church, that in all things **he might be pre-eminent:** this is His right for He is the beginning, presumably here with reference to the new creation, and the firstborn from the dead, as in v. 15 He was the firstborn of creation.

the body, the church: The figure chosen aptly illustrates how close is the relationship and vital the link between Christ and His Church. It exists only by His indwelling Spirit, operates by His power, and functions as His representative. But it is surely unscriptural to think of it as an extension of Christ's Incarnation, for His Incarnation was unique and He was sinless, which in experience the Church is not.

v. Christ and Reconciliation (1: 19-23)

Here again the pre-eminence of Christ is affirmed. **Fullness** is a thought not uncommon in both OT and NT, but if the heretical teachers were already employing this as a technical term to denote the totality of divine emanations, under whose power men were supposed to be living, it is peculiarly fitting that Paul should thus describe the Saviour. It is God's pleasure that all fullness, the full essence of deity, should reside in Christ, thus undermining their whole argument. Furthermore His purpose reached out to effect reconciliation, to end disrupted harmony and establish for sinful men peace with God, by the Saviour's sacrifice upon the Cross. Realizing as he does the extent of this cosmic discord (Rom. 8: 22) Paul sees that this reconciliation is far-reaching enough in its scope to embrace **all things,** though this must not be pressed to mean universal reconciliation irrespective of the will of man to accept God's offer. Of this reconciliation the Colossians have been a particular example, showing how great truths must be personally applied. Once they operated in an orbit of evil works resulting from their hostile attitude when they were estranged from God, but Christ's death has effected their reconciliation. Perhaps it was necessary to stress the reality of His Incarnation and its vital connection with atonement to correct the Colossian heresy. Christ did actually enter into the life of man and wrought out redemption as a historic fact in His body, and His purpose was to **present** them at the parousia **holy and blameless,** in fact 'justified by faith'. But this involves the present responsibility of holding fast, not being drawn away by false teaching. The certainty of the divine promise offers no grounds for human complacency: they are the genuine believers who persevere to the end, and their faith is a universal one.

vi. Paul's Ministry (1: 24-2: 7)

At the time of Paul's conversion a double truth was revealed: he was a 'chosen instrument' to evangelize the Gentiles, and this would involve suffering for his Master. The apostle here takes up both these thoughts. Perhaps to strengthen the link between himself and these unknown Christians he rejoices in his sufferings for the sake of the Lord's work and so in measure for them. The sufferings of Christ involved in His expiatory death are not here in view, for that work was complete and peculiar to the Lord Himself. But in the proclamation of the gospel the Church must suffer, and their sufferings are His also (Ac. 9: 4). Paul gladly has a share in this, a **divine office** in the economy of God, that he may preach to the full to unfold the mystery now revealed, that Gentiles with Jews may share in the wealth of this glorious manifestation, that Christ should dwell in their hearts; and this is a pledge of future glory also. He continues the work of instruction even after their conversion, for his object is their spiritual maturity. By repeated emphasis that this is for all, for **every man,** Paul refutes the gnostic claim of superior knowledge for the few, the initiates, though probably he looks to the parousia as the time of its realization. To this end he strives, as active as an athlete in the arena, but gladly acknowledging that it is the Lord's strength working within him.

26. the mystery: There is no reason to suppose that Paul borrows this term from the Greek mystery-religions, but rather from the OT (*e.g.* Dan. 2: 18 ff.). A mystery is not something which must be kept secret, but rather a concealed truth which God is pleased to unveil when the time is ripe. Thus the mysteries (RSV secrets) of the kingdom were revealed to the disciples, but not to the prophets preceding them (Mt. 13: 11–17). While the OT revealed something of God's blessing for Gentiles as well as Israelites, the method by which this would be accomplished was a mystery first revealed to Paul. In Colossians he shows that Christ indwells Gentile and Jewish hearts; in Ephesians is revealed the fact that in Christ Gentile believers are fellow-heirs with Jewish Christians.

2: 1–7. The apostle who at Miletus urged the Ephesian elders to watch over the church in their care shows his own deep concern for these converts unknown to him personally. Error is divisive, but his objective in prayer is their encouragement and harmony, for brotherly love is an indispensable condition for spiritual development (cf. Eph. 3: 18, 19; 4: 16). In this way they may be brought into the wealth of a full grasp of divine wisdom, a larger knowledge of God's revealed mystery, even of Christ Himself in whom divine wisdom is enshrined. This is the purpose of his letter, to prevent their being deceived by plausible arguments. Even in writing to strangers Paul can feel spiritually present with them, delighting in the solidity of their Christ-centred faith, a happier association than when with the Corinthian church he dealt with the disciplining of a defaulter (1 C. 5). He urges them, therefore, that as it was no mere tradition of words they received, but Christ Himself, so they must walk and live, their way of life and thought conforming to the way of Christ and centred in Him. With rapid change of metaphor he likens them to a tree rooted in Christ once for all, then to a building being erected on Him as foundation and consolidated in the faith. So doing they would remain true to the teaching of Epaphras and this should be done with thanksgiving.

2. God's mystery, of Christ: Probably the correct reading is that which has **Christ** in apposition to **God's mystery,** and the many

variations (discussed in Lightfoot, p. 252 f.) are explanations or modifications of this. In 1: 27 the mystery is Christ, **the hope of glory** indwelling Gentile hearts, here it is Christ as the incarnation of divine wisdom.

5. good order . . . firmness: As a military metaphor depicting their order and close phalanx resisting Gnostic infiltration this makes good sense (so Lightfoot and C. F. D. Moule). But the former term may describe national or domestic organization (cf. Abbott and also 1 C. 14: 40) while the latter may re-echo a Gnostic term denoting the barrier between the upper and lower realm (so F. F. Bruce, quoting H. Chadwick). It is also found in the LXX for the 'firmament'.

7. in the faith: Lightfoot prefers 'by their faith' in which case it would mean 'trust' rather than 'convictions'.

III. SAFEGUARDS AGAINST ERROR (2: 8–3: 4)
i. The Fullness of Christ (2: 8–10)

Here in vivid picture language Paul warns them against allowing anyone to carry them off as captives through specious, make-believe philosophy. Clearly the apostle condemns *false* philosophy, though surely he would have condemned any teaching relying upon inadequate human reason as the source of spiritual truth. His message was not 'man's gospel' (Gal. 1: 11), but theirs was **according to human tradition** which was their yardstick instead of Christ. It was according to the elemental spirits of the universe and not according to Christ, and this was fatal to it, for in Him resides all the fullness of deity and as such He must be the source and meaning of truth. In Christ they **have come to fullness of life,** an obvious correction of false teaching involving degrees of initiation or the need of ritual or mediating powers to share the *plērōma*. Christ is the head, not merely the sovereign but source of all power and authority, not merely preceding other powers (1: 17) but their conqueror (2: 15) and this must invalidate any claim of subjection to them.

8. elemental spirits: The word *stoicheia* originally meant things in a series, *e.g.,* the alphabet, and so the rudiments of knowledge (*e.g.* the A B C) and is so used in Heb. 5: 12. Then it came to mean 'the elements of the world' in the LXX and 2 Pet. 3: 10, and finally in Hellenistic syncretism 'cosmic spirits'. It occurs here, 2: 20 and Gal. 4: 3, 9. It seems possible from a reference to days and seasons (Gal. 4: 10) that they may have been regulating their religious life by observing the movements of the stars, with which they associated certain angelic powers, hence the interpretation accepted above, but C. F. D. Moule prefers 'elementary teaching' as the other meaning is later except for these possible NT references. If Gal. 4 is interpreted to mean merely Jewish holy days, then a relapse to elementary teaching makes good sense, but something personal still seems preferable.

9. bodily: Lightfoot seems to have grammatical support for his interpretation 'bodily' i.e. referring to the Incarnation, and the present tense 'dwells' need present no difficulty in its application also to His glorified body (Phil. 3 : 21). Other interpretations include 'corporately' rather than 'corporeally' or 'in totality', the complete embodiment in contrast to the supposed distribution among the intermediaries (C. H. Dodd and F. F. Bruce), or 'in reality' as opposed to the shadow (Arndt-Gingrich). Is it not possible that Paul intends a double meaning as seems occasionally true of John?

ii. Spiritual Circumcision (2: 11–12)
The theme of the remainder of the chapter is that of reality contrasted with the shadow. To the Jew circumcision was the outward sign of union, the entering into the covenant, though Paul (Rom. 2: 28, 29) is in line with the OT when he stresses that real circumcision is inward, that of the heart. So in the death of Christ, His real 'circumcision' (as it was also a 'baptism', Mk 10: 38) of which the literal circumcision had been a 'token-anticipation' (Bruce) the Christian, too, has a share. He is thus circumcised, that is to say there is the **putting off the body of flesh** or 'the old man', his old nature in its unregenerate state of rebellion against God. This 'circumcision' then is internal not external, of the whole not the part. As in Rom. 6, baptism is depicted as illustrating a burial to the old life with Christ and thus a sharing in His resurrection but it is through faith that this new life is imparted.

iii. Christ's Victory (2: 13–15)
Paul now passes on to results. Though previously dead, devoid of the principle of spiritual life through sin, and outside the covenant, believers are made spiritually alive, sharing Christ's life and completely forgiven. This is possible because of His cross where Christ dealt with the IOU, the legal bond of ordinances to which the Jew had agreed and to which even the Gentile's conscience had in some degree given assent (Rom. 2: 14, 15). This bond Christ took and cancelled by His death, nailing it to His cross as a challenge to the principalities and powers whom He had defeated and led in triumph, thus preventing their using this broken bond to intimidate the conscience.

13. made alive: Regeneration is a new moral and spiritual life now and it continues

through death, so it is both present and future.
14. nailing: There seems no evidence for the custom often referred to in this context that bonds were cancelled by being pierced by a nail. As there is no obvious change of subject from 'God' to 'Christ', it is understood that God in Christ was acting. The verb *apekdysamenos* could mean 'stripped Himself' of hostile powers assailing Him (so the Greek Fathers and Lightfoot) or 'stripped off' His body at the Cross (so the Latin Fathers and some modern writers) or simply **disarmed** or 'despoiled', the middle voice implying His interest in this action, and this seems most suited to the context.

iv. Christian Freedom (2: 16–19)
Here Paul briefly gives some indication of the beliefs and practices of the false teachers. Discussing first food and festivals he denies the necessity of asceticism. The Levitical law did prohibit certain foods, but not beverages, and the observance of certain times was obligatory. But Christ by His death has abrogated these legal demands, and to look to these is to prefer the shadow to the substance which is Christ Himself. The Letter to the Hebrews is in fact a detailed commentary on this verse (17). The second rebuke is directed against the **worship of angels,** mediating powers, which means that respect was paid to the inferior instead of to the Head. Christians are not to be condemned for not observing ritualistic rules by those who insist on subjection to angels on the strength of their alleged visions to which they pay an unduly high regard. For all their officious parade of humility, a humility in which one takes delight is but excessive pride arising from their unspiritual nature. In acting thus they fail to adhere to the Head who is Christ, and thus they promote disintegration instead of unity (cf. Eph. 4: 16). In such unity there is divine growth, as each in love plays its part.
18. In spite of the attractive idea of 'disqualify', *katabrabeuetō* should probably be taken to mean 'condemn' or 'decide against'. The AV negative must be omitted as in RSV. The translation of *embateuōn*, **taking his stand on** as RVmg and RSV, though doubted by C. F. D. Moule, does seem admissible (cf. F. F. Bruce quoting Sir William Ramsay).

v. Our Death with Christ (2: 20–23)
If indeed these Colossians are dead with Christ their lives should no longer be conditioned by interests in this world, restricted by what is after all only in 'the category of the perishable' (Lightfoot). Here religious prohibition has reached its climax: these believers have been told they must not handle, taste nor even touch certain things, rules of human origin, of the kind more appropriate for the development of

children than the conduct of free men. Superficially this may appear to have a form of wisdom in its apparent humility, though human traditions may mean the heart is far from God (Isa. 29: 13). In fact such asceticism far from being of any value serves only to indulge the flesh, the old unregenerate nature.

23. In this difficult verse *logos* has been taken to mean 'show' or **appearance** of wisdom, *pros* to mean 'against', i.e. to counteract or combat the fleshly desires.

vi. Our Life with Christ (3: 1-4)
The apostle now develops his ethical teaching, erecting, as is his custom, his moral superstructure upon a solid doctrinal foundation. The theme of the rest of the letter is a simple challenge to them to become experimentally what by God's grace they are: 'You are', he argues, 'raised with Christ; then let your thoughts and aspirations rise to the same level, your aims finding their end in Christ, your conduct characterized by heavenly wisdom. Sharing in His death, you also share His resurrection with a new life whose eternal perspective is something the world cannot understand. Because your life is bound up with Christ, His future manifestation will be yours also'. Paul writes in somewhat similar strain in Phil. 3: 19-20: there it is to rebuke sensuality, here asceticism.

IV. CHRISTIAN LIFE IN ACTION (3: 5-4: 6)

i. Discard the Old (3: 5-11)
5. Put to death: Paul's argument continues as follows: 'In spite of your heavenly life you are now living on earth, and so are in some degree of tension. There is indeed a place for Christian asceticism, but this is internal, not external, the renouncing of propensities belonging to the old life'. Five of these are named, immorality and impurity in deed, as well as in thought and desire, reaching their climax in covetousness equated with idolatry. Here Paul adopts the same pattern as the Sermon on the Mount, proceeding from outward deed to inner motive, culminating in the spirit of acquisitiveness making a god of gain. These are not dealt with by human striving but by death, a result of that incorporation with Christ described in vv. 1-4, and becoming experimental by faith (cf. Rom. 6: 6, 11). Failing that, continuance in evil practices characteristic of the old life of disobedience necessitates judgment, **the wrath of God,** no impulsive passion, but also no mere impersonal moral principle. It is God who acts in judgment (cf. Rom. 1: 18; Eph. 5: 6) against disobedience, a condition once true of them. Now they must put off the sins mentioned, like a discarded

cloak, the previous list (5) laying emphasis on sensuality, this one on uncharitableness which is quite out of keeping with the new life. Paul specially deals with the tongue (cf. Jas 3: 2-10) but he makes it clear it is not merely conduct or habits which have been put off: it goes deeper, it is the very self, **the old nature,** and they **have put on the new,** being renewed in the likeness of God as was the original intention (cf. Gen. 1: 27; 1 C. 15: 45; Gal. 3: 27). This renewal in mind and spirit results from incorporation with Christ: here all barriers go, whether racial, religious, cultural or social. The gospel removes all distinctions, so visibly symbolized by the dividing wall in the Temple (Eph. 2: 14).

5 ff. 'Put off', 'put on', 'be subject', 'watch and pray' are among the catchwords thought to have been used to sum up some early Christian teaching.

ii. Put on the New (3: 12-17)
As they have been chosen to be holy they must put on the garments of salvation, the new robe of character whose texture is sympathy, kindness, humility, meekness, patience, for they are the new Israel. These are the qualities to prevent friction and will help to settle their quarrels if any exist, their forgiveness being prompted by Christ's forgiveness to them, as is expected of them (Mt. 5: 9; Lk. 6: 36; Mt. 18: 33). Above all they must **put on love,** not an additional garment but the girdle to hold the others in place, **in perfect harmony** (*teleiotēs*). The apostle then refers to **peace,** which in the Ephesian letter has the function of the girdle here represented by love. These partial resemblances reveal not a different writer but the working of the apostle's mind along similar but not identical lines. Here peace, which in Phil. 4: 7 is to garrison the heart, is to arbitrate, to umpire, to discipline the mind to a decision where there is a conflict of motives or impulses, to promote a unity of purpose in a spirit of thankfulness.

16. They are also to allow **the word of Christ** to **dwell** in them, or more probably among them as a community, though of necessity it must dwell in the heart of each individual. In this way they will **in all wisdom** teach each other by means of **psalms and hymns and spiritual songs** having a didactic value (Eph. 5: 19). The new convert can easily imbibe some theology from carefully chosen hymns, and there are not lacking indications of such woven into the text of the NT. But this must be no mere external song of praise but accompanied by inward emotion, a matter of the heart.

17. Paul deals now with motives: whether in action or speech everything must be done in the name of Christ, in an attitude of thanks-giving to the Father. Mature Christians do not need codes of rules, merely this basic principle applied to various relationships, and these ap-plications are thought to be part of a fairly well-defined body of catechesis (cf. also Eph. 5: 22).

iii. Social Relationships (3: 18–4: 1)
The subjection of wives to husbands is indicative of a divine hierarchy (cf. also 1 Pet. 2: 18–3: 7) and what makes it remarkable is its stress on reciprocal duties, all stemming from the funda-mental relationship to the Saviour, for they must do what is fitting **in the Lord.** Children also and parents have mutual responsibilities, one of obedience, the other of forbearance. Perhaps because he has Onesimus in mind Paul deals with the obligations of slavery in more detail. Acknowledging the human distinctions of master and slave, he calls for no superficial service merely to catch the eye to win human favour, but urges undivided service from the heart done as unto Christ, for while in this world the slave-master relationship survives, to members of the Church there is a higher relationship embracing all under one Master from whom the reward will be received. Whatever their human standing all are sons to share the divine inheritance. While Eph. 6 expands the thought of reward, here a note of warning is emphasized, and there must be fair dealings for there will be no divine favour-itism either for unfaithful slave or unjust master.

iv. Prayer and Wisdom (4: 2–6)
Paul stresses the need of constancy in prayer, showing that a careful watch on past mercies will promote thanksgiving and a prayerful spirit (cf. Rom. 12: 12). Perhaps this call to vigilance was a recollection of the disciples' experience at the Transfiguration or their failure in Geth-semane. In their prayers Paul seeks a place for himself and his friends, for a **door for the word,** a door of opportunity, that he may with all needed courage and ability preach **the mystery of Christ,** which is indeed the cause of his imprisonment. Had he been content with a Jewish gospel, not embracing the Gentiles as part of the one Body, he might still have been free.

5 f. Here as in Eph. 5 there is the exhortation to redeem the time by buying up their oppor-tunities. There the reference is primarily to Christian prudence, here to the need to display a discreet sanctified conduct to silence any wrong impression among non-Christians. To this end their **speech** must not be vapid and insipid but **gracious,** wholesome and Christlike, since **salt** may signify either its preserving power or its flavour. It should, in fact, fit the person and the occasion.

V. CONCLUSION: PERSONAL GREETINGS AND CHARGES (4: 7–18)
The concluding greetings are more detailed than in Ephesians. Tychicus, a native of pro-consular Asia and perhaps of Ephesus (cf. Ac. 20: 4; 2 Tim. 4: 12), a faithful friend and colleague, accompanied Paul eastwards on his third missionary journey, probably as a church representative in connection with Paul's collec-tion for the poor in Jerusalem (Ac. 20: 4). Here he acts as Paul's messenger: later he is to be Paul's representative in Crete and Ephesus (Tit. 3: 12; 2 Tim. 4: 12). Here his purpose is to inform the Colossians concerning Paul's circumstances and to encourage them. With Tychicus he also sends Onesimus, now a **faithful and beloved brother** (see Intro-duction to Philemon): it is a wonderful illus-tration of the power of the gospel to cut across social barriers that he calls a slave **one of yourselves.** There follow greetings from six of Paul's companions, three Jewish, three Gentiles. Aristarchus the Thessalonian would be well known from his previous visits to Asia (Ac. 19: 29; 20: 4; 27: 2) though he may not have met the Colossians personally. Lightfoot prefers to interpret the title **fellow prisoner** as meaning spiritually a captive, as there are no known facts to explain it literally, and he thinks Aris-tarchus left Paul at Myra. If so, he must have rejoined him later. Instructions have already been given concerning the welcome of **Mark the cousin of Barnabas,** so clearly any misunder-standing arising from the second missionary journey has been removed. **11. Jesus . . . Justus** makes his sole appearance here, as one of those standing by the apostle in his present circum-stances. These three were the only Jews present to assist Paul in the work, and this line of demarca-tion furnishes the chief evidence that Luke was a Gentile. **12. Epaphras** comes next, one of their own number, a bondslave of Christ and hard worker, for praying is working. He wrestles in the intensity of his prayer for these three local churches, seeking their maturity of character and full dedication to the will of God. **14. Luke** is called **the beloved physician,** possibly a grateful acknowledgment of help received from his medical skill. Of **Demas** who has not yet defaulted little is known, but the absence of any word of praise may be an anticipatory hint of the cooling off of his enthusiasm. Greetings are also sent to the Christians in Laodicea and to **Nympha** in whose house the local church met, a state of affairs often true of NT churches, though these may have been smaller units within the larger fellowship of believers in any city. A charge is then given that after reading this letter at Colossae it is to be read at Laodicea

and conversely their letter is to be read to the Colossians. In thus giving to writings primarily local in their significance a wider, and ultimately a universal range may be seen the germinal idea of Scripture, as a body of authoritative writings. Finally there is a charge to **Archippus** (cf. Phm. 2): if passed on by a public reading of the letter in church it would no doubt gain in significance and solemnity, though it may well have caused some embarrassment, which was perhaps intended. Paul concludes his greeting in his own hand, which would prevent any thought of forgery. Pleading for a kindly remembrance in his imprisonment he leaves them a blessing, **Grace be with you.**

16. the letter from Laodicea: Presumably now lost, though some have identified it with

Ephesians which we assume to have been written later, others with Philemon. There is also an apocryphal Laodicean letter.

BIBLIOGRAPHY

ABBOTT, T. K., *The Epistles to the Ephesians and to the Colossians. ICC* (Edinburgh, 1897).

CARSON, H. M., *The Epistles to the Colossians and Philemon. TNTC* (London, 1960).

LIGHTFOOT, J. B., *The Epistles to the Colossians and to Philemon* [on the Greek text] (London, 1875).

MOULE, C. F. D., *The Epistles to the Colossians and Philemon* [on the Greek text]. *CGT* (Cambridge, 1957).

RADFORD, L. B., *The Epistles to the Colossians and Philemon. WC* (London, 1931).

SIMPSON, E. K. and BRUCE, F. F., *The Epistles to the Ephesians and to the Colossians. NLC* (London, 1957).

THE FIRST LETTER TO THE THESSALONIANS

PETER E. COUSINS

It was probably the winter of A.D. 49/50 when Paul and Silas, accompanied by Timothy, arrived in Thessalonica. Paul was making his second missionary journey, but in spite of his previous experience he had been badly shaken by his rough handling at Philippi (1 Th. 2: 2). Now the missionaries nerved themselves to face the challenge of Thessalonica. An important centre of communications and commerce, it had a Jewish community in which, as usual, the missionaries began their work. Three weeks passed, and Paul's preaching of a crucified Messiah whom he identified with Jesus bore fruit in the formation of a church containing some Jews and a larger proportion of Gentiles and women who had been regular worshippers at the synagogue. Angry at this blow to their own missionary work, some of the Jews instigated a riot during which an attack was made on the house where the missionaries were staying, and the owner, Jason, together with some of the converts, was taken before the authorities and made responsible for seeing that the trouble did not recur. In the circumstances it seemed wise to save the church from further trouble and the missionaries from danger, so all three moved on to Beroea. Following similar riots there, Paul separated from the other two, continuing to Athens and Corinth (Ac. 17: 1-15; 18: 1).

In Athens he was joined by Timothy, but not for long. Already Paul had tried to revisit Thessalonica, but had been hindered (1 Th. 2: 18). Now he sent Timothy to the young church, himself facing the loneliness of Athens because he felt the Thessalonians needed Timothy's help. From Athens to Corinth—and here Timothy rejoined him with news from Macedonia. On the whole, it was good (1 Th. 3: 6). So remarkable was the tone of this church that the news had spread to other areas of the evangelization of Thessalonica and the spiritual growth of the converts (1 Th. 1: 6-8; 3: 6; 4: 1, 9, 10). Yet the hostility that had driven the missionaries from the city continued, and Paul wished he could give encouragement personally, for some of the converts were easily depressed (1 Th. 4: 13-18;

5: 14). In addition, they were concerned about friends who had died and about the delay in the Lord's return. Paul's absence was being pointed to as a sign of a lack of concern for the Thessalonian church, and he and the other missionaries were the objects of a whispering campaign intended to show that they were no better than the normal run of magico-philosophical charlatans (1 Th. 2: 3-12, 17-20). Certain undesirable tendencies were developing. The Gentiles had not made a clean break with their formerly low sexual standards (1 Th. 4: 3-8). Some believers, presumably in response to the eschatological element in the apostolic preaching, had given up their jobs (1 Th. 4: 11 f.; 5: 14). It may have been the reaction of others to this group that had produced disunity (1 Th. 5: 13b). Certainly there was a tendency to give the elders of the church less respect than they deserved (1 Th. 5: 12 f.).

Such were the circumstances in which Paul wrote 1 Thessalonians. It was for a long time believed to be the first of his letters, but today many scholars, particularly in Britain, are inclined to award this position to Galatians. Its sole doctrinal distinguishing feature is its stress on eschatology, and more particularly its description of the translation from earth of believers at the *parousia* (see note on this word at 1 Th. 2: 19), which is unparalleled in the NT. Otherwise the letter shows signs of its early date (*e.g.* the vagueness of reference to church office-bearers in 5: 12) though by no means of an undeveloped theology. Indeed, the Thessalonians are assumed to have become familiar during Paul's stay with a surprising variety of doctrines. These babes in Christ were well fed! Paul's companions are repeatedly associated with him in the letter (cf. the frequent use of 'we'); another prominent feature of the letter is the insight provided, especially in chapter 2, into the motives of an ideal missionary team and their relationship with their converts. It is plain that one secret of Paul's success was his personal concern for the individuals among whom he worked. In this, as in other respects, this primitive document, a relic of the earliest days of the Church, speaks to and challenges us today.

ANALYSIS

I   GREETING (1: 1)

II   THANKSGIVING FOR THE THESSALONIAN CHURCH (1: 2-10)

III   THE EVANGELIZATION OF THESSALONICA (2: 1-16)

IV   PAUL AND THE THESSALONIAN CHURCH (2: 17-3: 13)

V   ETHICAL INJUNCTIONS (4: 1-12)

VI   THE PAROUSIA (4: 13-5: 11)

VII   FINAL EXHORTATIONS (5: 12-22)

VIII   CONCLUSION (5: 23-28)

I. GREETING (1: 1)

For **Paul, Silvanus and Timothy** see above. (Silvanus was the Latin form of Silas's name.) Morris points out that Paul's happy relationship with the Thessalonian church enables him to dispense with any such title as 'apostle'. The description of the church as **of the Thessalonians** and **in God the Father and the Lord Jesus** is unique, perhaps a sign that the apostle had not yet formed his style. Hogg and Vine comment, 'The first part marks the assembly at Thessalonica as non-heathen, the second as non-Jewish'. Whereas 'in Christ' is commonly used to show the complete union of the believer with his Saviour, **in God** is rare (Col. 3: 3). Its use here is a powerful incidental witness to the faith of the primitive Church in the full deity of the Son.

II. THANKSGIVING FOR THE THES-SALONIAN CHURCH (1: 2-10)

2. The difficulties he was experiencing at Corinth would increase Paul's joy in the strong faith of the Thessalonian converts. **constantly:** May qualify **mentioning** or **remembering**. It probably refers to both. **3. faith . . . love . . . hope:** Frequently linked in the apostolic Church (5: 8; Rom. 5: 2-5; 1 C. 13: 13; Gal. 5: 5 f.; Col. 1: 4 f.; Heb. 6: 10-12; 10: 22-24; 1 Pet. 1: 21 f.). Here the **work** is probably less that of believing than the works resulting from faith (Jas 2: 14-26). **labour:** The word implies toilsome effort; love is costly. **steadfastness:** Active, whereas patience (AV) is passive. It results from the Christian's certain **hope** in Christ (Col. 1: 26). **before . . . Father** is more naturally taken (with the Greek) at the end of this verse.

4-10. The Thessalonians' initial response to the gospel. 4 f. The free preaching of the gospel reveals those who are **chosen** by God.

Here as elsewhere election derives from God's love. Election to damnation (the 'double decree') is not found in the NT, however 'logical' it may appear to be. Rom. 9: 21 ff. is hypothetical; Paul significantly fails to state the doctrine. **for:** i.e. 'because'. **our gospel:** 'the gospel we preach'. The **power** experienced resulted neither from eloquence (1 C. 1: 17), personality (2 C. 10: 10), nor evil spirits, but from **the Holy Spirit. full conviction:** The same word (*plērophoria*) occurs in Col. 2: 2; Heb. 6: 11; 10: 22. Here it refers to the freedom felt by the preachers. **5b** looks forward to 2: 3-12. **6. you became imitators:** Cf. 1 C. 4: 16; 11: 1. The aorist indicates a decisive moment, while the emphatic *you* stresses that the election of the Thessalonians was shown in their experience as well as in that of the preachers. **the word:** Here, as most often in the NT, the gospel. **affliction:** Cf. Ac. 17: 1-10; 14: 22. **joy:** Part of the harvest of the Spirit (Gal. 5: 22), who enables believers to rejoice in spite of, even because of hardship (Jn 16: 22; Rom. 5: 3-5; 1 Pet. 4: 13). **7. example:** *Typos* originally means an imprint (Jn 20: 25), then an image (Ac. 7: 43), and so a pattern (Heb. 8: 5). **Macedonia and Achaia:** These two provinces comprised the whole of Greece. **8-10.** The gospel has **sounded forth** (perfect, indicating that the process continues) from them, throughout Greece, aided no doubt by Thessalonica's strategic position. Paul need never tell of their heroic faith (2: 14) for the story of the mission to Thessalonica is on the lips of Christians everywhere. (Prisca and Aquila had recently arrived in Corinth from Rome cf. Ac. 18: 2.) Morris suggests that the absence of Pauline vocabulary in vv. 9 f. shows that Paul is using the common terminology of the apostolic Church. **turned:** 'Conversion is always the voluntary act of the individual in response to the presentation of truth' (Hogg and Vine). **from idols:** They were largely Gentiles. Cf. Paul's preaching at Lystra (Ac. 14: 15 ff.). **to serve:** As slaves, in total devotion. **the living God:** An OT term contrasting Jehovah with idols who can do nothing (Isa. 41: 23 f.). **true:** Not *alēthēs* (truthful) but *alēthinos* (genuine) as in Jn 1: 9, etc. Again Paul refers to the Christian hope, which is rooted in the resurrection of Jesus Christ. **delivers:** A timeless participle equivalent to 'The Deliverer' (cf. Rom. 11: 26). **to come:** A present participle stressing the inevitability of the wrath. In the light of the general NT reference of **wrath** to God's total antagonism to sin, it seems unduly limiting to interpret it here of anything less than final judgment.

III. THE EVANGELIZATION OF THESSALONICA (2: 1–16)

1–6a. The Motives of the Missionaries. The ancient world was full of wandering 'philosophers' and 'holy men' who were greedy and unscrupulous. Some of Paul's enemies suggested that he was one of these, but he denies the charge. **1. in vain:** May mean 'fruitless', or 'devoid of purpose.' Paul insists that he and his fellows had a definite object in view, and attained it. **2.** Paul remembers both the physical pain of the flogging at Philippi and the insult offered him as a Roman citizen (Ac. 16). **had courage:** This verb is always used in the NT of the proclamation of the gospel and denotes freedom from stress (see Ac. 9: 27, etc.; Eph. 6: 20). **opposition:** *Agōn* is a term from athletics meaning 'a contest'; it implies strenuous activity. **3.** Paul rebuts three charges: (*a*) that the gospel was based on error, being a fallible human philosophy; (*b*) that it encouraged sexual immorality (this was true of much contemporary religion and was a common accusation against Christians); (*c*) that the methods used were underhand. **4.** Positively, he asserts the gospel is from God (so not erroneous); its ministers are not unclean but divinely attested; the methods used must withstand God's scrutiny. The words **approved** and **tests** are related. The root idea is of approving after carrying out tests. God has thus tried and attested the preachers. As Jer. 11: 20 says, they must reckon with a God who does scrutinize men; thus their responsibility is to 'please' (or serve) Him rather than men. **hearts:** As always in the Bible, not the emotions but the innermost life. **5.** He appeals to what the Thessalonians know of their methods and what God knows of their motives. **Flattery** here means any insincere use of words. Literally, Paul says that they have not 'come

to be (and continue) in a word of flattery'. He is speaking of a settled policy of deception about the true meaning of the message, designed, presumably, to gain adherents by false pretences. **greed** is *pleonexia*, lit. 'a desire to have more', 'insatiableness'. In the NT and elsewhere it is thought of as one of the worst of vices, and in Col. 3: 5 is called 'idolatry'. Had the missionaries been like many 'philosophers' of the day, their teaching would have been a mere pretext to conceal their greed. **6a.** Paul denies that his motive was to gain esteem and respect. He demonstrates this by referring to the missionaries' behaviour. The verse thus marks a transition to what follows.

6b–9. The Missionaries Supported Themselves. An apostle was a fully accredited representative. The Lord chose His apostles primarily to preach (Mk 3: 14). Paul asserts the privileges of apostleship but is more conscious of its responsibilities. **7. gentle:** Many MSS have 'babes' (*nēpioi* for *ēpioi*). The second part of the verse strikingly illustrates the missionaries' pastoral care. **8. affectionately desirous:** An unusual verb of uncertain origin. It expresses 'yearning love' (NEB) as of a mother-nurse, over the converts. **we were ready:** Better 'we chose'. Preaching the gospel involves giving the whole personality away. **9.** All Jewish boys learned a trade; no rabbi might earn his living by teaching the Law. Paul had trained as a tentmaker (Ac. 18: 3) and often supported himself thus. The Church is now rediscovering (what some Christians have never forgotten) the value of the presentation of the gospel by men who do not earn their living by it, as well as by those whose whole time must necessarily be devoted to that task. **labour and toil:** The first word implies wearying work, the second, the difficulty of the job. The word **burden** is related to **made demands** in v. 6. **10.** Again Paul appeals to the experience of the Thessalonians in order to refute slanders. **holy . . . righteous . . . blameless:** The first word possibly refers to goodness as seen by God, the second by man, and the third to its giving no cause for reproach ('devout, just and blameless' NEB).

11 f. The Missionaries' Behaviour was Blameless. Their ministry is described as directed in love to individual needs. Again Paul stresses the love shown to the converts. Two types of exhortation are mentioned; some needed encouragement (cf. Jn 11: 19, 31) and others stern warning. **12.** The preachers' aim was Christian living. The present continuous force of **calls** is important. Paul speaks less often than the synoptic gospels of the kingdom of God (but cf. Ac. 20: 25; 28: 31;

Rom. 14: 17; 1 C. 4: 20; 6: 9, 10; 15: 50; Gal. 5: 21; Eph. 5: 5; Col. 4: 11; 2 Th. 1: 5). It is not static, but God's rule over man, in action. Present in the world now, it will one day appear to all men and its glory be made plain.

13. The Missionaries' Message was from God. Though delivered by human agency the gospel comes from God. It is to be both **heard** and also **accepted**—the word is used of welcoming a guest. Such a welcome results in its becoming an active power that 'goes on working' in those who 'go on believing' (two timeless present tenses. cf. 1: 5).

14–16. Persecution. As Paul looks back on his experience and that of the church at the hands of his Jewish brethren, he sees that their present hostility is of a piece with their attitude throughout their history (cf. Stephen's speech in Ac. 7). His bitterness suggests that the persecution at Thessalonica, though carried on by Gentiles, was instigated by Jews (cf. Ac. 17: 5–9). They cannot escape God's judgment. Paul uses the OT metaphor of the cup of the wrath of God (Ps. 11: 6; cf. Gen. 15: 16). The inevitability of judgment is seen in his use of the aorist. The fall of Jerusalem both expresses and symbolizes this judgment, which awaits all who thus **displease God.**

IV. PAUL AND THE THESSALONIAN CHURCH (2: 17–3: 13)

17–20. Paul's Intended Visit. A new section begins here, extending to 3: 13, in which Paul speaks of his relationship to the Thessalonians. He begins by explaining that in spite of what enemies were suggesting, his failure to return was involuntary. **17. bereft:** Lit. 'made orphans'. Paul is ready to mix metaphors in expressing his love for the Thessalonians (cf. vv. 7, 10). They were out of sight but not out of mind. **endeavoured:** The word 'combines the ideas of speed and diligence' (Morris). Calvin comments: 'Our feeling of attachment must be strong when we find it difficult to wait even a very short time'. **desire:** The word (*epithymia*) usually indicates intense and evil passion. **18.** The first use in this letter of the first person singular emphasizes the depth of the apostle's emotion. It is useless to speculate on the nature of the repeated difficulties that hindered the visit. They were no doubt explicable by natural causes, but Paul does not take them as 'the Lord's will', rather seeing behind them the 'prince of this world'. **19 f.** Paul explains his desire to visit them by the fact that these converts are to be his pride at the **coming** (*parousia*). The word originally means simply 'presence' as in 2 C. 10: 10. But presence implies

'coming' and this is the general NT meaning, with special reference to the second coming of the Lord. In some documents it is used of the 'coming of a hidden divinity' in his cult, and of an official visit by a king or emperor. **crown:** *stephanos* is usually (not always) applied to the laurel wreath worn at a banquet or by the victor at the games.

3: 1–5. Timothy's Mission. Ac. 17: 14–18: 5 suggests that Paul was alone from the time when he left Thessalonica until Silas and Timothy joined him at Corinth. These verses show that Timothy (at least) met him in Athens, then left for Thessalonica, rejoining Paul in Corinth. The word **alone** in v. 1 and the parallel between **we sent** in v. 2 and **I sent** in v. 5 suggest that the plural here is not to be taken literally. **1.** Apparently the atmosphere of Athens preyed upon Paul (cf. Ac. 17: 16a) so that only his great affection for the Thessalonians made him choose to be **left . . . alone** (lit. as if abandoned or by a dead friend; cf. Gen. 42: 38 LXX). **2.** The importance of Timothy's mission is stressed by his being described as **God's servant.** A better MS reading is possibly 'God's fellow-worker'. He was to **establish** (lit. buttress) and **exhort** (*parakaleō*) them in order to strengthen their faith. **3.** Apparently their enemies were suggesting that their suffering proved the gospel to be false. Ac. 14: 22 explains why the Thessalonian converts knew better. **moved:** The Gk. may mean 'disturbed' or 'beguiled' (i.e. seduced away from the faith by those who were apparently showing sympathy). **4. we told you beforehand:** The continuous tense shows that the subject had been repeatedly mentioned. **5. I sent:** Paul's enemies had suggested that his failure to return showed lack of concern, hence he uses the singular and emphatic pronoun. **tempter:** Again Paul traces events to Satanic influence. The thought of temptation as testing is prominent here. It is significant that **had tempted** is indicative—Paul knows this is likely. In contrast, **would be in vain** is subjunctive, for he does not expect the converts to give in.

6–8. Timothy's Report. Paul's joy at hearing of the steadfast faith of the Thessalonians, their love, and their longing for him, has caused him to write immediately. **6. good news:** The word normally refers to preaching the gospel—so great was Paul's joy at what he heard. **7.** Paul is suffering physical hardship (**distress**) and persecution but is strengthened (cf. v. 2) by Timothy's news. **8. we live:** 'a breath of life to us' (Phillips, NEB). This passionate concern for his spiritual children is typical of Paul; it both demonstrates and explains his success as evangelist and pastor.

9 f. Paul's Satisfaction. His joy does not lead to self-satisfaction, but to thanksgiving ('What sufficient thanks can we repay?'—Lightfoot) and a realization that the converts' faith is not yet perfect.

11-13. Paul's Prayer. He seeks a blessing for himself (11) and for them (12) with the advent in mind. **11. direct** is a singular verb, for the Father and the Lord Jesus are one. A typical example of the way in which the doctrine of the Trinity is found 'in solution' throughout the NT, however rarely it may crystallize and become visible. **12. you** is emphatic, implying 'whether you come or not'. **increase** goes with **love** which may not be confined to Christians. **13. holiness:** The word used here implies a state rather than a process; though referring mainly to separation to God it connects with v. 12. The **saints** at the *parousia* are either angels (Dan. 8: 13; Mk 8: 38) or departed believers (Eph. 3: 18; 1 Th. 4: 16 f.); probably both are intended (cf. Weymouth, 'holy ones').

V. ETHICAL INJUNCTIONS (4: 1-12)

1 f. Introductory Exhortation. As usual, Paul devotes the last section of his letter to practical problems of Christian living. Timothy had doubtless described the needs of the Thessalonian church. **1. Finally** marks the opening of the closing section. Paul carefully avoids suggesting that the Thessalonians are at fault. But 'life is marked by either growth or decay' (Hogg and Vine). **2. instructions:** A military metaphor stressing their authoritative nature as coming **through the Lord Jesus** (cf. 1 C. 7: 10). **3-8. Sexual Purity.** Unlike the Jews, the Greeks had low standards of sexual morality: even religion was tainted by prostitution. Hence even so healthy a church as that at Thessalonica needed this exhortation, which Paul grounds in the revealed will of God, who both helps by the gift of the Spirit and judges those who despise this gift. **3. sanctification:** All who believe are 'sanctified' or set apart for God because He has chosen them for Himself. But this has implications for conduct. We must become what we are, and 'follow after sanctification' (Heb. 12: 14). Paul now brings out the implications for sexual relationships. **4. to take a wife:** Both words present difficulties. *Skeuos* ('vessel') is translated by RSV as 'wife'. This agrees with the use of the verb *ktaomai* ('take') in Ru. 4: 10; Sir. 36: 24 for marriage. And in rabbinical literature 'vessel' can mean 'woman' (1 Pet. 3: 7 is not a parallel). This, however, implies a low view of marriage, and it is better to follow Phillips and NEB in rendering *skeuos* as 'body'. (cf. 2 C. 4: 7; *Ep. Barn.* 7: 3; 11: 9). Papyri show that *ktaomai* can

mean simply 'to have', but here the sense may be 'to gain control'. 'Each of you must learn to control his own body' (F. F. Bruce, *An Expanded Paraphrase of The Epistles of Paul*). **5.** Christian behaviour is contrasted with that of the heathen (Jer. 10: 25; Ps. 79: 6; cf. Rom. 1: 18-25). This is marked by **passion** (a word implying desire suffered by helpless man) and **lust** (*epithymia*; cf. 2: 17) which is, by contrast, active and violent. **6.** 'All sexual looseness represents an act of injustice to someone other than the two parties concerned. Adultery is an obvious violation of the rights of another, but the same principle applies to pre-marital promiscuity. For the impure person cannot bring to the marriage that virginity which is the other's due' (Morris, *TNTC*). **transgress** may be intransitive or it may have **brother** as object and mean not overstepping his rights (Darby, *A New Translation*). **wrong:** To defraud covetously. Three reasons are given for purity. First is the divine judgment, seen both now and at the Last Day (2 C. 5: 10, etc.). This truth had been part of Paul's mission preaching. **7.** The second reason is that God's purpose in effectually calling man is a moral one. **8.** Thirdly, impurity contemptuously ignores the indwelling Spirit of God whom God continually gives (timeless present) to the believer.

9, 10a. Brotherly Love. This section is linked with the previous one by the thought of the Spirit's indwelling. Paul has already commended the Thessalonians for their love (1: 3; 3: 6). Here he uses a word, *philadelphia*, which outside the NT refers to love of the brother by birth. Its existence within God's family is a sign of divine paternity (Jn 13: 34 f.). **taught by God:** Cf. Jn 6: 45; Isa. 54: 13, thus fulfilled. **10a.** Love within a church inevitably expresses itself in a wider context.

10b-12. Honest Work. 2 Th. 3: 6-13 shows that some people, encouraged by the generosity of others, had given up work. One motive may have been the supposed nearness of the *parousia* and the need to proclaim it, but they had become idle busybodies, ignoring the truth that we show love for our fellow-men by serving them in daily work. **11. aspire:** Either 'seek earnestly' or (paradoxically) 'let it be your ambition'. Paul's advice is still relevant. 'If we cannot be holy at our work, it is not worth taking trouble to be holy at any other times' (Denney). Manual labour was despised by the Greeks, as by many (including some of the Carpenter's disciples) today. **12.** Two reasons are given for Paul's advice. Non-christians were being disgusted by these adventist busybodies and layabouts; also they were parasites on the church. **nobody** may be masculine (as RSV) or neuter: 'have need of nothing'.

VI. THE PAROUSIA (4: 13–5: 11)

13-18. The Dead in Christ. Although the mission preaching at Thessalonica had included a good deal about the *parousia* (cf. 2 Th. 2: 5), some questions had naturally remained unanswered. In particular the church (disturbed no doubt by recent deaths) wondered whether the glories of the great day were reserved for the living. Paul explains that dead Christians will share in the triumph, as in the resurrection of their Lord. Premillennialists of whatever school will tend to interpret **grieve** (13) as arising from a fear that the dead may not be raised until the second resurrection at the end of the millennium. Thus in v. 15 Paul explains that the blessing of the living will not **precede** that of the dead in Christ. Postmillennialists and amillennialists, however, point to **as others do who have no hope** in v. 13, saying that this implies a definitely pagan type of grief, i.e. the Thessalonians doubted whether their dead would be raised at all (cf. the error of the Corinthian church). V. 14 is explained as agreeing with this, for Paul points to the fact that Jesus both **died and rose again.** V. 17, it should be noted, speaks simply of being always **with the Lord** but does not specify whether the saints return to the earth with Him immediately, or after an interval, or whether the 'new heavens and earth' follow at once. **13.** The resurrection gave new force to the Jewish custom (1 Kg. 2: 10, etc.; Dan. 12: 2) of referring to death as 'sleep'. Phil. 1: 23 warns against arguing from the metaphor that the dead are unconscious. Pagan literature and the words of unbelievers today show an absence of the sure hope that characterizes Christian experience. Christians may **grieve** for their own loss, but not for the departed. **14.** The unspoken assumption is that believers, alive or dead, are 'in Christ' and thus share His glory. **through Jesus** may be taken (as in RSV) with **will bring** or with **asleep.** In this case the thought is probably not of martyrdom but that it is through Jesus that death has become sleep to His people. **15.** Paul refers to an otherwise unrecorded saying of Jesus, or possibly to a prophetic revelation. He classes himself with those **who are alive** but this is less an intellectual judgment than a spiritual attitude. **16.** Far from being at a disadvantage, the Christian dead will rise first. The Gk. suggests that either the three signals are one or at least that the **archangel's call** is identical with **the trumpet of God. cry of command:** Often

a military term (cf. Prov. 30: 27; Jn 5: 28). **archangel's call:** anarthrous, perhaps 'as of an archangel'. **trumpet of God:** Lightfoot points to Zech. 9: 14 as a warning against a literal interpretation. Among relevant OT references are Exod. 19: 16; Jl 2: 1 ff. (cf. v. 11); Isa. 27: 13. **17.** It is trivial to pander to curiosity by interpreting this verse in a materialistic manner. The Lord comes, and His people meet Him **in the clouds** (Mk 13: 26; cf. Dan. 7: 13), not as a vehicle but as a sign of glory and divine majesty. The air was thought of as the realm of demons, but their power has now been broken (Col. 2: 15). **to meet** is used in the papyri of the official reception given to a visiting governor, whom his citizens escort into the city from which they have come to meet him. The fact, not the location, of the Church's being with her Lord is stressed. **18.** The purpose of this teaching is practical, not the satisfying of idle speculation. Christians need not **grieve** (13) for they have God-given words of consolation, far transcending any human comfort.

5: 1-3. The Time is Uncertain. Paul now reassures those who feared they might not be ready for the *parousia*. He had already told them it would be unexpected and now simply repeats this, pointing out that unbelievers will be overwhelmed by it. **1. times and seasons** refer respectively to the length of time that will pass (*chronoi*) and the special character of the divinely appointed moments (*kairoi*) when God acts. **2. the day of the Lord** is an OT term for any occasion when God acts in a striking way to overthrow His enemies (cf. Isa. 2: 12) and for the final overthrow (cf. Jl 2: 31). It is the day of the Lord, as opposed to man, or the nations. The prophets insisted on its ethical implications (Am. 5: 18 ff.). In view of the fact that Jesus is called Lord throughout the NT it is unnecessary to distinguish between 'the day of the Lord' and 'the day of (our Lord Jesus) Christ' (1 C. 1: 8, etc.). **like a thief:** Cf. Mt. 24: 43. **3. travail** is often used in rabbinical writings (and *e.g.* Mt. 24: 8) of the sufferings preceding the establishment of the messianic age. Here the thought is of suddenness, or perhaps inevitability.

4-11. The Need to Watch. The word **night** leads to the thought of the moral darkness of the unbeliever. The believer must be ready to receive the salvation that the day of the Lord will bring to him. **5. sons of light:** This use of 'son' to indicate close connection or resemblance is a Heb. idiom (cf. sons of the prophets . . . of Belial . . . of perdition) and the Qumran community applied this title to themselves. **sons of the day** extends the thought;

the believer's sphere is the age to come. **6, 7.** As **sleep, keep awake,** and **be sober** are figurative, so presumably is **drunk.** From the literal nocturnal activities of 'sons of darkness' Paul draws the lesson that believers must be alert and self-controlled. **8.** As in Rom. 13: 12 f., Paul passes for no obvious reason to a military metaphor. The difference between these verses and Eph. 6: 13-17 (cf. Isa. 59: 17) warn against emphasizing details in applying the passage; Calvin comments (quoted by Morris in *NLC*): 'The man that is provided with faith, love and hope will be found in no department unarmed'. **9, 10.** Those who fear are reminded that the wrath is not for the believer. Salvation here (as in v. 8) includes all the believer's benefits in Christ. Its root in election is pointed by **destined,** and man's response by **to obtain.** V. 10 is the only plain statement in the two letters of the truth that Christ died for us; it also teaches that He shares His risen life and power with His people. **wake or sleep** is figurative for 'live or die'. The thought in this passage connects with 4: 13-18 rather than 5: 6. The apostle is not encouraging moral slackness. **11.** As in 4: 18, Paul expects practical use to be made of the truth; we notice his tactful conclusion.

VII. FINAL EXHORTATIONS (5: 12-22)

12 f. Attitude to Elders. It is plain from Ac. 14: 23 that Paul selected elders to guide the churches he founded, and so in Thessalonica. Inexperienced as they were, they may not have dealt tactfully with some of the problems mentioned. Here Paul's appeal to respect them is based, not on their formal office but on the service they render. He speaks gently—**we beseech**—and reminds believers that an elder's duty of leading and counselling (NEB) involves hard work. They are to be respected (lit. 'known' —perhaps 'acknowledged') and lovingly esteemed, not because of personal charm, but for the work they do. The injunction to **be at peace** is primarily, though not exclusively, addressed to the rank and file. **12. in the Lord:** The sole ground and limiting extent of authority in the church. **13. very highly:** Cf. 3: 10.

14 f. Mutual Responsibilities. Paul begins by thinking of the duties of elders, but imperceptibly is drawn to speak of the relationship between all believers. **14. idle:** Cf. 4: 11; 2 Th. 3: 6 f., 10 ff. The word *ataktos* and its cognates are used in the NT only in these places. Originally a military term, 'out of order', 'undisciplined', it came to be used of 'idle and careless habits' (Milligan). **fainthearted:** Cf. 4: 13; 5: 4, 9. **help:** The word implies

standing by another and is used in Mt. 6: 24. **15. seek to do good:** The stress is not on a moral ideal but on strenuously pursuing (*diōkō*) what benefits others. cf. Rom. 12: 21.

5: 16-22. Prayer and Spiritual Matters. Paul now gives advice about the Christian's personal relationship to God and to problems in the church and daily life. **16.** The Christian must rejoice even when persecuted (cf. v. 15). **17.** Unceasing prayer is the secret of continual joy. **18.** Thanksgiving will result from the realization gained in prayer that God's purpose is behind all circumstances. Although **this** is singular, it must refer to all three, prayer, rejoicing and thanksgiving. God's will is not remote or impersonal but is revealed **in Christ Jesus. 19.** To **quench the Spirit** might be to discourage the exercise of spiritual gifts, but it seems unlikely that such a tendency should exist in so young a church. At Corinth the opposite danger existed. Probably the emphasis is ethical, a warning against conduct which might stifle the Spirit's operation (cf. Eph. 4: 30). **20. prophesying:** 'the impassioned and inspired utterance of the deep things of God' (Lightfoot). Regarded at Corinth as inferior to speaking with tongues, prophesying may have been in danger of being undervalued at Thessalonica because of its abuse by second advent enthusiasts. **21. test everything:** The Christian must not uncritically accept—or reject—spiritual teaching but must be careful in all matters to distinguish the good and hold on to it. He will thus avoid 'evil in any form' (Phillips).

VIII. CONCLUSION (5: 23-28)

Only God Himself can give the strength necessary to obey the apostolic injunctions. Having prayed for this, Paul closes with three requests and a typical benediction. **23.** Although there is a reference to v. 13, the OT meaning of **peace** as prosperity and security is more prominent. Sanctification implies both separation for God, and its ethical result. A tri-partite nature of man is not necessarily implied here, for **be kept** and **sound** are singular. **sound** has sacrificial associations in the OT (Dt. 27: 6; Jos. 8: 31) and more explicitly in Philo. **24.** The fact that the Thessalonians have experienced the calling of God guarantees their final sanctification (Rom. 8: 29 f.). He is trustworthy. **25.** Paul never forgot his dependence on the prayers of others (cf. Rom. 15: 30; Eph. 6: 19; Phil. 1: 19). **26.** Kissing was a normal mode of greeting friends and became a sign of the mutual affection within the Christian brotherhood (cf. Rom. 16: 16; 1 Pet. 5: 14). Later it continued (to the

R

present day in some liturgies) as a ritual observance. In the West today, even the most conservative are content to substitute the handshake as a rule—an interesting example of how it is legitimate to reinterpret apostolic injunctions in the light of later conditions. The point in this verse, however, is that individual members of the church are to be kissed as a greeting from Paul. **27.** It is difficult to explain the severity (unparalleled in the NT) of Paul's language without knowing more of the circum-

stances. Did he fear that the elders might withhold the contents of his letter from some? Or (as seems more likely) is he ensuring that his words reach even the idlers and the downhearted referred to in v. 14? **28.** Paul ends his letters, normally written by an amanuensis, with a few words in his own hand; here the first person singular of v. 27 may mark the point. As usual, he replaces the conventional 'Farewell' of his day with a prayer for grace, thought of as fully expressed in the Lord Jesus.

THE SECOND LETTER TO THE THESSALONIANS

While few critics have doubted the authenticity of 1 Thessalonians, rather more have found difficulties in the Second Letter. Many of these are subjective, or disappear when the circumstances of the letter's writing are understood. Thus it is said that the style of 2 Thessalonians is formal, that it makes a greater use of the OT, that it is inconceivable that the same author should in so short a period write two letters showing such similarity. These arguments are no more convincing than the suggestions that 2 Thessalonians was written first (but see 2: 2, 15; 3: 17), or that it was intended for the Jewish and 1 Thessalonians for the Greek half of the church (in spite of Paul's insistence on the unity in Christ of Jew and Gentile).

There is more force in the objection that the eschatology of the letters is inconsistent. Ultimately it results from a misunderstanding, but a misunderstanding that has not been without its effect on theology. It is pointed out that the apocalyptic section, 2 Th. 2: 3–12, is without parallel in Paul's letters, not only because of its affinities with other apocalypses, but because it teaches that the second coming is to be preceded by signs. Elsewhere Paul speaks of the suddenness of the Lord's return; some scholars conclude that 2 Thessalonians is not Pauline. One way out of the difficulty has been to distinguish between a 'coming for the saints' at any moment and without preceding signs, and a 'coming with the saints' some years later, after the 'tribulation', which will be preceded by the signs listed in 2 Th. 2. If it is true, then Paul's handling of the situation at Thessalonica was surprising. The answer to those who believed that the day of the Lord had begun would, on this view, be simple.

Paul had only to point out that the saints would all have been raptured before the onset of the day of the Lord. Instead, he lists events that must precede it, without a hint that the Thessalonians would not be in the least affected by them. We are thus led to conclude that Paul saw no conflict between saying that the *parousia* was at hand, and that certain events must nevertheless precede it.

It is relevant to point out that Joel, centuries earlier, had said that the day of the Lord was *at hand* (1: 15; 2: 1; 3: 14.) When God leads men to think earnestly about the last things, He gives a sense of urgency to their thoughts. This will have been true of Paul. But secondly, as F. F. Bruce says (*NBC*, p. 1058), 'A distinction should be made between suddenness and immediacy'. Paul's insistence in 1 Thessalonians 'on the suddenness of the *parousia* had been understood to mean its immediacy'. Hence there was some agitation, and a continued refusal by a small group to work for their living. In these circumstances, it is plain why Paul wrote again within a few weeks (for he is still accompanied by Silas and Timothy) repeating so much that he had already said, but going into greater detail about the *parousia*, and showing that it could not have already begun, because the 'man of lawlessness' had not yet appeared. A greater number of OT references is inevitable, as the teaching given has its roots ultimately in the OT. On this view the resemblances and the differences between the two letters are simply explained, as is the apostle's insistence in 3: 17 on the genuineness of the letter as opposed to the falsity of others in circulation (2: 2) that contained different teaching.

ANALYSIS

I. GREETING (1: 1 f.)

These verses are identical with those beginning the First Letter (*q.v.*) with two exceptions. One is the description of God as **our Father** in v. 1. The other is the addition of the words following **peace** in v. 2. This formula is found in every Pauline letter except Col. and 1 Th. The equality of Father and Son is taken for granted.

II. PRAYER AND ENCOURAGEMENT (1: 3–12)

It seems likely that some at least of the Thessalonians had felt unworthy of Paul's commendation in the First Letter for he repeats this in emphatic terms. He encourages those who were faint-hearted in face of continued persecution, pointing out its purifying effect (5) and that it seals the doom of the enemies of God's people. The day of the Lord will mean judgment for these, but all (without exception) who have believed will then be glorified and enjoy rest. He prays they may then be found worthy, being strengthened by God's grace. **3, 4.** The Thessalonians' faith and love are singled out (cf. 1 Th. 1: 3) for commendation; their courage in facing persecution even leads Paul to boast of them. **are bound:** As a duty to God. **fitting:** In fairness to the Thessalonians. **4. we ourselves:** Emphatic; as founders of the church, they would have kept silent had not the behaviour of the Thessalonians been so remarkable. **faith:** Probably religious (the cause of the **steadfastness**) rather than moral (synonymous with it). **are enduring:** Note the present tense. **5–10.** Their steadfastness in suffering witnessed to the truth of the gospel, which includes the vindication of right and the

overthrow of evil. There will be rest for the saints when the Lord Jesus Himself is revealed in a dual role, as the judge of the ungodly and the source of the glory which will then be seen in believers. The premillennialist sees in these verses a description of the final judgment that will follow the rebellion at the end of the millennium. Some would make what is perhaps a rather over-elaborate distinction between the 'day of Christ' or *parousia*, understood as primarily concerning the Church (the 'coming for the saints') and the day of the Lord, or revelation of the Lord Jesus, understood as primarily concerning the world (the 'coming with the saints'). The post-millennialist and amillennialist, however, interpret them of the single crisis of the *parousia* and judgment. V. 7 seems to link the **rest** for afflicted believers with the revelation (*apokalypsis*) in wrath of the Lord Jesus. Premillennialists, who separate these by the millennium, regard the words from **and to . . . afflicted** as parenthetical. **5.** The RSV appears mistaken in translating **made worthy,** for *kataxioō* means 'to prove or account worthy'. Their steadfastness, itself a result of God's grace, shows they are truly his, and are suffering **for** (on behalf of) His kingdom, as are the missionaries. (The Gk. places 'also' before **are suffering.**) **6.** God's justice is seen, not only in his vindication of the righteous, but in retribution on their enemies. **7. with us:** A gentle reminder by the apostle of the missionaries' sufferings. **when . . . revealed:** Lit. 'in the revelation (*apokalypsis*)'. This word applied to the Lord's return stresses the unveiling of his glory and greatness. The phrase refers back to v. 6 (**repay with affliction**) as well as v. 7. Both are part of the *apokalypsis*, which is described in three ways, being **from heaven** (the unseen place of divine glory where the Lord is now enthroned); **with His mighty angels,** or better, 'with the angelic ministers of His power'; **in flaming fire,** a sign in the OT of God's majesty. The whole passage is reminiscent of the OT (cf. the RV references) and Paul does not hesitate to apply to Jesus words used in the OT of Yahweh. **8.** Divine vengeance is free from personal spite; the word here used is cognate with 'justice'. Two signs are mentioned: wilful ignorance of God (cf. Rom. 1: 18, 28), seen in all men; and disobedience to the gospel, here described with great dignity as **of our Lord Jesus. 9.** The **punishment** (lit. 'a just penalty') is said to be **eternal,** which means unending, whatever further meaning it may have. 1 C. 5: 5 and 1 Tim. 6: 9 show that **destruction** (Gk. *olethros*) is not annihilation but (as in NEB) 'ruin'. RSV adds **exclusion** (not in the Gk.) to bring out the meaning of the phrase **from . . . might.** To see the Lord's face and the glory of His might is here thought of as a privilege, whose loss is the chief punishment of unbelievers. But cf. Isa. 2: 10, 19, 21. **10.** The day of the Lord brings glory to Him by displaying the glory of His people (cf. Jn 17: 10; Rom. 8: 18 f.). **marvelled at:** By faith, believers have already seen Jesus glorified by the Father; but as faith gives place to sight they are 'lost in wonder, love and praise'. **because . . . believed:** A reminder that the Thessalonians will be included. **11. to this end** refers in general to the salvation the apostle has spoken of, or else to **made worthy** (5). Although the RSV is probably wrong in v. 5, here the slightly different verb (*axioō*) may well mean **make . . . worthy,** and Paul be praying that the Thessalonians will, by God's power, live a life that will deserve a favourable verdict. **12.** Cf. Isa. 66: 5 (LXX); Mt. 5: 16; Jn 17: 10, 22. **the grace:** 'the source whence all glorification springs' (Lightfoot). As a frequent title, the word **Lord** is best taken with **Jesus Christ,** not co-ordinate with **God.**

III. EVENTS PRECEDING THE PAROUSIA (2: 1–12)

1 f. The End is not Yet. Paul warns his hearers against teaching ascribed to him that the day of the Lord has begun. It is interesting to note that these verses associate **our assembling to meet Him** with **the day of the Lord. 1. concerning:** *hyper* here combines the meanings 'about' and 'in the interests of.' **coming:** *parousia.* **assembling:** The word is used in *e.g.* Mt. 24: 31; Heb. 10: 25. **2.** Two words are used to describe the unsettling effect of the teaching. It drives men 'from their

sober sense like a ship from its moorings' (Frame, ref. **shaken in mind**) and also produces a lasting state of disturbance. Paul, who is not quite sure what has happened, refers to three possible ways in which the false teaching may have reached Thessalonica. All are governed by **purporting to be from us:** They are (*a*) a reported divine revelation, (*b*) spoken teaching ascribed to the apostle, and (*c*) a letter, either forged or mistakenly attributed to him. It was being said that the series of events constituting the day of the Lord had begun to take place.

3–12. The Great Apostasy. Paul now outlines the events that must precede the day of the Lord—a widespread rebellion against God, directed by **the man of lawlessness.** He is supplementing teaching already given to the Thessalonians (5), which we do not possess. Hence 'this passage is probably the most obscure and difficult in the whole of the Pauline correspondence and the many gaps in our knowledge have given rise to the most extravagant speculations. It will be well . . . to maintain some reserve in our interpretations' (Morris, *NLC*). The **man of lawlessness** (as the better MSS read) is identical with the one spoken of by the early Church as 'antichrist' and regarded (in spite of 1 Jn 2: 18) as an individual to appear in the days immediately before the *parousia.* We need look no further for the origin of the idea than the book of Daniel (see 7: 25; 8: 9 ff.; 11: 36 ff.). These passages refer primarily to Antiochus Epiphanes, who in 167 B.C. installed in the Temple at Jerusalem the cult of Zeus, whose representative he claimed to be. That there is to be a further fulfilment is shown by the way in which the Lord takes the words of Daniel and applies them in Mk 13: 14 to the end-time. (His words are not exhausted either by Caligula's attempt to place his statue in the Temple or by the siege of Jerusalem.) This figure is placed in the general context of **the rebellion,** which is also spoken of in the eschatological discourse of Mk 13 as occurring in the last days. The word, *apostasia,* was used in secular Greek of a political revolt and in the LXX (cf. Jos. 22: 22) of rebellion against God. It is not stated whether **the rebellion** occurs among Jews, in the church, or is a general refusal by men to acknowledge the Creator's authority. Some interpreters understand these references to the man of lawlessness and the persecution elsewhere associated with him as phenomena existing throughout the whole of the Church's history (cf. 1 Jn 2: 18). Others expect an individual and specific fulfilment in the last days. Among these, some expect the 'translation' of the

Church to take place before the appearance of the antichrist and consequent persecution, while others believe that the Church will be on earth throughout this period. **3. is revealed:** Emphatic by position, and contrasted with the *apokalypsis* of the Lord in 1: 7. **son of perdition:** A Hebrew idiom, applied also to Judas Iscariot (Jn 17: 12), meaning 'doomed to destruction' (cf. v. 8). **4.** The 'lawless one' opposes Christ, rather than presenting himself as a false messiah, for he acknowledges no other authority than his own, whereas the Messiah is by definition subordinate to God. **the temple of God:** History shows this is not the temple of Herod. But Paul may have had in mind Gaius's attempt ten years previously to have his image set up in the Jerusalem temple. See Mt. 24: 15; Mk 13: 14. The Letter to the Hebrews appears to rule out the idea of a future temple with sacrificial worship. Some interpreters, however, understand this verse literally of a revived Jerusalem cultus taken over by antichrist, in which case the worshippers are said to be the people of Israel, and Gentiles converted by Jewish preaching. Although the term may mean the Church (cf. 1 C. 3: 16 f.) yet, as Morris (*NLC*) says, 'Would not the Church by that very fact (sc. its being dominated by the man of lawlessness) cease to be the *Christian* church?' It is probably best understood as a vigorous description of his claim to divine authority, the temple being the very centre and expression of God's sovereignty and presence among men. **5.** The continuous tense shows that Paul repeatedly gave instruction on this subject (cf. Ac. 17: 7). The Thessalonians should not need this recapitulation. **6 f.** Already present in the world is a secret lawless influence (cf. 1 Jn 2: 18) which will finally issue in the rebellion of the last days. But there existed also in the apostle's day a **restraining** power (well understood by his hearers, though not by us) which would prevent the revelation of antichrist so long as it continued to operate. This power is referred to in v. 6 as masculine and in v. 7 as neuter. It might grammatically be the Holy Spirit, but this idea is 'without support in other parts of the NT' (Hogg and Vine). Nor does this theory account for the apostle's mysterious way of referring to the subject. This objection also applies to the idea that the restraining power is an angelic being (cf. Dan. 10). Many understand the reference of a Roman emperor, seen as an individual (masc.) or as a personification of the empire (neuter). The best (though by no means certain) interpretation sees the Roman empire as symbolizing the God-given authority of government (Rom. 13: 1-6), which acts as a barrier against such unbounded claims as those made by the man of lawlessness. Paul dare not refer openly to the disappearance of the empire; hence his veiled language. **restraining:** The word may mean (*a*) to hold fast (1 Th. 5: 21); (*b*) to restrain (Lk. 4: 42); (*c*) to rule. **now** may indicate time (as RSV) or logical connection. **time:** *kairos* (see 1 Th. 5: 1). **7. mystery:** A secret too deep for human ingenuity (*Arndt*), often with the implication that it has been revealed by God. The forces of lawlessness, although operating beneath the surface of affairs, would not be revealed until the restraint of law and order disappeared. Then they would appear, embodied in the man of lawlessness. Lightfoot points out the contrast with 1 Tim. 3: 16. **he is out of the way:** Lit. 'he comes out of the midst'. Arndt-Gingrich show this is simply an idiom, meaning 'is removed'; cf. Kelly's note *in loco*. **8.** Paul passes over the career of the man of lawlessness, and gives no timetable of events, confining himself to asserting the great spiritual truth of the ultimate triumph of Christ. Again he speaks of the revelation (cf. vv. 3, 6) of antichrist, but if he is revealed, so too will the Lord Jesus shine forth (*epiphaneia*) when he comes (*parousia*). 'The radiance of his coming' (Phillips, NEB) will break the power of **the lawless one. slay . . . mouth:** Cf. Isa. 11: 4; Ps. 32: 6. No battle takes place. Morris aptly quotes Luther: 'A word shall quickly slay him'. **9, 10a.** Paul summarizes the 'ministry' of the antichrist, again bringing out the parallels with that of the Lord. First he stresses the principle behind it—the active power (*energeia*) of Satan. Then he describes the accompanying miracles. Three words are used, all applied elsewhere to the miracles of Christ. **All** points to their variety. As **power** miracles reveal superhuman might; as **signs** they teach some truth; as **wonders** they amaze men. **Pretended** in no way impugns the genuineness of the miracles; rather does it mean 'false', for the teaching of the 'signs' is a falsehood. Finally, the accompanying effects on men. The faint-hearted at Thessalonica are reassured—only those on the road to ruin (1 C. 1: 8) will be deceived. **10b-12.** In all this the justice and sovereignty of God are vindicated. Behind these verses lies the characteristic OT insight that all events, even the activities of the powers of evil, are ultimately in God's control (cf. *e.g.* 1 Chr. 21: 1; 2 Sam. 24: 1; 1 Kg. 22: 23). Men are doomed because they **refused to love the truth,** not even desiring it. Such moral delinquency exposes them to God's judgment. As in Rom. 1 God 'gives them up', so here in His sovereignty He allows them to be deceived, and they believe (lit.) **the lie** as opposed to **the truth.**

This has a moral as well as an intellectual reference (cf. 1 Jn 1: 6) so that their ultimate condemnation is not on intellectual grounds; not to **believe the truth** inevitably results in taking **pleasure in unrighteousness** (cf. Rom. 1: 32). A similar process may be seen in the OT when Pharaoh's heart is hardened first by himself, finally by the Lord. **sends:** The present tense both indicates the certainty of the prediction (prophetic present) and points to the present operation of this principle.

IV. THANKSGIVING AND EXHORTATION (2: 13-15)
The emphatic **we** seems to imply a return to the theme of 1: 3 f., as Paul encourages the faint-hearted: 'Now we, for our part, are bound . . .' The same Lord who will destroy the lawless one loves the Thessalonian believers. Their salvation is assured, because God Himself has both chosen them in eternity, and in due time **called** them **through** the **gospel.** It is logical, then, that they live accordingly. **13. from the beginning:** *ap' archēs,* to interpret this of the 'beginning' of the apostolic mission is not suitable in the context (cf. Rom. 8: 29 f., 1 Pet. 1: 2, both parallels to this passage as a whole). Nor does the variant reading 'first-fruits' (*aparchēn*) make such good sense, though equally well attested. **sanctification . . . and belief:** God's purpose includes both the Spirit's total activity and man's response. **14. to this:** i.e. salvation, further defined in the rest of the verse. **15.** Believers, secure in the purpose of God, should not be disturbed in either their beliefs or their behaviour as were some at Thessalonica. The present imperative of **stand firm** implies a continuous action; the word **hold** suggests a firm grasp. The verse reminds us that the Christian faith is derived from Christ Himself (tradition, *paradosis,* meaning something handed down; cf. 1 Tim. 6: 20; 2 Tim. 1: 12, 14) and not a subjective construction. At first it was passed on **by word of mouth,** but by the time of this letter was already being committed to writing (**by letter**). Today we possess the *paradosis* in the pages of the NT. No other tradition, oral or written, is binding on the Church.

V. PRAYER FOR THE BELIEVERS (2: 16 f.)
The structure of the Second Letter resembles that of the First (cf. 1 Th. 3: 11-4: 1). Paul realizes the power of evil, hence this prayer. The singular aorist participles (**who loved . . . gave . . .**) associate Father and Son in the crucifixion and Pentecost, which are the foundation of true Christian hope, the gracious gift of God. In Christian experience they bring **comfort** (or encouragement) and confidence (cf. 1 Th. 3: 2) which affect every aspect of life.

VI. A REQUEST FOR PRAYER (3: 1 f.)
The closing section (cf. 1 Th. 4: 1) opens with a request for prayer that the preaching at Corinth may prosper as it had at Thessalonica, both advancing (cf. Ps. 147: 15) and being approved of for its effect on men. Also for deliverance from a body of perverse and evil men. **faith:** Probably saving faith, rather than a body of belief.

VII. THE FAITHFULNESS OF GOD (3: 3-5)
The word **faith** speaks to Paul of the Saviour's reliability (3) so that he trustfully relies (4) on the converts' continued obedience (anticipating the requests of vv. 6-15). An awareness of God's love and the endurance of the Lord Jesus will **strengthen** them (cf. 1 Th. 3: 2). **3. evil:** Better, 'the evil one', Satan.

VIII. HOW TO TREAT THE IDLERS (3: 6-13)
The problem hinted at in 1 Th. 5: 14 has become serious. Paul refers to the missionaries' example (7-9) and teaching (6b, 10) to reinforce his injunction that the work-shy minority (11) be disciplined (6) until they obey the apostolic demand (12). **6-9.** Paul's insistence on the need to imitate him is a challenge to all preachers. For his reminder of the missionaries' behaviour see 1 Th. 1: 5 f.; 2: 5-12, and for his insistence on the apostolic right to support cf. 1 C. 9: 3-14. For **in idleness** and **idle** see 1 Th. 5: 14. **6.** We notice the appeal to the Lord's authority here and in v. 12. **keep away:** *stellō,* to furl a sail, retreat into oneself. But the offender is still a **brother** and the purpose of the withdrawal is his restoration to the shared life of the church when he ceases to sin against the brotherhood (cf. v. 13 and 2 C.: 7). **8.** Cf. 1 Th. 2: 9; Ac. 18: 3. **9. example:** Cf. 1 Th. 1: 7. **10.** This habitual (continuous tense) teaching agrees with that of the rabbis, who insisted that even a scholar must learn a trade, and not live by his study of the Law. The origin of the saying is unknown. **will not:** A deliberate refusal—those who *cannot* work must be helped. **11.** By a play on words Paul points out how the lack of occupation has demoralized the fanatics ('busybodies instead of busy'—Moffatt). Morris (*NLC*) drily conjectures: 'We may conjecture that they were trying to do one or both of two incompatible things, namely, to get their living from others, and to persuade those others to share their point of view about the

second advent, and so persuade them to stop working also'. **12.** Tactfully Paul (*a*) speaks of the layabouts in general terms (*b*) does not merely **command** but adds **and exhort,** and not 'by' but **in . . . Christ. quietness:** The inner calm that should characterize believers. **13.** This exhortation to the rest of the church 'never to tire of doing right' (NEB) may refer to the need to maintain a sympathetic attitude to the others or (taking it with vv. 14 f.) to take a firm line with them.

IX. CHURCH DISCIPLINE (3: 14 f.)

Those who had ignored the admonition of the elders (1 Th. 5: 14) must, if they now disobey the apostle's written word (as binding as if spoken) be taken note of in some unspecified manner. They must not be associated with. The same word is used in 1 C. 5: 9, 11, but there a more severe discipline is in view—'not even to eat' with the offender. Nor are the disobedient one whit less the people of God, but still 'of the family' (NEB).

X. CONCLUSION (3: 16–18)

Paul prays that all, including the idlers, may know God's peace (cf. 1 Th. 1: 1) and presence. He ends the letter, as was his practice (1 C. 16: 21;

Gal. 6: 11; Col. 4: 18, explicitly and **in every letter of mine**) by taking the pen from the amanuensis and writing a few words himself to prove the genuineness of the document (cf. 2: 2). The benediction (18) is identical with that of 1 Th. apart from the word **all.** Even here we may see Paul's care for those he had censured.

BIBLIOGRAPHY

BRUCE, F. F., 'Thessalonians', in *NBC* (London, 1953).

DENNEY, J., *The Epistles to the Thessalonians. EB* (London, 1892).

FRAME, J. E., *The Epistles to the Thessalonians. ICC* [on the Greek text] (Edinburgh, 1912).

HOGG, C. F., and VINE, W. E., *The Epistles to the Thessalonians* (London, 1914).

KELLY, W., *The Epistles to the Thessalonians* (London, 1893).

LIGHTFOOT, J. B., *Notes on the Epistles of St. Paul* [on the Greek text] (London, 1904).

MILLIGAN, G., *The Epistles to the Thessalonians* [on the Greek text] (London, 1908).

MORRIS, L., *The Epistles to the Thessalonians. TNTC* (London, 1956).

MORRIS, L., *The First and Second Epistles to the Thessalonians. NLC* (London, 1959).

NEIL, W., *The Epistles to the Thessalonians. MNT* (London, 1950).

VOS, G., *The Pauline Eschatology* (Grand Rapids, 1930).

THE PASTORAL LETTERS

ALAN G. NUTE

Despite the fact that it was only in the 18th century that the letters to Timothy and Titus began to be known generally as The Pastoral Epistles, it was actually in 1274 that Thomas Aquinas, referring to 1 Timothy, wrote, 'this letter is, as it were, a pastoral rule which the Apostle delivered to Timothy'. The term, though not technically accurate, does suffice to indicate that in these letters attention is directed to the care of the flock of God, to the administration of the church and to behaviour within it. Although the letters are addressed to Timothy and Titus and contain personal injunctions, they are clearly written for the benefit of the churches concerned.

Authorship

Doubt about the Pauline authorship of this group of letters was probably first expressed during the opening years of the last century. Particularly since the publication of P. N. Harrison's The Problem of the Pastoral Epistles (1921) debate on the subject has been greatly intensified.

In the main, the arguments against Pauline authorship rest on the historical situation, the type of false teaching condemned, the stage of church organization described, and the vocabulary and style.

It is readily agreed that the historical allusions (e.g. 1 Tim. 1: 3; 2 Tim. 1: 16, 17; 4: 13, 20; Tit. 1: 5; 3: 12) cannot be fitted into the framework of the Acts. Even allowing for the selective nature of Luke's record of Paul's activities, any attempt to find room there for the happenings described in the passages listed is futile. The well-known theory that a period of liberty followed the imprisonment with which the Acts concludes would accommodate these events and, in the light of the evidence available, appears not unreasonable. Certainly Paul was expecting release (Phil. 1: 25; 2: 23, 24; Phm. 22), and the atmosphere of the final paragraphs of Acts points that way rather than towards execution. Tradition supports the idea of a temporary period of freedom during which Paul engaged in further missionary labours and which was cut short only by his final imprisonment in Rome (1 Clement 5: 7; Eusebius,

Ecclesiastical History ii. 22. 1 f.). Some modern scholars also subscribe to this reconstruction of events (W. M. Ramsay, St. Paul the Traveller and Roman Citizen, 1920, pp. 360 ff.; R. St. J. Parry, The Pastoral Epistles, pp. xv ff.; D. Guthrie, NT Introduction: The Pauline Epistles, p. 212). As a theory it has as much likelihood as the one which makes Paul's activity, if not his life, terminate with the last chapter of Acts.

Considerable effort has been expended in an attempt to prove that the false teaching referred to in the Pastorals reflects 2nd century Gnosticism. On the other hand, many deny this, pointing out that Gnosticism must have had its origins in the 1st century, and that what is here condemned is much closer to incipient Gnosticism than to the fully-developed form of that heresy. Indeed, it is not easy to discern any essential difference between the errors reproved in these letters, and an amalgam of the Gnosticism refuted in Colossians and the Judaism combated in Galatians. The approach adopted is admittedly different, refutation is replaced by denunciation, to which is added guidance on the practical handling of the situation. This may well be explained by the fact that the letters are not addressed to churches but to apostolic representatives well acquainted with Paul's answers to these heresies, though still needing his advice about the way they should deal with them.

Further objection is made on the ground that the organization of the early Church could hardly have developed during the apostolic age to the degree here described. The position accorded to Timothy and Titus, as well as Paul's use of the term 'bishop', is said to reflect a monarchical episcopate, which it is known did not arise until the beginning of the 2nd century. It is obvious that Timothy and Titus exercised a larger authority than that of the normal New Testament elder, but this was clearly as representatives of the apostle rather than as monarchical bishops. Where the singular of the word 'bishop' occurs, it is undoubtedly used in a generic sense. Far from suggesting that one bishop should be appointed in each church, Paul emphasizes the plurality of 'elders in every town'. The argument that the church government described in the Pastorals is post-apostolic loses much of its weight when the teaching of these letters with regard to bishops and elders is compared with the references to such in Ac. 14: 23; 20: 17, 28; Phil. 1: 1; 1 Th. 5: 12, 13. Of particular interest is Paul's address to the Ephesian elders (*episkopoi*) inasmuch as they were actively responsible in that church prior to Timothy's assignment there. Finally, in connection with church organization, it will be well to compare the advice given in 1 Tim. 5 regarding widows, with Ac. 6: 1; 9: 39, 41.

Probably, however, the weightiest objection to Pauline authorship stems from the clearly discernible differences between the language and style of the Pastorals and that of other letters accepted as Paul's. This argument is set out forcibly in P. N. Harrison's work. He points out that a large number of words occurring in this group of letters have not made an earlier appearance in Paul's writings, and that some, indeed, are not found elsewhere in the NT. Moreover, some that have been used previously now bear a different meaning. For example, whilst the word 'faith' had earlier borne the meaning of 'trust', here it is used to describe 'the body of doctrine'. But the most outstanding stylistic deviation from the earlier Pauline letters is in the use of particles, those words in which individual style is so largely involved and which seem not subject to the same degree of change as a writer's vocabulary and general style. The difference between Paul's other letters in this regard is less than the difference between them all and the Pastorals. In addition, there is a conspicuous absence of certain prepositions and pronouns which characterize Paul's acknowledged writings. At first sight the argument arising from statistical analyses of the words used is impressive, but its force is diminished when other factors are taken into consideration. Full weight must be given to the not inconsiderable variation of vocabulary and style which occurs in his other letters. Change of both vocabulary and style can also be attributed to some extent to the purpose in the mind of the writer. He is dealing with situations essentially different from those tackled in earlier letters. Nor should the age of the writer be ignored, or the fact that he is addressing individuals and not churches.

The method of writing which was adopted must also be borne in mind. It seems probable that the author employed an amanuensis who was permitted a measure of latitude in the actual phrasing of the material dictated to him, the letter being subsequently scrutinized by the author, and on occasion, concluded and signed with his own hand (1 C. 16: 21; Col. 4: 18; 2 Th. 3: 17; Gal. 6: 11; cf. Rom. 16: 22 where the amanuensis adds his own signature). Indeed it is likely that with increasing years and the effect on health of the rigours of his service the apostle would depend more largely than ever before on the help an amanuensis would be able to give. This so-called 'editor-secretary theory' might well account in part for the different selection of words used. It might also supply a solution to the neat, somewhat pedestrian style which replaces the more familiar Pauline one where parentheses and anacolutha, like a series of explosions, shatter orthodox grammatical construction. Quite apart from these explanations it is probable that too great a reliance has been placed on linguistic arguments for the determining of authenticity, especially where these are based on statistical analysis.

It remains only to notice the hypothesis which suggests that fragments of genuine Pauline material were woven into the letters as we now have them by a close follower of his and were then issued under Paul's name. This is for some an attractive solution, but for many it is hardly satisfactory. They prefer to accept the *prima facie* claim which the letters make, to have been written by Paul. Again, despite all the attacks, there remains a complete absence of any positive external evidence against Pauline authorship, while, on the other hand, the numerous personal references in the letters possess a distinctively genuine ring. For a more detailed examination of these matters the student is referred to D. Guthrie, *NT Introduction: The Pauline Epistles* and the *Tyndale Commentary on the Pastorals*, J. N. D. Kelly, *The Pastoral Epistles* (A. & C. Black, 1963), and to articles by B. M. Metzger and E. Earle Ellis (see Bibliography, p. 530).

Purpose

It is clear that here the apostle is giving his two friends and trainees help and encouragement in connection with their responsibilities in the churches to which they have been sent. In the case of the letter to Titus he is obviously confirming in writing instruction already given orally (1: 5). This is probably true also with regard to the letters to Timothy. Paul is anxious for the preservation and communication of 'sound doctrine', and for the maintenance of proper order and becoming behaviour in the local churches. This is made the more pressing by the increasing opposition of false teachers and the uncertainty of his own future. He here makes wise provision for the day when the voice of apostolic authority will be silent. Timothy, in particular, receives exhortation to self-discipline and the cultivation of other personal qualities.

The atmosphere of 2 Timothy contrasts strongly with that of 1 Timothy and Titus. Martyrdom, now, seems imminent, and the apostle is anxious that Timothy should come to him as quickly as possible. He asks him to bring Mark with him, and also bids him fetch the cloak left at Troas together with the books and the parchments. Church organization and administration receive no mention, and matters of doctrine are barely touched upon. The personal note is dominant and Paul passes on to his young friend encouragement, advice and a solemn charge. This brief letter is permeated by a spirit of warm affection, and bears a clearly discernible note of urgency.

Value

The present-day relevance of these letters is anticipated by the writer when he refers to the characteristics of the 'last days'. He contends that the development of evil will demand from the people of God a determination to submit obediently to the Scriptures, which, he asserts, are adequate for every situation which may confront them. Foolish and 'senseless controversies' must be avoided, and error must be opposed with a positive presentation of the truth. Such truth Paul here enshrines in terse statements, some designated as 'faithful sayings' and affirmed to be 'worthy of full acceptance'. In this way the mischievous teaching of the legalists and others who upset the believers is reproved, and the principles upon which they are to be dealt with are set forth. Not least important in this connection is the guidance given for the ordering of church life; with the appointment of elders and deacons, and the provision of an adequate ministry of the Word of God. That it may prove difficult to implement these directions should not deter. Rather should the difficulty presented by the contemporary situation be regarded as a chief reason for endeavouring to follow out these things which the Spirit through the apostle has set down for all ages. The emphasis upon the deposit of truth, namely the faith contained in the gospel and in Scripture, indicates its continuing authority.

There may also be detected throughout, a constant demand for godliness of character and the prosecution of good works. Since a harmony is shown to exist between the foundation truths of the faith, proper order in the church, and piety of life, evidence of all three is declared essential for the maintenance of an effective witness.

THE FIRST LETTER TO TIMOTHY

ANALYSIS

I   GREETING (1: 1-2)

II   PAUL AND TIMOTHY (1: 3-20)
    i A reminder of the charge given (1: 3-11)
    ii Paul's experience of divine grace (1: 12-17)
    iii The charge reiterated (1: 18-20)

III   THE CHURCH AT PRAYER (2: 1-15)
    i Subjects for prayer (2: 1-7)
    ii Engaging in prayer (2: 8-15)

IV   RESPONSIBILITY IN THE CHURCH (3: 1-16)
    i The overseer (3: 1-7)
    ii The deacon (3: 8-13)
    iii Behaviour and belief—purpose in writing (3: 14-16)

V   DANGERS TO THE CHURCH (4: 1-16)
    i The apostasy described (4: 1-5)
    ii Timothy's role (4: 6-16)

I. GREETING (1: 1, 2)

As he has done on a number of earlier occasions, Paul opens this letter with an assertion of his apostleship, and, in this way, justifies the note of authority frequently sounded in the letter. This apostleship, so the writer claims, is his by divine command, its dual source being **God our Saviour** and **Christ Jesus our hope.**

The repeated occurrence of the former expression in the Pastorals, is in marked contrast to its almost complete absence elsewhere. Its use in these letters may well arise from a desire to encourage Timothy and Titus, for they face, on the one hand, strong opposition, and have to deal, on the other, with those in whose lives spiritual progress is slow. The reference to **Christ Jesus our hope** might also imply a further cause why they should be confident.

Timothy is affectionately addressed as one, who, in addition to having been brought to faith through Paul's instrumentality, gives proof of being a **true,** a 'genuine', **child.** Upon him is pronounced the threefold blessing of **grace, mercy, and peace,** and this is invoked from the Father and the Son conjointly. The bracketing of Christ Jesus with the Father twice in these opening verses is not without significance especially in the light of subsequent teaching in the letter concerning Christ as mediator (2: 5).

II. PAUL AND TIMOTHY (1: 3-20)

i. A reminder of the charge given (1: 3-11)

The commission previously given is here reaffirmed, for the task is one of great difficulty and is not lessened by Timothy's natural reticence. The apostle's representative in Ephesus obviously needs to be nerved for the fulfilment of his responsibilities. He will find, too, that critics will not be lacking, and the opportunity to appeal to such a charge, given him by Paul, might well prove useful.

The persons needing to be reproved (**charge** denotes a word of command) were mistakenly concentrating on **myths and endless genealogies,** probably of Jewish origin. **Myth** conveys the notion that these ideas were of their own inventing, lacking completely any foundation in the Scriptures of truth. **Genealogies** is used in a wider sense than that customarily accorded it, and describes fatuous and extravagant interpretations of OT history, possibly mingled with certain Gnostic philosophical notions. These are said to be **endless,** for those who wander along these strange by-paths find themselves in an interminable labyrinth, leading nowhere.

This state of affairs had arisen, it seems, from an ambition on the part of these men to be teachers. Lacking, however, the necessary understanding of the truth, as well as the ability to communicate it, they had turned aside to **speculations** and **vain discussion.**

Paul recommends two tests by which the hollowness of such false doctrine may be exposed. (a) *All teaching must be judged by what it produces.* In contrast to the irrelevance and fruitlessness of the speculative and vain, the true ministry, here designated **the divine training that is in faith** will issue in the noble quality of love. The steps by which it will reach this goal are here traced for us. Not being mere sentiment, nor unrelated to ethical standards, the love spoken of finds birth in a heart that is pure. This, in turn, results from a **good conscience,** which is itself the product of a **sincere faith** (5). These virtues vindicate the character of the true teaching. The 'wilderness of words' (v. 6 NEB) to which the other teaching tends is its obvious condemnation. (b) **Sound doctrine,** a term confined to the Pastorals, is *the standard by which all teaching is to be tested.* Healthy, and healthful in its influence, this doctrine was, by this time, well defined; its essential features being crystallized in **the glorious gospel of the blessed God** (11). **Any different doctrine** (3) would immediately stand out in contrast with the true doctrine, which consisted not in theological dogma but in apostolic teaching.

Against these standards Paul measures the false teaching of these whom Timothy must reprove. In ignorance they were expatiating on the law. Mingling it with fable and fanciful interpretation they misconstrued its true purpose. **We know** (v. 8 contrasts strongly with their confident assertions of v. 7) introduces a declaration of the nature as well as the proper function of the law. 'It is good', says Paul, in a phrase reminiscent of Romans 7. Inapplicable to the **just**, its primary purpose is to expose and condemn sin. Paul appends a catalogue of some of the glaring vices prohibited by the Mosaic law. So to preach the law as to make men aware of their sinfulness is to use the law aright: it is a use which accords with **the glorious gospel.** This he claims is no human invention, but the truth divinely **entrusted** to him as an apostle.

ii. Paul's experience of divine grace (1: 12-17)
The mention of the entrustment to him of the message of the gospel gives rise to a paragraph of praise. It commences with the simple—
I thank him (12) and reaches its climax in the noble doxology of v. 17.

Thanksgiving is first for inward strength to discharge the task allotted him. This Paul proceeds to relate to his commissioning by **Christ Jesus our Lord.** It was an appointment based on the divine foreknowledge that he would prove faithful, both as an apostle and a steward of the gospel. This exhibition of God's grace toward him is heightened, as he points out, by the fact that it was displayed to one who previously **blasphemed and persecuted and insulted him.** This spite, vented against the church, was nevertheless directed against the Christ Himself (Ac. 9: 4); even so, he records, **I received mercy.** The word suggests that this sovereign act of pity was utterly undeserved, and the phrase that follows does not negate this. Deeds of ignorance arising from blind unbelief afforded Paul no ground for claiming the mercy of God, but did place him within its range. His ignorance was culpable but not deliberate, and as such it called forth the divine compassion (cf. Lk. 23: 34; Ac. 3: 17). Where mercy is found, grace is not far distant, and here Paul tells of this grace which brought him, through incorporation into Christ Jesus, both faith and love.

The whole experience recalls to Paul's mind a **faithful saying** (15). Five of these occur in the Pastorals (1 Tim. 1: 15; 3: 1; 4: 9; 2 Tim. 2: 11; Tit. 3: 8), the formula not appearing elsewhere in the NT. Epigrammatic in form, these axiomatic truths of the Christian faith would be easily memorized. Being frequently repeated they soon became almost proverbial in the early Church. The saying Paul here quotes presents,

in language matched only by Jn 3: 16, the central fact of the gospel. It is, he emphasizes, **worthy of full acceptance.** He further magnifies the grace of God in declaring that it was lavished upon him, **the foremost of sinners;** a condition he further underlines by the use of the present tense—**I am.** The language appears extravagant, but here is neither rhetorical hyperbole nor sentimental self-depreciation. In deep humility Paul remembers his bitter opposition to Christ and His Church, and conscious of the enormity of his sin describes himself by this phrase (cf. 1 C. 15: 9; Eph. 3: 8). The exercise of mercy towards such an one as himself, Paul sees as a dramatic and convincing example of Christ's **perfect patience.** None need despair, either for themselves or for others. All who **believe in him** (this is an unusual construction conveying the thought of reposing faith in Christ the firm foundation) are brought into the life eternal.

The contemplation of these things calls forth the doxology of v. 17. It is ascribed to **the King of ages,** as the One who, in His sovereignty, is working out His redemptive purposes through all the ages. **Immortal, invisible, the only God:** He is not as man—mortal. He is not even visible to human gaze, neither can He be compared with 'gods many' for He is **the only God.**

iii. The charge reiterated (1: 18-20)
The subject introduced in v. 3 is resumed. Timothy is affectionately addressed as **my son,** and Paul reminds him that the fulfilment of the mandate given him is but the proper outcome of his initial call. The origin of that call is suggested by the phrase **the prophetic utterances which pointed to you** ('led the way to thee', RVmg). This may refer to a spiritual premonition granted to Paul as he approached Lystra on his second missionary journey, that Timothy, converted on an earlier visit, should share with him the burdens of his work for God. This was confirmed by prophetic utterances, possibly by some of Paul's company or, more probably, by the presbyters who, after conference with Paul, shared in Timothy's commissioning (4: 14). The recollection of such a call is calculated to inspire Timothy as he continues to **wage the good warfare.** For this fray it is imperative that he be 'armed with faith and a good conscience' (19 NEB). The emphasis is on the necessity of matching a firm faith with moral integrity (cf. 1: 5; 3: 9). This contrasts with such as Hymenaeus and Alexander, who **rejecting conscience . . . made shipwreck of their faith.** The order is significant. Where a consciousness of sin fails to lead to repentance and forgiveness, it produces an inconsistency in

life which is destructive of faith. Such conduct Paul castigates as blasphemy.

Hymenaeus (2 Tim. 2: 17) and Alexander were blatant examples of those who sought to divorce belief and behaviour. The stern disciplinary action exercised in their case was remedial in intention, as indeed such discipline must ever be. The expression **whom I have delivered unto Satan** might suggest adversities supernaturally inflicted (cf. 1 C. 5: 5; 11: 30; Ac. 5: 1–11), or simply excommunication. The phrase would then describe the removal of the person from the sphere where God rules, to that where Satan has sway.

III. THE CHURCH AT PRAYER (2: 1-15)
i. Subjects for prayer (2: 1-7)
Paul now proceeds to the particular items of the charge which he has just laid upon Timothy. **First of all** stresses the primary importance of public prayer, an importance further emphasized by the use of **I urge,** and also by the mustering of what are virtually synonyms to describe this exercise. It is more likely to be for the purpose of emphasis, than to provide a four-fold classification of prayer. These words do, however, suggest different aspects of prayer. **supplications:** A request arising from specific and urgent need. **Prayers** is a more general term. **Intercessions** combines the thought of a petition offered to a superior with the intimacy of the child/father relationship. It does not necessarily include the representing of the needs of others. **Thanksgivings** find their place here for expressed gratitude must ever be mingled with our prayers.

for all men: Prayer must never be parochial. The sectional interests of the heretical teachers must not be reflected in the prayer-life of the church. Instead, in its universal range will be included all who are in authority (cf. Rom. 13: 1–7; 1 Pet. 2: 13–17). The object stated is that life being lived under settled conditions, Christians shall discharge their daily duties and their Christian service with simple dignity and true piety. The prayer and its fulfilment are linked with the realization of God's gracious purpose in man's salvation (3, 4). This would obviously be furthered through the conduct described in v. 2 and the service listed in v. 7; both being assisted by conditions of peace and security.

V. 4 must not be pressed to support a numerical universalism. The expression **all men** tells us that salvation is for all, even as in v. 1 the phrase indicates that prayer must be made for all, that is, *without distinction*. On God's part is 'desire', on man's 'responsibility', the latter thought being conveyed by the phrase

come to the knowledge of the truth. This divine desire for man's salvation has found concrete expression, and the means for it has been provided as vv. 5 and 6 declare. The universality of the gospel is the concept which underlies these verses. **there is one God and there is one mediator:** Strait is the gate by which all must enter. **a ransom for all:** The work He accomplishes is of infinite value. As a mediator, the Saviour answers the need poignantly expressed in Job's wistful cry for a *daysman that might lay his hand upon us both* (Job 9: 33). The Saviour's incarnation was His qualification for the task—'himself man' (RV). As a ransom (*antilytron*) Christ fulfils the declared purpose of His incarnation—'The Son of man came . . . to give his life a ransom' (*lytron*) (Mt. 20: 28). The addition of the prefix *anti* extends the meaning from 'a price' to 'a corresponding price'. This is further illumined by the use of the preposition *hyper*, the effect of which is to underline the vicarious nature of Christ's sacrifice.

This is the testimony borne by Christ to God's desire that all men be saved, and Paul rejoices in being himself appointed a herald, an apostle and a teacher of this glorious truth.

ii. Engaging in prayer (2: 8-15)
Turning again to the matter of prayer Paul gives direction as to the spiritual qualities to be seen in those who draw near to God. Mention is made first of all of **the men,** as distinct from the women referred to in v. 9. 'Apparently all male members of the church had an equal right to offer prayer, and were expected to use their right' (C. K. Barrett, *The Pastoral Epistles,* p. 54). The prerequisite of holiness is not related to place, for prayer may be made **in every place,** but to the character of the one who prays. The standard of conduct demanded of such is conveyed by the phrase **holy hands,** and the disposition of the heart by a freedom from anger and inward argument (cf. Ps. 24: 3, 4; Jn 4: 21, 23.).

The adverb which introduces v. 9 *hōsautōs* seems somewhat inadequately rendered by the RSV—**also.** By the use of 'similarly' (Kelly) or 'so, too' (Knox) the demeanour of the women, as the integrity of the men (8), is related to the prayer-meeting. The responsibility placed upon women is that they be free from ostentation and display in matters of dress. Instead, those who would be known as Christian women should concentrate upon the apparel of **good deeds** (1 Pet. 3: 3, 4) and in this way 'adorn the doctrine'. But gradually the apostle leaves the subject of prayer to advise concerning the rôle of women in the church in general. The word **silence** (*hēsychia*, 13, 14) can hardly be intended in an absolute sense. In all probability the RV is the more accurate when it renders it 'quietness' (cf. 2 Th. 3: 12, also v. 2 of this chapter where the adjective *hēsychios* is appropriately translated 'quiet'). There is no question here of a ban of silence being imposed upon women, either in public prayer or in the gathering for instruction, where active dialogue would feature prominently. The intention is rather to forbid a self-assertive attitude, and to require that women be marked by restraint and a readiness to display the qualities of 'quietness' and **all submissiveness.**

When, however, it comes to the matter of teaching, Paul's tone becomes more authoritative. In addition to repeating his exhortation regarding 'quietness', he declares categorically, **I permit no woman to teach or to have authority over men.** This prohibition in no way contradicts Tit. 2: 2, 3 (see note). It relates to teaching in the church in the presence of men and to the fact that authority in matters concerning the church is not committed to women. The apostle's argument is founded on the initial relationship of man and woman (13, 14). The reason supplied by v. 13 is similar to that given by Paul in 1 C. 11; 8, in which passage the subject of the relationship of the sexes in the Christian church is developed in greater detail. A further plea for a submissive spirit is based on the fact that the woman in succumbing to deception revealed a tendency which disqualifies for leadership. It was when Eve acted in independence and took the initiative, refusing to remain but a help-meet for Adam, that sin entered.

The meaning of v. 15 has been oft debated. Clearly it suggests to the woman that she is not to think that her contribution is of negligible worth. The realization of her noblest instincts lies in the realm of motherhood (NEB), in which, provided **she continues in faith and love and holiness, with modesty** she will know that salvation which is 'achievement' in its highest sense. Her greatest work will be ever in the home, and her profoundest influence in the moulding of the children she bears. This verse can hardly be interpreted as a mystical allusion to the incarnation which appears to be the nuance of 'the child-bearing' (RV) and especially where Gal. 4: 4 is given as a cross-reference.

IV. RESPONSIBILITY IN THE CHURCH (3: 1–16)

i. The overseer (3: 1–7)

Having enjoined upon Timothy the responsibility of ensuring that the prayer-life of the church is ordered aright and that public worship is conducted with propriety, Paul proceeds to advise him concerning those upon whom responsible office in the church will devolve. Another 'faithful saying' introduces this section, though some early expositors attach it to the statement which precedes it (see NEB footnote).

In the light of the fact that the common, present-day meaning of the word 'bishop' bears no relation to the position Paul envisages when he refers to *episkopoi*, it seems regrettable that not only the RSV but also the majority of other recent translations have adhered to it. The RV mg gives more accurately 'overseer', but even this is not without certain ecclesiastical overtones. The idea underlying the word is that of a guardian, superintendent or leader. Instead of the **office of bishop** a stricter translation might provide us with the expression 'overseership' or with such a phrase as 'spiritual supervision and leadership'. Even so, the interpretation based on the omission of the word **office** should not be so weighted as to imply that it is the task which is all-important, and that formal recognition and acknowledged leadership may be ignored. That such were officially appointed, known, respected and obeyed is clear from such passages as 5: 17; 1 Th. 5: 12, 13; Heb. 13: 17; Ac. 20: 17. Quite obviously Paul is not commending an aspirant guilty of unworthy self-seeking, but rather one who is moved by a true desire for the welfare of God's people. The thought in mind is surely that one who desires to serve in this capacity, sets his heart upon **a noble task.** The responsibility involved is onerous, but its fulfilment highly satisfying.

The rest of the paragraph (vv. 2–7) is concerned with standards of character and conduct which should mark the overseer; any lack of these would disqualify for leadership in the church. It is clear that his life in the church cannot be considered as independent of his personal and domestic life. He must be known to be pure in conduct, disciplined in habits, balanced in outlook, and free from those sins that mark the society and the age in which he lives. It is improbable that Paul had polygamy in mind in using the expression **the husband of one wife.** Perhaps he deemed it advisable to recommend to men responsible for setting an example of strict personal discipline, that they refrain from remarriage on the death of a partner. For today, the phrase might be allowed a wider application, against a precipitate or injudicious remarriage. Further, if the elder enjoys the privilege of parenthood then his home life should have provided him with a training ground for the exercise of that fatherly care which he will be required to show towards the believers. Recent converts are deemed unsuitable for this task; it has its perils for which they would be ill-equipped. His reputation must stand high with outsiders; otherwise he will prove an easy prey to Satan's subtlety. The mention of **reproach** possibly suggests that failure in this respect might occasion slander on the part of the 'slanderer' (RSVmg.) Thus Paul gives a picture of the true leader. These verses must not be turned into a hard, uncompromising list of legal requirements; they are those spiritual and moral standards which God sets before any who would take up service for Him.

ii. The deacon (3: 8-13)

The word *diakonos*, found some thirty times in the NT, is customarily translated either *servant* or *minister*, and denotes one engaged in rendering some particular service. It is used to describe domestic servants, civil rulers, preachers and teachers, and in a general way to denote Christians engaged in work for their Lord or for each other. This has led many to the conclusion that Paul is not alluding to a specific group within the church, but to all who are active in Christian service of one form or another. On the other hand, the fact that the paragraph follows immediately the one relating to overseers certainly implies that the cases are parallel and that these **deacons** have recognized functions. Support for this view might also be adduced from Phil. 1: 1 where Paul sends greetings to 'all the saints in Christ Jesus who are at Philippi, with the bishops and deacons', which, apart from the passage under consideration, is the only place where the RSV translates *diakonos* by 'deacons', though it should be noted that in Rom. 16: 1 Phoebe is described as 'a deaconess of the church at Cenchreae'. Somewhat surprisingly the seven appointed 'to serve tables' (Ac. 6) are not designated by this term.

The very vagueness which obtains in connection with this matter may be taken as indicative of the latitude to be enjoyed, and accorded to others, in the ordering of church life. Whether the deacons be taken as a distinct class upon which devolves the responsibility of attending to those matters, administrative and financial, delegated to them or as those who in a general way serve Christ and His Church, the requirements outlined in these verses are equally apposite. In addition to the demand for moral and spiritual qualities similar to those set down for elders, Paul adds three things: (*a*) the desirability of submitting the deacon to a period of probation (10); (*b*) the need for the women who contribute to the service of the church to measure up to certain standards of character and behaviour (11); (*c*) the beneficial results accruing to the one who faithfully discharges his tasks as a deacon. This anticipates the possibility that some not called to leadership might view the work of a deacon with disdain (13).

iii. Behaviour and belief—purpose in writing (3: 14-16)

Paul having expressed the hope that he might soon visit Timothy, goes on to explain his object in **writing these instructions**. It is that he might provide apostolic guidance for the ordering of their church life. He employs three expressions to describe the church. (*a*) **the household of God** (*oikos*): It is the same word as is used in vv. 4, 5 and 12, and the thought is clearly that of the members of a family group. In this the RSV is more accurate than the AV and RV—*house*. (*b*) **the church of the living God**: If the previous phrase conveys the thought of intimacy, this one emphasizes dignity. Paul might have had in mind the lifeless idol revered at Ephesus in contrast to which the God whose *ecclesia* they are is the living God. The temple devoted to 'Diana of the Ephesians' was renowned for its massive pillars; they as a company of God's people constitute (*c*) **the pillar and bulwark of the truth**: Paul has discharged his responsibility as a custodian of the truth (2 Tim. 1: 12; 4: 7), Timothy must guard it too (6: 20; 2 Tim. 1: 14), but it must also be the task of the whole church. The RSV choice of the word **bulwark** by which to translate *hedraiōma*, is a happy one.

There follows a summary of the truth enshrined in what was undoubtedly part of an ancient Christian hymn. This truth the writer readily concedes is a **mystery,** that is, it was hitherto both unknown and unknowable, but has now been revealed. **Great . . . is the mystery**, it has been suggested, echoes the cry of Ac. 19: 28, 34.

By the pronoun **He** with which the hymn opens, is to be understood, Christ. The Greek reading which underlies the AV translation 'God' is almost certainly wrong. Three couplets of contrasts direct attention to the Saviour. The opening phrase tells of His incarnation. The pre-existent One **was manifested in the flesh** (cf. Jn 1: 14). In apposition to this is the statement—**vindicated in the Spirit.** Spelling the word **Spirit** with a capital letter the RSV denotes the Holy Spirit as the agent of Christ's vindication. If this is the case, then the mind is naturally directed to the climax of this vindicating work, namely the resurrection. If, however, the word should refer to His own human spirit, then we have the thought that throughout His whole career the Saviour knew an inner vindication; that His conscience gave a positive approval of every thought, word and deed. **The flesh**, to be understood here literally, would seem more likely to have in apposition to it the human **spirit**, whereas when used metaphorically, the divine.

The next couplet declares the extent of His renown. It is not easy to know what is intended by the phrase **seen by angels.** If the second line applies to the resurrection, then it would be best to follow a chronological sequence and see this as a reference to the angelic witnesses of His ascension, but it could be interpreted in a much wider sense. It will be remembered that in His birth, temptation, agony in the garden, resurrection and ascension He was 'seen of angels'. There follows the statement that He has been **preached among the nations.** Far beyond the narrow limits of Jewry has Christ been heralded. For Paul the universalism of the gospel had special appeal (cf. 2: 4 f.).

The final lines tell of His acceptance on earth and in heaven. **Believed on in the world** speaks of the triumph of His work in the hearts of men; **taken up in glory,** refers to the enthronement which was heaven's verdict in relation to Him and His accomplished mission.

Viewed entirely, the hymn arches from Bethlehem to the heights of heavenly majesty; the Saviour is seen as the object of angelic contemplation and the subject of apostolic preaching; and He is acclaimed as the One vindicated not only in His spirit, but also in the hearts of all who believe in Him.

V. DANGERS TO THE CHURCH (4: 1-16)
i. The apostasy described (4: 1-5)
As a **bulwark of the truth** the church must be aware of the evils which will array themselves against it. Paul claims that the consistent witness of the Spirit is that the situation will deteriorate. He may have had in mind OT prophecy, the teaching of Christ (*e.g.* Mt. 24: 11), or the illumination granted by the Spirit to NT prophets. By **later times** Paul is possibly referring to that period indicated by the phrase 'after my departure' which he uses in his address to the Ephesian elders (Ac. 20: 29 f.), though the expression could equally well be extended to cover all the succeeding days until the end of the age. The period will be characterized by apostasy. The underlying cause of this is traced to **deceitful spirits.** These contrast strongly with 'the Spirit of truth', the author of that 'sound doctrine' to which frequent reference is made in these letters. They introduce their **doctrines** through men described by Paul as pretentious **liars.** Their **pretensions** may well have consisted in claims to inspiration. **Whose consciences are seared** means either that their consciences have become insensitive, having been cauterized by persistent submission to evil influences, or that they bear the brand-mark of Satanic ownership. The particular form of error into which they lead their dupes is a false

asceticism. Probably it reflects the Gnostic heresy which regarded matter as intrinsically evil, and which found specific expression in recommending avoidance of marriage and abstinence from certain foods. Paul's answer relates particularly to **foods,** but the principles which govern it could easily be applied to the question of marriage. He gives it in three propositions: (*a*) That the divine intention in creation is not to deny these things to man, but to bestow them upon him. They are to be **received with thanksgiving** (3). This is true for all men, but is here applied specifically to **those who believe and know the truth.** (*b*) That everything God has created **is good.** This strikes at the root of the heresy (cf. Mk 7: 19; Ac. 10: 15). (*c*) That things are legitimately enjoyed by the Christian when they are **received with thanksgiving** (4). Guthrie points out that the word *apoblētos* (to be refused) occurs only here in the NT, and that it is used in the sense conveyed by Moffatt's translation: 'nothing is to be "tabooed" provided it is eaten with thanksgiving'. The ability to render sincere thanks to God for the gift received is the determining factor. The phrase **it is consecrated by the word of God and prayer** must not be taken to mean that the food itself is affected, but rather that thanksgiving to God for it, and enjoyment at meal-times of conversation on the Scriptures, imparts a sanctity to the occasion.

ii. Timothy's rôle (4: 6-16)
Having set before Timothy the difficulties likely to be encountered, Paul now advises him regarding his personal life and spiritual responsibilities. He must endeavour to counteract the heresies, but this must be done in a spirit of gentleness and humility. Later, Paul bids him speak with authority (11), but **put these instructions before the brethren** is a phrase which suggests the offering of advice rather than the peremptory laying down of the law.

For himself, it is essential that he should be **nourished on the words of the faith.** Considerable prominence is given in the Pastorals to the Word as God's agent in conversion, and the controlling factor in life and service. Here the use of the present participle reminds Timothy that though he has indeed **followed** them in the past, he needs still to feed his soul constantly upon **the words of the faith and of the sound doctrine.** He must studiously avoid being sidetracked from these centralities. Heretics concentrate on **godless and silly myths** and Paul, recognizing a perennial danger, warns the servant of God lest he become immersed in teachings which, lacking an adequate basis, prove futile in their outworking. Instead, says the apostle, continuing on a positive note, **train**

yourself in godliness. A favourite metaphor is introduced. The rigours of athletic training are contrasted with the self-discipline required of one who makes **godliness** his goal, so is the transient value of **bodily training** with the far more extensive and enduring benefits accruing from godliness. Its effects for good permeate every realm and are experienced both here and hereafter.

Authorities appear to be almost equally divided as to whether the familiar 'faithful saying' formula of v. 9 refers backward to v. 8 or forward to v. 10. One or other must have been in the mind of the apostle, but as it is well-nigh impossible to discern which, it seems not unreasonable to point out that it can be suitably applied to either, and particularly to the climax of each verse.

Once again Paul takes up the metaphor of the preceding section. **Toil and strive** tells of weariness endured and intense effort expended. The secret of perseverance of this tenacious quality is found in a **hope** which is **set on the living God.** He is the Creator and Preserver of **all men,** indeed He provides and offers *life* through His saving work to all. But by **those who believe,** these things are known and experienced in a special way.

The final paragraph of the chapter (11-16) assumes a more personal character. If, in answering the heretics, Timothy must adopt a quiet modest approach, in teaching the truths just enunciated he must **command.** By nature diffident, not overstrong physically, he needs to be encouraged to teach with authority. His comparative youth (probably he was in his late thirties) may lead some to treat him with a measure of suspicion, if not disdain. He must not allow himself to be intimidated. But as C. K. Barrett points out, 'a minister secures respect, not by the arbitrary use of authority but by becoming an example' (*op. cit.*, p. 71). Criticism is adequately silenced only by conduct, and true authority in the spiritual realm springs not merely from advancing years, but from a genuine piety. This must reveal itself in **speech and conduct,** both being governed by 'love, fidelity and purity' (NEB). These are the three great qualities required in the **minister of Christ Jesus.** V. 13 recommends three activities to which Timothy should give himself. The first is **the public reading of Scripture.** This had been an essential part of synagogue worship (Lk. 4: 16; Ac. 13: 15, 27; 15: 21), it was to form an equally important constituent in the worship of Christians. Out of it would flow the **preaching** (*paraklēsis*) and **teaching** (*didaskalia*). The ministry would consist in practical exhortation as well as doctrinal

instruction. For the exercise of these responsibilities due preparation must be made—**attend to,** but for their proper discharge nothing less than a divinely bestowed **gift** would avail. Such a gift Timothy had received. Its reception would ever be linked in his mind with the solemn occasion when the apostle and the elders of his home church had publicly attested their fellowship with him in his going forth with Paul to the work to which God had called him. This step had been the subject of **prophetic utterance** (cf. 1: 18) and it was undoubtedly this that gave them confidence in identifying themselves with Timothy by the laying on of hands. Paul had probably taken the lead in this act (2 Tim. 1: 6). In addition to the action signifying identification, it appears that it was the moment of the impartation of a **gift.** The references to the imposition of hands in the OT, the Gospels and the Acts seem frequently to combine the two ideas of identification and transference, though it need hardly be said that it is nowhere inferred that it lies within human power to *effect* the transference, whether of sins or of blessing. The laying on of hands was accompanied by prayer (Ac. 6: 6; 8: 15 ff.; 13: 3). In this case the blessing sought and subsequently bestowed by God, was a gift adequate to the task requiring to be performed. Reminding Timothy of this event, Paul exhorts him **do not neglect the gift.** It must be developed (cf. 2 Tim. 1: 6), and this will demand that he **practise these duties.** In fact, adds the apostle, **devote yourself to them.** Such concentrated effort will result in an obvious progress. V. 16 is in the nature of a summary. Timothy is reminded that he must keep under careful and constant scrutiny both what he is in himself, and what he teaches. Only thus will God's saving purpose be realized in his own life, and only thus will he bring to the same joy others also.

VI. REGARDING RELATIONSHIPS (5: 1-6: 21)

i. Seniors and juniors (5: 1-2)

In this chapter, the apostle turns to a new theme, that of personal relationships. The opening verses introduce the topic with words of general advice. The recommendations are addressed directly to Timothy, but are of wider application both to his day and ours. The word *presbyteros* is here rightly translated **older man.** Where the necessity of speaking straightly to such arises, care must be taken that there be no lack of courtesy. The **older man** must be treated with the deference accorded **a father.** **Older women** are to be regarded with that respect and affection which a **mother** has the right to expect from her children. With his male contemporaries Timothy is to enjoy that sense of freedom and friendship which exists between brothers. To the recommendation that he should regard the **younger women as sisters**, Paul adds the common-sense caveat that in this there should not be the slightest hint of impropriety.

ii. Widows (5: 3–16)
The plight of the widow in the 1st century can be gauged from the various references to widows in the Gospels and the Acts. By the time this letter was penned the Church had recognized its obligations and relief was being administered (Ac. 6: 1). The need had now arisen, however, to lay down certain principles regulating this whole question of the distribution of the Church's largesse to widows. It seems that certain widows may have been trading on their widowhood. Instead of supporting themselves from their own resources, or looking to their Christian relations for help, they were relying on the church for their support. Guidance is given to Timothy as to the way he should deal with this delicate situation.

First, Paul distinguishes between widows and **real widows** (3, 5). She is in the latter category who is left with no living relatives who can help her, whose faith reposes in God and expresses itself **in supplications and prayers night and day. Honour,** a word which stresses consideration or respect, but may include the thought of support, is to be accorded the one who is a widow 'in the full sense' (NEB); she is to be assisted financially (16).

Where the widow has believing relatives they should feel it incumbent upon them to minister to her need. The primary **religious duty** of a widow's **children or grandchildren** would be to find in this an opportunity of making some recompense to her. The final phrase of v. 4 echoes the fifth commandment. Paul states the truth negatively, and yet more emphatically in v. 8. Failure to make provision for **relatives, and especially for his own family** is equivalent to a denial of **the faith.** Indeed, inasmuch as pagans discharge their duties in this matter, to neglect this basic responsibility is to be **worse than an unbeliever.** A widow, however, may have means of her own. To use these in self-indulgence is to die to true life (v. 6; cf. Rom. 8: 6), and must exclude her from the church's aid. Timothy must give corrective ministry along this line (7).

The same subject continues in the paragraph which follows. Paul here recommends that certain of the widows receiving support be **enrolled** for specific work in the church. It seems clear that even if there was no 'roll'

(NEB) or 'official list' (J. N. D. Kelly) there was proper recognition. It would seem, as already inferred, that this was not a qualification for receiving relief, but was a condition for the discharge of certain tasks. The stipulations are that the widow must be over sixty, must not have remarried, and must have a reputation for **good deeds.** Her good works must have included the bringing up of **children,** for she may be required to act as foster-parent, and hospitality, for she may well be asked to engage in this service for the church. And altogether her life must have been marked by the humility that serves, though the task be menial, and by the devotion which seeks to relieve distress of every kind.

The advice not to **enrol younger widows** (11) suggests that these qualified for assistance, but were not suitable candidates for the recognized ministry accorded the older women. Apparently, the acceptance of a widow for service on behalf of the church implied that she would not remarry. It would be unfair to restrict a younger widow thus. In the early days of her widowhood she might impulsively desire to give herself wholly to Christian work, but in the event of an opportunity of remarrying she might regret the step taken. Then to renounce her 'calling' would be to stand self-condemned, her **first pledge** having been **violated** (12). Another reason is given. The tasks given the widow to perform might carry with them an inherent temptation, especially when it involved visiting other people's homes. This could easily lead to idleness, and produce mischievous results as spiritual conversation degenerated into gossip and as one desiring to help ended by becoming an interfering busybody. The older widow is presumed to have learned sufficient wisdom not to fall a victim to this peril. As for the **younger widows,** Paul recommends that the better course for them would be to remarry, and to take up again the responsibilities of family and home. In this way would the critic, human or Satanic, be silenced. Tragically enough, some of these younger widows had already 'taken the wrong turning and gone to the devil' (15, NEB). These verses should have been noted by subsequent un-Pauline advocates of celibacy. With v. 16 Paul harks back to vv. 4 and 8. The expression **believing woman** in the text, has the greater authority, though the marginal alternatives would seem to make better sense.

iii. Elders, and Timothy himself (5: 17–25)
Having set down the qualifications of the overseer (3: 1–7), Paul now turns to the responsible attitude which should be adopted towards him. He uses the synonymous term **elder,** and

though the word is the same as that translated **older man** in v. 1, it is clear that here it bears its technical meaning. The apostle's first recommendation is that there should be a realistic appreciation of the elder's personal needs. **Double honour** contains the two elements of respect and remuneration. 'That financial, or at any rate material, rewards are primarily intended cannot be evaded' (J. N. D. Kelly). As the assistance given to the widows was dependent on their meeting certain conditions, so those elders deserve not only respect but a suitable remuneration who are engaged in the demanding tasks of leadership (*proistēmi*—'rule', lit. 'to stand before'), **preaching and teaching.** This injunction is underlined by two quotations, one from Dt. 25: 4 and the other from words spoken by the Saviour (Lk. 10: 7). Paul may possibly have learned the latter from Luke himself, who in all probability had by this time completed his Gospel.

Next, the apostle advises Timothy to be wary of listening to **any charge** brought **against an elder,** 'for none are more liable to slanders and calumnies than godly teachers' (Calvin). He must insist on there being present two or three witnesses to corroborate the allegation (cf. Dt. 19: 15). Obviously this would prove an effective deterrent on the irresponsible gossip or the malevolent person. But where the **charge** is proven and the elder remains unrepentant, in that he persists **in sin,** the matter is sufficiently grave to warrant a public rebuke (20). It has been argued that this verse applies not only to elders, but to all who sin. The context would suggest that it is the elder who is in view. The sin of one holding the position of a leader is the more reprehensible, its effects the more serious, and if these effects are to be counteracted, public censure would seem to be the only course.

Timothy is now solemnly counselled to act with complete impartiality in the implementing of **these rules** (21). This will require moral courage and Paul seeks to impart this by expressing himself strongly on this question of being entirely free from biased judgment or prejudiced action.

Another peril of which Timothy is apprised by his mentor, is that of making rash appointments to office within the church. The advice, **do not be hasty in the laying on of hands,** immediately following the counsel regarding elders, suggests that Paul is warning Timothy against impulsively associating those with himself who would subsequently prove unsuitable. **The sins of some men are conspicuous:** He is not likely to be misled by such, **but the sins of others appear later** (24). To have made a wrong choice might mean that Timothy would

find himself involved in a measure of liability for the man's sins. He must exercise the greatest care. In his responsible position at Ephesus he, above others, must **keep** himself **pure.** His own life must be absolutely beyond reproach.

The obligations which have been placed upon Timothy are heavy, they have taken their toll of his health, which, in any case, had never been of the best. Paul inserts some words of kindly advice (23). They provide a salutary reminder that the servant of the Lord does not automatically enjoy a special immunity from common ills, nor can he expect to break the laws governing health with impunity. It is clear, too, that the command **keep yourself pure,** does not depend on a complete teetotalism for its fulfilment. Paul indicates the medicinal value of **a little wine.** Normal means to maintain physical fitness must be taken. Such an 'aside' as this also bears witness to the authenticity of the letter.

The admonition which follows, as already noted, is related to v. 22. Still the thought persists of Timothy's duty in connection with the appointment of elders. It would be inexcusable to incorporate in the leadership of the church one whose **sins** are **conspicuous,** whilst another, **conspicuous** for **good deeds,** would be a natural choice. But great discernment will be required where the true character of the individual is not so obvious. Some will only after a time reveal disqualifying traits. Others, in danger of being turned down, may subsequently show that they possessed in good measure the qualities of a first-class elder. Timothy must beware of making a rapid assessment, and arriving at a superficial judgment. First impressions are not always accurate. Where uncertainty exists caution will clearly be the wisest course. And yet Paul encourages his colleague; **good deeds,** though not always immediately discernible, 'cannot be concealed for ever' (NEB).

iv. Slaves (6: 1-2)

Quite a high proportion of the earliest communities of Christians were slaves. This accounts for the frequent exhortations directed to them in the NT letters. As has frequently been observed, nowhere do these exhortations assume political significance, and yet if fulfilled they must ultimately sound the death knell of this deplorable institution. Here Paul admonishes those slaves who have pagan masters to **regard** them as **worthy of all honour.** Failure to show proper respect would have the effect of bringing the name and truth of God into contempt and ridicule. Should the slave be fortunate enough to have for a master a Christian, he must not take advantage of this situation. The very fact that they are brothers in Christ should call forth increased respect. As far as **service** is concerned, it should be regarded as a privilege, and be in quality **all the better**, since **those who benefit** thereby **are believers and beloved.**

v. False teachers (6: 3-10)
Having been bidden to **teach and urge these duties,** Timothy is now warned of those who will contradict him. Two tests will reveal them as heterodox. (*a*) **the sound words of our Lord Jesus Christ:** It is improbable that this means precise sayings of the Saviour, but rather the healthful words which originate and centre in Christ. (*b*) **the teaching which accords with godliness;** namely the instruction which aims at promoting godliness. The character of these teachers is next exposed. They are to be distinguished by three things, conceit, contention and covetousness. Though he is swollen with **conceit,** such a man is written off with a curt phrase—**he knows nothing.** According to the NEB he is 'a pompous ignoramus'. Contentious, he wrangles over **words.** This arises from **a morbid craving for controversy. Morbid** (*noseō*), 'ailing', contrasts designedly with the **sound** or 'healthful' **words** of v. 3. This spirit of contention produces a host of evil things (4b). Such individuals are **depraved** in moral judgment and are **bereft of the truth.** They have only a commercial interest in the faith, and so add covetousness to their other sins.

This leads to a homily on the Christian's attitude to wealth. Taking up the phrase **godliness is a means of gain** as though it were their slogan, Paul concedes its truth, but only where it is utterly free of covetousness. **Contentment** (*autarkeia*) for the Stoic philosopher carried the sense of an independence of, and indifference to circumstances. For the Christian it bears a deeper meaning, *a satisfaction* with the situation ordained of God. The only other NT occurrence of the word is in 2 C. 9: 8 where the RSV renders it 'enough of everything' (cf. Phil. 4: 10-13). Reasons for contentment follow. The first, in the nature of a proverb (7), is reminiscent of Job 1: 21; Ec. 5: 15, and the parable of Lk. 12: 16-21. It emphasizes the futility of concentrating on that which is of a temporal nature only. Secondly, contentment requires the minimum for its sustenance, only **food and clothing.** Both are the subject of the Saviour's assurances (Mt. 6: 25-33). Thirdly, covetousness has tragic results. A. S. Way translates vv. 9 and 10: 'But they that crave to be rich fall into temptation's snare, and into many witless and baneful desires which whelm men in pits of ruin and destruction; for love of

money is a root whence spring all evils. Some have clutched thereat, have gone astray from the faith, and have impaled themselves on anguish manifold.' He then adds the interesting footnote: 'The metaphor . . . may be taken from the wild beast which, leaping at the bait hung over a pit, falls in, and is impaled on the stake below.' The determination **to be rich,** whatever the excuse offered to the soul, cannot but prove spiritually disastrous, and Paul thinks sadly of **some** who, through the **love of money,** have **wandered away from the faith.**

vi. The 'man of God' (6: 11-16)
The choice of this expression with its reminder of the OT prophet as God's man for the hour, would convey to Timothy both encouragement and challenge. Not content merely to **shun** the evils which Paul has been exposing, he must positively **aim at** those virtues in which the Christian's true wealth consists. It seems probable that with v. 12 Paul takes up again the metaphor from the games (cf. 4: 7-10). The contestant engages in the noble contest and is upheld and impelled by **faith.** To succeed he must **take hold of the eternal life.** Faith translates this future boon into a present blessing, it possesses its possessions. It is to this that Timothy was **called.** The occasion to which v. 12b makes reference has been variously suggested to be his baptism, his setting apart for the work of God, or perhaps his arraignment on some charge. Whichever is correct the appeal is that Timothy should live up to God's calling and his own public **confession.** To be faithful will be costly, and so Paul's appeal assumes the nature of a **charge.** The wording of v. 13 adds to its solemnity, but at the same time ministers encouragement. It is uttered in **the presence of God, and of Christ Jesus,** but it is God **who gives life,** and it is Jesus who did not deviate, for **in his testimony before Pontius Pilate** He **made the good confession,** though fully aware of its inevitable consequences.

There follows the substance of the **charge** (14). **The commandment** might apply specifically to vv. 11 and 12, or more generally to the injunctions laid upon him at his calling and by this letter, but is preferably to be taken in the widest sense as synonymous with 'the faith'. **Unstained and free from reproach** describes the condition in which **the commandment** must be kept, though the adjectives could refer to Timothy himself in the manner and motive of his execution of this duty. And all must be carried out in prospect of **the appearing of our Lord Jesus Christ.** In this reminder is cheer, for it hints at Christ's triumph; challenge is here too, for that day will be one of examination and testing. The thought of this glorious event which **at the proper time, will be made manifest** (cf. Mt. 24: 36; Ac. 1: 7), immediately occasions the most majestic doxology. Its theme is the incomparable glory of God. He is the **only sovereign,** His control over time and affairs is absolute. He is unique in His supremacy, **King** over all **kings, Lord** over all **lords. Alone** in possessing inherent immortality (cf. Jn 5: 26), He is also transcendent in holiness dwelling **in unapproachable light**—'too bright for mortal eye' (C. K. Barrett). To this One, **whom no man has ever seen or can see** (cf. Exod. 33: 17–23; Jn 1: 18) is ascribed **honour and eternal dominion,** a climax well suited to the theme of the doxology.

vii. The wealthy (6: 17–19)

It is as though the writer fears that his strong words regarding wealth in vv. 7–10 might be construed to imply that it is impossible for a man to be a Christian and **rich in this world.** This is automatically corrected by the advice given in these verses. Negatively, they are **not to be haughty,** ever a subtle temptation for the wealthy. Nor must they rely on **uncertain riches** (cf. Prov. 23: 4, 5). Instead, though affluent, they must **set their hopes on the God** who with lavish hand **furnishes us with everything to enjoy.** The contrast with the ascetic's view of God is obvious. Positively, Paul views these riches which could so easily ensnare, as a means of doing **good.** The very possession of wealth will enable them to engage in **good**

deeds, to be **liberal and generous.** With a rapid change of metaphor the apostle pictures this right use of money as treasuring up **a good foundation** for the day to come; thoughts which may well have their origin in the Saviour's Sermon on the Mount teaching. The final phrase of v. 19, which corresponds closely to **take hold of the eternal life** of v. 12, might well express a present blessing enjoyed by those who follow these injunctions.

viii. A final appeal (6: 20–21)

Paul seems almost reluctant to bring the letter to a close. The personal note in his appeal might indicate that he wrote these sentences with his own hand. Timothy is bidden to **guard** what has been **entrusted** to him. The deposit (*parathēkē*) of which he is the custodian is the Christian faith (see also 2 Tim. 1: 12, 14; cf. 2 Tim. 2: 2). In order rightly to execute this trusteeship he will need to **avoid** those teachings which despite the extravagant and arrogant claims made for them are empty and profane. The warning is further emphasized by the sad observation that **by professing** the false teaching **some have missed the mark as regards the faith.**

The letter concludes with a brief benediction which, as the plural pronoun **you** indicates, was addressed not to Timothy alone, but to all in the church at Ephesus and beyond who require divine grace for obedience to the truths declared herein.

THE SECOND LETTER TO TIMOTHY

ANALYSIS

V FINAL INSTRUCTIONS (4: 1-22)
   i A solemn charge (4: 1-5)
   ii Paul's circumstances and prospects (4: 6-18)
   iii Concluding salutations (4: 19-22)

I. GREETING (1: 1-2)

In accordance with the custom of the day, and in common with the majority of NT letters, the letter opens with the name of the writer, that of the recipient, and a greeting. Concerning himself Paul makes reference to his apostleship, for it is the basis of the authority he exercises. He hastens to add, however, that this apostleship is **by the will of God.** He was not self-appointed to this position, nor was he elected to it by others, nor was it his by hereditary right. In addition to looking back to his appointment as an apostle, he also declares the object of it to be **the promise of the life which is in Christ Jesus.**

Timothy is affectionately addressed as **my beloved child.** This arises from the fact that he was brought to faith through Paul's instrumentality; furthermore the years have forged a deep bond of friendship between the two men, which has been further strengthened by extensive fellowship in the work of God. The greeting Paul sends is identical with 1 Tim. 1: 2.

II. ENCOURAGEMENT TO TIMOTHY (1: 5-18)

i. To rekindle the gift (1: 3-7)

It seems likely that age and the knowledge that death cannot be far off combine to evoke in Paul's mind thoughts of the past, though memory, for him, is no mere nostalgic indulgence. It is made the cause for thanksgiving and the occasion of prayer. His own heritage is reason for gratitude to God, and he finds a parallel to it in Timothy's experience. For Paul the past contributed the example of his forebears who served God **with a clear conscience;** for Timothy the background was that of a godly **mother** and **grandmother** in whose lives there shone forth a **sincere faith.** Paul does not despise the religious life of his antecedents. Not as enlightened as he, yet they were true to the light they had, and that light was as the first streaks of dawn heralding the rising sun of righteousness which had now illumined the world. Similarly the **faith** of **Lois** and **Eunice** may initially have been Jewish rather than Christian, but had proved the foundation, for them, as for Timothy later, of that which makes 'wise unto salvation' (3: 15). The constant

prayer for Timothy to which the apostle gives himself, has added fervency as he recollects the **tears** his colleague shed when last they parted. These tears reflect to some degree the more demonstrative and uninhibited emotion of the day. But they also portray a personality, sensitive and affectionate. A reunion with Timothy would bring nothing but joy, and so Paul longs and prays for it **night and day** (cf. 4: 9, 21).

Another memory is of the time when Timothy had been commissioned to the work of God (see note on 1 Tim. 1: 18; 4: 14). It was on that occasion that Paul had publicly indicated his oneness with Timothy in the latter's dedication to the call of God, by the **laying on of . . . hands.** In response to this action God had imparted to Timothy a gift (*charisma*), a spiritual endowment. 'God never commissions anyone to a task without imparting a special gift appropriate to it' (Guthrie). Now he is exhorted to stir it into a flame (RVmg). The basic gift had been bestowed, but it needs to be developed. Indifference or fear might lead to its burning low, and so he is reminded that **God did not give . . . a spirit of timidity.** In these words Paul delicately administers the mildest of reproofs, softened still further by his choice of the plural pronoun **us.** Instead, he continues, the **spirit** is one of **power,** strength to discharge the task allotted; of **love,** without which all service is valueless; and of **self-control,** an essential in all who would influence others for God.

ii. To share in suffering (1: 8-14)

Timidity might easily degenerate into cowardice revealing itself in a reluctance to testify or suffer for the gospel's sake, or to be identified with the imprisoned apostle. The phrase **testifying to our Lord** emphasizes the testimony borne, 'the testimony of our Lord' (RV)—the message itself. To be **ashamed** of the message would lead to a failure in testimony, but he may count ever upon inward strengthening through **the power of God.** In the verses which follow, reasons are given why none need ever feel ashamed of this gospel (9, 10). Paul himself has not done so (11, 12), and Timothy must not (13, 14).

9, 10. Their own experience of the gospel and the power of God had meant salvation (cf.

Rom. 1: 16), a salvation which both delivered them from the past, and introduced them to a new life of holiness, for its calling is **a holy calling.** These are blessings which arise not from **works** of self-effort, but from the gracious **purpose** of God which centred **in Christ** 'before times eternal' (RV, cf. Eph. 1: 4). This purpose of grace, he asserts, has been revealed, and ultimately realized **through the appearing of our Saviour Christ Jesus.** It was through His manifestation (*epiphaneia*) in the incarnation that the work could be wrought which, at once, **abolished death and brought life and immortality to light.** His death has annulled for the believer the power and sting of death (cf. Heb. 2: 14, 15; 1 C. 15: 56, 57), and will finally annihilate it completely (1 C. 15: 26). His resurrection has not only brought from the realm of obscurity the truth of **life and immortality** (cf. the somewhat nebulous ideas found in the OT on this subject), but is itself the ground of admission to this life. Paul's exalted view of the gospel, its origin, outworking and achievements, lends strong support to his plea—**do not be ashamed then of testifying.**

11, 12. He himself has been unashamed of this gospel. For its promulgation he was appointed a **preacher,** to herald it forth, an **apostle,** to declare it authoritatively, a **teacher,** to instruct in its doctrines (see note on 1 Tim. 2: 7). Though this had entailed suffering, there is no sense of regret or repining, but only a joyous confidence in the One whom he has come to know intimately and trust implicitly. **I am sure,** he cries, **that he is able to guard. Until that Day** refers to the day of assessment and reward (cf. 1 C. 3: 13). Support for the alternative renderings **what has been entrusted to me,** and 'what I have entrusted to him' (RSVmg.) is fairly equally divided. The other occurrences of *parathēkē*, in 1 Tim. 6: 20 (see note), and in v. 14 of the present chapter, suggest the former to be the case. Either would be legitimate; taken together they represent both sides of one transaction. The truth and the propagation of it, together with the requisite gift divinely bestowed, comprise what God had entrusted to Paul; for their safe-keeping he entrusts them to God. Paul's exhortation (8) has been reinforced, first by his concept of the gospel, and now by his own example.

13, 14. In declaring the message Timothy must have before him Paul's teaching. He need not repeat it parrot-fashion nor slavishly imitate his mode of presentation, but while expressing it in his own idiom, he must adhere to the content of **sound words** (cf. 4: 3; 1 Tim. 1: 10; 6: 3; Tit. 1: 9; 2: 1). **pattern** (*hypotypōsis*): 'rough draft' (J. N. D. Kelly). This forms the

'deposit' of **truth,** it must be guarded by the power of the indwelling **Holy Spirit.** But its foes are not merely external, for any lack of **faith and love** on his part would leave him open to a charge of hypocrisy. Truth communicated other than in **the faith and love which are in Christ Jesus** remains unacceptable.

iii. To heed examples, bad and good (1: 15-18)

Timothy, in addition to being unashamed **of testifying to our Lord,** must also be unashamed **of me his prisoner.** A spirit of fear is not infrequently manifested in an unwillingness to associate with the people of God, though few of them could be as *persona non grata* as was Paul with the authorities of his day. Two examples are given, the first, of those who failed in this matter. The words **from me** suggest that the defection was from Paul personally, and it would be unfair to imagine a wholesale apostasy. Maybe the apostle's difficulties led him to take the rather sombre view that **all** had acted thus, and he appears particularly upset that **Phygelus and Hermogenes** were among them. Perhaps he had expected better treatment from them.

In contrast he places the loyalty of **Onesiphorus.** Paul and Timothy had probably both benefited from the ministrations of Onesiphorus **at Ephesus** (18b), but it had been one thing for him to assist them there, and wholly another for him to be identified with Paul at Rome. Having no illusion as to the very real danger involved, he yet acted with courage. It appears that it was not without difficulty that he tracked Paul down (17), but he was determined to find him, and having done so he showed himself entirely unashamed of Paul's **chains. He often refreshed me** is the veteran apostle's tribute to this unknown traveller. Present **mercy** upon his family (16), and **mercy** upon Onesiphorus **on that Day** (18, cf. 12) is Paul's ejaculatory prayer-wish. The references to his **household** in v. 16 and 4: 19, and to **mercy . . . on that Day,** have led some to conjecture that Onesiphorus was dead when this letter was written, whilst others have gone to the extent of constructing upon this flimsy foundation arguments for prayers for the dead. But the point is that the memory of his courageous friendship moves Paul still, and provides just the example he needs to illustrate his appeal to Timothy.

III. DIRECTIONS TO TIMOTHY (2: 1-26)
i. A call to endurance (2: 1-13)

With the expression **you then,** the pronoun being emphatic, Paul again addresses his appeal to Timothy. He must **be strong** (cf. 4: 17; 1 Tim. 1: 12) and this will be possible only as he draws upon the source of all inspiration and strength—'the grace of God which is ours in Christ Jesus' (NEB). The immediate duty for which strength is required is that of teaching the truth. Reference to this responsibility runs through the whole chapter, and recurs again and again in the letter. The sacred deposit of truth is only properly guarded when communicated to others. Timothy has Paul's example of this (1: 11-14; 2: 2a) and he in turn must select suitable men to whom the faith can be transmitted, faithful men capable of passing it on to yet others. The **many witnesses** may refer to those present on the occasion of his call (cf. 1: 6 *et alia*), but owing to the length of time which would have been required for full recital of Christian doctrine, it seems more likely that reference is being made to truths in general acceptance by the Church (cf. 3: 14).

Paul returns to his call for endurance, and three illustrations supply challenging standards for those engaged in Christian service. All three are popular metaphors with the apostle, and have appeared together before (1 C. 9: 7, 10, 24). *The soldier.* (*a*) He is willing to endure the rigours of arduous campaigns; v. 3 applies this. (*b*) He recognizes the impossibility of engaging in military service and maintaining a civilian occupation. So must God's servant place priority on his calling, and refuse to allow business or home to become a hampering entanglement. (*c*) His ambition is **to satisfy** his commander. Loyalty and devotion must be pre-eminently to the person of Christ. *The athlete* (5). The contest was subject to stringent rules which governed the training of the athlete as well as his participation in the games. No less must Timothy subject himself to personal disciplines, some of which may be alluded to in vv. 24 and 25, if his efforts are to be rewarded by the heavenly adjudicator. *The farmer* (6). The word **hard-working** (*kopiaō*) describes the **farmer.** For his patient efforts he is ultimately compensated by the joy of benefiting personally from the harvest. This could have an immediate and financial application (cf. 1 C. 9: 11), or a future and spiritual one (cf. 1 Th. 2: 19, 20). Without making too close an application of these matters Paul suggests that Timothy thinks them over, for he is confident that where there is careful meditation upon spiritual truth, there too is known divine illumination (7).

8. Remember Jesus Christ: Here is the great incentive of Christian service, and the central subject of the Christian message. Paul directs attention to two great facts concerning Him. He is the living, victorious Christ, **risen from the dead,** and He remains, what in time He became, the Man Christ Jesus **descended**

from David. The only other occurrence of this phrase in Paul's writings is in Rom. 1: 3. It is possible that in both places he is quoting from a commonly used summary of gospel facts. These truths were certainly central to Paul's preaching and for them he was prepared to suffer. Indeed he was **suffering**, as a fettered **criminal** (*kakourgos*; cf. Lk. 23: 32, 39), incidentally, a description ill-suited to the situation portrayed by the closing chapter of Acts. He rejoices that, whatever his condition, men cannot fetter divine truth, which is always free.

Next, Paul tells of the object which inspires his endurance. No hardship is considered too great when the blessing of those who are the chosen of God is involved. The goal before him is that **the elect** should **obtain the salvation** which belongs to those who are **in Christ Jesus,** a salvation which is itself the promise of **eternal glory.**

The section concludes with a quotation of an early Christian hymn, which Paul introduces with the 'faithful saying' formula. He uses these lines to emphasize still further his call to endurance. This may well have been an extract from a hymn sung at baptismal services, and if so it would remind Timothy of those basic principles of Christian life and service which the rite signifies. Behind v. 11 lies the teaching of Rom. 6; with v. 12a cf. Rom. 8: 17; and with v. 12b cf. Mt. 10: 33. The final line, possibly added by Paul, assures that **if we are faithless, he remains faithful** (cf. Rom. 3: 3). No action of His will ever conflict with His character, for **he cannot deny himself.**

ii. A call to concentration on essentials (2: 14-26)
Timothy must constantly set these truths before the believers at Ephesus, and at the same time **solemnly charge** them to **avoid disputing** over matters of little or no consequence. The danger was that the consideration of basic doctrine (*e.g.* vv. 8, 11-13, 19) might be replaced by **words** (14), **godless chatter** (16) and **talk** (17). This sort of thing says Paul, **does no good** in that it provides no food for the soul; instead it only **ruins the hearers,** for it unsettles and turns men away from the truth. Further, it results in progress in the wrong direction—**unto more and more ungodliness** (16). The persistent discussion of non-essentials is likened to a gangrenous condition where increasing areas of otherwise healthy tissue are insidiously eaten away. **Hymenaeus** (see note on 1 Tim. 1: 20) **and Philetus** are cited as glaring examples. In their philosophical disputings they had missed the way on a fundamental matter, **holding that the resurrection is past already,** and this in turn had the effect

of **upsetting the faith of some** (cf. 1 C. 15).

The situation was serious, and so in the centre of his description of this state of affairs Paul inserts positive advice to Timothy (15). A personal responsibility to **do your best to present yourself to God as one approved** is laid upon him. He must be determined to enjoy a constant sense of divine acceptance, both of himself and of his work. In particular, he must know this in his handling of **the word of truth.** The AV translation of this phrase has been used to warrant a treatment of Scripture quite other than that which Paul intended. The picture in his mind might have been a straight-cut furrow or road, or possibly a stone-mason achieving a perfect symmetry in his work. Both may lie behind this appeal for a straightforward, balanced exegesis of holy Scripture. This is the only answer to the empty and impious talk here condemned, and is the sole corrective to those heretical beliefs to which such talk leads.

Faced with these difficulties Timothy is given an encouraging reminder that **God's firm foundation stands.** The foundation can be read as the unassailable truth, or the work of God in the souls of genuine believers—members of that Church against which the powers of death shall not prevail (Mt. 16: 18). Paul wants Timothy to remember the twofold truth which stands as a permanent inscription upon this foundation. It tells that God alone possesses infallible discernment when it comes to knowing **who are his,** and that he who claims to be Christ's must give evidence of it by departing 'from unrighteousness' (RV). The story of Korah clearly lies behind these quotations, although the parallels between that mutiny and the heretical activity of Hymenaeus and Philetus must not be pressed too far. The first inscription is a direct quotation of Num. 16: 5. The second is a typical Pauline loose rendering. Here he changes the emphasis from separation from the wicked (Num. 16: 26) to 'forsake wickedness' (NEB).

The illustration that follows contains this thought of separation from evil. It is akin to 1 C. 3: 10-15 and, as there, the thought is that of personal responsibility. Paul is still concerned that Timothy shall be **approved, a workman** unashamed. That departure 'from unrighteousness', rather than separation from individuals, is Paul's intended meaning is plain, because vessels could hardly 'purge' themselves from other vessels, and in any case all vessels prove useful in the house, even though some are for less noble purposes. God's servant must follow such advice as is contained in vv. 22-24 and in this way purify himself so that he becomes **a vessel . . . consecrated,** set apart as **useful to the**

master of the house, ever **ready for any good work.** To equate the **great house** with 'christendom' is entirely arbitrary and wholly fails to regard the personal nature of the exhortation.

From illustration Paul turns to precise instruction. Negatively, Timothy must **shun youthful passions.** Included in these will be not only sensual desire, but proneness to intolerance, arrogance and so on, the very antitheses of the qualities Paul proceeds to recommend. To **righteousness, faith and love** (cf. 1 Tim. 6: 11) Timothy must add **peace,** and all these virtues are to be known and enjoyed in the company of true fellow-Christians. Again the apostle counsels him not to be drawn into pointless debates which only result in **quarrels.** Instead of being **quarrelsome** the **Lord's servant** must be **kindly to everyone**: the picture presented bears a striking resemblance to that portrayed by Isaiah in the Servant passages. As a teacher he must be **apt** (cf. 1 Tim. 3: 2), **forbearing,** that is showing tolerance and patience with the difficult, and where these become **opponents** he must correct them, though always in a spirit of **gentleness.** At the same time he will remember that greater forces are at work. **The devil** setting his **snare** intends to capture men for his fell designs, but God is working too. Through His servants He calls men to repentance and 'the acknowledging of the truth' (AV). This is the true knowledge (cf. 1 Tim. 2: 4; 2 Tim. 3: 7; Tit. 1: 1). It is extremely difficult to decide on the persons indicated by the two pronouns in the phrase **by him to do his will.** Above, they have both been made to apply to the devil. The alternative interpretation (RSVmg) is that those ensnared by the devil, exchange that state for a new captivity 'to the will of God', to which blessed servitude they are led 'by the Lord's servant' (see RV).

IV. THE LAST DAYS (3: 1-17)
i. Their characteristics (3: 1-9)
In proceeding to describe the conditions which will obtain in the world of **the last days** (cf. 1 Tim. 4: 1) the writer obviously has in mind the days which will end this present era, days immediately preceding the second advent of Christ. In a broader sense Peter, quoting Joel's prophecy, could announce at Pentecost that 'the last days' had begun (Ac. 2: 17). The features here depicted can be said then, to apply not only to 'the final age of this world' (NEB) but to Paul's day, to Timothy's and to every succeeding period of the Church's history (cf. 1 Jn 2: 18). The expression **times of stress** contains within it the thought 'of threat, of

menace, of danger' (Wm. Barclay, *The Daily Study Bible*, p. 209). The nature of the evils catalogued are certainly those which would produce such conditions for the Christian. They are **times of stress** inasmuch as their influence is adverse to spiritual life and occasion innumerable dangers for the child of God. The life of the ungodly is frequently corrupt, and the pressures exerted upon the believer are as a floodtide which runs strongly against him. There follows in vv. 2-5 a list of vices which constitutes a frightful picture of a world which has turned its back upon God. In a sense the first two, **lovers of self** and **lovers of money,** are the parent sins from which all the rest of the wretched brood are begotten. The first, the most 'natural' of sins, when persisted in and linked to the second, banishes God from the life. Where 'me and mine' is the principle which obtains, there remains little to restrain the evils here 'set out in a ghastly series' (Wm. Barclay, *op. cit.*, p. 211). The description is sufficiently plain not to require amplification. It culminates in a warning that these things may be found in the orthodox, religious person—**holding the form of religion but denying the power of it** (5). Where religious life consists in externals only, knowing no spiritual dynamic, the door is wide open to the entrance of such sins as these. The plain advice Paul gives to Timothy is condensed in the brief warning—**avoid such people.**

The apostle next envisages a situation which might easily arise. Not being allowed in the church, some of those already described, anxious to peddle their false religious wares, 'insinuate themselves into private houses' (NEB). Once in, they try to exert an influence on impressionable women, particularly by playing on their sensitive awareness of sin and spiritual shortcoming. The promises they hold out of a deeper **knowledge of the truth** beguile their dupes, who instead of realizing this knowledge, come ever more and more under the sway of these unscrupulous men (cf. Tit. 1: 11).

A historical analogy is found in the story of the Egyptian magicians who **opposed Moses.** No direct reference to these individuals is found in Scripture, though ancient Jewish legends, well known to Timothy, surrounded the events described in Exod. 7: 8-12. The parallel is not pressed, though it provides a useful illustration. They are **men of corrupt mind and counterfeit faith.** Their understanding is warped, and in consequence, the faith they hold is false. As Pharaoh's magicians were exposed to public ridicule, so these teachers must soon be revealed as impostors, their career will be short-lived (see *art.* 'Jannes and Jambres', *NBD*).

ii. The safeguards (3: 10-17)

It seems from the emphatic **now you** that it is with a measure of relief that Paul turns from this gloomy recital to address himself to his friend. Once again Timothy is reminded of that life and career to which he is no stranger. It provides an obvious example for him to copy. Paul first lists the principles which have governed his life (10). He has given himself to **teaching.** The apostle's clear setting-forth of Christian doctrine constituted his chief contribution to the life of the Church. **My conduct,** he claims, without immodesty, has testified to the truth taught. **My aim in life** will remind of that sense of purpose which dominated Paul's whole life. The heavenly vision had never been forgotten or disobeyed. **Faith, patience, steadfastness** continue to delineate the character which is set before Timothy as a model. As a craftsman demonstrates the perfect technique to his apprentice, and bids him observe and imitate, and yet is never thought guilty of egotism, so is Paul free from all trace of this fault as he reminds Timothy of these essentials.

The list of qualities in v. 10 continues in v. 11 with **persecutions and sufferings,** and in one sense these can be regarded as just as much the result of personal purpose as the rest. The example he has given consists in his determination to continue his work for God despite the afflictions which this must inevitably bring. Paul selects for mention those occasions which occurred immediately prior to Timothy's conversion, and which probably profoundly influenced him at the time. Paul rejoices to add **yet from them all the Lord rescued me.** On the one hand he encourages Timothy with this word, and on the other proceeds to warn him that every one who is determined **to live a godly life** must anticipate persecution (cf. Ac. 14: 22; 1 Th. 3: 4). This will be so because **evil men and impostors** (cf. v. 8) **will go on from bad to worse,** the whole situation deteriorating as men are carried along, and carry others along in a progressive course of deception.

The safeguard for the servant of God is to adhere staunchly to the truth imparted by trustworthy friends and founded upon the Scriptures. The opening words of v. 14 pair up with those of v. 10 and Paul now calls upon Timothy to **continue** ('abide', RV) **in what you have learned and have firmly believed.** Convictions must not be lightly jettisoned, for two reasons. First, because of the persons who taught him these truths; were they not reliable guides, people of spiritual stature and holy living? The appeal is probably primarily to Lois, Eunice and Paul himself; he would be ill-advised to forsake such mentors to follow the latest religious quack. Secondly, because such truths rest squarely upon the solid foundation of the Scriptures. From his earliest years Timothy has been **acquainted with the sacred writings** (15). Lois and Eunice had attended to that. These Scriptures, says Paul, are the source of all spiritual intelligence, and lead to **salvation** as **Christ Jesus,** the subject of them, is received by **faith.** The oblique reminder of his personal experience is intended to stimulate Timothy's confidence in the trust-worthiness of the Scriptural message.

The section concludes with a statement concerning the nature and value of the Scriptures. The apostle is concerned alone with the OT, but the principle he enunciates has its obvious application to the whole of Holy Writ. Considerable debate has centred around the opening phrase of v. 16, whether it should be rendered **All scripture is inspired by God** or 'Every inspired scripture has its use' (NEB, similarly RSVmg and RV). The difficulty arises from the absence of 'is' in the Greek text. If the word **scripture** is given its more restricted sense of Holy Scripture, which is the general meaning accorded it in the NT and that which fits well the preceding verses, then the first alone adequately expresses the truth. If *graphē* is taken to mean writings in general, then not only is the wording of the second translation accurate but necessary, and given this meaning the first would be palpably false. Space forbids extensive examination of this exegetical problem. The matter is carefully weighed by J. N. D. Kelly, D. Guthrie and others in their commentaries; cf. also B. B. Warfield, *Biblical Foundations* (Tyndale Press), chap. 2. As for the expression **inspired by God** (*theopneustos*, lit. 'God-breathed') the thought conveyed is that the writings under consideration are 'the product of the creative breath of God' (see *art.* 'Inspiration', *ISBE*).

The point Paul appears to be making is that Timothy, confident of Scripture's inspired nature, can rely upon it to be **profitable.** This profit lies first in the fact that it is the source of **teaching** ('doctrine', AV). It is the basis and test of true Christian belief. **For reproof** suggests that it not only points out error, but is also the agent to be used in refuting it. Following refutation, comes the necessity for indicating the right path—**for correction.** Moreover, it is able also to hold a man steady in this path—**training in righteousness.** The end product is **that the man of God** (cf. 1 Tim. 6: 11) **may be complete** ('efficient', NEB), adequate to the task, and **equipped for every good work,** equal to any opportunity which may arise for engaging in good works.

V. FINAL INSTRUCTIONS (4: 1–22)
i. A solemn charge (4: 1–5)
Paul has some final words of exhortation to give to Timothy. The very fact that they are addressed by one anticipating martyrdom to a younger colleague upon whom heavy responsibilities will soon devolve gives them an air of gravity. Their solemnity is further stressed by the manner of their introduction—**I charge you** (*diamartyromai*, cf. 1 Tim. 5: 21). It is not an expression Paul takes lightly upon his lips, he utters it **in the presence of God and Christ Jesus.** He speaks as one answerable for his words, and makes reference to the judgment. Timothy, too, must recognize that they are commands made with heaven's authority, and that an account will be required of him by **Christ Jesus who is to judge the living and the dead** as to his discharging of these obligations. Paul still further strengthens his appeal by reminding Timothy of the Saviour's **appearing, and his kingdom** which it will consummate. Life must be lived and service rendered in the prospect of these glorious events.

Of the fivefold duty which is Timothy's, conveyed to him in crisp imperatives, **preach** or herald **the word** is basic. So essential is this that he must regard no occasion as inopportune. He must adopt a varied approach—**convince, rebuke, exhort;** thus, as has frequently been suggested, addressing himself to reason, conscience and will. Men might be slow to learn, provocative in their refusal of the message; he must be **unfailing in patience,** nor must his preaching be divorced from **teaching.**

The situation envisaged by the apostle (3, 4) makes fulfilment of these directions doubly important. **Sound teaching** will be rejected, its demands being too great. Instead, **people, having itching ears,** desiring merely to be entertained, **will accumulate for themselves teachers** who will tell them only what they want to hear. **The truth** will still be taught, but they will **turn away from listening to it,** preferring to **wander into myths** (cf. 1 Tim. 1: 4; 4: 7; Tit. 1: 4).

Returning to Timothy (5a; cf. 3: 10, 14), Paul bids him not to be carried away by this state of affairs; rather he must stand his ground, willing to suffer if needs be. His responsibility is to **do the work of an evangelist.** Whilst the wording may imply that **evangelist** is not being used of the specific gift as listed in Eph. 4: 11 yet the exhortation consists in more than the duty resting upon every Christian to spread the gospel. A brief but comprehensive command, **fulfil your ministry,** concludes the paragraph.

ii. Paul's circumstances and prospects (4: 6–18)

Again, Paul's appeal to Timothy is reinforced by his example, but here the gravity of his position, vividly depicted, gives it increased point and power. Morbid thoughts or distressing fears are entirely absent as Paul confidently speaks of his death using imagery both glad and triumphant. Of the phrases chosen to describe the death which is regarded as imminent, the first is a drink-offering (cf. Phil. 2: 17). He states that his life is about to be poured out as a libation on an altar of sacrifice. The second, **the time of my departure,** is not unrelated to the picture of a ship about to weigh anchor, or a soldier preparing to strike camp (cf. Phil. 1: 23).

Reviewing his life for God the apostle can claim to have fulfilled his ministry. **The good fight** is frequently thought to represent the wrestling match, with **the race** continuing the metaphor of the athletic contest. **I have kept the faith** may well correspond to the earlier references to guarding the deposit (cf. 1 Tim. 6: 20; 2 Tim. 1: 12, 14). The perfect tense used in each case carries the sense of completion. For Paul, the end of life brings a quiet confidence that with the long struggle over, the course stayed to the end, the stewardship worthily discharged, **there is laid up . . . a crown of righteousness.**

'Tis no poor withering wreath of earth,
Man's prize in mortal strife,

but **a crown of righteousness.** The crown can hardly describe a reward consisting of righteousness inasmuch as righteousness is granted in response to faith alone, although the expression could mean the crown which is the reward of righteousness. Maybe, in view is a righteous crown, namely a reward consistent and just. It is more probable that the expression **a crown of righteousness** describes the anticipated righteousness, once imputed, soon to be known in reality. It will be received from **the Lord, the righteous judge.** No justice can be hoped for from his earthly judge; but on **that Day** of final assessment at Christ's appearing, says Paul, I shall not be alone in receiving a reward. **A crown** will be the lot of all whose lives have been controlled by the prospect of **his appearing** (cf. v. 1).

With v. 9 the apostle turns to personal requests. Earlier in the letter (1: 4) he had expressed his longing to see Timothy again, and now this is crystallized into a specific and urgent request, one which is repeated in v. 21. Much of what Paul has written was obviously put in writing in case his death should intervene before Timothy could complete the journey to Rome, but it does not make the visit unnecessary. Paul is lonely. Several factors have contributed to his solitariness. **Demas . . . deserted me:** Though previously a 'fellow-worker' (Col. 4: 14; Phm. 24) Demas had found the pull of **this present world** too great, especially when compared with the dangers and privations of life with Paul. The use in v. 10 as in v. 8 of the verb **love** suggests a deliberate contrast between Demas and all who love His appearing, and between this present age (RVmg) and the day of His appearing. Without reading too much into this act of Demas, it is clear that Paul felt his defection keenly. **Crescens** and **Titus** Paul has, in all probability, selflessly dispatched on missionary work, the former **to Galatia,** sometimes considered Gaul, and the latter **to Dalmatia.** As a result **Luke alone is with me** (11). The last of the band of faithful men who had accompanied Paul on his extensive journeys, he still loyally ministers to the aged apostle. **Mark** had 'made good' (Col. 4: 10), and Paul besides refusing to hold past failure against him, magnanimously writes of him as **very useful in serving me** and requests Timothy to 'pick up Mark and bring him with you' (NEB). Continuing the names of those dispatched elsewhere, Paul says that **Tychicus,** a trustworthy companion, and a frequent bearer of letters, has been **sent to Ephesus.** He could possibly have been the carrier of the present letter (*apesteila* being an epistolary aorist), as well as the person intended to relieve Timothy from his post for his visit to Rome. Lonely, and in prison, with winter drawing on (cf. v. 21), Paul remembers **the cloak,** a large, heavy cape-like garment which had been **left with Carpus at Troas** (13). He probably feels the need also of the mental and spiritual stimulus that **the books** and **the parchments** would provide. These personal requests attest the authenticity of the letter, and many critics of Pauline authorship, outstanding among them P. N. Harrison, have felt it necessary to ascribe them to fragments of genuine material incorporated by an unknown writer. The possibility of the survival of such a fragment, and the decision to incorporate it, would seem highly unlikely.

Rapidly moving from one matter to the next, Paul warns Timothy of **Alexander the coppersmith** (14). Either at his trial as a prosecution witness, or on some earlier occasion as one who had opposed the truth Paul proclaimed, Alexander had done the apostle **great harm.** Not personally vindictive, Paul leaves it to **the Lord** to **requite him** (Ps. 62: 12; cf. Rom. 12: 19), but promptly adds a common-sense warning to Timothy to keep out of his way. It is not possible to identify this Alexander with either of the men of that name referred to in Ac. 19: 33, 34 and 1 Tim. 1: 20, though interesting theories have been constructed by various commentators.

My first defence has been regarded by some as descriptive of an earlier trial. This enables the central phrases of v. 17 to be interpreted as referring to further missionary activity. It seems far more likely, however, that the 'first defence' relates to the preliminary hearing with which Paul's trial had opened. **No one** had come forward on this occasion to take his **part.** Disappointment but not bitterness is discernible as he recalls the experience. Reminiscent of Christ's prayer (Lk. 23: 34) and Stephen's (Ac. 7: 60) are Paul's words—**may it not be charged against them.** Their failure throws into relief the divine loyalty exultantly conveyed in the words, **But the Lord stood by me.** This had resulted in an inner strengthening, so that the occasion proved an opportunity to proclaim the word fully. It seems as if Paul looked back on this experience as the climax of his public heralding of the gospel, and if the terms in which he describes it are somewhat extravagant, this is understandable if they in fact refer 'to witness borne when on trial before the ruler of the whole pagan world' (C. K. Barrett). The reference to being **rescued from the lion's**

mouth describes Paul's delight at the favourable outcome of the preliminary hearing of his case. He is aware, however, that martyrdom is not far away (6–8), and so in v. 18 his thoughts turn to spiritual preservation and to the **heavenly kingdom.** He asserts his confidence in the Lord, and breaks into a doxology ascribing to Christ **glory for ever and ever.**

iii. Concluding salutations (4: 19–22)
Paul adds greetings to his friends and staunch associates **Prisca and Aquila,** and to **the household of Onesiphorus** (see note on 1: 16, 18). Timothy is informed of the fact that **Erastus,** a mutual friend, **remained at Corinth,** and that the illness of **Trophimus** had necessitated his being **left** behind **at Miletus.** (This interestingly enough, happened despite the presence of a doctor and an apostle in the company!) But it all adds up to loneliness for Paul, and so he repeats his request, 'Do try to get here before winter' (NEB), the added reference to approaching winter making his plea yet more urgent.

Paul conveys a few further personal greetings in which **all the brethren** join, and then concludes with a prayer for Timothy, **The Lord be with your spirit.** The latter part of the benediction is identical with the one which ends the first letter, the plural pronoun being used there also. It may be appropriated by all who read the letter—**Grace be with you.**

THE LETTER TO TITUS

ANALYSIS

I GREETINGS (1: 1–4)

II ELDERS (1: 5–16)
   i Their appointment, qualifications and responsibilities (1: 5–9)
   ii Their call to check false teaching (1: 10–16)

III CHRISTIAN BEHAVIOUR (2: 1–3: 11)
   i Sundry groups (2: 1–10)
   ii An appeal to the grace of God (2: 11–15)
   iii In society (3: 1–2)
   iv A further appeal to the grace of God (3: 3–7)
   v Final advice (3: 8–11)

IV PERSONAL MESSAGES AND GREETINGS (3: 12–15)

I. GREETING (1: 1–4)
Introduced among the many practical matters with which the writer deals in this letter are three short, but most valuable doctrinal statements. They happen to fall one in each chapter, the first being combined with the opening salutation.

Paul's designation of himself—**a servant of God** is unique, though he does refer to himself elsewhere as the 'bondslave of Jesus Christ'. A freeman, and proud of it, he nevertheless glories in his bondage to his heavenly Master. Again, he makes mention of his apostleship.

The phrase 'according to' (AV and RV) has occasioned some difficulty. It is probably intended to convey the thought—'in the interests of', 'to promote' or 'to secure', in which case it is aptly translated by the RSV as **to further.** The object before him is described, therefore, as the promotion of **the faith of God's elect** and may cover both the bringing to faith of those chosen of God, and the development of faith in those already His people. It also includes the leading of these to a recognition and apprehension of **the truth.** This knowledge, related to and producing piety, stands in marked contrast to v. 16. The ultimate goal for them and for him, is the **hope of eternal life.** This undoubtedly acts as a powerful incentive in his work, for it is a hope not vague or uncertain, but firmly grounded in the abiding purposes of the **God who never lies.** An antithesis to the lying Cretans is possibly intended (12).

The message which Paul bears had its origin 'before times eternal' (RV), but was declared **at the proper time,** in the incarnation and the divine self-revelation which was then introduced. The truth was unveiled, and its declaration was entrusted to the apostle. In each of the Pastorals he rejoices in this privilege (1 Tim. 1: 11; 2 Tim. 1: 11), and here he ascribes it, as in 1 Tim. 1: 1, to the direct **command of God.**

The opening paragraph forms, then, no mere apostolic salutation, but a majestic survey of the great purpose which spans the ages, which Paul as **a servant of God and an apostle of Jesus Christ** was called to advance.

The address to Titus in v. 4 tells that he had been brought to faith through Paul (cf. 1 Tim. 1: 2). It might also imply that he was displaying those spiritual traits which mark him as a true successor of the apostle. The several references to Titus in 2 Corinthians portray him as indeed a **true child in a common faith.** The RSV, in common with the RV, rightly omits 'mercy' from the prayer Paul utters for his colleague. The change from the title 'Christ Jesus our Lord' which occurs in parallel passages elsewhere, to **Christ Jesus our Saviour,** accords with the emphasis this letter places upon God's Saviourhood. Used of the Father and the Son, the expression may have been chosen with the intention of encouraging Titus as he faces an extraordinarily difficult situation in Crete.

II. ELDERS (1: 5-16)
i. Their appointment, qualifications and responsibilities (1: 5-9)
The impression created by the phrase **I left you in Crete** is that Paul and Titus had been labouring together on the island when the apostle felt it necessary to press on with his journeys. It is impossible to fit this into the brief call at Crete reported in Ac. 27: 7, 8, so it is assumed that this visit was made after release from the first Roman imprisonment (see Introd., p. 504). Affairs in the churches in Crete were far from satisfactory, but Paul could stay no longer. He gave Titus advice with regard to the ordering of church life, and, having left him, now writes to confirm his oral instructions and to provide Titus with an authoritative word for the execution of these duties. Churches without properly appointed **elders,** Paul regards as **defective.** Two things, however, should be observed: (a) that elders are not necessary for the *existence* of churches, and (b) that in keeping with advice he had given elsewhere (1 Tim. 3: 6; 5: 22) Paul refrained from acting prematurely in making appointments. Titus must now select and **appoint elders in every town.** The apostle specifies the need for a plurality of elders, and the definite appointment of them. He then proceeds to list the qualities required (see notes on 1 Tim. 3: 2-7). In his family-life the elder must show loyalty to his wife, and exercise spiritual discipline over his children. 'Faithful children' (AV, cf. similar idiom 1 C. 4: 17) may well represent the text with greater accuracy than the more restricted term **believers.** In this realm he must be **blameless,** as also in the church where, as a **bishop** (RVmg 'overseer'), he bears the responsibility of being **God's steward.** The five negative requirements which follow (7), list the faults which might easily have persisted in the Cretan Christians who, as yet, had not overcome the temperamental weaknesses of their race, a danger which exists in every age. Paul continues in v. 8 to enumerate the qualities which should have replaced the vices just listed. He specifies also, that the overseer **must hold firm to the sure word,** and in this insists that he is required to have not only a tenacious grip of the faith, but also a firm adherence to it in conduct. This equips and qualifies him to instruct in **sound teaching** (see note on 1 Tim. 1: 10), and also to deal with **those who contradict it.**

ii. Their call to check false teaching (1: 10-16)
The necessity for the high standards demanded of elders is now seen in proper perspective as Paul describes the characters, activities and teachings of those who oppose the work of God (10-16). In the main these opponents appear to be church members, for Titus is required to silence them (11), and Paul expresses the hope that being rebuked **sharply, they may be sound in the faith** (13). Behind them, however,

were teachers propagating **Jewish myths, men who reject the truth** (14). The members of the former group who are described as **insubordinate,** flout the authority of God's word and His appointed teachers. They talk freely but to no profit (cf. 1 Tim. 1: 6; 2 Tim. 2: 16) for they are **deceivers.** Jewish Christians form the more active section of these dissidents, perhaps because their national heritage produced in them a sense of superiority, or because of the freedom they had learnt in the synagogue in such matters. It is probable that the technique of these men was akin to that described in 2 Tim. 3: 6, that is, the private circulation of heresy. Certainly the disruptive effect of their teaching was particularly apparent amongst Christian families. Detecting that they subordinate truth to finance, Paul castigates their motives as mercenary and writes off their message as **what they have no right to teach.** He goes on to add that being Cretans they are but revealing national characteristics. In order to describe these, Paul tactfully quotes **a prophet of their own.** These lines, attributed to Epimenides (in a context from which another quotation is taken in Ac. 17: 28a), express a verdict with which Paul fully concurs. His statement implies an opinion based on a personal, and not too happy, experience. The purpose of the treatment of these men which the apostle now recommends, is a positive one, namely their recovery to spiritual health.

The dual source of the false teaching is said to be **Jewish myths** (cf. 1 Tim. 1: 4), and **commands of men** (cf. Col. 2: 21, 22). It was probably this amalgam of Jewish regulations and Gnostic asceticism that led Paul to quote the principle enunciated by Jesus (15a, cf. Lk. 11: 41). The inference here is that moral purity is unaffected by questions of ceremonial. J. N. D. Kelly makes the valuable observation that 'when modern people quote the apothegm, they usually take the word exclusively in the moral sense and deduce that the man who is himself pure need not fear contamination by anything impure. This is a dangerous half-truth, and far from Paul's meaning'. From this point Paul proceeds in phrases of strong condemnation to describe those responsible for these heresies. **Nothing is pure** for them, for the springs of thought and action are **corrupted.** They are **corrupt** in life, because **unbelieving** in heart. Their pretentious claim to **know God,** an expression which implies a semi-Jewish, semi-Gnostic origin, lacks any foundation for **they deny him by their deeds.** Paul rounds off his description of them with three stinging epithets, **detestable, disobedient,** useless **(unfit for any good deed,** cf. 2 Tim. 2: 21; 3: 17).

III. CHRISTIAN BEHAVIOUR (2: 1–3: 11)
i. Sundry groups (2: 1–10)
Cretans may be **liars,** and some of the believers **empty talkers, but as for you,** writes Paul to Titus, **teach what befits sound doctrine.** The **doctrine** must be **sound;** this is a recurring demand in the Pastorals (*e.g.* 1: 9; 1 Tim. 1: 10), but the emphasis that Paul makes here is that Titus should instruct them in the behaviour which accords with belief. Paul recommends that in doing this Titus should address himself separately to various groups.

Older men (2) because of the maturity expected of them, should be marked by restraint, seriousness of outlook and self-control. **Sensible** (*sōphrōn*) occurs in 1: 8 regarding the overseer— **master of himself,** and this quality is also demanded of three of the groups which follow, and of all in v. 12. The prominence of this requirement in this letter, and in those to Timothy (1 Tim. 2: 9, 15; 3: 2; 2 Tim. 1: 7), indicates the importance which the apostle attached to it. It is the 'sober-minded' (vv. 2, 5, 6, RV) who **control themselves** (6), so that with thoughts and passions held in check their resultant conduct is **sensible** (2, 5). To these general virtues, Paul adds the Christian qualities of **faith, love** and **steadfastness,** and these should not have degenerated with the passing years, but be **sound** still. **Steadfastness** is not so much a replacement for 'hope' in the triad, but is that aspect of hope required of the elderly.

Older women (3) are to be **reverent** in deportment, not only in the church, but generally; their behaviour revealing that they regard every part of life as holy. The negative commands may imply a connection between the devastating sin of slander and the tongue-loosening effect of **drink.** Thoughtless gossip indulged in on social occasions remains a prevalent evil. The danger should be overcome by occupation with private instruction in **what is good** and by the recognition of their duty to **train the young women** both by word and example.

Young women (4, 5), in character, must be **sensible** (see note on v. 2) and **chaste.** Paul's main recommendations for them relate to their home responsibilities. They are to be devoted to **their husbands and children,** to be **domestic** in that they recognize the home as their main sphere, and **kind.** Granted a new dignity by the ennobling influence of the gospel, they must not abuse their liberty but remain **submissive to their husbands** (cf. Eph. 5: 22; Col. 3: 18). Any failure in these matters would expose **the word of God** to contempt by the world.

Younger men (6), Titus must **urge**

('admonish' rather than 'request') **to control themselves** (*sōphronein*, cf. v. 2 note). Again, personal mastery of self is considered to be an essential quality.

There follows advice to Titus himself (7, 8), but the advice given has its relevance for all leaders and teachers in the Church. For his work to be effective it must be supported by a life which is **a model.** In addition, his teaching must be imparted with **integrity.** It is essential that there be no tainted motive, such as personal gain (cf. 1: 11), nor underhand method (cf. 2 C. 4: 2). The teacher must also be characterized by **gravity.** This serious attitude towards his task must spring from the conscious dignity of his calling, and yet be free from affectation. If to these standards he adds a message which is **sound,** one which leaves no possible loop-hole for censure, then any **opponent** will be shamed into silence (cf. Ac. 4: 13, 14).

Slaves (9, 10) constitute a special class regarding which the apostle advises Titus (cf. 1 Tim. 6: 1). The **submission** they are enjoined to show must be demonstrated by a sincere attempt 'to give satisfaction all round' (Moffatt). This must arise from a spirit of co-operation, for **they are not to be refractory.** Paul envisages the slave in his situation indulging in specious rationalizing of petty larceny, and therefore adds the words—**not to pilfer.** Instead, absolute **fidelity** must be his standard. To the negative reasons in vv. 5b, 8b which support his previous exhortations, the apostle now adds a positive one (10b). If these slaves are obedient to his counsel 'they will add lustre to the doctrine of God our Saviour' (NEB). There can be no loftier aim than this.

ii. An appeal to the grace of God (2: 11-15)
Having described 'the things which befit the sound doctrine' (RV), Paul now turns to the doctrine which makes the demand. There can be no divorce between the two, and this second of the three great doctrinal passages of the letter is given as the impulse and reason for all practical godliness.

The writer first refers to that most impelling of all motives—**the grace of God.** This spontaneous loving intervention of God in history has procured **salvation** for **all men. Grace** seen as a tutor **training us,** demands, negatively, that we renounce **irreligion and worldly passions,** that we have done with all 'godless ways' (NEB) and those desires which are dominant in the world that knows not God. Positively, it requires that the Christian's conduct **in this world** should be marked by personal self-control (cf. v. 2 note), uprightness relative to others, and godliness in place of **irreligion** towards God.

The **grace** which has **appeared** will find its consummation in **the appearing of the glory.** Both alike are powerful incentives to true Christian living, for the first promotes a response of gratitude while the second stimulates the sense of expectancy, denoted by the participle **awaiting.** The alternative translations of the rest of v. 13 are represented by the RSV text and margin. If the marginal rendering, which has the support of the earliest versions, is adopted, there is no need to understand two separate appearances of the Father and the Son, but rather that as Christ was the grace of God revealed (11), so will He be the manifestation of the glory of God. The text, declaring the true hope of the believer to be **the appearing of the glory of our great God and Saviour Jesus Christ,** bears attractive testimony to the deity of Christ. In favour of this translation it can be said that nowhere else in the NT is God the Father said to appear, nor is the adjective **great** used of Him. The most convincing argument, however, is the presence of only one definite article which has the effect of binding together the two titles.

A final appeal is made, this time to the redeeming act of Christ. **who gave himself for us:** These words of utter simplicity yet unfathomable profundity, tell of the price involved in ransoming men (cf. 1 Tim. 2: 6). The work was voluntary, substitutionary and infinitely costly. Its stated purpose must be regarded as having a dual aspect, namely Christ's achievement, and the Christian's obligation. (*a*) **to redeem: from** must be given the full meaning of 'right away from', and **all iniquity** must also be given its widest significance. (*b*) **to purify:** A sanctification which is complete in its formal sense (Heb. 10: 10, 14), and progressive in its ethical (Eph. 5: 25-27) is the goal of the Redeemer's work. *Saints* thereby become a people essentially His, who may be identified by their zeal for **good deeds.**

The command of v. 1 which inspired the detail of the succeeding verses, is reiterated (15), and is amplified by the additional stipulation that Titus **exhort and reprove** (cf. 2 Tim. 4: 2). His ministry must be exercised with **all authority,** and Titus must not allow anyone to **disregard** him (cf. 1 Tim. 4: 12). Whilst the letter itself would add to it, true authority would only derive from obedience to the exhortation of v. 7.

iii. In society (3: 1-2)
Paul proceeds to develop the theme of the Christian's obligation to be **zealous for good deeds** and bids Titus **remind them** of this responsibility, particularly in relation to society.

It would have been easy for the Cretan Christians to be restive under the Roman yoke, they must therefore be reminded of the need **to be submissive** and **obedient** to civil authorities (cf. Rom. 13: 1-7; 1 Pet. 2: 13-17). The final phrase of the verse recommends that they should be public-spirited, willing to co-operate in any effort for the common good. Paul continues in v. 2 to sketch the Christian character, which, if reproduced, will stand out like a beacon against the dark background of a pagan society.

iv. A further appeal to the grace of God (3: 3-7)

The appeal is made the more powerful by a portrayal of life as it was lived before the transformation wrought by the saving activity of the triune God. The description is general and Paul does not hold himself aloof from it. In listing seven vices he shows man at his worst, lacking spiritual intelligence, flouting God's law, deluded, enslaved by inner 'urges' and outward **pleasures,** malicious, envious and hateful. But man's depravity proves no obstacle to God. As **God our Saviour** He penetrated the darkness (cf. 2: 11) and shed upon mankind the light of His **goodness and loving kindness** (*chrēstotēs*—goodness of heart, benignity; *philanthrōpia*—love for man). The consequence, as Paul exultantly declares it, was that **he saved us.** This has been well defined as 'the inward application to particular men of the universal act of redemption' (C. K. Barrett). This, he continues, arose not as a result of **deeds done by us in righteousness,** but rather **in virtue of his own mercy.** The total lack of desert serves only to heighten the spontaneity of God's saving grace. The phrases Paul uses to describe the means by which this grace is mediated to the soul, follow closely Christ's teaching to Nicodemus (Jn 3: 3-8). It is possible that both found a common origin in Ezek. 36: 25-27. It has been suggested that the conjunction **and** (*kai*) which links the expressions **by the washing of regeneration and renewal in the Holy Spirit,** could bear the meaning 'even', the second clause thus becoming explanatory of the first (see C. F. Hogg, *What saith the Scripture?* p. 145 on Jn 3: 5; cf. W. E. Vine, *Expos. Dic. of N.T. Words,* s.v. 'Regeneration'). Whether or not it is taken thus, **the washing** and the **renewal** are obviously closely connected. Both the writers referred to above, associate **washing** with the Word of God, although this seems to lack any clear Scriptural support. If the assumption of a common source in Ezekiel is correct, then it is better to understand **the washing of regeneration** as signifying simply the cleansing wrought at new birth, though it may well

include the thought of baptism as the outward symbol of that inward cleansing. Guthrie points out that 'the whole passage is designed to exhibit the grandeur of the grace of God and many details, such as faith-appropriation' (and, we might add, the Scriptures and baptism) 'are omitted to serve that end'. The word **renewal,** especially, is forward-looking, linking the momentous event of **regeneration** with the consequent continuous operation of the indwelling Spirit (cf. Rom. 12: 2). **Washing** may be said to describe a change of condition, **regeneration** a change in status, and **renewal** a change of disposition. Each is attested by baptism, though none is conferred by it. Together they are the work of the **Holy Spirit . . . poured out** at Pentecost as a consequence of the Saviour's glorification (cf. Jn 16: 7; Ac. 2: 33). Using the pronoun **us** in the clause **poured out upon us** the apostle declares his belief in a present identification with the past phenomenon of Pentecost (cf. 1 C. 12: 13). The object of this tremendous work wrought in the sinner is that he **might be justified,** and the motivating force is summed up in the phrase **by his grace.** To the ideas of salvation, cleansing, justification, Paul adds, finally, that of **eternal life.** Already **heirs** and, in part, possessors of the inheritance, believers yet look forward **in hope** to its full enjoyment. Although the faithful saying would not be inappropriate to what follows, the RSV, in appending it to this paragraph, is most probably correct.

v. Final advice (3: 8-11)

The preceding declaration of God's grace in salvation has been given as an incentive to good works, and Titus is required to give emphatic teaching concerning these basic truths, so that believers may be stirred up to **apply themselves to good deeds.** The alternative translation 'enter honourable occupations' (RSVmg) might represent the technical meaning of the Greek verb used, but the general meaning of **good deeds** seems preferable. Presumably it is the truths taught that are **excellent and profitable,** for they are in clear contrast to the heretical teaching which is **unprofitable and futile** (9). The character of the false teaching which Titus must **avoid,** is presented in summary form and bears resemblance to that described in ch. 1 as well as elsewhere in the Pastorals (1 Tim. 1 and 6; 2 Tim. 2). Titus next receives counsel with regard to the **man who is factious,** the one who is an adherent and propagator of his 'self-chosen and divergent form of religious belief or practice' (Alford). As a schismatic he must be cautioned, but if after the second warning he remains unrepentant there must be no further contact with him (cf. Mt. 18: 15-17).

S

One who is unmoved by such treatment reveals himself to be completely **perverted** and stands **self-condemned.**

IV. PERSONAL MESSAGES AND GREETINGS (3: 12-15)

Paul is aware that the Cretan Christians are still immature, and he knows well enough that churches cannot become indigenous overnight. He, therefore, proposes to **send** either **Artemas or Tychicus** to relieve Titus. This casual note of uncertainty leaves an imprint of genuineness upon the letter. The **Nicopolis** referred to was probably a town in Epirus which Paul regarded as a suitable rendezvous, and a strategic centre for evangelism during the coming **winter.** A further movement into Dalmatia (see 2 Tim. 4: 10) would be straightforward from Nicopolis.

Of **Zenas the lawyer** we know nothing, though **Apollos** is well known. Generous hospitality must be shown them as they journey through Crete. The apostle adds a final word about **good deeds** (cf. v. 8 note), and possibly suggests that in this matter of hospitality, Titus should not shoulder the whole burden, but **let our people learn . . . to help cases of urgent need.** Thus they will never be **unfruitful.**

From the expression **all who are with me** it may be concluded that Paul was not at a place where there was a local church, but that he is journeying and these are his travelling companions. Alternatively, if he is with a church it suggests that Titus is unknown to its members. Greetings are sent to **those who love us in the faith,** which could mean either that their love is founded upon a sharing in the common faith, or that their love is sincere and loyal. There may be here a hint of coolness towards the dissident members. But if this is the case, the apostle concludes with a prayer which embraces all the Christians in Crete. He not only uses the plural pronoun which signifies that the letter is intended for other readers apart from the one to whom it is addressed (cf. 1 Tim. 6: 21; 2 Tim. 4: 22), but he adds the word **all.** On the qualities and achievements of **grace** Paul has in this letter written

panegyrics unsurpassed in all his writings; his longing for Titus and the saints in Crete he now compresses in this concluding word— **Grace be with you all.**

BIBLIOGRAPHY

Commentaries

BARRETT, C. K., *The Pastoral Epistles.* New Clarendon Bible (Oxford, 1963).

CALVIN, J., *The Second Epistle of Paul to the Corinthians; The Epistles of Paul to Timothy, Titus and Philemon.* Translated by T. A. SMAIL (Edinburgh, 1964).

EASTON, B. S., *The Pastoral Epistles* (London, 1948).

GUTHRIE, D., *The Pastoral Epistles.* TNTC (London, 1957).

HENDRIKSEN, W., *NT Commentary: Exposition of the Pastoral Epistles* (Grand Rapids, 1957; reprinted in 'Banner of Truth' series, London, 1959).

KELLY, J. N. D., *A Commentary on the Pastoral Epistles.* BNTC (London, 1963).

LEANEY, A. R. C., *The Epistles to Timothy, Titus and Philemon.* Torch Commentaries (London, 1960).

LOCK, W., *The Pastoral Epistles.* ICC [On the Greek text] (Edinburgh, 1924).

PARRY, R. ST. J., *The Pastoral Epistles.* [On the Greek text] (Cambridge, 1920).

SCOTT, E. F., *The Pastoral Epistles.* MNT (London, 1936).

SIMPSON, E. K., *The Pastoral Epistles.* [On the Greek text] (London, 1954).

SPICQ. C., *Saint Paul: Les Épitres Pastorales.* Études Bibliques [On the Greek text] (Paris, 1947).

Other Studies

HARRISON, P. N., *The Problem of the Pastoral Epistles* (Oxford, 1921).

HARRISON, P. N., 'Important Hypotheses Reconsidered: III. The Authorship of the Pastoral Epistles', *Expository Times* 67 (1955-56), pp. 77-81.

GUTHRIE, D., *The Pastoral Epistles and the Mind of Paul* (London, 1956).

METZGER, B. M., 'A Reconsideration of Certain Arguments against the Pauline Authorship of the Pastoral Epistles', *Expository Times* 70 (1958-59), pp. 91-94.

GRAYSTON, K. and HERDAN, G., 'The Authorship of the Pastorals in the Light of Statistical Linguistics', *New Testament Studies* 6 (1959-60), pp. 1-15.

ELLIS, E. E., 'The Authorship of the Pastorals: A Résumé and Assessment of Current Trends', *Evangelical Quarterly* 32 (1960), pp. 151-161, reprinted in *Paul and his Recent Interpreters* (Grand Rapids, 1961), pp. 49-57.

THE LETTER TO PHILEMON

ERNEST G. ASHBY

Onesimus, a slave of Philemon in Colossae, fled to Rome, re-imbursing himself at his master's expense. There meeting Paul, whether by deliberate choice in seeking help, or by apparent 'accident', he was converted, and sent back with this most sympathetic letter to ease his return. Such is the traditional and apparently correct view of the situation. But J. Knox has in brilliant style sought to re-interpret this, for he thinks the whole of Colossians is more or less overshadowed by Paul's concern about Onesimus. To him Archippus is the owner of Onesimus and the ministry he is to fulfil is to send him back to Paul. The letter comes via Philemon of Laodicea to Archippus at Colossae in whose house the church met, and this letter is therefore that mentioned in Col. 4: 16. The facts as we have them in our letter seem to rule out this interesting theory, but Prof. Knox is inclined to identify Onesimus with the Bishop of the church at Ephesus, also of the same name, to whom Ignatius wrote, and to think that he had a share in collecting the Pauline letters (J. Knox: *Philemon among the letters of Paul*, pp. 30, 38-47, 49-61, 82, 88).

It is a model handling of a delicate situation, neither infringing the rights of others nor compromising his own convictions. That there is no frontal attack on slavery was not due to fear of opposition, but such a method might well have had prejudicial results then for the slaves themselves. More important still he demonstrates that the best way to prevent evil is to apply a positive principle, and brotherly love must, and ultimately did undermine slavery.

ANALYSIS

I   GREETINGS (1-3)

II   THANKSGIVING (4-7)

III   THE APPEAL (8-22)

IV   CONCLUSION (23-25)

I. GREETINGS (1-3)

In this letter of entreaty Paul introduces himself not as an apostle but as **a prisoner for Christ Jesus,** and **Timothy** is included surely as a personal acquaintance of **Philemon** rather than, as some think, a witness in view of the somewhat legal nature of this correspondence. No doubt Philemon qualified for the title of **fellow worker** by his activities in the gospel during Paul's stay in Ephesus. It is generally assumed that **Apphia** was Philemon's wife, and perhaps **Archippus** was their son. To this household church Paul sends a message of grace and peace.

II. THANKSGIVING (4-7)

Every remembrance of Philemon in prayer moves Paul to thanksgiving for his practical Christianity shown in his faith in the Lord and his love to all his fellow Christians. He prays that Philemon's **sharing** of his faith, so described because faith is the root from which such beneficence springs, may be effective in promoting a full knowledge of all the blessings which through the gospel are the possession of Christians in their Lord. The help and relief thus ministered by Philemon has brought joy and encouragement to Paul.

5. Heb. 6: 10 does indicate that love to God is displayed in love to His people, but this verse is best explained as a chiasmus. This pairs off the internal and external terms of the sentence. Though the original speaks of **love** and **faith . . . toward the Lord Jesus and all the saints** it would then mean faith towards (i.e. in) the Lord and love to the saints **6. knowledge:** Possibly Philemon's, or those who share in his beneficence.

III. THE APPEAL (8-22)

Paul is indeed gracious in preferring a request to a command, in refusing to take what he desires without Philemon's **consent,** and in undertaking to make good the deficiencies of Onesimus. Waiving his right to make demands on Philemon, as the ambassador and prisoner of Christ he prefers entreaty, appealing as a father for his own **child** whom with consummate tact he now mentions for the first time. Doubtless **Onesimus** was doubly dear to him, his son in the faith over whom he had travailed (Gal. 4: 19; 1. C. 4: 15) and the child of his imprisonment thereby confirming the overruling providence of God. The apostle has begotten him as Onesimus (i.e. useful)— for so the case of the word may imply—a punning reference to his name indicating that now for the first time he was true to it. **now he is indeed useful** both to his master and to Paul but the latter sends him back, though it is like giving up part of his very self. The apostle admits his own inclination: he could have wished to have kept him, but decided against such arbitrary action, and perhaps **on your behalf** (13) is a hint that he assumes Philemon would wish that he should keep him. But he sends him back so that Philemon's hand may not be forced, and sees that perhaps in the providential ordering of God his friend suffered a temporary loss to experience the permanent gain of a brother beloved. This goes beyond the mystery religions where a slave was treated as a fellow man: to receive him **as a beloved brother** was bound to create problems when slavery was part of the very social structure of the day (cf. 1 Tim. 6: 2). Paul now makes his great appeal and offer. If Philemon regards him as an intimate friend, he is asked to forget all the misdemeanours of Onesimus and **receive him** with the same welcome as he would give to the apostle himself. An implied reason for such action has been given in recounting God's

hand at work in the life of the slave, but Paul also approaches it in business-like fashion. 'Debit me', he writes in the wording of business papyri, 'if there are debts'. In such gracious words he avoids actual reference to theft, though doubtless aware of it, and refers to his own autograph here, though this need not necessarily indicate he penned the whole letter. It is a legally signed IOU, but more of a gentleman's solemn assurance than meant to be a legally cognizable bond, for the reminder that Philemon owed his conversion to Paul would surely rule out any resort to law. But the offer is sincerely made and may imply Paul still had possession of some private property or could rely on Christian gifts to meet any need arising. In the light of the next statement, that it is really for a favour to **benefit** himself that he is pleading (20) there is virtually a certainty that Philemon will freely assent, and this Paul assumes (21). In fact the preservation of the letter confirms this: had the request been disregarded the letter would have been destroyed.

9. ambassador (*presbeutēs*): Though MS evidence favours 'old man' (*presbytes*), by that time the two words were virtually interchangeable, and the first fits the context well. **12. sending him back:** In other contexts this means 'refer back' i.e. to some other tribunal. Paul is referring the matter back to Philemon for his decision. **22.** Paul's hope of meeting Philemon may be a further inducement to comply with his request. If written from Rome it also indicates a change of plans as he had hoped to go on to Spain.

IV. CONCLUSION (23-25)

Epaphras their own evangelist is naturally singled out from the rest, and to call him **fellow prisoner** may only mean he is voluntarily sharing Paul's imprisonment. Concluding greetings come from the same friends as in Colossians, except for Jesus Justus who may have been, as Lightfoot suggests, a Roman Christian and included in the Colossian letter for his personal devotion to Paul. The letter concludes with a benediction.

BIBLIOGRAPHY

See Bibliography on Colossians.

KNOX, J., *Philemon Among the Letters of Paul* (New York, 1959: London, 1960).

MÜLLER, J. J., *The Epistles to the Philippians and to Philemon. NLC* (London, 1955).

THE LETTER TO THE HEBREWS

GERALD F. HAWTHORNE

In language and learning the letter to the Hebrews ranks first among NT writings. Its argument is as brilliant as its theme is exalted. From first to last the author skilfully weaves his rich vocabulary into two basic themes— that of admonition and doctrine, and he does so via a style of Greek which approaches that of the very best literature of the Koine period (330 B.C.-A.D. 330). Yet in spite of Hebrews' own intrinsic brilliance there is that about it which is still dark and mysterious—well-nigh inexplicable. Who wrote it? To whom was it written? When and why was it written? These are questions which still perplex today, and for which there yet seem to be no final answers. Nevertheless, they are important to consider because whatever answers are given to them will influence one's interpretation of the letter.

Authorship

The AV, following a tradition going back to the late second century, answers the question of authorship with its informative title, 'The Epistle of Paul the Apostle to the Hebrews'. But did Paul really write Hebrews? The evidence is not sufficiently conclusive to answer the question unhesitatingly. Nowhere within the body of the letter does the author identify himself—a fact which is most unusual if indeed Paul is its author. For every other letter of his not only bears his name but contains personal greetings to his readers, and includes a complimentary paragraph about them. Hebrews, however, contains none of these characteristic Pauline features. Nor do any of the oldest Greek manuscripts in existence today contain a title for the letter other than the simple unadorned caption, 'To Hebrews', and even this brief title may not have been part of the original draft, since none of these manuscripts go back beyond the second century A.D. All longer titles which identify the author and include historical statements concerning him are late additions and hence, without authority or value.

When it comes to the testimony of the early Church Fathers the matter is not so simple or so certain. The Western wing of the Church did not recognize Paul as the author of Hebrews nor Hebrews as canonical until late in the fourth century. But on the other hand, as early as A.D. 185 the Eastern Church (particularly that located in the great centre of learning at Alexandria) knew of a tradition which attributed the letter to Paul. Although some of these Alexandrian scholars questioned the reliability of this tradition, they did not, however, deny it.

The style of the writer of Hebrews is unique in the NT, and exhibits none of those peculiarities characteristic of Paul's letters. There are none of Paul's hebraisms in Hebrews, none of his anacolutha (sentences which begin in one type of grammatical construction and end in another which is not consonant with the first, or simply tail off without any end at all), none of that rapid change, none of that same fiery passion which drove Paul on to the second topic before he had finished the first, none of the characteristic Pauline formulae for introducing OT quotations. Rather the style of Hebrews is that of a studied scholar who works with a rich and varied vocabulary, choosing words with accuracy and care so as to produce the proper rhythmical cadences for his composition. The sentences are carefully formed and finished, each blending into the other with a delightful smoothness of transition reminiscent of the Greek rhetoricians. Yet with all of its precision the letter is not without its depth of feeling. There is the exulting spirit, the fiery oratory, the glowing doxology. But unlike the Pauline letters emotion never dictates the manner of expression. Hebrews has a style which reflects the purest Greek in the NT. Thus style, too, seems to point away from Paul as the author of Hebrews. Some early fathers of the Church recognized this fact but explained the difference in style by saying that it was because Paul wrote the letter in Hebrew and Luke translated it into Greek, or again, that the thoughts were the thoughts of Paul but another, perhaps one of his students, later put it in written form.

Strangely, however, even the thought of Hebrews seems unlike that of Paul. Some of the most frequently used words in Hebrews, words like 'priest', 'high priest', 'tabernacle' (Gk. *skēnē*), 'offer', do not occur even one time in any of Paul's letters, while on the

533

other hand many of the concepts stressed by Paul in the letters bearing his name find little or no emphasis in Hebrews. Only once is specific reference made in Hebrews to the resurrection of Christ (13: 10). Rarely does the author speak of 'righteousness'. Never does he use the word 'gospel'. But who can argue conclusively from this that Paul was indeed not the author? Does not subject matter dictate the themes for emphasis? And if Paul did have it in mind to cast the Lord Jesus in the role of priest, might he not have done it in just this very way? And the suppression of his name— could it not be, as Clement of Alexandria suggested, due to Paul's modesty, 'both for the sake of the honour of the Lord, "who being the Apostle of the Almighty was sent to Hebrews", "and because it was a work of supererogation for him to write to Hebrews, since he was herald and apostle of the Gentiles" '? (A. H. McNeile, *An Introduction to the Study of the New Testament*, 2nd rev. ed., 1953, pp. 236 f.).

Nevertheless, how the author says he learned the gospel seems to be a very strong argument against Pauline authorship. Could the same person who told the Galatians so vehemently that the gospel which he preached had not been communicated to him by any man— only by revelation from Jesus Christ—ever have written to the Hebrews that he had had it confirmed to him by those who heard the Lord Jesus (2: 3), that is, that he learned it second hand?

Who then wrote Hebrews? If not Paul, could it have been Barnabas? Barnabas was a levite (Ac. 4: 36) and thoroughly familiar with the priestly services. He was known as the 'son of encouragement' (Ac. 4: 36; cf. Heb. 13: 22). He was a companion of Paul (Ac. 13: 1 ff.), and there is very ancient tradition (Tertullian, who died after A.D. 220) which says that he was indeed its author. In more recent years, however, other names have been suggested. Luke, Priscilla, Silvanus are some of these. Apollos was Luther's intelligent guess. He was a Jew and an Alexandrian. He was eloquent and mighty in the Scriptures—'a gifted teacher and an ingenious exegete' (Ac. 18: 24). He was no doubt acquainted with Paul and possibly also with Timothy. His training (and especially the place where he had received it) would certainly have enabled him to write in the style and employ the thought-forms found in Hebrews.

Nevertheless, in the final analysis it is really necessary to confess humbly one's ignorance and say in the words of Origen, 'who wrote the epistle, in truth, God alone knows'. The question of authorship, however, is not really

as important now as it was in the early years of Hebrews' existence, for then authorship and canonicity were closely associated. Then Hebrews ran the risk of being excluded from the canon because there were real questions about who wrote it. Though the influence of the Eastern Church, claiming Pauline authorship for Hebrews, did help give the letter standing, yet in the final analysis its own intrinsic worth won for it the place it holds in the canon.

Audience

The second problem is very like the first in that it too is difficult to solve. To whom was Hebrews written? This question is complicated by the fact that there is no epistolary introduction which names the recipients. And although it does possess a letter-like conclusion in which the author expresses his hope of being restored to his readers (13: 19), and though it names a certain Timothy (13: 23) and sends along the greetings of those from Italy (13: 24) there is still insufficient evidence for saying positively who these readers were.

The classical answer to this question has been that they were a specific group of Jewish Christians living in Palestine, or Rome, or Alexandria, or possibly Ephesus, who had renounced their ancient religion with its elaborate external ceremony to embrace Christianity with its contrasting de-emphasis of the externals, and who now found the transition to be very difficult psychologically. They were wavering in their faith because of persecution and were in danger of abandoning Christianity in order to beat a retreat back to Judaism. One is encouraged to adopt this view by the fact that the letter bears the title 'To Hebrews', makes prolific use of the OT, refers to the 'seed of Abraham', alludes frequently to the fathers of the Hebrew religion—Moses, Aaron, Joshua—and discusses in considerable detail the Jewish sacrificial system. The force of this argument is considerably weakened, however, when one recalls the possibility of the title not being original, but rather a later addition to make this letter conform to the pattern set by other letters—'To the Romans', 'To the Galatians', etc., and when one is made aware of the possibility that the title, if original, may have been simply a symbolic designation denoting the Church as 'the pilgrim-people of God' (cf. 1 Pet. 1: 17). At least once in the OT the expression 'The Hebrew' (Gen. 14: 13 RSV), is translated by the Greek word *peratēs* meaning 'wanderer'. Perhaps then, 'To Hebrews' may have meant not necessarily 'To Jewish Christians' but 'to the wandering people of God', whoever they may be—an idea which the author develops throughout his letter but especially in 3: 7–4: 13 where he parallels 'the Christian Church with Israel on its wandering toward the promised land'. This idea reaches its climax in the stirring words 'Here we have no lasting city, but we seek the city which is to come' (13: 14; cf. E. Käsemann, *Das Wandernde Gottesvolk*, 1939). The argument for a Jewish audience exclusively, is further weakened by recalling that the OT was as much the Bible of Christians as it was of Jews. Thus its authority would be just as great for Christians as for Jews. Thus also the great leaders of the past would belong to the Gentile Church quite as much as to the Jewish. All these things coupled with the fact that Paul himself calls Christians the true seed of Abraham (Rom. 4: 16; Gal. 3: 29) tend to cancel out the arguments in favour of the letter's recipients being Jewish Christians only and should caution one against being too sure of his ability to identify them.

Others have suggested that the recipients of this letter were Jewish Christians influenced by a type of gnosticism similar to that which Paul encountered in Colossae—a gnosticism which taught that matter was evil, that there were emanations from the ultimate reality—angels—the lowest of which produced and controlled the material universe, and that asceticism (sometimes the very opposite—immorality) was the best course to follow if one wished to overcome the evil material world in which he found himself. This theory is based on such passages as Heb. 9: 10 and 13: 9, on the lengthy discussion of Christ's superiority to the angels, and on the author's insistence that matter is not evil—it was created by the Son of God (1: 2), who Himself partook of blood and flesh in the incarnation (2: 14).

More recent interpreters have turned aside from all such identification of its recipients as being Jewish to suggest that they might have been Gentile Christians or simply Christians without reference to whether they were Gentiles or Jews, whose problem was not one of wishing to return to Judaism but of drifting away from the living God (2: 1 with 3: 12). There is no mention of Judaism as such within the letter, and no trace of any tension existing between Gentile and Jew as often was the case in Paul's letters. The OT, used so frequently in Hebrews, was always the Greek translation, known as the Septuagint (LXX). Never did the author quote from the Hebrew text nor does he show any knowledge of it. This coupled with the fact that Hebrews, in spite of its many OT quotations, is the least Hebraic writing in the NT, even using religious vocabulary not derived from the LXX, certainly tells something about

the audience as well as the author. Such expressions as 'repentance from dead works and of faith toward God' (6: 1), and 'purify your conscience from dead works to serve the living God' (9: 14) seem certainly to indicate that they were not wholly Jewish, for in spite of his many failures the Jew did render service to and have faith in the living God. One notices, too, that the exhortations given in Hebrews are not warnings against relapsing into Judaism but are general exhortations to lead a life of faith (A. Wikenhauser, *Introduction to the New Testament*, 1958, p. 464). It is also significant that all the writer's references are to the *Tabernacle* services, not to the *Temple* activities of his day.

William Manson recently sought a fresh integration of Hebrews into the historical development of early Christian thought and life. He rejected the view that Hebrews was written to Gentile Christians, but at the same time he attempted to relate it to the Hellenistic movement within the early Church—a movement which, though Jewish in its backgrounds, had grasped the more-than-Jewish sense in which the office and significance of Jesus in history were to be understood. These Hellenists had 'perceived the universal range and bearing of the Christ-event' and had understood the full implications of being called by Christ. Hence, they were willing to accept the consequences of this call in terms of *world-wide evangelization* and were desirous of exhorting others to do the same. Manson's hypothesis is suggested by the similarities between the letter of Hebrews and the Sermon of Stephen who was the chief spokesman for the Hellenists (Ac. 6–7). He concludes, therefore, that the letter issued forth from the Hellenistic wing of the Church and was directed toward Christians of Jewish extraction who were still clinging to the Jewish ordinances and were 'hanging back from accepting the full consequences of their calling' (W. Manson, *The Epistle to the Hebrews*, 1951, ch. 1). Such a view as this accounts for the emphasis of Hebrews on Jewish ordinances, the Greek style of the letter, the absence of any specific warning against lapsing back into Judaism, and the strong urging to go on to perfection. It should be noted, however, that one serious objection to Manson's thesis is that for the Hellenistic Hebrew Christian, dietary and similar laws would have had more significance than the cultic ones used by the writer of Hebrews.

More recently some have suggested the possibility that the audience of Hebrews was a group of Jews who had formerly belonged to the Dead Sea Sect at Qumran. Perhaps they were priests of Qumran for 'only priests would have had sufficient intelligence and taste for this theology of sacrifice so that one could write an entire epistle dedicated exclusively to this theme' (C. Spicq, *L'Épître aux Hébreux*, 1953, I. p. 266). They had been converted to Christianity and had carried with them—to their own spiritual disadvantage—some of their former beliefs: (1) in two messiahs—one a priest, the other a king, with the priestly messiah superior to the kingly; (2) in the necessity for a temporary cessation of sacrifices, but also in the future restoration of these when the eschatological war would leave the elect of God triumphant (cf. F. F. Bruce, 'Qumran and Early Christianity', *NTS* 2 (1956), p. 187); (3) in the tremendous importance of angels whom they conceived to be the first-creatures of God—perhaps even 'sons of God'—the transmitters of the law, and those who in the final war would bring salvation to God's elect (see note on 1: 4; cf. also H. Kosmala, *Hebräer-Essener-Christen*, 1959).

No doubt there are other possibilities, but the variety of opinions displayed here is sufficient to show the difficulty of deciding who really did receive this letter originally. Perhaps it is not at all important to know who they were. For if Adolf Deissmann (*Light from the Ancient East*, chs. 2–3) is correct in saying that Hebrews is *not* a *letter* (defined by Deissmann as a non-literary composition designed only for a particular group without any thought of publication) but an *epistle*, that is, an artistic piece of literature carefully worked out in form as well as in content so as to present something literarily worthy of wide distribution, then the many hypotheses about the 'addressees' may be unnecessary—perhaps even misleading. Were it not for chapter 13 with its epistolary conclusion and the occasional reference to the readers (5: 11–6: 12; 10: 32–34; etc.), one would not at all suspect that Hebrews was a letter. It seems more like a written-down sermon intended for wide distribution, for the rhetoric is more that of pulpit oratory than prose composition and the author presents himself as a speaker rather than as a writer (Spicq, *Comm.* I, p. 18; see Heb. 2: 5; 6: 9; 8: 1; 9: 5; 11: 32). He himself terms his brilliant work a '*sermon* of exhortation' (Gk. *logos parakleseōs*, 13: 22). Thus, if it is necessary to assume that the author wrote originally to a particular group, it can be inferred that he did so only while seeing the whole Church. He wrote with ecumenical vision!

Destination and Date

The place where these recipients resided is, of course, connected with who they were and to some extent with who wrote to them. If they were Gentile Christians, or even Jewish Christians for that matter, they well might have resided in any of the cities of the Mediterranean area. Even Jews were found in almost every important centre of the world. If they were Jewish Christians beset by a gnostic heresy, some place in Asia Minor, perhaps Ephesus, would be a possibility. If they were priests from Qumran, then Antioch in Syria could have been the place. Alexandria also has been suggested because of the philosophic nature of the letter. Rome, however, has the strongest arguments in its favour. Here Hebrews was first quoted, perhaps as early as A.D. 95 by Clement of Rome in his letter to the Corinthian church. Hebrews also includes the expression 'those from Italy send you greetings' (13: 24), which, though ambiguous, at least links the readers with Italy in some positive way.

As to when the author wrote to his friends, this too is as uncertain as who the author was and who they were to whom he wrote. The only certain thing about the date of Hebrews is that it must have been written sometime before Clement's letter (see above), which is customarily dated about A.D. 95–96 (some date it as late as A.D. 120). Thus, A.D. 95–96 (or possibly A.D. 120) becomes the latest possible date for Hebrews. But how early could it have been written? Because Hebrews makes no mention of the destruction of the temple in Jerusalem—an event which the writer might well have capitalized upon in his emphasis on the end of the old dispensation and the dawn of the new—it is assumed by some that it must have been written before A.D. 70. Manson wishes to supplement this evidence for an early date by arguing that the letter's 'reiterated emphasis on the "forty years" of Israel's probation in the desert in chapters 3–4 makes transparent the date of the epistle to the Hebrews. Hebrews was written at a time when the fortieth anniversary of the dawning of salvation in Jesus (2: 3) was already at hand . . . therefore in the sixties of the first Christian century' (*op. cit.*, pp. 55–56). There is also the fact that Timothy was still living (13: 23) though this in itself is no certain argument for an early date, since it is not known that this Timothy was Paul's companion by that name. This much, however, seems to be clear, namely, that the letter was written not to recent converts but to those who had been Christians for some time, who, for the length of time since their conversion, should have been teachers (5: 12), who could be called upon to remember the 'former days', and the conduct of their leaders now deceased (13: 7).

In addition, 2: 3 indicates that the author and his readers were second generation Christians at least in the sense that they had not received the message originally from the Saviour. Thus it is possible to date Hebrews only loosely as having been written sometime between the middle of the first century and the time when 1 Clement was written—A.D. 95-96 (no later than 120).

Aim

The writer of Hebrews himself discloses the nature and purpose of his letter when he calls it a word of exhortation (13: 22). This means that the many paragraphs of warning and admonition interspersed throughout the work are not to be considered parenthetical but primary. The theological sections surrounding them are important only because they furnish the basis for these exhortations. The writer believes in the possibility of his readers being deceived by sin (3: 13), of drifting away from the message delivered by the Saviour (2: 1), of falling from their Christian profession (3:12; 6: 4-6; 10: 26 ff.) and his concern knows no bounds. For to turn from Christ is to turn from the living God and to renounce Christianity is to renounce the ultimate in divine revelation. There is nothing left but a fearful prospect of judgment (10: 27). From such a tragedy the writer wishes to preserve his readers, whoever they may be, whether they be persons careless of their heritage (2: 3), underdeveloped because of slothfulness (5: 11), indifferent to the importance of the Christian assembly (10: 25), pressured to give in by the dullness of daily life (10: 32-36), weary from the struggle—perhaps simply morally lax (12: 12), or influenced by diverse and strange teachings (13: 9). His course of action is simple and direct. It is to 'prove' that Christianity is the final and absolute revelation of God to man and that it alone discloses the only way of worshipful access to God (10: 19-22).

The writer does this by starting with the basic presuppositions, first, that the religion of the OT was the highest and best of all religions, because the one true God had revealed Himself to the Jews as He had to no other people, and second, that the OT constituted the inspired Scriptures containing this divine revelation. From such a basis he can prove that Christianity has superseded the OT religion simply by showing that this supersession was predicted in the Scriptures themselves. Thus it is that he uses many OT proof-texts to proclaim the surpassing excellence of the 'Son' to angels, Moses, Joshua, and Aaron, thereby asserting the transcendent character of Christ's revelation to that transmitted through angels, of His

priestly ministry to that inaugurated by Aaron, of the 'rest' He provides to that offered by Joshua, and of the new covenant established by Him to that mediated through Moses.

It is this understanding that keeps prompting the writer to use the adjective 'better', thirteen times, as well as many other comparative words, in describing Christianity over against Judaism. His descriptive vocabulary also includes such words as 'perfect', 'stable', 'genuine', 'eternal', when commenting on the new revelation in Christ in contrast to such words as 'fragmentary', 'shadowy', 'shakeable', etc., to describe the old. But at the same time the writer is careful to show that there is no discontinuity between the two revelations. The same God who spoke long ago is the One who has spoken in these last days. The promises made in the past are the very ones being fulfilled today. The old covenant, though a shadow, was nevertheless a true shadow of the real substance now here.

This then is his argument aimed at preventing professing Christians from turning away from God's revelation in Christ. For if Judaism, the highest and best of all religions, has now given way to Christianity, as promise must give way to fulfilment, then no other approach to God is worth considering. Surely then his readers will hold fast to their Christian confession if only they can be made to grasp this great truth!

One thing more needs to be said: The writer of Hebrews approaches the subject of salvation from what might be called the 'phenomenal' approach. He understands that it is entirely possible for any group of confessing Christians to be made up of a 'mixed-multitude'—those with and those without genuine faith. The only objective test to prove the reality of one's own commitment to the Lord Jesus, or the commitment of anyone else for that matter, is the test of perseverance—faith *made visible* by a loyalty which continues throughout life. That a vast multitude left Egypt under Moses proved nothing about the faith of that group. That only two men entered Canaan at the end of the journey did. So the warnings of Hebrews are real warnings intended to point up this possibility of a mixed-multitude existing and to point out the tragic and ultimate consequences of defection, not at all like the consequences of those who defected in the wilderness. But the encouragement offered in Hebrews is just as real: You may show to yourself and to the world that your confession was a real one by holding firm to it until the very end of life, and you may be sure of divine help in this determination to endure (4: 16).

S*

ANALYSIS

I. GOD'S FINAL REVELATION (1: 1-14)

i. Prologue (1: 1-4)

The first four verses of Hebrews comprise one long majestic sentence in the Greek, which befittingly serves to set forth the writer's grand theme—the transcendence of Christ as Revealer and Redeemer. The beauty and balance of it are sufficient proofs that there was no original epistolary beginning now lost.

The letter begins in such a way as to throw the nature of the earlier revelation into sharp contrast with that of the new. By stating that God spoke of old **in many and various ways** (1), the writer indicates that not only was the OT varied, and full and inspired, but also that it lacked finality, that at no one time in the past and through no one person, prophet or psalmist, nor through all of them together, did God fully disclose His will; whereas by the expression, **in these last days he has spoken** (lit. 'spoke', carrying with it the idea of 'once and for all'), he emphasizes the completeness and perfection of that revelation which now has come in this final stage of God's plan of redemption (cf. Isa. 2: 2; Dan. 10: 14). And there is good reason for drawing such a sharp contrast between the two revelations as the writer now makes clear: the old came **by** (lit. 'in') **the prophets,** but the new **by** ('in') **a Son** (1–2). In the first instance the prophets were mere human instruments of revelation, nothing more; in the second, one who is Himself God's Son, possessing His same nature, is the means by which that message comes. Thus the superiority of God's revelation in Christ is due not merely to the fact that it came last and at the end of an era, but to the 'transcendent character of the person, the rank, the status, and the authority of Him through whom and in whom it comes' (Manson, op. cit., p. 89). Two things should be observed from these opening remarks. First, the writer stresses the unity and continuity of the two revelations, which in essence are not two but one which culminates in Christ. The same God speaks **in these last days** as spoke **of old.** And secondly, he implies that whenever God does disclose Himself to man it is chiefly through man that He does it. 'In the prophets' and 'in a Son' are expressions which reiterate the principle that God communicates His truth through the human personality.

But it is not just in one who is son among many that God offers His final revelation. The expression, **by a Son** (2), therefore, inadequately conveys the writer's intent at this point. It is true that the Greek lacks both definite article and possessive pronoun, but this omission is due either to the rhythmic demands of the sentence or to the writer's desire to stress the quality of this ultimate word of His. The context demands that it be translated 'His Son', 'one who is Son' (B. F. Westcott, *The Epistle to the Hebrews,* 1889, p. 7), or 'the Son', for He must be thought of as Son 'incomparable and unique'. That this is so is demonstrated by the several expressions which immediately follow. They describe the Son as (*a*) author and goal of creation, in that He is **heir of all things** and the efficient cause of their creation, and as (*b*) Himself divine, in that **He reflects the glory of God and bears the very stamp of his nature** (3).

The word 'reflects' translates the Greek *apaugasma* which also has an active meaning of 'radiates' (cf. the translation of the NEB, 'The Son who is the *effulgence* of God's splendour'. Cf. also Wis. 7: 24 ff. where this word is used with the meanings 'reflect' and 'radiate' combined. The writer of Hebrews was no doubt familiar with this passage). By

means of this word the writer shows the divine origin of the Son, His resemblance to the Father and at the same time His personal independence (cf. Spicq, *Comm.* II. p. 7)—He reflects or radiates 'the Glory'. [Note: 'of God' is not in the Gk. Since 'the Glory' was particularly associated with God in the LXX, the expression came to be a surrogate for God (cf. 2 Pet. 1: 17). Perhaps it is used that way here—'the Son reflects (radiates) God'.] The expression, **bears the very stamp of his nature,** adds no new idea but enlarges upon the former, further defining the relationship existing between the Son and the Father. He is the 'exact representation of God's real being', and all the essential characteristics of God are brought into clear focus in Him: he that has seen the Son, has seen the Father also (cf. Jn 14: 9). This, together with the former statement, comprises one of the strongest claims for the deity of Christ found anywhere in the NT (cf. also Jn 1: 1–3; Col. 1: 15). It is strengthened by the assertion that He is **upholding the universe by his word of power** (3). One must not, however, picture the Son as an Atlas supporting in stationary fashion the weight of the world on His shoulders, for there is within the word 'uphold' (lit. 'bear', Gk. *pherein*) not only the idea of 'maintenance', but also of 'movement toward'. Thus the Son is described as one who both maintains 'the All' and who bears it forward to its final goal.

In the latter part of v. 3 there is a brief reference to that idea which really constitutes the main theme of the letter: the priest who made **purification for sins.** The writer of Hebrews understands the priestly service to be the essential activity of the Son, and the real reason for His coming to earth. This is reflected even in the form of the verb he uses to describe His work although the translation obscures it. When he talks about the beginning of the aeons he says that the Son **created** (lit. 'made', Gk. *epoiēsen*) them. When he approaches the subject of purification for sins he employs the same verb but gives it a different form—a form which implies greater interest or involvement in the action on the part of the subject (*poiēsamenos*). This idea is correctly reflected in the translation of the AV: 'when he had *by himself* purged our sins . . .'

Along with the basic themes of redemption and resurrection, that of the exaltation of Christ to the right hand of God was an essential element in apostolic preaching and teaching (Ac. 2: 34; Eph. 1: 20; Rev. 3: 21). When the writer of Hebrews states that the Son **sat down at the right hand of the majesty on high** (3), he shows that he is in accord with this traditional emphasis. But at the same time he uses this statement to stress the finality of the Son's work (cf. the note on 10: 12), and to show that the Son is at the same time the promised Messiah. [Note: this expression concerning the Son's exaltation to the right hand is a quotation taken from a messianic psalm (Ps. 110).]

It is just possible that verse 4 was occasioned by angel worship on the part of the audience, but not necessarily so. In the OT as well as in many apocryphal books angels played a very important role. They were looked upon as creatures in closest proximity to God (Isa. 6: 2 ff.), possibly even called 'sons of God' (cf. Gen. 6: 2 with Job 1: 6; 2: 1. Cf. also E. L. Sukenik, *The Dead Sea Scrolls of the Hebrew University*, pl. 53, fragment 2, 1. 3). They were also considered to be the mediators of the law (Ac. 7: 53; Gal. 3: 19; Heb. 2: 2). In any case, as the writer points out, the Son is superior to angels because, quite apart from His 'eternal nature', in His human rôle He earned by experience (this is the force of the expression **having become**) what was already His by personality—a **name . . . more excellent than theirs** (cf. Phil. 2: 5–11).

ii. Proofs for the Statements in the Prologue (1: 5–14)

In a fashion typical of this writer, the OT is now called upon to give validity to the statements he has made. For him the OT is inspired by God and wholly authoritative. Its pronouncement is final, no further argument is required. For him, too, there is a deeper meaning to the OT than the historical. It is the Christological. The Son, who is the Christ, is the key unlocking the true treasures of the ancient Scriptures. Thus, he feels free, in fact compelled, to apply to Christ the exalted language of the OT although it originally may have been spoken of another. By such an exegetical method it is quite an easy matter to establish the validity of his statements concerning Christ.

He begins the proof for his statement concerning Christ's superiority to angels with a quotation from Ps. 2: **'Thou art my Son, today I have begotten thee'** (5). Historically this may have been sung to an Israelite monarch on the day of his coronation (cf. H. H. Rowley, ed., *The Old Testament and Modern Study*, 1951, p. 167). Later it was interpreted messianically (cf. Ac. 4: 25 f.; 13: 33). It is in this Christological sense that the writer of Hebrews uses it to establish by it the fact that the Son was always Son (the 'Thou *art*' describing an essential and continuing relationship with the Father), that He nevertheless earned this title of Son at some moment in history (the '*Today* I have begotten thee' implying a particular 'time when'. Cf. Lk. 3: 22 (RSVmg); 9: 35; Rom. 1: 4 for possibilities as to when this was), and that He is infinitely superior to angels, **for to what angel did God ever say** such a thing (5)?

The writer continues piling up proof by adding a quotation from 2 Sam. 7: 14: **'I will be to him a father'** (5). These words were addressed originally by God to David and they concerned his son. But if the words were ever true of Solomon they are surpassingly more true of Christ. In fact, to the writer of Hebrews they find their ultimate fulfilment in Him. This passage was never applied messianically in Rabbinic literature, but there is now evidence from the Dead Sea Scrolls that some Jewish communities did so interpret it. The writer of Hebrews, however, never refers to Christ as the Son of David.

He continues his proof by combining Ps. 97: 7 with the Septuagint reading of Dt. 32: 43. [Note: The Septuagint (LXX) is the Greek translation of the Hebrew OT, and at Deut. 32: 43 it has a longer reading than that found in the Massoretic Text of the Hebrew. Because it is not in the Hebrew it is not in the English translations based upon them. Now, however, for the first time there is support for the longer reading in a pre-Massoretic Hebrew text found in the Dead Sea community of Qumran (cf. F. M. Cross, *The Ancient Library of Qumran*, 1958, pp. 182 f.).] His combination of these two passages results in a command for **all God's angels** to **worship him** (6). The interesting thing about this exhortation is that in both the Psalm and the Deuteronomy passage the 'Him' refers to God Himself. But because the writer has already made clear the community of nature that exists between the Father and the Son, he has no misgivings whatsoever in applying to the **first-born** what was said originally of the Father. The expression 'first-born' is a technical term which when here applied to Christ may mean that to the writer of Hebrews Christ is prior to and sovereign over all creation (cf. Lightfoot's note on Col. 1: 15), or it may mean that he simply intended it to be understood of Christ in His relationship to men who also are called 'sons of God' (2: 10; cf. also Rom. 8: 29).

The final proof of Christ's superiority to angels comes from Ps. 104: 4. By describing the angels as **winds** and **flames of fire** (7), the writer calls attention to their 'mutability, materiality and transitoriness' (Westcott, *Comm.*, p. 25), in contrast to the enduring qualities of the Son whose throne **is for ever and ever** (8). 2 Esd. 8: 21 f. shows by synonymous parallelism that this interpretation of the nature of angels is correct: 'Before whom the hosts of angels stand with trembling: at whose bidding they are changed to wind and fire'.

The second set of quotations is designed to substantiate the writer's statement concerning the Son as the radiance and stamp of deity (8–9). He begins with a quotation from Ps. 45 stating that the words of this Psalm were addressed in reference to the Son: **'Thy throne, O God, is for ever and ever'** (8). Historically, this Psalm probably was composed for and sung at the wedding of an Israelite king. As was common, the king, because of his intimate relationship to God as God's representative on earth, was on occasion made the recipient of such hyperbolic attributions as *'Elohim*, 'God' (cf. Ps. 82: 6 with Jn 10: 34; cf. also Rowley, *op. cit.*, pp. 167 f.). What was symbolically true of the ancient Hebrew monarch only by virtue of his office, the writer of Hebrews sees to be wholly true of Christ by virtue of His nature. The first part of this quotation is ambiguous in the Greek so that some translators are inclined to translate it 'God is thy throne' (cf. the RSV mg), yet it is clear both from the context of Ps. 45 and that of Heb. 1 that the vocative of address is intended—'Thy throne, O God'. There is the same ambiguity of construction in v. 9 so that the expression, **'God, thy God, has anointed thee'**, may also be translated 'O God, Thy God, has anointed Thee' (cf. Aquila's translation of the Hebrew psalm; so also NEB). This anointing came originally as a reward for righteousness and justice (9). Because the writer of Hebrews now applies this psalm to Christ and because he understands the life of Christ to have been a period of 'moral probation' (2: 18; 5: 8; etc.), it is most likely that he equates the anointing of Christ with His exaltation—a reward, no less, for the successful accomplishment of His mission on earth (cf. 2: 9). **Beyond thy comrades** (9) means beyond all those who have received the royal unction before and since.

Finally, the writer establishes the truth of his statement concerning the creative activity of the Son by an extended quotation from Ps. 102: 25-27 (10-13). Originally it outlined the creative power of God—**'Thou . . . didst found the earth in the beginning . . . the heavens are the work of thy hands'** (10), and His eternal qualities over against the creation's transient ones—**'they will perish, but thou remainest'** (11). Now, however, it is applied to the Son. The writer found this application an easy one to make because in the LXX, which he uses continuously, there was the insertion of the word 'Lord' into the text—

'Thou, *Lord*, didst found the earth . . .'—which does not appear in the Hebrew. 'Lord', of course, was the title the apostolic age most frequently gave to Jesus Christ.

The author climaxes his catena of OT quotations by again referring to Ps. 110 (cf. 1: 3). With it he describes God as entering the conflict to fight the enemies of His Anointed: **'Sit . . . till I make thy enemies a stool for thy feet'** (13). This quotation is not designed to show that the Son is impotent and unable to fight His own battles, but to make clear the identity of will that exists between Father and Son, and the respect the Father has for the Son (Spicq, *Comm.*, II, p. 2). Never could this be said of angels for they are mere **ministering spirits sent forth to serve . . . those who are to obtain salvation** (14). With this mention of 'salvation' the author closes his discussion concerning the cosmic dimensions of the Son, and moves on to a new topic—the rôle of Jesus in redemption on the plane of historical events.

II. GOD'S PROGRAMME FOR SALVATION (2: 1-18)

i. Warning and Exhortation (2: 1-4)

Before developing the theme of salvation the writer feels compelled to stop and issue a warning based upon the implications of his exegetical theology. This is in keeping with his method of interweaving exhortation with theology. Such 'digressions' are not to be thought of as the writer stepping aside from his main purpose. Rather he is laying bare his main purpose by means of them (cf. 13: 22).

The warning here may be the key to the understanding of the difficulty faced by those who first received the letter to the Hebrews. It seems to be a warning against neglect and indifference to the new revelation, against failure to appreciate it and to go on into its full benefits, against the possibility that we might **drift away from it** (1). The solution to the problem is moral exercise: **pay the closer attention to what we have heard** (1), which implies individual responsibility in the application of one's mind to the new revelation in such an extraordinary fashion that he obeys it with abandon.

The reason for this exhortation is to be found in the nature of this new revelation. The earlier **message** was **declared by angels** (2) and every sin of commission and omission (**transgression or disobedience**) was properly punished. But the new message of salvation **was declared . . . by the Lord** (3), who has been shown to be incomparably superior to angels. His message, therefore, is equally superior to that mediated by them, and neglect of it that much more culpable. It was never stated explicitly in the OT that the law was transmitted through angels, only implied (cf. Dt. 33: 2, LXX, and Ps. 68: 17, LXX), but it was nevertheless an axiom of Judaism (see Josephus, *Ant.* 15, 5. 3), and a belief of the Church (cf. Ac. 7: 53 and Gal. 3: 19).

Because the new revelation brought by the Son **was attested to us by those who heard him** (3) we have the certainty of a faithful tradition in which we can have the utmost confidence. The expression, 'was attested', translates the Greek *bebaioō* meaning 'make firm', 'establish', 'confirm'. Goodspeed thus more clearly expresses the idea contained here when he translates it: 'was guaranteed'. Here also is the hint that the author reckoned himself among those who received his 'authentic tradition' second hand from those who had actually heard the Saviour.

Verse 4 serves two purposes: (*a*) to show the place and purpose of miracles, namely to establish the authenticity of the NT message (God 'added His testimony' in miracle to show it had divine sanction) and (*b*) 'to emphasize the awful authority of "the things that were heard"' (F. D. V. Narborough, *The Epistle to the Hebrews*, 1930, p. 86). Not only was this message spoken by the Lord, it was visibly approved by God, and by charismatic gifts of the Holy Spirit. Father, Son, and Holy Spirit thus co-operated to produce this revelation of salvation. To drift from it or to treat it with indifference is the height of folly.

ii. The Outline of Salvation (2: 5–18)
This first section (5–9), which outlines the need for salvation and the means by which it is accomplished, becomes more intelligible if it is connected with 1: 14. Angels are **sent forth to serve . . . those who are to obtain salvation** (1: 14), **for it was not to angels God subjected the world to come** (2: 5). In these words the writer is saying that in spite of what may have been a temporary policy [Note: angels were believed to rule people (Dt. 32: 8, LXX; Dan. 10: 13; 12: 1) as well as stars and planets (1 Enoch 60: 15-21; 18: 13-16; Jubilees 2: 2)], it was not God's purpose to give angels sovereignty over His 'moral, organized system' (Gk. *oikoumenē*, Westcott, *Comm.* p. 42). This sovereignty He reserved solely for man as the writer's use of Ps. 8 shows so clearly (note the casual way in which he introduces this quotation: lit., 'someone testified somewhere', implying that to the writer of Hebrews the instrument is insignificant; it is really God who has spoken): **'Thou hast crowned him (man, the son of man) with glory and honour,**

putting everything in subjection under his feet' (7b f.). This then is the divine ideal (cf. Gen. 1: 26-28): man is to rule; the son of man who was made only a 'little less than God' (Ps. 8: 5, RSV) is destined to be sovereign, and nothing is to be left **outside his control** (8). It is at this point, however, that the need for salvation becomes crystal clear, for **we do not yet see everything in subjection** to man (8b). God's goal for man is not now being realized.

Yet divine purposes cannot be frustrated. Verse 9 reveals that God has provided a means of salvation. He has found a way to restore man to his place of sovereignty: **Jesus, who for a little while was made lower than the angels,** is now **crowned with glory and honour.** [Note: Here for the first time is the mention of the name 'Jesus'. It is a favourite designation, used by the writer of Hebrews thirteen times in his letter.]

In the present argument of the writer, the expression 'made lower than the angels', probably means little more than that the Eternal became human, for it is to be noted that this expression is borrowed from Ps. 8 (quoted above), and is the only one that says anything at all about the nature of man. Therefore, when the writer of Hebrews states that Jesus was made lower than the angels, he is simply saying, by means of scriptural phraseology, that the Son of God became incarnate as a man, that He assumed man's position. But this is a tremendously important statement, nevertheless, for in his thinking it was only in this act of self-identification with the human race that **by the grace of God** He was enabled to **taste death for every one** (9).

The prevalent idea of 'corporate solidarity' no doubt was in the writer's mind when he penned the foregoing statement: the redeemed together with the Redeemer 'constitute a unity and this unity is conceived in terms of substance: they and he belong to one body . . . What happens to the Redeemer, or happened while he tarried in human form on earth, happens to his whole body, i.e., not to him alone but to all who belong to that body. So if he suffered death, the same is true of them (2 C. 5: 14). If he was raised from the dead the same is true of them (1 C. 15: 20-22)' (cf. Rom. 5: 12, 18 f.; 1 C. 15: 45 f.; R. Bultmann, *Theology of the New Testament*, 1951, I, p. 299).

From this it now becomes clear that when the writer proceeds to say that Jesus was **crowned with glory and honour** (9) he understands this event to be far more extensive than the exaltation of Jesus' single self. For if it is true that Jesus has been exalted to the place of sovereignty, it is also true that they who are bound up with Him in one body likewise share in this exaltation. Thus it is that salvation is made complete, for what man had not been able to realize, namely his divinely appointed destiny of being sovereign, Jesus has, and man through Him.

Mention should be made of two other things: First, whether the Greek expression *brachy ti* be translated to show degree, i.e., 'a little lower than the angels' (AV), or to show time, i.e., 'a little while' (RSV, for which there is general support today), makes little difference, for it adds nothing at all to the writer's main argument. He seems to have included it primarily because it was part of a quotation he needed to show that Christ became what man was. Second, it is worth calling special attention to the fact that for the writer the exaltation (including that of man as well) came about only because of the suffering and death of Jesus. Nothing is said of His teaching as a means of human salvation. This, of course, is in keeping with the writer's emphasis upon the priesthood of Christ, and His self-sacrifice by which atonement was made (cf. 9: 14).

This next section (10–18) reiterates the great concept of the divine identifying with the human, and seeks to offer reasons why such a method of salvation was used by God. The first reason is suggested without the customary proof from Scripture, namely, that this particular method, which necessarily involved the perfecting of the Saviour **through suffering** (and death), **was fitting** to the one **for whom and by whom all things exist** (10). And not only is such a plan of redemption fully in keeping with the nature of God, but this description of Him as the final and efficient cause *of all things* lays bare two more essential truths pertaining to salvation: (*a*) that the suffering of the Redeemer was not accidental, but in accordance with the general plan of divine providence (Spicq, *Comm.*, I, *ad loc.*), and (*b*) that God Himself is the grand initiator of this redemptive process; it is He who has set all things in motion who has determined to bring **many sons to glory** (this being the key phrase, denoting the essence of salvation, cf. 7b and 9b) by perfecting their Saviour through suffering. The verb 'to perfect' (Gk. *teleioun*) means 'to complete a process', and by its use the writer has shown that Jesus became fully qualified to be the pioneer of man's salvation through the process of human suffering.

In v. 11 emphasis is again placed upon the self-identification of the Son with those He came to redeem, its completeness, and its *raison d'être*: **he who sanctifies and those who are sanctified have all one origin,** i.e., are inextricably bound up together. Hence, since suffering and death are so very much a part of humanity, it was impossible for it to have been otherwise with the Son who had graciously taken to Himself this same humanity. In making use of the verb 'sanctify' the author is not commenting on the moral character of its subjects, for it is primarily a technical term meaning simply 'to set apart'. It was often used of Israel (cf. Exod. 19: 14) who, by their sanctification, were set apart as the special people of God. Now those who have been redeemed by the death of Christ are given the same designation used of ancient Israel—a fact which may signify that the writer understands Christians to be the new people of God.

Now the writer turns to the Scriptures for proof (12–13). The identification of the Son with humanity was no afterthought of God. He had announced it through the prophetic voice of psalmist and seer: **I will proclaim thy name to my brethren . . . ,** and, **I will put my trust in him,** and finally, **I, and the children God has given me.** How complete then was this identification? The scriptural answer given to this question is that it was as complete as that which exists between brothers, or that which exists between father and child. It was as complete as 'community of nature' could make it. The first of these OT quotations comes from Ps. 22, a Psalm which earlier had been used by the Lord of Himself while He was on the cross (cf. Mt. 27: 46). Thus it was an easy matter for the writer to apply another part of that same Psalm to Him here. The last two quotations are from Isa. 8: 17 f. (LXX), and their words originally gave expression to that prophet's personal faith in God and his conviction that he and his sons symbolized the believing remnant of Israel. When applied to Christ they reveal that in assuming humanity to Himself He was required to live within those limitations in complete dependence upon God (cf. the note on 12: 2), and that He and His 'children' comprise the new community of God's believing people.

Not only was salvation by identification consonant with the nature of God, it was also necessary (14–18). For **since . . . the children share in flesh and blood** (the word order in the Greek, however, is 'blood and flesh'), that is to say, since they are human, the Son also in just the same way (Gk. *paraplēsiōs*, 'in absolutely identical fashion') had to partake **of the same nature** (14) if He was to get at their real problem—death. [Note: The two verbs, **share** and **partook,** reflect two different verbs in the Greek, the first 'marks the common nature shared among men as long as the race lasts'; the second 'expresses the unique fact of the incarnation as a voluntary acceptance of humanity' (Westcott, *Comm.*, p. 53).] By becoming human the Eternal Son made Himself susceptible to death. But the great paradox is that by death He destroyed (lit. 'rendered powerless') the devil **who has the power of death** (cf. Wis. 2: 24), and released once-and-for-all **all those who through fear of death were subject to lifelong bondage** (14, 15). The author does not here make clear how the death of Christ actually destroyed the power of the devil and released men from the fear he held them in, but he does so later on. Then he shows that Christ's death was of such a nature that it freed men from the guilt of their sin and their consciences from the dread of its consequences (cf. 9: 14; 10: 22).

Verse 16 is a summary. It shows that this salvation is intended for men not angels. The expression **is concerned** poorly translates the Greek verb *epilambanesthai* which means 'to take hold of', or 'grasp'. The idea is that God graciously laid hold of the **descendants of Abraham,** that is, all who like Abraham have faith in God (cf. Gal. 3: 29) in order to lead them from death to glory (cf. Jer. 31: 32 (38: 22, LXX); Isa. 41: 8 f. LXX). He has not done this for angels.

The method God designed for accomplishing this salvation is the priestly, for it was as **a merciful and faithful high priest** that Christ was to **make expiation for the sins of the people** (17). 'To make expiation' translates the Greek verb *hilaskesthai* which also carries the idea of 'to satisfy', 'appease', 'propitiate'. Here, however, with 'sins' as its object (cf. the Gk.) it most likely means 'wipe out', 'remove' rather than 'appease'. But, and again the writer returns to a much emphasized concept, the Son can be effective as a priest only by identification with those whom He is to represent. **Therefore he had to be made like his brethren in every respect** (17).

III. EXHORTATION AND WARNING (3: 1–4: 13)

i. Exhortation to Consider Christ as Superior to Moses (3: 1–6a)

The previous section ends with a description of Jesus as a **merciful and faithful high priest.** This now becomes the theme for the new discussion. But in reverse fashion the author treats first the faithfulness of Jesus and secondly His mercy (4: 14 ff.).

From the vantage point of theological truth, the author makes his appeal to **holy brethren, who share in a heavenly call** (1). The word 'holy' has the same root meaning as that of 'sanctify', and refers, therefore, to those set apart by God and for God, i.e., Christians (cf. note on 2: 11; Lev. 20: 26; 1 Pet. 2: 9). These Christians whose call or invitation is *from* heaven ... and *to* heaven' are now addressed directly for the first time. They are urged to **consider Jesus, the apostle and high priest,** the subject of their open confession, as being **faithful to him who appointed him** (1-2). And yet it is not that Christians are to fasten their attention upon Jesus as faithful merely, for **Moses,** who himself was looked upon as apostle (cf. Exod. 3: 10) and priest (Exod. 24: 6-8; cf. also Philo, *On the Life of Moses*, 2. 2-5), **also was faithful** (2; cf. Num. 12: 7). But they are to give careful and prolonged attention to the person and work of Christ because, by His very nature, He is completely 'other' and far greater than Moses. Moses was a faithful servant in God's house (2)—a mere witness, through the moral and ceremonial laws he established, to the gospel which was **to be spoken later** (5). But Jesus is God's Son set over that house, the 'creative agent' by whom it was built, who is Himself the gospel anticipated by Moses and the One by whom it was first declared (3, 5 f.; cf. also 1: 2; 2: 3). Verse 4 is difficult, and its difficulty is only slightly eased by the RSV putting it in parenthesis, for it is not wholly parenthetical. It has some connection with the reference to Jesus as builder in v. 3. Perhaps its meaning is that **every house is built by someone, but the builder of all things is God,** whose 'creative agent is Christ'. Or possibly its meaning may best be understood by translating the word 'God' as 'divine' since in the Greek the definite article is omitted: 'the builder (i.e., Christ) of all things is divine'.

It is worth noting that the expression **God's house** ('his house', AV) refers to the 'household' or 'family' of God and apparently describes the believing people of God in the OT and also in the NT, for the 'house' is the same in both. Moses was a servant in God's house, a house which Christ founded, over which He presides, and to which Christians belong—**we are his house**! (6). This passage argues strongly for a continuity between ancient Israel and the new 'Israel of God' (cf. Gal. 6: 16).

ii. Warning against Missing God's Promised Rest (3: 6b–4: 11)

6. We are his house if we hold fast our confidence and pride in our hope: This warning is directed to those who have 'confessed' themselves Christians. It is intended to show that true Christianity is proved by endurance, by continued confidence in and loyalty to Christ who is our hope (cf. Col. 1: 27). He does not belong to God's house who merely professes to do so. He belongs who continues believing 'to the end' (6 RSVmg, a reading which, though parallel to 3: 14, is probably genuine here in light of its wide textual attestation). Ps. 95, which is now quoted as the voice of the Spirit still speaking to Christians today (7-11), is intended by the writer to show that Israel's tragic loss was due to rebellion or unbelief—a failure to maintain an attitude of confidence and obedience throughout their journey from Egypt to Canaan—and as a warning to professing Christians not to make the same mistake. It thus serves to illustrate the principle already laid down, namely, that perseverance is indeed the proof of faith. Israel's initial exit, their 'baptism unto Moses', their participation in the spiritual food (cf. 1 C. 10: 1 f.), i.e., their observation of divine **works** (9), did not guarantee their entrance into Canaan. Some continued to believe God and entered Canaan but some rebelled and never experienced God's rest (11, cf. 16-19). The journey decided the vitality of their faith.

Therefore, since the Holy Spirit is still speaking and saying **'Today'** (7, 13, 15), **take care, brethren, lest there be in any** (one) **of you an evil, unbelieving heart, leading you to fall away from the living God** (12). The gravity of the situation is thus heightened by three things: (*a*) by the writer calling attention to the fact that it is God speaking and not man—**the Holy Spirit says** (7); (*b*) by his pointing out that this departure is from the **living God,** a favourite designation for God in Hebrews (9: 14; 10: 31; 12: 22; cf. also 4: 12; 11: 6), which pictures God as 'all alive', active in making Himself known to men, able to keep His promises and determined to execute His oaths (note: the warning against departing from the 'living God' does not sound like a warning against relapsing into Judaism), and (*c*) by his repeated use of the imperative (3: 12, 13; 4: 1, 11). The preventive for such a condition is to **exhort one another** (Gk. 'yourselves' stressing the 'unity of the Christian body') **every day** (13). This requires both individual and corporate responsibility. The expression **deceitfulness of sin** (13) describes sin as a seducer, and may be an allusion to that first sin when Eve was seduced by the serpent (Gen. 3: 13; cf. 1 Tim. 2: 14). Verses 12 and 13 together describe that process which happens deep within a man when there is not the constant strengthening of mutual exhortation—a process which initially is invisible to any observer. First the germ of

unbelief is allowed to sprout, then evil and God-defying thoughts begin to spread. These gradually dominate the entire attitude, until the whole character is changed. A new tendency is in control of the person involved. His basic response to God is NO. There is now no longer the YES of submission which he professed at his baptism (J. Schneider, *The Letter to the Hebrews,* 1957, pp. 31-32).

The writer reiterates in a more forceful fashion what he has said already (14), namely, that there is one simple test by which we can know whether or not **we share in Christ,** whether we are 'partakers of' or 'partners with' Him (Gk. *metochoi tou christou,* which itself has an ambiguity of meaning): Do **we hold our first confidence firm to the end?** [Note: the Gk. for 'confidence' is *hypostasis,* that firm support on which 'a man bases himself as he confronts the future' (J. Moffatt, *The Epistle to the Hebrews, ad loc.,* p. 48). Here it is the persuasion with which the Christian life began that God has spoken His ultimate word in Jesus Christ.] The desert experience of Israel (16-19) proves that 'this total-life picture is *the* criterion' by which one can tell objectively the reality of his faith. What is faith for the writer of Hebrews? Chapter 11 is his full discussion of the subject, but by comparing v. 18 here with v. 19 it is clear that he understands faith to be something closely akin to obedience or loyalty.

Chapter 4 continues the same warning against the possibility of failing to enter God's rest which was begun in 3: 6b. That there is such a rest the author proves in his typical exegetical fashion by a quotation from Gen. 2: 2: **'And God rested on the seventh day from all his works'** (4). That God wishes to share this rest and that the promise of entering this rest still holds good is proved by two other passages, both from Ps. 95. The first quotes God as saying that **'They shall never enter my rest'** (5). This is a concise statement compressing several ideas into one brief remark. God, who never desires a thing in vain, must have wanted to share His rest, else He would never have extended an invitation to men to join Him in it. But since He did, and since those whom He first invited **failed to enter because of disobedience** (6), and since God's purposes cannot be frustrated, the offer to enter into the enjoyment of His rest must still hold good. The writer then proceeds to use another part of Ps. 95 to prove this conclusion. God is still extending His invitation to men to join Him in His repose: **'Today, when you hear his voice, do not harden your hearts'** (7). By this 'Today' the writer understands that

God again is setting **a certain day** (7), defining 'a new period in which the rest is to be open and accessible'. **So then, there remains a sabbath rest for the people of God** (9). From this it is learned that the 'rest of God' must not be equated with Canaan for God's second and continued invitation has come through David who lived long after Joshua (Jesus, AV) had led Israel into the promised land (8). [Note: This attribution of Ps. 95 to David is found only in the LXX; it is not in the Hebrew text.] **Had** Joshua **given them rest, God would not** have spoken **of another day** (8). Thus the tragedy of unbelieving Israel is seen to be far greater than appeared on the surface. The greatness of their failure lay not merely in that they could not enter Canaan, but in that they also were irrevocably excluded from the eternal rest of God.

It is against this background—the possibility of an eternal rest and also of the possibility of failing to achieve it—that the writer makes his appeal: **while the promise of entering his rest remains, let us fear lest any of you be judged to have failed to reach it** (1). Here there is both severity and tender concern— severity, in the need for fear; tender concern in the 'cautious and delicate way' the writer expresses the possibility of failure: 'Lest any of you should seem to come short of it' (AV, in preference to the RSV or more specifically, 'should seem to have come short of it *in the judgment of others*'). Failure, the author goes on to explain, ever lies in unbelief. Mere hearing the good news is not enough. The gospel must **meet with faith in the hearers** (2, but cf. RSVmg for an alternate translation). When it does it becomes effective, **for we who have believed enter that rest** (3). Notice that the tense of the verb is present—'enter'. Thus God's rest is not wholly some future goal to be attained, but it is a present reality to be enjoyed. The author coins a word to describe it and calls it **a sabbath rest** (9, Gk. *sabbatismos*), **for whoever enters God's rest also ceases from his labours as God did from his** on the sabbath, i.e., the seventh day (10, cf. 4).

What is meant by 'ceases from his labour as God did from His'? Since it is impossible to conceive of God as resting from good works, the idea of God resting must mean that God worked without hindrance or tension with energy flowing from Him with calm steadiness (cf. Jn 5: 17; cf. also A. C. Purdy, 'Hebrews', *The Interpreter's Bible*, XI, p. 631). If this was in the writer's mind then 'ceases from his labours' describes that cessation from futile activity done in resistance to God, that is, from dead works (cf. 9: 14), to find rest in a life of complete

dependence upon Him—much like Paul's 'contrast of the life of faith in Christ and the life of performing the works of the law' (Narborough, *Comm.*, p. 95). Though it is true that God cannot rest from good works, yet the Hebrew verb (*shābath*, from which 'sabbath' comes) does mean 'to cease, desist, rest'. 'God rested', then, must mean that God desisted from what He had been doing, i.e., His creative activity. And when a man enters into God's sabbath-rest he too must desist from what he has been doing, in this case, attempting to work out his own salvation. 'More positively, we are justified in filling the word with meaning derived from the writer's dominant longing for a satisfying worship of God. This *rest* is peace in the assurance of an access to God unhindered by rites that cannot touch the conscience and made possible only by Christ's "purification for sins" that pollute and prevent our reaching the final goal of worship' (Purdy, *Comm.*, p. 631). Since then this is now available **let us therefore strive** (lit. 'give all diligence') **to enter that rest** (11).

iii. The Impossibility of Concealing Unbelief from God (4: 12–13)

Because unbelief is a matter of the heart it often escapes the notice of man but never of God whose word **is living and active, sharper than any two-edged sword** (12). It has the power to reach right through to the inmost parts of one's personality. It has the power to judge (Gk. *kritikos*) both the feelings and thoughts of the heart (cf. Wis. 18: 15 ff.). It is able to discern and decide on the moral value of a man. The expression 'word of God', may refer to that message of God spoken either through the prophets or by Christ and His apostles which in itself possesses a dynamic so great that when heard and retained it creates anew (cf. Rom. 1: 16), or it may simply be a circumlocution for God Himself, as was sometimes done. Notice that in v. 13 the 'word' is left behind and it is before God Himself we stand—completely exposed. What we really are now is **laid bare to the eyes of him with whom we have to do.**

With this the author concludes his lengthy warning and comes to the subject which is closest to his heart and which he has already touched upon twice before (1: 3b; 2: 17 f.)— namely the priesthood of Jesus.

IV. THE PRIESTHOOD OF JESUS IN-TRODUCED (4: 14–5: 10)

i. The Priest's Sufferings and their Meanings (4: 14–16)

From warning the author now turns to consolation and encouragement which he ties inseparably to the priestly work of Christ—a theme which in a very real sense constitutes the main burden of the letter. The life of faith, though difficult, is not devoid of external support: **we have a great high priest** (14) who can **help** us (16). And the greatness of this high priest is measured (*a*) by the fact that He **has passed through the heavens** into the very presence of God, as the ancient high priest passed through the veil into the holy of holies—the place of effective service for man, and (*b*) by the names assigned Him here: **Jesus, the Son of God.** These tell us that He is both man and God, both 'sympathetic and powerful'. Therefore, **let us hold fast our confession** (14). This exhortation is based upon the fact that our high priest, too, suffered and was tempted, for these experiences of the Saviour have great significance to us. They mean that there is an incentive for us to persevere, for although Jesus was tempted **in every respect . . . as we are** (15), He yet remained faithful to the end. They also mean that because He suffered and was tempted He can sympathetically understand what we are going through, appreciate our weaknesses, and do something to help (15-16). Therefore, **let us** continually **draw near to the throne of grace, that we may receive mercy and find grace to help in time of need** (16), and let us come **with confidence.** This is the first statement, to be repeated many times, indicating the ultimate results of Christ's priestly work—open access into God's presence for all who wish to come. The expression 'draw near' (used seven times in Hebrews) was a technical term employed in the LXX of the priests who alone were able to approach God in worshipful service. Now 'the right of priestly approach is extended to all Christians' (Westcott, *Comm.*, p. 108).

The writer of Hebrews emphasizes the divine character of this new high priest beginning as he does with a description of Him in His cosmic rôle as creator and Son of God, but he also stresses the reality of His humanity as does no other NT writer. He insists, for example, that the temptations of Jesus were not mock temptations—they were genuine: **in every respect** like ours. How can this be, if at the same time he were the Son of God? Would not His divine nature protect Him from the possibility of sinning? This question of the possibility of Christ's sinning has been debated for centuries and is not yet resolved to everyone's satisfaction. It cannot be discussed now. Nevertheless, assuming that it was impossible for Him to sin, because of the nature of His person, yet it is also possible to assume that He did not know this was the case. Mk 13: 32

implies that the Son, in His incarnate rôle, was not omniscient—there is at least one thing recorded there which He did not know. If, then, there was one thing He did not know, ignorance of other things was also possible, even this concerning whether or not He could sin. In any case, though Hebrews says He lived His life **without sinning** (15, Gk. *chōris hamartias*, lit. 'apart from sin', not meaning 'without the ability to sin' but 'without having in fact sinned'), it also makes clear that Jesus experienced temptations in just the same manner as we do and that this sinlessness was the result of 'conscious decision' on His part in the midst of intense struggle (cf. 5: 7-9). One must never suppose that His victory over temptation was 'the mere formal consequences of His divine nature'. Any interpretation of the person of Christ which in any way diminishes the force and genuineness of His temptations cannot be correct.

ii. The Priest's Qualifications (5: 1-10)

Now the writer turns to discuss the qualifications of the high priest (1-4). He sees only two of them to be significant enough to mention: (*a*) that the priest be human, **chosen from among men** (1), and (*b*) that he be appointed to his post by God (4). God ordained that the priest be a man (not an angel or some other celestial being) because the priest's main function is **to act on behalf of men in relation to God** (1), that is, stand 'on the Godward side' of men (A. Nairne, *The Epistle of Priesthood*, 1913, p. 146). Only man is **beset with** human **weakness** (2). Hence, only man can understand human weakness in such a way as to **deal gently with the ignorant and wayward** (2). Thus only when the priest is a man can man be assured that he is fully able to sympathize with his frailty and thus represent him fairly before God. [Note: In the days of the Aaronic priesthood the priest was constantly reminded of his own moral inadequacy (not physical inadequacy for he was to be without physical defects) by the need of constantly offering sacrifice **for his own sins as well as for those of the people** (3). Attention is never drawn to this part of the analogy when applied to Christ, for, as the writer has already stated, He was without sin.] The verb **deal gently** (2) translates a verb (*metriopathein*) which describes the mean between indifference and hypersensitivity. Understood in this way the priest is one who must not be apathetic to nor yet too easily affected by the problems of those he represents. The verb in other contexts, however, was associated also with such ideas as magnanimity and clemency. Hence, it also possesses the meanings of condescension, indul-

gence and generosity, making it almost synonymous with sympathy (Gk. *sympathein*). If this
meaning is accepted it rather describes the
priest as compassionate, a characteristic which
belongs to his very nature (Spicq, *Comm*. II,
pp. 108-9). Notice that the sacrifices to be
offered are for sins of ignorance and wayward-
ness (1-2), not for wilful sins (cf. Num. 15:
22-31).

Not only must the priest be human but he
must be ordained by God (4). This is an office
so important that no man has the right to
take the honour upon himself (4)—only God
possesses the prerogative of priestly appointment.
The precedent was set when Aaron was so
established in his office.

Having called attention to the qualifications
for the priesthood in general the writer now
applies them specifically to Christ in a manner
which shows the studied nature of his rhetorical
style. He treats these priestly qualifications in
reverse fashion (5-10). Firstly, he dispenses with
the divine call rather hurriedly. There is simply
the statement: **Christ . . . was appointed**
as priest (5), and the proof from Scripture: the
very one who earlier had said to Christ
'Thou art my Son' (Ps. 2: 7, cf. Heb. 1: 5),
now has said to Him **'Thou art a priest for
ever, after the order of Melchizedek'** (Ps.
110: 4).

Secondly, the writer discusses the humanity
of the priest but in far greater detail, for in his
thinking it is a subject which requires special
emphasis. He wishes to show most clearly
that Christ was truly human, that He truly
did know what it meant to suffer as a human,
that He truly did learn by experience what
total submission to God involved, so that as
a result He can be fully aware of our problems
and fully capable of sympathizing with us in
them. The writer does this with language
unparalleled in the NT for its intensity (7-8).
In the days of his flesh (7) 'should not be
pressed to imply that the writer thought Jesus
was no longer incarnate after his death and
exaltation' (F. F. Bruce, 'Hebrews', *Peake's
Commentary on the Bible*, newly revised, 1962,
ad loc.). We are not told what Christ asked for
in the **prayers and supplications** He made
with loud cries (lit. 'shouts') **and tears** (7),
but the language is suggestive of Gethsemane,
or of times similar to that recorded in Jn 12: 27:
'Father save me from (lit. 'out of') this hour!'
It can be inferred, therefore, that it was a prayer
for deliverance offered, nevertheless, in submission to the Father's will And **he was heard**
because of His submissiveness or **his godly fear**
(7). The one **who was able to save him from**
(lit. 'out of') **death** did deliver him out of

death by resurrection, though it was not His
purpose to save Him from dying.

Although he was a Son (8) means 'although
He was Son' (cf. the note on 1: 2), and by the
expression, **he learned obedience through
what he suffered,** the writer is saying that He,
now in the sphere of humanity, must, as must
all 'sons' (cf. 12: 7 ff.), learn what it means to
obey God when encircled by human sufferings
and temptations. If His sufferings and temptations were genuine (cf. the comment at the end
of ch. 4), then His obedience could have been
won only through struggle. Hence, the perfection (9) He achieved must of necessity be
a moral perfection, whose benefit extends far
beyond Himself to embrace in redemptive
fashion **all who** in turn **obey him** (9).

From the words the writer chooses for this
section, it seems clear that he intends to describe
this 'Son of God' in sharp contrast to the first
'son of God' (Adam, cf. Lk. 3: 38), who, when
put to the test, chose to disobey the divine
demand rather than submit to it, and who,
as a consequence, became the universal cause
of death rather than of life (cf. Rom. 5: 18 f.;
cf. also Heb. 10: 4-10). Jesus, on the other hand,
having obeyed completely **became the source
of eternal salvation** (9)—a salvation mediated
through His rôle as **high priest after the order
of Melchizedek** (10).

V. WARNING AGAINST THE FATEFUL CONSEQUENCES OF IMMATURITY (5: 11-6: 20a)

i. Possibility of Immaturity Leading to a Final Break with Christ (5: 11-6: 8)

It is the writer's purpose now to explore deeply
the meaning of Christ's priesthood. But because
this part of his sermon (Gk. *logos*, 11) is **hard to
explain** to those who are **dull of hearing** (11),
and infantile in their understanding of **the
word of righteousness** (13), he feels compelled
to postpone it until first he has stirred them out
of their lethargy. From this it is clear that the
problem Hebrews is attempting to resolve is
the problem of inactivity, of not persevering,
of dullness and spiritual immaturity. It is this
kind of attitude, insignificant as it may seem,
which if persisted in, slowly, almost imperceptibly leads one to break finally with Christ.
As the precaution against such a tragedy the
writer urges them to **have their faculties
trained by practice** so as to be able **to
distinguish good from evil** (14), to engage
in moral exercises, in the development of mental
habits by which they may become mature
(Gk. 'perfect'), i.e., able to appreciate **solid
food**—the significance of Christ's rôle as
priest, for example—and no longer require

milk—the **first principles of God's word** (12), or salvation's ABC's (cf. 1 C. 2: 1–3: 2).

Since, therefore, spiritual maturity (or immaturity) is largely a matter of the will, the writer urges them to **leave the elementary doctrines of Christ and go on to maturity** (6: 1). It is possible that the verb translated 'let us go on' should be given a passive meaning—'let us be carried along', for there is an ambiguity in meaning arising from the form of the Greek verb (*pherōmetha*). If the passive meaning is the true one 'the thought [would not be] primarily of personal effort, but of personal surrender to an active influence. The power is working; we have only to yield ourselves to it' (Westcott, *Comm.*, p. 145; cf. 2 Pet. 1: 21). The idea of **maturity** is consonant with that use of the word in 5: 14. It means those capable of understanding, appreciating and of being affected by 'the exposition of Christian truth with its higher development'.

The writer's summary of **elementary doctrines** from which Christians are to move on in the sense of building upon a foundation, falls into three groups of two each. The first is repentance and faith and has to do with the Christian's 'personal character'. This repentance is a radical reorientation of outlook which results in a turning away from **dead works** (1), that is, from all activity done in rebellion against God (cf. 9: 14). Faith, on the other hand, is both a trust set upon and an obedience rendered to God. The second group involves the 'outward ordinances' of the Christian society and is composed of (*a*) **instruction about ablutions,** or baptisms, which are plural, because instruction concerning Christian baptism required that it be set off against other baptismal rites either Jew or pagan, and (*b*) **the laying on of hands,** which act was 'the sequel and complement of baptism', and the symbol of ordination (cf. 1 Tim. 4: 14; 2 Tim. 1: 6; cf. C. J. Vaughan, *The Epistle to the Hebrews*, 1890, p. 103). The last group is eschatological and has to do with the Christian's 'connexion with the unseen world': **resurrection of the dead and eternal judgment** (2).

And move on we will **if God permits** us to do so (3). This statement of condition implies that some will not be able to advance, for by their own decisions they will have placed themselves beyond the range of God's permission. The writer now comes to the most solemn warning thus far in his letter as he shows the tragic end which may befall a person who has made his Christian 'confession', but who has failed to advance beyond a rudimentary knowledge of the implications of this confession, or of the ultimate significance of Jesus for the forgiveness of his sins.

The things listed here by the writer to describe the 'fallen' are most certainly things which characterize all true Christians. These **have once been enlightened** (4), an expression which could mean complete inner illumination—the God-given capacity to understand and respond positively to the Christian message (cf. Eph. 1: 18; 3: 9; 2 C. 4: 4). They also are those who **tasted the heavenly gift** (4). Now if Christ is this gift from above (cf. Jn 4: 10; Rom. 5: 15; 8: 32), and if 'tasted' means to have 'experienced' or 'come to know' in the fullest sense (cf. Arndt and Gingrich, *Greek-English Lexicon, geuomai;* cf. Heb. 2: 9), then obviously the writer had in mind a matter of grace and divine life procured by Christ and enjoyed fully by the Christian (the middle voice, *geuesthai*, marking more forcefully the personal character of the experience; cf. C. Spicq, *Comm.*, II, p. 150). Again, they are said to **have become partakers of the Holy Spirit** (4). This translation points to the fact that these may have been recipients of the Holy Spirit much the same as were the disciples of Jesus when He breathed on them (Jn 20: 22), or the Samaritans when the apostles laid their hands on them (Ac. 8: 17)—recipients of the essence of the Christian life (Rom. 8: 9b). Finally they are those who **have tasted the goodness of the word of God and the powers of the age to come** (5). They have experienced supernatural energies resulting from the work of Christ which are clear manifestations of the nearness (or the presence) of the messianic era (Ac. 2: 11 f.; cf. Spicq, *Comm.*).

Because this description of the 'apostate' indicates that he showed every sign of being a Christian, a very great many commentators have so understood him to be, i.e., a true Christian. The Shepherd of Hermas (*c.* A.D. 148) seems to have been the first to give this interpretation to Hebrews 6, though he tempers the 'no second repentance' theme, by allowing at least one more chance (Mandates, IV. 3).

It is necessary to point out, however, that these descriptive expressions are susceptible of more than one interpretation, and, in their less than 'ultimate' meaning, may be applied to 'professing' Christians as well as to 'genuine' believers. 'Enlightened' (4) is a term applied by Justin Martyr (d. *c.* A.D. 165; 1 *Apol.* 61: 12 f.) to the baptized—those who had given consent to the truth of the Christian catechism by their submission to baptism. It is just possible, therefore, that the writer of Hebrews used it in this sense also. At least the Peshitta (a fourth century Syriac translation) so understood the word, substituting, as it did, 'have gone down for baptism' for 'enlightened'. Moreover, several interpreters (cf. Spicq, *Comm.*, II, p. 150 for a list of these) understand the expression, 'tasted the heavenly gift' (4) to mean partaking of the Lord's Supper, 'the divine gift *par excellence*' (cf. Mt. 26: 26 ff., and especially Ac. 20: 11, Gk., where 'taste' is used *à propos* of eating the eucharistic bread). 'Partakers of' the Holy Spirit (4) may have the less ultimate meaning of 'partners along with' the Holy Spirit (cf. 2: 14; 3: 1, 14; 12: 8). And the last two expressions (5) may mean that these have seen the creative power of the preached Gospel and have themselves performed miracles (cf. Judas Iscariot).

To sum up: the writer, in composing such a list as this, may have intended to describe one who has all the ear-marks of Christianity and who yet is not a real Christian. The *one* proof of genuineness is a continuing loyalty which keeps faith to the very end. Just as all Israel left Egypt under Moses, crossed the Red Sea, ate the heavenly manna, observed the mighty acts of God, etc., giving all appearances of a people of faith, and yet only two entered Canaan, the rest falling dead in the desert, so it is possible that within the visible Church there may be those who have experienced all the advantages of Christianity, instruction, baptism, the Lord's Supper, manifestations of the Spirit, etc. (though it should be noted carefully that there is no gift of love mentioned in this list, cf. 6: 10), and who yet are capable of renouncing it all because the basic inner attitude, of which they themselves may not be fully aware, has become one of unbelief or disobedience, of an attitude of NO toward God. The situation here, then, may be analogous to that in Mt. 7: 21 ff.

In any case, if those who have been blessed in such an extraordinary fashion do **commit apostasy** (6, lit. 'fall by the wayside', Gk., *parapesontas*, an expression perhaps occasioned by the desert experience of ancient Israel), **it is impossible to restore them again to repentance** (4), **since they crucify the Son of God on their own account and hold him up to contempt** (6). 'Repentance' here is more than grief for past wrong done; it is a change of mind or attitude—a positive, affirmative act which accompanies the beginning of a new religious experience and moral life (Arndt and Gingrich, *Greek-English Lexicon*), rather than a mere negative turning away from sin. It refers to that disposition of mind toward Christ which prevailed when the confessing Christian was baptized, but which, through lack of moral exercise (5: 14), now has been

altered radically. And the truly terrible thing about this apostate attitude is that it is *humanly* (or psychologically) impossible to change it back, for it is not the result of a quick decision in a weak moment, but of a gradual hardening process within the mind which has crystallized now into a 'constant attitude of hostility towards Christ' (as the expressions 'since they crucify', etc., using the present tenses as they do, imply). Therefore all confessing Christians must stir up themselves and others lest continued immaturity in the Christian profession lead to eventual hostility toward Christ. Those who remain loyal to the end demonstrate that their confession was genuine.

Verses 7 and 8 contain a parable the interpretation of which is consistent with this emphasis of the writer upon perseverance as the real test of genuineness: the rain is to be equated with the five extraordinary blessings enumerated in vv. 4-5, and the earth with the readers of the letter. The rain is common to both good earth and bad, i.e., great spiritual blessings are common to all confessing Christians, those who truly believe and those who merely confess that they do. It is what the soils produce—the kind of lives the confessing Christians live—that makes visibly clear what their true nature is and what kind of seed is within them. And yet, as in the horticultural realm where soil which is of poor quality and poor content often cannot be distinguished immediately from the good (for after a rain even the bad ground *looks* promising with its myriads of verdant shoots), so it is within the visible Christian Church. All may have been well instructed, etc., and made their confession of faith, and given evidence of genuineness. But as time proves some soil to be bad and its produce **thorns and thistles** (8), or the reverse, so it does with those who claim to be Christians. The perseverance of the saints, on one hand, offers proof of the reality of their confession. The lack of it gives testimony to the opposite. The one receives God's blessing (7), while the other is **near to being cursed and its end is to be burned** (8). 'Near to being cursed' does not mean merely that judgment is threatening, and may be avoided by a subsequent and unexpected fertility of the land, but that it is inevitable (cf. the same construction found in 8: 13, *engys aphanismou*, where the disappearance of the old covenant means not that it is merely liable to disappear, but rather that its disappearance is certain; cf. also Mk 1: 15 with Mt. 12: 28). Nor is it proper to think only of the fruit of the land as being burned away, for the burning is actually the punishment visited upon the accursed land itself (cf. Gen.

19: 24; Dt. 29: 22). The expression 'whose end is to be burned' may be a Hebraism equivalent to our expression 'dedicated to destruction' (cf. Ps. 109: 13). It is simply the application of the principle set forth in 2 C. 11: 15: 'Their end will correspond to their deeds'—i.e., whatever happens to their fruit happens to them also (Spicq, *Comm.*, II, p. 156). In other words, the one who confesses to being a Christian and enjoys all the spiritual benefits attendant upon this confession, but who does not persist in his loyalty to Christ to the end, can only look forward to a fury of fire which will consume him in the day of judgment (10: 27); whereas the one who confesses to being a Christian and continues faithfully in this confession enjoys and will enjoy the blessing of God.

ii. Encouragement and Consolation (6: 9–20)

After the warning comes encouragement. This section begins with an assertion of the writer's confidence in his readers, whom he calls **beloved** only here in his letter (9). It is a confidence inspired by his knowledge of the character of **God** who **is not so unjust as to overlook** their **work** (10), and of their past and present life of **work** and **love** (note this important word; it is not 'labour of love' as in AV) shown for God's sake **in serving the saints** (10, cf. also 10: 32–34). The encouragement continues with the writer giving his reasons for such a severe warning. It was because of his passionate concern for the welfare of each individual Christian (11). It also was given so that they might demonstrate some excitement or **earnestness in realizing the full assurance of hope** (11), and so that they might not become dull (**sluggish,** 12), or so that they might be roused out of their dullness if they were that already (cf. 5: 11), and finally, so that they might be spurred on to be **imitators of those who through faith and patience inherit the promises** (12, cf. ch. 11), that is, of those who through continued obedient loyalty to God have already entered into the realization of His offer. 'Once again, continuance is emphasized as the proof of reality'. Once again, also, it is evident that spiritual lethargy, the danger of 'drifting away', indifference, and the like, are the sins combated in this letter.

The appeal to perseverance is now given incentive by assuring the reader of the absolute validity of the divine promise (13–20). Originally God made a promise to Abraham. To give him incentive to believe that the promise would be fulfilled, God, accommodating Himself to such a human custom as that of a man taking an oath by something greater than himself, thereby giving added assurance of the validity of his statement, **swore by himself** (13), since there was none greater by whom He could take such an oath. **And thus Abraham** was given every possible assurance that if he would patiently endure he would obtain the promise (15). Abraham did in fact obtain the promise (15), but, in the thinking of the writer, the scope of that promise was not exhausted in the earthly experience of this man. God not only had said to him, **'Surely I will bless you and multiply you'** (14, cf. Gen. 22: 17), but He also had said 'In your seed shall all the nations of the earth be blessed' (Gen. 22: 18). Now although there is here no quotation from Gen. 22: 18, nor any explicit reference to the fact that Abraham's 'seed' is Christ, yet like Paul (cf. Gal. 3: 16) the writer surely must have had it in mind for he envisions Christians as being **the heirs of the promise** made to Abraham (17). Consequently they, too, are interested in its validity. The fact that it involves **two unchangeable things**—the promise itself and the oath which rests on the very being of God—**in which it is impossible that God should** (ever) **prove false,** provides **strong encouragement** (18) for Christians to persevere while hoping for the ultimate fulfilment of that promise, i.e., the heavenly blessing to which even Abraham looked (cf. 11: 8–19).

This hope, is like **a sure and steadfast anchor of the soul** (19) which Christ has taken and dropped securely within the harbour. Actually the writer of Hebrews mixes his metaphors at this point, for he does not say 'harbour', as one might expect with 'anchor', but rather **inner shrine behind the curtain** (19). This anchor of hope ties the Christian securely to the place of God's presence, the heavenly world. This unexpected change in figure of speech is a neat rhetorical device to return the readers to the subject already begun— the priesthood of Christ (ch. 5). The veil was the inner curtain separating the holy from the most holy place. Christ has penetrated that veil and has gone into the holy of holies to work **on our behalf** (20). But He has done so as a forerunner (Gk. *prodromos*, used in classical literature of a scout reconnoitring, or of a herald announcing the coming of a king)—a word which implies that others are to follow, i.e., Christians too are to be brought into that same sacred area. This was indeed a startling statement, for though the ancient high priest was his people's representative he was never their forerunner—they were never allowed to follow him within the curtain. But the key-note of Hebrews is that the new high priest guarantees to every believer the privilege of confident access into this most holy place—the very presence of the living God, and it is summed up in one carefully chosen word: 'forerunner'. Jesus has 'gone that we may follow too' (F. W. Gingrich, 'Forerunner', Hastings' *Dictionary of the Bible*, rev. ed., pp. 303-4).

VI. THE PRIESTHOOD OF CHRIST (7: 1-10: 18)

i. After the Order of Melchizedek (7: 1-28)

The writer of Hebrews has mentioned Melchizedek several times already (5: 6, 10; 6: 20). Now he begins a full-blown discussion of him and his relation to Christ. Gen. 14: 17-20 provides the historical background, and serves several purposes: (*a*) to show the moral character of Melchizedek, (*b*) to demonstrate his greatness, and (*c*) to establish the existence of another order of priesthood than that of Aaron. Insight into his moral character is gained from an etymological study of his name and that of the city he ruled. Melchizedek is a name composed of two words which when translated mean **king of righteousness** (2). The name of his city, Salem, meant 'peace'. Hence, to the writer of Hebrews, Melchizedek was a king characterized by righteousness and his rule by peace (cf. Isa. 32: 1, 17). His greatness is seen from the fact that he blessed Abraham the patriarch (i.e., the father of us all) at a time when Abraham was second to none in the land—victor over Chedorlaomer and the kings who were with him, and from the fact that **to him Abraham apportioned a tenth part of everything** (2). Proof of the existence of another order than that of Aaron and his descendants lies in the fact that Melchizedek is **without father or mother or genealogy,** without **beginning of days** or **end of life** (3), expressions which in themselves probably mean no more than that there is no mention of father and mother, etc., in inspired Scripture. But by a principle of exegesis, that the silences of Scripture are as significant as its statements, the writer understands from such omission that Melchizedek was a solitary figure in history who possessed his priesthood in his own right, not by virtue of descent, 'who never assumed and never lost his office', hence, whose priesthood abides forever. Significantly, the writer of Hebrews does not identify Melchizedek with Christ, but says that he resembles **the Son of God** (3). Melchizedek thus was the facsimile of which Christ is the reality. Christ, therefore, is king of righteousness and peace in the fullest sense, and priest 'in likeness of', 'after the order of' Melchizedek (15), that is, priest forever!

In vv. 4-10 the writer continues to magnify the priesthood of Melchizedek. He does this by reiterating the fact that Abraham **gave him a tithe of** (the choicest of) **the spoils** (4) and in return received his priestly blessing (6). By accepting this rôle of 'tithed' and 'blessed', Abraham who 'owned the promises' doubly acknowledged his inferiority to Melchizedek (7). The writer further magnifies that mysterious priesthood by first calling attention to the fact that the levitical priests are superior to all other Israelites in that they alone **have a commandment in the law to take tithes from the people . . . , their brethren** (5), and then by showing that even **Levi himself, who receives tithes, paid tithes** to Melchizedek **through Abraham** (9). The levitical priests, then, though superior to the mass of Israel, are indeed inferior to Melchizedek, and their priesthood to his. Thus the writer's argument runs like this: The levitical priests are superior to the rest of the Israelites, because, though mortal, they, nevertheless, tithe their brethren; Levi is superior to the priests because he is their progenitor; Abraham is greater than Levi for he is father of them all; Melchizedek is greater than Abraham if for no other reason than that he both tithed and blessed Abraham; therefore, Melchizedek is greater than Abraham, Levi, the levitical priests and all Israel. The point of all this is, of course, to prove the ultimate superiority of Christ's priesthood, which by now is quite easy to do for the writer has already implied Christ's superiority to Melchizedek when he said that Melchizedek resembled the Son of God (3). Christ is greater than Melchizedek as the reality is greater than the facsimile. Therefore, Christ is greater than Abraham, Levi and all his descendants, and His priesthood, too, is greater than theirs.

Verses 11-28 deal now with this new order of priesthood and the need for it. First of all the writer points out that the new order was predicted (he returns to Ps. 110: 4), and it was predicted because **perfection** was not **attainable through the Levitical priesthood** (11). **Perfection** here means man's ability to draw near to God (cf. v. 19; 9: 9; 10: 22). The old order of priesthood could never effect such an approach, though this was the chief purpose of the priesthood, simply because it could never fully remove the sin which barred the way. Therefore, the new order was in the mind and plan of God even while the old was in full operation. This means that the old law and the old covenant (8: 7 ff.) also were provisional, and were destined to be set aside along with the priesthood, for the whole legal system 'turned upon the priesthood' since **under** (Gk. 'based upon') **it the people received the law** (11). Thus, **when there is a change in the priesthood** there is necessarily a change in the law as well (12). 'The high priesthood is like the keystone of the whole structure of the Mosaic Law; all the other regulations fell away of their own accord when the priesthood passed over to Christ' (E. F. Scott, *Comm., ad loc.*).

The need for such a radical change was great. It is obvious that the one of whom these things are spoken belonged to another tribe (13) to which priestly privileges did not belong. The writer understands the law to forbid one from any tribe other than that of Levi to serve at the altar (13). But it is evident that our Lord was descended from Judah (14) and that He nevertheless was destined to be priest, for He was the historical reality of the prediction of Ps. 110: 4—'a priest for ever' (15-17). Thus it is even more clear that since the law allowed only the sons of Levi to be priests it had to be abrogated to make way for this one who possessed a priesthood not by virtue of legal descent (which the writer calls bodily, meaning physical, mortal and concerned with externals), but by the power of an indestructible life (16). The emphasis here is upon the eternal qualities of His priesthood which are proven by the scriptural quotation in the following verse (17). Though the writer does not mention the fact that our Lord descended from David, he demonstrates, nonetheless, that Christ combines in Himself the offices of both king and priest—'of the tribe of Judah', and 'according to the order of Melchizedek'. [Contrast the concept current in the Qumran texts of *two* messiahs, one priestly, who was superior in rank, and one kingly (cf. *Manual of Discipline*, 9: 11, in the translation of A. Dupont-Sommer, *The Essene Writings from Qumran*, 1961). It is possible that Hebrews combats this idea in this careful exegesis of the meaning of Melchizedek.]

Verses 18-19 constitute a summary of the writer's argument concerning the supersession of the law. 19. the law made nothing perfect: that is, it brought no one to God, but the 'substitution' of a better hope ('of forgiveness and absolution') did (see Moffatt's comment on is introduced, *Comm., ad loc.*). Now it is possible for us to draw near to God (19), to worship truly, which to the writer of Hebrews is the fundamental element in redemption. For now man's relationship to God is no longer one of external ordinances simply, but it is an inward spiritual relationship which guarantees true communion with Him.

The ultimate superiority of Christ's priesthood is made even more clear in 20-25. Firstly, attention is called to the fact that God did not underwrite the old levitical priesthood as He did the new. They took their office without an oath (21). This means to the writer that it was only temporary—provisional. The priest 'after the order of Melchizedek', however, was confirmed in his office by an oath from God (21), hence His priesthood is eternal. This makes Jesus (note the name) the surety of a better covenant (22), for since the priesthood and the covenant are inextricably bound together (cf. note on 'covenant' in ch. 8), the covenant is only as permanent as the priesthood. Secondly, the multiplicity of the former priests in contrast to the one new priest also emphasizes the superiority of the latter. Previously death kept a priest from continuing in office (cf. v. 16); it made his work incomplete. But not so with the new priest—he holds his priesthood permanently, 'as one not to be transferred to another' (Gk. *aparabatos*), because he continues for ever (24, cf. also 13: 8). This brings the writer to the climax of this part of his priestly discourse. Because Christ's priesthood is inviolable and 'untransferable' he is able for all time to save those who draw near to God through him (25). [Note: (a) 'completely' better translates the Gk. *eis to panteles* (cf. Lk. 13: 11) than does the 'for all time' of the RSV. Thus, 'He can guarantee their total and final salvation' (F. F. Bruce, *Peake, ad loc.*); (b) the meaning and tense of the verb 'draw near' indicate that those who *constantly* come to worship God through Jesus Christ are the ones He is able to save.] Again, because Christ's priesthood is inviolable and 'untransferable' He is able to make continual intercession for us—uninterruptedly He can take up our case before God.

The final contrasts showing the superiority of Christ's priesthood to the levitical are made, firstly, between His personal character as priest and theirs: He was one who exactly suited our need, 'altogether pure within'; they were compelled to offer sacrifices daily, even for their own sins (27), and secondly, between the quality of His sacrifice and theirs: His was the offering up of Himself, a conscious willing victim, of such a nature that it need never be repeated, hence it was once for all (27); theirs was the sacrifice of unwilling, unthinking beasts whose blood could never take away sin (cf. 10: 1 ff.), hence it was a daily perpetual affair (27).

ii. Christ's Priestly Ministry and the New Covenant (8: 1-13)

From a description of the greatness of the priest the writer now turns to discuss, as the crowning part of his argument (Manson, *Epistle to the Hebrews*, p. 123), the greatness of

His ministry—a greatness which is due largely to the sphere in which this ministry is carried out. The high **point in what we are saying** (1) is not simply that **we have such a high priest** as that described in ch. 7, but that we have such a high priest **seated . . . in heaven** (1). For the writer of Hebrews the unseen world is the real world which faith takes with all seriousness (2, cf. 6: 20; 11: 1 f., 16; 12: 22), and the world of the phenomenal is but a copy and shadow of that reality (cf. Num. 24: 6, LXX, and Exod. 25: 9, 40). Thus when he states that Christ as high priest is in heaven, he is doing more than merely telling his readers where Jesus is now. He is telling them that His ministry is a 'real' ministry because its sphere of operation is the real world—**the sanctuary and the true tent which is set up not by man but by the Lord** (2, cf. vv. 5 f. for the scriptural proof for the existence of the heavenly sanctuary). Thus His ministry, as His person (ch. 7), stands in distinct contrast to that of the levitical priests. Their ministry was earth-bound. Hence **they serve a copy and shadow of the heavenly sanctuary** (5). They and their service, too, are but shadows cast by the good things which were to come, and not the very realities themselves (cf. 10: 1).

To review, the writer's argument seems to go like this: Christ is a high priest established so by God (ch. 7). Since 'the one task of a high priest is to offer sacrifice in a sanctuary', He also needed **to have something to offer** (8: 3) and a sanctuary in which to do it. But because there already were priests on earth **who offer gifts according to the law** (4), and because there was no room for Christ in the earthly sanctuary by virtue of His descent from Judah (cf. 7: 13), His sphere of priestly service must of necessity be heaven if He is to carry out the purpose of His office. This, then, means that **Christ has obtained a ministry . . . much more excellent than the old** (6). And as a corollary to this, the covenant He mediates is a better covenant than the former **since it is** (legally) **enacted** (Gk. *nenomothetētai*) **on better promises** (6).

The concept of 'covenant' plays an important rôle in Hebrews, used by the writer at least seventeen times. The Greek word for it is *diathēkē*, which in classical times meant 'disposition', 'testament' or 'will'. But this meaning is never given to the word in Hebrews (with the possible exception of 9: 15 f.). The writer's context for understanding *diathēkē* is not the classical world, but the world of the OT. There it was used by the LXX translators to convey the ideas contained in the Hebrew *berîth*—a word which usually meant a covenant or an agreement between two parties consenting to certain conditions set down for the purpose of attaining some object of mutual desire. Each party, then, was under obligation to fulfill his end of the bargain. Sometimes the covenant was sealed with the blood of a slain animal (Gen. 15: 1-10; Exod. 24: 5-8), which may have symbolized the deaths of those making the covenant—deaths which put them, figuratively speaking, in a position where they could do nothing to break the agreement entered in upon. [Note: in all likelihood the Hebrew verb 'to make a covenant', *kārath*, goes back to this very ritual, for it literally means 'to cut', i.e., to cut up an animal in order to seal the contract.] In addition to the external obligations each took upon himself in entering a covenant relationship, there was also a spiritual aspect to the ancient covenant—a pledge of loyalty or community of soul—which can best be represented by the expression, 'loyal love' or 'steadfast-love'.

The covenant between God and man, however, must never be thought of merely as a contract between two equal parties. Rather God is the sole initiator, who sets down the terms under which the agreement will go into effect. He then invites men to join with Him in it (cf. Heb. 8: 8-9 where God speaks and says 'I will establish' and 'I made'; cf. also Dt. 4: 13). Though God is the Senior Partner, so to speak, men, nevertheless, are free to respond, free to choose whether or not they will accept His invitation. If they do they become His worshipping people and He becomes their God (cf. Exod. 19: 5 f. with Heb. 8: 10).

There are many covenants mentioned in the OT and the covenant concept is a developing one, but the writer of Hebrews here seems to have in mind that covenant which was inaugurated at Sinai. The conditions under which it went into effect involved the keeping of the Law (cf. Exod. 24: 6-8; Dt. 4: 12 ff.; 5: 1 ff.; 1 Kg. 8: 21). The Law, however, was an external voice to the people and never really a part of them. Hence, they could not observe it without transgressing its ordinances. This was indeed a severe weakness of the old covenant but not its greatest, since within the covenant relationship the people really were not expected to be sinless. God recognized that 'to err is human' (Heb. 5: 2; 9: 7), and, therefore, provided for such human failure by inaugurating the sacrificial system for the covering of all those sins of ignorance and error done within the covenant. [Note: Wilful sins were another matter. They were basically sins against the covenant and involved wilful rebellion and unbelief. For such sins there was no sacrifice (cf. Heb. 10: 26).] It was at this point, however, that the real weakness of the old covenant became painfully obvious. Its sacrificial system, centring as it did in its high priest, could not even cope with those transgressions done within the covenant so as to give the people involved a sense of true forgiveness (Heb. 9: 15; 10: 4). Now, however, under the new covenant (though the conditions for its effectiveness are not here made explicit), there is provided a spontaneous inner correspondence to the expressed will of God by the inscription of His laws upon the human heart (Heb. 8: 10), and the complete forgiveness of sins by the priestly work of Christ. Now God's covenant people can draw near to Him with a cleansed conscience (Heb. 8: 12; 10: 21 f.). From the idea that the covenant is a relationship existing between God and His people maintained through atoning sacrifice, it is clear that the high priest becomes the central figure in it. He is the minister of atonement. The covenant relationship, therefore, is only as good as the high priest who administers it. The ministry of the ancient high priest was imperfect. Thus the old covenant also was imperfect and hence transitory (8: 13)—weaknesses which were recognized even by the old covenant itself, for from within it comes the prediction of a new one to take its place (8). But our high priest is Jesus the Son of God (4: 14), forever ordained to this office by an inviolable oath of God (7: 21), who continually ministers effectively in the unseen world of realities (8: 1 ff.). It is no wonder then, that the writer is so sure that the new covenant **is enacted on better promises** (8: 6; for this discussion see A. B. Davidson, *The Epistle to the Hebrews*, 1950, pp. 162 ff.; E. D. Burton, *Galatians (ICC)*, note on 'covenant' in the Appendix; G. Vos, *The Teaching of the Epistle to the Hebrews*, 1956).

From this it is clear that in the mind of the writer of Hebrews Jeremiah's prediction of the new covenant now has found its fulfilment in the Christian era. He does not look forward to some future time when this will be true. It is true now. The laws of God are written on the Christians' hearts (cf. Rom. 7: 22; 8: 4) and Christ is the perfect priest who makes it possible for God to **be merciful toward their iniquities,** and to forget their sin (8: 12). That this is so can be seen by comparing this passage with 10: 15 ff. where the writer again quotes this same prophecy of Jeremiah and says that the Holy Spirit is thus bearing witness to *us* in the statement, 'This is the covenant that I will make with *them* . . . says the Lord'. The 'house of Israel' (8: 8, 10), thus, becomes that

'Israel of God' Paul writes of in Gal. 6: 16. Verse 11, which seems not yet to have been fulfilled, can be understood as a powerful, perhaps poetic, way of expressing the idea that the Christian, as none before him, has been brought into an intimate and profound relationship with God so that his will conforms to the will of God 'by a direct personal communication of instruction and influence' (Vaughan, *Comm.*, p. 150).

iii. The Priestly Ministry of the Two Covenants Contrasted (9: 1-28)

The writer continues his contrast between the old and new covenants by a description, not of the temple at Jerusalem and its ritual service (which would have been particularly appropriate if the readers were 'Hebrews'), but of the wilderness tabernacle (cf. Exod. 25-31; 35-40) which had been the focal point of worship for the ancient 'wandering people of God'.

He refers to the tabernacle as **an earthly sanctuary** (1), which to him meant that it belonged to the imperfect world of shadows (as contrasted with the place where Christ serves, 8: 1-5). Thus at the outset the writer again calls attention to the essential and radical difference between the two covenants. The reference to the furniture within the tabernacle is, as the writer himself implies, of secondary importance to his present discussion, hence **of these things we cannot now speak in detail** (5). Suffice it to say that what seems to be a mistake with reference to the placing of the golden altar of incense (probably not 'censer' as AV), namely, behind the second curtain and in the holy of holies (3-4 contra Exod. 40: 26), may not be a mistake at all. It must be noted that the writer says there is a tent **called the Holy of Holies, having the golden altar of incense** (3-4). He does not say 'in which is the golden altar' as he did in describing the position of the furniture mentioned above in v. 2. The substitution of 'having' for 'in which' 'itself points clearly to something different from mere position'. It was probably intended to mean that the altar properly belonged to the holy of holies. 'The ark and the altar of incense typified the two innermost conceptions of the heavenly sanctuary, the manifestation of God and the spiritual worship of man. And thus they are placed in significant connection in the Pentateuch: Exod. 30: 6; 40: 5; cf. Lev. 4: 7; 16: 12, 18 (before the Lord)' (Westcott, *Comm.*, p. 247, cf. also 1 Kg. 6: 22). One should also note that though the tables of the covenant were indeed placed within the ark (Exod. 25: 16, 21) there is no explicit statement in the OT that the pot of manna and Aaron's rod were also put inside. Rather it is stated that they were laid up 'before the testimony' (Exod. 16: 34; Num. 17: 10). Perhaps the writer here is following a tradition which placed all within the ark in order to show that interposed between these symbols of Israel's rebellion (so Chrysostom: 'the tables of the covenant because he broke the former ones, and the manna because they murmured . . . and the rod of Aaron which budded because they rebelled') and a holy God **were the cherubim of glory overshadowing the mercy seat** (5), i.e., interposed between God and the people's sin was the place of atonement.

The author continues in vv. 6–10 to point out the symbolic nature of the ancient tabernacle, the very construction of which was the Holy Spirit's way of proclaiming that free access to God was impossible under the old covenant (8). Everyone, except the high priest (and even he but for one day in the year—the day of atonement, cf. Lev. 16), was shut out by a thick veil (and by ritual law) from the place where God visibly manifested His gracious presence— the holy of holies. **According to this arrangement** it is obvious, then, that the gifts and sacrifices which were offered did not perfect the conscience of the worshipper (9) for he was ever kept at a distance from God. They were wholly external, **regulations for the body** (10), and did not penetrate deeply enough into the moral realm to clear the conscience from its sense of guilt. And 'it is an axiom of the epistle that you cannot worship with a guilty conscience' (Narborough, *Comm.*, p. 115). These things, however, the tabernacle with its two tents, its symbolic furnishings and elaborate ritual, etc., were not valueless or wrong—only temporary for they were **imposed** (presumably by God) **until the time of reformation** (10), until the shadow should give way to reality.

That time has now come! The veil has been rent. What the ancient priesthood with its sacrifices and earthly sphere of operation could not accomplish, Christ was able to accomplish. As **high priest of the good things that have come** (11, not 'things to come' as AV), He has entered once for all (12) into **the greater and more perfect tent (not made with hands, that is, not of this creation)** (11). It was a heavenly tent He went into, being enabled to do so by virtue of (the meaning of the RSV 'taking', lit. 'through') **his own blood** (12). Thus, because of the merits of His person, the quality of His sacrifice, and the sphere of His ministry, Christ has secured *by himself* (and perhaps, 'for His own interest', Gk. *heuramenos*) **an eternal redemption** for us (12). The author does not state explicitly what this redemption is

from, nor does he say to whom the redemption price was paid, but this much at least may be inferred from the context: redemption means 'release' from a guilty conscience which was made possible only at great cost to the Redeemer.

The writer admits that the sacrifices belonging to the day of atonement (**the blood of goats and bulls**—cf. Lev. 16) and even the oblations offered on other occasions (**the ashes of a heifer**—cf. Num. 19), did have positive value. Though wholly external they provided ceremonial cleansing so that the defiled was not cut off from the covenant relationship with God (13). But he is willing to do this only that he might show the far greater effectiveness of Christ's sacrifice which was a 'conscious and willing' self-sacrifice, offered to God without moral blemish **through the eternal Spirit** (14). This last expression is a very difficult one. Some have interpreted it as meaning that Christ offered Himself to God 'after the power of an indissoluble life' (cf. 7: 16), that is to say, by virtue of His eternal nature. Others have understood it to mean that His sacrifice was of His own free will. Still others, that His sacrifice was offered on the spiritual plane and not on the ritual. Most probably correct is the view that as the Saviour depended upon the power and direction of the Holy Spirit to accomplish the will of the Father in all of His life, so He did in death. [Note: some early scribes must have understood it in this last sense because 'holy' appears with 'spirit' instead of 'eternal' in some ancient Greek and Latin manuscripts.] The effectiveness of the **blood of Christ** (14), is seen from the fact that it purifies the conscience (14)—it realizes in personal experience what all the other blood-sacrifices merely pointed to but could not effect.

The result of this cleansed conscience is release from **dead works** (see note on 4: 10) and the ability **to serve the living God** (14). **To serve** translates the Greek word *latreuein* which always means 'to carry out *religious* duties', 'to render service within a sanctuary' (Arndt and Gingrich, *A Greek-English Lexicon*). It is used several times in Hebrews, and at one point the one who thus 'serves' is called a 'worshipper' (9: 9). Thus **to serve the living God** really means that anyone whose conscience has been cleansed now may enter the holy of holies as a priest to render worshipful service to 'a God who is all life'.

Therefore (15), that is, because forgiveness of sins truly has been effected through the blood of Christ, as the cleansing of the conscience proves, **he is the mediator of a new covenant** —the one capable of guaranteeing that all **who are called** will **receive the promised**

eternal inheritance (15). But does 'the called' include only those believers living in the new age? What of those people of faith who lived under the old covenant (cf. 11: 8 ff., 13-16)? Are they left in their sins, since their institutions did not adequately cope with the sin-problem, removing it only ceremonially? The answer to this question is immediately forthcoming: the range of the effectiveness of Christ's death is so vast that it also **redeems them from the transgressions** (done) **under the first covenant** (15). The death of Christ is retroactive (cf. Rom. 3: 25 f.).

The phrase, **For where a will is involved, the death of the one who made it must be established** (16) may be translated differently from the RSV in two places: 'for' and 'will'. The 'for' could be the expansive 'now', since it appears to be the writer's intention to expand upon his statement concerning Christ as the mediator of the new covenant (cf. 15). He wishes to show that He is more than a mere intermediary between God and man; He is that very one whose death was required to ratify the covenant. The word 'will' (Gk. *diathēkē*) may also be translated by the word 'covenant'. It is true that *diathēkē* had as its basic idea 'will' or 'testament', but it must not be forgotten that the author of Hebrews had the meaning of this word mediated to him through the OT (the LXX), and that he never uses it in any other sense than 'covenant' anywhere else in his letter. This, coupled with the fact that v. 16 is an expansion of the idea begun in v. 15 where Christ is described as the mediator of a new covenant, makes it clear that the writer hardly intends to shift meanings with so little warning. What then do vv. 16-17 mean if the word 'covenant' is substituted wherever 'will' is found? It is important to notice that v. 16 does not say that he who makes the covenant must die, but that his death **must be established** (Gk. *pheresthai*, meaning 'brought forward', 'presented', 'introduced upon the scene', 'set in evidence'). Traditionally this was effected through the slaying of some animal 'introduced' by those entering into the covenant (cf. note on covenant, ch. 8). 'He who makes the covenant . . . is, for the purposes of the covenant, identified with the victim by whose representative death the covenant is ordinarily ratified. In the death of the victim his death is presented symbolically' (Westcott, *Comm.*, p. 265; cf. also pp. 298 ff.). Hence, the one who made the covenant is rendered (symbolically) incapable of doing anything to alter the covenant for in figure he has died. This is made clear in v. 17: **For a will** ('covenant') **takes effect only at death** (lit. 'is ratified over dead (bodies)'; cf.

Gen. 15: 7-21; Jer. 34: 18 f.), **since it is not in force as long as the one who made it is alive,** i.e., as long as he is not symbolically dead through the death of the covenant-ratifying victim. Thus the death of Christ, which was difficult for the readers of Hebrews to understand, was made meaningful to them by means of the covenant-concept and that which was required to put it into effect. God who made the covenant rendered the terms of the covenant unalterable, as far as He was concerned, by His death, not symbolically, but really, in the person of His eternal Son become man! [It is only proper to note, however, that this interpretation is rejected by many who see the plain sense of vv. 16, 17 to require the meaning of 'will' or 'testament' for *diathēkē*, for this is the only kind of covenant or settlement which has no validity so long as he who made it remains alive. *Pheresthai*, the Gk. verb rendered, *be established* (16) is then understood in the secular sense of 'be registered' or 'be produced as evidence', i.e., in order to secure probate of the will (F. F. Bruce; see also his remarks in *Peake's Commentary on the Bible*, rev. ed., p. 1015, where he takes note of Westcott's interpretation adopted here in this commentary, only to dismiss it. Cf. also C. Spicq, *Comm.*, *ad loc.*, who maintains that in Heb. 9: 15, 18-20 *diathēkē* means covenant in the same sense as in the OT but that the term means 'testament' in vv. 16-17). Such a change points out the twofold aspect of *diathēkē* namely as a covenant sealed in the blood of Christ and as a will or testament by which the dying Christ bequeathed to all believers the goods of salvation.]

The writer shows the correctness of this principle by a reference to what had already happened in Israel's redemptive history: **Even the first covenant was not ratified without blood** (18). When Moses had read the book of the covenant in the hearing of the people, he **sprinkled both the book itself** (not mentioned in Exod. 24: 6 ff.), **and all the people** (19), who, by the blood of the slain oxen, declared that they were now placing themselves in a position not to alter the terms of the covenant they had agreed to: *All that the Lord has spoken we will do, and we will be obedient* (Exod. 24: 7).

The meaning of blood, however, is not exhausted when explained as representing the death of those making the covenant. Blood was also required to cleanse away the sins done within the covenant relationship (cf. the note on 'covenant' in connection with ch. 8). Hence, the writer is led on by the force of the meanings of blood and of covenant to say that **under the law almost everything is** purified with blood, and without the shedding of blood there is no forgiveness of sins (22; for exceptions to this requirement of blood for cleansing cf. Lev. 5: 11-13; Num. 16: 46; 31: 50).

It appears strange that the writer should say that **heavenly things** had to be purified (23). It may simply be because he was compelled by his analogy to make such a statement, or perhaps he conceived the heavenly things as having incurred 'a certain defilement through contact with the sins that are absolved' in them (E. F. Scott, *Comm.*, *ad loc.*). In any case, having offered a better sacrifice than did His counterpart, **Christ has entered, not into a sanctuary made with hands, a copy of the true one, but into heaven itself, now to appear in the presence of God on our behalf** (24). His sphere of service is the true holy of holies, and He enters it by virtue of the one final sacrifice made by Him in history **at the end of the age** (26, cf. Gal. 4: 4; Eph. 1: 10)—the sacrifice of Himself. It is an offering so complete and so ultimate as never to be repeated again (26), a substitutionary offering which was effective in bearing away **the sins of many** (28). [Note: 'many' does not necessarily mean anything less than 'all' (cf. 2: 9 and Mk 10: 45 with 1 Tim. 2: 6); it comes into the NT as 'a legacy from Isa. 53: 11 f.' 'All' may be expressed by 'many' when the largeness of the 'all' is being stressed.] Because it was made at the end of this age, nothing stands between it and the full-realization of the age-to-come which will be inaugurated when Christ **will appear a second time, not to deal with sin but to save those who are eagerly waiting for him** (28).

iv. The Finality of Christ's One Sacrifice (10: 1-18)

In emphasizing the finality of Christ's sacrifice the writer, as has been his custom, contrasts it with the lack of finality found in the OT system of law and sacrifice. **The law,** he says, **has but a shadow of the good things to come** (1). It does not itself possess **the true form of these realities** (1). Consequently, because of its very nature—shadow and copy—it was incapable of perfecting any worshipper through its sacrifices (1). That is to say, no worshipper was ever brought 'into a real and enduring fellowship with God', for none fully lost his **consciousness of sin** (2). To the writer of Hebrews the very fact that sin-offerings were made continually, **year after year** (3, cf. Lev. 16) was itself proof that the institutions of the ancient order, though divinely ordained, were not final. To this argument the writer adds that even reason itself teaches that it is **impossible that the**

blood of bulls and goats, the involuntary death of irrational beasts, **should take away sins** (4); at best they were only visible symbols of something better to come.

But the one sacrifice God was pleased with, as the prophetic voice of the OT stressed again and again, was that of the conscious and willing dedication of a man's total life to do the divine will. **Consequently, when Christ came into the world, he said, 'Sacrifices and offerings thou hast not desired, but a body hast thou prepared me . . . Lo I have come** (lit. 'I am here') **to do thy will, O God'** (5-7). The writer is quoting from Ps. 40: 6 f., using the LXX which differs from the Hebrew in that it says, 'a body thou didst prepare for me', instead of 'mine ears hast thou opened'. As has been his custom, he now puts these words, originally spoken by another, into the mouth of Christ, for in the thinking of this writer 'where that is written of a *man*, which no *mere* man can satisfy, there lies under it a reference to One who is not man only' (Vaughan, *Comm.*, p. 190). Here, then, the words of the psalmist become the words of the incarnate Son, overheard as they were spoken to the Father. This Psalm implies that **sacrifices** (peace offerings) **and offerings** (cereal offerings), **burnt offerings and sin offerings** (5-6)—offerings of all types, were never decreed by God. [Note: the expression, **thou hast not desired,** of v. 5 really means 'thou hast not willed or purposed' such sacrifices. Cf. B. W. Bacon, *Journal of Biblical Literature*, 16 (1897) pp. 136 ff. for the meaning of 'desired', Gk. *eudokein*. It is significant in this connection, that the writer of Hebrews changes the LXX *ētēsas* of Ps. 40: 7, 'you asked', to this verb expressing divine will or purpose—*eudokēsas*.] They were but a stop-gap measure devised as a result of man's rebellion. What God has always wanted has been absolute loyal obedience to His will. Now at last that divine desire has been realized. The pre-existent Son became incarnate in accordance with the voice of prophecy (i.e., as it was written of Him **in the roll of the book,** 7) and announced 'His resolution to replace' the ancient sacrifices by His own obedience. By this gracious act He voluntarily identified Himself with humanity to such an extent that His life of total obedience to the Father, even to the point of dying on the cross (cf. Phil. 2: 8), becomes the ultimate act of obedience for all who acknowledge their identification with Him. Hence, because obedience is what God has eternally willed, with sacrifices introduced only as an interim measure on account of man's disobedience, and because man has now been made obedient by virtue of his identification with Christ (or the other way around), the whole system of sacrifice, therefore, has been abolished by the realization of the true will of God (9). This is clearly stated in v. 10 where the writer says explicitly, **by that will we have been sanctified through the offering of the body of Jesus Christ once for all.** This means that we have been 'set apart' ('sanctified') 'into the true condition for making our approach to God'—i.e., that of obedience—by means of the dedication of Jesus Christ to the will of God—a dedication which reached its climax in and was supremely proven by His death, the offering up of His body once for all. The Christian now stands perfected by means of the perfect obedience of Jesus Christ (cf. Rom. 5: 18 f.; Heb. 5: 8-9).

The finality of this supreme sacrifice is further heightened by other contrasts existing between Christ and the ancient priests. The latter **stands . . . at his service** (11), indicative of the fact that there is work still to be done; Christ on the contrary, sits **at the right hand of God** (12), signifying that His task has been accomplished. The ancient priest **offered repeatedly the same sacrifices which could never take away sins** (11); Christ, however, **offered for all time a single sacrifice for sins** (12). Thus Christ **has perfected for all time those who are** (being) **sanctified,** that is, He has cleared the conscience of the Christian from its sense of guilt and has brought him as a worshipper into the very presence of God (14). That this is so is proved by the Holy Spirit who witnesses through Jeremiah that the new covenant and forgiveness of sins have been promised **to us** Christians (15-17). Thus **where there is forgiveness . . . there is no longer any offering for sin** (18). The basic requirements for the full enjoyment of the covenant relationship have been wholly met—forgiveness of sin and a cleansed conscience.

VII. FINAL EXHORTATIONS TO PERSEVERANCE AND FURTHER WARNINGS AGAINST INDIFFERENCE (10: 19-12: 29)

i. Exhortation to Worship (10: 19-25)

Having concluded his great theological section on the priesthood of Jesus Christ, the writer returns again to the real purpose of his homily—exhortation and warning.

The first exhortation urges the Christian to take full advantage of the privilege of worship—of drawing near (22)—which is now available to him (19-22). The reasons given by the writer for his exhortation are twofold: (a) the confidence we now have **to enter the sanctuary** (19), and (b) the **great priest** we have **over the**

house of God (21). Here 'confidence' (Gk. *parrhēsia*, lit. 'outspokenness', 'openness') conveys the idea of an exulting boldness, a vivid sense of freedom from all fear when it comes to entering the sacred area of God's presence. This 'open access' has been provided **by the blood of Jesus** (19), **by the new and living way** of his flesh (in contrast to the RSV which identifies 'flesh' with 'curtain') **which he opened for us through the curtain** (20). In these words the writer is saying that every barrier to the presence of God has forever been torn down through the blood and flesh (cf. 2: 14 for this same order) of Jesus, i.e., through the true historical human experiences, including death, of the eternal Son who is the Christian's **great priest over the house of God** (21, cf. 3: 6). Not only has this one pulled aside the separating veil, but He is there personally to escort the worshipper into the sanctuary. True worship of God, therefore, is accomplished only through Jesus Christ and His atoning sacrifice (20 f.).

Having outlined the reasons for taking advantage of the Christian's right to worship, the writer now turns to describe the manner in which it is to be done: (a) The Christian is to worship with **a true heart** (22), that is to say, he is to come with sincerity in his innermost being, remembering the critical capabilities of the word of God (4: 12); (b) he is to worship **in full assurance of faith** (22), 'to have done with all doubt and misgiving', reflecting continuously on the basis for his faith—the person and work of Christ; (c) he is to worship with his heart **sprinkled clean from an evil conscience** (22), and (d) his body **washed with pure water** (22), that is to say, he is to assemble for worship only after he has gained a consciousness of sins forgiven through faith in the atoning work of Christ, and only after he has participated in Christian baptism (cf. 1 Pet. 3: 21 f.). These last two requirements for worship are cast in language suggestive of the ancient ritual performed at the ordination of the levite into his priestly service (cf. Lev. 8: 30; Exod. 29: 4; 30: 20; 40: 30), and are intended to show that the Christian stands in the high place of being a priest himself ordained for worshipful service to God.

The second admonition exhorts the Christian to **hold fast** (persevere in) **the confession of . . . hope without wavering** (23) which he made public at his baptism (cf. Justin, 1 *Apol.* 61: 1 ff.). The strong appeal for such perseverance is found to be in the great faithfulness of God who has made His promises irrevocable (cf. 6: 17; 11: 11; 13: 5 for this same concept).

Lastly, Christians are exhorted to consider

how they can **stir up one another to love and good works** (24). These things are of the essence of Christianity. Since their maintenance is dependent upon the mutual interaction of the Christian society, it is absolutely essential that one assemble himself with other Christians if he is to be assured of continued spiritual development. Any type of go-it-alone Christianity is unthinkable to the writer of Hebrews who deplores the fact that, in the face of the impending Day (25), there are those who neglect **to meet together** (25). Here in these exhortations are found the Pauline trinity of faith (22), hope (23), and love (24).

ii. Warning against Defection (10: 26–39)
The mention of the coming day of judgment and of the need for continuous mutual edification provides the writer with the necessary means of transition from exhortation to severe warning, very similar to that of 6: 4 ff. (26–31). Again, it appears to be a warning against the possibility of defecting from one's confession. There is no objective evidence that one who has made his Christian 'confession' and has been baptized is indeed a Christian, other than the daily perseverance in love and good works— a persistence in the very essence of what his confession implies (cf. 23–24). For the writer of Hebrews the definition of a true Christian is one who manifests 'a life-long allegiance to Christ' (cf. Jn 15: 2, 5; 10: 27; Rom. 11: 22). It *is* possible, implies the author, for one who has received **the knowledge** (Gk. *epignōsis*, 'full-knowledge') **of the truth to sin deliberately** (26, *hekousiōs*—a word which really means 'willingly', 'without compulsion'). It is possible for the 'baptized Christian' who has been thoroughly instructed in the truth of Christianity prior to his baptism to reach that place in his experience where through constant sinning (Gk. *hamartanontōn*) his attitude becomes one of continued conscious resistance to all that he has been taught. Then, because he has become psychologically hardened (cf. 3: 13) to the point where he sees no redeeming value in Christ's death, treating **the blood of the covenant by which he** (i.e., the confessing Christian, or perhaps Christ Himself) **was sanctified** as a common thing (29), there is for him, therefore, no more **sacrifice for sins** (26). He has rejected the only possibility of atonement. The only thing he can look forward to is a more fearful type of judgment than that inflicted upon the man who wilfully renounced the ancient covenant (27). The greater judgment is due to the fact that the covenant he has renounced is greater, for in this act he **has spurned the Son of God** (note the title), **profaned the blood of the covenant . . . ,**

and outraged the Spirit of grace (29). The writer closes this sombre warning with a reminder that **the living God** (31) does not threaten in vain: **I will repay,** says the Lord, and scripture (which cannot be broken) promises that **the Lord will judge his people** (30).

Nevertheless, in a fashion identical with 6: 9 ff. the writer brightens as he informs his readers that their past experience of perseverance in persecution is itself objective proof of the reality of their Christian confession (32–39). Wherever and whenever this persecution took place it did not result in martyrdom. It was rather the harassment of **being publicly exposed to abuse and affliction** (33), the distress of imprisonment and of the loss of property (34), which, nevertheless, is often more difficult to endure than death itself. They had persevered in all such abuses because of the certainty they had of **a better possession and an abiding one** (34, cf. 12: 26 f.).

Having endured under persecution, they must not now let down in the hum-drum of every day activities. The normal routine of life, uninterrupted by persecution, is often the real test of genuineness of one's Christian experience, for the very absence of trials and difficulties tends to promote spiritual drifting (2: 1), moral sluggishness and lethargy (5: 11), the slow imperceptible hardening of attitude (3: 13). Into just such a situation, comes the writer's 'word of exhortation' in order to rouse them from sleep and to advise them that they **have need of endurance** (or patience) even now **so that** they **may do the will of God and receive what is promised** (36). How long must they wait to receive the fulfilment of this promise? Not long. **For yet a little while** (lit., a very little while), **and the coming one shall come and shall not tarry** beyond the designated time (37). With these words, freely quoted from Isa. 26: 20 and Hab. 2: 3 f. LXX, the writer guarantees them with the certainty of prophecy of the soon return of their Lord ('the coming one'), and the realization of their hope. In addition, he has changed the sequence of Hab. 2: 4 so as to accentuate the fact that the one who is made righteous by God *lives* by faith, and so as to leave until the end that part which points up the danger of failure to persevere (38) as though he were reluctant to mention it again.

iii. Faith Defined and Illustrated (11: 1–40)
Since faith is such an important element in perseverance as the prophecy from Habakkuk shows, so much so that it constitutes the very dynamic by which the just shall live, the writer now turns his attention to a full exposition

of its meaning. He begins with a description: **faith is the assurance of things hoped for, the conviction of things not seen** (1). Now if this translation is accepted (note AV and Westcott, *Comm.*, p. 350, for an alternate possibility), then the writer has described faith, not as itself 'the substance of things hoped for', etc., but as an attitude of mind toward the future and the unseen that is determinative for personal conduct in the present. Faith, based as it is upon the firm word of God, is not at all a 'leap in the dark'. It assures one of the reality of the invisible world, and of its superiority to the visible, and thereby enables him to make the right choice in the moment of decision. Faith, therefore, is fundamental to perseverance, for perseverance is nothing more than a series of choices for the future and the unseen over against choices for present and transient things belonging to the phenomenal world. It was thus by faith that **the men of old received divine approval** (2), for they, as the author is about to demonstrate massively, were enabled by it to 'hold fast to the unseen in spite of the illusions and temptations of this passing world' (E. F. Scott, *Comm.*, *ad loc.*). Thus, there is seen again a continuity existing between the past and the present—a continuity of faith in the unseen which binds the two peoples together.

It is interesting to note that in illustrating his definition of faith he does so in roughly chronological fashion. He begins with the creation of the world. **By faith we understand that the world was created . . . that what is seen was made out of things which do not appear** (3). This statement is not intended to teach creation *ex nihilo*, or to say anything at all about the character of the prior substance from which the world was made. The writer's only point is that 'no purely physical explanation of the world is possible' (Westcott, *Comm.*, p. 353). Faith looks for its answers beyond that which is seen (1).

Next the writer calls many OT saints to witness to the meaning of faith. First in order he discusses those great heroes who lived before the flood (4–7). Abel **offered to God a more acceptable sacrifice than Cain** (4). The writer does not state in what way it was 'more acceptable' except to say that it was done in faith, and to hint at the possibility of it being a 'more abundant' (Gk. *pleiona*) offering than Cain's, a fact which would have indicated a fuller sense of God's claim upon his life than that evidenced by his brother (cf. Westcott, *Comm.*, p. 354). Notice that God accepted **his gifts** (4), not gift!

Proof for Enoch's faith lies in the fact that he

pleased God (5, cf. Gen. 5: 24, LXX, where the Hebrew text has 'walked with God'), for one cannot please God without a faith which clearly sees Him, the unseen, as a living reality, and as one who can intervene in history to reward **those who seek him** (6). The reward for Enoch's faith was translation—he **was taken up so that he should not see death** (5).

The meaning of faith as defined by the writer of Hebrews is most clearly illustrated from the life of Noah, of whom it was said that God warned him of **events as yet unseen** (7). His response showed that, though the flood was still future and perhaps unheard of, certainly unseen, he nevertheless was convinced of its reality because of the divine oracle. This conviction determined his course of action—he obeyed God. Thus he **became an heir of the righteousness which comes by faith** (7, a Pauline-like expression; cf. Rom. 3: 22; 4: 13; Heb. 10: 38).

Next in order as witnesses to faith were the patriarchs extending from Abraham down to Joseph (8–22). Abraham is the first and perhaps the greatest OT example of faith. To the writer of Hebrews Abraham proved his faith by his prompt response to God's call, although it was to go to a place with which he was totally unacquainted (8), and by the fact that he did not make a permanent home in this **land of promise** (9), **for he looked forward to the city which has foundations, whose builder and maker is God** (10). In much the same way as he did in chapters 3–4, the writer shows that the **land of promise** was for Abraham only a land of temporary promise. The real 'promised land' was the heavenly, the unseen, which, when made visible by faith, caused him to live as a pilgrim in this world. Faith is 'the conviction of things not seen'. **Isaac and Jacob, heirs with him of the same promise** (9), also shared his outlook on life.

According to v. 11 Sarah's faith is joined with Abraham's in a co-operative venture to produce a son. But there is no record of her faith in the OT—only of her incredulity at the promise of the Lord (Gen. 18: 12 ff.). In addition, the Greek expression translated **to conceive** (*katabolē spermatos*) is regularly used of the 'sowing' of the seed, of 'begetting' (Arndt and Gingrich, *Greek-English Lexicon*), rather than of 'conceiving'. Hence, it is most likely that the Greek should be translated, 'By faith he (Abraham) received power to beget *by* Sarah herself'. This alternate translation coincides with Rom. 4: 19 where Paul, too, ignores the faith of Sarah.

In good literary fashion the author breaks up his survey of redemptive history lest it

T

become monotonous, and pauses to summarize what he has been saying (13-16). There is a larger fulfilment to God's promises than that which can be realized on earth in the realm of the visible—**these all died in faith not having received what was promised** (13). Thus, though Abraham did get to Canaan—the promised land—and though Isaac was born to him in his old age, and in this sense the promises of God were realized, his faith not being totally unrewarded, it is also true that he did not receive what was promised, that is to say, he did not receive *the* promises (the literal translation of the Greek). *The* promises of God cannot be fulfilled short of that **better country, that is a heavenly one** (16). Recall that to the writer of Hebrews, the heavenly is the real world. The phenomenal world is but its shadow. Faith, the capacity to see that unseen sphere and to understand its superiority over the seen, compels the believer to choose for the former and against the latter. Thus it was that faith made the patriarchs live as **strangers and exiles on the earth** (13 f.) because they were **seeking a homeland** beyond earth's space-time limits (14). Hence, **God is not ashamed to be called their God** (16, cf. Mk 12: 26 f.). The writer arrives at this conclusion from the fact that while residing in the promised land the patriarchs still called themselves 'sojourners', 'pilgrims' (Gen. 23: 4; 24: 37; 28: 4; 47: 9). Faith, then, is the opposite of shrinking back; it is rather a pressing forward toward goals which are real although imperfectly seen. This, of course, is the whole theme of Hebrews, and it is compressed within the limits of one concept—faith.

The writer now returns to the faith of Abraham before going on to mention that of Isaac, Jacob, and Joseph (17-22). The supreme test of Abraham's faith was God's request that he offer up Isaac (17), **of whom it was said, 'Through Isaac shall your descendants be named'** (18). Abraham obeyed though 'the command of God seemed to clash with the promise of God', because **he considered that God was able to raise men even from the dead** (19, cf. Gen. 22: 5; here is another of the very few references to the writer's belief in the resurrection). Thus Isaac's 'resurrection' was 'by way of a parable' (RSV has **figuratively speaking,** 19) and became a type of the resurrection of Christ. Isaac, Jacob and Joseph combine, each in his own way, to illustrate again that faith is the assurance of things hoped for, the conviction of things not seen (20-22). The reference to Jacob's staff (21) where the Hebrew text mentions his 'bed' (Gen. 47: 31) is further proof of the writer's use of the LXX.

Next, the faith of Moses is dealt with (23-28). His faith, beginning as it did with his parents who by it gained 'some inkling of their child's destiny' (Josephus, *Ant.*, 11, 9, 3 cited by F. F. Bruce, *Peake's Comm.*, p. 1,017), compelled him to forfeit the immediate for the future, the seen for the unseen, to choose **ill-treatment with the people of God** (25), rather than **pleasures of sin** for a moment. **He considered abuse suffered for the Christ greater wealth than the treasures of Egypt** (26). This interpretation placed upon the Greek by the RSV means that Moses had 'faith in the God who would fulfil his purpose and his promise, a fulfilment which could come . . . only in the coming of Christ' (A. C. Purdy, *Comm.*, *ad loc.*; cf. 1 C. 10: 4). Literally translated, however, this verse says, Moses 'considered the reproach of the christ to be greater riches', etc., which could mean that Moses himself was happy to suffer that reproach which belongs to any anointed envoy of God sent to a world rebelling against Him. In other words, Moses suffered as God's christ, His anointed, for 'this reproach, which was endured in the highest degree by Christ Jesus (Rom. 15: 3), was endured also by those who in any degree prefigured or represented Him' (Westcott, *Comm.*, p. 372).

Finally, the writer briefly touches on the faith of those from the Exodus to Maccabean times (29-38), mentioning specifically the faith of 'the people' in crossing the Red Sea and conquering Jericho (29), and of Rahab the harlot (31) showing that 'strongholds tumble before faith and even the most disreputable are redeemed by it'. Then with time failing him, he summarizes the exploits of judges, prophets, kings, exiles, and martyrs, not, however, in strict chronological order, whose exploits are etched deeply in the annals of Israel's history. This is one of the most beautiful passages from the standpoint of style to be found in Hebrews; it is also the most moving. It serves magnificently to summarize the writer's concept of faith. It is that which drives one forward always, never allowing the luxury of retreat. It is 'venturesome action'. It is trust and confidence. It is obedience. It is endurance. Faith is seeing the invisible in clear focus, so that the present visible world loses its charm. One is thereby enabled to forfeit life itself, if necessary, in order to gain that better world to come (35b). It is quite likely that the background for much of this concluding summary comes from 2 Mac. 6: 18-7: 42. The writer considers the men and women mentioned there to rank with Gideon, Barak, Samson, David, etc., in witnessing to the meaning of faith. The reference to being **sawn in two** (37) may indicate an acquaintance with a legendary work entitled the *Martyrdom of Isaiah* where Isaiah was allegedly sawn asunder with a wood saw because he prophesied the coming redemption through Christ (cf. R. H. Pfeiffer, *History of the New Testament Times with an Introduction to the Apocrypha*, 1949, pp. 73-74).

And all these . . . did not receive what was promised (39), that is, they did not receive '*the* promise', the *messianic* promise. All of redemptive history, with its manifold partial fulfilments, moves on to its culmination in what might be called the Christ-event. That event was the capstone, the *teleiōsis* of history, therefore, the writer of Hebrews can say God has spoken ultimately in His Son, and He has done it 'in these last days' (1: 2). Thus the Christian is living in the age of fulfilment—God's promise has been realized in the coming of the Messiah. It is in this light that the words **God had foreseen something better for us** (40) are to be understood. How much greater, therefore, should be our faith, our loyalty to God, than that of the ancients. And yet, the expression, **that apart from us they should not be made perfect** (40) implies that the men of faith in the OT and those in the Christian era alike belong to one people of God who are *together* made perfect.

iv. Application of the Faith-principle to Life (12: 1-24)
The many heroes of faith enumerated in chapter 11 become to the writer an amphitheatre of spectators cheering the Christian runner on toward the goal. Indeed they are more than spectators; they are witnesses (Gk. *martyres*) interpreting the meaning of life to him. They encourage him by their own lives, which make clear the certain success of persistent participation, to **lay aside every weight, and sin which clings so closely** (1). This latter expression translates a Greek word, *euperistatos*, which is made difficult by the fact that there is little or no clue to its meaning from an etymological study. As it is translated in the RSV it describes the hampering effects of a clinging robe which then may refer to those sins of drifting, dullness, lack of spiritual exercise, or immaturity, which could lead one to lose the race of life. The earliest known Greek manuscript of Hebrews, however, gives a different word, *euperispastos*, which means, 'easily distracting'. This word fits in well with the figure of a runner whose eyes should be fixed only on the goal. That goal is **Jesus** (2), who participated in our human experiences. He is not only the object of faith's vision, but He is its greatest encouragement for He is its **pioneer and perfecter** (2). As pioneer,

He himself participated in believing (cf. 2: 13). He blazed the trail of faith for Christians to follow, for his human experience, like theirs, was controlled by faith and not by sight. But He is also faith's perfecter, for all that faith hopes for finds its consummation in Him. Jesus is a further example of encouragement to faith in that the endurance of the cross was the price He willingly paid **for** (Gk. *anti*) **the joy that was set before him** (2, cf. v. 16, where Esau's birthright was the price he paid for (*anti*) the single meal). Thus believers are encouraged to regard their sufferings (less, in any case, than Christ's) as a small price to pay for the prize to be secured at the end of the race set before *them*. Choosing the cross, however, resulted in Christ being exalted to **the right hand of the throne of God** (2). Because of His exemplary life, therefore, which included accepting the **hostility** of sinners **against himself**, Christians are encouraged to **consider him** (3), to study carefully His life of steadfast endurance so that in their experience they may be able to decide for the same path of suffering, if loyalty to God demands that, rather than the way of easy relief (3-4). Thus they will finish the race though weariness may tempt them to give out and quit. The life of Jesus, therefore, is a call to perseverance, for the contest is 'not a short dash to glory, but a distance race calling for endurance' (A. C. Purdy, *Comm.*, p. 739).

In the next section (5-24) the writer explains the meaning of suffering and hardship as the discipline (not 'chastisement' or 'punishment') of a loving Father (cf. 6), whose purpose in it is to educate (Gk. *paideuein*) his child. Thus in the case of the Christian, suffering is God's educational process by which he is fitted to share God's holiness (10). It is a necessary element in the Father-child relationship as the writer establishes from his book of proofs—the OT (Prov. 3: 11 f.), and from the analogy of human parenthood (8-9). If you are not being educated you are not a legitimate son (8). Since this is so, the proper attitude to take toward suffering is that of submission—**be subject to the Father of spirits** (a contrasting expression to that of **earthly fathers** and means 'spiritual Father'), **and live** (9). Discipline, though painful, later **yields the peaceful fruit of righteousness** (11), but only to those who exercise themselves through it, that is, 'those who have by practice acquired the capacity of reacting rightly to affliction' (Narborough, *Comm.*, p. 143, cf. 5: 14). These understand that the circumstances of their lives are dictated by God who directs their destinies through His unfailing omniscience, and whose all-loving nature actively promotes their highest welfare.

Along with the discipline of God, however, the writer urges self-discipline and the discipline which comes through 'the power of mutual influence' (12–17): **lift your drooping hands, and strengthen your weak knees, and make straight paths for your feet,** etc. (12 ff.). Here again he returns to the real problem facing his audience—dullness resulting in gradual drifting away from the living God. Only now he uses the figure of enfeeblement. 'Final failure', he warns them, 'comes from continuous weakening. The moral strength is enfeebled little by little' (Westcott, *Comm.*, p. 398). The admonitions in v. 14 are to the individual and seem to be an echo of the sermon on the mount (cf. Mt. 5: 8 f.). The expression 'to see the Lord' is a common OT way of describing 'acceptable worship' (cf. Isa. 6: 1 ff., Purdy, *Comm.*, p. 745).

The exhortations given in vv. 15 ff. are to the Church. The power of the corporate body is to make sure that no one of its members fails **to obtain the grace of God** (15), or to put it more correctly, that none may lack the grace of God, i.e., fall behind by 'not keeping pace with the movement of divine grace which meets and stirs the progress of the Christian' (Westcott, *Comm.*, p. 406). The Church is to guard against the growth of any 'root of bitterness', an expression which, coming as it does from Dt. 29: 18, probably means a person whose heart has been turned away from the Lord and who becomes 'a root bearing poisonous and bitter fruit', thereby causing trouble within the Christian community and defiling many besides himself (15). The Church is also to make sure that no second Esau arises among them, a person who is **immoral** (in a religious rather than a sensual sense) or **irreligious** (16), a person who does not value spiritual things (Gen. 25: 29 ff.). The writer warns that a decision like Esau's is irrevocable. **He found no chance** (Gk. 'place') **to repent, though he sought it** (i.e., 'to inherit the blessing' not the place of repentance) **with tears** (17).

Accept the discipline of God, the writer exhorts, and discipline yourselves, because as Christians you have far greater advantages than those under the old covenant, and the end of this present educational process is much more glorious than the previous. The old covenant was inaugurated at Mount Sinai, a mountain which could **be touched** (18), material and temporal. The new has been put into effect at **Mount Zion . . . the city of the living God, the heavenly Jerusalem,** the real world, spiritual and eternal (22, cf. Rev. 3: 12; 21: 2 ff.;

Gal. 4: 26 f.). The former was established in an atmosphere of dread. A blazing fire raged, darkness and gloom were everywhere. There was tempest and the sound of trumpet. People begged to hear no more (19, cf. Dt. 4: 11 f.; Exod. 20: 18; Dt. 5: 23 ff.; Exod. 19: 12 f.). Even Moses trembled with fear (21, but cf. Dt. 9: 19 and its context). But not so the new: there is about it an atmosphere of joy and peace and confidence, though at the same time awe. Here there is a festal gathering (Gk. *panēgyris*). Present at it are angels and the assemblage of saints, **the first-born who are enrolled in heaven** (23), 'no longer separated, as at Sinai, by signs of great terror, but united in one vast assembly' (Westcott, *Comm.*, p. 413). The **judge who is God of all** (23) is also there, and **the spirits of just** (righteous) **men made perfect** (23). Jesus is there, too, whose sprinkled blood **speaks more graciously than the blood of Abel** (24). Abel's cried for revenge; Christ's pleads for forgiveness. It is to this festal gathering that Christians are invited to come (Gk. *proserchesthai*, i.e., to come as a worshipper).

v. The Final Warning Against Refusing God (12: 25–29)

The contrast between the old covenant (which to the writer of Hebrews was the highest expression of all religions) and the new is as great as the contrast between terror and grace. Thus, if to refuse God's covenant made on earth (through Moses) meant death (25), to refuse God's covenant made from heaven (through Jesus) means far greater punishment. [Note: The refusal is not simply the refusal of a covenant, but of God who invites one to join Him in the covenant relationship (25).] For at Sinai **his voice then shook the earth** (26), but according to the prophecy of Haggai (2: 6) God now plans to shake the entire universe (cf. Mk 13: 31; 2 Pet. 3: 7) so that only those things belonging to an unshakeable order may remain (27, cf. Dan. 2: 44). Christians belong to just such a kingdom, one that cannot be shaken (28). It is, therefore, a cause for gratitude and worship and also for awe (28), for we must not forget that our God is a consuming fire (29, cf. Dt. 4: 24; Isa. 33: 14), who 'destroys all transient and temporal things in order that what is timeless and unchanging may emerge in full glory'.

VIII. PRACTICAL EXHORTATIONS, PASTORAL BENEDICTION AND PERSONAL GREETINGS (13: 1–24)

In a manner similar to that of Paul (cf. Rom. 12: 4 ff.; Eph. 5: 21 ff., etc.) the writer concludes his letter with practical instructions. Apparently he is following a catechetical outline which deals with Christian ethics and which was already well established within the early Church. His concern is that his readers exercise **brotherly love** (1), which means an active interest in the welfare of fellow-Christians, and that they **show hospitality to strangers** or travellers (2), which has its own compensations (cf. Gen. 18-19), and that they have a fellow-feeling with those who are **in prison** and the **ill-treated** (3) so as to provide for their needs for they, too, being human are susceptible to identical difficulties (3), and that they not only recognize the honourableness of marriage and the sacredness of sexual intimacy within the marriage bond, but also the wickedness of immorality and adultery (4), and finally, that they be content with what they have, keeping their minds free from avarice (5), for God is their helper and provider. The only intelligent response then to an understanding of such providential care is that given by the psalmist: **I will not be afraid** (6b).

The writer also gives his readers advice concerning the welfare of the Church. By recalling the faith-life of their leaders and the way they died, i.e., **the outcome of their life** (Gk. *ekbasis*), they will be stimulated to emulation (7). But the greatest of all patterns to imitate is Jesus Christ (8). 'Human leaders may pass away, but Jesus Christ, the supreme object and subject of their faithful teaching, remains, and remains the same: no novel additions to His truth are required' (J. Moffatt, *Epistle to the Hebrews, ad loc.*). The writer also warns against departing from the doctrines of their leaders, **led away by diverse and strange teachings** (9). What these were is not known. The writer merely mentions **foods** (cf. Col. 2: 16 ff.) and does not elaborate. Nevertheless, the point of his remark is to show that Christianity in its truest form is not regulated by externals; it is a matter of the heart **strengthened by grace**, by spiritual influences (9).

Verses 10 ff. are most difficult to interpret. They may mean that though Christianity is not dependent upon external things it does not therefore lack anything essential as one might be led to think. In fact, Christians really partake of the one altar which was barred to the worshippers of the old covenant. In the earlier dispensation the priests partook of all the sacrifices offered on the altars of Israel, except that one sacrificed on the Day of Atonement (Lev. 16: 27), for **the bodies of those animals whose blood is brought into the sanctuary . . . were burned outside the camp** (11). They could not be eaten by the priests, not even by

the high priest. We Christians, however (and here the contrast between the old and the new is again made great), partake of that very sacrifice of expiation—the sacrifice of the Day of Atonement by partaking of Christ, for He is its grand fulfilment (cf. Spicq, *Comm.*, II, p. 424). That Christ is indeed the antitype of this great sacrifice is now made even more clear by the writer in the words which follow: just as the body of the sacrificial animal, slain on the Day of Atonement, was taken **outside the camp** and burned, so Jesus was taken **outside the gate** to suffer for and sanctify His people by His death (11-12).

On the other hand, these verses may mean that Christianity is not at all determined by external things such as those sacrificial celebrations so essential to the old order. To prove this the writer points out that Christianity depends upon a sacrifice of which *no one* is allowed to partake—the sacrifice of atonement. Even the high priest, as great a figure as he was, was forbidden to eat of it (cf. Lev. 16: 27), for the law said that the bodies of those sacrificial animals *had* to be taken and **burned outside the camp** (11). Now, as the writer has already shown, Jesus is the fulfilment of that to which the sacrifice on the Day of Atonement pointed and that is why He, too, **suffered outside the gate** (12). Therefore, the service He requires 'does not consist in any kind of ritual meal. It consists rather in suffering the world's scorn and rejection along with Him' (cf. for this view Scott, *Comm.*, *ad loc.*).

There may be other views too. But whichever one is correct it is not necessary to see in the exhortation which is based upon it, **go forth to him outside the camp** (13), any command to leave Judaism or any other religio ~~licita~~ (in contrast to Manson, *Epistle to the Hebrews*, p. 151). It is more positive than that, meaning simply, you must identify yourself wholly with Jesus, though to do so may mean **bearing abuse for Him** (13). Such abuse is to be expected and is of no consequence, since this world is not our home; we seek the eternal city which is to come (14).

Since therefore, Christianity is not a matter of external ritual, **let us continually offer up a sacrifice of praise to God, that is, the fruit of lips that acknowledge his name** (15; cf. Hos. 14: 2; cf. also the prevalence of this concept of worship among the members of the Dead Sea Sect: *Manual of Discipline* 9: 3 ff.; 9: 26; 10: 6, 8, 14; *Hymn Scroll* 11: 5, in the translation of A. Dupont-Sommer, *The Essene Writings from Qumran*, 1961). Worship with the lips is not enough, however. It must be accompanied by good deeds (sharing, in particular, is singled out) which are also acceptable sacrifices with God (16).

In the writer's concluding words of advice there is an entreaty to be submissive to Christian leaders charged with the welfare of all souls under their care (17). There is also an exhortation to pray: **Pray for us . . . that I may be restored to you the sooner** (18 f.). This request for prayer may indicate that the writer is in prison, but not necessarily so.

Having made a request for their prayer, he now offers a prayer of benediction for them. It is magnificent in its style and meaning. Herein is contained the only explicit reference to the resurrection of Christ in the letter: God **brought again from the dead our Lord Jesus . . . by the blood of the eternal covenant** (20). The phrase 'by the blood of the eternal covenant' may have been taken from Zech. 9: 11. There the blood of the victim was that which consecrated the messianic alliance. If so, the writer is saying again that Christ, by virtue of His sacrifice, is made supreme mediator of the new covenant (cf. Spicq, *Comm.*, II, pp. 435 f.). His resurrection demonstrates conclusively that His sacrifice was accepted and that the covenant has been ratified. God now stands ready to equip us **with everything good that** we **may do His will** (21). He is ready to work within us so that we may not offer 'dead works' but that activity **which is pleasing in his sight** (21). And all this is accomplished through Jesus Christ. It is uncertain to whom the doxology is addressed: to God, or to Jesus Christ (21).

A personal greeting from the writer closes this **word of exhortation,** which he says was brief (22). He mentions that a certain **Timothy has been released,** or that he has already 'set out' on his trip, and that he himself fully intends to accompany him on his journey to them (23). The word of exhortation appears to have been written to the rank and file, not the leaders (24), or else this is a tactful way of addressing a community, including its leaders, of which he is no real part. **Those who come from Italy** (24) is the chief clue to the riddle of who the readers were, perhaps indicating

that it was sent to Rome. But since this expression is ambiguous, it may mean 'those of Italy' as well as 'those from Italy', indicating that it was written in Rome to Italians who were away from the capital city. The writer concludes with a second benediction: **Grace be with all of you. Amen** (25).

BIBLIOGRAPHY

BRUCE, A. B., *The Epistle to the Hebrews* (Edinburgh, 1899).

BRUCE, F. F., 'Hebrews', *Peake's Commentary on the Bible,* newly rev. (London, 1962).

BRUCE, F. F., *The Epistle to the Hebrews,* NIC (Grand Rapids, 1964).

DAVIDSON, A. B., *The Epistle to the Hebrews* (Edinburgh, 1882; reprinted 1950).

LENSKI, R. C. H., *The Interpretation of the Epistle to the Hebrews* (Minneapolis, 1956).

MANSON, W., *The Epistle to the Hebrews* (London, 1951).

MOFFATT, J., *A Critical and Exegetical Commentary on the Epistle to the Hebrews.* ICC (Edinburgh, 1924).

MONTEFIORE, H. W., *The Epistle to the Hebrews.* BNTC (London, 1964).

NAIRNE, A., *The Epistle of Priesthood* (Edinburgh, 1913).

NAIRNE, A., *Epistle to the Hebrews.* CGT (Cambridge, 1917).

NARBOROUGH, F. D. V., *The Epistle to the Hebrews* (Oxford, 1930; reprinted 1946).

PURDY, A. C., 'Hebrews', *The Interpreter's Bible,* XI (New York, 1955).

ROBINSON, T. H., *The Epistle to the Hebrews.* MNT (London, 1933).

RODDY, C. S., *The Epistle to the Hebrews* (Grand Rapids, 1962).

SCHNEIDER, J., *The Letter to the Hebrews* (Grand Rapids, 1957).

SCOTT, E. F., 'Hebrews', *Commentary on the Bible,* ed. A. S. Peake (Edinburgh and London, 1919).

SPICQ, C., *L'Épître aux Hébreux* (Paris, 1952), in two volumes, very complete, extensive bibliography Vol. I ch. 13.

VAUGHAN, C. J., *The Epistle to the Hebrews* (London, 1890).

WESTCOTT, B. F., *The Epistle to the Hebrews* (London, 1889).

WICKHAM, E. C., *The Epistle to the Hebrews,* 2nd ed. WC (London, 1922).

THE LETTER OF JAMES

T. CARSON

Character and Contents

James is the first of seven letters known as 'catholic' or 'general'. See separate article (pp. 124 ff.). Three of the principal features of the letter are: (*a*) the comparative lack of distinctive Christian doctrine, (*b*) its practical character, (*c*) the Jewish background. With regard to the first Martin Luther wrote: 'It teaches Christian people, and yet does not once notice the Passion, the Resurrection, the Spirit of Christ [but cf. 4: 5]. The writer names Christ a few times, but He teaches not of Him, but speaks of general faith in God'. He therefore regarded the letter as 'a right strawy epistle in comparison with the writings of Paul, Peter and John.'

Some have even suggested that it was originally a Jewish and not a Christian writing, but this judgment has not found much acceptance. It is discussed fully by Mayor.

But this lack of Christian doctrine is not as great as it might at first sight appear, for: (*a*) 'James in this one short letter reproduces more of the words spoken by Jesus Christ our Lord than are to be found in all the other letters of the NT taken together' (Liddon). (*b*) Twice James uses the expression 'Lord Jesus Christ' (1: 1; 2: 1). (*c*) He speaks of 'that honourable name by which you are called' (2: 7). (*d*) He applies to Christ the word 'glory' (2: 1), 'which surely involves the belief in the Resurrection and Ascension and even the Divinity of Christ' (Mayor). (*e*) He refers to the second coming (5: 7). (*f*) The word 'Judge' in 5: 9 refers to Christ. (*g*) The regeneration of the Spirit and the divine sovereignty in our salvation are alluded to in 1: 18. (*h*) The elders of the church are mentioned in 5: 14. (*i*) His readers are not only 'brethren' but 'my beloved brethren' (1: 16, 19; 2: 5).

The following points are also worthy of notice: (*a*) He appears to have unbelieving Jews in mind as well as believing. See below 'Readers and Place of Writing'. (*b*) The more distinctive teachings of Paul may never have been fully appreciated by James and certainly not at the early period when it is believed that the letter was written. See below, 'Date'. Even as late as

Ac. 21: 20 the Jewish Christians were all 'zealous for the law.' (*c*) James is by nature a moralist rather than a theologian. He is not so much concerned with the correct verbal expression of Christian truth as with its living expression. If he makes no reference to the Christian ordinances of baptism and the Lord's Supper, he is equally silent about the rites of Judaism. 'He wished to make the Christians better Christians, to teach them a truer wisdom, a purer morality . . . and he wished to convert the Israelites into being worthier members of the commonwealth of Israel before he could win them to become heirs of the covenant of the better promise' (F. W. Farrar, *The Early Days of Christianity* [London, 1900], p. 317). The concentration upon the ethical side may also help to explain the absence of express reference to the Cross and Resurrection, though they are implied in 2: 1, 7.

The Jewish background of the letter is evident from the following features: (*a*) The form of address: 'To the twelve tribes in the Dispersion' (see also below, 'Readers and Place of Writing') (1: 1). (*b*) The use of the word 'synagogue' (2: 2, see note). (*c*) The emphasis on law-keeping (2: 9-11; 4: 11). (*d*) The reference to the basic article of the Jewish faith (2: 19). (*e*) James calls Abraham 'our father' (2: 21), 'without a hint that it is to be understood in any but a literal sense' (Plummer). Cf. Rom. 4: 1. (*f*) God is spoken of under the Hebrew title 'Lord of hosts' (5: 4), a title which occurs elsewhere in the NT only in Rom. 9: 29 in a definite quotation. (*g*) Jewish forms of oaths are quoted (5: 12). (*h*) The anointing of the sick with oil (5: 14-15), which is not found in any other NT letter. (*i*) Several references to nature which 'point to Palestine as the place of composition' (Salmon). (*j*) James refers not only to the life of Abraham (2: 21, 23) but to Rahab (2: 25), the prophets (5: 10), Job (5: 11), and Elijah (5: 17), and it is noteworthy that in the other NT letters Rahab is mentioned only in Heb. 11: 31, Elijah in Rom. 11: 2 and Job not at all. (*k*) 'The sins and weaknesses which James denounces are the very ones for which Jesus scourged His countrymen, particularly the Pharisees . . . Among these are the superficial hearing of God's word . . .; pious prattle and profession instead of the practice of what they believe . . .; the disposition to dogmatise . . .; the failure to fulfil the real requirements of the law while paying devotion to its letter . . .; the getting of wealth without any thought of God, with the impossible attempt to divide their affections between God and earthly possessions . . .; the exercise of prayer without faith in God . . .; slandering and cursing of their neighbours . . .; and the taking of oaths too lightly' (Th. Zahn *Introduction to NT*, Eng. tr. [Edinburgh, 1909], pp. 90 f.). On the other hand, unlike the letters addressed to Gentiles, there are no warnings against idolatry and immorality and nothing is said of the relation of masters and slaves.

It is admitted that not all the above arguments have equal cogency, but when they are taken together, and especially when one considers the small compass in which they occur, the Jewish background is unmistakable. M. Dods went so far as to say that 'the epistle is Jewish in every line' (*An Introduction to the NT*, p. 190).

Other features are: (*a*) resemblance to the OT prophets (*e.g.* in ch. 5). James has been called the 'Amos of the New Testament' and his letter 'a golden bridge between the Old and New Testaments.' (*b*) Similarity to the Book of Proverbs. Many scholars also believe that there are echoes of the books of Wisdom and Ecclesiasticus. (*c*) Points in common with Romans, Hebrews, 1 Peter, Acts 15 and especially the Sermon on the Mount. (*d*) The letter is written in 'excellent Greek with great energy' (W. Kelly). See also below, 'Authorship'. There are several references to the LXX (cf. 2: 11; 4: 6; 5: 4). This is not surprising considering the number of Hellenists in the church at Jerusalem (cf. Ac. 6: 1). Cf. also the use of the LXX by James in Ac. 15: 16-18.

Authorship

The letter is said to have been written by 'James, a servant of God and of the Lord Jesus Christ', and it is addressed to 'the twelve tribes in the Dispersion', *viz.* to all the Jews outside Palestine. See below, 'Readers and Place of Writing'.

And who was this James? Had he been one of the Twelve, it would have been natural for him to call himself an apostle when addressing the Twelve Tribes, and there is in fact little reason for identifying him with either of the apostles of that name. But in the Acts and letters there is a James who stands out prominently, a pillar of the church in Jerusalem, whose position and character exactly suit the author of the letter. Though not one of the Twelve (cf. Mt. 13: 55; Jn 7: 5), he was the leader of Judaic Christianity,

and so the familiar James or Jacob required no further designation. (Cf. Ac. 12: 17; 15: 13; 21: 18; Gal. 2: 9, 12.) In Gal. 1: 19 he is called 'James the Lord's brother'. Though other explanations have been given, the natural meaning appears to be that he was a child of Mary and Joseph, born after Jesus. The subject is fully discussed by Mayor in his Introduction. See also the note on Mk 6: 3.

James was not a disciple during the Lord's lifetime (cf. Jn 7: 5), but Christ appeared to him after His resurrection (cf. 1 C. 15: 7). That may mark the time of his conversion.

Eusebius has preserved for us an account of the life and character of James by Hegesippus (2nd century), and while it contains manifest improbabilities, there is much in it that harmonizes with the NT references. He says that James was holy from his mother's womb, that he drank neither wine nor strong drink; he would go into the temple alone, and would be found there on his knees and asking for forgiveness for the people, so that his knees became hard and dry as a camel's. On account therefore of his exceeding justness, he was called 'Just' and 'Bulwark of the People'.

From 'the picture of James as a stern ascetic, so deeply impressed upon the memory of the early Church', and from the fact that tradition makes no mention of his descendants, Zahn inferred that he was probably unmarried. He argued that 1 C. 9: 5 could hardly include James, who was resident in Jerusalem, whereas the persons referred to were itinerant teachers. But the inference is doubtful. Though stationed in Jerusalem, James may have visited 'the twelve tribes in the Dispersion'.

Some have objected that the Greek is too good for such a man as James, but Mayor has pointed out that Galilee was studded with Greek towns, and there were ample opportunities to learn Greek, while others, *e.g.* Zahn, have shown that the Greek of the letter could not be confused with that of a classical writer. It is possible too that James may have used one of his Hellenist brethren as an amanuensis.

Readers and Place of Writing

The letter is addressed to 'the twelve tribes in the Dispersion'. Some have understood this to refer to Christians, whether Jews or Gentiles, as the 'new Israel', the Dispersion being referred to the scattering of the Christians that followed the death of Stephen (cf. Ac. 8: 1; 11: 19). 'But', as Hort remarked, 'this comes in very strangely at the head of a letter with no indication of a spiritual sense, and coupled with "in the dispersion"; and especially so from St. James' (p. xxii). His objection would apply even more to the view that the expression is purely symbolical, meaning Christians who are exiles from their home in heaven.

It has been argued that, as the 'Dispersion' in 1 Pet. 1: 1 includes Gentiles (which is the view of many scholars, but not all) it may also include them here, but Peter does not mention the twelve tribes and he does refer to the Gentiles (4: 3).

To the present writer the Jewish background (cf. above, 'Character and Contents'), the absence of any reference to the Gentiles and of anything distinctively applicable to them in the warnings, the position and character of James, and the form of address, make it clear that the letter is addressed to literal Jews (cf. also the note on 1: 1).

But are they believing Jews only or both believing and unbelieving? In favour of the first is the fact that in most of the letter James regards his readers as Christians, e.g. 1: 18; 2: 1, 7; 5: 7, 14. But on the other hand in 4: 1-4 he seems to be thinking of what took place among unbelieving Jews, and that is even clearer in 5: 1-6, where he predicts the judgment of those whom he addresses, and in v. 7 contrasts them with the brethren. It is to be noted also that in 2: 19 it is the fundamental article of the Jewish creed that is quoted.

Two conclusions seem possible. Either James is writing to believing Jews only and from time to time turns aside to address the unbelieving, as an OT prophet might address Tyre, Sidon or the Gentiles, or the letter is addressed to all Jews outside Palestine; but James, knowing that the letter will be chiefly read by the Christians, directs most of his remarks to them.

The second view seems preferable, for no restriction to believers is suggested by the 'twelve tribes' such as is found in 1 Pet. 1: 1-2, and the Book of Acts indicates that among the Jews there was not to begin with the open breach between believers and unbelievers that was found among the Gentiles (cf. Ac. 2: 46, 47; 3: 1, 11; 5: 12, 42; 6: 7; 17: 2; 21: 20-26). In fact as late as A.D. 80/90 in Palestine it was necessary to take special steps to bar believing Jews from the synagogue.

It has been objected that James had no authority to address all the Jews, but, if there is any truth in the account of Hegesippus, and even of Josephus, he was esteemed by all the people, and he might well have hoped that his voice would be heard beyond the bounds of the Church. One might compare the Sermon on the Mount, which was addressed firstly to the disciples, and secondly to the multitudes (cf. Mt. 5: 1-2; 7: 28-29).

While all Jews outside Palestine are included in the address, it is quite likely, as Hort suggested, that James had principally in view those of Syria

T*

beyond Palestine, and possibly Babylonia, and in Syria especially those of Antioch. Mayor thought that in contrast to Peter's letter to the western dispersion, James wrote for the eastern. The distribution of the letter may have occurred at one of the national feasts.

As to the place of writing, there can be little doubt that it was Jerusalem, the fixed residence of James, and that is in keeping with the Palestinian references in the letter.

Date

It is not easy to determine the exact date of the letter but certain limits can be set. (a) The scattering and persecution of the Christians would indicate that it was written after the martyrdom of Stephen (A.D. 36 or 37 or a little earlier according to some). (b) It was evidently written before the destruction of Jerusalem, as the oppression of the poor by the rich Sadducees ended with the war (A.D. 66-73) and James was looking forward to judgment (5: 1-5). (c) James, according to Josephus, was martyred in A.D. 62, according to Hegesippus about A.D. 68. As the account of the latter is late and in part legendary, the first is to be preferred. (d) Many scholars have dated the letter early, between A.D. 40 and 50 according to Mayor, before the Conference at Jerusalem (Ac. 15) and before the writings of Paul, thus making it the earliest NT document. One of the chief arguments for the early date is the lack of reference to the Gentiles and their relation to the Jewish law, a topic of special interest to James (cf. Ac. 15), and of great importance to Jewish believers (cf. Ac. 21: 18-25; Gal. 2: 11 ff.).

The case for the early date is set out fully by Mayor and is strongly advocated by Alford and Zahn. Their arguments appear convincing.

On the other hand some scholars, e.g. Farrar and Hort, believed that the letter was written near the end of James's life, after Paul had written Romans and Galatians. It has been argued that 'the epistle implies not only a spread of Christianity among the Dispersion, but its having taken root there some time' (Hort). Farrar's arguments are answered in detail by Mayor. On the relation between Paul and James see the note on ch. 2.

Some have ascribed the letter to an unknown writer of the second century who assumed the name of the Lord's brother. Hort however wrote that the view is based 'on very slight and intangible grounds'. And would not such a person have made more of the authority of James? G. H. Rendall, whose work *The Epistle of St. James and Judaic Christianity* is an excellent defence of the genuineness of the letter, considered that the lack of systematic teaching concerning Christ was 'one of the weighty,

James

indeed fatal, objections to assigning a late date to the epistle' (p. 88).

Canonicity

There are resemblances to the language of James in writers of the first and second centuries, as in Clement of Rome and especially Hermas, but the letter is omitted from the Old Latin Version and the Muratorian Fragment, both of the second century. The latter however also omits Hebrews and the Letters of Peter and the text is obviously corrupt.

The first known writer to quote the letter as Scripture and as written by James was Origen, the famous teacher of Alexandria (c. A.D. 185-254). 'From the third century the epistle begins to be . . . included in the canon, first of all in the Greek Church, then in the Latin, and finally in the Syrian Church' (Ropes, pp. 86-87). Early ignorance of the letter, especially in the west, may be explained by the fact that it was written to Jews of the Dispersion by a leader of Judaic Christianity, who spent his life in Jerusalem.

Even when it became more widely known, doubts were held concerning its canonicity because many were uncertain of the identity and authority of the writer, who did not claim to be an apostle. These doubts may also have been accentuated by the comparative lack of Christian doctrine and the apparent inconsistency with Paul's teaching.

Eusebius, at the beginning of the fourth century, classed it among the doubtful books, though he himself does not seem to have shared the doubts. By the end of the fourth century its canonicity was universally accepted until the time of the Reformation, and that view has commended itself to Christians generally. Luther's objection to the letter was based on the mistaken assumption that there was a conflict between James and Paul. See the notes on ch. 2. For further study of the question the reader is referred to the article on the General Letters and to D. Guthrie, *New Testament Introduction: Hebrews to Revelation* (London, 1962), pp. 60-63.

ANALYSIS

IV CONCLUSION, PATIENCE AND PRAYER (5: 7-20)

I. SALUTATION (1: 1)

1. James: See above, 'Authorship'. **servant** (i.e. bondservant) **of God and of the Lord Jesus Christ** (cf. Phil. 1: 1; Jude 1): Jude adds that he is the brother of (the more prominent) James. Though James was the Lord's brother, both here and in 2: 1 he gives Him His full title (cf. 2 C. 5: 16). Such words from a strict Jew, especially as he links the service of God and of Christ, are equivalent to a confession of His deity. **To the twelve tribes:** Cf. Mt. 19: 28; Ac. 26: 7 and above, 'Readers and Place of Writing'. Only Benjamin and Judah had returned from the Captivity to any great extent. Of the other tribes individuals could be identified from the genealogies. The Twelve Tribes were no longer a religious or political unity but in the eyes of God Israel was still one (cf. Ezr. 6: 17; Jer. 3: 18; Ezek. 37: 16-17; 48: 19; Rev. 7). **in the Dispersion:** The Jews were scattered throughout the civilized world (cf. Ac. 2: 5). The three main divisions of the dispersion were the Babylonian, Syrian and Egyptian (cf. Dt. 28: 25 (LXX); Jn 7: 35; 1 Pet. 1: 1 and above 'Readers and Place of Writing'). **Greeting:** Often rendered 'hail' or 'rejoice', found elsewhere in the NT, in this form only in Ac. 15: 23, in a letter probably composed by James, and in ch. 23: 26. In other forms it is the commonest Greek word for greeting (*e.g.* Lk. 1: 28).

II. INTRODUCTION, RELIGION IN A TIME OF TRIAL (1: 2-27)

i. The Sweet Uses of Adversity (1: 2-4)

The Christian is not to court trial (cf. Mt. 6: 13), but if he meets with it (cf. Lk. 10: 30 for the same word), he is to regard it with unreserved joy. 'Joy' in v. 2 is similar to 'greeting' in v. 1. This repetition of a word is characteristic of the letter (cf. 'steadfastness' in vv. 3 and 4 and 'lack' in vv. 4 and 5). **2. my brethren:** James addresses his readers as 'brethren' fifteen times, with the addition of 'beloved' three times. They were 'brethren' because they were fellow Israelites (cf. Ac. 13: 38) and also because they were fellow Christians. Women are of course included. **3. the testing of your faith produces steadfastness:** 'Testing' is the word used for 'crucible' in Prov. 27: 21 (LXX). Deissmann, however, following the papyri, both here and in 1 Pet. 1: 7, explained it as 'that which is genuine in your faith', but 'testing' seems to give better sense here. The AV gives 'patience', but the thought is rather 'endurance'. **4. And** (not 'but') **let steadfastness have its full effect** ('perfect work' AV): Endurance produces rich fruits in the lives of those who are spiritually exercised (cf. Lk. 21: 19, RV; Rom. 5: 3-4; Heb. 10: 36; 12: 1-3, 11; 1 Pet. 1: 6-7). 'Perfect' is found five times in the letter (cf. vv. 17, 25; 3: 2). **perfect and complete:** The first word indicates positive excellence (cf. Gen. 6: 9, LXX) and the second absence of defect (cf. Ac. 3: 16; 1 Th. 5: 23).

ii. Prayer for Wisdom (1: 5-8)

Wisdom is one of the great themes of the letter (cf. 3: 13-17). God is its source (cf. 1 Kg. 3: 9-12; Eph. 1: 17); He gives to all **generously, without reproaching** them for their unworthiness (cf. Mt. 5: 45). But we must **ask in faith,** for the doubter is like the restless sea (the first of the metaphors drawn from nature). No such **double-minded man, unstable** like a drunken man or a tossing ship (cf. Prov. 23: 29-34; Isa. 57: 20; Eph. 4: 14) **will receive anything from the Lord** (cf. Mt. 6: 22-24; 21: 21; Heb. 11: 6). **8. the Lord:** That is 'God' (cf. v. 5). So in 4: 10, 15; 5: 4, 10, 11, but in 5: 7, 14, 15 it is used of Christ. It is possible however that James may not always have sharply distinguished the Persons of the Godhead.

iii. The Rich Poor and the Poor Rich (1: 9-11)

The RV introduces v. 9 with 'but'. 'Far from being thus undecided and unsettled, the Christian should exult in his profession' (Mayor). The lowly or poor brother is to **boast in his exaltation** (9) or his 'high estate' (RV) as a Christian. The rich brother is to boast **in his humiliation** (10), for if a rich man is to be a Christian he has to be 'made low' (RV) (cf. Lk. 18: 25; 22: 26). He must learn the transitory nature of earthly things (cf. Ps. 49: 16-17). Some link these verses with v. 2, the meaning being that the poor brother is to rejoice in the benefits of trial, and the rich in its humbling effect, but the above interpretation is wider and deeper. Some again take the 'rich' to refer to the unbeliever, as elsewhere in the letter, but the meaning given is unsatisfactory, *e.g.* 'let the rich man, if he will, glory in his degradation', the words being ironical. For **scorching heat** (11) the RV gives 'scorching wind', which would refer to the burning wind which blew from the desert over Palestine (cf. Ezek. 17: 10; Jon. 4: 8; Lk. 12: 55). This was the view of Hort and Mayor, but Arndt and Gingrich prefer 'heat' (cf. Mt. 20: 12). **grass** here includes wild flowers (cf. Isa. 40: 6; Mt. 6: 30; 1 Pet. 1: 24).

iv. Trial and Temptation (1: 12-15)

12. the crown of life is promised to the man who **endures trial,** as it is to the martyr in Rev. 2: 10. A crown or garland was given as a reward in the Greek games. It was also 'a token of public honour for distinguished service, military prowess, etc., or nuptial joy or festal gladness, especially at the parousia of kings' (W. E. Vine). The figure is also found in the OT, *e.g.* in Ps. 21: 3; 89: 39; Prov. 4: 9; Zech. 6: 11-14. As a strict Jew James was probably not thinking of the reward at the games. It seems that **life** is here the crown. Eternal life is a gift (cf. Rom. 6: 23), possessed by all believers (cf. Jn 10: 28). It is also the end or crown of the believer's walk (cf. Rom. 6: 22; Gal. 6: 8); so here the crown is not so much a reward, as in 1 C. 9: 25, as an incentive, in contrast to vv. 10-11 (cf. Rev. 2: 10-11; 1 Th. 2: 19; 2 Tim. 4: 8; 1 Pet. 5: 4). Another less likely view is that **of life** refers to the permanence of the crown. **when he has stood the test:** RV gives: 'when he hath been approved'. 'Test' is similar to 'testing' in v. 3. **God has promised to those who love him:** Some MSS give 'Lord' and others omit. It has been thought that an unrecorded saying of the Lord is here referred to (cf. Ac. 20: 35), but there may be an expansion of OT promises, *e.g.* Dt. 30: 15-20. **to those who love him:** A general description of Christians (cf. 2: 5; Rom. 8: 28; 1 C. 2: 9; Heb. 9: 28).

James then passes from the outward trial to the inward trial or temptation, 'from our holy trials to our unholy ones' (W. Kelly). The former must be endured, the latter resisted. 'Tempt' and 'test' represent the same Greek word, which strictly speaking means 'to test'. Evidently there were those who said that God was the author of all things and was therefore responsible for our temptations but God is 'untemptable of evil' (Mayor), 'untried in evil' (RVmg). Evil

never finds an entrance into His heart and therefore He tempts no-one. In Gen. 22: 1 the meaning is 'to prove'. 'Satan tempts to bring out the bad; God tests to bring out the good' (W. H. Griffith Thomas). The true source of temptation is the evil heart within. First of all there is evil desire, which has a child called 'sin', **and sin when it is full-grown brings forth death** (15), spiritual death now and eternal death hereafter. The latter seems chiefly in view here in contrast to 'the crown of life' (v. 12). Cf. Gen. 2: 17; Ezek. 18: 4; Mt. 7: 13-14; Rom. 5: 12; 6: 21, 23; 7: 11-13; 8: 13; 1 C. 15: 56; 1 Tim. 5: 6. It has been suggested that behind the words **lured and enticed** (14) there is a picture of the hunter or fisherman luring his prey from its safe retreat. Others have thought that 'he probably pictured to himself the tempter desire as a harlot' (Hort). Satan is not here mentioned as a source of temptation, as in 3: 6; 4: 7, as that would only have provided the sinner with an alternative excuse.

v. God the Source of All Good Gifts (1: 16-18)

In vv. 16, 19 and 2: 5 'beloved' is added to 'brethren'. Such an address was unknown among the Jews (Knowling). The thought of 'deception' is found three times in the chapter (vv. 16, 22, 26), though the words are different in the Greek. Far from God being the author of evil, **every good endowment and every perfect gift is from above** (17). 'Endowment' and 'gift' are translations of the Greek *dosis* and *dōrēma*. Generally *dosis* is the act of giving and *dōrēma* the thing given, but here *dosis* is mostly taken to mean the concrete gift (a meaning attested as early as Homer but apparently not found in the papyri. See *MM*). Philo, an older contemporary of James, said that *dōrēma* was much stronger and involved the idea of magnitude and fulness, applying to it the epithet 'perfect', as James does here. For *dōrēma* RV gives 'boon'. The words are poetical in form and they may be a quotation from a Greek poet or a Christian hymn. Ropes therefore regarded the difference as purely rhetorical but Hort (and also Lightfoot) strongly maintained the distinction. He said that the second word usually implied free giving. He preferred the rendering: 'Every giving (of God) is good and every gift perfect from above' (or 'from its source'). NEB gives: 'All good giving and every perfect gift . . .' **17. Father of lights:** God is the fountain of all light in the physical, intellectual, moral and spiritual spheres (cf. Gen. 1: 3, 14; Ps. 27: 1; Jer. 31: 35). **with whom there is** (RV 'can be') **no variation** (cf. Gal. 3: 28 RV): The sun may change in its course but not God. **shadow due to change:** 'shadow cast by turning' (RV). Others give 'changing shadow'. James 'may have had chiefly in view either night and day, or the monthly obscuration of the moon, or even the casual vicissitudes of light due to clouds' (Hort); cf. Mal. 3: 6. Far from giving birth to sin, **of his own will he brought us forth** (same word as in v. 15) **by the word of truth** (18): Cf. Jn 1: 13; Eph. 1: 5, 11; 5: 26; 1 Pet. 1: 3, 23. James is no mere moralist but is at one with the other writers of the NT concerning the gospel of the grace of God. There is an excellent note in Alford (quoted from Wiesinger) on the evangelical implications of the verse. Some have applied the words to creation rather than regeneration, but 'begetting' and the 'word of truth' are rather the language of the gospel. **a kind of first fruits of his creatures:** In 1 C. 15: 20 'firstfruits' is used of Christ, here of Christians. Later the figure became more common, but here James introduces it apologetically with 'as it were' (Knox). Perhaps a small indication of an early date. 'Firstfruits' implies both priority and consecration. A redeemed Church is a pledge of a redeemed creation. As James is looking forward to the near return of Christ (cf. 5: 8), the meaning can hardly be that the early believers were the nucleus of the Church. Cf. Lev. 23: 10, 17; Dt. 26: 2; Rom. 16: 5; 2 Th. 2: 13 (RVmg); Rev. 5: 13; 14: 4. 'The substance of John's ministry is in verses 17, 18' (C. A. Coates).

vi. The Anger of Man and the Righteousness of God (1: 19-21)
19. Know this: Or 'You know this' (cf. RV). The knowledge of the new birth should lead to a new life. James warns against the sins of the tongue, a theme developed in ch. 3. With **quick to hear,** cf. Isa 50: 4; **slow to speak,** Ec. 5: 1-2; **slow to anger,** Eph. 4: 26-27. The words appear to refer primarily to anger in debate. The angry talker is not doing what is right in God's sight. Very likely his anger is but a cloak of bitterness. **20. work** is here 'practise' rather than 'produce', the same word as 'commit' in 2: 9 (cf. Ac. 10: 35; Heb. 11: 33). There is probably no thought here of a right standing before God, as we find in Paul's letters, *e.g.* Phil. 3: 9. Contrast Ps. 76: 10. **21. Therefore put away** (as a polluted garment) **all filthiness** (cf. 2 C. 7: 1) **and rank growth** ('abundant crop', Alford) **of wickedness:** Mayor preferred the 'overflow of wickedness,' as in the RV, the thought being that the evil within is not to be allowed to break out in hasty words or violent temper, for there is defilement in the overflow (cf. 3: 6 and Mt. 15: 18-19). The AV 'superfluity of naughtiness' is objectionable if it is taken to mean that James is advocating

the lopping off of the excrescence of evil, as if a certain amount would do no harm. Some translate 'the remainder of wickedness' (cf. Mk 8: 8), but it seems less natural. As in 1 Pet. 2: 1-2, the laying aside of the sinful tendencies is to be accompanied by the reception of the **implanted** (not 'engrafted') **word** (cf. the Parable of the Sower, Mt. 13), **which is able to save your souls.** The soul is the living principle and it is saved from death here and hereafter by the power of the Word (cf. v. 15 and also Mt. 16: 25-26; Lk. 6: 9; Heb. 10: 39; 1 Pet. 1: 9, 23; 2: 2, RV).

vii. Doers and Hearers (1: 22-25)
If one uses the Word only as a text-book, there will be no blessing but only self-deception. Cf. Mt. 7: 21-27; Lk. 11: 28; Jn 13: 17 and Rom. 2: 13, the only other place in the NT where 'doers' and 'hearers' are found together. **23. his natural face:** RVmg gives 'face of his birth'. Hort took it to mean 'the invisible face, the reflexion of God's image in humanity,' but this view seems too subtle.

The contrast appears to be a simple one. On the one hand is the careless man who looks at his natural face in a mirror. 'He glances at himself' (NEB). His face may be soiled, care-worn or wrinkled, but he goes away, and, becoming absorbed in other matters, soon forgets. On the other hand is the earnest man who 'looks closely' into the divine mirror, and, instead of going away 'lives in its company' (cf. Ps. 1: 2), and, instead of forgetting, 'acts upon it' (NEB). He is the man who will receive the blessing. **25. the perfect law, the law of liberty:** It is the divine law, interpreted and enriched by Christ (cf. Mt. 5: 17 ff.) and is therefore perfect. It is the 'law of liberty' (cf. 2: 12), which we obey, not because we have to, but because we want to, and in obeying which we find our true freedom (cf. Jn 8: 31-36). Any conflict between this teaching and Paul's (*e.g.* Rom. 6: 14; 7: 4) is only apparent (cf. Rom. 3: 31; 8: 4; 1 C. 9: 21). Even OT saints had an understanding of the 'law of liberty' (cf. Ps. 119: 45, 54).

viii. True Religion (1: 26-27)
26. religion, according to R. C. Trench, is 'predominantly the ceremonial service of religion', and James 'is not herein affirming, as we sometimes hear, these offices to be the sum total, nor yet the great essentials, of true religion, but declares them to be the body, the *thrēskeia*, of which godliness, or the love of God, is the informing soul' (*Synonyms of the NT,* § xlviii). **27. pure** is the positive side, **undefiled** the negative. The Jews were at times more careful of ceremonial defilement than moral (cf. Mk 7: 1-13). **before God and the Father:**

'our God and Father' (RV). If we know God as Father we shall be concerned about His children. **to keep oneself** (cf. the similar phrase in Ac. 15: 29, which was probably drafted or composed by James): Cf. also 4: 4; Ps. 68: 5; Isa. 58; Mt. 25: 36, 43; Mk 12: 40; 1 Tim. 5: 22; 1 Pet. 1: 19; 2 Pet. 2: 20.

III. SINS, SOCIAL AND SPIRITUAL (2: 1–5: 6)

i. Partiality to the Rich (2: 1–7)

1. show no partiality as you hold the faith of our Lord Jesus Christ: Some take this as a question: 'Do ye, in accepting persons, hold the faith, etc.?' (RVmg) but the prohibition is more in keeping with the writer's general style. Some too think that James means the faith that our Lord exemplified (cf. Heb. 12: 2), but Mk 11: 22; Ac. 3: 16; Gal. 2: 16, 20; Eph. 3: 12; Phil. 3: 9 suggest that the meaning is simply 'faith in'. For **Lord Jesus Christ** see 1: 1. 'Lord' is not repeated in the original before 'glory' and Bengel suggested that the meaning is 'our Lord Jesus Christ (who is) the glory', and that rendering has been accepted by Hort, Mayor and others (cf. Lk. 2: 32; Jn 1: 14; Rom. 9: 4; Heb. 1: 3; 9: 5; 1 Pet. 4: 14). A simple emendation would yield the attractive reading: 'the Lord Jesus Christ, our glory'. Mayor quotes evidence to show that the Shekinah, the Jewish name for the divine glory living among men, was used of God and of the Messiah, e.g. 'The Lord of the serving angels, the son of the Highest, yea, the Shekinah' (cf. Zech. 2: 5; 6: 13). In the synagogues the Jews worshipped according to their importance in human estimation (cf. Mt. 23: 6), but such behaviour was contrary to the example and teaching of our Lord (cf. Lk. 14: 12–14; 2 C. 8: 9; Phil. 2). **2. with gold rings:** It was not uncommon for several to be worn and it was a mark of wealth and social distinction (cf. Lk. 15: 22). **assembly:** Literally 'synagogue' (RV). It could refer to a company of Jewish Christians or to the building. The word may be another pointer to an early date, but the reference can hardly be to an ordinary Jewish synagogue, as the Christians could not be held responsible for the conduct there. It is **your assembly.** The thrice repeated **clothing** is the same word in the Greek, though different words are used in AV. So too with **fine:** AV 'goodly' and 'gay'. Ropes believed that the visitors are undoubtedly non-Christians (cf. v. 6), but it seems better, with Alford, to leave the reference general. **3. please** (so also NEB): Both AV and RV say 'in a good place'. It is literally 'beautifully' or 'excellently'. **4. have you not made distinctions . . .:** This is good sense but rather obvious. 'Are ye not divided in your

own mind?' (RV) is preferable. The same word as 'doubt' in 1: 6. **judges with evil thoughts:** Literally 'of evil thoughts'. Weymouth gives 'full of'. **5. poor in** ('as to' RV) **the world to be rich in faith** (cf. Lk. 12: 21; Rev. 2: 9): 'To be' is not in the Greek but is understood by RV, Hort and Mayor (cf. Eph. 1: 4). **heirs of the kingdom:** Cf. Mt. 5: 3; 1 C. 6: 9, 15, 50; Eph. 5: 5; 1 Pet. 1: 4. **which he has promised to those who love him:** Cf. 1: 12; Dan. 7: 18; Lk. 12: 31–32. **6. is it not they** ('themselves' RV) **who drag you into court:** The reference is to the rich, unconverted Jews dragging the poor Christians to the synagogue and heathen courts (cf. Mt. 10: 17–18; Ac. 4: 1–3; 9: 2; 12: 1–2; 16: 19). The persecutions are viewed as still continuing. 'The picture here exhibited well corresponds with that which is presented by Josephus and other Jewish authorities of the conditions of Palestine in the time following the death of our Lord' (G. Salmon, *Introduction to the NT*, p. 456). **7. Is it not they who blaspheme that honourable name by which you are called:** RVmg gives the literal rendering, 'which was called upon you', and the reference may be to the invocation of the name of Christ at baptism (cf. Ac. 15: 17; Gen. 48: 16). While 'blaspheme' could be used in reference to both God and man, 'a Jew would not be likely to associate blasphemy with any name less than a divine name' (Knowling). Cf. Lev. 24: 11; Ac. 26: 11; 1 C. 12: 3.

ii. The Royal Law (2: 8–13)

The expression **royal law** (8) has been variously interpreted: (a) as describing the law of love as sovereign over all others (cf. Mt. 22: 36–40; Rom. 13: 8–9; Gal. 5: 14); (b) as fitted for kings and not slaves (cf. vv. 5, 12); (c) as given by the King. The first is the commonest explanation but James may have had more than one thought in mind. 'Law' is not generally used of a single commandment, but it may be so used here because of the comprehensive nature of the command, or possibly it refers here also to the whole law of which the commandment is a part. **according to the scripture** is to be taken with what follows, not with 'fulfil'. **you do well:** Cf. Ac. 15: 29. **If you really fulfil:** RV gives 'Howbeit if ye fulfil', and the meaning appears to be that James makes no objection if their attitude to the rich is one of love, but if it springs from snobbery and self-seeking it is sinful. If the RSV rendering is adopted, which was that of Hort, the reference is rather to a general claim to fulfil the law. **9. commit** is the same verb as 'work' (1: 20). It is plain from Dt. 1: 17 that partiality is a breach of the law, and **whoever keeps the whole law but fails in one point has become guilty of all of it** (10). Augustine explained this by saying that the whole law hangs on the love of God and that every transgression is a breach of love. It is also true that the whole law expresses the divine will, and every breach is disobedience to that will.

In v. 11 the seventh commandment precedes the sixth, as in Lk. 18: 20 and Rom. 13: 9. This may have been due to LXX influence (for James and the LXX see above, 'Character and Contents'), as Mayor believed, or the order may have been simply due to the context, as Zahn held, the Jews being more particular about the seventh commandment than the sixth (cf. 4: 2; 5: 6 and cf. Mt. 19: 18-19 for an inversion involving the fifth commandment). James does not here say that the Christians were actually guilty of killing but see the note quoted from Alford on 4: 2. The commands quoted by James, which are the first two in the Decalogue relating to our duty to our neighbour, suggest that he did not have in mind the ceremonial side of the law. It has been thought that the words of Ac. 15: 24 were based on a misinterpretation of such teaching, as if James insisted on a literal observance of the whole Mosaic code. See also the comment on this passage in the article on the General Letters. **11. a transgressor of the law:** The expression occurs in an uncanonical saying of our Lord: 'O man, if thou knowest what thou art doing, thou art blessed; but if thou knowest not, thou art accursed, and a transgressor of the law' (Lk. 6: 4 fin., western text). **12. under the law of liberty:** Cf. 1: 25. This will be more exacting than a merely external law, because it will judge the heart and motive. The absence of the article before 'law' ('a law', RV), unlike 1: 25, emphasizes the character of the law. **13. For judgment is without mercy to one who has shown no mercy:** Cf. 2 Sam. 12: 5; Mt. 18: 21-35. **yet mercy triumphs over judgment:** The absence of a connecting particle in the Greek, the use of 'mercy' instead of 'merciful man', and the change to the present tense, all indicate that a universal truth is expressed. It is true of God's mercy that it triumphed at Calvary over His judgment, though not at the expense of His justice; it is true in the conversion of the sinner (cf. Lk. 18: 12-14); and it should also be true in our relationship with one another (cf. Lk. 6: 36-37).

iii. Faith and Works (2: 14-26)

This is the celebrated passage which was a stumbling-block to Martin Luther. He considered it impossible to reconcile Paul and James, but the difficulties will be seen to be more apparent than real if we note the following: (*a*) To James faith is as fundamental as to Paul. He begins and ends with faith and in the middle explains its true character (1: 3, 6; 2: 1, 5; 5: 15). It is James who says 'rich in faith' (2: 5). (*b*) To Paul works are as fundamental as to James (cf. Rom. 2: 5-11; Eph. 2: 10; 2 Th. 2: 17 and especially the Pastoral Letters). He recognizes that faith in itself can be unprofitable (1 C. 13: 2) and it is Paul who says 'rich in good works' (1 Tim. 6: 18). (*c*) The three basic words 'faith', 'justify' and 'works' are used differently in Romans 3-4 and in verses such as 14, 17 and 26 of James 2. In Paul faith is a living trust in God but in these verses it is a dead faith, mere belief unquickened by the Spirit of God. In Paul 'justify' means 'to acquit the sinner in the sight of a holy God' (see note on v. 18); in James it means 'to vindicate', 'to show to be righteous' before God and men. Then the works are different. In Paul they are works of the law, regarded as a ground of merit; in James works of obedience and love. 'The works Paul speaks about are those that precede faith, those of James, those wrought in faith' (Godet). Paul says 'a man is justified not by the works of the law but by the faith of Jesus Christ. James speaks of works without any mention of law and of faith without any mention of Jesus Christ' (Salmon). Paul's words in Rom. 2: 13 and Gal. 5: 6 are exactly the teaching of James. (*d*) Apart from the question of inspiration, it is against all probability that James should be attacking the teaching of Paul, for: (1) At the Conference of Jerusalem (Ac. 15) he supported Paul and the letter mentioned 'our beloved Barnabas and Paul' (v. 25), and in Gal. 2: 9 he gave to them 'the right hand of fellowship'. (2) There is much to be said for the view that James's letter was written before the letters of Paul (see above, 'Date'). Mayor and Zahn believed that Paul had the letter of James before him and developed the thought, but others, *e.g.* Knowling, have thought that the two writers may have simply used language that was current in early Christian circles (cf. Gal. 2: 16 ff.). (3) Some have held that James wrote after the writing of Galatians and Romans and that he had these letters before him. E. H. Plumptre however questioned whether those letters would have reached Jerusalem during James's lifetime, and, even if they did, there is no opposition, for 'a real antagonist would have followed St. Paul more closely, and come definitely into collision, which St. James never does' (Hort). Some believe that James is attacking an antinomian perversion of Paul's teaching. The main argument for this view is the language of vv. 21-26. It is pointed out that elsewhere in the NT it is only Paul who speaks of justification by faith (even Ac. 13: 39 being spoken by Paul), and there is the common reference to Abraham's faith. This however may not be conclusive, for 'justification by faith' is a natural way of expressing the truth of Gen. 15: 6. Our Lord spoke of justification (cf. Lk. 18: 14) and of being justified by words (cf. Mt. 12: 37) and of faith saving (cf. Lk. 7: 50), and Gal. 2: 16 ff. shows that justification by faith was a subject of discussion among the apostles quite early. Besides, 'the nature of faith and the special merit of Abraham's faith were subjects often discussed among the Jews' (Plummer).

And the view is not without other difficulties: (1) Jewish believers would not have been greatly influenced by Paul. (2) If, as some believe, James was also warning Gentile believers, it would surely have been fitting, especially in view of the strong language he was using, to make it clear that it was a perversion of the doctrine of the apostle of the Gentiles that he was attacking and not his true doctrine. (3) 'If v. 14 was based upon any formula at all, it must have been some such saying as the one so often used by Jesus, "Thy faith hath saved thee"' (Zahn). (4) James quotes the fundamental article of the Jewish faith, but 'the Pauline conception of justifying faith had its object, not in the unity of God, but in Christ, His death and resurrection' (Knowling, p. 59). (5) There is no mention of grace and no suggestion that those to whom James writes desire to do evil or continue in sin, as in Rom. 3: 8; 6: 1: there is simply an absence of desire for good works.

For reasons such as the above Zahn believed that 'it is a perversion of the Christian Gospel in general rather than Paul's expression of it that James has in mind'. It should be noted that not only Paul but NT writers generally protested against such abuses; *e.g.* 1 Pet. 2: 16; Jude 4; 1 Jn 1: 6.

A third possibility, which seems to have much to commend it, is that James has in view a Jewish attitude on the subject, and that view derives support from the fact that the passage speaks of faith in general and not of faith in Christ. 'It is the cold monotheism which the self-satisfied Pharisee has brought with him into the Christian Church, which he supposes will render charity and good works superfluous, that St. James is condemning' (Plummer). Cf. Jn 5: 39; Rom. 2: 17–29 (especially v. 17 'restest upon the law', RV).

(*a*) **The problem introduced (2: 14–20)**
In v. 14 James is not denying that the person has faith of a kind, but it is not saving faith. **Can his faith save him:** RV gives 'that faith'. **15. ill-clad:** Such is the force of the literal 'naked', AV and RV (cf. Mt. 25: 36, 43). **16. 'Go in peace . . . ':** A common Jewish farewell (cf. Gen. 26: 29; Mk 5: 34). **17. So faith:** Faith by itself is as ineffective as the previous words. **18. Show:**

James is concerned with the evidence of faith. It is a mistake however to think that he has in view justification before men only, as is shown by v. 14 and the illustration of Abraham (cf. Gen. 22: 12). In this verse the objector cannot be addressing James, who is commending works rather than faith. Some think he is addressing the one whom James is criticizing, but it is simpler, with Ropes, to regard 'you' and 'I' as equivalent to 'one' and 'another', a picturesque mode of indicating two imaginary persons (cf. Rom. 2: 1–5; 9: 19 ff.; 1 C. 15: 36). The meaning then is that the gifts of God are different: to one He has given faith, to another works. But James will not hear of that. The two are inseparable. So he challenges the objector to show genuine faith apart from works and he will demonstrate the reality of his faith by his works. In v. 19 James continues to address the objector. He refers to the central article of the Jewish faith, the unity of the Godhead. Godet quotes from the heretical *Clementine Homilies:* 'A monotheistic soul has the privilege above that of an idolater that even when it has lived in sin it cannot perish'. This is an extreme form of the error condemned by james. **Even the demons** (not 'devils', for there s but one devil) **believe—and shudder:** The word 'shudder' was 'specially used of awe of a mysterious divine power, as often of the adepts in the Greek Mysteries' (Hort). In v. 20 the AV gives 'dead' but the RSV reading **barren** is to be preferred. **you foolish fellow:** Literally 'empty', 'empty-headed, empty-handed, empty-hearted' (Plummer). It has been compared to the 'Raca' of Mt. 5: 22 (RSVmg) and the inference drawn that such precepts of the Sermon on the Mount refer more to the attitude of the heart that the letter of the Word.

(*b*) **Example of Abraham (2: 21–24)**
21. Was not our father Abraham justified by works, when ('in that' RV) **he offered his son Isaac upon the altar:** Paul deals with the same example in Rom. 4: 1–3 (cf. also Gal. 3: 6), but he denies that a man is justified by works. Paul however is referring to Abraham's initial justification recorded in Gen. 15: 6, James to his crowning act of obedience some thirty or more years later. James does not say that Gen. 15: 6 was contradicted or modified, but fulfilled, for **faith was** (all the time) **active along with his works** (22). So it came to full fruition and the reality of his early faith was demonstrated. 'Not for faith plus works does St. James plead, *but for faith at work,* living, acting in itself, apart from any value in its results' (Hort). **as** (RV 'for') **righteousness:** The translation of a Hebrew idiom where 'for' was equivalent to 'as' (cf. Rom. 2: 26). **23. and**

he was called the friend of God: Abraham is so called by the Arabs to this day (cf. Gen. 18: 17; 2 Chr. 20: 7; Isa. 41: 8; Jn 15: 15). Both the Hebrew and Greek words indicate not only companionship but love. 24. You see that (not 'how', AV) a man is justified by works and not by faith alone: Calvin wrote that 'it is faith alone that justifies, but the faith that justifies can never be alone', and another that 'good works are such that a man is neither justified by them nor without them.'

(c) Example of Rahab (2: 25)

There is a marked contrast between Abraham and Rahab. 'He is the friend of God, and she of a vile heathen nation and a harlot. His great act of faith is manifest toward God, hers toward men. His is the crowning act of his spiritual development; hers is the first sign of a faith just begun to exist' (Plummer). Rahab is one of the four women in the genealogy of Mt. 1. In Heb. 11: 31 her faith is commended, and certainly faith is revealed in Jos. 2: 9-11, for the Jordan still flowed between Israel and the Land. She was so well-known in Jewish tradition that there is no need to infer any literary connection between Hebrews and James.

A critic might dismiss the work of Abraham as murder and that of Rahab as treason, but that would be to ignore the historic setting. It is as true now as then that God is greater than family or nation.

(d) Conclusion (2: 26)

26. For as the body apart from the spirit is dead, so faith apart from works is dead: NEB omits 'for'. The words sum up the previous passage. If the comparison is to be pressed strictly, faith is here the body, and works the spirit, the opposite of our general conception. The thought would be that a barren orthodoxy needs obedience to give it life. Some think that James is comparing simply the co-operation of body and spirit on the one hand and faith and works on the other (cf. v. 22). Others have taken 'spirit' here to mean 'breath', which simplifies the comparison, but that is not the usual meaning in the NT (see however 2 Th. 2: 8; Rev. 13: 15). 'In v. 17 it was said that faith, if it have not works, is "dead by itself"; in v. 20 faith without works is barren; here at the end of the discussion faith without works is pronounced absolutely "dead", and so it is' (W. Kelly).

iv. Teachers and the Tongue (3: 1-12)

'Religious fluency, the lust of teaching, the rage for casuistical discussion, have in all ages been the characteristic feature of Pharisaic piety. The third chapter of the epistle is entirely devoted to attacking this fault' (Godet). Other references to the tongue are: Ps. 52: 2; 141: 3; Prov. 10: 18-21; 12: 18; 13: 3; 14: 23; 17: 27;

21: 23; 26: 20-22; Ec. 5: 2-3; Mt. 12: 33-37; 26: 73; Lk. 4: 22; Eph. 4: 15, 29-31; Col. 4: 6; 1 Tim. 5: 13; Tit. 2: 8. 1. Let not many of you become teachers: In NT churches teaching was not confined to a single channel (cf. Ac. 13: 1; 1 C. 14; 1 Pet. 4: 10-11). we who teach shall be judged with greater strictness: James links himself with those he warns (cf. 1 Jn 2: 1). The greater the light the greater the responsibility (cf. Am. 3: 2; Mk 12: 40; Lk. 20: 47). In v. 2 James turns from public speech to uncontrolled speech in general. A perfect control of the tongue would mean a perfect life. Even Moses and Paul failed here (cf. Ps. 106: 33; Ac. 23: 5). V. 4 begins with 'Behold' (RSV Look at), which is found in six places in the letter, 'a common interjection in James's native tongue' (Knowling). Two illustrations are given in vv. 3 and 4. With a bit we guide horses; by a very small rudder we guide great ships wherever the will of the pilot directs, 'even when' (Hort) they are driven by strong winds. 5. So the tongue, though small, boasts of great things: 'Boasts' suggests haughtiness (cf. Ps. 12: 3) and is used instead of 'does' to prepare for what follows; for the tongue is capable of great evil, just as a forest is set ablaze by a small fire! 6. And the tongue is a fire: Cf. Ps. 120: 4; Prov. 16: 27. It is an unrighteous world among our members: 'In our microcosm the tongue represents or constitutes the unrighteous world' (Mayor). staining the whole body: Often the effect the tongue has on others is emphasized but James emphasizes its effect on the person himself (cf. Mk 7: 21-23). The mere uttering of evil is defiling. setting on fire the cycle of nature: The last words are very difficult. The AV gives 'course of nature'; Alford 'the orb of the creation'; Plumptre 'the wheel of life from birth'. The last seems the simplest. Perhaps the tongue is compared to the axle from which a fire sets ablaze the whole course of human life. It is set on fire by hell. In 1: 14 James emphasizes that temptation comes from within; here he traces it back to its Satanic source. 'Hell' here is 'Gehenna', a word used elsewhere in the NT only by the Lord in the Synoptic Gospels. With vv. 7-8 cf. Gen. 1: 24; 9: 2; 1 Kg. 4: 33. The tongue is a restless (not 'unruly' AV) evil, full of deadly poison (cf. Ps. 140: 3). tame: In NT only elsewhere in Mk 5: 4. Here it is the tongue under Satanic control, there the whole man. Fortunately James did not say that God cannot tame the tongue. 9. Lord and Father (so also RV) is not found elsewhere. made in the likeness of God: Cf. Gen. 1: 26-27. While the divine image was marred it was not wholly obliterated. 'Absalom fell from his father's favour, but still the people recognized him as the king's son' (Bengel). Cf. 1 C. 11: 7; Col. 3: 10; Eph. 4: 24. **10. blessing and cursing:** The strong denunciations of our Lord (cf. Mt. 23) and of Paul (cf. Ac. 13: 10; 1 C. 16: 22; Gal. 1: 8), may seem opposed to this teaching, but they were based on truth and love, whereas the cursing James condemns springs from bitterness (v. 11, cf. Rom. 12: 14). In vv. 11 and 12 James draws two illustrations from nature to prove the inconsistency of blessing and cursing (cf. Mt. 7: 16-20; 12: 33-36). Some have thought that James is referring to the Dead Sea (called in the OT the Sea of Salt), which had both salt and fresh springs on its shores.

v. Wisdom, the False and the True (3: 13-18)
James returns to the subject of wisdom which he has already touched upon in 1: 5. He begins by pointing out that true wisdom is not intellectual only: it is shown by a **good life** (readers of the AV should remember that 'conversation', used here and elsewhere, has generally the archaic meaning of 'manner of living' or 'behaviour') and it is marked by meekness (cf. Mt. 5: 5; 11: 28), not pride. In this James is in harmony with the consistent Biblical teaching (cf. Job 28: 28; Ps. 25: 9), but he runs counter to much worldly wisdom. Wisdom and **understanding** (13) are here linked, as often in Scripture. 'The second word expresses personal acquaintance and thus experience' (Hort). The opposite of the meekness of wisdom is **jealousy and selfish ambition** (14). Cf. Gal. 5: 19-23. If these things characterize us, though we may boast of our wisdom, our whole life is a denial of the truth revealed in Jesus (cf. Eph. 4: 21). False wisdom is **earthly, unspiritual, devilish** (15). For 'unspiritual' RV gives 'sensual', and in the margin 'natural' or 'animal' and for 'devilish' RVmg gives 'demoniacal'. In other words it belongs to earth rather than heaven (cf. 1 C. 15: 48), to nature rather than the Spirit (cf. 1 C. 2: 14; 15: 44-46; Jude 19) and to demons rather than God (cf. 1 Tim. 4: 1). **16** gives proof of the previous statement (cf. 1 C. 14: 33). But true wisdom is heavenly in its origin, and it is **first pure, then peaceable** (17). It is pure in its essence and consequently in its manifestation it is peaceable (cf. Prov. 3: 17), **gentle** ('forbearing', Hort), **open to reason** ('easy to be intreated', AV and RV), **full of mercy and good fruits** (contrast 3: 8), **without uncertainty** ('partiality', AV and RVmg), or **insincerity.** If we take 'mercy' and 'good fruits' together we have 'Seven Pillars of Wisdom' (cf. Prov. 9: 1). **18. And the harvest of righteousness is sown in peace by those who make peace:** The 'fruit of righteousness' is sometimes taken to mean the 'product of

righteousness' (cf. Isa. 32: 17; Rom. 6: 20-22) but it seems to fit the context better if we interpret it as 'the fruit which is righteousness', and the verse is thus the complement of 1: 20. The words are an expansion of 'peaceable' and 'good fruits' in v. 17. Some link 'righteousness' and 'peace' (cf. Ps. 85: 10), and some give 'for' instead of 'by'. Cf. Prov. 11: 30; Am. 6: 12; Mt. 5: 9; Phil. 1: 11; Heb. 12: 11. Moffatt gives: 'The peacemakers who sow in peace reap righteousness'.

v. Selfishness and Worldliness (4: 1-4)
The first three verses should be linked with the closing verses of ch. 3. The causes of war and strife are not merely economic or intellectual but moral. As there were no civil wars at this time, James seems to have had primarily in mind 'private quarrels and lawsuits, social rivalries and factions and religious controversies' (Plummer); cf. Rom. 7: 23; 1 Pet. 2: 11. See too the comment in the article on the General Letters. In v. 2 Erasmus and others after him, without any MS authority, read 'envy' for **kill,** as 'killing' would rather follow than precede 'coveting'. The difficulty, however, is largely removed, if, as in RSV, a full-stop is placed after **kill.** Another difficulty is that 'kill' seems a strange word to apply to Christians. But here, as elsewhere, James appears to be looking beyond the bounds of the Church to the unbelieving Jews where assassination was not uncommon (cf. Mk 15: 7; Ac. 21: 38). Besides 'there is no saying how far the Christian portion of Jewish communities may have suffered themselves to become entangled in such quarrels and their murderous consequences' (Alford; cf. 2: 11). Some have taken the word figuratively (cf. Mt. 5: 21-22; 1 Jn 3: 15) like 'adultery' in v. 4. It is suggested that James had Sir. 34: 21, 22, in mind: 'The bread of the needy is the life of the poor; whoever deprives them of it is a man of blood. To take away a neighbour's living is to murder him; to deprive an employee of his wages is to shed blood'. Thus understood the words are an anticipation of 5: 4. The literal meaning, however, seems the more natural (cf. 2: 11; 5: 6), as the words are connected with 4: 1 rather than 5: 4, and, where a figurative sense is required, the context generally clearly indicates it. V. 3 gives us one of the hindrances to prayer, *viz.* selfishness (cf. 1: 8; Ps. 66: 18; Isa. 59: 1-2; 1 Pet. 3: 7). Worldly Christians are described as **Unfaithful creatures** (RV 'adulteresses') (4). Hort took the word literally, but the absence of the masculine and the charge of friendship with the world rather than the violation of the commandment (cf. 2: 11) point rather to a figurative meaning. James is writing in the manner of the OT

prophets (cf. Isa. 57: 3-9; Ezek. 23: 27 and especially the whole of Hosea and also Mt. 12: 39). With **the world** cf. 1 Jn 2: 16. The world has been defined as 'society as it organizes itself apart from God'. Note that in v. 4 instead of 'will be' and 'is' (AV) RSV gives **wishes to be** and **makes himself.**

vii. God a Jealous Lover and the Bestower of Grace (4: 5-6)

The interpretation of v. 5 is difficult. RV gives in the margin one variation for the first part and three for the second. However the following points seem clear: (a) The formula **the scripture says** normally introduces a quotation, but it may give the general sense rather than the exact words (cf. Jn 7: 38); (b) **the spirit which he has made to dwell in us** refers naturally to the Holy Spirit (cf. Rom. 8: 11; 1 C. 3: 16); (c) **yearns** in the NT is always used in a good sense, e.g. Phil. 1: 8; (d) It is true that the word used for 'jealousy' (*phthonos*) regularly and everywhere else in the NT has a bad sense, but as it was used of the jealous feeling of a lover towards a rival, it could understandably be used of the Spirit's desire to have us wholly for Himself. So the most satisfactory rendering appears to be the second in RVmg: 'That Spirit which he made to dwell in us yearneth for us even unto jealous envy.' This was also Mayor's view. The exact quotation has not been found. Perhaps James had in mind Dt. 32: 11, 19, which in the LXX speaks of God's yearning love and jealousy. There may be also echoes of other Scriptures (cf. Gen. 6: 3-5; Exod. 20: 5; 34: 14; Num. 35: 34; Isa. 63: 8-16; Ezek. 36: 27; Zech 1: 14; 8: 2). Some have recently found a Qumran parallel (*Manual of Discipline*, col. 4, lines 9 ff.) and it has been suggested that behind both quotations there may have been a targum or interpretative paraphrase of Gen. 6: 3. Such a high standard of devotion may seem beyond us, but God **'gives grace** (i.e. gracious help) **to the humble'** (6). The second part of v. 6 is from Prov. 3: 34 (LXX), except that **God** is used for 'the Lord' (cf. Isa. 57: 15; Job 22: 29; Lk. 1: 52-53; 14: 11; 1 Pet. 5: 5 and v. 10 of this chapter). For the use of the LXX cf. above, end of 'Character and Contents'.

viii. Exhortations to Wholehearted Devotion (4: 7-10)

The verbs in these exhortations are in the aorist tense, indicating that these things are to be done 'once for all as a settled thing for the soul' (W. Kelly). The first exhortation is to submit to God, which is a mark of true humility and a condition of successful resistance to the devil (cf. Eph. 6: 11; 1 Pet. 5: 9). **7. therefore:** I.e. because of God's character as explained in vv. 5 and 6. **8. Draw near to God:** Cf. Exod.

19: 22; Dt. 4: 7; Ezek. 44: 13; Zech. 1: 3; Heb. 10: 22. **Cleanse . . . purify:** Cf. Gen. 35: 2; Exod. 30: 17-21; Lev. 10: 3; Ps. 24: 3-4; 73: 13; 1 Tim. 2: 8. **sinners** is generally used of the openly ungodly, but here it is parallel with the 'double-minded' (cf. 1: 6, 8), and appears to be addressed to professing Christians 'to startle and sting' (Ropes), though here too the unconverted may be also in view (cf. 5: 20). **9. Be wretched:** AV and RV give 'Be afflicted'. Fasting may be included. **laughter:** Cf. Lk. 6: 25. Sometimes in the Bible laughter is a desirable thing (cf. Ps. 126: 2), but sometimes it is the shallow laughter of the fool (cf. Ec. 7: 6). In the NT it is never used in a commendable sense. With v. 10 cf. v. 6.

ix. Judging One Another (4: 11-12)

In v. 11 the RV omits 'evil' (cf. Rom. 1: 30; 2 C. 12: 20; 1 Pet. 2: 1, 12; 3: 16). **or judges:** Instead of AV 'and judgeth'. 'And' is simpler, for evil-speaking and judging are not strictly alternatives, but 'or' (which is found in the most ancient MSS) may suggest that in some cases the 'uncharitable act' is more prominent, in others the 'judicial assumption'. For **the law** see 2: 8. That the reference is to the command: 'Thou shalt love thy neighbour as thyself' seems plain from the reference to the **neighbour** in v. 12 (so RV and RSV instead of AV 'another'). The verse is found in Lev. 19: 18 and in v. 16 evil speaking is forbidden. The person who judges his brother disobeys the law, thus putting himself above it and treating it with contempt (cf. Mt. 7: 1-5; Rom. 14: 4-13). The three-fold repetition of 'brother' in v. 11 is calculated to emphasize the unbrotherliness of the conduct. **12. one lawgiver and judge:** Though Christ is called judge in 5: 9 'one lawgiver' points rather to God (cf. Isa. 33: 22; Mt. 10: 28; Jn 19: 11; Rom. 2: 16; 3: 6; 13: 1; Heb. 12: 23; 13: 4).

x. The Folly of Forgetting God (4: 13-17)

This section, as 5: 1-6, is sometimes taken to refer to unbelieving Jews, but there is nothing in it inapplicable to professing Christians. The Jews bent on trade are warned not to forget God, for they are of such a nature that they **do not know about to-morrow** (14). Their life is but a passing **mist** (cf. Job 7: 6; 8: 9; 9: 25-26; 20: 8; Ps. 39: 5; 78: 39; 90: 9; Isa. 38: 12; 1 Pet. 1: 24). There is a reading adopted by some editors: 'Whereas ye know not on the morrow of what kind your life shall be' but it gives a weakened sense, as they may not be alive on the morrow. **15. 'If the Lord wills, we shall live and we shall do this or that':** Of course the important thing is not a formula but the dependent attitude of mind. Sometimes Paul used one, and sometimes he dispensed with it (cf. Ac. 18: 21; 19: 21; Rom. 15: 28; 1 C. 4: 19, and Prov. 27: 1). It should be noted also that 'If the Lord wills' means more than 'If the Lord does not prevent'. We should be exercised about His will. **16. you boast in your arrogance:** 'Arrogance' is the same as 'vainglory' in 1 Jn 2: 16 (RV). RV here gives 'vauntings' i.e. their proud speeches. NEB says: 'You boast and brag'. The last verse is added to give point to the previous exhortations. **17. Whoever knows what is right to do and fails to do it, for him it is sin:** The words may refer especially to vv. 13-16, but they are of general application. James is not denying the possibility of a sin of ignorance, but he is emphasizing the seriousness of sinning against the light (cf. Lev. 4: 2; Lk. 12: 48; Jn 9: 41; 15: 22).

xi. The Judgment of the Rich (5: 1-6)
It seems plain that in this section James is denouncing ungodly Jews in the manner of the OT prophets (cf. Isa. 2: 7 ff.; Lk. 6: 24-25). The context (cf. v. 6) indicates that wealthy Jews rather than Gentiles are in view. There is no call to repent but an announcement of impending judgment, and v. 7 distinguishes the 'brethren' from those addressed here (see above, 'Readers and Place of Writing'). In vv. 2-3 three kinds of riches are mentioned, goods, garments and gold. Through hoarding and disuse the goods have rotted, the garments are moth-eaten and the gold is rusted (not literally, but it has become worthless) and their ruin is a picture and prophecy of the ruin of their owners (cf. Mt. 6: 19). **3. for the last days:** Literally 'in the last days' (RV). The last days are already upon them. The Christian is always in the last days (cf. 1 Jn 2: 18). The reference is to the last days before the Second Advent (cf. Isa. 2: 2; Hos. 3: 5; Ac. 2: 17; 2 Tim. 3: 1; 1 Pet. 1: 5), of which the destruction of Jerusalem was a partial fulfilment (cf. Mt. 24). In the war of A.D. 66-73 the wealthy (Sadducean) landowners of Judaea lost all the riches they had accumulated. **4. fields:** Cf. Isa. 5: 8. **cry out:** Cf. Gen. 4: 10; 18: 20; 19: 13; Dt. 24: 14-15; Mal. 3: 5. **Lord of hosts:** Apart from the quotation in Rom. 9: 29, only here in the NT. (In both places the Greek text retains Heb. *Sabaoth* instead of translating it; cf. AV, RV.) It occurs first of all in 1 Sam. 1: 3 and is found in the OT chiefly in the prophetic writings. It expresses God's omnipotence and supremacy. James uses it to assure the oppressed that they have a mighty protector. He may have had in mind Isa. 5: 9, where LXX retains 'Lord of Hosts' instead of translating, *e.g.* by 'the Lord All Sovereign'. (For the use of LXX see above, end of 'Character and Contents'.) **5. in a day of slaughter:** They are like animals gorging themselves on the very day of their

destruction (cf. Jer. 7: 32; Isa. 34: 2, 6). The best exposition of the text is Josephus's account of the destruction of Jerusalem. The aorist tenses in vv. 5 and 6 have been regarded as indicating the viewpoint of the day of judgment. RV and RSV however do not here distinguish from the perfect. **6. the righteous man** is a term elsewhere applied to Christ (cf. Ac. 3: 14; 7: 52; 22: 14) and some apply it to Him here, but, in the absence of any suggestion from the context, it seems better to apply it to righteous men generally (cf. Mt. 24: 35). James himself was known as 'the righteous' and his words are an unconscious prophecy of his own end. **he does not resist you:** The present adds vividness. It 'brings the action before our eyes and makes us dwell upon this, as the central point, in contrast with the accompanying circumstances' (Mayor). Some make this clause a question but the words seem a reminiscence of Mt. 5: 39 (cf. Isa. 53: 5-7).

IV. CONCLUSION, PATIENCE AND PRAYER (5: 7-20)
i. The Need of Patience (5: 7-11)
In view of the oppressions mentioned in vv. 3-6, James exhorts Christians to be patient until the coming of the Lord and he cites the farmer, the prophets and Job. 'Patience' or 'long-suffering' is mentioned four times and steadfastness' ('endurance', RVmg) twice in this section. According to Trench the first expresses patience in respect of persons and the second in respect of things (cf. 1 C. 13: 4, 7). James evidently shared with the other NT writers the conviction that the coming of the Lord was near (cf. Lk. 21: 31; 1 Th. 4: 13-18; Heb. 10: 25, 37; 1 Pet. 4: 7). **7. Behold, the farmer waits for the precious fruit of the earth, being patient over it until it receives the early and the late rain:** The rendering 'it receives' is generally preferred to AV and RVmg 'he receives'. The early and late rains are the rains of autumn and spring. The first germinates the seed; the second matures it. Some of the best MSS omit 'rain', and it has been thought that 'fruit' (which is found in some good MSS) should be repeated, but OT parallels (*e.g.* Dt. 11: 14; Jer. 5: 24; Jl 2: 23; Zech. 10: 1) favour the common rendering. The words naturally recall our Lord's comparison of the consummation of the age to a harvest (cf. Mt. 13: 39) and Joel's prophecy of the former and latter rain after God's judgment upon His enemies (2: 23), but it is unsafe to make a simple illustration the basis of prophetical interpretation. **8. Establish your hearts:** Cf. 2 Chr. 15: 7; 1 C. 15: 58. **9. Do not grumble** (RV 'murmur') . . . **the Judge is standing at the doors:** From v. 8 it appears that the Judge

here, unlike 4: 12, is Christ (cf. Mt. 7: 22–23; Jn 5: 22). **at the doors:** Cf. Mt. 24: 33; Mk 13: 29; Rev. 3: 20. **10. the prophets:** Cf. Mt. 23: 29–36; Ac. 7: 52; Heb. 11: 32–39. **in the name of the Lord:** I.e. as His representatives (cf. Jer. 11: 21; Mt. 7: 22 and v. 14). V. 11 is the only place in the NT where Job is referred to, though he is quoted in 1 C. 3: 19. **11. The steadfastness of Job** was evidently a familiar subject, perhaps in the teaching of the synagogue (cf. Job 1: 21; 2: 10; 13: 15). **the purpose of the Lord:** AV and RV 'end' is better, i.e. the end that the Lord brought to all his trials (42: 12–17). Some have referred the word to the Lord's death but the suggestion is at variance with the context and gives to 'the Lord' two different meanings in the verse. The reason why Christ is not mentioned as an example, as in 1 Pet. 2: 21, is probably because James has unbelieving Jews as well as believing in mind. (See above, 'Readers and Place of Writing'.) Knowling suggested that the reason might be that James wished to keep before the eyes of his readers Jesus as the Lord of glory.

ii. Oaths (5: 12)
The intention of this verse is not to forbid a Christian to take an oath before a magistrate, as is plain from the example of the Lord, who made no objection when the high priest virtually put him under oath (cf. Mt. 26: 63–64), nor to forbid oaths in circumstances of special solemnity (cf. Gen. 22: 16; Isa. 45: 23; Rom. 1: 9; Gal. 1: 20), but rather to discourage the use of oaths in the ordinary relationships of life and **above all** as an expression of impatience. See also the note on Mt. 5: 33–37.

iii. Prayer (5: 13–18)
(*a*) **Prayer and Singing (5: 13).** The true remedy for trouble is not complaining, far less swearing, but praying, and the true outlet for joy is not worldly frivolity but the singing of **praise.**
(*b*) **Prayer and Anointing (5: 14–15).** The following points are submitted to help in the understanding of this difficult and important passage: (1) The elders of the church are to be called. In NT times the care of the churches, under the Chief Shepherd, was regularly in the hands of elders (cf. Ac. 11: 30; 14: 23; 15: 2; 1 Tim. 5: 17; Tit. 1: 5; 1 Pet. 5: 1). So we have here no purely Jewish instructions, though there may have been Jewish elements present. It is noteworthy that anointing with oil is not prescribed for Christians in any other letter.
(2) The initiative lay with the sick person and the ceremony was in the privacy of the home and had little in common with modern healing movements.

(3) Among the Jews the rabbis were asked to pray for the sick and they sometimes visited them; so here the elders are sent for as those who are the most spiritual and have a care for the believers. It may surprise us that the physician is not sent for, but while such advice is given in Ecclesiasticus (38: 12–15), there was no system of medical education in Palestine in Bible times, and one reason for James's exhortation may have been to keep the Christians from resorting to heathenish incantations and superstitious practices (cf. Ac. 19: 13). Very likely also James is contemplating cases that a doctor could not help (cf. v. 15, note).
(4) Some believe that we have here the exercise of the miraculous gift of healing. The absence of any mention of laying on of hands (cf. Mk 6: 13; 16: 18) may not prove the contrary, but why not send for those who had the gift of healing rather than the elders? For it is plain from 1 C. 12: 28–30 that the gifts of government and healing were distinct, and the latter was not possessed by all. Even in the earlier period, before the conference at Jerusalem, the gift of healing was not exercised by the elders, as far as the records go, but by the Twelve, Stephen, Philip, Paul and Barnabas (cf. Ac. 2: 43; 3: 6; 5: 12–16; 6: 8; 8: 6–7; 9: 34, 38–40; 14: 3, 9, 10). Besides it is the prayer of faith that James emphasizes, and in connection with Elijah he stresses the fact that he **was a man of like nature with ourselves** (17).
(5) By many the oil is regarded as medicinal. It is pointed out that oil was a common remedy at the time (cf. Lk 10: 34) and that *aleiphō* ('anoint') is used only in a non-religious sense elsewhere in the NT. It should be noted, however, that Trench's dictum that *aleiphō* is the 'mundane and profane' and *chriō* the 'sacred and religious' word cannot be accepted without reservations; '*aleiphō* is a general term used for an anointing of any kind' (W. E. Vine). It is used occasionally in the Greek OT in a sacred sense and *chriō* is found in the papyri in a mundane sense. See Moulton and Milligan. (Besides *chriō* is never used literally in the NT.) But it seems plain that the oil cannot be purely medicinal, for the Holy Spirit would not sanction the belief that oil was a remedy for all diseases, and the words 'in the name of the Lord' suggest an invocation of the divine name (unlike Col. 3: 17; and cf. Ac. 3: 6; 19: 13; 22: 16). It is significant also that oil was used in Mk 6: 13, where the healing was plainly miraculous, and the emphasis here is on the healing power of prayer rather than of the oil. Besides the sickness may have been of the soul and not of the body. See (7) below. The best view seems to be that of Plummer, that the oil was 'a channel of divine power and an aid

to faith'. In some cases it would have medicinal value, in all cases it would give relief, and it would give confidence to those who attached healing virtue to it. Compare the use of clay and spittle in Jn 9: 6. Some have viewed the oil as purely symbolical, *e.g.* R. A. Torrey, who regarded it 'as symbol of the Holy Spirit in His healing power' (cf. Ac. 10: 38), and the anointing as 'an act of dedication and consecration', while Grotius viewed the oil as 'a token of that ease and joy that they should obtain from God'. There is doubtless truth in these views but, because of the common use of oil as a medicine, it seems impossible to rule out all reference to its therapeutic value.

(6) James does not contemplate failure, but the explanation appears to be found in the expression **the prayer of faith** (15), which is not a prayer that can be prayed at any time but only as it is granted by the Holy Spirit. It was not always granted to Paul (cf. 2 C. 12: 8; 2 Tim. 4: 20). The absolute statement of James is similar to promises made elsewhere (cf. Mk 11: 24). In all cases we must add 'if the Lord will'.

(7) Some have limited the application of the passage to cases where sickness is the result of a particular sin. Arguments for this view are: (*A*) the word used for 'sick' in v. 15 (but see note under (9)); (*B*) the mention of sins in v. 15; (*C*) the confession of sins in v. 16 (which, however, in the manner of James, is to be linked with the latter part of v. 15 rather than v. 14); (*D*) the disciplinary famine in the days of Ahab used as an illustration; (*E*) the recovery of the erring one in vv. 19-20.

It is plain that James contemplates the possibility that the trouble is primarily spiritual, and that should guard us against the view that oil here is a crude form of medicine, but, on the other hand, the use of the general term for 'sick' in v. 14 and the 'if' of v. 15 are arguments against the suggested limitation.

(8) Historically, Extreme Unction developed out of this rite, but the significance is entirely changed, for the Roman Catholic rite has death in view, not recovery.

(9) **14. pray over:** I.e. 'stretching the hands over' (Mayor). **anointing:** 'having anointed' (RV). **in the name of the Lord:** Cf. v. 10. **15. save** is used of physical healing as in Mk 5: 23. **sick** in vv. 14 and 15 represents two different Gk words. Some take the word in v. 15 to mean 'depressed in spirit' (cf. Heb. 12: 3) but as the article in v. 15 identifies the sick man of v. 15 with the one already referred to, it is doubtful if any distinction is intended. Mayor was not prepared to make a distinction. **raise him up** may suggest a serious illness, one that has not responded to ordinary measures.

(10) Many modern examples of the efficacy of the practice have been quoted, *e.g.* in R. A. Torrey's *Divine Healing* and H. P. Barker's booklet of the same name. In the latter a letter of J. N. Darby's is quoted to the effect that 'prayers for the sick, and healing as the result of the prayer of faith, were common among the brethren at the beginning. In the Great Cholera plague of 1832 this was so effective that the doctors were in consternation' (p. 24). Cf. J. N. Darby, *Collected Writings XXVI*, p. 396; *Letters* I, pp. 2 f., III, p. 210. Similarly, F. W. Newman's recovery from fever at Aleppo in 1831 was attributed by A. N. Groves to his anointing with oil, together with his companions' prayer of faith (H. Groves, *Memoir of Lord Congleton* [London, 1884], pp. 32 f.).

(11) However we interpret this passage, there is Biblical authority elsewhere for the use of means in sickness (cf. 2 Kg. 20: 7; 1 Tim. 5: 23). (*c*) **Prayer and Confession (5: 16). Therefore** (so also RV) links this verse with the previous one. James proceeds to give instructions to Christians generally. Even where the elders are not called, Christians should confess their sins one to another that they may be healed, whether in body as in Jn 4: 47 or in spirit as in Mt. 13: 15. **to one another** is fatal to the Roman doctrine of the confessional, which is a perversion of a wholesome practice. Nothing is said here as to the mode or place of such confessions. 'We need not suppose any reference here to a formal confession of sin, but merely to such mutual confidence as would give a right direction to the prayers offered by one for the other' (Mayor). The latter part of the verse, which is an encouragement to mutual confession, has been variously translated. The AV gives 'fervent prayer', a meaning which the word does not seem to bear, the RV 'in its working', the RSV **in its effects.** Perhaps the best view is that of Hort and Mayor, 'inwrought prayer', i.e. prayer prompted by the Spirit.

(*d*) **The Prayer of Elijah (5: 17-18).** The references to Elijah in Matthew are sufficient to indicate the place he occupied in Jewish thought (11: 14; 16: 14; 17: 3-4, 10-12; 27: 47, 49). The miracle-working Elijah might seem to belong to another world, but James assures his readers that he was **of like nature with ourselves** (cf. Ac. 10: 26; 14: 15; 1 Kg. 19: 4). He **prayed fervently** (so also RV), 'earnestly' (AV): Literally 'with prayer' (cf. Lk. 22: 15). His prayer is not actually mentioned in the OT but it is implied in 1 Kg. 17: 1 (cf. Gen. 18: 22; 19: 27; Jer. 15: 1). Here is Biblical authority for prayer for a change of weather, and in a letter which stresses the unchanging character of God (1: 17). The three and a half years are also mentioned by our Lord (Lk. 4: 25). In 1 Kg. 18: 1 it says that the rain came 'in the third year'. Some have therefore seen a discrepancy, but, as James Orr remarked, 'it is forgotten that in Palestine rain is not an everyday occurrence, as it is with us. The ground had already been dry for six months—since the previous rainy season—when Elijah stayed the rain by his word at the commencement of the new rainy season. If the cessation lasted till the third year thereafter, the total period of drought would necessarily be about three years and six months' (*The Bible Under Trial*, pp. 264-265). Cf. Dan. 12: 7; Rev. 11: 2-3; 12: 6; 13: 5. For the second prayer see 1 Kg. 18: 1, 42.

iv. Reclaiming the Wanderer (5: 19-20)
19. My brethren (so also RV): It is debatable whether these verses refer to the restoration of a truly regenerate person or the conversion of an unregenerate one. **wanders from the truth** may seem to favour the first view (but cf. 2 Pet. 2: 20-22), while **save his soul from death** and **cover a multitude of sins** appear to favour the latter, at least to one who holds the doctrine of the security of the true believer. Some have understood 'death' as loss of communion or physical death (cf. 1 C. 11: 30), but these views scarcely satisfy the terms used (cf. 1: 15, 21), and there is no evidence that physical death was the regular punishment of backsliding. The rendering **among you** instead of 'of you' (AV) should be noted. Perhaps 1 Jn 2: 19 is a parallel. It seems therefore that in their fulness the words apply only to the unregenerate (as is true also of Rom. 8: 13 and 1 Tim. 5: 6) but they have an application to a backslider. **the truth** is 'the sum and substance of the Apostolic teaching and preaching' (Knowling) (cf. 1: 18; 3: 14). This use is common in John's writings. With **sinner** (20) cf. 4: 8. AV gives 'hide a multitude of sins' but RV and RSV **cover**. There is evidently an allusion to Prov. 10: 12, which is quoted more fully, but not exactly, in 1 Pet. 4: 8. Some have thought that a proverbial saying is also behind the words. In Proverbs the meaning appears to be simply that if we love a person we hide his sins from men (cf. Gen.

9: 23), but here the thought is rather of forgiveness (cf. Rom. 4: 7). Some have referred the sins to the converter rather than the sinner, as if converting a sinner is a means of securing forgiveness for one's own sins, but, though such an idea may be found in Jewish writings, it is foreign to the NT, nor is it taught in Dan. 12: 3. It has been objected that to refer it to the sinner 'makes a bad anticlimax' but cf. Ps. 116: 8. The meaning is that 'the soul is not merely saved out of death, not merely rescued from peril, but blessed, Ps. 32: 1' (Knowling).

The letter ends abruptly, without benediction, perhaps in order to make the final words ring in the ear, perhaps also because it is not strictly a letter.

BIBLIOGRAPHY

ALFORD, H., *The Greek Testament*, Vol. IV, Part 1 (London, 1870).

CADOUX, A. T., *The Thought of St. James* (London, 1944).

CALVIN, J., *Commentaries on the Catholic Epistles*, Eng. tr. (Edinburgh, 1855).

DALE, R. W., *The Epistle of James* (London, 1895).

ELLIOTT-BINNS, L. E., *Galilean Christianity* (London, 1956).

GODET, F., *Studies in the New Testament*, Eng. tr. (London, 1876).

HORT, F. J. A., *The Epistle of James* (London, 1909).

KELLY, W., *The Epistle of James* (London, 1913).

KNOWLING, R. J., *The Epistle of St. James*. WC (London, 1904).

MAYOR, J. B., *The Epistle of St. James* (London, 1913).

MITTON, C. L., *The Epistle of James* (London, 1966).

PARRY, R. St. J., *A Discussion of the General Epistle of St. James* (Cambridge, 1903).

PLUMMER, A., *St. James and St. Jude*. EB (London, 1891).

PLUMPTRE, E. H., *St. James*. CBSC (Cambridge, 1878).

REICKE, B., *The Epistles of James, Peter and Jude*. Anchor Bible (New York, 1964).

RENDALL, G. H., *The Epistle of St. James and Judaic Christianity* (Cambridge, 1927).

ROPES, J. H., *St. James*. ICC (Edinburgh, 1916).

ROSS, A., *The Epistles of James and John*. NLC (London, 1954).

TASKER, R. V. G., *The General Epistle of James* TNTC (London, 1956).

THE FIRST LETTER OF PETER

G. J. POLKINGHORNE

1 Peter stands with 1 John as the only Catholic Letter whose authority was never doubted by the early Church. All our textual authorities contain Peter's name in the first verse. The Petrine speeches in Acts have clear parallels in thought and language. 2 Pet. 3: 1 implies the existence of a former letter, which may not, of course, be our letter (cf. notes there). Early non-canonical writings which show knowledge of 1 Peter include those of Barnabas, Clement of Rome, Hermas and Polycarp, to mention only the clearest testimony. Despite this array of support, Petrine authorship has been challenged. The main grounds are set out and briefly considered below:

1. **Language.** It is held that the language and style show learning and ability beyond the reach of a Galilean fisherman. While we cannot say what may be the possibilities of such a man as Peter in Christ and may also remember that he came from a bilingual area, we must concede that the excellent Greek of a literary type showing acquaintance with classical usage is not likely to have come from Peter, despite the occurrence of Semiticisms. We may recognize the truth of this objection without abandoning belief in Peter's authorship by accepting the hypothesis that Silvanus (cf. 5: 12) was more than postman or even amanuensis and was entrusted with considerable responsibility for the drafting and wording. Similarities with other parts of the NT in which Silvanus had part, such as Ac. 15: 23-29 and the Thessalonian Letters are cited in support of the suggestion.

Another facet of this problem of language is the dissimilarity in style between 1 and 2 Peter. As ancient a writer as Jerome (died A.D. 420) proffered the solution that two different amanuenses were used for the two works. Guthrie (*New Testament Introduction, Hebrews to Revelation*, p. 181), after careful consideration of the matter, concludes that 'the kind of relationship between the two Epistles does not prohibit the tradition of Petrine authorship from being maintained'.

2. **Persecution.** The many references to persecution, especially that in 4: 16 to suffering 'for the Name', are held to indicate a date after Peter's death when formal and official persecution of Christians for their mere profession was instituted. The answer to this is two-fold: first, that the persecution alluded to in the Letter is not necessarily formal and official, but probably only sporadic and unofficial: second, that Acts (*e.g.*, 5: 41; 11: 26) shows how early Christians were called upon to suffer for the Name alone.

3. **Dependence on Paul.** It is contended that the chief of the apostles would not rely so much on Paul's ideas, nor quote so extensively from his writings. We may dispute whether there is in fact quotation from Paul's writings (cf. below). Even so, the granting of common ground with Paul does not amount to conceding that this is inevitably fatal to Petrine authorship. Cannot Peter honourably accept that which God has revealed to his brother apostle? Nevertheless, some significant Pauline emphases are lacking, notably justification by faith, freedom from the Law, the New Adam, the work of the Spirit, and the concept of mystical union with Christ. Conversely, the references to the spirits in prison (3: 19) and the interpretation of the work of Christ in terms of the Isaianic Suffering Servant are non-Pauline. This is not to imply that there is divergence of doctrine, merely that there is individuality in presentation.

4. **Reminiscences of the Lord Jesus.** Peter, it is said, would have included far more reminiscences of the Lord Jesus than are found in this Letter. Just how many are requisite is not prescribed, but two considerations may be mentioned. First, that more allusions to the Lord's words and deeds are found here than in all Paul's letters. Second, that there may be more such allusions than we realize with only the four Gospels to guide us.

In conclusion, it may be said that the challenge to Petrine authorship is not considered strong enough to annul the plain ascription in the text. (Further information can be found in the works by Selwyn and Beare named in the Bibliography; also Guthrie, *New Testament Introduction, Hebrews to Revelation*.)

Literary Affinities

Peter quotes frequently from the OT, almost invariably from the LXX. As to the NT, besides the reminiscences of the Lord and the parallels with the Petrine speeches in Acts already mentioned, there are many similarities to the other Letters, especially Thessalonians, Romans, Ephesians, James and Hebrews. Scholars have debated, without agreed conclusions, the reasons for these latter similarities—did Peter quote from them, or they from him, or were they all quoting from other documents, *e.g.*, liturgies, hymns, catechisms, etc.?

Date

Selwyn is probably right in placing the writing of the Letter between the death of James, the Lord's brother, in A.D. 62 and the outbreak of Nero's persecution in A.D. 64. The former publicized the breach between Church and Synagogue and exposed Christians to persecution by removing them from special privileges allowed to the Jewish religion by the Roman authorities, while expectation of the latter formed the occasion of writing. Tidings of the commencement of the fiery trial appear to have reached the writer before he had finished the work and prompted the exhortation in 4: 12-19.

Place of Origin

Babylon (5: 13) cannot be the city on the Euphrates, which after A.D. 41 was very sparsely populated and with which Peter had no connection. Nor can a Roman garrison in Egypt be seriously considered. Rome must be meant, cf. Rev. 17 and 18, as was universally accepted until Reformation times. The symbolic designation would save trouble should the censor's eye light on the letter in transit.

Destination

The first verse lists the recipient churches, all in Northern Asia Minor, in a region for the most part not evangelized by Paul, who probably confined his activities to southern Galatia and Asia. The order is that in which the messengers bearing the letter would reach them. Some of the members may have been Jews, but many were Gentiles, as may be deduced from 1: 14, 18; 2: 9 f.; 4: 3 f. Peter addresses them now as one new man in Christ Jesus, the spiritual heirs of the promises to Israel.

Purpose of the Letter

Many scholars have regarded the work as a baptismal sermon later adapted to a letter. The baptismal address runs from 1: 3 to 4: 11, with the baptism taking place between 1: 21 and 22, while 4: 12-5: 14 is either an address to the general congregation after the ceremony or an addition at the time of compilation of the letter. Notes on 2: 2 ff.; 3: 21 and 4: 11 discuss some of the evidence usually cited. For a fuller consideration cf. *NBD* sub 1 Peter and Guthrie, *op. cit.* pp. 121-125.

To the present writer, it seems preferable to regard the references to baptism as incidental and the work as a circular letter written to Christians already enduring suffering and expected to be further tried, exhorting them to courage, hope and faithfulness and directing their hearts to the great Example of suffering meekly borne, the Lord Jesus Christ. 4: 12 f. may be taken as an epitome of the thought.

Throughout the letter, suffering is revealed as essential to Christianity. The Prophets predicted it for Christ (1: 11) whose cross was both redemptive and exemplary (1: 18 f.; 2: 21-24; 3: 18 f.): redemptive, in that the resurrection and glory that ensued for Him (1: 3, 21) spell secure salvation for His people (1: 5); exemplary, in that Christians must share both the shame and the glory (4: 13). Hence, suffering to Christians is within the will of God (4: 19)—though Satan may attempt to gain advantage by it (5: 8)—and can get glory to God (4: 16) especially by purifying their characters (1: 7); so that it must be embraced cheerfully (4: 13), the more so as it will be brief (5: 10). Therefore, they must submit, not merely to God's hand in discipline (4: 17; 5: 6) but also to human authorities (2: 13), doing right (3: 17) and viewing the endurance of persecution as a kind of spiritual sacrifice (2: 5) acceptable to God through Christ Jesus.

The development of ideas does not lend itself readily to a brief outline, but the following is proposed as a working basis for exposition.

ANALYSIS

I THE STATUS OF THE CHRISTIAN (1: 1-2: 10)
   i The Derivation of this Status from God (1: 1-9)
   ii The Permanence of the Christian Status in the Counsel of God (1: 10-12)
   iii The Holiness appropriate to the Christian Status (1: 13-21)
   iv Love as an Expression of the Christian Status (1: 22-2: 3)
   v The Priestly Status of the Christian (2: 4-10)

II THE SUBMISSION OF THE CHRISTIAN (2: 11–3: 12)

   i Introductory (2: 11 f.)

   ii The Christian's Civic Submission (2: 13-17)

   iii The Submission of Christian Slaves (2: 18-25)

   iv Wives and Husbands (3: 1-7)

   v A Final Word on Christian Submission (3: 8-12)

III THE SUFFERING OF THE CHRISTIAN (3: 13-4: 19)

   i The Manner of Endurance (3: 13-17)

   ii Christ's Righteous Suffering and Vindication (3: 18-22)

   iii Holiness of Conduct required of Christians (4: 1-7)

   iv Christian Conduct within the Brotherhood (4: 8-11)

   v The Fiery Trial (4: 12-19)

IV FINAL EXHORTATION AND GREETINGS (5: 1-14)

   i Exhortation to the Elders and their Younger Brethren (5: 1-5)

   ii A General Exhortation to Submission to God (5: 6-11)

   iii Final Salutation (5: 12-14)

I. THE STATUS OF THE CHRISTIAN (1: 1-2: 10)

Writing to Christians facing a 'fiery trial' (4: 12), the apostle directs their minds to the unshakeable bases of their status, the eternal purpose of God the Father, the historically completed work of Christ and the outwardly verifiable work of the Spirit. This concentration on objective fact accounts for the relative paucity of teaching about the more subjective aspects of the work of the Spirit. 'The tyrant's brandished steel and the lion's gory mane' may perchance diminish Christian joy, but they are powerless to cancel the divine election and the finished work of Calvary.

i. The Derivation of this Status from God (1: 1-9)

Frequently in this Letter, the Church is presented as the New Israel of God and parallels and contrasts with the position and experience of Israel of old are developed. The Church, like her predecessor, is both 'exiled and dispersed' in its earthly experience while 'chosen, destined, sanctified, obedient and sprinkled' in God's mercies. She, like the Jewish dispersion (Jn 7: 35; Jas 1: 1), is scattered in the world but united in herself, yet she enjoys the fulness of divine blessing. Indeed, the entire Trinity of the Godhead is shown to be active on her behalf. The rôle of God the Father is that of 'choice according to foreknowledge' (cf. RV). Foreknowledge is to be understood, as in Rom.

8: 28-30 and Eph. 1: 3-6, less as a passive 'knowing in advance' than an active 'taking note of', an eternal intention to bless. V. 20 and Ac. 2: 23 demonstrate that it was conceived and executed in Christ. God the Spirit acts to make effective the choice of the Father by calling the believer into the company of the redeemed. **Sanctified** means 'separated to the service of God' (cf. NEB 'hallowed to His service') rather than 'made Christlike', the term in scripture often having a different connotation from common theological usage. Similarly, **born anew** in v. 3 (cf. on 1: 23) is not primarily a reference to an individual's regeneration but a description of the formation of the New Israel. It recalls the prophecies of Isa. 66: 8; Ezek. 36 and 37, taken up by the Saviour Himself in Jn 3. God the Son provides the precious covenant blood. **Obedience** and **sprinkling with his blood** refer back to the establishment of the Mosaic covenant in Exod. 24: 7 f. and describe how the New Israel is similarly brought into relationship with God. As at that time the people promised obedience to the commands of the book of the covenant and were sprinkled with the sacrificial blood, so now the believer pledges his obedience to Christ and obtains the benefit of His blood. Once more, the thought is concrete, pointing to a known time when a decision to be obedient was made and the blood was appropriated, hence the term 'sprinkling' rather than 'shedding'.

The greeting in v. 2, combining the Greek 'grace' with the Hebrew 'peace', reflects the mixed character of the churches. This mixed company is welded into one new man by a process likened to a new birth by yet another fact beyond the reach of the persecutor, the resurrection of Jesus Christ. Thereby, they are brought, as were God's ancient people, into an inheritance, but into one which, because it is heavenly rather than earthly, is **imperishable, undefiled and unfading**, i.e., 'untouched by death, unstained by evil, unimpaired by time' (F. W. Beare).

A double security attaches to this inheritance. It itself is 'kept', the Greek perfect tense indicating a past act with abiding consequences, and 'ready' (cf. Jn 14: 2 for the Saviour's promise to make it ready), while believers are 'guarded', the present tense indicating a continuing process—'being guarded by the might of God'!

Therefore, the various trials allowed to reach them are not perilous, being designed simply to refine their characters as precious metals are refined, by fire. The **praise and glory and honour** of v. 7 may equally legitimately be taken as due to the kept Christian or the keeping God.

V. 6 anticipated the theme of joy which is now developed. There, the phrase **in this** is of uncertain import: it may refer to a specific antecedent, whether 'God' (3) or 'the last time' (5) or the whole circumstances of vv. 3–5, when the phrase is virtually a vague resumptive expression, 'and so'. The Greek phrase reappears in 3: 19 (RSV 'in which')—cf. note there—and 4: 4, where the RSV ignores it in translation.

What was ambiguous in v. 6 is made clear in v. 8. It is their confidence of seeing the unveiled glory of Christ that enables them to rejoice amidst their tribulations. Already their love for Christ and the sweetness of spiritual communion bring to their hearts a joy which is **unutterable** and **exalted** (better, with Alford, 'already glorified') and which is described as **the salvation of your souls.** As such, it is preparatory for the 'salvation ready to be revealed in the last time' (5) and akin to the 'guarantee of our inheritance' of Eph. 1: 14 and perhaps to the attained resurrection of Phil. 3: 11. Cf. also on 1 Pet. 4: 1, 7, 14.

ii. The Permanence of the Christian Status in the Counsel of God (1: 10–12)

One proof that the Christian's grace is indeed the eternal counsel and purpose of God is now adduced, in that **the prophets** spoke of it. Peter does not state that he refers to OT prophets, so that some commentators have interpreted his words to mean Christian prophets. V. 11 is then taken to concern the 'sufferings of the Christward road', i.e., the sufferings of Christians, not of Christ Himself; then v. 12 deals with the unity of Jew and Gentile in the Gospel, that is, 'they were not serving their own (Jewish) race, but you Gentiles'. Much simpler sense is obtained by understanding that OT prophets were intended. Frequently the sufferings and glory of Christ are coupled as here—cf. 3: 18; 4: 13; 5: 1—and v. 12 takes the meaning 'they were not serving their own generation, but the present one'.

Thus, the Spirit of God who spoke through the preachers who proclaimed the Gospel in Asia Minor had already spoken earlier in the OT. These prophets, realizing that the Spirit signified more by their words than they themselves could appreciate, scrutinized their writings for the deeper significance. Dan. 8: 15; 9: 2 f., is one example of this process in operation, while Isa. 53, quoted in 2: 22–25, is an instance of the type of prophesying in mind. Hence, the hopes of the OT are fulfilled in Christ: and the unity of the two Testaments is shown to include the ministry of the Holy Spirit and testimony to Christ.

So Peter introduces his major theme, which he himself learnt from his Master in Mk 8: 31–38 and to which he repeatedly returns (cf. 2: 21; 3: 14–22; 4: 12–19; 5: 1, 10) that, like Christ Himself, the Christian has to suffer on earth to be glorified hereafter. Many passages in the rest of the NT might be cited as teaching the same truth—*e.g.*, Ac. 14: 22; Rom. 8: 17 f.; 2 C. 1: 7; 2 Tim. 2: 12. Suffering for righteousness' sake, accordingly, is no unscheduled disaster overtaking the Christian without the wish of God. On the contrary, it is altogether of the warp and woof of His purposes—the very route by which the Son of His love wrought His wonderful redemption, the assured pathway whereby His many sons are to be brought to the glory.

iii. The Holiness appropriate to the Christian Status (1: 13–21)

Upon the doctrinal foundation thus laid, the apostle proceeds in typical NT fashion to raise up an ethical superstructure. The Christian must not allow pressure from outside to determine his behaviour. He must act according to the light within him. Particularly, he must be holy in all things (13–21) and, within the brotherhood of faith, loving (1: 22–2: 3).

The New Israel, as the Old, must be holy. For them, holiness is encouraged by hope (13), enforced by the character of God (14–17) and reinforced by the sacrifice of Christ (18–21).

Hope is more than a vague, amorphous aspiration. It requires that the loins of the mind be girded, that is, that the loose skirts of the flowing robe must be gathered into a belt for hard work or vigorous activity. Such was the condition in which the first Passover had to be eaten (Exod. 12: 11). In using the metaphor, maybe Peter recalled his Lord's words to him recorded in Jn 21: 18. Thus, abstaining from the enervating pleasures of the surrounding paganism in which they formerly indulged, they must direct their whole being to eternal matters.

No longer are they ignorant. They know the character of God. He is not merely holy, He is actually 'The Holy One' (cf. Isa. 12: 6; 41: 16), and that character they, in common with their predecessors under the Old Covenant, must reflect (Lev. 11: 44; 19: 2; 20: 7). Therefore, they must not presume that because they say 'Our Father' to God, their relationship as sons will make Him favour them in judgment. They must remember that His judgment is impartially based on deeds done. As those who must eventually render an account to Him (cf. Rom. 14: 12; 2 C. 5: 10), they must lead lives of reverence, that is, the fear of respect, not of terror.

Exile (17) is not the same word as is so translated in 1: 1 and 2: 11 but is similar to the word rendered 'aliens' in the latter passage.

A further incentive to right behaviour is introduced in vv. 18–21—the costly sacrifice of Christ. Their old way of life which their fathers had handed down to them is described as **futile** (RV 'vain'). Often in the OT, 'vanity' refers to idols—cf. Jer. 8: 19; 10: 14 f. RV—so that evidently Peter's readers had inherited pagan ways from their ancestors, an inference confirmed by 'lawless idolatry' in 4: 3. From these pagan ways they had been ransomed by blood so precious as to make gold and silver appear as corruptible things, whether they are symbols of human wealth or human religion (cf. Mt. 2: 11; Exod. 30: 11 ff.; Ezek. 7: 19). Logically, the word 'ransom' raises the question as to whom the price is paid, but in NT times, this aspect of the word is lost to view and nowhere in scripture is that question answered for the ransom provided by Christ.

The description of the Saviour as a **Lamb without blemish or spot** directs the mind to the injunctions of the Levitical law—cf. Lev. 22: 19 ff.—but what type of sacrifice was envisaged is not made plain. The Passover lamb (Exod. 12), as the sacrifice whereby Israel was delivered from bondage and separated to the Lord, is richly significant in the context. So also is the lamb of Isa. 53, the passage so largely quoted in 2: 22–25.

But the glory of the Saviour Himself now seizes the apostle's thoughts. Here is One who was eternally **destined**, literally 'foreknown', the centre of that great electing purpose of God mentioned at 1: 1. Such an expression implies the eternal Sonship of Christ, for which see Jn 1: 1–18; Phil. 2: 1–11; Heb. 1: 1–14, *inter alia*. This One was **manifested** at Bethlehem at the appointed time (cf. Gal. 4: 4) for our benefit. Not only did He pay the ransom price in His own blood, but also He was raised from the dead and **given glory**—a reference to His ascension (cf. Ac. 1: 6–11).

The last clause of v. 21 should be read as the RV, 'so that your faith and hope *might be* in God', showing the purpose behind this mighty display of divine grace.

Peter thus links the Christian's eternal hope, the holiness of God Himself and the person and work of Christ together to enforce a strong exhortation to right conduct. Six of the thirteen NT occurrences of the word translated 'conduct' (15) are in this short letter, proving how important he knew it to be. Cf. also the exhortations at 2: 9, 11 f.; 3: 16; 4: 3, 15.

iv. Love as an Expression of the Christian Status (1: 22–2: 3)

In keeping with the objective character of the teaching throughout the Letter, the love here enjoined is to be thought of as a practical virtue, a closing of the ranks under the fire of persecution. There is to be no deserting a brother who is punished, but since all are members of the family of God (cf. v. 17 above), they are to love one another earnestly and heartily. **Purified** is in the perfect tense, pointing to a past act of obedience which has enduring results. **Earnestly** recalls the prayers of the church for Peter in Ac. 12: 5, where the same Greek word is used, and the prayer of the Lord in Gethsemane, where Lk. 22: 44 uses a similar word. **Born anew,** as 1: 3, refers primarily to the work of God in making the whole church into one new man without by any means excluding the individual experience of each member. Once more, the concrete emphasis is apparent as the Word of God is described as the formal cause of their new life. Here is something that is **imperishable** (literally, incorruptible) living and abiding, whatever the persecutor may try to do.

2: 1 shows the negative implications of the command to love—everything disruptive is to be put away. **Malice** accordingly should be taken in the modern English sense of 'malevolence' in this context. In v. 16, the same Greek word is rightly rendered 'evil'.

Newborn babes (2: 2) is taken as evidence that the readers were new converts by the supporters of the theory that the work was originally a baptismal homily (cf. Introduction), in view of their aptness to the condition of those who have just been received into the church by baptism. But **pure spiritual milk** seems to be the dominant concept, especially in the light of the concluding vv. of the preceding chapter, and 'newborn babes' adds a touch of graphic realism. The absence of the definite article in the Greek before 'pure milk' suggests that it was a popular expression, with 'spiritual' inserted to ensure that it was taken metaphorically. Rom. 12: 1 also employs the same word (*logikos*) in the phrase 'spiritual worship'. It can also mean 'rational' or 'metaphorical' or, as the AV, 'of the word', which makes good sense in the context. The figurative use of 'milk' occurs also in 1 C. 3: 1 f. and Heb. 5: 12 f., but with the suggestion, which is absent from 1 Pet., that the mature believer should outgrow it. **Salvation** bears the meaning 'full spiritual development' and connotes the process of 'growing up' to it (cf. 2 Pet. 3: 18). This involves both the continual feeding on the Word commended here and the advancement beyond first principles implied in Corinthians and Hebrews.

V. 3 continues the thought of eating, **tasting the kindness of the Lord** being an allusion to Ps. 34: 8. The aorist tense of 'tasted' points back to a decisive moment of appropriation of divine grace. **Come to him** (4) also may be an echo of the LXX of Ps. 34: 5, the Hebrew having '*look to him*'. The same Psalm is quoted at greater length at 3: 10 ff. It is of interest that many scholars believe that Ps. 34 was used for catechetical and baptismal purposes in the early church.

v. The Priestly Status of the Christian (2: 4-10)

The richness of the Christian's status is now drawn out under the two analogies of the Church as a Temple, with Christ as its principal stone, and as a priesthood, though without the specific presentation of Christ as High Priest which is found in Hebrews. Notice that the thought is still of the corporate entity in which individuals participate as members. The frequent OT quotations show conclusively that the practices of the Hellenistic mystery cults are not the main sources of the writer's ideas.

(a) The Church as Temple (4-8)

For clarity of exposition, let us first note the OT scriptures quoted. For **come to him** cf. above on 2: 3. The other quotations are: Isa. 28: 16 in v. 6; Ps. 118: 22 in v. 7 (also quoted by the Lord Jesus in Mk 12: 10 whence Peter probably derived the teaching, cf. Ac. 4: 11); and, lastly, Isa. 8: 14 f. in v. 8. Compare the use of the first and last of these by Paul in Rom. 9: 33. On the principle enunciated in 1: 10-12, Peter applies the passages to Christ,

though doubtless they had other associations for their original writers and readers. Christ, the living Person, is the stone rejected by the builders, but chosen and precious (better, honourable) to God. Indeed, He is the chief corner stone of God's edifice. **Cornerstone** (6) (Gk. *akrogōniaios*) is derived from the LXX of Isa. 28: 16 and occurs here and in Eph. 2: 20 only in the NT. Both it and the **head of the corner** (7) might be either the bottom or the top stone of the corner of the building. Most probably they signify the stone at the extremity of the angle, from which the builders work both horizontally and vertically in setting and checking the walls. So is Christ the basis and standard on which God erects His building.

Into this building, Christians as living stones made alive by Christ (1: 3) are in the process of being incorporated (5), reading 'are being built', that is, the indicative rather than the imperative, the Greek being ambiguous. The figure is of God at work, erecting His building, stone by stone.

The nature of the building is suggested by **house** (5). Frequently in scripture, 'house' means 'temple', cf. Hag. 2: 3 and Mt. 21: 13. So here in Peter, the Church is presented as God's Temple, based on Christ and partaking of his preciousness or honour (7). The RV and NEB of vv. 6 f. make clearer than the RSV the connection between the great worth of Christ in the Father's estimation and the believer's appreciation of and blessing in Him.

Meantime (7 f.) those builders who have refused to use this stone in their building find that as it lies on their site it encumbers their operations by tripping them up. Such is the appointed portion of those who reject Christ, as Isa. 8: 14 f. predicts, especially of Israel after the flesh, endeavouring to continue as the people of God and to do His work while refusing His Messiah. It is noteworthy that the primary significance of Ps. 118: 22 was that the nations rejected Israel in their imperial schemes, but this mattered not, as God had His plans for His people. Later, however, Israel itself despised Christ (cf. Isa. 8: 14) and this was disastrous.

(b) The Church as a Priesthood (5, 9 f.)

Side by side with the metaphor of the Church as a Temple and the believers as stones built into it, Peter works out another analogy, that of the Church as a Priesthood. V. 5 introduces the theme, describing believers as a priesthood, or, with the NEB margin, as intended to perform 'the holy work of priesthood'. In vv. 9 f., he clarifies their position and function, showing what are the 'spiritual sacrifices' of the earlier verse. They include the submissive sufferings mentioned so often in the letter, but also the kind of sacrifice extolled in Heb. 13: 15, 'the fruit of lips that acknowledge his name'. So, they are to **declare the wonderful deeds** of God (9). The word rendered 'wonderful deeds' (Gk. *aretē*) can have the meaning 'moral excellence', as in 2 Pet. 1: 5, or 'manifestation of divine power', but 'praise', as in the Hebrew text of Isa. 43: 21, accords best with the governing verb 'declare', which certainly means a verbal declaration, in contrast, for example, to the silent testimony of 3: 1.

Several OT allusions enforce the exhortation and show conclusively that the author is thinking of the Church as the spiritual heir of God's ancient people. Significantly, the passages alluded to relate to important moments in the history of Israel. Exod. 19: 5 f. *'my own possession . . . a kingdom of priests . . . a holy nation'*, deals with the establishment of the Lord's covenant with the nation at Sinai; and Isa. 43: 20 f. *'my chosen people . . . declare my praise'* relates to the re-establishment of the national testimony after the Babylonian exile. In Christ, the Church comes into the good of these scriptures.

Out of darkness suggests that Peter's readers were formerly pagans, as Philo of Alexandria uses a similar expression regarding proselytes to Judaism. Moreover, Paul in Rom. 9: 24 ff. uses the quotation from Hos. 2: 23 to illustrate the calling of the Gentiles in Christ, although the prophet himself had in mind the restoration of Israel.

II. THE SUBMISSION OF THE CHRISTIAN (2: 11–3: 12)
Peter now turns from the status of the Christian in all its security and privilege to deal with the problems of right conduct in their present circumstances. The key-word is 'submit', Gk. *hypotassō*, which occurs six times in the Letter—2: 13, 18; 3: 1, 5, 22; 5: 5, not always, of course, in this section. (3: 22 has no reference to Christian conduct.)
i. Introductory (2: 11 f.)
As **aliens** (Gk. *paroikos*) they have no status as citizens in this world, a sombre contrast to their standing as regards heaven, Eph. 2: 19; while as **exiles** (Gk. *parepidēmos*) their stay is only transitory. Therefore, they are not to be conformed to the standards of conduct prevailing in the world, since these 'passions of the flesh' 'war against the soul', a statement hinting at the state of war between the prince of this age and God.

Flesh is used in an ethical sense for that which is opposed to the influence of the Spirit, a sense more common in the Pauline letters and not

found elsewhere in 1 Pet. **Soul** (Gk. *psychē*) on the contrary has a distinctively non-Pauline sense of the essential inward nature of man, without the adverse implication found, *e.g.*, in 1 C. 2: 14; Jas 3: 15; Jude 19 (cf. the *NBD* articles on these two words). **Gentiles** means not merely 'non-Jews' but also 'non-Christians', hence the NEB rendering of v. 12, 'Let all your behaviour be such as even pagans can recognize as good'. The word used for **see** (*epopteuō*) occurs only here and in 3: 2 in the NT. While the rendering given is legitimate, it could also be translated 'gaining insight by your good deeds'. **The day of visitation** may be the final judgment day (cf. 4: 7) or the occasion when disaster overtakes the persecutor himself, awakening him to the truth of the Christian's position, or the time of the Christian's suffering (cf. 4: 17).
ii. The Christian's Civic Submission (2: 13–17)
Every human institution, literally, 'every human creation' can be paraphrased, with Selwyn, as 'every fundamental social institution', i.e., the state (13–17), the household (18–25) and the family (3: 1–7). Wherever the Christian finds himself in relationship with other men, he must behave in accordance with his high calling.

The apostolic injunction of submission to the state probably arose from the temptation to rebellion occasioned by persecution. Such ill-treatment of well-doers was contrary to the divine intention for the state, fully set out in Rom. 13: 1–7 and briefly summarized here in the remark that the emperor is supreme. The preposition translated 'by' in v. 14 is literally 'through' (Gk. *dia*) and perhaps contains a hint that governors are commissioned by the emperor as God's vicegerent. This recognition of the source of imperial authority in no sense supports Emperor worship, but simply indicates that God as a faithful Creator provides for the proper government of His creatures. An undertone of culpability lies in the word translated 'ignorance' (15), so that the Christian's right conduct should produce conviction of sin in their slanderers. In v. 16, there is a deliberate contrast between 'free men' and 'slaves', which is the literal force of the word rendered 'servants'. Many Christians were in fact slaves (cf. the next section) but in Christ Jesus they had become God's free men. Even so, they must surrender their freedom to the will of God and enter into voluntary bondage. Christian freedom is not a veil for evil behaviour but a liberty to serve God. Rom. 6: 1 shows in what sense freedom might be abused, and Gal. 5: 13 suggests its right use.

Peter reveals his OT cast of thought by describing believers as a **brotherhood** (17), a word which occurs again in 5: 9 and nowhere else in the NT. It is evidently his synonym for 'church' (Gk. *ekklēsia*), which he does not use, possibly because it signifies a local congregation, whereas he writes to a group of gatherings (cf. the *NBD* article 'Church', especially regarding Ac. 9: 31). The absence of the word for church does not justify the conclusion that the thing is not found, nor the further conclusion that 1 Pet. was concerned with Jewish believers rather than Gentile-Christian churches (cf. Introduction).

iii. The Submission of Christian Slaves (2: 18-25)

The second fundamental social institution is the household, and the exhortation is addressed to the 'household slaves'. Evidently, many of these slaves were enduring persecution at the hands of unconverted masters, whose legal authority over them was virtually absolute. Once more (cf. on 2: 13) not revolt, or even flight, but submissive acceptance of unjust punishment is required, both out of respect for the master and of conscience toward God. **Mindful** (19) is better translated 'for conscience toward' as RV and cf. 3: 16. The expression translated **one is approved** (19) and **you have . . . approval** (20) is literally 'this is grace' (cf. RVmg and *Arndt* p. 885 (*b*) end of Section (*b*)). While one can hardly translate thus, the form of words suggests the thought that it is the inwrought grace of God that enables a slave to behave in this manner.

Peter does not condemn slavery in principle, not because 'the end of all things is at hand' (4: 7) but more probably because he expected believers to accept the sovereign will of God in whatever social position their lot is cast. This is surely the force of 'for the Lord's sake' in v. 13. The death-knell of slavery is implicit in the gospel, as events proved, and is sounded in such passages as Phm. 16 and Gal. 3: 28.

In vv. 21-25, the suffering of the Lord Jesus Christ Himself is cited to drive home the point. Note that though the sin-bearing and substitutionary aspects of the Cross are mentioned, they are not the primary concern. As in 1: 18-21, the Cross is referred to as an incentive to right conduct, so here it is shown to be exemplary. Quoting four passages from Isa. 53, Peter recognizes the Lord Jesus as the Suffering Servant of Jehovah (cf. Isa. 52: 13) and presents Him to other suffering servants as their Pattern. The word translated **example** (Gk. *hypogrammos*) means a tracing to be written over or an outline to be filled in. It was Jesus who taught this view of Himself to Peter—cf. Mk

10: 45 and Lk. 22: 37—and it forms the special insight of his presentation of the Lord. In three verses (22 ff.) all beginning with the same Greek word (*hos*, 'who', only fully represented in the AV), the comparison between the Servant and the servants is worked out.

In the first of them, the affirmation of the sinlessness of Christ (22) is significant as coming from a man who lived so closely to Him for so long and observed intimately His behaviour in times of terrible stress. It is mentioned to show that His suffering was innocent, as that of Christians must be (cf. 19 f.) if their patient endurance of punishment is to be valuable in God's sight or effective testimony before men. Similarly, the silence of the Sufferer (23) is a pattern for copying (cf. 'gentleness and reverence' in 3: 15). The RV 'committed' is preferable to the RSV 'trusted'. What is committed is left unsaid: it could be Himself, His cause or His enemies. The imperfect tenses of this verse imply an eye-witness's report, as though Peter mentally pictures the events happening and describes them in the language of Isa. 53. In the third of these verses (24), the sin-bearing of Christ has practical rather than theoretical implications. It is referred to that **we might die to sin** (NEB excellently, 'that we might cease to live for sin') and **live** for **righteousness.** The **tree** was the instrument of death for a slave and the **wounds** were the product of just such a scourging as Pilate administered to the Lord. How precious a reflection for those called upon to follow in His pathway of suffering! A further inference from v. 24 is that those slaves who are thus expected to suffer for Christ's sake are reminded that He suffered for theirs. The verse means that he bore as substitute the consequences of our sins on the cross, whether we accept the text or the margin of the RSV. Weymouth conflates the two thus: 'He carried the burden of our sins to the tree and bore it there'. Some commentators have expanded this conflation so as to teach that as Priest, Christ carried our sins up to the Cross and as victim, He bore them on the Cross, but this overloads the language. It is also doubtful how far ideas of the Levitical sacrificial system may be read into the verse, which is based on Isa. 53: 12. Certainly, it would be wrong to think of our sins as the offering made.

V. 25 shows that the purpose of Christ's suffering was accomplished and that now He superintends and protects those who live for Him, though He may call upon them to suffer for Him.

iv. Wives and Husbands (3: 1-7)

The third fundamental social institution is the family. Although six or seven verses are devoted to the exhortation of wives and only one to husbands, we may not deduce that Peter is anti-feminist. In fact, the gospel has proved the greatest force for the liberation of women that history has known (cf. Gal. 3: 28), as may be verified by comparing their lot in countries influenced and uninfluenced by Christianity.

The situation envisaged is that of a woman who has been won for Christ after her marriage to a pagan man—rather a more difficult situation than that of a male convert whose wife refused to become a fellow-believer. She is not therefore released from the duty of obedience (cf. on 2: 13, 18) but is required to submit to her husband, even though he may be unkind to her because of her new faith. Christlike conduct rather than perpetual preaching is prescribed as the method of winning her spouse. So, with a **gentle** (better, meek) spirit, she endures whatever is inflicted and with a **quiet** spirit, she gives no cause for offence, thus silently demonstrating the superiority of Christ. This is far more important than any cosmetic devices, such as hair style, jewellery or clothing, having the advantage of being precious in God's sight, whereas the other things at best appeal only to men. Just as elsewhere Abraham is cited as the father of the faithful, here Sarah, the mother of faithful women, is brought forward to strengthen the exhortation, since she actually called her husband 'lord' (Gen. 18: 12). Those who follow her example are rather her daughters than those who happen to be her physical descendants (6)—perhaps another indication that the readers of the letter were Gentiles by birth.

Let nothing terrify you (6) appears to be an allusion to Prov. 3: 25. A more exact translation is 'and are not put in fear by any intimidation', the intimidation being the husband's persecution.

Husbands are not exempt from instruction, though less is said because their problems are less pressing than those of wives at the mercy of unsympathetic husbands. They are to live **considerately** (RV 'according to knowledge') with their wives, three facts being taken into account. First, that the woman is the **weaker sex**, the Greek word actually meaning 'vessel', cf. 1 Th. 4: 4; 2 C. 4: 7, and hence unable to withstand his strength; second, that as God's creature she has equal right to life as the man, so that he must not make her life a misery; and third, that prayers must not be hindered. The force of this last injunction is that a man who fails to give his wife due consideration can hardly pray with her at family prayers.

In passing, it might be noted that no attention is given to the relation of parents and children as is done in Ephesians and Colossians.

v. A Final Word on Christian Submission (3: 8–12)

From the natural relationships of state, household and family, attention is now turned to the supernatural relationships within the brotherhood of faith, all the virtues listed in v. 8 being those that make for harmony in an assembly. Even if one member of the fellowship uses harsh words (9), he is to be answered in accordance with the example of the Master (2: 23) with blessing. Ps. 34 is quoted to enforce the exhortation, as also at 2: 3 (where see note). Its essential message is that the Lord uses Christians much as they use other people, so that if we wish blessing in our lives, we must speak and do right and peaceable things. This, equally with suffering (2: 21) and glory (5: 10), is the Christian's calling, cf. the Golden Rule in Mt. 7: 12 (cf. on 3: 14 below on the words for 'bless').

III. THE SUFFERING OF THE CHRISTIAN (3: 13–4: 19)

We now reach the most significant part of the letter, wherein the apostle tackles the practical problem confronting his readers, the problem of persecution. His standpoint differs from that of Hebrews and Revelation, which handle the same question. Hebrews warns its readers of the awful consequences of apostasy, even under the pressure of persecution. In Revelation, persecution has become an organized exercise by the imperial authorities and is shown to be demonic in origin, a manifestation of the eternal opposition of Satan to God. For Peter's readers, not only is there less enticement to abandon Christ than there was for the Hebrews, but also persecution is sporadic rather than systematic. Nevertheless, it was indeed a 'fiery trial' (4: 12) for them. Hence, Peter assures them of their inalienable standing in Christ as the Israel of God (1: 1–2: 10), counsels submission to every human institution (2: 11–3: 12) and, especially in the present section, points out the divine purposes of grace in their suffering. Throughout the letter, he reminds them that the Saviour Himself was called to walk the same road.

Up to 4: 12 ff., persecution is envisaged as a possibility, which may have been realized in some instances, but at that point it becomes an actuality, as Nero's policy makes itself felt from Rome to the uttermost parts of the Empire.

i. The Manner of Endurance (3: 13–17)

A note of surprise underlies v. 13. Having counselled his readers (9–12) that their calling is to peaceableness and blessing, he asks in effect, 'Whatever makes you think that you could possibly come to harm if you are zealous for good?' This reflects the general law and order of Roman society, whose officers were commissioned to promote morality (2: 14). Should it happen, however, that they be ill-treated—and the rare optative construction in the Greek for 'even if you do suffer' shows that the event is considered to be unlikely (contrast 4: 14, where the verb 'reproached' is in the indicative)—they would inherit the beatitude of Mt. 5: 10, 'Blessed are those who are persecuted for righteousness' sake'. Two words are used for **blessed** in the letter. The first (*eulogētos*), found in 1: 3, with a cognate form in 3: 9, focuses attention on the divine source of blessing; while the second (*makarios*), used in 3: 14 and 4: 14, as also in the Sermon on the Mount, concentrates on the happy result. NEB renders 'happy' in 1 Pet. 3: 14 and 4: 14.

In view of this blessedness, reverence for God, not fear of man, should characterize them (15). A significant variation is made in the passage from Isa. 8: 12 f. alluded to here. Where Isaiah has 'the Lord of Hosts', Peter substitutes 'Christ', demonstrating that for him, Christ was truly divine.

V. 15 also gives guidance as to their behaviour should they be called to account. They are not forbidden to defend themselves. **Defence** (Gk. *apologia*) might be a formal proceeding in a law court, as 2 Tim. 4: 16, or an informal self-justification, as 2 C. 7: 11. Here, the words 'always' and 'to anyone' point to the latter, as defendants would presumably be compelled to offer a defence in legal action. This suggests that the opposition was so far unofficial and supports the arguments for an early date. Two features of the method of self-defence are stressed. It must be done with **gentleness and reverence** (15), or, better, 'meekness and respect', since the two words rendered 'reverence' in the text are different in the Greek. Peter seems particularly anxious to restrain them from the sharp retort— cf. also 2: 23 and 3: 9. Further, their answer is to be backed by a good conscience (16), so that the accusers rather than the accused may be put to shame. The kind of slander that might be expected is evident from 4: 14. If, despite their defence and their good behaviour, they are made to suffer (17), they can be sure that it is the will of God, as it was in the case of the Lord Jesus, as the succeeding passage shows. The recurrence of the optative mood in v. 17 (cf. on v. 14) postulates a possibility of suffering rather than a probability.

ii. Christ's Righteous Suffering and Vindication (3: 18-22)

Doctrinally and linguistically, this is the most difficult and debated passage in the letter. The limits of a short commentary preclude a detailed discussion (for which see Essay I in Selwyn's Commentary, and C. E. B. Cranfield's article, 'The Interpretation of 1 Peter 3: 19 and 4: 6', *Expository Times*, Sept. 1958). We must be content to advance a view in the text and append a brief summary of other possible interpretations.

Happily, there is no obscurity in 3: 18 which speaks of the victory of Christ's innocent and vicarious suffering. He is designated **the Righteous One** (cf. 2: 22), a quotation from Isa. 53: 11, a chapter so frequently quoted by Peter both in the speeches recorded in Acts (cf. 3: 14) and this letter. Nevertheless, He **died for sins**. 'Suffered' (AV and RV), a less well-attested variant for 'died', would suit the context better, which may account for its existence (cf. also 2: 21). The line of comparison is similar to that in 2: 21-25 (see notes there) in that the emphasis is on the example of Christ, the Suffering Servant. Though righteous, yet He died 'for sins', which might be rendered 'as a sin-offering' as in Rom. 8: 3 and Heb. 10: 6, but the plural form in 1 Pet. militates against such a rendering. Further, He died **for the unrighteous** (cf. 2: 24) in which phrase the preposition *hyper* includes the idea of 'as a substitute for' as well as 'for the benefit of'.

A new note, absent from chapter 2, enters in the words **once for all**, a note of triumphant vindication implicit in the 'it is finished' from the Saviour's own lips on the Cross (Jn 19: 30). This is underlined by the statement **that he might bring us to God** wherein we learn that the purpose of the Father in the crucifixion was attained, the ultimate aim of all religion, accomplished only in the gospel. So, after His death, Christ is **made alive in the spirit.** 'The spirit' in this passage is not the Holy Spirit, but the spiritual aspect of the Lord's personality, cf. Rom. 1: 3 f. for a similar antithesis of the Lord's natures and 4: 2, 6 for an extension of the concept to ordinary men. Alford is worth quoting here: 'His flesh was the subject, recipient, vehicle, of inflicted death; His spirit was the subject, recipient, vehicle, of restored life'. V. 22 brings the note of triumph to its crescendo in the ascension of the risen Lord and His session at the Father's right hand. The Suffering Servant who in chapter 2 appears as the patient victim of rampant evil now is shown to be gloriously victorious.

The triumph of Christ after suffering is taken

U

as the clue to the enigmatic verses lying between 18 and 22. After His vindication, Christ went to rebellious angels in captivity and announced His victory over sin, death, and Satan. As to the words of the passage: **in which** need not necessarily mean 'in the spirit' but may be no more than a general resumptive expression 'and so' or 'in the course of which' (cf. on 1: 6). **Went** is the same word as 'has gone' in v. 22 and in both places equally signifies a definite journey. **Preached** means not 'evangelized' but rather 'heralded his triumph'; cf. Rev. 5: 2, where the same Greek word is translated 'proclaimed'. **The spirits in prison** are those 'sons of God' who sinned in Gen. 6: 2, i.e., angelic beings as in Job 1: 6; 2: 1; Dan. 3: 25, 28. 2 Pet. 2: 4 f. seems decisive for this interpretation, especially if the genuineness of that letter is accepted, since the imprisonment of sinning angels is immediately followed by a reference to the flood (cf. also Detached Note, below). Likewise, the mention of angels in v. 22 as subjected to Christ bears out the meaning we see in v. 19. **God's patience** alludes to the delay in the judgment of the flood while Noah preached (2 Pet. 2: 5).

As in the days of Noah a small minority of the faithful rode to safety in the ark, so the antitype of Noah's company, the Christians, likewise a tiny minority, are borne to safety through the waters of baptism. The inference from all this is that, as Christ was triumphant through suffering and as Noah's little group were vindicated by deliverance, so those who now suffer for righteousness' sake will finally be partakers of glory. This theme is taken up in chapter 4.

Many interpreters regard baptism as the theme of the whole letter (cf. Introduction). To these, **now** (21) indicates that baptism has just taken place. (A similar inference is drawn from the same word in 1: 12; 2: 10, 25.) This theory certainly makes the introduction of the idea of baptism at this point comprehensible. To others, it reads like a passing allusion, prompted by the mention of Noah and the waters of the flood. The essence of baptism is shown not to consist in the cleansing of the body, but in the soul's response to God. **Appeal** is not easy to translate. It probably means the clause in a contract containing a formal question to and consent of the parties contracting and thus signifies 'a pledge to God proceeding from a good conscience'. The response usually required of a candidate prior to baptism may have suggested the statement. Baptism is thus the glad and thankful confession to God that through the death, resurrection and ascension of

the Lord Jesus Christ, the believer rejoices in a cleansed conscience.

Detached Note—Some other Views of 3: 19-22

For the reader's information, three other views differing from the above (which is based mainly on Selwyn) are given:—

(*a*) The Spirit of Christ through Noah (Gen. 6: 3) preached to the men of that day, who rejected the message, perished in the Flood, and are now the spirits in prison. These same men are taken to be the 'dead' of 4: 6. This view fails to give a consistent sense to 'went' in 3: 19—cf. note above.

(*b*) The spirits in prison are all who have died without hearing the gospel, those of Noah's day being selected as representative. Between His death and resurrection, Christ went and preached the gospel to them. Once more, the 'dead' of 4: 6 are regarded as the same persons as the spirits in prison. A theory of a second chance for the unconverted after death is sometimes deduced from this view of the passage, but does not really follow from it.

(*c*) Calvin took the 'spirits in prison' to be Jews who had looked for Christ's appearing and the 'prison' to be the Law, despite the fact that the Flood so long preceded the giving of the Law.

iii. Holiness of Conduct required of Christians (4: 1-7)

Therefore in v. 1 resumes 3: 18, the intervening verses being in parenthesis. Peter again links doctrine with practice (cf. on 1: 13-21). The challenge is to equip ourselves with Christ's determination to do the will of God, whatever the cost (cf. 2: 21 for a similar appeal to the example of Christ). So, **whoever has suffered in the flesh has ceased from sin** must be understood, on the one hand, in the light of Christ's suffering and, on the other, in view of Peter's readers' liability to persecution. Not affliction in general, but the endurance of the world's hatred of Christ is what is in mind. Thereby is the dominion of sin broken in practical experience, because the saint who has boldly stood his ground and taken punishment for it is launched on a plane of living where sin is easier to overcome and more difficult to fall into (cf. Gal. 6: 17 for the actual experience). For him, henceforth, 'to live is Christ' (Phil. 1: 21). Rom. 6: 1-14 presents a similar teaching, though Paul goes to the root of the matter while Peter rests on the effect. Comparison should also be made with 1 Pet. 1: 8 f. (where see comments) and Phil. 3: 8-11.

As Christ (3: 18) was 'put to death in the flesh but made alive in the spirit', so (2) the Christian must here and now finish with human passions and live by the will of God. Specifically, all the foul practices associated with the heathen religion they once pursued must cease, however much surprise and abuse this may occasion from those with whom they once joined in these things. **Join them** (4) is literally 'run together with them' and conjures up a picture of people hastening out of their homes so as not to be late, when the signal for the idol festival is given. **Wild profligacy** (4) is a fair description of some of the rites associated with Greek deities. The kind of abuse that Christians received for their abstinence may be illustrated from Tacitus' description of them as 'haters of the human race'.

They may safely leave their detractors to God's judgment (5), as did their Saviour (2: 23). Some expositors regard the judge of this verse as Christ, but Peter throughout thinks of God in this capacity (*e.g.*, 1: 17; 2: 23; 4: 19). No ultimate inconsistency with such passages as Jn 5: 22 arises in view of the statements there (27, 30) indicating that the Son exercises judgment under the authority of the Father.

Difference of interpretation of 4: 6 has already been mentioned. The view taken here is that 3: 19-22 are parenthetic, so that the 'spirits in prison' of 3: 19 are not identical with the **dead** of 4: 6. Moreover, whereas the **dead** of 4: 5 are all deceased persons irrespective of character, those of the next verse are deceased Christians, about whom the early church was frequently exercised—cf. 1 Th. 4: 13; 1 C. 15: 29. Their judgment 'according to human standards' (RSV **like men**) lies both in the condemnation of v. 4 and in the fact of their death, which is the penalty of sin upon the human race (Rom. 5: 18, etc.). But, as their Lord was made alive in the spirit after death (3: 18) so they also **live in the spirit** 'according to God's standards' (RSV **like God**). The final assessment of a Christian life cannot be made with earthly data only; the facts of the after-life must be brought in to redress the balance.

This final assessment is not indefinitely remote, for **the end of all things is at hand** (7) and judgment has already begun at the house of God (17). Christ's incarnation marked 'the end of the times' (1: 20) and His crucifixion 'the judgment of this world' (Jn 12: 31). Hence, NT men lived in the consciousness that 'the end of the ages has come' (1 C. 10: 11), that the new creation had arrived (2 C. 5: 17), that they were already tasting 'the powers of the age to come' (Heb. 6: 5) in the experience of the Holy Spirit (Eph. 1: 13 f.). The unveiling of Jesus Christ was eagerly awaited as the consummation of their experience and hopes (cf. on 1: 6 ff.). The proximity of the 'end'

or 'goal' (Gk. *telos*) required that they lead lives which were controlled, abstemious, and prayerful (cf. v. 7, NEB: 'an ordered and sober life, given to prayer').

iv. Christian Conduct within the Brotherhood (4: 8-11)

Against the background of the abuse of godless men (4) and the imminence of Christ's appearing (7), the apostle renews his plea of 1: 22 for mutual love among Christians. Such love **covers a multitude of sins**—probably an allusion to Prov. 10: 12. Since only love within the brotherhood is under consideration, Mt. 18: 21-35 affords the surest guide to interpretation. Because God's love in Christ has made atonement for our many sins, we also, living by His forgiveness, must be forgiving to our brethren. In the governmental dealings of God, we receive in like manner as we give—cf. on 3: 8-12.

Hospitality is particularly mentioned (9) in view of the needs of those who had suffered the loss of goods through persecution (cf. Heb. 10: 34). It is at once a way of ameliorating their suffering and a demonstration of loyalty and solidarity which might have the consequence of exposing the giver to action by the persecutor, hence the necessity of specific exhortation.

A spiritual gift (10) (Gk. *charisma*) comes from God's grace (Gk. *charis*) and must be administered as the property of Another, that is, as a steward not a proprietor. Moreover, it is given for the benefit of the whole brotherhood, not for the possessor only. Speakers, therefore, are not free to advance their own opinions, but must speak the words of God (Gk. *logion*, 'divinely authoritative communication' cf. *NBD s.v.* 'oracle'). **Service** (Gk. *diakonia*) included waiting at table, as in Lk. 17: 8 and perhaps Ac. 6: 1-4, but extended to all forms of help to others and came to have the technical meaning within the church of 'deacon', cf. Rom. 16: 1; Phil. 1: 1, one who performs duties complementary to those of elders or bishops (cf. 1 Tim. 3: 1-13), whom Peter exhorts in the next chapter. Since God supplies the strength for such service, He must have the glory of it.

The doxology of v. 11 reads most simply as applying to Christ, though some scholars take it as addressed to the Father, on the grounds that glory would not be simultaneously ascribed both to and through Christ. Those who consider that the letter was originally two works would terminate the first, the Baptismal Homily, at the end of v. 11 and regard the doxology as evidence in their favour. This conclusion is precarious, however, as Westcott has shown that only three of sixteen NT doxologies terminate a letter.

v. The Fiery Trial (4: 12-19)
At this point, it seems that the writer received tidings of the aggravation of the situation of his readers through the flaring up of persecution (cf. on 3: 14). But the **fiery ordeal** is sent to 'prove' them as was explained in 1: 6 f., so that the latter end would be joyous, and three reasons for rejoicing are now advanced. First, (13) **in so far** (Gk. *katho*) indicates that in precise proportion as they share Christ's sufferings they will share His glory when it is revealed. No participation in the atoning work is implied in this sharing of suffering, but simply as in Col. 1: 24, the bearing of the burden of evangelism in the face of opposition. Secondly (14), they obtain the blessing and happiness (cf. on 3: 14) of the Presence of the Glory through the mediation of the Holy Spirit. 'Glory' only once in this letter (1: 24, an OT quotation) means 'honour'. Elsewhere, it refers to the divine splendour, especially at the unveiling of Jesus Christ. Here, it connotes that peculiar manifestation of God's presence, the Shekinah Glory (cf. *NBD s.v.* 'shekinah'). Exod. 40: 35 describes the first appearance of that glory on the Tabernacle, while Jn 1: 14 connects it with the incarnation. To the suffering Christian, the Spirit makes very real the presence of the glory of God in Christ. Thirdly (15-18), the hapless lot of the non-Christian in eternity makes all suffering for Christ's sake more than worthwhile.

The list of offences to be avoided (15) is two-fold: the initial three are criminal, and the fourth is more general. Only the latter two call for comment. **Wrongdoer** is of uncertain meaning: the NEB 'sorcerer' is as old as Tertullian, but hardly proven. The NEB margin, 'other crime', is nearer the mark. **Mischief-maker** also cannot be certainly defined— 'busybody', 'infringing the rights of others', 'concealer of stolen goods', 'spy', 'informer', or even 'agitator' are all possible. The Christian must not incur penalties for such deeds, but to suffer for the Name itself is not shameful. *Christianos*, meaning 'a partisan of Christ', occurs only twice elsewhere in the NT, Ac. 11: 26; 26: 28. These early uses of the word dispose of Ramsay's theory that the word pointed to a formal outlawing of Christians by the Emperor and hence to a late date for 1 Peter (cf. also *NBD*, p. 975). Although originally a nickname, it may be confessed to the glory of God.

The concept that **judgment begins at the house of God** derives from such passages as Am. 3: 2; Jer. 7: 8-15; 25: 29 f.; Ezek. 9: 6. It implies that the persecutions and afflictions of Christians are part of the displeasure of God at sin, but they come upon them rather to refine away the evil than to condemn (cf. 1: 6 f.). Similar teaching is found in Jn 15: 2; 1 C. 11: 31 f.; 2 Th. 1: 3-8. Because of these disciplinary acts of God, the righteous is saved **with difficulty** (not 'scarcely'), i.e., the path to life is arduous, as the Saviour Himself taught, Mt. 7: 13; Mk 8: 34; Mt. 24: 9-14. Even so, God is a faithful creator, who will keep the trial within bearable limits; cf. 1 C. 10: 13. Therefore, all can be safely entrusted to Him. To **entrust** means to deposit for safe keeping, as in Lk. 23: 46 and 2 Tim. 1: 12, a common practice before banks existed. Exod. 22: 7-9 and Lev. 6: 1-7 show how severely breach of trust was punished. If men could be relied on to guard possessions, much more can God be depended on to protect the souls of His people.

Here ends the argument proper of the Letter. Chapter 5 is a kind of prolonged salutation.

IV. FINAL EXHORTATION AND GREETINGS (5: 1-14)
No individual greetings are included, perhaps because Peter had no personal contact with the churches he addresses. But this conclusion does not necessarily follow, *e.g.*, Galatians also lacks individual greetings, yet Paul certainly knew the Galatian churches intimately. Vv. 12, 13 imply that Mark and Silvanus were known personally to the recipients.

i. Exhortation to the Elders and their Younger Brethren (5: 1-5)
Peter does not base his authority to address elders on his apostleship, an omission regarded by some commentators as evidence of pseudonymity. Surely, however, a forger would most certainly have stressed apostolicity otherwise there would be little purpose in using Peter's name, so that the omission is actually favourable to Petrine authorship. Three grounds of authority are in fact claimed. First, he is a fellow-elder, presumably of the church from which he is writing. Nowhere else in scripture does this word fellow-elder appear. Second, he has witnessed Christ's suffering. Thirdly, he expects to share in the glory yet to be revealed. In 1: 11 and 4: 13 he has already similarly linked the suffering and glory of the Lord.

Elder (Gk. *presbyteros*) is capable of many meanings. It can signify 'older' (as in Lk. 15: 25); 'men of old' (as Heb. 11: 2); a Jewish leader, whether local (Lk. 7: 3) or national (Ac. 4: 23), i.e., a member of the Sanhedrin. But here, as frequently in the NT, it must mean a 'leader of the church'. If the marginal reading of v. 2 is accepted, 'exercising the oversight' Gk. *episkopountes*, literally 'being a bishop', we observe a further instance of the NT practice of identifying the terms elder and bishop. Not all elders were older men—cf. 1 Tim. 4: 12. Their function is described as 'tending the flock of God', which involves the duties of shepherding, as outlined in such scriptures as Ps. 23 and Ezek. 34 and as commanded to Peter by the risen Lord in Jn 21. Three couplets of instruction are given to them. They must be volunteers (2) not pressed into service by other Christians. They must be eager or enthusiastic, not motivated by the salary offered by the church (cf. 1 Tim. 3: 3; 5: 17 f.). And they must be exemplary Christians, not lords of the flock, which is not theirs but God's. Men like this will receive a reward from the returning Lord—a crown which, unlike the laurel wreath awarded to a victor in the games or worn as a festive garland, was as unfading and immortal as the saint's inheritance (cf. 1: 4).

Younger members (5) are to be in subjection to the elders. The latter term might mean 'your seniors in age' but is best taken in the same sense as v. 1, 'the leaders of the church'. Humility is to characterize all. The word translated **clothe yourselves** signifies 'binding firmly on and wearing constantly', and maybe Peter in using it had in mind the towel wherewith Jesus girded Himself in Jn 13: 4. Prov. 3: 34 is cited from the LXX to prove that humility is the sure route to divine blessing.

ii. A General Exhortation to Submission to God (5: 6-11)

Many times throughout the letter, exhortations to submit occur—cf. especially 2: 11-3: 12. These are now brought to their final issue, as a matter of 'accepting your humiliations' (Selwyn), since they come ultimately from the mighty hand of God. Even the adversities they have experienced are within the ambit of His sovereign will for their lives. **In due time** (6) points on to the unveiling of Jesus Christ so often mentioned and to the salvation ready to be revealed then (1: 5). If meantime they are anxious, they may take comfort from Ps. 55: 22 and cast their anxieties upon Him who is a 'faithful creator' (4: 19). The second clause of v. 7 gains force if translated impersonally: 'It matters to Him about you'. God is not indifferent about His people's misfortunes. In the present, He will bear the anxiety; in the future, He will abundantly recompense.

If worrying is needless, watchfulness is emphatically required, and Peter repeats in revised wording the injunction of 4: 7: 'Be sober and stay awake!' Someone besides God has an eye on the Christian's progress. **Adversary**

and **devil** both translate the Hebrew, Satan. Adversary (Gk. *antidikos*) signifies an opponent in a lawsuit, as in Zech. 3: 1, where Satan stands ready to give evidence against Joshua. Devil, (Gk. *diabolos*) includes the idea of false accusation, reminding us that he is a liar and the father of lies (Jn 8: 44). Capable of masquerading as an angel of light (2 C. 11: 14), to Peter's readers he prowls around like a roaring lion, attempting through the activities of the persecutors to devour them. Consistently, the NT exhorts resistance to him—v. 9 and Jas 4: 7; Eph. 6: 11. V. 9 mentions one strengthening consideration, that the whole brotherhood in the world confronts the same problem. F. W. Beare's translation of the clause is: 'Showing yourselves able to fulfil the same meed of suffering as your brotherhood in the world'. Thus, the courage of one church confirms that of another.

But the surest source of strength is found (10) in the personal interest of God and His promise of eternal bliss. It is His purpose that the suffering shall be little, whether in duration or extent, and that the glory shall be eternal (cf. also Rom. 8: 18 and 2 C. 4: 17). The glory to which we are called is His, and He Himself (an emphatic pronoun) will **restore,** that is, 'make complete or perfect', a word used of setting a broken bone and of equipping or arranging a fleet of ships. It brings the double thought of providing all that is needful to get them through the trials and of repairing the damage received in action. Moreover, He will **establish,** i.e., make steadfast, and **strengthen,** i.e., give all needed power. The additional word 'settle' in the margin has good manuscript authority, but adds little to the sense. NEB takes it with the preceding word 'strengthen you on a firm foundation'.

A further doxology (11, cf. 4: 11) follows, before the words of greeting.

iii. Final Salutation (5: 12-14)

We may envisage Peter now taking the pen from Silvanus to write a short salutation himself, as did Paul from his amanuensis at 2 Th. 3: 17 and Gal. 6: 11.

In the Introduction mention has been made of the suggestion that Silvanus played a large part in the composition of this Letter. **To you** (12) comes in the Greek immediately after the name of Silvanus, which suggests a close link between him and the recipients. Peter testifies his confidence in him as he sends him off with the letter. Probably, he is the same person who assisted Paul in 1 Th. 1: 1 and 2 Th. 1: 1. In Ac. 15-18, he is called 'Silas', which appears to be a Greek form of the Hebrew name, while Silvanus is the Latinized form, more appropriate for use in Rome.

The doctrine of the letter is similarly authenticated: it is **the true grace of God** and they must **stand fast in it.** Whatever part the amanuensis may have played, the apostle takes full responsibility for the teaching.

For **Babylon** see Introduction. In thus designating Rome by the name of the city of captivity of ancient Israel, Peter reminds his readers afresh that they, as the Israel of God, are exiles in a foreign land (cf. 1: 1).

Mark, Peter's interpreter or dragoman, according to Papias, is the composer of the second Gospel. His presence with Peter enhances the likelihood that he is writing from Rome.

The **kiss of love** (14) is not promiscuous, men kissing only men and women only women. Indeed, as a token of love between the sexes it does not occur in the NT. Rather is it a kind of formal greeting, akin to the modern Western handshake, and is still so used in some countries. At one time, it was part of the ritual of public worship in churches.

Lastly comes the greeting, not, as 1: 2 'grace and peace', but simply the Hebraic **peace** signifying that fulness of well-being that only God in Christ gives.

BIBLIOGRAPHY

Commentaries;

BEARE, F. W., *The First Epistle of Peter* [on the Greek text] (Oxford, 1961).

CRANFIELD, C. E. B., *I and II Peter and Jude. TC* (London, 1960).

SELWYN, E. G., *The First Epistle of St. Peter* [on the Greek text] (London, 1946).

STIBBS, A. M., and WALLS, A. F., *The First Epistle General of Peter. TNTC* (London, 1959).

THE SECOND LETTER OF PETER

DAVID F. PAYNE

2 Peter is undoubtedly one of the least read of the NT documents. And yet it purports to come from the pen of an outstanding apostle, Peter himself, whose first letter is widely prized and loved. Small wonder, perhaps, that so many commentators have denied that Peter could ever have written it. The traditional or stated authorship of many books of the NT has been challenged by some scholars; but scholarship as a whole, with few dissentient voices, has denied flatly that this letter emanated from its stated author, 'Simon Peter, a servant and apostle of Jesus Christ' (1: 1).

The fact has to be faced that the case against the apostolic authorship is strong; answers can be found to most of the arguments raised, it is true, but there is no denying that the cumulative effect of these arguments is considerable.

The chief points at issue are as follows. If Peter was the author, how is it that the style, the language, and the treatment are all so different from those of 1 Peter? Secondly, why should a writer of Peter's calibre and authority have borrowed so much from the Letter of Jude? Thirdly, if the apostle was martyred in Nero's reign (as there is good reason to believe), in the middle sixties A.D., how is it that 2 Peter presents features which point more naturally to a date no earlier than A.D. 90? There is, moreover, no certain reference to the letter in early Christian writings till Origen (early third century), and for many years afterwards there were leading churchmen who expressed doubts about the apostolic authorship. On the other hand, the fact remains that the letter was ultimately included in the NT canon, whereas a number of spurious works bearing Peter's name were firmly excluded from it.

There is no doubt that the style and diction of 2 Peter are rather different from those of the first letter, as many commentators have demonstrated; but there are also some close similarities, which must not be ignored (cf. E. M. B. Green, 2 Peter reconsidered, pp. 11 ff.). (Indeed, it is currently reported that a linguistic comparison of the two letters, made with a computer, reveals clear affinities of style between them.) While it is possible that some unknown author of 2 Peter borrowed much from 1 Peter, it is equally possible that the same man produced both letters, but employed a different secretary. It is widely believed that Silvanus influenced the shape of 1 Peter (cf. 1 Pet. 5: 12); he had no hand in 2 Peter. The argument about the different treatment of the two letters is even less convincing: there are again certain similarities, in any case, and the differences may well have been dictated by the very different needs of those to whom the letters were written; there is no certainty that both letters were written to the same people. Cf. Green, op. cit., pp. 14-23.

The relationship with Jude is puzzling. 2 Peter 2 is so close to the Letter of Jude that nearly all scholars are agreed that one writer borrowed from the other. The probability is that Jude is the original, though there can be no certainty. But would an apostle have utilized another, lesser, man's letter? The answer is that he might have done, for all we know to the contrary; perhaps Jude's letter was widely used as a tract attacking a certain heresy, and Peter, when obliged to counter similar false teachings, found it convenient to re-echo, embody or adapt many of Jude's arguments.

The nature of the heresy, it has been argued, demands a second century date. The false teachers scoffed at any thought of the second coming of Christ; and they contended that since faith in Christ sufficed to save a man, Christians could live as profligate lives as they wished. It is true that such views had their heyday in the second century, but there is evidence that such heretical tendencies began at an earlier date (cf. 1 C. 15: 12, e.g.); the second element in these teachings probably began as a perversion of Paul's gospel (cf. Rom. 3: 8; 6: 1, 15). Cf. Green, op. cit., pp. 25 f.

But the clearest indication of a late date, in the opinion of many, is 2 Pet. 3: 15 f., where the writer seems to know of Paul's letters as a collection, and moreover to view them as equally authoritative with OT Scripture. The available evidence suggests that Paul's letters were not brought together and circulated as a collection before c. A.D. 90. However, it is conceivable that the writer of these two verses was referring not to any collection of letters, but simply to all Paul's letters he himself knew of.

Paul may well have written many more letters than those that were preserved in the NT. Secondly, Paul himself viewed his writings as fully authoritative; Peter may well have considered that his fellow-apostle's letters were as much God's Word as any part of the OT.

As for the patristic evidence, it cannot in the nature of the case rule out an early date for 2 Peter; arguments from silence are notoriously precarious.

These considerations by no means prove that Peter himself did write our Letter, but they serve to show that the case against apostolic authorship is not so conclusive as is often supposed. Indeed, some features of the Letter point to a relatively early date. For instance, it is noticeable that despite the mention

of Paul's letters, practically no quotations from them or allusions to them occur in 2 Peter; this fact might suggest that none of Paul's writings were available to the writer, nor could he quote them from memory. Or again, the emphasis in the Letter on the imminence of the return of Christ is a frequent feature of the NT documents, but figures relatively little in second century works.

Calvin's assessment of the evidence was that the Letter was truly Peter's, 'not that he wrote it himself, but . . . one of his disciples composed by his command what the necessity of the times demanded' (J. Calvin, *The Epistle to the Hebrews and the First and Second Epistles of St. Peter*, tr. W. B. Johnston, p. 325). Some such view may appeal to many as best suiting the evidence and resolving the difficulties.

ANALYSIS

I   SALUTATION (1: 1–2)

II   A CHALLENGE TO ZEAL (1: 3–15)

III   THE CERTAINTY OF GOD'S PROMISES (1: 16–21)

IV   WARNING AGAINST FALSE TEACHERS (2: 1–22)

V   GOD'S FUTURE PLANS (3: 1–10)

VI   PRACTICAL LESSONS AND CONCLUSION (3: 11–18)

I. SALUTATION (1: 1–2)

This is a general letter, i.e. it is not addressed to any specific church or group of churches; but 3: 1 tells us that Peter had written to his readers once before, so no doubt he did have a particular church or area in mind. V. 1 may imply that the readers were Gentiles, Peter emphasizing that they had **obtained** (the Gk. verb *lanchanō* implies lack of any merit) **a faith of equal standing;** under the New Covenant, Jewish birth gave a status of no special privilege (cf. Gal. 3: 28). Alternatively, he means that the faith of apostles has no more validity than that of other Christians. **Our God** seems to be a title of the Lord Jesus Christ. **2.** Cf. 1 Pet. 1: 2; Jude 2.

II. A CHALLENGE TO ZEAL (1: 3–15)

The message of the letter opens with a positive declaration of what God has given the Christian. Much of the phraseology of v. 3 recalls gnostic concepts and claims (for a brief account of them, cf. Green, *op. cit.*, pp. 25 f.), against which Peter puts up the basic Christian truth that **divine power,** true **knowledge** (the Gk. word *epignōsis* implies *full* knowledge), and all that stem from them, are the gifts of God, unmerited and but for His grace unattainable. It is uncertain

whether **to** or 'by' (RSVmg) **his own glory and excellence** (or 'might'; cf. NEB) is to be understood. Either makes good sense.

5–8. In a passage very reminiscent of the teaching of James about faith (cf. Jas 2: 14–26), Peter now indicates the Christian's responsibility: God has acted, and man must cooperate. Cranfield compares Phil. 2: 12 f. It is probable that the Christian virtues Peter proceeds to list are not intended as a systematic progression, though certainly **love is** the crown of them all. The word **virtue** (the same as that rendered 'excellence' in v. 3) has here the usual sense of moral uprightness. **Godliness,** says Cranfield, 'denotes the attitude and behaviour of the man who is truly God-fearing'. All these virtues are to be possessed and fostered (see v. 8 in NEB); the word **abound** is in Gk. a present participle, denoting constant increase. **9.** Any Christian who does not **make every effort to supplement** his **faith** in these ways is described as forgetful and **shortsighted.** Peter recalls the significance of conversion (and probably baptism); **old sins** means those committed prior to conversion.

10 f. God's saving acts have future reference and relevance. Note the emphasis, once again, on God's initiative and man's response; both are essential, or the Christian may **fall** (literally, 'stumble'). Cf. Jude 24.

11 concludes this paragraph, by outlining the Christian's hope, in terms recalling Jn 3: 5. The word **kingdom** is much more common in the Gospels than elsewhere in the NT, but the concept is found throughout, as this verse testifies (cf. Ac. 20: 24 f.). It may be that the term was generally avoided outside Jewish circles, for fear that Gentiles would misinterpret it, and view Christian teaching as seditious.

12. Reminders of the truth are often salutary: cf. Jude 5. Peter has already indicated the proneness of human beings to forgetfulness (9); and he is the more concerned because of his approaching death.

13 f. The reference here is most probably to our Lord's prediction in Jn 21: 18, in which case the point of the allusion is the fact and manner of Peter's death, and not the imminence of it (which Peter could now doubtless gauge for himself). In any event, the word **soon** should perhaps be translated 'swift' (i.e. 'sudden'), as in 2: 1. Mayor and Cranfield, however, maintain that the writer is not referring to Jn 21 but to some other experience, presumably a vision. The word **body** is literally a 'tent'—a clear reminder that life is but a pilgrimage. Cf. 2 C. 5: 1–5, a passage Peter may have in mind. Death is a **departure**; the Gk. word is *exodos*, used similarly in Lk. 9: 31. Evidently the transfiguration story was in Peter's mind, as the rest of the chapter makes patent. **15.** It seems clear that Peter is alluding here to some written 'reminder' available to his readers. He may mean this Letter itself; but an attractive suggestion is that the writer means the Gospel of Mark, which early tradition tells us was the written record of much of Peter's own preaching.

III. THE CERTAINTY OF GOD'S PROMISES (1: 16–21)

Peter now moves to a consideration of the truth of the second coming; he lays a foundation for it by stressing the historical and undeniable fact of the transfiguration of our Lord. The apostolic predictions of the return of Jesus were not **myths**, i.e. 'human speculations and inventions' (Cranfield). Peter, with James and John, had had a preview of the **majesty** of Christ, on the mount of transfiguration; thus he was in a position to certify **the power and coming** (i.e., 'the coming in power'; cf. Mk 13: 26). **17. 'This is my beloved Son, with whom I am well pleased'**: The margin gives a more accurate rendering, and the NEB is better still—'This is my Son, my Beloved, on whom my favour rests'. Peter

omits the additional 'listen to him!' of Mt. 17: 5, Mk 9: 7, and Lk. 9: 35. In other respects, the wording of the heavenly saying most nearly approximates to Matthew's account of it, but there are some slight differences in the Gk. The apocryphal 'Petrine' literature chose to follow 2 Pet. 1: 17 in preference to any of the Gospels. This fact, together with the fact that 2 Peter is here independent of the Gospels, is good evidence that these verses do emanate from the apostle himself. **18,** and indeed the whole paragraph, constitutes a claim to have witnessed the transfiguration glory of Christ, a claim which can only be viewed as fraudulent unless it derives from Peter himself. **19.** The transfiguration not only gave assurance of future realities, but it also served to confirm OT predictions. Peter now draws the moral, that having such a certain hope for the future, the Christian must regard this present life as transient; he uses a new simile (cf. the metaphor in v. 13).

20 f. This passage makes it clear that certain false teachers had been guilty of misusing OT prophecy. Peter therefore stresses that just as the OT Scriptures were God-given, through the Holy Spirit, in the first place, so too their interpretation must come from God and be guided by the Holy Spirit. 1 Pet. 1: 10–12 similarly states that the OT prophets had not been independent when they wrote. The word **men** is placed in an emphatic position in the Gk. sentence, as the NEB rendering 'men they were' indicates well; the point is made that the OT, though admittedly penned by human writers, was no human production. (The RSV text of v. 21 is preferable to the margin.)

Much discussion has centred round the phrase 'private interpretation' (AV) in v. 20, a phrase which, isolated from its context, is capable of several meanings: it might mean that individual passages of Scripture are not to be interpreted on *their* own, but that Scripture is to be compared with Scripture; or it might mean that Scripture is not to be subjected to **one's own interpretation**, i.e. highly individualistic viewpoints. There is much truth in both of these sentiments, doubtless, but neither is what Peter says, if we consider the context: it is not to other Scriptures nor to other people that Peter would refer us, but to the Holy Spirit. Just as the biblical authors in the first place could not have written what they did but for the Holy Spirit's activity in and through them, so no reader can properly interpret the OT prophecies without the Holy Spirit's guidance. This truth might well be applied to the interpretation of any part of the Bible, but OT predictions were what Peter was specifically discussing.

IV. WARNING AGAINST FALSE TEACHERS (2: 1-22)

This chapter, especially the first 18 verses, is very closely akin to the bulk of the Letter of Jude (see Introduction). The outstanding points of similarity are the denunciation and description of false teachers; the reference to Israel's rebelliousness; and the mention of fallen angels, Sodom and Gomorrah, and Balaam. It seems most probable that one of the two writers utilized the other's letter, when facing the same problem, that of the danger of heretical and vicious teachers appearing in the churches. Evidently the heresy in question was of much the same character; in vv. 2, 10-22 Peter gives us some description of the false teachers.

1. Peter indicates first that history is repeating itself; **false prophets** are a permanent danger to God's people. By **the people** he means Israel of old; cf. Dt. 13: 1-5. He re-echoes the prediction of the Lord Jesus Christ recorded in Mt. 24: 4 f., 23 f. (and cf. 2 Tim. 3: 1-9), which may explain the future tense here; the present tense in v. 13 makes it plain that the heretics were already active. Alternatively, the future tense here may imply that the present trends are bound to occur and to continue, or may give warning that the heretics already active elsewhere will soon make contact with the readers. Whatever professions the false teachers may make, in effect they are **denying the Master who bought them;** their actions deny His work, together with His lordship and ownership. And sad to say, these men will not be altogether unsuccessful (2). **3.** One of their methods is now exposed; their **false words,** or sheer fabrications' (NEB), stand in sharp contrast to the Gospel truths, which apparently they perversely described as 'myths' (to judge by 1: 16).

4-9. Like Jude (vv. 5-7), Peter uses three well-known examples of God's punishment of the wicked and presumptuous. First he recalls **the angels** who **sinned,** probably an allusion to Gen. 6: 2 (see the commentary on Jude 6). They were **cast into hell** (literally, Tartarus, the Gk. name for the very lowest hell); **pits** represents the better MS reading, preferable to the 'chains' of the AV. Another warning example, that of **Sodom and Gomorrah** (6), is likewise utilized by Jude as well; but where Jude draws attention to the Israelites who disbelieved God in wilderness days, Peter makes use of another OT incident, the **flood,** drawn from Gen. 6-9. Evidently this was one of Peter's favourite OT passages (cf. 1 Pet. 3:

20). The description of **Noah** as **a herald of righteousness** is derived from current Jewish thought (cf. Josephus, *Ant.* I. iii. 1; Jubilees 7: 20-39); the concept is in turn taken from Gen. 6: 9. Peter agrees fully with Jude about the punishment of the lawless and wicked, but he shows a further concern, not mentioned by Jude: he stresses the goodness of God in rescuing His own. While **the ancient world** perished, God **preserved Noah;** while **Sodom and Gomorrah** were **condemned to extinction, he rescued righteous Lot** (who is not mentioned by Jude).

9. The moral of the preceding verses is pointed (**if . . . if . . . if . . . then**). It is not clear whether in this verse Peter means **punishment** in this life or in the intermediate state (cf. Lk. 16: 19-31); but the latter is more likely, since Peter mentions **the day of judgment** rather than 'the day of their death' or some similar phrase.

10-22. In this passage the writer reverts to a consideration of the false teachers and a description of them. Two of their characteristics, in particular, link up with the OT examples he has just recalled; they are lustful and presumptuous. They **despise authority** in general, and that of Christ in particular (cf. v. 1); Jude 8 accuses such men of despising angelic authority, and Peter now proceeds to the same thought.

11. By contrast, angelic beings do not use arrogant language against **them.** This pronoun, in context, can only mean the heretics; but this verse epitomizes Jude 9, where it is explicitly stated that Michael the archangel did not revile Satan. Several commentators conclude, therefore, that the writer here has been over-concise, and really means that fallen angels (rather than the heretics) were not reviled. More probably, however, Peter has extended Jude's thought, and maintains that angels do not arrogantly address any of their opponents, whether angelic or human.

12. The outspoken denunciation of the heretical teachers beginning with this verse is very like Jude's. This particular verse has several verbal contacts with Jude 10 (*e.g.* the phrase **irrational animals**), but the thoughts are Peter's own. He is not discussing the time or manner of the death of the heretics when he says they **will be destroyed in the same destruction** as the brute creation; his point is that just as **animals** are **born to be caught and killed,** those who wilfully act like them will suffer the same natural and predictable fate.

13. The statement that the false teachers will one day find themselves **suffering wrong for their wrongdoing** must mean that they will receive the same treatment from others that they have meted out to others. Cranfield suggests that the phrase might be rendered 'being cheated of the profits of their wrongdoing'; Balaam (cf. v. 15), at any rate, certainly failed to get his expected profits, perishing miserably (cf. Num. 24: 11; 31: 8). But the heretics, without a glance at the future, in the meantime delight to carouse 'in broad daylight' (NEB)—shamelessly turning the Christian fellowship meals into riotous drinking-parties. The word **dissipation** represents the Gk. *apatais* (literally 'lusts' or 'deceits'), and is very probably a play on words by Peter, recalling Jude's mention of *agapais*, 'love feasts' (cf. Jude 12), although his readers can scarcely have appreciated this. Numerous Gk. MSS of 2 Peter, however, read *agapais*, no doubt influenced by Jude's use of the word.

14. Nor are the evil men's vices those of the table only. Sexual licence was another hallmark of their characters, as Peter declares in a phrase reminiscent of our Lord's own words recorded in Mt. 5: 28. Moreover, their **hearts** are **trained in greed;** here is a striking metaphor from the gymnasium, difficult to reproduce in English, although NEB's 'past masters' gets near it. The final exclamation, **Accursed children!,** reproduces (both in Greek and English) a Semitic turn of phrase, literally 'children of cursing', and the word 'children' gives a wrong implication in English; the sense is simply, 'they are accursed', as Barclay renders it. The following verse makes it clear that the deceivers, not those duped by them, are thus described.

15 f. Peter again turns to the OT for an example, **Balaam;** see the commentary on Jude 11. Peter has selected one of three examples used by Jude, but has expanded it considerably. It is the love of gain exhibited by the heretics that Peter was most keenly aware of. The mention of the **dumb ass** is devastatingly sarcastic: not only are the false teachers on a level with brute beasts, but their own prototype had stooped so low as to be rebuked by one!

17. Cf. Jude 12 f. These men have no value, no goal, and no future.

18. Worst of all, they are not content with indulging their own **licentious passions;** they delight in seducing new converts into similar behaviour. Sexual immorality was rife in much of the world of Peter's time, and it frequently took considerable time and patience to inculcate Christian ethics in those young in the faith. To such young, unstable Christians the heretical teachers applied themselves assiduously, with foolish **boasts** and specious promises of **freedom.**

19. This verse recalls Paul's words in Rom. 6: 16 and Gal. 5: 1, 13; an appreciation of what Christian freedom really consists of, is vital.

20–22. V. 20 recalls Mt. 12: 43 ff. It is disputed whether this final section of the chapter refers to the false teachers themselves or to those misled by them. The former view seems preferable; if so, the passage indicates that the heretics had been orthodox Christians in the first place. The strict warning implicit in these verses is thus reminiscent of several passages in Hebrews (especially 6: 4-8; 10: 26-31). **22.** Peter concludes his denunciation by remarking that the evil men 'exemplify the truth of the proverb' (Mayor) of the dog (cf. Prov. 26: 11) and of the sow (a proverb to be found in the ancient Story of Ahikar, 8: 18).

V. GOD'S FUTURE PLANS (3: 1-10)
Peter again points out that what he is saying is nothing new, but is simply a **reminder** of what the readers had been told long before; v. 1 is therefore resumptive of 1: 12 f. He is addressing those readers of **sincere mind,** *i.e.* those who had not been led astray by the heretical teachings. It is natural to take the statement that this is his **second letter** as alluding to 1 Peter; this is possible, but it is more probable that Peter had written a letter to the recipients of 2 Peter of which we know nothing. Since our letter does not name his readers, there can be no certainty.

2 f. Peter insists that the doctrine of the second advent has the strongest possible support, from **prophets, apostles** and **the Lord** Jesus Himself. The phrase **your apostles** is unique in the NT (the nearest parallel is in Rom. 11: 13); Peter may well mean that his readers could and should lay claim to the apostles and their doctrines, while disowning the pseudo-Christians and their pernicious teachings. Jude too mentions the apostles in his parallel passage (Jude 17 f., *q.v.*); Peter, however, mentions prophets as well. He has spoken of them already (1: 19-21), of course, and besides, he is making the valid point that all the testimony of Scripture (*i.e.* OT Scripture) supports the orthodox Christian views. **3.** The apostolic predictions of God's purposes included the statement that **scoffers** would arise. Jude 18 mentions this, and Peter expands the thought, clarifying the actual claims of these mockers. Jesus and the early church taught the imminence of the second coming; as time passed, there were evidently some who first doubted and then scoffed at the whole idea. But it was no embarrassment to the orthodox, who (like Peter in this chapter) continued firmly to maintain its imminence (or rather its suddenness). The scoffers argued—perhaps using Ec. 1: 1-11 as scriptural support—that all things had always continued unchanged on earth, and might be expected to remain unchanging. Numerous commentators have taken the mention of **the fathers** to refer to the first generation of Christians; this interpretation would make good sense (and incidentally rule out an early date for the letter), but 'fathers' without further description is more naturally applied to the patriarchs. This latter interpretation makes equally good sense, and has the support of the allusions which immediately follow, allusions not to events of the life of Christ, but to Genesis, the creation and the flood stories.

5. Peter's first reply to the scoffers is that the world we live in has not always existed, and has not proved consistently stable. In the Gk., **the word of God** is in emphatic position; God's spoken word alone had sufficed to change the whole shape of the universe (cf. Gen. 1), and logically His promise for the future must be equally effective and capable of fulfilment. The world had been created **out of water,** certainly, but it is not absolutely clear what Peter meant by **by means of water.** It was not an uncommon view in the ancient world that water was the first principle of the material world; but there is no need to suppose that Peter's remark has other than a biblical basis. Possibly he is recalling Ps. 24: 1 f., but the Psalmist's language is highly pictorial; more probably he has Gen. 1 still in mind, as indicating that the very dividing of the waters produced the dry land (cf. Gen. 1: 6-10).

6. The phrase **through which** again presents problems of interpretation and translation: in the best MSS, the pronoun is plural, and must presumably refer back to the waters just mentioned, despite the fact that the phrase **with water** appears later in this verse. Note the NEB rendering.

7. Flood had once proved disastrous to mankind; **fire,** says Peter, is the world's fate in store. This concept was widely held in Jewish (and indeed some Greek) circles at the time, but this is the only NT passage to express it. OT passages such as Jl 2: 30; Zeph. 3: 8, and Mal. 4: 1 lie behind the concept, and in view of their pictorial character, one wonders whether Peter is to be taken literally here. Hell is frequently depicted in terms of fire (cf. Mt. 25: 41; Mk 9: 43; Rev. 20: 9 f.); in this respect the imagery may derive from the use of the name Gehenna, properly applied to a valley just outside Jerusalem associated with idolatrous sacrifices by fire. Cf. also Mt. 13: 40-42; Jn 15: 6. Whether or not Peter is to be taken literally, his two chief points are plain, that the world is transient and that the wicked await judgment and punishment.

8 ff. Peter proceeds to meet the possible objection, why the delay? He first cites Ps. 90: 4, paraphrasing and expanding it; it is not simply that God counts a thousand years as practically nothing, but further, that God does not view time by human standards at all. He is eternal; 'the eternal order is other than that of time' (A. McNab). So there is no 'delay' by divine standards; but if there is one to the human mind, then it has a clear purpose—and Peter suddenly makes a frontal attack on the scoffers, **The Lord . . . is forbearing toward you** (not 'us', as the Received Text [see article 'Text and Canon'] and the AV read). This constitutes the third argument against those who mock; God is graciously giving rebellious men time for **repentance.** Finally, Peter reiterates his firm conviction, his confident certainty, that **the day of the Lord will come;** the emphasis is on its sudden and unexpected arrival rather than its imminence. The facts and imagery of v. 10 are drawn from various earlier passages of Scripture, to be found in both Testaments. By **the elements** he may mean the heavenly bodies (so RVmg), but more probably the material elements, or the elemental substances, of this world. The **loud noise** will be the sound of fire; alternatively, the phrase may simply mean 'with great suddenness'. Everything on earth **will be burned up** (Gk. *katakaēsetai*): NEB's 'will be laid bare' represents what is probably the better text. The verb (Gk. *heurethēsetai*) would normally mean 'will be found', however, and the possibility exists that a negative has dropped out of the text. To insert a negative would give excellent sense (**the works** upon earth 'will not be found', *i.e.* will disappear) and has some slight textual support. Alternatively, the variety of readings might be explained if they are replacements for an original *heuthēsetai* ('will be burned') from the rare verb *heuō*, attested in poetry with the meaning 'singe' and cognate with Lat. *urō* ('burn').

VI. PRACTICAL LESSONS AND CONCLUSION (3: 11-18)

Peter now draws his conclusions; he is not giving a blueprint as to the manner in which God will fulfil His purposes, but rather laying stress on the certainty that He will do so, on the suddenness with which He will act, and on the fact that total destruction awaits everything useless and godless. Biblical predictions consistently demand not only our belief but more particularly behaviour compatible with our creed. So Peter demands **lives of holiness and godliness** from all Christians, who should be expectantly **waiting for** God to act, and 'earnestly desiring' (cf. RSVmg) that He will do so. But the Gk. word Peter uses, *speudō*, should really be rendered **hastening,** in the way that both RSV and NEB understand it. (The AVmg is to be followed; AV text wrongly inserts the word 'unto', giving quite a different sense, and one which Peter never intended.) This is a striking suggestion, implying that men can in some way speed up God's plans, and it does not commend itself to all commentators; nevertheless it may well be correct, and it would link up well with v. 9: since God delays to give men time to repent, their speedy obedience will shorten the interval prior to **the day of God. 13.** The Gk. verb here translated **wait for** (used three times in vv. 12-14) means rather 'to expect', 'to look out for'. The Christian's hopes and expectations are not, however, centred on the threat of the world's fate, but on God's **promise** of **new heavens and a new earth** (cf. Isa. 65: 17; 66: 22; Rom. 8: 21; Rev. 21: 1). **14.** In view of the absolutely righteous character of the universe-to-be, the Christian's present duty is clear. Peter is here particularly concerned with the Christian's behaviour within the local church: all must be harmonious (**at peace**), but at the same time any **spot or blemish,** in the shape of the pseudo-Christians (cf. 2: 13), must be eradicated. Truth and grace must be preserved within the church in equal measure. See too the commentary on Jude 24.

15 f. The first part of v. 15 is very concise, and presents at first sight an equation, **forbearance=salvation:** the sense is that God's forbearance is intended as an opportunity for men to be saved. This brief sentence epitomizes Peter's statement in v. 9.

In mentioning **Paul,** Peter is presumably not thinking merely of his fellow-apostle's similar doctrine of the purpose of God's forbearance (cf. Rom. 2: 4, for instance), but of all he had said about the second coming. Such a statement by Peter is perhaps evidence that Paul wrote far more letters than were preserved for posterity in the NT. Paul himself was aware that his teaching about justification by faith could be misrepresented and abused.

Since he argued that good works could not save anyone, men so minded were able to twist this doctrine to mean that good works did not matter at all. Paul emphasized several times (cf. Rom. 6: 1, 15; Gal. 5: 13) that such a view was totally improper, and a very caricature of his own doctrines. By his reference to Paul, Peter is able to claim yet further support for the views he has expressed, and to stress once again, briefly, the vital importance of a correct interpretation of Scripture (cf. 1: 20).

17 f. Peter concludes the letter with a final word of warning, a final word of exhortation, and a brief doxology. His characterization of the heretics as **lawless** shows clearly the antinomian nature of the false teaching: *i.e.* those who held it viewed themselves as under no obligation whatever to any laws, maintaining, indeed, that no laws applied to them. The true Christian, by contrast, is to **grow** (literally, 'increase') **in the grace and knowledge of our Lord;** thus Peter recalls his opening thought (cf. 1: 5-7) that the Christian life cannot be static. The only way to be sure of avoiding **the error of lawless men** is to tread single-mindedly the path of divine and Christ-like virtues.

The phrase **the day of eternity** possibly indicates the writer's familiarity with Hebrew or Aramaic turns of speech; 'the eternal day' would be the English equivalent, but it is difficult to improve on the simple AV rendering: 'To him be glory both now and for ever. Amen'.

BIBLIOGRAPHY
Commentaries
BIGG, C., *St. Peter and St. Jude* [on the Greek text]. ICC (Edinburgh, 1902).

CRANFIELD, C. E. B., *I and II Peter and Jude*. TC (London, 1960).

GREEN, M., *2 Peter and Jude*. TNTC (London, 1968).

JAMES, M. R., *2 Peter and Jude* [on the Greek text]. CGT (London, 1912).

KELLY, W., *The Epistles of Peter* (London, 1923).

MAYOR, J. B., *The Epistle of Jude and the Second Epistle of Peter* [on the Greek text] (London, 1907).

WEISIGER, C. N., *The Epistles of Peter* (Grand Rapids, 1962).

For a thorough defence of the apostolic authorship.

GREEN, E. M. B., *2 Peter Reconsidered* (London, 1961).

THE LETTERS OF JOHN

R. W. ORR

This commentary proceeds upon the belief, once universally held, that these letters are the work of the Apostle John, and that the Fourth Gospel and the Revelation are from the same writer. There is no definite claim within the writings that this is so: the view is based upon the ancient testimony of the Church, upon certain internal indications, and the use in the writings of a common stock of ideas, vocabulary and style, and upon biographical data concerning John drawn from Scripture and tradition, providing a reasonable framework, as they do, for such activity.

Many scholars draw a different conclusion from the evidence, attributing the work, at least in part, to a 'Johannine school'. The different views, and the evidence upon which they are based, are presented by Dr. Donald Guthrie in his *New Testament Introduction* (Tyndale Press, 1962).

A conjectural outline may be made of the last third of the life of the Apostle John, into which the Johannine literature may be fitted. At the latest, he cannot have continued to make his home in Jerusalem much longer than the commencement in A.D. 66 of the Jewish War which ended in the destruction of Jerusalem in the year 70. Before that event, James the Lord's brother and Peter—who together with John had formed the leadership of the early disciples (Gal. 2: 9)—had both met death in martyrdom, as also Paul, and John was left alone.

At that time, the church in Ephesus, founded by Paul, was being troubled with teachers

bringing a Jewish form of that arid speculation and wrangling, which was beginning to make false claim to the name of *gnōsis* (that is *knowledge*, 1 Tim. 6: 20). To meet that emergency, Paul had put that church under a mild martial law, so to speak, with Timothy in authority over the local elders (1 Tim. 1: 3; 4: 11; 5: 17-22). But with Paul now dead, and Asia fast becoming the focus of two dangerous movements (Emperor-worship and gnosticism) which in fact came near to strangling the life of the Church in the next century, John took up residence in Ephesus. John would at that time be in his mid- or late sixties, and for close on thirty years, until his death about the end of the century, Ephesus remained his home. It was a convenient centre for pastoral supervision of the province, including the well-known seven churches of the Revelation. Roads joined them all, and from a point twenty miles up the hill road from Ephesus, a compass of eighty miles would take in all seven, and the island of Patmos as well.

This framework provides a setting for the whole body of John's writings, which the historian Eusebius (A.D. 265-340), following Irenaeus (c.140-202), affirms were composed in Ephesus. The Revelation does not concern us here. The Fourth Gospel, its apparent simplicity inwrought like figured damask with subtle symmetries and patterns, is manifestly a growth of many years of meditation and teaching. The Letters draw upon the same stock of material, and there are fairly strong indications of the priority in time of the Gospel.

THE FIRST LETTER OF JOHN

It may well be that at the time of the publication of the Fourth Gospel in written form, the First Letter was composed—though only for the churches of Asia—as an epilogue or covering pastoral letter, pointing out the practical

application of the Gospel to their lives and in their circumstances. This does not rule out the possibility of a crisis in the Asian churches at that time, perhaps linked with the publication of the Gospel, determining to a great extent the contents and tone of the Letter.

C. H. Dodd (*The Johannine Epistles*, MNT, 1946) suggests that the First Letter was called forth by the crisis referred to in 1 Jn 2: 19 'They went out from us'. 'They' were men of influence in the churches of Asia, with prophetic and teaching ability, and had been attempting to introduce an 'enlightened' and 'advanced' doctrine of the kind which came to be known as *gnostic*. The Church, however, with her intuitive sense of what belonged and what could not belong to the gospel which she had received, had rejected the new teaching, and its prophets had no option but to leave the fellowship of the churches.

The Gnostic's pride was in his knowledge (the root *gnō-* is the parent, or at least a relative, of our English *know* and of the Scots *ken*). Ideas were the great thing, rather than historic facts upon which faith is built. The concrete actualities of the Incarnation and the Resurrection were laughed out of court as childish literalism, and the man who had been initiated knew the spiritual meaning of these 'myths'—an attitude which has prominent contemporary exponents. This 'knowledge' was not for all, but for the select few who had been initiated. It set them in a special class far above common humanity, and emancipated them from the morality which governed the unenlightened. Concerning certain of their sects it is reported, 'They do whatever they please, as persons free, for they allege that they are saved by grace'; and again, 'The law, they say, is not written for kings' (quoted in Law, *Tests of Life*, p. 226). One leading idea was that matter is evil, and is not the creation of God. And so it was unthinkable that the Word should become flesh,

and the Incarnation was denied. Cerinthus, a heretical teacher in Asia at that period, taught that 'the Christ' came upon the man Jesus at his baptism, and left him before his crucifixion. All these denials of the Gospel are firmly dealt with in the First Letter.

So also are the false claims to spirituality which those teachers made. It is worse than idle to say, as those teachers were saying, '*We are in the light*', unless sin is being confessed and put away; the claim '*We know God*' is utterly incredible unless the heart is resolutely set to obey God's commandments. John takes the Christian vocabulary which is being abused by those false teachers, 'disinfects' it, fills it with its true Christian content, and restores it to Christian use.

Such appears to have been the occasion which called forth the encyclical which we know as the First Letter, and sent it round the churches of the province of Asia.

But it has permanent value, because the crisis of that hour is always with us. Like those originally addressed, most of us are not new to Christianity, but generations of Christian profession lie behind us, with all the confusion that is found when membership of the church may be motivated by social custom rather than conviction. The clean strong winds of the Letter separate chaff from wheat, or at least show us the lines along which one may test himself, may learn from his own behaviour whether or not he is a true Christian. This very practical letter is ours today as 'the condensed moral and practical application of the Gospel' (Westcott, *The Epistles of St. John*, p. xxx). 'The Gospel gives us the theology of the Christ; the Epistle, the ethics of the Christian' (Plummer, *CGT*, p. 36).

ANALYSIS

Additional Note on Analysis:

'Probably few commentators have satisfied themselves with their own analysis of this Epistle; still fewer have satisfied other people' (A. Plummer in *CGT*).

Although there is very clear linkage between the *sections* of each part—the leading idea of one section being found in the closing words of the previous section—there is no such linkage between the different *parts*; the only exception being in the Epilogue. The connecting words are: *commandments* 2: 4 and *commandment* 2: 7; *born of him* 2: 29 and *children of God* 3: 1; *by the Spirit* 3: 24 and *test the spirits* 4: 1; *faith* 5: 4 and *witness* 5: 7. On the literary structure, see note on *introversion* in section VI. (p. 616)

I. PROLOGUE (1: 1-4)

The general sense of the paragraph is: Our apostolic witness concerns the Lord Jesus, that eternal One who 'was in the beginning with God', and is yet truly man; that 'Word' concerning whom we have written again that 'in him was life'. The life, of course, is in Him as God's Son; and He it is, in His incarnation, who has brought it to light. That testimony which is our regular ministry among you has as its aim your sharing in the life in which we also partake, a life which means fellowship with God and with His people. Now we are writing this further letter in order to bring our ministry to its full practical realization among you: a result which will be a matter of great joy for us.

Our understanding of this difficult passage depends upon the sense assigned to the phrases **the beginning** and **the word of life**. The former may be understood in the sense which it bears in the prologue of the Fourth Gospel, (B) *from all eternity*, as also in the LXX of Hab. 1: 12; or as (b) *the beginning of Christ's ministry* (Lk. 1: 2; Jn 15: 27). **The word of life** may also have the sense it bears in the other prologue (in which case it should be spelt *Word* as in AV and RV), that is (W) *the personal Logos*; otherwise (w) *the life-giving gospel*. There is no precise biblical example of (w), Phil. 2: 16 being the only similar usage; and none of the partial parallels (Mt. 13: 19; Ac. 20: 32; 2 C. 5: 19) is Johannine. Ac. 5: 20, quoted by ASV to support this sense, is quite different. The alternatives are therefore, in brief: (BW) the interpretation we have adopted; (Bw) *Proclaiming as we do Jesus as the eternal Word, we bring you the life-giving gospel;* (bW) *We who have companied with Jesus from the beginning proclaim to you that He is the eternal Word of God, in whom is life;* and (bw) *It is out of first-hand experience as those who have companied with the Lord Jesus from the beginning that we give our apostolic testimony concerning the life-giving gospel.*

It is difficult to decide, but the sense given first (BW) is preferred because the prologue of the Letter seems to be an intended parallel to the prologue of the Fourth Gospel. The weight of contemporary scholarly opinion is for that given last (bw), but even so it seems strange that RSV does not give a place even in the mg to the Logos tr. which their predecessors had in the text.

Westcott teaches that **from the beginning** is contrasted with, rather than corresponds with, 'in the beginning' (Jn 1: 1)—it is ambiguous, and it claims that the Christian revelation is in some sense as old as creation (pp. 5, 51); and that **the word of life** corresponds with the revelation of the whole message of God to man which both proclaims and imparts life, i.e., the gospel. But the teaching of the Letter is not about the word of God as scripture; rather is it centred in the person and work of Christ. It might be well to summarize the NT use of *logos*, leaving aside the verse under discussion. (i) The personal Word of God: Jn 1; 1, 14; Lk. 1: 2 (?); Rev. 19: 13; (ii) The utterances of God or of Christ: frequently; about 28 times in Jn and 4 times in 1 Jn (1: 10, 2: 5, 7, 14); (iii) Word, reason, etc.: somewhat less frequently; 6 times in Jn and once in 1 Jn (3: 18); (iv) account, Lk. 16: 2; Heb. 4: 13. It will be seen that in the Fourth Gospel it is only in the prologue that 'word' signifies the personal Logos; thus strengthening the view that it is in this special sense in which it is used in the corresponding prologue of the Letter.

1. That which (neuter, not the masculine *Him who*): i.e. *we proclaim the things concerning our Lord's pre-existence, and the things which we ascertained by actual hearing, seeing and touch concerning the Logos* **with our** own **eyes. . . with our** own **ears.** The latter phrases are quite emphatic, and no simple reader would seek another meaning. Those who believe that the writer was not the apostle but a later writer of the Johannine school regard the claim of first-hand observation as being made for the Church as a whole, the apostles being the eyes, ears and hands of the Church. **have heard . . . have seen:** Perfect tense—the words and deeds of the incarnate Logos though witnessed long ago are still present with the writer. The tense now changes to aorist for **have looked upon and touched.** The change was marked in

RV by omitting *have* in the second pair, but is now disguised, as in AV. The significance is that the *looking* and *touching* are not general, but refer to the occasion of the Resurrection when, in John's account, they *looked* intently to see the significance of the empty grave-cloths (Jn 20: 6), the two angels (20: 12), and Jesus Himself standing (20: 14). The unusual word *touch* (with only two other NT uses) is the Lord's word in resurrection, '*Handle* me and see' (Lk. 24: 39). Thus the claim to have tested the objective reality of the Incarnation extends to experience of the Risen Lord also. This is important as perhaps the only allusion to the Resurrection in the Letter. (But see also on 4: 2 f.)

2. the life was made manifest: In the Fourth Gospel, alluded to in the prologue as the background of the Letter, the divine life was manifest in the person of Jesus; the Letter deals with the same divine life, in the believer. If the life —eternal life—is truly present, it also will come into manifestation; and through the Incarnation, eternal life has already been manifested in understandable human terms. **the eternal life . . . was with** (*pros*) **the Father** (as in Jn 1: 1 2): i.e. *in relation with:* eternal life, wherever found, is of the nature of that fellowship.

3. that which we have seen and heard we proclaim: Not in the Letter but in the Gospel. The habitual sense of the present tense may be understood here: *we make it our business to proclaim.* Readers are thus informed that this letter is supplementary to the basic witness of the Gospel. **also to you** is an improvement on *to you also* (AV, RV), the contrast being not between the present readers and others, but between the apostle and all those he addresses. His aim as an evangelist is to bring his hearers into **fellowship with us,** that is, the **fellowship** which we enjoy **with the Father and with his Son.** The phrase may be taken as typical of the constantly recurring echoes of the Fourth Gospel in this letter. In the paschal discourse the Lord had declared, 'I am the way, and the truth, and the life' (Jn 14: 6). Replying to the third question from the disciples, the Lord expanded the third term of that great saying, explaining the inwardness of spiritual life as a divine-human fellowship. 'If a man love me, he will keep my word, and my Father will love him, and we will come to him and make our home with him' (Jn 14: 23). Then follows, in ch. 15, the parable of the True Vine, an illustrated expansion of the saying 'I am . . . the life'. This is a large part of the background of the Letter. In the title God's **Son Jesus Christ** another important matter finds expression in the prologue: that the

human Jesus is one and the same as the Son of God, the Christ.

4. Having completed his brief summary of the Fourth Gospel as the basis for the Letter, the apostle now declares, like another John, that the consummation of fellowship in Christ of his readers will leave him more than contented (Jn 3: 29). More than that, in language drawn from the parable of the True Vine, he will share in the very **joy** of God. 'These things I have spoken to you, that my joy may be in you, and that your joy may be full'. Joy, the fruit of abiding in Christ second only to love (Jn 15: 9; Gal. 5: 22), becomes full or **complete** when the life of fellowship reaches practical and conscious realization: fruit both abundant and abiding. Allusions to the Fourth Gospel recur constantly in the Letter; the reader will find study of the parallels most instructive.

II. GOD IS LIGHT (1: 5–2: 6)

the message we have heard from him is possibly an actual saying of Jesus, repeated by Him at various times (see on 'have heard', 1: 1). The same expression in 3: 11 introduces a saying recorded in the Gospel. (Cf. Jn 21: 25 for the abundance of unpublished material; Ac. 20: 35 for a saying not recorded in the gospels; Jn 7: 38 for a reference which is difficult to identify.) But whether a direct saying or not, it summarizes one aspect of Jesus' teaching about God. For this 'message' consider Mt. 5: 43-48, especially v. 45. The 'message', **God is light, and in him is no darkness at all,** is comparable with another dominical saying, 'God is spirit, and those who worship him must worship in spirit and truth' (Jn 4: 24).

Light is the frequent accompaniment of God's presence. The Shekinah, the manifestation of God's presence, was seen as a blaze of glory; and when the incarnate Word dwelt among men, there was a glory as of the only Son from the Father (Exod. 40: 34; Jn 1: 14). The word carries a rich complex of meaning. Light is the medium of perception, and therefore of truth and of revelation (Ps. 43: 3). Light is outgoing and self-communicating, and so light is the medium of fellowship and of love. Supremely it is **he** who **is in the light,** the Father and the Son in eternal, loving fellowship (Jn 1: 2, 18). The 'light of life' is the salvation which Christ brings (Jn 8: 12). And light, which cannot co-exist with or yield to darkness, is the symbol of ultimate victory (Jn 1: 5). Judgment consists of 'bringing to light the things now hidden in darkness' (1 C. 4: 5), whether they be good or evil (Mt. 10: 26). In contrast, **darkness** represents the realm of Satan, with ignorance, enmity, guilt, and the nether gloom in which the wicked await the day of judgment (Jn 3: 19). Of these meanings, it is chiefly **fellowship** which is in view here, with its dark contrast of enmity, opposition and separation. In respect of God, light will signify *source* rather than *emanation* of rays; but even so, radiance is inseparable from its source, giving aptness to the figure in its Christological relation (Heb. 1: 3, RV). With Isa. 33: 14 f. as background and Heb. 12: 29 as a parallel, the **light** takes on the character of *the Devouring Fire*, much in the sense of J. S. Stewart's words 'It is possible to sing, "Jesus the very thought of Thee . . ." without having once asked ourselves if there are not things in our life and character that that holy Presence, if it once came anywhere near us, would burn to shreds' (*The Gates of New Life*, 1937, p. 25). The foundation of true ethics is in the knowledge of the character of the God to whom we are answerable.

6. The exhortation proceeds upon this revelation of God's character to expose false claims to spirituality, probably made brazenly by the heretical teachers of 2: 19, but in some degree making their appeal to all Christians. **If we say** [direct speech with quotation marks is used in 2: 4 and 4: 20. Some such arrangement might helpfully be extended to cover all of the supposed watchwords of the heretics —1: 6, 8, 10; 2: 4, 6, 9; 4: 20—though 2: 6, 9 are in indirect speech in Greek.] **we have fellowship with him:** 'Fellowship' being the sharing of the divine life and communion of the Father and the Son (Jn 14: 23; 1 Jn 1: 3), and 'him' being here equivalent to 'God'. ['He', etc. is frequently used in the Letter by way of emphatic reference to Christ as The Person (*e.g.* 1: 5; 2: 8, 12; 4: 17, 21), but it is sometimes ambiguous whether God or Christ is meant (*e.g.* 2: 13, 25, 27; 3: 19, 24; 4: 13). This is strong testimony to John's belief in the unity of Father and Son; statements made of the one can often be used interchangeably of the other.] **while we walk in darkness:** Our actual conduct being such that out of shame and fear we conceal our deeds, and are not living in frank and loving fellowship with fellow Christians—then we are both speaking and acting out falsehood; 'our words and our lives are a lie' (NEB).

7. The result of **walking in the light** is not stated, as one might expect from the logical progress of the sentence, to be that we have fellowship with God, but (in the manner of the Letter, the right foot, so to speak, is not simply brought level with the left, but is placed clear ahead) our fellowship with God finds expression in **fellowship with one another** which has already (1: 3) been seen to be essentially

the same things as fellowship with God. **and the blood of Jesus:** The life of the Lord's servant given up in death as an offering for sin (Isa. 53: 10). **his Son:** Jesus who died on the cross was God's Son even at that time (despite Cerinthus: see Introduction). **cleanses us:** A benefit in which John includes himself. This continually repeated cleansing is distinguished in Jn 13: 10 from the initial complete 'bath' of regeneration. (See Mt. 11: 28 f., 'the two rests'; Mt. 18: 22-35, 'the two debts' for similar distinction between the abiding reality and its practical daily realization.) Yet the repeated cleansings are confirmation that the initial bath was received, as well as being its practical fulfilment. The man who feels no need to come for the 'cleansing' has never had the 'bath', and has no part in Christ. **from all sin:** From sin of every kind.

8. If we say: The second false claim (see on 1: 6). **we have no sin:** That the root principle of sin has been eradicated from our heart—another claim of the gnostic heretics—we are not simply mistaken, but **we deceive ourselves** and have only ourselves to blame for having gone astray: an even worse situation than the failure in 1: 6. Westcott, however, teaches that the false plea of v.8 is that sin does not cleave to him who commits it; it is a mere accident, and not a continuous principle.

9. If we confess: Bring into the light of God, with what that may involve in terms of fellowship with one another. **our sins:** The actual offences arising from sin the principle. **he is faithful and just and will forgive:** The RV rendering 'faithful and righteous to forgive' is perhaps better, as what is in question is not God's character, but the character of the action. God forgives, and that consistently with His own character and in righteousness (Rom. 3: 21-26).

10. If we say we have not sinned (see on 1: 6) our course in deceit is complete; we deny the whole testimony of God's word, and the need for His redemptive activity.

2: 1. The teaching of 1: 7-10 might be open to perverse misinterpretation: 'I may as well commit sin since everyone else does. God will forgive me; what else is He for?' Hence the caution that the writer's purpose is **so that you may not sin: . . . but if any one does sin:** Both verbs are aorists: acts of sin rather than a sinful course of life are in view. **we have:** Logic demands 'he has', but the apostle breaks the grammatical concord to include himself in the gracious provision. **an advocate** (a pleader defending the accused in court): This is the best general tr. of *Paraclete*, found only here and in Jn 14-16, a title of the Holy Spirit and (by implication, Jn 14: 16) of Jesus; though 'Comforter', 'Helper', and 'Counsellor' rightly indicate the breadth of the spectrum of meaning. The Holy Spirit is God's Advocate, instructed by the Father and the Son, within our hearts; here the Lord Jesus is our Advocate, representing our interests and pleading our cause before God. But the phrase is rather **with the Father**— with (*pros*, see on 1: 2) the One who sustains a relation of intimacy with our Advocate and of grace toward us. This present ministry of the Lord Jesus is illustrated in Lk. 22: 31 f. and Jn 17; see also Rom. 8: 26 f., 34 for the intercession of the two Advocates. Though our restoration depends upon our confession (1: 9), the ministry of the Advocate does not.

2. Not only does He plead our cause: He is in Himself, by virtue of his life offered up in death (1: 7) **the expiation for our sins,** the sacrifice which restores fellowship (see on 1: 7). The death of Christ, in a manner which was prefigured by the levitical sin offering (Lev. 4), breaks down the barrier which sin has erected between God and man. **the sins of** is not expressed, but is perhaps implied. **for . . . the whole world:** Life for the world through individual appropriation of Christ in His death is taught in Jn 6: 51. Cf. Mk 10: 45; Jn 1: 29; 3: 16; 4: 42; 11: 51 f. God loves the whole world, and Christ died for its sake; in this lies the balance to the concentration in the Letter upon love within the boundaries of the Christian brotherhood (3: 16; 5: 1). Love learnt within the boundaries will be exercised outside; in this way the love proves to be divine (Mt. 5: 44-48). The expiation is the righteous basis for God's present forbearance in respect of a rebellious world (cf. Rom. 3: 25); and in any case, all those who are about to be called are at present in 'the world' (Eph. 2: 3).

3. And by this we may be sure: A characteristic phrase of the Letter (2: 3, 5, 29; 3: 19, 24; 4: 2, 6, 13; 5: 2) marking the intention of offering a series of tests by which the reader may discover whether or not he has eternal life (5: 13). In the first three, the tr. is 'be sure', for the remainder the translators lapse into 'know'. The flow of the argument would call for the statement that the proof of knowing God is in not sinning; John characteristically advances beyond that to the positive **keep his commandments.** The high-sounding 'fellowship with God' (1: 6) has down-to-earth expression in obedience, and that to actual commandment.

4. See on 1: 6. **5. love for God:** This selects rightly and helpfully the appropriate sense of the wide phrase 'the love of God'. The practical realization ('perfection', as our writer would say) of love for God is not found in transports of mystical adoration, but in obedience, in walking **in the same way in which he** (i.e. Jesus) **walked** (6).

III. THE COMMANDMENT (2: 7-17)

This new section is prepared for in 2: 3, where the matter of 'not sinning' is advanced to its positive aspect of 'keeping his commandments'. In this section, the view of 'his commandments' is narrowed to the supreme commandment which includes all others, that of love (Mt. 22: 36-40; Rom. 13: 8 ff.): love for our brother (7-11) and love for the Father (15-17). An interjected lyrical address (12-14), in terms of particular affection, celebrates the marvels of redeeming love as the basis of a call to moral earnestness. **the old commandment which you had from the beginning** is undoubtedly 'that you love one another even as I have loved you' (Jn 13: 34). Recall to the original gospel, in both its doctrine of the Incarnation and the Atonement, and its commandment of love, is the apostle's method of dealing with the crisis brought by the new teaching. The **beginning** might be the beginning of Christ's ministry (Jn 15: 27), but in view of 2: 24; 3: 11 and 2 Jn 6, more probably = the beginning of your Christian faith. (This does not necessarily fix the sense of the word in 1: 1, in a writer who is capable of using one word in three distinct senses in one sentence ['truth' in 2 Jn 1, 2,—*q.v.*].) In a wider sense, the commandment is **old**: it is found in the Old Testament (Lev. 19: 18), and indeed it is a primal law of creation. Its correlative in the physical world was formulated by Newton, 'Every body attracts every other body with a force proportional to its mass', with the other principle in impressive proximity, 'To every action there is an equal and opposite reaction'. The principles by which the physical universe coheres are thus 'figures of the True', of love, and of justice, corresponding with the two great theological affirmations which dominate the Letter, **God is love** and **God is light**— though nature shows the more austere and—so to speak—mechanical aspects: grace comes by Jesus Christ. It is nevertheless **a new commandment.** In Mt. 22: 37-40 the whole of the law and the prophets is declared to depend upon the two commandments of love to God and love to one's neighbour. But in constituting a new Society, the Lord promulgated a new commandment as the principle of its order, the commandment of love to the brotherhood— while at the same time confirming the first two commandments. This commandment is **true in him,** its great exemplar, **and,** in a different degree, true **in you.** (For a similar distinction between the senses in which a term may be applied to Christ and to His people, see Mt. 17: 27; Jn 20: 17.) The principle of love is true in our case because into our experience Christ has come, **the true light** which enlightens every man **is already shining** in our hearts, and our **darkness is passing away.**

9. Light is the medium of perception and recognition, of understanding and fellowship; and **he who says he is in the light** (see on 1: 6) **and hates his brother** actually knows nothing of these things: he is still in unregenerate man's native sphere (Eph. 2: 1 ff.; cf. Exod. 10: 22 f.).

10. the light in which **he who loves his brother abides** still primarily signifies fellowship, but with all that is involved in a holy fellowship, a fellowship which is 'with the Father and with his Son Jesus Christ'. RSV text takes the remainder of the sentence to mean that **there is no cause for stumbling** in the light: a statement which is grammatically and logically unexceptionable, but which would seem too obvious to require saying. It is better to follow the margin, and to understand the phrase of the one who loves his brother: he abides in the holy fellowship, and has within him no tendency to be suddenly provoked to sin, and thus to become a cause of offence. The Gospel background of 2: 9–11 is in Jn 11: 9 f. and 12: 35.

11. hates: Not simply *dislikes:* the malign, hellish contrast to divine love, actively wishing evil to its object. Such a person is in Satan's realm of **darkness** and enmity; he is incapable of discerning the true nature of his own actions or the destiny for which he is preparing himself. Psychologically and spiritually, hatred blinds its subject just as surely as love illumines. It is characteristic of John to disregard the blurred colour of a human situation, and to insist upon the stark black and white of the underlying spiritual principle. His function is not that of a judge, weighing all the factors (Prov. 21: 2), but that of a teacher elucidating the essential spirit of a matter, indeed showing things clearer than they are in actual fact. The either/or necessity of love and hate is well illustrated in Mk 3: 1-6.

12-14. Turning again to his beloved 'children', the apostle breaks out into ecstatic congratulation of them upon their place in the family of God, all the more marvellous in contrast with the darkness just considered. The brief prophetic lyric consists of two stanzas each of three lines, the change from the formula **I am writing** to **I write** being simply, it seems, a device to distinguish the two stanzas. In this way the repeated sequence of **children, fathers,** and **young men** stands out significantly. The

idea that the first series, introduced by 'I am writing', refers to the Letter, while the 'I write' (literally 'I wrote') series refers to the Gospel, has nothing to commend it. The same 'I write' is used in 5: 13, referring to the Letter. All those whom the apostle addresses in the Letter are his **little children** (2: 1 etc.), and so it is improbable that **fathers** and **young men** represent different age-groups; it rather belongs to Christian experience to combine the innocence (through grace) of infants with the maturity of fathers and (this being the main point) the moral earnestness of youth. The natural order of address would be children, young men, fathers; the addresses to young men, being displaced from their natural order, are emphatic; and the purpose of the section is to be found in them. Some scholars, however (with Westcott), regard the words as indicating different age groups.

12, 13. As **little children,** Christians enjoy the primary boon of having their **sins forgiven,** and that **for his sake** (2: 2), and of **know**ing God as **Father.**

13, 14. As **fathers,** Christians **know him who is** ('and has been', NEB) **from the beginning,** that is, the Eternal.

13, 14. The addresses to Christians as **young men,** which would come logically between the other two, but brought to the end for emphasis, declare that the middle term between simple forgiveness and mature apprehension is that high and earnest resolve which is youth's noblest trait: standing firm, giving serious heed to the written **word of God,** and pressing on to subdue **the evil one.**

15. Divine love, the subject of the commandment, is always in danger of being crushed out by a rival love, **the love of the world.** 'Worldliness' is identified with love of **the things in the world.** Yet when we enquire what may be the 'things' which are 'worldly', we find that 'things' do not exist in this connection except as a necessity of English translation; the 'things in the world' being its spirit, its tone, its values. Worldliness consists of attitudes: the three characteristic attitudes of the world being *sensuality, materialism,* and *ostentation* (C. H. Dodd).

16. The phrase **lust of the flesh** is plain enough, signifying the notion that desires and appetites have a right to insist upon fulfilment without reference to any superior law. The **lust of the eyes** is the spirit of the world in putting supreme value upon things which can be seen (as opposed to the value which faith puts upon the unseen—2 C. 4: 18), and the consequent greed to obtain them. The **pride of life** is probably 'ostentatious pride in the possession of worldly resources' (Plummer in *CGT*), as the word tr. **life** is commonly used in the sense of 'means of life' (*e.g.* 3: 17; Mk 12: 44).

17. Yet death is the termination as well as the tendency of these things, and not only the individual but the world itself has the sentence of death upon it, and is already moving toward its dissolution. **but he who does the will of God,** who obeys the commandment of divine love, shares the very life of God, and **abides for ever.**

IV. THE RIVAL ANOINTINGS (2: 18-29)

It is in this section and in section VI that the crisis which may have occasioned the Letter comes into clear view (see Introduction and note on 1: 6). The falsity of the new teaching is expressed in a play of words difficult to put into English, but which we shall understand better if we keep in mind that *Christ* means *Anointed*. Jesus is the Christ; His people share his life (Jn 14: 19 f.), and are in a derived but true sense 'christs', and do his works, having a *chrisma* (**anointing,** 2: 20, 27) from Him (cf. Jn 14: 12; 20: 21 ff.). It was well known that the end of the age would be heralded by the appearance of the **antichrist;** but, says John, his spirit is already abroad in the world. Those false teachers are his people and share his spirit; they are **antichrists,** and their initiation (the rival anointing—the anti-baptism, one might almost say) into this new teaching is no true *chrisma*, but an *antichrisma* which blinds them (2 Th. 2: 9-12).

18. John has been widely censured for his declaration that **it is the last hour.** A moderate statement of the view is that made by Jelf, quoted in *CGT* p. 106: 'The only point on which we can certainly say that the Apostles were in error, and led others into error, is in their expectation of the immediate coming of Christ, and this is the very point which our Saviour says is known only to the Father'. But this is a superficial view, and one which shows little regard for the teaching of the Lord Himself as to the recurring nearness of the End (Mt. 10: 23; 16: 27; 24: 14, 30; 25: 13), let alone sympathy with the regular apostolic teaching (1 C. 1: 7; 1 Th. 1: 10; Jas 5: 7 f.; 1 Pet. 1: 13). John and his readers were living in *an eschatological hour*, electric with movements of the unseen principalities which might burst into sight at any time. Jerusalem had fallen, and antichristian Rome was already closing in mortal combat with the Church. These were the days of the eighth emperor, Domitian; would he prove to be the Antichrist, 'the eighth king' of Rev. 17: 11? (See p. 658.) Even from our point of time, John's assessment

was correct. There are periods when the End draws obviously near, though in course of time the crisis subsides and recedes. The periods of the rise of Islam, the Reformation, the Napoleonic Wars, and the present age, are examples of epochs heavy with destiny. In one such 'last hour' the End will suddenly break into its irreversible course: this realization braces Christians to special preparedness at such times (*e.g.* 1 C. 7: 26). If it be asked if John had all this in view, the answer must be 'not at all likely'. Prophets speak better than they know (1 Pet. 1: 10 ff.), and John had good reason to think about his day, as we do of ours, that it is *the* last hour; though his word here is literally '*a last hour*'.

It was a regular part of Christian expectation, though for prudential reasons passed on more by way of oral teaching than of written instruction (**you have heard** cf. 2 Th. 2: 5), that the appearance of the sinister figure of **antichrist** would herald the end (cf. 'the little horn' of Dan. 7, 'the man of lawlessness' of 2 Th. 2: 3, and the 'beasts' of Rev. 13). Exalting himself above every object of worship, he will deny that Jesus is the Son of God incarnate. But now, says the apostle, this teaching has already appeared in Christian circles; 'the rebellion' (2 Th. 2: 3) has already begun; and with the rising of **many antichrists** what hinders the appearing of Antichrist himself? It should be noted that John's reading of his contemporary situation goes no further than this, and commentators need have no fear in leaving us under his teaching. [Antichrist: one who assuming the guise of Christ opposes Christ—to be distinguished from 'false Christs' (Mt. 24: 24), i.e. messianic pretenders. Origen taught that 'all that Christ is in reality, Antichrist offers in false appearance; and so all false teaching which assumes the guise of truth, among heretics and even among heathen, is in some sense antichrist. The Incarnation reveals the true destiny of man in his union with God through Christ; the lie of Antichrist is that man is divine apart from Christ'. Abbreviated from Westcott, pp. 69, 90.]

19. The secession of the antichristian teachers, marking their apostasy from the truth, serves however a solemn but necessary purpose. It was not only a divine providence to limit their opportunity for mischief, but it also demonstrated that **they all are not of us,** or, as NEB has it, ' so that it might be clear that not all in our company truly belong to it'—a salutary warning for every church. Apostasy on the part of those in formal church membership can and does occur, but only in those who never were truly Christ's.

20. you (emphatic) **have been anointed:**
The suggestion being that 'they' also had their
anointing—probably the rite of initiation into
their gnostic circle, admitting them to the
esoteric teaching. 'You, no less than they, are
among the initiated' (NEB). The 'anointing'
bestowed by Christ as **the Holy One,** is the
Holy Spirit, by virtue of which **you all know.**
This tr. is preferable to AV, RV. The knowledge
of the truth is not the privilege of a select
few, but of all God's people (Jn 18: 20; Col.
1: 28; Heb. 8: 11); this is a strong attack upon
the position of the heretics.

21. The appeal to the common faith of the
Church is based on the convictions of v. 20:
the Church knows intuitively what belongs
to her historic faith (**the truth**), and will recognize and reject any foreign elements as a **lie.**
Prophets will no doubt weigh the utterances
of other prophets (1 C. 14: 29), but the final
judgment is that of the whole congregation.
22. The antichristian lie which is being countered
is the denial that **Jesus is the Christ** and **the
Son** of God (see Introduction).

24. This denial is incompatible with **what
you heard from the beginning**—the original
gospel which is now being corrupted—and
by its very nature this denial renders impossible
that fellowship, that abiding in the Son and in
the Father, which (25) is the very nature of
eternal life (Jn 14: 23; 17: 3). **26.** 'So much
for those who would mislead you' (NEB).

27. the anointing (v. 20)—the Holy Spirit,
that *chrisma* which makes us *Christians*—**abides**
(Jn 14: 16) and **teaches** (Jn 14: 26). It is thus an
impertinence, and worse, that people should
come along and **teach** new doctrine. The
Christian teacher, from this point of view,
simply reminds his brethren of what they
already know (at least in principle), clarifies
their thinking and directs it into practical
channels. The Holy Spirit will teach them to
recognize what belongs and what does not
belong to the gospel when they hear it (Jn 10: 5).
The word **abide** (27 f.) recalls again the figure
of the True Vine (Jn 15: 1–11); the ambiguous
reference of **him** may be defined by taking it
as 'God in Christ'. The phrase **shrink from
him in shame** (at his *parousia*), taken from
old commentators, fills out well the sense of
the Greek 'be ashamed from him'. Cf. *Hamlet:*
'. . . started like a guilty thing upon a fearful
summons'.

29. Even before making his dramatic transition in 3: 1 to the subject of *the children of God,*
John's mind has already moved to that realm
of thought, and he declares by way of anticipation that God's children will be recognized by
righteous conduct—the standard of conduct

being the character of God Himself, and therefore expressed in obedience to *His will.* See
note on 4: 7. The 'son of thunder' takes a solid
piece out of the heart of his next section to
hurl as a parting shot at the apostate teachers
in their *self-will.*

V. THE CHILDREN OF GOD (3: 1–24)
(i) The divine nature is manifested in being
like Christ (1–3); more specifically, in (*a*) doing
right (4–10), and (*b*) loving the brethren (11–18).
(ii) It is by such practical obedience that we may
obtain reassurance and confidence (19–24). The
central thought of the chapter echoes clearly
the Lord's teaching in Jn 8: 39–47: 'If God were
your Father you would love me . . . your will
is to do your father's desires . . . you do not
believe me'—illuminating by contrast the three
marks of eternal life: love, obedience and belief.

1. See what love: For devotional use we
are better with 'Behold what manner of love',
a tr. which held the field until RSV. The force
of **what** is 'how glorious' (*Arndt*). The purpose
of God's love is that we should become his
children (*children* signifying the sharing of
nature, with the possibility of development;
as against *sons*—not used by John except in
Rev. 21: 7—emphasizing privilege and likeness
of character: cf. Rom. 8: 14, 16). This is already
true, and is no empty title, for **so we are** in a
vital sense, by regeneration (Jn 1: 12 f.). We
may perhaps interpret quite strictly the declaration that **The reason . . . the world does not
know** (i.e. recognize) **us** to be God's children
is that **it did not** recognize **him** as God's Son.
The world would then be following out the
course of wilful blindness noted in Mt. 21: 23–27
and Jn 12: 35–40. But it seems better to follow
the thought of Jn 8: 39–47, and to understand
that **the reason** is the same in both cases: on
account of radical disparity of nature, the world
has not the capacity for recognizing the divine.

2. The **now** and the **not yet** are both true,
and express the tension which exists between
the ideal holiness and glory belonging to men
who have become God's children, and their
actual observable condition of failure and distress.
It is not yet manifest (to the world) **what we
shall be;** but of course Christians know,
because they have overheard their Lord praying
for them (Jn 17: 24 ff.). However unlikely
it seems, the dull chrysalis will yet take the air
as a butterfly; and all intelligent people know
that it will be so. **we shall be like him** when we
see Him at His parousia (1 C. 15: 51).

3. This hope of ultimate conformity to the
moral likeness of Christ is a powerful motive
to diligent moral cleansing here and now, and
is one channel by which the implanted divine

nature achieves progressive conformity of the indwelt life with its own law of being.

4. For any one at all (**Every one,** including those who imagine that being saved by grace they are above mere literal obedience) to commit sin is to flout the law, and therefore the will, of God.

5. But Christ is the antithesis of all sin (**he appeared to take away sins,** and He personally is free from sin). That is to say, everyone who sins is a rebel against (*a*) God, by refusing submission to His law; (*b*) the work of Christ, directed as it is to the removal of sins; and (*c*) the character of Christ as the Holy One of God. So—and this is the intended conclusion of the reasoning—**No one who abides in him sins.** Here the verb 'to sin' is in the present indicative, with the sense of continued or habitual action. By contrast, the two occurrences of the same verb in 2: 1 are in the aorist, signifying isolated sins. No Christian can continue in disobedience as his way of life: it is a moral impossibility. [It should be noted, however, that Law (*op cit.* p. 219) protests strongly that the point of the argument is missed when one relies, with Westcott, as we have done, upon the *habitual* sense of the verbs 'to commit sin' and 'to do righteousness' in this paragraph. While unable to follow Law here, we may yet avoid undue reliance upon the habitual sense, as though it meant that we are at liberty to make occasional excursions into sin, provided we do not become domiciled there—an unchristian position close to that of Rom. 3: 8.]

7. 'Righteous is as righteous does' (to adapt a common saying); but it is obvious that there were teachers around with a sophisticated theory of salvation which left plenty of room for illicit behaviour. John was neither the first to encounter this, nor the first to declare that such people try to **deceive** you (1 C. 6: 9 f.; Eph. 5: 6). He states flatly **No one born of God commits sin;** and if this statement, with its verb in the present tense, seems strong, it is good to note that if the verb had been aorist, it would have been even stronger. It would then have read: 'No one born of God commits a sin . . . and he cannot commit a sin, because he is born of God'. This would be manifestly contrary to experience; contrary also to the testimony of the Letter itself (1: 8, 10). The explanation of this moral necessity is couched in the form of a strong figure. The word tr. **nature** (lit. 'seed', Gk. *sperma*) introduces the analogy of human begetting; cf. C. H. Dodd's tr., 'A divine seed remains in him'. The reason that Christians cannot live a life of sin is that the principle of divine life has been implanted within them by God, and life develops

according to that principle. God is their Father, and their true nature accords with this, the deepest truth of their personality.

8, 10. 'All mankind is God's children by creation: as regards this a creature can have no choice. But a creature endowed with free will can choose his own parent in the moral world. The Father offers him "*the right to become a child of God*" (Jn 1: 12), but he can refuse this and become a child of the devil instead. There is no third alternative' (Plummer in *CGT*, p. 128). Correspondence between spiritual parentage and moral character means that attitudes and actions betray our spiritual nature. Then at the end of the paragraph, the next subject (brotherly love) is introduced, in the Johannine manner.

11. The commandment **that we should love one another** goes back to Christ Himself (Jn 13: 34), to **the beginning** of the gospel. See note on 2: 7.

12. The reference to Cain, the only allusion in the Letter to the OT, is deeply significant. Adam had been warned that in the day of disobedience he would die; yet in fact it seemed that the serpent's word was true: he 'lived' a long life and became the father of humanity. He gave to his wife—was it in perverse bravado? —the name of 'Eve': the mother of all 'living'. In their first-born, Cain, was manifested the nature of that 'life'. Cain was not master but slave of passion, and his very worship was unacceptable to God. In Cain is seen the horrifying nature of hatred: **he murdered,** and that **his brother. And why did he murder him?**— 'Much might be said on both sides. It takes two to make a quarrel'. The apostle has no time for this kind of moral sluggishness which refuses to see ultimate principles; and brushing aside all possible secondary and contributory causes he declares that the sin was Cain's. Cain could not bear the contrast of **his brother's righteous** deeds with **his own deeds** which **were evil,** and the first murder became a monument to self-love, as the cross was to become the demonstration of divine love. Not only the world is shown in the story of Cain, but in a sense the Church too. The seed of Seth was the appointed representative of the slain Abel—and if we understand the first two verses of Gen. 6 aright, the two seeds are actually called the children of God and the children of men. Such is the background to the apostle's thought as he moves from the 'righteous brother' (with no doubt the ever-present consciousness of the Son of Man slain out of envy by the children of men—Jn 1: 11; Mt. 27: 18) to (13) **the brethren,** and from Cain to **the world** which **hates you.** See also Jn 8: 37–47.

14. Hatred is the realm of death, love the realm of life; and assurance **that we have passed out of death** (*out of . . . into* is more decisive than the AV *from . . . unto*. It is no 'to and fro' movement: we have made the passage once for all: Jn 5: 24) **into life** (and—significance of perfect tense—we remain there) is conveyed by our consciousness of brotherly love. The unregenerate man **remains in death,** which is thus implied to be his native realm. Hating his brother, he is in heart **a murderer** (Mt. 5: 21 f.), and this attitude is incompatible with **eternal life.** In visiting condemned murderers, I have met despair of God's pardon because of this verse—and without cause (Mt. 12: 31a; 1 C. 6: 9-11; 1 Jn 1: 7).

16. '*The second John three sixteen*'. We know what 'love' in its lower meanings is: physical attraction, natural affection and friendship; but we would be totally unacquainted with *agapē*, the divine **love,** were it not that **he** took frail flesh and died for our sake. That love which has made us rich has also made debtors of us (a rather stronger word than **we ought**) to lay down our lives, as our Lord laid down His. **to lay down** one's **life** for the sake of another is to set oneself to seek the good of that person at all cost, even at the cost of life itself. Cf. Christ's cross and the disciples' cross (Mt. 16: 21-25). One might perhaps expect that the indwelling divine love would constrain us to die *for His sake:* but what would be remarkable in our loving Him who has done us nothing but good? Divine love goes further: it is love to the undeserving, the unthankful, even the rebellious (Jn 3: 16; Mt. 5: 43-48; Rom. 5: 6-8). **the brethren,** in their foolish and sinful weakness so truly *our* brethren, are the proper objects of our self-sacrificing love. If our love cannot encompass them, how shall it prove to be that divine *agapē* which reaches out to the world?

17. Few of us are called to die for our brethren. But in smaller things we may show the same spirit, and share whatever we have of **the world's goods** with a **brother in need** (Lk. 16: 11).

18. love in word may be genuine enough, but is not fulfilled **in deed.** Love **in speech** consists of hypocritical utterances with no **truth** in it. We are to beware lest our love stop at mere talk, or even prove downright insincere.

19. By this, that is, by 'love in deed and truth' we may reassure our hearts in God's presence that we belong to the Lord (a matter of value to the spiritual physician as well as to the general reader. (For 'being **of the truth'** see Jn 18: 37.) When conscience (**our hearts**) brings its accusations, we may appeal to the higher and final tribunal of Omniscience:

'Lord, you know everything; you know that I love . . .' (Jn 21: 17). But it should be noted that it is a record of actual deeds of self-sacrifice done out of unfeigned love which constitutes this sign of indwelling divine life, and not simply the feeling of adoration toward the Infinite, which so easily passes for 'love of God'. Tests, to be worth anything, have to be applied on a level available to inspection and observation. **21 f. if our hearts do not condemn us:** The accusations of conscience either having not arisen or having been silenced, then we have liberty in prayer and joy in answered prayer. **23.** The **commandment,** which is so often summed up as 'trust and obey' (Rom. 6: 17; 16: 26) is given in the form, 'believe and love' **—believe . . . in Jesus . . . and love one another.** In both forms it is the same faith which works through love (Gal. 5: 6), for the commandment in which all obedience is summed up is the new commandment of love. For obedience, love and belief, here found in one verse, as the three manifestations of eternal life, see on 4: 7. Then, in the manner of the Letter, the section is rounded off by an anticipation of the next section: **by this we know—** another of the series of tests as to whether or not we possess life—by the gift of the Holy **Spirit.**

VI. THE RIVAL SPIRITS (4: 1-6)

Having accomplished his central purpose of providing practical means of identifying the children of God, John begins to retrace his course of thought—the literary structure of *introversion* which enters into the pattern of the Fourth Gospel (F. Madeley, 'A New Approach to the Gospel of St. John,' *EQ* July-Sept. 1961; R. W. Orr, *The Witness,* July 1962)—and of Rev. also (R. G. Moulton, *The Modern Reader's Bible,* pp. 1708 f.).

1. The **many false prophets** who **have gone out into the world** (where they really belong) are probably the same people as 'the many antichrists' who 'went out from us' (2: 18 f.). They spoke as prophets by inspiration, and that mere fact was sufficient to ensure them a large following. But Christians forgot, and still do, that we live in a whirlpool of spiritual influences, by no means all of which are holy or divine. We must **test** the utterances, and thereby **the spirits** which inspire them. Not all that appears to be supernatural is genuinely so—there is deliberate deceit and there are delusions—and even after eliminating the spurious, there must be careful discernment as to the source of inspiration, **whether of God** or of the devil.

2 f. The test prescribed is quite comprehensive. The witness of **the Spirit of God,** and therefore of **every spirit** which is **of God,** is to **Jesus,** the historical man of Nazareth; that He is the **Christ,** the Saviour-King foretold in OT type and prophecy; that this Jesus the Messiah *came* —implying his pre-existence—**in the flesh** (Jn 1: 14): the actuality of the Incarnation; rather, that He **has come** in the flesh, and is still truly man: the permanence of the Incarnation, implying the Resurrection. The 'confession' is thus a Christian creed in brief compass. It might be better rendered as 'Every spirit which confesses Jesus as Christ come in the flesh is of God' (Law, *op. cit.*, p. 94 n.)—a tr. which leads on smoothly to the converse.

3. every spirit which does not confess Jesus (as Christ come in the flesh) **is not of God.**

4-6. Beliefs and utterances which are disloyal to the person of Jesus as recorded and interpreted in the apostolic testimony are inspired, not by the **spirit of truth** (the Holy Spirit, Jn 14: 17) but by the **spirit of error.** The spirit which will animate the Antichrist is a spirit which the world finds congenial. Right belief as to the person of Jesus is based upon the apostolic testimony, and John holds the high ground of being one of the primary witnesses appointed by God. **We** (the apostles) **are of God.** He is not here contrasting the apostles with other Christians, but with the new teachers (**they** of v. 5). The apostles received the Spirit to enable them to bear their witness, basic to the very existence of the Church; other Christians are enabled by the same Spirit to believe the apostolic witness: **whoever knows God listens to us** (i.e. listens and obeys: cf. Mt. 18: 15 f.). Prophets and teachers are therefore to be judged by their doctrine; and doctrine is to be judged, not by its emotional quality and strength, but by its agreement with the apostolic testimony to Jesus.

VII. GOD IS LOVE (4: 7-5: 5)

The latter part of the Letter is dominated by the great affirmation *God is love,* as the earlier part is by *God is light* (1: 5). The practical corollary of **God is love** is that **he who abides in love abides in God** (4: 16). 'Abiding in love' is the ruling thought of this section, just as 'abiding in the light' (2: 10) was earlier seen to be necessarily the condition of those who abide in the God who is light. The section also contains the main part of two series of tests (noted by Law, *op cit.*, p. 186 n. and p. 279): they may conveniently be shown together here.

	Obedience	Love	Belief
Tests of being children of God	2: 29	4: 7	5: 1
Tests of abiding in God	3: 24	4: 12	4: 15

Considering the human mind in its three functions of intellect, emotion and will, we see that it is renewed in all its parts by the indwelling of God: the intellect is enlightened to believe, the emotions are kindled to love, and the will is turned and strengthened to obey.

7. 'Jerome tells us that during St. John's last years "Little children, love one another" was the one exhortation which, after he had become too old to preach, he never ceased to give. "It is the Lord's command", he said, "and if this be done, it is enough" ' (quoted by Plummer in *CGT*, pp. 128 f.). **love is of God:** *Agapē* whether manifested in God or in man, is of divine origin (see on v. 9), being God's own nature; **and he** (*every one:* this 'test of life' is more clearly seen to be such if this tr. is retained). **who loves** (not of course every one who feels the force of natural affection or physical attraction or the warmth of friendship, but he through whom courses the divine love) **is born of God:** Perfect tense: literally 'has been born of God'. The divine begetting preceded the love: love is an activity of the implanted eternal life, and is therefore a proof that the life is present. This significance of the perfect tense is important also in the other two signs given of our being children of God (2: 29; 5: 1— see table above). **and knows God:** Love, 'the eyes of the heart' is the organ of perception of God and of His counsels (Eph. 1: 18). Cf. music, which might be studied as a branch of applied mathematics, resulting in interesting and valuable insights, but is really known only through a love of music.

9 f. We would have had no notion of what *agapē* is—the love divine, all loves excelling— but for the amazing facts of the Incarnation and the Atonement. We could conceive of the Lord the Almighty sitting in His heaven, contemplating with serene detachment the self-ruin and extinction of his creatures: such is a God created by man in his own image. But that God should involve Himself in man's ruin, and Himself suffer their disgrace and pain and bereavement! The **expiation** (see on 2: 2) due to Himself, God Himself provided, and that by sending **his only son** (the willing suffering of the Father is as truly manifest as that of the Son; Gen. 22: 2; Rom. 8: 32), that **we,** despite all **our sins**—rebellious as well as unworthy—might receive the supreme gift of life. This is love.

11. The proper response to divine love is to show love which has something of the divine character of self-sacrifice for the unregarding: God, the giver and forgiver, cannot be loved in that way: our brother can, especially if he has not first loved us.

12. Men have seen God manifest as man (Jn 14: 9); but God as God, **no man has ever seen** nor can see (Jn 1: 18; 4: 24; 1 Tim. 6: 16); that kind of vision of God is a fruitless aim to pursue. But the gracious presence of God making His home within us is experienced when **his love is perfected in us,** that is, when the divine life expresses itself in actual deeds motivated by love, for the good of others. Here is a practical demonstration of eternal life (see table at the beginning of this section).

13. The love of God was manifest not only in sending His own Son, but also in giving **us of his own spirit** in order to quicken faith within us.

14. The primary work of the Spirit among men was to create the apostolic testimony to Jesus, teaching the apostles the meaning of what they had **seen,** and enabling them to **testify** as to the person of Jesus, that He is the **Son of the Father** (Jn 1: 14), and as to His work, that He is **the Saviour of the world** (Jn 4: 42).

15. By the same Spirit does each believer make his confession unto salvation (1 C. 12: 3), belief in the heart and confession upon the lips being proof that God by the Spirit dwells within.

16. It is by this further gracious action of God that the Incarnation and Atonement become good to us, and **we know and believe.**

God is love, and he who abides in love abides in God, and God abides in him. This is the great affirmation in its full form, consisting of a theological statement followed by a practical corollary, comparable with Jn 4: 24 and 1 Jn 1: 5. The utterance **God is love** has been hailed as 'the summit of all revelation', 'the innermost secret of existence' (Law, *op. cit.*, p. 70); 'the touchstone of all theology'. True, but what if revelation, like Hermon, has more than one summit? *God is spirit*— Eternal Spirit — Himself the ever-springing source of all that He requires. *God is light*— Eternal Light, Everlasting Burnings—seeking fellowship with Himself which must have the moral quality of sincerity and obedience. *God is love*—Eternal Love—and fellowship in His life will be manifested in the likeness of His love, shown even to the unloving. God is The Person, and relations with him are personal: *agapē* is His own nature and the ground of His activity, and those who are habitually motivated by *agapē* are in the fellowship of His life. The mutual indwelling of Vine and branches is in view (Jn 15: 5): only in the Gospel it is the relation to Christ which is in view, while in the Letter it is the relation to God in Christ.

17. One great practical result (or 'perfection' as our writer would say) is **confidence for the day of judgment. for** interprets correctly the compressed idea of confidence *now* as we anticipate the day of judgment: a confidence which will not forsake us when that day actually comes. The ground of confidence is **in this,** in the fellowship of love with God and with the brethren. If **we,** here and now **in this world** are **as he is**—if there is evidence that the divine nature is implanted within us, expressing itself in loving the brethren and in a forgiving spirit and in seeking at cost the good of the unworthy after the pattern of His life— then there is solid ground for confidence that it is because He has given us eternal life. Not of course that our love is the ground of confidence, any more than our trust or our obedience: it is the sign that we belong to Him who is the Saviour. This verse should be read along with 3: 18-20.

18. perfect love: Love which reaches beyond word and speech to deed and truth cannot provide any occasion for **fear,** because he who loves is abiding in the light (2: 10), and is therefore being cleansed by the blood of Jesus from all sin (1: 7), and is doing what pleases Him (3: 22). More than that, love 'in deed and truth' **casts out fear** which is already present, by the confidence it gives of fellowship with God in the life eternal. Some, however, understand the love spoken of to be that love which on God's side is already full, and which we are exhorted to make our own in full measure, thus casting out its dark negation of slavish fear. Bengel remarks that men may pass through diverse conditions: without either fear or love, in fear and without love, in both fear and love, finally reaching love without fear. What has **fear . . . to do with punishment**? Fear is the foretaste, the earnest, of the punishment which conscience anticipates; but the believer can appeal from the fallible interim sentence of conscience to the judgment of Him who knows all things, on the ground of already having been granted the spirit of love, earnest of the fulness of eternal life.

19. We love (*him* [AV] is properly omitted: all activity of love, whether to man or God, is meant) because all true love comes from God, and is His gift.

20. But **if any one says** (see on 1: 6), '**I love God**', imagining that his religious feelings of adoration and gratitude are of a higher order than 'love in deed and truth', while at the same time he **hates his brother,** consciously wishing him evil, **he is a liar**—he is telling and living a lie, and would realize that it is so if only he would stop to consider. For **the brother whom he has seen,** in all his sinful weakness, is the appointed receptacle for the divine love which he professes to be receiving (Mt. 25: 40).

5: 1 carries on the thought of 4: 21, that to love God involves loving God's children, but v. 2 carries us to new ground: that love for the brethren is no mere indulgent kindness, but is holy love, grounded in and regulated by **love to God,** and obedience to **his commandments,** desiring the highest good of the beloved, and finding (as *agapē* always does) its pattern in Jesus. 'For their sake I consecrate myself, that they also may be consecrated in truth' (Jn 17: 19). **3 f.** The apostle looks to the moral struggle required if we would live the holy life of love, and finds the guarantee of overcoming strength in **whatever is born of God.** The neuter (not 'whoever') emphasises not personal strength, but the fact of birth from God. Then, in vv. 4 f. he anticipates the next section by introducing the idea of **faith** or belief. He who believes is an overcomer: his faith is a manifestation of the life of God which must prevail. 'Belief in Christ is at once belief in God and in man. It lays a foundation for love and trust towards our fellow men. Thus the instinctive distrust and selfishness which reign supreme in the world are overcome' (*CGT, ad loc.*).

VIII. THE TESTIMONY (5: 6-12)

The apostle keeps his aim closely in view, that his readers may be brought into conscious enjoyment of fellowship in eternal life. We have already seen (4: 13-16a) that even though the objective grounds of reconciliation are prepared—the Incarnation and the Atonement—yet the work of the Holy Spirit is required to bring the individual into life. This section shows the strength of the grounds for believing in the Son of God and in the love of His atonement, and thus sharing in the fellowship of life.

6. This Son of God **is he who came** (cf. the technical title of the Messiah as 'he who comes' or 'he who is to come': Mt. 11: 3 etc.) **by** (better, through) **water,** quite literally, at His baptism, **and blood,** almost as literally, at His death (see *Arndt* on *dia*). The emphatic denial and affirmation which follow, show that some were teaching that the Christ came only through water, and not through blood. This was the error of Cerinthus (see Introduction), who taught that 'the Christ' came upon Jesus at His baptism, but left Him before His passion: thus denying a true incarnation and atonement. No, says the apostle, He who passed through the water was Jesus Christ, and he who passed through the blood was the same Jesus Christ.

For the explanation of John's reference to the water and the blood, one turns naturally to the emphatic recital of the miraculous issue of blood and water from the side of the slain Saviour (Jn 19: 34 f.). There is good reason for understanding the flowing blood of that narrative to signify the propitiatory power of the death of Christ (Jn 6: 52-57), and the water to signify the gift of the Spirit, after the manner of the water from the smitten rock (Jn 7: 37 ff. with Exod. 17: 6; 1 C. 10: 4). Thus, although there is basic correspondence in the ideas involved, a direct reference from 1 Jn 5: 6 to Jn 19: 34 would not be appropriate; the passages point to the same eternal verities rather than to each other—similar to the relations between the 'bread of life' discourse of Jn 6 and the Lord's Supper. The reversal of the terms **water and blood** rather than 'blood and water', as well as corresponding to the historical sequence of the baptism and the passion, may also serve as a warning that no direct reference is meant. In His baptism, Jesus committed Himself publicly to the path of the suffering Servant of the Lord, and, numbered already with transgressors, he went down symbolically into the water of death, like Jonah into the 'belly of Sheol' (Jon. 2: 2). Then in His symbolic resurrection, He saw heaven opened and the Spirit of God descended. In short, the *idea* of the Passion was represented in His baptism (Lk. 12: 50); and for the heretical teachers, ideas were everything. The symbolism of the baptism would suffice: they would see no need for the grim actuality of the timber and the nails and the blood. The water, yes; but not the blood. So by two great actions Jesus proved to be the Christ: at the deliberate and solemn inauguration of His public ministry; and when, pouring out his soul to death, he bore the sin of many in the fulfilment of prophetic scriptures (Isa. 53: 12).

7 f. The Holy **Spirit,** who descended like a dove upon Him, makes a third witness, completing the full number of witnesses which the law might require (Dt. 19: 15). Their testimony is in agreement: that Jesus is the Christ, the Son of God. The present tense may well be significant: **There are three witnesses,** still bearing their concurrent testimony to Jesus: the Spirit, whose gracious ministry in teaching, witnessing and helping is a known fact in the Church's life; and the water of Christian baptism and the blood of the communion cup—permanent memorials of the Lord's baptism and of His death. And it is undoubtedly true that the two sacraments have great evidential value. 'The fact that from apostolic days the Church has met to break the bread and drink the cup is a continuing testimony to the truth of Jesus' interpretation of the significance of his own death as a means of ratifying a new covenant between God and man. The eucharistic action, the fact that it has been performed numberless times by every generation of Christians since the first, is more impressive testimony than any documentary evidence: "as often as ye eat this bread and drink the cup, ye proclaim the Lord's death till he come"(1 C. 11: 26)' (A. Richardson: *An Introduction to the Theology of the NT*, 1958, p. 365).

Textual criticism has done a service in excising 5: 7 of the AV. The *Three Heavenly Witnesses* appear in no Gk. MS before the 15th century. The latter part of v. 6 was moved up by the Revisers to make the new v. 7.

9. We all **receive the testimony of men**—daily life could not go on otherwise—how much rather **the testimony of God**?—the historic testimony of the baptism and death of His Son with the attestation of His Spirit, and the continuing testimony of the Spirit and the sacraments in the Church.

10. Moreover, every believer has first-hand experience of this threefold testimony within himself: it is the Spirit who works within him faith, and enables him to make the good confession that Jesus is the Son of God; he has been baptized in the name of the Son of God; and the pledge of life eternal through His death is renewed within him as often as he takes the sacramental cup. To disbelieve the historic and continuing testimony is nothing short of blasphemy.

12. **He who has the Son** making His home within him (Jn 14: 23) **has life**; while **he who has not** is pointedly reminded that it is **the Son of God** whom he has refused to receive; he remains in fallen man's state of death (1 Jn 3: 14).

IX. EPILOGUE (5: 13–21)

The body of the Letter, written to enable Christians to **know** with assurance that they **have eternal life,** has been brought to a fitting conclusion in 5: 12. How then shall the Christian employ himself in his glad confidence?—by bringing his brothers into the same state. With this, and with a summing-up of the doctrinal results of the Letter, the brief epilogue concludes the Letter.

13 ff. Comparison of the purpose of the Letter as declared at its commencement (1: 3 f.) and at its conclusion (5: 13) shows that joyful fellowship with the Father and the Son and with the people of God is one and the same thing as the assurance of eternal life; this **confidence** brings childlike frankness and assurance in prayer.

16. What then is the will of God in accordance with which we are to pray? Nothing less than this, that men be brought into, and abide in, the fellowship of the divine life (Jn 1: 13; 1 Th. 4: 3; Jas 1: 18). **If** therefore **any one sees his brother committing . . . a . . . sin**—and it may well be that the reading of the Letter has sharpened the perception of sin in others as well as in oneself—**he will ask** by way of intercessory prayer (not an imperative: a Christian will spontaneously do this), **and God** [The word *God* is supplied by the translators instead of *he* to simplify a sentence which (in English) has three 3rd person pronouns in a row. The reader will however gather from the margin that it is also possible to consider the person who prays as being the one who gives life, in a secondary, instrumental sense; one engaged in such a ministry being indeed a life-giving agency in respect of his brother. John's colleague James ended his Letter on just the same note (Jas 5: 19 f.)] **will give him**—will grant to the intercessor in answer to his prayer—**life** for the brother concerned.

The difficult matter of **mortal sin** ('sin unto death') remains to be discussed. Under the Old Covenant, sin which was deliberate and presumptuous, knowing the Lord's will and of set purpose flouting that will and reviling the Lord, was **mortal**: no sacrifice would avail (Num. 16: 30). Similarly, in the NT, wilful rejection of the witness of God, and open-eyed apostasy from Christ, if persisted in, will carry the offender over the line beyond which repentance and therefore forgiveness is impossible (Mt. 12: 31 f.; Heb. 6: 4-6). The difficulty in this interpretation of the matter is how to reconcile it with the offender's being called a **brother.** In answer it may be pointed out that narrowly considered the 'brother's' sin in v. 16 is not mortal; however, the word 'brother' may be used as involving a judgment of charity in a case of doubt, as often it must. There is something to be said for the view of this matter which finds **mortal sin** illustrated in Ananias (Ac. 5), the immoral man of 1 C. 5: 1-5, and the 'many' of 1 C. 11: 30 who died under God's displeasure. These may all have been believers, whose 'spirit will be saved in the day of the Lord Jesus'; and it seems that even the gross offender of 1 C. 5 continued to be the object of the prayers of the congregation (2 C. 2: 5-11; but see pp. 418 f.).

Since in this Letter *life* is considered as fellowship with God and with His people, **mortal sin** may signify any such action as deliberately repudiates that fellowship. In some cases, such action would be apostasy, showing that the sinner never belonged to the Lord; in others it would be a serious act of rebellion on the part of a carnal Christian, removing him from the fellowship of the church and delivering him for the destruction of the flesh to Satan's power (1 C. 5: 5).

Even in desperate cases, prayer is not forbidden but neither is it enjoined; and there cannot be confident assurance that the request will be granted. Even in the case of 'non-mortal' sins, it is some quite serious matter which is in view; the offender is in no frame of mind to confess his own sin even though his **life**—his conscious fellowship with the Father and with his brethren —has been suspended.

The answer to such a prayer would be a conviction of his guilt sent upon the offender, and the consciousness of access to God for confession, resulting in restoration to the fellowship which is life indeed.

There are at least three situations for which the apostle's remarks about mortal sin provide in advance a possible answer. (*a*) 'Elder, why don't you restore those antichristian teachers (2: 19) by your prayers?' (*b*) 'I have prayed long and earnestly for So-and-so's restoration. Why is he not restored?' (*c*) 'Since a sinning brother can be reclaimed by prayer, I decided that I could safely venture upon a certain little excursion into sin that I had set my heart upon, knowing that my brethren could be counted upon to pray me back again.'

The godless chatter and contradictions of the self-styled gnostics, ever learning and never able to come to the knowledge of the truth (1 Tim. 6: 20; 2 Tim. 3: 7), are finally silenced by the concluding threefold shout of triumphant certitude, summing up not only the Letter, but in a sense the New Testament, of which it is the last major writing. It might be possible to regard the Three Certitudes as consisting of the gnostic false claims duly 'disinfected' and now returned to Christian use. The ideas in the gnostic watchwords (listed in the note on 2: 4) are explicitly present here, perhaps excepting 4: 20.

18. We are not only born by God's grace, but kept by Christ's power. **does not sin** denotes habit, without denying the exceptional occasion of committing a sin. In **He** (with capital) **who was born of God,** the translators give us considerable help at some cost of their professional principles: they make up our mind for us that Christ is meant and indicate this by a quite exceptional use of the capital letter (contrast 'him' and 'his' in v. 20). The sense of the verse turns upon whether **him** (RV, RSV) or 'himself' (AV, ASV) is to be read after **keeps,** the manuscript evidence being rather equally balanced. Law prefers the latter, and finds the sense, 'He that was begotten of God taketh heed to himself', but it leads him into supposing that the divine begetting might not necessarily be of continuing efficacy. The verse then means that Christians cannot live a sinful life, because God's Son guards God's children (Jn 17: 12, 15), and **the evil one** (Satan) does not lay hold of them. As in Jn 20: 17 **touch** does not convey the proper sense. Satan may indeed *touch* God's children, but cannot hold on to them.

19. Satan not only lays hold upon the **whole world;** it is wholly within his grasp. The world is still the world that crucified Christ, and we are decisively with Him in the fellowship of the life of God.

20. The Son of God has come (and that *to abide*—such is the force of the verb) **and has given us understanding**—spiritual intelligence and the capacity to receive divine knowledge are in the gift of the Spirit (Jn 14: 26; Col. 1: 9)—**to know him who is true**—the real and living God. Even more, **we are in him**—the real and living God, as branches in the Vine, being in Christ (Jn 15: 1; see Col. 3: 3; 1 Jn 4: 16 note).

20. This God (though it could mean *this Jesus*—one of John's ambiguities: see on 1: 6) **is the true** i.e. real and living **God . . . and** this is **eternal life:** To know Him and to be in Him, in the fellowship of the Father and the Son.

21. Little children, keep yourselves from the **idols**—from the gods constructed out of human speculation, the gods without life, the substitutes for the truth.

THE SECOND AND THIRD LETTERS OF JOHN

The First Letter has been thought of as an encyclical sent round a group of churches very much like, perhaps even identical with, the 'seven churches' of the Revelation (Rev. 1: 11). The Second and Third Letters, however, are true letters addressed to particular persons or groups. We have already noted the early opinion that the Letters were all written in Ephesus; the destination of the Second and Third would be somewhere (indeed anywhere, as far as the indications go) within the province of Asia, to which the aged apostle's labours were probably confined in his old age.

The Second and Third Letters are obviously a matched pair: (1) the writer calls himself 'The Elder', a usage confined entirely to these two letters; (2) the letters, of much the same length, conclude with the promise of a visit, prefaced by a remark about disinclination to rely upon mere letter-writing.

It is possible that, as is usually held, the two letters are simply examples of the apostle's pastoral correspondence, with no other connection between them; cf. Plummer's view that these last writings of the Apostle John were written respectively 'to a Christian lady and a Christian gentleman regarding their personal conduct' (CGT, p. 58). But the fact that they have been preserved together (or indeed at all) suggests that they are more closely related, and of more general interest, than Plummer's view indicates. We have also the interesting fact that toward the end of the second century, Irenaeus knew of only *two* letters of John. It is difficult to imagine how such slight-seeming works as these letters could have survived to gain universal recognition unless they were present in the Johannine corpus from the beginning—and that means together. A matched pair of letters could presumably be counted as one (thus making up Irenaeus's total of two letters) in the same way as in some psalters, Pss. 1 and 2, which are separate and contrasting compositions, are counted together as 'the first psalm' (Ac. 13: 33 in 'Western' MSS). If this line of reasoning is sound, we may expect to find a common purpose in the Letters. This commentary suggests a reconstruction of the situation in which the Letters were written: the reader will of course recognize the element of conjecture.

The reconstruction stands thus: In one of the Asian churches, an elder (Diotrephes) had become enamoured of the new gnostic teaching. [Note however Guthrie's sage comment (op. cit., p. 220): 'Gnostic tendencies might well have fostered such an exhibition of pride as is seen in his love of the pre-eminence, but Gnostics were not the only ones addicted to arrogance, and it is not necessary to appeal to heretical views to account for a failing which is all too often the accompaniment of orthodoxy'.] He had of course to reckon with strong conservative resistance from those who held to the original gospel, headed by the Apostle John himself in Ephesus. But our Diotrephes was an able man of forceful character, and succeeded, not only in dominating his fellow-elders to the

point that he became monarchical bishop with power to excommunicate his opponents, but even in throwing off the authority of the aged apostle.

John wished to appeal to the church in its peril, but the only constitutional approach left was Diotrephes himself. Would Diotrephes read the Apostle's letter to the church? At least the attempt could be made, and it might perhaps elicit a loyal response. But those were perilous times, and it would not be an unknown thing, in those days any more than ours, for a disaffected Christian to turn over an incriminating letter to the non-christian civil authorities, and to procure prosecution of the writer for provoking a disturbance. John would write, but he would avoid names and addresses: the church would be 'an elect lady', and he himself 'the Elder'—which to an uninformed reader might simply mean, in an affectionate sense, 'the Old Man'. And of course John kept a copy of the letter.

It fell out as expected, and the report was brought back that Diotrephes had suppressed the letter (or at least had denied its authority); but it was well to have made the attempt. Now John wrote to a trusted believer (Gaius) in that same church, censuring Diotrephes in terms which left no doubt as to his unsuitability as a church leader. At the same time Gaius, and with him Demetrius, is furnished with a testimonial of unreserved confidence. The Apostle hopes to visit the church, but in the meantime the church has a chance to set her own house in order. Let her take the hint, and throw off the domination of this unspiritual autocrat in favour of the joint administration of these two well-proved men. Failing this, the Apostle will be obliged on his visit to use the less satisfactory method of dealing with things by personal authority (cf. 1 C 4: 18-21), bringing Diotrephes to book and reorganizing the church. Below is a summary of the two Letters from this point of view, the matter in italics being what may be read 'between the lines'.

Summary: 2 John

1-3. John to the church at A.

4. I am happy to learn of the good state of doctrine and behaviour of some of your number, *but I am concerned about the remainder*.

5. With this situation in mind, here is my message for you: Remember the command of the Lord Jesus, that we love one another. *In the fellowship of love, the present danger of schism will be avoided*.

6. The fellowship will be preserved only if we hold by the original gospel as our rule of life.

7. I write in this way because of the danger to the fellowship from heretical teachers: they deny the fundamental truths of the gospel.

8 f. Beware of this danger from among your own selves; beware of anyone who leaves the original gospel to go in for this 'advanced' teaching, which is definitely antichristian.

10 f. Beware too lest this heresy come to you from outside; refuse church fellowship and any appearance of approval in such cases.

12. There is more to be said than I care to put down in black and white; I hope to visit you some time.

15. Greetings from the church here.

Summary: 3 John

1–8. To Gaius, *of the church* at *A.* I am happy to record my unreserved approval of you as a Christian leader, particularly in your care of the travelling preachers.

9–11. I wrote a short note to the church at A., *of which I attach a copy*, but Diotrephes will have none of it. He is an evil man, that Diotrephes, especially in the way he obstructs the travelling preachers whom you help so much; and he is no example to follow. If I come, I shall bring him before the church for discipline, *though it would be better for the church to deal with him now herself.*

12. I would have entire confidence in you and Demetrius *to succeed Diotrephes jointly in the leadership of the church, if the believers see fit.*

13–15. In the meantime this letter will suffice *to let you and the church know what I wish you to do. Let me find it done when* I visit you soon.

THE SECOND LETTER OF JOHN

1 f. The elder: The simple and solitary dignity of the last surviving apostle of Christ. The epithet is appropriate to the purpose of the Letters, dealing as they do with church leadership (cf. 1 Pet. 5: 1). **to the elect lady:** Better *to an elect lady:* there are many such. In ordinary address the significance would be *eminent* (Rom. 16: 13), but the Christian reader would understand it to mean that the **lady** is *chosen by God* (Eph. 1: 4 f.). For another example of personification of a church as an **elect lady** (also apparently for security reasons) see 1 Pet. 5: 13. (On the other view of the Letter *to the elect Kyria*, Kyria = 'Lady' being the Gk. equivalent of *Martha*.) The **children** are the members of the church (for use of an associated figure to denote constituent members, cf. 'bride' and 'guests', Rev. 19: 7, 9). **whom** is plural, denoting the lady and her children (as also the **you** etc. of vv. 6, 8, 10 and 12. The **you** of vv. 4, 5, and 13 is singular, indicating the lady alone). **truth** is used in three distinct senses in one sentence: paraphrase: **whom I love** (i) in sincerity, **and not only I but also all who know** (ii) the gospel, **because of the abiding presence of** (iii) Christ by the Spirit. **All who know the truth** love the local church (this statement could hardly be made of an individual lady). This whole address to the church is of surpassing beauty.

6. this is the commandment as you heard from the beginning, that you follow love: The last word is simply *it*, referring to either *love* or, more likely, *the commandment.*

Taking the latter, paraphrase 'Love is the commandment, just as you heard from the beginning, for you to make your rule of life' (see NEB).

7. who will not acknowledge the coming of Jesus Christ in the flesh: Perhaps better: 'who do not confess Jesus as Christ coming in the flesh'; cf. 1 Jn 4: 2. But for the latter ref. with the perfect participle (see note *ad loc.*) one might think that the new teachers were simply denying the historic Incarnation. But the contrasting use here of the present participle (which, as in English, has frequently future significance: *e.g.* the 'who is to come' of Rev. 1: 8) may suggest that the heretics were taking the logical next step in denying the personal return of the Lord Jesus at the end of the age. Both beliefs stand or fall together.

8. The mg reading, being harder, is more likely. Paraphrase: 'By failure on your part you will throw away the results of our labour among you; but by steadfastness you will reap its full harvest' (2 C. 12: 14 f.).

9. Any one who goes ahead: The 'advanced' teachers of v. 7, and probably Diotrephes of 3 Jn 9, contrasted with those who **abide** in the original gospel. **the doctrine of Christ:** The confession of 'Jesus as Christ coming in the flesh' (7).

10. into the house on our interpretation of 'the elect lady' will mean 'into church fellowship'. Commentators have been embarrassed by the apparent churlishness of this verse in forbidding the common courtesy of hospitality to heretics. *E.g.* Plummer: 'The greatest care will be necessary before we can venture to act upon the injunction here given to the Elect Lady' (*CGT*, p. 183). C. H. Dodd simply declines to heed the injunction. If however we understand church fellowship to be the matter in question, the difficulty disappears: the **greeting** will signify church approval or commendation. In any case, 1 C. 5: 11 is not a true parallel, as those in view there are not people with wrong beliefs (who *may* benefit from meeting people with right beliefs), but immoral men whose behaviour is in flagrant opposition to what they themselves acknowledge to be right.

11. work (lit., *works*): Better than AV 'deeds', as including doctrine, which was where the danger actually lay.

13. The **elect sister** is the church from which John wrote, presumably Ephesus. This verse forbids that interpretation of the Letter favoured by some early commentators, in which the *elect lady* is the universal Church.

THE THIRD LETTER OF JOHN

1. Gaius is already known to the church as **the beloved.** The apostle adds his own endorsement: **'I love** him also in sincerity'.

2. The graceful address is well rendered in RSV. The AV 'above all things', conveying the unfortunate impression that prosperity and good health are rated above everything else, is rightly contracted into **all,** and attached as subject to **may go well with you.** Supply 'just as' before **I know.**

4. than this: Prefer *than these* (i.e. these reports from the brethren), that you, as one of **my children** (in a pastoral relation: cf. 1 Tim. 1: 2; contrast Phm. 10) *walk in,* as daily habit, rather than **follow . . . the truth,** the gospel and commandment of the Lord Jesus.

5. especially to strangers: 'Yes and strangers at that': the more difficult and therefore more praiseworthy form of hospitality (Heb. 13: 2; Mt. 25: 35).

6. send them on their journey: 'Help on one's journey with food, money, by arranging for companions, means of travel, etc.' (*Arndt*); cf. Rom. 15: 24; 1 C. 16: 6, 11. **as befits God's service:** Even more—*worthily of God,* whose servants they are.

7. they have set out: Rather: *they went out,* leaving the reference applicable to their whole course of life as well as to that particular ministry . . . *for the sake of the Name:* this phrase of reverential awe (cf. the note at 1: 6 on *he*) should be preserved (Lev. 24: 11; Ac. 5: 41). The accepting of spontaneously proffered assistance from non-christians has good precedent (Ac. 28: 2, 7, 10), and we may tr. 'they went forth from the heathen taking nothing'. I.e., in becoming Christians, and more particularly preachers, they surrendered rights of ownership and of inheritance in their heathen families.

They might have insisted upon their rights, but for the sake of the Name they did not (Phil. 2: 5-11)—a renunciation still called for today in non-christian countries.

8. One of the ways in which the church fulfils her calling to spread **the truth** is by supporting such. This statement prepares the way for showing the failure of Diotrephes in a serious light.

9 f. something (depreciatory): Just a short note: a suitable description of 2 Jn.

10. The objection has been made that Gaius cannot have belonged to the same church as Diotrephes, otherwise he would not have needed to be told about the conduct of Diotrephes. The objection would be valid only if this were a purely private letter—but there are no purely private letters in the NT. The Letter is a formal indictment of Diotrephes as well as a testimonial for Gaius and Demetrius.

12. the truth itself: The Spirit speaking through believers, probably by way of prophecy (cf. Ac. 13: 2; 1 Tim. 1: 18). Demetrius is not, any more than Gaius, simply the apostle's nominee: his worth is independently and widely recognized. Commentators have regarded Demetrius as the bearer of the letter, or as a travelling preacher being commended to the hospitality of Gaius.

14. For the promise of a visit as a spur to immediate compliance, see Phm. 21 f. **soon:** This is now added to the half-promise of 2 Jn 12: a slight indication that 3 Jn is later than 2 Jn.

15. individually: This tr. disguises the echo of Jn 10: 5, where the Good Shepherd calls his own sheep *by name,* an example for undershepherds, and a good closing note for The Elder's pastoral correspondence.

BIBLIOGRAPHY

BROOKE, A. E., *The Johannine Epistles*. ICC [On the Greek Text] (Edinburgh, 1912).

DODD, C. H., *The Johannine Epistles*. MNT (London, 1946).

FINDLAY, G. G., *Fellowship in the Life Eternal* (London, 1909).

HOWARD, W. F., *Christianity according to St. John* (London, 1943).

LAW, R., *The Tests of Life* (London, 1909).

PLUMMER, A., *The Epistles of St. John*. CGT [On the Greek text] (Cambridge, 1886).

ROSS, A., *Commentary on the Epistles of James and John*. NIC (Grand Rapids, 1954).

STOTT, J. R. W., *The Epistles of John*. TNTC (London, 1964).

WESTCOTT, B. F., *The Epistles of John* [On the Greek text]. (London, 1892; reprinted, Abingdon, 1966).

V

THE LETTER OF JUDE

DAVID F. PAYNE

This Letter tells us nothing about the author, save that his name was Jude (Gk. 'Judas') and that he had a brother called James. It is quite possible that both men are otherwise completely unknown to us, but there is nothing inherently improbable in the widely held and traditional view that the writer was one of the sons of Joseph and Mary, mother of our Lord (cf. Mk 6: 3; Ac. 1: 14). His brother James became the recognized leader of the Jerusalem church.

Such verses as 3 and 17 give the impression that the Letter was written at least a generation after the earliest apostolic preaching. A date as late as A.D. 70-80 is generally acceptable— Jude, if a younger brother of Jesus, could well have lived till then. If, however, it is agreed that 2 Peter was written after this Letter (and if the genuine apostolic authorship of 2 Peter is allowed), then clearly Jude's letter must have been in existence at least two or three years before Peter's martyrdom (usually considered to have taken place in the persecution by Nero, A.D. 64). A date in the early sixties A.D. is not impossible; but the evidence for the date of Peter's death is slender, and if the apostle in fact lived into the following decade, the usual dating of Jude's letter need raise no problems. The free use Jude makes of non-canonical literature points on the whole to a first century date, since thereafter various heretical teachers began to produce apocryphal and subversive works, and the church leaders gradually came to feel themselves obliged to discard books which, however wholesome, did not have full authority as Scripture. Even

so, 1 Enoch retained its popularity into the third century.

If the writer was the son of Joseph and Mary, the Letter will probably have been written in Palestine; but the Letter itself gives no hint where it was penned. Nor does it mention by name the intended recipients of the letter; it is a truly 'general' letter, though no doubt sent to one particular church in the first place.

The purpose of the Letter was to counter certain heresies which were arising inside the churches. The false teachings were evidently of an antinomian character. Antinomianism was one manifestation of gnostic thought; men of this persuasion viewed all matter as evil, and everything of a spiritual nature as good. They therefore cultivated their own spiritual lives, while allowing their 'flesh' to do just as it liked, as if they had no responsibility for its misdeeds; with the result that they were guilty of blatant immorality of all kinds.

Most of this brief letter is strikingly similar to 2 Pet. 2: 1-3: 3, so much so that it is usually thought that one writer must have borrowed from the other. Probably Jude is the earlier Letter; but see the introduction to 2 Peter for further discussion.

There are possible allusions to the Letter of Jude in early second century writings, but the Muratorian Canon (late second century) gives the first mention of it by name. It was not accepted in all quarters till relatively late, no doubt because of its extreme brevity and its use of books from the OT pseudepigrapha.

ANALYSIS

I SALUTATION (1-2)

II THE DANGER (3-4)

III THE DANGEROUS MEN (5-16)

IV PRACTICAL ADVICE (17-23)

V DOXOLOGY (24-25)

I. SALUTATION (1-2)

Jude describes himself in a truly humble way, recognizing himself as **a servant** (literally, 'slave') **of Jesus Christ,** and as insignificant in comparison with his brother **James.** He does not name those to whom he wrote; he describes them as **called, beloved . . . and kept**—a reference to the Christian's past, present and future. His wish for them is that God's **mercy, peace, and love** may be theirs in increasing measure.

II. THE DANGER (3-4)

Jude relates his purpose in writing; **the faith** is in danger; by 'the faith' he means primarily the whole body of the truths of the Gospel. Paul outlines such a creed for us in 1 C. 15: 1-11. Faithful Christians must always defend these truths vigorously against dilution or perversion; **once for all** indicates that the Gospel truths are immutable—cf. Gal. 1: 6-9. The word **delivered** means 'handed down', and is used of traditions: the only immutable traditions Christians have are the truths of the Gospel. The chief enemies of the truth, from the earliest days of the church, were men who 'wormed their way in' (NEB), though inwardly opposed to the Gospel and all it implied, men destined (**designated**) for **condemnation,** not salvation. Such false brethren in Jude's time were characterized by **licentiousness;** Rom. 6: 1 describes the outlook of such pseudo-Christians. Jude regards such an antinomian attitude as equivalent to a denial of the Lord Jesus Christ. (It is uncertain whether **Master** here refers to God the Father or to the Son; but the Gk. construction seems to favour the latter.)

III. THE DANGEROUS MEN (5-16)

Jude knows his readers are **fully informed** of the stories recalled in vv. 5-7; he wants to **remind** them of the implications. The three groups named had all been at one time signally favoured; they had all been guilty of presumption, lack of faith, or gross immorality; and they had all paid a dreadful penalty. The first and third examples are biblical (cf. Num. 14; Gen. 19); but the second of them, that of the fallen **angels,** is drawn from non-canonical books such as 1 Enoch (chapters 6-10), although the basis of the apocryphal details may well have been Gen. 6: 1-4. Such apocryphal books were evidently well known and appreciated by Jude's readers, and so he could confidently appeal to them as well as to Scripture. Books of this sort might not be truly inspired nor authoritative, but their moral lessons in particular were wholesome and worth heeding. **6. Position** renders a Gk. word which usually means 'dominion' (cf. NEB); perhaps it includes both ideas in this context, i.e. position and status, and so 'domain' would be a convenient translation of the word. **7.** The **fire** which destroyed **Sodom and Gomorrah** Jude describes as **eternal.** It had permanent effects, to be sure; but probably the fires of hell (cf. Mk 9: 43) were in the writer's mind.

Jude's contemporary false brethren ignored such signal examples, and were equally guilty of sexual immorality and presumptuous behaviour against God's own authority and that of the angels of His appointment. **8.** The phrase **in their dreamings** may suggest that these men claimed that their actions were justified by certain visions they had received. Cf. Dt. 13: 1-5. With their arrogance Jude contrasts the behaviour of a very **archangel** when challenging Satan himself: **Michael** would not speak arrogantly even to **the devil.** The source of this allusion is no longer extant, but Origen (*De Princ.* iii. 2. 1) informs us that it was a work called *The Assumption of Moses;* the actual wording of the rebuke, however, derives ultimately from Zech. 3: 2.

10. Attention is again drawn to the licentious behaviour of the pseudo-Christians. Furthermore, they are typified by a general lack of spirituality (with **Cain**), by ungodly motives and avarice (like **Balaam**), and by rebellion against divine authority (like **Korah**). **Balaam's error,** too, points to immorality and false worship (cf. Num. 31: 16; Rev. 2: 14). Such men are certainly **blemishes,** perhaps dangerous 'reefs' (RSVmg); the former interpretation seems more natural, but either is possible, since the Gk. word *spilades* is ambiguous. The term **love feasts** denotes the fellowship meals of the early church, in the course of which the Lord's Supper was often celebrated (cf. 1 C. 11: 17-34); evidently these men had permeated to the very centre of Christian church fellowship, some of them probably gaining positions of leadership, for **looking after themselves** means literally 'shepherding themselves' (see NEB's paraphrase).

12-14. The striking metaphors that follow are largely self-explanatory. **Twice dead** probably means firstly dead in sins (cf. Eph. 2: 1), and after professing conversion, still dead to good works (cf. Jas 2: 17, 26). The final metaphor, **wandering stars,** is an allusion to the Book of Enoch, again (18: 12-16; 21: 1-6). Jude goes on (vv. 14 f.) to give a citation from 1 Enoch 1: 9. V. 14 may imply that Jude actually believed that the patriarch Enoch had himself written the book bearing his name; but this is not the only possibility. The phrase describing Enoch is not Jude's own, but is again drawn from the pseudepigrapha (cf. 1 Enoch 60: 8). It may be that Jude was simply arguing from grounds he knew to be acceptable to his readers or opponents. We might compare Paul's use of Gk. poetry when addressing an Athenian audience (Ac. 17: 28). At any rate, the general statements drawn from the Book of Enoch, and the inferences from them, are authenticated here and elsewhere in the NT. **16.** Jude sums up his description of the false brethren by stressing their three chief characteristics; his opponents were rebellious, licentious, and motivated by their own advantages.

IV. PRACTICAL ADVICE (17-23)

True Christians in such circumstances must be very careful, obviously; but they need not be alarmed, because the presence of evil men had been foreseen and foretold (cf. Mk 13: 5 f., 21-23; Ac. 20: 29 f.; 2 Th. 2: 3-12; v. 18 is probably Jude's epitome of the apostolic teaching on this point). False Christians are bound to create factions within a local church (cf. v. 19); vv. 20-23 show the true brethren what are their responsibilities in such adverse

circumstances. Note that those of wavering faith (v. 22) need kindness and help: some MSS read **convince,** others 'pity' (cf. NEB). But the true Christian must never be complacent nor instil complacency in such vital matters.

There are several textual problems in vv. 22 f.; the general sense is plain, however. The earlier mention of Sodom and Gomorrah may have reminded Jude of Am. 4: 11, of which the phrase **snatching them out of the fire** is reminiscent.

V. DOXOLOGY (24-25)

Jude reminds his readers of their bright hope and present help. The phrase **without blemish** may recall v. 12, although the Gk. words are not connected; it is in any case a metaphor from the OT sacrificial system (cf. Lev. 1: 3, etc.).

BIBLIOGRAPHY

JONES, R. B., *The Epistles of James, John and Jude* (Grand Rapids, 1962).

KELLY, W., *Lectures on the Epistles of Jude* (London, 1912).

WOLFF, R., *A Commentary on the Epistle of Jude* (Grand Rapids, 1960).

See also the books listed at the end of the commentary on 2 Peter.

THE REVELATION TO JOHN

F. F. BRUCE

Origin, Character and Purpose

The Book of the Revelation—or, as it might well be called, the book of the triumph of Christ —was composed and sent to seven churches in the Roman province of Asia at some point between A.D. 69 and 96 to encourage them, and their fellow-Christians everywhere, with the assurance that, despite all the forces marshalled against them, victory was theirs if they remained loyal to Christ.

Whereas before A.D. 60 an apostle like Paul could count on the benevolent neutrality, if not the positive protection, of the imperial power in his evangelization of the Roman provinces, the relation between the empire and the church changed radically in the 60's, and for two and a half centuries thereafter Christianity had no right to exist in the eyes of Roman law. So long as Roman law regarded Christianity as a variety of Judaism, Christianity profited by the status which Judaism enjoyed as a permitted cult (*religio licita*); but when the distinction between the two became plain to the imperial authorities Christianity was left destitute of any legal protection. Nero's attack on the Christians of Rome in A.D. 64 may have been due to personal motives of malice and self-protection (against the popular rumours which blamed him for setting the city on fire); but later emperors maintained a more official hostility against a movement which was suspected of being subversive and anti-social in tendency and a revolutionary ferment within the body politic.

Various reactions to this change of policy on the part of the empire may be recognized in the New Testament. Luke endeavours to refute popular prejudice by writing an orderly account of the rise and progress of Christianity, dedicated to a member of the official class in Rome. Peter urges his readers to live in such a way as to 'put to silence the ignorance•of foolish men' and, if called upon to suffer as Christians, to glorify God under that name (1 Pet. 2: 15; 4: 16). The author of Revelation reminds his hard-pressed readers that, long drawn out as the campaign may be in which they are engaged, the decisive battle has already been won, and final victory is therefore assured. Their only means of resisting the assaults of their enemies is by faithful con-

fession, suffering and, if need be, death. But this is only reasonable, for it was precisely thus that their Leader won the decisive battle. Jesus, not Caesar, is the one to whom all power has been given; Jesus, not Caesar, is Lord of history; and in His sovereignty and triumph His faithful followers share already in anticipation and will share fully at His parousia.

The symbolism in which this message of hope was conveyed to Christians whose cause, by all outward reckoning, was doomed to annihilation, was easier for them to understand than it is for us. Apocalyptic was a familiar literary form to Jews and Christians in the first century A.D., however foreign it may be to readers in the twentieth. Much of it goes back to Old Testament imagery (*e.g.* the plagues of Egypt in Exodus and the visions of Ezekiel and Daniel); even if occasionally we seem to have lost the key altogether, the main outlines of the message are clear enough.

Earlier apocalyptic passages in the New Testament throw some light on Revelation— especially Mk 13 and its Synoptic parallels and 2 Th. 2: 1-12—although they lack the exuberant imagery of the seer of Patmos.

The framework of Revelation is provided largely by successive heptads (series of seven). Some commentators have seen further heptads in the book, where the number seven does not expressly appear; but their findings have not commanded general agreement. Apart from the letters to the seven churches (2: 1-3: 22), the principal heptads are the three judgment-series, the seals (6: 1-8: 5), the trumpets (8: 6-11: 19) and the bowls containing the seven last plagues (15: 1-16: 21). These heptads are parallel to some extent, the trumpets and the bowls especially so. But all of them are marked by what A. M. Farrer calls 'cancelled conclusions'; the final and irrevocable judgment, which we expect to be executed in the last member of each heptad, is regularly deferred—in confirmation of the Bible's uniform witness to God's reluctance to press His 'strange work' to a full end.

The main division of the book falls between chapters 11 and 12. The seventh trumpet announces the time for final judgment and reward; then in a series of tableaux (12: 1-20: 15) the main themes of the visions of 4: 1-11: 19 are presented afresh. In the visions of 4: 1-11: 19 and in some of the following tableaux, the seer views things on earth from the vantage-point of heaven, to which he is caught up in ecstasy in 4: 1. Here he enjoys the privilege which Christian enjoyed in the Interpreter's House, when he was led about 'to the back side of the wall, where he saw a man with a vessel of oil in his hand, of the which he did also continually cast, but secretly, into the fire'—so that it burned 'higher and hotter' for all the endeavours of the man in front of it to quench it by pouring water on it.

The seer's name was John (1: 4, 9; 22: 8); he received his visions in the Aegean island of Patmos, to which he had presumably been exiled in the course of repressive action by the authorities against the Christians in the province of Asia. His identity with any other John of the New Testament cannot be proved; as early as Justin Martyr (died A.D. 165) he was identified with the apostle of that name. Revelation certainly comes from the same environment as the other Johannine writings. Whatever differences there are between this book and the Fourth Gospel, both present one who is called 'The Word of God' and 'The Lamb of God' saying to His followers, 'In the world you have tribulation; but be of good cheer, I have overcome the world' (Jn 16: 33); whatever differences there are between it and the First Letter of John, both encourage the people of Christ with the assurance: 'This is the victory that overcomes the world, our faith' (1 Jn 5: 4).

Revelation in the Church

In Asia Minor Rev. was accepted from the outset, so far as we can tell, as a work possessing divine authority. In Rome and the west it was also acknowledged from an early date. There are possible echoes of it in the *Shepherd of Hermas* and the *Epistle of Barnabas* (c. A.D. 100). Papias, bishop of Phrygian Hierapolis (c. A.D. 130), evidently knew and used it. Unfortunately Papias's references to it are lost, with the bulk of his *Exposition of the Dominical Oracles;* but Eusebius ascribes to him a statement about the millennium almost certainly based on Rev. 20: 1-6; Andreas of Caesarea (6th cent.) says that he bore witness to the credibility of the book; and there is reason to believe that Victorinus of Pettau (d. 303), the earliest Latin commentator on Rev., drew upon Papias. Papias interpreted the millennium of Rev. 20 as a golden age on earth, and embellished his description of it with features drawn from Jewish sources.

Fragments of exposition of Rev. appear in Justin Martyr (d. 165) and Irenaeus (c. 180);

Melito of Sardis (c. 170) and Hippolytus of Rome (c. 200) wrote complete commentaries on it. It is listed in the Muratorian Canon, a Roman catalogue of NT books (c. 190). The Montanists, who arose in Phrygia c. 150, and combined adventist and pentecostal fervour, attached high value to Rev.; by way of reaction to them the Alogoi, and more particularly Gaius of Rome (c. 200), rejected it and ascribed its authorship to the heresiarch Cerinthus. Hippolytus replied to this aberration of criticism with his *Chapters against Gaius and Defence of John's Apocalypse.* Apart from Gaius and the Alogoi, and of course Marcion and his followers, the authority of Rev. was not seriously questioned in the west.

At Alexandria Dionysius (c. 260) denied its apostolic authorship on grounds of style and language, in a reply which he wrote to another Egyptian bishop, Nepos, who had interpreted the visions of the book (especially the millennium) in a judaizing sense—perhaps following Papias. The allegorizing methods of the school of Alexandria gradually displaced the eschatological interpretation of Rev., although the latter is still maintained in the commentary of Victorinus of Pettau. The Donatist Tyconius (c. 390), who adopted these allegorizing methods, treated the millennium as the interval between the first and second advents of Christ. His interpretation was taken over by Jerome and Augustine, and became normative in the church for the next eight centuries.

Eusebius of Caesarea (c. 325) followed the lines laid down by Dionysius of Alexandria. He includes Rev. among the books generally acknowledged by the churches of his day, but makes no secret of his own antipathy to it and his personal inclination to class it among the 'spurious' works. His example no doubt influenced the churches of the east against the canonical recognition of the book. While Athanasius of Alexandria in 367 included it in his list of canonical works, it is omitted from the lists drawn up by Cyril of Jerusalem (d. 386), Gregory of Nazianzus (d. 389), the Synod of Laodicea (360) and the *Apostolic Constitutions* (c. 380). Indeed, Amphilochius of Iconium (d. 394) says that most (in Asia Minor and Syria, presumably) regarded it as spurious. The school of Antioch, too, largely ignored it in this period, and it was not included in the Syriac Bible until 508. The Armenians do not appear to have accepted it until the 12th century. By that time its canonicity was universally acknowledged except among the Nestorians, who have never accepted it.

A revival of the eschatological interpretation

of Rev. set in around 1200, especially with Joachim of Floris, under whose influence many in Europe of the 13th and 14th centuries looked eagerly for the new age which would deliver them from the evils which they saw to be rampant in church and state. It is to this period that we can trace the identification of the Papacy with Antichrist, an identification which later commended itself to Luther and other Reformation leaders. Luther was one of the first to interpret Rev., from ch. 4 onwards, as a prophetic survey of church history. Calvin did not write a commentary on Rev. as he did on all the other NT books—perhaps because the grammatico-historical study which he would have produced would have been out of step with prevalent trends.

But a partial return to the exegesis of Hippolytus and Victorinus, an exegesis partly contemporary-historical and partly eschatological, appears in the sixteenth century in the works of the Reformer Theodor Bibliander and of the Jesuits Francisco Ribera and Luis de Alcazar. In many respects they differed one from another: Bibliander maintained the identification of the Papacy with Antichrist, which the Jesuits did not; Ribera's interpretation was predominantly eschatological (in a futurist sense) while Alcazar's was predominantly contemporary-historical (preterist). They also retained elements of the church-historical method in accordance with their varying points of view. Hugo Grotius (1583-1645) followed them, with two important departures of his own: he was the first Reformed exegete to give up the identification of the Papacy with Antichrist, and he held that some of the visions of Rev. reflect the period before, and others the period after, the fall of Jerusalem in A.D. 70. He may thus be regarded as the pioneer of the literary-critical approach to the book.

No important contribution to the exegesis of Rev. was made by those who concentrated on its numerics—whether J. A. Bengel in Germany or Joseph Mede, Sir Isaac Newton and William Whiston in England—eminent as these exegetes were in other fields of study. The book itself has suffered in its reputation from the extravagances of some of its interpreters, who have treated it as if it were a table of mathematical conundrums or a divinely inspired *Old Moore's Almanack*. Extravagant interpretations of Rev. have been stimulated especially by times of international tension and war, such as the French Revolution and Napoleonic Wars (1789-1815) or the two world conflicts of this century. But the book has always spoken its message most clearly to readers who were involved in the same kind of situation as those to whom it was first addressed.

Throughout the age of persecution at the hands of imperial Rome, for well over 200 years after its publication, Rev. spoke its central message unambiguously to the majority of Christians, even if they were rather vague about some of the symbolism. The identity of the beast from the abyss was not in doubt, nor was there any doubt about the victory which awaited those who were faithful unto death. With the peace of the church in the early 4th century this clear insight into the message of the book was inevitably obscured. But it has returned in other persecuting ages.

In more comfortable times Rev. may be degraded to the unworthy status of a book of puzzles, a battleground for conflicting schools of interpretation, or it may be briefly dismissed as a putrid backwater, cut off from the main stream of Christian faith and life. But 'when tribulation or persecution arises on account of the word', the book becomes once more what it really is, a living word from God, full of encouragement and strength to those who find that 'all who desire to live a godly life in Christ Jesus will be persecuted'. Christians in our own day who have to suffer for 'the word of God and the testimony of Jesus' under régimes which set themselves 'against the LORD and his anointed' have no difficulty in identifying Antichrist or in finding themselves in the company of those who 'come out of the great tribulation'. Above all, this book reminds them that He with whom and for whom they endure these things is the triumphant Lord of history, and that His victory is theirs.

ANALYSIS

Prologue (1: 1-8)

First Division: Visions of Conflict and Triumph (1: 9–11: 19)

I   THE INAUGURAL VISION (1: 9-20)

II   THE LETTERS TO THE SEVEN CHURCHES (2: 1-3: 22)
    i The Letter to Ephesus (2: 1-7)
    ii The Letter to Smyrna (2: 8-11)
    iii The Letter to Pergamum (2: 12-17)
    iv The Letter to Thyatira (2: 18-29)
    v The Letter to Sardis (3: 1-6)
    vi The Letter to Philadelphia (3: 7-13)
    vii The Letter to Laodicea (3: 14-22)

III   A VISION OF HEAVEN (4: 1-5: 14)
    i The Throne-room of God (4: 1-11)
    ii 'Worthy is the Lamb' (5: 1-14)

IV   THE BREAKING OF THE SEVEN SEALS (6: 1-8: 5)
    i-iv First Four Seals: The Four Horsemen (6: 1-8)
    v Fifth Seal: The Cry of the Martyrs (6: 9-11)
    vi Sixth Seal: Day of Wrath (6: 12-17)
    Interlude before the Seventh Seal (7: 1-17)
      a) The Sealing of the Servants of God (7: 1-8)
      b) The Triumph of the Martyrs (7: 9-17)
    vii Seventh Seal: Preparation for the Trumpets (8: 1-5)

V   THE BLOWING OF THE SEVEN TRUMPETS (8: 6-11: 19)
    i-iv First Four Trumpets (8: 6-12)
    The Three 'Woes' (8: 13)
    v Fifth Trumpet (9: 1-12)
    vi Sixth Trumpet (9: 13-21)
    Interlude before the Seventh Trumpet (10: 1-11: 14)
      a) The Angel with the Little Scroll (10: 1-11)
      b) The Two Witnesses (11: 1-14)
    vii Seventh Trumpet (11: 15-19)

Second Division: Tableaux of Conflict and Triumph (12: 1–22: 5)

I   THE WOMAN, THE CHILD AND THE DRAGON (12: 1-17)
    i The Birth of the Child (12: 1-6)
    ii The Downfall of the Dragon (12: 7-12)
    iii The Assault on the Woman and her other Children (12: 13-17)

II   THE TWO BEASTS (13: 1-18)
    i The Beast from the Sea (13: 1-10)
    ii The Beast from the Earth (13: 11-18)

III   FIRST FRUITS, HARVEST AND VINTAGE (14: 1-20)
    i First Fruits (14: 1-5)
    ii Angel Proclamations (14: 6-13)
      a) An Eternal Gospel (14: 6-7)
      b) The Fall of Babylon (14: 8)
      c) The Doom of Apostates (14: 9-11)
      d) The Bliss of the Faithful Departed (14: 12-13)
    iii Harvest (14: 14-16)
    iv Vintage (14: 17-20)

IV THE SEVEN LAST PLAGUES (15: 1-16: 21)

    i Introduction of the Seven Angels and Victory Song of the Redeemed (15: 1-8)

    ii The Outpouring of the Seven Plagues (16: 1-21)

V BABYLON THE GREAT (17: 1-19: 5)

    i The Scarlet Woman (17: 1-18)

    ii Dirge over Babylon (18: 1-24)

    iii Exultation over Babylon (19: 1-5)

VI THE MARRIAGE OF THE LAMB (19: 6-10)

VII THE HOLY WAR (19: 11-21)

VIII THE BINDING OF SATAN AND REIGN OF THE MARTYRS (20: 1-6)

IX GOG AND MAGOG (20: 7-10)

X THE LAST ASSIZE (20: 11-15)

XI THE NEW HEAVEN AND NEW EARTH (21: 1-8)

XII THE NEW JERUSALEM (21: 9-22: 5)

Epilogue (22: 6-21)

    i Attestation by the Angel (22: 6-7)

    ii Attestation by John (22: 8-11)

    iii Attestation by Jesus (22: 12-16)

    iv Invocation, Invitation and Response (22: 17-20)

    v Benediction (22: 21)

Prologue (1: 1-8)

i. Preamble (1: 1-3)

1. The revelation of Jesus Christ, which God gave him: The Greek word here translated 'revelation'—*apokalypsis*—has given its name to this whole genre of literature, called 'apocalyptic'. The common feature of apocalyptic literature is an unfolding of matters generally unknown, such as the heavenly regions or the events of the future, by someone who has been granted a special revelation of these things by God, either directly or through an intermediary, such as an interpreting angel. The most outstanding example of this literature, apart from the present book, is the OT book of Daniel. But this work is unique in that the revelation is communicated by God, not to any mortal man but to Jesus Christ, risen from the dead and exalted in glory. In many apocalypses the revelation is contained in a heavenly book—the scroll of destiny already written on high, or, as it is called in Dan. 10: 21, *the book of truth*. That this is true of the present revelation is made plain in 5: 1 ff., where Jesus takes the book or scroll from the right hand of God. **to show to his servants what must**

soon take place: The subject-matter of this revelation comprises the events of the future—the near future. The argument that Gk. *en tachei* implies that the events will not take place 'soon', but will be completed speedily once they begin, cannot be sustained; it is not what the original readers of the work would have naturally understood. **he made it known by sending his angel to his servant John:** The interpreting angel appears from time to time in the book (cf. 17: 1, 7; 19: 9 f.; 21: 9 ff.; 22: 6 ff., 16), but much of the revelation recorded takes the form of visions seen by John. **2. who bore witness:** A solemn affirmation of the reliability of John's record of all that he saw. **to the word of God and to the testimony of Jesus Christ:** Here these words sum up the subject-matter of the revelation; they recur with a somewhat different force in verse 9. **3. Blessed is he who reads aloud the words of the prophecy, and blessed are those who hear, and who keep what is written therein:** This double beatitude conveys a direction that the book should be read publicly at church meetings—primarily, but not exclusively, in the seven Asian churches named below—and that its contents should receive careful

v*

attention from the hearers and exercise a decisive influence on their way of life. **the time is near:** Reinforcing the 'soon' of verse 1.

ii. Greetings and Doxology (1: 4-7)

4. John to the seven churches that are in Asia: This apocalypse is not pseudonymous. Who this 'John' was we cannot be sure; he was self-evidently a prophet (cf. 19: 10; 22: 9) and gives his credentials in verse 9. He does not claim to be an apostle; Justin Martyr, towards the middle of the 2nd century, makes this claim for him (*Dialogue with Trypho*, 81), and it may well be right. The 'seven churches' are identified in verse 11. The province of Asia was evangelized during Paul's Ephesian ministry, A.D. 52-55 (Ac. 19: 10), and all seven of John's churches may have been founded then. While the reasons for selecting these seven are the local conditions described in the seven letters (2: 1-3: 22), the symbolic use of the number seven throughout the book suggests a symbolic significance here; while the messages are primarily for the seven churches named, they are relevant also to the churches everywhere. **Grace to you and peace:** A common epistolary greeting in the NT combining Greek and Hebrew salutations. The terms which follow are trinitarian in substance, though not in form. **from him who is and who was and who is to come:** That is, the Eternal One; the designation is used by John as an indeclinable nominative, in whatever construction it may be found. We may regard it as John's rendering of the ineffable name Yahweh, or of the fuller expression in Exod. 3: 14, *I am who I am.* **from the seven spirits who are before his throne:** Formally this expression (cf. 4: 5; 5: 6) resembles 'the seven angels who stand before God' (8: 2), but actually it denotes the Holy Spirit in the plenitude of His grace and power. At an early stage in the exegesis of this book the expression was associated with the seven designations of the Spirit of the LORD in Isa. 11: 2, LXX: *the spirit of wisdom and understanding, the spirit of counsel and might, the spirit of knowledge and godliness, the spirit of the fear of God* (so Victorinus of Pettau *ad loc.*). Cf. the lines in the *Veni Creator:*

> Thou the anointing Spirit art
> Who dost thy sevenfold gifts impart.

'Before his throne' or 'before the throne' occurs repeatedly in Rev. as an expression for the presence of God in His heavenly temple (cf. 4: 5 f., 10; 7: 9, etc.). **5. and from Jesus Christ the faithful witness:** This collocation of Christ with the Eternal One and the sevenfold Spirit is noteworthy, and consistent with the portrayal of Him throughout the book. In a day when so many of His people, like John himself, were suffering because of 'the testimony of Jesus' (1:

9; cf. 12: 11), it would encourage their fidelity to be reminded that Jesus Christ was 'the faithful witness' *par excellence.* The same expression is used of Antipas (2: 13). **the first-born of the dead, and the ruler of kings on earth:** An echo of Ps. 89: 27, where God appoints David (and, by implication, the son of David) *the firstborn, the highest of the kings of the earth.* Here the title 'the first-born' is related to Christ's status in resurrection, as in Col. 1: 18 (cf. 1 C. 15: 20; also Rom. 8: 29). The 'crown rights of the Redeemer' on earth are twofold: He who is 'the head over all things for the church, which is his body' (Eph. 1: 22 f.), is also 'the ruler of kings on earth'; it was good that John's readers should be reminded that their Lord, for whose sake they were persecuted, was also Lord over Caesar, their persecutor, even if Caesar did not acknowledge Him. **To him who loves us and has freed us from our sins by his blood:** The reading 'freed' (Gk. *lysanti*) is better attested than the later 'washed' (Gk. *lousanti*). 'Washing in blood' is not a biblical image (7: 14 is an exception, but there it is robes that are washed). **6. and made us a kingdom, priests to his God and Father:** Israel in the wilderness, after the experience of redemption from Egypt, was called to be a *kingdom of priests* to God (Exod. 19: 6; the construction **a kingdom, priests** in our present passage is apparently a literal reproduction of the Hebrew phrase there). (Cf. Isa. 61: 6, where they are called *the priests of the Lord* after a later redemption.) So the NT people of God, having been freed from their sins, are similarly designated 'a kingdom and priests' (cf. 5: 10; 20: 6; 22: 5; also 1 Pet. 2: 9). The incorporating of these words in a doxology without explanation suggests that the royal priesthood of Christians was already a thoroughly familiar concept. Those who shared their Priest-King's suffering were called to share His intercession and sovereignty (cf. verse 9, also Lk. 22: 28-30; Rom. 8: 17; 2 Tim. 2: 12). **7. Behold, he is coming with the clouds:** The clouds, associated with a theophany or symbolizing the divine presence, are derived from Dan. 7: 13, where *one like a son of man* (cf. verse 13 below; also 14: 14) comes *with the clouds of heaven* (cf. Mk 13: 26; 14: 62 and parallels; 1 Th. 4: 17). **every eye will see him, every one who pierced him:** Cf. 'then they will see . . .' in Mk. 13: 26 and parallels, and 'you will see . . .' in Mt. 26: 64 || Mk 14: 62; but more particularly the language echoes Zech. 12: 10, applied to Christ in Jn 19: 37, *they shall look on him whom they have pierced.* **and all tribes of the earth will wail on account of him:** In Zech. 12: 10 ff. all the families of Israel mourn over the pierced one, but here (as in Mt. 24: 30) all the families of mankind mourn. The annually repeated lamentation *for Hadad-rimmon in the plain of Megiddo* (to which the OT prophet compares the mourning over the pierced one), never finished and always fruitless, has now been swallowed up by penitent tears for a victim pierced once for all, never to be struck again.

iii. The Divine Authentication (1: 8)

8. I am the Alpha and the Omega (cf. 21: 6): That is, the beginning and the end, or the first and the last, 'alpha' and 'omega' being the first and the last of the 24 letters of the Greek alphabet. This assertion by the Eternal God of His names and titles, authenticating the following revelation as His, is the more striking in view of the freedom with which in the sequel the same titles are applied to Christ (cf. verse 17; 22: 13). In this title there may also be a suggestion of the principle that 'the end shall be as the beginning', which is amply illustrated in Rev. (cf. *e.g.*, 2: 7; 22: 1-4 with Gen. 2: 8 ff.). **the Almighty:** Of the 10 NT occurrences of this divine title (Gk. *pantokratōr*), 9 are in Rev. (the remaining one is in 2 C. 6: 18). In LXX it usually represents Heb. *tseba'oth* in the title *Yahweh ('elohe) tseba'oth,* 'LORD (God) of hosts', except in Job, where it represents *Shaddai.*

First Division: Visions of Conflict and Triumph (1: 9-11: 19)

I. THE INAUGURAL VISION (1: 9-20)

9. I John, your brother: Whether he had apostolic status or not, he lays no claim to it here, but puts himself on a level with his readers. **who share with you in Jesus the tribulation and the kingdom and the patient endurance:** The placing of 'kingdom' between 'tribulation' and 'patient endurance' is eloquent of the firmness of Christian hope (see on verse 6 above), and also of the general NT insistence that 'through many tribulations we must enter the kingdom of God' (Ac. 14: 22; cf. 6 above). **the island called Patmos:** A small island in the Aegean Sea, some 37 miles W.S.W. of Miletus. **on account of the word of God and the testimony of Jesus:** This could mean that he had gone to Patmos to receive the revelation (cf. verse 2), or to preach the gospel, but its traditional, and much more probable, meaning is that he had been banished to Patmos because of his Christian witness—to hard labour in the quarries on the island, according to Victorinus of Pettau (d. 303). Eusebius (*HE* iii. 20. 9) states, on the authority of 'the account given by men of old among us', that he was released from his banishment under Nerva (emperor A.D. 96-98) and took up his abode in Ephesus.

10. I was in the Spirit: Literally 'I became in spirit', i.e. was caught up in prophetic ecstasy—the same experience as Ezekiel describes by saying *the hand of the Lord was upon me* (Ezek. 3: 22, etc.). **on the Lord's day:** On the *kyriakē hēmera,* i.e. the day belonging to the Lord (Latinized as *dies dominica,* whence it has passed into the romance languages). This name was appropriately given to the first day of the week as the day of Christ's triumph, when he was 'designated Son of God in power . . . by his resurrection from the dead' (Rom. 1: 4). The expression is also reminiscent of the OT 'day of the LORD'—the day of Yahweh's vindication of His cause and victory over all opposing forces; the day of Christ's resurrection (and the first day of every week on which it is commemorated) may properly be called 'the day of the Lord'. It was the 'D-day'—the decisive action—which guarantees the future 'V-day', the celebration of final victory. And the supper of the Lord, specially associated with the first day of the week (so much so that it is denoted by the same adjective *kyriakos,* 1 C. 11: 20), brings together and actualizes the past and future day of the Lord. **a loud voice like a trumpet:** A fitting prelude to the appearance of the exalted conqueror (cf. Ps. 47: 5). It is not the Son of man's own voice that is so described; His voice 'was like the sound of many waters' (verse 15). **11. Write what you see in a book:** Probably indicating a roll of papyrus. **send it to the seven churches:** The order in which the seven cities are named is that in which a messenger would visit them one by one, starting at Ephesus, going north via Smyrna to Pergamum, and then turning in a south-easterly direction to visit Thyatira, Sardis, Philadelphia and Laodicea. **12. seven golden lampstands:** As verse 20 shows, these symbolize the seven churches mentioned. There is a deliberate departure here from the more familiar figure of the seven-branched lampstand of Israel's sanctuary, in order to emphasize the separate responsibility of each local church to bear its own witness to its Lord. The lamp is a natural symbol of witness-bearing (cf. Jn 5: 35; Phil. 2: 15 f.). **13. in the midst of the lampstands one like a son of man:** The separateness of the lampstands is emphasized by the fact that the Lord is seen walking among them (cf. 2: 1). The expression *one like a son of man* is based on Dan. 7: 13, where it means 'one like a human being' (cf. Dan. 8: 15; 10: 18; Ezek. 1: 26) in contrast to the wild beasts seen by Daniel earlier in his vision. To Dan. 7: 13 also our Lord's use of the title 'the Son of man' is to be traced. Here the 'one like a son of man' is plainly identified with the risen and glorified Jesus,

clothed with a long robe and with a golden girdle round his breast: In other words, He wears the full-length high-priestly robe for which the same Greek word *podērēs* (lit. 'reaching to the feet') is used in the LXX of Exod. 28: 4; 29: 5, together with the sash or 'girdle' for which Greek *zōnē*, as here, is used in the LXX of Exod. 28: 4, 39. Here the sash is of gold, as befits a royal priest. In these introductory verses of Rev., then, Jesus is portrayed in His threefold office as prophet, king and priest— as the recipient of God's revelation (verse 1), as 'ruler of kings on earth' (verse 5) and as the wearer of the high-priestly vestments (verse 13). **14. his head and his hair were white as white wool, white as snow:** This is also reminiscent of Dan. 7, but there it is the Ancient of Days that is so described (verse 9) while here it is the risen Christ. This wholesale transference of the divine attributes to Jesus is characteristic of Rev., but by no means peculiar to it in the NT; it attests the spontaneous recognition by the church of apostolic days of the deity of Jesus. It may be a relevant point that the older Gk. version of Dan. 7: 13 says that the *one like a son of man* came *as the Ancient of Days;* this in turn may throw light on the prompt conviction of blasphemy which followed Jesus' application of the language of Dan. 7: 13 to Himself in reply to the high priest's question at His trial (Mk 14: 61–64). **his eyes were like a flame of fire:** Like the celestial visitant of Dan. 10: 6, whose eyes were 'like flaming torches'. The figure recurs in a similar context in 19: 12. **15. his feet were like burnished bronze:** Better: 'his legs' (so *podes* is rightly translated in 10: 1); cf. Dan. 10: 6, *his arms and legs like the gleam of burnished bronze* (see also Ezek. 1: 7). **his voice was like the sound of many waters:** This figure, suggesting the sound of a rushing torrent after heavy rain, recurs in 14: 2 and 19: 6, of the voice of the heavenly host. In Ezek. 43: 2 the sound of the coming of the glory of the Lord is so described. **16. in his right hand he held seven stars:** Without an interpretation one would naturally think of the seven planets known to the ancients (cf. Philo's and Josephus's explanation of the seven-branched lampstand); to hold them in one's hand was a symbol of dominion over heaven and earth. In the light of the whole tendency of Rev. this general interpretation is apt in the present context, for universal sovereignty certainly belongs to Christ; but the stars are given a special interpretation in verse 20. **from his mouth issued a sharp two-edged sword:** Cf. 19: 15. The sword is the word of God (cf. Heb. 4: 12; also Eph. 6: 17); for its proceeding from the mouth of the Son of man cf. Isa. 11: 4, where the Messiah *shall smite the*

earth with the rod of his mouth, and with the breath of his lips he shall slay the wicked. The sword in the NT application is the gospel, which proclaims grace to those who repent and put their faith in God, with the corollary of judgment on the impenitent and disobedient (cf. Jn 3: 36). **his face was like the sun shining in full strength:** So, on the mount of transfiguration, 'his face shone like the sun' (Mt. 17: 2). **17. When I saw him, I fell at his feet as though dead:** A vision of divine glory can be conveyed, if at all, only in symbolism. That the language of John's vision of Christ in glory is symbolical is clear enough, especially in the detail of the sword proceeding from His mouth. A notable OT parallel is the vision of God in Ezek. 1: 4 ff. John, like Ezekiel, falls on his face before the glory, and like Ezekiel is raised to his feet. It is the man who has fallen prostrate before God and been raised to his feet by God who can henceforth look the whole world in the face as the fearless spokesman of God. Cf. Dan. 8: 17; 10: 9, 15; and the three disciples on the mount of transfiguration (Mt. 17: 6). **he laid his right hand upon me:** Cf. Dan. 8: 18; 10: 10, 18. **Fear not:** Another echo from Matthew's transfiguration narrative (Mt. 17: 7). Cf. also Lk. 2: 10; Mt. 28: 5; Ac. 18: 9; 27: 24. **I am the first and the last:** Cf. 2: 8; 22: 13. The titles of the God of Israel (cf. verse 8) are also borne by Christ, who in exaltation has received from God 'the name which is above every name' (Phil. 2: 9). *I am the first and I am the last; besides me there is no god,* says Yahweh in Isa. 44: 6 (cf. 41: 4; 48: 12); but there is no title which He does not now freely share with His crucified and glorified Son. **18. and the living one; I died, and behold, I am alive for evermore:** The RSV punctuation, which (following RV) attaches 'the living one' closely to the preceding words, is inferior to that of AV which attaches the phrase, in accordance with the natural sense, to what follows. Render with NEB: 'and I am the living one; for I was dead and now I am alive for evermore'. As the one who conquered death in death's own realm He is pre-eminently 'the living one'; 'Christ being raised from the dead will never die again; death no longer has dominion over him' (Rom. 6: 9; cf. 2 Tim. 1: 10). **I have the keys of Death and Hades:** That is, His authority extends throughout the realm of death. Therefore His people, who were threatened with death for their loyalty to Him, need not fear that death will separate them from His love; He who died and came to life again is Lord of the dead as of the living: 'so then, whether we live or whether we die, we are the Lord's' (Rom. 14: 8 f.; cf. Heb. 2: 14 f.). **19. write what you see, what is and what is** to take place hereafter: What John saw embraced both the situation already in existence and things which still lay in the future. The division is twofold, not threefold. One of the chief problems of exegesis in Rev. is to distinguish those elements in the visions which symbolize 'what is' from those which symbolize 'what is to be hereafter'. See note on 4: 1. **20. the seven stars are the angels of the seven churches:** Christ, who holds these stars in His right hand, is therefore the Lord of each local church. The angels of the churches should be understood in the light of the angelology of Rev.—not as human messengers or ministers of the churches but as the celestial counterparts or personifications of the various churches, each of whom represents his church to the point where he is held responsible for its condition and behaviour. We may compare the angels of nations (Dan. 10: 13, 20; 12: 1) and of individuals (Mt. 18: 10; Ac. 12: 15). **the seven lampstands are the seven churches:** See note on verse 12 above.

II. THE LETTERS TO THE SEVEN CHURCHES (2: 1–3: 22)

The letters to the churches follow an easily recognized pattern. The risen Christ, designating Himself by one of His titles, addresses the 'angel' of the church with the words 'I know'; there follows a brief description of the condition of the church with appropriate commendation or reproof, promise or warning. Each letter ends with the exhortation 'He who has an ear, let him hear what the Spirit says to the churches' preceding or following a word of encouragement for him 'who conquers'—i.e. the Christian who maintains his confession steadfastly, without prevarication or compromise, even (if need be) to death itself.

The letters give a vivid impression of Christian life in the province of Asia some decades after the evangelization of the province by Paul and his colleagues (A.D. 52–55). Pressure is being brought to bear on the Christians to be less unyielding in their negative attitude to such socially approved activities as emperor-worship and the like, to be less insistent on those things which distinguish their way of life so sharply from the civilization in the midst of which they live. The pressure might take the form of active persecution, as at Smyrna and Pergamum, or the more subtle and less easily resisted form of continued emphasis on the advantages of just so much conformity to paganism as to make life a little more comfortable.

i. The Letter to Ephesus (2: 1–7)

Ephesus, at the mouth of the Cayster, was an ancient Anatolian city colonized by Ionian Greeks. At this time it was the greatest commercial city of Asia Minor and capital of the province of Asia; it retained its free constitution under the Romans, with its own senate and civic assembly. It was widely renowned as the home of the cult of Ephesian Artemis (a local manifestation of the great mother-goddess of Asia Minor), whose temple there was one of the seven wonders of the world. The Ephesian church dated from Paul's three years' residence in the city (Ac. 20: 31).

John's association with Ephesus is perpetuated in the place-name *Ayasolúk*, a corruption of Gk. *hagios theologos*, 'the holy divine'.

1. The words of him who holds the seven stars in his right hand, who walks among the seven golden lampstands: For these titles see 1: 16, 13. His 'walking' among the lampstands may imply an inspection of their condition, one by one. **2. I know your works:** Cf. verse 19; 3: 1, 8, 15. **you cannot bear evil men:** Cf. the 'evil-workers' of Phil. 3: 2 (and 2 C. 11: 13); here probably they are those who would lower the Christian standard of conduct. **have tested those who call themselves apostles but are not, and found them to be false:** Cf. 2 C. 11: 13: 'false apostles, . . . disguising themselves as apostles of Christ'—but here the false apostles are more likely to be antinomian than Judaizing. Ignatius, in his letter to the Ephesians (c. A.D. 115), commends them because they refused a hearing to visitors who taught evil doctrine. **4. I have this against you:** Cf. verses 14, 20. **you have abandoned the love you had at first:** So penetrating a diagnosis, especially of people who have just been praised for 'enduring patiently' and not growing weary (verse 3), bespeaks uncommon spiritual insight and long and intimate acquaintance with the church addressed. For all their commendable endurance, the fervour of their original love—their 'love toward all the saints', as the longer text of Eph. 1: 15 puts it—had waned. And nothing—no amount of good works or sound doctrine—can take the place of *agapē* in a Christian community; unless there was a change of heart and a return to the original works of love, that church's days were numbered; its lampstand would be removed (verse 5). That the church of Ephesus paid heed to this warning is a fair inference from the testimony of Ignatius, who commends it for its faith and love. **6. Yet this you have:** This is to your credit. **you hate the works of the Nicolaitans:** This word means 'the followers of Nicolaus'—whether Nicolaus the proselyte of Antioch (Ac. 6: 5), as was held by the Church Fathers from Irenaeus and Clement of Alexandria (c. A.D. 180) onwards, or some other

Nicolaus, cannot be determined. They appear to have relaxed the conditions laid down by the apostolic letter of Acts 15: 20, 29. (See verses 14 f., 20.) **7. I will grant to eat of the tree of life, which is in the paradise of God:** That is, I will give him eternal life. The origin of the imagery is recognizably Gen. 2: 8 f.; 3: 22. The tree of life in the Eden of Genesis was the terrestrial counterpart of the tree of life in the Eden above. Cf. 22: 1 f.

ii. The Letter to Smyrna (2: 8–11)
Smyrna (modern Izmir) was an ancient Greek colony, destroyed by the Lydians in 627 B.C. It was refounded by Lysimachus, one of the successors of Alexander the Great, in 290 B.C. From 195 B.C. onwards Smyrna maintained relations of firm friendship with Rome. Its tutelary deity was the 'Sipylene Mother', a local phase of Cybele. The letter to the church in Smyrna, while the shortest of the seven, is also the most warmly commendatory.

8. the first and the last, who died and came to life: An echo of 1: 17 f. **9. those who say that they are Jews and are not:** The true Jew is one whose life is praiseworthy in God's sight (cf. Rom. 2: 28 f.). The Jewish community in Smyrna, because of its slanderous attacks on the Christians, had shown itself unworthy of the name 'Jew'; they were rather, by virtue of their opposition to the gospel, **a synagogue of Satan** (cf. 3: 9). (Satan means 'adversary', as its Greek equivalent *diabolos* means 'slanderer' or 'false accuser'; cf. 12: 9 f.) Several decades later, the Jews of Smyrna played a prominent part in the attack on Polycarp, bishop of Smyrna. **10. the devil is about to throw some of you into prison:** The devil used the imperial authorities as his instruments (cf. 13: 2, where the imperial wild beast is energized by the dragon). Imprisonment was not a punishment in itself, but a prelude to trial and sentence. **for ten days you will have tribulation:** For a prolonged but not unlimited period. Well-known episodes in the history of the Smyrnaean church are the martyrdom of Polycarp (A.D. 156) and that of Pionius (A.D. 250). **the crown of life:** The Smyrnaean Christians' garland won for endurance and victory in the spiritual contest would be eternal life—the promise is the same as that to Ephesus in verse 7, though the imagery is different. The imagery here is suggested by 'the crown of Smyrna', the circle of colonnaded buildings on Mount Pagos, which overlooked the city. **11. the second death:** Final judgment, the alternative to eternal life (cf. 20: 14; 21: 8).

iii. The Letter to Pergamum (2: 12–17)
Pergamum means 'citadel' (Gk. *pergamos*); the city was so named from its commanding position overlooking the Caicus valley, and the name survives in modern Bergama, which lies in the valley below. It was the capital city of the Attalid dynasty whose kingdom, bequeathed to Rome in 133 B.C., became the province of Asia.

12. who has the sharp two-edged sword: For this title cf. 1: 16; it is appropriate here because of the severity of the language of verses 14-16. **13. where Satan's throne is:** Three explanations of this expression have been offered, for Pergamum boasted (*a*) a throne-like altar to Zeus on the citadel; (*b*) the temple of the healing god Asklepios, before which stood an image of the god in association with a gigantic snake, which might have reminded Christians of the serpent in Eden; (*c*) the earliest shrine of the provincial cult of Rome and Augustus, established there in 29 B.C. In view of other allusions in Rev. to the imperial cult, this is most probably the reference here. **in the days of Antipas my witness, my faithful one:** Cf. 1: 5; 3: 14, where Christ Himself is 'the faithful witness'. Who Antipas was, or in what circumstances he died, we do not know; evidently his death lay some considerable way back in the past. A passage like this marks the beginning of the transition of the meaning of Gk. *martys*, from 'witness' to 'martyr' (cf. Ac. 22: 20). **14. the teaching of Balaam:** A reference to the apostasy of Baal-peor (Num. 25: 3 ff.) which was instigated by Balaam (Num. 31: 16); it involved fornication or ritual prostitution as well as idolatry. Here the Nicolaitans and their followers (verse 15) are described as holding his teaching. From this it has been thought by some that the Nicolaus after whom the latter were called (cf. verse 6) was simply Balaam, whose name (derived from Heb. *bala'*, 'devour', and *'am*, 'people', so as to yield the meaning 'devourer of the people') was translated by Gk. Nicolaus ('conqueror of the people'); but this is improbable. There was evidently a tendency by this time to dismiss the requirements of Ac. 15: 20, 29, as a dead letter, including those which forbade the eating of meat sacrificed to idols and the contracting of marital unions prohibited by the law of Israel (Lev. 18) but countenanced by pagan custom. Such a relaxation would have reduced the social differences between Christians and their pagan neighbours. It is possible, however, that more than this is involved—something amounting to a token participation in pagan worship. **16. the sword of my mouth:** The self-fulfilling word of divine judgment (cf. verse 12). **17. the hidden manna:** An abundant compensation for abstention from idol-food. As the tree of life had its heavenly archetype (verse 7), so has the manna which Israel ate in the wilderness. There was among the Jews a considerable body of teaching about this manna, hidden in heaven, which would be revealed at the end time and given as food to the faithful (so, *e.g.*, 2 Bar. 29: 8). It is called *the bread of the angels* (Ps. 78: 25) or 'the bread of God' (Jn 6: 33); in the light of the teaching about the bread of life in Jn 6: 27 ff. we can recognize the 'hidden manna' as yet another expression for eternal life. **a white stone, with a new name written on the stone:** The meaning of this gift is uncertain, but it may denote an inscribed pebble (Gk. *psēphos*) serving as a ticket of admission to the heavenly banquet. The 'new name', according to 3: 12, is Christ's (cf. 22: 4). **which no one knows except him who receives it:** Purveyors of magical amulets knew how important it was that a name of power should be kept secret; the power of Jesus' name is not to be commanded by magic arts, but is known in the experience of His servants.

iv. The Letter to Thyatira (2: 18-29)
Thyatira was founded by Seleucus I about 300 B.C. as a garrison city. Its other NT mention is as the birth-place of Lydia, the seller of purple, Paul's first convert in Philippi (Ac. 16: 14).

18. **who has eyes like a flame of fire, and whose feet are like burnished bronze:** From 1: 14 f.; here, as in 1: 15, 'legs' would be preferable to 'feet'. 19. **your latter works exceed the first:** Up to this point Thyatira's commendation exceeds that of Ephesus, whose love had waned to a point where a return to her first works was called for. 20. **you tolerate the woman Jezebel, who calls herself a prophetess:** That she not only called herself a prophetess but was recognized as such by her associates (called in verse 22 'those who commit adultery with her') and followers (called in verse 23 'her children') is certain (we may recall the Montanist prophetesses who were active in the following century in Phrygia). Her name was not really Jezebel, but she is described here as 'that Jezebel of a woman' because her relaxation of the terms of the apostolic decree or further compromises with paganism (cf. verse 14) placed her in the succession of the OT Jezebel, whose Baal-cult was marked by idolatry and ritual prostitution. 21. **I gave her time to repent:** Her activity had evidently gone on for some time, and previous warnings had been unheeded; now sickness and plague will fall as a judgment on her and her votaries. 23. **and I will strike her children dead:** Literally, 'I will kill her children with death', where 'death' may mean 'pestilence', as in the second occurrence in 6: 8. **I am he who searches mind and heart:** Cf.

Ps. 7: 9; 26: 2; Jer. 20: 12. Once again, the attributes of God are shared by Christ. **I will give to each of you as his works deserve:** The constant principle of divine judgment in Scripture; cf. 20: 12; 22: 12; also Ps. 62: 12; Mt. 16: 27; Rom. 2: 6, etc. 24. **the deep things of Satan:** As there is a heavenly wisdom which explores 'the depths of God' (1 C. 2: 10), so a counterfeit wisdom promises to open up 'deep things', as they are called—'deep things, indeed', says the speaker, 'but deep things of Satan'. The reference is probably to some form of Gnostic teaching. **I do not lay upon you any other burden:**—i.e., than those imposed by the Council of Jerusalem; the very language of Ac. 15: 28 is echoed. 25. **until I come:** His coming is a visitation of judgment upon the unfaithful (verses 5, 16), but of reward for the faithful. 26-27. **I will give him power** (Gk. *exousia*, 'authority') **over the nations, and he shall rule them with a rod of iron:** Cf. Ps. 2: 8 f.; Messiah's dominion (cf. 12: 5; 19: 15) is shared with His victorious followers. 'Rule' is literally 'shepherd' (*poimainein*); the shepherd's staff is a protection for the sheep but a weapon of offence against their enemies. **even as I myself have received power from my Father:** Cf. Ps. 2: 8; Mt. 11: 27; 28: 18; Lk. 22: 29. 28. **I will give him the morning star:** This must be understood in relation to 22: 16 (*q.v.*), where Jesus calls Himself 'the bright morning star'—an allusion, perhaps, to the royal 'star . . . out of Jacob' foretold by Balaam in Num. 24: 17. The conquering believer, it is implied, is to share the royal rule of his conquering Lord (cf. 3: 21).

v. The Letter to Sardis (3: 1-6)
Sardis was the capital of the ancient kingdom of Lydia, overthrown by Cyrus in 546 B.C. By Roman times it had lost its former greatness, and it never recovered from a great earthquake which devastated it in A.D. 17.

1. **who has the seven spirits of God and the seven stars:** Cf. 1: 4, 16. **you have the name of being alive, and you are dead:** The church partook of the character of the city, 'whose name was almost synonymous with pretensions unjustified, promise unfulfilled, appearance without reality, confidence which heralded ruin' (W. M. Ramsay). Quite evidently compromise with its pagan environment had so eroded the witness of the church in Sardis that it was a Christian church in name only. Revival and repentance are urgently called for; otherwise there is no future for the church. 3. **if you will not awake, I will come like a thief, and you will not know at what hour I will come upon you:** This language, describing the suddenness of Christ's coming in

judgment, appears in several parts of the NT (cf. 16: 15; Mt. 24: 43; Lk. 12: 39; 1 Th. 5: 2; 2 Pet. 3: 10); here it is specially apt in view of the history of Sardis, which had been captured suddenly more than once when its steep citadel was scaled at points where such access was thought impossible. **4. you have still a few names in Sardis:** A minority in the church had refused to follow the compromising ways of the majority; since on earth they had kept their garments 'unstained from the world' their reward will be white robes in glory, meet for the companions of their Lord (perhaps there is an allusion here to the principal trade of Sardis —the manufacture and dyeing of woollen garments). This is the incentive held out in this letter to the overcomer, together with the promise: **I will not blot his name out of the book of life; I will confess his name before my Father and before his angels** (5). This promise recalls Mt. 10: 32 f.; Lk. 12: 8 f. The 'book of life' appears here, but not in the other places where it is mentioned in Rev. (13: 8; 17: 8; 20: 12, 15; 21: 27) to include at first all whose names are on the membership roll of a local church on earth, but those whose membership is but nominal have their names deleted— i.e. the Lord declares that He never knew them (cf. Lk. 13: 25, 27). Elsewhere in Rev. those whose names are in the book of life are those who steadfastly resist the temptation to apostasy and who therefore stand in God's great day.

vi. The Letter to Philadelphia (3: 7–13)
Philadelphia received its name in memory of Attalus II, king of Pergamum (159-138 B.C.) who was called Philadelphus ('lover of his brother') because of his devotion to his brother and predecessor, Eumenes II. The earthquake of A.D. 17 devastated Philadelphia as it did Sardis; out of gratitude to the Emperor Tiberius for relief given after the earthquake the city renamed itself Neocaesarea, but the name Philadelphia quickly reasserted itself.

The letter to Philadelphia, like that to Smyrna, contains no word of blame. The Philadelphian church, though small and weak, has maintained its Christian allegiance in spite of the hostility of the synagogue.

7. the holy one, the true one: These two titles are given to God separately in 1 Jn 2: 20 and 5: 20; and together in Rev. 6: 10. Here they are designations of Christ (cf. Mk 1: 24; Jn 6: 69; Ac. 3: 14). **who has the key of David:** In Isa. 22: 22 *the key of the house of David* is laid on the shoulder of Eliakim, so that *he shall open, and none shall shut; and he shall shut, and none shall open.* That is to say, Eliakim is appointed chief steward or grand vizier of the royal palace in Jerusalem. Here,

however, the same language is used to designate Jesus as the Davidic Messiah—not as chief steward but as Prince of the house of David (cf. Heb. 3: 2-6). **8. I have set before you an open door:** An opportunity for witness (cf. 1 C. 16: 9; 2 C. 2: 12). **9. the synagogue of Satan:** Cf. 2: 9, in the letter to Smyrna. **I will make them come . . . and learn that I have loved you:** They will acknowledge that the despised church of Philadelphia is the true congregation of the people of God in that city. **10. my word of patient endurance:** 'My word' of verse 8 is here made more specific as Christ's command to endure patiently for His sake, an essential element in the gospel (cf. 2: 10 b; Mt. 10: 22 b; Mk 13: 13 b; Jn 15: 18 ff.; 16: 1 ff., 33). **the hour of trial which is coming on the whole world, to try those who dwell upon the earth:** This is the visitation portrayed in the successive series of judgment-visions from 6: 1 onwards, which is directed against the 'earth-dwellers'—a recurrent expression in Rev. which excludes the people of God, perhaps because the latter are of heavenly citizenship, members of the New Jerusalem. Cf. Lk. 21: 35. Against this visitation the faithful servants of God, among whom the members of the Philadelphian church are plainly included, are 'sealed' (7: 2-8). In the interpretation of Rev. it is important to distinguish between the tribulation which comes by way of divine judgment on the ungodly (as here) or on unfaithful Christians (as in 2: 22) and that which comes in the form of persecution upon the faithful (as in 2: 10; 7: 14). **11. I am coming soon:** As to the Ephesians (2: 5), Pergamenes (2: 16), Thyatirans (2: 25), and Sardians (3: 3); but to the Philadelphians His coming brings unmitigated blessing, provided that the expectation of it nerves them to maintain their loyalty and not forfeit their crown (cf. 2: 10 b). **hold fast what you have:** Cf. 2: 25, where the faithful souls in Thyatira are similarly exhorted. **12. a pillar in the temple of my God; never shall he go out of it:** The metaphor apparently undergoes a sudden change; the pillar upholding the roof or pediment becomes a worshipper or ministrant in the shrine; but the point may be that this pillar will never be moved from its base, like so many pillars in earthquake-stricken Philadelphia. **I will write on him . . . :** As overcomer he has a triple name inscribed on him—the name of God, who owns him for a son; the name of the city of God, among whose burgesses he is enrolled; the name of Christ his Lord. Cf. 2: 17; 14: 1; 22: 4. **the city of my God, the new Jerusalem . . . :** That is, the commonwealth of saints; see 21: 2 f., 9 ff., with Ps. 87 as OT background.

vii. The Letter to Laodicea (3: 14–22)
Laodicea, founded by the Seleucid king Antiochus II (261–246 B.C.) and called after his wife Laodice. The church there is mentioned in Col. 2: 1; 4: 13 ff., as one of the churches of the Lycus valley, alongside those of Colossae and Hierapolis; all three were probably planted by Epaphras during Paul's Ephesian ministry. The Laodicean church is marked neither by steadfast loyalty nor by active disloyalty, but by a comfortable self-satisfaction which made it incapable of bearing true witness to Christ.

14. the Amen: The one in whom the revelation of God finds its perfect response and fulfilment (cf. 2 C. 1: 19 f.). A connection with Heb.'*amon* in Prov. 8: 30 (RSV 'master workman') has been suggested by some interpreters because the final part of this triple title of Jesus, **the beginning of God's creation,** comes from the same context, from Prov. 8: 22 (cf. Col. 1: 15 ff.). Jesus speaks here in the rôle of Divine Wisdom. **the faithful and true witness:** Cf. 1: 5. **15. you are neither cold nor hot:** The choice of the figure of lukewarmness to characterize the Laodiceans' ineffectiveness or lack of zeal may have been suggested by their city's water supply, drawn from the hot springs at Denizli to the south, which was still tepid after flowing for five miles in stone pipes—unlike the cold water which refreshed their neighbours at Colossae or the hot water whose healing properties were valued by those of Hierapolis. Cf. M. J. S. Rudwick and E. M. B. Green, 'The Laodicean Lukewarmness', *ExpT* 69 (1957–58), p. 176. **17. I am rich, I have prospered, and I need nothing:** The church of Laodicea evidently took character from the city as a whole, which was renowned for its wealth. When it was destroyed by an earthquake in A.D. 60, the citizens declined assistance from Rome and rebuilt their city from their own resources. But, however admirable this independence might be in material things, in the spiritual realm self-sufficiency means destitution; a church's true sufficiency must come from God (cf. 2 C. 3: 5), who alone supplies spiritual riches, clothing and health (verse 18). **18. white garments:** Laodicea was famed for the manufacture of black woollen cloaks called *laodicia;* the black sheep from which the wool was obtained have survived locally to our own day. **to keep the shame of your nakedness from being seen:** Cf. 16: 15. **salve to anoint your eyes:** There was a famous medical school near Laodicea where 'Phrygian stone' was powdered to produce collyrium (Gk. *kollyrion*, here translated 'salve'), which appears to have been mixed with oil and applied to the eyes as an ointment.

19. Those whom I love, I reprove and chasten: From Prov. 3: 12 (cf. Heb. 12: 6). **be zealous and repent:** This is the fifth call to repentance in these letters (cf. 2: 5, 16, 21; 3: 3); Smyrna and Philadelphia alone require no such call. Laodicea's repentance would involve the replacement of complacency by zealous concern. **20. Behold, I stand at the door and knock:** Christ has no place in the life of the Laodicean church, and seeks admission; even if the church as a whole pays no heed to his call, those members who do will enjoy mutual fellowship with Him. The language is reminiscent of Jn 14: 23. **21. I will grant him to sit with me on my throne, as I myself conquered and sat down with my Father on his throne:** Cf. Jesus' promise in Lk. 22: 28–30 to those who had 'continued' with Him in His 'trials'. Their conquest, like His, is won by way of suffering and death (5: 5 f.; 12: 11); those who suffer with Him reign with Him (2 Tim. 2: 12). The same promise has been made in other words at the end of the letter to Thyatira (2: 26–28). Christ's being seated on His Father's throne is His exaltation to the right hand of God, of which He spoke in His reply to the high priest (Mk 14: 62) and which was from the beginning proclaimed in the apostolic preaching and in the church's confession (Ac. 2: 33 ff.; 5: 31; Rom. 8: 34; Eph. 1: 20; Col. 3: 1; Heb. 1: 3 etc.; 1 Pet. 3: 22). 'The highest place that heaven affords/Is his, is his by right'; but participation in His sovereignty is granted to His people (cf. Eph. 2: 6). **22. what the Spirit says to the churches:** To other churches than the seven, no doubt, the seven being representative of all; and, *mutatis mutandis*, to the churches of the twentieth century as plainly as to those of the first.

III. A VISION OF HEAVEN (4: 1–5: 14)
In OT prophecy only those can learn the divine purpose who are admitted to *the council of the* LORD *to perceive and to hear his word;* then they are in a position to proclaim confidently what He will do (Jer. 23: 18, 22). So John learns the course of coming events by being rapt in ecstasy to heaven. His description of heaven falls into two parts, characterized respectively by the hymn of praise to God as Creator (4: 11) and by that addressed to Christ as Redeemer (5: 9 f., 12, 13 b).
i. The Throne-room of God (4: 1–11)
1. an open door: Cf. Ezek. 1: 1, *the heavens were opened, and I saw visions of God.* **the first voice . . . like a trumpet:** That of 1: 10. **Come up hither:** The heavenly ascent is a well-marked feature of prophetic ecstasy; cf. 2 C. 12: 2 ff. **what must take place after this:** Cf.

1: 1, 19. Chapters 4 and 5 provide the setting for the panorama of 'what must take place', portrayed from chapter 6 onwards in the parallel judgments of the seals, trumpets and bowls (see first note on 7: 1-8). **2. I was in the Spirit:** Cf. 1: 10. **a throne stood in heaven:** The vision of the throne-room of God (the heavenly archetype of the holy of holies in the earthly sanctuary) has OT antecedents such as 1 Kg. 22: 19; Isa. 6: 1 ff.; Dan. 7: 9 ff.; but there are here additional features peculiar to Rev. **3. he who sat there appeared like jasper and carnelian:** Cf. Exod. 24: 10; Ezek. 1: 26 ff. Words cannot describe the divine glory; those who have seen it in ecstasy, like Ezekiel and John, can give but a general impression of how it impressed them. **a rainbow that looked like an emerald:** Cf. Ezek. 1: 28; the mention of the rainbow may recall the covenant of Gen. 9: 12 ff. **4. twenty-four thrones:** Cf. the 'thrones' of Dan. 7: 9, occupied by assessors at the divine judgment (but see a closer parallel to this in 20: 4). **seated on the thrones were twenty-four elders:** These may constitute the order of angel-princes called 'thrones' in Col. 1: 16; they are perhaps the celestial counterpart of the 24 orders of priests in 1 Chr. 24: 4 ff., since they discharge priestly functions before the throne of God (5: 8). **5. From the throne issued flashes of lightning:** Cf. 8: 5; 11: 19; 16: 18. Lightning is a regular feature of OT theophanies (cf. Exod. 19: 16; Pss. 18: 8, 12 ff.; 77: 18; 97: 4; Ezek. 1: 4, 13; Hab. 3: 4). **voices and peals of thunder:** Cf. the 'seven thunders' of 10: 3 f. **seven torches of fire, which are the seven spirits of God:** Cf. 1: 4; also Ezek. 1: 13. **6. a sea of glass, like crystal:** This heavenly sea (cf. Gen. 1: 7; Pss. 104: 3; 148: 4) is the archetype of the 'molten sea' in Solomon's temple (1 Kg. 7: 23 ff.), which is commonly taken to represent the cosmic flood, over which God *sits enthroned as king* (Ps. 29: 10). **four living creatures:** These are closely akin to the 'four living creatures' (cherubim) of Ezek. 1: 5 ff.; 10: 1 ff. (symbols of the storm-winds upbearing the chariot-throne of God in His progress through the heavens); but they have also some of the features and functions of the seraphim of Isa. 6: 2 f. They represent the powers of creation in the service of the Creator. **full of eyes:** Like the living wheels of the chariot-throne in Ezek. 1: 18, a token of the divine omniscience (cf. also Zech. 4: 10 b). **7. the first living creature like a lion . . .:** Each of Ezekiel's living creatures had the four heads (more strictly 'faces') of a man, a lion, an ox and an eagle (Ezek. 1: 10); here each living creature has one head only, but between them the four symbolize the principal

divisions of the animal creation. **8. each of them with six wings:** Like the seraphim of Isa. 6: 2. **day and night they never cease to sing** (lit. 'say'): The hymn of the living creatures is the first part of the hymn of the seraphim (Isa. 6: 3), the name of God being amplified by the title of 1: 4. The hymns of Rev. are worthy of careful study (cf. 4: 11; 5: 9 f.; 7: 15-17; 11: 17 f.; 15: 3 f.; 19: 6); the context in which they appear implies that the praise of the church on earth is an echo of the liturgy of heaven. The unceasing praise of the living creatures is the voice of creation glorifying its Creator, and is accompanied by the adoring homage of the 24 angel-princes, as they too proclaim their great Creator's praise, and **cast their crowns before the throne** (10) in acknowledgment that all sovereignty is His. The hymn of praise to God for the wonders of creation echoes the language of many of the Psalms (*e.g.* Pss. 19: 1-6; 104). But all OT worship points on to Christ, in whom it meets its fulfilment; hence the vision of heaven in chapter 4 is incomplete without the scene unfolded in chapter 5.

ii. 'Worthy is the Lamb' (5: 1-14)
1. a scroll written within and on the back: This is the scroll of destiny containing the 'revelation' of 1: 1, but its contents must remain a mystery and not a revelation until it is unsealed. The fact that it contains writing outside as well as inside may suggest the amplitude of the revelation it contains; but more probably the writing outside is a copy or summary of the writing inside. But the writing inside is the legal document, and only when it is exposed and read can its contents be validly implemented. **sealed with seven seals:** Like a will or other official instrument under Roman law, which required to be sealed by seven witnesses. The seals could be properly broken only by someone with due authority to do so. In this instance the person authorized to break the seals will be marked out by that very fact as lord of history and master of the world's destiny. **4. I wept much:** As well he might, for unless the seals were broken and the scroll opened and read, the divine purpose of judgment and blessing for the world must remain unfulfilled. Man in the beginning was appointed God's viceroy over the world (Gen. 1: 26, 28; Ps. 8: 6 ff.), but has proved unequal to his responsibility. Now the 'Proper Man' appears, and *the will of the* LORD *shall prosper in his hand* (Isa. 53: 10). **5. one of the elders said to me:** Cf. 7: 13 for one of these angel-princes acting as a guide or interpreter to John. **the Lion of the tribe of Judah, the Root of David:** Two titles of the Davidic Messiah; the former is based on

Gen. 49: 9, and the latter (cf. 22: 16) on Isa. 11: 10, where the coming prince of the house of David is called 'the root of Jesse' (cf. Isa. 11: 1; 53: 2). **has conquered, so that he can open the scroll:** Christ's victory on the cross, although at the time it seemed to be defeat, guaranteed the accomplishment of God's purpose in the world. **6. between the throne and the four living creatures:** A clearer rendering than 'in the midst of the throne . . .' **I saw a Lamb standing, as though it had been slain:** Paradoxically, the conqueror announced as a lion is seen as a slaughtered lamb. Only in the Johannine writings of the NT is the title 'the Lamb' applied to Jesus. In Jn 1: 29, 36 John the Baptist calls him 'the Lamb (Gk. *amnos*) of God'—primarily (in view of the paschal emphasis of the passion narrative in Jn) with reference to the Passover victim (cf. the simile in 1 Pet. 1: 19), although an allusion to Isa. 53: 7 (and perhaps to Gen. 22: 8) may also be recognized. In Rev. the reference is primarily to the *lamb led to the slaughter* of Isa. 53: 7 (that Rev. uses Gk. *arnion* and not *amnos* is of no great consequence here). Later in Rev. 'the Lamb' becomes a permanent title of Christ with no sacrificial emphasis; thus in 7: 17 the Lamb is a shepherd and in 19: 7 ff.; 21: 9 ff. the Lamb is a bridegroom whose bride is a city. Here, however, the sacrificial connotation is essential: Christ's sacrifice *is* His victory. The moment is that of His appearance in heaven, fresh from the suffering and triumph of the cross. **with seven horns and with seven eyes:** Denoting plenitude of power and wisdom. **the seven spirits of God:** Cf. 1: 4. **sent out into all the earth:** Cf. Zech. 4: 10 b. **8. each holding a harp, and with golden bowls full of incense:** This participial phrase refers to the elders alone. **which are the prayers of the saints:** Cf. 8: 3 f. The elders perform priestly functions in heaven. **9. and they sang a new song:** New in comparison with the ancient song of creation in 4: 11 (cf. Job 38: 7). **Worthy art thou . . .:** The advent motifs with which Roman emperors were acclaimed included such terms as 'Worthy art thou' and 'Worthy is he to inherit the kingdom'; but only one is worthy to exercise world sovereignty, and He has won that right by His obedience and blood. **didst ransom men for God:** The elders are not the objects of redemption, as is implied by the inferior reading of AV ('hast redeemed us')—inferior in spite of its presence in *Codex Sinaiticus* (which is rather inaccurate in Rev.). So in verse 10 read (this time with the support of *Sinaiticus*): **hast made them** (not 'us') **a kingdom and priests:** Cf. 1: 6. **and they shall reign on earth:** The textual

evidence is fairly evenly divided between this reading and the present tense (RV: 'they reign upon the earth'). The latter reading emphasizes that believers, even while suffering persecution on earth, have already been made 'a kingdom and priests' to God, reproducing here below the eternal worship of heaven. The former reading points on to their coming reign with Christ (20: 4); hence J. N. Darby renders 'they shall reign over the earth' (i.e., from heaven). **11. myriads of myriads and thousands of thousands:** Cf. Dan. 7: 10. The hymn of praise to the Lamb is taken up in ever widening circles; from the elders it is taken up by all the heavenly host (verses 11 f.), and from them by all creation (verse 13; Phil. 2: 9-11), while the praise of creation to God and the Lamb is sealed by the word and adoring action of those in closest proximity to the divine throne (verse 14).

IV. THE BREAKING OF THE SEVEN SEALS (6: 1-8: 5)

As Christ takes the scroll of destiny and proceeds to break one seal after another, the 'unveiling' properly begins. His action in heaven determines events on earth. Since He is envisaged as taking the scroll in A.D. 30, it is not surprising to find a rather close correlation between the first six seals and the forecast of the immediate future to be fulfilled within a generation, presented in the eschatological discourse of the Synoptic Gospels (Mk 13: 5 ff. and parallels). Invasion, civil war, scarcity, widespread mortality, persecution and earthquake are announced: 'this must take place, but the end is not yet' (Mk 13: 7). The seven seals, like the seven trumpets which follow them, fall into two divisions of four and three, with an interlude before the seventh. The breaking of the first four seals unleashes the four horsemen of the Apocalypse, each of whom rides into the arena at the summons of one of the living creatures. These may recall the four horsemen of Zech. 1: 8 ff.; 6: 1 ff., sent by Yahweh to patrol the earth; but their function is more sinister by far. 'The messianic games begin with the usual race in four colours. But it is not the usual race, it is the apocalyptic death-race, a frightful game in which the heavenly Imperator mocks the defiant and fearful heart of the Roman false Christ. All hopes and promises of the imperial rule are shattered; all the fears of the Roman world are realized' (E. Stauffer, *Christ and the Caesars*, p. 184). The appearance of the horsemen marks 'the beginning of the sufferings' which herald the winding up of the age (Mk 13: 8).

i. The First Seal (6: 1-2)

1. I heard one of the four living creatures say, . . . 'Come!': Summoning the first horseman (cf. verses 3, 5, 7), not issuing an invitation to John (as AV 'Come and see' suggests). **2. a white horse, and its rider had a bow:** One long-established interpretation understands this of the victorious progress of the gospel, the rider on the white horse being Christ, as in 19: 11. But the analogy of the other horsemen, and the fact that this horseman is equipped with a bow (like the mounted archers of the Parthian army), suggests rather invasion from beyond the eastern frontier of the Roman Empire. **a crown was given to him:** A suitable token for one who **went out conquering and to conquer.**

ii. The Second Seal (6: 3-4)

4. bright red (Gk. *pyrrhos*): The blood-red colour of the horse is in keeping with the mission of its rider, which is to sow strife and slaughter on earth—civil war this time rather than foreign invasion: such civil war as had recently been experienced during the 'year of the four emperors' (A.D. 68-69).

iii. The Third Seal (6: 5-6)

5. a black horse: The colour of this horse is not specially significant: it is scarcely the discoloration caused by famine (cf. Lam. 4: 8), for scarcity, high prices and rationing, rather than famine, are implied by the proclamation of verse 6. **its rider had a balance in his hand:** An indication that bread must be sold and eaten *by weight* (Lev. 26: 26; Ezek. 4: 10, 16). **6. A quart of wheat for a denarius, and three quarts of barley for a denarius:** The 'quart' is a *choinix*, a dry measure slightly greater than a litre. In the 5th century B.C. a *choinix* of grain was a fair daily ration for a Persian soldier or a Greek slave; for a Greek soldier twice as much was thought suitable. The denarius (a Roman silver coin weighing $\frac{1}{8}$ oz., rather less than a shilling in size; cf. Mk 12: 15) was a labourer's daily wage in Palestine in A.D. 30 (according to the parable of Mt. 20: 2); the announcement is thus to the effect that a man's daily wage would buy just enough wheat for one, or just enough barley for three —appreciably more than the siege-rations of Ezek. 4: 10, but at a price up to ten times as high as in normal times. **but do not harm oil and wine:** This injunction is evidently addressed to the horseman; the olive and vine are to be spared at this stage, but they too will suffer with other trees when the winds of wrath are unleashed against them (7: 1, 3; 8: 7).

iv. The Fourth Seal (6: 7-8)

8. a pale horse: A livid, corpse-like colour is implied (Gk. *chlōros*, usually translated 'green',

as in 8: 7; 9: 4). **its rider's name was Death, and Hades followed him:** Death and Hades (Sheol) appear in synonymous parallelism in OT (*e.g.* Hos. 13: 14), but in Rev. they are personified as two allied but separate beings (cf. 20: 13 f.). **they were given power** ('authority' Gk. *exousia*) **over a fourth of the earth:** Four kinds of death are specified, by which a quarter of mankind is wiped out. **with sword:** In continuation of verse 4. **with famine:** The scarcity of verse 6 has been intensified. **with pestilence:** Lit. 'with death' (as, possibly, in 2: 23). Cf. Jer. 15: 2 with Ezek. 5: 12 for this restricted sense of 'death'. Plainly what is required here is a particular form of death, not death in general. **by wild beasts of the earth:** These would multiply in territory devastated and depopulated by war, famine and plague.

v. The Fifth Seal (6: 9-11)

9. I saw under the altar: John is still in heaven 'in the Spirit'; the 'altar' is therefore the altar of incense in the heavenly temple, on which the prayers of saints are offered to God (8: 3 f.). The souls of the praying martyrs are accordingly pictured as beneath the altar from which their prayers ascend. **10. O Sovereign Lord** (Gk. *despotēs*): Their prayer for vindication is addressed to God upon His throne (cf. Lk. 18: 7). **those who dwell upon the earth:** See note on 3: 10. **11. a white robe:** A token of their blessedness (cf. 7: 9, 13 f.). **rest a little longer, until the number . . . should be complete:** The persecution, launched in A.D. 64, must run its course. But when the full tale of the martyrs is made up, the prayers of the saints on the altar fall in judgment on the earth (8: 5).

vi. The Sixth Seal (6: 12-17)

12. a great earthquake: A recurrent sign of divine visitation in the Bible (Exod. 19: 18; Zech. 14: 4 f.; Mt. 27: 51). **the sun became black as sackcloth, the full moon became like blood:** For the darkening of the heavenly bodies on the day of the LORD cf. Isa. 13: 10; Ezek. 32: 7 f.; Jl 2: 10; 3: 15; but more particularly Jl 2: 31, quoted by Peter on the day of Pentecost as part of the prophecy fulfilled at that time (Ac. 2: 20). Peter's hearers could remember the preternatural darkness at noon on Good Friday, seven weeks before; whatever darkened the sun on that day may well have caused the paschal full moon to rise blood-red. That was the day of the LORD in realized eschatology, the day when this feature of apocalyptic symbolism was for once experienced in sober fact. **13. the stars of the sky fell to the earth:** Cf. Mk 13: 25: The collapse of established authority is meant. **as the fig-tree sheds its winter fruit:** The simile resembles that in Isa. 34: 4, where on the day of the LORD the host of heaven is compared to *leaves falling from the fig-tree.* The 'winter fruit' (Gk. *olynthos*, as in Ca. 2: 13, LXX) is the green fig which appears before the leaves, and which readily falls off when the wind blows. **14. the sky vanished like a scroll that is rolled up:** From Isa. 34: 4. **every mountain and island was removed from its place:** A complete convulsion of heaven and earth is implied; the use of such language to describe political upheaval is well established in biblical prophecy. Cf. the picture of chaos-come-again in Jer. 4: 23-26, where the desolation caused by foreign invaders is intended. **15. Then the kings of the earth . . . hid in the caves:** We have here an echo of Isa. 2: 10, 19, where men *enter the caves of the rocks and the holes of the ground, from before the terror of the* LORD, *and from the glory of his majesty, when he rises to terrify the earth.* But John elaborates the picture by enumerating the successive ranks of men, from **kings** to **every one, slave and free,** who seek refuge thus on the day of wrath. **16. calling to the mountains and rocks, 'Fall on us':** From Hos. 10: 8; but the best commentary on the present passage is found in our Lord's words to the 'daughters of Jerusalem' on the Via Dolorosa (Lk. 23: 30), where He applied Hosea's language to their plight during the forthcoming siege and destruction of their city. If the same crisis is in view here, the first six seals span the forty years up to A.D. 70. **the wrath of the Lamb:** A daring paradox, on which A. T. Hanson's book *The Wrath of the Lamb* is an extended commentary. **17. the great day of their wrath has come, and who can stand before it:** Cf. Jl 2: 11. This 'wrath' is the retribution which must operate in a moral universe such as God's universe is; even if we call it 'retribution' rather than 'wrath' to exclude the intemperate passion which is so rarely absent from our anger, yet it is not a principle operating independently of God, but it is the response of His holiness to persistent and impenitent wickedness. It is indeed His *strange work* (Isa. 28: 21) to which He girds Himself slowly and reluctantly, in contrast to His proper and congenial work of mercy; but where His mercy is decisively repudiated, men are left to the consequences of their freely chosen course. If here the wrath of God is also 'the wrath of the Lamb', it is because that wrath is not detached from the cross; indeed, it is best understood in the light of the cross.

Interlude before the Seventh Seal (7:1-17)
(*a*) **The Sealing of the Servants of God (7: 1-8)**
From this point on to the end of ch. 11 John describes visions of the end, 'what is to take place hereafter', seen by prophetic perspective as the immediate sequel to his own day. **1. four angels . . . holding back the four winds of the earth:** The winds are winds of judgment for they are restrained from harming earth, sea and trees until God's elect are sealed (verses 2, 3). **2. another angel, . . . with the seal of the living God:** The seal with which God's servants are to be sealed (cf. 9: 4) is elsewhere called His name (see notes on 14: 1; 22: 4). **3. till we have sealed the servants of our God upon their foreheads:** This sealing is based on Ezek. 9: 4, where those inhabitants of Jerusalem who deplore her abominations have a mark (the X mark of the Hebrew letter *tau*) put on their foreheads to safeguard them in the impending judgment on the city. So here the faithful are sealed against the great day of divine wrath. **4. a hundred and forty-four thousand sealed, out of every tribe of the sons of Israel:** The followers of Christ are here viewed as the true 'Israel of God'; and the number indicates the sum total of the faithful; this is emphasized by the breaking down of the number among the twelve tribes (cf. 21: 12). **5. twelve thousand sealed out of the tribe of Judah:** The unusual order of the tribal names here may have a special significance; but if so, it escapes us. Judah, however, is doubtless placed first because Christ belonged to it (cf. Gen. 49: 10; Heb. 7: 14). **6. twelve thousand of the tribe of Manasseh:** It is strange to find Manasseh listed separately, since the **tribe of Joseph** (embracing Ephraim and Manasseh) is listed in verse 7. On the other hand, the tribe of Dan is omitted. It may be thought that Dan originally stood where Manasseh now stands, but such a conjecture is unsupported by any evidence. It was held by many early expositors from Irenaeus onwards that Dan is omitted because Antichrist is to come from that tribe—a belief based by Irenaeus on the LXX version of Jer. 8: 16. But this roll-call of the tribes is schematic; we are not dealing with a census tribe by tribe as in Num. 1: 20 ff.; 26: 5 ff., and need not be over-concerned about the inclusion of Manasseh or the exclusion of Dan.
(*b*) **The Triumph of the Martyrs (7: 9-17)**
9. a great multitude which no man could number: The Christian Clement of Rome and the pagan Tacitus both describe the victims of Nero's persecution as 'a great multitude'; how much greater, then, must be the full complement of Christian martyrs! **from all tribes and peoples and tongues:** John certainly does not confine his vision to Jewish Christians. These martyrs, having already glorified God in death, have no need to be sealed against the eschatological judgment like the 'servants of our God' in the preceding episode; yet in either case we

are reminded that the Israel of God knows no national frontiers. **standing before the throne and before the Lamb:** Now that their number is complete, they no longer remain 'under the altar' (6: 9) but stand in the presence of God; to the **white robes** of blessedness (cf. 6: 11) are now added the **palm branches** of victory. But they ascribe their victory to God and to Christ (verse 10); the Lamb's conquest (5: 5) is also theirs. **10. Salvation** (Gk. *sōtēria*) has the fuller sense of 'victory'; cf. the synonymous parallelism of victory, salvation, righteousness in Ps. 98: 1–3; Isa. 59: 16 f. **11. they fell on their faces before the throne and worshipped God:** The triumph of the martyrs elicits similar praise to that which hailed the triumph of the Lamb in 5: 8–14; rightly so, because their triumph is His, and won in the same way (cf. 12: 11). **13. one of the elders addressed me:** Acting as interpreter, as in 5: 5. **14. These are they who have come out of the great tribulation:** Lit., 'these are the comers (Gk. *erchomenoi*) . . .'; the present participle may be timeless, or may have imperfect force here: 'these are they who came . . .' It is plain that they are not still in process of arriving; their number is complete. This **great tribulation** is different from that of 2: 22, from the 'hour of trial' of 3: 10, and from the wrath against which the elect were sealed in verses 3–8; in all these places it is divine judgment against the wicked that is in view. It must also be distinguished from the tribulation predicted in Mk 13: 19, which fell on Judaea and Jerusalem in A.D. 70. The tribulation of our present passage is the persecution of the followers of Christ which broke in such intense malignity in John's day and continues until the ultimate triumph of Christ. (We western Christians may forget too easily that the present day is one of intense and large-scale persecution of the church.) **they have washed their robes and made them white in the blood of the Lamb:** A vivid way of saying that their present blessedness and their fitness to appear in the presence of God have been won for them by the sacrifice of Christ. **15. serve him** (Gk. *latreuō*): Priestly service is implied (cf. 20: 6; 22: 3). **within his temple:** Since the heavenly dwelling-place of God described in 4: 2 ff. is itself His temple, this phrase is practically synonymous with 'before the throne of God'. **will shelter them with his presence:** Lit. 'will tabernacle over them'; the verb is *skēnoō*, as in Jn 1: 14. RSV rightly sees an allusion to the divine *shekinah*, God's presence in glory among His people (cf. 21: 3). **16. They shall hunger no more . . .:** The blessedness of the glorified martyrs is elaborated in language

derived from Isa. 49: 10, where Yahweh guides the liberated exiles home. **17. the Lamb in the midst of the throne will be their shepherd:** In Isa. 49: 10 it is Yahweh who takes pity on His people and leads them (cf. Isa. 40: 11); here it is Christ who acts as shepherd (cf. Jn. 10: 11 ff.). Plainly 'the Lamb' is here used as an established title of Christ, with no stress on the original figure as there is in 5: 6. **he will guide them to springs of living water:** Cf. Ps. 23: 2 as well as Isa. 49: 10. **God will wipe away every tear from their eyes:** In Isa. 26: 8 this promise refers to the new age when God *will swallow up death for ever* (cf. 1 C. 15: 54); it is repeated below in 21: 4.

vii. The Seventh Seal (8: 1–5)
The fearful expectation of the sixth seal (6: 15–17) is due to be realized with the breaking of the seventh. **1. there was silence in heaven for about half an hour:** 'Half an hour' is the duration of the silence as it appeared to John's consciousness in the vision. All heaven breathlessly awaits the final act of divine judgment. **2. the seven angels who stand before God:** Gabriel identifies himself as one of these (Lk. 1: 19); cf. Tob. 12: 15, where Raphael describes himself as 'one of the seven holy angels who present the prayers of the saints and stand before the presence of the glory of the Holy One.' The names of all seven appear in 1 Enoch 20: 2–8 as Uriel, Raphael, Raguel, Michael, Sariel, Gabriel and Remiel: 'the archangels' names are seven'. **and seven trumpets were given to them:** As the Jewish new year was inaugurated with the blowing of trumpets (Lev. 23: 24; Num. 29: 1), so the day of the LORD is heralded by the eschatological trumpet-blasts (cf. Isa. 27: 13; Jl 2: 1; Mt. 24: 31; 1 C. 15: 52; 1 Th. 4: 16). **3. another angel came and stood at the altar:** For the altar cf. 6: 9. **he was given much incense to mingle with the prayers of all the saints:** Better: 'he was given much incense to offer, consisting of the prayers of all the saints'. So in verse 4 **the smoke of the incense** consists of **the prayers of the saints.** The preposition 'with' represents the Greek dative case, which, however, is used in these two verses as the equivalent of the Heb. *le* of definition. In 5: 8 the incense is identified with 'the prayers of the saints', and so it is here. **5. the angel took the censer and filled it with fire from the altar and threw it on the earth:** So in Ezek. 10: 2 ff., after the sealing of the godly in Jerusalem, burning coals are taken from the chariot-throne of God (cf. Ezek. 1: 13) and scattered over the city. But here it is the prayers of the saints that fall in judgment on the earth: the cry 'How long?' of 6: 10 is answered at last. **peals of thunder,**

loud noises, flashes of lightning, and an earthquake: Such as marked the theophany on Sinai (Exod. 19: 16 ff.); see note on 4: 5.

V. THE BLOWING OF THE SEVEN TRUMPETS (8: 6–11: 19)

i–iv. The First Four Trumpets (8: 6–12)

The first four trumpets are blown in swift succession and each lets loose on mankind a plague paralleled in the Exodus narrative of the plagues of Egypt, but more deadly in its effect. The last three trumpets announce calamities more frightful still, the three 'Woes' of verse 13. The fifth and sixth involve not merely natural disasters, like the first four, but demonic assaults on the human race. The seventh trumpet, like the seventh seal, is preceded by an interlude. The **hail and fire, mixed with blood** (7) which follows the first trumpet, may be compared with the seventh plague of Egypt (Exod. 9: 22 ff.); the admixture of blood may have been suggested by a climatic phenomenon of Mediterranean lands (H. B. Swete), but is more probably a purely apocalyptic portent (cf. Jl 2: 30, *blood and fire . . .*). The **great mountain, burning with fire,** which **was thrown into the sea** when the second trumpet sounded (8), so that **a third of the sea became blood** (8) recalls the first plague of Egypt (Exod. 7: 17 ff.), but the undrinkable character of the fresh water, which is a feature of the first Egyptian plague (Exod. 7: 24), is paralleled in the effect of the **great star** called **Wormwood** (Gk. *apsinthos*), which fell on **a third of the rivers and fountains of** (fresh) **water** after the third trumpet-blast (10 f.). The darkness which follows the fourth trumpet-blast is reminiscent of the ninth Egyptian plague (Exod. 10: 21 ff.); it is caused, however, by no mere passing sandstorm like Egypt's *darkness to be felt*, but by a disturbance of the heavenly luminaries (cf. Lk. 21: 25 f.). These four plagues destroy one-third respectively of earth, sea, fresh water and natural light.

These four judgments remind us that the sin of man can and does adversely affect the rest of creation in a way that reacts disastrously upon his own life. John would have agreed with all that Paul says about the creation's bondage to frustration and decay (Rom. 8: 20 f.), and he later expresses the same hope as Paul's for that 'revealing of the sons of God' which will liberate creation from this bondage, when he envisages the manifestation of the new Jerusalem, the glorified community of the people of God, accompanied by the appearance of 'a new heaven and a new earth' (Rev. 21: 1 f.). But first judgment must work itself out to the bitter end.

The Three 'Woes' (8: 13)

It is not only in man's natural environment that the repercussions of his sin are felt; that same sin unleashes demonic forces, uncontrollable by man, which bring woe after woe upon him. This is what is symbolized in the judgments which follow the next trumpet-blasts, preceded as they are by the **Woe, woe, woe** proclaimed against **those who dwell on the earth** (see note on 3: 10) by the **eagle . . . as it flew in mid-heaven** (13). **Eagle** and not 'angel' is the best-attested reading here; an eagle as heavenly messenger, although not found elsewhere in canonical scripture, appears in other apocalyptic writings (cf. 2 Esd. 11:1) and in Christian apocrypha. That each of the three 'woes' announced by the eagle refers to one of the three remaining trumpets is made clear by 9: 12 and 11: 14.

v. The Fifth Trumpet (9: 1–12)

As in the sequence of the seals, so in the trumpets the fifth and sixth are described at greater length than the first four. **1. a star fallen from heaven to earth:** Probably a fallen angel (cf. 12: 4), possibly identical with Abaddon-Apollyon, the angel of the abyss (verse 11). In 1 Enoch 86: 1 'a star fell from heaven' refers to the first fallen angel, who was followed by other 'stars' (see notes on 12: 4, 9; 20: 1–3). **he was given the key of the shaft of the bottomless pit:** It would have been better if RSV (following RV) had translated Gk. *abyssos* by 'abyss' in Rev., as it does in Lk. 8: 31 and Rom. 10: 7. The abyss is the abode of demons, as in Lk. 8: 31; it is pictured here as a hollow place in the heart of the earth, communicating with the upper air by means of a shaft or well (Gk. *phrear*), the cover of which is locked. **3. from the smoke came locusts on the earth:** We recall the Egyptian plague of locusts, so dense a swarm *that the land was darkened* (Exod. 10: 15), and the plague of locusts foretold by Joel, *like blackness . . . spread upon the mountains,* and bringing *a day of darkness and gloom, a day of clouds and thick darkness* (Jl 2: 2). But the locusts now seen by John are no ordinary locusts, but demon-locusts from the abyss; unlike ordinary locusts they leave the vegetation alone but with the sting of their scorpion-tails they torment those men who did not receive the seal of God in their foreheads (cf. 7: 3). The repeated mention of **five months** (5, 10) as the term of their activity has been explained by the five-months' life cycle of certain species of natural locust. **6. men will seek death, and will not find it:** Bodily death would afford an escape from physical pain, but not from the torment of an evil conscience. **7. In appearance the locusts were**

like horses arrayed for battle: Cf. Jl 2: 4, *their appearance is like the appearance of horses:* but what is a bold simile in the description of Joel's locusts takes shape in John's vision, and is further elaborated in verses 7-10. **9. like the noise of many chariots:** Cf. Jl 2: 5, *as with the rumbling of chariots.* **11. They have as king over them the angel of the bottomless pit:** This 'angel of the abyss' is possibly the fallen 'star' of verse 1. **his name in Hebrew is Abaddon:** Abaddon (lit. 'destruction') occurs 6 times in the Hebrew Bible (Job 26: 6; 28: 22; 31: 12; Ps. 88: 11; Prov. 15: 11; 27: 20) as a poetical synonym for Sheol, death, or the grave; here it is given personal force ('the destroyer') and glossed by Gk. *Apollyon,* the present participle of the verb *apollymi* ('destroy')— perhaps with a side-glance at the god Apollo, who in certain phases of his activity symbolized destructive forces.

vi. The Sixth Trumpet (9: 13-21)
13. a voice from the four horns of the golden altar: Perhaps the voice of the angel who was seen offering incense there in 8: 3. The heavenly incense-altar is equipped with horns like its earthly copy (Exod. 30: 2 f.). **14. Release the four angels who are bound at the great river Euphrates:** The Euphrates (cf. 16: 12) is significant as the eastern frontier of the Roman Empire, beyond which lay the Parthian menace (see note on 6: 2). These demon-horsemen with their mounts, hitherto held in leash, are now let loose like avenging furies upon the Roman provinces at **the hour, the day, the month, and the year** appointed (15). **15. to kill a third of mankind:** The demon-locusts were prohibited from killing men, but the demon-cavalry are more lethal: the first four trumpet-plagues blasted one-third of nature, and now **a third of mankind** is massacred. **16. twice ten thousand times ten thousand** (lit. 'two myriads of myriads'; cf. 5: 11): To express the product of these numbers prosaically as 'two hundred thousand thousand' (AV) is to lose their evocative overtones. **17. And this was how I saw the horses in my vision:** The colours of the riders' breastplates, **the colour of fire and of sapphire** (lit. 'hyacinth') **and of sulphur,** correspond respectively to the **fire and smoke and sulphur** which issue from the horses' mouths, thus denoting their demonic nature (cf. 14: 10 f., 19: 20, etc.), and destroy **a third of mankind** (18). The horses' lion-like heads (17) and serpent-like tails (19) further emphasize their destructive power. However symbolically they may be portrayed, there is no doubting the reality of those demonic forces which thrive on men's unbelief and are bent on their ruin; but those who are allied to

their Conqueror are immune against their malignity. **20. The rest of mankind . . . did not repent:** Plague and similar disasters, which bring out the best qualities in some people bring out the worst in many others. Samuel Pepys speaks of the Plague of London (1665) as 'making us more cruel to one another than if we are dogs'; Thucydides made a similar observation in the Plague of Athens over 2000 years earlier. God has pledged His ready pardon wherever a glimmer of repentance is shown, but what if men persist in impenitence?

Interlude before the Seventh Trumpet (10: 1–11: 14)
(*a*) **The Angel with the Little Scroll (10: 1-11)** Although the **mighty angel** whom John now sees **coming down from heaven** has features which recall the vision of Christ in 1: 13 ff., especially **his face . . . like the sun** (1), he is not to be identified with Christ. Holding **a little scroll open in his hand** (2)—for its character and contents see notes on verses 8-11— he bestrides the narrow world like a colossus, and his voice, **like a lion roaring,** awakens **the seven thunders** (3). The **seven thunders** (cf. the sevenfold *voice of the* LORD in Ps. 29) are a further heptad of divine visitations, like the seals, trumpets and bowls, but the revelation which they convey (unlike that contained in the **little scroll**) is not ready to be revealed yet, so John is commanded to **seal up** their utterance and **not write it down** (4; cf. Dan. 12: 4 and contrast Rev. 22: 10). (The late S. H. Hooke has suggested that what John was forbidden to write down on this occasion was later divulged in Jn 12: 31 f.) The colossal angel then swears by God that there will be **no more delay** (6; RSV gives the true sense of Gk. *chronos* here, whereas it is obscured by the AV rendering 'that there should be time no longer'); the purpose of God will now advance swiftly to its fulfilment, at the seventh trumpet-blast. **7. the mystery of God:** The hidden purpose, 'kept secret for long ages' (cf. Rom. 16: 25), had been **announced to his servants the prophets** (cf. Am. 3: 7), but even so knowledge of the time when it would be accomplished had been withheld from them (cf. Mk 13: 32). **10. I took the little scroll from the hand of the angel and ate it:** A similar visionary experience is recorded by Ezekiel (Ezek. 2: 8–3: 3). To eat the scroll is to assimilate its contents; the prophet digests the divine revelation himself before communicating it to others. Ezekiel's scroll was *as sweet as honey* in his mouth (Ezek. 3: 3), although *there were written on it words of lamentation and mourning and woe* (Ezek. 2: 10); John similarly records that he found the little scroll **sweet as honey**

in my mouth, because it contained God's word (cf. Pss. 19: 10; 119: 103; Jer. 15: 16), but since that word was a word of judgment, he found it bitter to digest, just as Ezekiel, after eating his scroll, *went in bitterness* to communicate its contents to the exiles at Tel-abib (Ezek. 3: 14). The contents of John's little scroll are apparently represented by Rev. 11: 1-13, originally a separate and earlier apocalypse now incorporated in John's record and reinterpreted by him. **11. You must again prophesy:** Having digested the contents of the little scroll he must now make them known to others.

(b) **The Two Witnesses (11: 1-14)**

1. I was given a measuring rod like a staff: This fragmentary vision is reminiscent of Ezek. 40: 3 ff., where, however, it is the interpreting angel and not the prophet himself who measures the temple of the new commonwealth, as in the measuring of the new Jerusalem in Rev. 21: 15 ff. No details are preserved here of the dimensions of **the temple of God and the altar and those who worship there. 2. do not measure the court outside the temple; leave that out, for it is given over to the nations:** The apocalypse contained in the 'little scroll' probably referred to the literal city and temple of Jerusalem, and reflected the interval between July 24 and August 27, A.D. 70, when the Romans under Titus were in occupation of the outer court of the temple but had not yet taken the holy house itself. A term of **forty-two months** is prescribed for their occupation of the city (cf. Lk. 21: 24); this is the traditional apocalyptic term of Gentile domination, derived from Dan. 9: 27; 12: 7 (where its primary reference is to the period of the defilement of the temple by the 'abomination of desolation' set up by Antiochus IV from 167 to 164 B.C.). It is identical with the **one thousand two hundred and sixty days** of v. 3 (cf. also 12: 6, 14; 13: 5), during which the **two witnesses** exercise their ministry, **clothed in sackcloth,** the rough garment of hair traditionally associated with prophets (cf. 2 Kg. 1: 8; Zech. 13: 4; Mk 1: 6). The original reference is to the ministry in Jerusalem of a latter-day Moses and Elijah (cf. Dt. 18: 15 ff.; Mal. 4: 5 f.; Mk 9: 4 f., 11 ff.), which is terminated by their martyrdom at the hands of the occupying Roman power. Their martyrdom brings relief to the people whose consciences had been disturbed by their call to repentance; but this relief is short-lived, for after **three and a half days,** during which their dead bodies are publicly exposed in the city, they are raised to life and taken up to heaven (9-12). Their translation is the signal for **a great earthquake** (13), which causes havoc to the city and its inhabitants, so that the survivors are moved to confession and repentance.

But this little apocalypse is now to be re-interpreted in the light of the new context which it acquired by its incorporation in John's Apocalypse, especially in the light of ch. 13. The temple is now the people of God; the measuring of the worshippers (1) is analogous to the sealing of the servants of God in 7: 3-8. The external approaches to this spiritual temple may be assaulted and trodden down by pagan imperialism as some Christians yield to the temptation to compromise with idolatry and so deny Christ. But the true dwelling-place of God is immune from earthly invasion; the church's life is 'hid with Christ in God' (Col. 3: 3) throughout the period of tribulation and loyal confession, symbolized by the three and a half years of verses 2 and 3. The two witnesses now become symbolic figures for the church in its royal and priestly functions, as is suggested by the two metaphors by which the witnesses are designated in v. 4, **the two olive trees and the two lampstands which stand before the Lord of the earth.** In Zech. 4: 2 f., 11-14, where they originally appear, these figures denote Zerubbabel the governor, prince of the house of David, and Joshua the high priest, *the two anointed ones.* **5. fire pours from their mouth and consumes their foes:** Cf. Elijah's power in 2 Kg. 1: 10, 12; the fire from heaven which consumed the men who came to take him came from his mouth in the sense that it fell upon them at his word (cf. Lk. 9: 54). **6. They have power to shut the sky, that no rain may fall:** A further point in common with Elijah (1 Kg. 17: 1); moreover, **the days of their prophesying** (cf. verse 3) last as long as Elijah's drought did (cf. Lk. 4: 25; Jas 5: 17). **they have power over the waters to turn them into blood:** As Moses had (Exod. 4: 9; 7: 17 ff.). **and to smite the earth with every plague:** Perhaps a reference to the nine other plagues of Egypt (cf. 8: 7 ff.; 16: 2 ff.). **the beast that ascends from the bottomless pit:** Indicating demonic origin and character (cf. 9: 1 ff.). This beast from the abyss reappears in 13: 1 ff. and 17: 3 ff., where he is plainly the persecuting Roman Empire, or else the imperial antichrist of the end-time in whom the power and malignity of the persecuting empire are finally embodied and brought to a head; it is this latter sense that is uppermost here. The Gk. word for this **beast** is *thērion*, 'wild beast', as distinct from *zōon*, which is used for the 'living creatures' (AV, unfortunately, 'beasts') of 4: 6 ff. **will make war upon them and conquer them:** Similar language is used of the assault on the saints by the *little horn* of Dan. 7: 21

(cf. Rev. 13: 7). **8. their dead bodies will lie in the street of the great city which is allegorically called Sodom and Egypt:** Jerusalem is called Sodom because of her un-righteousness in Isa. 1: 10; but why is she also called Egypt here? Perhaps because Egypt is an apt symbol for the oppression of the people of God. **where their Lord was crucified:** This points to Jerusalem rather than Rome. Jesus was crucified by Roman law, but even in apocalyptic language this can scarcely be expressed by saying that He was crucified in Rome. Yet Rome has its advocates in this context—most recently J. Munck, who thinks of Peter and Paul as the two witnesses. It might be said that Jesus suffered in His followers when they were put to death in Rome, but 'where also' (AV, RV) distinguishes Him from His witnesses, and presents Him as being crucified personally in the city where they subsequently were martyred. However, we must distinguish our two levels of interpretation—the earlier one, in which **the great city** is Jerusalem: and the later one, in which it is, more generally, the world which has rejected first Christ and then His people. The **three and a half days** (9, 11) during which the witnesses' bodies lie exposed to public gaze, before their resurrection and ascension to heaven, may designedly correspond to the duration of their ministry in the ratio of a day to a year. **10. those who dwell on the earth:** Cf. 3: 10. The phrase here is synonymous with **men from the peoples and tribes and tongues and nations** (9), and confirms the more general interpretation of **the great city** as the whole earth. The **two prophets had been a torment** to them, because the witness of the godly is a condemnation to the ungodly (cf. 1 Kg. 18: 17). The language of v. 11 echoes Ezek. 37: 10. **12. Come up hither:** This is the plural equivalent of the summons to John in 4: 1; but here the rapture of the resurrected martyrs to heaven is described, and described in language reminiscent of that in which Luke records the ascension of Christ (Ac. 1: 9); cf. 1 Th. 4: 17. **13. the rest . . . gave glory to the God of heaven:** Unlike the survivors of 9: 20 f., these turn to God as a result of their experience of His judgments.

14. The second woe has passed: This sentence marks the end of the interlude; it resumes the trumpet visions where they were broken off in 9: 21. The **third woe** is heralded by the blowing of the last trumpet.

vii. The Seventh Trumpet (11: 15-19)
The last trumpet is followed by the proclamation that **the kingdom of the world has become the kingdom of our Lord and of his Christ, and he shall reign for ever and ever** (15).

The sovereignty of God has never ceased, but now it is universally manifested and acknow-ledged; at last the time has come for the full realization of the divine purpose that in Jesus' name 'every knee should bow, . . . and every tongue confess that Jesus Christ is Lord' (Phil. 2: 10 f.). **17. who art and who wast,** but no longer 'who art to come' (as in 1: 4, 8; 4: 8); the Coming One has now come. **thou hast . . . begun to reign:** The proper rendering of the ingressive aorist *ebasileusas*. (The aorist of *basileuō* is used differently in 19: 6.) **18. The nations raged:** Cf. Ps. 2: 1. **thy wrath came:** Divine judgment and reward (especially judg-ment) have been present in abundance in the previous stages of John's vision, but they reach their climax at the seventh trumpet. The climax of judgment is to be elaborated in the vision of the seven bowls (15: 5 ff.); the climax of reward in the vision of the new Jerusalem (21: 9 ff.). Preparation is made for the vision of the seven bowls by the opening of the heavenly sanctuary (Gk. *naos*)—implying the revelation of God's hidden counsel—with attendant thunder-peals and lightning-flashes (19) such as preceded the sounding of the seven trumpets (8: 5). **the ark of his covenant was seen:** This is the first mention of the ark in Rev.; it is the archetype of the ark in the Mosaic tabernacle and Solomon's temple. Its exposure now is a token that God will fulfil to the last detail His covenant-promises to His people.

We are now carried back to the beginning of the story of salvation: a new series of visions or tableaux portrays significant figures and episodes from the course of events outlined in chapters 5-11.

Second Division: Tableaux of Conflict and Triumph (12: 1-22: 5)

I. THE WOMAN, THE CHILD AND THE DRAGON (12: 1-17)
i. The Birth of the Child (12: 1-6)
1. a great portent (Gk. *sēmeion*, 'sign') **appeared in heaven:** Cf. 12: 3; 15: 1. **a woman clothed with the sun, with the moon under her feet:** Cf. Ca. 6: 10. The precise source of this imagery cannot be determined; various partial parallels from the ancient Near East are adduced by commentators. The woman is no individual human being, but the celestial counterpart of an earthly com-munity; the fact that she wears **on her head a crown of twelve stars** (cf. Gen. 37: 9) marks her out as being the true Israel, from which the Messiah was born. One of the Qumran hymns similarly pictures the faithful community as a woman enduring birth-pangs until she

brings to birth a man child, *a wonder of a counsellor* (quoting Isa. 9: 6, where this is one of the titles of the Davidic prince of the four names). John sees no discontinuity in the life of the true Israel before and after the birth and exaltation of Messiah; the faithful remnant of the old Israel was the nucleus of the new. **2. she was with child and she cried out in her pangs of birth:** Cf. Isa. 7: 14; Mic. 5: 3. **3. a great red dragon, with seven heads and ten horns:** This is Leviathan, the primaeval dragon of chaos, whose overthrow by God in the beginning (Ps. 74: 14; Isa. 51: 9) and at the end-time (Isa. 27: 1) is declared in various OT writings. That his heads (Ps. 74: 14) were seven in number is attested in the Ugaritic texts, where he is called 'the accursed one of seven heads'. His **ten horns** are probably borrowed from the fourth beast of Dan. 7: 7 (cf. Rev. 13: 1; 17: 12). Here he is identified with the serpent of Eden and with Satan (verse 9). **4. His tail swept down a third of the stars of heaven:** Cf. Dan. 8: 10, where the *little horn* (Antiochus Epiphanes) casts *some of the host of the stars* down to the ground and tramples upon them. This may refer to Antiochus's discouraging the worship of certain deities in favour of Olympian Zeus, whose manifestation on earth he claimed to be. But here (whatever the source of the imagery may have been) the reference is probably to the angels who were involved in Satan's fall (cf. 9: 1; also verse 9 below). For the third part of the stars cf. 8: 12. **5. she brought forth a male child, one who is to rule all the nations with a rod of iron:** These words from Ps. 2: 9 identify the child with the Davidic Messiah (cf. 19: 15); in 2: 27 they have already been applied to the overcoming confessor, but they are applicable to him only by virtue of his association with the Messiah (cf. verse 11 below). **her child was caught up to God and to his throne:** It is strange that the ascension of Christ is here presented as the immediate sequel to His birth, but it would not be less strange if the child represents the people of Christ, or Christ with His people. John is using ancient material, which he re-moulds so that its elements tell the gospel story, but its elements evidently included nothing that could be reinterpreted of the events between Christ's birth and ascension. There are admittedly exegetical problems here whose solution escapes us. **6. and the woman fled into the wilderness:** A reference to the flight of the Palestinian church in A.D. 66, at the outbreak of the Jewish revolt; according to Eusebius, she found a refuge in the territory of Pella beyond Jordan—but did some members settle in the wilderness of Judaea? The true Israel of whom Christ was born lives on, according to the seer, in the Palestinian church; Christians elsewhere are **the rest of her offspring** (v. 17). **where she has a place prepared by God:** Cf. Isa. 26: 20. **one thousand two hundred and sixty days:** Cf. v. 14; 11: 2 f.; 13: 5. During this period of Satanic wrath the woman is safe, while her children are persecuted; the Palestinian church escaped the most hostile attentions of the imperial power during the first-century campaign against the Christians of Rome and Asia Minor.

ii. The Downfall of the Dragon (12: 7-12)
7. Now war arose in heaven: Satan's fall from heaven 'as lightning' (Lk. 10: 18) is here portrayed in pictorial terms. Jesus' ministry involved his overthrow, for his kingdom could not stand against the inbreaking kingdom of God, and he received his *coup de grâce* through the cross, the crown of Jesus' ministry (cf. Col. 2: 15). In the early Christian hymn-book curiously called the *Odes of Solomon* (Ode 22) Christ, speaking of His triumph over death, addresses God as the One 'that overthrew by my hands the dragon with seven heads: and thou hast set me over his roots that I might destroy his seed'. **9. that ancient serpent:** Cf. Gen. 3: 1 ff.; also Isa. 27: 1. **who is called the Devil and Satan:** Gk. *diabolos* ('calumniator') is the equivalent of Heb. *satan* ('accuser'); in OT Satan appears as chief prosecutor in the heavenly court (Zech. 3: 1 f.; cf. Job 1: 6 ff.; 1 Chr. 21: 1), hence he is called in verse 10 **the accuser of our brethren.** Thanks to the victory of Christ, however, he is the principal target of the challenge: 'Who shall bring any charge against God's elect? It is God who justifies; who is to condemn?' (Rom. 8: 33 f.). The victory of Christ and the downfall of Satan are celebrated in the triumphal shout of vv. 10-12. In Christ's victory the victory of His people is included (cf. Rom. 8: 37; 1 C. 15: 57; 2 C. 2: 14). As He conquered by His passion (Rev. 5: 5 f.), so they in turn conquer the dragon **by the blood of the Lamb and by the word of their testimony, for they loved not their lives even unto death** (11). But the dragon's downfall means an intensification of his malignant activity on earth, during the brief interval before he is put out of harm's way (cf. 20: 1 ff.).
iii. The Assault on the Woman and her other Children (12: 13-17)
14. the woman was given the two wings of the great eagle that she might fly from the serpent into the wilderness: Cf. Exod. 19: 4, where God speaks thus of Israel's escape from Egypt into the wilderness: *I bore you on eagles' wings and brought you to myself* (cf. also Dt. 32: 10-12). **a time, and times, and half a time:**

This variant designation of the 1260 days of verse 6 is derived from Dan. 7: 25; 12: 7. **15. The serpent poured water like a river out of his mouth after the woman:** This may refer to some incident of the war of A.D. 66-73 no longer identifiable which threatened to cut off the church's escape. The reference might, indeed, be to a literal flood, like that which prevented the Jews of Gadara from escaping across the Jordan from the Romans in March, A.D. 68 (Josephus, *War* iv. 433-436); but a literal flood would scarcely be spoken of as 'like a river'. **16. the earth opened its mouth and swallowed the river:** For the personification of earth cf. Gen. 4: 11; Num. 16: 30. **17. the dragon . . . went off to make war on the rest of her offspring:** Frustrated in his attack on the Palestinian church, the dragon stirs up fierce persecution against Christians in other parts of the empire. That Christians are meant is shown by the fact that they not only **keep the commandments of God** but also **bear testimony to Jesus**—the very activity for which John was in exile (1: 9; cf. 19: 10). **And he stood on the sand of the sea:** The bulk of later manuscripts read 'I stood' (Gk. *estathēn*), and link the clause to what follows in 13: 1 (so AV); but **he stood** (Gk. *estathē*) is right; the subject is the dragon, not the seer, who is still viewing the earthly scene from his heavenly vantage-point.

II. THE TWO BEASTS (13: 1-18)

i. The Beast from the Sea (13: 1-10)

1. I saw a beast rising out of the sea: This **beast** is the persecuting Roman Empire. We may think of it as rising in its home, the city of Rome, far west across the Mediterranean Sea from Patmos; but **sea** means more than this: 'the beast from the abyss', as it is called in 11: 7, is thrown up, like other chaotic forces of evil, by the cosmic deep (cf. Dan. 7: 2 f.). **with ten horns and seven heads:** The **ten horns** (cf. 12: 3) are derived from Dan. 7: 7, where the fourth beast in Daniel's vision of judgment is so equipped. The horns of Daniel's fourth beast (Dan. 7: 24) are ten Hellenistic rulers, between Alexander the Great (332-323 B.C.) and Antiochus IV (175-163 B.C.); for their significance in Rev., cf. 17: 12-14. The **seven heads** are derived from the dragon (12: 3), signifying that the beast's authority is received from him (v. 2); but they are further explained in terms of the seven hills of Rome (17: 9) and seven Roman emperors (17: 10). **with ten diadems upon its horns:** Indicating their royal character. **and a blasphemous name upon its heads:** Indicating the claims to divine honour made by or on behalf of the Roman emperors. **2. the beast that I saw was like a leopard:** Like the

third beast of Dan. 7: 6. **its feet were like a bear's:** The second beast of Dan. 7: 5 was *like a bear.* **its mouth was like a lion's mouth:** The first beast of Dan. 7: 4 was *like a lion.* Thus John's beast, while it is mainly a representation of Daniel's fourth beast, has features drawn from Daniel's first three beasts. **3. One of its heads seemed to have a mortal wound:** A reference probably to Nero, who committed suicide on June 9, A.D. 68. **its mortal wound was healed:** When Nero, deposed by the senate in A.D. 68, committed suicide to escape the ignominious death to which that body had condemned him, many of his eastern subjects (among whom he had enjoyed great popularity) refused to believe that he was really dead. For some twenty years after his death, therefore, the belief persisted that he had not really died but gone into hiding, probably beyond the Euphrates, and that he would return one day at the head of an army of Parthians to recover his dominions and rule once more as emperor. Several opportunists profited by this widespread belief to set themselves up as pretended Neros. After 88, the last year in which one of these pretenders is known to have arisen, the belief that Nero was still alive was generally given up; but it was replaced by the belief that one day Nero would return from the dead and regain his sovereignty. This later belief in a *Nero redivivus,* which can be traced right on almost to the end of the second century, was not only a subject of hope to pagans in the eastern empire, but also a subject of dread to Christians, who identified *Nero redivivus* with the last antichrist. The persecuting rage of the empire had already been experienced by John and his fellow-Christians, but when the imperial beast is embodied in the revived ruler who had previously received a **mortal wound**—an embodiment still future to the seer—that persecuting rage will reach an unprecented intensity. **5. a mouth uttering haughty and blasphemous words:** Cf. Dan. 7: 8; 11: 36, **forty-two months:** The duration of the *little horn's* authority in Dan. 7: 25. **7. it was allowed to make war on the saints and to conquer them:** An echo of Dan. 7: 21 (cf. Rev. 11: 7); this conquest consists in the infliction of bodily death on them, but the ultimate victory is theirs (15: 2). World-wide power is exercised by the beast, and world-wide worship paid to it. Cf. 2 Th. 2: 3 f., where the 'man of lawlessness . . . opposes and exalts himself against every so-called god or object of worship (cf. Dan. 11: 37), so that he takes his seat in the temple of God, proclaiming himself to be God.' **8. all who dwell on**

earth (cf. 3: 10) are here identified as those **whose name has not been written before the foundation of the world in the book of life of the Lamb that was slain.** RSV makes it plain, as AV and RV do not, that **before the foundation of the world** refers to **written**, not to **slain** (cf. 17: 8; also 3: 5; 20: 12, 15). **10. The endurance and faith of the saints** are rooted in their recognition of the sovereignty of God over the world of mankind; His righteous retribution and reward will assuredly be manifested in due course (cf. Hab. 2: 3 f.; also Mt. 26: 52).

ii. The Beast from the Earth (13: 11–18)
ii. I saw another beast: Thus the unholy trinity of dragon, beast and false prophet is completed. As the true Christ received His authority from the Father (Mt. 11: 27; 28: 18; Jn 13: 3), so Antichrist receives authority from the dragon (verse 4); as the Holy Spirit glorifies the true Christ (Jn 16: 14), so the false prophet glorifies Antichrist (verse 12). **which rose out of the earth:** John on Patmos may have in view the neighbouring mainland of Asia Minor, where the cult of Rome and Augustus flourished (cf. 2: 13). The second beast is the embodiment of this cult, or its priesthood, in its final development. It looks as harmless as **a lamb,** but its real nature is revealed when it opens its mouth, for it speaks **like a dragon.** The imperial worship which was fostered already in provincial Asia would spread over the world, and the final intensification of imperial persecution would be accompanied by world-wide pressure of every form, psychological and economic, to worship the divinity of Caesar. The mighty works and 'pretended signs and wonders' which, according to Paul, attend the parousia of Antichrist and seduce unbelievers (2 Th. 2: 9 f.) are manipulated by this second beast, who acts as Antichrist's Minister of Propaganda. The **image of the beast** (14 f.) recalls the 'abomination of desolation standing where he ought not' (Mk 13: 14, RV). The economic boycott of nonconformists (16 f.) is almost startling in its prophetic clarity. The **mark** stamped **on the right hand or the forehead,** where Jews wore their phylacteries (cf. Dt. 6: 8), is **the name of the beast** worshipped by those who receive it —an unholy travesty of the seal stamped on the foreheads of the servants of God (7: 3; 14: 1; cf. 22: 4). **18. This calls for wisdom:** Similarly the prophecies of Daniel were conveyed in symbolical terms which required divine enlightenment for their elucidation: *none of the wicked shall understand; but those who are wise* (the *maskilim*) *shall understand* (Dan. 12: 10). **let him who has understanding reckon the number of the beast:** The beast is embodied

in the emperor, and it is one of the emperors whose 'number' is to be reckoned. **for it.is a human number:** Lit., 'the number of a man', i.e. the total numerical value of the letters in some person's name, when spelt in the Greek, or possibly in the Hebrew, alphabet. This reckoning of the numerical value of words and names was a riddle-game among the Greeks and Romans (as in the frequently quoted Greek graffito from Pompeii, 'I love the girl whose number is 545'); among the Jews (who called it 'gematria') and some early Christians it was treated as a matter of mystical significance—as in the *Sibylline Oracles* (i. 328), where the appropriateness of 888 as the numerical value of the name of Jesus in Greek is pointed out. There is nothing mystical about the present passage; the seer's use of gematria could be a precaution against a charge of sedition if the name of the individual were spelt out in full. **its number is six hundred and sixty-six:** So successful was the seer's precaution that the solution of his riddle had been forgotten by the time of Irenaeus (A.D. 180) and remains uncertain to this day. One must hope that the original readers of Rev. understood his allusion. To complicate the matter there is a variant reading 616, but this may have been a deliberate change in order to identify the 'beast' with Gaius Caesar (spelt in Greek). Gaius's attempt to have his image erected in the Jerusalem temple in A.D. 40 marked him out as belonging to the authentic succession of Antichrist. A popular explanation of the true reading, 666, takes it as the sum of letters in 'Nero Caesar', as spelt in Hebrew or Aramaic (precisely the required spelling appears on an Aramaic document of Nero's reign from the Wadi Murabba'at, in Jordan). Another attractive suggestion is that John had in mind a type of coin circulating in the province of Asia, on which the abbreviated style of Domitian in Greek ('Emperor Caesar Domitian Augustus Germanicus') yields the total 666. But complete certainty is unattainable. George Salmon's 'three rules' for making any desired name yield the required total are still carried out in deadly seriousness by earnest Bible readers who imagine that John was really referring to the latest nine days' wonder in world politics of the 20th century. The three rules are: 'First, if the proper name by itself will not yield it, add a title; secondly, if the sum cannot be found in Greek, try Hebrew, or even Latin; thirdly, do not be too particular about the spelling' (*Introduction to the NT*, 1889, p. 253).

III. FIRST FRUITS, HARVEST AND VINTAGE (14: 1–20)
The series of tableaux in ch. 14 may be summed

up under the heads of first fruits (1-5), harvest (14-16) and vintage (17-20), the first fruits and harvest being separated by four angelic proclamations (6-13).

i. First Fruits (14: 1-5)

1. on mount Zion stood the Lamb: That is, on the heavenly Zion (cf. Heb. 12: 22), since He and His 'fair army' appear **before the throne and before the living creatures and before the elders** (3; cf. 4: 2 ff.; 7: 9 ff.). The fact that His 144,000 companions have **his name and his Father's name written on their foreheads** suggests their identity with the 144,000 servants of God who are sealed on their foreheads in 7: 3 ff.; while the fact that they **follow the Lamb wherever he goes** (4) links them also with the white-robed multitude of 7: 9 ff. (cf. especially 7: 17). The scene has a noteworthy parallel in 2 Esd. 2: 42 ff., 'I, Ezra, saw on Mount Zion a great multitude which I could not number, and they all were praising the Lord with songs.' Ezra goes on to describe how in their midst stood 'the Son of God, whom they confessed in the world.' **2. I heard a voice from heaven**—or 'a sound from heaven'. For **the sound of many waters** cf. 1: 15; 19: 6; for **the sound of loud thunder** cf. 19: 6, and for **the sound of harpers playing on their harps** cf. 5: 8; 15: 2. The sound which John hears is the **new song** (3) of redemption, accompanied by the music of heaven. It is not a different song from the 'new song' of 5: 9 f., except that now it is sung in the first person, as only those can sing it who have themselves been **redeemed from the earth. 4. they are chaste:** Lit. 'they are virgins'—an exceptional use of Gk. *parthenos* in the masculine. The term has usually been interpreted here of celibacy, as though these men had, in Christ's words, 'made themselves eunuchs for the sake of the kingdom of heaven' (Mt. 19: 12). In that case we might compare Paul's injunction in view of the 'impending distress': 'let those who have wives live as though they had none' (1 C. 7: 26, 29). Cf. E. Stauffer: 'There is here no suggestion either of human impotence on the one side or of successful monkish achievement on the other. The reference is to the genuine heroism of those who are called for the sake of a unique situation and commission.' But this implies that married men have 'defiled themselves with women'— something so contrary to the uniform biblical teaching on marriage (cf. Heb. 13: 4) that it is unlikely to be introduced incidentally in so thoroughly 'Hebraic' a book as this. More probably the reference is to people who have been, in the language of the Pastoral Letters, 'the husband of one wife'. **these have been redeemed from mankind as first fruits for**

God and the Lamb: The first fruits are the earnest of the much greater harvest to come (cf. verses 15 f.): as Paul speaks of his first converts in Asia and Achaia as the 'first fruits' (Gk. *aparchē*) of these provinces, so John thinks of these 144,000 as the first instalment of redeemed humanity, presented as a living sacrifice to God and to Christ. **5. in their mouth no lie was found:** The same testimony was borne to their Master (1 Pet. 2: 22; quoting Isa. 53: 9). **they are spotless:** Cf. the white robes of 7: 9, 13 f.

ii. Angel Proclamations (14: 6-13)

(a) **An Eternal Gospel (14: 6-7)**

6. another angel: This phrase appears six times in this chapter, but it would have been more consistent with English idiom to render it on its first appearance here by 'an angel' (Gk. *allos* in a sequence like this is used for both 'one' and 'another'). **flying in midheaven:** Cf. 8: 13. **with an eternal gospel to proclaim to those who dwell on earth:** The earth-dwellers are here designated by a different verb from that used in 3: 10, etc.; for this use of Gk. *kathēmai* (lit. 'sit') cf. Lk. 21: 35. The gospel which is preached to them calls for submission to God as Creator and Judge rather than faith in Christ as Saviour and Lord. **7. Fear God and give him glory:** Cf. 11: 13. To give God glory may imply making confession to Him, as in Jos. 7: 19. **the sea and the fountains of water:** Salt water and fresh water are here distinguished; the Creator has power over both, as the second and third trumpet-judgments showed (8: 8 f., 10 f.).

(b) **The Fall of Babylon (14: 8)**

8. Fallen, fallen is Babylon the great: This proclamation echoes such OT passages as Isa. 21: 9; Jer. 51: 8; it is elaborated in the dirge over Babylon in ch. 18. **she who made all nations drink the wine of her impure passion:** Cf. Jer. 51: 7; Rev. 17: 2, 4. For 'passion' we should probably render 'intoxication' here (as also in v. 10; 16: 19; 18: 3; 19: 15), Gk. *thymos* having here the sense borne by Heb. *chemah* in Isa. 51: 17, 22; Jer. 25: 15; Hab. 2: 15.

(c) **The Doom of Apostates (14: 9-11)**

The third angel follows with a loud warning of the divine judgment which will fall on anyone who **worships the beast and its image,** or receives 'the mark of the beast' **on his forehead or on his hand** (9: cf. 13: 15-17). The warning may be intended for all mankind, but it is especially directed at apostate Christians (cf. Heb. 6: 4-6). It may be a mitigation of the fierceness of their judgment that it is endured **in the presence of the holy angels and in the presence of the Lamb** (10); to be judged in His presence is less intolerable than to be banished from His presence unjudged. Yet would their anguish not be rendered the more acute by the very presence of the one whom they have denied by their apostasy? **11. the smoke of their torment goes up for ever and ever:** The language is drawn from the description of the overthrow of the cities of the plain under the rain of brimstone and fire; cf. Gen. 19: 24, 28; Isa. 34: 9 f.; Jude 7.

(*d*) **The Bliss of the Faithful Departed (14: 12–13)**
On the other hand, those who maintain their confession steadfastly and resist the blandishments and intimidation of the antichristian power, even at the cost of life (12; cf. 13: 10), are pronounced **blessed** in their death by a further **voice from heaven,** because they **die in the Lord** (13). The seer is commanded to write down this beatitude, for the encouragement of those who **henceforth** suffer as martyrs of Christ. The heavenly voice is confirmed by the Spirit: for apostates and faithful confessors alike it is true that **their deeds follow them;** but whereas this means tribulation for the former, it means rest after suffering for the blessed. The **labours** from which they rest are the troubles they endured, not the works which they accomplished.

iii. **Harvest (14: 14–16)**
14. seated on the cloud one like a son of man: The language is derived from Dan. 7: 13 (cf. Rev. 1: 13), where *one like a son of man* comes with the clouds of heaven to receive from the Ancient of Days universal and everlasting dominion; this is He to whom the Father has also given 'authority to execute judgment, because he is the Son of man' (Jn 5: 27). Once again (as in 11: 15 ff.) we are brought to the final judgment: as in Mt. 13: 39, 'the harvest is the close of the age'. In Mt. 13: 39 ff., however, 'the reapers are angels', sent by the Son of man to 'gather out of his kingdom all causes of sin and all evildoers'; here the Son of man is himself the reaper, and his angel-servants are absent from the picture. **15. Put in your sickle:** Cf. Jl 3: 13a (to which the present passage ultimately goes back); Mk 4: 29.

iv. **Vintage (14: 17–20)**
At the grain-harvest the grain is gathered into barns, although the tares and chaff are burned. But this vintage-scene symbolizes unmitigated judgment: this is perhaps why the angel who gathers the vintage receives his orders from **the angel who has power over fire** (18), fire being another judgment-symbol (cf. Mt. 3: 11 f.; 1 C. 3: 13 ff.). The use of the vintage as a judgment-symbol probably goes back to Joel 3: 13 b; it also recalls Isa. 63: 1-6, where the conqueror over Edom has his garments all

stained with the lifeblood of his enemies whom he has trampled underfoot as grapes are trodden in the wine press (cf. Rev. 19: 13, 15). So here **the vintage of the earth** is trodden so unrelentingly in **the great wine press of the wrath of God** (19) that blood flows bridle-high for a distance of **one thousand six hundred stadia** or furlongs (20). We may rephrase this measurement as 200 miles, but if we do so we miss the symbolic completeness of 1600, which is the square of 40. Yet the remark that the vintage was trodden **outside the city** (20) may remind us of one who absorbed in His own person the judgment due to mankind, and did so outside the city (cf. Jn 19: 20; Heb. 13: 12).

IV. THE SEVEN LAST PLAGUES (15: 1-16: 21)
i. **Introduction of the Seven Angels and Victory-Song of the Redeemed (15: 1-8)**
1. I saw another portent in heaven: Cf. 12: 1, 3. **seven angels with seven plagues:** Cf. verse 6, which is apparently anticipated by verse 1. But before more is said about the seven angels, John describes another vision of the beatified martyrs. **2. a sea of glass mingled with fire:** Cf. 4: 6; the fire which is added here may symbolize the judgment about to be consummated in the seven last plagues. **those who had conquered the beast:** This is the true sense; RV 'them that had come victorious from the beast' is more literal, but the Greek here imitates a Hebrew construction (literally 'to conquer from'), translated 'prevailed over' in 1 Sam. 17: 50. They had conquered by refusing to worship **the beast and its image** or to be sealed with **the number of its name** (cf. 13: 15-17; 14: 9-11). **standing beside the sea of glass:** Or perhaps 'on the sea of glass' (AV); the preposition *epi* is ambiguous. In either case, they stand before the heavenly throne (cf. 7: 9). **with the harps of God in their hands:** Cf. the harpers of 14: 2. This company recalls the 144,000 of 14: 1 ff.; but now their song is called **the song of Moses, the servant of God, and the song of the Lamb** (3). **The song of the Lamb** is probably 'Worthy is the Lamb' (5: 12); **the song of Moses** refers not only to the hymn of praise for redemption in Exod. 15: 1-18 but also to the judgment-song of Dt. 32, for in verses 3 f. we can discern clear echoes of Dt. 32: 4:

The Rock, his work is perfect;
for all his ways are justice.
A God of faithfulness and without iniquity,
just and right is he.

But the song of verses 3 f. is a cento of passages from various places in OT. **Great and wonder-**

ful are thy deeds: Cf. Pss. 104: 24; 111: 2; 139: 14. **O Lord God, the Almighty:** Cf. 4: 8 (echoing Isa. 6: 3). **Just and true are thy ways:** Cf. Ps. 145: 17. **O King of the ages:** Or 'Eternal King'; cf. Jer. 10: 10. The strongly attested variant reading, 'O King of the nations' (margin) is due to the influence of Jer. 10: 7, *Who would not fear thee, O King of the nations?* A much more weakly attested variant is 'King of saints' (AV). **4. thou alone art holy:** Cf. Pss. 86: 10; 99: 3, 5, 9. **All nations shall come and worship thee:** Cf. Ps. 86: 9. **5. the temple of the tent of witness in heaven was opened:** The opening of the sanctuary, denoting the unfolding and fulfilment of God's purpose, recalls 11: 19, and may well be a resumption of it, after the 'signs' and other visions which have intervened. In that case, just as the breaking of the seventh seal was the cue for the blowing of the seven trumpets (8: 1 ff.), so the blowing of the seventh trumpet is the cue for the emptying of the seven bowls of wrath on earth. **6. robed in pure bright linen:** They are vested in priestly garments for their terrible liturgy. The remarkable variant 'stone' (Gk. *lithon*) for 'linen' (Gk. *linon*) is preferred by some on the principle that the more difficult reading is more likely to be original; it has been explained in terms of the stones in the high-priest's breastplate, or of the description of the king of Tyre in Ezek. 28: 13, *every precious stone was your covering.* But the weight of the evidence favours 'linen' here. **their breasts girded with golden girdles:** Like the Son of man (1: 13). **7. seven golden bowls full of the wrath of God:** A contrast to the golden bowls containing the prayers of the saints (5: 8), and yet the out-pouring of wrath on the earth-dwellers is the response to those prayers (6: 10; 8: 3 ff.). **8. the temple was filled with smoke from the glory of God:** The cloud envelops the divine *shekhinah* as in Exod. 40: 34 f.; 1 Kg. 8: 10 ff.; Isa. 6: 4. Long deferred though God's judgment may be, when once it is begun it proceeds with terrible swiftness. The seven receptacles of His wrath are not narrow-necked 'vials' (as in AV), from which the contents trickle slowly, but wide, shallow bowls, whose entire contents splash out immediately when they are upturned. But while the strange and swift work is going on, the sanctuary is inaccessible; the meaning may be that the time for intercession is past.

ii. The Outpouring of the Seven Plagues (16: 1–21)

There is a remarkable parallelism between most of the seven trumpet-judgments of chapters 8-11 and the last plagues of chapter 16. In the first form of each series the earth, sea, fresh water and sun are respectively affected; but the present judgments are more severe than their 'trumpet' counterparts; where the former judgments affected one-third of the area in question, these affect the whole. The sixth plague in the present series, like the sixth trumpet-judgment, affects the Euphrates; and the emptying of the seventh bowl, like the blowing of the last trumpet, is followed by a proclamation from heaven. We may also be struck by the resemblances between these 'last plagues' and the plagues of Egypt. Unpalatable as the work of judgment may be, it is inseparable from a moral universe. 'Is God unjust to inflict wrath on us?' asks Paul. 'By no means!' is his reply. 'For then how could God judge the world?' (Rom. 3: 5 f.). Symbolical as the details of these plagues are, they denote terrible realities. More terrible than the plagues them-selves, however, is the way in which those on whom they fall are but hardened in their impenitence.

1. I heard a loud voice from the temple: The voice of God Himself. **pour out on the earth:** Here 'earth' is used in a general sense, and is not restricted to the dry land, as it is in verse 2. **2. foul and evil sores:** Like the Egyptian plague of boils (Exod. 9: 8 ff.). **3. the sea ... became like the blood of a dead man, and every living thing died that was in the sea:** A more wholesale judgment than the similar one of 8: 8 f. **4. the rivers and the fountains of water . . . became blood:** As in the first plague of Egypt (Exod. 7: 17 ff.). **5. the angel of water:** The various natural elements and forces are all placed under the control of their appropriate angels in Jewish literature of this period; cf. the four angels who controlled the four winds in 7: 1, and the angel of fire in 14: 18. **Just art thou in these thy judgments:** The hymn of vv. 5 f. strikes the same note as that of 15: 3 f., and similarly echoes Moses' song of Dt. 32. **thou who art and wast, O Holy One:** Even in 1611 there was no justification for the AV reading 'which art, and wast, and shalt be'; all the earlier English versions read 'holy' and have no knowledge of 'shalt be' (which resulted from a misreading of Gk. *hosios*, 'holy', as the future participle *esomenos*). **6. It is their due:** The same Gk. words as are rendered 'they are worthy' in 3: 4—'a terrible antithesis' (H. B. Swete). **7. I heard the altar cry:** The incense-altar responds with an Amen to the angel's affirmation of divine righteousness; why the altar? Perhaps because it was witness to the martyrs' prayer of 6: 10. **8. the sun . . . was allowed to scorch men with fire:** Contrariwise, when the fourth trumpet sounded, one-third of the sunlight (and of the light of the other luminaries) was darkened. **9. they did**

not repent and give him glory: Unlike those who survived the earthquake of 11: 13; but cf. 9: 20 f. and the note there. **10. The fifth angel poured his bowl on the throne of the beast:** Presumably on Rome; the centre of world-power is now attacked. **its kingdom was in darkness:** Cf. the ninth plague of Egypt (Exod. 10: 21 ff.). **men gnawed their tongues in anguish:** Hardly on account of the darkness, but because of the continuing pain of the previous plague, which was aggravated by the darkness. **11. and cursed the God of heaven . . . and did not repent:** A repetition of verse 9. **12. the great river Euphrates . . . was dried up:** After the blowing of the sixth trumpet four demon-angels bound at the Euphrates frontier were released to invade the Roman Empire. Now, across the dry bed of the river, **the kings from the east** (a reference to the Parthians and their allies) may invade the Roman provinces unimpeded. But worse than this overrunning of ordered civilization by the incursion of alien armies is the perversion of the minds of those in authority by demonic powers, operating on a world-wide scale to engulf humanity in ultimate catastrophe. These demonic powers are here pictured as the **three foul spirits like frogs** (13) from the mouths of the unholy trinity. The picture may be suggested by the second plague of Egypt (Exod. 8: 2 ff.); but this is a plague infinitely more destructive. The kings of the whole world—not only the invaders from the east but the rulers of the Roman Empire and the outer barbarians (cf. 17: 12 ff.)—are gathered **for battle on the great day of God the Almighty** (14), the day when His cause is finally vindicated.

15. Lo, I am coming like a thief: This parenthetic announcement by Christ (cf. 3: 3) is no accidental displacement: 'the day of the Lord will come like a thief in the night' (1 Th. 5: 2; cf. Mt. 24: 43 f.). **Blessed is he who is awake, keeping his garments:** The soldier who is alert and prepared for a sudden attack or call to action will not lose time by looking for his clothes or incur disgrace by *fleeing away naked in that day* (Am. 2: 16; cf. Mk 14: 52). Spiritual alertness is here enjoined, 'for you know neither the day nor the hour' (Mt. 25: 13). **that he may not go naked and be seen exposed:** According to the Mishnah, the captain of the temple in Jerusalem went his rounds of the precincts by night, and if a member of the temple police was caught asleep at his post, his clothes were taken off and burned, and he was sent away naked in disgrace. Cf. 3: 18.

16. And they assembled them: The subject is the three demonic spirits of verses 13 f.; AV 'he' is due to the singular verb *synēgagen*, but the verb is singular because the subject is neuter plural. **at the place which is called in Hebrew Armageddon:** Better: 'Har-Magedon', which could be interpreted in Hebrew as 'Mount Megiddo'—the spelling Megiddon appears in Zech. 12: 10 and *Magedōn* in the LXX of 2 Chr. 35: 22. Megiddo was the scene of many a decisive battle in antiquity, as in more recent times. The difficulty with this, however, is that there is no 'Mount Megiddo'; Megiddo was the name of a city which gave its name to the pass which it commanded. An alternative suggestion, which is not without difficulties of its own, is that the reference is to Heb. *har mo'ed, the mount of assembly* of Isa. 14: 13: the place of divine assembly has its demonic counterpart. In any case, it is on no ordinary battlefield that these kings and their armies are mustered for the eschatological conflict. The sequel to their mustering is described in 19: 19. **17. It is done:** The last plague has now been poured out. Cf. 21: 6. **18. flashes of lightning, loud noises, peals of thunder:** Such as followed the blowing of the seventh trumpet (11: 19). **a great earthquake:** More disastrous than that of 11: 13. **19. The great city was split into three parts:** Cf. 11: 8; perhaps it is the world-city rather than Jerusalem. It is not Rome, which receives separate mention as **great Babylon** (cf. 14: 8); what is said of her here is amplified in 17: 1-18: 24. **20. every island fled away, and no mountains were to be found:** Compare the result of the breaking of the sixth seal (6: 14); see also 20: 11. **21. great hailstones . . . dropped on men from heaven:** Compare the Egyptian plague of hail (Exod. 9: 22 ff.); but these hailstones, **heavy as a hundredweight,** are no ordinary ones; in the general convulsion of nature a rain of meteorites may be pictured. But it produces no repentance, even for the time being, as the hail in Egypt did.

V. BABYLON THE GREAT (17: 1-19: 5)

One of the angelic announcements of ch. 14 proclaimed the fall of 'Babylon the great'; and later, when the seventh bowl of judgment was emptied, 'God remembered great Babylon, to make her drain the cup of the fury of his wrath' (16: 19). The judgment of great Babylon is now portrayed in a further vision.

i. The Scarlet Woman (17: 1-18)
1. one of the seven angels who had the seven bowls: Cf. 15: 7; 21: 9. **the great harlot:** For similar descriptions of other cities cf. Nah. 3: 4 (Nineveh); Isa. 23: 15 f. (Tyre); Ezek. 23: 5 ff. (Samaria). Jerusalem herself is so portrayed in Ezek. 16: 15 ff.; 23: 11 ff. **who is seated upon many waters:** The language is

W

borrowed from Jer. 51: 13, where the literal Babylon dwells 'by many waters'; for its present meaning cf. verse 15. **2. with whom the kings of the earth have committed fornication:** Have concluded political and economic treaties. **with the wine of whose fornication the dwellers on earth have become drunk:** Cf. 14: 8; the reference is to Rome's domination of the Mediterranean world. **3. And he carried me away in the Spirit:** For this language of prophetic ecstasy cf. Ezek. 37: 1; 40: 1 f. **a woman sitting on a scarlet beast:** The beast is patently the beast from the sea of 13: 1 ff.; the imperial city is maintained by the empire. The colour of the beast, like the woman's finery (4), bespeaks Rome's ostentatious splendour. **4. holding in her hand a golden cup:** Cf. Jer. 51: 7, where the literal *Babylon was a golden cup in the Lord's hand, making all the earth drunken.* **5. and on her forehead was written a name of mystery:** Lit., 'a name, a mystery'; the name she bears (as Roman harlots wore their names on their foreheads) is not to be understood literally, but allegorically: **Babylon the great** is read, but 'Rome' is meant (cf. verses 9, 18). **mother of harlots and of earth's abominations:** A reference to the concentration of idolatry, superstition and vice in the imperial city; cf. Tacitus's description of Rome as the place 'where all the horrible and shameful things in the world congregate and find a home' (although Tacitus, unlike John, includes Christianity among these things). **6. drunk with the blood of the saints and the blood of the martyrs of Jesus:** A reference to the persecution of Christians in Rome, beginning with Nero's assault on them after the great fire of A.D. 64. **7. I will tell you the mystery of the woman:** In apocalyptic, revelations are made in symbols which remain mysteries until the appropriate interpretation is supplied; cf. Dan. 2: 18 ff.; 4: 9 ff.; 5: 5 ff.; 7: 15 ff. **8. The beast that you saw:** The beast is described as in 11: 7; 13: 3, 8. While the beast is the empire, the interpretation oscillates between the empire and its personification in the persecuting emperor who after his mortal wound comes to life again as the last Antichrist (cf. v. 11). **it was and is not and is to come:** A profane parody of the divine name of 1: 4, etc. **9. This calls for a mind with wisdom:** Cf. 13: 18. **the seven heads are seven hills on which the woman is seated:** Even if the imperial police missed the reference to Rome elsewhere in the vision, the proverbial **seven hills**, the *septimontium*, could not be mistaken. Rome was at first a conurbation of seven hill-settlements on the left bank of the Tiber, the principal settlement being that on the Palatine hill. **10. they are also seven kings:** Seven Roman emperors (Gk. *basileus* is used in this sense in Jn 19: 15; Ac. 17: 7; 1 Pet. 2: 13, 17). **five of whom have fallen:** If we reckon from the first emperor, these would be Augustus (27 B.C.-A.D. 14), Tiberius (A.D. 14-37), Gaius (37-41), Claudius (41-54) and Nero (54-68). **one is:** Probably Vespasian (69-79); the three emperors Galba, Otho and Vitellius, who ruled in quick succession at Rome during the 18 months between Nero's death and the capture of Rome by Vespasian's troops on December 21, A.D. 69, hardly come into the reckoning from the viewpoint of the eastern provinces. In them Vespasian's authority was undisputed after his proclamation at Alexandria on July 1, A.D. 69. (His accession to the imperial throne had been predicted two years previously by Josephus, who regarded Vespasian as destined to fulfil part of the messianic prophecies.) **the other has not yet come, . . . he must remain only a little while:** Titus, Vespasian's successor, reigned for only two years (A.D. 79-81). **11. As for the beast that was and is not, it is an eighth:** Here again we have the oscillation between the empire (the beast) and the emperor (one of the heads) who embodied its power at any one time (cf. 13: 3, 12). At the end the power of the persecuting empire will be embodied in the imperial Antichrist, who **belongs to the seven,** presumably in the sense that he is a reincarnation of one of them. It was natural for commentators from the second century onwards to identify him with Domitian (81-96), successor to his brother Titus, and to envisage him as a second Nero. But John is not thinking of Domitian (whose traditional reputation as a persecutor of the church rests on a very modest historical foundation), but of a demonic potentate, *Nero redivivus* (see note on 13: 3). **it goes to perdition:** Cf. 19: 20. Antichrist is designated 'the son of perdition' in 2 Th. 2: 3. **12. The ten horns** have a different significance from that of their prototypes on the nameless beast of Dan. 7: 7. They represent **ten kings** who are yet to arise as allied dependants of Rome in making **war on the Lamb** (13 f.), but who subsequently, in concert with the people of the empire itself, turn and rend her (15). They cannot be identified with known historical characters. The city of Rome was indeed sacked in 410 by the Goths, who had entered into alliance with the emperor; but it is doubtful if John would have regarded that event as a fulfilment of his vision. By that time Rome had long since capitulated to the sovereignty of Christ. Particular announcements of judgment in Scripture are regularly liable to be averted by timely repentance (cf. Jer. 18: 7 f.; Jon. 3: 10). Even so, John reminds us, with reference to the empire that he knew best, that imperial dominion does not endure, and that any power which sets itself *against the* LORD *and his anointed* (Ps. 2: 2) signs its own death-warrant. **14. the Lamb will conquer them, for he is Lord of lords and King of kings:** Cf. 19: 11-21 for details of this eschatological victory, and 19: 16 for the Lamb's title. **those with him are called and chosen and faithful:** In 19: 14 they are described as 'the armies of heaven, arrayed in fine linen, white and pure.' **16. they and the beast will hate the harlot:** The imperial allies and provinces unite in this annihilating attack on **the great city which has dominion over the kings of the earth** (18).

ii. Dirge over Babylon (18: 1-24)

The theme of great Babylon's downfall is continued, but it is now presented in terms of the destruction of a great mercantile city. In John's day Rome was the centre of world commerce—'Rome was the whole world, and all the world was Rome' (Spenser)—and what is here portrayed is not merely the doom of an ancient city, but the sure collapse of all human organization, commercial and otherwise, that leaves God out of its reckoning:

> *Lo, all our pomp of yesterday*
> *Is one with Nineveh and Tyre!*

First, a mighty and resplendent angel (v. 1) announces the fall of Babylon (v. 2) in language drawn from Isa. 21: 9 (cf. Rev. 14: 8); 13: 21 f., and Jer. 51: 8, where the desolation of Babylon on the Euphrates is vividly portrayed. For the language of verse 3 cf. 14: 8; 17: 2. It might seem unnecessary to mention that Babylon of ch. 18 is identical with Babylon of ch. 17, were it not that some commentators have tried to make a distinction between them. **3. the wealth of her wantonness:** 'Wealth' represents Gk. *dynamis* ('power'), which is used here in the extended sense of Heb. *chayil* ('might', 'wealth'). Next, another voice from heaven calls upon the people of God to leave the doomed city, in language drawn from Jer. 50: 8; 51: 6, 45; Isa. 48: 20; 52: 11 f., lest they **take part in her sins** and **share in her plagues** (4). **5. for her sins are heaped high as heaven:** Cf. Jer. 51: 9. **6. Render to her as she herself has rendered:** A statement of the principle of retribution in human history which recurs throughout the Bible; cf., with special reference to Babylon, Ps. 137: 8; Jer. 50: 15, 29. **7. A queen I sit, I am no widow . . .:** These and the following phrases are quoted from Isa. 47: 7 ff., where the plight of captive Babylon is depicted. **8. in a single day:** Cf. Isa. 47: 9, *in a moment, in one*

day: cf. also verses 10, 17, 19 below ('in one hour'). **for mighty is the Lord God who judges her:** Cf., in similar contexts, Isa. 47: 4; Jer. 50: 34. John's transference of older prophecies to suit new conditions may encourage modern readers (although they can lay no claim to his prophetic gift) to apply the *principles* of John's prophecy to the present day, where they are applicable to it. But it is one of the oddities of the history of biblical interpretation that Christian communities have been so prone to identify one another with the apocalyptic Babylon; it is too easy and agreeable to apply the denunciations of Scripture to others and claim the blessings for oneself. **9. the kings of the earth . . . will weep and wail over her:** The laments in verses 9-19 by rulers and merchants who grew prosperous by their commerce with the great city echo the dirges over Tyre in Ezek. 26: 17-19; 27: 25-36. **10. Alas! alas! thou great city, thou mighty city:** Cf. Ezek. 26: 17. **11. the merchants of the earth weep and mourn for her:** Because the city's fall deprives them of so inexhaustible a market for their wares. **cargo of gold, silver, jewels and pearls . . .:** Cf. the catalogue of Tyrian merchandise in Ezek. 27: 12 ff. **13. slaves, that is, human souls:** Lit. 'bodies, and souls of men'. The change in construction suggests that 'souls (lives) of men' is in apposition to 'bodies'. Cf. Ezek. 27: 13, where *the persons of men* (Heb. *nephesh 'adam*) is in LXX *psychai anthrōpōn*, the same expression as John uses here. There is good Hellenistic evidence for taking 'bodies' in the sense of 'slaves'. **17. all shipmasters and seafaring men, sailors and all whose trade is on the sea, stood far off:** Cf. Ezek. 27: 29, *The mariners and all the pilots of the sea stand on the shore.* In Ezekiel the fall of Tyre is depicted as the foundering of a great merchant-man, laden with goods from many lands, *in the heart of the seas* (Ezek. 27: 25); here the spectators come to witness and mourn over the disappearance of a great city in a gigantic conflagration, and they keep their distance because of the intense heat (verses 9 f., 15, 17 f.); cf. Abraham's view of the burning cities of Sodom and Gomorrah in Gen. 19: 27 f. **20. Rejoice over her, O heaven:** This is not the malignant delight which some take in the discomfiture of their enemies, but a call to rejoice in the judgments of God. There is unmistakable pathos in the dirge over Rome, just as there was in the dirge over Tyre which it echoes, and we need not suppose that either Ezekiel or John did not feel this pathos at heart. But *when thy judgments are in the earth, the inhabitants of the world learn righteousness* (Isa. 26: 9). In the judgments of God, rightly considered, the people of God can properly rejoice, but they will 'rejoice with trembling', remembering that His judgments begin with His own household (1 Pet. 4: 17; f. Ezek. 9: 6; Am. 3: 2). **21.** The angel's action in throwing **a stone like a great millstone . . . into the sea** in token of Rome's annihilation recalls the acted prophecy which Jeremiah commanded Seraiah to carry out at Babylon in 593 B.C. (Jer. 51: 59–63). The angel now takes up the dirge with its heavy refrain **no more** (cf. Ezek. 26: 21; 27: 36). The activities and recreations of city life will come to a full stop, and great Babylon will vanish as though she had never been. **22. the sound of harpers . . . shall be heard in thee no more:** Cf. Ezek. 26: 13 (of Tyre). **23. the voice of bridegroom and bride shall be heard in thee no more:** Cf. Jeremiah's similar language with regard to Jerusalem (Jer. 7: 34; 16: 9; 25: 10). **24. in her was found the blood of prophets and of saints, and of all who have been slain on earth:** Cf. our Lord's similar words about Jerusalem's impending expiation of 'the blood of all the prophets, shed from the foundation of the world' (Lk. 11: 50; Mt. 23: 35). It is not for her wealth and commercial enterprise that the great city is doomed. If prosperity is no proof of divine approval, neither does it arouse divine envy. But godlessness brings on its own nemesis, and where godlessness is conjoined with the unconscionable exploitation of the underprivileged and the persecution of the righteous, nothing but timely and wholehearted repentance can avert the death-sentence. Where, however, the sins of civilization reach their utmost limit and there is no further room for repentance, the judgment falls with the decisiveness of the 'great millstone' of v. 21.

iii. Exultation over Babylon (19: 1–5)
1. I heard . . . the mighty voice of a great multitude in heaven: The collapse of godless rebellion and oppression on earth gives rise to jubilation in heaven. For mortal men the vindication of God's righteousness is a sobering spectacle, even when it is most welcome, for there is none who is not liable to His judgment in some degree: 'If thou, O LORD, shouldst mark iniquities, Lord, who could stand?' But saints and angels in heaven with purified vision see this lower world in the light of God's glory, and their praise need not be disturbed by uneasy reflections.

VI. THE MARRIAGE OF THE LAMB (19: 6–10)
6. Hallelujah! For the Lord our God the Almighty reigns: This is the keynote of the whole book. Though the enemies of God rage against His people like savage beasts and great

Babylon exults in her insolence, He remains supreme, 'keeping watch above His own' and ready to call His foes to account when their rebellion has passed the point of no return. The present tense **reigns** represents the Gk. aorist *ebasileusen* (cf. 11: 17), which here follows the LXX of Ps. 93: 1, etc., where the aorist serves as the equivalent of the Hebrew perfect (RSV, *The* LORD *reigns*). **7. the marriage of the Lamb has come, and his Bride has made herself ready:** The ancient motif of the sacred marriage is introduced towards the end of the apocalyptic drama. For the messianic bridal theme cf. Jn 3: 29 (the figure of speech appears more generally in Mt. 25: 1 ff.; Mk 2: 19 f.; 2 C. 11: 2; Eph. 5: 25 ff.). The Lamb is the Messiah: the Bride is the messianic community (cf. 21: 2, 9 ff.). **8. it was granted her to be clothed with fine linen, bright and pure:** Cf. the white garments of the multitude in 7: 9 ff. The **fine linen** represents 'the sum of the saintly acts of members of Christ, wrought in them by His Spirit' (H. B. Swete). **9. the angel said to me:** The interpreting angel of 1: 1 (cf. 17: 1; 21: 9). **Blessed are those who are invited to the marriage supper of the Lamb:** While the beloved community is the Bride, its individual members can be envisaged as wedding guests. Cf. the pious remark in Lk. 14: 15. **These are true words of God:** This assurance is repeated in 21: 5; 22: 6. **10. You must not do that:** Cf. 22: 9. Bearing Col. 2: 18 in mind, we may recognize a warning to the Asian churches against angel-worship. **I am a fellow-servant:** 'Angels, though greater in might and power' (2 Pet. 2: 11), do not share the divine nature but are 'ministering spirits sent forth to serve' (Heb. 1: 14). **Worship God:** Cf. Mt. 4: 10 ‖ Lk. 4: 8, quoting Dt. 6: 13. **the testimony of Jesus is the spirit of prophecy:** Here NT prophecy is meant; for a similar statement about OT prophecy see 1 Pet. 1: 10 f. (cf. Jn 5: 39; Ac. 10: 43).

VII. THE HOLY WAR (19: 11–21)
11. I saw heaven opened: Cf. 4: 1; Ezek. 1: 1. **a white horse:** A symbol of victory, as in 6: 2. **He who sat upon it is called Faithful and True:** This horseman is different from the first horseman of ch. 6; he is the conquering Messiah, the 'faithful and true witness' of 3: 14. **in righteousness he judges and makes war:** Cf. Isa. 11: 4. The theme of the holy war of the end-time (already announced in 16: 14, 16; 17: 14) recurs frequently in apocalyptic; its features were well established, but John resolutely bends them, recalcitrant as they may be to his purpose, to serve as symbols of the victory of

the Lion of the tribe of Judah who conquered by his death (5: 5 f.). **12. His eyes are like a flame of fire:** Cf. 1: 14; 2: 18. **on his head are many diadems:** More than the dragon's seven (12: 3) or the imperial beast's ten (13: 1); they represent the universal allegiance which He receives (5: 11-13). **he has a name inscribed which no one knows but himself:** Cf. the secret name given to the overcomer in 2: 17. Here the mystery of the person of Christ is suggested (cf. Mt. 11: 27 ‖ Lk. 10: 22); this name is apparently neither of the revealed names of verses 13, 16. **13. He is clad in a robe dipped in blood:** For 'dipped' (Gk. *bebammenon*, from *baptō*) some early manuscripts and versions read 'sprinkled' (Gk. *rerantismenon*, from *rhantizō*). The picture is drawn from Isa. 63: 1-3, but there the conqueror's *crimsoned garments* are dyed with the blood of his Edomite foes. This is one of the recalcitrant features of the imagery which John re-shapes to portray the gospel of the Christ who triumphed by the shedding of His own blood. **and the name by which he is called is The Word of God:** A notable point of contact with the Johannine Gospel (cf. Jn 1: 1-14). **14. the armies of heaven:** The 'called and chosen and faithful' of 17: 14. **arrayed in fine linen, white and pure:** Cf. verse 8. **on white horses:** Cf. verse 11; they share their Leader's victory (cf. 12: 11). **15. From his mouth issues a sharp sword with which to smite the nations:** From Isa. 11: 4; cf. 1: 16; 2: 16. The sword symbolizes the irresistible power of His word of judgment and grace. **he will rule them with a rod of iron:** From Ps. 2: 9; cf. 12: 5 (also 2: 27). **he will tread the wine press of the fury of the wrath of God the Almighty:** From Isa. 63: 2 f., 6; cf. 14: 19 f. **16. on his thigh:** On the assumption that a Semitic original underlies John's Greek, it has been conjectured that Heb. or Aram. *regel* ('leg') has inadvertently replaced an original *degel* ('banner'). **King of kings and Lord of lords:** This name of universal dominion (cf. 17: 14) resembles the designation of Israel's God in Dt. 10: 17; to Christ is given 'the name which is above every name' (Phil. 2: 9), and world dominion is His. **17. an angel standing in the sun:** From which vantage-point he can be heard by all the birds of the air. **Come, gather for the great supper of God:** This ghastly picture is drawn from Ezek. 39: 17-20. The battle of Armageddon, once joined, is quickly won; the powers that militated against God and His people suffer final and irreparable destruction. Cf. the fate of Daniel's fourth beast, whose dead body was *given over to be burned with fire* (Dan. 7: 11). But here the creatures which embody imperial force and

emperor-worship are **thrown alive into the lake of fire that burns with brimstone** (20) —John's symbol for 'the second death' (cf. 20: 14; 21: 8). With verse 21, these words emphasize the completeness of the overthrow of the enemies of God. From first to last Rev. is the book of the triumph of Christ. It was by no material weapons, but by the power of the gospel, that Christ conquered the pagan Roman Empire; by that same power He has continued to conquer in history, and will conquer to the end. The analogy of Scripture discourages the idea that Christ, having conquered thus throughout preceding ages, will change His weapons for the final struggle and have recourse to those which He rejected in the day of temptation in the wilderness.

VIII. THE BINDING OF SATAN AND REIGN OF THE MARTYRS (20: 1-6)

The subordinate powers of evil having been destroyed, only Satan remains to be dealt with. An angel from heaven—not the fallen angel of the abyss (9: 1, 11)—chains him and locks him in the abyss **for a thousand years** (1-3). Cf. 1 Enoch 88: 1, where one of the principal archangels 'seized that first star which had fallen from heaven, and bound it hand and foot, and cast it into an abyss', into which the other fallen stars were then thrown bound (see note on 9: 1). Satan's consignment to the abyss is clearly later than his expulsion from heaven (12: 9); that preceded the rise of the beast and false prophet, whereas this follows their destruction. The thousand years of Satan's imprisonment in the abyss are surely identical with the thousand years of verse 4, during which the risen martyrs reign with Christ.

In some phases of Jewish eschatology 'the days of the Messiah', introduced by the appearance of Messiah on earth, were expected to precede the age to come. The duration of these days was variously estimated (cf. the 400 years of 2 Esd. 7: 28 f.); the estimate of a thousand years was related to Ps. 90: 4 (cf. 2 Pet. 3: 8). But for Christians the Messiah had already come, and with His exaltation to God's right hand His reign had already begun (5: 6 ff.; cf. 1 C. 15: 24-28). The millennial period of vv. 4-6, however, does not commence with the enthronement of Christ but at a later point, with the resurrection of the martyrs to share His throne (cf. 3: 21). **4. I saw thrones:** Cf. Dan. 7: 9, *thrones were placed*. **seated on them were those to whom judgment was committed:** Cf. Dan. 7: 22 (RV), *judgment was given to the saints of the Most High* (cf. also 1 C. 6: 2 f.). In verse 4 **the souls of those who had been beheaded for their testimony to Jesus** and for the word of God (cf. 1: 9; 12: 11) are probably identical with all who had not worshipped the beast or its image and had not received its mark (cf. 13: 15 ff.). No longer 'under the altar' (6: 9), they are glorified with Christ (as we have already seen in 14: 1 ff.; 15: 2). They came to life: The correct translation of the Gk. aorist *ezēsan*. and reigned with Christ a thousand years: It is not said, and perhaps not even implied, that earth is the place where they reign with Him (see note on 5: 10), although earth certainly enjoys a blessed respite during this period of the binding of Satan (verse 3). 5. The rest of the dead did not come to life again until the thousand years were ended: Cf. verses 12 f. This is the first resurrection: That is, the resurrection of those who came to life again in verse 4. 6. Over such the second death has no power: See note on verse 14. they shall be priests of God and of Christ, in addition to reigning with Christ; cf. 1: 6; 5: 10.

IX. GOG AND MAGOG (20: 7-10)
The binding of Satan is a restraint on evil, but does not extirpate it. A brief spell of renewed devilry intervenes between the thousand years and the last judgment. Satan, released from the abyss, resumes his deception of the nations, and finds obedient tools in Gog and Magog: Here, as in Ezek. 38: 1 ff., and in several other (but not all) places where Gog appears in Jewish literature, his attack comes between the messianic age and the establishment of the new Jerusalem. Whereas Ezekiel places *Gog, of the land of Magog* (Ezek. 38: 1) in his precise geographical setting (Asia Minor), together with his subject-allies (from north, east, and south-west of the Fertile Crescent), the geographical delimitation disappears here, and the reference comprises the marginal forces of evil from the four corners of the earth (8). (In the *Sibylline Oracles* iii. 319 f., the 'land of Gog and Magog' is located 'in the midst of the rivers of Ethiopia'.) Again, whereas in Ezek. 38: 1 Magog is the territory of which Gog is ruler, Gog and Magog here, as in Sibylline and Rabbinic literature, are parallel names, used together as a symbol of the world-powers opposed to God. their number is like the sand of the sea: Cf. Gen. 22: 17; 1 Sam. 13: 5, etc. for the simile; Ezekiel describes Gog's army as *a cloud covering the land* (Ezek. 38: 16). 9. they marched up over the broad earth (lit. 'the breadth of the earth'): From Hab. 1: 6, where a Chaldaean invasion is similarly described. surrounded the camp of the saints and the beloved city: Cf. for the latter phrase Pss. 78: 68; 87: 2. Some have thought of a new foundation on the site of the

old city 'which is allegorically called Sodom and Egypt' (11: 8); we need not think, however, of a walled and built-up city (cf. Ezek. 38: 11, 14), but rather of a community of the true Israel, encamped, as earlier Israel once was, in the wilderness. Not the resurrected confessors, but the mother-church of 12: 13 ff., which had been protected against her enemies in the persecution under the 'beast', should probably be identified as the target of this attack. fire came down from heaven and consumed them: Cf. Ezek. 38: 22 (and more generally Gen. 19: 24 ff.; 2 Kg. 1: 10, 12). 10. the devil who had deceived them was thrown into the lake of fire and brimstone: This must be 'the eternal fire prepared for the devil and his angels' of Mt. 25: 41. The 'adamantine chains and penal fire' which Milton envisages as Satan's dungeon at his primaeval fall are assigned to him by John at the end of time. where the beast and the false prophet were: Cf. 19: 20. This clause has no verb in Gk.; it might be slightly better to supply 'were cast' (cf. NEB 'had been flung') than 'were', since the two earlier prisoners are evidently still there, for, together with their new companion, they will be tormented day and night for ever and ever. Since the beast and the false prophet are figures for systems rather than individual persons, the permanent destruction of evil is evidently meant.

X. THE LAST ASSIZE (20: 11-15)
11. I saw a great white throne and him who sat upon it: In Dan. 7: 9 *one that was ancient of days took his seat* as judge at the final assize. But in Rev. 1: 13 ff. the *one like a son of man* shares the features of Daniel's Ancient of Days; and since, according to Jn 5: 27, the Father 'has given him authority to execute judgment, because he is the Son of man', we may think of the Son of Man as seated on this throne (cf. Mt. 19: 28; 25: 31). from his presence earth and sky fled away: Cf. Isa. 34: 4; Mk 13: 31; 2 Pet. 3: 10. But the language here serves chiefly to underline the awesome majesty of the Judge and the judgment. 12. I saw the dead, great and small, standing before the throne: These are 'the rest of the dead' of verse 5; now they too have been raised. books were opened: As in Dan. 7: 10, these are the records of men's lives; cf. Wis. 4: 20 (of the wicked): 'They will come with dread when their sins are reckoned up, and their lawless deeds will convict them to their face'. the book of life: Cf. 3: 5; 13: 8; 17: 8. the dead were judged by what was written in the books: The last assize is conducted with scrupulous justice; if salvation is always by grace, divine judgment

is always according to men's works (cf. 2: 23; 22: 12; Rom. 2: 6, etc.). **13. the sea gave up the dead in it:** Death at sea, with no monument to mark the spot where one's body lay, was thought of as a terribly desolate fate. In some Jewish circles resurrection was thought of as possible only for those buried on dry land. **14. Death and Hades were thrown into the lake of fire:** Death and Hades are personified as in 6: 8. The gospel proclaims Christ as the 'Death of death, and hell's destruction'; in 1 C. 15: 26 death is viewed as 'the last enemy to be destroyed' by Him, but in 2 Tim. 1: 10 faith sees Him as the One who, by His own death and resurrection, has already 'abolished death and brought life and immortality to light through the gospel.' **This is the second death:** Perhaps because it befalls men who have been raised from the 'first' death (cf. Heb. 9: 27). **15. if any one's name was not found written in the book of life, he was thrown into the lake of fire:** It is curious exegesis that would infer from this that all who appear at the last assize are consigned to perdition. True, those who have committed apostasy and worshipped 'the image of the beast' have no place in the book of life (13: 8); but the dead who stand before the throne include all mankind from earliest days. The scene which John paints here, with its vivid and sombre hues, is unforgettably impressive; it is not intended to gratify curiosity about eschatological details but to challenge the reader with a reminder of the One to whom the final account must be rendered.

> *O may we stand before the Lamb,*
> *When earth and seas are fled;*
> *And hear the Judge pronounce our name*
> *With blessings on our head!*

XI. THE NEW CREATION (21: 1-8)

1. I saw a new heaven and a new earth: He sees the fulfilment and transcendence of the promise of Isa. 65: 17; 66: 22. The way has been cleared for the emergence of this new creation 'in which righteousness dwells' (2 Pet. 3: 13), by the abolition of evil and the passing of the **first heaven and the first earth** before the advent of the divine Judge (20: 11). **the sea was no more:** The sea was to the Jews a symbol of separation (not, as to the Greeks, a means of communication); moreover, throughout the Bible it symbolizes restless insubordination (cf. Job 38: 8-11; Ps. 89: 9; Isa. 57: 20), and in Rev. 13: 1 it casts up the system which incarnates hostility to God and His people. Naturally, then, there is no room for it in the new creation. **2. I saw the holy city, new Jerusalem:** The glorified community of

the people of Christ (cf. Gal. 4: 26; Heb. 12: 22). **coming down out of heaven from God:** Cf. 3: 12. It is thus emphasized that the church is 'the city . . . whose builder and maker is God' (Heb. 11: 10), not a voluntary association of men. Hitherto the glorified saints have been seen in heaven with Christ (cf. 14: 1 ff.; 15: 2). **prepared as a bride adorned for her husband:** Cf. Isa. 62: 4. The beloved community is both city and bride (cf. verses 9 ff.; 19: 7 f.). **3. a great voice from the throne:** Cf. 16: 17; 19: 5. Now the voice proclaims the eternal consummation of the blessings of the gospel. **the dwelling** (Gk. *skēnē*, 'tent') **of God is with men. He will dwell** (Gk. *skēnoō*, as in Jn 1: 14) **with them:** Cf. Exod. 25: 8. So it was when the Word became flesh and pitched his tabernacle among men; so it is in the renewed earth because of the presence of the redeemed community, reflecting the glory of God (v. 23). **they shall be his people, and God himself will be with them:** The covenant blessings promised in Jer. 31: 33; Ezek. 37: 27; Zech. 8: 8 are now extended world-wide. **4. he will wipe away every tear from their eyes:** The consolation enjoyed by the martyrs in 7: 17 is now enjoyed by mankind, in fulfilment of Isa. 25: 8. **death shall be no more,** because it has been destroyed in the fiery lake (20: 14; cf. again Isa. 25: 8). **the former things have passed away:** Cf. Isa. 42: 9; 2 C. 5: 17; both these passages are also echoed in the divine proclamation of verse 5. **Behold, I make all things new:** 'If anyone is in Christ', says Paul, 'he is (or 'there is') a new creation' (2 C. 5: 17); now, through those who are elect 'in Christ' God communicates His blessings to the world (cf. Rom. 8: 18-25). To the same effect James writes: 'Of his own will he brought us forth by the word of truth that we should be a kind of first fruits of his creatures' (Jas 1: 18). Cf. 14: 4. **Write this:** Cf. 19: 9 (also 22: 6) for the confirmation. **6. It is done:** Cf. the utterance at the outpouring of the last bowl of wrath (16: 17). **I am the Alpha and the Omega:** Cf. 1: 8 (also 22: 13). **To the thirsty I will give water without price from the fountain of the water of life:** An application of Isa. 55: 1 in the light of Jesus' invitation in Jn 7: 37 f. Cf. 22: 1. The free offer of the gospel sounds clearly and repeatedly in the last two chapters of Rev. **7. He who conquers . . . :** Here are summed up the blessings promised to the victorious confessors in the letters to the seven churches (2: 7, 11, 17, 26 ff.; 3: 5, 12, 21). The words of 2 Sam. 7: 14, applied to Christ in Heb. 1: 5, are here applied to Christ's loyal followers. **8. But as for the cowardly, the faithless . . . :** Characteristically, John's catalogue of those who are excluded from the blessings of the new creation begins with those who through fear have denied the faith in face of persecution. His universalism is eschatological, but not retrospectively effective.

XII. THE NEW JERUSALEM (21: 9-22: 5)

9. one of the seven angels: Cf. 17: 1. The holy Jerusalem is revealed to the seer either by the same angel, or by one of the colleagues of the angel, who previously showed him the spectacle of great Babylon. **the Bride, the wife of the Lamb:** With a sovereign disregard of rules against mixing metaphors, the beloved community is portrayed as both bride (cf. 19: 7 f.) and city (21: 10 ff.). **in the Spirit he carried me away to a great, high mountain:** Cf. the *very high mountain* from which Ezekiel in vision saw *a structure like a city* (Ezek. 40: 2). **11. having the glory of God:** John ransacks the resources of language and metaphor—jewels, gold and pearls—to describe the indescribable glory which the holy city reflects (cf. Isa. 26: 1 f.; 54: 11 f.; 60: 18 ff.). **12. on the gates the names of the twelve tribes of the sons of Israel were inscribed:** The beloved city is thus marked out as the true Israel or people of God; this is emphasized by the recurrence of the number twelve and its multiples throughout the description of the city. Cf. the number of the elect in 7: 4 ff.; 14: 1 ff. **14. twelve foundations, and on them the twelve names of the twelve apostles of the Lamb:** The true Israel is the *new* Israel, as indeed Jesus implied when 'he appointed twelve, to be with him, and to be sent out . . .' (Mk 3: 14; cf. the implication of Mt. 19: 28; Lk. 22: 30); it comprises all the faithful of Old and New Testament times alike. **15. a measuring rod of gold:** Ezekiel's angelic mentor had *a line of flax and a measuring reed* for a similar purpose (Ezek. 40: 3; cf. also Zech. 2: 1 f.; Rev. 11: 1). **16. The city lies foursquare:** Like Ezekiel's city (Ezek. 48: 16) and the heavenly *ekklēsia* in Hermas, *Vision* iii. 2. 5; but John's city is a cube, like the holy of holies in Solomon's temple (1 Kg. 6: 20) and the heavenly Jerusalem in the Talmud tractate *Baba Bathra* 75b (we are scarcely intended to envisage it as a pyramid). **twelve thousand stadia:** The measurement is symbolic, and its significance would be lost if it were re-stated as 1500 miles. Ezekiel's foursquare city was built on a side of 4500 cubits, approximately a mile and a quarter. **17. a hundred and forty-four cubits** is probably the thickness of the wall; such a height would be disproportionately small for so high a city. But this might be irrelevant when such schematic numbers are in question. In any case, the **man** whose measurements are used

as the scale of reference here is, like the 'man' of Ezek. 40: 3 ff., an angel. **19. The foundations of the wall of the city were adorned with every jewel:** The twelve precious stones mentioned in verses 19, 20 are reminiscent of those in the high-priestly breastplate, engraved with the names of the twelve sons of Israel (Exod. 28: 17-21); nine out of the twelve appear in both lists (though not in the same order), and perhaps John intends to reproduce all twelve of the earlier list, though we cannot be sure because of the possibility of choosing a variety of Greek equivalents for some of the Hebrew words. According to Philo and Josephus, the twelve jewels on the breastplate were believed by some Jews in the first century A.D. to represent the signs of the zodiac; R. H. Charles points out that, in this case, the sequence of the signs is reversed in John's list, as though to suggest that the divine purpose upsets the basis and findings of pagan astrology. **21. the twelve gates were twelve pearls:** The pearly gates, like the city foursquare itself, are applied in popular hymnody to heaven; but John uses this language to convey some idea of the splendour of the glorified people of God. **22. I saw no temple in the city**—because God and the Lamb together constitute the city's holiness, and it is itself God's dwelling-place on earth (v. 3). **23. the city has no need of sun or moon:** Cf. Isa. 60: 19 f.; there, as here, *the LORD will be your everlasting light, and your God will be your glory;* but here (as from ch. 5 onwards) the Lamb is seen in the closest association with God. **24. By its light shall the nations walk:** Cf. Isa. 60: 1-3. In the Bible the election of some does not imply the damnation of others, but rather their blessing. The AV wording, 'the nations of them which are saved', represents an inferior reading, but is sound exegesis. **the kings of the earth shall bring their glory into it:** Cf. Isa. 60: 5 ff.; Ps. 72: 10 f. **25. its gates shall never be shut by day:** Cf. Isa. 60: 11, where they stand open day and night, but such language would be inappropriate in the present context, for **there shall be no night there**—no intermission of the glory of God's presence. **26. they shall bring into it the glory and the honour of the nations:** Cf. Isa. 60: 11 (*the wealth of the nations*); Hag. 2: 7 (*the treasures of all nations*). The glory of the church is incompatible with a dead-level uniformity; the variety of national contributions helps to make up her many-splendoured life. **But nothing unclean shall enter** the city; **the Lamb's book of life** is her burgess-roll.

The opening verses of ch. 22 depict the new creation as Paradise restored, with the serpent banished. the curse abolished. and access to the tree of life continually open to all. **1. the river of the water of life, bright as crystal, flowing from the throne of God and of the Lamb:** Cf. the life-giving river of Ezek. 47: 1 ff. which rises beneath the eastern threshold of the temple and flows down the Kidron valley to sweeten the water of the Dead Sea (see also Zech. 14: 8, *living waters shall flow out from Jerusalem*). **2. through the middle of the street of the city:** Cf. Ps. 46: 4, where the *river whose streams make glad the city of God* is God's own presence (see also the *place of broad rivers and streams* in Isa. 33: 21). **the tree of life:** Cf. Gen. 2: 9; 3: 22; Rev. 2: 7. The Paradise motif suggests that the river of water of life may have a further antecedent in the river which flowed out of Eden in Gen. 2: 10. The tree of life and the river of life are both symbols of the eternal life brought near in the gospel. **twelve kinds of fruit:** Cf. Ezek. 47: 12, *they will bear fresh fruit every month.* **the leaves of the tree were for the healing of the nations:** Cf. Ezek. 47: 12, *their fruit will be for food, and their leaves for healing.* The saving benefits of the gospel promote the well-being of all aspects of personal and communal life. **3. there shall no more be anything accursed:** The sentence of Gen. 3: 17 is cancelled; the curse cannot survive in the presence of God. **his servants shall worship him:** The verb is Gk. *latreuō*, as in 7: 15. **4. they shall see his face, and his name shall be on their foreheads:** In the words of 1 Jn 3: 2, they are 'like him', because they 'see him as he is'. Here and now the sanctification of believers consists in their being progressively conformed to the likeness of God by the power of the Spirit, as they reflect the divine glory revealed to them in the face of Christ (cf. 2 C. 3: 18–4: 6); John describes the climax of that process, for the beatific vision involves the perfect glorification of those who receive it. Cf. 3: 12, 'I will write on him the name of my God, . . . and my own new name.' **5. they shall reign for ever and ever**—sharing in the eternal 'kingdom of our Lord and of his Christ' (11: 15). Cf. Dan. 12: 3.

Epilogue (22: 6–21)

i. Attestation by the Angel (22: 6–7)

6. These words are trustworthy and true: Cf. 19: 9; 21: 5. **The Lord, the God of the spirits of the prophets, has sent his angel to show his servants what must soon take place:** Cf. 1: 1; 22: 16. Here Jesus Himself seems to be identified with 'the God of the spirits of the prophets' (cf. the end of 19: 10). **7. I am coming soon:** The angel apparently speaks in the Lord's name. Cf. verses 12, 20.

Blessed is he who keeps the words of the prophecy of this book: A repetition of the beatitude of 1: 3. Keeping the words involves not only retaining them in memory but regulating one's life by them, especially maintaining one's Christian confession without compromise.

ii. Attestation by John (22: 8–11)

8. I John am he who heard and saw these things: Cf. 1: 1, 9. He affirms that the visions of Revelation were his authentic experiences and not literary inventions. The angel's repudiation of the homage which John attempts to pay him (verses 8b, 9) follows 19: 10 closely. **10. Do not seal up the words of the prophecy of this book, for the time is near:** Daniel was commanded to seal up the record of his visions *until the time of the end* (Dan. 12: 4, 9), because centuries were to elapse between the third year of Cyrus (Dan. 10: 1) and the fulfilment of the visions which bear that date; but no such time-lag is envisaged here (contrast 10: 4). The problem of the postponement of the parousia (as commonly understood) is thus underlined. Because the time is short, there will be but little opportunity for repentance and change: the wicked are confirmed in their wickedness, the righteous in their righteousness (verse 11; cf. Dan. 12: 10).

In the Christian doctrine of the Last Things however, the imminence of the end is moral rather than chronological; each successive Christian generation, for aught that is known to the contrary, may be the last generation. In that sense the time is always near (1: 3); it is therefore the path of wisdom for believers to be ready to meet their Lord. When He comes and institutes the final judgment, the verdict will be that which men by their attitude to God and their way of life have already incurred for themselves (cf. Jn 3: 18). Till then the 'water of life' remains available to whosoever will, as verse 17 makes plain.

iii. Attestation by Jesus (22: 12–16)

The Lord announces His swift advent, to recompense **every one for what he has done** (12). The principle has already been laid down in 2: 23; 20: 12; cf. also 1 C. 4: 5; Eph. 6: 8; Col. 3: 23–25. **13. I am the Alpha and the Omega, the first and the last, the beginning and the end:** A combination of 1: 8, 17b; 21: 6. **14. Blessed are those who wash their robes:** Cf. 7: 14. An inferior, though well-attested, variant reads 'Blessed are those who keep his commandments' (this could have arisen in the copying of a rather faded Greek text). Those who are excluded from the city (v. 15) belong to the categories already indicated in 21: 8, 27 (cf. 1 C. 6: 9 f.; Gal. 5: 19–21). Verses

14 and 15 may be a parenthesis between the two parts of Jesus' attestation in verses 13 and 16; it has frequently been suspected that the closing paragraphs of Rev. have suffered some primitive dislocation. **16. I Jesus have sent my angel:** Cf. 1: 1; 22: 6. **the root and the offspring of David:** For the former title see 5: 5. His eternal being (verse 13) and His Davidic descent are set in paradoxical juxtaposition; cf. Mk 12: 35-37; Rom. 1: 3 f. **the bright morning star:** Cf. 2: 28. The *star . . . out of Jacob* or *sceptre . . . out of Israel* foretold by Balaam (Num. 24: 17) was primarily a reference to David and his conquering career, and is therefore transferred, not inappropriately, to great David's greater Son. In the Qumran texts Num. 24: 17 is a recurring *testimonium* of the messianic warrior of the end-time. Another NT reference to Christ as the morning star may be detected in 2 Pet. 1: 19 (where the word is *phōsphoros*, 'light-bringer'; here *astēr . . . prōinos* is the expression used).

iv. Invocation, Invitation and Response (22: 17-20)
17. The Spirit and the Bride say, 'Come': This 'Come' (singular) is addressed to the Lord. We may regard the Spirit as indwelling the beloved community and inspiring it to respond thus to the Lord's promise of verse 12, or we may take the Spirit to be the Spirit of prophecy, in which case **the Spirit and the Bride** 'is practically equivalent to "the prophets and the saints" ' (H. B. Swete). **let him who hears say, 'Come':** Every one who listens to the reading of the book (cf. 1: 3) must at this point break in with his personal response: 'Come!' The Aramaic form of the invocation, *Marana-tha*, 'Our Lord, come' (1 C. 16: 22) was retained even in Greek-speaking churches, especially at the celebration of the Eucharist. This we gather from the *Didache* (c. A.D. 100) where, strikingly enough, *Marana-tha* is immediately preceded by the call: 'If any man is holy, let him come; if any man is not, let him repent' (*Didache* 10: 6). So here the invocation to the Lord is closely associated with the invitation to the outsider, **let him who is thirsty come, let him who desires take the water of life without price** —take it, as 21: 6 declares, from the Alpha and Omega, to whom all power is given. In a book so full of judgment, it is exhilarating to find the gospel invitation extended so plainly and freely at the end. No assessment of the Christian quality of Rev. is adequate which does not give full weight to these words. If 'let him who

desires' (AV 'whosoever will') is felt by some to present a problem, it is a problem imported from outside; it does not arise from the context. The blindest idolater, the fiercest persecutor, were he Nero himself—and might we add the most abject apostate?—may come if he will and accept the full and free benefits which the gospel provides. **18. I warn every one:** The warning not to add to or subtract from the words of the prophecy (verses 18 f.) echoes Dt. 4: 2; 12: 32. It was not intended for textual critics who prefer longer or shorter readings in this or any other book of the NT! **20. He who testifies to these things**—Jesus Himself, 'the faithful witness' (1: 5). His repeated 'Surely, I am coming soon' is His reply to His people's invocation (v. 17), and evokes from them the further call: **'Amen. Come, Lord Jesus!'** So, in *Didache* 10: 6, *Marana-tha* is confirmed by *Amen*.

v. Benediction (22: 21)
The final benediction has a form familiar in NT letters; our early witnesses to the text oscillate between the longer reading **with all the saints** and the shorter readings 'with the saints' (RV) and 'with all' (AV 'with you all' reproduces a later and inferior reading).

BIBLIOGRAPHY

BECKWITH, I. T., *The Apocalypse of John* (London, 1919).

CAIRD, G. B., *The Revelation of St. John the Divine*. BNTC (London, 1966).

CHARLES, R. H., *A Critical and Exegetical Commentary on the Revelation of St. John* [On the Greek text]. ICC (2 vols. Edinburgh, 1920).

FARRER, A. M., *The Revelation of St. John the Divine* (Oxford, 1964).

HENDRIKSEN, W., *More than Conquerors* (London, 1962).

KELLY, W., *Lectures on the Book of Revelation* (London, 1874).

KIDDLE, M., *The Revelation of St. John*. MNT (London, 1940).

LANG, G. H., *The Revelation of Jesus Christ* (London, 1945).

McDOWELL, E. A., *The Meaning and Message of the Book of Revelation* (Nashville, Tenn., 1951).

NEWTON, B. W., *Thoughts on the Apocalypse*[3] (London' 1904).

PEAKE, A. S., *The Revelation of John* (London, 1919).

PRESTON, R. H., and HANSON, A. T., *The Revelation of Saint John the Divine*. Torch Commentaries (London, 1949).

RAMSAY, W. M., *The Letters to the Seven Churches of Asia* (London, 1909).

SWETE, H. B., *The Apocalypse of St. John* [on the Greek text] (London, 1906).